# Dav of Cheste Carolina and His Descendants 1772-1989

## by

## Katharine Tolle Kell
## and
## Philip James Graham

With Introduction in 2008
by Sam Sloan

## ISHI PRESS INTERNATIONAL

# David Graham
## of Chester County, South Carolina and His Descendants 1772-1989

by Katharine Tolle Kell and Philip James Graham

Copyright © 1990 by Katharine Tolle Kell
and Philip James Graham
4402 Maple Avenue
Bathesda, Maryland 20814

First Printing 1990 in Birmingham, Michigan

Second Printing April, 2008 by
Ishi Press International

All rights reserved according to International Law. No part of this book may be reproduced by any mechanical, photographic or electronic process nor may it be stored in a retrieval system, transmitted or otherwise copied for public or private use without the written permission of the publisher or authors.

ISBN 0-923891-07-2
978-0-923891-07-7

Ishi Press International
1664 Davidson Avenue, Suite 1B
Bronx NY 10453
USA
917-507-7226

Printed in the United States of America

## Publisher's Foreword

Publisher's Foreword

The picture on the cover of this book is of William Graham (1801-1882) who was the grandson of David Graham and is my great-great-grandfather. The Grahams have consistently maintained high levels of reproduction and have enjoyed long life spans. David Graham (1731-1800), who arrived in America in 1772, had eight children. His son Andrew Graham (1753-1821) had twelve children. His son William Graham (1801-1882) had twelve children. His son Samuel Graham (1848-1931) had eight children. His daughter Mary Graham (1879-1856), who was my grandmother, had six children. Multiply that out and you will see how we have been able to flood this place with Grahams.

This book is a genealogical database and family history of 6,897 members of the Graham Family, consisting of David Graham and his three children who arrived in Charleston South Carolina on the ship *Pennsylvania Farmer* in 1772, and their descendants.

The 6,897 descendants listed in this book are a drop in the bucket compared to the actual number, because the main typist and compiler, Katharine Kell, stopped typing in most cases when the daughters married and had children who did not carry the Graham name. I have added as appendices to this book the family histories of some of these daughters. These were sent in by relatives most likely to be included in a future update to this book.

One story or legend in our family is that we are related in some way to the famous sea captain John Paul Jones. I heard this when I was a child and other distant branches of the Graham Family have heard this too. It turns out that this is true as is shown in the first appendix to this book.

Katharine Kell died on October 23, 1992 at age 69. She was my Fourth Cousin. Her co-author, Philip James Graham, is my Fourth Cousin One Generation Removed, which means that he is one-half generation further away. I know this because I have my own genealogical database in my computer which calculates these things. I am a newcomer to this field, having only started in 1991, but my family tree database in my computer has 13,589 names in it. Most of the names in this book are not included.

## *Publisher's Foreword*

This book was originally self-published in 1990. Although the cost of printing was $4,038.06 for 250 copies, the book was distributed free of charge or in some cases sold to family members. I did not find out about the existence of this book until about 1997. By then, there were no more available. Since I mention this book several times in my genealogical database online, I constantly receive requests from distant relatives for copies of this book, and I have to inform them that there are none available.

In 2006, I asked the surviving author, Philip James Graham, for permission to reprint this book. He readily agreed and sent me the original camera-ready copy. However, the size and weight of the original book is too big for easy distribution. I wanted to reduce it to a manageable size. I could not figure out how to do it. Fortunately, Pamela McCallum of Scituate, Massachusetts came to the rescue and agreed to scan the entire book for me and to reduce the margins so that it would fit in a 6 x 9 book, which is the preferred size for many books. Pamela McCallum did a wonderful job. I could never have done it myself or, if I had tried to do it, it would have taken me several months. As you will see, she even made the gutter margins wider than the outside margins, which are vitally important to open and read a soft-cover book of 700 pages.

As the introduction states, this book is the result of more than 15 years of research by the two authors. They originally started their research independently of each other, and eventually they found each other, and decided to collaborate.

The book was published in 1990. It was self published through the services of a local bookbinder in Birmingham, Michigan, where Katharine Kell, who had typed the manuscript, lived. It was self published on 8 3/8 x 11 paper, which seems to be a standard size for Family History Books of this nature. The bill from the printer came to $4,038.06 which, I believe, was paid by Mrs. Kell.

Mrs. Kell died on October 23, 1992 at age 69. Her husband, Joseph Cass Kell, died on January 24, 1993 at age 80. Thus, it fell to the co-author, Philip James Graham, who was born December 4, 1954, to become the guardian of this manuscript.

## Publisher's Foreword

In 1991, I started my own independent research, not into my own family but into the family of President Thomas Jefferson because I was writing a book called *"The Slave Children of Thomas Jefferson"*. Although I am not a member of the LDS, in 1991 I traveled to Salt Lake City to learn their techniques for gathering genealogical data. I bought the first edition of their Personal Ancestral File or "PAF" program that had just come out and I started gathering and entering data on the family tree of Thomas Jefferson. As an aside, I put my own very limited Family Tree on disk. I knew little about my own family history. I only knew the names of three of my grandparents, one of whom was Mary Graham (1879-1956).

I sent a floppy disk with my data on it to the LDS in Salt Lake City, Utah, with about 1200 names on it of relatives of Thomas Jefferson and about 12 names on it of my own relatives. As a result, everybody in my database was assigned an Ancestral File Number by the LDS.

Required reading for anybody interested in this book is *"Scotch-Irish migration to South Carolina, 1772: (Rev. William Martin and his five shiploads of settlers)"* by Jean Stephenson ISBN 0806348321 . That book provides passenger lists for the five boatloads of settlers led by Rev. William Martin. The five ships were *"James and Mary"*, *"Lord Dunluce"*, *"Pennsylvania Farmer"* (the ship on which the Grahams sailed), *"Hopewell"* and *"Free Mason"*. There were approximately 1,100 members of the group, all of whom attended Rev. Martin's Church in Atrium, Northern Ireland. They were all fleeing the turmoil and fighting that had taken place between the Catholics and the Protestants in Northern Ireland (not unlike the fighting that is still taking place today). They had been promised free land in South Carolina.

Most of the Graham Family did not stay long in South Carolina. Being farmers, they started moving Westward. My own branch moved to Kentucky, then to Indiana, then to Illinois, then to Iowa, where my Grandmother Graham was born.

A question that often comes up concerns a number of famous people named Graham who remained the area and did not go West. These include The Reverend Billy Graham (born November 17, 1918) , United States Senator from Florida Robert Graham (born November 9, 1936), who was briefly a presidential candidate, and Editor and Owner of the

## Publisher's Foreword

Washington Post Philip L. Graham (1915-1963), among many others.

I have never been able to prove that any of these people are our relatives. On the other hand, I cannot prove that they are not our relatives either. One person who has written me believes that there were two Graham Brothers in Ireland. One brother, David Graham, was the ancestor of all of us poor Grahams, whereas the other brother was the ancestor of all those rich Grahams. Due to the difficulties in obtaining any original family records from Northern Ireland, it has not proven possible to prove or disprove any of this. Numerous relatives have gone over there and searched, and none have found anything conclusive.

This book by Katharine Kell also contains an important article about the history of Scot Irish Immigration, explaining how the Scots arrived in Ireland in the first place. After King Henry VIII (1491-1547) changed the official religion of the Church of England, so that he could divorce his wife rather than chopping off her head as had previously been his custom, Ireland remained Catholic. England had conquered but could not control Ireland, but they were able to push the Catholics out of Northern Ireland and settle Scots there to replace them. This resulted in the wars which have continued to this day. However, the Scots eventually rebelled under English Rule, rebellions broke out and those who chose not to fight but quit moved to America. This explains the boatloads of 1,100 settlers that arrived in Charleston South Carolina on December 19, 1772, their departure from Ireland having been delayed to give the farmers time to sell their crops.

This also explains how I got here, being one of those Scot-Irish.

The five ships that came in 1772 were among the last to arrive in this way, because right after that the American Revolutionary War broke out. For many years thereafter, no more ships from Ireland were allowed to sail from Ireland to America, until the Titanic.

The Graham Family joined with zest into the American Revolutionary War, because they hated the British. A little remembered fact is that fighting continued in South Carolina even after Cornwallis had surrendered in Virginia. David Graham and his two sons joined in the fighting (on the American side).

## Publisher's Foreword

A problem has arisen for those descendants who want to join the *"Daughters of the American Revolution"*. The rosters of the names of the soldiers fighting include David Grimes and Andrew Grimbs. Also, the rosters of the ships arriving in 1772 list David Grimbs and Andrew Grimbs. The problem has been to prove that David Grimbs and Andrew Grimbs are the same persons as David Graham and Andrew Graham who are our relatives. This book contains documentary proof on pages 52-59 that these are the same persons and, as I understand it, the DAR will now accept us as members.

Another problem is that at least one researcher clams that Andrew Graham was born in 1720, not in 1753, and thus when he died in 1821 he was 101 years old. The debates on this subject have been hot and heavy. I express no opinion on this subject but refer the reader to my website and to my page on worldconnect.rootsweb.com where the debate is outlined:

http://www.samsloan.com/pafn33.htm#575

Another problem is that Andrew Graham, son of David Graham, had the same bad habit as I have, which is getting married. Andrew Graham had either three or four marriages and either two or three of his wives were named Margaret. These include Margaret Coulter, Mary Chesnut, Margaret Phillips and another wife just named Margaret. Andrew Graham had twelve known children and ever since researchers have been debating the subject of which child came from which wife. The stakes in this are high, because at stake here is the right TO CLAIM MEMBERSHIP IN THE BRITISH ROYAL FAMILY. This of course is very important because everybody wants to be a member of the British Royal Family, of course, and this has led to endless debates.

This issue arises because the mother of Margaret Coulter was Mary Stuart who, it is claimed, was a descendant of the Stuart Family, one of the Royal Families of England, through one of the concubines of either King James IV (1473-1513) or King James V (1512-1542) of Scotland.

King James IV and King James V of Scotland had another bad habit, which is having lots of mistresses, numbering around twenty each, and having lots of bastard kids. Both of these kings had short lives and died

## Publisher's Foreword

in battle, but left things to remember them by. Mary Stuart is said to have been descended from one of them, but nobody has been able to establish which one, or even if the relationship is true at all.

Seriously, being the bastard child of a King of England or Scotland still makes one a member of the British Royal Family in spite of the illegitimacy. Whenever someone wants to claim descent from British Royalty they usually claim descent from King Edward I or King Edward III. Those are both safe claims to make because they are regarded as relatively good kings and they both had lots of kids. If the truth were known, probably all of England is descended from King Edward I (1272-1307), except for the recent immigrants. However, if you want to know the real truth, we are all probably descended from King John (1164-1216). King John was the grand champion of them all when it came to having mistresses and bastard kids but, since he is regarded as a bad king, indeed the worst king England ever had, nobody wants to claim descent from him.

An interesting coincidence is that according to page 362 of this book, Katharine Kell, the author, has a son, Matthew Kell, who has won several trophies in chess tournaments. Since I was a member of the Executive Board of the United States Chess Federation, I looked him up to see if this was really true. To my great surprise, it really was true. More than that, he has almost the same rating as me. He was rated 1939. I was rated 1955. There must be a generic factor at work, since he is my fourth cousin, one time removed.

I have been trying to contact him or any of the children of Katharine Kell because I have been hoping that the original computer files that were used to create this book might be available somewhere. If I had those files, I could have reprinted this book a year ago. Even now, if I had those files, I could update the data with the next generation, the births and deaths of our family members that have been born or died since 1990. If anybody knows how to contact Matthew Kell or any of the other children of Katharine Kell, please let me know.

Sam Sloan<br>
Bronx NY USA<br>
April 2, 2008

# PREFACE

The Graham genealogy is the result of almost fifteen years of research and was begun tentatively by each of the authors before they begun corresponding in 1983. Since then the genealogical facts have acquired mainly by plodding persistence, though sometimes by luck, and always the acquisition has been accompanied by a feeling of pleasure in learning something new about the Grahams. Many miles have been driven in pursuit of the facts, many letters exchanged, but also many new friends have been made for which the authors are grateful.

We are indebted especially to Velores Koll Graham and to Lyle Graham Wimmer for their enthusiastic support and for the great amount of information they have sent to us.

Others we wish to thank are Persis (Peggy) Moss Blachly, Arlene Probst Blackwell, James L. Buckley Jr., Ruth Josephine Graham Butler, Lorna Howard Cline, Margaret Shannon Cross, Rae Graham Darner, Charlotte Graham, Dr. David Tredway Graham, Elvina Erickson Graham, Evarts Ambrose Graham Jr., Kathryn Patterson Graham, the late Wilmer Trumbull Graham, David A. Gwinn, Elizabeth Caldwell Hallam, Alvin K. Krug, the late Nancy Avery Kuhl, Erma Graham McCallum, Sarabelle Talbot O'Daniel, Carol L. Olmstead, Margaret Graham Parker, Martha Paton, Marsha Hoffman Rising, Bernice Vitosh Ruyle, Vivian Cooper Shannon, Raymond Rodell Simpson Jr., James A. Smith, and Dellawayne Gleghorn Watson.

We are also indebted to the genealogists with whom we worked, chiefly Brent H. Holcomb of South Carolina and Frances T. Fox of Kentucky. Others have been Elmer 0. Parker, Barbara Langdon, and Mary Boulware of South Carolina, Margaret Mason of Kentucky, Audrey Gilbert of Ohio, Ethel Trego of Illinois, Wilma Symonds of Iowa, Martin W. Beerman, of Nebraska, and Pat Manusov of California.

Finally, we wish to thank the many librarians and clerks who have been generous with their time and assistance.

# CONTENTS

Preface .................................................... i

Introduction ........................................... 1

  1. The Scottish Background ........................ 1

  2. The Ulster Years ................................ 7

  3. The Rev. William Martin and the Migration to America.    14

  4. South Carolina    19

  5. The Revolutionary Period in the Carolina Backcountry    29

  6. Early Spelling Variants of the Name Graham    34

First Generation    61

Second Generation    65

Third Generation    95

Fourth Generation    236

Fifth Generation    304

Sixth Generation    396

Seventh Generation    459

Eighth Generation    492

Notes    509

Bibliography    542

Index    557

# APPENDICES

**Family of John Paul Jones** .................................................... 623

**Descendants of Andrew Graham**                  626

**Descendants of Jean Graham and Samuel Adams**     637

**Descendants of Elizabeth Graham Gleghorn**         644

**Descendants of Alexander Chestnut**               647

**Emigration Led by Rev. William Martin in 1772**     655

**Jennet Graham Mills**                             659

**Notes to Mills**                                   665

**Descendants of John Popham**                       670

**Children of John Stevenson & Mary Coulter**         678

**Descendants of William Gartin**                    682

**Descendants of David Graham (1788-1844)**          702

# INTRODUCTION

Although the authors have made no attempt to trace the Grahams of the present study to their Scottish roots, certain traditions concerning the origin of the Graham clan may be mentioned. One doubtful tradition is that early in the fifth century, A.D., the first known Graham, called *Graym, Gramus,* or *Graem,* breached the Roman wall between England and Scotland, and the wall at that spot became known as "Graem's Dyke." The reason this story is doubtful is that Graem, if he existed at all, would probably have been a Pict or a Celt, and the Grahams most likely were Anglo-Saxon or possibly Danish. To be sure, the etymology of the name has been the subject of fanciful conjecture by those who have sought a Celtic connection. They have pointed to a parallel with the Gaelic gruamach, `sullen,' `morose,' `gloomy.' But others, more logically though still fancifully, have seen a parallel with the Anglo-Saxon grim or gram, `furious,' `fierce,' `angry,' passionate.' In mundane fact, the name probably means `home of Gray' which is purely Anglo-Saxon, unromantic, and utilitarian.[1]

The first Graham to come to prominence was William de Graham, a name suggesting a Norman origin. In 1128 William witnessed the Charter of the Abbey of Holyrood by Scotland's King David I, and the king awarded him lands at Dalkeith. In 1237 Sir David Graham of Dalkeith was awarded land near Montrose on the North Sea, and almost a century later, in 1325, his descendant, also named David, was created the Lord of Montrose. Gradually these Montrose Grahams became dominant. In 1504 the then clan chief, William Lord Graham, was created the Earl of Montrose, and in 1612 James, the fifth Earl, became the Duke of Montrose. From him is descended the present Duke of Montrose who is also the chief of the Clan Graham.[2]

But not all present-day Grahams are descended from the Grahams of Montrose. Other branches of the Graham family during the late middle ages were located at Stirling, Menteith, Dundee, and on the Esk River which flows into Cumberland, England's border county. Grahams also lived elsewhere, and although there is a tradition that the Grahams in the present study are descended from the Grahams of Montrose, no proof of that tradition is known. The Grahams in the present study could have been descended from any of the several branches.

## 1. The Scottish Background

By the late middle ages, the people of Scotland consisted of two main ethnic groups, the Highland and the Lowland Scots, who had certain traits in common but who differed from each other in language, blood, and social structure. The Highland Scots, living in the mountainous Northwest, were a mixture of Celtic Scot, Irish, and Pict, and the language they spoke was Gaelic. Their society was based mainly on the clan system, modified by feudalism, in

## Introduction Page No. 2

which they gave loyalty to their clan chiefs. The highlands had few towns and almost no industries, but great families ruled there among which were those named Campbell, Cameron, Fraser, MacPherson, MacDonald, Mackay, MacLeod, Mackenzie, MacGregor, and Macrae. These were the people who were largely responsible for the colorful usages associated with the Scots--the bagpipe and the tartan. These people were also uncouth and ferocious compared with the Lowlanders, and they often carried on extensive clan feuds in addition to embarking on frequent plundering, murderous raids into the lowlands. To the Lowland Scots they were lawless, savage, uncivilized, and contemptible, although it should be noted that the Lowland and Highland Scots differed in pugnacity only by degree.[3]

They differed more markedly in other ways. For one thing, the Lowland Scots were mainly Anglo-Saxon, and they retained their Anglo-Saxon tongue. For another, their social structure was feudal, not clan-based.. Allegiance was nominally given to the king (although he usually had to take it by force) who granted land to the nobility. Equal in rank to the nobles were the clergy who also were often more wealthy and powerful. Further, a few free merchants lived in the towns, a few skilled workmen plied their trades, and other social gradations existed down to the lowest peasants. But in ancient times the Lowlanders had been conquered by the Highlanders, and before they were driven back they left with the Lowlanders a profound sense of allegiance to the clan. Thus, kinship was very important in the lowlands even though the social structure was feudal, and among the great families there were those named Armstrong, Johnstone, Kerr, Maxwell, Stewart (Stuart), Douglas, Scott, Wallace, Elliott, Hamilton, and Graham. Another inheritance from the Highlanders was their inclination to make war. Thus, also, the Lowlanders fought not only with the Highlanders and among themselves but also with the English on the border, and if the Lowlanders regarded the Highlanders as savage, the English regarded all the Scots as barbaric.[4]

The English had good reasons for their assessment: squalor was everywhere, lawlessness abounded, and the kings seemed unable to control their unruly nobles. For example, when King Robert III died in 1406 (born c. 1340) he was succeeded by his twelve-year-old son James I (1394-1437) whose uncle, Robert Stuart, immediately spirited the boy out of the country to keep him safe from the plotting factions. Returning to Scotland in 1424, James ruthlessly set about restraining the nobles by imprisoning many, executing others, and confiscating their lands. Retaliation was therefore in order, and Sir Robert Graham of Stirling plotted with two members of the Stuart clan to murder the king who had gone with his court to a monastery at Perth to spend Christmas. Sir Robert Graham together with a Thomas Chambers and Sir John Hall and his brother gained entry to the monastery. Hearing the noise they made, the king hid in a vault but was soon discovered by the Halls who, however, were overpowered by the king. Sir Robert Graham then entered the vault and

## Introduction Page No. 3

mortally wounded the monarch. The Halls stabbed him repeatedly. Within six weeks the murderers were caught, viciously tortured, and executed. It is said that before he was allowed to die, Robert Graham was forced to watch his son being disemboweled.[5]

James I was succeeded by his son James II (1430-1460) who also being only a boy was protected by members of the Douglas family. By 1452, James II had grown to manhood and resolved upon a firm rule, but he was displeased by certain bonds which the Earl of Douglas had made with the Earls of Crawford and Ross. Therefore, James called Douglas to the castle at Stirling and ordered him to break the bonds. Douglas refused, so the king stabbed him.. The attending nobles then fell upon Douglas and killed him. Civil War broke out, and the king's forces marched upon Douglas's land, burning and destroying everything within reach. Douglas's title and land, being forfeited to the crown, were conferred upon the Earl of Angus.[6]

The above instances of violence were not rare; they constituted a way of life in Scotland and continued until modern times. James III (1452-1488) was eventually killed by plotting nobles. James IV (1473-1513) invaded England and was killed at the battle of Flodden as were most of his followers. James V (1512-1542) also waged war against England, was routed with his army at Solway Moss, and died soon after. His daughter, Mary Queen of Scots (1542-1587), was an infant when he died and was sent by her mother to France where she was reared. When she returned in 1561, the court was in great turmoil, and the nobles forced her to abdicate in 1567. She fled to England where, because of her plotting, Queen Elizabeth I (1533-1603) eventually had her executed. Nonetheless, Elizabeth declared her son, James VI (1566-1625), heir to the throne of England which he assumed as James I of England when Elizabeth died. He also determined to end the warfare in Scotland particularly on the English border where among the great families who lived and marauded there were the Grahams of Esk bordering Cumberland. These Grahams had settled in that fertile country in about 1300 and by 1550 were the largest clan in the area. By 1552 they held thirteen border towers and could muster five hundred fighting men when they felt it necessary which was often. Naturally, they incurred jealousy among those who coveted their lands, and among those who did so was the English Earl of Lancaster. When James I came to the English throne, Lancaster persuaded him that the Grahams of Esk were the true trouble makers on the border which could be made safe simply by removing them. Accordingly, James ordered his forces to march upon them. Some were hanged, others deported, others impressed into foreign service; in general, they were banished and dispossessed. Nonetheless, some came back, reversing the spelling of their names, and Mahargs or McHargs are said to live in Scotland today.

Because of this continual strife, most of the Scottish people led lives of penury. The mass of the people, who were superstitious and illiterate, lived in

# Introduction Page No. 4

hovels made of stone or turf, chinked with straw, with holes in the roofs instead of chimneys. The floors were bare ground, and fireplaces were in the middle while ox hides formed the doors. Cattle were kept in the huts with the families and were tied to stakes at one end. Sanitary conditions were wholly absent, and disease and epidemics raged. Farming methods were primitive and difficult on the rocky soil, even in the relatively fertile lowlands, and the staple crops, oats and barley, were grown from the poorest of grain. Wheat bread was unknown until modern days. Despite the hardship, the Scots' diet seems to have been adequate during the good years since oats and barley were supplemented by milk, butter, cheese, fish, and a few vegetables, but frequent crop failures and raiding enemy clans meant disaster.[8] Still, there is little evidence to suggest that the people understood the causes of their poverty or even that they were greatly dissatisfied much before about 1525, and if they accepted their lot it may have been that they had never known otherwise. Chiefly, though, they were fiercely proud of their clans and gave unquestioning loyalty to their clan chiefs. The men also served as the chiefs' fighting forces and did their own share of killing, plundering, and cattle theft. As a mark of their general acceptance of their lives, it is instructive to note that Scotland never witnessed a parallel to England's Peasants' Revolt of 1381.

    Dissatisfaction began to grow in the first part of the sixteenth century with the early stirrings of the Protestant Reformation in Scotland. The Roman church had come there in the twelfth and thirteenth centuries and at first did much good work in education and caring for the sick and poor. But gradually, as throughout Europe, the church became corrupt so that by 1500 the Scottish kings and powerful nobles controlled it through appointments to high ecclesiastical offices. Politics ruled, not religious purpose. To cite a few among many examples, three of James V's illegitimate children were endowed with church appointments while they were infants. A member of the Gordon clan with no theological training became the Bishop of Aberdeen, and the Hamiltons acquired the abbeys of Paisley and Arbrouth. Celibacy, if heard of, was ignored: Archibishop Hamilton had three children, Cardinal Beaton had five, and the Prior of Saint Andrew's (later the Bishop of Moray) had ten. Some of the ordinary clergy, though not all, were illiterate and could barely stumble through mass, and some of the nuns, though again not all, were wanton. Indulgences were sold, parishes were empty and neglected, and widows and orphans were bilked of their meager possessions. Further, the church was extremely rich -- it owned more than a third of the total national wealth -- so that it seemed to the populace that the worldly, prosperous clergy strutted, unmoved and uncaring, among the distressed poor. Despite the misery, the church sternly exacted tithes no matter how destitute the lay members.[9] One resentful parishioner, though not destitute, rebelled. He was a fisherman and employed workers. When the church's representative came to collect the man's tithe, he instructed his workmen to throw every tenth fish back into the sea and told the churchman to look for his tithe there. The man was burned at the stake.[10]

Introduction Page No. 5

Throughout this sorry period the truly pious among the clergy and nobility as well as among the growing middle class increasingly protested conditions in the church, and brave priests preached reform from their pulpits. Many of them were executed. But James V was supported by the Catholic hierarchy which thus constituted a mighty bloc in his battles with the nobles; therefore, the king was deaf to Protestant complaints. Not surprisingly, then, it was the opposition by the self-seeking nobles which led to the church's eventual downfall, not the pious alone who effected it. The reasons were political. Historically, Scotland had allied herself with France because of her hatred of England, but during James V's reign the nobles came to see that alliance with Catholic France did little to benefit then while alliance w!th Protestant England could do much. Also, the great wealth which England's Henry VIII (1491-1547) had acquired by confiscating Catholic property was noted with considerable interest.[11] It did not take much persuasion for the worldly nobles to join their pious brothers in support of the Protestant Reformation once they saw the potential gain.

James' successor, Mary Queen of Scots, was only six days old when re died, and her mother, Mary of Lorraine-Guise (1515-1560) sent the baby to France where she was reared. Mary of Guise, acting as regent, continued Scotland's alliance with France and arranged her daughter's marriage to the dauphin, a marriage which angered many Scots. It also angered Henry VIII who had intended to marry his son to Mary Queen of Scots and therefore sent an army in 1545 to lay waste to Edinburgh and its environs. Mary of Guise further continued her husband's policy of suppressing Protestantism, and the resulting upheaval kept Scotland in civil war throughout the regency. The church also continued to burn heretics. One of them was the saintly George Wishart (c. 1513-1546), an effective speaker who preached at various places in Scotland. In time he was captured and turned over to the powerful Cardinal Becton who had him burned at the stake in front of Saint Andrew's. Three months later Wishart's supporters broke into the castle of Saint Andrew's where the cardinal was staying and killed him. The Protestants then took possession of the castle, others joined them, and they withstood the subsequent siege for a year or until French forces arrived with cannons, bombarding the Protestants into submission. Those of good birth were imprisoned; the others were made galley slaves in France which meant that they were jailed with the worst criminals.[12]

At this point the fiery and uncompromising John Knox (c. 1513-1572)[13] appeared on the scene. Knox had been among the Protestants in the castle at Saint Andrew's and was a galley slave for nineteen months. During the siege he began to preach with such effect that the others urged him to assume leadership, but the surrender put a temporary stop to that. After he was released he went to England where he was a royal chaplain and helped prepare The Second Book of Common Prayer. But in 1553 with the succession of the Catholic "Bloody" Mary

(1516-1558) and her ensuing persecutions of the Protestants, Knox fled to Geneva where he came into contact with John Calvin (1509-1564), the leader of the French Protestants. Calvin's teachings affected Knox profoundly. Not only did Calvin reject papal authority as well as that of cardinals and bishops, but also he held that mass and transubstantiation were idolatrous. The only sacraments were baptism and the Lord's Supper, and the only source of divine truth was the Bible. Therefore, everyone was his own bishop or king, and everyone was also obligated to read and know the Bible and teach it to his children. Another of Calvin's teachings was the Doctrine of Predestination in which grace existed but free will did not. God predestined everyone from eternity to be saved or damned, and those who were saved were the Elect, although no one in this life could know of his destiny in the after.[14]

Knox became Calvin's disciple, and when Knox visited Scotland briefly in 1555 and was allowed to preach privately, he preached Calvinism, converting many. He soon returned to Geneva, but he had made so deep an impression that he became the chief adviser to the Scottish Protestant nobles though he was still in exile. In 1557 the lords formed the first covenant by which they made a solemn oath to stand together in defense of their religion, and in 1559 Knox was back in Scotland, preaching impassioned sermons to multitudes. Following his sermons at Perth and Saint Andrew's, mobs destroyed the monasteries. In 1559 France sent troops whereupon England joined Scotland as an ally. The French were defeated, a treaty was made in 1560, and with that treaty Protestantism triumphed in Scotland. Civil war continued throughout the remainder of the sixteenth century and through the Stuart and Cromwell periods in England, and the Presbyterian Church, which is what the reformers wanted, had to fight for its existence until 1688, but by 1560 the country itself was Protestant.[15]

Much which was ugly marked the early Scottish Protestant church. The God about whom the ministers thundered from their pulpits was the vengeful Old Testament one, not the forgiving New. Perceived signs and omens were regarded with superstitious fear, and protracted witch hunts were carried out. Music and art in churches, no matter how sublime, were deemed idolatrous. But politically, Calvinism was revolutionary; so was the Presbyterian form of church government which appeared later. Together, they rejected not only the Roman church but also the English Episcopal one because it was Roman in structure. Calvinism also placed great importance on individual responsibility since all should read the Bible, and Presbyterianism eventually would carry the concept of individual responsibility further. In the future the structure of each congregation would be self-governing: the congregation would call its own ministers and elect its own elders and deacons from among its members, and this importance placed on the individual would inevitably lead to the early stirrings of the idea of equality (although in no sense was the church then democratic and would not be so for several centuries). Finally, Calvinism stressed the need for universal education, the sole purpose of which was to enable everyone to read and understand the scriptures. While this stress on education cannot possibly be construed as an aim to create well-rounded human beings who were conversant on many subjects, it nonetheless opened a way, for the first time in human history, for everyone to acquire an education – indeed, acquiring an education was everyone's stern duty.

What say be said, then, about the mass of the Scots at this time? First, they had few worldly goods and lived in squalor; second, they were accustomed to violence and warfare and fought often for their beliefs and for what they wanted; third, they hated both the Roman Catholic Church and the Church of England; and fourth, their grim religion made them dour, joyless, and indifferent to beauty. But it should be added that the Scots' religion gave them a belief in individual responsibility and an awareness of the importance of education. These were the two great positive concepts which they carried with them when they migrated first to Ulster, then to America.

## 2. The Ulster Years

In the late middle ages and early modern times, the Irish were even more backward and poverty-ridden than the Highland Scots. England had conquered the island without any great difficulty in the Twelfth Century when the Pope granted to Henry II of England (1133-1189) the "Lordship of Ireland", and what his forces found there was hardly more than a group of loosely bound tribal kingdoms consisting of mostly semi-nomadic peoples. Tribal warfare kept the country politically unstable, manufacturing was non-existent, little trade was carried on and that only in a few coastal settlements, and intellectual developments elsewhere in Europe were unknown. The Christian church had been established in Ireland by the fifth century, and until the Viking invasions, beginning in the eighth century, the Irish monks led Europe in learning and missionary activity. By the time of Henry II, however, the Irish church had become overlaid with Celtic ways. Henry, who was a Norman and granted his fellow Normans land in Ireland, attempted to bring the Irish church more in conformity with the church in the rest of Europe. But his reforms were only partially successful (although many Normans stayed and intermarried with the native Irish), and in time the church became as corrupt as it was everywhere else before the Reformation. When the threat of Reformation did arise, however, the newly formed order of Jesuits targeted Ireland especially as a country to be saved for the church. Accordingly, they poured in by the dozens, earnestly teaching, giving succor to the poor, and preaching to the Irish in their own tongue. The Jesuits kept the Irish in the Catholic fold. They also gave the Irish a sense of nationalism which they had hitherto not possessed, and because of the Jesuits' zealous work, Irish nationalism became inextricably mixed with Catholicism. Thus, by the mid-sixteenth century to be Irish meant to be Catholic. Not only was England the hated foe, but also Protestantism. What had once been the Irish versus the English now became Ireland and Catholicism versus England and Protestantism, and during the sixteenth century, as the English monarchs increasingly sought to impose the Church of England upon Ireland, the Irish resisted with increasing violence as they also resisted English secular impositions. The Irish "problem", therefore, became one of considerable worry in the English court.[16]

At the time, Ireland was divided into four provinces: Connaught in the Northwest, Munster in the Southwest, Leinster in the Southeast, and Ulster in the Northeast. All the provinces showed unrest by the late sixteenth century which meant that the English had to keep a standing army there (who, incidentally, lived off the Irish thus angering them further). But the greatest troublemaker and the most Gaelic was Ulster which lay just a few miles across the North Channel from Scotland. Although Ulster did have a substantial Scottish coastal settlement brought in by the MacDonnell clan, it was the stronghold of several powerful and rebellious Irish leaders the chief of whom were the Earls of Tyrone and Tyrconnell. They initiated one uprising after another, and Queen Elizabeth I (1533-1603; ruled 1558-1603) came to see that Ulster was the main obstacle to the pacification of the rest of Ireland. In the 1570's Elizabeth tried to plant an English colony in Northeast Ulster, but the attempt failed largely because not enough settlers could be found. Then in 1595 Hugh O'Neill, the Earl of Tyrone, marshaled his men and in 1598 won a great victory at the battle of Yellow Ford. The rebellion spread throughout the country, and in September 1601 four thousand Spanish troops arrived as Irish allies. The English under Lord Mountjoy soon routed the Spanish and turned their fury back onto the Irish, destroying crops, homes, and livestock as well as fighting in the fields. The Irish finally surrendered a little more than a year later, December 1602. They were unaware that Elizabeth was mortally ill, and when O'Neill made his "abject submission" to the English crown on 30 March 1603, Mountjoy did not tell him that she had died six days earlier. Later O'Neill regretted not having held out longer, but it is doubtful that the outcome would have been different.[17]

Nonetheless, the Earls of Tyrone and Tyrconnell were allowed to retain their lands though otherwise stripped of power, and an uneasy period of sporadic lawlessness ensued. Soon after 1603 England did establish courts, counties, and towns in Ulster which was the most backward of the four provinces from the English point of view. The counties were Antrim, Down, Armagh, Monaghan, Cavan, Fermanagh, Tyrone, Donegal, and Coleraine (later renamed Londonderry); some of the newly established towns were Belfast, Bangor, Newry, Charlemont, Dungannon, and Strabane. But the Irish chiefs maintained large groups of armed followers with the result that much plundering and banditry occurred. Inevitably, the Earls of Tyrone and Tyrconnell were suspected of formenting the unrest, perhaps unjustly, and when they received a summons to London in August of 1607 they determined to flee

## Introduction Page No. 9

the country which they did on 3 September 1607, taking many supporters with them, never to return. It was this "flight of the earls" which discouraged the Irish rebels The province was now open for settlement.[18]

In 1610 the new King of England, James I (1566-1625), adopted the idea of a "plantation" of settlers in Ulster. The land was to be divided into tracts of 1,000, 1,500, or 2,000 acres to be granted to Scottish English Protestants known as "undertakers" who would let the land to tenants. The undertakers were to live on their land and rent only to Protestant settlers; Catholics were specifically excluded. The Catholics who remained in Ulster were to be transported to less desirable ares of the province, and a law was passed forbidding the English and Irish to intermarry. Since the counties of Antrim and Down already had large Protestant populations, and Monaghan posed no threat for other reasons, the counties to be planted were the remaining six: Tyrone, Londonderry, Fermanagh, Armagh, Cavan, and Donegal. The plan was immediately successful. Ulster had been prostrated by years of bitter warfare, many areas being depopulated, so that the plantation scheme went forward almost without hindrance. Lowland Scots and Northern English poured into the province, attracted by the promise of cheap land and wishing also to escape the poverty prevailing in the larger island. Within a comparatively short time, the land was transformed into thriving farming communities and would soon support industried in wool and linen. Also, a period of peace ensued after the flight of the earls, and Ulster's growing prosperity was relatively unhampered by civil strife for more than thirty years.[19]

But during this period, Irish anger smoldered so that what seemed to be a sudden flareup in the fall of 1641 was in fact the result of decades of growing fury. In late October 1641 the Irish seized Newry, Charlemont, Dungannon, Lisburn, and other towns in Ulster. A long war thus began, and in it the Irish were vicious beyond anything the Scots had hitherto witnessed. Those Protestants who could not reach safety were massacred; those who did find haven told horrifying tales of atrocities. In the next few years the Irish initiative slowed, the Protestants held and even made headway, but the fighting continued because the Protestants received little help from England which was engaged in its own civil war. Finally, in 1649 Oliver Cromwell (1599-1658) came with his legions who with cold efficiency committed fresh atrocities and eventually quelled the rebellion. Cromwell then dictated the following policies: the Irish, particularly those in the towns, were to be transported to Connaught in Northwest Ireland; a massive effort was to be made to plant Ulster and Leinster with more Protestants; and a resolute attempt would be undertaken to eradicate Catholicism entirely. In the 1650's these orders were carried out to a large extent. Thousands of Catholics were transported, thousands of Protestants were brought in, and the few remaining Catholic churches were destroyed, their priests declared outlaws. Peace was again established but at a frightful price, and although the Catholics had great hopes when the monarchy was restored in

1660, their expectations came to nothing. In the meantime, the Protestants' abhorrence of Irish Catholics became almost palpable. It is not difficult to discern in these seventeenth-century events the origins of the twentieth-century strife in Northern Ireland.[20]

The political turmoil more or less quieted after 1660, remaining so throughout the rest of the seventeenth century and through most of the eighteenth. Also, the terrible restrictions against the Catholics lessened under the wise policies of William III (1650-1702; ruled 1688-1702). By 1700 Catholic churches and schools were tolerated, priests fulfilled their duties, and Catholic lawyers practiced in the courts. But other forces were at work to cause dissatisfaction, not among the Catholics, but among the Presbyterians. It should be noted that the Presbyterians never constituted a majority in Ulster; in fact, by 1715 they amounted to only about one-third of the total population. Another third were Anglicans, and the remainder, despite Cromwell's efforts, were Catholics. But the Anglicans were scattered throughout the province while the Presbyterians were concentrated near the port cities of Belfast, Londonderry, Portrush, and Larne. Because of this concentration, they controlled their own civic affairs as well as their own religious activities, and their churches were strong. By 1688 they had five presbyteries with more than eighty ministers and about one hundred congregations. As the civil unrest quieted at the end of the seventeenth century, however, the High Church, which had the strong support of Queen Anne (1665-1714; ruled 1702-1714), turned its attention to eliminating the dissenters. Queen Anne's position was not unusual; most European rulers thought it wise for all their subjects to worship in the same way, but it was a matter of considerable resentment to the Presbyterians who regarded themselves as good citizens.[21]

In 1703 the High Church succeeded in getting parliament to pass the odious "Test Act" by which all holders of office in Ireland were required to take the communion of the established church. Theoretically aimed at Catholics, this act was soon used by the Anglicans against the Presbyterians. City aldermen in Ulster's Presbyterian areas were turned out, usually to be replaced by incompetents, and military commissions were denied. Other repressive acts followed: Presbyterians were not allowed to teach in schools; their doctors and lawyers were not allowed to practice; their ministers were banished, and the marriages and baptisms which they had performed were declared illegal.. Many men were prosecuted for "cohabiting" with their wives, while their children were called bastards. Further galling was that the Presbyterians were forced to pay tithes to support the Anglican clergy, and even more embittering was the comparative leniency with which the Catholics were treated during Queen Anne's time. Anglicans seemed to regard Catholics as wayward brethren whereas Presbyterians were heretics. Fortunately for the Presbyterians, however, the repression did not last long. After the more lenient Hanovers came to the throne in 1714, the Test Act was seldom enforced. By the time of George II

(1683-1760; ruled 1727-1760), Presbyterian marriages were declared legal, and by 1755 Presbyterians could again hold commissions. But not until 1782 was the act, itself, repealed – a continuing irritation to the Ulster Scots. [22]

The Ulster Scots had subtly changed by this time. For one thing, they were no longer entirely Scottish; they were a new ethnic group comprised not only of Scots but also of Northern English, Welsh, and French Huguenots who had fled to Ireland after the Edict of Nantes was revoked in 1685. The Ulster Presbyterians had also changed in other ways. They now thought of Ireland as their home, not Scotland, and when they later migrated to America it was "swate ould Ireland" they recalled, not Scotland's bonnie braes. Then, too, their religion had hardened, due as much to their convictions as to the threat posed by Anglicans; and their church, which was of vital importance, became the absolute arbiter of human conduct. Their hatred of Catholics had intensified with the intermittent wars, and the atrocities turned the Ulsterites into cold-blooded fighters. Finally, the economic events of the eighteenth century completed the formation of this new race who in America came to be known as the Scotch-Irish. For, it was England's policy in handling Ireland's economy which forced thousands to emigrate to the new world. At the time the policy was standard toward the colonies; now it seems astonishingly short-sighted.[23]

Ireland's greatest problem in the eighteenth century was lack of capital, a problem which England fostered by crippling Irish industries and taking wealth out of the country without replacing it. For example, during the slow recovery after the seventeenth-century wars, Ireland developed an excellent woolen industry, the only industry of any consequence which Ireland then had, but since it competed with England's woolen industry, it was destroyed. In 1699 the British parliament enacted a law prohibiting Ireland from exporting wool to any country but England, thus ensuring that the British manufacturers could buy the wool low and sell it abroad high. By 1710 the Irish woolen industry was a memory. Later Ireland established a brewing industry which relied upon imported hops; therefore, England enacted a series of laws preventing the Irish from buying hops from anyone but England, and the prices they charged ruined the Irish breweries. A growing glass industry was similarly destroyed, as was one in hemp, and there was even talk of prohibiting fisheries along the Irish coast except in British made vessels. The only industry which was allowed to thrive was one in linen manufacturing, but even that was hampered when England declared that Ireland could export only white and brown linens; colored linens were forbidden. Also, the restrictions against other industries led to an unhealthy reliance upon linen, especially in Ulster where most of the linen manufacturing took place. Further, the price of linen increased only moderately during the eighteenth century while rents and other costs soared.[24]

Another aspect of England's economic policy in Ireland was the method of leasing land. When the Scottish and English tenants migrated to Ulster they found mostly wilderness which they cleared and cultivated. But the terms of the leases were usually for only a few years, and as the leases came to an end the landlords doubled or even tripled the rents and continued doing so as subsequent leases expired. On the Stewart lands in County Down, for example, the rents increased by more than 600% between 1720 and 1770. Also, some of King James's conditions for settlement--that the land promoters live on the land and rent only to Protestants--were abandoned by the eighteenth century, and not only were Catholics allowed to rent land but also much of it was owned by absentee English landlords who usually lived in London, never having seen their Irish property. Thus, a great amount of money which might have been turned back into the Irish economy instead flowed out. Ulster was less troubled by absenteeism than were other parts of Ireland, but it had another problem in the unscrupulous land agents who were hired by the landlords to collect the rents. Of course, these land agents charged more than they had been authorized to do and pocketed the difference. Later a system arose whereby the tenants had to submit written bids to the land agents and could bid only once, and because the tenants feared losing the land on which they had lived for many years they had to bid high. Their fears were compounded by the fact that Catholic families sometimes banded together to bid on the land, and by pooling their capital they could bid higher than the Protestants could. Also, a tendency grew for the landlords to lease their land in large blocs. These blocs were then sub-leased which, in turn, were broken into further sub-leases and so on until as many as five different leases were involved. Each of the middlemen took his share in the transactions. Finally, added to these problems were frequent inflation, low wages, and natural disasters such as crop failures. When the crops failed, famine usually resulted because the rack-renters kept the tenants at a hand-to-mouth existence.[25]

    Nonetheless, in the early and middle years of the eighteenth century Ulster had certain advantages which the other provinces lacked. One was that the linen industry was centered there thus providing an amount of money in circulation. This, in turn, led to a small but rising middle class, non-existent elsewhere in Ireland, and this class sent their sons to Scottish universities to be trained as doctors and ministers. Another advantage was the "Ulster Custom" which was never written as a statute but was nevertheless observed. According to this custom a tenant was recognized as having certain rights of ownership. He could sell his rights, subject to the landlord's approval, and if a landlord wished to evict a tenant he had to pay the tenant at the going rate of the land. Later the tendencies of landlords to lease their lands in blocs nullified the custom, but at the time it did lead to certain side benefits. First, it was to the interest of the tenant to improve his land in order to be able to sell his rights at a higher price, and most did improve their land. Travelers to Ulster almost always commented on its prosperous appearance. A second benefit was that the Ulster Custom gave the tenant a certain sense of self-reliance and pride of place as illustrated by one noteworthy example: during the Seven Years War between England and France

(1756-63), the French landed a force on the coast of County Antrim in 1760, and the speed with which thousands of armed Ulstermen spontaneously arose to protect Belfast and rout the French was impressive. The French sailed away a week later. But still another benefit, perhaps the most significant, resulted from the Ulster Custom: some tenants could acquire cash if they wished to emigrate to America.[26]

Surprisingly, very little migration from Ulster took place in the seventeenth century and the first years of the eighteenth, but by 1718, when the first leases began to expire, the emigration began in earnest. The great majority of those who migrated were Presbyterians, and the causes of their going were economic, not religious, although religious oppression may have been a secondary motivation during the early periods. Before 1718 the number of those who left was probably less than 1,000, but in 1718-20 about 2,600 went, and in 1725-1729 about 10,500 left. The reasons were clear. Drought and crop failures with resultant famines occurred at the same time the first leases expired with a consequent rise in rents. During the next forty years the emigration continued to act as a barometer of Irish economic lift. Rack-renting, low wages, inflation, drought, crop failures, famine -- all these factors, either singly or in combination, signaled new floods of emigration. It is estimated that during the forty-year period from 1730 to 1770, between 50,000 and 70,000 people migrated.[27]

But the most concentrated period of migration was during the four years of 1771-74 when rack-renting skyrocketed. In County Down renewed leases tripled the rent; in County Londonderry they doubled it. Lord Donegall's estate in County Antrim was a special case. In 1770 he wanted ready cash, so he kept the rents at their former level but assessed fines amounting to £100,000 as compensation. These fines, were three or four times the rent, were far beyond the ability of anyone to pay, and the tenants were evicted or their leases were turned over to middlemen. Many tenants then erupted into violence, forming an outlawed group called the "Hearts of Steel" or the "Steelboys" who slaughtered the landlord's cattle and destroyed the property of the new tenants. The unrest soon spread to other areas of Ulster where new bands, also under the name of "Hearts of Steel", slaughtered cattle, destroyed property, and fought open battles with the troops sent against them. Eventually the rebellion was quelled, resulting in great bitterness on the part of the tenants. But the obvious response of many was to emigrate: 7,700 people sailed from Irish ports in 1771, 9,300 in 1772, 12,300 in 1773, and 8,300 in 1774, a total of 37,600 in all, and when they went they carried with them a hatred of the English which George Washington would come to appreciate.[28]

## 3. The Reverend William Martin and the Migration to America

The Graham family of the present study may have been among the unfortunate tenants on Lord Donegall's estate. The reason it is thought so is that they were probably parishioners of the church at which the Rev. William Martin was the pastor at the Kellswater congregation in County Antrim. Another family belonging to the church were the Stephensons who, according to a story handed down through the generations and recounted by Jean Stephenson, had cousins among Donegall's tenants. The story is as follows: the cousins, whose name was Beck, had not been able to pay their rent, and early in 1772 a land agent came to collect it at the very time Mrs. Beck was giving birth with great difficulty to her first child. Mr. Beck, who was tall, strong, and heavy, picked up the agent and literally threw him out of the house. The agent's neck was broken when he hit the ground. Mrs. Beck and her baby died; Mr. Beck disappeared, and nothing more is known of him. The following Sunday, so the story goes, Reverend Martin gave one of the impassioned sermons for which he was noted. In it he referred with great eloquence to the religious persecutions which their forefathers had endured not only in Ulster but also in Scotland and England in earlier days; he detailed clearly their present economic distress as well as the reasons for it, concluding that their condition would only worsen; and he then proposed that the entire congregation migrate with him to South Carolina.[29] Whether or not Ms. Stephenson's family story is correct cannot be ascertained as she comments, but it does furnish evidence that the Grahams may have been among the many families who were tenants of Lord Donegall, and, if so, they had overwhelming economic reasons for emigrating.

The Rev. William Martin was an unusual man. Born on 16 May 1729 near Ballykelly, County Londonderry, he was the son of a prosperous merchant named David Martin. David Martin, who was a pious Covenanter, sent his son to the University of Glasgow from which young William was graduated in 1753. He then studied theology under the Rev. John McMillan and was licensed in Scotland by the Reformed Presbyterians on 10 October 1756. On 13 July 1757 he was ordained at Vow on the lower Bann River in County Antrim and installed as pastor of societies which were called Ballymoney although many of them were far from the town of that name. The presbytery was large in area and included congregations south as well as north of Lough Neagh, so in 1760 the societies were divided into two at the Bann which flows both north and south of Lough Neagh. Martin, who had a choice, picked the Kellswater congregation in the eastern part and lived for many years at Bangor which is located almost at the mouth of Belfast Lough on its south side.[30] He soon became active in Covenanter church government, officiating at several ordinations and performing other duties. But he was thoroughly aware of economic conditions and by 1772 had probably been thinking of migrating to America for some time. Also, he received a call from a group in South Carolina, and according to tradition an "incident" occurred which led him to urge his entire congregation to accompany him. Whether or not the incident had to do with Ms. Stephenson's story about the Becks is not known. What is known is that most of Martin's congregation, plus members of other Presbyterian congregations in the area, did go, and Martin acted as an agent for one of the ships which transported the parishioners.[31]

Even the average passage to America was an ordeal which was not to be undertaken lightly. The usual length of time for the voyage was about seven to nine weeks, and a period of calm on the ocean could increase the time considerably, resulting in reduced rations. The rations, themselves, generally seem to have been adequate, but they were monotonous at best. One ship owner advertised in 1775 that the provisions for each "full" fare per week were six pounds of beef, six pounds of bread or oatmeal, one pound of butter or a pint of treacle or molasses, and fourteen quarts of water. "Half" fare (that is, provisions for children between two and twelve years old) meant half these amounts. Sometimes potatoes were included, and rum was sold on board. Added to the discomfort resulting from this diet were overcrowding and cramped quarters. Since it was to the captain's interest to transport as many people as he could, the usual practice was to double them in the berths whenever possible. Often about twelve people occupied every seven berths, the standard measurements of which were five feet ten inches long by eighteen inches wide. Also, the ships had two and sometimes three tiers of berths, and the space between them was usually less than two feet. The height between the decks was seldom more than five feet, and there were no portholes. During bad weather the passengers had to stay in these quarters for days or even weeks at a time so that frequent sickness and occasional deaths resulted.[32] None but the desperate would have undertaken such an ordeal, which is a measure of the desperation Reverend Martin's parishioners must have felt.

Five ships had to be engaged to transport Martin's party which included about 1,100 people. (The exact number of people is not known; see below.) The ships sailed at different times from different ports, and, as was customary, the times of sailing were delayed for various reasons. In the order of their departure, these ships were the *James and Mary*, *Lord Dunluce*, *Pennsylvania Farmer* (the ship on which the Grahams sailed), *Hopewell*, and *Free Mason*.

*James and Mary*, 200 tons, was first advertised to sail on 15 April 1772. The time of departure was later changed to 10 July then 8 August; finally, it sailed from Larne on 25 August and arrived at Charleston on 16 October. Smallpox broke out during the passage, and five children died. Therefore, upon arrival the ship was quarantined for more than seven weeks near Sullivan's Island.[33]

*Lord Dunluce*, 400 tons, was first advertised to sail on 15 August 1772. Later the departure time was changed to 20 September, then 22 September; it finally sailed from Larne on 4 October, arriving at Charleston on 20 December. This was the ship on which Martin sailed and for which he was one of the agents. Smallpox also broke out on this ship, and one man plus several children died. The ship was quarantined for only fifteen days, however, because the captain "made application to a friend."[34]

*Pennsylvania Farmer*, 350 tons, was first advertised to sail to Philadelphia on 20 September 1772. Later the destination was changed to Charleston. On 11 September the sailing time was postponed until 6 October to allow the farmers to sell their crops. It was again postponed to 10 October and finally sailed from Belfast on 16 October, arriving at Charleston on 19 December 1772. This was the only one of the five ships which advertised single berths. Passengers in addition to the Grahams included those named McDill, McKee, Mebin (Maben), McCollough, Wiley, and Brown.[35]

*Hopewell*, 250 tons, was first advertised to sail on 15 August 1772. The date was postponed to 15 September then to 1 October and 5 October. The ship finally sailed from Belfast on 19 October and arrived at Charleston on 23 December, "all in perfect health."[36]

*Free Mason*, 250 tons, was first advertised to sail on 20 August 1772. This was later changed to 1 September, 10 September, and 20 September. Finally, it sailed from Newry on 27 October and arrived at Charleston on 22 December. In their advertisement the agents said this ship was "remarkably lofty between decks."[37]

Presumably, as each group arrived in Charleston they waited for the others, although where so large a group lodged is an interesting question which cannot be answered. South Carolina had a land grant policy, and on 6 January 1773 most of the heads of families and single adults in Martin's party went together before South Carolina's General Assembly to request land. Thus, an invaluable listing of their names exists in South Carolina's records. They were listed according to the ships on which they had sailed, and each list began with the names of those few who could pay the fees of about £5 per hundred acres followed by the names of those who could not pay (called "poor persons"). Most could not pay. The policy was to give warrants for one hundred acres to every unmarried adult man and woman and one hundred acres to every married man plus fifty acres apiece for each member of his household, including servants. It should be emphasized, however, that these lists did not constitute a complete listing of every family in Martin's party; also, estimating the number of people in it simply by noting the amount of acreage warranted to each applicant is not possible. First, not every adult in the group who was eligible for land went before the South Carolina General Assembly to request it. Some had bought their

land before migrating, others after. Second, in some cases the men who
engaged in certain service occupations such as that of smiths did not
take up all the land to which they were entitled because they had no
need for it. Therefore, the amount of acreage in their warrants did
not indicate the number of people in their households.[38] Nonetheless,
it can probably be said with fair accuracy that the number of people in
Martin's group amounted to about 1,100, and they must have expected to
settle together as a community.

Unfortunately, that was not to be. Perhaps because of the great
number of people in this group, they did not all receive warrants for
land in the same area. They were simply split up. The South Carolina
authorities had been having considerable difficulty with the backcountry Scotch-Irish who already lived in the province, and the authorities
may have deemed it prudent to separate this large new group. Whatever
the reasons, Martin's people were scattered all over South Carolina, a
disappointment to them. Those who had some money bought land in the
areas where they wished to live, but others had no choice so the group
as such no longer existed.[39]

Other concerns soon took their attention, however, the first of
which was to acquire final title to their land. The method of acquisition was in three stages. (1) The man or woman had to go before the
South Carolina General Assembly to apply to the governor and council
for a warrant. As noted above, the members of Martin's party completed
this step on 6 January 1773. (2) The applicant then took his warrant
to the surveyor general who ordered a survey of the land available.
The survey usually took place within a few months, and when the plat
was finally made it was certified by the surveyor general. Two copies
were made of the plat. One remained with the surveyor general; the
other was sent to the secretary of the province. (3) The secretary
then prepared the final grant which the governor eventually signed in
the presence of the council.[40]

Four Grahams received warrants. David Graham, who was able to pay
the fees, applied for four hundred acres. His three oldest children,
Andrew, Jean, and Matthew, who could not pay, received warrants for one
hundred acres apiece which meant they were single adults. The Grahams'
warrants were for land in what was later southeast Chester County, and
among others in the group whose warrants were for land in the same area
were those named Jamieson, Cherry, McQuiston, Fairy, Maben, Strong,
Wiley, Brown, McCreight, Harbison, and Stinson (Stevenson)--some of
which names appear later in this study. The Rev. William Martin's
warrant was also for land in Chester County.

At this point an account of Martin's subsequent career should be
given.[41] He acquired four hundred acres on his warrant and later
bought a square mile on which he built a stone house. He also preached
at various places and was invited to supply a congregation called
Catholic Presbyterian Church which was located about fifteen miles

southeast of the town of Chester. (By that time Presbyterians had divided into several groups such as the Reformed, Associates, Burgers, and others, and Catholic Presbyterian Church was named so because its founders intended that all Presbyterians should be able to worship there.)[42] But Martin was a firm member of the Reformed Presbyterians, also called Covenanters, and it had been the Covenanters in the area who had extended the call to him while he was still in Ireland. Therefore, in 1774 Martin and the other Covenanters withdrew from Catholic and built a meeting house about two miles east. Apparently, however, Martin had a drinking problem which was to haunt him all his life. The first we hear of it was in 1777 when his congregation dismissed him for intemperance. Still, he was a powerful speaker and had many supporters who soon built him a new church nearby.

The Revolutionary War broke out in 1775, and increasing bitterness arose between the Patriots and Loyalists in the area, but not until the fall of Charleston in May 1780 and the British invasion of the backcountry did the area become a battlefield. In June 1780 Martin preached another of his impassioned sermons, and immediately after the service the men in his congregation formed two companies who joined the American forces. The British then burned the Covenanter meeting house and took Martin prisoner while he was in the act of preparing a second sermon urging resistance to England. He was taken to Camden then to Winnsboro to be tried before Lord Cornwallis who ordered that Martin be released. Perhaps a condition of his release was that he not return to his former area which in any case was extremely dangerous for both sides. Whatever his reasons for not going back, he went to Mecklenburg County, North Carolina, where he remained until the British surrendered at Yorktown. He then returned to present Chester County and again took charge of Catholic Presbyterian Church.

In 1784 the Reformed and Associate Presbyterians united under the name of The Associate Reformed Presbyterian Church, but Martin refused to go in with them and remained a Covenanter. A year later he was dismissed from Catholic, again on a charge of drunkenness, although there were some who claimed the real reason for his dismissal was his refusal to join the Associate Reformed Presbyterians. In fact, the debate over his dismissal continued for many years after he died. It was often pointed out that drinking liquor was a common practice at the time and was even considered healthful, while offering it to a visiting clergyman was a gesture of courtesy. Many of Martin's contemporaries said they had never seen him drunk. Even so, the official reason for Martin's dismissal was "intemperance." At any rate, he did not suffer long from this rebuff. He was in demand as a speaker and preached at schools, meeting houses, and homes not only in present Chester County but also in present Fairfield, Lancaster, and Abbeville Counties, even in North Carolina and in Georgia. Also, it is said that his congregation built him another church east of the one which the British had destroyed. But the charge of drunkenness did not die. In 1793 Martin became part of a three-man committee to supervise the Reformed Presby-

terian Church in America. The other two men, the Rev. James McGarragh,
recently from Ireland, and the Rev. William King, recently from Scotland, were considerably younger than Martin who, therefore, probably
resented their suggestions. Also, all three men held firm opinions.
Rancor resulted, and Martin withdrew from the committee just as the
other two men were preparing charges against him. Later McGarragh,
himself, became intemperate and was suspended in 1795; King died in
1798, so Martin was left alone for a time. In 1798, however, the
Reformed Presbytery was reorganized at Philadelphia, and ministers were
sent to South Carolina to put the church affairs in order. Eventually
seven charges were brought against Martin, including drunkenness and
slave holding, and he was removed from ministerial office on 1 March
1801. Still, he continued preaching until shortly before his death.
His stone house was destroyed in a fire in 1804, so he moved to a log
cabin nearby. On 25 October 1806 he died of a fever which resulted
after he fell off a horse. He was buried near his cabin.

He had been married three times. He first married in Ireland Mary
___ who died perhaps about 1770 or earlier. In about 1771, also in
Ireland, he married Jennet Cherry who gave Martin his only child,
Nancy, who married John McCaw of York County, South Carolina, and had
at least one child of her own. (Although Nancy died before her father
wrote his will on 3 June 1805, he bequeathed money to her in it--a
comment on the state of his mental health.) Martin's third wife, whom
he probably married in South Carolina, was Susannah Boggs, described in
Martin's will as "a woman who calls herself my wife . . . whom I came
unto certain promises to and she to me as husband and wife before
witnesses. . . ."[43] Probably, as Mary Wylie Strange commented, this
testy description constituted the words of an old man who was broken in
body and mind. But in his younger days, as William Melancthon Glasgow
earlier wrote, Martin had been "a large, fine-looking man, a proficient
scholar, an eloquent preacher, and an able divine."[44]

### 4. South Carolina

When the Grahams and the others of Martin's group arrived in what
later became Chester County, two disturbing issues greeted them. The
first concerned the character and manner of the Scotch-Irish already
there; the second was the political situation and the animosity with
which these backcountry people regarded the authorities and the wealthy
plantation owners in the coastal regions.

The Scotch-Irish in what was later Chester County were mostly
descendants of those who had migrated down the frontier from Pennsylvania. In 1718 as the Ulster Presbyterians first began to sail for
America in considerable numbers, they went initially to New England
where they soon learned they were not welcome. Nor did they wish to
remain when they discovered that a requirement for owning property was

membership in the Congregational Church. Most of the Scotch-Irish soon left, although some did establish settlements in Maine, Vermont, and western Massachusetts. Other Ulster immigrants went to New York, Maryland, and South Carolina, but after 1720 most of them sailed directly to Philadelphia or to New Castle, Delaware, and from there traveled overland to Pennsylvania. The reason they went to Pennsylvania was not only that the colony had a policy of religious toleration, but also that it had some of the most fertile and accessible land in America. As soon as possible after arriving, the immigrants headed for the frontier where the available land was located and where they usually became squatters since few could pay for their land at first. Many were indentured servants, however, and had to remain near the coast in order to fulfill the terms of their contracts, but they, too, generally headed west when they were free. By 1750 the Scotch-Irish lived all along the Pennsylvania frontier and had learned to be fiercely independent and self-reliant. They also were fierce Indian fighters, and the Indians returned the savagery in kind. Outlaw gangs of whites further terrorized the more peaceful among the backwoodsmen, and, since they received little help from the Quaker authorities in the East, the backwoodsmen established their own justice. Thus, the American frontiersman, later famed in American folklore, had come into being. In time these people, perhaps feeling crowded and certainly feeling restless, began to turn south, migrating down The Great Wagon Road east of the Appalachians into Virginia, the Carolinas, and Georgia. In the Carolinas they met other Scotch-Irish Presbyterians who had landed at Charleston and from there traveled to the backcountry.[45]

Many remarkable traits have been ascribed to the American frontiersman. In addition to being independent and self-reliant, he was said to be courageous, fearless, aggressive, hardy, honest, democratic, and fair-minded. He was an outstanding marksman and could dispatch a raccoon, a wildcat, or an Indian with equal ease. He could hold his liquor and his tongue, too, if necessary, though he would rather tell about his abilities: he could outdrink, outride, outshoot, outfight, and outwrestle any man alive. Nonetheless, he was pious, and he established churches and schools which he protected from godless enemies. He had "the Bible in one hand, a rifle in the other, and a scalping knife at the belt."[46] In time the image of the frontiersman in the popular imagination included both the heroes and the villains of American folklore--the Andrew Jacksons and Davy Crocketts as well as the Hatfields and McCoys--and what the heroes and villains had in common were most of the traits listed above, the difference being that the villains were neither honest nor pious. Nor were they particularly adept at outriding, outfighting, outwrestling, outshooting, or outdrinking. In short, the villains were lesser men than the heroes though of the same type.

In sober fact, the Scotch-Irish frontiersman in pre-Revolutionary days differed considerably from this mythic figure. Where they remained settled they established churches and schools and generally

became good citizens. But characteristic of most of them was their
restlessness. Indian style, they would move into new areas, kill the
trees by girdling them, plant between the trees, and be gone before
they fell.[47] The restlessness amounted almost to a compulsion and
affected even those who were prosperous. One family named Pettigrew
sailed from Ulster to Delaware in 1740 and bought a 300-acre tract in
Pennsylvania where they became well established and could have remained. But after a few years they moved to western Virginia and in
1768 to Long Cane Creek in South Carolina, then sparsely populated.
Three years later they moved again but this time only a mile farther
out. In 1745 two brothers named Pickens were justices of the peace in
Augusta County, Virginia, thus seeming to be settled citizens. In 1751
they moved to the Waxhalls in South Carolina and nine years later to
the Savannah Valley. In three generations the Boone family moved from
Bucks County, Pennsylvania, to the Shenandoah, to western North Carolina, and finally to Kentucky where they helped found Boonesborough.[48]
Nor did this restlessness stop at the end of the eighteenth century.
In two generations of the Graham family in the present study, one
branch moved from County Antrim, Ulster; to Chester County, South Carolina; to Todd County, Kentucky; to Preble County, Ohio; and finally to
Warren County, Illinois. These examples were multiplied many times
over. One result of this restlessness in the early and mid-eighteenth
century was that certain "civilizing" influences occasionally fell
away, and a few frontiersmen became hunters rather than farmers.
Crèvecoeur wrote of the latter:

> I must tell you, that there is something in the proximity of
> the woods, which is very singular. . . . The surrounding
> hostility immediately puts the gun into their hands; . . .
> once hunters, farewell to the plough. The chase renders them
> ferocious, gloomy, and unsociable; a hunter wants no neigh-
> bour, he rather hates them, because he dreads the competition.
> . . . That new mode of life brings along with it a new set of
> manners, which I cannot easily describe. These new manners
> being grafted on the old stock, produce a strange sort of law-
> less profligacy, the impressions of which are indelible. The
> manners of the Indian natives are respectable, compared with
> this European medley. Their wives and children live in sloth
> and inactivity; and having no proper pursuits, you may judge
> what education the latter receive. Their tender minds have
> nothing else to contemplate but the example of their parents;
> like them they grow up a mongrel breed, half civilised, half
> savage. . . .[49]

Actually, Crèvecoeur probably overestimated the number of frontiersmen
who became isolated hunters. According to the records, most of them
were farmers, settled in communities, and seldom lived farther away
than five or six miles from their nearest neighbors. Perhaps because
of this proximity, they developed other traits. In addition to being
restless, they sometimes lived in squalor, sometimes drank to excess,

and often were quarrelsome. Again quoting Crèvecoeur:

> Out of twelve families of emigrants of each country [that is, Scottish, German, and Scotch-Irish], generally seven Scotch will succeed, nine German, and four Irish. . . . [The Scotch-Irish] love to drink and to quarrel; they are litigious, and soon take to the gun, which is the ruin of everything; they seem beside to labour under a greater degree of ignorance in husbandry. . . .
>
> It is in consequence of this straggling situation, and the astonishing power it has on manners, that the back settlers of both the Carolinas, Virginia, and many other parts, have been long a set of lawless people; it has been even dangerous to travel among them.[50]

Another to comment on the backwoodsmen of the Carolinas was the Rev. Charles Woodmason, an Anglican clergyman who felt he had a calling as a missionary to the frontier and who therefore traveled many miles in the backcountry in 1766-1768. He kept a journal and in it often commented on the squalor he encountered. Undoubtedly he exaggerated, and his account should not be taken at face value, but probably there was enough truth in what he wrote to give some indication of frontier conditions. For example, in May 1768 he said:

> . . . In many Places they have nought but a Gourd to drink out off [sic] Not a Plate Knive or Spoon, a Glass Cup, or any thing--It is well if they can get some Body Linen, and some have not even that. They are so burthen'd with Young Children, that the Women cannot attend both House and Field--And many live by Hunting, and killing of Deer--There's not a Cabbin but has 10 or 12 Young Children in it--When the Boys are 18 and Girls 14 they marry--so that in many Cabbins You will see 10 or 15 Children. Children and Grand Children of one Size--and the mother looking as Young as the Daughter.[51]

Woodmason also often commented on what he perceived as the great amount of moral looseness in the backcountry. On 25 January 1767 he wrote in his journal:

> For thro' want of Ministers to marry and thro' licentiousness of the People, many hundreds live in Concubinage--swopping their Wives as Cattel, and living in a State of Nature, more irregularly and unchastely than the Indians--I therefore made Public Notice ev'ry where be given, that whoever did not attend to be legally married, I would prosecute them at the Sessions--and that all who had liv'd in a State of Concubinage on application to me, I would marry Gratis--Numbers accepted of my Offer, and were married, and then I baptiz'd their Children. . . .[52]

In 1768 he wrote of an immoral and drunken teacher:

> The Schoolmaster . . . having been drunk for some days past--I gently chid Him for such Misdemeanour--for which he gave me such horrid abuse, that but for the Bystanders, I should have caned Him--and was about to whip a Strumpet whom he keeps for her Lewdness and Prophaneness--but was prevented. And yet there is a Magistrate here--but he is a Presbyterian-- So are these Wretches. Instead of this Magistrate punishing these worthless Sinners he protects them--[53]

Being a devout Anglican, Woodmason was unable to find good in anyone not of that faith and was particularly biased toward the Scotch-Irish Presbyterians whom he called "the most lowest vilest Crew breathing."[54] They retaliated, as he reported:

> I had appointed a Congregation to meet me at the Head of Hanging Rock Creek--Where I arriv'd on Tuesday Evening [in February 1767]--Found the Houses filled with debauch'd licentious fellows, and Scot Presbyterians who had hir'd lawless Ruffians to insult me, which they did with Impunity--Telling me, they wanted no D___d Black Gown Sons of Bitches among them --and threatening to lay me behind the Fire, which they assuredly would have done had not some travellers alighted very opportunely, and taken me under Protection--These Men sat up with, and guarded me all the Night--In the Morning the lawless Rabble moved off on seeing the Church People appear, of whom had a large Congregation. But the Service was greatly interrupted by a Gang of Presbyterians who kept hallooing and whooping without Door like Indians.[55]

In December 1767 Woodmason again burst out:

> This Day we had another Specimen of the Envy Malice and Temper of the Presbyterians--They gave away 2 Barrels of Whisky to the Populace to make drink, and for to disturb the Service--for this being the 1st time that the Communion was ever celebrated in this Wild remote Part of the World, it gave a Great Alarm, and caus'd them much Pain and Vexation. The Company got drunk by 10 oth [sic] Clock and we could hear them firing, hooping, and hallowing like Indians. Some few came before the Communion was finish'd and were very Noisy. . . .[56]

In short, if we are to accept Crèvecoeur's and Woodmason's accounts, the Scotch-Irish in the backcountry when the Grahams arrived were a drunken, clamorous lot who were shiftless, immoral, unschooled, godless, and generally contemptible. Probably to some extent there was truth to this, and the Grahams must have felt greatly dismayed at first. But there was considerably more to these backcountry people than Crèvecoeur and Woodmason were willing to perceive. For, although

these Scotch-Irish were rough and unmannerly and owned few worldly
goods, most of them were neither godless nor unschooled. They established churches and schools all along the frontier from Pennsylvania to
Georgia, and, while it is true that many of the churches did not have
ministers, and some schools taught only reading, it is clear that the
frontier people were very aware of the importance of education and
religion. If they could not procure teachers, they taught their children themselves. Also, they sent constant appeals for ministers to the
Scottish and Irish Presbyteries, and since few responded they welcomed
the circuit riders who came briefly, preached in barns or fields, performed marriages and baptisms, then moved on.[57] Woodmason, himself,
often commented, though with disapproval, on the considerable number of
itinerant preachers of various sects who had come through the backcountry. He also noted, again with disapproval, that the Scotch-Irish
Presbyterians had built a meeting house at Waxhall and had a minister.[58] Further, as was seen in Section 3 above the Chester County
Presbyterians had built the Catholic Presbyterian Church designed for
all Presbyterians, and enough Covenanters were among them by 1770 to
withdraw and send a call to the Rev. William Martin. Actually, Presbyterian churches were fairly numerous in the South Carolina backcountry
relative to the number of people. York, Lancaster, and Abbeville
districts each had four by 1772; Chester, Laurens, Union, Newberry, and
Kershaw each had two; and Sumter and Spartanburg each had one.[59]

But if the character of the people whom the Grahams encountered
dismayed them at first, they were probably more disturbed by the political situation and the anger with which the backcountry people viewed
the authorities in Charleston, then the capital. South Carolina had
problems which differed from those in other colonies. Established as a
proprietorship in 1663, it was successful as a business venture from
the beginning, but while the proprietors' chief purpose was to make
money, they also gave some thought to the colony's social structure.
Since they viewed New England as dangerously democratic, they set out
to pattern Carolina after England with a landed aristocracy plus
tenants and yeomen farmers. The landed aristocracy was readily established; tenants and yeomen farmers were harder to find, so the landowners turned to slave labor thereby introducing a major problem which
was to haunt Carolinians for many years. Other worries came from
Indian attacks, often in alliance with Spanish, and since the landowners were greatly outnumbered by their slaves, it was highly possible
that the slaves would turn against their masters when the Indians and
Spanish attacked. (In fact, the slaves did so.) Therefore, the landowners urged the proprietors not only to send more Protestant farmers
to populate the backcountry in order to form buffer communities between
the landowners and the Indians, but also to send soldiers and military
supplies and build frontier forts. The proprietors were absentee landlords, however, and by 1700 their only interest was making money, so
they did virtually nothing to help. In the meantime, additional
problems arose. Although there was an elected assembly, the judicial
system was presided over by a single judge who answered only to the

proprietors and was thus capable of nullifying any actions which the
assembly might take. Also, courts were held only at Charleston which
meant that most people had to travel great distances to appear there.
Another complaint was that the proprietors had done nothing to establish churches and schools, and although religious freedom had been
extended to all Protestants in 1696, two laws were enacted in 1704
which made the Anglican church the official one. The laws also forced
dissenters to pay taxes for the Anglican church's support and required
that all members of the assembly take oaths of conformity to the
Anglican faith.[60]

In 1719 the proprietors were overthrown, and South Carolina became
a royal colony, but its social and political structure of a ruling
aristocracy remained; so did the dominance of the Anglican church, the
problems with the slaves, the difficulties resulting from having courts
only in Charleston, and the threat of Indian attacks. To address the
latter problem, the authorities encouraged the immigration of backcountry settlers by adopting a bounty system in 1732 whereby settlers were
granted free land and tools. In time the bounties were paid for by
taxes on slave importations, and the system was continued with minor
changes until 1768 when the bounties were dropped because of abuses.
Free land was still granted, however, usually at the rate of fifty
acres for each member of the household. Later this allotment was
changed to one hundred acres for the head of the household and fifty
acres apiece for each household member.[61]

By the mid-eighteenth century, the backcountry began to fill up,
but it had problems of its own due largely to the arrogance of the
aristocracy. One problem was the threat of Indian massacres, and in
1757 the people living between the Broad and Saluda rivers petitioned
the assembly for enough money to build a fort. The aristocratic assembly refused, saying, "Other inhabitants living in the back settlements
have, heretofore, erected small forts to defend themselves against the
inroads of the Indians, without ever applying to the government of this
province to defray any part of the expense; and as the granting of the
sum prayed for by the petitioners, though but a small one, may be a bad
precedent by opening a door to great impositions from people who live
so very remote, we can not agree to make provision for the same."[62]
One may imagine the resentment which the petitioners felt when they
read these words, especially when they learned that at the same sitting
the assembly voted large sums for repairs and construction at Charleston, Georgetown, Port Royal, and Dorchester. Further, in 1765 the
aristocrats actually asked the backwoodsmen to be in readiness to save
the plantations if the slaves should rebel.[63]

Other causes for resentment were the tax rates. Although the
authorities at Charleston would not help the backcountry people at the
threat of Indian massacres and expected those same people to come to
their aid if the slaves rebelled, the authorities taxed the backcountry
people at the same rate as the wealthiest planters in the tidewater

region.  Yet, the backcountry people had to travel far to take their
produce to market while the planters had only a short distance to go.
Constant appeals for adjustments in the tax rates brought no change and
seldom even a response.  In 1766, for example, a petition for redress
in the tax rates was tabled at a session of the assembly while the
members went on to consider the complaints of Charleston's dray owners
against traffic regulations.[64]

Still other causes for resentment were that the backcountry had no
courts and no way to take legal action other than in distant Charleston, and they had no representation in the assembly not only because
the voting places were too far away but also because few people in the
backcountry even knew where to vote.  Further, by 1775 the backcountry
probably had almost four times as many whites as the tidewater region
did.  (South Carolina is the only colony for which census figures and
other population guides for the whites do not exist; the population
estimates before the Revolution are based on other sources, and conservative estimates show that by 1775 the backcountry whites outnumbered
the tidewater whites by almost four to one.  The 1790 census showed
clearly that by then the backcountry had almost four times as many
whites as the tidewater area did.)  In view of the unfair taxes, this
was truly taxation without representation to the frontier people.[65]

Finally, added to all these problems were white terrorist gangs
who ranged freely because there were no courts and no legal machinery
except at Charleston.  They stole livestock and goods, destroyed crops
by riding over them, ransacked stores, turned families naked into the
woods and burned their houses, tortured men Indian fashion to make them
tell where they had hidden their valuables, raped women, and threatened
or murdered anyone who tried to stop them.  Repeated appeals brought no
help from the Charleston authorities who in any case regarded all frontiersmen as ruffians, and by 1767 the backwoodsmen were driven beyond
endurance.  Early in 1767 they spontaneously organized into vigilante
groups called Regulators and went after the outlaw gangs.  By October
1767 the governor heard reports that Regulators were not only burning
the houses of those who harbored criminals but also were talking of
marching on Charleston.  This latter possibility was especially
alarming to the council since they knew that the frontiersmen greatly
outnumbered the tidewater whites, many of whose able-bodied men were
occupied in keeping the slaves under control.  Therefore, the governor
issued a proclamation ordering the Regulators to disperse and sent a
regiment to the Saluda region to enforce the order; also, the Court of
General Sessions convicted criminals and Regulators alike.  In short,
Charleston did its best to inflame the backcountry further.[66]

At this point the Rev. Charles Woodmason threw his weight behind
the Regulators and on 7 November 1767 wrote a long, eloquent, and carefully detailed petition to the assembly over the signatures of four
well-to-do planters on behalf of the backcountry people.  This document, plus the threat of a march on Charleston, seemed to produce

results. The assembly voted for courts and a vagrancy act and sent two companies of soldiers to the backcountry for three months. Most of the soldiers were Regulators, so the movement had an air of official sanction. In fact, however, the Regulators soon learned that the court bill did not provide county and circuit courts and included provisions which almost certainly would make the bill unacceptable to the king. Meanwhile, Regulators continued to be arrested. Outraged, a large number of them met at the Congarees in June 1768 and adopted the "Plan of Regulation" which denied the jurisdiction of Charleston's courts in the backcountry. In July and August the Regulators continued to hold meetings and even engaged in armed battles with the military forces sent to arrest their leaders. By September 1768 the backcountry settlers not only continued to claim that Charleston's courts had no jurisdiction there, but also refused to pay their taxes and again talked of marching on Charleston. The lieutenant-governor then announced that an election for a new assembly would be held on October 4 and 5, and this time the settlers made a point of learning where to vote. Early in October several hundred of them set off for the polls on the coast, some traveling as far as 150 miles. No doubt the tidewater planters and their families anticipated the worst from this frontier horde, but the Regulators were orderly, probably to the surprise of many aristocrats. The Regulators succeeded in electing candidates, but the lieutenant-governor postponed the new assembly until the return of the governor who was in England. When he returned in mid-November with the news that the court bill had been disallowed, he said a few vague words about addressing the problems in the backcountry and, several days later, dissolved the assembly. Thus, the backcountry still had no courts and no voice in the elected body.[67]

Confrontations, arrests, and imprisonments continued, and in February 1769 the governor, who was determined to suppress the rebellion by any means, summoned a backcountry magistrate to act as an informant. The magistrate named some of the leading Regulators and told of one Musgrove whom the Regulators had whipped and driven from his home. Arrest warrants were then issued for twenty-five Regulators whose names had probably been supplied by Musgrove, and a Joseph Coffell, known in the backcountry as a thief and a scoundrel, was commissioned to execute the warrants. Coffell appointed Musgrove as his major. Musgrove then recruited men among the outlaw gangs, set out to arrest some Regulators while plundering homes, and succeeded in capturing nine men named in the warrants. Other Regulators immediately surrounded them, however, thus preventing Musgrove from taking the prisoners to Charleston. At this juncture the governor and council asked Charleston's Light Infantry to intervene but they refused, and it must have seemed to the authorities that anarchy prevailed. At about the same time, a new assembly election was to take place on 7 and 8 March 1769, and the backwoodsmen set off again to elect representatives, but word came of Coffell's actions, so they hurried back. Also, a rumor circulated that the governor had deliberately called the election to draw the men away from their homes so that Coffell's and

Musgrove's men might rape and plunder freely.[68]

Probably at no time in the Regulator movement was the backcountry fury at a higher pitch. As Woodmason wrote:

> . . . The Commotion which this rais'd in ev'ry Part, is not to be expressed--The People were about to march downward and destroy all the Plantations of those Gentlemen whom they thought in the Plot--And it was with difficulty they were restrain'd. . . . But they could not be prevented from maltreating ev'ry Bailif that came into the Country to serve Process--They drove off many--and came to Resolutions of not suffering Process of any kind to be serv'd till Courts of Justice among themselves take place. . . .[69]

Later a few of Musgrove's men did make it to Charleston with five prisoners, and perhaps the governor and council thought these prisoners were enough to save face. Also, three prominent backcountry planters had been sent to Charleston to convince the authorities of their mistake in commissioning Coffell. Nonetheless, the authorities haughtily took their time about disavowing the man although they finally did so, and the planters hurried back to find the Regulators on the verge of civil war. Fortunately, the planters were able to give written proof that Coffell and his men were now without authority, and the civil war was thereby prevented, but a profound hatred toward the tidewater aristocracy remained.[70]

In June 1769 the governor toured the backcountry, and when he returned to Charleston he urged the council to pass a circuit court bill. The bill was passed speedily, the governor sailed with it to England in July, and word came in December that the king had approved it. The bill established seven court districts and provided for courts to meet three times a year at Charleston district and twice yearly at Georgetown, Cheraws, Camden (which included later Chester County), Ninety Six, Orangeburgh, and Beaufort districts. One requirement, however, was that the courts could not be established until jails and courthouses were built, so another long delay took place. Part of the delay was caused by the assembly, some of whose members were petulantly angry that Britishers rather than Carolinians were appointed as judges. Not until late 1772 was the new court machinery in place and operating. Meanwhile, many Regulators were released from prison, others were restored to their offices or given commissions, and pursuits of the remaining outlaws were carried out. After the courts opened, the new judges and lawyers gave highly favorable reports of the backcountry people, reports which probably did not please the tidewater aristocracy who still were contemptuous of the frontier settlers. For their part, the settlers did not forget their grievances against the tidewater aristocrats. After the Revolutionary War broke out, many settlers rejoiced when they heard a rumor that British men-of-war were about to seize Charleston.[71] The Grahams must have been astonished.

5. The Revolutionary Period in the
   Carolina Backcountry [72]

It has sometimes been said that the Scotch-Irish, "without exception," were Patriots during the Revolution.[73] In South Carolina that was hardly the case. Deeply angry at the tidewater aristocrats and having no quarrel with the king who had given them their lands, many backwoodsmen were not persuaded when the Charleston merchants and others exhorted them to protest the Stamp Act or the tax on tea. The Stamp Act, which required stamps on all legal documents, commercial papers, newspapers, pamphlets, almanacs, cards, and dice, affected the backwoodsmen very little, if at all, and few of them, if any, drank tea. Further, the backwoodsmen must have appreciated the irony in the cry of "Taxation without Representation!" which the tidewater planters and merchants raised. To bring the backcountry out of its indifference, the Charleston revolutionaries sent William Henry Drayton and the Rev. William Tennant to explain why American liberties were threatened. Drayton headed the Provincial Congress's Secret Committee, and Tennant was a dissenting minister with a large following, but they met with limited success in the backcountry.

In June 1776 a British invasion by sea was repulsed when the British fleet could not get past the famous "Palmetto Fort" which the Charlestonians built on Sullivan's Island to protect the city. Thus, until 1780 the main theater of the war was in the North. But it would be a mistake to think the South Carolina backcountry was completely peaceful during the intervening period, for, if the backcountry contained Loyalists (Tories) it also contained Patriots (Whigs). Many Whigs, such as the Grahams and others in Martin's party, were newcomers who had taken no part in the Regulator movement and, because of their Ulster experiences, had every reason to hate England. Tensions between the factions grew. Even before 1776 a battle between Tories and Whigs occurred at Ninety Six when in November 1775 some Tories captured a load of ammunition which was being taken to the Cherokees as part of their hunting allowance. This allowance was necessary to keep peace with the Indians, and the Council of Safety sent a detachment under Major Andrew Williamson to retake the ammunition. Before Williamson could organize his forces, the Tories attacked, and the ensuing battle lasted three days, ending in a truce. In December the Council of Safety ordered Col. Richard Richardson to call up the Camden militia to pursue the Tories who had captured the ammunition. In what was later called the "Snow Campaign," Richardson and his men tracked the Tories to their camp, killed several, and took the rest prisoners. Later the prisoners were paroled, but anger grew, and Tories and Whigs began taking vengeance on each other.

For a time the frontiersmen were distracted by a threat from the Indians. The Cherokees were angry not only because of being deprived of their ammunition but also because of white encroachment on their lands, and in 1776 some of the hot-headed among them banded with hot-

headed members of other tribes to embark on a frontier massacre from
Virginia to Georgia, killing every white man, woman, and child they
found. Indian uprisings were always a matter of immediate concern to
the whites. Also, rumors circulated on both sides during the Revolution that the enemy intended to incite the Indians against the opposition, and, in fact, the French had done that against the outlying
English settlements during the French and Indian War two decades
earlier. The horrors which resulted then were not forgotten, and when
this new Indian threat appeared in 1776 the whites reacted instantly.
In South Carolina Williamson organized a militia which destroyed
Cherokee towns, crops, and animals. Frontiersmen in the other states
reacted similarly; they scalped, then killed, Indian men, women, and
children, captured and sold others into slavery, and destroyed every
possible means of sustaining life in the Cherokee country. In South
Carolina the Cherokee country included the extreme northwest counties
of present Greenville, Pickens, and Anderson. Finally, on 20 May 1777
a treaty was made with the Cherokees which forced them out of their
lands, and the whites rushed into and settled the newly ceded terri-
tories. No doubt this was harsh treatment of a tribe, most of whose
members were decent, honorable, and friendly to the whites, but it
should be remembered that the whites were squaring off against each
other and wanted no repeat of the atrocities which occurred during the
French and Indian War.

Aside from the Indian problems, South Carolina generally maintained an uneasy peace during the interval from 1776 when Charleston
repulsed the British and 1780 when Charleston fell to them. To be
sure, confrontations erupted between Whigs and Tories, and tarring and
feathering incidents occurred, but the state as a whole remained
reasonably quiet, though restlessly so. During that time South Carolina wrote a constitution in which the General Assembly, or Congress,
was to consist of a lower and an upper house both of which were to be
elected. The tidewater region still had the largest number of dele-
gates, thus continuing the unfair representation. The president, who
was stripped of his veto power, was to be chosen by both houses, and
the courts remained unchanged from their formation in 1769. Surprisingly, due to the eloquence of the Rev. William Tennant the Anglican
Church was disestablished, thereby eliminating a problem which had
annoyed non-Anglican Carolinians since the time of the proprietors. No
longer would taxes be used to pay the Anglican clergy. The "established religion" in South Carolina was simply Protestantism.

The war, however, seemed to be at a stalemate. In 1778 Sir Henry
Clinton, leader of the British Army, decided on a new tactic for ending
the conflict. His plan was to land forces in the South and march them
north through the Carolinas and into Virginia in order to trap Washington between the northern and southern British armies. He also counted
on support from Loyalist citizens. In December 1778 Gen. Augustine
Prevost seized Savannah and in May 1779 laid siege to Charleston. The
inept American Gen. Benjamin Lincoln then pursued Prevost who escaped

with little difficulty, and the ease with which Prevost had reached
Charleston encouraged Clinton in his plan. He attacked from both sea
and land in March 1780, and, due largely to General Lincoln's poor
handling of the Carolina troops, Charleston fell on 12 May. Thus began
real warfare in South Carolina.

At this point South Carolina was confused and demoralized and with
wise judgment the British could have kept her neutral for the remainder
of the war. Instead, in three months the Patriots' will to fight was
thoroughly aroused because of British policies, and the will to fight
was particularly aroused in the backcountry.

What happened was that Clinton put Gen. Charles Cornwallis in
command and prepared to sail back to his headquarters in New York, but
before leaving he ordered that American regulars be imprisoned while
the militia be freed on parole on condition that the paroled militia
take arms against rebels if required to do so. On 1 June 1780 Clinton
extended pardons to everyone but those still rebelling, but on 3 June
he did an about-face. He abolished the freed status of paroled prisoners for all except those in Charleston and proclaimed that anyone
who did not declare allegiance by 20 June would be deemed an enemy,
subject to the severest punishment. By this order he alienated thousands who otherwise would probably have been submissive. Also, one of
Cornwallis's officers, Banastre Tarleton, committed the first of many
atrocities which were to inflame the Patriots. Cornwallis had sent
Tarleton after the retreating American Col. Abraham Buford. On 29 May
1780 Tarleton overtook Buford near present Lancaster and attacked with
fury. Buford's men surrendered and asked for quarter, but Tarleton's
men continued the slaughter. The Whigs were outraged when they heard
of the massacre, and "Tarleton's Quarter!" later became a battle cry.
Nor was this the only outrage. Presbyterian ministers such as the Rev.
William Martin were arrested and their churches burned. Whigs were
hanged even after declaring allegiance. Neighbors murdered neighbors.
Women and children were turned into the woods and their houses burned.
In present York County an iron works which employed one-hundred Scotch-Irish Patriots was destroyed along with its out-buildings and the workmen's houses.[74] In present Fairfield County a Tory named Colonel
Phillips, who was with Tarleton at Little Rocky Creek, broke into the
home of Patriot Archibald McClurkin against whom Phillips probably had
a grudge. Although McClurkin was near death from smallpox, Phillips
dragged him to a tree and hanged him.[75] On 15-16 August the Americans
under Gen. Horatio Gates were badly defeated at the Battle of Camden.
Cornwallis then issued an order to hang any member of a militia who had
once fought with English forces and later joined the Patriots. The
hangings began immediately. Faced with such threats the frontier
Patriots, who now were defending themselves, their families, and their
homes, instantly took up arms, formed militias, and engaged in guerilla
warfare. Thus, what the Stamp Act, the tea tax, and the exhortations
of the tidewater aristocrats could not accomplish in five years,
British policies did within three months.

After Horatio Gage's defeat at Camden, Washington sent in Gen. Nathaniel Greene, a careful tactician who technically never won a battle in the Carolina campaign but who made victory so costly for the British that in effect he won every engagement. Among his commanders was Andrew Pickens who later distinguished himself at Cowpens. Two others were Thomas Sumter, the "Gamecock," and Francis Marion, called the "Swamp Fox" because he was too wily to be caught and escaped into swamps where he could not be tracked. These men with their militias constantly struck at the British outposts and supply lines, keeping Cornwallis so occupied with guerrilla harassment that months passed before Clinton could put into action his plan to have Cornwallis march north. By the time Cornwallis did so, the French fleet was in Chesapeake Bay, and instead of trapping Washington, Cornwallis was himself trapped. Therefore, it may be said that the delaying actions in South Carolina led directly to Washington's triumph.

Not all the actions were guerrilla harassments; some were open battles. On 19 August 1780 at Musgrove's Mill in the southern point of present Spartanburg County, the Patriots were forced to fight which they did with great skill against British regulars twice their number. The Patriots took the field, no doubt to the astonishment of the British. Then on 7 October occurred the famous Battle of Kings Mountain just south of the North Carolina border in present York County. The North Carolinians and Tennesseeans had heard that Lieutenant-Colonel Patrick Ferguson intended to attack them in their mountains. Instead of waiting for that event, they decided to march upon Ferguson and attack wherever they found him. Ferguson unwisely chose to make camp on a Kings Mountain plateau, although at the time it seemed to be a good choice of ground. The North Carolina and Tennessee militiamen were soon joined by infantry from South Carolina and Virginia so that the Patriots had about 1,000 men to the Loyalist 1,100. (It is interesting to note that except for Ferguson all the combatants at Kings Mountain were Americans; Ferguson's troops were mostly Loyalists from New York and New Jersey.) The Patriots tethered their horses about a mile down the slope, proceeded upwards Indian file, and surrounded the Loyalists before they were aware of it. Hiding behind trees and being superb marksmen, they picked off the redcoats with deadly accuracy. Ferguson was killed trying to escape. After the remaining Loyalists surrendered, the slaughter continued as Patriots cried, "Tarleton's Quarter!" Finally, the officers stopped the killing.

At one o'clock in the morning of 9 November 1780, The British attacked Sumter while he was camped in the southwestern part of present Chester County. He escaped to present Union, and on 20 November Tarleton pursued him, having been sent by Cornwallis who was then in Winnsboro. Sumter's adroitness led Tarleton to attack too soon, and the British were again defeated. Another stunning British defeat came on 17 January 1781 at Cowpens in present Spartanburg County when the Virginia Patriot Gen. Daniel Morgan, with brilliant strategy, achieved an overwhelming victory against Tarleton after only one hour of fighting.

Morgan had the able assistance of Andrew Pickens, and together their
tactics were simple and deadly. Morgan placed his men in the center of
the line and told them to fire two rounds then fall back. Pickens
stationed his men at the sides behind trees or in the tall grass. As
Morgan's men fired then retreated, Pickens' men shot at the onrushing
redcoats, aiming particularly for the officers. Finally, Tarleton's
troops refused the command to charge, and he fled with the few men he
had left. Tarleton, whose force numbered more than 1,000 before the
battle, lost at least 750 men in killed or wounded. Morgan, whose
force numbered about 950, lost 12 killed and 60 wounded.

The battles of Kings Mountain and Cowpens were the most dramatic
and important of the war in South Carolina, but probably Cornwallis did
not realize their significance as he continued to fight his way toward
Virginia. What these battles did was to give new heart to the uncon-
quered Patriots. The guerrillas under Sumter, Marion, and Pickens
increased in daring as they cut off British supplies, captured outposts, and killed British officials. Cornwallis was being stung to
death and did not know it. He decided to go after Greene who was then
in North Carolina, and on 15 March 1781 they clashed in savage fighting
at Guilford Courthouse near Greensboro. Greene retreated, and Cornwallis technically won the battle but suffered so many losses in wounded
and exhausted men that he had to lead his troops to Wilmington near the
coast in order for them to recuperate. Thus, he was further delayed in
his move north. In the meantime, Cornwallis put Lord Rawdon in command
at Camden. Greene returned to South Carolina, and on 25 April 1781
Rawdon almost captured him at his camp on Hobkirk Hill near Camden.
Greene escaped, but Rawdon soon learned that he and his men were isolated because Marion had taken all of a protecting ring of British outposts. Rawdon had to evacuate Camden and return to Charleston. The
British post at Ninety Six held out longer, but after the Patriots
besieged Ninety Six it, too, was evacuated in late June, leaving the
post at Eutaw Springs the only one which the British held in the backcountry. There, Greene attacked on 8 September and had almost won the
battle when his troops fell into confusion probably because they
stopped to plunder for food and rum. He had to retreat, but again the
British losses were so heavy that they had to abandon the post and
return to Charleston. By the time Cornwallis marched to Yorktown--to
his defeat on 17 October 1781--the only South Carolina territory he
held was Charleston.

After Cornwallis's surrender at Yorktown, the war was over almost
everywhere but in South Carolina. Since 1779 both sides had been
killing prisoners with no pretense at trials, and, now, fresh atrocities broke out as Patriots retaliated against Tories. Again, neighbors
murdered neighbors, women as well as men. Tories were caught and tortured, then killed. Homes were plundered, then burned. In April 1784
twelve prominent Tories who had formerly fled to the safety of Charleston returned to their homes on Fishing Creek in present Chester County.
The Whigs there gave them twenty days to leave. They remained, and,

soon after, eight of them were killed. The four who were spared were allowed to carry the news to other Tories.[76] On 7 November 1784 a judge at Ninety Six pardoned one of the most villainous of the Tories who had been brought to trial. Relatives of people whom the man had killed waited until the judge left then fell upon the Tory and hanged him.[77] One Tory who escaped was Colonel Phillips who had dragged Archibald McClurkin from his sickbed and hanged him. Phillips returned to Ulster where one of McClurkin's brothers stalked and shot him.[78] But these examples are only a few among thousands. Several voices were raised on behalf of moderation, notably that of Christopher Gadsden, but it seemed that the fury had to spend itself out. In time, of course, the fury did spend itself, and South Carolina gradually returned to normal after a terrible war and the dreadful convulsions of its aftermath. It has been estimated that the war cost South Carolina well over eleven million dollars. Only Massachusetts, with three times South Carolina's white population, paid more, and that by only some forty thousand.[79] The cost in lives and suffering can never be calculated.

Three Graham men, perhaps four, were actively involved in the Revolution. David Graham, the father, provided food and blacksmith services for the Patriots. Andrew Graham, David's oldest son, fought in at least two militias and provided beef for them. David also probably had a son named Matthew who may have fought and been killed, although no evidence of his doing so has been found. Almost nothing is known about Matthew except that he must have died between 1775 and 1778, and, given the events of the time, it seems possible that he was killed by some Tory. The Graham who was most deeply involved, however, was David's son James who was drafted in December 1778 at the age of seventeen, marched with the Patriots all over South Carolina, and was active in pursuing Tories after the war (see his testimony concerning his war record on pages 54-56).

### 6. Early Spelling Variants of the Name *Graham*

Probably the greatest obstacle to Graham research in South Carolina has been the name's spelling variations. These variations were not discovered until recently, and doubtlessly their existence explains the fact that a comprehensive Graham family history has not hitherto been compiled. Formerly, researchers knew from the federal censuses that the Grahams came from South Carolina. Researchers also were aware that the first known Graham, Andrew, moved from South Carolina to Todd County, Kentucky, where he died in 1821. Andrew's first known land deed in Kentucky was in 1809; therefore, he must still have been living in South Carolina when the 1790 and 1800 censuses were taken. An Andrew Graham was listed in the 1790 federal census of Lancaster County, South Carolina, but that Andrew was soon revealed to be someone other than the ancestor who moved to Kentucky. Besides, several documents showed that the ancestor Andrew must have lived in Chester County, not Lancaster County, and therein lay the problem because although an Andrew Graham was listed in the 1800 federal census of Chester County, he was not listed in the 1790 one. Yet, he is known to have been in Chester County at least as early as 1775 because a record was found stating that in 1790 he sold one hundred acres there which he had originally received in a colonial grant in 1775. To deepen the mystery, no colonial grant was found for an Andrew Graham in Chester County. Further, although the names of Andrew's father, David, and Andrew's siblings were soon learned through the discovery of David's will, and documents concerning them were found in Chester County, they also could not be traced. Added to the puzzle was the statement that Andrew had been born in Ireland--a statement made by Andrew's only children who lived long enough to be included in the 1880 census (the first to list parents' places of birth). Yet, no passenger records for David Graham or Andrew Graham or for Andrew's known siblings could be found. A book by Janie Revill with the promising title, *A Compilation of the Original Lists of the Protestant Immigrants to South Carolina, 1763-1773*, listed no one named Andrew or David Graham.

Gradually, through a suggestion by Barbara R. Langdon and Elmer O. Parker, Certified Genealogists of Columbia, South Carolina, the realization came that spelling variants must have existed for the name *Graham*. One name often found in the Chester County records was *Grimes*, and, in fact, men named David, Andrew, and James *Grimes* were listed there in the 1790 census. Ms. Revill's book was consulted again and this time yielded the names David *Grimbs*, Andrew *Grumbs (sic)*, Jean *Grimbs*, and Matthew *Grimbs* as passengers on the ship *Pennsylvania Farmer* in late 1772.

In time, proof that the Graham name was first often written as *Grimes* or *Grimbs* was found in three sets of documents, copies of which were acquired. First, the land which Andrew *Grimbs* received in 1775 was clearly described in the grant; in 1790 Andrew *Graham* sold the land which had been granted to him, and its description in the deed of sale matched the description in the grant to Andrew *Grimbs* in 1775. Also in this deed, Andrew is generally referred to as *Graham* except in one passage, and in that passage he is called *Grimes*. Second, David Graham's audited Revolutionary accounts contained two documents dated less than a month apart; in the first, he was called David *Grimes*, in the second, David *Graham*. Finally, in James Graham's audited Revolutionary accounts there is a letter dated 1785 in which the writer stated that James's Accounts Audited bore the name James *Grimes* whereas James signed his name to the Order for his Indent as James *Graham*. Many years later, James applied for a pension and was refused at first because of the spelling variation.

It should not be inferred that the spellings were consistently *Grimes* or *Grimbs* until some time after 1790 then changed suddenly to *Graham*. In 1773 David, as *Grimbs*, was warranted land in Chester Coun-

ty, and in 1774, also as *Grimbs*, he was cited in a deed to Richard
Jamieson, but his Revolutionary War Accounts Audited generally cited
him as David *Graham* with the exception of the instance mentioned above.
In 1785, as David *Graham*, he bought land in Chester County, but in
1786, as David *Grimes*, he served on the county's grand jury. Also, as
seen above he was listed as David *Grimes* in the 1790 census, but in his
will dated 1795 he was David *Graham*. Andrew, as *Grimbs*, was granted
land in Chester County in 1775, but his Revolutionary War Accounts
Audited generally cited him as *Graham*. In 1785, as *Graham*, he
witnessed the will of John Caskey, but in 1786, as *Grimes*, he was a
witness in a court case. He also often served on the county jury.
Before about 1787 he was listed as Andrew *Grimes*; after 1787 he was
Andrew *Graham*. In summary, the change in the spelling was gradual, but
it may generally be said that the Graham name was spelled as such soon
after the 1790 census was taken. Before that time it was often spelled
*Grimes* or *Grimbs*, and these spelling variants probably explain the
silence on the Grahams' family history before the present time.

The following are photocopies of South Carolina documents which
show the spelling variants of the Graham name. Every effort has been
made to secure clear copies, but it should be remembered that most of
the documents are more than two hundred years old. Pages are torn and
the ink sometimes barely legible. Nonetheless, the important passages
can be discerned.

The first photocopy, consisting of three pages, is taken from
South Carolina's Council Journal, pp. 13, 13B, and 14. The pages do
not represent a passenger list; they are a listing of the people who
had recently arrived in Charleston from Ireland and who went before the
South Carolina General Assembly to request land. The figures next to
the entries give the amount of acreage warranted to each applicant, the
practice being to warrant one hundred acres to each adult male and one
hundred acres to each adult unmarried female. An adult married male
was also assigned an additional fifty acres apiece for each member of
his household, including servants. Single adults could be as young as
fourteen years old. Those who could pay the fees of about £5 per hundred acres were listed first; those who could not pay the fees were
listed next. David Graham (*Grimbs*), whose name appeared on the first
page of the list of people who had sailed on the *Pennsylvania Farmer*,
could pay the fees. Andrew *Grumbs*, Jean *Grimbs*, and Matthew *Grimbs*
could not pay the fees and were listed close to the end on the third
page. Each was assigned one hundred acres which signified that each
was a single adult and eventually would receive the land as grants.

Note the names Matthew and William Mebin on the second page and
Martha and Mary Meabin on the third. Andrew's daughter Mary later
married an Andrew Maben.

## Lord Charles Greville Montagu Governor

| | Acres |
|---|---|
| 9th January 1768 Alexander Douglas | 300 |
| George Thomson | 100 |
| John Beard | 250 |
| Mary Shepherd | 100 |
| William Spends | 400 |
| Joseph Gray | 250 |
| Robert Matthews | 300 |
| Elizabeth Matthews | 100 |
| Margaret Matthews | 100 |
| Janet Patterson | 100 |
| James McCauley | 100 |
| Robert Alexander | 150 |
| Alexander Craig | 100 |
| John Thomson | 150 |

In South Carolina

Ordered that the Secretary do prepare Warrants of Survey as prayed for by the several Petitioners.

A List of Passengers arrived from Ireland in the Ship Pennsylvania Farmer and this day Petitioned for Land viz.

| | Acres |
|---|---|
| John Logue | 400 |
| James Moore | 300 |
| James Phillips | 250 |
| John Smith Senior | 250 |
| Francis Patterson | 250 |
| David McCright | 150 |
| William McCright | 400 |
| David McCright | 200 |
| William Young | 300 |
| William Riley | 350 |
| Thomas Prince | 350 |
| Archibald Todd | 250 |
| David Grimbo | 400 |

In South Carolina

## His Excellency The Right Honorable

| | | |
|---|---|---|
| 6 July 1772 | Nathaniel McDill | 500 |
| | John Cochran | 100 |
| | Samuel McGee | 100 |
| | John Smith Junr | 100 |
| | James Fairy | 100 |
| | David Dunn | 100 |
| | William McKeen | 100 |
| | James McCreight | 100 |
| | Ann Young | 100 |
| | Francis Arbuthnot | 450 |
| | Hugh Wear | 350 |
| | Samuel Jamble | 300 |
| | James Harbinson | 150 |
| | William Brown | 450 |
| | Moley McRoy | 150 |
| | Robert Caldwell | 450 | In South Carolina |
| | Thomas Scott | 300 |
| | Samuel Hall | 150 |
| | Andrew Spence | 300 |
| | Robert Spear | 350 |
| | Mary Kieston | 200 |
| | James McMaster | 250 |
| | James McConaghy | 100 |
| | John Sprowl | 100 |
| | David Miller | 300 |
| | James Mann | 200 |
| | James Barber | 250 |
| | Matthew Mehan | 150 |
| | William Mehan | 200 |
| | John McCory | 100 |
| | Alexander Gaston | 100 |
| | John Sinton | 100 |
| | James Walker | 100 |
| | John McChesney | 100 |

## Lord Charles Grenville Montagu Governor

| | | |
|---|---|---|
| 6th June 1753 | James Hill | 100 |
| | Alexander McCauley | 100 |
| | Elizabeth Allan | 100 |
| | Mary Leak | 100 |
| | Samuel Logue | 100 |
| | Agnes Wilson | 100 |
| | Elizabeth Wilson | 100 |
| | Agnes Harbison | 100 |
| | Mary Gaston | 100 |
| | Jean Young | 100 |
| | Mary Ann McCartney | 100 |
| | Mary Strawn | 100 |
| | William Hill | 100 |
| | John Miller | 100 |
| | Elizabeth Miller | 100 |
| | James Spence | 100 |
| | Mary Spence | 100 |
| | Jean Spence | 100 |
| | Jean Todd | 100 |
| | Martha Meabin | 100 |
| | Mary Meabin | 100 |
| | John Blear | 100 |
| | John Brown | 100 |
| | William Brown | 100 |
| | John Barber | 100 |
| | Andrew Grimke | 100 |
| | Jean Grimke | 100 |
| | Matthew Grimke | 100 |
| | William Caldwell | 100 |
| | Robert Caldwell | 100 |
| | Jane Caldwell | 100 |

In South Carolina

On this and the next page are photocopied documents concerning the land which Andrew *Grumbs* was warranted on 6 January 1773 and which was eventually granted to him. The first is a plat dated 1 July 1773 and is located in *Colonial Plats*, Volume 16, page 243; the second, which is the final grant dated 17 March 1775, is in *Royal Grants*, Volume 35, page 301. The land is described as follows: "a tract of land containing one hundred acres situate in Craven County on a branch of Rockey Creek bounded NE by James Knox's land SE by Francis Hendersons land SW by Benjamin Mitchells land NW by Lard Burns's land the other sides by vacant land. . . ." Chester County was later formed from Craven County. Note that Andrew is called Andrew *Grimbs* in these documents, not Andrew *Grumbs*.

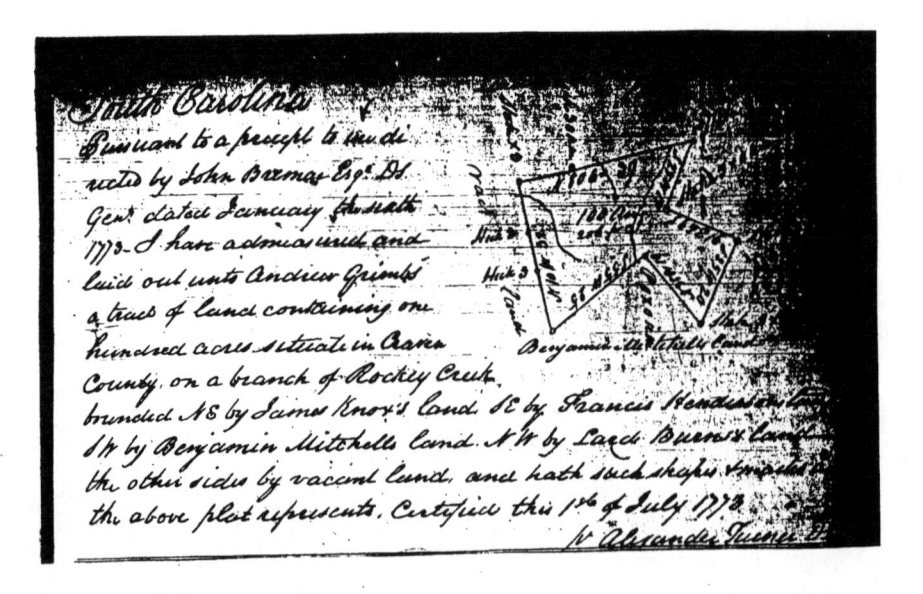

**SOUTH-CAROLINA.**

307

**GEORGE** the *Third* by the Grace of God, of GREAT-BRITAIN, FRANCE and IRELAND, KING, Defender of the Faith, and so forth; TO ALL TO WHOM THESE PRESENTS shall come Greeting: KNOW YE, THAT WE of our special Grace, certain Knowledge and mere Motion, have given and granted, and by these Presents, for us our heirs and successours, DO GIVE AND GRANT unto *Andrew Grimbs his* heirs and assigns, a plantation or tract of land containing *One hundred acres, situate in Craven County, bounding North East on James Knox's Land, South on Francis Henderson's Lands, South West on Benjamin Mitchell's Land, North West on Lard Burns Land; the other sides on Vacant Land*

And hath such shape, form and marks, as appear by a plat thereof, hereunto annexed: Together with all woods, under-woods, timber and timber-trees, lakes, ponds, fishings, waters, water-courses, profits, commodities, appurtenances and hereditaments whatsoever, thereunto belonging or in anywise appertaining: Together with privilege of hunting, hawking and fowling in and upon the same, and all mines and minerals whatsoever; saving and reserving, nevertheless, to us, our heirs and successours, all white pine-trees, if any there should be found growing thereon; and also saving and reserving, nevertheless, to us, our heirs and successours, one tenth-part of mines of gold and silver only: TO HAVE AND TO HOLD, the said tract of *One hundred* acres of land and all and singular other the premises hereby granted unto the said *Andrew Grimbs his* heirs and assigns for ever, in free and common soccage, the said *Andrew Grimbs his* heirs and assigns yielding and paying therefor, unto us, our heirs and successours, or to our Receiver-General for the time being, or to his Deputy or Deputies for the time being, yearly, that is to say, on the twenty-fifth day of March, in every year, at the rate of three shillings sterling, or four shillings proclamation money, for every hundred acres, and so in proportion, according to the number of acres, contained herein; the same to commence at the expiration of two years from the date hereof. Provided always, and this present Grant is upon condition, nevertheless, that the said *Andrew Grimbs his* heirs or assigns, shall and do, yearly, and every year, after the date of these presents, clear and cultivate at the rate of three acres for every hundred acres of land, and so in proportion according to the number of acres herein contained; AND ALSO shall and do enter a minute or docket of these our letters patent in the office of our Auditor-General for the time being, in our said Province, within six months from the date hereof; AND upon condition, that if the said rent, hereby reserved, shall happen to be in arrear and unpaid for the space of three years from the time it shall become due, and no distress can be found on the said lands, tenements and hereditaments hereby granted; or if the said *Andrew Grimbs his* heirs or assigns shall neglect to clear and cultivate yearly and every year, at the rate of three acres for every hundred acres of land, and so in proportion, according the number of acres herein contained, or if a minute or docket of these our letters patent, shall not be entered in the office of our Auditor-General for the time being, in our said Province, within six months from the date hereof, that then and in any of these cases, this present Grant shall cease, determine and be utterly void and the said lands, tenements and hereditaments hereby granted, and every part and parcel thereof, shall revert to us, our heirs and successours, as fully and absolutely, as if the same had never been granted. PROVIDED ALSO, if the said tract containing *One hundred* acres of land or any part thereof, hereby mentioned to be granted unto the aforesaid *Andrew Grimbs* shall happen to be within the bounds or limits of any tract or tracts of land which have been granted, to be granted in any grant or grants signed by the Governour of the Province of North-Carolina, on or before the fourth day of June in the year of our Lord one thousand seven hundred and seventy-two, that then this grant shall be utterly null and void, any thing herein contained to the contrary notwithstanding.

Given under the Great Seal of our said Province.
WITNESS The Honble Will<sup>m</sup> Bull Esq<sup>r</sup>

Governour and Commander in chief in and over our said Province, this
*Seventeenth* Day of *May*
Anno Dom. 17*75* In the *Fifteenth*
*William (L. M. S.) Bull*
Signed by his Honor the Lieutenant Governor
And hath thereunto A plat thereof annexed

*John Bremar Deputy*

30

On 5 January 1790 Andrew *Graham* sold the land which he, as Andrew *Grimbs*, had received in the grant shown on the previous page, and the deed of sale, which appears on the next three pages, is recorded in Deeds Book B, pages 576-578. The description of the land in the deed, which matches the description in the grant, reads as follows:

> Whereas in and by a Certain grant bearing date the seventh Day of March in the year of our Lord one thousand seven hundred & seventy five under the hand of his excellency the right Hono[ra]ble William Bull Esquire Lieutnenant Governor in & over the state of So. Carolina & the great seal of the State for that purpose appointed did give & grant unto Andrew Graham a Plantation or tract of Land containing one hundred Acres situate in Chester County on the waters of Rocky Creek and bounded north East on James Knoxes land Sou East on Frances Hendersons Land So West on Benjamin Mitchells land North West on Lard Burnses land the other sides on Vacant Land & hath such shape form & marks as appears by a Platt thereof to the said Grant. . . .

The only discrepancy is the date of the grant which is given here as 7 March 1775. The actual date was 17 March 1775.

Note that except in one spot in this deed Andrew is referred to throughout as Andrew *Graham*. The exception occurs on the second page in the ninth line from the bottom. There, he is called Andrew *Grimes*.

43

This Indenture made this fifth day of January in the year of our Lord one thousand seven hundred & ninety and in the fourteenth year of the Independence of america between Andrew Graham & Margaret his wife of the County of Chester & State of So Carolina of the one part and David Burns of the County & State aforesaid of the other part Whereas in and by a certain grant bearing date the seventh day of March in the year of our Lord one thousand seven hundred & seventy five under the hand of his excellency the right Hon'ble William Bull Esquire Lieutenant Governor in & over the State of So Carolina & the great Seal of the State for that purpose affixed did give & grant unto Andrew Graham a Plantation or tract of Land containing one hundred acres situate in Chester County on the waters of Rocky Creek and bounded North East on James Knox's Land So East on Francis Henderson's Land So West on Benjamin Mitchell's Land

South West on said Burns' land the other sides on Vacant Lands & hath such shape form & marks as appears thereof by a Platt thereof to the said Grant annexed as in & by the said Pratt & Grant bearing date duly Recorded in the Secretaries Office of the said State reference thereunto had may more fully appear Now this INDENTURE WITNESSETH that the said Andrew Graham & Margaret his wife for and in Consideration of the sum of fifteen pounds Sterling to him in hand well & truly paid at & before the sealing & delivery of these presents the receipt whereof they do hereby acknowledge to be well contented satisfied & paid hath granted bargained & sold aliened conveyed released conveyed & confirmed & by these presents do grant bargain & sell alien release convey & confirm unto the said Laird Burns in his actual Possession being by virtue of a bargain & sale for one whole year by Indenture bearing date the day next before the date hereof and by force of the Statute for transferring uses into Possession and to his Heirs and Assigns forever all the said Plantation or tract of land of one hundred acres together with all & singular the Houses out Houses Edifices buildings Barns Stables Gardens Orchards Woods underwoods Timber & timber trees meadows Pastures Lakes ponds fishings ways Waters & Watercourses paths passages liberties priviledges profits benefit claim and demand whatsoever of him the said Andrew Graham and Margaret his wife of into or out of the said premises & every part thereof & every part thereof & all said Evidences Escripts & Writings whatsoever touching or concerning the Premises & every part thereof TO HAVE & to hold the said Plantation or tract of one hundred acres as aforesaid with every the Premises & appurtenances thereunto belonging herein before granted released conveyed & confirmed unto the said Laird Burns his Heirs & Assigns forever they the said Andrew Graham & Margaret doth hereby for themselves their Executors Administrators & Assigns Covenant promise & agree to & with the said Laird Burns his Heirs & Assigns in Manner & form following, Viz that they the said Andrew Graham & Margaret his wife now & untill the Execution of these presents shall stand seized of a good sure perfect & indefeasible Estate of Inheritance in fee simple of & all the said Plantation of one hundred acres & land with the rights privileges & appurtenances Hereditaments & premises & Everything thereunto belonging or appertaining & hath in themselves good right full power & lawfull authority times hereafter peacably and quietly have hold use occupy possess & enjoy the said Plantation or Tract of one hundred acres of Land with every the Premises & Appurtenances thereto belonging without any manner of hindrance molestation hindrance molestation or Denial of them the said Andrew Graham & Margaret his wife their Heirs & Assigns or of all & every other person or persons whatsoever And lastly the said Andrew Graham and Margaret his wife ~~himself & assigns~~ for themselves their Heirs Executors Administrators the said Plantation or tract of Land Containing one hundred acres with the Premises & appurtenances unto the said Lord Burns his Heirs & Assigns against them the said Andrew Graham & Margaret his wife their Heirs & Assigns & all & every other person or persons whatsoever shall & will warrant & forever defend by these presents In Witness whereof the said Andrew Graham and Margaret his wife hath hereunto set their hands & seals the day & year first above written Signed Sealed

and Delivered in presence of us —

Samuel Henderson

Margaret  her  McConnell
          mark

Andrew Graham (seal)

Margaret  her  Graham (seal)
          mark

The two documents on the following page are from David Graham's Revolutionary War Accounts Audited 3144B.  In the first, dated 26 June 1781, he is referred to as David *Grimes*.  In the second, dated less than a month later--13 July 1781--he is called David *Graham*.

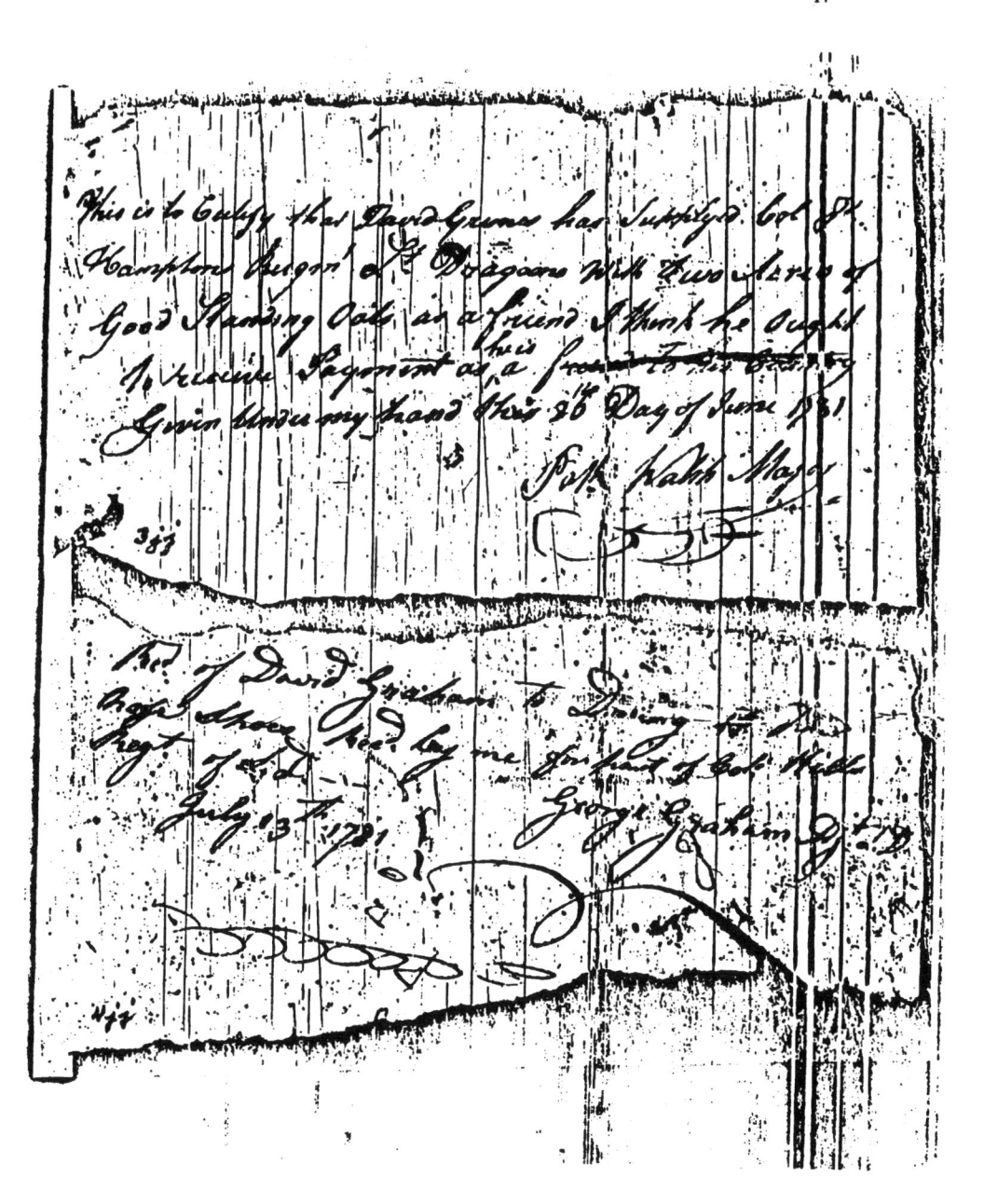

This is to Certify that David Graves has Supplyed Col. Jn.
Hamptons Regmt. of Light Dragoons with Two Acres of
Good Standing Oats as a friend I think he Ought
to receive Payment as a friend to his Country
Given under my hand this 26 Day of June 1781

Pett. Wakie Major

Recd. of David Graham to Serving the
Regt. of &c. [illegible] by me Inspect of Col. Will
July 13th 1781
George Graham

The next two pages give copies of documents in James Graham's Revolutionary War Accounts Audited 3030. On the first page appears the name "James Graham's"; this is immediately followed by "(or Grimes)." The second page is a copy of a letter recommending a payment to James. The writer says an order for payment had previously been made "in the Name of James Grimes--in this Name his Accounts Audited, but he has signed his Name to the Order for his Indent [as] James Graham which is his proper Name. . . ."

James Graham's
(no Grimes)
Orders presented
by Wm Maund
See Entry Book
May 28th 1792

Rejected

was [illegible] 27 May 1785
by [illegible] no 321 [illegible]
for £56
[illegible]
by [illegible]

Gentlemen,  High Hills 4th July 1788

When I was last in Town in [illegible], I apply'd for an Indent on an order of James Graham, which was due him for 12 Months' Service in of Colo. Maham's State Legion; By some means I left the Paper in the Treasury without getting the Indent thereon, the paper here on it laying before a Committee of the House in this there appears to have been a mistake, he having taken a Copy of his Service (wrote by Capt. Stevens who writes in the Aud. Genl. Office) in the name of James Grimes, in this name the Account is credited, but he has signed his name to the order for his Indent, James Graham which is his proper name. Should [illegible] particular kind of you to settify your files on this head by shewing this to Capt. Stevens in order that you may be [illegible] in sending the Indent, which should amount to £56. Sterling

Your [illegible] respectfully

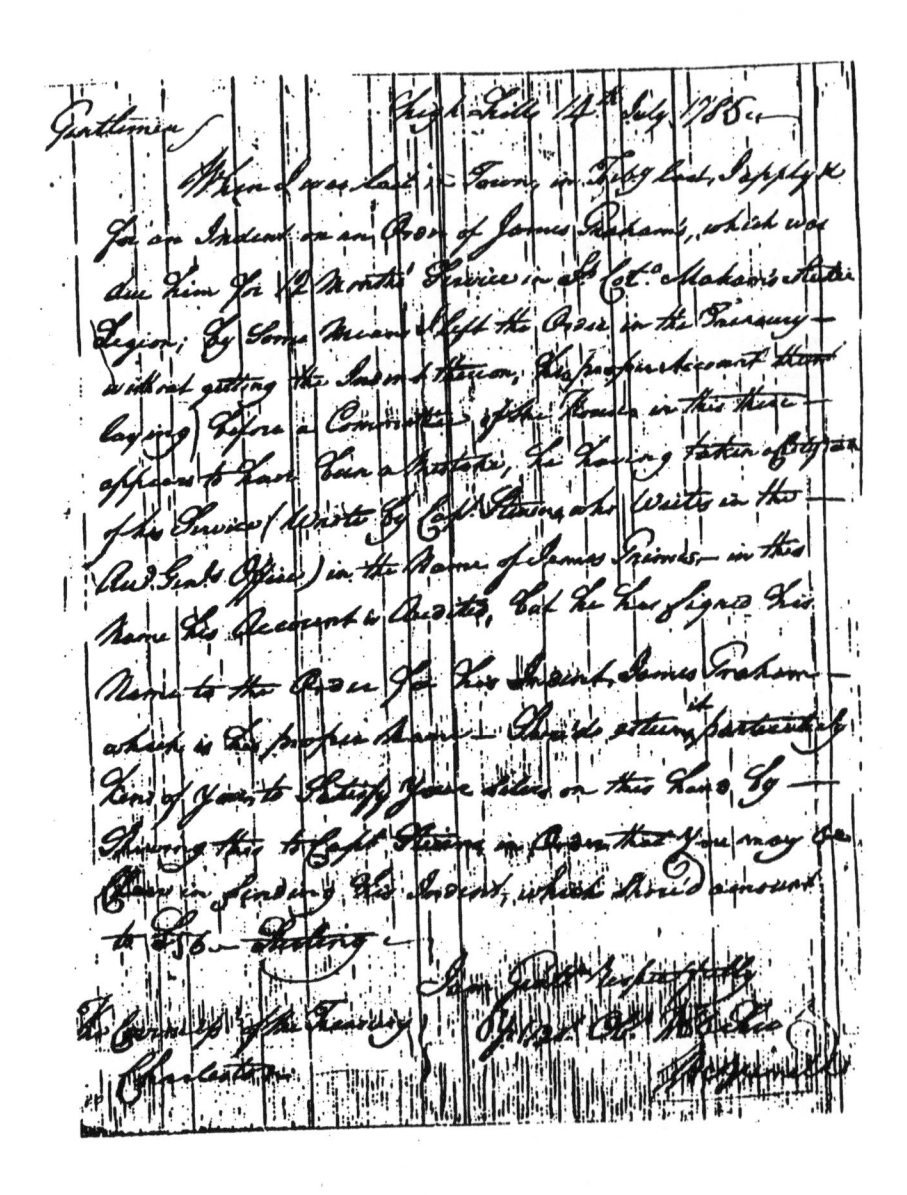

The Commissioners of the Treasury
Charleston

During the Revolutionary War both Andrew and James fought in more than one militia. The first in which they fought was that of Capt. Alexander Turner's company in the Upper Battalion of Samuel Richardson's Regiment under the command of Major Joseph Brown. The following page is a copy of the militia's roster as of 21 December 1778. The document is located in the Andrew Richardson Papers in the South Caroliniana Library at the University of South Carolina. (Permission to reproduce the document has been granted by the university.) Andrew and James are listed one after another and are called *Grimbs*.

Other names should be noted, particularly those of John Dick, Thomas McClorken, and John *Madill* (McDill).

A Return of Capt. Alexander Turner's company of Militia Belonging to The Upper Battalion of Colonel Richardson's Regiment who Marched the 7th Inst. under the Command of Major Joseph Brown Esq. Now in Camps Near Monks Corner

Officers and Privates

| Names &c. | Guns | Ammunition |
|---|---|---|
| Alexander Turner Capt. | Gun | None |
| John Dick Serj. | do | |
| Willm. Bokenberry Private | | |
| James Wilson | | |
| John McGluskan | | |
| James Stinson | Gun | |
| Mathew McGluskan | Gun | |
| John Madill | Gun | |
| Alexr. Chesnut | Gun | |
| Andrew Grimbo | Gun | |
| James Grimbo | Gun | |
| Denry Castles | | |
| Henry McClelland | | |
| Thomas McGluskan | | |
| Hugh McDonald | Gun | |

Dec. 21. 1778

Although James Graham had difficulty in receiving a Revolutionary War pension because of the spelling variant, he eventually did so in 1833. The following document from his pension records (S21786) consists of his testimony concerning his war participation. As will be noted, he said, "In the beginning of the month of December 1778, being Seventeen years of age, I was drafted under Capt. Alexander Turner, Major Brown and Brigadier Genl. Richardson. . . ." The roster of this company is reproduced on the previous page, and on the roster James is listed as James *Grimbs*. His brother is listed as Andrew *Grimbs*.

The State of South Carolina } ss
Chester District.

On this Second day of April, one thousand eight hundred and thirty three, personally appeared in open court, before the Honorable Richard Gantt one of the Judges of the court of General Sessions and common Pleas of said District and State, now sitting, James Graham, a resident of Chester District, and State of South Carolina aged Seventy two years, who being first duly sworn according to law, doth, on his oath, make the following declaration, in order to obtain the benefit of the act of Congress passed June Seventh, one thousand eight hundred and thirty two.

That he entered the service of the United States under the following named officers and served from the year 1778 to the year 1782 as herein stated – "In the begining of the month of December 1778, being Seventeen years of age, I was drafted under Capt. Alexander Turner, Major Brown and Brigadier Genl. Richardson, we lay at Monk's Corner some time and proceeded to the quarter house near Charlestown, from thence we crossed the Edisto River, through Jacksonborough to the town of Purrysburgh, where we fell under the command of General Lincoln, who I believe had his head quarters at that place, we remained at Purrysburgh until my term of service expired – about the first March 1779 when I returned home, immediately on my return home I was called out with all those leable to do duty, under the command of Capt. Turner and Lieutenant Col. Brown we marched to Orangeburgh, where we lay a considerable time, and then marched to Black Swamp, the British troops being after us, we were compelled to retire to Charlestown, where I believe, we remained six months, if not longer."

"In the begining of the year 1781 I was attached to Capt. John Turner's Militia Company, under Col. Lacy, we joined General

Sumter, and marched to the Congaree Fort, which we besieged for some time — we were compelled to abandon the siege and marched towards Charleston — on our route we met a party of the enemy — killed and took nearly the whole of them — we then crossed the Santee River and had an engagement with the enemy — Gen.<sup>l</sup> Sumter retreated — we then marched to Kings-Tree on Black River, from thence to the Waxsaw where we were dismissed."

"In the month of March 1781 a small party under the command of Lieutenant James Kennedy attacked a party of Tories at the plantation of old James Wylie, in this District, on Rocky Creek — we routed them through the old fields — they returned, and owing to superior numbers, they compelled our party to leave the field, after killing one of our men, Samuel Wylie, the son of old James Wylie — we killed a Tory by the name of — Fair."

"In the month of May 1781 I was attached to Capt. John Turner's company under Col. Hampton — we marched to the Congaree Fort, after besieging it a short time — the enemy surrendered to Col. Lee and I returned home."

"In the month of July 1781 I again started out with Capt. Turner, and left the company to drive cattle for General Green's army, which occupied my time about one month."

"In the month of February 1782 under the command of Capt. Turner, we marched to Orangeburgh and fell under the command of Major Wallis. we guarded the jail containing Tory prisoners about two months — In the month of May 1782 under the command of Major Hanna we hunted the woods on the Edisto River for about two months, for Tories." This was the last of my Revolutionary services. I now live in the same neighbourhood that I lived in during the Revolutionary War.

Deponent further says he has no written discharge and hereby relinquishes every claim whatever to a pension or annuity except the present, and declares his name is not on the pension role of the Agency of any State or Territory.

Sworn to and subscribed
the day and year aforesaid
in open Court
    T. Roseborough D. Ch.

                James Graham

The State of South Carolina }
Chester District       } I, George Gill, Sr, aged Seventy two years do hereby certify that I was personally acquainted with the above named James Graham in the time of the Revolutionary War.

                                  Geo Gill

Sworn to and subscribed
the day and year aforesaid
in open Court
    T. Roseborough D. Ch.

The State of South Carolina }
Chester District       } We, J LeRoy Davies a clergyman residing in the District of Chester and George Gill Sr residing in the same place hereby certify that we are well acquainted with James Graham, who has subscribed and sworn to the foregoing declaration; that we believe him to be Seventy-two years of age; that he is reputed and believed, in the neighbourhood where he resides, to have been a soldier of the Revolution, and that we concur in that opinion.

                          J. LeRoy Davies
                          Geo Gill

Sworn, and subscribed
the day and year aforesaid
in open Court
    T. Roseborough D. Ch.

The photocopy above is from Andrew Graham's Accounts Audited 3024. In this document dated 27 April 1785 Andrew is called *Graham* and is listed as a member of John Turner's Company. Other members of the company were John Dick and Thomas McClorken both of whom were also members of Alexander Turner's company in 1778 as listed in the roster on page 52 above. In the 1778 company Andrew Graham was listed as Andrew *Grimbs*. Because most Revolutionary War soldiers were members of several consecutive militias during the war, it may be assumed that John Dick, Thomas McClorken, and Andrew Graham/*Grimbs* fought at different times in the companies of both Alexander Turner and John Turner.

On the last two pages in this section are affidavits in James Graham's Accounts Audited 3030. One was signed by Thomas McClorken, the other by John McDill (*Madill*). Both men testified to having served with James during the Revolution, and both were listed with James and Andrew *Grimbs* in Alexander Turner's company in 1778.

So Carolina } personally came Thomas McClerken who
Chester District } be the subscribing Justice and being duly
sworn sayeth he was aquainted with James Grahm from
a boy that he knew that he was Early called out in to the
Servis in the Revulutionary War that he Beleves he was a
Good Soulder his first trip was in 1770 at
Jiuresburge he was Next in 1779 at Orengburg & at Black
Swamp and then Retreated with General Moultry in to
Charlstown he was then under Brid General Richerson and
Major Genl Lincon afterward he joined Sumpter & was with
him in the troop called the hounds he was also at the takeing
of Fodar fort he was then out under Col<sup>o</sup> Winn under gener
al green at the high hills then at Orengburg he was in
all the Battels in thos campains and at several Surmeges
of a Smaller Nature but Equaly Dangrus and still Behav
ed well he is Now grown old and Destetute of land & Spon
Says he has two small negroes of Six or Eight
Years of age — Sworn to the 2<sup>nd</sup> Nov<sup>r</sup> 1829
before David Jamieson JP }  Thomas McClerken
13<sup>oo</sup>

State of So Carolina } personally appeared John M. Gill before me the
Chester District    } subscribeing guides
and being sworn sayeth I was acquaint with James Grimes
as asolder the time of the revolutionary war and that he served
with me in the american serves and Can aform that he was
a good whig and I belive a true frend to this Country and he
bore the carector of a good soldger and that few exceled him in
turning out to do duty his first trip was in the year 1778 and
in the begining of the year 1779 to Purringbury under
the Comand of brigader Ritcheson and major Lincoln
the next sumer flowing out at orrengbury and towards
blake swamp and there the brutish drove them into Chearlston
and afterwards he gained general Sumter and was with him in
the trip Calld Sumters rounds nixt he was at the taking
of fridays fort nixt he was at orrs out I belive under general
Green and had Colonel Wins for Colonal nixt he served a campain
at Orengbury and then he was another trip out on Edisto Chara-
Pee he was with Sumter in the indon land   John M Gill
sworn before me this 19th day of oct 1827

John Moffat J.P.

## FIRST GENERATION

1-1 DAVID GRAHAM (also written *Grimbs* and *Grimes*) was born probably in County Antrim, Ireland,[1] died in Chester County, South Carolina, between 2 April 1795 and 18 November 1800 (dates of writing and probate of his will); married, probably in Ireland, JANET ___ who died in Chester County, South Carolina, 1800-9. Because there seems to have been a difference of several years in the ages of David's fourth and fifth children, it is thought that Janet may have been a second wife.

For a discussion of *Graham* spelling variants, see the Introduction, Section 6.

David and his family were among the five shiploads of settlers led by the Rev. William Martin from Ulster to South Carolina in late 1772. (See the Introduction, Section 3.) The ship David and his family took was the *Pennsylvania Farmer*[2] which left Belfast on 16 October 1772 and arrived at Charleston on 19 December 1772.[3] On 6 January 1773 David and most of the other heads of families in the group went before the South Carolina General Assembly to request land grants. Some of them, such as David, could pay the fees of about £5 per 100 acres; most could not pay and were assigned the land as bounty. In a Colonial Plat certified 5 April 1773, David (as David *Grimbs*) was warranted 400 acres in an area of Craven (later Chester) County; this tract was bounded by the lands of Joseph Carley, Jasper Rodgers, Jonathan Smith, Thomas Hickling, Jonathan Lee, and Mary Miller (Vol. 18, p. 327). There is no record of David's having paid for the land, however, so apparently he did not want it. (It was later granted to a John McQueen.) Nonetheless, David did buy land at about that time in Craven (Chester) County. This is known because in 1774 he was mentioned (as David *Grimbs*) in a deed assigning a 250-acre tract to Robert Jamieson, another of the group led by the Rev. William Martin. In this deed David was named as one of those whose land bounded Jamieson's (certified 6 June 1774; Vol. 19, p.

489). Others whose lands bounded Jamieson's were Robert Coulter, John Caskey, Thomas Huston, and Mary Coulter--most of whom were later connected with the Grahams. Robert and Mary Coulter were future in-laws of David's son 2-1 Andrew, and John Caskey was the future father-in-law of David's granddaughter 3-13 Julianna.

David had a Revolutionary War record. Specifically, he provided food and blacksmith services for the Patriots (Accounts Audited 3144B) and on 9 May 1785 was awarded £15 to be paid by 1787 at an annual interest of one pound, one shilling. In David's audited Revoluntionary accounts is a document dated 26 June 1781 in which he is cited as David *Grimes* while in another document dated less than a month later, 13 July 1781, he is cited as David *Graham*. Both documents are reproduced on page 47 above.

He is known to have been living in Chester County in 1785 because on 19 September of that year he (as David *Graham*) witnessed the will of John Caskey. Others who witnessed the same will were David's sons 2-1 Andrew and 2-5 John. Later David was also an appraiser of John Caskey's estate, the inventory having been signed and dated 21 September 1786.[4] On 5/6 October 1785 David (as *Graham*) bought 150 acres on a branch of Rocky Creek, Chester County, for £30 from Arthur Hicklin of Lancaster County, South Carolina (recorded 29 August 1820; Book T, p. 265).[5] After Chester County was formed on 24 March 1785, David (as *Grimes*) was called to serve on the county's grand jury during its October session of 1786.[6]

In the 1790 census David was listed in Chester County as David *Grimes*, and his sons were listed as Andrew *Grimes* and James *Grimes*. Shortly thereafter, the change of the name to *Graham* was apparently complete because no documents after that time have been found citing the Grahams as *Grimes* or *Grimbs*.

David and his family were members of Catholic Presbyterian Church in Chester County. Presumably, he and his wife lived in Chester County for the remainder of their lives. He was a blacksmith.

David's will, written and proved in Chester County, is transribed as follows verbatim:

In the Name of God amen--the Second day of April
1795 I David Graham of Chester County Pinkney district, &
State of South Carelina, Blacksmith, being Verry Weake of
Body, but of Perfect Mind & Memorey, thanks be given unto
God, therefore Calling unto mind the Mortallitey of my
Body & knowing that it is Appointed for all Men once to
die, do Make & ordain this my last Will & testament, that
is to Say, first & princiably of all I Give & Recommend
my Soul into the hands of Almighty God that give it, & my
Body I Recomend to the Earth, to be Buried in a Christan
& Desant Manner at the Discreschon of my Executors
hereafter Named & Nothing Dobting but at the Jennarel
Resureccton, that I Shall Recive the Same, Again, by the
Mighty power of God & as tuching Such Worldly Estate
Wherewith it hath pleased God to Bless me with in this
Life, I Give Devise & Dispose of the Same in the fol-
lowing Manner & form,------ Imprimis first & princi-
abley of all I Allow all my Lawfull debtes & Remander to
be paid by my Executors & 2 ly I Give & Bequeth to my
Well Beloved Wife Jenat Graham her Bed & Bed Cloase &
also A lawfull Mintance off the plantation What my
Executors thinks Suficent during Life & to be Buried
desantly at death by John & Marey 3 ly I Give & Bequeth
to my Well Beloved son Andrew my 2 ferring Books[7] & 4 ly
I Give & Bequeth to my Well Beloved daughter Jean Adams
Wife to Samuel Adams S4 & d8 pence sterl. & no more 5 ly
I Give & Bequeth to my Well beloved Son James Graham S4 &
d8 & no more 6 ly I Give & bequeth to my Well beloved
daughter Jinat Boys Wife to david Boys S4 & d8 & no more
& 7 ly I Give & bequeth to my Well Beloved Son John
Graham all my Smith tools & A sertin Bay horse & Saddle &
A sertin Black Meer Coalt formerly Called his Black Coalt
& 8 ly I Give & bequeth to my Well beloved daughter
Margret my old Black Meer & Saddle & two Cows & Calves
her Such of all About the house & her Equall Share of all
the Bed Cloase that is the third of them & likewise
Thirty Pounds Sterling to be paid to her in hand cash by
John & Marey & allso her third of all my Books Excepting
my House Bible that I allow to John & all the Remainder
of my property not Mentioned I Allow to be Equally
devided Between John & Marey & I do herby Constitute Make
& ordain James Chesnut & Andrew Graham & John Graham my
Sole Executrix of this my Last Will & Testament & I do
herby utterly disalow & Revoake & disanul all & Every
other former Tistaments Wills Leagises & bequests &
Executors by me in any ways before Named Willed &
bequethed Ratifying & Confirming this & no other to be my

Last Will & Testament in Wittness Whereof I have herunto
Set my hand & Seal the day & Year Above Written---

Signed Sealed published & Pronounced
& Declared by the Said David Graham
as his last Will & Testament
in the presants of us
the Subscribers                              David Graham (Seal)

James Chesnut
James Willson
James Boyd

This document was proved on 18 November 1800 and was recorded in Book B, p. 101. It is located in Apartment No. 21, Package No. 315.

After David died, his widow, Janet, probably lived with her children 2-5 John and 2-7 Mary neither of whom was married. Since John died in 1809 and did not mention his mother in his will, it is thought that Janet died before 1809.

The following are the known children of David Graham. The first four children may have been by a wife whose name is not known, but the last four children were probably by Janet:

2-1 Andrew, b. Ireland, *c.* 1753
2-2 Jean (Jane), b. Ireland, 1754-8
2-3 Matthew?, b. Ireland
2-4 James, b. Ireland, 1761
2-5 John, b. Ireland, before 1767
2-6 Jennet (Jane), b. Ireland, *c.* 1769
2-7 Mary, b. Ireland or South Carolina
2-8 Margaret, b. South Carolina, 1775-80

1-1 David                                                                                      2-1

## SECOND GENERATION

2-1 ANDREW GRAHAM (also written *Grumbs*, *Grimbs*, and *Grimes*),[1] born probably in County Antrim, Ireland, *c.* 1753, died in Todd County, Kentucky, between 11 March and May 1821 (dates of writing and probate of his will); married (1) in Chester County, South Carolina, MARGARET COULTER, born probably in County Tyrone, Ireland, died in Chester County, South Carolina, 1792-6, daughter of Robert Coulter and Mary Stuart;[2] Andrew married (2) probably in Chester County, *c.* 1797, MARGARET ___ (Mills?), born Ireland 1770-4, died Henderson County, Illinois, after 1840, perhaps a daughter of William Mills and Martha ___.[3]

For a discussion of the spelling variants of the name *Graham*, see the Introduction, Section 6.

Andrew, listed in the South Carolina Council Journal as Andrew *Grumbs*, came to America with his parents and siblings on the ship *Pennsylvania Farmer*[4] which left Belfast on 16 October 1772 and arrived at Charleston, South Carolina, on 19 December 1772.[5] He was part of the Rev. William Martin's group of five shiploads of settlers. (See the Introduction, Section 3.) On 6 January 1773 he went with the others before the South Carolina General Assembly to request land and on 17 March 1775, as Andrew *Grimbs*, received the single-person's grant of 100 acres. The land was in Craven (later Chester) County on Rocky Creek and was bounded by the lands of James Knox, Francis Henderson, Benjamin Mitchell, and Laird Burns (Royal Grant, Vol. 35, p. 307; and Colonial Plats, Vol. 16, p. 243--see pages 40 and 41 above).

Andrew may have married Margaret Coulter shortly before he received his land since their first child, Elizabeth, could have been born as early as 1775. On 6 February 1773 Margaret had been warranted 100 acres as a single person in Craven County on Rocky Creek on land bounded by that of Mary Ann Coulter (Margaret's sister) and Joseph Carley, other boundaries vacant (Colonial

Plats, Vol. 14, p. 202). Margaret had the following siblings: (a) Archibald, born Ireland, c. 1753, died Todd County, Kentucky 1824; (b) Mary Ann, died Todd County, Kentucky, c. 1825, married John Stevenson; (c) Elizabeth, married ___ Kell; and (d) Robert Stuart, born County Tyrone, Ireland, c. 1760, died Madison County, Illinois, 1821, married in South Carolina, c. 1798, Margaret Fleming. Both Archibald and Robert S. had Revolutionary War records,[6] and both, plus Mary Ann, received warrants in Craven County, South Carolina (Colonial Plats, Vol. 14, pp. 202-3).

During the Revolution Andrew fought in militias and provided beef for them, and on 24 May 1785 he filed a claim in the amount of 1 pound, 11 shillings, 5 pence sterling for his services.[7] One militia he fought in was that of Capt. John Turner in Colonel Winn's regiment. Another was that of Capt. Alexander Turner belonging to the Upper Battalion of Colonel Richardson's Regiment under the command of Major Joseph Brown. Among those in the company were his brother 2-4 James as well as James Willson, John Madill, Alexander Chesnut, and John, Matthew, and Thomas McClurken--all names associated with the Grahams.[8]

During the war Andrew's name appeared on at least one land document: on 27 October 1779 he witnessed a deed of sale from Samuel and Frances Fulton to Robert McCullough (Book E, pp. 168-170). After the war Andrew's name appeared often on deeds and other documents in Chester County: (1) on 19 September 1785, Andrew Graham and Archibald Coulter were named as executors of the will of John Caskey, witnessed by Andrew as well as his father, David, and brother John;[9] (2) July 1786, Andrew *Grimes* was paid 10 shillings for four days in court as a witness for Thomas McClurkin in his suit against John Holeman;[10] (3) 5 January 1790, Andrew and Margaret Graham sold to Lard (sic) Burns, for £15, 100 acres granted to Andrew *Grimbs* on 17 March 1775 (Book B, pp. 576-8); (4) 7 May 1791, John Cameron sold to Andrew Graham 200 acres on Rocky Creek, Chester County (recorded 23 July 1799, Book G, pp. 94-7); (5) 3 July 1791, Andrew and Margaret Graham sold to Hugh McMillian 100 acres warranted to Margaret Coulter in 1773 (Book E, p. 263); (6) January 1792, Andrew Graham gave an indenture of lease and release to Lard (sic) Burns (Order Book B, p. 167);[11] (7) 22 November 1792, Andrew Graham and Robert Caskey witnessed two deeds of sale to John McKee from Matthew and Jenny McClurkin (Book F, pp. 142-6); (8) 28 November 1794, Andrew Graham, James Brown, and James Chesnut were witnesses to the will of Thomas McDill of Chester County;[12] (9) 25 January 1797, a release from Andrew Graham to Hugh McMillen;[13] (10) 24 January 1797, Andrew Graham, Matthew McClurkin, and John Mabin were named as witnesses to the will of David Weir;[14] (11) 25 January 1799, Andrew Graham was paid

1-1 David                                                                                                                    2-1

for three days at court as a witness on behalf of James Boyd in his suit against William Reedy and David Bell;[15] (12) 9 May 1799, Andrew Graham, his son Matthew Graham, and his son-in-law Adam Mills were witnesses to two deeds of sale to another son-in-law, John Gleghorn (Book W, pp. 3-5); and (13) 24 July 1799, Andrew Graham, James Cooper, and Adam Mills appeared in court as witnesses to the will of John McKee.[16] John McKee was probably the future father-in-law of Andrew's third son, Robert C. Graham.

Andrew also served on the jury in the Chester County court at the January and July terms of 1787 and the July term of 1799, and in two court cases he acted as foreman of the jury.[17] (Before July 1787 he was listed as Andrew *Grimes* in the court records; after that time he was called Andrew *Graham*.) Also, in April 1790 Andrew was one of the men appointed as overseers for the construction of a north-south road beginning at the York County line on the North and continuing to Fairfield County on the South. Andrew's section was large: it began near Bull Run which is near the center of the county and continued south to the Fairfield County line.[18] In September 1792, however, Andrew was relieved of his duty as overseer, and William Reedy was appointed in his stead.[19] It is thought that Andrew's wife, Margaret Coulter, became ill or died at about this time, and her illness or death may have accounted for his being released from duty.

It is not known when Andrew and Margaret ___ (Mills?), his second wife whom he married c. 1797, moved to Kentucky, although they probably did so late in 1805. The earliest known land purchase by Andrew in Kentucky was in September 1809, but Andrew sold 200 acres in Chester County on 24 October 1805 to John McClurkin for $900 (Book L, p. 249--incidentally, in this deed Andrew indentified himself as a blacksmith as was his father before him). The land which Andrew sold in 1805 was that which he had bought from John Cameron in 1791 after selling his and his first wife's land grants, and because no land sale by Andrew has been found in Chester County dated later than 1805 it is assumed that those 200 acres represented his total holdings there. Andrew's name did appear on two other documents after he sold his land: he proved two land deeds to his son-in-law John Gleghorn on 1 November "1806." Since these deeds were not recorded until 17 October 1825 (Book W, pp. 3-5), and, as mentioned above, no other land sale by Andrew dated later than 1805 has been found in Chester County, the date "1806" was probably an error on the part of the recording clerk, and the actual date of Andrew's proof of the two deeds was 1 November 1805.

Whenever it was that Andrew and Margaret moved to Kentucky,

they were preceded by Andrew's daughter and son-in-law Janet and Adam Mills whose second child was born in Kentucky in 1803. Andrew's son Matthew and his wife, Jennette, may also have moved to Kentucky shortly after they were married in about 1804. As was the custom when whole families migrated, Adam and perhaps Matthew may have returned briefly to South Carolina in 1805 to guide Andrew and his family to the area of Kentucky where they eventually settled. Eight of Andrew's ten children then living went with them (the ones who remained in South Carolina were 3-1 Elizabeth Graham Gleghorn and 3-5 David), and perhaps, also, they traveled in a group of several other families who may well have included those named McKee, Coulter, Maben, Brown, Wilson, and Chesnut. These Chester County families are known to have moved to Logan/Christian/Todd Counties, Kentucky, where Andrew lived.

An explanation of the formations of the Kentucky counties of Logan, Todd, and Christian is necessary in order to make clear Andrew's various legal transactions there. These three counties are contiguous, east to west, and they were all part of Logan County when it was formed at the time Kentucky became a state in 1792. (At that time Logan County was large, including many more subsequent counties than these three.) In 1796 Christian County was formed from Logan, and in 1819 Todd County was formed literally between the two, taking some of the western part of Logan and some of the eastern part of Christian.[20] Therefore, Andrew's various legal affidavits in these three counties reflect only the fact that he probably lived in the same general area during the entire time despite the name of the county he lived in at any given time. The general area in which he lived was the south-central part of present Todd County.

The following are known deeds in Kentucky bearing Andrew's name: (1) on 1 September 1809, Griffin and Margaret Dickerson of Christian County sold to Andrew Graham of Logan County 129 acres on the Elk Fork of the Red River in Logan County for $387 (Book B, p. 573); (2) 20 April 1811, Andrew witnessed a deed of land sale from Bartley and Polly Pitts to William McKee (Book C, p. 261); (3) 6 October 1812, Andrew bought 210 acres adjoining his first tract on the Elk Fork of the Red River in Logan County for $250 from Beverly A. Allen, witnessed by his son Matthew Graham and son-in-law Adam Mills (Book C, p. 561); (4) 1 January 1818, Andrew Graham of Christian County sold to Cornelius Hall of Logan County 238 acres "on both sides of the Elk Fork of the Red River on which said Graham lived on the first day of January 1818" (this included parts of both tracts bought from Dickerson and Allen--Book M, p. 108); (5) 29 August 1819, Andrew Graham, formerly of Logan County, now of Christian County, sold to Samuel Smith 90 acres on the Elk

Fork of the Red River, witnessed by William McKee and Adam Mills (this was part of the purchase from Beverly Allen in 1812--Book G, p. 378); and (6) 23 October 1820, Finis and Margaret Ewing of Todd County sold to Andrew Graham of Todd County 340 acres for $2,210 on Reins Lick Creek, bounded by lands of Widow Shanklin, James Johnson, Joseph Roberts, and Samuel Jameson (Book A, p. 49). The Widow Shanklin (Frances Gartin Shanklin) was the future mother-in-law of Andrew's daughter 3-7 Martha. Finis Ewing was later a founder of The Cumberland Presbyterian Church.

The land which Andrew sold to Cornelius Hall in 1818 came under legal dispute on 20 November 1819 when Hall sued Andrew, charging that fifty acres of the land Andrew sold to him was claimed by a man named Smith Lofland. Testimony in the case showed Lofland to be a malicious prankster, however. Lofland had been with Andrew and Hall when the land was surveyed prior to the sale, and he had made no claim to it at that time except for about an acre near the creek. Also, a John Cross testified that he had considered buying Andrew's land before Hall bought it, that he (Cross) had gone to see Lofland to inquire about any claim and Lofland said he had none, and that Lofland then stated he had once run through Andrew's land with his compass only to "pester the old man." The case was dismissed at the November term of 1820 (Logan County, Kentucky, Court Records E-C-9 #177).

The 1819 Tax List showed that Andrew had 340 acres of "second rate land" with a total value of $2,955.

By the time Andrew and his family moved to Kentucky, the Indians were no longer a menace in that part of the country. Even so, conditions were primitive as the following excerpts indicate. They are from a series of articles written by Urban Ewing Kennedy and published by *The Todd County Witness* beginning in 1872. Kennedy was born in Lincoln County, Kentucky, in 1799 and in 1809 brought by his parents to Todd County where he lived out his life. His articles afforded a rare view of the time and place:

> The only water mill was John Carson's, where Reames and Bradshaw's mill now stands. This was the first water mill built in Todd; she only had one pair of runners, and, when we had wheat to grind, we had to turn the bolt by hand; and a jocular old fellow, when enquired of how the new mill was doing, answered firmly, "She is doing a brisk business, for, as soon as she gets one grain smashed, she hops instantly on another." We had some horse-mills, and hand-mills, and some times beat our

meal in mortars. There were settlements along the Elkfork; Millens, Cunninghams, Coulters, Grahams, Chesnuts; and after a few years Daniel N. Russell moved into the neighborhood. All these and many others were Seceders, and Covenanters of the strictest sect, and most excellent citizens. The old stock have all gone to their rewards, and their children and grandchildren make the best of Cumberland Presbyterians, "having been taught the scriptures from their youth." All down the creek, where spots of timber grew, the first settlers pitched their cabins. . . . In this neighborhood, lived Uncle Jimmy Allen, first Coroner of Todd, and auctioneer general for all this country. He was of Irish origin. He cried all the sales of this new region. He would proclaim the terms and commence to sell, with a bottle of whisky in his left hand and his cane in his right hand. . . .

The religious customs and training of that early day was quite different from the present. The Old School Presbyterians under the ministry of McGready, Temple, and W. K. Stewart, whose church and center was old Rockbridge, two miles above Elkfork, and the well known and remembered Peter Cartwright, one mile and a half east of Hopkinsville. These were all the Methodist preachers I knew in that early day. There were others, no doubt, but as a small boy, my circle of acquaintances was very limited. . . . John Graham [a Methodist minister unrelated to Andrew], about this time, who was surrounded by the Seceders, Covenanters, had a public debate with Samuel Brown, a very talented minister of the Seceders of Elkfork.

Mr. Brown affirmed the doctrines of election and reprobation, and Mr. Graham denied, and advocated the doctrines of free grace and a possible salvation for all men. Both were men of talent, and they carried on for days their altercations, and being but a boy I didn't remember to hear the finality of the matter, more than as at the present time, both sides claiming the victory; for the O. S [Old School] Presbyterians, Covenanters and Seceders were for Brown, and the Methodists and Cumberland Presbyterians for Graham. The peculiarities of the Seceders were the undeviating principles of catechising their rising posterity in the fundamental doctrines of their church, keeping sacredly the Holy Sabbath, all preparations made the day or week previous, nothing to

be transacted only works of necessity; all of which I
think is a characteristic of true Christianity. They
were generally men of excellent character, and stuck
close to their creeds and doctrines. They would not
sing on the Lord's day, and think but the pure psalmody
of the sweet singer of Israel, saying "I'll have none of
your wriggling ditties, but give me the sweet, pure,
sweet psalmody that David made in Swate ould Ireland."

Well, they are all gone now to their reward, and
many of them are resting in the city of the dead that
surrounds the Seceder church, called Hopwell [Hope-
well]; here lie the parents and relatives of the best
citizens of Todd.

The exact date of Andrew's death cannot be determined. The
only facts known are that he wrote or dictated his will on 11
March 1821 and that it was proved during the May court session of
1821. Probably, he died not long after his will was written. The
following is a verbatim transcription of the will:

In the name of God Amen March the 11th Eighteen hundred
& twenty one. I Andrew Graham of Todd county & State of
Kentucky being very Sick & weak of body but of perfect
mind & memory Thanks be to god. Therefore Calling to
mind the mortality of my Body & knowing that it is
appointed for all men once to die do make & constitute
this to be my last Will & Testament that is to Say
principally & first of all I give & recommend my Soul
unto god who gave it & my body I Recommend to the Earth
to be buried in a decent & Christian manner at the
Discretion of my Executors nothing doubting but at the
general Resurection I shall receive the same again by
the mighty power of God touching Such worldly estate
whereof it has pleased god to bless me in this life I
Give devise & dispose in the following manner Viz, I
will & bequeath my plantation containing near five
hundred acres to my three Sons William M. Graham Thomas
Graham & Andrew to be equally divided between them
according to the valueation my Sone Andrew is to have
his part laid off in the middle lot so as to include all
my improvements also the Timber part of my land I wish
in the Division to be equally divided between my three
sons if any of them should die in their non age the
land to be divided between the surviving heirs my son

1-1 David                                                              2-1

William is to have the mare which he calls his & is to
pay thirty dollars to to [sic] my wife and Daughter[s]
at the expiration of two years from this date which
money is to be equally divided between my wife & three
daughters my wife Margret is to have a decent support
off my farm  after paying my Just Debts all the balance
of my property is to be equally divided between my wife
& three daughters (to wit) my wife Margret & Martha
Margaret & Nancy my 3 daughters my wifes part at her
death is to be equally divided between my three daughters above mentioned  my widowed daughter Mary Maben is
not to be disturbed in her possesion which she may
choose to keep them or untill the land is sold  my
book[s] to be equally divided to all the above mentioned
except my son Andrew is to have my large bible for his
share of Books.  I will & bequeath to Elizabeth Graham
one Dollar also to the heirs of Jennet Mills deseased
one dollar also to Mathew Graham one dollar also to Mary
Maben one dollar also to David Graham one dollar also to
Robt. C. Graham one dollar  with respect to my negro man
Sandy my will is that my Executors should have the power
of choosing his master[?]  if he must be hired out with
I wish to be awarded if possible all the profits arri-
sing from sd negro is to be divided equally divided
[sic] between my wife & three daughters above mentioned
(to wit) Martha Margret & Nancy  I likewise make & ordain my two sons Mathew Graham & Robt C Graham and William McKee the sole executors of this my last will &
Testament & I hereby ___ & ___ all former wills & Testaments in witness whereof I have hereunto set my hand &
seal this 11th day of march 1821

                                    Andrew Graham (seal)
Signed sealed in presence of
Joseph C. Frazer
Hugh Brown
[Will Book A, p. 15.]

   On 9 February 1829 Margaret, Martha, Margaret Jr., and Nancy
emancipated the slave, Sandy (Deed Book E, p. 445).  On this
latter document all the women signed their names except Margaret
Senior who signed with an X.  In the 1850 census of Todd County,
Sandy (born Kentucky, c. 1805) was listed in the household of
Thomas Bradshaw (born Virginia, c. 1799) and his wife, Sarah (born
Virginia, c. 1802), both white.  Also in the household was Isaac
Chesnut (black; born South Carolina, c. 1818).

Following Sandy's emancipation, Margaret moved with most of her children to Morgan County, Illinois. Before leaving Todd County, however, she signed two more deeds. On 1 May 1828 she and her son 3-8 William M. and his wife sold 75 acres on the West Fork of the Red River to Andrew Alexander for $300 (Book E, p. 205), and on 2 October 1830--the last confirmed date on Margaret in Todd County--she and her son 3-12 Andrew sold 46 more acres on the West Fork of the Red River also to Andrew Alexander for $200 (Book F, p. 407). Both sales were of land which William M. and Andrew had inherited from their father. Since Margaret and three of her children, 3-7 Martha, 3-8 William M., and 3-11 Nancy, are known to have moved to Morgan County at about that time, it is thought that two other children, 3-10 Margaret Jr. and 3-12 Andrew, also moved there. The one who remained in Todd County was 3-9 Thomas.

Margaret bought fifteen acres in Morgan County, Illinois, then sold them on 13 October 1835 in the following deed:

This Indenture made and entered into this thirteenth day of October in the year of our Lord one thousand eight hundred and thirty five by and between Margaret Graham by her attorney in fact William M. Graham and Ezekiel Popham and Nancy Popham his wife late Nancy Graham of the County of Morgan and State of Illinois of the first part and Peter Akers of the said County and State of the second part Witnesseth that the said Margaret by her attorney in fact William M. Graham and said Ezekiel and Nancy his wife for and in Consideration of the sum of one hundred and twenty five Dollars to them in hand paid by the said Akers the receipt whereof is hereby acknowledged. . . . [The fifteen acres were in the northwest quarter section of T15 R10W.] In testimony whereof the said parties of the first have hereunto set their hands and Seals the day and year first above written. . . .

      Wm. M. Graham
      in fact for
      Margaret Graham
      Ezekiel Popham
      Nancy Popham (Book I, p. 216)

Margaret then moved with her children 3-8 William M. Graham and 3-11 Nancy Graham Popham to Henderson County, Illinois, where they joined the South Henderson Presbyterian Church on 26 May 1836.[21] In the 1840 census she was listed in the household of her son-in-law Ezekiel Popham, and she probably died a few years later.

Children of Andrew Graham and (1) Margaret Coulter, all born probably in Chester County, South Carolina:

3-1 Elizabeth, b. c. 1775-7
3-2 Jennet, b. c. 1777-9
3-3 Matthew, b. 17 January 1780
3-4 Mary, b. c. 1784
3-5 David, b. c. 1787
3-6 Robert C., b. 11 July 1792

Children of Andrew Graham and (2) Margaret ___ (Mills?), the first four probably born in Chester County, South Carolina:

3-7 Martha, b. 23 August 1798
3-8 William Mills, b. 26 September 1801
3-9 Thomas P., b. 18 October 1803
3-10 Margaret, b. 1804-7
3-11 Nancy C., b. probably Kentucky, c. 1807-8
3-12 Andrew W., b. Kentucky, c. 1809

2-2 JEAN (JANE) GRAHAM ADAMS, born probably in County Antrim, Ireland, 1754-58, died in Chester County, South Carolina, perhaps 1820-2; married SAMUEL ADAMS, born in Ireland, died Chester County, South Carolina, 1822-7, son of John Adams and ___. (Jean was called "Jean" in her father's will, 1795, but "Jane" in the will of her brother 2-5 John, 30 August 1809.) Jean seems to have been listed with Samuel in the 1820 census of Chester County, but she was not mentioned in the will of her sister 2-7 Mary, 21 January 1822, although her husband and two of her children were. Therefore it is thought that she died in 1820-2. She may have been Samuel's second wife.

Jean came from Ireland with her parents and siblings on the ship *Pennsylvania Farmer* which left Belfast on 16 October 1772 and arrived at Charleston, South Carolina, on 19 December 1772.[22] They were part of the Rev. William Martin's group of five shiploads of settlers. (See the Introduction, Section 3.) With her brothers 2-1 Andrew and 2-3 Matthew, she went before the South Carolina General Assembly on 6 January 1773 to request land,[23] and on 17 March 1775 she and her brothers were each granted 100 acres in Craven County which later (1785) became Chester County (Vol. 35, p. 303). Jean's tract was on a branch of Rocky Creek and was bounded only by Samuel Fulton's land, the other sides being vacant. Jean could have been only fourteen years old in 1773 since the practice was to warrant land to children that young.[24] More likely, however, she was about eighteen to twenty years old.

1-1 David                                                                                                2-2

Jean was called Jean *Grimbs* on her land grant. For a discussion of the spelling variants of the name *Graham*, see the Introduction, Section 6.

Samuel's parents came to South Carolina before 15 July 1768 on which day his father, John, received a grant of 350 acres (see below). During the Revolution Samuel served first as a lieutenant then as a captain under Col. Edward Lacey and fought in the Battle of Congaree Fort among others. He also served as a horseman for 380 days in 1780-1.[25]

After the war Samuel sued a John Carson in the April court of 1786 (Book A, p. 73); two years later, April 1788, Carson sued Samuel, but the case was dismissed in October of the same year (Book A, p. 324, and Book B, p. 17). In June 1793 Samuel was a member of a petit jury.[26]

Samuel's father, John, died intestate in 1800-10, and Samuel inherited his father's land by primogeniture. When Samuel died, 1822-7, the land seems to have been divided among Jean's and Samuel's four younger children who in 1837 sold one-fifth of it for $900 to their brother, John, who already lived on the land. In any case the deed is puzzling:

> We Martha Adams Mary Adams Samuel A. Adams and David Adams for and in consideration of the sum of nine hundred dollars to us paid by John Adams of Chester District . . . do grant bargain sell & release unto the said John Adams that plantation or tract of land where he now lives containing one hundred & ten acres more or less . . . on the part of the division of the land belonging to the Estate of Samuel Adams decd and certify the A.D. 2d & 3d days of March 1827 bounded on Daniel McWilliams land & land belonging to the Estate of the decd Robert McCullough decd, Wm Curries[?] land and on the line and N54½ ___ by part No. 2d of this division now set apart to Mary Adams it being the one fifth part of the land belonging to the estate of Samuel Adams decd originally granted to John Adams the 15th day of July A.D. 1768 for 350 acres and the above described fifth part of which we do hereby convey to the aforesaid John Adams. . . . In witness whereof we have hereunto set our hands & seals this 29th day of March A D 1837 . . . (Deeds, BB, 317-8).

This document was signed by Martha Addams (*sic*), Mary Addams, Samuel A. Addams, and David Addams, and was witnessed on 10 May

1837 by John McWilliams. Nearly thirty years later the heirs of John Adams sold his share (see below under 2-2A John Adams).

Jean and Samuel had five known children, all born probably in Chester County, South Carolina:

A. John Adams, b. 12 August 1785
B. Martha Adams, b. 1786-94
C. Mary Adams, b. 1786-94
D. Samuel A. Adams, b. 1786-94
E. David Adams, b. 1794-1800

---

A. John Adams,[27] born Chester County, South Carolina, 12 August 1785, died Perry Township, Monroe County, Indiana, 4 January 1853, buried United Presbyterian Cemetery in Bloomington Township, Monroe County; married in South Carolina, Mary Simpson, born Chester County, South Carolina, c. May 1792, died Perry Township, Monroe County, Indiana, 3 April 1878, buried Clear Creek Cemetery, Monroe County.

In about 1835 John and his family left South Carolina and moved first to Franklin County, Illinois, where they remained only a short time. They then moved to Perry Township, Monroe County, Indiana, where they lived out their lives. On 1 April 1869 Mary and four of her children sold the land in Chester County, South Carolina, which John and his siblings had inherited from their father and which they owned jointly (see above). In the Chester County deed of sale (Book QQ, pp. 186-8), the land was described as 134 acres, "said tract of land being the estimated portion to which we are entitled in a certain tract of land situated in Chester County, South Carolina, formerly held and possessed by David Adams, Martha Adams, Mary Adams, Samuel Adams, and John Adams as copartners consisting of 430½ acres. . . ." The tract was sold to Hugh White of Chester County for $893.34. The grantors named in the deed were Mary Adams, widow of John Adams; Joseph and Minerva J. Adams; David and Mary Johnston (*sic*); Joseph and Jane Harrell; and David and Indiana Adams.

In the 1860 and 1870 censuses Mary was listed in the household of her son David. Mary is said to have had nine children only six of whom are presently known:

1. Mary Adams Johnson, born South Carolina, c. 1825, died probably in Monroe County, Indiana, after 1880; married in Monroe County, 4 March 1847, David Johnson (Book B, p. 124), born South Carolina, c. 1822, died Monroe County,

1-1 David 2-2A1a

Indiana, between 2 March and 26 May 1877 (dates of writing and probate of his will). David was in the 1870 census of Monroe County, and in the 1880 one Mary was listed there as a widow. In the 1860 census a Jane Johnson (born South Carolina, *c.* 1820) was listed with them, probably David's sister or sister-in-law. Also listed with them were two children who may have been children of Jane: Mary C. Johnson, born Illinois, *c.* 1845, and George Johnson, born Indiana, *c.* 1846. Known children of Mary and David, all born in Monroe County, Indiana:

a. Martha J. Johnson, born *c.* 1848

b. Mary Johnson, born *c.* 1850

c. Emma Johnson, born *c.* 1853

d. Robert R. Johnson, born *c.* 1857. In the will of his father, Robert was described as infirm and unable to care for himself.

e. Frank N. Johnson, born July 1860, died after 1910; married in Monroe County, Indiana, *c.* 1888, Zera Vilula Denton, born Indiana, May 1865, died after 1910, daughter of ___ Denton (born Maryland) and Elvira ___ (born Tennessee, October 1827, died after 1910). Listed with Frank and Zera in the 1900 and 1910 censuses of Monroe County were Zera's mother, Elvira, and her brother William Denton (born Indiana, January 1849). Children of Frank and Zera, all born in Indiana: (**a**) Mary Emily Johnson, born November 1889; (**b**) Elvira Norine Johnson, born November 1891; (**c**) Hester Katharine Johnson, born February 1894; and (**d**) Mildred L. Johnson, born October 1895.

f. William G. Johnson, born May 1864; married probably in Monroe County, Indiana, *c.* 1889, Sarah Ellen Stipp, born January 1870, daughter of George Stipp (born Indiana, November 1824, died 1900-10) and ___ (born South Carolina, died before 1900). According to the 1910 census, Sarah had had nine children six of whom were living. Known children: (**a**) Mary A. Johnson, born January 1891; (**b**) Clara M. Johnson, born April 1893; (**c**) Lucy E. Johnson, born March 1897; (**d**) Florence Johnson, born November 1899, died before 1910; (**e**) Olive Johnson, born *c.* 1901; (**f**) Bertha Johnson, born *c.* 1904; and (**g**) Frances Johnson, born *c.* 1906.

g. Samuel Ellison Johnson, born *c.* 1872

2. David Adams, born South Carolina, 4 October 1821, died in Perry Township, Monroe County, Indiana, 27 May 1885, buried Clear Creek Cemetery, Monroe County, Indiana; married, perhaps *c.* 1851, Indiana McQueen, born Bartholomew County, Indiana, 26 November 1831, died 28 August 1912, buried Clear Creek Cemetery, Monroe County, Indiana, parents born in Kentucky. Indiana was listed with her children George and Sallie in the 1900 census. In the 1910 census she was listed in the household of her son George who by then was married. Also in that census Indiana said she had had nine children only four of whom were living. Known children, all born in Monroe County, Indiana:

   a. ___ Adams, died 15 June 1852(?), buried Clear Creek Cemetery, Monroe County, Indiana.

   b. Mary M. Adams, born Monroe County, Indiana, *c.* 25 August 1860, died 19 September 1861, aged 1 year, 25 days, buried Clear Creek Cemetery, Monroe County, Indiana.

   c. William Adams, died at the age of 6 days, 14 September 1861, buried Clear Creek Cemetery.

   d. ___ Adams, died in infancy, unnamed.

   e. Emma Adams Rhorer, born in May 1865; married, *c.* 1893, Alvin K. Rhorer, born in Indiana, October 1859, son of Henry C. Rhorer (born in Kentucky, *c.* 1828) and Martha ___ (born Kentucky, *c.* 1835). Child: Russell Rhorer, born Indiana *c.* 1897.

   f. Sarah (Sallie) Adams Perring, born March 1868; married, after 1900, Clinton Perring. In the 1900 census she was listed with her mother and brother George and was a teacher.

   g. George Adams, born November 1871; married (1) *c.* 1903, Myrtle Prince, born Indiana, *c.* 1881, died after 1910; (2) Bertha Waldron. For several years George was a trustee of Perry Township, Monroe County, Indiana. Known child by his first wife: Grace Adams, born Indiana *c.* 1905.

1-1 David 2-2A2h

h. Laura Adams Deckard, born September 1873; married Charles Deckard, born Indiana, September 1872. According to the 1910 census Charles was a merchant in a general store. Known children: (a) Elma Deckard, born 1898-9, married Eugene Daniels; (b) Ethel Helen Deckard, born 13 September 1900, married Leonard L. Clifton, born 14 January 1889, died 30 June 1976; (c) Lawrence Deckard, born c. 1906; and (d) David Deckard, married Frances Kelly.

3. Joseph Adams, born South Carolina, September 1823, died probably in Perry Township, Monroe County, Indiana, after 1900; married in Monroe County, 18 December 1850, Minerva Jane Whisenand (Book B, p. 214), born Indiana, c. 1832, died probably Monroe County, Indiana, before 1900. Known children:

a. Elizabeth J. (Lizzie) Adams, born Indiana, c. 1853

b. John S. or L. Adams, born Indiana, October 1854; married Sarah F. ___, born Indiana, October 1854. In the 1910 census Sarah said she had had seven children only five of whom were living. Known children: (a) Burt R. Adams, born March 1878; (b) Ola Adams, born September 1881; (c) Myrtle Adams, born September 1885; (d) Joseph S. Adams, born March 1887; (e) Blanche Adams, born December 1890; and (f) Jessie E. Adams, born September 1892.

c. Wilford C. Adams, born Indiana, July 1858; married Bridget Sherlock, born Indiana, April 1862, daughter of Stephen Sherlock (died Monroe County, Indiana, 1898) and Malinda ___. Known children, all born Indiana: (a) John L. Adams, born July 1893; (b) Ed C. Adams, born January 1895; (c) William Joseph Adams, born April 1897, married Jessie Deckard; (d) Carrie E. Adams, born August 1899, married Dr. ___ Shepp; and (e) James Adams, born c. 1903.

d. Joseph Edgar Adams, born Indiana, c. 1861

e. William H. Adams, born Indiana, April 1863; married in Monroe County, Indiana, 16 March 1887, Laura B. Helms (Book 7, p. 433), born Indiana, March 1869. Known children, all born Indiana: (a) Richard F. Adams, born September 1889; (b) Allie C. Adams, born June 1892; and (c) Roy L. Adams, born December 1893.

f. Bancroft Adams; married Amanda Clark. Children: (a) Guy Adams, married Mary Deckard; (b) May Adams; (c) Walter Adams; and (d) Perry Adams.

g. Pink L. Adams Todd, born Indiana, October 1869; married ___ Todd. In the 1900 census Pink, but not her husband, was listed with her son in her father's household in Perry Township, Monroe County, Indiana. Also in that census she said she had had two children only one of whom was living. Known child: Charley E. Todd, born Indiana, March 1898.

h. Evart B. Adams, born Indiana, c. 1873

4. Jane Adams Harrell, born South Carolina, 15 February 1829, died Monroe County, Indiana, 14 January 1905, buried Christian Church Cemetery at Smithville, Monroe County; married in Monroe County, 2 April 1862, Joseph Harrell, born Virginia, 7 March 1826, died Monroe County, Indiana, 29 October 1899, buried Christian Church Cemetery, Monroe County, son of James Harrell and Mary Thrasher. Joseph had married (1) Jane Holland and had one child by her: Arthusa J., born Indiana, c. 1859. Children of Jane Adams Harrell:

   a. John P. Harrell, born Indiana, April 1863, died ___; married Amanda ___, born in Indiana, October 1865, died ___. Known children: (a) Edward Harrell, born August 1888; (b) Maud Harrell, born February 1891; and (c) Ethel Harrell, born March 1899.

   b. Samuel Harrell, born Indiana, April 1866, died ___; married Susie ___, born February 1870. Known children: (a) Lena M. Harrell, born January 1897; (b) Ralph K. Harrell, born September 1898; and (c) Marshall Harrell, born February 1900.

   c. Tabitha Harrell, born Indiana, c. 1868, died after 1880 and before 1900; probably unmarried.

   d. William O. Harrell, born May 1870, died ___; perhaps unmarried. In the 1900 census of Monroe County, Indiana, he was listed in his mother's home and was single.

5. Isabella Adams, born South Carolina, c. 17 October 1831, died Monroe County, Indiana, 20 February 1862, aged 31 years, 4 months, 3 days, buried Clear Creek Cemetery,

Monroe County; unmarried.

    6. Alexander Adams, born South Carolina, 5 June 1832, died 26 October 1857, buried United Presbyterian Cemetery in Bloomington Township, Monroe County, Indiana; perhaps married in Monroe County, 11 October 1856, Susannah Woodman.

B. Martha Adams, born Chester County, South Carolina, 1786-94, probably died or moved away before 1850; unmarried. She was named in the will of her uncle 2-5 John, 30 August 1809.

C. Mary Adams, born Chester County, South Carolina, 1786-94, probably died or moved away before 1860; unmarried. She was named in the will of her aunt 2-7 Mary, 21 January 1822.

D. Samuel A. Adams, born Chester County, South Carolina, 1786-94, probably died or moved away before 1860; unmarried. He was named in the will of his aunt 2-7 Mary, 21 January 1822.

E. David Adams, born Chester County, South Carolina, 1794-1800, probably died or moved away before 1860; unmarried.

2-3 MATTHEW (MATHEW) GRAHAM (*Grimbs*), born probably in County Antrim, Ireland, died in South Carolina, 1775-8. It is not known beyond question whether 1-1 David Graham had a son named Matthew because no one of that name is mentioned in David's will (1795). On the other hand, a Matthew *Grimbs* was named immediately after 2-1 Andrew *Grumbs* and 2-2 Jean *Grimbs* on the list of people who had recently come from Belfast on the *Pennsylvania Farmer* and who on 6 January 1773 went before the South Carolina General Assembly to request land. (For a discussion of the spelling variants of the name *Graham*, see the Introduction, Section 6.)

    On 17 March 1775 (the same day on which Andrew Grimbs and Jean Grimbs were granted their land), Matthew was granted 100 acres in Craven (Chester) County on Rocky Creek. Matthew's land was bounded by lands of Samuel Willson, John McDonald, and Alexander Turner, the other sides vacant (Vol. 35, p. 294). His name also appeared on two other documents: on 6 January 1773 William Fairy was warranted 200 acres in Chester County, and the land he later received in his grant by then was bounded by that of Matthew *Grimbs*, William Boyd, David Chesnut, John Pike, and Elisha "Garets." On the same day, John Smith was warranted 250 acres in Chester County, and the land he later received in his grant by then was bounded by that of Matthew *Grimbs*, Elisha Garret, William

Hood, Thomas Hickling, and Jasper Rogers.[28] Nothing more about Matthew appears in the records after 1775, however, so it is thought that he died soon after. Andrew named his first son Matthew, born 17 January 1780; perhaps the son was named for a deceased brother.

As to what happened to Matthew's land, Brent H. Holcomb comments:

> If he [Matthew] died intestate . . . prior to 1791 in South Carolina, his land automatically descended to his eldest son. If he had no son, then his widow and daughters (if any) were to sell the land and divide the proceeds. If he had no children, his eldest <u>brother</u> would receive any real estate, and his widow none. If he sold the land and recorded the deed prior to 1785, the deed would have been in Charleston deed books. If he sold it after 1785 and recorded the deed, it should be recorded in Chester County deed books. We have not found any record of this land.[29]

2-4 JAMES GRAHAM (also written *Grimes* or *Grimbs*), born probably in County Antrim, Ireland, 1761, died Tipton County, Tennessee, 1837, buried next to his daughter Esther in the Salem A.R.P. Church Cemetery near Atoka, Tipton County, Tennessee; married, *c.* 1782?, ESTHER ___ who was still alive in 1826 but died probably before 1835 in Chester County, South Carolina.

For a discussion of the spelling variants of the name *Graham*, see the Introduction, Section 6.

James's life seems to have been beset with difficulties and confrontations. For example, although at the age of seventeen he joined the Patriots during the American Revolution and served in various militias from 1778 to 1782, he was denied a pension when he first applied for it in 1827 because of the spelling variant of the name *Graham*. His name appeared in most of his war records as *Grimes*. (See the Introduction, pages 54-56, for his testimony concerning his war record.) Not until 7 August 1833 was the pension granted (S21786).[30]

One passage of genealogical interest in the lengthy hearings on James's pension concerned his responses to inquiries about his background. He said, "I was born in Ireland in the year 1761 and emigrated to Charleston in the year 1772 afterwards settled where

I now live [Chester County]. . . . My father had a book containing the family ages which I have seen but cannot say at this time what became of it. . . . I was living in Chester District at the same place that I now live when called into service . . ." (recorded Spring Term, 1833).

James also was involved in an unusually large number of legal actions: (1) in October 1786, James sued a John Holeman, but the case was dismissed (Book A, p. 156); (2) October 1787 and April 1788, a John Farriss sued James perhaps for slander, and again the case was dismissed (Book A, pp. 285 and 321); (3) April and October 1788, a Robert Smith sued James also perhaps for slander, but this time James lost and was fined 29 pounds 3 shillings 4 pence (Book A, p. 328, and Book B, pp. 17-8); (4) July 1789, James then sued Robert Smith in a case which continued until June 1791; James finally won and was awarded 21 pounds 9 shillings 5 pence (Book B, pp. 53, 109, and 152); (5) January 1789, Elijah Nunn sued James, and the case was dismissed at James's costs (Book B, p. 20); (6) 30 January 1794, James then sued Elijah Nunn and Sampson Noland for debt, and the defendants had to pay 19 pounds 12 shillings (Book B, p. 255); (7) October 1789, James Crawford sued James for debt, and in the puzzling decision in October 1790 the judgment would be "according to specialty when all the Credits shall be made fully appear for the Balance" (Book B, pp. 58 and 105); and (8) In June 1792, a George Kenedy sued James for slander, and in June 1793 the jury found for Kenedy who was awarded 45 shillings and costs (Book B, pp. 195 and 233).[31] James must have become thoroughly familiar with the Chester County court house because he also served on the jury in July 1789 and in January and April 1791.[32] Even James's wife, Esther, appeared in one record: on 29 January 1792 she was called as a witness in a slander case brought by William Reedy against David Graham.[33] This David may or may not have been 1-1 David; another unrelated David Graham lived in Chester County at that time. William Reedy may have been the father or a brother of the Reedy who later married a daughter of James and Esther.

On 19 June 1802 James appointed John Harbison to collect from John Dougherty "all such sum or sums of money Debts and dues whatsoever which now are due and owing unto me the said James Graham . . . Together with the Interest on the same. . . ." Apparently, James had been awarded the money in a court action; the amount was unspecified in this document (Book I, pp. 62-3). Also in 1802 James sued a Joseph Weir, and on 23 December 1802 the jury found for Weir at a cost to James of $36.52. The only record of this case appeared in the Docket Abstracts for the Court of Common Pleas (no page numbers).

Nothing was found on James in the court records from 1802 until April 1820 at which time he (or perhaps his son James Jr.) served as the foreman of a jury in the case of Alexander Cabeen versus Lewis E. Wilson (Court of Common Pleas, Book G, p. 3). In the Spring Term of 1821 James won a case for debt against John Kelly and was awarded $40.45 plus interest from 8 December 1817 and costs. On 31 October 1821 James was indicted by the state for "Bastardy"; the case went to trial during the following spring term, and on 26 March 1822 the jury found him innocent (General Session Minutes, Fall Term 1821 to 1838). Nothing more has been found on this provocative case. James was already involved in another one, however. In March 1821 Sheriff Thomas R. McClintock sued James for trespass, trover, and conversion of "one Still with its head and worm of the value of one Hundred and fifty dollars." McClintock sued for one thousand dollars. Specifically, McClintock stated that one day he

> lost the said still with its head and worm which said still with its head and worm afterwards on the same day came into the hands and possession of the said James Graham by finding yet the said James Graham well knowing the same to be the proper goods and chattels of the said Thomas R MClintock as Sheriff and of right to appertain to him as Sheriff though requested hath not delivered the same to the said Thomas R MClintock but afterwards at the same time and place converted the same to his own use to the damage of the said Thomas R MClintock one thousand dollars and therefore he brings suit. . . .

This case dragged on for four years, and the records are not clear on how it was decided. On 28 March 1825 a jury which was called "the jury numbered (2)" decided for the defendant, but apparently the case was not concluded then because on 24 October 1825 another jury called "the jury numbered (1)" decided for the plaintiff and awarded him $49.50. James also had to pay the court costs amounting to $46.22 (Book J, pp. 51-3).

Of course, not all the records on James pertain to court actions. On 28 April 1800 he witnessed a land sale by his brother-in-law Edward Blackstock to Archibald McQuiston (Deeds Book H, pp. 7-9). James also owned slaves--how many is not known, although in the 1790 census two slaves were listed in his household. On 5 December 1795 he sold a negro boy named Lampoon for £30 to a James McKeown (Book D, p. 415), and on 25 August 1824 he sold a black woman and her child, both named Letty, to Thomas McClintock for $250 (Book V, p. 114). It seems unlikely that this Thomas McClintock was the Sheriff Thomas McClintock who was suing

James at the time.

James also bought and sold a fair amount of property. On 24 November 1800 he paid £100 sterling to William Reedy and his wife, Isabel, for 100 acres in Chester County to be signed over to James's sons 3-15 David and 3-16 James Jr. The land was on Rocky Creek on the road from Fishing Creek to Charleston. Originally it had been part of a 200-acre tract bought by Micajah Piggot, then sold to Jasper Rogers, then to William Stroud, then to John Caskey (father-in-law of James's daughter Julianna), then to William Reedy (Book T, pp. 74-5). Many years later, 3-15 David sold his joint ownership in the land to his brother, 3-16 James Jr., a sale which led to a long court case instituted by David's wife, Elizabeth. See the story under 3-15 David Graham.

Others of James's land transactions included the following: on 29 September 1814 he bought 103 acres in Chester County from Joseph Caskey (Book T, p. 158). Joseph was probably a brother of Thomas Caskey who married James's daughter Julianna. On 25 November 1822 James bought 100 more acres in Chester County from Thomas and William McLuce, "otherwise called T. and W. McLuce, Merchants," for $114.38. This land was described as situated "on Turkey Creek whereon William Love now lives bounded on the West by Turkey Creek and land belonging to John R. Love, on the South by land belonging to the Estate of Samuel Love, on the East by land now claimed by W. Farley, and on the North by land belonging to the Estate of Col. Joseph Brown which was seized and taken as the property of the aforesaid William Love by Thomas R. McClintock Esquire Sheriff of Chester District and by him to us the said T & W McLuce conveyed . . ." (Book U, p. 274).

In the 1827 hearings on his Revolutionary War pension, James said he owned no land. He must have sold it recently because on 25 September 1824 there was a land sale from Jesse Sampson to David Graham (perhaps 3-15), and the land was described in the deed as bordering the land of James Graham among others (Book W, p. 406).

The claim that James's land bordered the land sold in this deed may have reflected only the fact that James merely lived on the land, and it was actually owned by others. Two subsequent deeds mentioned "Captain" James Graham's land as bordering the land described in the deeds. One was dated 6 January 1825, the other 16 January 1832, and both concerned property owned by Edward Blackstock, James's brother-in-law (Book Y, pp. 470-2).

Finally, on 9 October 1832 James signed over his entire

1-1 David                                                                2-5

remaining property in a gift deed to his daughter and son-in-law 3-17 Esther and Alexander Smith (Book Z, pp. 63-4).

In 1836 Esther and Alexander Smith moved to Tipton County, Tennessee, and, according to a descendant, took James with them even though he was seventy-five years old then. When Esther and Alexander moved to Tennessee, they were part of a general family migration which also included most of the children and grandchildren of James's daughter Julianna.

Known children, all probably born in Chester County, South Carolina:

3-13 Julianna, b. *c.* 1783?      3-16 James Jr., b. *c.* 1793
3-14 ___ (girl) b. *c.* 1785?    3-17 Esther, b. 1797
3-15 David, b. 1788-92

2-5 JOHN GRAHAM, born probably in County Antrim, Ireland, *c.* 1767 or earlier, died Chester County, South Carolina, between 30 August 1809 and 1 December 1809 (dates of writing and probate of his will); unmarried. The date of his birth is established at about 1767 or earlier because he witnessed with his brother 2-1 Andrew and his father, David, the will of John Caskey dated 19 September 1785. John would have had to be at least eighteen years old to witness a legal document.

On 22 September 1795 a John Graham (perhaps unrelated to the Graham family in this study) received a deed of conveyance from Samuel Lowrie, and on 31 October 1796 a John Graham and a William Graham entered security for court costs in a lawsuit by William Rice versus Sherwood Nance. A John Graham sued Charles Atterberry on 1 February 1799 and was awarded $4 plus costs. A John Graham also served on a jury on 16 April 1799.[34] The 1800 census of Chester County, South Carolina, showed two men named John Graham; therefore, these law cases may have referred to the unrelated man of that name.

For several years John was an elder in the Catholic Presbyterian Church in Chester County, serving until his death in 1809.[35] He and his sister 2-7 Mary inherited most of their father's property.

John's will is transcribed verbatim as follows:

      In The Name of God Amen. -------

1-1 David                                                                    2-6

I John Grahams of Chester District State of South Caro-
lina Being Sick of Body; But Sound of Memory & Judgment;
& Calling to mind that it is Appointed for All men once to
die-  Therefore I do hereby make & ordain this as my last
Will & Testament in Manner & form following this 30th Day of
Augt in the Year of our Lord one Thousand eight Hundred &
Nine; That is to Say

First I leave & Commit my Soul to the Hands of Almighty
God who gave it; and my Body to my friends & Executors to be
Decently Buried----  Secondly (after the full payment of all
my Just & Lawful Debts) I leave & Bequeath to my Niece Martha
Adams the Sum of one Hundred Dollars to be taken equally off
the whole of my Estate & paid her by my Executors

Thirdly I leave & Bequeath to my Brother Andw Grahams
the Sum of one Dollar and no more-------

Fourthly.  I leave & Bequeath to Jane Adams Wife of
Samuel Adams the Sum of One Dollar & no more

Fifthly.-----I leave & Bequeath to Jennet Boyse formerly
the Wife of David Boyse the Sum of one Dollar & no more

Sixthly I leave & Bequeath to my Brother James Grahams
the Sum of one Dollar & no more-----

Seventhly, I leave & Bequeath the whole of the Remainder
of my whole estate equally Betwixt my two Sisters Mary
Grahams and Margret Grahams by an equal Division------

Ninthly,[36] and lastly I leave Constitute and Ordain
James Chesnut and Robert Hamilton the Soal Executors and
Administratores of this my last Will and Testament  Given
under my Hand & Seal ths Day & Year above written

Robert Wilson                       his
Samuel adams[?]              John   T   Grahams    L.S.
John willson                       mark

This document was proved on 1 December 1809 and recorded in Book
D, p. 434. It is located in Apartment No. 21.


2-6 JENNET (JANE, JENNY) GRAHAM BOYSE, born probably in County Antrim,
    Ireland, c. 1769, died Preble County, Ohio, 10 March 1849 (aged

four score years), buried Hopewell Cemetery, Preble County; married, probably in Chester County, South Carolina, DAVID BOYSE, born perhaps in Ireland, *c.* 15 July 1763, died Union County, Indiana, 22 July 1827 (64 years and 7 days), buried Hopewell Cemetery, Preble County, Ohio.[37]

Jennet and David may have been separated for a time. In her father's will, 2 April 1795, she was named as "Jinat Boys Wife to david Boys." But in the will of her brother 2-5 John, 30 August 1809, she was mentioned as "Jennet Boyse formerly the wife of David Boyse," and in the will of her sister 2-7 Mary, 21 January 1822, Jennet was cited in one section (as "Jane Boyse") while in a separate section appeared mention of "David Boyse of the state of Ohio." Nonetheless, in David's own will, 25 June 1827, he spoke of Jennet as his "beloved wife Jenny" and left all his property to her and their daughters.

Mary Graham's will shows that David moved to Ohio as early as 1822. He is known to have been in Preble County, Ohio, by 1824 because he bought land there from a Martha Foster on 1 June 1824 (Book 6, p. 136). Later that year he sold the land and moved across the Ohio border to Union County, Indiana: there is a record of a mortgage deed dated 31 December 1824 with a payment made on 16 April 1825 by Miers Miller of Preble County, Ohio, to David Boyse of Union County, Indiana (Book 6, p. 245). David and Jenny finally sold the land to Miers Miller on 31 December 1825 (Book 6, p. 311). David died in Union County, Indiana, 22 July 1827, where his will is recorded. Jennet and her daughters probably moved back to Preble County although Jennet, herself, did not die until 10 March 1849. She and David are buried together in the Hopewell Church cemetery, Preble County. On her tombstone her name is inscribed "Jennet Graham, wife of David Boyse."[38]

David was a Revolutionary War veteran, serving 184 days in the militia under Capt. John Norwood during the period from April 1781 to December 1782.[39]

Children, both probably born in Chester County, South Carolina:

A. Mary Margaret Boyse, b. 1795

B. Elizabeth Boyse, b. *c.* 1798?

---

A. Mary Margaret Boyse Wilson (Molly P. or Molly Peggy),[40] born probably in Chester County, South Carolina, 1795, died Preble

County, Ohio, 1853, buried Hopewell Cemetery, Preble County; married in Preble County, 1841, Matthew Wilson, born Ireland, *c.* 1780, died Preble County, Ohio, 24 June 1863, buried Hopewell Cemetery, son of John Wilson and Martha ___ (born Ireland *c.* 1758, died Preble County, Ohio, 10 December 1845, buried Hopewell Cemetery, Preble County). Matthew had married (1) in Christian County, Kentucky, 9 March 1809, Jane or Jennet McQuiston (died 1837) and moved to Preble County, Ohio, in *c.* 1829, about the same time that 3-3 Matthew and 3-6 Robert C. Graham moved there with others from Kentucky. Matthew Wilson was a brother of Jennette Wilson who married 3-3 Matthew.

On 29 December 1851 Mary Boyse Wilson, her husband, Matthew Wilson, and her sister, Elizabeth Boyse, all of Preble County, Ohio, sold some land there to 4-3 John W. Graham, a cousin of Mary and Elizabeth (Book 39, p. 605).

B. Elizabeth Boyse, born probably in Chester County, South Carolina, *c.* 1798?, died ___; probably unmarried.

2-7 MARY GRAHAM, born perhaps in County Antrim, Ireland, died in Chester County, South Carolina, between 21 January 1822 and 7 October 1822 (dates of writing and probate of her will); unmarried.

She and her brother 2-5 John inherited most of their father's property. After John died she then inherited half of his estate, and on 13 January 1819 she sold all her inherited property for $700 to Captain Edward Blackstock, husband of her sister 2-8 Margaret (Book T, p. 262). Also on 13 January 1819 Mary, her sister Margaret Graham Blackstock, and Margaret's husband, Edward, sold a slave named Dick to Robert Hamilton for $2,000 on condition that Hamilton emancipate Dick after eleven years of service (Deed Book V, pp. 64-5).

Mary's will is transcribed verbatim as follows:

In the name of God Amen.
I Mary Grahams of Chester District and State of Carolina being Sick of body, but of sound mind and memory; and calling to mind that it is appointed for all men once to die-- Therefore I do hereby make Constitue and publish this my last will and testament in manner and form following, this 21st day of January, in the year of our Lord one thousand eight hundred and twenty two that is

1-1 David 2-7

to say First I leave and commit my soul to the hands of Almighty God who gave it. And my body to the hands of my friends to be decently burried. Secondly I allow all my lawful debts or Just demands to be paid in the first place off my estate------- Thirdly I leave and bequeath to my Niece Mary Adams daughter of Samuel Adams the Sum of Fifty dollars and no more----- Fourthly I leave and bequeath to Samuel Adams Junior Son of Said Samuel Adams forty dollars. Fifthly I leave and bequeath to Samuel Adams Senr the sum of ten dollars to purchase religious books for his children--and also a feather bed and bolster------- Sixtly I leave and bequeath to my Niece Molly Peggy Boyse daughter of David Boyse of the State of Ohio the sum of Sixty Dollars Sevently I leave and bequeath to Elizabeth Boyse daughter of said David Boyse Forty Dollars-- Eeghtly I leave to my Sister Jane Boyse Ten Dollars-- Ninthly I leave twenty Dollars to my brother James Grahams to purchase Religious books for his children-- Tenthly I leave to my niece Esther Grahams daughter of James Grahams twenty dollars,-- Eleventhly I leave to my Niece Elizabeth Gleghorn Twenty Dollars To purchase Religious books for her children-- Twelfthly I leave to my Nephew David Grahams Blacksmith fourteen dollars to purchase Religious books for his family. and to Jane Grahams daughter to said David Grahams Ten Dollars-- I also leave ten dollars or more if it is my part to repair the Graveyard where my father and mother and other friends are burried------- Thirteenthly I leave and bequeath the whole of the Remainder of my whole Estate to my Sister Margaret Blackstock to be at her own Disposal-- Lastly I Leave constitue and ordain Robert Hamilton and Alexander Skelly sole Executors and Administrators of this my last will and testament. Given under my hand and seal this day and year above written

Signed Sealed and Acknowledged        her
in presence of        Mary O Grahams
Bextun[?] Mcalster        mark
James Boyd
Alexander Skelly

This document was proved on 7 October 1822 and was recorded in Book G, p. 421. It is located in Apartment No. 22, Package No. 317.

1-1 David  2-8

2-8 MARGARET GRAHAM BLACKSTOCK (Peggy), born Chester County, South Carolina, 1775-80,[41] died probably in Chester County after 8 December 1835; married in Chester County, c. 1816, CAPTAIN EDWARD BLACKSTOCK (Ned), born County Down, Ireland, 1760-70, died Henderson County, Illinois, 20 December 1846.[42] This was Edward's second marriage, his first to Elizabeth Wilson (born Ireland, c. 1762, died Chester County, South Carolina, 1 October 1815, age 53, buried next to her father in Hopewell Cemetery, Chester County), daughter of John W. Wilson who cited Edward Blackstock as a son-in-law in his will, 14 August 1812.[43] Elizabeth Wilson was probably related to Jennette Wilson who married 3-3 Matthew Graham and to Matthew Wilson who married 2-6A Mary Margaret Boyse. Elizabeth and Edward had one known child, Edward Blackstock Jr. In the Chester County, South Carolina, Deeds Books there is a document dated 22 August 1815 in which Thomas Walker of Chester County gave a negro girl aged three years to his daughter Jennet Blackstock, wife of Edward Blackstock Jr. of Tennessee (Book R, p. 143).

Edward came to America on the ship *Irish Volunteer* which left Ireland on 25 September 1792 and arrived at Charleston, South Carolina, on 25 December 1792.[44] He was in the company of his mother and two siblings, the Rev. William Blackstock and Jane Skelly, wife of Alexander Skelly. Their father had died in Ireland as did another sibling, Samuel. On 17 April 1804 Edward became a naturalized citizen, and, interestingly, he took his citizenship oath on the same day and at the same place as did Andrew Crawford, father of Mary Crawford Gleghorn who married the oldest son of 3-1 Elizabeth Graham Gleghorn [Naturalized Citizens (1802-1832), Book A, pp. 12-14].

In the War of 1812 Edward was a sergeant in Duffy's Rifle Infantry, and on 9 February 1818 he was awarded land in Illinois for his war services.

Edward was well liked and well respected in Chester County. The Blackstock post office, of which he was the postmaster, and the once prosperous town which subsequently grew around it in Chester and Fairfield Counties, South Carolina, were named in his honor. They were established probably in the first decade of the nineteenth century, and the town still appears on maps.

Further evidence that he was well liked appeared in the mild tones of the few court cases in which he was implicated. (It was a litigious age, and the fact that Edward was involved in very few such cases testifies again to the esteem in which he was held.) In October 1807 a Benjamin Boyd sued Edward for debt. Boyd, who was the surviving executor of the will of one William W. Turner of Charleston, claimed that Edward owed Turner's estate $2,059.89; Boyd also sued for an additional $500 for "his damage." Boyd's evidence was conclusive, and on 3 April 1809 the jury found for him but instead of the $500 damage they awarded him one shilling plus $27.75 court costs (Court of Common Pleas, Book C, pp. 132-137). In November 1806 William Brown sued Edward for assault and battery, and the case was "settled by the parties" (Court of Common Pleas, no page number or title). In the fall term of 1814, James Adace(?) sued Edward for a reason which is illegible on the Common Pleas docket. The judgment was by default and was "referred to the clerk to assign the damages."

Of Edward's land deeds only the following are known. He must have bought a considerable amount of land in Chester County during the 1790's because on 28 April 1800 he sold 236 acres for $708 to Archibald McQuiston. This deed was witnessed by his brother-in-law 2-4 James Graham as well as by James Chesnut and Samuel Faris (Book H, p. 7). On 14 August 1800 Edward bought 150 acres for £100 sterling from Christopher Thompson (Book H, p. 66). On 13 January 1819 Edward bought for $700 all the land which his sister-in-law 2-7 Mary had inherited from her father and her brother (Book T, p. 262--the amount of the land was unspecified, but it probably included well over 200 acres). On 6 January 1825 Edward sold 14½ acres for $50 to James Miller (Book Y, pp. 471-2), and on 16 January 1832 Edward sold 14½ more acres for $50 to Peter Wilson Jr. (Book Y, pp. 470-1).

On 13 January 1819 Peggy and her sister 2-7 Mary sold a slave named Dick for $2,000 to a "trusted friend," Robert Hamilton, with the proviso that Hamilton emancipate Dick eleven years later (Book V, pp. 64-5). Edward Blackstock's name was mentioned in the deed.

Edward also appears to have been a man of mild intemperance as well as one of strong conscience. On 26 June 1833 at a session of the Hopewell Church in Chester County, he voluntarily appeared and confessed to drinking too much although he had not been cited by the church for doing so. He vowed that with divine assistance he would quit drinking altogether.[45]

Of some interest is a letter which Edward wrote in 1834 to his sister, Jane Skelly, who then lived in Illinois. This letter is in the possession of Dale Edmiston of Americus, Kansas:

> March South Carolina Chester District March 22nd 1834
> Dear Sister G.C. Youers of 31st of Decr last I
> rcd which gave us great pleasure to hear that you ware

1-1 David

all well. We are all in the land of the Living for
which I desire to thank the God of all our mercies. It
is six weeks past last tusday since Peggey was taken ill
of a plurecy, all persons that seen her for the first
three weeks had no hops of her recovery, She was two
weeks in a State of insensabilety She is now abel to
walke through the ___ and we have now hops of her
recovery, the rest of our friends here is well as for
aught I know, plese Excus heast [haste?] I have nothing
new to inform you of but what the bearer Mr Archabald
McClorkan Can let you know, I am glad to hear that ___
has got maried to a man of the Character that Mr. Dickey
has perhaps I may have Seen him but I do not remmber of
it plese to tell him I would be glad to get a letter
from him remember us to him and famely and Alexander
Skelley and famely Samuel and famely ___ and fanely and
to all my old friends as you have opertunety, Tell
Peggey I am obliedged to her for writing to me and I am
glad to heare you are all pleased with that part of the
Contry I ad no more but remaines your loving Brother
and Sister--
      Edward and Peggey Blackstock
Mrs. Jain Skelley

P.S. Plese to write to us as afften as passabel. I
think long to heare from you all
          E.B.

 On 8 December 1835 Margaret and Edward sold 162 acres to
Robert White for $1,600 (Book AA, p. 428). Margaret may have died
soon after, and Edward then moved to Warren County, Illinois,
where he was listed in the 1840 census. He bought land there from
James Boyd in a deed dated 6 March 1837 (Vol. 3, p. 413). The
part of Warren County where he lived became Henderson County in
1841, and in December 1844 he sold some land in Henderson County
to James H. Carmicle (*sic*; Book 2, p. 203).

 Many years later, on 4 July 1885, the South Henderson United
Presbyterian Church held ceremonies during which the speakers
reminisced about early Henderson days. One speaker was the Rev.
J. A. P. McGaw, born 4 February 1834, who told about his boyhood
in the church and included the following story:

 There was an old Mr. Blackstock who came from South
 Carolina, bringing with him two women of African des-
 cent, who had been slaves. Their names were Rose and
 Emma. They were members of the church; and, being the

only people of color in the neighborhood, they were
quite conspicuous. Mr. Blackstock used to ride a very
sleek, fat horse to church. One day as he was riding
down the hill from the church his horse was attacked by
yellow jackets, and came pretty near throwing the old
man. He amused himself in his old age in making wills,
Col. Henderson being his scribe for that purpose. I
believe, however, his last "last will and testament" was
written by Preston Martin [father-in-law of 4-31 Mary M.
Graham], at that time a justice of the peace. On being
asked why he did not employ Col. Henderson, he said,
"Henderson don't believe there is any de-vil." Col.
Henderson had one day spoken in the hearing of Mr.
Blackstock of the view held by some persons that the
devil spoken of in the Bible is simply a personification
of the evil principle in human nature, and has no
personal existence. Mr. Blackstock got the idea into
his head that this was the Colonel's own view, and hence
could no longer trust him to write his will.[46]

In 1839 and 1841 Edward deeded some land to Rose and Emma
(called Amy in the deed), the black women mentioned above, and
said he did so for "love and affection" (Book 1, p. 487). In his
will dated 20 December 1846 he left $100 apiece to them, naming
them as Rosana Blackstock and Emaline Foster (Henderson County
Probate Records). Later Rosana sold the land for $75 to J. Burn-
sides (Book 2, p. 580).

Appearing in the session minutes of the South Henderson
Presbyterian Church is a series of entries concerning Rosana. On
8 April 1843 Rosana Blackstock, who had been "previously suspended," was restored (p. 21). On 6 May 1844 the council again
considered a case involving Rosana who had been charged with
cohabiting with "a certain individual" without marriage while
falsely claiming that she was in fact married. A committee of two
was appointed to look into the matter. On 10 May 1844 the committee was expanded to include 3-8 William M. Graham (p. 22), and on
11 May 1844 the council ordained that the case of Rosana Blackstock be disciplined (p. 24) although the nature of the discipline
was not stated.

Margaret's name is not mentioned in either the 1837 deed in
which Edward first bought land in Henderson County or the deeds
giving land to Rosana and Emma. It is therefore thought that
Margaret died before Edward moved to Illinois. She had no known
children.

THIRD GENERATION


CHILDREN OF 2-1 ANDREW GRAHAM
AND (1) MARGARET COULTER


3-1 ELIZABETH GRAHAM GLEGHORN, born Chester County, South Carolina, 1775-77, died probably in Lincoln County, Tennessee, 1830-40; married in Chester County, c. 1794, JOHN MATTHEW GLEGHORN, born Ireland, 1770-75,[1] died probably in Lincoln County, Tennessee, 1830-40.

Although John did not apply for citizenship until 7 April 1814, he had actually migrated to America many years earlier-- August 1790--and soon made his way to Chester County, South Carolina.[2] A tradition among some of his descendants is that he was a blacksmith, and, if so, he may first have worked for Elizabeth's father, Andrew Graham, who was a blacksmith. In any case, John prospered and by 9 May 1799 was able to buy almost 125 acres in two separate deeds. In the first deed, he bought 24½ acres from John Stedman for £40 sterling. The land was described as "situate in Chester County on the head branches of Rockey Creek adjoining a tract of one hundred acres originally granted to John Watson and hath such shape form and marks as appear by a plat thereof to the original grant. . . ." This deed was witnessed by John's father-in-law, Andrew Graham, and brothers-in-law Matthew Graham and Adam Mills. On 1 November "1806," (probably 1805) Andrew Graham proved the deed although it was not recorded until 17 October 1825 (Book W, p. 3). The second deed, dated 9 May 1799, was from John Watson to John Gleghorn. In this deed Watson sold Gleghorn 100 acres also for £40 sterling, and this land was described as "situate in Chester County on the head branches of Rockey Creek bounded on all sides by vacant land when surveyed and hath such shape form & marks as appears by a plat thereof to the original grant . . . ." This deed was witnessed by Andrew Graham, Jeremiah Walker, and

William Joyner, and Andrew also proved it on 1 November "1806" (probably 1805--recorded 17 October 1825, Book W, pp. 4-5). The reason it is thought that the correct date was 1805 is that Andrew probably moved to Kentucky late that year.

On 8 October 1801 John bought fifty adjacent acres in Chester County from John Bell for $100. The tract was described as "being in Chester District on the waters of Rockey Creek bounded to the S. E. by John Gleghorn N. E. by John Bell and N. W. by John Bell and Hugh Brown being on the S. E. Side of a tract of land belonging to the Said John Bell." This deed was witnessed by Robert Strong, Alexander Boyd, and James Strong (recorded 17 October 1825, Book W, p. 4).

Among Elizabeth's and John's neighbors were Matthew and Jennie (McKay) Elder and their ten children. One of the children, Matthew Elder Jr. (1813-1892), later told his "autobiography" to his daughter Mary J. Elder who transcribed it. Her transcription included a rare account of daily lives in Chester County in 1823 and was probably a close reflection of the lives led by Elizabeth and John, themselves:

No labor saving machines were then in operation, granering [sic] hundred[s] of bushels of grain in a few hours. In close hot suffocating barns, the grain was taken off the straw with flails or the feet of horses. The straw was then taken off by hand and by rakes and the grain separated from the chaff by running it through a coarse and fine riddle kept constantly in motion before a domestic fan turned by hand. Putting a crop of 150 bushels through this process occupied, perhaps eight or ten days.

The peaches and apples from the large orchards were taken to the distillery, put into large troughs and by the application of mauls, pounded into fragments. In this changed condition they were thrown into barrels and when sufficiently rotten by a process of [dis]tillation converted into brandy. Almost every family had more or less of this fiery stuff.

The surplus produced was all hauled to Charleston, Columbia or Camden in wagons and all the merchandise and grocers used in the up country brought back in the same vehicle, a trip to Charleston occupying three weeks and to Columbia or Camden each a week. The price of hauling to Charleston per hundred was two dollars "down" and

2-1 Andrew

from one dollar fifty, to one dollar seventy-five "up."
A wagoner never slept half the night keeping up his
fire, cooking his meals, greasing his wagon, feeding,
cudding and brushing his horses occupying more than half
his time, and when he lay down on the cold wet ground,
how much would he--could he sleep?[3]

Matthew also gave a brief sketch of domestic life as it existed in his parents' household:

> He had two little brothers yo[u]nger than himself,
> and no domestic event ever produced a deeper or more
> lasting impression on his boyish intellect than the care
> manifested by his good mother, in training these diminu-
> tive mortals. At a certain hour every night, the [spin-
> ning] wheel and cards were put aside, the thread care-
> fully reeled from the spools, the hanks suspended on the
> wall, the floor nicely swept, the three children called
> to her side where they repeated the Lord's Prayer, and
> answered a few questions from Brown's Cathechisms for
> children. The paternal head of the family then sung a
> Psalm or part of one, read a portion of scripture and
> offered a prayer. In a short while everything in the
> miniature Temple of Industry was silent as thought,
> except the tick-tick of the old Seth Thomas that occu-
> pied a position on the wall.
>
> During the winter everything was moving early. The
> fires were made, the feeding done and worship over be-
> fore the dawn of day. In summer, the first ray of light
> that appeared in the East was the signal for leaving the
> bed.[4]

In 1825 John and Elizabeth decided to leave South Carolina,
and in a Chester County deed dated 18 October 1825 John sold
159-9/10 acres for $1,060 to Robert Boyd (Book W, p. 59). The
following winter, 1825-6, he and Elizabeth moved with all their
children to Lincoln County, Tennessee. Since it is known that
their oldest son, Samuel, settled on Cold Water Creek in the
western part of Lincoln County,[5] it is assumed that John and
Elizabeth also settled there. They probably lived out their lives
in Lincoln County.

Elizabeth had twelve children, several of them twins, and all born in Chester County, South Carolina:

A. Samuel Gleghorn, b. 19 November 1795
B. Andrew Gleghorn, b. *c.* 1798
C. Margaret(?) Gleghorn, b. 1795-1804
D. Jane(?) Gleghorn, b. 1800-4
E. Mathew Gleghorn, b. *c.* 1802
F. John Gleghorn, b. *c.* 1810
G. James Gleghorn, b. *c.* 1810
H. David Gleghorn, b. 1810-15
I. Sarah Gleghorn, b. *c.* 1814
J. Robert Gleghorn, b. *c.* 1814
K. Elijah Gleghorn, b. *c.* 1818
L. William Gleghorn, b. *c.* 1820

While in Lincoln County, Tennessee, many of these children plus one grandchild married members of the Gault family, grandchildren of William Gault (1735-1803) and Rebecca Coffee of Virginia.[6] The Gaults and their allied families had moved to Tennessee probably in the 1810's. In the following chart, the three Gault siblings named--Thomas, Grace, and Nancy--were among the thirteen children of William Gault and Rebecca Coffee:

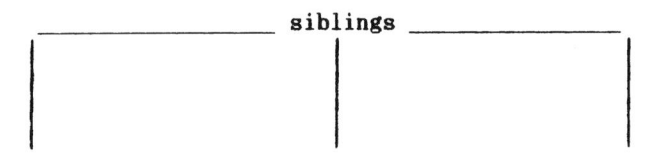

siblings

Thomas Gault m. Sarah Apeling: children:

-William Gault m. 3-1I Sarah Gleghorn

-Henry Calvin Gault m. 3-1A2 Mary Ann Gleghorn

Grace Gault m.
(1) James Johnson;
(2) John Wilson;
children:

-Rebecca Johnson m. 3-1B Andrew Gleghorn

-Mary Johnson m. 3-1G James Gleghorn

-Ursula Wilson, m. 3-1J Robert Gleghorn

-Susan C. Wilson m. 3-1K Elijah Gleghorn

-Eliza L. Wilson m. 3-1L William Gleghorn

Nancy Gault m. John Clark Taylor; child:

-Huldah Taylor m.
(1) 3-1H David Gleghorn

2-1 Andrew                                                                  3-1A

In the early 1850's, most of the Gleghorn descendants moved to Arkansas. The only ones who remained in Tennessee were 3-1A Samuel and his family plus one daughter of 3-1B Andrew who had married one of Samuel's sons. In the late 1860's, several Gleghorns then moved from Arkansas to Texas.

A. Samuel Gleghorn, born Chester County, South Carolina, 19 November 1795, died in Lincoln County, Tennessee, 3 December 1883, buried Bethel Cemetery; married in Chester County, South Carolina, 16 February 1819, Mary Crawford, born Chester County, 12 March 1792, died Lincoln County, Tennessee, 23 September 1879, buried next to her husband in Bethel Cemetery, only child of Andrew Crawford (born Ireland, died Chester County, South Carolina, c. 1832) and ___.[7] In his naturalization papers, 17 April 1804, Andrew Crawford testified that he had sailed to America from Ireland in October 1791, landing at Charleston in December 1791. Andrew became a citizen on the same day and at the same place as Edward Blackstock, husband of 2-8 Margaret Graham Blackstock [Naturalized Citizens (1802-1832), Book A, pp. 12-14].

At the age of sixteen, Mary joined the Hopewell Church in Chester County and continued her church involvement for the remainder of her life. She and Samuel moved to Tennessee in the winter of 1825-6, settling on Cold Water Creek. Later they had a home on Swan Creek.[8]

Since Mary was an only child and her mother died when she was young, she inherited all her father's property in Chester County and had to sell it through Chester County agents. In one series of letters and deeds, 26 November 1833 to 1 January 1834, she and Samuel sold 117 acres in Chester County for $506 to George McCormick who was representing Samuel, John, and Sarah McCormick. The land was on Sandy Creek and was bounded by lands of Robert Strong, deceased, Samuel McKeown, and Samuel, John, and Sarah McCormick (Book Z, pp. 320-23). In another series of letters and deeds, 17 October 1843 to 18 November 1843, Mary and Samuel sold an additional 100 acres for $480 to Jesse Gouis of Chester County. The land was on a branch of Rocky Creek and was bounded by lands of the Widow Read, the Widow Boyd, Robert Hamilton, ___ Elders, and Jesse Gouis (Book FF, pp. 126-9).

Probably due to these sales and to Samuel's industriousness, he and Mary prospered in Lincoln County. In the 1860 census Samuel gave his total assets as over $25,000 which were considerably higher than those of any one of his neighbors. In his will, written on 6 August 1878 and proved on 27 December 1883, Samuel mentioned all five of his children:

1. Andrew C. Gleghorn,[9] born Chester County, South Carolina, *c.* 1820, died of drowning in 1897 (age 77 years, 1 month); married (1) on 23 January 1849, Sarah A. White (Sally), born in Tennessee, *c.* 1826, died Lincoln County, Tennessee, 15 October 1874; (2) on 6 February 1879, Sallie A. Hines, born 1838, died near Blanche, Tennessee, 7 December 1912. Andrew was a ruling elder in his church for twenty years and was also fairly active in community affairs. Children:

    a. Samuel Wiley Gleghorn, born Tennessee, 18 November 1849, died 5 April 1873; married in Lincoln County, Tennessee, 18 December 1869, Mary Poindexter, born Tennessee, *c.* 1850, died ___, daughter of W. H. Poindexter and Sallie W. ___.[10] Samuel and Mary were married by J. B. Tigert. Child: Sallie (Lila), born Tennessee, *c.* 1872.

    b. Robert Young Gleghorn, born Tennessee, *c.* 1851, died Chisholm County, Texas, 1897; married, 9 September 1875, Sallie Hampton, born Tennessee, *c.* 1856. They were married by A. S. Sloan, MG. Known children: (**a**) Jennie R., born 2 June 1876, married Porter Bailey; (**b**) Maud G., born 30 July 1878, married Alex Patterson; (**c**) Leila May, born 1879, married Henry Hawks; (**d**) Thomas Urban, born 6 March 1881, married Effie Hogue; (**e**) Robert A., born 13 May 1883, married Bertha Haley; (**f**) Ralph, born 20 December 1885, married Lillie Owens; (**g**) Minnie, born 17 May 1887, married Fred Coffee or Joffyees; (**h**) Ola, born April 1889, died young; (**i**) Theodore, born July 1891, married Ollie Crawford; (**j**) Claude, born 1893, died 1950, unmarried; (**k**) Sadie, born 25 February 1895, married (1) Gus Boling, (2) Gene N. Burrell; and (**l**) Jesse, born 18 August 1897, married Bertha Greer.

    c. William Wood Gleghorn, born Tennessee, *c.* 1854, died ___; married Retta Pincard. They lived in Texas. Known children: (**a**) William Francis; (**b**) Lillian, married ___ Bowles; (**c**) Robert L.; (**d**) Beulah, married ___ Henson; and (**e**) Wood.

2-1 Andrew                                                              3-1A1d

    d.  Margaret Gleghorn, born Tennessee, c. 1856

    e.  Andrew Gleghorn, born Tennessee, c. 1858, died ___; married Lizzie Williams. Known children: (**a**) Rosaline; (**b**) Sallie, married ___ Fox; (**c**) Clark, unmarried; (**d**) Belle, married ___ Herring; and (**e**) Helen, married ___ Parker.

    f.  J. A. (or Plesants) Gleghorn, born Tennessee, c. 1864, died ___; married Frances Resinover. Known child: James Douglas, married Tommie Terrell.

    g.  Sallie Gleghorn Carpenter, born Tennessee, c. 1866, died in Tennessee, 21 December 1897; married Dr. C. C. Carpenter. Known child: Lili Bell, married ___ Turley.

    h.  Joseph Crawford Gleghorn, born 26 August 1879, died August 1941; married, December 1900, Rebecca Elizabeth Bowling, born 8 February 1878, died 17 May 1947. Children: (**a**) Annie Lee, born 1902, married ___ Mills; (**b**) Albert Edward, married Gertrude ___; (**c**) John Diemer, died young; (**d**) Arthur Ransom; (**e**) Lucy Belle, married ___ Pickle; and (**f**) Margaret Lorene, married ___ Ledford.

    i.  John Diemer Gleghorn

2.  Mary Ann Gleghorn Gault,[11] born Chester County, South Carolina, 20 November 1822, died Lincoln County, Tennessee, September 1879; married in Lincoln County, 8 December 1840, Henry Calvin Gault (called Andy), born Tennessee, 20 November 1820, died Lincoln County, Tennessee, 12 December 1901, son of Thomas Gault and Sarah Apeling. Mary Ann and Henry were married by Samuel S. Ralston, MG. Henry's mother, Sarah Gault, was listed in his household in the 1860 census of Lincoln County, Tennessee. In the 1880 census Henry was listed in the household of his son Henry Jr. On 26 December 1882 Henry married (2) Elizabeth Anderson, daughter of John Anderson. Mary Ann's children:

    a.  Samuel Bryson Gault, born 22 October 1841

    b.  William Thomas Gault, born 8 January 1845, died ___; married ___. Known children: (**a**) Lloyd; (**b**) Lois, married ___ Wade; (**c**) Fred; and (**d**) Myrtle, married ___ Welch.

c. Nancy E. Gault, born 10 June 1847, died 19 October 1848.

d. Sarah Ann Gault Tate, born 23 December 1848, died ___; married ___ Tate. Known children: (**a**) Pearl, married ___ Shelton; (**b**) Pressley; and (**c**) Arch.

e. Martha Jane Gault Tate, born 13 March 1852, died ___; married ___ Tate. Known child: J. Norman who lived in Blythe, California.

f. John Wood Gault, born 19 September 1854, died 1922; married Elizabeth Porter, born ___, died 31 October 1890. In the 1880 census he was listed in the household of his brother Henry. Known children: (**a**) Robert Lee; (**b**) Agnes, married ___ Cowley; and (**c**) Tom.

g. Henry Calvin Gault Jr., born 28 February 1857, died ___; married (1) in February 1877, Mary A. ___, born 10 August 1856, died 22 July 1881; (2) on 15 April 1882, Mary Elizabeth ___, born 16 September 1865, died 1 June 1916. Listed in Henry's household in the 1880 census were his father and his brothers John and Lewis. Known children: (**a**) Albert; (**b**) Maggie, married ___ Moyers; (**c**) Hubert; (**d**) Herbert; (**e**) Frederick; (**f**) Carl; (**g**) Charlie; (**h**) Maude, married ___ Rainey; (**i**) Frances, married ___ Allen; and (**j**) Johnnie Mae, married ___ Bell.

h. Mary Emma Gault Jobe, born 17 April 1860; married James Kelly Jobe, son of Samuel Jobe and Mary ___. Known children: (**a**) Zederick; (**b**) Velma, married ___ Parks; (**c**) Florette, married ___ Ray; (**d**) Virgil; (**e**) Frank; (**f**) Ozella, married ___ Holly; (**g**) Alvin Leon; and (**h**) Grady George.

i. Lewis S. (or Davis) Gault, born *c.* 1863, died ___; married ___. Known children: (**a**) Clarence; and (**b**) Macie, married ___ Ipock.

3. Nancy F. Gleghorn Jobe,[12] born Chester County, South Carolina, *c.* 1825, died 2 December 1896; married in Lincoln County, Tennessee, 17 January 1848, John H. Jobe, born Tennessee, 1826, died ___, probably son of Samuel Jobe (born North Carolina, *c.* 1777) and Rebecca ___ (born Tennessee, 1794). Children, all born in Tennessee:

a. Samuel Jobe, born c. 1849; married, c. 1870, Nancy A. ___, born Tennessee, c. 1851. Known children: (**a**) Will; (**b**) Joseph; (**c**) Riley; (**d**) Walter S.; (**e**) Eugene; (**f**) Sallie, married ___ Caughron; (**g**) Mary Dale; and (**h**) Nancy Elizabeth, married ___ McFerrin.

b. Mary R. Jobe Nerren (Molly), born c. 1852; married ___ Nerren. Known children: (**a**) John; (**b**) Ben; and (**c**) Maggie, married ___ Clark.

c. Elizabeth Jane Jobe, born c. 1854; unmarried.

d. John H. (Harvey?) Jobe, born c. 1856. Listed in the 1880 census of Lincoln County, Tennessee, was a "Harvey Job," perhaps the John H. Jobe who was Nancy's son. Listed with him was "Young Job," perhaps John's brother P. Y.

e. P. Y. Jobe (boy), born c. 1857. See John above.

f. James L. Jobe, born c. 1859

g. Nancy Laura Jobe, born c. 1863

h. Arlena L. Jobe, born c. 1867

i. L. M. Jobe (boy), born c. 1876

4. Elizabeth B. Gleghorn Dickey,[13] born Lincoln County, Tennessee, 2 April 1829, died Lincoln County, 15 October 1874; married, 11 August 1853, John S. Dickey, born North Carolina, 25 April 1825, died 8 November 1855. They were married by T. W. Parkerson. Known children:

    a. Samuel Dickey, born Tennessee, c. 1854

    b. Mary Jane Dickey Kidd, born Tennessee, c. 1857; married ___ Kidd.

    c. Thomas A. Dickey, born Tennessee, October 1859; married ___. Known children: (**a**) Thomas Edgar; and (**b**) Martha D., married ___ Martin.

    d. J. C. Dickey (boy), born Tennessee, c. 1862

    e. R. N. Dickey (boy), born Tennessee, c. 1866

f. Elizabeth Anna Dickey Rowell, born ___; married ___ Rowell. Known children: (**a**) Knox Russell; (**b**) Minnie R., married ___ Reville; and (**c**) Mary Elizabeth, married ___ Gardner.

5. Samuel W. Gleghorn,[14] born Lincoln County, Tennessee, 20 February 1832, died Lincoln County, 3 August 1908; married in Lincoln County, 11 April 1867, 3-1B5 Sarah Susan Gleghorn (Sallie), born Lincoln County, 30 October 1841, died Lincoln County, 22 January 1909, daughter of 3-1B Andrew Gleghorn and Rebecca Johnson. They were married by A. S. Sloan, MG. On 10 November 1862 Samuel enlisted in the Confederate Army, Company C, 41st Tennessee Infantry, was taken prisoner near Jackson, Mississippi, in July 1863, sent to Camp Morton, Indianapolis, and was finally released on oath, 11 May 1865. At that time he was described as being 5 feet 8 inches tall and had blue eyes, dark hair, and a fair complexion. Children, all born in Tennessee:

   a. Chalmers A. Gleghorn, born 25 January 1868, died 6 April 1945; probably unmarried.

   b. Thomson S. Gleghorn, born 15 October 1871, died 25 July 1916, probably unmarried.

   c. Mary Rebecca Gleghorn Atkins, born c. 1874, died at the birth of twins who also died; married ___ Atkins.

   d. Samuel Moses Gleghorn, born 5 July 1875, died 6 August 1913; probably unmarried.

   e. Martha E. Gleghorn, born 14 October 1877, died in Lewisburg, Tennessee, 19 October 1955; unmarried. When Martha died, her will was legally declared invalid on the grounds that she had been *non compos mentis* when she wrote it. Since her siblings had all died and left no heirs, her estate was divided among the heirs of her father's siblings.

B. Andrew Gleghorn, born Chester County, South Carolina, c. 1798, died Lincoln County, Tennessee, soon after 17 August 1850 when his will was written;[15] married in Tennessee, Rebecca Johnson, born ___, died perhaps before 1850, daughter of Grace Gault and (1) James Johnson.[16] The reason it is thought that Rebecca died before 1850 is that she was not listed with Andrew in the 1850 federal census.

Many of Andrew's children moved first to Hempstead County, Arkansas, c. 1851, then to Fulton County, Arkansas, before 1860. By 1870 they had moved elsewhere. Known children:

1. John Wiley Gleghorn,[17] born Lincoln County, Tennessee, 13 January 1830, died 12 July 1899, buried Humphries Cemetery, Fulton County, Arkansas; married in Hempstead County, Arkansas, 9 January 1857, Rosanna G. Brooks, born Tennessee, c. 27 June 1829, died 17 July 1899 (69 years, 11 months, 20 days), buried Humphries Cemetery, Fulton County, Arkansas. In the 1880 census John and Rosanna were listed in Izard County, Arkansas, where in the same year he bought land in the northeast area: T18N R8W S11. Children:

   a. James Lavelle Gleghorn, born Arkansas, 21 October 1860, died 9 September 1944, buried Humphries Cemetery, Fulton County, Arkansas; married in Fulton County, c. 3 September 1889, Lavona A. Herriott, born 8 March 1871, died 13 February 1944, buried Humphries Cemetery, daughter of George R. Herriott and Elizabeth Catherine Ross. At some time James and Lavona moved to Izard County, Arkansas, where in 1894 he bought T18N R8W S1. Children, all born in Wiseman, Izard County, Arkansas: (a) Tersie Elgivia Gleghorn Brawley, born 6 September 1891, died Springfield, Missouri, 29 April 1955, married, 19 April 1909, James Harvey Brawley, born Agnes, Fulton County, Arkansas, 13 August 1886, died Springfield, Missouri, 15 December 1950, son of Hugh P. Brawley and Mary E. ___; (b) Austin Wiley Gleghorn, born 27 January 1894, died Springfield, Missouri, 5 March 1972, married Bertha Bell Chadwick, daughter of C. A. Chadwick and Nancy Mendona Wagoner; (c) Archie Vernile Gleghorn, born 17 September 1896, died Fulton County, Arkansas, 23 July 1980, married, 18 January 1920, Dellaphine Johnson, born Fulton County, 28 January 1900, died Fulton County, 26 December 1982, daughter of Samuel David Johnson and Eliza T. Godwin; (d) James Ellis Gleghorn, born 19 August 1898, died Springfield, Missouri, 29 January 1982, married c. 2 January 1920, Edythe Myrtle Oldfield, born Wiseman, Arkansas, 19 August 1902, died Springfield, Missouri, 4 June 1977, daughter of James Pinkney Oldfield and Mary Kent; (e) Hugh Elmer Gleghorn, born 1 September 1900, died Salinas, California, 1985, married, 24 November 1928, Audie Artie Lee Bell, born Wiseman, Arkansas, 7 September 1905, died Porterfield, California, 26 December 1977, daughter of Joseph Plummer Bell and Allie Elizabeth Darrell; **(f)** Letha Stella Gleghorn Richardson, born 6 September 1902, died after 1987, married, 25 October 1919, Tollye James Richardson, born Sidney, Arkansas, 3 August 1898, son of John Richardson and Fannie McElmurry; **(g)** Earl Edgar Gleghorn, born 4 June 1905, died after 1987, married, 19 September 1926, Mary Evelyn (Evalee) Shannon, born Mountain View, Arkansas, 19 February 1906, daughter of John Burton Shannon and Isophene Gray (Earl and Evalee are the parents of Dellawayne Gleghorn Watson who supplied the data on her grandparents' descendants); **(h)** Kilbert Vance Gleghorn, born 24 February 1907, died 20 December 1921; **(i)** Troy Roscoe Gleghorn, born 24 March 1909, died 7 August 1960, married, 12 July 1942, Opal Elzona Reeves, born Fulton County, Arkansas, 13 March 1916, daughter of Charles Reeves and Hester Grissom; **(j)** Loma Janette Gleghorn Chadwick, born 20 October 1911, died after 1987, married, 26 February 1930, Boyce Asberry Chadwick, born Morriston, Arkansas, 22 December 1910, son of C. A. Chadwick and Nancy Mendona Wagoner; and **(k)** ___ (girl) died infancy.

b. Sarah G. Gleghorn, born Arkansas, *c.* 1865, probably died young. She was listed with her parents in the 1880 census of Izard County, Arkansas, and may have died soon after.

c. Rebecca Elgiva Gleghorn Moser, born Arkansas, June 1868, died 1930, buried Humphries Cemetery, Fulton County, Arkansas; married, 25 July 1889, Cephas Wesley Moser, born November 1869, died 1937.

d. Janette Gleghorn Oldfield (called Net), born Arkansas, ___, died ___, buried Humphries Cemetery, Fulton County, Arkansas; married Allen Oldfield.

2. Elizabeth Jane Gleghorn Andrews,[18] born Lincoln County, Tennessee, *c.* 1833, died ___, buried Wiseman Cemetery, Izard County, Arkansas; married in Hempstead County, Arkansas, 9 September 1852, Joshua Rucker Andrews (called Bud), born *c.* 1831. They were married by John M. Whiteside, JP. In the 1860 census they were listed in Hempstead County, Arkansas. Children, all born in Arkansas:

a. Sarah Andrews Williams, born *c.* 1850; married Richard

2-1 Andrew  3-1B2b

Williams.

b. John Andrews, born c. 1852

c. Ann Andrews, born c. 1854

d. Jane Andrews, born c. 1856

e. Tilitha C. Andrews Montgomery; married John P. Montgomery.

f. Ulysses Hiram Grant Andrews; married Cordillia Soden.

g. Frank Andrews; unmarried.

h. Delbert Rucker Sherman Andrews; married Rebecca M. Bell.

i. Mary E. Andrews Williams; married Vincent Garner Williams.

3. Hugh Gleghorn,[19] born Lincoln County, Tennessee, c. 1836, died probably in Fulton County, Arkansas, ___; married in Hempstead County, Arkansas, 12 April 1855, Jennette Farris Brooks, born Tennessee, c. 1832, died 1899. They were married by Hugh's cousin 3-1G1 James J. Gleghorn, JP (Book A, p. 218). Hugh and Jennette were listed in Fulton County, Arkansas, in the 1860 census. Listed with them was Hugh's sister 3-1B7 Rebecca. Also in 1860 he bought land in the northeast area of Izard County, Arkansas--T18N R7W S15--but whether he and Jennette moved there is not known. During the Civil War Hugh served as a private in the Confederate Army, New Company B, 27th Arkansas Infantry, and was discharged with a disability on 18 March 1863. After Hugh died, Jennette may have married (2) in Fulton County, W. Ferguson, born North Carolina, c. 1809. Children of Hugh and Jennette, all born in Arkansas:

   a. Andrew J. Gleghorn, born 22 December 1855, died 5 April 1895; unmarried.

   b. Canaan Elonzo Gleghorn, born 27 July 1857, died 6 February 1937; married, 19 November 1890, Narcissus Jane Lampkin (Jennie), born Mississippi, 20 November 1867, died 21 June 1947. In the 1900 census they were listed in Izard County, Arkansas. Known children: (**a**) Golda A. (boy), born January 1893; and (**b**) Terry

M. (boy), born July 1898.

c. Cobburn(?) Gleghorn (girl), born *c.* 1859

d. Walker Gleghorn, born *c.* 1862

4. Mary Elender Gleghorn Smith,[20] born Lincoln County, Tennessee, *c.* 1838, died ___; married in Hempstead County, Arkansas, 23 May 1854, William A. Smith, born Mississippi, *c.* 1834, died ___. They were married by John M. Whitesides, JP. In the 1860 census they were listed in Hempstead County, Arkansas. No children were listed with them.

5. Sarah Susan Gleghorn,[21] born Lincoln County, Tennessee, 30 October 1841, died Lincoln County, 22 January 1909; married, 11 April 1867, her first cousin 3-1A5 Samuel W. Gleghorn, son of 3-1A Samuel Gleghorn and Mary Crawford. In the 1860 census of Fulton County, Arkansas, Sarah was listed in the household of her brother 3-1B1 John. For her children, see under 3-1A5.

6. Martha Minerva Gleghorn Nelson, born Lincoln County, Tennessee, *c.* 1842, died ___; married in Hempstead County, Arkansas, 11 February 1859, James S. Nelson, born *c.* 1840.[22]

7. Rebecca Gleghorn, born Lincoln County, Tennessee, *c.* 1844. In the 1860 census of Fulton County, Arkansas, she was listed in the household of her brother 3-1B3 Hugh.

8. Ursula Gleghorn, born Lincoln County, Tennessee, *c.* 1845

9. Elgiva Gleghorn Wiseman,[23] born Lincoln County, Tennessee, *c.* 1847, died ___; married John Wiseman. In the 1860 census of Fulton County, Arkansas, she was listed in the household of her brother 3-1B1 John.

C. Margaret(?) Gleghorn, born South Carolina, 1795-1804. A Margaret Gleghorn, aged 65(?) and born in South Carolina, was listed in the household of Frank F. and Elizabeth Wilson in the 1860 census of Fulton County, Arkansas. It is likely that 3-1 Elizabeth Graham Gleghorn would have named a daughter Margaret since that was her mother's name. Perhaps this Margaret was that girl. She was listed in her parents' household in the 1830 federal census of Lincoln County, Tennessee, but nothing more has been found on her.

2-1 Andrew                                                                    3-1D

D.  Jane(?) Gleghorn, born South Carolina, 1800-1804. On 25 March
    1822 in Chester County, South Carolina, a Jane Gleghorn was
    indicted for perjury although the circumstances in the case
    were not given. Probably she was a daughter of John and
    Elizabeth (Graham) Gleghorn. The case continued until 14 July
    1823 when a jury found her innocent (General Session Minutes,
    Fall Term 1821 to 1838). She was listed in her parents'
    household in the 1830 federal census of Lincoln County,
    Tennessee, but nothing more has been found on her.

E.  Mathew (Matthew) Gleghorn,[24] born Chester County, South Caro-
    lina, c. 1802, died near Hope, Hempstead County, Arkansas, 14
    September 1869, buried Forest Hills Cemetery, Bodcaw, Hemp-
    stead County; married probably in Lincoln County, Tennessee,
    c. 1830(?) Martha Smith (called Matty), born Chester County,
    South Carolina, c. 1806, died Bodcaw, Hempstead County, Arkan-
    sas, 11 August 1885, daughter of William Smith (born Ireland,
    c. 1760, died probably in Hempstead County after 1860) and
    ___, born c. 1765. Listed with Matthew in the 1830 census of
    Lincoln County, Tennessee, were two women, one aged 15-20, the
    other 20-25. The older one was probably Matty, but it is not
    known who the younger one was. In the 1840 census, Matthew
    and Matty were listed in Fayette County, Tennessee, and in
    1850 they moved to Hempstead County, Arkansas, where they
    lived out their lives. During the trip to Arkansas their
    sixth child, William, died and was buried at the side of the
    road. At first they were squatters in Hempstead County, but
    Matthew soon built a log house and cleared three acres of
    land; the state then gave him a deed for 160 acres. Matty's
    father, William Smith (aged 100) was listed with them in the
    1860 census. In 1880 Matty was listed with her daughter Mary.
    Their listing came immediately after that of Matty's son Baron
    (Barney). Children, all born in Tennessee:

    1.  Eliza Gleghorn Crews, born Tennessee, 1834-5, died at
        Bodcaw, Hempstead County, Arkansas, 14 January 1892 (aged
        57 years), buried Forest Hills Cemetery, Hempstead County;
        married in Hempstead County, 23 January 1855, Robert M.
        Crews, born Tennessee c. 1831, perhaps son of E. Crews
        (born North Carolina, c. 1805) and Sarah L. ___ (born
        Tennessee, c. 1808). Eliza and Robert were married by
        Barry W. Yates, JP. In the 1860 federal census of Hemp-
        stead County, they were listed immediately after her
        parents. With them were the following children:

        a.  Martha J. Crews, born Arkansas, c. 1856

b. Albert M. Crews, born Arkansas, *c.* 1858; unmarried.

c. William Crews

2. Jane or Jeannette Gleghorn Smith, born Tennessee, 7 September 1837, died Bodcaw, Hempstead County, Arkansas, 20 September 1915; married in Hempstead County, 1 March 1855, James A. Smith (Book A, pp. 211-2), born Tennessee, *c.* 1833, died Bodcaw, Arkansas, 18 September 1879, son of Clement Smith (born North Carolina, *c.* 1803, died Bodcaw, Arkansas, *c.* 1869) and Nancy ___ (born North Carolina, 9 June 1812, died Bodcaw, Arkansas, 3 October 1890, buried Forest Hills Cemetery, Hempstead County). Jane and James were married by Barry W. Yates, JP. During the Civil War James fought for the Confederacy in Company C, 20th Arkansas Infantry, and was captured at the siege of Vicksburg, Mississippi. Jane later drew a CSA widow's pension. Known children, all born near Bodcaw, Hempstead County:

   a. Alice Smith Scott, born *c.* 1855, died Rosalie, Texas, 1925; married, 7 December 1871, William Walter Scott, born 30 April 1852, died Rosalie, Texas, 27 July 1936. Alice and William were the great-grandparents of James L. Buckley Jr. who furnished much of the information on the Gleghorns. Children, both born in Bodcaw, Arkansas: (a) Ida Delaney Scott Russell, born 15 October 1872, died Idabel, Oklahoma, 25 June 1956, married in Bodcaw, 21 December 1890, Jasper Newton Russell, born Covington County, Alabama, 11 October 1861, died Idabel, Oklahoma, 17 March 1925; and (b) Emma Valerian Scott Owens, born 21 October 1875, died in Bodcaw, Arkansas, 9 September 1943, married Dock Owens.

   b. Nancy E. Smith, born *c.* 1857

   c. Edwina Smith Beckham; born *c.* 1858; married Solomon D. Beckham.

   d. Etta Smith Skinner, born 1862; married George Skinner.

   e. John Calvin Smith, born 21 October 1864, died Bodcaw, Arkansas, 14 June 1928, buried Forest Hills Cemetery; married Mary E. Russell, born Covington County, Alabama, 25 September 1868, died Bodcaw, Arkansas, 19 March 1931, buried Forest Hills Cemetery.

   f. Ann Smith, born 1868; unmarried.

2-1 Andrew          3-1B2g

g. Mary Lou Smith Skinner, born 27 September 1870, died Bodcaw, Arkansas, 25 June 1939; married John W. Skinner. Known children: (a) Una; (b) Maude; (c) Idell; (d) Dewey (girl); (e) Bonnie Fay; (f) Lester; (g) Clinton; (h) James Pascal; and (i) Grace.

3. Martha Gleghorn Campbell, born Tennessee, 29 September 1839, died Bodcaw, Arkansas, 25 January 1877, buried at Forest Hills Cemetery, Hempstead County; married in Hempstead County, 5 February 1857, James H. Campbell, born Alabama, 4 October 1819, died 21 July 1899, buried Forest Hills Cemetery, Hempstead County. They were married by John Mouser, JP. James was listed in the 1880 census of Hempstead County. Children, all born in Arkansas:

   a. Orville Campbell, born c. 1858, died 1896; unmarried.

   b. Valerian Campbell Sawyers (girl), born c. 1860, died 1896; married ___ Sawyers.

   c. Udora J. Campbell, born c. 1862, died 1944; unmarried.

   d. Martha Emma Campbell, born c. 1865, died 1945; unmarried.

   e. Sarah J. Campbell, born c. 1868, died 1889; unmarried.

   f. Joseph M. Campbell, born c. 1872; married Allie Wiggins.

   g. Pamelia or Emma C. Campbell, born c. 1875, died 1934; unmarried.

4. James Andrew Gleghorn,[25] born Tennessee, 27 August 1840, died Bodcaw, Arkansas, 11 June 1927, buried Forest Hills Cemetery, Hempstead County, Arkansas; married in Hempstead County, 16 August 1866, Margaret Melvina Hamilton, born Arkansas, c. 1846, died 3 January 1913, daughter of A. W. Hamilton (born Tennessee c. 1816) and Elizabeth ___ (born Tennessee c. 1817). They were married by the Rev. Neill Munn (Book B, p. 106). They lived in Hempstead County, Arkansas. Inscribed on James's tombstone is "Co. D, 24th Inf. C.S.A."

   In 1850 James' parents moved with their children from Fayette County, Tennessee, to Hempstead County, Arkansas. On the way, James' five-year-old brother William died and was buried at the roadside. This was an event which James never forgot, and many years later his grandson, Thomas Irwin, took him back to the burial site. Many years after that, Thomas Irwin wrote to James L. Buckley Jr., on 15 November 1976:

> My Grand Father was 10 years old at that time [when his brother William died]. He talked so much about it that I carried him to the spot where he thought he [William] was buried in 1927 which was 77 years later. We walked about 15 ft. and I found the tombs of 2 babies. There was no marker of William ever put to his grave.

Children:

a. Mary Elizabeth Gleghorn, born 20 August 1867, died 30 May 1929; unmarried.

b. Martha Ann Gleghorn, born 18 December 1868, died August 1947; unmarried.

c. John Matthew (or Andrew) Gleghorn, born 25 February 1871, died 28 November 1905; married Lillie Moxley. He and his brother Count Pulaski were killed by a negro who later was hanged for the dual murder.

d. Sarah Frances Gleghorn Piercy, born 27 November 1873, died 18 June 1944; married Roger Piercy.

e. Thomas Levi Gleghorn, born 7 October 1874, died 23 April 1937, buried Forest Hills Cemetery, Hempstead County, Arkansas; married Susan Paralee Brightwell, born 30 March 1887, died 1968, buried Forest Hills Cemetery, Hempstead County. Children: (**a**) Thomas Irwin, born 2 February 1905; (**b**) Otis, born 25 March 1907, twin to next; (**c**) Olis, born 25 March 1907, twin to former; (**d**) Edna, born 28 March 1910; (**e**) James Andrew, born 15 November 1915; (**f**) Vera, born 15 May 1916; (**g**) Guynell, born 4 June 1919; and (**h**) Ernest Milton, born 29 April 1924.

f. Lou Isabelle Gleghorn Crank, born 1878, died ___; married Joe Selone Crank, born 1876, died 1938.

g. Count Pulaski Gleghorn, born 1885, died 28 November 1905; unmarried. He and his brother John were killed by a negro who later was hanged for the murder.

    h. Ruth Angeline Gleghorn, born ___, died 11 July 1916.

    i. Emma Odell (or Idell) Gleghorn Stark, born 12 February 1890, died 24 July 1951, buried Forest Hills Cemetery, Hempstead County, Arkansas; married S. N. Stark, born 1883, died 1962, buried Harmony Cemetery, Hempstead County.

5. John C. Gleghorn, born Tennessee, 1843, killed in the Civil War.

6. William Gleghorn, born 1845, died 1850 en route with his family from Tennessee to Arkansas. His death made a great impression on his older brother 3-1E4 James Andrew. See the story above under James' entry.

7. Count Pulaski Gleghorn (twin to next), born 5 January 1847, died Bodcaw, Arkansas, 18 June 1875 (aged 28 years, 6 months, 13 days), buried Forest Hills Cemetery, Hempstead County, Arkansas; married c. 1870, Mary ___, born Arkansas, c. 1854. They were listed in the 1870 census of Hempstead County, Arkansas.

8. Baron DeKalb Gleghorn (called Barney, twin to above), born 5 January 1847, died Bodcaw, Arkansas, 1903; married Ellen A. Powell, born Arkansas, 15 March 1852, died 6 December 1881, buried Forest Hills Cemetery, Hempstead County, Arkansas, daughter of Hiram Powell (born Alabama, c. 1813) and Sarah R. ___ (born Tennessee, c. 1819). In the 1880 census Baron and Sarah were listed in Hempstead County, Arkansas; Baron, widower, was listed in Hempstead County in 1900. Known children, all born in Arkansas:

    a. Sarah Vida Gleghorn Jones, born 13 October 1872, died 7 August 1917, buried Forest Hills Cemetery; married Lee Jones.

    b. Hiram Matthew Gleghorn, born 8 October 1874, died 15 January 1954; married Frances ___.

    c. Albert Edward Gleghorn, born 14 June 1877, died 1940, buried Forest Hills Cemetery, Hempstead County.

    d. Count Pulaski Gleghorn, born May 1879, died 1913; unmarried.

> e. Luther L. Gleghorn (boy), born October 1881, died 1954.
>
> 9. Mary Coborn Gleghorn Richard, born 30 March 1850, died Bodcaw, Arkansas, 1922; married William Richard. Known children:
>
>> a. James Albert Richard, born 1884; married Estelle Cox.
>>
>> b. Fred Richard, born 1886; married Lila Ewing.
>>
>> c. Gordon Richard; married Ora Powell.
>>
>> d. Carl Richard, born 1892; married Flossie Powell.

F. John Gleghorn,[26] born Chester County, South Carolina, c. 1810, died in Greene County, Arkansas, April 1866, buried at the Gainesville Cemetery, Greene County; married in Lincoln County, Tennessee, Sciscilda Coleman (Sisley), born South Carolina, c. 1816, died probably in Marion County, Arkansas, after 1891. Although Sisley was born in South Carolina, she was reared in Alabama. She and John first lived in Lincoln County, Tennessee, then in 1842 moved to Independence County, Arkansas, arriving on the first steamer which sailed up the White River in that county. In 1859 they moved to Greene County, Arkansas, where they owned a farm near Gainesville. During the Civil War John fought for the Confederacy in Captain Morgan's company, Marmaduke's brigade. He was wounded in 1863. After he died in 1866, Sisley lived with her younger children in Greene County and in the 1870's moved to Marion County, Arkansas, where she was said to be living in 1889. Sisley had twelve children:

> 1. Rhoda E. Gleghorn Pool, born Tennessee, c. 1834, died ___; married Samuel Pool, born Tennessee c. 1837. In the 1880 census they were listed in Searcy County, Arkansas. Listed with them were the following children, all born in Arkansas:
>
>> a. Mary C. Pool, born c. 1863
>>
>> b. Ann E. Pool, born c. 1865
>>
>> c. James W. Pool, born c. 1869
>>
>> d. Daniel Pool, born c. 1872

2-1 Andrew                                                          3-1Ple

e.  John W. Pool, born c. 1878

2. David W. Gleghorn, born Tennessee, c. 1835, died young.

3. Stephen C. Gleghorn,[27] born Tennessee, c. 1836, died probably in Cleburne County, Arkansas, 20 January 1908; married (1) probably in Greene County, Arkansas, c. 1866, Nancy J. ___, born Arkansas, c. 1847, died ___; Stephen perhaps married (2) M. E. ___. He and Nancy were listed in the 1870 census of Greene County, Arkansas, but at some time they moved to Cleburne County and were living there when Stephen applied for a veteran's pension in 1904. He had fought for the Confederacy during the Civil War, enlisting in November 1861 as a private. On 24 July 1862 he was made a second sergeant, and on 6 November 1862 he was a second lieutenant. He served in Company A, 31st Arkansas Infantry, and Company K, 7th Missouri Cavalry. On 28 November 1863 he requested a furlough to visit his father in Greene County, Arkansas, and on 1 February 1864 was mistakenly listed as AWOL. The charge was dropped on 25 May 1864. He applied for his pension on 14 August 1904, and after he died his wife, "M. E." Gleghorn, applied for a widow's pension on 7 August 1908. His army record says he was 5 feet 9 inches tall and had blue eyes and light hair. Known child:

a.  Mary C. Gleghorn, born Arkansas, c. 1867

4. Lucretia M. Gleghorn Jones, born Tennessee, c. 1838, died ___; married William Jones who died before 1891.

5. Melissa Gleghorn Pool, born Tennessee, c. 1840, died ___; married, c. 1861, John A. Pool, born Arkansas, c. 1842. Known children, all born in Arkansas:

a.  Colman J. Pool, born c. 1862

b.  George A. Pool, born c. 1867

c.  Granville M. Pool, born c. 1877

d.  Walter L. Pool, born c. 1878

e.  Robert T. Pool, born February 1880

6. John Mobley Gleghorn,[28] born Independence County, Arkansas, 10 December 1843, died ___; married, November 1863,

Mary M. Arnold, born Tennessee, c. 1846, died Clay County, Arkansas, November 1887. John enlisted in the Confederate Army on 20 November 1861, served until 16 December 1862 when he was discharged with a disability at Readyville, Tennessee, reenlisted on 10 April 1863, and finally surrendered at Shreveport, Louisiana, 8 June 1865. After he and Mary were married, John was a farmer in Greene County until February 1871 when they moved to Clay County, Arkansas, where he farmed rented land until January 1881 at which time he bought 325 acres. He raised mostly corn plus some cotton and also bred stock. Although he was a staunch Democrat, he never ran for office. He is said to have done much to build up his county and to help others make a start by furnishing them with land and grain. His wife, Mary, was active in the Methodist Episcopal Church. Children, all born in Arkansas:

a. William Gleghorn, born 1864, died before 1891

b. Mary J. Gleghorn, born 1865

c. Luther L. Gleghorn, born 1866, died before 1891

d. John T. Gleghorn, born 1871, died before 1891

e. Lindsey C. Gleghorn, born November 1873, died before 1907; married in Clay County, Arkansas, 4 February 1894, Minnie Porter, born Kentucky, March 1876. In the 1900 census they were listed in Clay County, Arkansas. Children: (a) Luther, born Arkansas, March 1895; (b) John; (c) Ellen or Eileen, born Arkansas, November 1896; (d) Ruby, born Arkansas, February 1900; and (e) Edith. After Lindsey died, Minnie married (2) in Clay County, c. 1907, Charles Lethem. Later she married (3) ___ Bell and moved to Knobel, Arkansas.

f. Etta Gleghorn (called Hattie), born 1876

g. Walter Gleghorn, born 1879, died before 1891.

h. Amanda Gleghorn, born 1881

i. Lucy Anna Gleghorn, born 1884, died before 1891.

j. James R. Gleghorn, born Arkansas, November 1885. In the 1900 census he was listed with his father in Clay County, Arkansas.

2-1 Andrew                                                3-1P7

7. Sarah E. Gleghorn, born Arkansas, *c.* 1844, died before 1891.

8. William B. Gleghorn, born Arkansas, *c.* 1848, died before 1891.

9. James K. P. Gleghorn, born Arkansas, August 1849, died after 1900; married, *c.* 1870(?), Caroline ___, born Arkansas, August 1846. In the 1900 census they were listed in Greene County, Arkansas. Known children, all born in Arkansas:

   a. Etta Gleghorn, born *c.* 1872

   b. Nancy Gleghorn, born *c.* 1875

   c. Ellen Gleghorn, born *c.* 1877

   d. John Gleghorn, born March 1880, died ___; married, *c.* 1897, Docksey D. ___, born Arkansas, November 1878. In the 1900 census they were listed in Greene County, Arkansas. Listed with them were the following children: (**a**) Willie J., born Arkansas, *c.* 1898; and (**b**) Lucy E., born Arkansas, *c.* 1899.

   e. Mary S. Gleghorn, born April 1882

   f. Jiney (Jane?) M. Gleghorn, born January 1884

   g. Charley E. Gleghorn, born November 1889

10. Hardy C. Gleghorn, born Arkansas, *c.* 1853, died before 1891. In the 1870 census he was listed in the household of C. C. Gramling of Greene County, Arkansas, and was working as a farm laborer.

11. Louis C. Gleghorn, born Arkansas, *c.* 1856, died before 1891.

12. Marietta A. Gleghorn Gouch (Mary), born April 1860, died ___; married David Gouch.

G. James Gleghorn,[29] born Chester County, South Carolina, *c.* 1810, died probably in Arkansas after 21 March 1859; married in Lincoln County, Tennessee, Mary Johnson, born Tennessee *c.* 1809, died ___, daughter of Grace Gault and (1) James Johnson. In the early 1850's James and Mary probably moved to Fulton

County, Arkansas, then later moved to Hempstead County, Arkansas. Since his will was dated 21 March 1859, he probably died soon after. In it he left everything to his wife. In the 1860 census of Fulton County, Arkansas, Mary Johnson Gleghorn was listed in the household of her son Matthew. Children:

1. James Johnson Gleghorn (usually called Johnson), born Tennessee, *c.* 1831, died Parker County, Texas, 16 October 1887, buried Marlow Cemetery; married in Lincoln County, Tennessee, 8 October 1850, Margaret Ann Jones,[30] born Tennessee, 1832, died Texas, 1892-3. At some time they moved to Hempstead County, Arkansas, where he was a justice of the peace and in 1855 and 1857 presided at the weddings of his cousins 3-1B3 Hugh Gleghorn and 3-1B1 John W. Gleghorn. On 19 June 1862 Johnson enlisted in the Confederate Army, serving as a private in Company E, 33d Arkansas Infantry, and was discharged with a disability on 27 September 1863. Later he and his wife moved to Texas. Known children:

    a. Eliza Ann Gleghorn Wright, born 25 April 1853, died 27 February 1920; married (1) William A. Hancock, born 1851, died 1883; (2) on 6 July 1885, George Anderson Wright, born 23 January 1853, died 20 November 1932.

    b. Luther Gleghorn, born *c.* 1854

2. Matthew Gleghorn, born Tennessee, *c.* 1837, died Navarro County, Texas, 18 March 1882; married in Hempstead County, Arkansas, 5 April 1855, Mary Elizabeth Brooks (Book A, p. 214),[31] born Lincoln County, Tennessee, 6 October 1836, died Fluvanna, Scurry County, Texas, 28 November 1914. Matthew and Mary were married by John M. Whitesides, JP. In the 1860 census they were listed in Fulton County, Arkansas; listed with them was Matthew's mother. On 27 July 1862 Matthew enlisted as a private in the Confederate Army, Company F, 10th Missouri Infantry (which later became Company M, 38th Arkansas Infantry). He was taken prisoner at New Orleans on 26 May 1865 and parolled at Shreveport, Louisiana, 8 June 1865. In the 1880 census Matthew and Mary were listed in Navarro County, Texas. Known children:

    a. Coleburn Gleghorn, born Tennessee, *c.* 1856

    b. Evaline Gleghorn Sewalt, born 1856; married on 1 January 1874, L. L. Sewalt.

2-1 Andrew    3-1G2c

   c. James Gleghorn, born Tennessee c. 1858, died ___; married in Texas, c. 1880, Nancy ___, born Texas, c. 1863. They were listed in his parents' household in the 1880 census of Navarro County, Texas.

   d. Frances Gleghorn Patterson (called Parlee?), born Arkansas, April 1860; married, 2 March 1876, James Patterson, born Alabama, c. 1841. They were listed in the 1880 census of Navarro County, Texas. Listed with them were his mother, Louiza (age 60), his sister-in-law P. E. Gleghorn (age 29), his niece Josephine Gleghorn (age 7), and his nephew Dolphes(?) Gleghorn (age 2). The identities of P. E. Gleghorn and her children are not known.

   e. Vernila V. Gleghorn (boy), born Arkansas, c. 1866, died in Baird, Texas.

   f. Asa Vibran Gleghorn, born Texas, 3 December 1873 (twin to next), died 12 December 1946; married, 18 December 1894, Clarissa Belle Scott.

   g. Warren Gleghorn, born Texas, 3 December 1873, died c. 1880-1 (twin to above).

   h. Elbert Gleghorn, born Texas, c. 1877

3. Rebecca E. Gleghorn Wilson, born Tennessee, c. 1838, died ___; married in Hempstead County, Arkansas, 22 June 1854, Samuel S. Wilson of Ouachita County, Arkansas (Book A, p. 194).[32] They were married by John M. Whitesides, JP. Later they moved to Texas.

4. Mary Gleghorn, born c. 1840

5. Andrew Walker Gleghorn, born c. 1842. From 9 November until 9 December 1861, Andrew served as a 30-day volunteer in the Confederate Army, Capt. Perry Clayton's Company, Arkansas. He also served as a private in New Company B, 27th Arkansas Infantry, 28 February to 13 October 1863; in Company H, Crawford's Regiment of the Arkansas Cavalry, 31 December 1863 to 29 February 1864; and later was in Company B, Ford's Cavalry Battalion, Missouri. On 11 May 1865 he surrendered. He was described as being 5 feet 10 inches tall and had blue eyes, light hair, and a light complexion. Later he lived in Navarro County, Texas.

6. Jno T. or F. Gleghorn (written either John or Jonathan), born *c*. 1844. A J. F. Gleghorn was listed as having served in the Confederate Army, Company B, Ford's Battalion, Missouri Cavalry, perhaps this Jno T. or F. Later he lived in Spring Hill, Navarro County, Texas.

7. Eliza Ursula Gleghorn, born 20 January 1847; married 3-1K4 William Andrew Gleghorn, born Lincoln County, Tennessee, *c*. 1845, son of 3-1K Elijah Gleghorn and Susan C. Wilson. For children, see 3-1K4 William.

8. Abraham Gleghorn, born *c*. 1849. He lived in Wrightsboro, Gonzales County, Texas.

H. David Gleghorn,[33] born Chester County, South Carolina, 1810-1815, died Lincoln County, Tennessee, 1838-39; married in Lincoln County, *c*. 1835, Huldah Taylor, born Tennessee, *c*. 1818-1819, died ___, daughter of Nancy Gault and John Clark Taylor. After David died, Huldah was listed with her children in the 1840 census of Lincoln County. She then moved to Sparta, Randolph County, Illinois, to be near her brothers who lived there. In about 1856 Huldah married in Randolph County (2) James C. Brown whose first wife had died; James, himself, died a few years later. Huldah had one child by James: Marion H. Brown (boy), born *c*. 1857.

Huldah's granddaughter, Lyda Perkins Sproul, later wrote in a letter to a relative:

> My maternal grand-mother, Huldah Taylor, married David Gleghorn . . . who died in his early twenties leaving Huldah with 3 little daughters. . . . Huldah decided to come North to this locality, where two of her brothers lived. This incurred the wrath of the Gleghorns who said if she took David's children North they would not help in any way or have anything whatsoever to do with them. They have kept their word and are still keeping it. Letters receive no answer, and the county clerks give the same "stock" reply--"all records were destroyed during the war between the states."

Children:

1. Nancy E. Gleghorn Edmiston, born Lincoln County, Tennessee, *c*. 1836, died ___; married John Edmiston, a farmer of Parsons, Kansas.

2. Sarah Eliza Gleghorn Porch, born Lincoln County, Tennessee, c. 1837, died in the early 1860's; married, in the early 1860's, Dr. ___ Porch of Mississippi and died a few months later.

3. Mary Susan Gleghorn Perkins, born Lincoln County, Tennessee, c. 1839, died in Sparta, Randolph County, Illinois, 1921; married, in 1857, Jeremiah Clifford Perkins (Jerry), born Kaskaskia, Illinois, 1838, died ___, son of Ephraim Perkins (1809-1888) and Idile Buatte (1814-1894). Known child:

   a. Lyda Perkins Sproul; married C. E. Sproul. They lived in Sparta, Illinois.

I. Sarah Gleghorn Gault (Sallie), born South Carolina, c. 1814, died before 1880; married in Lincoln County, Tennessee, c. 1836, William Gault, born Tennessee, c. 1819, died ___, son of Thomas Gault and Sarah Apeling. In the 1860 census they were listed in Union Township, Fulton County, Arkansas. William married (2) Jane L. ___, born Tennessee, c. 1838, and they were listed in Izard County, Arkansas, in the 1880 census. Listed with them were his son Thomas and his granddaughter Margaret Steavenson (sic), born Arkansas, c. 1862. Children of Sallie and William, all born in Tennessee:

1. Sarah Gault, born c. 1838

2. Eliza Gault, born c. 1840

3. James H. Gault, born c. 1841, died ___; married Elizabeth ___, born North Carolina, c. 1845. At some time he enlisted in the Confederate Army and surrendered on 11 May 1865. At the time he was described as being 5 feet 9 inches tall and had blue eyes, light hair, and a fair complexion. In the 1880 census he and Elizabeth were listed in Izard County, Arkansas. Known children, all born in Arkansas:

   a. William O. Gault, born c. 1868. In 1896 he bought land in Izard County, T18N S8 7W.[34]

   b. John C. Gault, born c. 1870. In 1895 he bought land in Izard County, T18N S10 RW.[35]

   c. Mary E. Gault, born c. 1876

d. Sarah E. Gault, born c. November 1879

4. Robert Gault, born c. 1843

5. Thomas C. Gault, born c. 1845. He enlisted in the Confederate Army and surrendered on 11 May 1865. At that time he was described as 5 feet 7 inches tall and had blue eyes, light hair, and a fair complexion. In the 1880 census he was listed with his parents in Izard County, Arkansas.

6. Jno W. Gault (John or Jonathan), born c. 1848, died ___; married Martha T. ___, born Alabama, c. 1850. He enlisted in the Confederate Army and surrendered on 11 May 1865. At the time he was described as 5 feet 8 inches tall and had blue eyes, light hair, and a fair complexion. In the 1880 census he and Martha were listed in Izard County, Arkansas; living with them were his nieces Francey Heasen, age 18, and Sarah Heasen, age 15, both born in Alabama as was his wife. Probably they were his wife's nieces. He and his wife had no known children.

J. Robert Gleghorn,[36] born Chester County, South Carolina, c. 1814, died Wrightsboro, Gonzales County, Texas, 26 October 1905; perhaps married (1) in Lincoln County, Tennessee, c. 1837, ___ who died 1849-50; married (2) in Lincoln County, c. 1852, Ursula Wilson, born Tennessee, 19 July 1819, probably died in Texas, 27 January 1893, daughter of Grace Gault and (2) John Wilson. The reason it is thought that Robert had a wife before Ursula is that he and his first five children were listed in the 1850 census of Lincoln County, Tennessee, but no wife was listed. In the early 1850's Robert and Ursula moved to Hempstead County, Arkansas, and in about 1875 they moved to Gonzales County, Texas, where they were listed in the 1880 census. Living with them in Texas were their daughter Mary E. and her husband. Children:

1. John A. Gleghorn, born Lincoln County, Tennessee, c. 1838. On 16 June 1862 John and his brother William enlisted in the Confederate Army, Company C, 24th Arkansas Infantry. His last military record is dated December 1862, but he may have served longer.

2. William B. Gleghorn, born Lincoln County, Tennessee, c. 1840, died at an army post in Arkansas about February 1863. On 16 June 1862 William and his brother John enlisted in the Confederate Army, Company C, 24th Arkansas

Infantry. On 13 February 1863 his father filed a claim on his behalf as listed in a Register of Claims of Deceased Officers and Soldiers from Arkansas.

3. Melissa Ellender Gleghorn Tyree, born Tennessee, *c.* 1844, died ___; married in Hempstead County, Arkansas, 5 July 1866, John B. Tyree, born *c.* 1844. They were married by the Rev. William J. Scott (Book B, p. 103).[37] In about 1875 they moved with her parents and several siblings to Gonzales County, Texas, where they were listed in the 1880 census. Known children:

   a. S. M. Tyree (girl), born Arkansas, *c.* 1867

   b. R. G. Tyree (boy), born Arkansas, *c.* 1869

   c. D. F. Tyree (boy), born Arkansas, *c.* 1872

   d. J. H. Tyree (boy), born Arkansas, *c.* 1874

   e. J. J. Tyree (boy) , born Texas, *c.* 1875

   f. M. U. Tyree (girl), born Texas, *c.* 1878

   g. J. D. Tyree (boy), born Texas, October 1879

4. Margaret C. Gleghorn Lackland, born Lincoln County, Tennessee, *c.* 1845; married in Hempstead County, Arkansas, 10 May 1866, John W. Lackland (or Lacklin), born Arkansas, *c.* 1840. They were married by Neill Munn, JP (Book B, p. 104).[38] In the 1880 census they were listed (as Lackland) in Gonzales County, Texas. Listed with them were the following children:

   a. Martha Lackland, born Texas, *c.* 1871

   b. Robert A. Lackland, born Texas, *c.* 1874

   c. Mary Lackland, born Texas, *c.* 1876

   d. Maggie Lackland, born Texas, *c.* 1879

5. Elizabeth J. Gleghorn (Betsey), born Lincoln County, Tennessee, *c.* 1849

6. Benj. E. Gleghorn, born Arkansas *c.* 1853

7. Martha H. Gleghorn Gee, born Arkansas, c. 1854; married in Hempstead County, Arkansas, 12 May 1870, John A. Gee, born 12 April 1847, son of John H. Gee. They were married by the Rev. F. Sanders.[39]

8. Henry B. Gleghorn, born Arkansas, c. 1858; probably married in Gonzales County, Texas, c. 1877, L. A. \_\_\_, born Texas, c. 1860. An H. B. Gleghorn and wife, L. A., were listed in Gonzales County, Texas, in the 1880 census. Listed with them were the following children:

   a. Ida Gleghorn Kifer,[40] born Texas, c. 1878; married Lee Kifer. Known child: Howell Brassell Kifer, born 29 January 1901, died 26 July 1965, married Ella Heinemeyer.

   b. Frank Gleghorn, born Texas, c. 1879

9. Mary E. Gleghorn May, born Arkansas, c. 1859; married, c. 1878, W. G. May, born Tennessee, c. 1856. In the 1880 census of Gonzales County, Texas, they were listed in the household of Mary's parents. Known child:

   a. M. D. May (girl), born Texas, October 1879

K. Elijah Gleghorn,[41] born Chester County, South Carolina, c. 1818, died before 1860; married in Lincoln County, Tennessee, 12 December 1839, Susan C. Wilson, born Tennessee, c. 1821, daughter of Grace Gault and (2) John Wilson. Elijah and Susan were married by Samuel S. Ralston, MG, and since they were married on the same day and by the same minister as Elijah's brother William and Susan's sister Eliza, they probably had a joint ceremony. In the 1860 census of Hempstead County, Arkansas, Susan was listed with her sons John and William. Children:

1. David Gleghorn, born Lincoln County, Tennessee, c. 1840, died in Arkansas, 9 March 1862. In the 1860 census of Fulton County, Arkansas, he was listed in the household of his uncle 3-1L William Gleghorn. On 4 September 1861 he enlisted in the Confederate Army, serving in Company A, 21st Arkansas Infantry (later changed to Company C, 14th Arkansas Infantry). From 1 September to 30 November 1861, he was reported sick; then he was listed as present from the end of November until 31 January 1862. He died the following March.

2. Eliza Jane Gleghorn Lambright, born Lincoln County, Tennessee, 1842; married in Hempstead County, Arkansas, 12 February 1857, Josiah M. Lambright, born 1838. They were married by John J. Whitesides, JP.

3. John H. Gleghorn, born Lincoln County, Tennessee, c. 1843; married (1) ___; (2) Martha ___, born Arkansas, c. 1850. This was also Martha's second marriage, her first to ___ Brown by whom she had a son named Scott Brown, born in Texas, c. 1869. (Scott was listed with them in the 1880 census of Navarro County, Texas.) On 9 November 1861 John enlisted in the Confederate Army, serving as a 30-day volunteer in Capt. Perry Clayton's Infantry Company, and was discharged on 9 December 1861. On 28 February 1863 he reenlisted in Company H1, Arkansas Cavalry (which subsequently became New Company B, 27th Arkansas Infantry) and was recorded, probably incorrectly, as having deserted on 13 October 1863. In any case, he was a sergeant in Company H, Crawford's Regiment, Arkansas Cavalry, 31 December 1863 to 29 February 1864. Where he was from that time until his surrender on 11 May 1865 is not known. At his surrender he was described as being 5 feet 8 inches tall and had blue eyes, light hair, and a fair complexion. In the 1880 census he and Martha were listed in Navarro County, Texas. Known child:

   a. Matthew Gleghorn, born Texas, c. 1869

4. William Andrew Gleghorn, born Lincoln County, Tennessee, c. 1845; married, 6 February 1868, 3-1G7 Eliza Ursula Gleghorn, born Lincoln County, Tennessee, 30 January 1847, died Navarro County, Texas, 22 February 1879,[42] daughter of 3-1G James Gleghorn and Mary Johnson. During the Civil War William enlisted in Company B, Ford's Battalion, Missouri Cavalry, and surrendered on 11 May 1865. At that time he was described as 5 feet 10 inches tall and had blue eyes, light hair, and a fair complexion. In the 1880 census he was listed in Navarro County, Texas. Known children:

   a. John Gleghorn, born Texas, c. 1869

   b. Lee Gleghorn (boy), born Texas, c. 1872

   c. Martha Gleghorn, born Texas, c. 1875

5. Thomas F. Gleghorn, born Lincoln County, Tennessee, c.

1847; married, c. 1864, Cassander ___, born Arkansas, c. 1845. They were listed in the 1870 census of Fulton County, Arkansas. Known children:

    a. Martha Gleghorn, born Arkansas, c. 1865

    b. Jane Gleghorn, born Arkansas, c. 1867

    c. Moses Gleghorn, born Arkansas, c. 1868

L. William Gleghorn,[43] born Chester County, South Carolina, c. 1820, died probably in Izard County, Arkansas, before 1880; married in Lincoln County, Tennessee, Eliza L. Wilson, born Tennessee c. 1822, died ___, daughter of Grace Gault and (2) John Wilson. William and Eliza were married by Samuel S. Ralston, MG, and since they were married on the same day and by the same minister as William's brother Elijah and Eliza's sister Susan they probably had a joint ceremony. In c. 1874 William and Eliza moved to Izard County, Arkansas, where he bought land--T18N R8W S1--and in the 1880 census of Izard County, Eliza was listed in the household of her daughter Mary and son-in-law Jacob Bookout. Children:

1. ___ Gleghorn (girl), born Lincoln County, Tennessee, 27 April 1841, died Lincoln County, 3 November 1848.[44]

2. Young McCoy Gleghorn (called Y. M.), born Lincoln County, Tennessee, c. 1844, died 1884;[45] married, c. 1864, Harriet C. ___, born Arkansas, c. 1845, died after 1909. Y. M. enlisted in the Confederate Army, Company B, Ford's Battalion, and surrendered on 11 May 1865. At the time he was described as being 6 feet tall and had blue eyes, light hair, and a fair complexion. In the 1880 census he and Harriet were listed in Izard County, Arkansas. Later the part of Izard where they lived joined Fulton County, Arkansas, which was the location of Harriet's address when she applied for a widow's pension on 5 August 1909. She probably still lived on the same farm, never having moved at all. Known children:

    a. Eliza J. Gleghorn, born Arkansas, c. 1865

    b. William G. Gleghorn, born Arkansas, October 1868 (twin to next?), died ___; married, c. 1897, Mary E. ___, born Arkansas, November 1871. In the 1900 census, they were listed in Izard County, Arkansas. Listed with them were the following children: (a) Eldee, born October 1898; and (**b**) ___, born March 1900.

    c. Sarah Gleghorn, born Arkansas, *c.* 1868 (twin to above?)

    d. John Y. Gleghorn, born Arkansas, 1872

    e. Logan H. R. Gleghorn, born Arkansas, February 1874, died ___; married, *c.* 1900, Nancy E. ___, born Arkansas, May 1882. In the 1900 census they were listed in Izard County, Arkansas. Children: (**a**) Arvel, born 1900; (**b**) Walter V., born 1902; (**c**) Maggie; (**d**) Bernard, born 1911; (**e**) Ralph, born 1913; (**f**) Noble, born 1916; (**g**) Homer, born 1918; (**h**) Claris, born 1920; (**i**) Christine, born 1922; and (**j**) Rosa Lee, born 1927.

    f. Alfred S. Gleghorn, born Arkansas, *c.* 1875

    g. Mary C. Gleghorn, born Arkansas, *c.* 1879

3. Rachel Gleghorn, born Lincoln County, Tennessee, *c.* 1847, died before 1860.

4. William Gleghorn, born Lincoln County, Tennessee, February 1850

5. Elizabeth Gleghorn (Betsey), born Arkansas, *c.* 1853

6. Eliza Gleghorn, born Arkansas, *c.* 1856

7. Delina Gleghorn, born Arkansas, *c.* 1858

8. Mary L. Gleghorn Bookout, born Arkansas, *c.* 1863, died ___; married probably in Izard County, Arkansas, *c.* 1878, Jacob Bookout, born Arkansas, *c.* 1857. They were listed in the 1880 census of Izard County. Listed with them was Mary's mother, Liza H., and the following child:

    a. William H. Bookout, born Arkansas, *c.* 1879

3-2 JENNET GRAHAM MILLS,[46] born South Carolina, 1777-79, died Christian County, Kentucky, *c.* 1817; married in Chester County, South Carolina, *c.* 1798, ADAM MILLS, born Ireland, died Todd County, Kentucky, between 20 February 1823 and 21 October 1823, perhaps a son of William Mills and Janet McKee.

On 27 November 1795 Adam bought 92 acres on the Sandy River in Chester County, South Carolina, for £20 sterling from Joseph Boyd who had originally received it as part of a 482-acre grant in 1791. The land which Adam bought bordered tracts owned by Charles Boyd and James Wylie, and the deed was witnessed by John Kennedy, Alexander Boyd, and Adam's father-in-law, Andrew Graham. Andrew also proved the deed on 1 January 1798 (Book F, pp. 139-40). Adam sold this same land on 9 February 1798 (Book N, pp. 66-7), and on 10 August 1798 he bought another tract--104 acres on the Sandy River from Benjamin Wham for $180. This deed was also witnessed by Adam's father-in-law, Andrew Graham, as well as by Andrew Crawford whose daughter, Mary, later married Samuel Gleghorn, son of Andrew Graham's oldest child, Elizabeth Graham Gleghorn. Andrew Graham proved this latter deed of sale on 29 October 1804 (Book K, pp. 239-41) which was about a year prior to the time that he and his family moved to Kentucky.

Adam and Jennet (Graham) Mills had already moved there when Andrew proved the deed. On 9 February 1798 Adam sold his 92 acres in Chester County for £20 sterling to Molly Bean (Book N, pp. 66-7), and on 1 December 1798 Adam obtained a 100-acre grant on Beaver Dam Creek in Logan County, Kentucky, but he and Jennet did not move there until about 1801-2. Their first child was born in South Carolina in *c.* 1800; their second was born in Kentucky in 1803. On 2 December 1804 Adam received another grant of 100 acres on Beaver Dam Creek (Book 3, p. 477), and on 14 August 1805 he received 400 acres in Christian County, Kentucky (Book 7, p. 53). Adam and Jennet are known to have been in Logan County on 17 August 1812 when Adam bought a twelve-year-old black girl named Aggy from Elijah Carnal (Book C, p. 488). On 21 April 1815 Adam and Jennet sold 155 acres on the Elk Fork of the Little River in Christian County to a John Moore (Book E, p. 254). On 20 October 1817 Bouneres Roberts bought from Adam two tracts of 100 acres each in Logan County; the tracts had been patented in the name of Adam Mills, Assignee of Frederick McLenden, on Beaver Dam Creek, Elk Fork of the Red River (Book F, p. 70). On 22 December 1817 Adam sold 380 acres on the Elk Fork of the Little River to Robert Ellis of Christian County (Book H, p. 294), and on 1 October 1818 Adam bought some land on Spring Creek in Christian County from James and Margaret Manion (Book I, p. 509), land which he sold to Curtis Pendleton on 22 March 1820 (Book K, p. 661).

Jennet died in about 1817 and Adam about seven years later. Adam's will, dated 20 February 1823 and recorded 14 February 1825 in Todd County, Kentucky (Book A, pp. 233-4), is transcribed verbatim as follows:

2-1 Andrew 3-2

In the name of God amen, I Adam Mills of Todd County and state of Kentucky, being of perfect mind and memory, thanks be to God, therefore calling to mind the mortality of my body and knowing that it is appointed for all men once to die, do make and ordain this my last Will and Testament as followeth (___) I give and recomend my Soul to the hands of God who gave it, and my body I recomend to the Earth to be buried in a decent Christian manner at the discretion of my executors, Nothing doubting that at the general Resurection I shall receive the same again, by the mighty power of God.

And as touching such wordly [sic] Estate wherewith it has pleased God to bless me in this life, I give devise and dispose of the same in the following manner and form that is to say I give and bequeath to my son William Mills one dollar and no more, I likewise bequeath to my daughter Nancy Mills, now Knox, one dollar and no more, and after all my just debts is paid, I allow my property all to be Sold, my land Negro and all and the price to be equally divided betweixt my three sons, Andrew Robert and David, and my two Daughters Jiney and Polly, I likewise constitute make and ordain William Harlan Robert C. Graham and Mathew Graham ___ ___ Sole executors of this My last Will and Testament, and I do revoke, dissanull, and renounce all former Wills Legacys and bequests, by me in any ways Made ___. And do ratify and confirm this and No others as my last Will and Testament, in witness whereof I have hereunto Set my hand and Seal this twentieth day of February in the year of our lord One thousand eight hundred and twenty three

in presence of            Adam Mills (seal)
William McKee
      his
Barnet   X  Jeter
      mark

The will was proved on 14 February 1825, and the following men were appointed trustees of Adam's estate: 3-3 Matthew Graham, Matthew Wilson (brother-in-law of 3-3 Matthew), and William Mills, Adam's oldest son. On 1 November 1825 the trustees turned over a parcel of land on the West Fork of the Red River to Adam's younger children, David G., Jane M., and Mary M. On 24 April 1826 Adam's executor, 3-6 Robert C. Graham, sold 178 acres of Adam's estate to Lucy Adams for $1,051.50; the tract was described as adjoining lands of John McKee, John Brown, John Gray, William Mills, Colonel

Jeffries, William McKee, and Presley Polluck (Book D, pp. 167-9). Adam's son William Mills (*q.v.*) handled the remaining 178 acres.

Children:[47]

A. William Mills, b. South Carolina, *c.* 1800
B. Hannah (Nancy) Mills, b. South Carolina, 1803
C. Andrew Graham Mills, b. Kentucky, *c.* 1805
D. Robert Mills, b. Kentucky, 9 March 1809
E. David Graham Mills, b. Kentucky, 1811
F. Jane McKee Mills, b. Kentucky, *c.* 1812?
G. Mary M. Mills, b. Kentucky, *c.* 1815?

---

A. William Mills,[48] born probably in Chester County, South Carolina, *c.* 1800, died probably in Holly Springs, Marshall County, Mississippi, 1870-80; married (1) in Kentucky, ___, who died after 1826; (2) in Warren County, Mississippi, 23 April 1835, Minerva G. Elliott, born in Virginia, *c.* 1807, died probably in Holly Springs, Marshall County, Mississippi, 1860-70.

In a puzzling series of deeds in Todd County, Kentucky, William sold then bought more than once the same 178 acres inherited from his father. On 21 October 1823 he sold the tract to his brother-in-law James Knox for $1,200 (Book B, p. 144); on 5 November 1823 William bought back the same land from Knox for $1,400 (Book B, p. 426). At some time he apparently secured a mortgage on it from the Bank of the Commonwealth of Kentucky with George T. Scott and John Lewis as co-signers. On 1 September 1824 William again sold the tract to Henry B. Montague for $1 in hand and $553 to be paid to the bank (Book C, p. 115). Montague seems to have defaulted, however; on 18 November 1825 William deeded the land to 3-3 Matthew Graham and Matthew Wilson to be held in trust for William's youngest siblings, David G., Jane M., and Mary M., the amount specified as $1,000 (Book D, p. 74). Finally, until at least 1856 the land was managed by 3-9 Thomas P. Graham as agent for the estate of Adam Mills. Thomas grew mainly tobacco on the land and paid an annual tax on it.

Some sort of altercation must also have occurred earlier between William and his brother-in-law James Knox who had first bought the land: on 12 March 1825 William appointed Willis Reeves to sign any bond or injunction in a suit "which

I am about to institute in Chancery in Todd County Circuit
Court wherein I am complainant and James Knox and others are
defendants" (Book C, p. 269).

William moved to nearby Simpson County, Kentucky, in 1823
although there is a Todd County deed dated 29 August 1826 in
which he is identified as living in Todd County, Kentucky. In
the deed he bought 59-3/4 acres on headwaters of Spring Creek
in Todd County from John and Polly Dicus for $300 (Book D, p.
269).

After his parents died, William seems to have assumed the
responsibility for his siblings. In the late 1820's he moved
to Warren County, Mississippi, taking at least his two
youngest siblings, Jane and Mary, with him. He lived there
until the mid 1850's.

William was a planter and was referred to as "Judge
Mills." Perhaps he was a justice of the peace since he performed
several marriage ceremonies in Warren County, Mississippi,
in 1833-4. By the time of the 1860 census, he was in
Holly Springs, Marshall County, Mississippi, where he was
listed as a banker with property and personal assets of
$70,000. Listed immediately after his household was that of
Jane McDowell who probably was a younger sister (3-2F). Also
in Jane's household were 3-2G Mary Mills who was another
sister, and 3-2B8 Margaret Knox, daughter of still another
sister, 3-2B Hannah who died in 1845. In the 1870 census of
Holly Springs, Marshall County, Mississippi, William was
listed as a merchant. Listed with him were Rowena Knox
Benton, daughter of 3-2B Hannah, and Rowena's two children,
plus David and Edward McDowell, sons of 3-2F Jane.

Known children, as named in the 1850-70 censuses:

1. Samuel D. Mills,[49] born Kentucky, c. 1826, died before
   1886; married, c. 1858, Martha Bonner, born Alabama, c.
   1838, died probably in Waco, Texas, c. 1910. In the 1860
   federal census, Samuel and Martha were listed in his
   father's household, and Samuel was a bookkeeper. After
   Samuel died, Martha moved to Waco, Texas, where she was
   listed in the city directories until 1910.

    a. Mary M. Mills Baker; married in Waco, Texas, 14 January
       1886, Waller S. Baker, born Lexington, Fayette
       County, Kentucky, 30 March 1855, perhaps died in Waco,
       Texas, c. 1913, son of John H. Baker and Amanda Saun-

ders who moved to McLennan County, Texas, in 1839. Waller was graduated from Baylor University in 1875 and was admitted to the Texas bar in 1876. In 1884 he was elected chairman of the Democratic Executive Committee of his county and in 1887 was elected to the state senate. He was a presidential elector in 1893 and became chairman of the state Democratic committee in 1892. According to the Waco, Texas, city directories, Waller also had several successive law partners. In 1888 he was in partnership with Albert C. Pendergast. By 1896 his partner was Louis W. Campbell. By 1900 the partner was Stephen P. Ross, by 1904 it was Cullen F. Thomas, and by 1910 it was John W. Baker who perhaps was Waller's son. By the time of the 1913 Waco city directories, Waller was no longer listed.

2. Andrew Graham Mills,[50] born Mississippi, 1838, died Galveston, Texas, 25 March 1894; married in Galveston, Lucy Ballinger, born in Galveston, 1852, died Galveston, 1936, daughter of William Pitt Ballinger (born Kentucky, c. 1828) and Halley ___ (born Alabama, c. 1830). William Pitt Ballinger was a lawyer who moved to Texas in 1847. Andrew was also a lawyer. During the Civil War Andrew was a major in the Confederate Army in Forest's Brigade, and immediately after the war he moved to Galveston at the request of his uncles Robert and David Graham Mills who lived there and wished to have him as an associate in their cotton and banking firms. Later he was one of the organizers of the Galveston Cotton Exchange and was its secretary from its founding in 1873 until his death in 1894. In the 1900 census Lucy and her son were listed in the household of her sister-in-law Carry Ballinger.
Child:

   a. Ballinger Mills, born Galveston, Texas, 2 January 1879, died ___; married in Galveston, Evy Sampson Waters, daughter of Lodd M. Waters. Ballinger was graduated from Yale in 1899 then attended Harvard's law school and the University of Texas, receiving his LLB in 1901. Eventually he became a noted lawyer and philanthropist in Galveston. Child: Ballinger Mills Jr., born Galveston, 21 August 1914.

3. David G. Mills, born Mississippi, c. 1848

B. Hannah (Nancy) Mills Knox, born Union County, South Carolina,

2-1 Andrew 3-2B1

1803, died 1845; married in Christian County, Kentucky, 22 December 1819,[51] James Knox Jr., born 1792, died 1870, son of James Knox (born Ireland) and Jane McElroy (born Ireland). James Knox Sr. is said to have been a nephew of Gen. Henry Knox of Revolutionary War fame and a descendant of John Knox (*c.* 1513-1572), the founder of Scottish Presbyterianism (see the Introduction, Section 1).[52] Hannah and James moved to Lincoln County, Missouri. Children:

1. William James Knox, born Christian County, Kentucky, 20 October 1820, died in San Francisco, 1867.

2. Mary Jane (Janet) Knox Hill,[53] born Todd County, Kentucky, 20 January 1824, died 25 April 1902; married in Lincoln County, Missouri, 20 February 1840, Malcolm Henry Hill, son of Alexander Hill (born Georgia) and Nancy Henry (born Tennessee). They moved to Texas before 1876. In the 1900 census Mary was listed in the household of her daughter Nannie Hill Thompson in Johnson County, Texas. Children:

    a. James Henry Hill, born Missouri, March, 1841; married Mary L. Randall, born Alamaba, October 1847. In the 1900 census, they were listed in Hill County, Texas. Known children, as listed in the 1900 census: (**a**) Mary A., born Texas, January 1869; (**b**) Nannie L., born Texas, 1870; and (**c**) Minnie A., born Texas, September 1885.

    b. Mary Hill Brown (Molly); married Joseph C. Brown.

    c. Nannie Hill Thompson, born Texas, August 1851; married, *c.* 1874, Knox Thompson, born Texas, March 1849. In 1900 they were living in Johnson County, Texas. In 1907-12 they were listed in the city directories of Cleburne, Texas. He had a real estate business. Known children, as listed in the 1900 census: (**a**) Rowena, born Texas, October 1875; and (**b**) Mary K., born Texas, January 1882.

    d. Minnie Jane Hill Allen; married Clement H. Allen.

    e. Mattie Hill Powell; married Charles H. Powell.

    f. David C. Hill; married Lucerne ___.

    g. Rowena Benton Hill Ramsey, born January 1867; married Judge William F. Ramsey,[54] born Bell County, Texas, 25

October 1855. William was graduated from Tehuacana Institute in 1876 and was admitted to the bar on 4 July 1877. He was part of several law firms and was also a member at the Democratic state conventions, 1882-90, and a presidential elector in 1884. He was also a Mason and served on the school board. In 1907-17 he and Rowena were listed in the city directories of Cleburne, Texas. Known children, as listed in the 1900 census of Johnson County, Texas: (**a**) Sam, born January 1891; (**b**) Mildred, born May 1894; (**c**) Benton, born October 1896; and (**d**) Knox, born August 1899. William's marriage to Rowena was his second, his first to Emma Johnson who died 1 April 1885. She had one child: Felix, born November 1878.

3. Virginia Knox, born perhaps in Kentucky, died probably in Mississippi, 1861.

4. Rowena G. Knox Benton, born Missouri, *c.* 1830?; married in Marshall County, Mississippi, 10 May 1860, Samuel Hart Benton,[55] born Missouri, *c.* 1824, died Atlanta, Georgia, 1864. Samuel, a nephew of Senator Thomas Hart Benton of Missouri, was a lawyer and a representative to the state legislature from Holly Springs, Marshall County, Mississippi. During the Civil War he entered the Confederate Army as captain of a company raised in Marshall County, then became a colonel, and finally was a brigadeer-general. He was severely wounded at the Battle of Atlanta, 22 July 1864, and died in a hospital soon after.[56] Benton County, Mississippi, was named in his honor when it was formed on 15 July 1870.[57] In the 1870 federal census of Marshall County, Mississippi, Rowena and her children were listed in the household of her uncle 3-2A William Mills. Children, as listed in the 1870 census:

   a. Samuel Hart Benton Jr., born Mississippi, *c.* 1861

   b. Willie Benton (girl), born Mississippi, *c.* 1864

5. Nannie Knox Jack,[58] born Lincoln County, Missouri, *c.* 1834?; married, 1857, Colonel Thomas McKinney Jack, born San Felipe de Austin, Texas, 19 December 1832, died Galveston, Texas, 26 August 1880, son of William H. Jack (born Georgia, died Texas, 1844) and Laura Harrison (born South Carolina, died Texas, 1877). Thomas attended Georgetown College, Kentucky, and Yale from which he was graduated in 1853. He then studied law with his brother-

in-law Judge Ballinger with whom he entered into a lifelong partnership after being admitted to the bar in 1854. In 1856 he was elected chief justice of Galveston County, serving two years, and in 1858 was appointed to fulfill an unexpired term in the legislature. In 1860 he was chosen as a presidential elector for Breckenridge and Lane. When the Civil War broke out in 1861, he entered the 8th Texas Cavalry as a private but within a few months became a first lieutenant and aide-de-camp to Gen. Albert Sidney Johnston who was mortally wounded at the Battle of Shiloh and, it is said, died in Thomas's arms. Thomas was then made a major and was assigned to the staff of Gen. Leonidas Polk who also, it is said, died in Thomas's arms during the Battle of Kennesaw Mountain. He became a colonel in 1864, and in 1865 he accompanied his uncle Gen. James E. Harrison to Galveston for the formal surrender. Resuming his legal profession after the war, Thomas was a delegate to the 1880 Democratic national convention, but shortly after returning from the convention he died of pneumonia. Children:

a. David M. Jack, born Texas, *c.* October 1859

b. Laura H. Jack Davidson, probably born Texas; married Robert V. Davidson.

c. Hallie B. Jack, born Texas, *c.* 1867

d. Thomas M. Jack Jr., born Texas, *c.* 1872

6. Minnie Knox Hutchings,[59] born Missouri, March 1836; married in Galveston, Texas, 18 June 1856, John Henry Hutchings, born North Carolina, 2 February 1822, died in Galveston, 31 March 1906. Minnie was a ward of her uncle 3-2D Robert Mills who lived on a ten-acre site in Galveston in what later became Kempner Park. When Minnie was married, Robert gave her the west part of this estate and built a home on it as a wedding gift. John Henry moved to Galveston in 1845 and formed a partnership in the mercantile business with John Sealy in 1847. Later they took in George Ball, and the new firm, called Ball, Hutchings and Company, became well known in Texas. After the war John Henry expanded his civic interests, becoming director then president of the Galveston City Company. He also originated the plan to make Galveston Harbor accessible to oceangoing vessels and helped establish a regular line of ships between Galveston and New York. Another of his enterpri-

ses was his financial support in the founding of the Gulf, Colorado, and Santa Fe Railway. He was said to have been an amateur gardener of note. According to the 1900 census, Minnie had nine children only seven of whom were then living. Known children:

 a. Mary M. Hutchings Spencer, born Texas, *c.* 1857; married J. S. Spencer, born New Jersey, *c.* 1844. Known child: John H. Spencer, born Texas, 1880.

 b. Robert M. Hutchings, born Texas, *c.* 1860

 c. Frances Hutchings Byrne, born Texas, *c.* 1862; married C. R. Byrne.

 d. John H. Hutchings Jr., born Texas, September 1863

 e. Minnie K. Hutchings Harris, born Texas, *c.* 1865; married John W. Harris, son of Judge John W. Harris.

 f. Sealy Hutchings, born Texas, *c.* 1870; married, *c.* 1891, Mary ___, born Texas. He became president of the Hutchings-Sealy National Bank of Galveston. Known children: (**a**) John H., born August 1892; (**b**) William L., born April 1894; (**c**) Mary, born February 1896; (**d**) Commadore, born January 1898; (**e**) Elizabeth, born December 1899; and (**f**) Sealy Jr., born after 1900. Sealy Hutchings Jr. eventually inherited the property given to his grandmother by her uncle and ward, 3-2D Robert Mills.

 g. George B. Hutchings, born Texas, November 1872; married in 1899, Lelia C. ___, born Virginia, July 1878.

 h. Rebecca Hutchings Belknap, born Texas, *c.* 1875; married W. B. Belknap.

7. Lucy Knox Wright, born Missouri; married Wilbur Ward Wright.

8. Margaret Knox Dennis, born Missouri *c.* 1840; married Col. D. Newton Dennis. After Margaret's mother died, Margaret was taken in by her aunt 3-2F Jane Mills McDowell and was listed in Jane's household in the 1850 and 1860 censuses.

C. Andrew Graham Mills,[60] born Todd County, Kentucky, *c.* 1805, died 1835; probably unmarried. In the late 1820's Andrew

moved to Brazoria, Texas, where he engaged in merchandizing
and sea-going.  In 1830 his brother 3-2D Robert Mills joined
him, and, since Andrew was more interested in sea-faring,
Robert built up the business.  In 1832 Andrew and Robert
fought in the battle of Velasco against the Mexicans.  Andrew
is said to have been lost at sea in 1835.

D. Robert Mills,[61] born Todd County, Kentucky, 9 March 1809, died
Galveston, Texas, 13 April 1888, buried Episcopal Cemetery;
married probably in Galveston, Elizabeth McNeel who died with
her first baby in childbirth.  He took in his niece 3-2B6
Minnie Knox and became her ward.  Robert attended Cumberland
College, 1826-27, and in 1830 joined his next older brother,
3-2C Andrew G., in Texas where they established a mercantile
business in Brazoria.  After Andrew died in 1835, Robert's
younger brother, 3-2E David G., joined him, and their two
subsequent careers became inseparable.  See the paragraphs on
their company following the next entry.

E. David Graham Mills, born Todd County, Kentucky, 1811, died
Galveston, Texas, 27 February 1885, buried Episcopal Cemetery
in Galveston; unmarried.

## THE COMPANY OF ROBERT AND DAVID GRAHAM MILLS

After 3-2C Andrew Graham Mills died in 1835, 3-2D Robert
Mills was joined in Brazoria, Texas, by his younger brother
3-2E David Graham Mills.  At first their firm was called R.
Mills and Company but was soon changed to R. and D. G. Mills.
In 1849 they moved to Galveston where Robert built up their
commission and banking business while David ran their vast
land holdings.

In addition to other activities, Robert was a partner of
Mills, McDowell and Company of New York and of McDowell, Mills
and Company of New Orleans, each of which dealt in a huge
cotton and sugar shipping industry as well as an importing
one.  The company of R. and D. G. Mills was also in effect a
bank, dealing in exchange and credit to customers, because
Texas then lacked banks.  The notes issued by R. and D. G.
Mills became currency known as "Mills Money" and were said to
have been as negotiable as gold in Texas and New Orleans.

Meanwhile, David was equally successful in managing the
land operations.  By the time of the Civil War, R. and D. G.
Mills owned four large cotton and sugar plantations which

included about 3,300 acres under cultivation plus another 100,000 acres of unimproved land. They also owned an additional 100,000 acres scattered throughout the state. They were the largest slave owners in Texas and emancipated about eight hundred after the war.

The Civil War broke them. Although they were said to have been worth from three to five million dollars before the war, and they redeemed currency as late as 1868, they were bankrupt by 1873. Their last years were spent in poverty and dependence upon relatives.[62] Nonetheless, according to the Galveston city directories they maintained their business as R. and D. G. Mills, Cotton Buyers, until at least 1885. Their office was located on Strand avenue in Galveston.

F. Jane McKee Mills McDowell, born Todd County, Kentucky, *c.* 1812?, died after 1860; married, *c.* 1838, James R. McDowell, born Ireland, *c.* 1811, died perhaps in Madison Parish, Louisiana, 1855-60. In the 1850 federal census, they were listed in Madison Parish, Louisiana, where he was a planter and was worth $118,940. In the 1860 census, Jane and her children, but not James, were listed in Holly Springs, Marshall County, Mississippi, together with 3-2G Mary and 3-2B8 Margaret Knox. Jane gave her worth in 1860 as $812,000. Her listing in the census came immediately after that of 3-2A William Mills. Children:

1. Jennette McDowell (Jane), born Mississippi, *c.* 1839

2. James McDowell, born Mississippi, *c.* 1841

3. William McDowell, born Mississippi, *c.* 1843

4. Rose McDowell, born Mississippi, *c.* 1845

5. Edward McDowell, born Louisiana, *c.* 1847; married in Marshall County, Mississippi, 13 February 1871, Katherine Bonner.[63] In the 1870 census he was listed in the household of his uncle 3-2A William Mills in Holly Springs, Marshall County, Mississippi. He was a clerk in a store.

6. Mary McDowell (Polly), born Louisiana, *c.* March 1850

7. Eliza McDowell, born Louisiana, *c.* 1853

8. David McDowell, born Louisiana, *c.* 1855; married in Marshall County, Mississippi, 23 May 1877, Ruth Bonner.[64] In

2-1 Andrew                                                                3-2G

the 1870 census he was listed in the household of his
uncle 3-2A William Mills in Holly Springs, Marshall
County, Mississippi.

G. Mary M. Mills (Polly), born Todd County, Kentucky, c. 1815?;
probably unmarried. She was listed in the household of her
sister 3-2F Jane Mills McDowell in the 1850 census of Madison
Parish, Louisiana, and in the 1860 census of Holly Springs,
Marshall County, Mississippi.

3-3 MATTHEW GRAHAM,[65] born Chester County, South Carolina, 17 January
1780, died Henderson County, Illinois, 8 May 1854, buried South
Henderson Cemetery; married probably in South Carolina, c. 1804,
JENNETTE WILSON (Jane), born South Carolina or Ireland, 12 May
1783, died Henderson County, Illinois, 2 June 1843, buried South
Henderson Cemetery, daughter of John Wilson and Martha ___ (born
Ireland c. 1758, died Preble County, Ohio, 10 December 1845,
buried Hopewell Cemetery, Preble County).[66] Jennette was called
"Jane" in most church and legal records but "Jennette" on her
tombstone. Her brother Matthew Wilson married (2) Mary Margaret
Boyse, daughter of 2-6 Jennet Graham Boyse.

In about 1804 Matthew and Jennette migrated to Kentucky
where they probably had obtained land although no record of it is
presently known. On 9 May 1818 Matthew bought three tracts from
Gideon Mimms--150 acres on the Elk Fork of the Red River in Christian County, 13 adjoining acres, and 20 acres on Spring Creek
(Book I, p. 475). The 1819 tax list showed that he had 183 acres
of "second rate land" with a value of $2,796. On 1 December 1822
the state granted him 160 more acres on Beaver Dam Creek in Logan
County (Book 7, p. 50). Then on 21 September 1822, for $1,800,
Matthew and Jennette sold 160 acres on both sides of the Elk Fork
of the Red River to W. B. Scott of Todd County; this land had
first been patented to Matthew, "assignee of Frederick McClendon,"
on 19 January 1809 (Deed Book B, p. 62); and on 17 September 1828
Matthew and Jennette sold 183 more acres to Horatio Muir. Some of
the land (163 acres) was described as being on the Elk Fork of the
Red River and was part of a survey patented in the name of James
Meek and part of J. B. Campbell's survey; 20 more acres sold were
on Spring Creek bordering lands of Shadrack Mims and Allen McFail
(Book E, p. 305).

In 1828-29 Matthew and Jennette were among a migration of
several families from Kentucky to Preble County, Ohio, which had
already been settled largely by people from Chester County, South

Carolina. On 23 September 1829 Matthew bought the southwest quarter, section 3, T3 R1E, in Israel Township, Preble County, from George R. and Elizabeth Brown (recorded 12 June 1830, Book 11, p. 4). Matthew and Jennette did not remain long in Preble County, however; seven years later they sold the same land to Peter C. King (recorded 29 February 1836, Book 18, p. 430) and moved to Illinois.

In June 1836 Matthew and Jennette moved to what later became Henderson County, Illinois (formed from Warren County in 1841) where they lived for the remainder of their lives. On 23 July 1836 they joined the South Henderson Presbyterian Church. On 1 August 1836 Matthew bought land from his youngest half-brother 3-12 Andrew W. for which Matthew paid $800 (Book 2, p. 533). In 1837 and 1838 he bought additional land from Archibald McKinney (Book 5, p. 251, and Book 6, p. 523). On 23 January 1844 he bought 37½ acres from Sheriff Henderson (Book 1, p. 517), and on 10 November 1847 he bought 160 more acres from John Alstyne of New York City (Book 4, p. 110).

Jennette died in 1843; in the 1850 federal census of Henderson County, Matthew was listed in the household of his younger daughter, Margaret. He sold some land in 1852 and 1853 (Book 7, pp. 209 and 580) and died intestate in 1854.

Children of Matthew Graham and Jennette Wilson, all born in Todd County, Kentucky:

4-1 Martha W., b. 23 June 1805
4-2 Andrew, b. 1807
4-3 John W., b. 16 November 1809
4-4 Robert C., b. 1811
4-5 William Mills, b. 5 March 1814
4-6 Margaret, b. 1816
4-7 Wilson M., b. 1818
4-8 David, b. 12 April 1821
4-9 James Harvey, b. 23 April 1823
4-10 Archibald Young, b. 27 June 1826

3-4 MARY GRAHAM MABEN,[67] born South Carolina, *c.* 1784, died Todd County Kentucky, 1830-35; married in Chester County, South Carolina, *c.* 1803, ANDREW MABEN, born ___, died Kentucky, 1810, son of John Maben (died Chester County, South Carolina, 15 January 1819, aged 94 years, buried Hopewell A.R.P. Cemetery)[68] and ___.

Mary and Andrew moved to Kentucky in 1805 probably in the company not only of Mary's parents but also of others from Chester County. The others may well have included other Mabens as the

2-1 Andrew

following excerpt from a Todd County history indicates:

> The first authentic settlement in this region [Elkton area, Todd County] that we have any record of was in 1809. In that year Henry Maben came to this district and settled on the farm now owned by his children Matthew and Elizabeth Maben, both of whom are now [1884] over seventy years of age. He landed in Charleston, S. C., and lived there some eight or ten years, and then moved to Chester County, S. C., where he remained until his departure for the West. Upon his arrival here, he settled five miles south of Elkton in the fine grove of timber which still forms part of the Maben estate. He first entered 150 acres, which he afterward increased to 550 acres, and here he resided until his death, which occurred in 1840. While he was living in South Carolina, he enlisted in the Revolution and was under Gen. Washington. It is said that many were the hours he spent in relating stories of this great man to his listening children. Of his descendants but two are now living. A third child, Thomas Maben, was a soldier in the war of 1812, and was with Gen. Jackson at the battle of New Orleans. Returning to this county he resided here until his death in 1872.
>
> Accompanying Maben to the then "Wilderness of Kentucky" were several other sturdy yeomen of South Carolina. They were Archibald Cogell, James McKee and Isaac Bean. Cogell settled on part of the farm now owned by Matthew Maben, where he lived many years. Both he and his family have now passed away. McKee lived in the same neighborhood for twenty-five years and then moved to Ohio, where he remained a short time and then moved to Illinois, where he died. Bean settled on the farm now owned by Alex Chestnut, where he resided until his death in 1840.[69]

The James McKee mentioned above may have been a brother of Martha B. McKee who married 3-6 Robert C. Graham.

The Mabens probably came to America in 1772. On 6 January 1773 the South Carolina General Assembly, which heard requests for land grants, listed five people named "Maybean" as among those who had recently come from Ireland in the ship *Lord Dunluce*. They were Grizell, Henry, John, Thomas, and Elizabeth Maybean. At the same council meeting (6 January 1773), Matthew and William Mebin and Martha and Mary Mebin also petitioned for land. These latter

Mebins had come from Ireland in the ship *Pennsylvania Farmer* which was the same ship and same voyage that brought 1-1 David Graham (*Grimbs*) and his family.[70] As can be seen above, the name was variously spelled *Maben, Mebin, Mayben,* and *Maybean*.

Mary and Andrew had three children:

A. Sarah Maben, b. South Carolina, 9 July 1804
B. Margaret Maben, b. Kentucky, 26 October 1806
C. Jane or Jennet Maben, b. Kentucky, 7 December 1808

---

A. Sarah Maben Chesnut (Sally),[71] born Chester County, South Carolina, 9 July 1804, died Todd County, Kentucky, 30 January 1835; married, 4 October 1821, "Captain" John Chesnut, born South Carolina, 25 July 1796, died Todd County, Kentucky, 14 January 1873, son of Alexander Chesnut (1759-1809) and Sarah Meek (1766-1831). Sarah's and John's marriage was performed by a justice of the peace (Book A, p. 6). John married (2) *c.* 1836, Ruth Vance, born 7 November 1812, died 1 January 1873, daughter of John Vance.

On 15 April 1830 Sarah's husband, John Chesnut, instituted a suit in the Chester County, South Carolina, Court of Equity on behalf of himself, his wife, her sisters, and their husbands (Equity Bill No. 41A 1830). The case concerned interest which Chesnut and the others felt was due to the women from the estate of their grandfather, John Maben (spelled *Mayben* in the suit) who had died in Chester County on 15 January 1819. In his will, dated 25 May 1817, John left one-third of his estate to his widow, Eleanor (his second wife), and the remainder to his granddaughters, Sarah, Margaret, and Jane or Jennet Maben, the money to be given to each granddaughter as she came of legal age. John Maben also named as his executors his wife, Eleanor, plus James Strong Jr. and Robert Strong Jr. Later Eleanor refused to qualify as executrix, and, since James and Robert did so, they were the executors whom John Chesnut and the others sued in 1830.

The estate was fairly large: in addition to land, it included slaves, livestock, furniture, tools, and corn, plus cash and promissory notes. All the real and personal property was sold at auction according to the terms of the will, and as the two older granddaughters, Sarah and Margaret, came of age the executors paid each her legacy which amounted to

$800 apiece after costs. When the youngest granddaughter,
Jane or Jennet, came of age, however, her husband, Andrew
Gartin, who had traveled to South Carolina in January of 1830
to accept his wife's legacy, would not do so when he learned
that the money had accrued no interest. (Later Andrew regretted his action and asked for the money, but the Strongs
refused to give it to him.) Apparently, Andrew then returned
to Kentucky and conferred with his brothers-in-law whereupon
they instituted their suit in April of 1830. The three brothers-in-law were John Chesnut who married Sarah in October
1821, James T. V. Thompson who married Margaret in June 1825,
and Andrew Gartin who married Jane or Jennet in August 1828.
The names of the brothers-in-law and the dates of the
marriages were established in the case.

In their reply the executors, James Strong Jr. and Robert
Strong Jr., testified with some indignation that no interest
had accrued on the money because it had been neither invested
nor used by themselves; it had simply been kept locked away
until each granddaughter claimed her portion. The executors
had been willing and able to pay Andrew Gartin his wife's
legacy, but Andrew had refused it.

The case then moved back and forth between Chester County, South Carolina, and Todd County, Kentucky, with testimony
recorded at each location. In Todd County the witnesses were
Henry Maben, Thomas Maben, James McKee (probably a brother of
Martha B. McKee who married 3-6 Robert C. Graham), William
Shanklin (future husband of 3-7 Martha Graham), the Rev.
William K. Stewart (who performed the marriages of Margaret
and Jane or Jennet Maben), and 3-4 Mary Graham Maben (mother
of the three sisters). Mary gave not only the date of their
moving to Kentucky but also that of her husband's death (1810)
and the birth places and birth dates of her three daughters:
Sarah was born in South Carolina on 9 July 1804, Margaret was
born in Kentucky on 26 October 1806, and Jane or Jennet was
born in Kentucky on 7 December 1808.

In South Carolina the lawyers for the sisters and their
husbands tried unsuccessfully to prove that the money had in
fact been lent out. One person they subpoened was James McClurkin (perhaps the father of the James M. McClurkin who
married 3-13A2 Rosanna Hindman), but McClurkin did not appear.
Alexander Smith (husband of 3-17 Esther Graham Smith) did
appear and testified that he had served McClurkin with a
subpoena, and that he (Smith) "has been inform'd and so he
believes that James M Clurkin stated to Robert Hamilton that

he had paid to the defendants [James and Robert Strong] interest on this estate, the amount not stated, nor does this deponant know the amount. . . ." Whether Robert Hamilton was subpoened is not given in the records.

Some time before 1834, Robert Strong died, leaving only James Strong as the defendant.

The Maben women and their husbands lost the case, and James Strong paid Jane or Jennet her legacy of $800. In a long-winded though clearly stated opinion dated 1834, the judge, William Harper, said that no evidence was given to support the claims and none to believe that the Strongs had done anything other with the money than what they had testified--stored it under lock and key. The claimants also had to pay the court costs and, presumably, the fees of the law firm they had hired in Chester County, that of Clarke and McDowell. The claimants had asked for interest on Jane's estate from the time the Strongs had refused to give it to her husband until the time they did so, and that interest the judge did award to Jane, but nothing more, and nothing more to her sisters.

Children of Sarah Maben and John Chesnut Jr.:

1. A. Washington Chesnut, born c. 1823, still living near Paducah, Kentucky, in 1884.

2. Jane Chesnut, born c. 1825, died before 1884.

3. Mary E. Chesnut Duncan, born 5 January 1827, died 13 November 1861, buried Chesnut Cemetery, Todd County, Kentucky; married Jeptha Duncan.[72]

In the 1850 census of Todd County, Kentucky, John Chesnut was listed with his second wife and the above three children. Also listed were five more children the oldest of whom was born c. 1837.

B. Margaret Maben Thompson,[73] born Todd County, Kentucky, 26 October 1806, died Clay County, Missouri, 1849, buried near Liberty, Clay County; married in Todd County, 14 June 1825, James Turner Vance Thompson (known as James T. V. or J. T. V. Thompson), born Lincoln County, North Carolina, 27 July 1793, died Clay County, Missouri, 15 February 1872, buried with Masonic honors near Liberty, Clay County, son of Gideon Thompson and ___. Margaret and James were married by the Rev. William K. Stewart. James had married (1) in Todd County, 25

April 1822, Ruth Roberts who died soon after. After Margaret died he married (3) in Clay County, Missouri, 23 April 1850, Emily Warner Drew, born Todd County, Kentucky, *c.* 1820, died Clay County, Missouri, 6 January 1899.

On 13 August 1827 James T. V. Thompson was appointed guardian of Margaret's younger sister, Jane (Court Order Book C, p. 309), but since Jane married Andrew Gartin in 1828 James's guardianship was short-lived, and he made a brief accounting to the court, saying, "no estate come to hand" (Will Books A, p. 412, and B, p. 144). By that time, however, he and Margaret had moved to Missouri. He had owned land in "John Gray's plan of the Town of Elkton" in Todd County and sold it in a series of deeds (Books B, p. 180, C, p. 167, D, p. 34, and H, pp. 179-80). In the last deed dated 10 October 1833 to Daniel M. Kittinger, James was stated to be living in Clay County, Missouri. Actually, according to his autobiography which was later printed in the *Liberty Tribune* of Clay County in 1870, he and Margaret bought land there in 1826.

For James's involvement in the South Carolina court case on behalf of his wife and her sisters, see above under 3-4A Sarah Maben Chesnut. The suit, which concerned interest that James and his brothers-in-law felt was due to the women from their grandfather's estate, was instigated in 1830.

Although James was primarily a farmer, he contributed much public service. He was a justice of the county court, 1830-34, a member of the state senate, 1834-42 and 1856-61, and a delegate to every Democratic convention from 1826 to 1861. He was also a presidential elector in 1844, 1848, and 1860.

Among his business activities were the accumulation of about 6,000 acres plus many slaves and the construction of the "Thompson House," the largest hotel in the state outside of Saint Louis. He also actively supported the construction of the Kansas City and Cameron railroad, the organization of the Clay County Agricultural and Mechanical Association, the building of the Presbyterian church at Liberty in Clay County, and the founding of William Jewell College. He donated the grounds for the college.

During the Mexican War he pledged money, horses, and supplies. During the Civil War he espoused the southern cause and worked in the state senate to have Missouri join the South. In May 1861 he joined the forces of Gen. Sterling

Price in the latter's Missouri campaign and early in 1862 was captured at the Battle of Pea Ridge. After a few weeks' imprisonment in Saint Louis, he was released, but by that time he was close to financial ruin and had a stroke which left him partially paralyzed. It was also said that his mental powers had been weakened.

His biographer described him as physically large and powerful, with a dark complexion and dark hair, "black and piercing" eyes, and an habitual expression of "intensity, wariness, and thought." He was "extreme in affection as well as in hate."

Children of Margaret and James T. V. Thompson:

1. Mary Jane Thompson DeCourcey, born ___, died before 1878; married in Clay County, Missouri, 8 November 1842, T. W. W. DeCourcey of Kentucky. They were married by the Rev. John Edwards.

2. Eliza Thompson Shrader, born Missouri, c. 1829, died 15 November 1863; married in Clay County, Missouri, 19 June 1847, Stephen Ross Shrader, born Kentucky, c. 1824, died ___. They were married by the Rev. R. H. Jordan. Stephen was a business partner with Richard P. and Addison P. Evans, but the firm was dissolved by mutual consent on 6 January 1860. During the Civil War Stephen joined a military company called the "Mounted Rangers" which met every Wednesday evening at the Armory in the Thompson House, his father-in-law's hotel, and on 17 October 1862 he was among those who signed loyalty oaths. The Compiled Service Records of Confederate Soldiers lists him as a lieutenant-colonel and quartermaster in the 5th Division of the Missouri State Guard. Children:

    a. Margaret Shrader Beauchamp, born Missouri, c. 1848, died Elyria, Nebraska, 14 November 1891; married, 19 March 1868, C. R. Beauchamp. She had five children.

    b. Minnie Shrader Lanneau, born Missouri, c. 1851, died ___; married, 7 March 1871, A. S. Lanneau.

    c. James W. Shrader, born Missouri, c. 1854

    d. Fannie Shrader Roll, born Missouri, c. 1856, died ___; married, 22 March 1877, Henry E. Roll, born Missouri, c. 1853, died in Kansas City, Missouri, August 1895, buried Elmwood Cemetery, son of F. X. Roll. Fannie and Henry were married by the Reverend Maderia. They lived in Kansas City where he died by committing suicide. Children: (a) Edward, born c. 1878; and (b) Harry, born c. 1882.

    e. Harry Shrader, born Missouri, c. 1857, died in Atchison, Kansas, 9 December 1880; unmarried.

3. Sarah Thompson Lincoln (Sally), born Missouri, c. 1832, died after 1878; married in Clay County, Missouri, 13 May 1847, Robert Lincoln, born ___, died in Clay County, Missouri, October 1876, son of Col. George Lincoln. They were married by the Rev. A. H. F. Payne. Known children:

    a. George Lincoln, born Missouri, c. 1849

    b. Stephen Lincoln, born Missouri, c. 1852

    c. Lucy Lincoln Smith, born Missouri, c. 1854, died ___; married in Clay County, Missouri, 9 October 1873, James Smith. They were married by the Rev. James Via. One of the attendants was Lucy's aunt Maggie Thompson.

    d. James Lincoln, born Missouri, c. 1858

4. Minerva Thompson Gant, born Missouri, c. 1834, died in Hopkinsville, Kentucky, July 1898; married in Clay County, Missouri, 8 December 1857, Henry C. Gant, born Kentucky, c. 1833. They were married by the Rev. John G. Fackler. Henry was a druggist in Liberty, Missouri. In about 1866 they moved to Kentucky. Known child:

    a. James D. Gant, born Missouri, c. 1859

5. David R. Thompson, born Missouri, c. 1836, died before 1878.

6. Samuel Thompson, born Missouri, c. 1838, died March or April 1875.

7. Robert Thompson, born c. 1840, died February 1875. His obituary in the *Liberty Tribune* said he "was putting up a window curtain at the residence of his mother and was reaching up to drive a nail when he stopped, exclaiming 'give me the camphor or something, I believe it will kill me,' and expired in a few minutes."

8. Margaret Thompson (Maggie), born *c.* 1844, died March 1876; unmarried.

9. James P. Thompson, born *c.* 1846, died before 1878.

James T. V. Thompson had two children by his first wife both of whom died young. He had three children by his third wife: a girl who died young; John Drew Thompson, born *c.* 1853; and Anna R. Thompson, born *c.* 1855, married Professor James Love.

C. Jane or Jennet Maben Gartin, born Kentucky, 7 December 1808, died Barry, Clay County, Missouri, 30 September 1876;[74] married, 11 August 1828, Andrew Kincaid Gartin, born Greenbriar County, Virginia, 31 December 1805, died Barry, Clay County, Missouri, 21 March 1875,[75] son of Richard Gartin (born Spotsylvania County, Virginia, *c.* 1760, died in Todd County, Kentucky, *c.* 1815) and Anna Kincaid, and cousin of William Gartin Shanklin who married 3-7 Martha Graham; probably also related to Sally Gartin who married 3-8 William M. Graham. Jane's and Andrew's marriage was performed by the Rev. William K. Stewart, a Presbyterian minister.[76]

For Andrew's involvement in the South Carolina court case on behalf of his wife and her sisters, see above under 3-4A Sarah Maben Chesnut. The suit, instigated in 1830, concerned interest which Andrew and his brothers-in-law felt was due to their wives from their grandfather's estate.

Andrew's parents moved to Todd County, Kentucky, in about 1809, and when Andrew's father died in about 1815 Andrew inherited a considerable amount of land. On 21 May 1836 he and Jane sold approximately 270 acres to Daniel and Fanny Culbertson for $1,300 (Book J, p. 467). Also, Andrew's siblings left Todd County probably shortly before this time, and on 18 June 1836 six of them plus their spouses deeded their interests in their father's land in Todd County to Andrew for $50 each. They were John and Polly (Gartin) Cordry, Nathaniel and Clementine Gartin, Elizabeth Gartin, Richard and Anna Gartin, and William Gartin; they all then lived in Cooper County, Missouri (Book K, p. 3). Another brother, Elijah, moved to Oktibbeha County, Mississippi, where he was living on 21 September 1836 when he and his wife, Ann, sold their interest in the estate to Andrew for $58 (Book K. p. 1).

It is not known when Jane and Andrew moved to Clay County, Missouri, although Vivian Cooper Shannon, a great-granddaugh-

ter, believes it was in about 1838. They were definitely in
Missouri by 1840 when Andrew bought all of the southwest
quarter of T52 R33 in Clay County.[77] Jane's sister and her
husband, Margaret and James T. V. Thompson, already lived in
Clay County near Liberty, and in 1841 William Gartin Shanklin
(Andrew's cousin) and his wife, 3-7 Martha Graham Shanklin,
who was Jane's half-aunt, moved to nearby Platte County,
Missouri. For a short time 3-12 Andrew W. Graham may also
have lived near them.

Andrew's and Jane's land in Clay County abutted the
Platte County line, and it is said that Andrew built a large
brick house which straddled the Clay/Platte County line. Some
of their grandchildren were born in the house but in different
rooms with the result that some were born in Clay County,
others in Platte County.

Western Missouri was primitive at the time. The
following excerpt concerning the period is from a pamphlet
published by Barry Cemetery, Platte County, Missouri, as
quoted by Vivian Cooper Shannon:

> The cemetery was church-founded around 1840--a
> rough and ready time for the people of Barry Commu-
> nity. The township had been established as an
> Indian Trading Post and remained part of Indian
> Territory until 1837.
>
> Throughout those early years, pioneers passed
> through Barry on the Oregon Trail which followed the
> path that is now Barry Road.
>
> Just to the west of the cemetery, on Barry
> Road, stands an old stone well where pioneers
> stopped for their last drink of courage before
> crossing over the edge of civilization. Today a
> sign on the well imparts a chilling message: "Drink
> well, for you may never return."
>
> First, there were skirmishes with the Indians.
> Then came the Mormons, traveling to Missouri in
> search of their Promised Land. Their arrival
> stirred up local resentment and trouble ensued.
> Next came the tensions of the Civil War.

During the Civil War Andrew owned and ran a business in
buying and selling mules. He also owned slaves and emancipa-

ted about twenty of them after the war.

The following is from Andrew's obituary as it appeared in the *Liberty Tribune*, 2 April 1875:

> The deceased was born Dec. 31st., 1805 in Greenbriar Co., VA--at the age of three years moved with his parents to Todd Co., KY, where he married in 1828 and in Oct. about 10 years later, moved to Clay Co., MO., where he lived until his death. He was one of those lion willed men to whom no obstacle was too great to try to overcome--a man of indomitable energy, unflinching perseverance--actively engaged as a "trader" and had at one time in his life amassed a considerable fortune. As a "trader" and dealer in stock, he was liberal to a fault and a man whose loss is deeply felt by the many who had business with him. Whatever may have been his faults and foibles, no one can justly say he ever intentionally wronged them or oppressed the poor by grinding them to the dust with low prices when they were necessitated to sell--but that he paid liberally for that in which he speculated. Kind, generous and hospitable--his place in the community will be hard to fill.
>
> In his impulsive generosity and friendship, he unfortunately endorsed largely for friends before the war, and then in the Great Revolution, he paid thousands on security debts, reducing his once fine estate to almost nothing.

Vivian Cooper Shannon writes, "I don't know why I came to be so lucky as to inherit a set of six silver teaspoons--the fiddle back design. So shapely, but thin and polished to a nice patina, with the initials J. G. monogramed on the handles."

Children:[7][8]

1. Richard Maben Gartin, born Kentucky, 1829; married Emily Rankin. Child:

    a. James Gartin

2. Mary Frances Gartin Evans, born Kentucky, 1832, died 1898; married, 16 April 1850, Richard Parker Evans, a merchant.

They were married by the Rev. E. S. Dulin.[79] Children:

    a. Lucy Evans Wickersham; married ___ Wickersham.

    b. John Evans (Johnny); unmarried.

    c. Belle Evans Hines; married William Hines.

    d. Annie Evans Leach; married John Leach.

    e. Richard Evans (Dick); married Ida Norris.

    f. Margaret Evans (Maggie); unmarried.

    g. Sallie Evans Hackett; married Ollie Hackett.

    h. George Evans

    i. Virgie Evans (girl), died at about 8 years.

3. James William Gartin, born 1834; married in Clinton County, Missouri, 6 June 1858, Mary Frances Miller.[80] Children:

    a. Annie Gartin Walkup; married James Walkup.

    b. Archie Gartin, died while a young man.

    c. Charles Gartin; married Bess Seaton.

    d. Fannie Gartin Walkup; married George Walkup.

    e. Thomas Gartin; married (1) Clara Schuster, later divorced; (2) Lillie ___.

    f. Elva Gartin LaFollette; married Charles LaFollette.

    g. Emma Gartin Dekin; married Elmer Dekin.

    h. John Gartin, died infancy.

4. Margaret Elizabeth Gartin Lowe (Maggie), born 1837, died 1905; married, 4 June 1861, Percival Greene Lowe of Colorado Territory. They were married by the Rev. W. C. Barrett.[81] Children:

    a. Wilson Lowe

b. Percival Greene Lowe Jr.

c. Jennie Lowe McCormick; married Lloyd McCormick.

d. Nellie Lowe Wilson; married Samuel Wilson.

5. Sarah Jane Gartin Funk (Sally), born Missouri, *c.* 1839; married, 31 August 1858, John A. Funk,[82] son of John Funk (died 1861) and Nancy Rice and brother of Jacob Funk who married Sally's sister Annie. Children:

   a. Mattie Funk, born 1863, died 1923, buried Barry Cemetery; unmarried.

   b. Harry Funk; married Lydia Richardson. No children.

   c. Pink Funk (boy); unmarried.

   d. Lute or Lutie Funk Rosier; married Asa Rosier. Children: (**a**) Richard; (**b**) Russell J., born *c.* 1900, died Columbia, Missouri, 14 February 1983; (**c**) David; (**d**) Vincent; and (**e**) a daughter who died in infancy.

6. Eliza Ann Gartin Funk (called Annie),[83] born Missouri, 1841, died Platte County, Missouri, 1917, buried Barry Cemetery, Clay County, Missouri; married in Clay County, 24 December 1861, Jacob R. Funk, born Jessamine County, Kentucky, 31 December 1833, died 1918, son of John Funk (died 1861) and Nancy Rice and brother of John A. Funk who married Annie's sister Sally. Annie attended the Clay Seminary. Jacob left Kentucky in 1855 and, after traveling to Salt Lake City and Mexico, settled in Clay County, Missouri, where he bought a farm in 1862 and an additional one in 1879. He and Annie were prominent members of the Cumberland Presbyterian Church. Children:

   a. Mary Funk (Mamie), born *c.* 1864, died in 1886 at 22 years; unmarried.

   b. Annie Laurie Funk, born 1866, died 1949; unmarried.

   c. Sallie Funk Larimer; married David Larimer.

   d. Gillie Funk; married Annie Jenkins.

   e. Emma Funk Frasier; married Frank Frasier.

f. Earl Funk; born 1876, died 1927; unmarried.

7. George Gilmer Gartin (Gillie), born 1843, died 1921; married Margaret Ann Davis. Children:

   a. Nellie Leach Gartin Stucky, born near Barry, Clay County, Missouri, 11 January 1873, died Butler, Missouri, 1 July 1852, buried Oak Hill Cemetery; married, 6 October 1893, Claiborn Stucky. Child (adopted): Betty Ellen, married Howard Kahman and had Howard and Jerry.

   b. George Gilmer Gartin Jr., born Barry, Clay County, Missouri, 21 March 1875, died Las Vegas, Nevada; married in Bates County, Missouri, 1 January 1906, Maude Patrick. Children: (a) Frank Wilson, born Bates County, Missouri, 29 January 1908, died Independence, Missouri, 8 December 1980, married Kate Gore, born Kentucky, no children; (b) Margaret Virginia, born Cass County, Missouri, 14 December 1910, died Sun City, Arizona, 28 January 1981, married (1) Bud Parker, (2) Hugh W. Fraser, no children; (c) Howard Patrick, born 10 February 1914, married (1) Frances Atchison and had Carol Lee, born 2 December 1937, John Patrick, born 3 March 1939, and Paul Michael, born 30 May 1941; married (2) Enid Elizabeth Keeny and had James Andrew, born 18 July 1945, died of diabetes, 21 August 1966; (d) George Gilmer III, born Bates County, Missouri, 14 December 1916, married (1) Gladys Wilson, since divorced, (2) Imogean Hiatt and gained two stepsons; and (e) Betty Rose, born Independence, Missouri, 13 November 1922, died 16 June 1923.

   c. Jane Gartin, died infancy.

   d. Margaret Ann Gartin, born 31 August 1881, died Butler, Bates County, Missouri, 30 May 1950, buried Oak Hill Cemetery; unmarried.

   e. Mary Emeline Gartin, born Platte County, Missouri, 22 July 1883, died 11 July 1960, buried Oak Hill Cemetery; unmarried.

   f. Virginia May Gartin Cooper (Jennie), born Barry, Clay County, Missouri, 12 April 1886, died near Nevada, Vernon County, Missouri, 28 January 1937, buried Newton Cemetery, Nevada, Missouri; married near Ballard, Bates County, Missouri, 5 February 1907, DeWitt T. Cooper, born near Harrisonville, Missouri, 14 May 1886, died near Nevada, Missouri, 13 March 1950, buried Newton Cemetery. Children: (**a**) Gilmer DeWitt Cooper, born near Aaron, Bates County, Missouri, 8 April 1908, died at a hospital in Fort Scott, Kansas, 24 September 1959, buried Newton Cemetery, Nevada, Missouri; married (1) 17 February 1934, Marie Mitts, soon divorced; (2) Jestina Jewell Webb (her second marriage), born 12 March 1915, and had James Orville (stepson, born 21 February 1935); Elizabeth Mae (born 5 November 1936, married Rae Gene Jones and had Ronald, born 9 November 1954, and Becky Joann, born 24 November 1955); and Rhonda Kay (born 11 November 1954, married Kenneth Gene Cartwright, and had Anthony Webb, born 18 November 1975, and Timothy Ray, born 20 November 1977); (**b**) Thelma Virginia Cooper Merritt, born near Creighton, Bates County, Missouri, 19 October 1911; married at Nevada, Missouri, 25 August 1935, Forest Edward Merritt and had Forest Eugene (born 16 December 1937, unmarried); and (**c**) Vivian Elizabeth Cooper Shannon, born near Dayton, Cass County, Missouri, 29 August 1919, married near Nevada, Missouri, 17 April 1938, Orville Lynwood Shannon, born near Washburn, Missouri, 29 February 1916, son of Lynwood Shannon and Margaret Barker, and had Margaret Ann (born near Nevada, Missouri, 21 October 1941, married at Springfield, Missouri, 23 September 1962, Quincy Rae Cross, born Vernon County, Missouri, 23 October 1930, and had Ray Lynn, born Nevada, Missouri, 6 February 1964, and Matthew Shannon, born Nevada, Missouri, 27 December 1967); and Beverly Louise (born near Nevada, Missouri, 23 April 1943, married (1) at Willard, Missouri, 8 September 1968, Melvin Humphrey, divorced; (2) 7 March 1969, Jack Edward Freitag, divorced 1970; (3) 5 August 1978, Robert Melvin Teter, divorced 1979; Beverly had Elizabeth Ann Freitag, born 13 January 1970).

8. Martha Virginia Gartin Barnes (Mattie), born 1847; married James Matthew Barnes. Children:

   a. Roy Barnes (R. G.)

   b. Jamie Barnes (J. H.)

c. Patsy Barnes

d. Mary Barnes

e. Guy Barnes

f. Azel Barnes (A. D.)

9. John Andrew Gartin, born 1849, died 21 August 1849.[84]


3-5 DAVID GRAHAM, born Chester County, South Carolina, c. 1787, died perhaps in York County, South Carolina, 1830-40; married, perhaps before 1810, ELEANOR MCCREIGHT (Nelly), born Ireland c. 1785, died probably in South Carolina, after 1860, daughter of Robert McCreight (died York County, South Carolina, 1828-29) and Nancy ___.

David was a blacksmith as was his father.

David was mentioned in the Todd County, Kentucky, will (1821) of his father, 2-1 Andrew, as were Andrew's other children, but no David Graham was listed in the federal censuses of Todd, Christian, or Logan Counties, Kentucky, and no deed records have been found there concerning him despite the fact that most of Andrew's other children moved to that area. It is assumed, therefore, that David remained in South Carolina when the others migrated. He did not remain in Chester County, however.

Probably he was still in Chester County when his father and siblings left: the deed dated 24 October 1805 by which Andrew sold his land in Chester County prior to moving was witnessed by David and proved by him on 25 October 1805 (Book L, p. 249). David and Eleanor may have been in Chester County as late as 6 January 1813 when David sold land there, although it seems more likely that they had moved to York County before that time and that David was finally selling his holdings in Chester. In the deed he sold 100 acres for $400 on Rocky Creek to Samuel Ferguson as witnessed by William Hemphill and John Coulter (proved 28 July 1813; Book Q, p. 92). Also, this deed included a dower release signed by Eleanor on 16 February 1813.

The will of Eleanor's father, Robert McCreight, written 5 August 1828 and proved in York County on 27 July 1829, named his oldest daughter as "Eleanor McCreight alias Graham," and on a list of contra credit dated 23 July 1832 David Graham is mentioned as a claimant against the estate (York County Probate, Case 29, File

1211).

David and his wife seem to have been associated with his cousin 3-15 David (son of 2-4 James) and 3-15 David's wife, Elizabeth. The latter David (3-15) married in 1819 and had a stormy marriage which ended in permanent separation after three years. David (3-15) and Elizabeth also lived in York County, and there may have been a family connection between Elizabeth and Eleanor (Nelly), wife of 3-5 David. In a deed recorded and proved in Chester County on 17 September 1823, 3-15 David Graham of York County sold to his brother, 3-16 James Graham Jr., 100 acres in Chester County, witnessed by a David Graham (probably 3-5) among others. This sale caused Elizabeth, wife of 3-15 David, to go before the York County court to request alimony. One of the witnesses she called on her behalf was Nelly (Eleanor) Graham, probably the wife of 3-5 David. (See the full story under 3-15 David.)

David (3-5) is not listed in any 1840 South Carolina census although he is listed in the York County census of 1830; it is therefore thought that he died in 1830-40. Sadly, in the 1850 and 1860 censuses Nelly was listed in the county poor house.

In the will (1822) of David's aunt 2-7 Mary, she mentioned "My Nephew David Grahams Blacksmith" and left him money to buy religious books for his family. The only child of David whom Mary mentioned was Jane. According to the 1830 census, he and Nelly had seven children, three boys and four girls. The only known child is the following:

4-11 Jane


3-6 ROBERT C. GRAHAM, born Chester County, South Carolina, 11 July 1792, died in Spring Grove Township, Warren County, Illinois, 25 May 1863, buried Spring Grove Cemetery;[85] married in Christian County, Kentucky, 19 March 1812, MARTHA B. MCKEE, born probably in Chester County, South Carolina, 25 December 1787, died probably in Monmouth, Warren County, Illinois, 21 October 1882 (age 94 years, 9 months, 26 days), buried Spring Grove Cemetery, Spring Grove Township, Warren County, Illinois,[86] daughter of John McKee (born Ireland) and Nancy ___ (Collins?; born probably in Ireland, c. 1748, died Preble County, Ohio, 10 December 1832, buried Hopewell Cemetery, Preble County).[87] Robert's and Martha's marriage was performed by the Rev. Ben H. Reeves and was witnessed by Robert's brother 3-3 Matthew.[88] Martha's mother, Nancy, was listed with

Robert and Martha in the 1830 census of Preble County, Ohio.

This branch of the McKee family migrated in 1783-7 from Ireland to South Carolina. Known siblings of Martha B. were James, William, and John (the latter born in Ireland c. 1783), all of whom migrated from South Carolina to Todd County, Kentucky. Other siblings may have been Samuel Collins McKee and Susanna. They may have been related in some way to the Brown family, and Martha B. McKee's middle name may have been Brown. On her marriage license, the clerk wrote her name as follows: "Martha Bro-McKee"; that is, he wrote for her middle name "Bro" then crossed out the "r" and the "o." Whatever their relationships in the eighteenth century, however, the McKees were descended from the Mackay clan whose ancestral home was in the Scottish highlands in the northern part of Scotland near the present town of Bettyhill on the ocean. They were true Celts with a recorded history dating from the fourteenth century.[89]

On 25 October 1815 Robert C. bought land on the Elk Fork of the Red River in Todd County, Kentucky, from James McGill of Bedford, Tennessee (Book E, p. 408). The 1816 tax list showed that Robert owned 290 acres of "second rate land" with a total value of $1,280. In 1817 this value increased to $2,420, and in 1820 it was $3,180. The 1817 tax list also showed one black person, perhaps his father's slave, Sandy. The black was not on the 1820 tax list.

Robert and Martha were members of the Hopewell Presbyterian Church in Todd County of which Robert was a trustee together with James Chesnut and James McQuiston, and on 25 September 1820 the trustees bought one acre for the church from James Graham (no relation) for $5 (Book A, p. 117).

In the late 1820's several families, including Robert's and Martha's, moved to Preble County, Ohio, which already contained a large settlement of Scotch-Irish from South Carolina. Robert disposed of their land in Todd County in two deeds: on 28 March 1829 they sold 275 acres on the Elk Fork of the Red River to James Porter (recorded and dower relinquished on 7 April 1829 in Book F, p. 16); and on 4 April 1829 they sold an additional tract to Moody Grubbs for $500, "being land whereon said Grubbs now lives" and known as "Christopher Carpenter's old place" (Book F, pp. 17-18). They then moved to Preble County, Ohio, and on 19 February 1830 Robert bought 160 acres, T7 R1E S33, in Dixon Township from James and Margaret Giles for $1,100 (Book 13, p. 102). On 2 April 1832 Robert bought more land, the south half of T7 R1E S34, for $375 from John and Mary Pinkerton (Book 13, p. 101).

They did not remain long in Ohio, however. In early 1839 Robert and Martha moved again, this time to Monroe County, Indiana, where they were living on 24 April 1839 when they sold their land in Preble County to a Daniel Kendley for $4,400 (Book 25, p. 362). Earlier, on 16 March 1839, Robert had bought eighty acres in Richland Township, Monroe County, Indiana--the east half of northwest S36 T9 R2W--which was near Bloomington (Book G, p. 328). In the 1850 federal census, Robert gave the value of his total assets as $2,400 which was somewhat higher than those of his neighbors. Hence, Robert was a modest man of means.

He was also an individualist. He and Martha were members of the Associate Reformed Presbyterian Church, the mainstream of the Presbyterian Church at the time and a highly conservative group who regarded any travel on Sunday other than church-going as sinful. In fact, such non-religious activity was deemed a church offense, subject to admonishment or censure through church trial. Robert was admonished on 23 September 1843 for driving his wagon on a Sunday, not to church.[90] He seems, further, to have been a stubborn man with a high sense of moral rectitude: he later became involved in a church scandal which included his daughter Paulina (or Polina) and her in-laws. The following account comes from the records of Union Church, Monroe County, Indiana, of which Robert and his family were members, as reported by Prof. James Albert Woodburn, a descendant of another Union Church member:

### THE GRAHAM CASE--GOSSIP AND SLANDER

Another unique case of discipline, and from the nature of the circumstances, one of the most troublesome of all, was a slander case. Robert [Hemphill] had married Polina [Graham], and Robert's mother [Jennet] and his brother Andrew were accused by Polina's father [Robert C. Graham] of saying some hard things about her. This caused Andrew and his mother to complain to the session of unchristian treatment. They accused Polina's father of slander for saying that they (Andrew and his mother) were trying to ruin Polina's character. The identical words which the father was accused of using were these: "You, Mrs. H., are the very woman that broke covenant between man and wife and have been doing it." Andrew and his mother were asked if they were guilty of talking about Polina, and they said, "No." Then Mr. G. was asked if he was prepared to make any acknowledgments, and he said, "No." The parties were informed that they should stay back from the approaching communion, and the whole matter was laid over for future consideration. (May 2, 1844) It was later decided that Mr. R. G. should be rebuked and that public announcement thereof be made to the congregation. He appealed to the presbytery against this decision. The presbytery sustained the session, with this difference, that he be "admonished instead of rebuked." Mr. G. appeared and was admonished. Polina being rebuked for imprudent conduct, appealed to the presbytery, but when the presbytery sustained the session, Polina appeared and submitted to censure. (October 22, 1844) Polina's father was not satisfied with this disposition of the case. He was evidently one of the contentious kind with a hankering after church litigation. Nearly two years later, January 21, 1846, we find a bill of charges preferred against him by the Union Session:

"1. He has neglected to attend upon the preaching of the word since October 22, 1844, with the exception of a very few days, and that generally [when] some other person officiated besides the regular pastor of the congregation, nor has he since that time partaken of the Lord's supper, though it has been dispensed semi-annually since that time.

"2. He has neglected and virtually refused to pay his subscription of eight dollars for the support of the gospel in Union Congregation, for 1844.

"3. It is reported that some time last fall, or this winter, he drove his wagon coming from market on the Sabbath day.

"Done by order of the session,
"John Moffet, Clerk."

"Mr. G. being interrogated as to the truth of the charge, admitted it, and being called upon to give his reasons for neglect of ordinances as set forth in the first charge, and being asked why he thus acted, replied that he felt aggrieved at the action of the session in his daughter's, and in his own case also, which had been before the session; and one occasion of his grief was that the session insisted on and did ask witnesses living in the very neighborhood of her defamers how her character stood. And another grievance was the spirit manifested in both cases not to let us exculpate ourselves from the charges tabled against us."

"Under the Second charge Mr. G. answered that if his case was not adjusted he would lay in a claim against the moderator of some $2.50 or $3.00, which he once paid to Mr. Boyce when a subscription was got up to assist him in finishing his studies; also a claim of $5.00 which he says he paid to Mr. Moffet shortly after he came to this place to help the congregation out of debt.

"The session having considered the reasons given by Mr. G. in his defense and also the testimony of Mr. John D. Whiseand in regard to Mr. G's answer to the first charge, as insufficient, because--first, they do not know that the question put by the session and objected to by Mr. G. was an improper one, and even admitting it to have been so, it was not the ground of her suspension, and Mr. G. should remember that it is human to err but Divine to forgive. And because, secondly, we regard Mr. G. as making an unreasonable excuse for his conduct when he says a spirit was manifested not to let him and his daughter exculpate themselves. This we think unreasonable when it is remembered that the session spent twelve or fourteen days on these two cases, and Mr. G. had their action reviewed by a higher court; and as it respects the charge made as an offset to his subscription, the session thinks it is a thing almost unheard of for men to expect any pecuniary reward for what they have voluntarily given for charitable purposes.

"As to his travelling on the Sabbath, they are of the opinion his situation was somewhat critical and a kind of necessity drove him to it, and that should he acknowledge before the session his sorrow for the occurrence they would forgive him this offense.

"The session do therefore resolve as in their judgment the only means of removing the offense, that Mr. R. C. G. be and thereby [is] suspended from the enjoyment of sealing ordinances in this church till such time as he shall give signs of Repentance or Reformation, and that whenever he shall do this by returning to his Duty in the church and confessing his faults in these Respects we feel Disposed to Reverse this Decision, and to treat him as a Brother."

Such were the church problems in the country congregation in this vicinity seventy years ago [this was

2-1 Andrew

written in 1910]. Days and weeks of trouble and trial because of some neighborhood gossip about a frisky lass, or because Paulina G.'s mother-in-law was not fond of her.[91]

If this affair seems foolish now, it should be remembered that at the time one penalty for such admonishment and censure was social and economic ostracism--not a pleasant fate in a small community. Also as events proved, the rift and bitterness ran deep, too deep for healing. In the 1850 census of Monroe County, Paulina, who had divorced Robert Hemphill in 1846, was listed with her parents, and her former husband was in jail, his condition labeled "insanity."

Perhaps because of this scandal, Robert and Martha eventually sold their eighty acres in Monroe County on 31 August 1853 to a David Cathcart (Book Q, p. 129). They then moved to Spring Grove Township, Warren County, Illinois, where on 14 November 1855 Robert bought 160 acres, T10N 2W S21 (Book 24, p. 572). On 20 January 1857 he and his son-in-law William Robison bought a lot in the town of Monmouth (Book 25, p. 790), and on 19 May 1858 Robert granted a mortgage for $543 to his son 4-16 Andrew (Book 5, p. 313). Robert and Martha were listed with their youngest daughter, Sarah, in the 1860 census of Warren County. Sarah had married a man named William C. Whisenand who probably was related to the John D. Whiseand who was a witness in the case above. Robert died in 1863. In the 1870 and 1880 censuses of the town of Monmouth, Warren County, Martha was listed in the household of her daughter and son-in-law 4-17 Mary S. and William A. Robison. Martha died there, nearly 95 years old, in 1882.

In his will dated 2 July 1859, Robert named his wife and his surviving children; his sons-in-law, John Glenn, James Small, William Whisenand, and William Robison; and some of his grandchildren: Edward Glenn, Nancy Small, Robert A. Graham, Robert F. Graham, and Martha J. Hemphill who was Polina's daughter. To Martha J. Hemphill Robert bequeathed $100, the greatest single monetary bequest in his will. Children, all but the youngest born in Todd County, Kentucky:

4-12 Margaret C., b. *c.* 12 January 1813

4-13 John McKee, b. 28 April 1816

4-14 Nancy C., b. 1817-20

4-15 Paulina Jane, b. *c.* 1822

4-16 Andrew Edward, b. 29 May 1824

4-17 Mary Susan, b. 4 July 1829

4-18 Sarah E., b. Preble Co., OH, 1 July 1831

CHILDREN OF 2-1 ANDREW GRAHAM
AND (2) MARGARET ___ (MILLS?)

3-7 MARTHA GRAHAM SHANKLIN, born probably in Chester County, South Carolina, 23 August 1798, died Platte County, Missouri, 26 August 1887, buried Second Creek Cemetery, Platte County;[92] married in Morgan County, Illinois, 3 November 1831, WILLIAM GARTIN SHANK-LIN,[93] born Virginia, 4 July 1802, died Platte County, Missouri, 27 May 1891, buried Second Creek Cemetery, Platte County,[94] son of Joseph Shanklin (born perhaps Virginia, died Christian County, Kentucky, 1815) and Frances Gartin (born Virginia, c. 1770, died Syracuse, Morgan County, Missouri, after 1850). William Gartin Shanklin was a cousin of Andrew Kincaid Gartin who married 3-4C Jane Maben and probably also a cousin of Sally Gartin who married 3-8 William M. Graham. Martha and William are buried in a common plot with their older daughter, Nancy, their son, Robert, and Robert's wife and daughter.

After their marriage in Morgan County, Illinois, Martha and William, together with his mother and his living siblings, moved first to Cooper County, Missouri, where they were living on 10 January 1837 when William, his mother, and his siblings sold the land they had inherited from William's father in Todd County, Kentucky, to John Foster for $400 (Book K, p. 10). Soon after, William and Martha moved to nearby Morgan County, Missouri, and finally in 1841 to Platte County, Missouri, where William was a farmer owning 192 acres in Carroll Township, S21 T52N R33W.[95] Listed in their household in the 1850 and 1860 censuses was a Nancy Graham, born in Missouri c. 1849. This Nancy was probably a daughter of Martha's brother 3-12 Andrew W. whose wife had died in 1850 and who was said to have gone to California in 1852.

Martha and William had three known children, all born in Missouri:

A. Nancy Shanklin, b. 1832
B. Margaret Elizabeth Shanklin, b. 6 June 1835
C. Robert Gilbert Shanklin, b. 28 November 1839

---

A. Nancy Shanklin, born Missouri, 1832, died 1912, buried in the same plot as her parents in Second Creek Cemetery, Platte County, Missouri;[96] unmarried.

B. Margaret Elizabeth Shanklin Hardesty,[97] born Missouri, 6 June 1835, died 12 August 1912, buried Second Creek Cemetery;

married (1) in Platte County, Missouri, 12 March 1863, Thomas (or Thompson) Pierce Hardesty, born Jefferson County, Virginia, 2 February 1821, died Platte County, Missouri, 6 September 1876, buried Second Creek Cemetery; (2) on 5 February 1879, the Rev. T. B. (Zeke) Ricketts. Ricketts was not listed with Margaret in the 1880 census although a Fanny Ricketts, aged 17, was. (Fanny was probably Ricketts' daughter by a previous marriage). Margaret was buried beside her first husband, and her tombstone is inscribed "Margaret Elizabeth Hardesty." Children, all born in Missouri:

1. Martha V. Hardesty Callicotte (Mattie), born *c.* 1865; married, 20 February 1883, Joseph W. Callicotte, born Missouri, *c.* 1858, son of Henry Callicotte (born Russell County, Kentucky, 27 May 1827) and Mary Ann Murray (born Boyle County, Missouri, *c.* 1826). Children:

    a. Frances Callicotte Graves (Fannie); married Gilbert Graves.

    b. Cliff Callicotte

    c. George Callicotte

2. Lily Olivia Hardesty, born 6 September 1866, died 6 April 1955, buried Second Creek Cemetery; unmarried.

3. William Richard Hardesty, born 23 May 1869, died 24 December 1951, buried Second Creek Cemetery; married, 12 December 1895, Fannie McIlvain Slaughter, born Missouri 10 December 1871, died 10 July 1926, buried Second Creek Cemetery, daughter of Edward C. Slaughter (born Missouri, *c.* 1846) and Belle A. ___ (born Kentucky, *c.* 1846). Children:

    a. Thomas Edward Hardesty, born 11 November 1896, died ___; married Opal Robertson. Children: (**a**) Billy M., born 7 April 1923, married Deloris Lillihaug; and (**b**) Martha Jane, born 24 November 1925, married Leonard Mayo.

    b. Hazel Frances Hardesty, born 4 March 1898, died ___; unmarried.

    c. Richard Hobart Hardesty, born 23 August 1901, died ___; married (1) Verda Wills who died young; (2) Ruby Callahan. Children: (**a**) son, born 1925, died infancy; and (**b**) Rosetta David Hardesty (adopted); married Howard Boeger.

    d. Hope Hardesty, born 12 May 1903, died ___; unmarried.

    e. Milton Park Hardesty, born 15 June 1905, died 21 July 1848; unmarried.

    f. Lois Hardesty Holmes, born 27 September 1907; married Howard Holmes. No children.

    g. John Clay Hardesty, born 24 December 1911; married Willa Dee Hunt. Children: (**a**) LaDel, born 17 July 1940, married Harold Stephens; and (**b**) Richard D., born 17 January 1945.

    h. Lowell Slaughter Hardesty, born 29 November 1913; married Delvena Anderson. Children: (**a**) Lowell S. Jr., born 21 December 1939?, married Kae Field; (**b**) Billy Sherwin, born 7 April 1941; and (**c**) Sharron Zelena, born 17 November 1943.

4. Charley Hardesty, born 1874, died at 10 days, buried Second Creek Cemetery.

C. Robert Gilbert Shanklin, born Missouri, 28 November 1839, died 1929, buried with his wife in the common plot with his parents in Second Creek Cemetery, Platte County, Missouri; married, 2 November 1871, Martha Virginia Bohannon (Jennie), born 1848, died 6 September 1917.[98] Child:

1. Harriett May Shanklin Lincoln (Hattie), born Missouri, 1873, died in the 1950's, buried Second Creek Cemetery in the same plot as her parents and grandparents; married, late in life, Walter Lincoln. No children.

3-8 WILLIAM MILLS GRAHAM,[99] born probably in Chester County, South Carolina, 26 September 1801, died Winterset, Madison County, Iowa, 28 January 1882, buried Winterset, Iowa; married (1) in Todd County, Kentucky, 23 December 1823, SALLY C. GARTIN (Book A, p. 13), born Kentucky, 29 November 1798, died during a cholera epidemic near Jacksonville, Morgan County, Illinois, 29 July 1833 (said to have been pregnant when she died), perhaps a daughter of Richard Gartin (born Spotsylvania County, Virginia, c. 1760, died Todd County, Kentucky, c. 1815) and Anna Kincaid.[100] Sally may have been a sister of Andrew Kincaid Gartin, who married 3-4C Jane Maben, and a cousin of William Gartin Shanklin who married 3-7 Martha Graham. The epidemic which killed Sally was virulent; many people died in it.[101] William married (2) in Morgan County, Illinois, 13 March 1835, JANE POPHAM, born Virginia, 12 April 1809, died 14 December 1893, buried Winterset Cemetery, Winterset, Iowa.[102] Jane Popham may have been a sister of Ezekiel Popham who married 3-11 Nancy C. Graham.

On 30 January 1824 William sold land on Rains Lick Creek in Todd County, Kentucky, to Charles Deeds for $200 (Book B, p. 437). On 1 May 1828 he and his mother sold 75 acres to Andrew Alexander for $300, witnessed by 3-12 Andrew W. Graham and Samuel Boone who was probably a grand-nephew of Daniel Boone (Book E, p. 205). Finally William and his brother 3-12 Andrew sold 15 more acres to Garland McAllester for $50 (Book F, p. 139).

William and his first wife left Todd County, Kentucky, in 1829 and moved to an area near Jacksonville, Morgan County, Illinois, where his mother and most of his siblings joined him in 1830. On 28 and 30 November 1829, William acquired two different public domain land tracts in S6 T15 R10W totaling 181.64 acres.[103] Later he bought part of southwest S32 T16 R10. His land bordered that owned by Ezekiel Popham, his future brother-in-law. On 6 June and 27 August 1835, William sold his land in Morgan County (Vol. J, pp. 1 and 79) and moved with his second wife and children to Warren County (now Henderson County), Illinois, where a month earlier, 29 July 1935, he had bought land in Gladstone Township and eventually built a stone house there which is still standing (Book 29, p. 528).

His known negotiations at that time in Warren (Henderson) County are as follows. In 1836 he bought a tract from C. Ward and sold the land soon after to Cyrel Ward and H. E. Haley (Book 3, pp. 285, 288, and 298). He then bought land from Levi Brede and on 2 August 1837 sold land to Isaac Brooks or Brock who had also just bought land from 3-12 Andrew W. (Book 4, pp. 74 and 269, and Book 5, p. 85). On 11 June 1838 William bought 400 acres from his brother 3-12 Andrew W. for $225 (Book 6, p. 89). On 10 October 1849 William bought a tract from John Rankin (Book 4, p. 233); and on 9 April 1852 he sold small tracts for one dollar each to his sons 4-21 Andrew R. and 4-22 Robert C. (Book 6, pp. 394 and 395). Also on 9 April 1852 he sold a large tract for $1,200 to his son-in-law Thomas G. Allison, husband of 4-20 Nancy (Book 6, p. 393).

In the early 1830's while he was still in Morgan County,

Illinois, William was an elder in the Jacksonville Presbyterian Church and in 1834 helped people in Warren County found their South Henderson Presbyterian Church.[104] (Henderson County was formed from Warren County in 1841.) After William and his family moved to Warren County, he and his wife joined the South Henderson Church on 26 May 1836. Jane, who had been reared as a Baptist, converted to William's church and was baptized at the Sunday service on 27 May 1836. On 28 August 1837 William was chosen a ruling elder, a post he held for more than thirty years, and he was a delegate to the first meeting of the Presbytery of Illinois. On 2 March 1854 the congregation voted to build a new stone church, and William's name was the first to be listed on the committee of five to oversee the construction. He also donated stone from his quarry for the new building.

In 1860, however, he seems to have had some trouble with the church. In the session minutes of July 1860, a lengthy account was given of "difficulties existing" between William and Mr. W. J. Hutchinson; the differences were settled after much committee work (pp. 98-101). At the same time the church clerk, a man named Mekemson, charged William with scandal and in 1859 with having kept back from the accessor his money on interest and some hogs which were subject to taxation (p. 101). On 17 August 1860 the session minutes recorded that William was not guilty of scandal but that "private rebuke" be administered to him and that public announcement of the same be given from the pulpit before the congregation. William requested time to consider the action (p. 107). On 26 October 1860 William acceded, and the session then delivered the "private rebuke." The next Sunday, 28 October 1860, the following statement was read from the pulpit: "Mr Wm M Graham having acknowlege the sin of keeping back his money on interest from taxation & haveing made suitable acknowlegement of his guilt & given satisfactory evidence of penitence, & haveing received a rebuke by the session, has been restored to the previlages of the church & to the exercise of his office as Ruling Elder in this congregation" (pp. 110-1).

During the Civil War five of William M.'s sons fought in the Illinois 10th Infantry, and all survived.

In December 1870 William and Jane moved to Winterset, Madison County, Iowa, where he built a stone house at East 616 Court Street. Their sons 4-25 Matthew J. and 4-30 Samuel A. had already moved to Madison County. The following is from an obituary on William which appeared in the *Winterset Chronicle*:

The whole community was startled on Saturday evening by the death of Mr. Graham. He was in his accustomed pew of Sabbath last, and we met him on the street on Wednesday and could not help thinking how stout and hearty and cheery he was for a man over 80. He took a severe cold on Wednesday evening and rapidly grew worse until the end came. . . . Blithe of heart as a boy he conducted his affairs with the same energy up to the last, was as deeply interested in the prosperity of his church, and at the same time when it seemed as though he had many years before him, selected a lot in the cemetery, ordered improvements to his mind and urged them to a speedy completion, remarking that he hoped to occupy it before spring. He came to his grave "in full age like a shoot of corn in his season. . . ."

After he died Jane continued to live in the stone house, and after she died the house was willed to the church to be used as a manse.

Children by (1) Sally Gartin:

4-19 Martha Ann, b. Kentucky, 23 September 1824
4-20 Nancy Ellen, b. Kentucky, 23 November 1825
4-21 Andrew Richard, b. Illinois, 10 May 1829
4-22 Robert Culbertson, b. Illinois, 10 January 1831

Children by (2) Jane Popham, all born in Henderson County, Illinois:

4-23 James Thomas, b. 8 October 1836
4-24 William Alexander, b. 26 September 1837
4-25 Matthew Joseph, b. 12 November 1838
4-26 Sarah Jane, b. 3 September 1840
4-27 John Mills, b. 27 March 1842
4-28 David McDill, b. February 1843
4-29 Mary Margaret, b. 30 December 1844
4-30 Samuel Allison, b. 18 March 1848

3-9 THOMAS P. GRAHAM,[105] born Chester County, South Carolina, 18 October 1803, died Todd County, Kentucky, 21 May 1889, buried Duerson Cemetery on Simmons' Place which is in Todd County close to the Christian County border; married in Todd County, 19 November 1832, MARY P. WADDILL, born Virginia, 9 August 1803, died Todd County, 1 December 1888, buried Duerson Cemetery, daughter of Granville Waddill (born Virginia, c. 1779, died Todd County, 1857) and ___.

Thomas and Mary are buried in the same cemetery as their son Granville W. and daughter Joanna Duerson. They were married by J. H. Boone who was probably related to the Rev. William Boone, pastor of the Zion Baptist Church in Todd County. This church split in 1833, and Reverend Boone and others formed the Zion Christian Church which included among its officers a "Mr. Graham" who may have been Thomas.

After Thomas's father died, John McKee (brother-in-law of 3-6 Robert C.) was appointed Thomas's guardian. Thomas was still in school, and there is a record dated 16 March 1822 of 3-6 Robert C. paying $10 from his father's estate to Robert E. Acock for Thomas's schooling. Later that year, 23 November 1822, Robert C. again paid $3.56 from the estate for a lot bought by Thomas from William Greenfield. When Thomas came of age, he signed a receipt which said, "Recd of John Mckee $680.11 which is the full amount of all my state march 11th 1825" (Will Book A, pp. 257-8). Most likely this receipt was for the income on the 120 acres which Thomas had inherited from his father. He sold the land on 3 August 1830 to Samuel Boone who was probably a grand-nephew of Daniel Boone (Book F, pp. 367-8).

Thomas was the only one of Andrew's children to remain in Todd County when the others moved away beginning in 1829. Until at least 1856 he was the administrator of the estate of Adam Mills, husband of Thomas's half-sister 3-2 Jennet. The estate, which was on Spring Creek near a tract owned by his father-in-law, consisted of 178 acres; Thomas paid the taxes on it and raised mostly tobacco. No record of his paying the taxes after 1856 has been found, however. Since his father-in-law, Granville Waddill, died at about that time, Thomas and his family may have moved to Granville's land.

Granville left money to Thomas's wife, Mary, and her daughters, but the money was to be held in trust by Mary's brother, Joseph Waddill, and was not to be administered by Thomas who had already been advanced $500. Also, Mary was not to repay the $500 to the estate from her inheritance (Book I, p. 534; recorded 13 July 1857).

Joseph Waddill had no children when he died in May of 1888, and he named as his heirs his sisters as well as his wife. Mary inherited 71 acres on the West Fork of the Red River in Todd County (Book 16, pp. 579 and 593), but since Mary, herself, died in December of the same year the property was added to her estate which, in turn, was inherited by her children. The children sold their interests in the land to various buyers (see the children's entries).

Granville Waddill, Mary's father, was something of a personage in Todd County where he was said to have been generally well read and an excellent historian.

Children of Thomas and Mary as listed in the censuses, all born in Todd County, Kentucky:

4-31 Eliza Ellen, b. September 1834
4-32 Granville Waddill, b. 17 July 1835
4-33 Robert M., b. c. 1839
4-34 Lucy Ann, b. c. 1841
4-35 Mary M., b. 20 August 1843
4-36 Joanna, b. 1 September 1845


3-10 MARGARET GRAHAM (Peggy), born probably in South Carolina, 1804-7. Nothing more has been found on her. She may have moved to Morgan County, Illinois, c. 1830 with her mother and siblings and died there during the 1833 cholera epidemic which killed Sally C. Gartin, first wife of 3-8 William M. Graham.


3-11 NANCY C. GRAHAM POPHAM, born probably in Kentucky, c. 1807-8, died perhaps in Linn County, Oregon, after 1860; married (1) in Morgan County, Illinois, 17 October 1833, EZEKIEL POPHAM, born ___, died Salem, Champoeg County, Oregon, 20 August 1847, probably related to Jane Popham who married 3-8 William M. Graham as his second wife; Nancy and Ezekiel were married by Edward Tankersley, JP.[106] Nancy perhaps married (2) in Salem, Oregon, August 1847, John McGregor, born New York, c. 1805, died in Linn County, Oregon, September 1851.[107]

Nancy and her first husband were named as co-owners of fifteen acres in Morgan County, Illinois, where her mother had apparently bought the land when the family moved there from Todd County, Kentucky, in about 1830.[108] They sold the fifteen acres in 1836 when they moved, together with Nancy's brother 3-8 William M. and his family, to Warren (Henderson) County, Illinois. There, they all joined the South Henderson Presbyterian Church on 26 May 1836.[109] In Warren County, not Morgan County, there is a deed dated 18 March 1836 in which Ezekiel Popham of Morgan County sold land to John Lovett also of Morgan County (Book 2, p. 191). Nancy's mother was listed with Ezekiel and Nancy in the 1840 census of Warren County.

In the late 1840's Nancy and Ezekiel took one of the wagon trains over the Oregon Trail perhaps in the company of other families with whom the Grahams were associated in Illinois and Kentucky and who are known to have gone to Oregon. These families included those named Findley (Finley), Ritchie, and Shanklin.[110] In 1847 Ezekiel claimed 640 acres in Champoeg County, Oregon, and his neighbor to the north was William Finley. Ezekiel said he intended personal occupancy on 17 June 1847.[111] (Or perhaps he was granted the land on 17 June 1847 and said at that time that he intended personal occupancy.)

Two months later, Ezekiel was killed in a fight over his son. The following account of the affair is taken from a microfilm at the Library of Congress of *The Spectator* (of Oregon City), 2 September 1847, p. 2, col. 4:

> Allow me through your columns to give the public some information respecting the death of Ezekiel Popham. On the 22nd inst, I had an inquest held over the body of the deceased, Ezekiel Popham. It appeared from evidence given to jury, that the deceased came into the building where Jos. Holman, a native of the Sandwich Islands, (Jimo), and John H. Bosworth were at work, and Mr. Popham asked who had been whipping his child. Bosworth said he had. Witness, busily engaged at work, did not hear much of their conversation, but on hearing a noise as if they were in a scuffle, turned round and saw Mr. Popham lying on the floor, but did not know how he came there. Witness then assisted him in getting to his feet, after which Mr. Bosworth struck Mr. Popham twice. Witness thinks the first lick was with the open hand on the face, and the second lick with the fist on the neck, said Popham staggered back a short distance, picked up a stick, and was in the act of raising when he dropped on the floor dead.
>
> The jury [after] deliberating on this testimony, required [that a] post mortem examination should be [made on] the body, where upon Drs W. J. Bai[ley] and J. W. Boyl proceeded to examine the body. After which, reported to the jury as follows: "It is our belief that the deceased, Ezekiel Popham, before death had been laboring for a length of time, from an organic affliction of the heart and great vessels of the pulmonary tissues, and in consequence of the arterial excitement produced by the quarrel with John H Bosworth, produced a rupture of the pulmonary artery, and consequently fol-

lowed by immediate death." Whereupon the jury returned a verdict, that they believed that "the death of Ezekiel Popham was occasioned in consequence of a scuffle and fight between said Popham and John H Bosworth, and also from several blows received from said John H Bosworth, in the town of Salem, Champoeg county, Oregon on Friday the 20th day of August 1847". Signed by 12 jurymen.

I hereby certify the above to be a summary account of the proceedings. . . . J. M. Garrison, J.P.

No record has been found that Bosworth was indicted. He was formerly of Lexington, Kentucky, and was a son of David H. Bosworth. Earlier in 1847 (27 May) he was among those who at an Oregon City meeting were accused of claims jumping. In 1847-8 he was a rifleman in a company formed to fight the Indians. On 22 May 1848 he married Susan B. Looney of Champoeg County, and on 28 May 1850 he died in Oregon City after a "long illness" of four months.[112]

Shortly after Ezekiel died, Nancy may have married (2) John McGregor.

A year after they were married (if they were), John McGregor had a harrowing experience with a bear, as indicated in the following article which appeared in the *Oregon Spectator*, Thursday, 24 August 1848, p. 3, col. 6:

To the Editor of the Oregon Spectator

Sir- On Sunday morning last, as a Mr Jno McGregor was crossing a skirt of timber, from the south end of the French prairie towards the northeast point of the prairie, adjoining Mill creek, while in the brush a short distance south of lake La Biche, he was attacked by a large male bear & most shockingly mangled. After the beast had bitten him in a number of places severely, he seized him by the left breast and tore out a piece of flesh of the size of man's hand, when Mr McGregor ceased to struggle, & turned over upon his face, & the voracious bear left him, probably for dead. As soon as McGregor found that the beast had gone, he arose and made the best of his way to the nearest house, being nearly four miles, which he reached nearly exhausted with loss of blood and fatigue. It is believed that the man will recover.

2-1 Andrew                                                              3-11A

Your obedient servant,    L. H. Judson, Salem Mills,
August 8, 1848

John did recover, although he died three years later, September 1851, at the home of James Garbrough. He also owned land: T14S R14W S6 and S7 and T14S R5W S1 and S12 in Linn County, Oregon.[113] Nancy paid the taxes on his land in 1852 and was listed as the administrator of his estate in 1854.[114] Nancy and her children were not listed in the 1870 census of Linn County.

Children, all by (1) Ezekiel Popham and all born in Illinois:

A.  J. Ann Popham (?), b. c. 1834
B.  James Popham, b. c. 1835
C.  William Thomas Popham, b. c. 1840

---

A.  J. Ann Popham (?), born Illinois, c. 1834. She was not listed with Nancy and Ezekiel Popham in the 1840 census of Warren County, Illinois, but it seems possible that the census taker made an oversight.

B.  James Popham, born Illinois, c. 1835

C.  William Thomas Popham, born Illinois, c. 1840, baptized at the South Henderson Presbyterian Church, 1 June 1840.


3-12 ANDREW W. GRAHAM, born probably in Logan County, Kentucky, c. 1809, died ___; married ___ (Gartin?) who died c. 1850. The reason it is thought that Andrew's wife may have been a Gartin is that she named her son Andrew Gartin Graham.

Andrew was a minor when his father died in 1821, and Hugh Brown was appointed as his guardian (Book A, pp. 199 and 288, and Book B, p. 105). Hugh Brown was a witness to his father's will and may have been related to Martha B. McKee Graham, wife of 3-6 Robert C.

On 30 October 1829 while still in Todd County, Kentucky, Andrew and his brother 3-8 William M. sold "15 acres from the creek bank corner [of] Robert Stokes[?] and 15 acres from the creek bank corner [of] Shanklin" to Garland McAllester for $50 (Book F, p. 139). On 2 October 1830 Andrew and his mother sold 46 acres on the West Fork of the Red River to Andrew Alexander for

2-1 Andrew                                                              3-12

$200 (Book F, p. 407). Finally, on 27 August 1831 Andrew sold land on Rains Lick Creek to James Millen for $75 (Book G, p. 212).

He may then have moved to Morgan County, Illinois, where three of his siblings and his mother are known to have moved. In the mid-1830's, however, he was living in Warren County, Illinois, where in 1836 he bought the southwest quarter of S26 T10N R5W for $200 from Elenor and Sarah Cochran (Book 2, p. 381). A few months later, 1 August 1836, he sold the same land to his oldest half-brother 3-3 Matthew for $800 (Book 2, p. 533). He soon bought more land from Peter Steward and James Watt (Book 4, pp. 225 and 256) which in 1837 and 1838 he sold variously to Isaac J. Brooks, James Makimson, and 3-8 William M. Graham at a total profit of at least $1,525 (Book 4, p. 269 and Book 6, pp. 89 and 130).

Andrew then moved to Clay County, Missouri, where on 28 August 1838 he bought the east half of the southeast quarter of T52 R33.[115] He was joined then or a short time later by James T. V. and 3-4B Margaret (Maben) Thompson and by Andrew and 3-4C Jane (Maben) Gartin all of whom bought land near him. Andrew Gartin was also a cousin of William Gartin Shanklin who married 3-7 Martha Graham; in 1841 William G. and Martha (Graham) Shanklin moved to Platte County, Missouri, which is next to Clay County.

Some time before 1845, Andrew is known to have moved to Clinton County, Missouri (next to Clay and Platte), where his children were born. In about 1850 his wife died, and in about 1852 he is said to have gone to California. An obituary which appeared on his son, Andrew Gartin Graham, in the *Oquawka Spectator* (Henderson County, Illinois), 20 August 1902, said that Andrew G. was born in Clinton County, Missouri (1847), that his mother died when he was three, and that his father went to California when he was five.

In 1858 Andrew Gartin Graham and his sister Mary M. were taken in by their older cousin 4-22 Robert C., son of 3-8 William M. Their younger sister, Nancy, was probably taken in by their aunt 3-7 Martha Graham Shanklin of Platte County, Missouri.

Known children, all probably born in Clinton County, Missouri:

4-37 Mary M., b. 15 April 1846        4-39 Nancy, b. *c.* 1849
4-38 Andrew Gartin, b. 6 Janu-
     ary 1847

## CHILDREN OF 2-4 JAMES GRAHAM
## AND ESTHER ___

3-13 JULIANNA GRAHAM CASKEY,[116] born South Carolina, c. 1783?, died Chester County, South Carolina, 1848, buried Hopewell A.R.P. Church Cemetery; married THOMAS CASKEY, born South Carolina, 1783, died Chester County, South Carolina, 19 October 1840, buried Hopewell Cemetery (next to the grave of his brother-in-law James Graham Jr.), son of John Caskey (died 1785) and Esther ___ (died 1796).

In the April 1807 Court of Common Pleas in Chester County, Thomas sued Samuel Moffet and William Curry, innkeeper, for assault and battery, the details in the case not given in the record. The case finally went to the jury during the October session of 1808, and they decided for Thomas. They also put the entire guilt on William Curry, acquitting Samuel Moffet entirely. Curry had to pay $20 to Thomas plus the court costs which amounted to $61.37 (Common Pleas, Book C, pp. 25-9).

In 1826 Thomas was appointed guardian of Julianna's brother 3-15 David Graham. (See the story under David's entry.)

After Thomas died Julianna and four of her children plus their spouses deeded 121½ acres to her son James Caskey, "in consideration of the knowledge we have of its being the intention and design of the aforesaid Thomas Caskey, deceased." James already lived on the land which was bounded by tracts owned by Samuel McCaw, Hugh White, and men who were identified only by their last names--Archer, Miller, McAlilly, and Wallace. Julianna signed with her mark. Others who signed were her children Elizabeth Caskey, Joanna Caskey, John Caskey and his wife, Agnes, who also signed with her mark, and Hugh and Esther Mills (Deeds Book CC, pp. 430-1).

In her will dated 24 September 1844 and proved 18 July 1848, Julianna bequeathed most of her estate to her youngest son, Thomas. On the same day she made her will, she also deeded to Thomas 131 acres for $360.25. The land was described as "on the waters of Bullskin of Rockey creek, on both sides of the Rocky mount road, and bounded by lands of Saml. Hamilton and others" (Book FF, p. 73).

Many years before Julianna died, her father, her daughter Mary, and Mary's family moved to Tipton County, Tennessee, as did her sister and brother-in-law Esther and Alexander Smith and their children. In the 1850's and 1860's, most of Julianna's remaining children and grandchildren also moved there. Among other Chester County families who moved to Tipton County, Tennessee, were those named Strong, Wiley, McQuiston, McClerkin, and McDill.

Children of Julianna and Thomas Caskey, all born in Chester County, South Carolina:[117]

A. Mary Caskey, b. 9 September 1805
B. Rosanna W. Caskey, b. 1808
C. John Caskey, b. c. 1810
D. James Caskey, b. c. 1812
E. Esther Caskey, b. c. 1814
F. Elizabeth Ellen Caskey, b. c. 1820
G. Joanna Caskey, b. c. 1823
H. Thomas Caskey Jr., b. 1824

---

A. Mary Caskey Hindman, born Chester County, South Carolina, 9 September 1805, died near Brighton, Tennessee, 6 July 1879, buried Salem A.R.P. Church Cemetery; married in Chester County, South Carolina, c. 1826, William Hindman, born Fairfield County, South Carolina, 27 August 1805, died Tipton County, Tennessee, 21 July 1871, buried Salem A.R.P. Church Cemetery, son of James Hindman and Sarah ___. In South Carolina they were members of the Hopewell A.R.P. Church until 1838 when they decided to move to Tennessee. On 18 October 1838 William sold his 231 acres in Chester County, South Carolina, to Andrew J. Boyd; Mary signed the dower release on 11 November 1838 (Book BB, p. 408). They then moved to Tipton County, Tennessee, where Mary's aunt and uncle 3-17 Esther and Alexander Smith had gone a year earlier taking Mary's grandfather James with them. Mary and William first settled about three miles east of the present town of Brighton, and during the following spring, 16 April 1839, they joined the Salem A.R.P. Church. In 1844 they moved to another farm three miles west of Brighton, but they remained life-long members of the Salem Church. Children:

1. James Grimes (sic) Hindman, born Chester County, South Carolina, 9 November 1827, died Tipton County, Tennessee, 1 January 1888, buried Salem A.R.P. Church Cemetery; married (1) in Tipton County, Tennessee, 2 February 1858, Sarah Jane Lynn, born Portersville, Tennessee, 10 March 1840, died 27 August 1862, buried Salem Church Cemetery, daughter of John Lynn and Elizabeth McQuiston; (2) in Tipton County, Tennessee, 10 November 1863, Sarah Elizabeth Baird, born Tennessee, 17 December 1844, died 22

December 1909, daughter of William Baird and Nancy Jane McQuiston. James became a member of the Salem A.R.P. Church on 30 April 1847. His first wife, Sarah Jane, joined on 20 July 1855 and her son John on 4 August 1877. James, Sarah Jane, John A., and William P. Hindman all died on the family farm which was a few miles south of Brighton.

Children by (1) Sarah Jane Lynn, both born in Tipton County, Tennessee:

a. John Alexander Hindman, born 14 November 1858, died in Tipton County, 17 May 1878, buried Salem A.R.P. Church Cemetery.

b. William P. Hindman, born 8 January 1862, died in Tipton County, 6 July 1878, buried Salem A.R.P. Church Cemetery.

Children by (2) Sarah Elizabeth Baird, all born in Tipton County, Tennessee:

c. James H. Calvin Hindman, born 14 October 1864, died near Brighton, Tennessee, 20 December 1926; married in Tipton County, 11 December 1895, Mary Elizabeth Bell, born Chester County, South Carolina, 1 November 1860, died 1 June 1937, daughter of Robert Brown Bell and Margaret Ann Barnes. Mary's parents moved from South Carolina to Tipton County, Tennessee, in 1886-7. James joined the Salem A.R.P. Church on 21 August 1885, and after he and Mary were married he transferred to the Brighton A.R.P. Church. After their son died in 1917, they moved to Covington, Tipton County, where they joined the A.R.P. church there and James became an elder, but just before he died they returned to Brighton. Child: James Robert Hindman, born near Brighton, Tennessee, 23 March 1897, died of influenza during World War I while aboard ship off the coast of France, 7 October 1917, first buried in the American Cemetery in Brest, France, reburied on 11 June 1920 in the family plot at the Salem Church Cemetery in Tipton County, Tennessee. James had been a member of Company H, 57th Pioneer Infantry. The service was attended by members of the Tipton County American Legion Post No. 67 and other ex-servicemen.

d. Lindsay S. Hindman (called Linn), born 14 April 1867,

killed in a train accident in Tipton County, 23 February 1925, buried Salem A.R.P. Church Cemetery; married in Tipton County, 24 December 1923, Mrs. Martha Eleanor Moore Huffman (called Ella), born 10 September 1870, died 5 August 1958, daughter of John Alexander Moore and Mary Jane McClerkin. Ella had married (1) William Alexander Huffman (1867-1908) by whom she had two sons: Hugh Marion Huffman (1902-1985) and Fentress Maban Huffman (1904- ). The night Linn died he had been walking home after an evening spent at the house of his uncle Hugh Baird. Double tracks of the Illinois Central Railroad passed behind his farmhouse. It is thought that while he was watching a northbound train he stepped on the southbound tracks without noticing an approaching southbound train. His brother discovered his body lying between the tracks, and he was buried the next morning. No children.

e. Clemmie Euphemia Hindman, born 24 January 1872, died in Tipton County, Tennessee, 16 August 1892, buried Salem A.R.P. Church Cemetery; unmarried.

f. Luther Ebenezer Hindman, born 4 December 1874, died Tipton County, Tennessee, 17 May 1957, buried Salem A.R.P. Church Cemetery; married, 15 October 1919, his first cousin Margaret Ann Baird, born 3 October 1884, died Tipton County, 18 November 1977, buried Salem Church Cemetery, daughter of John Lindsay Baird and Sarah Ann McQuiston. On 4 September 1891 Luther joined the Salem A.R.P Church. Later he transferred to the Brighton A.R.P. Church but returned to Salem after he and Margaret were married.

2. Rosanna Wilson Hindman McClerkin (called Rhoda), born Chester County, South Carolina, 16 November 1829, died Brighton, Tipton County, Tennessee, 20 March 1899, buried Salem A.R.P. Church Cemetery; married, 18 September 1850, James Martin McClerkin, born South Carolina, 1 December 1824, died Tipton County, Tennessee, 27 February 1904, buried Salem Church Cemetery, son of James M. McClerkin and Sarah Lathan. (James' niece Elizabeth Martha McClerkin married Rhoda's brother 3-13A3 Alexander Sidney Hindman.) Soon after Rhoda and James were married, they settled on a farm just west of Brighton, Tennessee. James joined the Salem A.R.P. Church on 1 July 1843, Rhoda on 30 April 1847. Children, all born near Brighton, Tennessee:

a. ___ McClerkin, unnamed infant buried in the family plot in the Salem A.R.P. Church Cemetery.

b. Mary Elizabeth McClerkin McLaughlin, born 3 November 1853, died of pneumonia at Atoka, Tennessee, 7 March 1879, buried Salem A.R.P. Church Cemetery; married, at Tipton, Tennessee, 18 March 1874, William R. McLaughlin, born 4 April 1852, died 9 October 1938, son of John McLaughlin and Margaret Wilson. William was a depot agent at Atoka during the 1870's and 1880's. They had only two children both of whom died in infancy and were buried at Salem A.R.P. Church Cemetery. William married (2) ___ and moved to Georgia.

c. Sarah E. B. McClerkin, died 18 June 1858 at the age of two, buried Salem Church Cemetery.

d. Martha Jane "Mattie" McClerkin Simpson, born 1 September 1858, died Memphis, Tennessee, 28 June 1943; married ___ Simpson. They had children.

e. Samuel T. McClerkin, born November 1861, died Tipton County, Tennessee, 6 May 1903, buried Salem A.R.P. Church Cemetery; married (1) in Tipton County, 23 March 1887, Mary Frances Adkinson, born 15 July 1865, died in Tipton County, 16 February 1888, daughter of James Adkinson and Mary ___; (2) in Tipton County, 26 December 1894, Ivy B. Hamilton, daughter of James Wylie Burgess Hamilton and Mary Jane Cotton. Child by (1) Mary Frances Adkinson: (a) Willie Irene McClerkin McLister, born 24 January 1888, died 1967, married Dr. Waldo Alexander Leno McLister, born 6 March 1889, died 1954, son of Dr. William Alexander Leno McLister and Effie Della Dewese; Samuel's children by (2) Ivy B. Hamilton: (b) Lorena McClerkin Jones Allison, born c. 1895, died Corpus Christi, Texas, 10 May 1957, married (1) ___ Jones, (2) Al Allison; (c) ___ McClerkin (boy), born and died January 1898; (d) Herbert H. McClerkin, born 1899, died after 1957, at one time lived in or near Greenbriar, Arkansas; and (e) Eva E. McClerkin (called Missy).

f. William E. McClerkin, born 9 February 1863, died 1 November 1865, buried Salem Cemetery.

g. James Calvin McClerkin, born 1866, died Tipton County, Tennessee, 22 October 1898, buried Salem Church Cemetery; married in Tipton County, 22 November 1886, Margrete Donna Easley (called Maggie), born 27 September 1870, died 12 August 1940, daughter of James Daniel Easley and Mary Jane Pickard. Maggie married (2) George Adkinson whose first wife had died. Children of James and Maggie: (a) Sidney Ernest McClerkin (called Ernest), born 21 August 1887, died 5 February 1960, married (1) 21 July 1909, Gussie Price, born 9 December 1888, died 2 December 1927, (2) Mrs. Sloan; (3) Ola Williams McClerkin (1891-1979), widow of Ernest's brother Moffatt; (b) J. M. McClerkin, died young; (c) Charles Moffatt McClerkin (called Moffatt), born 2 September 1892, died 14 August 1945, married, 22 December 1910, Ola Williams, born 12 November 1891, died 10 December 1979, who married (2) Moffatt's brother Ernest after Moffatt died; (d) Inez McClerkin Williams Tennant, born 21 October 1893, died San Pedro, California, 21 March 1983, married (1) 2 June 1909, James Thomas Williams, born Palestine, Arkansas, 8 September 1888, died Memphis, Tennessee, 1961, divorced in May 1924 and Inez married (2) 29 August 1924, Odie Ernest Tennant, born 29 March 1881, died Granada Hills, California, 20 August 1969; (e) Eva McClerkin, born 1895, married ___ Ashby and moved to Florida; and (f) James Calvin McClerkin Jr., born 9 December 1898, died Memphis, Tennessee, 10 March 1978, married in Tipton County, 25 September 1918, Annie Pearl Turnage, born 8 June 1897, died Covington, Tennessee, 19 February 1975, daughter of John Altha Turnage and Mittie Florence George.

    h. Alice McClerkin, born near Brighton, Tennessee, 24 November 1868, died 18 August 1876, buried Salem A.R.P. Church Cemetery.

3. Alexander Sidney Hindman, born Chester County, South Carolina, 10 December 1832, died Brighton, Tipton County, Tennessee, 9 October 1910, buried Salem A.R.P. Church Cemetery; married in Tipton County, 29 March 1860, Elizabeth Martha McClerkin (called Mattie), born Tennessee, 15 April 1842, died Tipton County 10 June 1927, buried Salem Church Cemetery, daughter of John Maban McClerkin and Ann McQuiston. After their marriage Alexander and Mattie settled on a farm which is presently part of the Tipton County Penal Farm at Brighton. Alexander's father deeded 95 acres of the farm to him as a gift in January 1859. In the 1860's a school, known as the Marshall School, was

built on Alexander's farm. Later he was a school trustee and donated two acres to the board, including the land on which Marshall School stood. Children, all born near Brighton, Tennessee:

a. Mary Annette Hindman McQuiston (called Annie), born 11 February 1861, died of cancer in Bloomington, Tennessee, 13 November 1918, buried Salem A.R.P. Church Cemetery; married in Tipton County, 21 April 1904, James Andrew McQuiston, born Tennessee, 3 April 1846, died Tipton County, 9 January 1922, son of William H. McQuiston and Jane Wilson Allen. James had married (1) Mary Lina Hart (1856-1892). He was a deacon in the Brighton A.R.P. Church and served as church treasurer for many years. No children.

b. James F. Hindman, born 13 July 1863, died 15 October 1864, buried Salem A.R.P. Church Cemetery.

c. Thomas Knox Hindman, born 18 July 1865, died at the Frayser Rest Home in Memphis, Tennessee, 25 March 1957, buried Salem A.R.P. Church Cemetery; unmarried. He farmed with his brothers and lived most of his life on his father's farm near Brighton, Tennessee. At one time he was a director of the Planters Bank in Atoka.

d. Sidney Allen Hindman, born 12 February 1868, died in a hunting accident near Brighton, Tennessee, 4 November 1921, buried Salem A.R.P. Church Cemetery; married in Tipton County, 4 January 1905, Rosa Amanda Miller, born 6 November 1871, died 4 November 1905, daughter of the Rev. John Gardner Miller and Martha Jane Williams. Rosa died only ten months after she and Sidney were married, and he never remarried. He farmed with his brothers near Brighton and was a deacon at the Brighton A.R.P. Church. He was killed while hunting about 400 yards from his house when he tripped on an exposed root, causing his gun to discharge with a fatal shot to his left side.

e. John Hemphill Hindman (called Hemp), born 13 August 1870, died 10 November 1949, buried Salem A.R.P. Church Cemetery; married in Tipton County, 31 December 1903, Sarah Eunice Forsythe (called Eunice), born August 1873, died near Brighton, Tennessee, 21 November 1912, buried Salem A.R.P. Church Cemetery, daughter of Joseph Forsythe and Margaret Elizabeth Sherrill. Hemp and Eunice were members of the Brighton A.R.P. Church. Children: (a) Martha Elizabeth Hindman Tinkler, born 20 July 1905, died 3 March 1965, married Neil Douglas Tinkler, born 21 August 1905, died 28 June 1977, son of David Rainey Tinkler and Martha Lenore Strong; Martha was a high school English teacher at Brighton; (b) James Hemphill Hindman, born 1907, died of a heart attack at Bartlett, Tennessee, 1958, buried Salem Church Cemetery, married Alice Randolph; he was a football coach at Bartlett, Tennessee; and (c) Joseph Alexander Hindman, born 28 February 1910, died 4 February 1912, buried Salem Cemetery.

 f. William Cecil Hindman, born 27 September 1872, died 30 July 1959, buried Salem A.R.P. Church Cemetery; unmarried. He was a farmer in partnership with his brothers near Brighton, Tennessee, and their farm was mentioned in a pamphlet, *Covington and Tipton County, Tennessee, Illustrated* (1915) published by the *Tipton Record*: "[The] Hindman brothers own a splendid farm about two miles from Brighton. In addition to their general farming interests, they are successfully raising pure breed Jersey cattle, Cheviot sheep and Poland China hogs. They also raise considerable port for market." The pamphlet also included photographs of the two-story, frame, antebellum home of the Hindman family.

 g. Maude Eveline Hindman, born 29 August 1877, died at the Coleman Nursing Home in Arlington, Tennessee, 26 June 1953, buried Salem A.R.P. Church Cemetery; unmarried. She lived with her brothers on the family farm near Brighton, Tennessee. In 1953 she and her surviving brothers, Thomas and William, sold their home and moved to the Coleman Nursing Home.

4. Elizabeth Julia Ann Hindman McCormick, born Chester County, South Carolina, 18 January 1835, died near Munford, Tipton County, Tennessee, 8 September 1906, buried Salem A.R.P. Church Cemetery; married in Tipton County, 29 August 1855, Nathaniel Rainey McCormick, born Chester County, South Carolina, 22 March 1830, killed in a train accident at Covington, Tipton County, 15 February 1888, son of Samuel McCormick and Mary Rainey. Nathaniel moved to Tipton County with his parents in 1850. After he and Elizabeth were married, they first lived near Brighton and in 1880 moved to a farm about two miles southwest of Mun-

ford, Tipton County. Their heirs still own the farm, but the original log house was sold to Mike Mize in the early 1980's. Mize reassembled the house on his property east of Atoka and restored it to its original appearance. Nathaniel died after trying to flag a train at Covington near the depot. The train caught his long coat, pulling him beneath, and he died from the injuries a few hours later. Children, all born in Tipton County, Tennessee:

a. Margaret Rosetta Ann McCormick Billings, born 13 June 1856, died near Munford, Tipton County, Tennessee, 4 September 1933, buried Bethel Cumberland Presbyterian Church Cemetery; married in her father's house near Munford, 30 January 1883, Washington Franklin Billings, born 22 October 1853, died near Munford, 2 January 1908, buried Bethel C.P. Church Cemetery, son of George Washington Billings and Jane L. Walker. They lived on a farm a few miles southeast of Munford. Children: (a) ___ Billings (boy), born and died 30 June 1884, (b) Ruth Estelle Billings, born 21 August 1886, died January 1986, buried beside both her husbands in Forest Hill Cemetery, Memphis, Tennessee, married (1) on 20 December 1911, Dr. William Franklin Posey, (2) Walter Winfield Lyles; (c) Carl Rainey Billings, born 24 July 1888, died ___, buried Bethel C.P. Church Cemetery, married Mrs. Oma Lee King Lightfoot, born 14 October 1901, died Munford, Tennessee, 18 June 1989, Oma married (3) John Beaver; (d) ___ Billings (boy), born 29 June 1894, died 30 June 1894; and (e) Paul King Billings, married Massie Norman.

b. William Thomas McCormick (called Tom), born 8 November 1857, died June 1932, buried Munford Cemetery; married in Tipton County, 10 November 1898, Lilly Ada McBride, born 1865, died 1954, buried Munford Cemetery, daughter of William White McBride and Mary Ann Eliza Larimore. For several years during the early 1900's, Tom served as Tipton County's circuit court clerk. Child: ___ McCormick (girl), born 22 September 1899, died 26 September 1899.

c. Laura Eudora McCormick Smith, born 7 September 1859, died May 1945, buried Bethel C.P. Church Cemetery; married in Tipton County, 18 December 1889, Edward Scott Smith, born 1860, died 1932, buried Bethel C.P. Church Cemetery, son of John Alexander Smith and Jerusha D. Walker, and brother of Wyatt Andrew Smith who married Laura's sister Ollie. They lived on a farm near Tipton, Tennessee. Children: (a) Myrtle Clyde Smith, born 1894, died 1968, married John Walter Bomar; he ran a store at Munford for many years; (b) Roger B. Smith (twin to next), born 14 October 1896, died 14 January 1926, unmarried; he clerked at the G. D. McNair store, Tipton, where he also slept and was found shot to death one morning; and (c) Rodney Smith (twin to above), born 14 October 1896, died Gulfport, Mississippi, ___, married Rosie Mae Sawyer.

d. John Wesley McCormick, born 1 March 1861, died Memphis, Tennessee, 22 September 1945, buried Helen Crigger Cemetery, Munford, Tennessee; married in Tipton County, 28 November 1894, Lucy Ophelia Yancey, born 15 August 1876, died 13 May 1967, buried Helen Crigger Cemetery, daughter of Rufus William Yancey and Martha Bernice Gailor. In the early 1900's John and Lucy moved to Memphis where he was a member of the police department. Children: (a) Clifton T. McCormick, born April 1896, died January 1980, married Sadie ___ and lived in Nashville; and (b) Sadie Mary McCormick, born 26 March 1901, died in Florida, 1 September 1987, married William Horace McDonald and lived in Daytona Beach, Florida.

e. James Rainey McCormick, born 17 November 1862, died of pneumonia and malaria in Covington, Tennessee, 4 November 1902, buried Bethel C.P. Church Cemetery; married in Tipton County, Tennessee, 16 November 1892, Margaret J. Faires, daughter of William J. Faires and Elizabeth ___. Children: (a) ___ McCormick (boy) born and died on 12 September 1894; (b) ___ McCormick, (girl) born and died on 15 February 1898; and (c) Faires Rainey McCormick, born 31 August 1901, still living in 1989, married (1) Virgin (*sic*) McCalla, born 19 March 1899, died 10 July 1963, Faires married (2) Mrs. Helen Lyles Childress, daughter of Walter Winfield Lyles.

f. Claudius "Claude" McCormick, born 30 September 1864, died 26 December 1935, buried Helen Crigger Cemetery, Munford, Tennessee; married Winnie Norris, born 4 August 1881, died 26 December 1969, buried Helen Crigger Cemetery. Claude farmed his parents' land and lived in the old family home. Children: (a) Norris Rainey McCormick, born 10 October 1906, still living in 1989, married at Covington, Tennessee, 26 December 1939, Margaret Ann Furgerson (*sic*), daughter of W. Lanier Furgerson and Marguerite Hewitt; Norris taught agriculture at Brighton High School for more than forty years; (**b**) Mary Julia McCormick, born 1 November 1908, still living in 1989, married Luther Allen Fredrickson, born 21 October 1907, died 1 March 1979, buried Rose Hill Cemetery, Sardis, Mississippi; they moved to Sardis in the early 1930's; (**c**) James Wilmer "Red" McCormick, born 1911, died 1975, married Margie Simonton; and (**d**) Claude Hindman McCormick, born 22 August 1919, married Virginia Ruth Murphy, daughter of Hilliard Murphy.

g. Mary Willetta McCormick, born 16 September 1866, died 9 August 1868, buried at the Samuel McCormick family plot in the Salem A.R.P. Church Cemetery.

h. Othello Stewart McCormick, born 14 September 1868, died 3 September 1948; married in Tipton County, 24 March 1920, Mrs. Margaret Lucile Witherington Abernathy (called Lucile), born 6 December 1885, died 2 December 1968, daughter of Dr. James Barney Witherington and Mary Agnes McLaughlin. Lucile had married (1) William Mortimer Abernathy (died 1912) and had one child, William Mortimer Abernathy Jr. (1909-1976). After Othello and Lucile were married, they lived briefly at the old McCormick home southwest of Munford, Tennessee, then moved to the old J. S. Dickerson home on Tipton Road in Munford. Children: (**a**) Mary Agnes McCormick, born 2 May 1921, married her first cousin once removed John Walter "Jack" Bomar Jr., son of John Walter Bomar and Myrtle Clyde Smith; and (**b**) James Stewart McCormick, born 10 October 1926, unmarried.

i. Leslie Ernest McCormick, born 24 June 1870, died of pneumonia on 17 December 1896, buried Salem A.R.P. Church Cemetery; unmarried.

j. Olive Estelle McCormick Smith (called Ollie), born 13 May 1873, died in Barrettville, Tennessee, 19 January 1957, buried Bethel C.P. Church Cemetery near Tipton; married on 30 October 1901, Wyatt Andrew Smith, born 31 March 1871, died 26 April 1944, buried Bethel C.P. Church Cemetery, son of John Alexander Smith and Jerusha D. Walker and brother of Edward Scott Smith who married Ollie's sister Laura. Ollie and Wyatt were married in a buggy under a tree in the Bethel C.P. Church yard. At first they lived on a farm near Barrettville and in about 1905 moved to another farm just east of Barrettville. They were members of the Richland A.R.P. Church at Rosemark. Children: (**a**) Leslie Ernest Smith, born 7 September 1902, died 25 May 1986, married Ida Mai (*sic*) Liles; (**b**) Harry Avant Smith, born 5 January 1904, died of pneumonia on 5 January 1919; (**c**) Goldie Smith, born 12 August 1906, still living in 1989, married John McLauglin; (**d**) ___ Smith (boy), born and died 6 February 1909; (**e**) Velna Smith, born 30 September 1911, still living in 1989, married James Archie Wallace; (**f**) Pauline Smith, born 6 July 1913, still living in 1989; married John Leon McCullough; and (**g**) Maggie Lura Smith, born 20 May 1916, married in Hernando, Mississippi, 30 August 1956, Gilbert Austin Brown, born 19 July 1921.

5. Sarah Smith Hindman McCormick, born Chester County, South Carolina, 20 August 1837, died Brighton, Tipton County, Tennessee, 12 July 1879, buried Salem A.R.P. Cemetery; married in Tipton County, 23 January 1861, George Newton McCormick, born Chester County, South Carolina, 17 August 1838, died Brighton, Tennessee, 17 July 1911, son of Samuel McCormick and Mary Rainey. For most of their married lives, Sarah and George lived on a farm about two miles southeast of Brighton, and at one time George owned a half interest in a cotton gin in the town. Sarah died of puerperal fever twelve days after giving birth to twins who themselves died soon after. George married (2) on 7 February 1883, Nancy Moffatt McClerkin, born 12 August 1853, died 7 December 1913, daughter of John Maban McClerkin and Ann McQuiston. Nancy and George had four children: ___ McClerkin (boy), born 1 September 1884, died 8 November 1890; Grover Newton McCormick, born 1885, died 1968, a Memphis lawyer and a Tennessee state legislator at one time; Allen Moffatt McCormick, born 8 August 1888, died September 1890; and Lucia Earle McCormick, married Jesse Clyde Stancill.

Children of Sarah and George:

a. N. Bate McCormick, born 1862, died 1947, buried Salem A.R.P. Church Cemetery as are his wife and children; married Laura Kate Paine, born 1870, died 1930. In February 1886 N. Bate McCormick was graduated from

the Memphis Hospital Medical College. Later he
practiced in Millington, Shelby County, Tennessee.
Children: (a) Laura Fenner McCormick, born 27 July
1895, died 29 July 1902; and (b) B. M. McCormick, born
3 November 1902, died 1 November 1910.

b. William Samuel McCormick (called Sam), born 10 March
1864, died 1941; married in 1890, Ora Burrow, born
1867, died 1928, daughter of Robert Freeman Burrow and
Martha Phillips. Sam was a physician in Arlington,
Shelby County, Tennessee. When he first moved there
in 1884, he practiced in a one-room log cabin. After
he married he moved to a house three miles north of
Arlington but returned to the town in 1919 and lived
on Greenlee Street. In 1930 ill health forced him
into partial retirement. For many years he was a
member of the Shelby County Court and served as its
chairman for four years. Children: (a) Sam Eva
McCormick, born 1892, died ___, unmarried; (b) Rudolph
B. McCormick (twin to next), born 18 August 1894, died
___, married Mildred Durr; and (c) Ralph N. McCormick
(twin to above), born 18 August 1894, died ___,
unmarried.

c. Oscar Bingham McCormick, born 26 May 1866, died
Bloomington, Tennessee, 13 November 1930; married in
Tipton County, Tennessee, 20 November 1889, Mary Cockrell (called May), born 31 August 1868, died of a
heart attack on 19 December 1924, daughter of Thomas
E. S. Cockrell and Sarah Tipton. May's fatal heart
attack occurred while she was shopping with her daughter Ruth in the Tennessee Hardware Company in Covington. Oscar was a farmer. Children: (a) Fay McCormick, born 22 May 1891, died 12 July 1891; (b) Charles
McCormick, born December 1892, died October 1920,
married Clara McCullough; (c) Katherine McCormick,
born 1894, died 1976, married in Tipton County, 15
August 1917, James Fred Blanchard, born 14 June 1892,
died 2 July 1952; (d) Mary Ruth McCormick (called
Ruth), born 21 February 1901, died 1 January 1976,
married (1) Edgar Whitehorn (called Jack), (2) Thomas
McDow; (e) Marvin Edward McCormick (called Bill), born
1903, still alive in 1989, married on 23 November
1924, Mary Lila Byrd, born 1 August 1904, still alive
in 1989, daughter of Theo Harris Byrd and Lillian
Smith; (f) Oscar William McCormick (called Jab), born
___, still alive in 1989, married (1) Elizabeth Cox,

(2) Pearl ___; and (g) Carl Winsett McCormick (called Ted), married Ivee Sheppard, and lived in Sacramento, California.

    d. Lorenzo Thomas McCormick, born 11 June 1868, died 14 April 1875, buried Salem A.R.P. Church Cemetery. Lorenzo's tragic death occurred when he was with his father and brothers who were in a field burning a twenty-foot stump. The flaming stump collapsed suddenly, fell on Lorenzo, and crushed his skull, killing him instantly. It is said that his father's hair turned gray soon after.

    e. ___ McCormick (boy), born 29 March 1870, died 9 April 1870.

    f. Estes Venoy McCormick, born September 1875, died Memphis, Tennessee, 1950, buried Salem A.R.P. Church Cemetery; married, 1911, Robbie Moffatt Moore, born 31 January 1876, died 20 January 1970, buried Salem A.R.P. Church Cemetery, daughter of John Alexander Moore and Mary Jane McClerkin. Until December 1946, Estes and Robbie lived on the old G. N. McCormick farm about two miles southeast of Brighton. They then moved to Kenwood Street, Brighton, to a house bought from the Wade Williamson estate. Estes was a charter stockholder in the Brighton Savings Bank and was a long-time member of its Board of Directors. In June 1948 Estes was among nine stockholders who established the Brighton Grocery Company, Inc., which was built on the site of the old Majestic Hotel on Main Street in Brighton. The same building now houses the Handy Center. In his youth Estes was an outstanding baseball player. He continued to be an avid sports fan throughout his life and also enjoyed hunting and fishing.

    g. ___ McCormick (boy and twin to next), born 1 July 1879, died 16 July 1879.

    h. ___ McCormick (girl and twin to above), born 1 July 1879, died 18 July 1879.

6. Thomas Stewart Hindman, born near Brighton, Tennessee, 2 February 1840, died 20 August 1916, buried Salem A.R.P. Church Cemetery; married in Tipton County, 15 November 1876, Margaret Rosanna McCullough, born Tennessee, 10

March 1853, died 17 October 1897, buried Salem A.R.P. Church Cemetery, daughter of Robert Boyd McCullough and Elizabeth Moore. Thomas first joined the Mount Paran A.R.P. Church but in 1896 transferred his membership to the Brighton A.R.P. Church. Children, all born in Tipton County, Tennessee:

a. Ardelle Hindman Goodlett, born 22 October 1877, died 22 June 1970, buried Salem A.R.P. Church Cemetery; married in Tipton County, 1 January 1919, Gordon Goodlett, born 22 September 1885, died 29 December 1959, buried Salem Church Cemetery. Gordon was reared near Nashville, Tennessee, and moved to Tipton County in 1908. He was a farmer, livestock raiser, and painter. In 1946 he moved to Memphis, Tennessee, but returned to Tipton County before he died. Child: Dudley Kenneth Goodlett, born and died 13 October 1920.

b. William Stuart "Willie" Hindman, born 7 October 1879, died in Brighton, Tennessee, 18 October 1959, buried Munford Cemetery, Covington, Tennessee; married in Randolph, Tennessee, 27 December 1905, Susan Bertha Campbell (called Bertha), born 9 March 1880, died 31 December 1974, buried Munford Cemetery, Covington, Tennessee, daughter of Samuel Campbell and Ada Barton. Willie was a farmer and livestock dealer. He was also a member of the Brighton A.R.P. Church and served as a deacon. His wife, Bertha, was a life-long member of the New Salem (Flatwoods) Methodist Church. Children: (a) Leroy Earl Hindman (called Jack), born 7 October 1906, killed in World War I on 11 July 1943, buried Munford Cemetery, Covington, Tennessee; (b) Ada Rose Hindman, born 15 January 1908, still alive in 1989, married, 24 November 1937, William Brown Anthony, born 16 July 1903, still alive in 1989, son of Thomas Bascom Anthony and Margaret Elizabeth Whitley; Ada Rose was a teacher; (c) Gerald Paul Hindman, born 29 January 1910, still alive in 1989, married Ruth Sacra; and (d) Willie Bertha Hindman (called Willie B.), born 21 November 1911, died 6 November 1975, buried Munford Cemetery, Covington, Tennessee, unmarried; at first she was a teacher then became a businesswoman.

c. Alice Mai (*sic*) Hindman Bell, born 14 December 1881, died Memphis, Tennessee, 18 May 1858, buried Salem A.R.P. Church Cemetery; married, 14 October 1928,

William Sinclair Bell, born Pottsville, Pope County, Arkansas, 29 September 1868, died Russellville, Pope County, Arkansas, 23 December 1948, buried Pisgah Cemetery in Russellville, son of Ewart Adams Bell and Rebecca Susan Dickey. When Alice married William, he was a widower with four children. He was an accountant and had the title of Chief Deputy Sheriff of Tax Collection in Pope County, a job he held for more than twenty-five years. He and Alice lived in Russellville, and after he died she returned to Tipton County, Tennessee, where she lived out her life.

d. Cora Lee Hindman McGowan, born 20 February 1884, died during the World War I flu epidemic, 28 September 1918, buried Salem A.R.P. Church Cemetery; married at her father's home west of Brighton, 21 December 1909, Joseph Beaty McGowan, born Tipton County, 26 February 1884, died 23 September 1951, buried Salem A.R.P. Church Cemetery, son of William Oliver McGowan and Margaret J. English. Children, all born Tipton County: (a) Mary Grace McGowan, born 21 October 1910, still alive in 1989, married on 10 October 1929, Francis Baird; (b) Justin Berve McGowan, born 15 October 1912, still alive in 1989, married ___; and (c) Laurie Thomas McGowan, born 5 October 1915, still living in 1989, married on 24 December 1942, Dorothy Watts.

e. Robert Olien Hindman (called Olien), born 29 September 1886, died Brighton, Tennessee, 24 December 1972, buried Salem A.R.P. Church Cemetery; married, 30 March 1915, Gracie Pauline Smith (called Pauline), born Brighton, Tennessee, 23 November 1888, died Covington, Tennessee, 15 December 1965, buried Salem A.R.P. Cemetery, daughter of Augusta Washington Smith Jr. (called Tude) and Lizzie Almeta Vashti McLister. Olien and Pauline lived most of their lives in a frame house on the northeast corner of Woodlawn and Old Highway 51 in Brighton. They were members of the Brighton A.R.P. Church. Children: (a) Agnes Nell Hindman, born 6 September 1915, died 23 March 1969, married Alexander Baxter Cashion, born 29 October 1914, died 11 October 1981, son of James Futhey Cashion and Margaret Elmina McLister; and (b) Robert Orrell Hindman, born 19 November 1917, married Willie Durham; they live in Memphis.

f. Charles Estes Hindman, born 1889, died in Bolivar,

Tennessee, 1959, buried Salem A.R.P. Church Cemetery; unmarried. He was a farmer and a member of the Brighton A.R.P. Church.

g. Myrtle Roselle Hindman Escue, born 2 October 1893, died Brownsville, Haywood County, Tennessee, 22 November 1981, buried Salem A.R.P. Church Cemetery; married on 12 June 1916, Albert James Escue, born ___, died 1 January 1969, buried Haywood County, Tennessee. Myrtle and Albert lived most of their married lives in Brownsville, Tennessee. Child: Albert Hindman Escue, born 4 April 1917, died 22 June 1919, buried Salem A.R.P. Church Cemetery.

h. Thomas Sidney Hindman, born 9 May 1896, died of a heart attack in Brighton, Tennessee, 16 July 1957, buried Munford Cemetery, Covington, Tennessee; married (1) on 18 June 1919, Bessie Mai (*sic*) Clements, born 2 June 1897, died after childbirth at Saint Joseph Hospital in Memphis, Tennessee, 12 February 1920, buried Salem A.R.P. Church Cemetery, daughter of Benjamin Lafayette Clements and Magnolia Zuritha Roberts; Thomas married (2), 28 November 1924, Nora Elaine Gee, born 12 August 1897, died 10 October 1962, buried Munford Cemetery, Covington, Tennessee, daughter of James R. Gee and Mary Ophelia Ashe. Thomas was a World War I veteran. For many years he lived in Memphis where he worked at the Continental Baking Company. Also, in about 1935 he joined the Lindsay Memorial Presbyterian Church and was a deacon. His fatal heart attack occurred while he was changing a tire at his farm near Brighton. Thomas's first wife, Bessie, was graduated from Tennessee Normal (now Memphis State), and in 1918-19 she taught at Brighton High School. Child by (1) Bessie: Thomas Sidney Hindman Jr., born Memphis, Tennessee, 11 February 1920, died as did his mother at St. Joseph Hospital in Memphis, 12 February 1920, buried in his mother's arms in the Salem A.R.P. Church Cemetery.

7. Mary Joanna Hindman McCormick (called Dannie), born near Bloomington, Tennessee, 10 November 1842, died Shelby County, Tennessee, 1919, buried Salem A.R.P. Church Cemetery; married in Tipton County, Tennessee, 9 February 1875, John Leander McCormick, born Chester County, South Carolina, May 1846, died Hansonhurst, Tennessee, 1923, buried Salem A.R.P. Church Cemetery, son of Samuel McCor-

mick and Mary Rainey. At first, Dannie and John were members of the Salem A.R.P. Church in Tipton County but transferred to the Richland A.R.P. Church at Rosemark in 1887 when they moved to that area. Children, all born in Tipton County, Tennessee:

a.  Lomas Everett McCormick, born January 1876, died Covington, Tennessee, 14 July 1941, buried Salem A.R.P. Church Cemetery; married Cora Jemima McQuiston, born ___, died 5 March 1934, buried Salem A.R.P. Church Cemetery, daughter of Thomas Chisolm McQuiston and Calpuria Raymond. Lomas and Cora first lived near Rosemark, Tennessee, but moved to Covington c. 1910 where he ran a hardware store and later owned and ran a dairy behind his home on Tipton Street. They were members of the Covington A.R.P. Church in which Lomas was a deacon and at one time a Sunday school superintendant. Children, all born near Rosemark, Tennessee:  (a) Willard Carroll McCormick, born 2 March 1903, died at Memphis, Tennessee, 16 February 1958, married Blanche Lofton, born 20 August 1903, died Covington, Tennessee, 2 March 1989, daughter of John Lofton and Effie Ford; and (b) Everett Raymond McCormick, born 2 December 1905, died Covington, Tennessee, 3 October 1976, married in Covington, 9 December 1930, Elizabeth Fuqua Teasley, born 1909, still living in 1989, daughter of Dr. John Osburn Teasley and Annie Mae Fuqua.

b.  Viola Gertie McCormick, born 20 January 1878, died Tipton County, Tennessee, 17 January 1881, buried Salem A.R.P. Church Cemetery.

c.  Roscoe Marvin McCormick, born Tipton County, Tennessee, 25 July 1880, died Millington, Tennessee, 16 November 1942, buried Kerrville Cemetery at Kerrville, Tennessee; married Alta Simmons, born 30 October 1881, died 15 December 1964. They lived most of their lives near Millington, Tennessee, and were members of the Richland A.R.P. Church. No children.

d.  ___ McCormick (boy), born 24 September 1882, died 25 November 1882, buried Salem A.R.P. Church Cemetery.

e.  Nancy Grace McCormick Moffatt; married Willard Erskine Moffatt. Children: (a) James Erskine Moffatt; and (b) John Hindman Moffatt.

f. Clarence L. McCormick (called Jock), born January 1886, died March 1925; married Agnes McCalla, born near Rosemark, Tennessee, 1888, died Kerrville, Tennessee, 19 June 1924. Child: ___ McCormick, died on the day of its birth.

8. Jane Helen Hindman Caskey (called Helen), born Tipton County, Tennessee, 20 December 1844, died Tipton County, 20 May 1915, buried Salem Cemetery; married her first cousin 3-13D4 James Caskey Jr. See their children under his listing.

B. Rosanna W. Caskey Gourley, born Chester County, South Carolina, 1808, died ___; married in Chester County, Robert Gourley, born c. 1808, died ___. They remained in Chester County and at first were members of the Smyrna Associate Presbyterian Church. On 4 May 1844 they switched to the Catholic Presbyterian Church and in 1847 became charter members of Upper Catholic Presbyterian Church which later became Pleasant Grove Presbyterian Church. Known children, all born in Chester County, South Carolina:

1. Mary Gourley, born c. 1831, died after 1884; probably unmarried. She lived in Chester County, South Carolina, with her uncle 3-13C John Caskey until he died.

2. James Gourley, born c. 1834, died after 1884.

3. John Gourley, born c. 1838

4. Hugh Caskey Gourley, born 1844, baptized at Catholic Presbyterian Church in Chester County, 2 June 1844.

5. Elizabeth Rosanna Gourley, born 1847, baptized at Catholic Presbyterian Church in Chester County, 30 May 1847.

C. John Caskey, born Chester County, South Carolina, c. 1810, died in Chester County after 1883; married Agnes Marion (called Nancy), born c. 1808, died in the 1850's, daughter of William Marion and Jennet Stewart. John was a member of the Catholic Presbyterian Church in Chester County until 4 November 1866 when he was dismissed "to join some Presbyterian Church in the West whither he is about to move." Probably, he moved to Tipton County, Tennessee, with the children of his deceased brother 3-13D4 James, but he soon returned to Chester County where he was listed in the 1870 census. His wife was a charter member of Upper Catholic Presbyterian Church which later became Pleasant Grove Presbyterian Church. The only deed found on them in Chester County was dated 23 February 1846. In it John, Agnes, and Rosey Marion (Agnes's sister) sold ten acres to Robert Brice Jr. for $100. The land was on Rocky Creek and was bounded by tracts owned by John Caskey, Robert Bryce, and William Brice. Agnes and Rosey signed with their marks, and Agnes signed the dower release on 3 March 1846 (Book FF, pp. 165-6). No children.

D. James Caskey, born Chester County, South Carolina, *c.* 1812, died in Chester County in the 1860's, buried Hopewell Church Cemetery; married *c.* 1834, Letitia Wilson, born South Carolina, *c.* 1813, died Chester County, mid-1860's, buried Hopewell A.R.P. Church Cemetery. After he died most of his children moved to Tipton County, Tennessee, where his older sister 3-13A Mary Hindman and her family had moved in 1837. Children:

1. Thomas Caskey, born Chester County, South Carolina, December 1834, died Chester County, 1900-10; married in Chester County, *c.* 1866, Matilda Wallace, born Chester County, January 1841, died after 1910, daughter of William Wallace and Sarah Knox. At first, Thomas was a teacher, but he soon turned to farming. In November 1857 he joined the Hopewell Church and in July 1861 switched to the Salem A.R.P. Church in Tipton County, Tennessee, where he had moved with his brothers John, William, R. Calvin, and James Caskey Jr. during the winter of 1860-1. When the Civil War broke out, he returned to Chester County in order to enlist there in the Confederate Army (Company H, 24th South Carolina Regiment). After the war he remained in Chester County. Children, all born in Chester County:

    a. William Caskey, born *c.* 1868, died *c.* 1896 at the age of about twenty-eight years.

    b. Sarah Caskey, died at the age of about four years,

    c. James Joseph Caskey, born January 1873, died after 1924; unmarried. He was a blacksmith.

    d. Hugh W. Caskey, born *c.* 1876, died after 1924; unmarried.

    e. Mary B. Caskey Tennant, born February 1878, died after 1924; married in Chester County, *c.* 1908, Henry O. Tennant, a widower with three children. They lived near Blackstock, South Carolina. Known child: William Thomas Tennant, born c. 1909.

    f. ___ Caskey. Nothing more is known of this child.

    g. Elizabeth Caskey (called Bessie), born September 1882, died in Chester County, South Carolina, 18 October 1917; unmarried.

2. William Caskey, born Chester County, South Carolina, March 1836, died Gibson County, Indiana, 1920, buried Montgomery Cemetery, Oakland City, Indiana; married in Chester County, South Carolina, 10 February 1859, Mary Jane McWilliams, born Indiana, May 1843, died Gibson County, Indiana, 1926, buried Montgomery Cemetery in Oakland City, Indiana, daughter of David C. McWilliams and his first wife, Elizabeth ___. William and Mary Jane were married by the Rev. Robert Wilson Brice. In the winter of 1860-1, William and Mary Jane moved with William's brothers John, Thomas, R. Calvin, and James Caskey Jr. to Tipton County, Tennessee, where their aunt 3-13A Mary Caskey Hindman lived. In July 1861 they joined the Salem A.R.P. Church, and on 18 October 1862 William enlisted as a private in the Confederate Army, Company C, 12th Tennessee Cavalry. Later he changed his allegiance and joined the Union Army in Company G, 56th Volunteer Infantry. In the early 1870's William and Mary Jane moved first to Illinois then to Gibson County, Indiana, where others from Chester County, South Carolina, also lived. Children:

    a. James Arthur Caskey, born Tipton County, Tennessee, 1862, died Gibson County, Indiana, 1955, buried Archer Cemetery, Princeton, Indiana; married Tabitha Wilhite, born 1866, died 1929. Children, all born in Gibson County, Indiana: (a) Ora E. Caskey, born 15 July 1892, died 5 June 1984, buried Archer Cemetery, unmarried; (b) Arthur W. Caskey, born 1898, died 1950, buried Archer Cemetery, unmarried; (c) Margaret Caskey Peva, born 1900, married ___ Peva; (d) Clarence E. Caskey, born 3 September 1904, died 12 August 1978, buried Augusta Cemetery, Augusta, Indiana, married Carmi Norrick; and (e) Ernest B. Caskey, born 26 April 1907, died 20 August 1974, buried Archer Cemetery, unmarried.

    b. Mary R. Caskey McClaery (sic), born Tipton County, Tennessee, c. 1869, died ___; married John McClaery.

They lived near Evansville, Indiana. Known child: Carl McClaery.

c. David C. Caskey, born Tipton County, Tennessee, May 1871, died 1960, buried Montgomery Cemetery, Oakland City, Indiana; unmarried.

d. Sarah Caskey, born Illinois, c. 1873, died Gibson County, Indiana, after 1880 but while still a child, buried Eden Cemetery near Oakland City, Indiana.

e. Robert Nelson Caskey, born Gibson County, Indiana, 1875, died ___; married Della ___. Children, all born in Gibson County, Indiana: (**a**) Oma Olive Caskey Bent, born 6 February 1900, died October 1976, married George Bent, born 1898, died 1970, both buried Walnut Hill Cemetery, Fort Branch, Indiana; (**b**) Harvey Turner Caskey, born 27 August 1902, died 2 January 1984, buried Shiloh Cemetery in Hazelton, Indiana, married Alta McRoberts; (**c**) Harold H. Caskey, born 3 May 1904, still living in 1989, married, 3 May 1924, Ruth L. May; (**d**) Elvis Adrian Caskey, born 14 June 1910, died October 1972, married Dana Miley; (**e**) Erma Estal Caskey Meier, born 11 March 1912, still living in 1989, married Otto Meier; (**f**) Rosa Cleutis Caskey West, born 2 August 1914, still living in 1989, married Artmer West; (**g**) Eula Mae Caskey Schoonover, born 4 February 1916, still living in 1989, married Richard Schoonover; (**h**) Odelia Clarris Caskey, born 6 September 1919, died 20 September 1919; and (**i**) Imogene Caskey Brown, born 13 March 1921, still living in 1989, married Robert Brown.

f. Alice B. Caskey Burns, born Gibson County, Indiana, 3 August 1878, died 9 April 1977, buried Spurgeon Cemetery, Spurgeon, Indiana; married Frank Burns, born 28 March 1869, died 10 October 1917. Children: (**a**) Paul Burns (twin to next), born 10 July 1904; (**b**) Basil Burns (twin to above), born 10 July 1904; (**c**) Flora Burns, born 1908, died 1968; and (**d**) Carl Burns, born 1916, died 1929.

g. William G. Caskey, born Gibson County, Indiana. He lived in or near English, Indiana.

h. Thomas L. Caskey, born Gibson County, Indiana, 17 June 1883, died 1979; married Daisy O'Nell, born 31 March

1883, died 1918. Known children: (**a**) Glenn Caskey, born 6 April 1904; (**b**) Lidy Jane Caskey; and (**c**) Howard C. Caskey, born 1 November 1909, died 1 January 1910.

3. John Caskey, born Chester County, South Carolina, 1837, died after 1882; unmarried. During the winter of 1860-1, he moved with his brothers Thomas, R. Calvin, William, and James Caskey Jr. to Tipton County, Tennessee, and on 18 October 1862 he enlisted in the Confederate Army in Company C, 12th Tennessee Cavalry.

4. James Caskey Jr., born Chester County, South Carolina, 14 November 1838, died Tipton County, Tennessee, 1 July 1894, buried Indian Creek Cemetery in the Holly Grove Community, Tipton County; married in Tipton County, 8 December 1861, his first cousin 3-13A8 Jane Helen Hindman (called Helen), born Tipton County, 20 December 1844, died Tipton County, 20 May 1915, buried Indian Creek Cemetery, Tipton County, daughter of 3-13A Mary Caskey and William Hindman. In the winter of 1860-1, James moved with his brothers Thomas, William, R. Calvin, and John to Tipton County where they settled in the Sixth Civil District. James joined the Salem A.R.P. Church in July 1861, and Helen joined in 1870. In the 1870's they moved to the Holly Grove Community where James's aunt 3-13E Esther Caskey Mills lived as did his uncle 3-13H Thomas Caskey Jr. After Thomas died James bought Thomas's farm and homestead where James and Helen lived out their lives. Children:

  a. Mary Joanna Caskey Baskin (called Dannie), born Tipton County, Tennessee, 5 October 1862, died Tipton County, 6 December 1905; married in Tipton County, 17 August 1880, Andrew Jackson Baskin, born November 1862, died Tipton County, 26 August 1910, son of David Jefferson Baskin and (1) Louisa Adkinson. Children: (**a**) Ruth Eveline Baskin Murphy, born 12 December 1883, died 28 October 1952, married, 10 October 1899, Michael Francis Murphy, born 17 August 1872, died 21 October 1939; (**b**) Edward Lorenzo Baskin, born 1884, died 26 September 1958, married in 1910, Mrs. Geneva Gatlin Sarten (called Eva), widow of Dixie Sarten whom she had married in 1907; (**c**) Gertrude Baskin Gillihan, born *c.* 1891, died 22 September 1920, married on 28 September 1910, William H. Gillihan, son of Andrew Jackson Gillihan and Sarah Katherine Brewer; (**d**) Julia Baskin Wade Smith, married (1) on 4 October 1914, J. Warren

Wade, later divorced, (2) Samuel Edward Smith who was born ___, died April 1940; (e) John Franklin Baskin, born 2 May 1898, died 22 March 1977, married on 24 December 1923, Etta Pearlee Yount, born 31 August 1905, still living in 1989, daughter of James Malachi Yount and Mary Etta Shipp; (f) Ernest Baskin, born 4 July 1900, died 24 October 1949, married on 27 September 1925, Minerva Irene Griggs, born 14 August 1909, died 9 September 1979, daughter of Henderson Pickard Griggs and Vera Victoria Gillihan; (g) ___ Baskin, died infancy; and (h) ___ Baskin, died infancy.

b. Sarah Letitia Caskey Gwinn, born Tipton County, Tennessee, 18 March 1865, died Tipton County, 4 May 1941, buried Indian Creek Cemetery; married in Tipton County, 16 January 1885, 3-13E1b Hugh Alonzo Gwinn, born Tipton County, 4 March 1861, died Tipton County, 12 March 1927, buried Indian Creek Cemetery, son of Robert McLennan Gwinn and 3-13E1 Mary Anna Mills. Sarah and Hugh lived in the Holly Grove Community in Tipton County until the mid-1910's when they lived a few years in Mississippi County, Arkansas. In the late 1910's they returned to Tipton County where they lived briefly in the Oak Grove Community then returned to Holly Grove in the mid-1920's. Children, all born in Tipton County, Tennessee: (a) Annie Mae Gwinn Fryer, born 28 November 1885, died Covington, Tennessee, 20 December 1974, married, 22 September 1923, William Edmon Fryer, born Saline County, Illinois, 6 September 1886, died 31 March 1966, son of Richard Fryer and Mary Jane Reed; (b) Robert Lee Guinn (*sic*; some family members spelled their names *Guinn*, not *Gwinn*), born 4 November 1887, died 11 July 1867, married, 18 November 1911, Eula Agnes Huffman, daughter of John Franklin Huffman and 3-13E2e Rosanna Mills; (c) Modenia Pearl Gwinn Mills, born 2 September 1889, died May 1975, married Charles Fred Mills; (d) Henrietta Guinn (*sic*), born 3 July 1891, died of pneumonia at Saint Joseph Hospital, Memphis, following a kidney operation, 19 April 1925, unmarried; (e) Amanda Arene Gwinn Thompson (called Mandie), born 30 August 1893, died Covington, Tennessee, 6 December 1960, married in Marion, Arkansas, 23 August 1930, John L. Thompson (called Jack), born ___, died June 1932; (f) Melvin Alton Gwinn, born 31 March 1896, died Memphis, Tennessee, 27 July 1970, married, 25 February 1917, Lillie Mae Goforth, born 3 June 1899, died 25

February 1964, daughter of William Monroe Goforth and Sarah Catherine Coats; (g) Estes McLennan Guinn (*sic*, called Shorty) born 27 August 1898, died Covington, Tennessee, 20 May 1968, unmarried; (h) Reatha Dawsie Gwinn, born 16 November 1901, died in Covington, Tennessee, 30 January 1979, unmarried; (i) Samuel Arnold Gwinn, born 19 December 1904, died in Covington, Tennessee, 30 October 1976, married, 15 November 1924, Beryl Inez Walton, born 1 September 1907, still living in 1989, daughter of George Anderson Walton and Annie Maria Ladd (Samuel and Beryl were the grandparents of David A. Gwinn who provided the information on the descendants of 3-13 Julianna Graham Caskey); and (j) George Olien Gwinn, born 2 April 1906, died 15 June 1907, buried Indian Creek Cemetery.

c. William Francis Caskey, born Tipton County, Tennessee, 28 September 1867, died young.

d. Logan S. Caskey, born Tipton County, Tennessee, 24 January 1870, died 12 April 1873.

e. Ella Florence Caskey Lawrence (called Florence), born Tipton County, Tennessee, 15 September 1873, died Tipton County, 7 October 1952, buried Indian Creek Cemetery; married in Tipton County, 16 December 1901, Thomas Jefferson Lawrence, born Canada, 3 June 1872, died Tipton County, Tennessee, 19 December 1949, buried Indian Creek Cemetery. In 1888 Tom's parents moved to the United States, settling in Buffalo, New York, and in 1896 he left home to travel south. When he reached Tennessee he stopped for the night in the Holly Grove Community of Tipton County where he slept in a barn belonging to William Amos Rose. Rose found Tom in the morning, invited him to breakfast, and persuaded him to stay as a boarder. He did so until 1901 when he married Florence and moved to the James Caskey Jr. farm which Tom and Florence later bought after James's widow died. A self-educated man, Tom read law and in December 1917 became the magistrate of Civil District #2. Subsequently, he served many terms on the county court, retiring in 1948. He also was a member of Tipton County's school board, 1921-30, and was a member of the county's Democratic executive committee, serving once as chairman. Other memberships included those in Woodmen of the World, Knights of the Pythias, and the Liberty Lodge #265 of the

Independent Order of Odd Fellows. When he retired in 1948, Dr. John Marion Crigger, another long-time member of the court, said, "Although I have frequently been on the opposite side from the retiring justice, I have never doubted his honesty and convictions." Dr. Crigger added that he would miss Tom's "thundering voice." Tom and Florence were members of the Holly Grove Cumberland Presbyterian Church. They had one adopted child: James Gayle Kinney Lawrence (son of Florence's first cousin once removed, 3-13D9b(a) Eula G. Lockart and her husband, Thurman Kinney) born 18 July 1910, killed in Tipton County, 4 March 1949, buried Helen Crigger Cemetery, Memphis, married (1) 24 December 1927, Bernice Irene Gay, (2) 28 February 1932, Lena Frances Huggins, and (3) Marie Delancy who murdered him.

f. Euphemia R. Caskey, born Tipton County, Tennessee, 12 December 1874, died 4 May 1878.

g. ___ Caskey (girl), born and died in Tipton County, 11 December 1876.

h. Edward A. Caskey, born Tipton County, 5 April 1879, died 18 January 1882.

i. ___ Caskey (boy), born Tipton County, 19 September 1881, died 15 October 1881.

j. Rosetta Pearl Caskey Miller, born Tipton County, 2 February 1883, died 24 December 1961, buried Walton Cemetery; married, 25 March 1919, Walter Bairt Miller, born 28 February 1884, died 6 May 1971, buried Walton Cemetery, son of John M. Miller and Sarah Ann Bringle. They were members of the Oak Grove Baptist Church. No children.

k. ___ Caskey (boy), born and died in Tipton County, 18 March 1887.

5. Letitia Jane Caskey, born Chester County, South Carolina, 1840, died Chester County, mid-1860's; unmarried. On 13 November 1857, she became a member of Hopewell A.R.P. Church in Chester County.

6. Robert Calvin Caskey (called Calvin), born Chester County, South Carolina, August 1842, died Tipton County, Tennes-

see, 30 October 1916, buried Salem A.R.P. Church Cemetery; unmarried. During the winter of 1860-1, Calvin migrated with his brothers Thomas, William, John, and James Caskey Jr. to Tipton County, Tennessee, and on 1 March 1862 he enlisted in the Confederate Army, serving as a private in Company K, 51st Tennessee Infantry. In February 1863 he was wounded near Shelbyville, Tennessee, but soon recovered only to be captured near Nashville on 16 December 1864. After the war he went to Chester County, South Carolina, then returned to Tipton County, Tennessee, where he lived for the remainder of his life. When his parents died he reared his younger siblings. He also helped rear his niece 3-13D12a Ethel Caskey Griffin, and after she died he helped rear her children.

7. Joseph S. Caskey, born Chester County, South Carolina, 1843, died perhaps in Gibson County, Indiana, after 1882; unmarried. He enlisted in the Confederate Army, Company H, 24th South Carolina Infantry. After the war he moved with his younger sisters to Tipton County, Tennessee, and in the 1870's went with his brother 3-13D2 William to Gibson County, Indiana.

8. Francis Mc. Caskey (called Frank), born Chester County, South Carolina, c. 1845, died during the Civil War in or near Dalton, Georgia; unmarried. He enlisted in the Confederate Army, Company H, 24th South Carolina Infantry.

9. Joanna Caskey McWilliams (called Anna), born Chester County, South Carolina, 9 June 1846, died Tipton County, Tennessee, 30 August 1923, buried Indian Creek Cemetery; married in Tipton County, 21 January 1869, Pressly Boyce McWilliams, born Indiana, 8 June 1846, died Tipton County, Tennessee, 2 November 1918, buried Indian Creek Cemetery, son of David C. McWilliams and Elizabeth ___, and brother of Mary Jane McWilliams who married Joanna's brother 3-13D2 William Caskey. Joanna and Pressly were married by the Rev. James Hemphill Strong. Pressly enlisted in the Confederate Army, serving in Company A, 1st South Carolina Heavy Artillery Regiment. After the war he moved to Tipton County, Tennessee, where his sister Mary Jane McWilliams Caskey lived. On 7 August 1869 Pressly and Joanna joined the Salem A.R.P. Church and in the 1870's moved to Holly Grove Community where they joined the Holly Grove Cumberland Presbyterian Church. Children:

   a. ___ McWilliams, died infancy

b. Mary Eva McWilliams Lockart born Tipton County, Tennessee, 14 August 1872, died Tipton County, 27 August 1907, buried Indian Creek Cemetery; married in Tipton County, 5 March 1890, James Edward Lockart, born 21 August 1864, died 30 March 1957, buried Munford Cemetery, Covington, Tennessee, son of John B. Lockart and Jane Stephenson. James had married (1) on 4 December 1887, Allie Wiseman, daughter of Isaac Wiseman and Emaline Smith; James married (3) Mrs. Mary Anna Gay Ralph. Children of James and Mary Eva: (a) Eula G. Lockart Kinney, married Thurman G. Kinney, son of Obadiah Kinney and Willie Tipton Greggs; (b) ___ Lockart, died infancy; (c) Edith Lockart Peregoy, born 3 August 1896, died Tiptonville, Tennessee, 25 September 1973, buried Munford Cemetery in Covington, Tennessee, married at Atoka, Tennessee, 31 January 1914, Ernest Payne Peregoy; and (d) Annie Jane Lockart Smith Williams, born 31 May 1899, died Camden, Tennessee, 23 September 1983, buried Munford Cemetery, married (1) Prentiss Lionel Smith, son of David H. Smith and Sarah Wiseman, later divorced, (2) William Percy Williams.

c. Walter Alexander McWilliams, born Tipton County, Tennessee, 2 December 1873, died 2 March 1924, buried Indian Creek Cemetery; married, 18 November 1896, Minnie Lee Jeans, born 27 March 1875, died 28 May 1955, daughter of George W. Jeans and Minerva Ann Ladd. Children: (a) George Pressley McWilliams, born 21 December 1897, died 29 December 1966, married, 17 December 1922, Bessie Maude Huffman, born 18 January 1904, still living in 1989, daughter of John Franklin Huffman and 3-13E2e Rosanna Mills; (b) Robert J. McWilliams, born 7 July 1899, died 5 December 1929, married Ola Lee Baskin, daughter of Joseph Edgar Baskin and Lillie Mai (sic) Tanner; (c) Mary McWilliams Deen, married Robert Deen; (d) Velma McWilliams Winham Clark, born 24 May 1905, died 13 July 1984, married (1) Allen Winham, (2) Dr. James Whyte Clark, born 13 September 1890, died 6 September 1976; (e) Norma McWilliams Whitaker, married Ernest Whitaker; and (f) Ruth McWilliams Winham, married Lloyd Winham.

d. Nancy Beatrice McWilliams Dawson, born Tipton County, Tennessee, 22 November 1875, died 15 October 1898; married, 4 December 1894, Nicholas Caskey Dawson, born 24 January 1871, died 27 February 1907, son of Jesse Franklin Dawson and Martha Agnes Mills.

e. Clyde (*sic*) McWilliams Mills (girl), born Tipton County, Tennessee, 22 September 1878, died 11 March 1902; married 3-13E2b Hugh Jackson Mills, born 20 May 1867, died 6 August 1907, son of John Samuel Mills and Cynthia Catherine Baskin.

f. John Flenniken McWilliams, born Tipton County, Tennessee, 31 December 1881, died 11 February 1954, buried Indian Creek Cemetery; married in Tipton County, 10 April 1905, 3-13E2k Grace Eulayla Mills, born 8 September 1884, died 12 July 1961, buried Indian Creek Cemetery, daughter of John Samuel Mills and Cynthia Catherine Baskin. Children: (**a**) ___ McWilliams (boy), born 15 June 1905, died 20 June 1905, buried Indian Creek Cemetery; (**b**) Clyde McWilliams, born 25 August 1906, died 15 April 1907, buried Indian Creek Cemetery; (**c**) Ernest Elvin McWilliams, born 19 July 1908, still living in 1989, married Dollie Irene Abernathy, born 1 March 1908, died 29 June 1972, daughter of Joseph William Abernathy and Alva Radie Baskin; (**d**) Bryce Wesley McWilliams, born 29 November 1909, still living in 1989, married his first cousin Thelma Louise McWilliams, daughter of 3-13D9h James Warren McWilliams and Oma Bertha Rose; (**e**) Olvi Grace McWilliams Rose, born 3 September 1913, still living in 1989, married in Mississippi, 14 November 1942, Erskine Lee Rose, born 26 October 1907, died 5 December 1945, son of Henry Haskell Rose and Nan Wiseman; and (**f**) Anna Elizabeth McWilliams Owen, born 16 October 1917, still living in 1989, married Riley Burton Owen, born 1 July 1914, died 18 February 1976, son of Richard Lofton Owen and Effie F. Melton.

g. ___ McWilliams, died infancy.

h. James Warren McWilliams, born Tipton County, Tennessee, 18 September 1886, died Tipton County, 14 March 1956, buried Indian Creek Cemetery; married in Tipton County, 11 June 1911, Oma Bertha Rose, born 24 May 1891, died 3 February 1943, daughter of Henry Haskell Rose and Nan Wiseman. Children: (**a**) Ola Ivine McWilliams Taylor Yarbrough (called Toppy), born 20 March 1912, died 1986, married (1) in 1930, Ammon Taylor, later divorced, (2) Elgrim Wesley Yarbrough, born 13 August 1904, died 22 December 1987; (**b**) Kirby Thurso McWilliams, born 6 July 1915, died 23 April 1974, married Anna Laura Pinner; (**c**) Margie Lorene McWilliams Dawson, born 25 October 1916, died 15 July 1982, married Robert Terrell Dawson (called Chicken); (**d**) James Haskell McWilliams, born 7 May 1918, died 11 December 1918, buried Indian Creek Cemetery; (**e**) Thelma Louise McWilliams, born 11 December 1919, still living in 1989, married her first cousin Bryce Wesley McWilliams, born 29 November 1909, still living in 1989, son of 3-13D9f John Flenniken McWilliams and 3-13E2k Grace Eulayla Mills; (**f**) Malcomb McWilliams, born 7 August 1921, died early 1980's, married Tabatha Wilson; (**g**) Anna May McWilliams Killabrew, born 4 June 1924, still living in 1989, married William Killabrew; (**h**) Pauline McWilliams Graff, born 21 October 1925, still living in 1989, married Charles Graff; and (**i**) Christine McWilliams Hinton, born 15 September 1927, still living in 1989, married Walt Hinton.

10. Margaret W. Caskey Lynn, born Chester County, South Carolina, 15 July 1848, died Tipton County, Tennessee, 21 January 1889, married in Tipton County, 2 January 1871, James Alexander Lynn, born Chester County, South Carolina, c. 1843, died Tipton County, 19 March 1900, buried Salem A.R.P. Church Cemetery, son of John P. Lynn and Rosanna Adams. Margaret and James were members of the Bloomington A.R.P. Church at Bloomington, Tennessee. After she died he married (2) on 20 November 1890, Jane V. Jackson, born October 1854, died 26 September 1920. On 6 August 1893 James transferred to the Salem A.R.P. Church where he is buried. Children of Margaret and James:

   a. Rosanna Adams Lynn, born Tipton County, Tennessee, 21 October 1871, died 8 September 1875, buried Salem A.R.P. Church.

   b. Martha Estelle Lynn McDougal, born Tipton County, Tennessee, ___, died Randolph County, Illinois, ___; married in Tipton County, 15 November 1899, William J. McDougal. Martha joined the Salem A.R.P. Church on 31 August 1891. After her marriage she and her husband moved to Sparta, Randolph County, Illinois. Children: (**a**) James H. McDougal, married Bertha T. Wilson; and (**b**) Harold McDougal (called Pat), married Lucille Miller.

   c. Elmer J. Lynn, born Tipton County, Tennessee, ___, died Randolph County, Illinois ___; married in Tipton County, 25 September 1901, Emma Adell McDougal. After

- d. ___ Lynn, born Tipton County, Tennessee, ___, died infancy, buried Salem A.R.P. Church Cemetery.

- e. ___ Lynn (girl), born Tipton County, Tennessee, 1879, died infancy, buried Salem A.R.P. Church Cemetery.

- f. William D. Lynn, born Tipton County, Tennessee, 17 September 1883, died 6 October 1884, buried Salem A.R.P. Church Cemetery.

- g. John C. Lynn, born Tipton County, Tennessee, June 1888, died 1912, buried Salem A.R.P. Church Cemetery; unmarried.

11. Mary Ann Caskey Waters, born Chester County, South Carolina, 23 January 1850, died Tipton County, Tennessee, 30 July 1898, buried Indian Creek Cemetery at Holly Grove, Tipton County; married in Tipton County, January 1888, John Y. Waters, born 20 October 1858, died 6 January 1897, son of Thomas Waters and Elizabeth ___. Child:

    - a. ___ Waters (girl), died infancy, buried Indian Creek Church Cemetery.

12. Sarah Caskey, born Chester County, South Carolina, 1852, baptized at the Hopewell A.R.P. Church in Chester County, March 1852, died Tipton County, Tennessee, after 1880 and before 1900. Child:

    - a. Ethel Caskey Griffin, born Tipton County, Tennessee, 13 March 1879, died Tipton County, 13 June 1913; married in Tipton County, 23 November 1893, William Richard Griffin, born 22 September 1873, died 25 January 1927. Ethel was reared mainly by her uncle 3-13D6 R. Calvin Caskey, and after she died he also helped rear her children. Ethel and William joined the Walnut Grove Cumberland Presbyterian Church on 28 July 1893. Children: (a) ___ Griffin, died infancy; (b) Bertha Mae Griffin Fleming, born Tipton County, 13 March 1898, died 1987, married in Tipton County, 11 April 1918, Herman Marshall Fleming, born 22 October 1892, died 20 July 1960; (c) Lucille Griffin Harrington Gilpin (called Lucy), born Tipton County, 3 March 1902, died Long Beach, California, 30 May 1979, married (1) ___ Harrington, (2) ___ Gilpin; and (**d**) Maurice Griffin.

13. Martha Elizabeth Caskey Wilson (called Lizzie), born Chester County, South Carolina, 23 January 1857, baptized at the Hopewell A.R.P. Church in Chester County, March 1857, died Covington, Tennessee, 30 March 1917, buried Munford Cemetery in Covington; married at Walnut Grove, Tipton County, Tennessee, 9 February 1887, a distant cousin, William Harvey Wilson, born Tipton County, 25 September 1855, died 17 April 1937, son of William L. Wilson and Nancy McCarroll. Shortly after moving to Tennessee with others of her family, she joined the Mount Paran A.R.P. Church in Tipton County, and after her marriage she transferred to Walnut Grove Cumberland Presbyterian Church. William became a member of that church on 16 October 1881 and was a deacon. In the mid-1890's he and Lizzie moved to Covington where they joined the A.R.P. church there. Children:

   a. ___ Wilson (boy, twin to next), born and died in Walnut Grove, Tipton County, Tennessee, 12 September 1888.

   b. Maude Leona Wilson Boswell (twin to above), born Walnut Grove, Tipton County, Tennessee, 12 September 1888, died Memphis, Tennessee, 10 March 1921, buried Munford Cemetery, Covington, Tennessee; married in Tipton County, 22 June 1911, Dr. Everett Aredus Boswell, born Fayette County, Tennessee, 30 January 1886, died Canal Point, Florida, 9 April 1962, buried Shiloh Cemetery near Garland, Tennessee, son of John Wesley Boswell and Mary Josephine Crouch. Everett married (2) Hazel Luttrell. Child of Maude and Everett: Dorothy Louise Boswell Walk, born Covington, Tennessee, 30 March 1912, still living in 1989, married Claude L. Walk, born 20 November 1911, died 24 November 1987, son of Oscar Clyde Walk and Jerusha Walk.

   c. ___ Wilson, born and died in Walnut Grove, Tipton County, Tennessee, 21 May 1890, buried Indian Creek Cemetery at the Holly Grove Community.

E. Esther Caskey Mills, born Chester County, South Carolina, *c.* 1814, died Tipton County, Tennessee ___, buried Indian Creek Cemetery, Tipton County; married in South Carolina, Capt. Hugh McClellan Mills, born South Carolina, *c.* 1818, died Tipton

County, ___, buried Indian Creek Cemetery, son of John Mills and Anna ___. In Chester County they were members of the Hopewell A.R.P. Church which Esther joined in September 1834. The only deed found on them in Chester County was dated 4 September 1850. In it Hugh sold 87 acres to Samuel A. Wylie for $870. The land was on Rocky Creek and was bounded by tracts owned by Archibald Hood, the Rev. Robert Bryce, Moses H. Robinson, and David McWilliams. Esther signed the dower release on 7 September 1850 (Book GG, pp. 702-3). In 1851 Esther and Hugh moved to Tipton County, Tennessee, settling in the Holly Grove community. Most of their descendants still live there. Children:

1. Mary Anna Mills Gwinn, born Chester County, South Carolina, April 1841, died Tipton County, Tennessee, 30 March 1915, buried Indian Creek Cemetery; married in 1856, Robert McLennan Gwinn (called Mac), born South Carolina, 28 November 1834, died near the Pisgah community, Tipton County, Tennessee, 4 May 1921, buried Indian Creek Cemetery, son of William Gwinn and ___. Mac served in the Confederate Army, Company C, 12th Tennessee Cavalry. His father was listed with them in the 1880 census of Tipton County. Children, all born in Holly Grove community, Tipton County:

    a. Sarah Amanda Gwinn Huffman (called Mandie), born May 1857, died Memphis, Tennessee, 17 February 1928, buried Indian Creek Cemetery; married in Tipton County, 2 November 1874, William Coleman Huffman (called Bill Kid), born Tipton County, August 1855, died in Eastern Arkansas while logging, 3 March 1905, buried Indian Creek Cemetery, son of William Alexander Huffman and Julia Ann Catherine Banks. They lived most of their married lives in or near Brighton, Tennessee. Children: (a) Ardelle Huffman Kehoe, born 19 April 1879, died Memphis, July 1964, married in Memphis, 1917, Christopher J. Kehoe; (b) Lindsey Banks Huffman, born 6 August 1883, died Memphis, 1 August 1953, married in Tipton County, 24 December 1903, Cora Otho Morrison, born 30 November 1885, died 15 February 1960, daughter of John Gray Morrison and first wife, Clemmie E. Cole; (c) William Vernon Huffman, born 11 May 1890, died 6 November 1964, married Thelma Marshall, born 8 May 1898, died 3 March 1971, daughter of James Archibald Marshall and second wife, Mary Blanche Gladden; (d) Nora Lee Huffman Smith, born 19 November 1892, died 29 October 1959, married in Tipton County,

25 March 1908, Norman Everett Smith (called Joe), born 21 January 1883, died 19 December 1977, son of Augusta Washington Smith Jr. (called Tude) and Lizzie Almeda Vashti McLister; (e) Neverette Lafayette Huffman, born 7 March 1894, died in Brighton, 8 May 1946, married in Tipton County, 3 September 1921, Annie Mae Marshall, born 18 January 1902, died Memphis, 3 January 1986, daughter of James Archibald Marshall and Mary Blanche Gladden; (f) Minnie Clyde Huffman, born 1896, died 1970, married James Carl Huffman, born 26 June 1887, died 31 January 1954, son of Hugh George Huffman and Nancy Elizabeth Marshall; and (g) Lynn Udall Huffman (called Mike), born 15 August 1899, died 11 July 1972, married Jimmie Commer.

b. Hugh Alonzo Gwinn (called Lonza), born 4 March 1861, died 12 March 1927; married 3-13D4b Sarah Letitia Caskey. For their listing see under Sarah's entry.

c. Martha Ellen Gwinn, born 8 January 1862, died while a young woman, buried Indian Creek Cemetery.

d. William Thomas Gwinn (called Tom), born 6 April 1868, died Holly Grove, 3 July 1919, buried Indian Creek Cemetery; married in Tipton County, 21 October 1888, Sarah Jane Baskin, born Holly Grove, 22 May 1870, died 4 May 1950, buried Indian Creek Cemetery, daughter of John Henry Baskin (called Pecked-Eyed John) and his second wife Mahala Jane Kelley. Children: (a) Roscoe Malanthan Gwinn, born 9 February 1890, died Holly Grove, 22 October 1918, married in Tipton County, 16 February 1911, Sarah Eugenia Belle Anglin, daughter of Andrew Jackson Anglin and Alice Eugenia Goins; (b) Russell Wardlow Gwinn, born 12 February 1891, died Holly Grove, 19 October 1918, married in Tipton County, 27 May 1912, Alice Alda Dickey, born Holly Grove, 18 September 1894, died Holly Grove, 14 October 1918, daughter of William Henry Dickey and Laura Ann Myers; (c) Lillie Maude Gwinn Griggs, married in Tipton County, 25 September 1910, Oscar Griggs; (d) Ollie Leno Gwinn Deen, born 15 April 1895, died Memphis, 5 February 1973, married at Holly Grove, 25 September 1910, Elbert Lee Deen, born 16 July 1887, died Millington, Tennessee, 7 May 1972, son of Jeremiah Deen and Susan Townsend; (e) Regie Littleton Gwinn (called Litt), born 18 July 1896, died 31 December 1967, married at Holly Grove, 30 September 1917,

Robbie May Blankenship, born Holly Grove, 20 April 1899, still alive in 1989, daughter of Bascom Cannon Blankenship (called Babe) and Malinda Catherine Mills; (**f**) Bessie B. Gwinn Billings, born 23 December 1900, died 29 January 1924, married Leslie Billings (called Jack), son of W. W. Billings; (**g**) Beulah Bell Gwinn, born 29 January 1902, died 19 October 1903; and (**h**) Eula Dell Gwinn Evans, born 29 January 1902, still alive in 1989, married Claude Evans.

e. Mary Jane Gwinn Baskin Moore, born c. 1872, died ___, buried Elmwood Cemetery, Memphis, Tennessee; married (1) in Tipton County, 16 September 1888, Abner L. Baskin, born Holly Grove, March 1868, died Memphis, October 1906, buried Munford Cemetery, Covington, Tennessee, son of John Henry "Pecked-Eyed John" Baskin and second wife, Mahala Jane Kelley; Mary Jane married (2) in Memphis, James Moore. Mary Jane and her first husband had at least seven children, three dying in infancy. Known children: (**a**) Lelia E. Baskin Starnes, married Thomas Talmadge Starnes; (**b**) Leslie E. Baskin, married (1) Georgia Williams, (2) Elizabeth Coe; (**c**) Faye Elnora Baskin Davis, born 14 October 1895, died in Memphis, January 1979, married, November 1912, Oscar Gibson Davis, born 26 July 1888, died in Memphis, 6 June 1979, son of Thomas Gibson Davis and Alice Laurence; and (**d**) Ruth Aola Baskin Davis Acers, married (1) Joseph Jefferson Davis, son of Thomas Gibson Davis and Alice Laurence, (2) ___ Acers.

f. Julia Ann Gwinn Evans (called Jule), born May 1876, died Dyersburg, Tennessee, 15 March 1921, buried Indian Creek Cemetery; married in Tipton County, 15 January 1896, Andrew Jackson Evans, born Tipton County, 16 June 1866, died Dyersburg, 26 August 1966, buried Indian Creek Cemetery, son of Absalom Hendricks Evans and Eliza ___. Child: Roger McClellan Evans, born Holly Grove, 21 November 1896, died Dyersburg, 29 June 1983, married Mrs. Rebekah Ricketts.

g. Margaret E. Gwinn (called Mag), born January 1879, died Holly Grove, 13 March 1926, buried Indian Creek Cemetery; unmarried.

h. James McClellan Gwinn, born 22 July 1884, died Covington, Tennessee, 20 October 1962, buried Munford Cemetery, Covington; unmarried.

2. John Samuel Mills, born Chester County, South Carolina, 15 January 1845, died Holly Grove, 3 July 1925, buried Indian Creek Cemetery; married in Tipton County, Tennessee, Cynthia Catherine Baskin, born Holly Grove, Tennessee, 3 August 1847, died Holly Grove, 19 February 1912, buried Indian Creek Cemetery, daughter of Andrew Jackson Baskin and Cassanna Dacus. Children, all born in Holly Grove:

   a. Malinda Catherine Mills Blankenship (called Catherine), born 3 October 1865, died Holly Grove, 21 December 1933, buried Indian Creek Cemetery; married in Tipton County, December 1881, Bascom Cannon Blankenship (called Babe), born Arkansas, June 1857, died Oak Grove community in Tipton County, 29 September 1934, buried Mount Carmel Cemetery, son of Thomas C. Blankenship and Mary Ellen Huffman. This was Babe's second marriage, his first to Martha Ellen Huffman, daughter of William Alexander Huffman and Julia Ann Catherine Banks. Catherine and Babe were divorced in 1916. Children, all born in Holly Grove: (<u>a</u>) Leve Bruce Blankenship, born 8 May 1883, died ___, married Alva Wortham, daughter of Brent Heath Wortham and Ruth Curtis; (<u>b</u>) Eda Carlton Blankenship, born 4 April 1885, died Holly Grove, 26 September 1897; (<u>c</u>) Eupha Olivia Blankenship Hise, born 3 August 1887, died January 1955, married Marvin Augustus Hise, born November 1882, died 6 June 1914, son of William Hamilton Hise and Martha Elizabeth Ladd; (<u>d</u>) Marvin Bascom Blankenship, born 24 February 1890, died 7 January 1981, married in Tipton County, 8 December 1912, Effie E. Baskin, born 3 February 1893, died 15 January 1971, daughter of Hugh Andrew Baskin and Mary Alice Huffman; (<u>e</u>) Bradie Ethel Blankenship McPeak, born March 1893, died August 1915, married in Tipton County, 12 March 1911, Clarence McPeak; (<u>f</u>) Embry Owen Blankenship, born February 1895, died Memphis, 7 April 1959, married Nettye English; (<u>g</u>) Vesper Cornelius Blankenship, born 21 February 1897, died 15 September 1973, married (1) in Tipton County, 13 November 1921, Jessie Farmer, born c. 1900, died 1 April 1926, daughter of Otey Quintard Farmer and Lou Anna Baskin, (2) Lillian Margaret Edmiston; (<u>h</u>) Robbie May Blankenship Gwinn, born 20 April 1899, still alive in 1989, married Regie Littleton Gwinn, born 18 July 1896, died 31 December 1967, son of William Thomas Gwinn and Sarah Jane Baskin; (<u>i</u>) Ottis Hartley Blankenship, born 29 March 1903, died 11 September 1972, married (1) in Tipton

County, 24 January 1921, Lavenia Frances Owen, born Oak Grove community, 8 November 1900, died 8 September 1942, daughter of Richard Lofton Owen and Effie F. Melton, (2) Mrs. Ardelle Wiseman Bogue; and (j) Iris Blankenship Schmitz, married ___ Schmitz.

b. Hugh Jackson Mills, born May 1867, died Holly Grove, 6 August 1907, buried Indian Creek Cemetery; married in Tipton County, 21 December 1899, 3-13D9e Clyde (*sic*) McWilliams, born Holly Grove, 22 September 1878, died Holly Grove, 11 March 1902, buried Indian Creek Cemetery, daughter of Pressly Boyce McWilliams and Joanna Caskey. Child: John Vernon Mills, born Holly Grove, 1901, married in Tipton County, 17 April 1926, Margaret Helen Leach, born 1906, died 1955, daughter of Oscar Samuel Leach and Anna Mahala Huffman.

c. John Manuel Mills, born 10 February 1869, died Holly Grove, 11 November 1948, buried Indian Creek Cemetery; married in Tipton County, Mary Agnes Whitesides, born Liberty community, Tipton County, 25 September 1875, died Memphis, 8 October 1959, buried Indian Creek Cemetery, daughter of William Ross Whitesides and Sarah E. Wright. Children, all born at Holly Grove: (a) Randall Sidney Mills, born 8 October 1893, died Tacoma, Washington, 12 December 1983, married Eula C. Richardson, born 15 September 1894, died 10 November 1958, daughter of Clayton Mancel Richardson and Emma Lee M. Boshears; (b) Eura Grace Mills Baskin (called Eudell), born 17 August 1895, died 31 May 1980, married in Tipton County, 12 December 1920, Efford Jackson Baskin, born 19 April 1894, died 7 February 1960, son of Andrew Jackson Baskin and Telitha Ann Lavelle; (c) Erskine Lee Mills, born 3 September 1897, died 7 August 1960, married (1) Julia Elbert Burton, born 5 November 1899, died 16 November 1940, (2) Mrs. Lois Miller Goforth; (d) Leno Ross Mills, born 3 January 1901, died 23 July 1964, married in Tipton County, 19 January 1924, Willie Martha Fleming, born Oak Grove, 31 March 1906, still alive in 1989; (e) Ernie M. Mills (called Poolie), born 9 May 1903, still alive in 1989, married at Marion, Arkansas, 27 February 1927, Beatrice Mae Dailey, born Lauderdale County, Tennessee, 2 July 1905, died Covington, Tennessee, 15 April 1982, daughter of Jesse Dailey and Ida Laskey; and (f) Cecil Derwood Mills, born 10 June 1910, died Covington, 18 June 1987, married (1) in Tipton County, 24 December

1928, Cleffie Blackwell, (2) Nora Elizabeth Tracy.

d. Sidney C. Mills born 16 July 1870, died Holly Grove, 9 April 1895, buried Indian Creek Cemetery; unmarried.

e. Rosanna Mills Huffman, born 12 March 1872, died Brighton, 18 January 1933, buried Indian Creek Cemetery; married in Tipton County, 22 April 1891, John Franklin Huffman, born Tipton County, 13 July 1862, died Covington, 10 March 1945, buried Indian Creek Cemetery, son of William Alexander Huffman and Julia Ann Catherine Banks. Children, all born in Holly Grove: (a) Albert Huffman, born 3 August 1893, died Holly Grove, 2 September 1894, buried Indian Creek Cemetery; (b) Eula Agnes Huffman Guinn, born 24 January 1895, died 10 June 1929, married in Tipton County, 1 August 1911, Robert Lee Guinn (sic), born 4 November 1887, died 11 July 1967, son of Hugh Alonzo Gwinn and Sarah Letitia Caskey (3-13D4b); (c) Raymond McDonald Huffman, born 23 December 1898, died Covington, 15 February 1985, married in Tipton County, 8 July 1923, Nina Elmo Fortner, born Bride community, Tipton County, 9 November 1902, died Covington, 31 March 1982, daughter of James Henry Fortner and Edna Elmo Bradley; (d) Johnnie Lloyd Huffman, born 9 September 1901, died Holly Grove, 29 March 1904, buried Indian Creek Cemetery; and (e) Bessie Maude Huffman McWilliams, born 18 January 1904, still alive in 1989, married in Holly Grove, 17 December 1922, George Pressly McWilliams, born Holly Grove, 21 December 1897, died Holly Grove, 29 December 1966, son of 3-13D9c Walter Alexander McWilliams and Minnie Lee Jeans.

f. Ada Frances Mills, born 12 April 1874, died 11 June 1909; married, 16 January 1898, 3-13E3b George McClellan Baskin. See their listings under George's entry.

g. Yerby Samuel Mills (called Sam), born 10 May 1876, died Holly Grove, 4 October 1954, buried Indian Creek Cemetery; married in Tipton County, 22 December 1898, Mamie Love Williams, born Tipton County, 13 September 1875, died Memphis, 11 February 1956, buried Indian Creek Cemetery, daughter of Richard Williams and Sarah Roane. Children, all born in Holly Grove: (a) Ina Katherine Mills Goforth Rose, born 7 October 1899, died 23 May 1955, married (1) in Tipton County, 14 February 1917, Russell Leon Goforth, born Holly Grove,

11 June 1896, died 15 November 1921, son of William
Monroe Goforth (called Boss) and Sarah Catherine
Coats, (2) Oscar Lafayette Rose, born Holly Grove, 8
August 1888, died 24 October 1954, son of James F.
Rose and Sarah Elizabeth Hargett; (**b**) Julia Christine
Mills Dickey McLister, born 27 June 1901, died 1988,
married (1) in Tipton County, 22 December 1920, Aubrey
Earl Dickey, born Holly Grove 9 August 1899, died 12
February 1955, son of William Henry Dickey and Laura
Ann Myers, (2) Lucius Quintus Cincinnatus Lamar McLister (called Luke Faucett McLister), son of John Chisolm McLister and his second wife, Emily Caroline
Faucett; (**c**) Glen Roane Mills, born 30 August 1903,
still alive in 1989, married Sue Gray; (**d**) Richard
Thurso Mills, married in Tipton County, 22 December
1928, Alice Mae Faulk; (**e**) Sarah Elizabeth Mills
Taylor, born 19 October 1908, still alive in 1989,
married, 22 December 1928, Joseph Jasper Taylor
(called Buck), born 15 March 1908, still alive in
1989, son of Joe Robert Taylor and Lucinda Martin; (**f**)
Ruth Elaine Mills, born 4 November 1910, died Holly
Grove, 10 September 1920, buried Indian Creek Cemetery; and (**g**) Blanche Ladell Mills Whitehorn, born 28
March 1919, married Stanley Wilson Whitehorn, son of
Nelson Franklin Whitehorn and Bessie Davis.

h. Lora Lee Mills Morton, born 13 September 1878, died
Holly Grove, 5 February 1941, buried Indian Creek
Cemetery; married in Tipton County, 19 December 1901,
Andrew Jackson Morton, born Tipton County, 22 September 1879, died Holly Grove, 6 February 1941, buried
Indian Creek Cemetery, son of William H. Morton and
Eveline Cannon. Children, all born at Holly Grove:
(**a**) Floyd Morton, born 17 September 1902, died 6
December 1920, buried Indian Creek Cemetery; (**b**) Finis
Earl Morton, born 16 December 1905, died 19 July 1962,
married in Pisgah community, Tipton County, 24 November 1923, Letitia Elizabeth Glass (called Tishie),
born 10 November 1905, died 12 August 1987, daughter
of James Glass and Mary Jane Raynor; and (**c**) Lytle
Edgar Morton, born 9 August 1910, died 19 January
1980, married at Marion, Arkansas, 20 December 1930,
Callie B. Swindle, born 11 February 1915, daughter of
Thomas Elijah Swindle and Mary Viola McAlister.

i. Slonney Egnes (*sic*) Mills Griffith, born 30 June 1880,
died 3 March 1963, buried Indian Creek Cemetery; mar-

ried in Tipton County, 19 December 1905, John Jacob Griffith, born 1878, died 1932, buried Indian Creek Cemetery, son of Charles Francis Griffith and Sarah Frances Smith. Children, all born at Holly Grove: (a) Beulah Egnes (sic) Griffith Abernathy, born 13 October 1906, died at Memphis, 9 August 1984, married George Tipton Abernathy, later divorced, son of Joseph William Abernathy and Alva Radie Baskin; (b) Hugh Jacob Griffith, married Gertrude Carter; (c) Nannie Autry Griffith Cates, born 21 June 1910, married at Burleson, Tennessee, 17 September 1927, Herbert Raspis Cates, born 10 October 1905, died 17 May 1983, son of George Alexander Cates and Artie Lee Baskin; (d) Cynthia Frances Griffith Martin, married Welton Martin; and (e) Zuma Griffith, born 1919, died at Holly Grove, 12 October 1920, buried Indian Creek Cemetery.

j. Donnie Mills, born Holly Grove, 20 July 1882, died Covington, Tennessee, 24 February 1967, buried Indian Creek Cemetery; married his first cousin Oma Edna Baskin, born in Tipton County, 20 March 1888, died 19 December 1954, buried Indian Creek Cemetery, daughter of Yerby Baskin and Eliza Jane Baskin. Children: (a) Basil Farris Mills, born 25 March 1911, died 16 October 1962, married Myrtie Flowers; (b) Y. B. Mills, born 27 August 1914, married in Marion, Arkansas, 18 October 1941, Ardella Geneva Massengill; and (c) Bonnie Sue Mills.

k. Grace Eulayla Mills McWilliams, born 8 September 1884, died 12 July 1961; married in Tipton County, 10 April 1905, 3-13D9f John Flenniken McWilliams. For their listing see under his entry.

l. Alton Ellis Mills, born 24 November 1888, died Holly Grove, 10 December 1974, buried Indian Creek Cemetery; married in Tipton County, 10 April 1911, Bertha Grace Rose, born Holly Grove, 21 October 1892, died Covington, 20 March 1969, buried Indian Creek Cemetery, daughter of James F. Rose and Sarah Elizabeth Hargett. Children, both born at Holly Grove: (a) Clifton Woodrow Mills, born 11 February 1913, died 24 August 1953, married at Brighton, 9 December 1933, Velma Louise Zenar, born near Munford, Tennessee, 18 June 1913, daughter of James Ollie Zenar and Lillie Mae Hanks; and (b) Trilby Renee Mills Dacus, born March 1917, died at Memphis, 9 December 1959, married James

Leon Dacus, born July 1913, died at Covington, July 1964, son of Henry Franklin Dacus and Bessie Forrest Etheridge, James married (2) Mrs. Odell Adkins Cousar.

3. Julianna Ellen Mills Baskin, born Chester County, South Carolina, 16 May 1847, died Holly Grove, Tennessee, 24 November 1907, buried Indian Creek Cemetery; married in Tipton County, Tennessee, George M. Dallas Baskin (called Dallas), born Holly Grove, 31 January 1844, died Holly Grove, 18 February 1929, buried Indian Creek Cemetery, son of Andrew Jackson Baskin and Cassanna Dacus. Dallas was a farmer and later owned and ran a general store at Holly Grove in partnership with his sons. He and Julianna were members of Holly Grove Cumberland Presbyterian Church. After she died he married (2) in Tipton County, 22 March 1911, Mrs. Sarah Elizabeth Hargett Rose, widow of James F. Rose; divorced in 1923. Children of Julianna and Dallas, all born in Holly Grove:

   a. Hugh Andrew Baskin, born 26 November 1865, died Holly Grove, 13 July 1936, buried Indian Creek Cemetery; married in Tipton County, 2 February 1887, Mary Alice Huffman, born 1867, died 1900, buried Indian Creek Cemetery, daughter of William Alexander Huffman and Julia Ann Catherine Banks. Children, all born at Holly Grove: (**a**) Dallas Alexander Baskin, died young; (**b**) Julia Edna Baskin Rose, born October 1891, died 15 July 1923, married in Tipton County, 6 December 1913, Walter Elmore Rose, born Holly Grove, 3 November 1889, died Holly Grove, 9 May 1951, son of Samuel Sparks Rose and Lula Wiseman; (**c**) Effie E. Baskin Blankenship, born 3 February 1893, died 15 January 1971, married in Tipton County, 8 December 1912, Marvin Bascom Blankenship, born Holly Grove, February 1890, died 7 January 1981, son of Bascom Cannon Blankenship and Malinda Catherine Mills; (**d**) Ottis B. Baskin (called Beebe), born September 1895, died in California, 18 February 1961; (**e**) Chesley Baskin, died young; and (**f**) Warner Baskin, died young.

   b. George McClellan Baskin, born 2 March 1868, died 14 December 1933, buried Indian Creek Cemetery; married in Tipton County, 16 January 1898, his first cousin 3-13E2f Ada Frances Mills, born Holly Grove, 12 April 1874, died Holly Grove, 11 June 1909, buried Indian Creek Cemetery, daughter of John Samuel Mills and Cynthia Catherine Baskin. Children, all born in Holly

Grove: (a) Lee Amy Baskin Goforth, born 25 October 1898, died 11 November 1979, married in Tipton County, 28 December 1919, Alvin Pearl Goforth, born Holly Grove, 1 November 1893, died 5 November 1950, son of William Monroe Goforth (called Boss) and Sarah Catherine Coats; (b) Irene Baskin Evans, born 24 September 1900, died 12 November 1978, married Marvin Ollie Evans, born 1 December 1898, died 24 September 1961, son of John H. Evans and Elizabeth Dacus; (c) Georgia Mae Baskin Bennett, born 7 July 1903, died 19 July 1970, married Dave Bennett, born 3 May 1907, died 20 November 1972; (d) Du Pree Baskin (called Slick), born 24 July 1905, died 14 August 1978, married Ruby Estelle Taylor; and (e) Ermine E. Baskin, born 3 June 1908, died July 1909, buried Indian Creek Cemetery.

c. ___ Baskin (girl), died infancy.

d. Leona Baskin Rose, born 29 October 1878, died at Covington, Tennessee, 13 January 1962, buried Indian Creek Cemetery; married in Tipton County, 22 December 1904, Edward Wilson Rose, born Brighton, 7 September 1879, died Brighton, 3 February 1958, buried Indian Creek Cemetery, son of William Jordan Rose and Mary Sue Wilson. Children, all born at Holly Grove: (a) Eunice Ellen Rose Shamblee, born 21 September 1907, died 31 May 1989, married Harvey Lee Shamblee, born 8 May 1898, died 7 May 1968; (b) ___ Rose, died infancy; (c) ___ Rose, died infancy; and (d) E. L. Rose, born 18 April 1916, died 1979, married Katie Robertson, born 1911, died 1973.

4. Rosanna Jane Mills Dawson, born Chester County, South Carolina, 27 January 1851, died Atoka, Tennessee, 4 July 1933, buried Indian Creek Cemetery; married in Tipton County, Tennessee, 19 December 1869, William Bradley Dawson (called Brad), born Tipton County, 25 July 1849, died Atoka, 13 August 1911, buried Indian Creek Cemetery; son of William B. Dawson and Eliza Jane ___. Brad was a farmer and later had a store at Holly Grove, moving it to Atoka soon after 1900. Rosanna and Brad had eleven children three of whom died in infancy. Known children, all born in Holly Grove, Tipton County:

a. Naomi O. Dawson Blankenship Stebbins (called Daught), born 27 November 1872, died 11 February 1947, buried Indian Creek Cemetery; married (1) in Tipton County,

14 September 1890, Thomas L. Blankenship, born Arkansas, December 1871, died Tipton County, Tennessee, 25 December 1911, son of Thomas C. Blankenship and Mary Ellen Huffman; Naomi married (2) R. H. Stebbins. Children of Naomi and Thomas: (a) Vergie Ola Blankenship Glenn, born 1896, died in Memphis, 14 July 1964, married Walter B. Glenn, born 1893, died 1963; (b) Ruba Garner Blankenship (called Rube), married, 22 August 1920, Myrtle Belle Rose, daughter of Samuel Sparks Rose and Lula Wiseman; (c) Thomas Blankenship, married Josie ___; (d) Robert O. Blankenship; and (e) Parrish Blankenship, married Ruby Notgrass (sic).

b. William Lafayette Dawson (called Fayette), born 4 June 1878, died Millington, Tennessee, 25 August 1960, buried Kerrville Cemetery, Kerrville, Tennessee; married at Holly Grove, Tennessee, 9 September 1897, Ardella Jane Brown (called Della), born 15 February 1879, died 16 January 1957, buried Kerrville Cemetery, daughter of Moore E. Brown and Martha Abigail Lockart. Children: (a) William Bradley Dawson; (b) ___ Dawson, died infancy; (c) ___ Dawson, died infancy; (d) Edris Veleter Dawson, born 26 June 1903, died 25 August 1925, married Louis Crenshaw; (e) Zona Brown Dawson; and (f) Pawnee Bill Dawson, born Atoka, Tennessee, 5 April 1907, still alive in 1989, married in Munford, Tennessee, 2 October 1937, Ony Grace Joiner, born 1913, died 1982, daughter of Joe and Lula Ethel James Joiner.

c. Liza Emma Dawson Morton, born 21 July 1880, died Memphis, 28 November 1967, buried Indian Creek Cemetery; married Tipton County, 23 December 1896, John E. Morton, born 4 August 1873, died 25 November 1941, buried Indian Creek Cemetery, son of William H. Morton. Known children: (a) Estes C. Morton, born 2 January 1898, died 1981, married Ruby ___, born 9 December 1908, died 16 February 1967; (b) Elsie Jane Morton, married Roy Stinson; (c) ___ Morton, died young; (d) Dessie M. Morton, born 12 November 1903, died 1 October 1915; (e) Robbie Morton Black, married George Black; (f) Theodore Morton; (g) Edna Earle Morton Cobb, married Jake Cobb; and (h) George "Boot" Morton.

d. Saphronia Ann Dawson Massie (called Frone); married in Tipton County, 14 December 1902, George W. Massie, born 1874, died 1 January 1934, buried Salem A.R.P.

Church Cemetery. No children.

e. Eicy (*sic*) Dawson

f. Pearl Dawson

g. Trotty Mae Dawson Isom, born 21 December 1890, died Brighton, Tennessee, 9 April 1954, buried Salem A.R.P. Church Cemetery; married in Covington, 7 November 1910, Nathaniel Isom, born Idaville, Tennessee, 26 November 1885, died Brighton, 23 March 1971, buried Salem A.R.P. Church Cemetery. Children: (**a**) Vera Dawson Isom Phillips, born 29 January 1912, still alive in 1989, married on 20 September 1932, Walter David Phillips (called Deedee), born 22 June 1906, died 21 May 1969; (**b**) Emma Jane Isom Bridges, born 6 August 1914, still alive in 1989, married on 14 September 1946, J. P. Bridges; (**c**) Lena Mae Isom Grigsby, married J. T. Grigsby; (**d**) Mary Elizabeth Isom; (**e**) Autry Jeanette Isom Hanks, married James Hanks; (**f**) Margaret Cathleen Isom Lyles, married Thomas Lyles; (**g**) Nathaniel Isom Jr.; and (**h**) William Bradley Isom.

h. Robert Clifton Dawson, born 15 January 1893, died 22 April 1971; married in 1909, Clemmie Adkinson, daughter of Joseph Franklin Adkinson and Adaline Geneva Delashmit. Child: Willard H. Dawson, born 22 August 1917, died 13 April 1985; married at Saint Matthews Episcopal Church in Covington, 10 September 1950, Catherine Sherrod (called Kate), daughter of Fredrick Shelton Sherrod and ___.

5. Martha Agnes Mills Dawson (called Nan), born Tipton County, Tennessee, February 1855, died 21 September 1908, buried Indian Creek Cemetery; married in Tipton County, 19 January 1871, Jesse Franklin Dawson, born Tipton County, 11 April 1851, died 8 July 1921, buried Indian Creek Cemetery, son of William B. Dawson and Eliza Jane ___. Children:

   a. Nicholas Caskey Dawson (called Caskey), born Holly Grove, 24 January 1872, died 27 February 1907, buried Indian Creek Cemetery; married (1) in Tipton County, 4 December 1894, 3-13D9d Nancy Beatrice McWilliams (called Beatrice), born Holly Grove, 22 November 1875, died Holly Grove, 15 October 1898, buried Indian Creek Cemetery, daughter of Pressly Boyce McWilliams and

Joanna Caskey; Caskey married (2) Florence Alma Rose, daughter of James F. Rose and Sarah Elizabeth Hargett. Child (by first wife, Beatrice): Boyce Wesley Dawson, born 13 July 1895, died 2 February 1950, married in 1919, Mattie Bessie Smith, daughter of George Thomas Smith and Dora Peyton Rice.

b. Cora Ellen Dawson Cates Fleming, born 24 March 1875, died 4 June 1961; married (1) in Tipton County, 2 September 1897, Thomas V. Cates, born October 1873, died 8 September 1905, son of William Bloomer Cates and Margaret Jane Huffman; Cora married (2) Don F. Fleming. Children of Cora and Thomas: (**a**) Robbie Brathan Cates Ashe, married Floyd Walker Ashe; (**b**) Elma Fay Cates Deen, born 26 May 1902, still alive in 1989, married in Brighton, 15 February 1920, Melville Ostress Deen, born 26 July 1887, died 12 September 1971, son of Jeremiah Deen and Susan T. Townsend; (**c**) Alice May Cates; and (**d**) Virginia Inez Cates Erwin, born 7 October 1905, still alive in 1989, married Robert Porter Erwin.

c. LeRoy Dawson, born 1877, died 1966; married Mrs. Ida Wortham Walton, born 1871, died 1949, daughter of Nathaniel Wortham and Henrietta Smith and widow of William Davis Walton Jr. who was born 10 July 1869, died 17 September 1917. No children.

d. Sarah Arleta Dawson Lavelle, born 1880, died 1958, buried Smyrna Cemetery, Burleson, Tennessee; married in Tipton County, 7 October 1896, James Nathan Lavelle, born 1873, died 1953, son of James Franklin Lavelle and Telitha Ann Hartsfield, buried Smyrna Cemetery, Burleson. Children: (**a**) Alton H. Lavelle, born 22 September 1897, died 13 June 1898; (**b**) Telitha Agnes Lavelle Murphy, born 18 October 1899, died 21 August 1983, married on 8 February 1919, Dutes Eugene Murphy, born 16 August 1897, died 7 February 1965; (**c**) Bridgett Lavelle Smith, married Theo Smith; (**d**) M. A. Lavelle, born 6 October 1904, died April 1908; (**e**) Manon Franklin Lavelle, born 9 August 1907, died 5 May 1951, married on 28 July 1928, Eurania Marie Tennessee Burlison, daughter of John Edward Burlison and Docia Myrtle Evans; (**f**) Mary Sue Lavelle, born 8 October 1909, died 1925; (**g**) James N. Lavelle, married Marion Roberge; (**h**) Nelle Lavelle Glaze, married Alvin Glaze; (**i**) Alice Marie Lavelle Fleming, married Thomas

Fleming; and (j) Jessie B. Lavelle, born 19 April 1921, died 3 February 1984, unmarried.

e. Nola Jane Dawson Douglas, born 18 July 1882, died at Ripley, Tennessee, 2 July 1981, buried Munford Cemetery, Covington, Tennessee; married William Spencer Douglas, born 15 July 1879, died 13 June 1955, buried Munford Cemetery, son of William Douglas and Claryce Roane. No children.

f. Onie Frances Dawson Lavelle, born 9 February 1885, died 7 May 1949, buried Smyrna Cemetery, Burleson, Tennesee; married in Tipton County, 30 March 1903, Olien Renshaw Lavelle, born 30 November 1881, died 23 January 1934, buried Smyrna Cemetery, son of Thomas Lavelle and his second wife, Martha Catherine Baskin. Children: (a) Herman Glenn Lavelle, born 2 February 1904, still alive in 1989, married Robbie Merritt, daughter of Robert W. Merritt and Ella Jane Gwinn; (b) James Elbert Lavelle, born 18 July 1906, died 4 March 1975, married his father's first cousin Effie Elzoria Baskin, born 4 October 1904, died 10 December 1986, daughter of Olien Walter Baskin and Josephine Maddox; (c) Lawrence Roscoe Lavelle, born 11 September 1908, died 2 August 1986, married Pattie Mai (*sic*) Cousar; (d) Marshall Eudell Lavelle, married Nellie Joiner; (e) Roy Elton Lavelle, born 10 December 1912, died 21 October 1986, married Veda Mae Fleming; (f) Gladys Virginia Lavelle Richardson, born 26 February 1916, married Warner Leon Richardson; and (g) Herbert La Von Lavelle, born 27 August 1919, died October 1968, married Eris Huffman, daughter of Turner Elbert Huffman and Lillian Vaughan.

g. Estelle Dawson Hathcock, born 22 November 1887, died May 1910, buried Munford Cemetery, Covington; married William Thomas Hathcock, born 28 October 1885, died 18 April 1965, son of James Hathcock and Lula Hodges. He married (2) Kitty Mae Kinney. Estelle had one child: Vivian Hathcock Curle, born 7 November 1907, still alive in 1989, married Avery A. Curle.

h. Willie Ethel Dawson Hathcock, born 1 December 1890, died Covington, Tennessee, 30 June 1986, buried Tipton County Memorial Gardens at Covington; married in Tipton County, October 1912, James Cecil Hathcock, born 1894, died 1971, son of James Hathcock and Lula

Hodges.  Children:  (**a**) James W. Hathcock, married Miskel Huffman; (**b**) Louise Hathcock, married Vernon "Nick" Bungle, son of Sidney B. Bungle and Lou Ada Joy; and (**c**) Werdner Hathcock Coats Smith, married (1) Adrian Coats, (2) Don Smith.

    i. Hugh Leslie Dawson, born 11 November 1893, died 22 September 1921, buried Munford Cemetery at Covington; married Annie Elizabeth Hathcock, buried Munford Cemetery, daughter of James Hathcock and Lula Hodges. Child: Hugh Leslie Dawson Jr., born 4 September 1920, married, 4 October 1949, Mary Sam Shelley, daughter of M. H. Shelley and Marie Chapman.

F. Elizabeth Ellen Caskey Mills, born Chester County, South Carolina, *c.* 1820, died Tipton County, Tennessee, in the 1870's; married John Lyles Mills, born South Carolina, *c.* 1823, died Tipton County, Tennessee, in the 1870's. Elizabeth joined the Hopewell A.R.P. Church in Chester County on 12 May 1836 and switched to another Presbyterian church in the early 1850's. In 1854-5 she and John moved to Tipton County, Tennessee, and joined the Salem A.R.P. Church on 5 May 1855. When they moved to Tennessee, they were accompanied by Elizabeth's brother 3-13H Thomas Caskey Jr. Children:

1. John C. Mills, born Chester County, South Carolina, *c.* 1851, died Tipton County, Tennessee, 1875-1880; married in Tipton County, Mary E. Solomon. No children.

2. Mary Jane Mills Cox, born Tipton County, Tennessee, 1856, died Tipton County, early 1880's; married George W. Cox, born Tipton County, 24 March 1835, died probably in Tipton County after 1910, son of James R. Cox and Judith ___. George enlisted in the Confederate Army and served as a sergeant in Company B, 7th Tennessee Cavalry. Child:

    a. Nancy G. F. Cox, born Tipton County, Tennessee, December 1877, died after 1910; unmarried. She was named for her father's sister Nancy G. F. Cox.

G. Joanna Caskey, born Chester County, South Carolina, *c.* 1823, died at the home of her sister 3-13A Mary Caskey Hindman in Tipton County, Tennessee, July 1879, buried Salem A.R.P. Church Cemetery; unmarried. She joined the Hopewell A.R.P. Church in Chester County in September 1839. In 1867 she moved to Tipton County, Tennessee, and joined the Salem A.R.P. Church on 4 April 1868. She lived with her sister Mary.

H. Thomas Caskey Jr., born Chester County, South Carolina, 1824, died Tipton County, Tennessee, 1882; unmarried. In 1854-5 he moved with his sister and brother-in-law 3-13F Elizabeth (Caskey) and John Lyles Mills to Tipton County, Tennessee, where at first he ran a general store at Bloomington. In 1867 he settled in the Holly Grove community and lived on a farm which he ran until his death.

3-14 ___ GRAHAM REEDY (girl), born South Carolina, c. 1785?, died probably Chester County, South Carolina, before 1826; married ___ REEDY. This girl's brother 3-16 James Jr. died in 1826 and in his will bequeathed not only his cloak to "my nephew John Reedy" but also "what he hath in his Hands of my Estate at this time." Since James did not name John's mother in his will, although he named each of his other siblings, it is thought that she died before he wrote it. Nothing more has been found on her. Known child:

A. John Reedy

3-15 DAVID GRAHAM,[118] born Chester County, South Carolina, c. 1788-1792, died probably in Chester County after June 1844; married in York County, South Carolina, 4 March 1819, Elizabeth ___.

    Three Chester County court cases establish the year of David's birth as between 1788 and 1792. In the first which was dated 1808, David, "by Robert Caskey his next friend," sued James Chesnut for malicious practice (Index to Court Records, untitled and unpaged; no further information was found on this case). The fact that David needed a "next friend" indicated that he was under the legal age. The other two court cases were dated 19 May 1813 and 27 December 1813. In the first, David sued Jane McWilliams, in the second he sued John and David McWilliams, and in neither case did he need a "next friend" (Docket Abstracts, Court of Common Pleas, no page numbers and again no further information was found on these cases).

    Two other cases concerning David were located in Chester County. On 16 May 1815 he and Samuel Adams (perhaps his cousin 2-2D) sued Thomas McDill (Docket Abstracts, Court of Common Pleas, no page numbers and no further information found). Finally, in the spring term of 1817 David sued James Boyd, John Boyd, and Alexander Walker for debt, and the judgment was "by default and referred to the Clerk to assess the damages."

In 1819 David was married in York County where he lived at least until 1823. A deed of sale was recorded in Chester County and proved on 17 September 1823 in which David, "of York District," sold to his brother, 3-16 James Jr., 100 acres in Chester County. The land was described as being on the road leading from the south fork of Fishing Creek to Charleston and was part of a 200-acre tract sold by Micajah Piggot to Jasper Rogers, then to William Stroud, then to the late John Caskey. The deed was witnessed by Peter Wilson, Thomas Caskey (husband of David's sister 3-13 Julianna), and David Graham (perhaps 3-5). It was proved by Peter Wilson and Thomas Caskey (Book U, p. 503). Another deed dated 25 September 1824 showed that David had returned to Chester County by that time. In it Jesse Simpson sold 100 acres to David for $600. The land bounded that of his father, James Graham, who also witnessed the deed (Book W, p. 406).

The reason David returned to Chester County is that his marriage had been stormy and had ended in permanent separation within three years. A few months after David sold his 100 acres to his brother on 17 September 1823, David's wife, Elizabeth, who was living with her father in York County, went before the York County Court of Equity (9 January 1824) to request alimony. In her deposition she testified that during the three years she had lived with David he had physically beat and verbally abused her several times, even threatening to kill her, and at David's request she had returned to her father's home before the birth of her last child. Since that time David had contributed nothing to her support or to that of their children, and her father could ill afford to maintain them. Further, because David had sold the land in Chester County she believed he was planning to move to parts unknown. Finally, she knew that David was well situated financially, not only because of the land sale in Chester County, but also because several people owed him money, and a man named Thomas Williams was collecting the money on David's behalf. She also wanted Thomas Williams to be made accountable for the money he collected and to be enjoined from giving it to David.

In his official reply on 14 June 1824, David testified that Elizabeth had been pregnant when he married her, that he had then believed it was his child, but that he had come to believe the child was another man's. During their marriage she had frequently left his home and children for no cause to return to the home of her father who lived nearby, and at one time she had left him for two months during which time her father came to his house and "abused him very much" as well as drove off the cattle which the father had given him. He had never cursed or struck his wife except once. At that time he, though not Elizabeth, had been

invited by a neighbor to spend an evening and he wished to go, but
she refused to give him his clothes and tried to throw a basin of
suds at him whereupon he slapped her, an act he regretted. It had
been Elizabeth's own wish to go to her father's home to have her
last child; he had gone there himself when the baby was born.
After two months she had still not returned, so he went to his
father-in-law's house and offered his horse to Elizabeth to ride
home, but she and her father "abused him very much" while her
father "refused to let her sleep in the same bed with him and
forced a whip out of defendants [David's] hand, broke it to
pieces."

During the next two years, lists were made of David's
holdings and debtors, and witnesses were called. One of them was
Nelly Graham (probably Eleanor, wife of 3-5 David), but the
witnesses' testimonies do not appear in the record. Then in late
1826 David's brother, 3-16 James Graham Jr., was dying and wrote a
will dated 24 September 1826. In it James left $10 and most of
his clothing to David, adding that he also left David half of the
balance of his estate after all bills had been paid "on condition
that he becomes of a right mind and is in need of it to be left in
the Hands of my Father to give to my brother as he think best and
Should my brother never become of a right mind I give and bequeth
[h]is part to my Father to do with as he thinks best. . . ." The
will was proved on 20 October 1826.

A few months earlier, the Chester County, South Carolina,
Court of Equity recorded the following on 15 June 1826:

> We the committee and Jury aforesaid having been sworn
> and impanneled do make the following return. 1st
> [First] we find that David Graham is deranged or that he
> is a lunatic. We believe him to have some lucid inte-
> rests; We believe him to be between thirty and forty
> years of age; and we believe Chester District is his
> place of residence, & we believe [him] to have personal
> and real estate to the amt. of two thousand Dollars and
> that he has been insane and incapable of attending to
> his concer[n]s of life for upward of three or four years
> past; and from all this testamony adduced we have no
> doubt but that this Said David Graham is a lunatic and
> incapable of attending to his concerns of life. . . .

This document was signed by fifteen men.

Soon after, the court appointed David's brother-in-law Thomas
Caskey (husband of 3-13 Julianna) as David's guardian and on 13

August 1827 ordered Thomas to pay Elizabeth $120 annually in two half-yearly payments. On 28 June 1828 the court changed Elizabeth's settlement to an outright payment of half of David's estate after all debts had been paid.

Apparently, however, Thomas Caskey retained the title to a 175-acre tract in Chester County which had been awarded to Elizabeth, and the land was rented for a time with the proceeds supposed to go to her. But as she testified later, the trustee for her estate, a James M. Harris, turned over to her only a third of the actual rent money and pocketed the remainder, eventually absconding with the rest of the available money in David's estate. Also, the house on the rented land had burned down, making the land no longer rentable. Therefore, with the aid of a new trustee named T. W. McNeel, Elizabeth petitioned the court in 1832 to be allowed to sell the land, saying it was lying idle and unproductive and that she was in great need.

The case dragged on until 27 June 1836 when Elizabeth repeated her petition and requested that Thomas Caskey show cause why the land should not be sold. Thomas was directed to do so, and he replied that in order to save the land for David's children he had paid James M. Harris $600 for it, retaining the title, and had otherwise fully complied with the court's directions concerning Elizabeth's settlement. Because one of David's children had died, and Thomas would not acknowledge that Elizabeth's oldest child was David's, David had only one remaining child, and to that child Thomas was willing to execute a title at any time. Nonetheless, he was not willing that the land be sold.

Thomas Caskey died on 19 October 1840. In June of 1844 Elizabeth again petitioned the court to be allowed to sell the land, and this time Thomas's son John Caskey responded. In a deed dated 24 June 1844, he said, "I the committee of David Graham the Husband of Elizabeth Graham am satisfied that the petitioner is in extream want and therefore consent as such committee that the prayer of the petitioner be granted."

Nothing more is known of David, Elizabeth, or her children after this time although a D. Graham, aged "53," was listed in the household of 3-13B Robert and Rosanna (Caskey) Gourley in the 1850 census of Chester County, South Carolina. (Censuses were not always correct about ages.) If "D. Graham" was this David, Rosanna Caskey Gourley was his niece, daughter of 3-13 Joanna Graham Caskey.

Children, all born in York County, South Carolina:

2-4 James                                                                    3-16

4-40 Mary H., b. *c.* 1819         4-42 Martha Ann, b. *c.* 1822
4-41 ___, b. *c.* 1820


3-16 JAMES GRAHAM JR., born Chester County, South Carolina, *c.* 1793, died Chester County, 28 September 1826 (age 33), buried Hopewell Church Cemetery, Chester County;[119] unmarried.

James had several land dealings during his short life. On 29 May 1819 he and James Boyd sold 144 acres on Little River in Chester County to James McKinstry for $534 (recorded 31 July 1819, Book T, p. 37); and in a deed proved 17 September 1823, James's brother, 3-15 David, of York County sold to James 100 acres on Rocky Creek on the road leading to Charleston (Book U, p. 503). This sale led to a long court case involving David and his estranged wife (see under 3-15 David).

Two other land purchases were as follows: on 2 October 1821 and 5 August 1822 James bought a total of 175 acres for $245. The two sales were of land previously owned by John Trussell and sold at auction by Sheriff Thomas R. McClintock presumably for non-payment of taxes. The 1821 sale to James was by Henry Carter and included 52 acres on which Trussell then lived. James paid $25 for it (Book U, pp. 9-10). The 1822 sale to James was by David McCalla and included 123 acres for $220 (Book U, pp. 212-3). Probably, James allowed Trussell to continue living on the land.

James also owned land in Alabama, as was revealed during the settlement of his estate.

James's will, which is of some interest, is transcribed verbatim as follows:

In the Name of God Amen I James Graham Jioner [Junior] of the District of Chester and State of South Carolina being sick of body but of Sound and disposing mind memory and understanding praised by God for the Same do make this my last will and Testament in manner and form folowing Viz First I Recommend my soul to god who gave it and my body to the dust to be decently buried- and as to my worldly Estate In the first place I allow all my Just debts to be paid-- Secondly I geave and bequeth unto my Sister and Brotherinlaw Alexander Smith and Esther Smith one Nigroe girle named Loosey and the remander of my property both Real and personal as also my land In the State of the Alabama I alow to be Sold at

Public Sale as soon after my deceas as my Executors may
think best and the Moneys arising from the sales of said
estate I give and bequeth to my aged Father Two Hundred
Dollars also I give and bequeth to my aged Mother one Hundred
and Twenty Dollars- and to my Brother Thomas Caskey
Three Hundred Dollars- and I give to my Niece Mary Caskey
Ten dollars and to my Nice Rosahah Caskey I bequeth Ten
dollars and to my Nephew John Caskey I bequeth Ten dollars
and to my Nephew James Caskey I give Ten Dollars and to my
Nephew John Reedy I give and bequeth my Cloake and what he
hath in his Hands of my Estate at this time and to my Brother
David Graham I give and bequeth Ten Dollars-- and the
remainder of my estate in Notes I alow to be placed in the
hands of my Executors for Colection which is to the amount
of about seven or Eight Hundred Dollars and I alow after
the above bequethed part is paid off I alow the balance of
my Estate one Half to my Sister Esther Smith and my Brotherinlaw
Alexander Smith and the other Half I give and
bequeth to my Brother David Graham on Condition that he
becomes of a right mind and is in need of it to be left in
the Hands of my Father to give to my brother as he think
best and Should my brother never become of a right mind I
give and bequeth [h]is part to my Father to do with as he
thinks best and I Give and bequeth to my brotherinlaw
Alexander Smith all my Farming Tools and my Clothing  I
give and bequeth to my Father my Black Bumlezet Coat and
to Alexander Smith I give and bequeth my Black Broad Cloth
Coat and the balance of my body Clothing I give to my Brother
David Graham  And I do hereby Constitute and appoint
Edward Blackstocks [husband of James's aunt 2-8 Margaret]
John Douglas Executors of this my last will and Testament
hereby Revoking and making void all and every Will or
Wills at any time heretofore by me made do alow this to be
last will and testament

    In Witness whereof I have Set my hand and affixed
my Seal this Twenty fourth day of September A D 1826 and
Fiftyeth of american Independence    Signed Sealed Declared
and published by the above named James Graham Juner as and
for his last will and Testament in the presence of us who
at his Request and in his presence have Subscribed our
names
John Douglas
Peter Wilson                                 James Graham (L. S.)
Josiah Miller
[Probated 2 October 1826; recorded in Book H, p. 323
(Apartment 22, Package 323)]

Among the items for sale in James's estate were a six-volume encyclopedia, twenty-one issues of *Evangelical Witness*, and *Smiley's Geography and Atlas*, all bought for $24 by Alexander Smith, husband of James's sister 3-17 Esther. Other items included six volumes of Latin classics and five volumes of Greek classics bought by Hugh McWilliam for $10. Thomas Caskey, husband of James's sister 3-13 Julianna, bought a copy of *Butler's History* for $1.00, and James's mother, Esther, bought his Bible for 50¢.

James's land was not sold until 1832 and 1833. On 20 August 1832 James's father, James Graham Sr., bought the Alabama tract for $170 on behalf of his grandson James Graham Smith who was a minor (son of James's youngest daughter, 3-17 Esther). The land consisted of 166-87/100 acres and had been sold to James Jr. at a public auction held in Huntsville, Alabama (Book F, pp. 42-3). Finally, on 29 July 1833 Alexander Smith bought the remaining land for $800. It consisted of 195 acres in Chester County and was bounded by lands of James Miller Jr., James Sloan, Robert Wilson, and Thomas Caskey (Book F, pp. 228-9).

3-17 ESTHER GRAHAM SMITH,[120] born Chester County, South Carolina, 1797, died near Bloomington, Tennessee, 30 April 1864, buried Salem A.R.P. Church Cemetery near Atoka, Tipton County; married in Chester County, *c.* 1826, ALEXANDER SMITH, born County Antrim, Ireland, 1796, died Tipton County, Tennessee, 13 August 1870, buried Salem A.R.P. Church Cemetery.

On 1 November 1819 Alexander migrated from Ireland to South Carolina where he became a naturalized citizen on 18 April 1825. He and Esther were probably married in about 1826 shortly before her brother James Jr. died. James bequeathed half his estate to them as well as a negro girl named Loosey. James also bequeathed his farming tools and a black broadcloth coat to Alexander, and at James's subsequent estate sale Alexander bought many additional items including a six-volume encyclopedia, twenty-one issues of *Evangelical Witness*, a clock, a barrel, six chairs, a hog, a frying pan, a large pot, four bags, and some brushes and razors.

Esther's father, who had been involved in many legal actions, deeded all his remaining property to her in a gift deed dated 9 October 1832 (proved 21 June 1833, Book Z, pp. 63 and 64). A month after the proof, 29 July 1833, Alexander bought the remaining Chester County property in James Jr.'s estate for $800. The property consisted of 195 acres and was bounded by lands of James Miller Jr., James Sloan, Robert Wilson, and Thomas Caskey (Book F, pp. 228-9).

A few years later Alexander and Esther decided to move west, and on 6 August 1836 they sold 194 acres on Rocky Creek in Chester County to Moses H. Robinson for $1,550. The land was described as bounded by lands of Thomas Caskey, William Wilson, Margaret Miller, James Miller, and Peter Wallace (Book AA, pp. 469-70). Esther signed the dower release on 24 August 1836, and they probably left South Carolina soon after. They moved to Tipton County, Tennessee, taking Esther's father along.

In Chester County Esther and Alexander had been members of Hopewell A.R.P. Church. On 16 April 1837 they joined the Salem A.R.P. Church in Tipton County.

Esther and Alexander had four children:

A. James Graham Smith, b. South Carolina, 18 September 1828
B. Jane Wallace Smith, b. South Carolina, c. 1832
C. John C. Smith, b. South Carolina, 15 October 1835
D. Alexander H. Smith, b. Tennessee, c. 1836-38

---

A. James Graham Smith, born Chester County, South Carolina, 18 September 1828, died Troy, Obion County, Tennessee, 4 August 1905; married in Tipton County, Tennessee, 3 January 1854, Sarah Eliza Allen, born May 1834, died 4 March 1899, daughter of William Allen (1796-1832) and Elizabeth ___ (1802-1865). In 1850 James went to Mississippi where he taught school. In May 1853 he moved to Troy, Obion County, Tennessee, where he taught at the Westbrook Academy and studied law under Judge S. W. Cochran. James was admitted to the Obion County bar in 1857 and eventually became esteemed as a lawyer throughout western Tennessee although he consistently refused to run for office. He and his wife were members of the Associate Reformed Presbyterian Church of Troy where James was an elder, led the singing, and taught Sunday school. He also was the chairman of the Board of Trustees of Obion College and was a school director for his district. When Western Tennessee was occupied by the North during the Civil War, he refused to sign the oath of allegiance and was imprisoned at Saint Louis for the duration. He was known as "Major Smith" and was also called "The Nestor of the Bar." Children:

1. Mary Jane Wallace Smith Crockett, born Troy, Tennessee, 3

October 1854, died 12 August 1944; married, 16 March 1871, Harry Hill Crockett, born 1850, died 7 March 1890. He was a Mississippi River boat gambler. Children:

a.  Cora Crockett Inman, born 21 December 1871, died 21 August 1946; married on 26 May 1896, John Inman. Children: (a) William Inman, born 26 February 1897, died 7 March 1897; (b) Harry Hill Inman, born 10 April 1901, died 27 June 1901; and (c) Ethel Lee Inman Hall, married Spencer Hall.

b.  Sarah Crockett King, born 3 September 1873, died 21 April 1965; married Walter B. King, born 1873, died 26 January 1940. No children.

c.  Lee Crockett Oates, born 3 March 1876, died 1 February 1958; married, 19 February 1899, the Rev. Dr. James Lee Oates, born 8 April 1873, died 2 April 1943. Children: (a) Louise Wallace Oates; (b) Pauline Oates; (c) Ruth Oates Currie, married Hugh Currie; and (d) Elizabeth Crockett Oates James, married Jock Tettus James.

d.  David Crockett, born 1 August 1878, died 18 June 1928; married, 2 June 1901, Ida Mae Tucker, born 10 June 1884, died 28 December 1970. Child: Paul Smith Crockett, married Katherine Hellis.

e.  James Smith Crockett, born 9 February 1881, died 16 September 1963; married, 26 February 1904, Cora Hogue, born 1882, died 1926, daughter of James Hogue and Jemima Moffatt. No children.

f.  Bessie Eudora Crockett Hayes, born 17 October 1883, died ___; married, 16 September 1902, Professor Samuel Banks Hayes, born 10 April 1872, died 14 November 1947. Children: (a) James Graham Hayes, born 25 April 1904, married, 5 June 1935, Alice Shankle; (b) Samuel Banks Hayes Jr., born 28 June 1906, married on 6 July 1935, Priscilla Alden Bailey; and (c) Eleanor Estelle Hayes, married Thomas Earl Digby.

g.  Paul Allen Crockett, born 17 July 1886, died ___; married, 12 May 1907, Mary Farrester. Children: (a) Thomas Hill Crockett, born 26 March 1908, married Bessie Tucker; (b) Mildred Crockett, born 11 September 1913, drowned in the Obion River on 17 January 1930;

and (c) Paul Allen Crockett Jr., born 12 June 1917, Married Julie Fox.

h. Harry (?, sic) Wallace Crockett Cunningham (girl), born 1 May 1890, died ___; married, 18 January 1911, John Talmadge Cunningham, born 19 June 1888, died 6 July 1963. Children: (a) Bob Hill Cunningham, born 22 October 1911, married Montell Hooper; (b) John Talmadge Cunningham Jr., born 27 December 1913, married Virginia Water; and (c) David Crockett Cunningham, born September 1919, died 31 May 1963, married Helen DeWitt.

2. Frances Bonner Hill Smith Maxwell (called Bonnie), born Troy, Tennessee, 2 June 1856, died 26 August 1934; married, 24 March 1875, John Basil Maxwell, born Henry County, Tennessee, 21 April 1851, died Troy, Tennessee, 5 September 1901. John moved to Troy in 1868 and for a time was the editor of a newspaper, *The Troy Times*. He was also once a deputy county court clerk of Obion County, Tennessee. Children:

a. Jennie Smith Maxwell, born Troy, Tennessee, 15 January 1876, died 7 July 1886.

b. Basil Bright Maxwell (called Jack), born Troy, Tennessee, 4 February 1878, died 8 November 1973; married, 4 September 1892, Lantye Turnage. Child: John Basil Maxwell.

c. Augusta Maxwell (called Gussie), born Troy, Tennessee, 15 November 1879, died 17 March 1893.

d. Luther Maurice Maxwell, born Troy, Tennessee, 17 July 1882, died 19 November 1967; married Lela Buchanan.

e. Martha Willie Maxwell McDaniel, born Troy Tennessee, 24 September 1887, died 3 February 1975; married, 6 December 1906, Hurdle E. McDaniel, born 23 July 1884, died 9 December 1966, son of Fountain P. McDaniel and Melissa Ann Inman. Children: (a) Hurdle E. McDaniel Jr., born 1914, married Virginia Blair; and (b) Howard Maxwell McDaniel, born 1919, married (1) in 1942, Frances Boyd, (2) in 1975, his first cousin Rebecca Hill Riddick, daughter of Prentice Riddick and 3-17A2g Medora Wallace Maxwell.

f. Fitz Lee Maxwell, born Troy, Tennessee, 10 March 1890, died 26 October 1964; married Neva McGregor. Children: (**a**) Frances Cooper Maxwell; and (**b**) Beth McGregor Maxwell.

g. Medora Wallace Maxwell Riddick, born Troy, Tennessee, 7 December 1892; married Prentice Riddick. Children: (**a**) Rebecca Hill Riddick McDaniel, married, 1975, her first cousin Howard Maxwell McDaniel, son of Hurdle E. McDaniel and 3-17A2e Martha Willie Maxwell; and (**b**) Patricia Maxwell Riddick.

h. Howard Stonewall Maxwell, born Troy, Tennessee, 6 June 1895, killed 18 June 1918 in Belleau Wood, France, during World War I.

i. John Bonner Maxwell, born Troy, Tennessee, 15 October 1897, died ___; married in Dyersburg, Tennessee, Mary Elizabeth House of Dresden, Tennessee. Children: (**a**) John Bonner Maxwell Jr.; and (**b**) Howard Stonewall Maxwell.

3. John William Alexander Smith (called Will), born Troy, Tennessee, 26 September 1858, died at the home of his daughter in Paducah, Kentucky, 11 March 1940; married in the Troy A.R.P. Church, 17 April 1889, Sunie Montgomery Pressly, born Starkville, Mississippi, 17 April 1869, died Troy, Tennessee, 15 June 1939, daughter of the Rev. Dr. David Pressly (1820-1891) and Sarah Brown Peden (1827-1883) and sister of the Rev. Thomas Peden Pressly who married Will's sister Dora. Will was a part-owner of the Troy Roller Mills which manufactured Helen of Troy flour. He was also a mason and an elder at the Troy A.R.P. Church. Sunie was graduated in 1887 from Due West Female College, South Carolina. Children:

    a. Louie Pressly Smith Trobaugh, born Troy, Tennessee, 10 January 1894, died 4 July 1972, buried Smith Cemetery at Troy; married John Chester Trobaugh, born 16 January 1890, died 20 March 1932. Children: (**a**) William Smith Trobaugh, born 27 June 1920, married, 11 April 1942, Elizabeth Gertrude Rhode; (**b**) Jesse Densmore Trobaugh, born 24 January 1922, married Mary Ellen Fleming, born 17 January 1925, died 21 October 1961; and (**c**) Sue Boyd Trobaugh Davidson, born ___, married, 20 August 1953, Harold Gordon Davidson (called Hal).

b.  Eudora Belle Smith Riddick, married in her father's home at Troy, 27 June 1918, Sidney Orton Riddick who died in Paducah, Kentucky, 5 May 1947. Children: (a) Elizabeth Kathryn Riddick Eudaukas, born 9 July 1919, married Peter Eudaukas; and (b) Dorathy (*sic*) Riddick, born 19 February 1922, died 27 October 1928.

c.  Alexander Densmore Smith (called Allie), born 9 January 1905, still living in Troy, Tennessee, in 1989; married, 21 December 1934, Margaret Lavinia McDaniel, born 28 March 1909, still living in 1989. Children: (a) James Allen Smith, born 23 March 1936, married Margaret Louise Durham (called Tiny), daughter of Hannah W. Durham and Ruby Peeler (James Allen Smith provided most of the information on the descendants of 3-17 Esther Graham Smith); and (b) John Densmore Smith, born 7 October 1938, unmarried.

d.  James Calvin Smith, born 25 November 1908, still living at Troy, Tennessee, in 1989; married, 26 June 1935, Hattie Mae Blakely of Ora, South Carolina, born 7 April 1906, died 25 March 1982. He is a minister and served at the Troy A.R.P. Church, 1968-1974. Children: (a) Nancy Suzanne Smith Elleat, born 24 April 1937, married the Rev. Robert Beever Elleat Jr; and (b) Harriett Elizabeth Smith Linderman, born 26 August 1938, married the Rev. Clifton Earl Linderman.

4.  Dora Augusta Lantha Smith Pressly,[121] born Troy Tennessee, 20 September 1860, died 15 April 1890, buried Smith family cemetery, Troy; married, at Troy, 25 December 1877, the Rev. Thomas Peden Pressly, born near Starkville, Mississippi, 15 January 1853, died 10 May 1923, son of the Rev. Dr. David Pressly (1820-1891) and Sarah Brown Peden (1827-1883), and brother of Sunie Pressly who married Dora's brother Will. Thomas was graduated from Erskine College, Due West, South Carolina, in 1872 and from Erskine's theological seminary in 1875. In the same year, he was licensed to preach by the Memphis Presbytery at the Salem A.R.P Church, Tipton County, Tennessee, and was ordained in 1876. He then became the pastor at the Troy A.R.P. Church, serving there until his death. After Dora died he married (2) on 22 December 1892, Mrs. Elizabeth Stephens Bittick, widow of James Bittick and daughter of Jerry Stephens and Martha Ann Taylor. Children of Dora and Thomas:

a.  James Wallace Pressly, born Troy, Tennessee, 12 March 1879, died 4 November 1931; married at his father's home, Martha Belle Bittick, born 1881, died 1972, daughter of James Bittick and Elizabeth Stephens. (Martha Belle's mother married (2) James's father.) In 1898 James was graduated from Erskine College, Due West, South Carolina, and later owned and operated Pressly and Company in Troy, Tennessee. He also once owned an insurance agency. He was an elder in his father's church. Children: (a) Peden Bittick Pressly, died at four months on 5 March 1906; (b) Elizabeth Stephens Pressly Nichols, married, 24 August 1934, James Edward Nichols; (c) Belle Bonner Pressly Gahlgren, married David M. Gahlgren; (d) Dr. Thomas James Pressly, a professor of history at the University of Washington, married Lillian Cameron; and (e) James Wallace Pressly Jr., born 23 December 1911, died 28 December 1914.

b.  David Peden Pressly, born Troy, Tennessee, 8 January 1881, died Utica, New York, 20 October 1934, buried Troy Cemetery, Tennessee; unmarried. David was graduated from Obion College at Troy and from Erskine College, Due West, South Carolina, in 1901. He then entered the theological seminary at Erskine, was ordained in 1903, and was licensed by the Memphis Presbytery on 30 June 1903. He began his ministry at Princeton, Missouri, later going to the Mount Zion A.R.P. Church, Missouri, then the Brighton, Tennessee, A.R.P. Church, 1908-11. He also helped establish the Brighton Savings Bank and the Brighton High School of which he was the first principal, 1909-12. After leaving Brighton he taught at a school in Saint Louis. Later he switched from the Associate Reformed Presbyterian Church to the United Presbyterian and preached at churches in Florida, New Jersey, and New York. In 1933 while at his home in Pattersonville, New York, he experienced a nervous collapse from which he never recovered.

c.  Sarah Bonner Pressly Nichols, born Troy, Tennessee, 4 March 1883, died 2 January 1968; married at her father's home in Troy, 4 September 1907, Herbert Sharpe Nichols, born 1886, died October 1946. Herbert taught at the Agricultural and Mechanical College at Starkville, Mississippi. Children: (a) Col. Thomas Eugene Nichols, married Elizabeth Sale, daughter of

Dr. William Henry Wooten Sale and Laura Kate Sanford (called Lollie); and (b) Herbert Sharpe Nichols Jr., born 24 January 1912, married Elizabeth Long.

5. Luther Andrew Densmore Smith, born Troy, Tennessee, 8 January 1862, died 19 June 1933; married (1) on 16 September 1891, Blanch Ott; (2) on 19 February 1897, Anna Polk Faulk, born 19 August 1870, died in Picayunne, Mississippi, 3 October 1967 at the age of 97, daughter of Joel Benjamin Faulk, and Elizabeth Dixon Faris.

   Child of Luther and (1) Blanch Ott:

   a. James Ott Smith, born 30 July 1893, died 12 July 1894.

   Children of Luther and (2) Anna Faulk:

   b. Joseph Allen Smith, born 7 April 1898, died Biloxi, Mississippi, 11 May 1972; unmarried. He was a World War I veteran.

   c. Wallace Graham Smith, born 14 August 1899, died ___; married, 3 November 1928, Marie Bias, born 25 August 1906, died 25 March 1940. When a young man, Wallace moved with two friends, Maxey Moffatt and Guy Hughes, to Williamson, West Virginia, where Wallace lived out his life. He and Marie had two children.

   d. Faris Montgomery Smith, born 12 October 1905, died 27 July 1987; unmarried.

6. Fitz James Lee Smith, born Troy, Tennessee, 16 October 1864, died ___; married, 14 November 1901, May Anderson, born 1872, died 31 March 1944. He was a lawyer practicing at Union City, Tennessee. Children:

   a. ___ Smith (girl), born and died 30 August 1902.

   b. J. G. Smith, born 1905, died 1924, buried Union City, Tennessee.

B. Jane Wallace Smith, born Chester County, South Carolina, c. 1832, died Troy, Tipton County, Tennessee, 21 November 1889; unmarried. She joined the Salem A.R.P. Church on 30 April 1847. After her parents died she moved to Troy to live with her brother Major James Graham Smith.

C. John C. Smith, born Chester County, South Carolina, 15 October 1835, died Troy, Tennessee, 27 May 1852, buried in the Troy Cemetery; unmarried. He joined the Salem A.R.P. Church on 10 March 1852.

D. Alexander H. Smith, born Tipton County, Tennessee, c. 1836-8, died at an asylum in Nashville, Tennessee, 7 October 1897, buried Troy, Tennessee; unmarried. In 1860 he was graduated from Erskine College, Due West, South Carolina, and soon enlisted in the Confederate Army, Company G, 51st Tennessee Infantry.

## FOURTH GENERATION

### CHILDREN OF 3-3 MATTHEW GRAHAM AND JENNETTE WILSON

4-1 MARTHA W. GRAHAM MCDILL,[1] born Todd County, Kentucky, 23 June 1805, died in Henderson County, Illinois, 12 May 1841 (35 years, 10 months, 19 days), buried South Henderson Cemetery; married in Preble County, Ohio, 12 or 13 October 1830, SAMUEL MCDILL (brother of Martha who married 4-2 Andrew), born Preble County, Ohio, 13 August 1807, died Henderson County, Illinois, 6 October 1866, buried South Henderson Cemetery, son of James McDill (born December 1769, died 21 November 1854, buried South Henderson Cemetery) and Margaret Chesnut (born c. 1779, died 2 August 1847, buried South Henderson Cemetery). Martha's and Samuel's marriage in Preble County, Ohio, was performed by the Rev. Alexander L. Porter; her younger sister, 4-6 Margaret, married a grandson of this minister.[2]

In 1836 Martha and Samuel moved to Warren County, Illinois, and the area where they lived became Henderson County in 1841. Soon after moving there, Samuel bought land from Martha's brother 4-2 Andrew in S7 T10 R4 Biggsville Township (Book 2, p. 176) where he lived for the remainder of his life. Samuel was a farmer and a ruling elder in the South Henderson United Presbyterian Church. He married (2) in Henderson County, 12 or 14 December 1842, Nancy Findley, born Clark County, Indiana, 27 December 1816, died 23 June 1897, buried South Henderson Cemetery, daughter of Alexander Findley (died 1817) and Agnes B. Ritchie (born Westmoreland County, Pennsylvania, 11 May 1795, died Halsey, Oregon, 28 September 1880).

Children of Martha and Samuel, the first three born in Preble County, Ohio, the other two in Warren (Henderson) County,

3-3 Matthew, 2-1 Andrew                                                4-1A

Illinois:

A. James Chesnut McDill, b.     D. Andrew Thomas McDill, b.
   1 August 1831                   2 July 1837
B. Martha Jane McDill, b.       E. Margaret E. McDill, b.
   14 April 1833                   20 July 1839
C. Matthew Harvey McDill, b.
   7 April 1835

---

A. James Chesnut McDill,[3] born Preble County, Ohio, 1 August 1831, died in Georgia, 19 June 1864, buried South Henderson Cemetery; married, 22 June 1854, his second cousin Sarah McQuiston, born Ohio, 1 February 1832, died near Biggsville, Illinois, 2 June 1902, buried South Henderson Cemetery, daughter of James McQuiston (born 15 October 1797, died Preble County, Ohio, 24 November 1869) and Margaret McDill (born 1798, died Henderson County, Illinois, 29 July 1861). James and Sarah were married by the Rev. James C. Porter.

During the Civil War James was a corporal in the Volunteer Infantry, Company G, 84th Illinois Regulars, and was killed in a skirmish at Kennesaw Mountain, Georgia. Sarah married (2) in Henderson County, 25 April 1872, Hugh R. Reynolds, born near Statesville, North Carolina, 12 November 1812, died 8 January 1896. After Hugh died, Sarah found herself in difficult circumstances and on 3 March 1901 reapplied for the widow's pension she had received after James was killed. When she, herself, died a year later, she was buried by James's side in South Henderson Cemetery. Children:

1. ___ McDill (girl), died infancy, 11 March 1857

2. Martha Elizabeth McDill Cochran (Lizzie), born probably in Henderson County, Illinois, 7 November 1859, died 1940, buried Biggsville Cemetery; married, 7 November 1883, William H. Cochran, born Illinois, 15 February 1862, died 1943, buried Biggsville Cemetery, son of John D. Cochran (born South Carolina, 25 June 1819, died 15 August 1896, buried Biggsville Cemetery) and Rachel Jane ___ (born Ohio, 30 November 1827, died 23 November 1900, buried Biggsville Cemetery). William was a farmer in Biggsville Township, Henderson County, Illinois. Children:

    a. James Wilbert Cochran (Bert), born 27 January 1886, died 1951; married, 1 May 1914, Naomi Godfrey, born

1887, died 1955. Child: Clarence Wilbert Cochran (Bill), born 1923, died 1981, married Jane Menely, and had Jan, born 1948, Kathy, born 1951, and Karen, born 1952.

    b. Frank Cochran, born 27 January 1888, died infancy, twin to next.

    c. Francis Cochran, born 27 January 1888, died infancy, twin to above.

    d. John Roy Cochran, born 8 December 1888, died 1952, married, 27 December 1912, Mabel Johnston, born 25 September 1889, died 1961. Children: (**a**) John Roy Jr., born 1914, died 1966, married Ruth Miller and had Donald Earl, born 1939, Stuart Allen, born 1942, Kenneth Miller, born 1946, and Suzanne, born 1950; (**b**) William Keith, born 24 July 1916, married Eloris Puckett and had Lynn, born 1943, Boyd, born 1946, and Norma, born 1949; (**c**) Loren Lee, born 1919, married Dorothy Pendarvis and had Katherine, born 1946, and Gary, born 1948; and (**d**) Paul, born 14 November 1924, married Donna Johnson and had Steven, born 1963, Christina, born 1964, Andrew, born 1965, and David, born 1967.

    e. Walter Raymond Cochran, born 1 August 1891, died 1964, buried Biggsville Cemetery; married, 14 April 1914, Pearl L. Myers, born 15 June 1889, died 1964, buried Biggsville Cemetery.

    f. ___ Cochran, died young

    g. ___ Cochran, died young

Sarah McQuiston had one child by her second husband: Margaret Jane Reynolds, born 20 October 1873, died 8 April 1944, buried South Henderson Cemetery.[4]

B. Martha Jane McDill, born Preble County, Ohio, 14 April 1833, died Preble County, 21 October 1834, buried Hopewell Cemetery, Preble County.[5]

C. Matthew Harvey McDill, born Preble County, Ohio, 7 April 1835, died December 1857 (22 years, 8 months, 3 days), buried South Henderson Cemetery, Henderson County, Illinois;[6] probably unmarried.

3-3 Matthew, 2-1 Andrew                                                        4-1D

D.  Andrew Thomas McDill,[7] born near Biggsville, Henderson County,
    Illinois, 2 July 1837, died of lobar pneumonia in Nashville,
    Tennessee, 29 January 1914, buried South Henderson Cemetery,
    Henderson County, Illinois; married at Knoxville, Knox County,
    Illinois, 25 November 1865, Elizabeth Emma Gowdy (called
    Emma), born *c.* 1838, died probably in Nashville, 9 March 1919.
    Andrew was graduated from Monmouth College in 1862 and served
    in the Civil War as a sergeant in Company G, 84th Illinois
    Infantry, enlisting on 19 June 1862, and mustered out on 18
    June 1865. He then attended Monmouth Seminary, was licensed
    by the Monmouth Presbytery, 10 April 1867, and ordained by the
    Chicago Presbytery as pastor at Ross Grove, Leland, Illinois,
    1868-70. From 1870 to 1871 he was a pastor in Kossuth County,
    Iowa, and 1871-76 was president of Amity College at College
    Springs, Iowa. Later he was a pastor at Washington, Iowa,
    1876-78, Chicago, 1878-81, and Philadelphia, 1881-83. He also
    edited and published *The Olive Plant, The Little Preacher,* and
    *The Young Christian Instructor,* 1880-85. From 1893 until 1901
    he was an editor and publisher at Santa Ana, California, and
    finally retired to Nashville, Tennessee. In 1906 he applied
    for a veteran's pension, stating he was blind in his right
    eye, and "the left eye will never be better." He also had
    kidney and bladder trouble. At the time of his enlistment, he
    was described as being 5 feet 9½ inches tall with a light
    complexion, gray eyes, and dark hair. In 1906 this descrip-
    tion was changed to 5 feet 8½ inches tall, dark complexion,
    brown eyes, and black hair. In Nashville he and Emma lived
    with their son Lee and his family. Children:

    1.  William Wilson McDill, born Monmouth, Illinois, 23 Novem-
        ber 1866, died of throat and lung diseases in Beaumont,
        California, 30 May 1888; unmarried.

    2.  Lee Harvey McDill, born College Springs, Iowa, 27 Febru-
        ary 1873, died ___; married perhaps in Colorado, *c.* 1891,
        Ray ___, born Arkansas, *c.* 1873, died ___. In the 1910
        census of Nashville, Tennessee, Lee and his family were
        living at 1604 Woodland Street, and his parents lived with
        them. Lee was a superintendant in a life insurance
        office. According to the census Ray had had six child-
        ren only four of whom were living. Known children:

        a.  Ray McDill (girl), born Colorado, *c.* 1893

        b.  Ora McDill (girl), born Colorado, *c.* 1895

        c.  Noveen McDill, born Colorado, *c.* 1897

d. Quintin McDill, born Tennessee, c. 1903

E. Margaret E. McDill (Maggie),[8] born 20 July 1839, died 14 December 1908, buried Monmouth Cemetery, Illinois; unmarried. Maggie was graduated from Monmouth College in 1862, taught at a school near Biggsville, Illinois, until 1870 and at Central School in Monmouth until 1876, and finally taught for twenty-six years at Harding School in Monmouth, retiring in 1902. When she first moved to Monmouth, she lived with her uncle 4-8 David Graham who died in 1894. She then made her home with David's daughter 5-29 Clara Graham McCoy, widow.

Samuel McDill also had children by his second wife: John Alexander, born 1844, died 1908; William J., born 1846, died infancy; Lydia Agnes, born 1848, died 1906; Robert Ross, born ___, died 1851; Martha Caroline, born 1851, died 1854; and Samuel Findley, born 1857, died 1915.

4-2 ANDREW GRAHAM,[9] born Todd County, Kentucky, 1807, died Henderson County, Illinois, 1848, buried South Henderson Cemetery; married (1) in Warren County, Illinois, 18 May 1837, MARTHA MCDILL (sister of Samuel who married 4-1 Martha), born Preble County, Ohio, 16 December 1812, died Henderson County, Illinois, 3 December 1838, buried South Henderson Cemetery, daughter of James McDill (born December 1769, died 21 November 1854, buried South Henderson Cemetery) and Margaret Chesnut (born c. 1779, died 2 August 1847, buried South Henderson Cemetery); Andrew married (2) in Henderson County, Illinois, 22 April 1841, RACHEL ANN DAVIS, born Virginia, 1814, died 1895, buried South Henderson Cemetery, daughter of David W. Davis (born 1779, died 8 September 1867, buried South Henderson Cemetery) and Hannah F. ___ (born 1791, died 1870, buried South Henderson Cemetery). When Andrew married Rachel he acquired the first marriage license ever issued in Henderson County which had just been formed from Warren County.

In 1829 Andrew moved with his parents from Kentucky to Preble County, Ohio, and in August 1835 he moved to what later became Henderson County, Illinois, where he settled on S7 T10N R4W with his brother-in-law Samuel McDill. On 21 March 1836, Andrew sold his share to Samuel and others and bought a section nearby (Book 2, pp. 176 and 177; Book 3, p. 568; and Book 7, p. 634). Andrew's second wife, Rachel, finally deeded the land to their son William on 24 January 1891 (Book 46, p. 11).

On 4 January 1842, on behalf of the South Henderson Presby-

3-3 Matthew, 2-1 Andrew                                                      4-3

terian Church which Andrew had joined on 23 July 1838, he, along
with John McDill and others, bought a small tract for $1.00 from
William R. Jamison (Book 1, p. 138).

After Andrew died in 1848 his brothers 4-5 William M. and 4-7
Wilson M. were appointed guardians of his children (Book E, p.
74). In the 1860 census Rachel and her children were listed in
T10N 10W Biggsville. On 1 September 1868 Rachel married (2)
Daniel Gordon who died on 23 October 1884 (75 years, 6 months, 7
days). Daniel had married first Jane P. ___ who died on 18 March
1848 (32 years, 6 months, 28 days). Daniel was buried beside Jane
in the South Henderson Cemetery while Rachel was buried next to
Andrew, and her gravestone is inscribed "Rachel A. Graham."

Children, all by (2) Rachel Ann Davis and all born in Henderson County, Illinois:

5-1 William B., b. 9 January 1842
5-2 David Wilson, b. 11 June 1843
5-3 Martha Jane, b. April 1845
5-4 Matthew Young, b. 1847, d. 1848

4-3 JOHN W. GRAHAM,[10] born Todd County, Kentucky, c. 16 November 1809,
died Monmouth, Warren County, Illinois, 8 January 1900, buried
Monmouth Cemetery; married in Preble County, Ohio, 15 November
1837, GRIZZELLA W. MILLIGAN, born Adams County, Ohio, 14 October
1816, died Monmouth, Illinois, 31 October 1874, buried Monmouth
Cemetery, daughter of John Milligan (born c. 1780, died 1823) and
Jane Mitchell (born c. 1794, died 1827). John and Grizzella were
married by the Rev. Jeremiah Morrow.

Until about 1861 John was a farmer in Israel Township, Preble County, Ohio, although at first he and Grizzella owned lot 17
in the town of Fairfield, Ohio. They sold the lot on 21 November
1839 to Silas Glover for $2,000 (Book 27, p. 109). On 11 March
1848 John bought from John Milligan (probably his brother-in-law)
part of the southwest quarter of S22 T6 R1E in Preble County for
$3,000 (Book 36, p. 380). After John Milligan died, John and
Grizzella deeded, on 7 April 1851, 1.95 acres of the land they had
inherited to the Hopewell United Presbyterian Church (Book 41, p.
532), and on 2 April 1851 they sold a large tract--the south half
and part of the north half of the southwest quarter of S22 T6
R1E--to George Ramsey for $5,280 (Book 39, p. 116). Apparently,
they then moved to Henderson County, Illinois, where they joined
the South Henderson United Presbyterian Church in August 1851

3-3 Matthew, 2-1 Andrew                                                    4-4

(Church Register). They soon changed their minds, however, and returned to Ohio where on 29 December 1851 they bought land in Preble County from John's first cousin once removed 2-6A Mary Boyse Wilson and her husband and sister, Matthew Wilson and Elizabeth Boyse (Book 39, p. 605). On 9 April 1853 John and Grizzella deeded the northeast corner of the northwest half of S22 T6 R1E to the Fairhaven Turnpike Company (Book 41, p. 476), and on 6 June 1854 they sold the southwest quarter of S22 T6 R1E to William McBride for $1,459 (Book 42, p. 337). On 24 May 1858 John and Grizzella sold the land they had bought from 2-6A Matthew and Mary (Boyse) Wilson and Elizabeth Boyse to Robert Rock (Book 47, p. 496), and finally on 19 March 1861 they sold the remainder of their S22 T6 R1E to Robert M. Wilson (Book 50, p. 382).

In about 1861 they moved to the town of Oxford, Butler County, Ohio, where they bought the in-lots 15 and 16. These lots were part of the land granted to Miami University which had leased it at an annual rent of $3 for each lot. John and Grizzella lived there until 13 February 1866 when they sold the lots to Mary McCracken for $2,200 (Book 73, pp. 274-5) and then moved again to Illinois, this time to Monmouth, Warren County. John's certificate of transfer to the Second United Presbyterian Church in Monmouth was dated 27 October 1866. He worked as a clerk and perhaps as the marshall of Monmouth in 1871. In the 1874-5 Monmouth city directory, he was listed as the baggage master at the railroad station.

This family suffered a singular amount of tragedy: two of the seven children died in infancy, three others died in their early manhood, and still another in 1874, the year in which their mother died. By 1893 John, retired, was boarding with his niece 5-33 Fannie Graham (later Herbert). His only surviving child, Mitchell M. who was unmarried, had moved to Carrollton, Missouri.

Children, all born in Preble County, Ohio:

5-5 John Milligan, b. 31 March 1839
5-6 William Andrew, b. 3 February 1841
5-7 Mitchell Matthew, b. 14 April 1843

5-8 Harvey Wilson, b. 3 September 1845
5-9 Frank Y., b. 14 July 1848
5-10 David W., d. at 6 months
5-11 ___ (boy), d. infancy

4-4 ROBERT C. GRAHAM,[11] born Todd County, Kentucky, 1811, died Louisa County, Iowa, 13 December 1878, buried Forest Home Cemetery, Henry

3-3 Matthew, 2-1 Andrew                                                4-4

County, Iowa; married MARTHA RITCHIE, born Illinois, c. 1830, died
Henry County, Iowa, 1866, buried Forest Home Cemetery.

In 1836 Robert and his parents moved from Preble County,
Ohio, to Warren (Henderson) County, Illinois, where they joined
the South Henderson Presbyterian Church on 23 July 1836. At some
time Robert and his wife moved to an area near Mount Pleasant,
Henry County, Iowa, where he bought a farm. There, his wife and
children predeceased him. He, himself, died at the home of his
brother 4-9 Dr. J. Harvey Graham in Louisa County, Iowa, although
he is buried beside his wife and sons in Henry County.

In his will, dated 8 July 1878 and proved 15 January 1879,
Robert bequeathed his mare and colt and some personal effects to
J. Harvey. His remaining property was left in equal shares to J.
Harvey, to his living brothers, John W. and David, to the heirs of
his deceased brother William M., and to the heirs of his other
deceased brother A. Y.

In October 1879 Robert's brother-in-law Harvey A. Ritchie
entered a claim of $100 against Robert's estate. The claim is of
some interest:

Question 1. State your name, age, residence occupation.
And were you in this life time acquainted with Robert C.
Graham late of Henry County Iowa?

Answer   Harvey A. Ritchie, 52. Wheatland Yuba County,
California, Carpenter. I was, he was a brother-in-law of
mine.

Question 2  State what if anything you know relating to
the borrowing by Said Graham, or loaning by H. A. Ritchie
of any money--giving time when place when, amount loaned,
under what circumstances, what if anything was said as to
the said Loan by Graham when the same was to be repaid &
how repaid, when the same was to mature, How if at all the
money was to be sent or paid by Graham to Ritchie. And
any and all other matters you may know concerning said
loaning--

Answer--  I loaned the said Robert C. Graham on the
Twenty-fourth day of July AD, 1870, at my Ranch, about 4
Miles North of Wheatland, in the County of Yuba State of
California, the Sum of One Hundred ($100.00) dollars gold
coin of the United States of America. He wanted the money
to pay his way home (to Mount Pleasant Iowa.) I Handed

him the Money, & he (Graham) said--"What shall I do about the payment of this money,--Shall I Send it back to you when I get home-- I (Ritchie) said "No Keep it until I Call for it." And the understanding between us, was that whenever I called or asked him for the money he was to pay me ___ in California, I never call on him for the money-- until since his death and I understood the payment was to be line gold coin, as currency was then at a big discount.

Question 3-- State any other matter or thing you may know of advantage to either parties concerning the Claim of H. A. Ritchie. . . .

Answer-- When he got to Corning Iowa he (Graham) wrote me a letter, which has since been lost, and in that letter he made this statement. Our fair from Sacramento to Omaha was _0$ in Green Backs, and from Omaha to Mt Plesant was 12$ you see that after paying our board on the way it about uses up the Hundred dollars. The reason he wrote so, was, that I only gave him the Hundred dollars & told him that was all I could do for him, & he must get home on that. I think my Brother H. D. Ritchie was in the room at the time. I gave each of them 100$, to return home with that same day.

Harvey A. Ritchie

The following are the children of Robert and Martha, both born in Iowa:

5-12 William, b. *c.* 1852      5-13 John H., b. *c.* 1857

4-5 WILLIAM MILLS GRAHAM,[12] born Elkton, Todd County, Kentucky, 5 March 1814, died Monmouth, Warren County, Illinois, 5 December 1863, buried Monmouth Cemetery; married in Butler County, Ohio, 15 September 1842, ELIZABETH A. ROBISON (or Robeson), born Ohio, 24 February 1822, died 22 February 1883, buried Monmouth Cemetery. They were married by the Rev. David McDill.

William was graduated from Miami University in 1838 (in the same class as that of his first cousin 4-13 John McKee Graham) and attended the Allegheny, Pennsylvania, and Oxford, Ohio, seminaries. He was licensed as a Presbyterian minister by the First Ohio Presbytery on 15 April 1841 and ordained by the Illinois Associate Reformed Presbytery. Later he went in with the United Presbyterians.

3-3 Matthew, 2-1 Andrew                                                    4-6

On 18 May 1849 William and his brother 4-7 Wilson M. were appointed guardians of the children of their late older brother 4-2 Andrew who had died in 1848 (Book E, p. 74).

William served as pastor of Union Congregation, Sparta, Illinois, 18 June 1844 until 10 September 1847, and of Virginia Grove and Harrison, Louisa County, Iowa, 10 July 1850 to 11 April 1860. He was at Spring Grove Church (later called Gerlaw), Warren County, Illinois, 11 October 1860 to 4 April 1863, and died at Monmouth, Warren County. His will was dated 8 September 1863, proved 16 February 1864; in it he named his brother Wilson M. (incorrectly cited therein as Matthew Wilson Graham) as his executor. Children:

5-14 Laura, b. IL, October 1846
5-15 Harriet E., b. IL, 20 June 1850
5-16 Martha E., b. IA, 1853
5-17 William I., b. IA, 17 August 1854
5-18 Robert, died young
5-19 John M., perhaps b. IA, 22 August 1860
5-20 Clinton W., b. IL, June 1863


4-6 MARGARET GRAHAM PORTER,[13] born Todd County, Kentucky, 1816, died Henderson County, Illinois, 21 May 1861, buried South Henderson Cemetery; married, 28 March 1848, ALEXANDER L. PORTER, born Preble County, Ohio, 24 November 1821, died 29 December 1901, buried South Henderson Cemetery, son of Hugh Porter and Eleanor Brown (1797-1885) and grandson of the Rev. Alexander Porter. Margaret's father, Matthew, was listed with her in the 1850 federal census.

In 1836 Margaret moved with her family from Preble County, Ohio, to Warren County, Illinois, where she and her parents joined the South Henderson Presbyterian Church on 23 July 1836 (Church Register). On 30 May 1841 she and seven other young people were reprimanded by the church for "promiscuous dancing"; they agreed to discontinue the practice (Session Minutes).

Alexander attended Miami University, Ohio, then went to Henderson County, Illinois, in 1840 where he taught school for a time. Later he was elected school treasurer for his township, a post he held for more than eighteen years, and finally he became a school director. He also farmed and in 1845 drove the first reaper ever run in Henderson County. On 19 June 1845 he joined the South Henderson Presbyterian Church.

After Margaret died Alexander married (2) on 15 May 1862,

Mrs. Sarah Graham Cameron, widow, born Huntington County, Pennsylvania, 31 January 1833, died 8 February 1902, buried South Henderson Cemetery, daughter of James Graham (no relation) and Nancy Wilson. Sarah had married (1) in Henderson County, 17 December 1858, William A. Cameron who died on 27 October 1859, age 22 years, buried South Henderson Cemetery; Sarah had one child by her first husband: Elizabeth (Lizzie) Anderson Cameron, born Illinois, 1859.

On 13 April 1871 Alexander was dismissed from his church because he was moving to Olena, a nearby town in Henderson County.

Children of Margaret and Alexander, all born in Henderson County, Illinois:

A. Lauretta L. Porter, b. c. 1849
B. ___ Porter, d. infancy
C. Alice Ellen Porter, b. c. 1850
D. William R. Porter, b. c. 1852
E. Wilson Graham Porter, b. 14 March 1854
F. John Porter, b. 15 November 1855
G. Frank M. Porter, b. c. 1857

---

A. Lauretta L. Porter Postlewaite, born Illinois, c. 1849, died ___; married in Henderson County, Illinois, 23 February 1871, James F. Postlewaite, born Illinois c. 1846, died ___, son of John J. Postlewaite (born Pennsylvania, c. 1815) and Isabel ___ (born Pennsylvania c. 1818). In the 1880 federal census, Lauretta and James were listed in Mercer County, Illinois. He was a farmer. Children:

1. Edward Hugh(?) Postlewaite, born Illinois c. 1872

2. Frank Postlewaite, born Illinois c. 1874; married Margaret ___.

3. Margaret(?) Elizabeth Postlewaite (called Bessie), born Illinois, c. 1876

4. Russell Postlewaite

B. ___ Porter, died infancy

C. Alice Ellen Porter McDougall, born Illinois, c. 1850, died ___; married in Henderson County, Illinois, 7 September 1886,

3-3 Matthew, 2-1 Andrew                                              4-6C1

John W. McDougall, born Argyle, New York, son of Daniel
McDougall and Martha Stevenson (Book C, p. 51). In the 1880
census of Henderson County, Illinois, Alice was listed as a
school teacher. Children:

1. Frederica McDougall Sympson, born 1888; married C. Sympson. Child:

   a. Robert F. Sympson, born 1927

2. Frances McDougall Maxwell, born 1890; married Dr. James
   Maxwell. Children:

   a. Jean Maxwell, born 1922

   b. Martha Maxwell, born 1925

   c. Ellen Maxwell, born 1929

   d. Howard Maxwell, born 1930

D. William R. Porter, born Illinois, c. 1852; married Marella
   ___. They lived in Oregon. Child:

   1. Anna Porter

E. Wilson Graham Porter, born Illinois, 14 March 1854, died 4 May
   1923, buried South Henderson Cemetery.

F. John Porter, born Illinois, 15 November 1855, died 19 December
   1928, buried South Henderson Cemetery; probably unmarried. He
   was listed in his father's house in the 1880 census of Henderson County. In 1910 he was still living in the same house and
   with him were his half-siblings Anna Mary and James E. Porter.
   Living next door to him was another half-sister, Lulu K.
   Porter Lant. He was a farmer.

G. Frank M. Porter, born Illinois c. 1857, died Burlington, Iowa,
   30 August 1944 (Probate Record, Box 1002); married in Gladstone, Illinois, 25 April 1894, Marietta (Mary) Lynn, born
   Illinois, c. 1864, daughter of Alexander Lynn (born Illinois,
   c. 1838) and Sarah Ann Appleby (born Iowa, c. 1844). Frank
   and Mary were married by the Rev. Andrew Renwick of the South
   Henderson United Presbyterian Church (Book C, p. 91). In the
   1910 census they were listed in Gladstone Township, Henderson
   County. With them was Mary's father, Alexander Lynn, who was

a widower. Frank was a mail carrier. Child:

1. Margaret Porter Futch, born Illinois, *c.* 1897; married Wilton Futch. Children:

    a. Wilton Futch Jr., born 1929

    b. Franklin R. Futch, born 1932

Alexander L. Porter had children by his second wife: Anna Mary, born 15 March 1863; James E., born *c.* 1866; and Lulu K., born *c.* 1872, married Charles E. Lant.

4-7 WILSON MATTHEW GRAHAM,[14] born Todd County, Kentucky, 1818, died Oquawka, Henderson County, Illinois, 11 or 19 May 1871, buried Oquawka Cemetery; married in Rushville, Schuyler County, Illinois, 18 September 1849, ELVIRA JANE WILSON (called Jane), born Kentucky, March 1830, died probably in Evanston, Illinois, 24 March 1919, buried Oquawka Cemetery.

Wilson joined the South Henderson Presbyterian Church on 24 March 1841 (Church Register). On 5 September 1843 he bought lot 15, block 66, in Oquawka for which he paid $150 (Book 3, p. 137), and on 26 March 1850 he bought a third of lot 2, block 72, also in Oquawka, paying $400 (Book 4, p. 397). On 13 March 1850 he and his wife sold lots 2 and 3 of block 36 in Oquawka for $600 to Robert Moir, father of John Moir who married their daughter Jessie (Book 6, p. 570).

In 1843 Wilson served a term as the Henderson County recorder. In the 1860 census he was listed as a merchant in Oquawka, and in the 1870 census he was a farmer in Henderson County. Also listed with them in 1860 and 1870 was Sarah Wilson, born Kentucky *c.* 1800, probably Jane's mother. Jane had a brother named John M. Wilson who petitioned the court on 19 June 1871 in the matter of the estate of Wilson M. Graham.

On 18 May 1849 Wilson and his brother 4-5 William M. were appointed guardians of the children of their late brother 4-2 Andrew who had died in 1848 (Book E, p. 74).

The following is from an obituary on Wilson which appeared in *The Oquawka Spectator*, 18 May 1871:

Died--In Oquawka, on the 11th, after a brief illness of ulcer in the stomache, Mr. Wilson M. Graham, aged 52 years. . . . Coming to this place from Ohio when he attained his majority, he had resided here ever since, and had always been a prominent and influential citizen. Of a genial and cheerful temperament; scrupulously honest and honorable in his business relations; a Christian; and a most exemplary husband and father; he has gone to his reward, leaving, we venture to say, not an enemy behind. In 1850, Mr. G. was a companion of the writer on a trip across the Plains to California, and passed through that ordeal which tries men as does nothing else, esteemed and honored by all his comrades.

In the 1880 census Jane was listed in Oquawka with three of her children: Carrie, Maude, and Willie. She was listed alone in the 1900 Oquawka census, but later she lived with her daughter Maude Graham Montgomery in Evanston, Illinois. Children, all born in Oquawka, Illinois:

5-21 Jessie E., b. January 1852
5-22 John, b. October 1853, d. 1855
5-23 Carrie Susan, b. October 1856
5-24 Gertrude S., b. 1858, d. 1863
5-25 Sally, b. 1861, d. 1863
5-26 Maude M., b. 1864
5-27 William W., b. 1866


4-8 DAVID GRAHAM,[15] born Todd County, Kentucky, 12 April 1821, died Monmouth, Illinois, 17 January 1894, buried Monmouth Cemetery; married in Warren County, Illinois, 3 November 1846, ELIZABETH BROWN, born 8 July 1826, died 19 May 1891, buried Monmouth Cemetery, daughter of the Hon. John Brown (1795-1870) and Elizabeth Porter.

David lived for a time in Henderson County, Illinois, where he joined the South Henderson United Presbyterian Church on 19 June 1846; his wife joined on 14 April 1849 (Church Register). The following deeds are recorded for David in Henderson County: he sold land to Peter Mundorff in 1843 (Book 2, p. 43) and bought 320 acres from Joshua A. More for $275 on 13 July 1844 (Book 2, p. 51). He bought land from Marie W. Smalley on 20 November 1847 (Book 3, p. 294). He also bought land in 1848 (Book 3, p. 126). He and his wife sold land in 1848 and 1850 (Book 3, p. 467, and Book 7, p. 82).

On 2 February 1868 the South Henderson United Presbyterian

Church dismissed him to Monmouth where they had moved in 1867.

The following is from David's lengthy obituary as it appeared in *The Monmouth Daily Review*, Wednesday, 17 January 1894:

>The angel of death paid a silent visit to one of Monmouth's most prominent homes last night and removed from this life David Graham, one of the best known and highly respected citizens of Warren County. For the past six months Mr. Graham has been confined to his home, and for the most of time to his bed. . . . At 12 o'clock last night the end was apparent, and the family was summoned to his bedside. The end came shortly after 1 o'clock.
>
>Since his removal to Monmouth in 1867, the deceased has almost continually been prominent in business circles and public affairs. As a member of the Second United Presbyterian church he has for years been a trustee of the church property, and has borne much of the responsibility connected with the affairs of this congregation. For years also he has held the honored position as a member of the senate of Monmouth College, and was until his death one of its trustees. Endowed with a large competency and enjoying much of this world's good, he has given liberally and has shown himself on many occasions one of the philanthropists of the city. The college campus on which Monmouth College now stands is a gift to that institution from him and his brother, the late [4-10] A. Y. Graham.
>
>In other affairs more public he has occupied honored positions. He has served as a member of the city council for a number of terms and as a member of the city school board for a number of years, has ably assisted in directing the educational affairs of the city. In business circles he was also prominent both as a capitalist and a merchant and farmer. He was a stock holder in the National Bank of Monmouth and one of its directors. The old dry goods business firm of Graham & Co. was founded by him 25 years ago. Five years ago he retired from active business as a member of this firm and since then has lived a retired life. He was the owner of several hundred acres of fine land in Henderson county, and in partnership with his son, James A. Graham, owned the famous Graham stock farm. He was also the owner of several large tracts of land in Warren County. . . .

3-3 Matthew, 2-1 Andrew                                                                    4-9

Another obituary on David appeared in *The United Presbyterian* (the official organ of the United Presbyterian Church), on 25 January 1894, p. 12. It gave much the same information as above and added that on the day of his funeral Monmouth College dismissed after the first hour, and faculty and students attended the funeral to pay homage. One reason they did so is that David had joined with his brother 4-10 A. Y. Graham in donating land for Monmouth College, as was mentioned in the obituary above. For more on the donation, see 4-10 Archibald Young Graham.

David served on Monmouth's city council in 1869-71, 1873-4, and 1876.

Children, probably all born in Biggsville, Henderson County, Illinois:

5-28 Elizabeth Jane, b. 8 February 1849
5-29 Clara Cecilia, b. 18 April 1851
5-30 James Andrew, b. 16 or 18 May 1855
5-31 Mary Louisa, b. April 1857
5-32 Ralph Walter, b. 1859, d. 1861
5-33 Frances Mabel, b. 11 May 1867


4-9 JAMES HARVEY GRAHAM (called Harvey),[16] born Todd County, Kentucky, 23 April 1823, died in Morning Sun, Louisa County, Iowa, 12 June 1897, buried Elmwood Cemetery; married in Morning Sun, Preble County, Ohio, 4 May 1847, MARY JANE BROWN, born Preble County, Ohio, 12 December 1822, died Greeley, Colorado, 21 July 1916, buried Elmwood Cemetery, Louisa County, Iowa, daughter of Nathan Brown (born South Carolina, 13 February 1792, died Malvern, Iowa, 27 March 1883) and Elizabeth Mitchell (born Kentucky, 22 July 1796, died Monmouth, Illinois, 29 May 1859).

James attended the academy at Morning Sun, Ohio, and with his cousin 4-16 Andrew E. took medical training at the Ohio Medical College, 1848-49. He practiced briefly at Oxford, Ohio, probably having apprenticed himself to an experienced doctor, then went to Henderson County, Illinois, where he and his wife were listed in the 1850 census. They joined the South Henderson United Presbyterian Church on 13 April 1850 (Church Register). Later they moved to Morning Sun, Iowa, then to Grandview, Iowa, where they were listed in the 1870 census. After a few years they returned to Morning Sun, Iowa, where he continued in practice until his death. He was a ruling elder in the United Presbyterian Church at Morning Sun. In the 1910 census of Louisa County, Iowa, Mary Jane was listed with her son Dales Young. At some time she moved to Greeley, Colorado, probably to live with her daughter Mary Ellen, where she died. Her body was shipped back to Morning Sun for burial beside that of her husband.

The following is from an obituary on Harvey as it appeared in *The United Presbyterian* on 8 July 1897:

> He was of Scotch-Irish descent, his forefathers being among the early settlers in South Carolina, from which state they removed to Kentucky. His father was a pronounced abolitionist, and, on account of his opposition to slavery, felt compelled, like many others, to leave the slave-holding community and move North. With his family he removed to Morning Sun, Ohio. . . . Dr. Graham was never a strong man, physically. On account of lung trouble he found it necessary to seek a change of climate, so, with his wife and child he came west and settled two miles south of the place where Morning Sun, Iowa, was afterwards built. He immediately united by letter with the United Presbyterian church of which his brother, Rev. W. Mills Graham, was then pastor. . . . He was elected a ruling-elder, April 8, 1861, and faithfully fulfilled the duties of his office.
>
> Dr. Graham was the father of eight children, of whom all are living save one, who died in infancy. One son entered the ministry, Rev. E. B. Graham, editor of the Midland; another engaged in real estate transactions, two are engaged in the practice of medicine. Of his daughters, one married a minister of our denomination, Rev. James A. Kennedy, and two are married to business men in Marshalltown, Iowa, and Tarkio, Missouri. On May 4, last, Dr. Graham, with his wife, celebrated their golden wedding, and for a few weeks afterwards he seemed to be in fairly good health, but about three weeks ago he showed signs of failing strength and passed peacefully away on Saturday, June 12, aged 74 years.

Children:

3-3 Matthew, 2-1 Andrew                                                4-10

5-34 Clara Jane, b. Oxford, OH, 14 May 1848
5-35 Edwin Brown, b. Oquawka, IL, 25 January 1851
5-36 William Franklin, b. Morning Sun, IA, 3 January 1854
5-37 John Mitchell, b. Morning Sun, IA, 26 June 1857
5-38 Laura Elizabeth, b. Morning Sun, IA, 14 January 1859
5-39 Mary Ellen, b. Morning Sun, IA, 19 August 1861
5-40 Wilson Thompson, b. Morning Sun, IA, 15 October 1863
5-41 Dales Young, b. Morning Sun, IA, 17 February 1866

4-10 ARCHIBALD YOUNG GRAHAM (called A. Y.),[17] born Todd County, Kentucky, 27 June 1826, died Monmouth, Warren County, Illinois, 23 September 1876, buried Monmouth Cemetery; married in Henderson County, Illinois, 7 April 1852, CATHARINE THIEROLF, born New York, 13 June 1834, died Monmouth, Illinois, 21 May 1871, buried Monmouth Cemetery, daughter of Johannes George Thierolf (born Alsace-Lorraine, Germany, 12 May 1802, died Henderson County, Illinois, 4 December 1850) and Catharine Crist (born Alsace-Lorraine, Germany, 28 January 1805, died Henderson County, Illinois, 5 August 1886), both buried in the South Henderson Cemetery.

In the 1850 census A. Y. was listed in the household of William J. and Nancy Hutchinson. Earlier, on 29 October 1846, he joined the South Henderson Presbyterian Church. His wife joined on 27 October 1855 (Church Register), and she was baptized as an adult on the day she joined.

On 29 January 1851 A. Y. sold a small tract for $25 to Ben. L. T. Bourland of Peoria (Book 5, p. 134), and on 3 March 1854 A. Y. and Catharine sold another small tract to Benjamin Hutchinson of Henderson County (Book 8, p. 408). In late 1859 or early 1860, they moved to Monmouth, Illinois, where they were listed in the 1860 census.

A. Y. actively supported the establishment of Monmouth College in 1853 and was a member of its board of trustees in 1856-7 and 1860-71. In 1860 he and his brother 4-8 David donated to the college its choice of over ten acres, the proceeds from the sale of which to go to a building fund for the college. The lots were sold for $3,360 at a public auction in August 1861, and through the generosity of many subscribers a new building was constructed in the spring of 1863 at a cost of $18,500. The building was fifty by eighty feet and was four stories high; it contained fifteen rooms plus a large basement.

Another of A. Y.'s and Catharine's projects was the founding of the Second United Presbyterian Church of Monmouth which was organized at their home on 25 October 1862 with nineteen charter members. A. Y. was an elder in the church. The members held their services at the college chapel until 1866 then built their own church structure a little south of the college. By 1877 their membership had increased to 375.

Children--the first four were probably born in Henderson County, Illinois; the last four were born in Monmouth, Illinois:

5-42 Jane Wilson, b. 18 April 1854
5-43 Nancy M., b. November 1855
5-44 Elmira E., b. 25 June 1857
5-45 Harvey Milligan, b. 5 August 1859
5-46 Edwin Young, b. 1862
5-47 Andrew Archie, b. 1865
5-48 Mary Louise, b. March 1870
5-49 Willie, d. infancy

## CHILD OF 3-5 DAVID GRAHAM AND ELEANOR MCCREIGHT

4-11 JANE GRAHAM, born Chester or York County, South Carolina. She was named as a daughter of David in the will of her great-aunt 2-7 Mary. Nothing more is known of her.

## CHILDREN OF 3-6 ROBERT C. GRAHAM AND MARTHA B. MCKEE

4-12 MARGARET C. GRAHAM GLENN,[18] born Todd County, Kentucky, 12 January 1813, died in Iowa, 16 August 1852 (29 years, 7 months, 4 days); married in Monroe County, Indiana, 18 June 1840, JOHN GLENN, born South Carolina, 6 June 1817, died probably in Henderson County, Illinois, 25 July 1881 (64 years, 1 month, 19 days), buried Monmouth Cemetery, perhaps a son of John Glenn and Nancy ___. In the 1860 census of Henderson County, an Agnes Glenn was listed in

3-6 Robert C., 2-1 Andrew                                                4-12A

John's household, probably his sister, not a second wife. She was not listed there in the 1870 census.

On 8 October 1837 while John was still living in Monroe County, Indiana, and before he and Margaret were married, he was deeded 60 acres there by John and Nancy Glenn who perhaps were his parents (Book G, p. 173). This tract was probably the same as the land he sold on 18 November 1851, described as 60 acres in Clear Creek Township, S3 T7 R1W (Book O, pp. 157-8). At that time John and Margaret moved to Iowa where she died shortly after. He then returned to Monroe County, Indiana, but soon moved to Henderson County, Illinois, where on 8 March 1855 he bought two tracts from the Caldwells for $75 each (Book 9, pp. 277 and 278). On 5 April 1856 John bought an additional tract also from the Caldwells for $375 (Book 10, p. 603). On 10 November 1860 John bought still another tract from 4-10 A. Y. and Catharine Graham (Book 17, p. 506). On 26 February 1862 he granted a mortgage to Booth Nettleton; the mortgage was canceled on 29 August 1862 (Book 2, p. 144). Then, on 3 November 1869 John sold some land to an Elizabeth Appleby for $125 (Book 29, p. 416). After John died (intestate), his three younger children sold their inherited shares of the land to their oldest brother, James Harvey Glenn, in a deed dated 8 September 1881 (Book 36, p. 387).

John's sister Agnes Glenn, who died in Monmouth on 19 January 1906 (born South Carolina, 16 June 1823), left a will dated 20 September 1901. In it she bequeathed her album to John's and Margaret's daughter Sarah A., furniture to her sister Martha Metlock, and the remainder of her property equally to John's and Margaret's four living children. James Harvey Glenn, oldest child, was the executor.

Children, all born in Monroe County, Indiana:

A. Martha Ann Glenn, b. 5 October 1841
B. James Harvey Glenn, b. November 1843
C. Theophilus (Thomas) M. Glenn, b. 13 May 1846
D. Edward G. Glenn, b. 19 April 1848
E. Sarah Adeline Glenn, b. 1850
F. ___ Glenn, d. infancy


A. Martha Ann Glenn, born Monroe County, Indiana, 5 October 1841, died Monroe County, 6 February 1848, buried United Presbyterian Cemetery in Bloomington Township, Monroe County.

B. James Harvey Glenn, born Monroe County, Indiana, November 1843, died Long Beach, California, 11 July 1923 (his probate record, #3090, is in Warren County, Illinois, and in it his residence is given as Warren County; perhaps he was visiting in Long Beach when he died), buried Monmouth Cemetery; married in Henderson County, Illinois, 25 October 1875, Cora Loraine Small,[19] born Illinois, May 1855, died 1934, buried Monmouth Cemetery.

James fought in the Civil War in Company G, 30th Illinois Infantry, enlisting on 18 October 1864 and mustered out on 17 July 1865. His company took part in Sherman's March through Georgia. On 2 September 1890 he applied for a veteran's pension, and on 26 February 1925 Cora applied for a widow's pension.[20]

Shortly after they were married, James and Cora lived a few years in Piper City, Ford County, Illinois, where his brother Theophilus also lived and where at least two of Cora's children were born. After James's father died, however, his three siblings sold their shares of their inherited property to him on 8 September 1881 for $9,000 (Book 36, p. 387), so James and Cora probably moved to Henderson County at that time. On 29 February 1892 they sold the property to Leroy Rezner for $12,000 (Book 43, p. 493). In the 1900 census they were listed in Monmouth, Warren County--he gave his occupation as retired farmer--and in 1910 he and his wife were still living there.

Children, as listed in the federal censuses, all born in Illinois:

1. Mary Ellen Glenn Miller, born Ford County, Illinois, c. 1876; married in Monmouth, Warren County, Illinois, 6 April 1898, J. Ed Miller, born Adams County, Ohio, c. 1862(?), son of George E. Miller and Esther A. Eckman. Mary Ellen and Ed were married by W. T. Campbell (Book E, p. 65). According to their marriage license, Ed was a civil engineer. By the time Mary Ellen's father died (1923), she and Ed lived in Nampa, Idaho. Known children, as mentioned in her father's will:

    a. George Miller

    b. Clarence Miller

2. Sarah Annabel Glenn Weed, born Ford County, Illinois, c.

3-6 Robert C., 2-1 Andrew                                               4-12B2a

1877; married in Monmouth, Warren County, Illinois, 26
October 1899, Robert H. Weed, born Colona, Henry County,
Illinois, c. 1875, son of Samuel H. Weed and Mary J.
Davidson. They were married by the Rev. Daniel H. Weed, a
Presbyterian minister (Book E, p. 86). According to their
marriage license, Robert was a horticulturist. When
Sarah's father died in 1923, she and Robert were living in
Parma, Idaho. Known children, as mentioned in her
father's will:

   a. Frances A. Weed

   b. Elizabeth M. Weed

3. Cora Margaret Glenn, born perhaps in Ford County, Illinois, September 1880; probably unmarried. She was listed with her parents in the 1900 census and was a dressmaker. In the 1922 Monmouth city directory, she was still a dressmaker and was living with her parents. Her father named her as the executrix of his will, 1923.

4. John Albert Glenn, born probably in Henderson County, Illinois, November 1882; married Helen N. ___. He lived in Scranton, Pennsylvania, at the time of his father's will, 1923, and was a civil engineer. Known child:

   a. Helen Elizabeth Glenn (called Betty). She was listed in her parents' home in the 1936 city directory of Scranton, Pennsylvania, and was a student.

5. Harvey Edward Glenn (called H. Edward), born probably in Henderson County, Illinois, January 1887, died after 1943; married in Warren County, Illinois, 3 February 1910, Nelle E. Roberson or Robinson,[21] born ___, died after 1943. They were listed in the 1943 Monmouth city directory, and his occupation was given as farming. Known children:

   a. John H. Glenn; married Lorene D. ___. They were listed in his father's home in the 1943 Monmouth city directory, and his occupation was given as driver for the Strand Baking Company. Lorene was a deputy county clerk.

   b. Harvey Edward Glenn Jr. (called Edward). In the 1943 Monmouth city directory, he was listed in his parents' home, and his occupation was given as factory worker.

c. Ruth E. Glenn. In the 1943 Monmouth city directory, she was listed with her grandparents, James H. and Cora Glenn, and was a teacher.

d. Elizabeth Glenn, probably died before 1923.[22]

6. Addie Viola Glenn Bonney, born probably in Henderson County, Illinois, July 1888; married ___ Bonney. She was called Addie Viola Bonney in her father's will, 1923, and lived in Atlantic, Iowa. Known children:

a. James H. Bonney

b. Adeline L. Bonney

7. Ruth Small Glenn, born probably in Monmouth, Warren County, Illinois, October 1896; perhaps unmarried. She was living in Monmouth, Illinois, at the time her father made his will, 1923.

C. Theophilus (Thomas) M. Glenn, born Monroe County, Indiana, 13 May 1846, still alive on 20 September 1901 when his aunt Agnes Glenn mentioned him in her will of that date; married in Lyman Township, Ford County, Illinois, 21 February 1878, Elizabeth Mosher, born New York, 13 December 1853, daughter of Alexander Mosher and Elizabeth ___. In 1870 Theophilus moved to Ford County where he established a farm in Brenton Township. In 1888 he moved to Piper City, Ford County, although he retained ownership of the farm. Children:

1. Elsie Glenn, born Illinois c. 1879

2. Jessie Glenn (girl), born Illinois, March 1880

3. Emma Glenn, died infancy

4. Edward M. Glenn

5. Theophilus M. Glenn Jr.

D. Edward G. Glenn,[23] born Monroe County, Indiana, 19 April 1848, died probably in Omaha, Nebraska, 14 December 1903, buried Forest Lawn Cemetery, Omaha; married, before 1890, Elizabeth Drennan, born Illinois, c. August 1859, died of lobar pneumonia in Omaha, 4 January 1946, buried Forest Lawn Cemetery, daughter of the Rev. Philip Drennan (born Pennsylvania, c. 1825, died east of Council Bluffs, Iowa, 10 March 1912, buried

3-6 Robert C., 2-1 Andrew

Forest Lawn Cemetery, Omaha) and Nancy I. ___ (born Pennsylvania, died Omaha, 8 February 19__, age 87, buried Forest Lawn Cemetery). Edward was graduated from Monmouth College in 1862. In the 1880 census of Henderson County, he was listed in his father's household and was a teacher. In about 1889 he moved to Omaha where he was listed as a real estate agent in the 1889-94 city directories. The 1895 Omaha city directory gave his address as Millard, Nebraska, which is a few miles west of Omaha. By the time of the 1898 city directory, however, he was back in Omaha and was again a teacher. His name did not appear in the directories in 1899 or 1900. In 1901 he was a clerk, and in 1903 (his last listing) he was a bookkeeper. After he died the Omaha city directories showed that Elizabeth lived in her father's home until about 1926 when she moved to the Fontennelle Boulevard Home for the aged. Known child:

1. Edward P. Glenn, born 22 April 1890, died 28 April 1890, buried Forest Lawn Cemetery, Omaha, Nebraska.

E. Sarah Adeline Glenn (called Addie), born Monroe County, Indiana, 1850, died 1924; unmarried. She was listed in her father's household in the 1880 census. By 1889 she was living with her brother Edward in Omaha, Nebraska, and was listed in the city directory as a dressmaker. She was not listed for several years beginning in 1895 but returned in 1902 and was then a clerk in Hayden Brothers Department Store. By the following year she was a clerk at Farnsley Drug Store but returned to Hayden Brothers in 1904. After 1912 Addie was no longer in the Omaha city directory.

F. ___ Glenn, died infancy


4-13 JOHN MCKEE GRAHAM,[24] born Todd County, Kentucky, 28 April 1816, died South Pasadena, California, 28 December 1893, buried Mountain View Cemetery, Altadena, California; married in Butler County, Ohio, 14 April 1842, NANCY SOPHIA YOUNG (called Sophie), born Ohio, 7 October 1822, died Pasadena, California, 13 March 1897, buried beside her husband in Mountain View Cemetery. John's and Sophie's marriage was performed by the Rev. J. Claybaugh.

John was graduated from Miami University, Ohio, in 1838 (the same class as that of his first cousin 4-5 William M.) and atten-

3-6 Robert C., 2-1 Andrew                                                          4-14

ded the Allegheny and Oxford Seminaries. He was licensed by the
First Ohio Presbytery (Associate Reformed) on 15 April 1841 and
ordained as pastor at Mount Pleasant in Monroe, Butler County,
Ohio, 22 June 1842, where he served until 8 June 1847. Later he
went in with the United Presbyterians. On 12 June 1844 he bought
two-fifths of an acre from a Joseph Baird in Butler County where
he and Sophie lived until 23 June 1847 at which time they sold the
land to Samuel L. Stewart for $800 (Book 16, pp. 671-2). John was
then the pastor at Broad Albin in Perth, Fulton County, New York,
11 January 1848 to 9 December 1857; at Elmira in Stark County,
Illinois, 30 December 1857 to 18 November 1865; and at Harrison in
Wapello, Louisa County, Iowa, 11 April 1876 to 9 October 1879. He
was also on the Board of Trustees of Monmouth College, 1857-8, and
was its financial agent, 1865-6. On 17 March 1864 he obtained two
separate mortgages, one from James H. Holmes for $950, the other
from James M. Whisnand for $735 (Book 9, pp. 12 and 13). In the
1870 census he was listed in Monmouth, Warren County, Illinois,
and in the 1880 census he was listed in Morning Sun, Louisa County, Iowa. In 1885 he retired to South Pasadena, California, where
he eventually died from the effects of an accident in which one of
his legs had been broken. John's and Sophie's son Donald preceded
them to the Los Angeles area.

On 15 August 1893 their son R. Alexander filed a petition on
behalf of his mother, Sophie, who was said to be an "incompetent
person" (probably senile). Sophie had an interest in the estate
of a Margaret Young, deceased, of Henderson County, Illinois.
Cash payments from Margaret's estate were subsequently made on 28
December 1893, 10 January 1894, 28 January 1895, and 19 March 1897
(Los Angeles Probate #2920).

Known children:

5-50 Edward Young, b. Ohio 19 May 1843
5-51 William Francis Claybaugh, b. Ohio 15 May 1845
5-52 Donald M., b. New York c. 1848
5-53 Robert Alexander, b. New York 1850
5-54 John McKee Jr., b. New York c. 1852
5-55 Ella, b. New York c. 1854
5-56 Margaret, b. New York c. 1857-8
5-57 Anne E., b. Illinois c. 1863


4-14 NANCY C. GRAHAM SMALL, born Todd County, Kentucky, 1817-20, died
probably in Monroe County, Indiana, 1848-49; married in Monroe
County, 4 March 1847, JAMES SMALL.[25] Nancy was not in the 1850

census of Monroe County. On 29 August 1850, however, a James Small, unmarried, was listed in the household of Joseph Small (born Ireland, age 68), perhaps James's father. This James was born in Ireland, c. 1821. In the 1860 census of Monroe County, there was a James Small (born Ireland c. 1821) whose wife was Matilda R. ___, born Ireland, c. 1825, perhaps a second wife. If so, and if this James was the husband of Nancy, she died 1848-49. She had one known child, as mentioned in the will of her father:

A. Nancy J. Small, born Monroe County, Indiana, March 1848, died probably in Monmouth, Illinois, after 1904; unmarried. Listed in the household of 3-6 Robert C. (Nancy C.'s father) in the 1850 census of Monroe County, Indiana, was a two-year-old child named Nancy J. whose last name was not given. If her mother had died and her father had returned to (or remained in) his father's house where there was no one competent to look after a two-year-old,[26] it seems probable that her mother's parents would have taken in the child. Also, in the household of James Small in the 1860 census there was a twelve-year-old girl named Anna J., perhaps Nancy J. Three other children were in the household: twin boys, age 5, and a one-month-old girl. Because of the seven-years' difference in ages between Anna (Nancy?) J. and the twin boys, it seems possible that Anna (Nancy?) J. was Nancy C. Graham's daughter, and the twin boys were children of James Small's second wife. In the 1900 census of Monmouth, Warren County, Illinois, Nancy was listed in the household of her aunt 4-17 Mary S. Graham Robison. Nancy, who was specifically named as Mary's niece, was a dressmaker and was unmarried. She had moved there as early as 1890-91 and was listed with Mary in the city directory of that year. In 1904 she was still listed in the city directory. Nothing more is known of her.

4-15 PAULINA JANE GRAHAM HEMPHILL (also spelled Polina and Pauline),[27] born Todd County, Kentucky, c. 1822, died probably before 1853 and certainly before 1859 (her father did not mention her in his will of that date); married in Monroe County, Indiana, c. 1839, ROBERT HEMPHILL, born South Carolina, c. 1814, died 29 July 1855, buried United Presbyterian Cemetery in Bloomington Township, Monroe County, Indiana, son of William Hemphill (born 1768, died Chester County, South Carolina, 30 August 1832, buried Hopewell Cemetery) and Jennet McQuiston (born Ireland, 1778, died Monroe County, c. 1842). Paulina and Robert were divorced on 19 January 1846.

Robert Hemphill had a brother named Andrew. Paulina's father, 3-6 Robert C., accused both Andrew Hemphill and his mother, Jennet McQuiston Hemphill, of coming between Paulina and her husband and of trying to ruin Paulina's reputation. The Hemphills complained to the church of Robert's unchristian accusation, and the affair resulted in open scandal by 1844. (See the story under 3-6 Robert C.) In the 1850 census of Monroe County, Indiana, Robert Hemphill was listed in jail in Bloomington, his condition called "insanity." In the same census Paulina and her daughter were listed with her parents. Nothing more is known of her. It is probable that she died before her parents moved to Warren County, Illinois, in 1853. Child:

A. Martha Evaline Hemphill Montgomery,[28] born Monroe County, Indiana, 15 September 1839, died of pneumonia and senility, 5 May 1926; married at Monmouth, Illinois, 14 August 1862, John H. Montgomery, born New Vernon, Mercer County, Pennsylvania, 4 May 1836, died of heart failure and senility at Pawnee City, Pawnee County, Nebraska, 3 July 1920, buried Pawnee City, son of Archibald Montgomery (born New Vernon, Mercer County, Pennsylvania, c. 1804) and Margaret Carnahan (born New Vernon, Pennsylvania, c. 1812). Martha and John were married by the Rev. David Wallace, president of Monmouth College.

Martha joined the South Henderson United Presbyterian Church in Henderson County, Illinois, on 30 April 1856, but it is not known with whom she was living since her grandparents had moved to Warren County, Illinois, in 1853. In the 1860 census, however, Martha was listed in the household of her aunt 4-17 Mary S. Graham Robison in Monmouth, Warren County, Illinois. Martha attended Monmouth College. Her husband, John, also attended Monmouth College as well as Monmouth Seminary, and on 21 July 1862 he enlisted as a sergeant in the army, serving until 21 May 1864. After the Monmouth Presbytery licensed and ordained him on 26 January 1864, he re-entered the army on 24 May 1864 as chaplain of the 16th USCI, a black troop. Unfortunately, he suffered a serious illness although he was misleading about the nature of the illness when he wrote to the pension office on 14 February 1888. At that time he said the open-air speaking while teaching had resulted in laryngitis and finally a slight throat hemorrhage, forcing him to resign on 1 October 1865. What happened was that on a hot July or August afternoon in Chattanooga, Tennessee, he experienced a severe sun stroke, causing his captain to testify later that he was "raving like a maniac and seemed to be suffering great pain in his head. . . . [Later] he seemed to be dazed and at times insane." After he resigned, as his wife's aunt 4-17 Mary S. Robison wrote on 8 December

1887, he was "both a physical and mental wreck, [and] after his return he had to be placed in the Insane Asylum at Jacksonville Ill. Since that time, [he] has been better and worse but not recovered."

Despite John's affliction he continued in his calling and even published two works: *The Unity of the Church* and *The Christian*. He was the pastor at Elmira, Stark County, Illinois, 1866-73; at Biggsville, Henderson County, Illinois, 1875-83; and at Vermillion and Lone Grove, Nebraska, 1885-7. He and Martha also lived at Junction City, Kansas, 1883-4, and at Conroy, Iowa, probably 1906-7. Their chief address, however, was Pawnee City, Nebraska, where they were living by 1903 and again after 1907. At the time of John's enlistment he was described as 5 feet 11-3/4 inches tall with light brown hair, blue eyes, and a light complexion. When Martha died in 1926, she was still living in Pawnee City probably with her daughter Pauline.

Children:

1. David Wallace Montgomery, born Illinois, 9 August 1864, died after 1929; married Mary B. ___ who died after 1944. He became a Presbyterian minister and in 1920 was living at Fresno, California. His last listing in the Fresno city directory was in 1929; Mary's last listing was 1944.

2. Charles A. Montgomery, born Illinois, 16 November 1867, died 1 June 1911

3. Alfred Celastus Montgomery, born Illinois, 28 February 1870

4. Mary Pauline Montgomery (called Pauline), born Illinois, 3 October 1872; probably unmarried. Pauline made the funeral and other arrangements when her mother died in 1926. At the time, she was called Pauline Montgomery.

5. Margaret (or Marguerite) J. Montgomery Barnett (Maggie), born Illinois, 11 November 1875; probably married, *c.* 1898, Charles H. Barnett, born New York *c.* 1875, son of ___ Barnett (born New York) and ___ (born New York). The informant for the data on John H. Montgomery's death certificate was a C. H. Barnett, probably a son-in-law. Charles H. and Marguerite J. Barnett were listed in the 1900 and 1910 censuses of Pawnee County, Nebraska. He was a farmer. Known children, as listed in the censuses:

a. Florence B. Barnett, born Nebraska, August 1899

b. Harold M. Barnett, born Nebraska, c. 1904

4-16 ANDREW EDWARD GRAHAM,[29] born Todd County, Kentucky, 29 May 1824, died Richland, Rush County, Indiana, 23 December 1897; married (1) in Decatur County, Indiana, 28 March 1851, MELCENA MARGARET GILLESPIE, born Greensburg, Indiana, 27 March 1827, died Richland, Rush County, Indiana, 15 February 1882, daughter of Dr. Jesse M. Gillespie (born Pennsylvania, 1805, died Greensburg, Decatur County, Indiana, 1833) and Catharine Collier Hopkins (born McBride's Creek, Nicholas County, Kentucky, 16 May 1803, died Greensburg, Decatur County, Indiana, 9 July 1886); Andrew married (2) in Lancaster, Jefferson County, Indiana, 22 February 1887, a widow, Mrs. CORNELIA B. MCCONNELL (Book 15, p. 524), born Pennsylvania, May 1835. She had married (1) George W. McConnell, born Ohio, c. 1822, died probably in Noble County, Indiana, after 1880.

Andrew attended Indiana University in 1847-8 and, accompanied by 4-9 James Harvey, attended the Ohio Medical College in 1848-9. At the time, medical training often consisted of young medical students taking what courses they could then apprenticing themselves to older, experienced doctors. Later they passed tests which qualified them to practice. Apparently that is what Andrew and his cousin Harvey did.

The following is from an obituary on Andrew which appeared in the 1898 Transactions of the Indiana State Medical Association:

Dr. Graham was of Scotch-Irish stock. His parents at an early period of history left the State of his birth [Kentucky] and settled at Morning Sun, in the State of Ohio. When he was fifteen years of age the family concluded to make Indiana their home, and made one in Bloomington. His education was obtained in the State University. He had a cousin living in Morning Sun, Ohio--Dr. Graham [4-9 James Harvey]--with whom he studied medicine and attended lectures in the medical college of Ohio--Cincinnati--during the session of 1848-9. The following spring he located in a village called Richland, Rush County, Ind., and, spending the summer there, left in the fall of 1849, that place, not knowing that he should ever return again. However, in the early beginning of the year 1851 he came back to adjust some business, and through the influence of friends was prevailed to remain

3-6 Robert C., 2-1 Andrew

and resume the practice of medicine. Thus he took his residence again and there remained continuously until he came to his death, December 23, 1897. He soon acquired the confidence of the people of his neighborhood, and thus inducted into a fair average income derived from his practice, and which he continued to maintain with creditable success. . . . In 1851 he was joined in marriage to Miss Melcena M. Gillespie, of Greensburg, Ind., by whom he brought to maturity four children, all of whom are living in Colorado, two sons and two daughters. [His son] Robert F. Graham, M.D., is practicing medicine in Greeley, Col. The mother of these children died in 1882. He married the second wife in 1887, who survives him, and she continues to reside in the old home. In religion a Presbyterian--U.P.; in politics a republican. . . . He was a member of Rush Medical Society. . . . Professionally, he was essentially a general practitioner. . . .

Prepared by John Moffett, M.D., Rushville, Ind.

Andrew's house in Richland, a large, square, red-brick, two-story structure, is probably still standing. His daughters were married there. Also, the distinguished Prof. James Albert Woodburn of Indiana University roomed there shortly after he had been graduated from the "Centennial Class" of 1876. In the same class were Andrew's son Robert F. and the brother of the future husband of Andrew's daughter Martha. (The brother was George Banta, the publisher.) Woodburn later wrote to Andrew's daughter Katharine (Kate) that he could never forget the time he lived there when a "green and callow youth" and she had put up lunches for him when he went forth to teach children "their ABC's."

It is said that during the Civil War Andrew's patients came to him in a group to ask him not to enlist because they wanted him there to look after the women and children.

Children, all born in Richland, Rush County, Indiana:

5-58 James Gillespie, b. 6 February 1852
5-59 Robert Francis, b. 23 April 1853
5-60 Katharine M., b. 11 April 1855
5-61 Andrew Edward Jr., b. c. 1857, d. 16 January 1871
5-62 Martha Evelyn, b. 5 May 1861

4-17 MARY SUSAN GRAHAM ROBISON,[30] born Todd County, Kentucky, 4 July 1829, died of paralysis in Monmouth, Illinois, 4 or 5 March 1905; married in Richland, Rush County, Indiana, 19 September 1854, WILLIAM ALEXANDER ROBISON, born Nicholas County, Kentucky, 14 September 1826, died Monmouth, Illinois, 11 December 1900, son of John(?) Robison (born Ireland, died before 1850) and Magdaline ___ (born Ireland or Scotland, died after 1850).

After Mary and William were married in Rush County, Indiana (where his mother and her brother Andrew lived), they remained there for a year and in October 1855 moved to Monmouth, Warren County, Illinois, where they lived for the rest of their lives. On 20 January 1857 William and his father-in-law, 3-6 Robert C. Graham, bought lot 1, block 41, in "the old town plat" in Monmouth (Book 25, p. 790). On 24 June 1889 Mary and William gave a mortgage on the lot to J. L. Young (Book 25, p. 494). Their son, John, finally sold the lot on 8 May 1908 to Mary M. Findley (Book 108, p. 427).

Listed with Mary and William in the 1860 census was Martha Hemphill, daughter of Mary's sister 4-15 Paulina. Mary's mother was with them in the 1870 and 1880 censuses, and Nancy J. Small, daughter of Mary's sister 4-14 Nancy, was with them in 1900. According to the city directories, Nancy had moved there as early as 1890-91.

The following is from an obituary on William in the *Monmouth Daily Review*, 12 December 1900:

> W. A. Robison, for almost fifty years an influential resident of Monmouth, finished his life of activity at 9:15 o'clock last evening. A stroke of paralysis, which he suffered on Monday night of last week, was the direct cause of death. . . .
>
> William Alexander Robison was born in Nicholas Co., KY, Sept. 10, 1826. When he was 14 years of age, he moved to Richland, Ind. with his parents. There he married Miss Mary S. Graham on Sept. 19, 1854. In October of the next year they came to Monmouth. His trade was a cabinet maker and, with his brothers H. C. and J. C. Robison, he operated a sash and door factory for several years. Then for a time he was a contractor and builder. When the Weir Plow shops began to grow, he became a foreman of the woodworking room and remained for 18 years. 17 years ago he was elected Justice of the Peace and opened the office which he filled ever since. He did a

real estate and insurance business in connection and was for one term the police magistrate for the city. He was one term an alderman and for many years a member of the school board.

When he first came to Monmouth, Mr. Robison joined the Presbyterian Church. His wife, however, was a Charter Member of the 2nd United Presbyterian Church and he soon joined the same church. He was ordained and installed a member of the Session June 10, 1865, and at the time of his death, was the oldest member in point of service. He was Superintendant of the 2nd United Presbyterian Sabbath School for a number of years, and later a teacher in the School, and in all his Church work was faithful and conscientous.

The surviving members of the family are Mrs. Robison, the widow, and Dr. John A. Robison, of Chicago, the only child living, one son having died in infancy. Dr. Robison was here last week but was called home. He returned last evening before his father died. The brothers and sisters are J. C. Robison, Mrs. J. C. Frew of this city, and Mrs. Louisa McCorkle who arrived last night from Alabama. H. C. Robison, a brother, died a few years ago.

In various legal documents their name was written either Robison or Robinson, but on his death certificate it was Robison, and his son's name was spelled the same. Mary was mentioned in the will of her brother 4-16 Andrew. Children:

A. John Albert Robison,[31] born Richland, Rush County, Indiana, 26 July 1855, died Chicago, 18 October 1942, buried Rosehill Cemetery; married in Chicago, 19 May 1890, Adeline Jessie Pyott-Love (called Jessie), born Illinois, December 1861, both parents from Scotland.

John was graduated from Monmouth College in 1877 and from Rush Medical College in 1880. He began practicing in Chicago in partnership with Dr. John P. Ross. From 1880 to 1888 John was the attending physician in the throat and chest department at the Central Free Dispensary, in 1884-8 he was an attending physician at the Cook County Hospital, and in 1890-2 he was a professor of material medica and therapeutics at Woman's Medical College and lecturer in the same branch at Rush Medical College. He was also a consulting physician to the Presbyterian and Mary Thompson Hospitals, director of the Chicago

Tuberculosis Institute, and attending physician at the Tribune Hospital at Algonquin, Illinois. In February 1911 he was appointed first lieutenant in the United States Medical Reserve Corps. He was a member of the Illinois State Medical Society, Chicago Medical Society (at one time its president), and the American Medical Association.

It is not known whether John and Jessie had children.

B. ___ Robison (boy), died infancy. This boy never appeared in a census.

4-18 SARAH E. GRAHAM WHISNAND,[32] born Preble County, Ohio, 1 July 1831, died Piper City, Ford County, Illinois, 25 October 1872 (41 years, 3 months, 24 days), buried Brenton Cemetery, Ford County, Illinois; married in Bloomington, Indiana, 1854, WILLIAM C. WHISNAND, born Bloomington, Indiana, 13 May 1834, died Warren County, Illinois, 26 April 1907 (72 years, 11 months, 13 days), buried Glendale Section of Monmouth Cemetery, perhaps a son of Isaac Whisnand and Anna ___. William married (2) Margaret Pope, born Kentucky, c. 1839, died after 1910.

In 1855 Sarah and William moved to Henderson County, Illinois, where she joined the South Henderson United Presbyterian Church on 10 June 1855 (Church Register). She was dismissed on 30 April 1856 when she and her husband moved to Spring Grove Township, Warren County, Illinois, where William was a farmer. In the 1860 federal census, Sarah's parents were listed with them. Later in 1860 Sarah and William moved to Piper City, Ford County, Illinois, and William was then a postmaster. Not until 29 January 1867 did they sell their land in Warren County; they sold it to Ephraim P. Allen (Book 48, p. 332). At some time William became a minister and was listed as such on his death certificate. In the mid-1870's after Sarah died, he went to North Dakota where he did home mission work among the Indians. He retired to Monmouth in 1901. His second wife, Margaret, was listed there in the 1910 federal census. Sarah's children, all born in Illinois:

A. James C. Whisnand, b. 24 January 1856
B. Lucy A. Whisnand, b. 29 August 1858
C. Martha M. Whisnand, b. c. 1862
D. William E. Whisnand, b. c. 1864
E. Mary B. Whisnand, b. c. 1867
F. Robert B. Whisnand, b. c. 1869

A. James C. Whisnand, born Henderson County, Illinois, 24 January 1856, died Warren County, Illinois, 8 October 1857 (1 year, 8 months, 14 days), buried Spring Grove Cemetery, Spring Grove Township, Warren County, Illinois. A lamb is engraved on James's tombstone.

B. Lucy A. Whisnand, born Warren County, Illinois, 29 August 1858, died Piper City, Ford County, Illinois, 16 September 1874 (16 years, 18 days), buried Brenton Cemetery, Ford County, Illinois.

C. Martha M. Whisnand, born Piper City, Ford County, Illinois, c. 1862, died before 1907.

D. William E. Whisnand, born Piper City, Ford County, Illinois, c. 1864. He moved to Wenatchee, Washington, and nothing more is known of him.

E. Mary B. Whisnand, born Piper City, Ford County, Illinois, c. 1867, died before 1907.

F. Robert B. Whisnand, born Piper City, Ford County, Illinois, c. 1869. He moved to Hope, North Dakota, and nothing more is known of him.

CHILDREN OF 3-8 WILLIAM M. GRAHAM
AND (1) SALLY C. GARTIN

4-19 MARTHA ANN GRAHAM HUTCHINSON,[33] born Todd County, Kentucky, 23 September 1824, died in Monmouth, Warren County, Illinois, 24 February 1896, buried Kirkwood Cemetery, Warren County; married in Henderson County, Illinois, 26 March 1842, SAMUEL HUTCHINSON, born Patterson, New Jersey, 19 or 28 June 1816, died Warren County, Illinois, 18 February 1886, buried Kirkwood Cemetery, son of James C. Hutchinson (born County Antrim, Ireland, 1790, died Henderson County, Illinois, 1852) and Sarah Delamater. Samuel was a farmer and auctioneer and was called "Colonel" Hutchinson, for what reason is not known. He and Martha lived in Biggsville Township, Henderson County, where they built a large house. Their daughter Sarah was married there in 1864. (It is said they rushed to finish the house for the wedding.) The last descendant to live in it was their grandson Fred Hutchinson whose widow finally sold it in 1978 and moved to California. The following is from a biography of Samuel in *History of Mercer and Henderson Counties*, II, 1367:

> During his residence in this county Mr. Hutchinson took an active part in its business affairs. His great circular wolf hunt organized and carried out was the means of ridding the county and its early settlers of a number of these audacious and sneaky pests. On that occasion many more scalps might have been taken but for the excitement created over the twenty or thirty deer which were also surrounded. Mr. Hutchinson affirms that he brought into this county the first combined reaper and mower that did successful work (though the writer was informed that Seth Oaks was the first to introduce that kind of a machine into this township if not in the county). In 1879 Mr. Hutchinson moved to his pleasant home in Monmouth, especially to secure needed rest for his wife.

Children, all born in Henderson County, Illinois:

A. Ellen Hutchinson, b. 26 February 1843
B. Sarah D. Hutchinson, b. 26 September 1844
C. Elizabeth Jane Hutchinson b. 27 January 1848
D. Samantha Hutchinson, b. 11 March 1850
E. Mary Hutchinson, b. 10 April 1852
F. William Graham Hutchinson, b. 15 June 1854

---

A. Ellen Hutchinson McDougall,[34] born Henderson County, Illinois, 26 February 1843, died Henderson County, 20 May 1864; married in Henderson County, 26 February 1861, John H. McDougall, born Washington County, New York, 4 May 1829, son of James McDougall and Ellen Bain. John was a farmer and stock raiser. He married (2) in Henderson County, 10 May 1866, Maggie Thompson. Children of Ellen and John:

1. Luetta McDougall Salter (Lottie), born 20 October 1861, died 12 July 1882; married David Parker Salter (Marriage Book C, p. 24), born Illinois, November 1860. David married (2) *c.* 1890, Josephine ___. In the 1900 census of Biggsville, Henderson County, Illinois, David was listed with his second wife and the following children: Gertrude, born May 1891, Guy P., born August 1894, George N., born July 1896, and Margaret, born March 1899. Child

of Lottie and David:

a. Sarah Ellen Salter

2. John McDougall, born 19 April 1864, died 9 September 1864.

B. Sarah D. Hutchinson Firoved, born Henderson County, Illinois, 26 September 1844, died Monmouth, Warren County, Illinois, 22 February 1928; married in Henderson County, 27 December 1864, William Firoved, born Hoguestown, Cumberland County, Pennsylvania, 10 February 1839, died Hale Township, Warren County, Illinois, 17 February 1911, son of Simon Firoved (born Pennsylvania, 26 July 1810) and Isabella Sprout (born Pennsylvania, 24 August 1821). Sarah and William were listed in Hale Township, Warren County, in the 1870 and 1880 censuses. He was a farmer and stockman. Children:

1. Horace Edgar Firoved, born Hale Township, Warren County, Illinois, 31 January 1866, died Hobson, Montana, 8 December 1923, buried Monmouth, Illinois; married, 18 April 1894, Rose Linda Smith of Waterford, Pennsylvania, born 13 September 1866, died Monmouth, Illinois, 2 April 1932. They moved to Hobson, Montana, where he died, and his widow brought his body back to Monmouth where she, herself, later died. Children:

    a. William Glenn Firoved, born Hale Township, Warren County, Illinois, 12 October 1895, died Coldbrook Township, Warren County, Illinois, 6 November 1956, buried Monmouth Cemetery; married, 22 January 1919, Loure Ethel Salzmann of Ainsworth, Nebraska, who died in Beardstown, Cass County, Illinois, 2 August 1983, buried Monmouth Cemetery. William was a farmer, dairy man, and hog raiser. Children: (a) Wilma Alene Firoved Pilger, born Hobson, Montana, 1 January 1921, married 13 June 1943, Vernon Dale Pilger, born 9 June 1920; they live near Beardstown, Illinois, where he is a hog raiser; children: Sue Athone, born 28 March 1947, married Tom Swigert, born 16 April 1948, and lives in Evanston, Illinois; and Theodore Robert, born 8 December 1948, married Sara Carter Lang and had Emilie Kate, born 13 March 1981, and Britta Noel, born 8 December 1982; (b) Robert Eugene Firoved, born Hale Township, Warren County, Illinois, 7 August 1922, married in Arvin, California, 13 June 1948, Leona Permenter; children: Jeffrey (adopted), born 8 October 1945, William Glenn, born 16 July 1950, Susan

3-8 William M., 2-1 Andrew 4-19B1b

Elizabeth, born 15 July 1952, and Roberta Lynn, born 28 November 1958; and (c) Edna Mae Firoved Hawkinson, born Monmouth, Illinois, 22 August 1934, married, 22 August 1954, Newton Watkins Hawkinson, born Galesburg, Illinois, 11 February 1933; he is with Standard Oil in Kennewick, Washington; children: Thomas Newton, born 13 March 1961, and John Edgar, born 14 March 1963, married, 16 July 1983, Cynthia Hinckley.

b. Bruce Melvin Firoved, born Hale Township, 28 April 1897, died Pinellas Park, Florida, 18 February 1977; married Margaret Burns, born 2 February 1890, died Hale Township, 17 September 1934. Child: Donald Bruce Firoved, born Hobson, Montana, 21 February 1919, married Iris Long; they live in Saint Petersburg, Florida.

2. Nettie May Firoved Herdman, born Hale Township, Warren County, Illinois, 7 November 1867, died 26 September 1963; married in Warren County, Illinois, 17 June 1891, John N. Herdman, born Monmouth, Illinois, 21 May 1866, died 11 August 1958, son of James H. Herdman (born Pennsylvania, c. 1834) and Emma J. Mitchell (born Ohio c. 1839, died 23 May 1911). They were married by Thomas G. Herdman, MG (Book D, p. 199). Nettie was graduated from Monmouth College in 1888. In the 1910 federal census, she and John were listed in Monmouth, Illinois, where he was a merchant selling plumbing. Nettie had no known children.

3. Anna Belle Firoved Talbot, born Hale Township, Warren County, Illinois, 5 June 1872, died 25 November 1950; married, 20 November 1907, William Cole Talbot, born Lumpkin, Georgia, 28 August 1872, died 24 March 1936. He was the owner of the Maple City Furnace Company in Warren County, Illinois. Child:

a. Sarah Belle Talbot O'Daniel (now written Sarabelle), born 10 June 1911; married, 31 August 1935, James Arrell O'Daniel, born 11 September 1906. James is a mechanical engineer. He, Sarabelle, and their son own a business called the Maple City Steel Supply Company, Monmouth, Illinois. Child: John William O'Daniel, born 25 May 1945; married, 10 May 1969, Janine Allen, born 6 May 1948, and had Meghan, born 12 February 1974, John Andrew, born 19 August 1975, Emily, born 26 March 1977, and James Charles, born 11 April 1980.

4. Nellie Pearl Firoved White, born Hale Township, Warren County, Illinois, 17 June 1875, died Monmouth, Illinois, 29 August 1971; married, 27 December 1899, George E. White, born near Waynesburg, Pennsylvania, 13 May 1869, died in the old Firoved home, Hale Township, Warren County, Illinois, 19 January 1950. Child:

   a. Sarah Dorothy White Saville, born 7 August 1904; married in Waterloo, Iowa, 27 October 1928, Edgar Stevenson Saville, born Monmouth, Illinois, 27 January 1903, died in the Galesburg hospital, 2 March 1977. He was a coach and a rural mail carrier. Child: Mary Ann Saville Bulen, born Canton, Illinois, 8 May 1933; married Donald Elden Bulen and had Harold Edgar, born 21 May 1956, Barbara Sue, born 23 March 1959, George Embree, born 26 January 1962, Donald Elden Jr., born 22 November 1963, and Cynthia Louise, born 25 February 1967.

5. Frank Merle Firoved, born Hale Township, Warren County, Illinois, 22 October 1878, died Coldbrook Township, Warren County, 9 October 1933; married in Warren County, 26 October 1898, Nancy McLaughlin, born Hale Township, Warren County, 20 March 1876, died Monmouth, Illinois, 12 November 1937, daughter of Joseph McLaughlin (born Ireland, c. 1831) and Mary ___ (born Ireland c. 1838). Child:

   a. Mary Louise Firoved Bruington, born Hale Township, Warren County, Illinois, 21 January 1908; married, 25 November 1926, Everett Manfred Bruington, born Coldbrook Township, Warren County, Illinois, 8 May 1906, died Galesburg, Illinois, 21 November 1975, son of Elmer Bruington (born Illinois, c. 1872) and Mina ___ (born Illinois, c. 1877). Everett was a farmer, county commissioner, and president of a school board. Children: (a) Donna Joan Bruington Dowden, born Monmouth, Illinois, 11 April 1935; married, 28 December 1957, John Lee Dowden, born 6 April 1934; they live in Conrad, Iowa, where he raises pure-blood cattle and hogs; children: Nancy Elizabeth, born 11 March 1959; Steven Howard, born 25 May 1961, married, on 26 May 1984, Kristie Holm; and Sally Jo Ann, born 27 September 1965; and (b) William Elmer Bruington, born 22 June 1940; married Marci Myers; children: Todd Steven, born California, 27 May 1966, and Jennifer Marie, born California, 18 June 1968.

C. Elizabeth Jane Hutchinson Woods, born 27 January 1848, died Kansas City, Missouri, 3 January 1935, buried Kirkwood, Illinois; married, 16 May 1865, Isaac Woods, born 9 October 1842, died Independence, Missouri, 4 January 1917, buried Kirkwood, Illinois. Children:

1. Arthur Wilburg Woods, born 10 March 1870, died Washington state, 3 September 1941; married, 27 September 1893, Mabel Mitchell, born ___, died 14 December 1899. Child:

    a. Melville L. Woods, born 21 July 1895; married Dora ___. He lived in Bellingham, Washington. No children.

2. Samuel Delois Ebard Woods, born 29 April 1877, died 2 April 1951; married (1) 4 April 1900, Mae Hills who died in childbirth as did her baby; (2) 5 February 1907, Lulu Meyers. He was a physician and director of a state mental hospital at Oswatamee, Kansas. Child:

    a. Helen Mildred Woods Darnell, born 2 December 1910, died 9 August 1965; married, 7 November 1840, Morris Darnell. Child: Samuel, born 1945.

3. Ross Herman Hutchinson Woods, born 27 December 1882, died near San Diego, California, 22 July 1965; married, 17 October 1906, Edith Gertrude Meyers, born 1 May 1888, died 16 October 1956. Children:

    a. Virginia Woods Forbes, born 24 September 1909; married 31 January 1928, George Forbes, born 8 January 1908. They lived in El Cajon, California, but traveled in the winters and gave travelogue programs. They also occasionally worked on Indian reservations. Children: (a) Robert Lewis Forbes, born 20 August 1928, married, 7 Decemeber 1947, Lila Jeannine Kirk, born 17 May 1929, and had Michael Ross, born 3 October 1948, and Merrill Lewis, born 1 August 1950; and (b) Donald George Forbes, born 18 January 1931, married, 8 January 1951, Hazel Aileene Plant and had Randolph George, born 24 August 1953, Ronald Dale, born 29 November 1954, Donna Aileene, born 6 June 1956, Marla Edith, born 10 July 1957, and Tonya Malyn, born 30 October 1961.

    b. Randolph H. Woods (Mike), born 10 July 1914; married, 23 November 1937, Helen Vroman, born 29 October 1918.

Child: Gretchen Marie Woods Bergman, born California, 30 October 1938, married, 3 August 1957, Fred Herman Bergman and had John Michael, born 10 October 1958, and James Eric, born 11 April 1961.

D. Samantha Hutchinson McCoy, born 11 March 1850, died 1933, buried Kirkwood, Illinois; married, 6 February 1868, William McCoy, born Ohio, 10 December 1836, died probably in Kirkwood, Illinois, 24 January 1916, son of James McCoy (born Pennsylvania) and Mary Creswell (born Pennsylvania).[35] Children:

1. Laura Ethel McCoy Oaks, born 15 October 1870, died 14 May 1950, buried Kirkwood, Illinois; married, 17 October 1888, John Marshall Oaks, born 4 October 1867, died Monmouth, Illinois, 7 November 1942, buried Kirkwood, Illinois. He was a dentist practicing in Kirkwood. Children:

    a. Hazel Mae Oaks Smith, born Kirkwood, Illinois, 14 September 1889, died Jackson, California, 9 January 1962; married, 5 January 1910, Harry Glen Smith, born 27 February 1890, died Monmouth, Illinois, 2 August 1945. Children: (a) Janice Oaks Smith Welch, born 31 October 1913; married, 11 June 1934, James William Welch, born Henderson County, Illinois, 22 July 1914; they live at Pine Grove, California; children: Sharon, born 2 November 1939, married in Nevada, 26 November 1955, Richard Lungren and had John, born 2 February 1958, and Angela Lucile, born November 1960; and James William Jr., born 10 December 1952; (b) John Willis Smith, born Monmouth, Illinois, 15 November 1916; married, 4 July 1939, Maxine Hoy, born 15 August 1922, died Colton, California, 4 December 1977; children: Michael Hoy, born 6 April 1959; and Andrea Lucile, born November 1960, married ___ Kileen; and (c) Harry Glen Smith Jr., born Monmouth, Illinois, 12 March 1922; married, 17 January 1943, Edith Christine ___; children: Susan, born 17 May 1944, and Richard, born 19 August 1952.

    b. Helen Lucile Oaks Oyler, born Warren County, Illinois, 29 December 1893, died Warren County, 20 October 1941; married, 25 November 1916, James Lloyd Oyler, born 7 October 1892, died 23 September 1951. Child: Martha Ann Oyler Fouad, born Monmouth, Illinois, 26 January 1928; married in Alexandria, Egypt, 26 January 1952, Youssel Fouad; children: Miriam, born 16 September 1957, Sarah, born 12 February 1960, and Hesham, born

3-8 William M., 2-1 Andrew   4-19D1c

16 December 1962.

 c. William Seth Oaks, born Warren County, Illinois, 31 October 1897; married, 7 March 1918, Lorena Margaret Hook, born Hedrick, Iowa, 12 November 1900, died February 1984. Children: (a) Donna Jane Oaks Erickson, born Kirkwood, Illinois, 3 June 1919; married, 11 June 1941, John Wilbur Erickson, born 20 September 1919; they live at Edmonds, Washington; children: Linda Rae, born 7 December 1945, Paula Sue, born 1 July 1948, and Eric William, born 28 August 1958; (b) Patricia Rae Oaks Thompson, born Monmouth, Illinois, 18 January 1925; married, 9 July 1943, Harold Glen Thompson, born 11 April 1925, died before 1984; child: Carol Jane, born 8 May 1946, married James W. Moore; and (c) Laurence Roger Oaks, born 16 January 1935; married (1) Nancy A. Black, (2) Karen Jane Sellers, born 18 April 1939; children by Nancy: Susan Lynn, born Boise, Idaho, 27 November 1956, and Margaret Ann, born Boise, Idaho, 12 December 1957; children by Karen: William Laurence, born 20 September 1962, Jayne Elizabeth, born 8 February 1964, Melissa Noel, born 18 December 1968, and Stefanie Kay, born 9 September 1971.

2. Louella Mae McCoy McDougall, born 16 May 1872; married Pear McDougall. Child:

 a. Clifford McDougall; unmarried.

E. Mary Hutchinson Wallace, born 10 April 1852, died c. 1922; married, 28 December 1871, John Cal Wallace. They lived in Los Angeles. Child:

1. Clyde Wallace; married ___. Child:

 a. LeRoy Wallace

F. William Graham Hutchinson, born 15 June 1854, died of diabetes on 7 April 1902;[36] married 20 September 1876, Mary E. Swinney. They lived and died in the red brick house which his father built in 1864 in Rozetta Township, Henderson County, Illinois. Children:

1. Flora Beatrice Hutchinson Clark, born 3 September 1877, died 9 February 1954, buried Kirkwood, Illinois; married Louis Lee Clark, born 31 October 1877, died 2 August 1955.

3-8 William M., 2-1 Andrew                                                4-19F1a

Children:

    a. Barbara Elizabeth Clark Woods, born 22 December 1903, died 16 December 1924; married Clarence J. Woods, born 16 February 1904. Child: Dorothy June Woods Ward, born 18 June 1924; married Merrill J. Ward, born 21 June 1903, died 4 April 1965; children: Merrill Craig, born 2 October 1952, and Janel Evelyn, born 22 June 1957.

    b. James William Clark, born 5 February 1905; married Adah Bess Snyder, born 1 September 1909. Children: (<u>a</u>) Gerald Lewis Clark, born 13 March 1934; married Beverly Darlene Sprout and had Bradley Dean, born 17 October 1958, Brian Lee, born 14 November 1961, and Brenda Kay, born 24 October 1964; and (<u>b</u>) William Dean Clark, born 1 May 1941; married Virginia Ann Livingston, born 13 July 1943 and had Tara Lynn, born 9 April 1964, and Amy Dawn, born 26 April 1965.

    c. Maria Louise Clark Maxwell, born 10 May 1907; married Howard Earl Maxwell, born 21 August 1905. They live in Henderson County, Illinois. Child: Henry Lee Maxwell, born 1 September 1930; married Barbara Ann Hughes, born West Virginia, 5 January 1930, and had Thomas H., born 24 October 1956, and William H., born 1 July 1960.

2. Samuel William Hutchinson, born 1 November 1878. He lived in the West.

3. Harley Ephraim Hutchinson, born 24 February 1881; married \_\_\_\_. They lived near Fresno, California. Children:

    a. Graham Hutchinson. He lived in Ventura, California.

    b. Mildred Hutchinson. She lived in Idaho.

    c. Donald Hutchinson

4. Mary Ruby Hutchinson Hess, born Kirkwood, Illinois, 20 March 1883, died 31 March 1967; married in Warren County, Illinois, 25 June 1907, Theola Melville Hess, born Tilden, Nebraska, 14 January 1885, died 23 January 1946, son of T. M. Hess and Mattie Allen. They were married by the Rev. D. E. Hughes (Book E, p. 213). Children:

a. Theola Melville Hess Jr., born 10 September 1908; married Louise Torley, born 12 May 1908. They live in Michigan. Child: Thomas Hess, born 26 October 1936.

b. Allen Hutchinson Hess, born 9 July 1910; married, 2 February 1928, Opal Anderson, born 16 April 1909. Children: (**a**) James Hutchinson Hess, born 13 April 1929; (**b**) Billie Allen Hess (girl), born 31 March 1931; (**c**) Betty Hess, born 24 August 1933; (**d**) Richard Lee Hess, born 12 January 1937; and (**e**) Linda Ruby Hess, born 11 September 1940.

c. Marian Ruby Hess Earp, born 5 September 1912; married, 2 January 1932, Wayne Earp, born 6 December 1907. Children: (**a**) Gerald Earp, born 3 October 1932; (**b**) Donald Earp, born 17 August 1934; and (**c**) Marilyn Joyce Earp, born 18 November 1940.

5. Martha Elizabeth Hutchinson Campbell, born Kirkwood, Henderson County, Illinois, 22 April 1885, died in Kirkwood, 12 February 1954, buried Kirkwood Cemetery; married in Kirkwood, 1 September 1910, Joseph Clyde Campbell, born Henderson County, Illinois, 1889, died 1921, son of J. W. Campbell and Sarah ___. They were married by the Rev. Thomas C. Pollack (Book C, p. 170). Joseph was a farmer. Children:

   a. Madeline Mary Campbell, born 1 November 1911, died June 1940.

   b. John Hutchinson Campbell, born 24 October 1915; married (1) Evelyn Bailey; (2) Judith McKnight. Children by Evelyn: (**a**) John Hutchinson Campbell Jr., born 28 October 1939; and (**b**) Dennis Paul Campbell, born 3 August 1942; child by Judith: (**c**) Brian Earl Campbell, born 30 April 1966.

6. Frederick McCoy Hutchinson, born 9 February 1887, died 8 September 1972; married, 18 February 1912, Myrl Elizabeth Sprout, born 18 October 1890, died in California, 20 January 1981. Fred lived and died in the house which his grandfather Samuel Hutchinson built in 1864. Fred's widow sold the house and moved to California to live with her daughter Lillian. Children:

   a. Mary Ruby Hutchinson Morrissey, born 27 October 1915; married William Thomas Morrissey, born 9 July 1907.

3-8 William M., 2-1 Andrew                                              4-19F6b

Children: (a) David William Morrissey, born 8 June 1949; and (b) Fredrick Joseph Morrissey, born 27 May 1951.

b. Lillian Elizabeth Hutchinson Lipes, born 5 January 1920; married Gerald Lipes, born 22 October 1914. They live in California. Children: (a) Barbara Jean Lipes, born 1 July 1939; (b) Bonnie Jane Lipes, born 20 March 1941; (c) Jerry Edgar Lipes, born 11 March 1944; and (d) Betsy Joe Lipes, born 23 January 1947.

4-20 NANCY ELLEN GRAHAM ALLISON,[37] born Todd County, Kentucky, 23 November 1825, died in Monmouth, Illinois, 10 December 1876; married in Henderson County, Illinois, 29 March 1848, THOMAS G. ALLISON, born Washington County, Pennsylvania, April 1817, died Stronghurst Township, Henderson County, Illinois, 3 or 8 September 1868, buried Monmouth Cemetery, son of Hugh Allison and Hannah McBride. Thomas was a farmer. On 9 April 1852 he bought land in Henderson County from his father-in-law, 3-8 William M., for $1,200 (Book 6, p. 393), and on 3 August 1854 he bought additional land from his brother-in-law 4-22 Robert C. and Mary Graham (Book 8, p. 572).

Children, all born in Stronghurst Township, Henderson County, Illinois:

A. Sarah Maria Allison, b. 27 December 1848
B. Martha R. Allison, b. 1856
C. William E. Allison, b. 15 March 1861

---

A. Sarah Maria Allison Baird, born Stronghurst Township, Henderson County, Illinois, 27 December 1848, died Omaha, Nebraska, 30 January 1944, buried Forest Lawn Cemetery, Omaha; married in Monmouth, Illinois, 11 July 1872, William Baird, born Carthage, Illinois, 7 July 1848, died Omaha, 22 July 1923, buried Forest Lawn Cemetery, Omaha, son of James Baird (born Scotland) and Mary Jane McAdam (born Scotland). William was a lawyer. They lived awhile in Carthage, Illinois, and in 1887 moved to Omaha. The following is from an obituary on William which appeared in Omaha's *Morning World Herald*, 23 July 1923, p. 1:

> For thirty years, Mr. Baird was an outstanding figure among Omaha attorneys. His ability in corpo-

ration, real estate and probate law was generally recognised and, in addition, his personal and professional integrity was respected in an unusual degree.

Mr. Baird was born on a farm near Carthage, Illinois, July 19, 1948. . . . He was educated in a rural school and in public schools of Carthage. Later he was graduated from Monmouth College, Illinois, in 1873, having worked his way through that institution. In 1873 he was admitted to practice of law in Illinois.

In 1887 Mr. Baird came to Omaha and formed a law partnership with L. D. Holmes and John C. Wharton. Later the firm became Wharton & Baird. In 1906 the firm was dissolved when Mr. Baird took his two sons into a partnership that was broken only by his death. . . . .

Mr. Baird's devotion to his profession was only surpassed by his interest in religion. He was a member of the Central United Presbyterian church ever since he came to Omaha and for many years he taught bible class there. He was also, for a number of years a member of the governing board of Monmouth college, a United Presbyterian school. Always a thorough student of the bible, Mr. Baird was the author of several booklets on religious topics, particularly in explanation of the revelations of the bible. One of the principle tenets of his faith was a belief that the church should never engage in politics.

In 1903 Sarah and William took in Sarah's uncle 4-21 Andrew R. Graham, a childless widower. Children:

1. Mary Ellen Baird Patton, born Carthage, Illinois, 18 August 1874, died in Omaha, Nebraska, 15 February 1958, buried Forest Lawn Cemetery, Omaha; married in Omaha, c. 1901, Paul Harsha Patton, born Harshaville, Ohio, 3 October 1873, died Omaha, 9 April 1950, buried Forest Lawn Cemetery, son of Carey S. Patton (born Ohio 1840, died 1909) and Hannah Elizabeth Harsha (born Ohio 1847, died 1915). Paul was an engineer and supervisor for the Bell Telephone. They lived first in Carthage, Illinois, then in Omaha and were members of the United Presbyterian Church. In the 1910 federal census of Omaha, they were

listed in the household of her parents; Mary said she had had two children only one of whom was living. Child:

a. Sarah Elizabeth Patton Moss (called Elizabeth), born Omaha, 17 March 1903; married in Omaha, 15 May 1926, the Rev. Mervyn Elroy Moss, born Irvona, Pennsylvania, 15 November 1895, died Kallispell, Montana, 17 October 1950, buried Junction City, Kansas, son of James Harry Moss (1856-1950) and Mary Sophia Hunter (1866-1941). Mervyn was a chaplain's assistant during World War I, 1917-19. In 1923 he was graduated from Coe College, Iowa, and in 1926 from the McCormick Theological Seminary. Also in 1926 he was ordained by the Kittannaning Presbytery. He and Elizabeth then served as missionaries in Rezaiah, Iran, 1926-34, where their children were born. Later Mervyn was the minister at the First Presbyterian Church of Junction City, Kansas, 1934-42; associate pastor at the First Presbyterian Church in Portland, Oregon, 1942-48; and minister of the Presbyterian church in Kallispell, Montana, 1948 until his death in 1950. Elizabeth was graduated from Coe College, Iowa, in 1925, and after her husband died she published a novel, *The Iranian*, in 1952. She also wrote many short stories and poems. Later she served as director of education at the First Presbyterian churches in Ridgewood, New Jersey, Sioux Falls, South Dakota, and Hood River, Oregon. At present she is living at the Benedictine Nursing Center, Mount Angel, Oregon. Children, all born in Iran: (a) Mary Ellen Moss, born 15 January 1928, died 15 November 1928; (b) Persis Ann Moss Blachly (Peggy), born 13 September 1929, married in Portland, Oregon, 26 July 1950, Arthur Theodore Blachly; and (c) Paul Mervyn Moss, born 24 August 1931, died Junction City, Kansas, 23 January 1942.

2. Edgar Allison Baird, born Carthage, Illinois, 28 November 1876, died Omaha, Nebraska, 13 March 1963, buried Forest Lawn Cemetery, Omaha; married Alice Frank Kennard, born 15 March 1889, died 15 October 1962, buried Forest Lawn Cemetery, Omaha. Edgar was a lawyer in partnership with his father and brother in Omaha. Children:

a. Edgar A. Baird Jr.; married Bette ___.

b. Sarah Lee Baird; married Truman Morseman.

c. Thomas Patton Baird. At the time of his father's death in 1962, Thomas was living in Princeton, New Jersey.

3. Claire James Baird, born Carthage, Illinois, 17 December 1878, died at Colorado Springs, Colorado, 13 August 1947, buried Forest Lawn Cemetery, Omaha, Nebraska; married Adele McHugh, born 10 February 1888, died 28 May 1963, buried Forest Lawn Cemetery. Claire was a lawyer in partnership with his father and brother in Omaha. Children:

   a. Barbara Baird McMartin; married Dr. W. J. McMartin. Children: (a) Ray; and (b) Richard.

   b. William James Baird, born ___, died September 1981, buried Forest Lawn Cemetery, Omaha, Nebraska; married Grace Staves. Children: (a) Jane, married ___ Funk; (b) Lynn, married ___ Garson; and (c) William James Jr.

   c. Janet Baird, deceased; unmarried.

   d. Adele Baird Wood (called Happy); married and divorced Ted Wood. She lives in Eugene, Oregon, and has a son and a daughter.

B. Martha R. Allison Dugdale (Mattie), born Stronghurst Township, Henderson County, Illinois, 1856, died Pawnee County, Nebraska; married, after 1885, William Dugdale, born ___, died 10 March 1920. Child:

1. Allison Dugdale; married Helen Davis. He was a physician. Children:

   a. Grant Dugdale

   b. Eunice Dugdale Knight; married and divorced ___ Knight. Child: Anne.

C. William E. Allison, born Stronghurst Township, Henderson County, Illinois, 15 March 1861, died 10 March 1870.

4-21 ANDREW RICHARD GRAHAM,[38] born Morgan County, Illinois, 10 May 1829, died at Omaha, Nebraska, 11 September 1910 (87 years, 4 months, 1 day), buried Forest Lawn Cemetery, Omaha; married (1) in Henderson County, Illinois, 21 March 1850, MARY ANN MCQUOWN, born Kentucky or Virginia, 1 November 1826, died 5 April 1891, buried South Henderson Cemetery, daughter of Arthur O. McQuown (born Washington County, Virginia, 4 September 1803, died Biggsville, Illinois, 28 February 1884, buried South Henderson Cemetery) and Nancy S. Smith (born Tennessee, 16 August 1803, died 24 July 1846, buried South Henderson Cemetery); Andrew married (2) in Monmouth, Illinois, 13 July 1893, KATE ANDERSON PIERSON (or PEARSON), born Sweden, c. 1838, her second marriage (Marriage Records Book D, p. 231). On 4 July 1898 Andrew wrote in his pension records that he and Kate had separated in April 1894. In the 1900 census of Monmouth, Illinois, he was listed as living alone, but in 1910 a Mrs. A. R. Graham arranged for his burial in Forest Lawn Cemetery in Omaha.

Andrew was a farmer and a clerk. On 7 February 1853 he bought 80 acres in Henderson County for $200 from John Reed (Book 7, p. 137), on 17 February 1854 he bought more land from James and Elizabeth McDill for $150 (Book 8, p. 239), on 3 August 1854 he bought additional land from his brother and sister-in-law 4-22 Robert C. and Mary Eliza for $800 (Book 8, p. 513), and on 18 June 1856 he bought still more land from Robert C. and Mary Eliza (Book 12, p. 107). Finally, on 27 June 1859 he bought lot 2, block 4, in the town of Oquawka for $850 from Gideon and Sarah Russell (Book 14, p. 219). Then, on 21 October 1865 he and his wife sold land to John Prince (Book 23, p. 408), and on 28 October 1868 they sold another tract to John McQuown (Book 26, p. 533).

During the Civil War Andrew was a sergeant in the Illinois 10th Infantry, Company E, enlisting on 20 August 1861, and mustered out on 14 September 1864. His pension papers say that at the time of his enlistment he was 5 feet 10 inches tall and had a light complexion, gray eyes, and brown hair.

Andrew seems to have moved a number of times. On 13 April 1850 he joined the South Henderson United Presbyterian Church while his wife joined on 9 August of the same year. Later they were dismissed to Biggsville. On 27 March 1858 the South Henderson Church again received them, and on 24 August 1873 they were again dismissed (Church Register). His pension records say he lived in Biggsville, Illinois, until the fall of 1870; in Madison County, Iowa, until the spring of 1884; in Henderson County, Illinois, until the fall of 1888; in Monmouth, Illinois, until the summer of 1903; and finally in Omaha, Nebraska, until his death in 1910. When he was in Henderson County, he lived with J. H. M. McQuown and did farm work. In 1888 he suffered two sun strokes

3-8 William M., 2-1 Andrew

and was thereafter unable to work. When he moved to Omaha, he lived with his niece 4-20A Sarah M. and her husband, William Baird. Andrew had no known children.

4-22 ROBERT CULBERTSON GRAHAM,[39] born Morgan County, Illinois, 10 January 1831, died of chronic interstitial nephritis in Walton, Harvey County, Kansas, 5 November 1915, buried South Henderson Cemetery, Illinois; married in Henderson County, Illinois, 21 September 1853, MARY ELIZA MCDILL, born Ohio, 2 January 1835, died 4 October 1919, buried Biggsville Cemetery, Henderson County, daughter of Robert McDill (born 20 September 1803, died 22 June 1890, buried South Henderson Cemetery) and Mary Porter (born $c.$ 1806, died 22 August 1886, buried South Henderson Cemetery).

During the Civil War Robert fought in Company E, 10th Illinois Infantry, enlisting on 24 May 1861, and mustered out on 13 August 1864. He dislocated his ankle while in the service and for the rest of his life suffered from the resultant rheumatism, often having to use crutches and no longer able to farm. He therefore moved to Biggsville, Illinois, where he ran a grocery but sold out in 1875 and was unable to do anything for a year. In May 1877 he and Mary moved to a location near Abilene, Kansas, and in 1884 they moved to Walton, Kansas, where he did limited farming.

While in Henderson County he and Mary were members of the South Henderson United Presbyterian Church. They took in their young cousins 4-37 Mary M. and 4-38 Andrew G. after their mother died and their father went to California. Robert's pension record says that at the time of his enlistment he was 5 feet 11 inches tall and had a fair complexion, blue eyes, and light hair. Child:

5-63 ___ (boy), stillborn
1 October 1871

CHILDREN OF 3-8 WILLIAM M. GRAHAM
AND (2) JANE POPHAM

4-23 JAMES THOMAS GRAHAM (called Thomas),[40] born Henderson County, Illinois, 8 October 1836, baptized South Henderson Presbyterian Church, 7 August 1837, died Summerfield, Marshall County, Kansas, 30 January 1921; married in Henderson County, Illinois, 24 February 1859, MELISSA JANE GILCHRIST, born Iowa or Missouri, 7 October 1842, died Summerfield, Marshall County, Kansas, 13 April 1915. Melissa's father died when she was an infant and her mother when she was two. Her grandparents cared for her, and when they died

3-8 William M., 2-1 Andrew

died she was reared by her aunt, Mrs. John Hutchinson of Henderson County, Illinois.

On 8 April 1859 Thomas and Melissa joined the South Henderson United Presbyterian Church, and on 12 December 1869 they were dismissed to Winterset, Iowa (Church Register). Interestingly, Melissa was baptized as an adult in Henderson County on 19 April 1859. In 1871 they moved to Adair County, Iowa, and in 1884 to Richland Township, Marshall County, Kansas, where they owned a farm and raised stock. Later they retired to Summerfield, Marshall County, Kansas. It is said that they moved to Kansas in a covered wagon with their (then) nine children. He was a farmer, stockman, and carpenter. He was also a Sunday school teacher and helped establish spelling bees, ciphering matches, and literary societies.

The following is from a letter, 28 January 1986, from 5-71B Lorna Howard Cline, granddaughter of James Thomas. Apparently Mrs. Cline copied it from material written for a reunion on 9 October 1949 of alumni of the Barklow School, District 113, Richland Township, Marshall County, Kansas:

J. W. Beacham boarded at Graham's just east of the schoolhouse on the north side of the road for the five days of the week. At one time he asked Mrs. Graham to serve him pie at breakfast. That created some wonderment among the Graham children, for while they did have pie at times and it was considered a luxury, they never ate pie for breakfast.

Each of the nine Graham boys had a "yell" which he let out the minute he got out of bed and out of doors, and his neighbors for a mile or more around could tell when each boy had emerged from his bed, and would say, "Well, Pete Graham just got up!" Or maybe it was John, or Doc, or Will, or Dick, or one of the others. . . .

Then to end the series in the spring was a big entertainment exhibition, it was called. Mr. Thomas J. [James Thomas] Graham, affectionately called "Uncle Tommy," would send for plays of an hour and a half to two hours long, and after deciding which one to use, would assign the parts. Seldom was it that anyone refused the part that had been assigned to him. Uncle Tommy copied all of the parts by long hand, and sometimes complained that "sitten" was about ["]played out" -- at which time he might snitch a pillow from the bed for chair bedding. . . .

Uncle Tommy, with volunteer help, built the stage and put up wires across the front of the room for stage curtains and for dressing rooms on either side of the stage, the curtains being made of flowered calico 3 cents - 5 cents a yard. These were made by Mrs. Graham who kindly offered to do her bit at home since she was kept busy cooking three square meals a day for her family of nine boys "and each boy with a sister," as Uncle Tommy once told a nosy inquirer. The "props" all came from homes in the neighborhood, and Mother Hubbard's cupboard had nothing on some of the homes when an exhibition was about to be put on. The blackboards in the front of the room were covered with bed sheets. Conard's organ was toted over to the school house in a lumber wagon for the programs until the Graham's moved closer to the school house, then theirs was used. In most cases [5-71] Iva Graham was the organist.

Children, the first five born in Illinois:

5-64 Alva Edson (called Al), b. 25 December 1859
5-65 Andrew Richard (Dick), b. 18 October 1861
5-66 William Mills, b. 27 December 1863
5-67 Harry Wilford (Had), b. 14 March 1866
5-68 John Gilchrist, b. 10 October 1868
5-69 Lawrence William (Pete), b. IA, 4 August 1871
5-70 James Thomas Jr. (Doc), b. IA, 16 June 1874
5-71 Iva Lenore, b. IA, 13 December 1876
5-72 George Washington, b. IA 10 December 1878
5-73 Frank Irwin, b. KS, 21 December 1885

4-24 WILLIAM ALEXANDER GRAHAM,[41] born Henderson County, Illinois, 26 September 1837, died Summerfield, Marshall County, Kansas, 15 July 1929, buried Summerfield Cemetery; in his pension record, 4 May 1898, William said he was a "widdower," and in the 1900 federal census he said he was divorced, but on 3 March 1921 a Sophie Graham (age 66), who lived in Berryville, Arkansas, testified to the pension board that she was his wife. No other record of a marriage has been found.

During the Civil War William fought in Company E, 10th Illinois Infantry, enlisting on 30 August 1861, and discharged 21 December 1863; he immediately reenlisted and was mustered out on 4

July 1865. He was a farm worker and day laborer and moved around a great deal. In 1870 he was listed in the federal census of Henderson County, Illinois (he was living alone), but by February 1882 he was living in Winterset, Iowa. His pension record gives the following subsequent addresses: about 1882, Pueblo County, Colorado; September 1891, Barry, El Paso County, Colorado; May 1893, Pueblo, Pueblo County, Colorado; September 1895, Monte Vista, Rio Grande County, Colorado; May 1896, Rocky Ford, Otero County, Colorado; (in the 1900 census he was listed in Pueblo City, Pueblo County, Colorado); March 1905, Nims City, Nebraska; September 1905, Dawson, Richardson County, Colorado; December 1906, Spaulding, Union County, Iowa; September 1907, Jasper County, Missouri; May 1912, Topeka, Kansas; March 1921, Berryville, Carroll County, Arkansas; and, finally in August 1926, Summerfield, Marshall County, Kansas. When he was living in Carroll County, Arkansas, Sophie testified that he was unable to work, needed help with his personal grooming, and was almost totally confined to his bed. By 4 August 1926 when William was living in Summerfield, Kansas, he was under the care of a Dr. V. R. Vincent who stated that William was completely disabled at that time.

His gravestone has a GAR marker on it. According to his physical description at the time of his enlistment in 1861, he had a dark complexion, brown hair, and gray eyes, and was 5 feet 5¼ inches tall; later his height was given as 5 feet 3 inches tall. He had no known children.


4-25 MATTHEW JOSEPH GRAHAM (called Joe),[42] born Oquawka, Henderson County, Illinois, 12 November 1838, died of cardiac failure and senility at Winterset, Iowa, 10 January 1937 (98 years, 1 month, 28 days), buried Winterset Cemetery; married in Henderson County, Illinois, 23 October 1865, MARY ELLEN ANDERSON, born 13 January 1847, died 10 August 1931, buried Winterset Cemetery, Iowa, daughter of John Anderson and Sophia ___.

During the Civil War Joe fought in Company E, 10th Illinois Infantry, enlisting on 30 August 1861, and mustered out on 14 September 1864. He took part in Sherman's March through Georgia. At the time of his enlistment, he was described as 5 feet 3 inches tall and had a dark complexion, hazel eyes, and brown hair. Apparently he sustained a throat injury while in the service, since his pension file contains several sworn statements to the effect that he was unable to speak above a whisper for about two months. The injury did not occur in battle.

After the war he lived for a few years in Illinois then moved to Madison County, Iowa, where he bought a quarter section in Douglas Township. The following is from an obituary on Joe in *The Winterset News*, 14 January 1937:

> In 1869 Mr. Graham came to Iowa, shipping his household goods to DeSoto, then the nearest railway point to the new home. From DeSoto the shipment was hauled by wagon to the farm.
>
> Mrs. Graham and her infant son George came to Iowa when Mr. Graham had completed the one-story, three room frame house that he had built on the farm eight and a half miles northwest of Winterset. Much of her journey to her new home was made by stage coach, entering the state at Dubuque.
>
> Built on the prairie, where the tall grass grew luxuriantly, the little home soon became the mecca for many of the Indians who roamed the prairie country demanding food. Like other Iowa pioneers, Mr. and Mrs. Graham and their family endured the severe blizzards, the many privations and discomforts of those early days in this sparsely settled section of Iowa.
>
> Slowly the farm was brought under cultivation, the two groves and the orchard and building improvements changing the place year by year. In 1883 Mr. Graham built a new home for his family. . . . In 1892 [*sic*; should be 1893] the family moved to Winterset.
>
> Mr. Graham bought a general merchandise stock on the west side of the square where the Graham stores are now located, and after three years retired from the business.

His subsequent life appears to have been uneventful although very long with the attendant illnesses of extreme old age. On 28 October 1925 when Joe was almost 87, his doctor, C. B. Hickenlooper, testified that Joe was unable to take care of normal household chores and had a failing mental condition. After his wife died in 1931, he lived with his daughter Mabel Eva and her husband, Leo Percival. The Percivals, who were well off, employed a maid. Also, one of Joe's sons, probably Frank L., stayed with the Percivals to help care for his father and applied to the federal government for an official burial flag after his father died. Joe died intestate with almost no equity left in the

3-8 William M., 2-1 Andrew 4-26

homestead. He and his wife are buried in the same plot as his
parents in Winterset Cemetery, Iowa, and inscribed on Joe's
tombstone is "Civil War Veteran."

According to the 1900 census, Mary Ellen had eight children
one of whom had died. Known children, as listed in the 1880 and
1900 censuses, all but the first born in Iowa:

5-74 George Mills, b. IL, 26 July 1868
5-75 Charles Wesley, b. 25 October 1870
5-76 Frank Leonard, b. 18 August 1873
5-77 Lee Anderson, b. 6 August 1875
5-78 Mabel Eva, b. 8 October 1879
5-79 Myrtle Ida, b. 8 January 1881
5-80 Ada Lenore, b. 23 July 1886


4-26 SARAH JANE GRAHAM MUNDORFF,[43] born Henderson County, Illinois, 3
September 1840, baptized South Henderson United Presbyterian
Church, 28 March 1841, died of a cerebral hemorrhage and senility
in San Jose, California, 20 March 1936 (95 years, 6 months, 17
days), buried Oak Hill Memorial Park, San Jose; married in Henderson County, Illinois, 26 October 1865, BENJAMIN FRANKLIN MUNDORFF,
born Lancaster County, Pennsylvania, 23 June 1835, died San Jose,
California, 29 August 1917, son of David Mundorff (born Lancaster
County, Pennsylvania, c. 1814, died Dallas County, Iowa, 1884) and
Sarah Stailey (born Pennsylvania, c. 1815, died after 1888).
Sarah and Benjamin were married by the Rev. James A. P. McGaw.

Sarah joined the South Henderson United Presbyterian Church
on 2 December 1854. Benjamin taught school a short time and
worked as an agent for a New York publishing house. When the
Civil War broke out, he enlisted on 30 August 1861 in Company E,
10th Illinois Infantry, the same company in which his future
brothers-in-law served. At the time of his enlistment, he was
described as 5 feet 4 inches tall and had a light complexion,
hazel eyes, and dark hair.

While in the service he sustained some accidental injuries.
On 17 December 1863 when his company was bivouced near Mission
Ridge about seven miles from Chattanooga, Tennessee, Benjamin and
the other men in his outfit were seated, eating supper, when the
men in another outfit cut down a tree which fell toward Benjamin,
knocking him to the ground, injuring his shoulder and arm, and
breaking his left leg three inches above the ankle. He was discharged because of this disability on 28 April 1864, but since his
leg had never been set properly it bothered him for the remainder

3-8 William M., 2-1 Andrew                                                        4-26A

of his life as did his arm and shoulder.

After he recovered he worked in a lumber company until 1869 at which time he and Sarah moved to Madison County, Iowa, where they lived for three years. In 1872 they homesteaded a tract in Osceola County, Iowa, living there for five years, and in 1877 they moved to Yankee Hill Precinct, Lancaster County, Nebraska. The following is an account of their trip, as given in *Portrait and Biographical Album of Lancaster County, Nebraska* (1888):

> He made the journey hither from Iowa with his family in a wagon drawn by one team of horses and two ox-teams, the journey consuming twenty-six days. Rain fell the greater portion of this time and they camped out wherever night overtook them. Upon their arrival here they slept in their covered wagon until October, when Mr. Mundorff put up a small house.
>
> Mr. Mundorff, upon coming to this county, purchased eighty acres of land from Burlington & Missouri River Railroad Company, for which he paid $10 an acre. Some discouraged settler had broken a few acres and then abandoned it. Aside from this there had been no attempt at improvement.

Sarah and Benjamin prospered in Nebraska, living on their eighty-acre farm in Lancaster County for many years. Benjamin held various local offices including that of school director. They were members of the Methodist Episcopal Church. According to Sarah's death certificate, they moved to California in about 1907, probably retiring there, and were in San Jose by 1911. After Benjamin died in 1917, Sarah lived with her daughter, Florence, in San Jose.

Children, all born in Iowa:

A. Florence Estella Mundorff, b. 15 November 1866
B. David Franklin Mundorff, b. 28 July 1869
C. William Mills Mundorff, b. 15 November 1871
D. Arthur Aaron Mundorff, b. 23 June 1873

---

A. Florence Estella Mundorff Jackson, born Iowa, 15 November 1866, died after 1936; married George O. Jackson. He was a carpenter in San Jose, California. Known children:

3-8 William M., 2-1 Andrew                                              4-26A1

1. Alice B. Jackson Fuller; married Hiram Clyde Fuller. They were listed in the city directories of San Jose, California, 1926-35. In 1930-1 he was a county agricultural inspector; by 1935 he was a plumber.

2. Clara M. Jackson Mentz, died after 1977; married Walter T. Mentz who died probably in San Jose, California, 1970-2. They were listed in the San Jose city directories from 1926 until 1970. In 1972 Clara was listed as his widow. Before her marriage Clara was a stenographer. Walter was a carpenter. Known children:

   a. Elizabeth Mentz

   b. Barbara J. Mentz. In the 1943 city directory of San Jose, California, she was listed as an employee of Hester Dairy; in 1947 she was a clerk at V. J. Lawrence Company. She lived with her parents.

B. David Franklin Mundorff, born Iowa, 28 July 1869, died after 1936; perhaps unmarried. In 1900 he was renting a farm in Lancaster County, Nebraska, and in 1910 he was a hired man on the farm of a John C. Kern or Korn. Since he witnessed his mother's declaration for a widow's pension in San Jose, California, on 17 September 1917, he had probably moved there. He was listed in the San Jose city directory in 1918. When his mother died in 1936, he was living in Colby, Kansas.

C. William Mills Mundorff, born Iowa, 15 November 1871, died 17 January 1927, buried Pleasant Hill Cemetery, Lancaster County, Nebraska. In the 1900 census of Lancaster County, Nebraska, he gave his occupation as student.

D. Arthur Aaron Mundorff, born Iowa, 23 June 1873, died after 1942; married Elma ___. When his mother died in 1936, he was living in Lincoln, Nebraska, where he was a carpenter. He and his wife were listed in the Lincoln city directories from 1913 through 1942. Known children:

   1. Maude M. Mundorff. She was listed with her parents in the 1918 and 1920 city directories of Lincoln, Nebraska. Nothing more is known of her.

   2. Verna M. Mundorff. She attended the Lincoln School of Commerce and worked at Rudge and Guenzel Company, 1926-9; O'Shea-Rodgers Motor Company, 1930-38; and Farmers Mutual Insurance Company, 1939- . Her last listing in the Lin-

coln city directories was in 1942. Perhaps she moved away.

3. Ethel Mundorff. From 1929 until 1933 she was listed in the Lincoln city directories as a stenographer. She was not listed after 1933.

4. T. Dean Mundorff. He was a geologist and by 1935 was a chairman at the State Department of Roads and Irrigation.

4-27 JOHN MILLS GRAHAM,[44] born Biggsville, Henderson County, Illinois, 27 March 1842, died Bonner Springs, Kansas, 24 November 1926, buried Springfield, Kansas; married (1) probably in Henderson County, Illinois, 15 August 1866, ELIZA AMELIA COWDEN, born Biggsville, Illinois, 4 February 1851, died probably in Kansas, 23 March 1900, daughter of George W. Cowden (1827-1864) and Eunice M. Signor (1830-1855); Eliza's brother George Henry Cowden married 5-28 Elizabeth Jane Graham. John Mills married (2) c. 1907, ANNA J. ___, born Illinois, c. 1854. This was also Anna's second marriage.

John attended Monmouth College, Illinois, in 1861-2, and on 6 August 1862 he enlisted in Company G, 84th Illinois Infantry, discharged as a sergeant on 8 June 1865. On 12 December 1890 he applied for a veteran's pension. He has a GAR marker on his gravestone.

On 20 May 1871 John joined the South Henderson United Presbyterian Church and was dismissed on 23 December 1873 (Church Register). He and Eliza then moved to Winterset, Madison County, Iowa, and in 1884 they moved to Marshall County, Kansas. In 1887 they moved to Humboldt, Richardson County, Nebraska, but they returned to Kansas before the 1900 census was taken. Eliza died in March of 1900, and John was listed as a widower in the 1900 census of Summerfield, Marshall County, Kansas. He was still listed there with his second wife in the 1910 census. He was a carpenter.

John's children were all by (1) Eliza Cowden. It is said that Eliza had fourteen children one of whom died unnamed in infancy. Known children:

3-8 William M., 2-1 Andrew                                                   4-28

5-81 Effie Jane, b. IL, 16 April 1869
5-82 Jessie Leonora, b. IL, 9 June 1870
5-83 Mae Belle, b. IL, 17 October 1871
5-84 Robert Cowden, b. IA, 17 April 1873
5-85 George Henry, b. IA, 26 October 1874
5-86 Oley Mills, b. IA, 3 June 1876
5-87 Florence Ella, b. IA, 8 March 1878
5-88 Harry Popham, b. IA, 12 April 1880
5-89 David Albert, b. IA, 23 December 1881
5-90 Myrtle Iva, b. KS, 4 July 1884
5-91 Araminta Signor, b. KS, 15 April 1886
5-92 Frank Harrison, b. NE, 1 January 1888
5-93 Roy, b. NE, 12 July 1891

4-28 DAVID MCDILL GRAHAM, born Henderson County, Illinois, February 1843, died Henderson County, 23 June 1849 (6 years, 3 months, 28 days), buried South Henderson Cemetery.[45]


4-29 MARY MARGARET GRAHAM, born Henderson County, Illinois, 30 December 1844, baptized South Henderson United Presbyterian Church, 14 April 1845, died 1 December 1936, buried Chariton Cemetery, Lucas County, Iowa; married in Henderson County, Illinois, 4 October 1866, her first half-cousin once removed 5-51 WILLIAM FRANCIS CLAYBAUGH GRAHAM, born Ohio, 15 May 1845, died Winterset, Iowa, 29 July 1935, buried Chariton Cemetery, Lucas County, Iowa. See their listing under 5-51 William Francis Claybaugh Graham.


4-30 SAMUEL ALLISON GRAHAM,[46] born Biggsville, Illinois, 18 March 1848, died Afton, Iowa, 1 October 1931, buried Orient, Iowa; married at the United Presbyterian Church near Macksburg, Iowa, 3 June 1869, ELIZABETH GRACE THOMSON, born Stranraer, Scotland, 25 May 1851, died Afton, Iowa, 12 June 1932, buried Orient, Iowa, daughter of Samuel Thomson (born Scotland, 1815, died Madison County, Iowa, 1903) and Elizabeth MacRobert (born Scotland, 1814, died Madison County, Iowa, 19 February 1879). Samuel and Elizabeth were married by the Rev. T. C. McKahn. Elizabeth's family migrated to America in 1856, living first at Oquawka, Henderson County, Illinois, then moving to Madison County, Iowa, in 1867.

Samuel's grandson, Lyle Graham Wimmer, writes:

Being the baby of the family, Samuel probably found that things gravitated his way rather easily. His father gave him a quarter section of land at about the time of his marriage at age twenty-one. He was an affable and sociable person, too credulous and trusting of others regarding business transactions. Also, he wasn't a succesful farmer, eventually losing his original property. The family moved to farms in adjacent Adair County, near Macksburg, Iowa, but because farming wasn't his forte the family moved to Orient in about 1893. It soon became clear that he was much better at being a salesman and dealing with the public. He became part owner and operator of a grain storage elevator and bought animals and hogs for meat packers.

When I was a child my mother and I visited my grandparents annually. Grandpa would be around and then he wouldn't. He just faded away. In later years my mother gave me the answer to some of his quiet disappearances: Grandma disliked tobacco. It never occurred to me that Grandpa's ever-present cigars were enjoyed away from home. Ah, well! I would catch up with him at the office or the general merchandise store. I especially liked the elevator where a gasoline engine powered the bucket conveyor which lifted the grain to the bins. An endless vertical wide belt with hand holds and foot cleet moved rapidly up and down through close-clearance appertures at each floor level. I used to ride that belt the full height of the elevator building, and I don't know why I wasn't mangled by missing the grip of the hand hold. But, boy! was that fun!

One of my most treasured memories is of a 26-page booklet that Grandma Elizabeth handcrafted and pasted together with hundreds of clippings of amusing incidents and jokes. She sent this to me at Fort Shaw, Montana, when I was thirteen and convalescing from surgery which was necessary because of an accident.

Samuel and Elizabeth lived the last several years of their lives in a small home in Orient, Iowa, adjacent to the home of their youngest daughter, Jennie, and her husband, Claude Bishop.

Children:

5-94 William Allison, b. 30 December 1870
5-95 Thomas Edward, b. 3 March 1872
5-96 Robert Culbertson, b. 18 August 1873
5-97 Lillie Maude, b. 30 June 1877
5-98 Elizabeth Mary, b. 13 June 1879
5-99 Jane Grace, b. 9 February 1883
5-100 Walter Nelson, b. 13 October 1885
5-101 Samuel Roscoe, b. 19 July 1888

## CHILDREN OF 3-9 THOMAS P. GRAHAM AND MARY P. WADDILL

4-31 ELIZA ELLEN GRAHAM, born Todd County, Kentucky, September 1834, died probably in Todd County, 1900-10; unmarried. Eliza lived with her parents until they died and probably continued to live in their house afterwards. When her uncle Joseph Waddill died in 1888, he left property to Eliza's mother who lived only a few months longer so the property was added to her estate which Eliza and her siblings inherited. Eliza seems to have sold her share of the estate in two separate deeds: on 11 December 1890 she deeded 58 acres to L. W. Duerson (brother-in-law of Eliza's sister 4-36 Joanna) for $116 (Book 17, pp. 512-3), and on 22 July 1891 she and her brother Robert M. sold another tract to a D. M. Townley for $700 (Book 18, pp. 180-1). The latter deed was also recorded in Ballard County, Kentucky, where Robert M. lived. Eliza was listed in the 1900 census of Todd County but not in the 1910 one. It is therefore thought that she died before 1910.

4-32 GRANVILLE WADDILL GRAHAM,[47] born Todd County, Kentucky, 17 July 1835, died in Pembroke, Christian County, Kentucky, 16 June 1905, buried in the Duerson Cemetery on Simmons' place, Todd County; married (1) in Todd County, 23 February 1874, SARAH M. BURRUS (Sallie), born Kentucky c. 1850, died in Todd County, Kentucky, before 1879, daughter of Charles R. (or B.) Burrus (born Kentucky c. 1824, died before 1886) and Zerilda ___ (born Kentucky c. 1821); Granville married (2) in Todd County, 8 October 1879, HELLEN NORA BURRUS, born Kentucky, 24 July 1851, died in Dallas, Texas, 1938, buried Laurel Land Cemetery, daughter of Charles Henry Burrus (born Kentucky, 17 November 1820, died 20 August

1872) and Frances Shelton Sanders (born North Carolina, 20 March 1825, died 19 September 1897). Granville is buried in the same cemetery as his parents and sister Joanna. Charles R. (or B.) Burrus and Charles H. Burrus were probably first cousins, grandsons of Robinson Burrus who came to Kentucky from Virginia in *c.* 1810. Charles R. (or B.) Burrus is listed in the censuses as C. B., but in at least two deeds he is called C. R.

In the 1870 census Granville was listed in the household of his uncle Joseph Waddill, and in the 1880 census Granville and his second wife were listed as boarders in the household of W. H. Wakefield in Todd County. On 25 December 1880 Granville bought 1¼ acres on Davis Mill Road from his former parents-in-law, C. R. and Zerilda Burrus (Book 11, p. 537), and on 19 April 1886 he signed another deed stating he was "justly indebted" to Zerilda in the amount of $100 and "for further consideration of the sum of $400 cash paid by said Burrus to Graham party." The description of the land in this deed matched the one in the former deed except that on the land "Graham has erected a cottage." Shortly after this time Granville and his second wife moved to nearby Pembroke in Christian County, Kentucky, and on 23 February 1887 they sold the above property to G. M. Mimms for $375 (Book 16, pp. 301-2).

Granville's uncle Joseph Waddill died in 1888 leaving 71 acres to Granville's mother who died soon after. Her children sold their interests in various deeds, Granville's being on 10 June 1889 to R. C. Jamison of Pembroke (Book 16, pp. 593-4).

On 1 October 1890 Granville bought land on Jackson Street in Pembroke where he established a tobacco factory. He bought the land from T. D. and Geneva Jameson for $530 cash plus $275 in promissory notes. The land was described as all of lot 64 and 100 feet of lot 63 in "R. C. Jameson's addition to the Town of Pembroke" (Book 79, p. 309). On 1 June 1895 he bought more of lot 63 from R. J. and Jewel Carrot for $200 (recorded 7 February 1899, Book 98, pp. 294-5). Both lots were eventually sold in various deeds. On 16 December 1898 Granville and Hellen sold part of it to James H. Wade for $600 (recorded 8 January 1902, Book 100, p. 133), and on 12 December 1899 they sold more of it to W. W. Eddins for $100 (Book 100, p. 228). Granville became partially paralyzed in June 1901, dying in June 1905, and on 23 October 1905 Hellen and her children sold the remainder in two separate deeds: a small part was sold to W. C. Whitlow for $150 (Book 113, p. 143), and the bulk of it was sold to Wallace Dickinson (or Dickerson) for $1,350 (Book 118, p. 390). Hellen then moved to Dallas, Texas, where at least two of her children lived, and in the 1910 census of Dallas she was listed with her children Thomas and Rena on Fleming Avenue. Finally, on 8 May 1920 Hellen and her children signed a deed of release to W. H. Payne of Pembroke for the money owed by Dickinson (or Dickerson--Book 156, p. 111). Hellen died in Dallas.

Granville was a life-long member of the Christian Church and taught a Sunday school Bible class for many years. Hellen was also active in the church and when she moved to Dallas became a member of Oak Cliff Christian Church.

Children, all by (2) Hellen Nora Burrus and all born in Kentucky:

5-102 Thomas Burrus, b. 11 July 1880
5-103 Charles Waddill, b. 10 October 1881
5-104 Rena Mary, b. 25 August 1883
5-105 Nora Davis, b. 2 September 1885

4-33 ROBERT M. GRAHAM,[48] born Todd County, Kentucky, c. 1839, died before 1900; married in Todd County, 3 September 1869, MARTHA E. HILTON, born Kentucky, March 1838, died probably before 1910, daughter of George Hilton (born Virginia, c. 1810, died before 25 September 1880) and Elizabeth Ann Davis (born Kentucky, c. 1814, died before 1860).

Robert and Martha moved to Ballard County, Kentucky, soon after they were married. On 25 September 1880 Martha gave her power of attorney to Robert to settle her father's estate in Todd County (Book 10, p. 581), and on 17 May 1889 his in-laws Andrew Hilton and Claude E. Hilton appointed Robert, "our former guardian," to collect money due to them from the estate of Mrs. S[usan] O. Floyd, "our aunt," in Todd County (Book 16, p. 574). Susan O. Hilton Floyd was the wife of E. B. Floyd.

Robert's uncle Joseph Waddill died in 1888 leaving 71 acres to Robert's mother who, herself, died a few months later. Her children therefore inherited the land, selling it in separate deeds. Robert and his older sister, Eliza, sold their interests jointly on 22 July 1891 to D. M. Townley for $700 (Book 18, pp. 180-1).

In the 1880 census of Ballard County, Robert and Martha were listed in Barlow District No. 5 with a black servant named Jones Waddel, age 14. In the 1900 census Martha was listed as a widow. Listed with her was her daughter, Georgia, also a widow.

Known children, both born in Kentucky:

5-106 Georgia A., b. October 1870

5-107 Thomas R., b. April 1874

4-34 LUCY A. GRAHAM, born Todd County, Kentucky, *c.* 1841, probably died young. She was listed with her parents in the 1860 census of Todd County but not in the 1870 one, and no record has been found that she was married.

4-35 MARY M. GRAHAM DANIEL (called Mollie),[49] born Todd County, Kentucky 20 August 1843, died 29 May 1911, buried Camp Cemetery, Todd County; married, 19 November 1868, WILLIAM B. DANIEL (Book B, p. 281), born Kentucky, 2 September 1832, died 7 April 1903, buried Camp Cemetery, Todd County. This was William's second marriage, his first to Jane Millen in 1862 (Book B, p. 191).

Children, all born in Kentucky:

A. Joanna Daniel, b. September 1869
B. Inez P. Daniel, b. November 1874
C. Richard Edward Daniel, b. August 1877
D. Horace Daniel, b. December 1878
E. Robert L. Daniel, b. 26 June 1880

---

A. Joanna Daniel Anderson, born Kentucky, September 1869; married, 15 October 1891, William F. Anderson (Book E, p. 6). Known children:

1. Clara Anderson, born Kentucky, November 1892

2. Mary Anderson, born Kentucky, April 1895

3. Odessa Anderson, born Kentucky, February 1899

B. Inez P. Daniel Duerson, born Kentucky, November 1874; married, 11 December 1907, Lawrence W. Duerson (Book F, p. 110), born Kentucky, October 1846, son of Thomas Duerson (born Virginia, *c.* 1796, died after 1870) and Eleanor G. Waddill (born Virginia, *c.* 1807, died after 1870), and brother of Granville Duer-

3-9 Thomas P., 2-1 Andrew                                              4-35C

son who married 4-36 Joanna. Lawrence and Granville Duerson
were grandsons of Granville Waddill who was the great-grand-
father of Inez. This was Lawrence's second marriage, his
first to Mary O. ___ who died before 1900 and is buried in the
Duerson Cemetery. Lawrence was the administrator of the estate of Inez's great-uncle Joseph Waddill (Book of Settlements 1, p. 444). It is not known whether Inez had children.

C. Richard Edward Daniel, born Kentucky, August 1877; married,
30 October 1912, Ruth B. Anderson (Book F, p. 118). Known
children:

1. Annie Ruth Daniel, born December 1878, died 1918, buried
Camp Cemetery, Todd County, Kentucky.

2. Leona Belle Daniel, born 1917, died infancy, buried Camp
Cemetery, Todd County.

D. Horace Daniel, born December 1878

E. Robert L. Daniel, born 26 June 1880, died 1 December 1910,
buried Camp Cemetery, Todd County, Kentucky.


4-36 JOANNA GRAHAM DUERSON,[50] born Todd County, Kentucky, 1 September
1845, died Todd County, 19 June 1933, buried with her parents and
brother Granville in the Duerson Cemetery, Todd County; married in
Todd County, 20 July 1874, GRANVILLE DUERSON, born Kentucky, September 1844, died 1925, buried Duerson Cemetery on Tress' Shop
Road and Trenton Road, son of Thomas Duerson (born Virginia,
c. 1796, died after 1870) and Eleanor G. Waddill (born Virginia,
c. 1807, died after 1870), and brother of Lawrence Duerson who
married 4-35B Inez Daniel. Joanna and Granville were first
cousins.

On 21 November 1876 Granville and Joanna sold 39½ acres to
her uncle Joseph Waddill for $1,188.95 (Book 9, pp. 28-9), and on
18 May 1889 Granville bought 116 acres at auction for $3,969. In
his will, dated 11 August 1886 and proved on 13 November 1925, he
left his entire estate to his wife, also naming her as executrix
(Book N, p. 194). Joanna died a few years later. In her will,
dated 3 December 1928 and proved on 10 July 1933, she left her
property and personal possessions equally to Joanna Anderson (wife
of W. F. Anderson), Inez Duerson (wife of L. W. Duerson), Ed
Daniel, and Horace Daniel (Book N, p. 310). All these heirs were
children of Joanna's sister Mollie.

3-12 Andrew W., 2-1 Andrew

Joanna Graham Duerson had two children both of whom died young. Neither child appeared in a census.

### CHILDREN OF 3-12 ANDREW W. GRAHAM
### AND ___

4-37 MARY M. GRAHAM MARTIN,[51] born probably in Clinton County, Missouri, 15 April 1846, died perhaps in Iowa, after 1908; married in Henderson County, Illinois, 27 or 28 February 1861, ANDREW W. MARTIN, born Henderson County, Illinois, 7 June 1838, died 15 February 1908, buried Biggsville Cemetery, Henderson County, son of Judge Preston Martin (born Bourbon County, Kentucky, 25 October 1804, died 30 June 1898, buried Biggsville Cemetery, Henderson County, Illinois) and Ann Taylor (born Alexandria, Virginia, 28 February 1803, died Biggsville, Illinois, 16 December 1880, buried Biggsville Cemetery).

After Mary's father went to California, she and her brother were eventually taken in by 4-22 Robert C. Graham.

Andrew W. Martin served in the Civil War in Company K, 84th Illinois Volunteer Infantry, and on 12 April 1879 he applied for a veteran's pension. Mary applied for a widow's pension on 23 March 1908.

On 26 July 1861 Mary and Andrew joined the South Henderson United Presbyterian Church. From August 1867 until August 1870 they lived in Iowa, according to Andrew's testimony for the army records of his brother-in-law Andrew G. Graham, then returned to Henderson County. On 28 March 1884, however, the South Henderson Church dismissed them again to Iowa. Andrew, but not Mary, was listed in the 1900 census of Linn Township, Marshall County, Iowa. He was in the Iowa Soldier's home. Andrew was a farmer.

Children, all born in Illinois:

A. Dorinda J. Martin, b. 1861
B. Annie B. Martin, b. c. 1863
C. Samuel P. Martin, b. c. 1865
D. John B. Martin, b. c. 1872
E. Ida M. Martin, b. c. 1874

A. Dorinda J. Martin McIntosh (called Jennie or Jane), born Illinois, 1861, died 1943, buried Biggsville Cemetery, Henderson County, Illinois; married in Henderson County, 5 October 1887, John M. McIntosh (Marriage Records, Book C, p. 22), born 1857, died 1926, buried Biggsville Cemetery, son of ___ McIntosh (born Scotland) and ___ (born Kentucky). He moved to Henderson County in 1883 and bought 156 acres near Biggsville. Children:

1. Maude McIntosh, born Illinois c. 1883. In the 1910 federal census she was listed in her parents' household and was a music teacher.

2. Dean McIntosh, born Illinois c. 1890

3. Marjorie McIntosh, born Illinois, 1891, died 1962, buried next to her parents in Biggsville Cemetery; unmarried.

4. Jack McIntosh, born Illinois, c. 1907

B. Annie B. Martin, born Illinois, c. 1863

C. Samuel P. Martin, born Illinois, c. 1865

D. John B. Martin, born Illinois, c. 1872

E. Ida M. Martin, born Illinois, c. 1874

4-38 ANDREW GARTIN GRAHAM,[52] born Clinton County, Missouri, 6 January 1847, died Biggsville, Illinois, 18 August 1902, buried Biggsville Cemetery, Henderson County, Illinois; married at Smith Creek Church near Rozetta, Henderson County, Illinois, 8 December 1869, MARTHA CAROLINE FRANCIS (called Caroline), born Ohio, 16 March 1849, died 13 December 1928, buried Biggsville Cemetery. Andrew and Caroline were married by the Rev. Samuel Millen.

After Andrew's father went to California, Andrew and his sister were eventually taken in by 4-22 Robert C. Graham. Andrew enlisted in Company H, 11th Illinois Cavalry on 26 November 1861 and was discharged on 30 September 1865. His pension record shows that while in the army he experienced considerable illness from dyspepsia, vomiting, and diarrhoea, illnesses from which he suffered intermittently for the remainder of his life. Also while in the army, he was mistakenly diagnosed as having syphilis--a diagnosis he firmly denied in a subsequent deposition--and later examinations showed no trace of the disease. The cause of his death in 1902 was "catarrh of stomach."

On 30 May 1870 Caroline joined the South Henderson United Presbyterian Church, the same church which her sister-in-law Mary Graham Martin and her husband joined later the same year. There is no record of Andrew's joining. Caroline was dismissed on 24 August 1872, and later they both joined the Cumberland Presbyterian Church.

The following is from an obituary on Andrew which appeared in the *Oquawka Spectator*, 20 August 1902:

> Mr. Graham was born January 6, 1847 in Clinton County, Missouri. His mother died when he was three years old and when he was five years old his father went to California. He had little chance to attend school when a child but acquired a fair education by his own efforts. In 1858, he came to Henderson County. Shortly afterward the war broke out and he enlisted when a little less than 16 years in November, 1861, in Company H, 11th IL Cav. He was in such desperate engagements as the battles of Shiloh and Corinth and did valiant service to his country. After serving out his term he came home and enlisted, serving altogether nearly four years. His health never recovered after his army experiences and much of his life since he has been an invalid. Mr. Graham was postmaster in Biggsville for years and had served one term as county treasurer.
>
> He was married December 16, 1869 to Miss Martha C. Francis. . . .

When Andrew died in 1902, his occupation as given on his death certificate was that of janitor. Martha was listed as a widow in the 1910 federal census of Henderson County, Illinois; she said she had had five children only three of whom were living.

Children, all born in Henderson County, Illinois:

5-108 ___ (boy), b. 11 November 1870, d. January 1871
5-109 Frank Mills, b. 7 October 1873
5-110 Charles Inman, b. 9 September 1876
5-111 Mary F., b. 24 September 1880, d. 9 December 1880
5-112 Russell Alexander, b. 24 April 1885

4-39 NANCY GRAHAM, probably born in Clinton County, Missouri, c. 1849. In the 1850 and 1860 censuses of Platte County, Missouri, a Nancy Graham was listed in the household of 3-7 Martha Graham Shanklin, older sister of Nancy's father, Andrew W., whose wife had died c. 1850 and who went to California c. 1852. It is thought that this Nancy was Andrew's daughter. Nothing more is known of her.

CHILDREN OF 3-15 DAVID GRAHAM
AND ELIZABETH ___

4-40 MARY H. GRAHAM, born York County, South Carolina, c. 1819. Nothing more is known of her.

4-41 ___ GRAHAM, born York County, South Carolina, c. 1820, died before 1836.

4-42 MARTHA ANN GRAHAM, born York County, South Carolina, c. 1822. Nothing more is known of her.

# FIFTH GENERATION

## CHILDREN OF 4-2 ANDREW GRAHAM
## AND RACHEL ANN DAVIS

5-1 WILLIAM B. GRAHAM,[1] born Henderson County, Illinois, 9 January 1842, died probably in Rice County, Kansas, 1922; married (1) in Henderson County, 7 January 1864, MARTHA A. MCDILL, born Preble County, Ohio, 10 April 1842, died Henderson County, Illinois, 18 October 1875, buried South Henderson Cemetery, daughter of Robert McDill (1803-1890) and Mary Porter (1806-1886); William married (2) in Henderson County, 17 January 1878, MARGARET WALLACE, born Belmont County, Ohio, 1839, daughter of David Wallace (born Ohio) and Fanny C. Ross (born Pennsylvania).

The following is from the *History of Mercer and Henderson Counties* (1882):

> William B., the eldest son [of 4-2 Andrew] is now on the home successfully engaged in farming and stock raising. His education was mostly received in the common schools of this county's early history, though it was extended by a few terms at Monmouth and Oquawka. . . . [He and his wife] are members of the [South Henderson] United Presbyterian church, and since 1870 he has been an elder in the same. On his farm he has erected a very substantial stone residence.

After William remarried, his new wife, Margaret, joined the South Henderson United Presbyterian Church on 10 May 1878. In 1891 they were dismissed to Sterling, Rice County, Kansas, where they were listed in the 1900 and 1910 censuses. In 1900 he was a butcher; by 1910 he was no longer working. Children by (1) Martha A. McDill, all born in Henderson County, Illinois:

4-2 Andrew, 3-3 Matthew, 2-1 Andrew          5-2

6-1 Mary Frances b, 10 October 1864

6-2 Robert A., b. July 1869
6-3 William Wilson, b. 1872

Child by (2) Margaret Wallace:

6-4 Ross W., b. Biggsville, IL, 6 January 1879


5-2 DAVID WILSON GRAHAM,[2] born Biggsville, Henderson County, Illinois, 11 June 1843, died Chicago, 9 February 1925; married in Chicago, July 1877, IDA ANSPACH BARNED, born Pennsylvania, January 1850, died Chicago, 1948.

David joined the South Henderson United Presbyterian Church on 29 March 1861 (Church Register). He then served in the Civil War in the 83d Illinois Volunteers, 1862-1865, was promoted to corporal on 31 May 1865, and was mustered out on 26 June 1865. On 27 February 1879 he applied for a veteran's pension, and after he died Ida applied for a widow's pension on 26 February 1925.

When David returned home after the Civil War, he entered Monmouth College from which he was graduated in 1870 and took a master's in 1873. In 1872 he earned his M.D. at Bellevue Hospital Medical College. In 1884 he became a surgeon at the Presbyterian Hospital, Chicago. Subsequently he was a consulting surgeon at the Evanston Hospital, professor of surgery at Rush Medical College, surgeon at the Cook County Hospital and Wesley Hospital, and professor of anatomy (1877-82) and of surgery (1883-98) at Woman's Medical College. He was also a lieutenant-commander and surgeon at the Illinois Naval Reserves and was a frequent contributor to medical journals. He was a member of the American Medical Association, president (1894) of the Illinois State Medical Society, president (1885) of the Chicago Medical Society, and president (1906-7) of the Chicago Surgical Society. He also belonged to the Chicago Pathological Society. In 1910 Monmouth College awarded him an honorary doctorate. David and his wife were members of the Third Presbyterian Church at Ashland Boulevard and Ogden Avenue in Chicago.

Ida served as president of the women's board at the Presbyterian Hospital for ten years.[3] Children, both born in Chicago:

6-5 David Barned, b. 9 April 1879

6-6 Evarts Ambrose, b. 19 March 1883

5-3 MARTHA JANE GRAHAM MCMILLAN,[4] born Henderson County, Illinois, April 1845, died 19 April 1910, buried South Henderson Cemetery; married in Henderson County, 28 May 1870, ROBERT T. MCMILLAN, born Illinois, November 1835, died 1916, buried South Henderson Cemetery, son of John McMillan and ___.

Martha attended Monmouth College, Illinois, 1862-64. In the 1900 census Robert was listed as a farmer in Biggsville, Henderson County, Illinois. Inscribed on his tombstone is "Co. K 84th Ill. Infantry."

Children, all born in Henderson County, Illinois:

A. Anna Mary McMillan, b. 5 November 1871
B. Jessie Belle McMillan, b. 9 January 1873
C. Laura McMillan, b. 1876
D. Edward Andrew McMillan, b. May 1880
E. Walter Wilson McMillan, b. May 1882

---

A. Anna Mary McMillan (Minnie), born Henderson County, Illinois, 5 November 1871, died 15 February 1887 (15 years, 3 months, 10 days), buried South Henderson Cemetery.

B. Jessie Belle McMillan Whiteman, born Biggsville, Illinois, 9 January 1873, died 1947; married, 30 November 1898, Alexander Francis Whiteman (Frank), born Henderson County, Illinois, 8 December 1871, died 1954, son of Henry Miller Whiteman and Elizabeth McDill. Frank was a farmer and stock raiser. In the 1900 census they were listed in Gladstone Township, Henderson County, Illinois. Children:

1. Harold McMillan Whiteman (Mac), born Illinois, 18 October 1899; married (1) Esther Fordyce; (2) on 17 April 1937, Lillian Potter, born 6 March 1906, daughter of Frank Potter and Violet Black. Mac was a farmer. Children:

    a. Frank Potter Whiteman, born 1940, died infancy.

    b. David Whiteman, born 1944; married Marianne Marine. Children: (**a**) Kirk David, born 1970; and (**b**) Garth (Toby), born 1972.

    c. Dean Whiteman, born 1946; married Marilyn McNichol. Child: Jennie L., born 1974.

2. Wendell Francis Whiteman, born 29 April 1901; married on 19 April 1924, Lucille Zimmerman, born 29 June 1901, daughter of Thomas Zimmerman and Irene Thomas. Wendell was a banker in Monmouth, Illinois. Children:

   a. Donald Graham Whiteman, born 22 May 1926; married Joan Weakly. Children: (**a**) Thomas Graham, born 1952, died 1971; (**b**) Wendy Laine, born 1954; (**c**) Nancy Allison, born 1956; and (**d**) Douglas Scott, born 1959.

   b. Ralph Edwin Whiteman, born 12 February 1928; married Louise Brown. Children: (**a**) Cyndy Louise, born 1952, married Thomas Burke; (**b**) Laurie Patrice, born 1954; and (**c**) Cheri Kay, born 1956.

   c. Richard Whiteman, born 1942; married Harriet Sutherland. Children: (**a**) Charles R., born 1969; and (**b**) Amanda, born 1972.

3. Edith Pauline Whiteman, born 29 January 1903, died 1978. She was in government service in Washington, D.C.

4. Robert Henry Whiteman, born 29 July 1905; married on 12 February 1927, Sarah Elizabeth Keister, born 27 March 1908, daughter of George Keister and Ethel Elliott. Robert was a banker in Monmouth, Illinois. Children:

   a. Barbara Joyce Whiteman Garland, born 25 November 1927; married Edward Garland. Children: (**a**) Edward Olin, born 1953; (**b**) Robert Henry, born 1954; and (**c**) Sara Jan, born 1959.

   b. Connie Lee Whiteman, born 18 September 1930, died 14 December 1931, buried Biggsville, Illinois.

5. Russell Edward Whiteman, born 6 June 1907; married on 6 September 1937, Opal Eaton, born 15 May 1906, daughter of G. E. Eaton. Russell was in government service in Biggsville, Illinois. Children:

   a. Constance Jeanne Whiteman Smith, born 17 May 1938; married (1) Alvin Wilson; (2) Donald Bitle; (3) George B. Smith. Children: (**a**) Robert Todd Wilson, born 1960; and (**b**) Alicia Bitle, born 1963.

   b. James Neal Whiteman, born 26 December 1939; married Frances Stratton. Children: (**a**) Elizabeth Susan, born 1962, married Donald Washburn and had Kristopher, born 1981; and (**b**) James, born 1964.

    c.  Scott Whiteman, born 1944

    d.  Michael Whiteman, born 1946; married Carol ___. Children: (**a**) Angela, born 1972; and (**b**) Teresa, born 1973.

6. Margaret Josephine Whiteman Kelly, born 1 November 1909; married, 22 December 1935, John R. Kelly, born 14 July 1910, son of Owen Kelly and Ollie Smith. Children:

    a.  Rollyn Graham Kelly (called Skip), born 1943; married Diana Berlin. Children: (**a**) Melinda, born 1967; (**b**) Shannon, born 1978; and (**c**) Brian, born 1980.

    b.  Susan Jane Kelly Hamilton, born 1945; married Kent Hamilton. Children: (**a**) William Todd, born 1965; and (**b**) Amy, born 1969.

7. Howard Graham Whiteman, born 6 February 1915, died 13 October 1918.

C. Laura McMillan Fuller, born Henderson County, Illinois, 1876, died 1945; married in Henderson County, 29 December 1896, Harvey Fuller, born Illinois, c. 1872, died 1953, son of Jerome Fuller and Grace Martin. Laura and Harvey were married by the Rev. R. H. McHenry (Book C, p. 105). In the 1910 federal census of Biggsville, Henderson County, Harvey was listed as a quarryman in a stone mine. Children:

1. Dean G. Fuller, born 1898, died 1912.

2. Donald G. Fuller, born 1899; married Frances Mahaffey. Child:

    a.  Marvin L. Fuller, born 1927; married Mary Opstad. Children: (**a**) Tom; (**b**) Fritz; and (**c**) Mia.

3. Guy Clifford Fuller, born 1900, died 1981; married Ethel Hartsock. Children:

    a.  James Fuller, born 1940 (twin to next); married Toni Spann. Children: (**a**) Michael, born 1967; and (**b**) Laura, born 1969.

4-2 Andrew, 3-3 Matthew, 2-1 Andrew                                  5-3C3b

   b. Jane Fuller Harrison, born 1940 (twin to above); married Wilkes Douglas Harrison. Children: (**a**) Will Durham, born 1968; and (**b**) Anita Jane, born 1975.

4. Martha Lois Fuller Stott, born 1902; married Brooke Stott.

5. Harry Fuller, born 1903, died 1959; married Lola Mock. Children:

   a. Dean G. Fuller, born 1927; married Patricia Peters. Children: (**a**) Pamela, born 1953; (**b**) Richard, born 1954; and (**c**) David, born 1957.

   b. Johanna Fuller Franklin House, born 1929; married (1) Willard Franklin; (2) Arnold House. Children: (**a**) Laura Sue Franklin, born 1950; and (**b**) Catherine Ann House, born 1958.

6. Paul J. Fuller, born 1905; married Marcella Gombert. Children:

   a. Jack Fuller, born 1928; married Judith McKechnie. Child: Catherine, born 1967.

   b. Sally Jo Fuller Dahltorp, born 1939; married Bruce Dahltorp. Children: (**a**) Timothy, born 1961; and (**b**) Jeff, born 1967.

7. George H. Fuller, born 1907; married Myra Tucker. Children:

   a. Cornelia Fuller Beaver, born 1934; married Jack Beaver. Children: (**a**) John Thomas (Jay), born 1961; and (**b**) Todd, born 1963.

   b. ___ Fuller; married Helen Scheder(?).

   c. Janet Ruth Fuller Doudna, born 1940; married William Doudna. Children: (**a**) Laura Ann, born 1960; and (**b**) William Scott, born 1966.

   d. Karen Fuller Crosby, born 1943; married James Crosby. Children: (**a**) Jeff, born 1960; (**b**) David, born 1962; and (**c**) Carrie, born 1964.

8. Ruth F. Fuller Brown, born c. June 1909; married Craig L. Brown. Child:

4-2 Andrew, 3-3 Matthew, 2-1 Andrew

      a. David McMillan Brown, born 1937; married Edna Atkin. Children: (**a**) Rhonda, born 1959, married ___ Mink and had Candace, born 1978; and (**b**) Craig, born 1967.

  9. Rachel G. Fuller Pollaschek, born 1911; married Fred Pollaschek.

 10. Everett McM. Fuller, born 1913; married Eileen Gans. Child:

      a. Stuart M. Fuller, born 1946; married Lois Nelson. Children: (**a**) Jason, born 1969; (**b**) Byron, born 1972; and (**c**) Tiffanie, born 1976.

 11. Dick G. Fuller, born 1916; married Elizabeth Boise. Child:

      a. Cassandra Fuller Friedman, born 1944; married Gerold Friedman. Children: (**a**) Bart, born 1964; and (**b**) Brian, born 1968.

D. Edward Andrew McMillan (E.A.), born Henderson County, Illinois, May 1880, died in the 1950's; married Florence Watson. In 1911 he was living in Macomb, Illinois. Later he moved to Monmouth where he was a dry cleaner. Children:

  1. Graham W. McMillan, born 1916; married Mary Ross, born 1915. Children:

      a. Elizabeth McMillan Hohlfeldt, born 1947; married David Hohlfeldt. Children: (**a**) Erin Elizabeth, born 1973; and (**b**) Bradley, born 1978.

      b. Mary Andrew McMillan, born 1951

  2. Jane McMillan Leslie, born 1918; married William J. Leslie. Children:

      a. William J. Leslie Jr., born 1941, died 1959.

      b. Charles Leslie, born 1942; married Susan O'Neal. Children: (**a**) Stacie, born 1968, died 1970; (**b**) Bill, born 1970; (**c**) Joe, born 1972; and (**d**) David, born 1973.

      c. Thomas Harold Leslie, born 1946; married Mildred Kindle. Child: Steven, born 1972.

4-2 Andrew, 3-3 Matthew, 2-1 Andrew                           5-3D2d

    d. Margaret Jane Leslie Ingalls Thormod, born 1951;
       married (1) David Ingalls; (2) Gary Thormod. Child-
       ren: (a) Jennifer Ingalls, born 1970; and (b) Tyler
       Thormod, born 1976.

  3. Patricia McMillan Knapp, born 1921; married H. D. Knapp.
     Children:

    a. Jane Elizabeth Knapp Clanahan, born 1947; married
       Steven Clanahan.

    b. Ann Knapp, born 1948; married ___. Children: (a)
       ___; (b) Elizabeth Ann, born 1973; and (c) Anthony
       Patrick, born 1977.

    c. John Knapp, born 1950

    d. Gail Knapp Harley, born 1952; married Robert Harley.
       Child: Sarah Jane, born 1980.

E. Walter Wilson McMillan, born Henderson County, Illinois, May
   1882, died 1950; married Mary Ethel Senseman. He lived in
   Monmouth, Illinois. Child:

  1. Robert McMillan, born 1916; married JoAnne Green.
     Children:

    a. Michelle McMillan, born 1952

    b. Steven McMillan, born 1956

    c. Wendy McMillan, born 1960


5-4 MATTHEW YOUNG GRAHAM,[5] born Henderson County, Illinois, 1847,
    baptized South Henderson United Presbyterian Church, 13 September
    1847, died 1848, buried South Henderson Cemetery.

## CHILDREN OF 4-3 JOHN W. GRAHAM
## AND GRIZZELLA W. MILLIGAN [6]

5-5 JOHN MILLIGAN GRAHAM, born Preble County, Ohio, 31 March 1839, died Morning Sun, Preble County, Ohio, 17 June 1863, buried Hopewell Cemetery, Preble County;[7] unmarried. He was graduated from Miami University in 1858 and was licensed as a minister of the United Presbyterian Church, but he died a few years later.

5-6 WILLIAM ANDREW GRAHAM, born Preble County, Ohio, 3 February 1841, died Oxford, Butler County, Ohio, 7 November 1863, buried Hopewell Cemetery, Preble County;[8] unmarried. He was graduated from Miami University in 1863 but died within a few months.

5-7 MITCHELL MATTHEW GRAHAM (called Mike),[9] born Morning Sun, Preble County, Ohio, 14 April 1843, died of Bright's disease in Carrollton, Missouri, 23 June 1917, buried Oakhill Cemetery; unmarried.

While a student at Miami University, Oxford, Ohio, where he was a member of Phi Delta Theta, Mitchell (Mike) enlisted as a private in Company A, 86th Ohio Infantry, serving from 28 May 1862 until 25 September 1862 when he returned to college. There, one of his professors who was a captain re-formed the company as Company K, 86th Ohio, and Mike reenlisted as a corporal, serving from 26 June 1863 until 10 February 1864 when he again returned to college. At his enlistment he was described as 5 feet 8 inches tall with blue eyes and light hair. When he was mustered out, he was described as 5 feet 9½ inches tall and had blue eyes, light hair, and fair complexion.

He was an artist and a photographer, living variously at Oxford, Ohio, until 1866; Monmouth, Illinois, until 1872 or 1874; Galesburg, Illinois, until 1876 or 1877; Carrollton, Missouri, until 1879; Salina, Kansas, until 1882; and finally Carrollton again where he eventually died. In about 1892 he slipped, fell on a sidewalk, and injured the third and fourth fingers of his right hand, ultimately causing them to contract and thus hampering his work. By 1907 he was a janitor at the Wilcoxson and Company Bank in Carrollton although he still gave his occupation as painter. While there he suffered an assault which resulted in a serious hip injury: during a street fair he was working at the bank which had

left its doors open so that people might come in and sit down. A
man sat on the steps near Mike, "began to block guard," and
indulged in "vile talk" whereupon Mike called the police. Later
that night the man attacked Mike, knocking him to the brick pavement, and thus causing him to break his hip. The following is the
testimony of Russell Kneisley, a witness to the incident:

> My age is 39, am an attorney at Law, address Carrollton
> Carroll Co Mo. I know the claimant Mitchell M. Graham,
> commonly known as "Mike Graham." Have known him ever
> since he has resided in Carrollton, Mo. He drinks some
> but not to excess. I never saw him drunk in my life.
> . . . I was present at the time he was assaulted by a
> man named Jack Saunders on October 4th 1906. It was at
> night between eight and 9 o'clock. I was in company
> with claimant at the time. . . . Saunders had a brick
> or stone or some other instrument in his hand, struck
> claimant right on the jaw or face. Claimant was not
> fighting with Saunders. It was not the impact of Saunders brick that caused the damage but his striking the
> brick pavement. We were having a street fair here in
> town at the time. I had free tickets to all the concessions and took claimant with me. His hip was broken
> by the fall. We placed him on a cot and brought him to
> the Wilcoxson's Bank where he stays. Dr. R. T. Cook was
> called and attended him. Claimant was absolutely not to
> blame in any way for it. He is such a quiet inoffensive
> old gentleman that I don't believe he ever had a quarrel
> in his life with anyone. He was insensible until he was
> attended by the doctor and brought upstairs to his own
> room. I prepared papers for a suit against Saunders for
> damages, but he and his ___ [mother?] came in and paid
> $100 and the doctors bill.


5-8 HARVEY WILSON GRAHAM, born Israel Township, Preble County, Ohio,
3 September 1845, died of diphtheria in Cedar Rapids, Iowa, 8
October 1869, buried Monmouth Cemetery, Warren County, Illinois;
married perhaps in Wisconsin, c. 1867, MARTHA AMANDA GLENN, born
Randolph County, Illinois, 29 May 1850, died probably in Beaumont,
California, 16 March 1888, daughter of the Rev. James Wilson Glenn
(born Saratoga County, New York, 28 August 1821, died Marissa,
Illinois, 18 June 1879) and Mary Ann Clendenin (born Randolph
County, Illinois, 12 October 1821, died Marissa, Illinois, 6
September 1872).

4-3 John W., 3-3 Matthew, 2-1 Andrew

On 4 July 1863 at the age of eighteen, Harvey enlisted in Company A, 167th Regiment of the Ohio National Guard under Capt. James Stewart and served until 8 September 1864. His company did mostly guard duty in West Virginia.[10] His army records described him as being 5 feet 11 inches tall with gray eyes, light hair, and a fair complexion. After the war he attended Miami University, 1865-6, where he became a member of Phi Delta Theta, then went to Monmouth College from which he was graduated in 1867. The following is an excerpt from his graduation oration which was entitled "The Work of Science":

> The antiquities of Greece and Rome speak to us in the eloquence of their beauty and grandeur of their former greatness and civilization. Those crumbling ruins, those solitary pillars, those broken columns all tell their tales of former times. So other nations that have passed away have left behind the relics of their existence. As of nations so of individuals. Each human being that has lived, acted, passed away, has left some relic of his life. Some effects exist today which belong to the chain of which his life was a link. Some influence is felt; some things are not as they would have been without his existence. And as each one of us must extend some influence, must leave some relic of our existence behind us, surely then it is our duty to see that it will be one which will be for good and not for evil.

Harvey died before his son was born. After he died, Martha moved in about 1872 to Marissa, Saint Clair County, Illinois, where she joined the United Presbyterian Church on 1 November 1872. On 4 September 1873 she married (2) Joseph W. Elder, born in South Carolina, July 1848, died probably in Beaumont, California, after 1900. Martha and Joseph moved to Beaumont in about 1888, and she died soon after. Their children, all born in Marissa, were Eva May, born 1874; Ada Glenn, born June 1876; Joseph Ross, born 7 August 1883; and Robert B., born August 1886.

Child of Harvey and Martha:

6-7 Harvey Wilson Jr., b. Randolph
      Co., IL, 20 December 1869


5-9 FRANK Y. GRAHAM, born Preble County, Ohio, 14 July 1848, died of tuberculosis in Monmouth, Illinois, 2 December 1874, buried Monmouth Cemetery; married in Monmouth, 30 October 1869, JANE E.

MCGAW, born Ohio, 1850. He attended Miami University and later was a clerk and bookkeeper in Monmouth. He and Jane had no known children.

5-10 DAVID W. GRAHAM, died at 6 months, buried Hopewell Cemetery, Preble County, Ohio.[11]

5-11 ___ GRAHAM (boy), died in infancy, buried Hopewell Cemetery, Preble County, Ohio.[12]

## CHILDREN OF 4-4 ROBERT C. GRAHAM
## AND MARTHA RITCHIE [13]

5-12 WILLIAM GRAHAM, born Iowa, c. 1852, died Henry County, Iowa, 1877, buried Forest Home Cemetery, Mount Pleasant, Henry County, Iowa, in same plot as his parents and brother; probably unmarried.

5-13 JOHN H. GRAHAM, born Iowa, c. 1857, died Henry County, Iowa, 6 May 1874, buried Forest Home Cemetery, Mount Pleasant, Henry County, Iowa, in same plot as his parents and brother.

## CHILDREN OF 4-5 WILLIAM MILLS GRAHAM
## AND ELIZABETH A. ROBISON [14]

5-14 LAURA GRAHAM ORR, born Illinois, October 1846, died in Fort Morgan, Colorado, 14 August 1918;[15] married in Warren County, Illinois, 12 October 1870, SAMUEL Y. ORR, born Indiana, April 1843. Laura was graduated from Monmouth College in 1869 and went to Morning Sun, Iowa, where she was a teacher. In the 1880 census of

4-5 William M., 3-3 Matthew, 2-1 Andrew                                5-14A

Morning Sun, Samuel was listed as a wagon maker. Children, all born in Iowa:

A. Eva Orr, b. c. 1872          C. Leila Orr, b. 1877
B. Marian Orr, b. c. 1874       D. William Graham Orr, b. December 1879

---

A. Eva Orr, born Iowa, c. 1872

B. Marian Orr Wilson, born Iowa, c. 1874; married Dr. C. S. Wilson or Willson. He was a physician. Children:

   1. Leila Wilson Scott, born 1895; married C. M. Scott. Children:

      a. Frank Scott, born 1919; married Mary Hanson. Child: Carol A. Scott, born 1940.

      b. Marian Scott, born 1921

      c. Carolyn Scott, born 1923, died infancy.

   2. Eugene Wilson, born 1897, died 1925; married Lillian Gibbs. Child:

      a. Eula J. Wilson, born 1923

   3. Paul M. Wilson; married Claire Hanson.

C. Leila Orr, born Iowa, c. 1877, died 1897.

D. William Graham Orr, born Iowa, December 1879; married Myrtle Sald. Children:

   1. William Graham Orr Jr., born 1916; married Aileen Fike.

   2. Robert Orr, born 1919

5-15 HARRIET E. GRAHAM (Hattie), born Henderson County, Illinois, 20 June 1850, died Monmouth, Illinois, 12 April 1917, buried Monmouth Cemetery; unmarried. She was listed with her mother in the 1870 and 1880 censuses of Monmouth, Illinois. In the 1910 census of Monmouth, she and her sister Martha were listed together in the

4-5 William M., 3-3 Matthew, 2-1 Andrew                                         5-16

same household.


5-16 MARTHA E. GRAHAM (Mattie), born Morning Sun, Louisa County, Iowa, 1853, died 1938, buried Monmouth Cemetery; unmarried. She was listed with her mother in the 1870 and 1880 censuses of Monmouth, Illinois. In the 1910 census of Monmouth, she was listed with her sister Harriet and was a clerk.


5-17 WILLIAM I. GRAHAM, born Iowa, 17 August 1854, died 21 October 1865, buried Monmouth Cemetery.


5-18 ROBERT GRAHAM, died young


5-19 JOHN M. GRAHAM, born perhaps Iowa, 22 August 1860, died of tuberculosis, 26 September 1880, buried Monmouth Cemetery.


5-20 CLINTON W. GRAHAM, born Illinois, June 1863, died Spokane, Washington, 1923; married, c. 1891, NINA CANNON, born Illinois, February 1865, died after 1940. Clinton was a conductor for the Spokane Street Railway, and according to the city directories his and Nina's address was 2119 Gardner. Nina's last listing was in 1940. No children were mentioned with their listings in the 1900 and 1910 censuses, but in the 1922 city directory a Glenn F. Graham was listed in their home. Glenn married Mina or Mena ___. In 1923-8 Glenn was a clerk, and in 1933-6 he was a solicitor at the city dye works. He has not been identified.

## CHILDREN OF 4-7 WILSON M. GRAHAM
## AND ELVIRA JANE WILSON [16]

5-21 JESSIE E. GRAHAM MOIR,[17] born Oquawka, Henderson County, Illinois, January 1852, died 1942, buried Oquawka Cemetery; married in Henderson County, 15 May 1873, JOHN MOIR, born Oquawka, 2 March 1850, died of tuberculosis, 13 October 1876, buried Oquawka Cemetery, son of Robert Moir (born Scotland, 30 October 1824, died Oquawka, Illinois, 1904), and Mary Nichol (born New York, September 1826). The following is from John's obituary in the *Oquawka Spectator*, Thursday, 19 October 1876, p. 1:

> The subject of this notice was the eldest son of Robert Moir, of this city. . . . A liberal education had just conducted him to the threshold of public life, on which he entered with the brightest prospects of success, giving evidence of being possessed of special business talents. . . . Disease laid hold upon him several years ago. Hoping to be benefitted by a change of climate, he spent the winter of 1874 in Florida. In the spring he returned, somewhat benefitted, and again resumed his business; but his strength again failing him, he started for Colorado in May last. For a time it seemed as if he would be restored to health, but disease had taken too strong a hold upon him, and soon did it accomplish its sudden, rapid work. He returned home on the 20th of September last, when he took his bed and was never able again to leave the house.

Jessie, widow, was listed in Oquawka in the 1880 and 1900 federal censuses, and by 1908 she had moved to the home of her daughter, Mabel Moir Lockwood, who lived in Peoria, Illinois. Jessie may not have lived permanently with her daughter, however, because she was not listed in the Peoria city directories after 1936. Children, all born probably in Oquawka, Illinois:

A. John G. Moir, b. 12 April 1874
B. Robert Moir (twin to next) b. 17 May 1876
C. Mabel M. Moir (twin to above), b. 17 May 1876

---

A. John G. Moir, born probably in Oquawka, Illinois, 12 April 1874, died 12 July 1901, buried Oquawka Cemetery. He was listed as a dry goods clerk in the 1900 census of Henderson County, Illinois.

   B. Robert Moir (twin to next), born probably in Oquawka, Illinois, 17 May 1876, died 13 July 1889.

   C. Mabel M. Moir Lockwood (twin to above), born probably in Oquawka, Illinois, 17 May 1876, died 1953; married in Oquawka, 15 November 1905, James Edwin Lockwood, born Burlington, Iowa, 1868, died 1928, buried Oquawka Cemetery, son of G. A. Lockwood and Sarah Kidmore (Marriage Book C, p. 150). Mabel's and James's marriage was witnessed by her uncle 5-27 William W. Graham. By 1908 Mabel and James were living in Peoria, Illinois. According to the city directories, in 1910 James was the treasurer and general manager of King Light Company, a position he held until 1919 or earlier when he became the vice-president of the State Trust and Savings Bank. By 1928 he had his own business, J. E. Lockwood and Company which dealt in loans, and after he died Mabel carried on the business herself. By 1931 she had taken in an associate, Grace M. Taylor, who continued the business after Mabel retired. Mabel's mother, Jessie, lived with her until at least 1936. Known children:

     1. Robert Lockwood, born 1906, died 1925.

     2. Jane Lockwood

5-22 JOHN GRAHAM (Johnnie), born Oquawka, Henderson County, Illinois, October 1853, died 4 November 1855, buried Oquawka Cemetery.

5-23 CARRIE SUSAN GRAHAM CAMPBELL, born Oquawka, Henderson County, Illinois, October 1856, died 1930, buried Oquawka Cemetery; married in Oquawka, 25 March 1885, ALEXANDER FERGUS CAMPBELL (called Gus), born Westmoreland County, Pennsylvania, 20 May 1853, died 1913, son of Mungo D. Campbell and Mary Ann Maben.

    Gus had a varied career.[18] He was reared in Monmouth, Illinois, where at age 13 he learned to be a moulder at a foundry. At 15 he became a clerk in the Monmouth post office, and at 20 he entered the railway mail service on the Chicago, Burlington, and Quincy railroad where he worked for the next 13 years. He then entered the newspaper business, and in 1888 he and Carrie moved to

4-7 Wilson M., 3-3 Matthew, 2-1 Andrew                                5-24

Chicago where he was in charge of the circulation department of the *Chicago Times* until 1895. Following this he went into law enforcement and was a captain, then inspector, of the Chicago Police Department until 1904. After that he was a commissioner for Chicago Underwriters' Association. When he and Carrie moved to Chicago, they lived for a short time with her cousin 5-2 David W. Graham at 672 West Monroe. Gus was a Republican and a member of St. Andrew's society. Carrie and Gus had no children.

5-24 GERTRUDE S. GRAHAM, born Oquawka, Henderson County, Illinois, 1858, died 30 December 1863, buried Oquawka Cemetery. Gertrude died on the same day that her sister Sally died.

5-25 SALLY GRAHAM, born Oquawka, Henderson County, Illinois, 1861, died 30 December 1863, buried Oquawka Cemetery. Sally died on the same day that her sister Gertrude died.

5-26 MAUDE M. GRAHAM MONTGOMERY, born Oquawka, Henderson County, Illinois, 1864, died probably in Evanston, Illinois, after 1948; married in Oquawka, 30 April 1890, WILLIAM TEEL MONTGOMERY, born Gibson County, Indiana, 12 August 1843, died probably in Evanston, Illinois, *c.* 1920-1, son of Isaac Montgomery and Mary Teel.

William[19] was orphaned at the age of ten and was reared by an uncle in Gibson County, Indiana, where he first worked on his uncle's farm, then as a clerk in a Princeton, Gibson County, hotel which his uncle had bought. In 1861 he enlisted in the army, serving until the end of the war. In 1865-8 he attended and taught school then began to study medicine with Dr. William T. Kirk of Atlanta, Illinois. After he was graduated from Rush Medical College, Chicago, in 1871, he interned at Cook County Hospital, 1871-3. In 1873 he married his first wife, Mettie McCague, who died in 1880. He was a general practitioner until 1888 at which time he began to specialize in eye and ear diseases. He was appointed oculist and aurist at Cook County Hospital, 1875; professor of ophthalmology and otology at Women's Medical College, Chicago, 1879; and surgeon of Illinois Charitable Eye and Ear Infirmary, 1880, of which he became the president of the Board of Trustees. Later he was an oculist at the Presbyterian Hospital. He was a Republican and a Presbyterian. After he and Maude were married in 1890, they lived at 567 West Congress in Chicago then moved to Evanston, Illinois, in about 1902. William's last listing in the Evanston city directories was in 1920-1, Maude's last in 1948. Maude had no known children.

5-27 WILLIAM W. GRAHAM (Will),[20] born Oquawka, Henderson County, Illinois, 1866; married KATHERINE(?) ___. He lived in Seattle, Washington, or Portland, Oregon, and had a lumber business. His wife was a writer, living on the south side of Chicago, and was a good friend of Mary Burrell Graham, wife of 6-5 David B. Will and Katherine may have been divorced or at least separated for many years. They had no known children.

## CHILDREN OF 4-8 DAVID GRAHAM AND ELIZABETH BROWN

5-28 ELIZABETH JANE GRAHAM COWDEN (called Lizzie),[21] born in Biggsville Township, Henderson County, Illinois, 8 February 1849, died Monmouth, Illinois, 2 December 1926; married at Monmouth, 7 April 1871, GEORGE HENRY COWDEN (called Henry), born Henderson County, Illinois, 5 May 1849, died 1931, son of George W. Cowden (born Preble County, Ohio, 10 April 1827, killed at Resaca, Georgia, 20 August 1864) and Eunice M. Signor (born Lawrence County, New York, 13 July 1830, died Henderson County, Illinois, April 1855). After the deaths of his parents, Henry was reared by his uncle Dr. James C. McDill who lived in Biggsville. Henry's sister Eliza married 4-27 John M. Graham.

Elizabeth was graduated from Monmouth College in 1870. When her father died in 1891, she inherited a large portion of his estate including a farm west of Biggsville, and she and her husband lived on it for several years. They also gave land for a school which became known as Cowden School. As her children grew, however, Lizzie decided to move into Biggsville so that the older children could attend the town high school; Henry commuted to the farm. Their granddaughter Betty Hallam writes that their home in Biggsville was a beautiful stone house which is still standing. Later they moved to Monmouth where they built a three-story house at 821 East Second Avenue, and Henry still commuted to the farm for a time. The third floor of the home, known as the "boys'

4-8 David, 3-3 Matthew, 2-1 Andrew          5-28A

dorm," subsequently housed many friends and relatives who lived there while enrolled at Monmouth College. After Henry retired from farming and no longer commuted, he entered politics and served on the city council for a term. He was also a member of the Modern Woodmen of America and of the Mystic Workers of the World. He and Lizzie belonged to the Second United Presbyterian Church where she taught Sunday school. Lizzie was also a member of several church societies and of the Monmouth Women's Club.

According to her granddaughter, Lizzie was a "tiny, spare woman" and had a "dry humor." Once, at dinner when she served a meat pie, she felt a dog under the table; lifting the pie crust and peering inside, she said at the same time, "How did that dog get in here?"

Henry was mild-mannered, jovial, and gentlemanly and was often perplexed by the events around him. After Lizzie died he lived with his daughters Margaret and Bess who were unmarried. Children, all born in Henderson County, Illinois:

A. Clara Cowden, b. May 1872
B. Margaret Louise Cowden, b. September 1875
C. George Glenn Cowden, b. July 1877
D. David H. Cowden, b. July 1879
E. Jessie Elizabeth (Bess) Cowden, b. September 1881
F. Ralph W. Cowden, b. August 1883
G. Mary Mabel Cowden, b. December 1884
H. Arminta Amelia Cowden, b. 15 March 1887
I. Earl W. Cowden, born December 1888

---

A. Clara Cowden Bowen, born Biggsville, Henderson County, Illinois, May 1872, married in Oquawka, Illinois, 18 June 1902, Fred A. Bowen, born Henderson County, c. 1874, son of Warren Bowen and Sarah Vinning. They were married by J. A. Renwick, MG (Book C, p. 134). Fred had various jobs among which was insurance adjusting. At one time he and Clara moved briefly to Kansas, leaving their children with Clara's parents, but they soon returned. They lived in an apartment owned by 5-33 Fannie Graham Herbert on South Eighth Street in Monmouth. Children:

1. Marjorie Elizabeth Bowen, born Monmouth, died in infancy.

2. Everett Bowen, born Monmouth, Illinois, died before 1988; married (1) Esther Patton; (2) Edith Hardesty. After

Everett married Edith, they moved to San Antonio, Texas. Edith was a researcher for the DAR. Child by Esther:

  a. Richard Bowen; married Patricia Maxey. He is an advertising salesman and lives in Chattanooga, Tennessee. Children: (a) Michelle, married (1) ___ Nelson, (2) Bruce Waugh, and had Melissa Nelson and Aaron Waugh; (b) Gina, married Greg Filter; (c) Douglas, married Susan ___; (d) Deborah; (e) Brian Robert; and (f) Jennifer.

3. Robert Cowden Bowen, born Monmouth, Illinois; married Dorothy Breiner. They live in Palm Harbor, Florida. Children:

  a. Sally Ann Bowen Coupal, born 1939; married Laurent Coupal, born 1926. She is a social worker in Tampa, Florida. Children: (a) Renee, born 1965; and (b) Melissa, born 1968.

  b. David Bowen, born 1943; married Betty Landshur, born 1945. They live in Palm Harbor, Florida, where he works for Honeywell Corporation. Children: (a) Heidi Elizabeth, born 1973; and (b) A. J., born 1981.

  c. Mary Elizabeth Bowen Cooper, born 1943; married Ward Cooper, born 1944. They live in Tampa, Florida, where she is in government work. Children: (a) John Edward, born 1967; (b) Katherine Jean, born 1972; and (c) David Cass, born 1973.

  d. Jane Louise Bowen Van Overmeiren, born 1949; married Frank Van Overmeiren, born 1947. Frank was a Dutch foreign exchange student. He and Jane have lived abroad a great deal and now live in Calgary, Alberta, Canada. Children: (a) Robert Serge, born 1970; and (b) Ileanna Marissia, born 1972.

B. Margaret Louise Cowden, born Henderson County, Illinois, September 1875, died probably in Monmouth, 1962; unmarried. Margaret was graduated in home economics from Bradley University, Peoria, Illinois. She taught in a Nevada mining town called Tonepah and at a mission school in Hawaii. By 1900 she was a teacher in or near Biggsville, Henderson County, Illinois. Later she was a teacher in Monmouth and lived with her sister Bess in the Cowden home.

C. George Glenn Cowden (called Jack), born Henderson County, Illinois, July 1877, died perhaps in Detroit, 1956; married Lillian Dale. In the 1900 census he was listed as boarding at the home of 5-33 Fannie Graham in Monmouth, Illinois. Later he and his wife moved to Detroit where he worked in the circulation department of a newspaper. Children:

1. George Dale Cowden, born 1916; married Laura Flowers. He worked in a Detroit department store and now lives in a Detroit suburb. Child:

    a. Suzanne Carrol Cowden, born 1955

2. David Graham Cowden, born 1918; married Arlene Coburn. He worked with General Electric. Children:

    a. Holly Cowden, born 1956

    b. Laurie Cowden, born 1958

    c. Billy Cowden, born 1960

    d. Nancy Cowden, born 1965

D. David H. Cowden, born Henderson County, Illinois, July 1879, died probably in Monmouth, 1956; married Mary Jones. He farmed awhile with his father then moved to Monmouth where he was a carpenter.

E. Jessie Elizabeth Cowden (called Bess), born Henderson County, Illinois, September 1881, died 1973; unmarried. She was an office worker and enjoyed traveling, often going on fishing trips in the North.

F. Ralph W. Cowden (called Doc), born Henderson County, Illinois, August 1883, died probably in Tucson, Arizona, 1957; married Elsie Parker. Doc got his nickname from a school play. After he was graduated in law from the University of Michigan, he returned to Monmouth where he was a lawyer and, briefly, a politician (state's attorney). Elsie was his secretary. They retired to Tucson, Arizona, in 1949. Children, all born in Monmouth, Illinois:

1. Martha Elizabeth Cowden Buckler, born 1920; married Leonard Buckler. He was an airplane pilot for a company and was killed in a crash. Martha lives in Tucson where she is retired from a brokerage house.

4-8 David, 3-3 Matthew, 2-1 Andrew                                    5-28F2

   2. Robert Parker Cowden, born 1921; married Janet Burmeister.
      Both Robert and Janet are retired from the Bell Telephone
      Company. They live in Tucson.

   3. Marian Frances Cowden Lewis (called Dee or Dee Dee), born
      1927; married James O. Lewis, deceased. He was in the
      automobile industry. Dee now lives in San Antonio, Texas,
      where she golfs and does sculpting. Children:

      a. William Lewis, born 1952; married ___. They live in
         Dallas, Texas, where he is a medical doctor. They
         have three daughters.

      b. Scott Lewis, born 1956; married ___. He works in
         retail sales and now lives in Temple, Texas. Child:
         Sean.

   4. Jo Anne Cowden Ludwig, born 1928; married (1) Richard
      Snodgrass, (2) John Ludwig. She is a secretary at a
      brokerage firm in Tucson, Arizona. Child:

      a. Michael Snodgrass. He lives in Oregon.

   5. Ralph W. Cowden Jr., born 1930; married Norma Murphy.
      They live in Memphis, Tennessee. Children:

      a. John Cowden, born 1951

      b. Debbie Cowden, born 1954

      c. Ralph W. Cowden III, born 1956

G. Mary Mabel Cowden Riegel (called Mabel), born Henderson County, Illinois, December 1884, died 1968; married in Monmouth, Warren County, Illinois, 21 June 1923, Robert Edgar Riegel, born Reading, Pennsylvania, c. 1897, died ___, son of Lewis Edgar Riegel and Florence Edna Witherhold. They were married by Thomas H. Mitchell, MG (Book G, p. 8). Mabel was graduated from Monmouth College and taught history in Illinois and at Central High School in Omaha, Nebraska. Later she attended the graduate school at the University of Wisconsin where she met her husband who was probably working on his doctorate there. He became a professor of history at Dartmouth and wrote several books on the American westward movement and on women's suffrage. He and Mabel traveled extensively and were enthusiastic golfers and bridge players.

4-8 David, 3-3 Matthew, 2-1 Andrew                                              5-28H

H.  Arminta Amelia Cowden Caldwell (called Minta), born Henderson
    County, Illinois, 15 March 1887, died in Monmouth, 24 May
    1964; married in Monmouth, 1 January 1922, 5-42A George Graham
    Caldwell, born 16 December 1886, died 27 November 1960, son of
    5-42 Jane (Jennie) Wilson Graham and Francis Marion Caldwell.
    Minta was graduated from Monmouth College and taught school
    briefly in Illinois and Iowa. Later she and her sister Mabel
    went to Omaha, Nebraska, where Minta taught typing and short-
    hand. George was a railway mail clerk. After he and Minta
    were married, they lived with Minta's mother in Monmouth.
    When he was not on the railroad, he was an avid reader of
    travel books. Child:

    1. Elizabeth Jane Caldwell Hallam (called Betty), born Mon-
       mouth, Illinois, 30 April 1927; married in Monmouth, 18
       June 1949, David Milton Hallam, born Monmouth, 16 March
       1922, son of George Milton Hallam (born Monmouth, 22
       October 1877, died Monmouth, 29 March 1964) and Anna Robb
       (born Vernon, Iowa, 21 February 1893, died Monmouth,
       Illinois, 27 July 1965).

       Betty was graduated from Monmouth College in 1949.
       While still in college and for a time thereafter, she
       worked as a reporter then as society editor for the
       *Monmouth Review Atlas.* From 1966 to 1988 she taught
       English and journalism at Warren High School near Monmouth
       and is now a substitute teacher. She is a member of Delta
       Kappa Gamma, an honorary teachers' sorority; the Monmouth
       Fortnightly Club; Faith United Presbyterian Church in
       which she has held synod offices; the Sleepy Eye Club in
       which she is the national secretary-treasurer; the War-
       man's Antique Guide in which she is on the board; the
       Crimson Clan, a Monmouth College alumnae group in which
       she was the president, 1986-8; and a Republican women's
       organization. Her first home was the house in which
       President Ronald Reagan lived when his father worked at a
       shoe shop in Monmouth.

       Betty's husband, David, was graduated in 1945 from
       Monmouth College and did graduate work at Northwestern
       University. He was a real estate broker for many years,
       the county assessor for ten years, and since 1979 a bank
       appraiser. He is a past president of the Rotary Club,
       president of Monmouth Chamber of Commerce, chairman of the
       City Planning Commission, a member of the Monmouth Econo-
       mic Development Committee, an elder in Faith United Pres-
       byterian Church, and a board member of the Sleepy Eye

Club. He is also active in the Republican party.
Children:

a. David Mark Hallam (called Mark), born Monmouth, Illinois, 2 August 1952; unmarried. Mark was graduated from North Central College, Naperville, Illinois, in 1972, and is working toward a degree in banking. He has been employed at several banking institutions and now is a vice-president for Harris Bank and Trust in Naperville. He received an award from the Naperville Jay Cees. He lives in Aurora, Illinois, a suburb of Chicago.

b. John Robb Hallam, born Monmouth, Illinois, 12 June 1954; married in Gainesville, Florida, 6 July 1985, Laura Terry, born Hartford, Connecticut, 18 March 1955, daughter of James Terry (born Florida) and Dorothy ___ (born Georgia). This was Laura's second marriage, her first to ___ Nixon. John attended the University of Kansas for two years and was graduated from the University of Illinois in 1976. He was in the master's program at Iowa State and is now earning a doctorate in the psychology of marketing at the University of Florida, Gainesville. He has been a senior analyst for Info-Tech, a contact person for departments of transportation throughout the country, and is now a senior analyst for Shands Hospital, Gainesville. While working at Info-Tech, he was among those investigating collusion in bidding for highway construction and maintenance and for other projects in the various states. In his church work he was involved in establishing a Presbyterian national mission at Gainesville and worked on its building program. Laura attended schools in Jacksonville, Florida, and later worked with the Sunshine State Games, coordinating races and other events before olympics competition. She is active in her church and in the Brownie Scouts. She and John are enthusiastic supporters of the Florida Gators. Children, both born in Gainesville, Florida: (a) Erika Leigh, born 19 August 1981, daughter of Laura and her first husband (John adopted Erika); and (b) Sean Caldwell, born 28 October 1986.

c. Charles Timothy Hallam (called Tim), born Monmouth, Illinois, 6 January 1963; married at Milwaukee, Wisconsin, 25 January 1986, Cynthia Lea Fillman, born Monmouth, Illinois, 25 June 1965, daughter of William

Fillman and Martha Kersey. Tim was graduated from Monmouth College in 1985 and is now working with computer business machines in Peoria, Illinois. He and Cynthia are sponsors of a church high school group. Children, both born in Monmouth, Illinois: (**a**) Allyson Sarah, born 1 November 1986; and (**b**) David William, born 21 February 1988.

    d.  Peter Graham Hallam, born Monmouth, Illinois, 19 March 1965. In 1987 he was graduated from North Central College, Naperville, Illinois, where he was the president of the student body for two terms and received a leadership award as an outstanding senior man. He won a Chicago bar association scholarship and is now a student and a research assistant to the dean at John Marshall Law School in Chicago.

I.  Earl W. Cowden, born Monmouth, Illinois, December 1888, died probably in California, ___; married Ruth Roland. Earl served in World War I and met his wife while he was stationed at Fort Des Moines. After they were married, they moved to California with her parents where the family established a retail business. Later Earl and Ruth lived in Woodland Hills, California, near Los Angeles. Child:

    1.  Roland Cowden, born 1922; married Dorothy Smith. He works in electronics and has taught courses on that subject. He and Dorothy are now partly retired and live in northern California. Children:

        a.  Rosalind Marian Cowden, born 1954

        b.  Matthew William Cowden, born 1956

5-29 CLARA CECILIA GRAHAM MCCOY,[22] born Illinois, 18 April 1851, died 13 June 1916, buried Monmouth Cemetery, Warren County, Illinois; married, 19 October 1877, ALBERT GALLATIN MCCOY, born Calcutta, Columbiana County, Ohio, 7 May 1849, died of tuberculosis in Greeley, Colorado, 11 November 1887, buried Monmouth Cemetery. Albert's attending physician in Greeley was 5-59 Dr. Robert Francis Graham.

    Albert was graduated from Monmouth College in 1874 and Clara in 1875. Albert then attended the Allegheny Seminary and was licensed by the Des Moines Presbytery on 16 June 1875, ordained by

4-8 David, 3-3 Matthew, 2-1 Andrew                                          5-29A

the Monongahela Presbytery as pastor of the Seventh Presbyterian Church of Pittsburgh which he served from 26 September 1876 until 31 December 1878. He was then an editor of *Christian Instructor*, Chicago, 1879-82, and received a Ph.D. from Indiana University in 1884. After he died in 1887, Clara returned to Monmouth where she lived for the remainder of her life. In the 1900 census she was listed as the owner of a boarding house. She had four boarders one of whom was her first cousin 4-1E Maggie McDill, the teacher. Children:

A. Albert Gallatin McCoy Jr. b. October 1879
B. Clara Elizabeth McCoy, b. July 1882
C. James A. McCoy, b. March 1885
D. Hugh W. McCoy, b. August 1886

A. Albert Gallatin McCoy Jr., born October 1879, died 1921, buried Monmouth Cemetery.

B. Clara Elizabeth McCoy Kirkpatrick Mench (called Beth), born Monmouth, Illinois, July, 1882, died 1918, buried Monmouth Cemetery; married (1) in Monmouth, Illinois, 15 September 1908, Gilbert Edgar Kirkpatrick, born Scioto, Illinois, c. 1873, died before 1916, son of Francis Asbury Kirkpatrick and Elizabeth Lowe (Book E, p. 231); Beth married (2) perhaps in San Diego, California, Jack L. Mench. When Clara married her first husband, Gilbert, he gave his residence as San Diego, California, and was working in hardware. At the time of her mother's death in 1916, Beth and her second husband, Jack, lived in Memphis, Tennessee. She was named as Elizabeth McCoy Mench on her tombstone. She had no known children.

C. James A. McCoy, born March 1885, died 1937; married (1) Estelle ___, died 1934; (2) Patsy ___.

D. Hugh W. McCoy, born August 1886, died 1926, buried Monmouth Cemetery.


5-30 JAMES ANDREW GRAHAM,[23] born 16 or 18 May 1855, died Kansas City, Missouri, 19 March 1937, buried Monmouth Cemetery, Warren County, Illinois; married, 22 February 1883, MARY EMMA MARTIN, born New Jersey, 21 December 1857, died Kansas City, Missouri, 17 October 1943, buried Monmouth Cemetery.

The following is James's obituary as it appeared in *The Monmouth Review*, Saturday, 20 March 1937:

Word was received in Monmouth today of the death of James A. Graham, of Loxley, Ala., former Biggsville farmer and horse man and later deputy sheriff of Warren county, who passed away at 10 o'clock last night at the home of his daughter Mrs. Linna Graham Beard, in Kansas City, Mo. Mr. and Mrs. Graham had been visiting at the Beard home for about 10 days when Mr. Graham was taken ill.

Mr. Graham was born in Biggsville, May 18, 1858 [sic], where he grew to manhood. He was married February 22, 1883, to Miss Mary Martin of New Jersey and for many years they made their home on a farm near Biggsville where Mr. Graham was engaged in the breeding and training of fine horses. Mr. and Mrs. Graham were the parents of four children, two sons, David and James, both deceased, and two daughters, Mrs. Beard of Kansas City, and Mrs. Beth Brooks of Midlothian (Chicago). In addition to his daughters, Mr. Graham is survived by his widow and one sister, [5-33] Mrs. Fannie Herbert, of Monmouth. Three other sisters, [5-28] Mrs. G. W. Cowden, [5-31] Mrs. Minnie Bryson, and [5-29] Mrs. Clara McCoy and one brother, [5-32] Ralph, preceded him in death.

After farming near Biggsville for a number of years, Mr. and Mrs. Graham moved to the state of Virginia about the turn of the century and after living in the South several years they returned to Monmouth. [They were listed in Monmouth in the 1910 federal census.] Mr. Graham was appointed deputy sheriff and served under Sheriff Ira Dilley. A number of years ago they moved to Loxley, Ala., where Mr. Graham carried on farming operations.

Mr. Graham was one of the organizers of the Monmouth Driving Park Association which was started in 1892. The association provided racing attractions at the annual Warren County Fair here in the 90's the track being south of what is now Fairlawn addition south of West eleventh avenue from D street to the railroad tracks. Mr. Graham was the first secretary of the association being associated with William Hanna, R. Lahann, W. S. Holliday, and C. L. Buck [probably the father of Dora Buck who married 5-36 William F.].

4-8 David, 3-3 Matthew, 2-1 Andrew     5-31

The body will arrive in Galesburg at 4:15 o'clock Sunday afternoon and funeral services will be held Monday after at 2:30 o'clock at the home of [5-28A] Mrs. Fred Bowen, 221 South Eighth street. Burial will take place in Monmouth Cemetery.

After James died, Mary Emma moved to the home of their daughter Melinda (Linna) Beard in Kansas City where Mary died five years later. Children, all born in Biggsville, Illinois:

6-8 David, died young
6-9 Mary Elizabeth, b. 16 October 1887
6-10 Melinda E., b. 3 January 1890
6-11 James H., b. c. 1896

5-31 MARY LOUISA GRAHAM BRYSON (called Minnie),[24] born April 1857, died 1935; married in Warren County, Illinois, 10 November 1880, WILLIAM B. BRYSON (Book D, p. 43), born Xenia Township, Ohio, August 1854, died 17 April 1931, son of James Bryson (born Pennsylvania, c. 1815) and Nancy A. ___ (born Ohio, c. 1828). Will was graduated from Monmouth College in 1876. He and Minnie lived near Xenia, Greene County, Ohio, where he was a farmer. Children:

A. William Graham Bryson, b. November 1881
B. ___ Bryson, died infancy
C. James Robert Bryson, b. June 1884
D. David B. Bryson, b. July 1896

A. William Graham Bryson (called Graham), born November 1881, died probably before 1958; married in Warren County, Illinois, 3 October 1907, Jessie Edith Graham (no relation--Book E, p. 217). They lived in Xenia, Ohio, where in the 1924-8 city directories he was listed as a member of the Xenia Township trustees. By 1943 he was an investigator and case worker for the state aid for the aged. He was not listed after 1958. Children:

1. Mary Elizabeth Bryson, born 1908

2. Sara Frances Bryson Morgan, born 1913; married W. Gerald Morgan. Children:

   a. William Morgan

   b. ___ Morgan, died young

c. Elizabeth Morgan

B. ___ Bryson, died infancy

C. James Robert Bryson, born June 1884, died 1929; married Mary Fay.

D. David B. Bryson, born July 1896; married Elizabeth Brower. Child:

1. James Bryson, born 1940


5-32 RALPH WALTER GRAHAM, born 1859, died 1861.


5-33 FRANCES MABEL GRAHAM HERBERT (Fannie),[25] born 11 May 1867, died Monmouth, Illinois, 11 February 1942; married in Warren County, Illinois, 1 July 1902, JOHN BUNYAN HERBERT, born Cambridge, Ohio, 14 September 1852, died Monmouth, Illinois, 19 May 1927, son of John T. Herbert and ___. John B. Herbert had married (1) in 1889, Rena Giddings who died in 1900.

Before she was married, Fannie took in boarders among whom was her uncle 4-3 John W. Graham, a widower who had been boarding at Fannie's house in Monmouth since at least as early as 1893 and who probably died there in 1900. According to the 1900 census, Fannie had two other boarders one of whom was 5-28C George Cowden.

Fannie's husband, John, was a musician and a medical doctor. The following is from his obituary in the Monmouth *Daily Review Atlas*, 20 May 1927, pp. 1 and 8:

> John Bunyan Herbert was the son of Mr. and Mrs. John T. Herbert, and was born at Cambridge, Ohio, September 14, 1852. The following year his parents moved to Monmouth, and this city has been his home ever since. At the age of sixteen he was graduated from Monmouth College and had the distinction of being the youngest to have that honor.
>
> When he was but fourteen his intense love of music led him to make it a serious study, and his devotion to the art he loved impelled him to give it every spare moment. After his graduation from college, his father,

inclined to ignore his son's musical tastes and preferences, urged him to prepare for the medical profession and he entered the Hahnemann Medical College at Chicago. While there he persisted in his devotion to music and sang in one of the church choirs. After three years of study he was granted the degree of M.D., and returned to Monmouth where he practiced successfully for several years. . . . Not despising the medical profession, Dr. Herbert loved music more and even while busy as a physician did not let a day pass without writing one or more exercises in composition and harmony. He worked practically unaided and his first real encouragement came to him when he found one of his songs printed, without the change of a single note, in one of the books edited by P. P. Bliss. In 1875 Dr. George F. Root and his son Prof. Frederick W. Root, conducted a Normal in Monmouth and the young physician availed himself of the opportunity to intensify his study of music. The friendship then formed with the two instructors proved to be lasting, and after they left Monmouth harmony lessons were conducted by mail. Dr. Herbert also studied with P. P. Bliss and others and in 1878 his first published work, "Chapel Anthems," appeared. That year he abandoned his medical practice and determined to give his entire time and attention to music. . . .

In addition to his work as editor and composer, Dr. Herbert has long been known for his ability as teacher and leader. In January 1903[?], he conducted a Normal at Birmingham, Ala., and the following year did similar work at Waco, Texas, returning there for ten years in succession. For the past five years a Normal has been conducted at Hartford, Ark., the pupils registering from six or eight different states. . . . He was a member of the Ninth Avenue United Presbyterian Church, and his service there was never perfunctory. As leader of the choir he was glad to serve. . . .

Among John's other publications were the following: *Herbert's Harmony and Composition* (1897), *The Quartet Queen (Collection of Quartets, Glees, Choruses, Anthems, and Part Songs)* (1899), and *How to Write an Accompaniment: Helps and Hints for Students and Young Composers* (1903).

The following is from Fannie's obituary which was also in the Monmouth *Daily Review Atlas*, 12 February 1942, p. 1:

The passing of Mrs. Fannie G. Herbert, announcement of whose death was made in the Review Atlas yesterday, ended a life of unusual activity and influence. The daughter of David and Elizabeth (Brown) Graham, she was born near Biggsville May 11, 1867. Of a family of six children, she was the youngest and the last to survive. One sister-in-law, Mrs. James Graham, is the only member of the family left.

She attended Monmouth College for a few years and in 1902 married Dr. John B. Herbert, well known throughout the country as singer and composer. She took unusual interest in Bible study and conducted classes while attending evangelistic meetings with Dr. Herbert, and also in her home church.

Dr. Herbert's death in 1927 made a profound change in her life, and for a considerable period after his going she lived in Ohio with close relatives, returning to Monmouth in 1939. With the exception of that interval, practically the whole of her life had been spent in Monmouth, her family coming to the home on South Eighth Street when she was only six months old and where she continued to live.

During the year before Fannie died, the Rev. A. E. Belstrom and his family lived in an apartment at her home. Fannie had no known children.


CHILDREN OF 4-9 JAMES HARVEY GRAHAM
AND MARY JANE BROWN [26]


5-34 CLARA JANE GRAHAM KENNEDY,[27] born Oxford, Butler County, Ohio, 14 May 1848, died Louisa County, Iowa, 6 May 1927, buried Elmwood Cemetery, Morning Sun, Iowa; married at Grandview, Louisa County, Iowa, 12 August 1874, JAMES ARMSTRONG KENNEDY, born Harrison, Louisa County, Iowa, 27 January 1848, died Louisa County, Iowa, 2 February 1926, buried Elmwood Cemetery, Morning Sun, Iowa, son of William Kennedy (1810-   ) and Mary C. ___ (1812-   ).

Clara was graduated from Monmouth College in 1873. James

4-9 J. Harvey, 3-3 Matthew, 2-1 Andrew                                    5-34A

took a master's from Monmouth College in 1873 then attended the
seminary at Xenia, Ohio. He was licensed by the Keokuk Presbytery
on 14 June 1876 and ordained by the Indiana Presbytery. He was
the pastor at Madison, Indiana, 1878-83; Second United Presbyterian Church at New Wilmington, Pennsylvania, 1884-91; First United
Presbyterian Church at Philadelphia, Pennsylvania, 1891-93; Second
United Presbyterian Church at New Concord, Ohio, 1893-1906; the
United Presbyterian Church at Little York, 1906-10; North Bend,
1910-12; stated supply at College Corner, 1913-14; Ainsworth,
1915-19; service 1920-23; and stated supply at Beulah and Mumford,
1923-26. Westminster College conferred a doctor of divinity
degree upon him in 1905. Children:

A. Edwin J. Kennedy, b. June 1875
B. William Graham Kennedy, b. October 1879
C. Mary Kennedy, b. 1885
D. Joseph Paul Kennedy, b. 1887

---

A. Edwin J. Kennedy, born Iowa, June 1875; married Zelma Ackley, born Michigan, c. 1882. He was a physician and practiced in Biggsville, Illinois. In the 1910 federal census of Biggs-ville, he was listed with his wife and the following children:

1. Patricia Kennedy, born Ohio, 1907; married Dell ___.

2. Paul Kennedy, born Ohio, c. December 1909

B. William Graham Kennedy, born October 1879; married Elsie Dorimus(?). Child:

1. Joan B. Kennedy, born 1919

C. Mary Kennedy, born 1885, died 1887.

D. Joseph Paul Kennedy, born 1887, died 1892.


5-35 EDWIN BROWN GRAHAM,[28] born Oquawka, Henderson County, Illinois, 25 January 1851, died Sioux City, Iowa, 7 September 1898, buried Prospect Hill Cemetery, Omaha, Nebraska; married in Keokuk, Iowa, 1 June 1876, ELIZA M. LOURIE, born New York, September 1852, daughter of ___ Lourie (born New York) and ___ (born New York).

The following is from an obituary on Edwin which appeared in

*The United Presbyterian*, 15 September 1898, p. 4:

Rev. Edwin Brown Graham, editor of The Midland and stated supply at Sioux City, Iowa, died of heart failure, Sept. 7 [1898] in the 48th year of his age. The news of his death came as a shock, for it was not known that his health was in any measure impaired. No particulars have as yet been received.

Mr. Graham was born Jan. 25, 1851, at Oquawka, Ill. He was a graduate of Monmouth College in the class of 1874, and of the Xenia Theological Seminary. He was licensed by Keokuk Presbytery, April 13, 1876, and ordained and installed by the same presbytery, Sept. 6, 1876, as pastor of Birmingham, Iowa. He retained this pastorate till April 5, 1880, when he removed to Omaha, Neb., and was the pastor of the First church of that city from May 13, 1880, to Sept. 21, 1888.

He is best known from his connection with The Midland, of which he was editor from 1885 till his death. He had his own ideas of what a religious newspaper ought to be, and he spared no time or pains to bring The Midland up to his ideal. He was a rapid, vigorous, and incisive writer. He was a great lover of brevity, and often so condensed his thoughts that they seemed abrupt. He dealt largely in humor, and though his wit sometimes stung there was no venom in it. He was fearless and persistent in advocating what he believed to be right in Church and State, and if he was one of a small minority, this fact seemed to inspire him to more earnest efforts. He was in many respects a natural editor, and he will be missed in the editorial fraternity of our Church.

His "Chalk Talks" were delivered in different parts of the Church, and made him many friends, for he excelled in his readiness with the crayon and pencil. In 1879 he published a small volume of 48 pages on "The Conscious Existence of the Soul After Death." Three years afterwards he published a novel, "In the Coils," [1882; it had three editions] which he asserted to be mainly founded on facts, and in which he severely arraigned the Masonic fraternity as hostile to the best interests of the individual, the family, the Church, and the State. This volume had a very considerable circulation, but it deserved a much larger one.

Mr. Graham continued to reside in Omaha till about the beginning of 1895, when he removed to Chicago, and soon after transferred the publication office of his paper to that city. In September last he was appointed stated supply at Sioux City, Iowa, and he was a resident of this place at the time of his death. After entering upon his duties as stated supply, he did not write as much as formerly for the columns of The Midland, but he was its responsible editor.

We have not always agreed with Mr. Graham in the opinions he held and policies he advocated. On more than one occasion we have crossed swords, but there was no bitterness on the one side or the other. He was an honorable antagonist as well as a genial companion.

When Edwin was living in Omaha and first began to publish *The Midland*, he was listed in the city directory as Graham and McNary, job printers over 722 North 16th. McNary was W. P. McNary.

In the 1900 census of Sioux City, Iowa, Edwin's widow, Eliza, was listed as a dressmaker. Since she was no longer listed in the city directories after 1903, it is assumed that she moved elsewhere. Children, all born in Iowa:

6-12 Mary Clara, b. March 1877
6-13 Laura, b. January 1879
6-14 Edna, b. 1882, d. 3 July 1882
6-15 Ella, b. 1884, d. 14 April 1884
6-16 Lois, b. November 1892

5-36 WILLIAM FRANKLIN GRAHAM (called Frank),[29] born Morning Sun, Louisa County, Iowa, 3 January 1854, died of cancer at Atlantic, Iowa, 8 August 1927, buried Atlantic Cemetery, Atlantic, Iowa; married (1) in Monmouth, Illinois, 3 February 1881, DORA A. BUCK, born Illinois, c. 1859, died 1885, daughter of Cyrus L. Buck (born Vermont, c. 1830) and Julia A. ___ (born Ohio, c. 1836); Frank married (2) in Washington County, Iowa, 21 June 1887, JANE A. WILSON (Jennie), born Iowa, December 1858, died 1931, daughter of ___ Wilson (born Ohio) and ___ (born Ohio).

The following is from Frank's obituary as it appeared in the *Atlantic* [Iowa] *News Telegraph*, 8 August 1927, p. 1:

Dr. Graham was graduated from Monmouth college in 1877 and from Rush Medical college at Chicago in 1881.

4-9 J. Harvey, 3-3 Matthew, 2-1 Andrew                                       5-37

Soon thereafter he located in Atlantic where he had lived ever since and engaged in the practice of his profession. He was a pioneer practitioner of Cass county. He was married to June [sic] A. Wilson at Washington, Ia., June 21 1887. His wife survives him with their children, Wilson H. Graham, employed by a telephone company at Grand Island, Neb., Xenophon A. Graham, with the same company at Minden, Neb., and Mrs. Mary M. Easton of Iowa City.

Dr. Graham was one of a family of eight children of Dr. and Mrs. J. H. Graham, pioneers of Louisa county, Ia. He is survived also by two sisters, [5-38] Mrs. Hugh McConnell of Marshalltown, Ia., [5-39] Mrs. T. T. Wilson, Denver, Colo., and a brother, [5-40] Wilson T. Graham, Omaha. [5-41] Dr. D. Y. Graham, another brother, died at Morning Sun last week.

Dr. Graham was active and interested in whatever was of an uplifting nature and for the good of his home city. He had a wide acquaintance and his genial disposition endeared him not only to his family and near friends but especially to those to whom he administered in the sick room. The community has lost a good man by his passing and Atlantic a loyal citizen.

Children, all by (2) Jennie Wilson and all born in Atlantic, Iowa:

6-17 Lessie Jane, b. 7 March 1889
6-18 Wilson Harvey (or Harvey Wilson), b. 30 September 1890
6-19 Xenophon Alexander, b. 13 November 1892
6-20 Mary M., b. 26 February 1902

5-37 JOHN MITCHELL GRAHAM, born Morning Sun, Louisa County, Iowa, 26 June 1857, died 17 August 1859.

5-38 LAURA ELIZABETH GRAHAM MCCONNELL, born Morning Sun, Louisa County, Iowa, 14 January 1859, died probably in Marshalltown, Marshall County, Iowa, after 1941; married in Morning Sun, Iowa, 9 November 1880, HUGH MCCONNELL, born Pennsylvania, September 1849, died probably in Marshalltown, Iowa, c. 1929, son of ___ McConnell (born Pennsylvania) and Martha ___ (born Pennsylvania c. 1810).

Laura was graduated from Monmouth College in 1877. In the 1880 census of Louisa County, Iowa, Hugh was listed as a dry goods merchant living in the town of Morning Sun. In about 1893 he and Laura moved to Marshall County, Iowa, where they were listed in Marshalltown in the 1900 census. Subsequent city directories of Marshalltown showed that from 1894 until about 1902 Hugh was the secretary of Whitton, Carr, McConnell Company, wholesale grocers. By 1902 he was a partner in Cady and McConnell Company which dealt in wholesale notions. By 1906 he was a travel agent and by 1922 a traveling salesman. His last listing in the city directories was in 1928, Laura's last in 1941. Children:

A. Martha Theresa McConnell b. August 1881
B. Mary Edna McConnell, b. 1883, d. 1889
C. Luther Graham McConnell, b. September 1885
D. Marjorie Belle McConnell, b. 1895, d. 1896

A. Martha Theresa McConnell (called Theresa), born August 1881, died after 1958; unmarried. Her last listing in the Marshalltown, Iowa, city directories was in 1958.

B. Mary Edna McConnell, born 1883, died 1889.

C. Luther Graham McConnell, born September 1885; married Helen Slagle. He lived in Marshalltown, Iowa, until about 1911 when he moved elsewhere. At first he was a clerk then a bookkeeper at Marshall State Bank. Children:

1. Graham S. McConnell, born 1915; married Laura Brown. Child:

   a. Sarah McConnell, born 1943

2. Mary McConnell (twin to next), born 1917

3. Helen McConnell (twin to above), born 1917

4. John S. McConnell, born 1924

5. David G. McConnell, born 1926

D. Marjorie Belle McConnell, born 1895, died 1896

5-39 MARY ELLEN GRAHAM WILSON,[30] born Morning Sun, Louisa County, Iowa, 19 August 1861, died Greeley, Colorado, 13 September 1940, buried Linn Grove Cemetery, Greeley, Colorado; married probably in Morning Sun, Iowa, 26 January 1887, THOMAS TRIMBLE WILSON, born Iowa, *c.* 1861, died after 1940. In the 1880 census a Thomas Wilson (born Iowa *c.* 1860) was listed in the town of Morning Sun, Iowa, perhaps Thomas Trimble Wilson. He was living with his parents, Prof. James H. Wilson (born Pennsylvania, *c.* 1830) and Esther J. ___ (born Ohio, *c.* 1835).

The following is an obituary on Mary Ellen which appeared in *The Greeley Daily Tribune*, Saturday, 14 September 1940, p. 1:

> Mrs. Mary Ellen Wilson, 79, wife of T. T. Wilson of 811 Twelfth Street, died at the Greeley hospital late Friday night following an illness of more than a month. Mrs. Wilson was the third person to die of encephalomyelitis during the present epidemic.
>
> Born in Morning Sun, Ia., Aug. 19, 1861, Mrs. Wilson was married Jan. 26 1887, to T. T. Wilson who brought her to Greeley as a bride. During her residence here she had been active in the First Presbyterian Church and numerous clubs.
>
> Survivors include her husband, two children, Mrs. Richard Hughes of Denver and Harvey Wilson of Long Beach, Calif., and four grandchildren, Dorothy and Richard Hughes of Denver, and Graham and Eugene Wilson of Long Beach. One sister, Mrs. [5-38 Laura] McConnell, lives in Marshalltown, Ia.
>
> Dr. R. F. Graham [5-59], who died Friday, was a second cousin of Mrs. Wilson's.

At some time, Mary Ellen and Thomas moved to Tarkio, Missouri, where they were living when their son, Harvey, was born in 1893 and when Mary Ellen's father died in 1897. In 1900-1910 they returned to Greeley, and according to the 1910 federal census Thomas was an editor of a newspaper. Children:

A. Mabel Elizabeth Wilson,
   b. Colorado, 1888

B. Harvey Alexander Wilson,
   b. Missouri, 1893

---

A. Mabel Elizabeth Wilson Hughes, born Greeley, Colorado, 1888,

4-9 J. Harvey, 3-3 Matthew, 2-1 Andrew	5-39A1

died probably in Denver after 1970; married Richard Hughes, born ___, died probably in Denver after 1945. In the Denver city directories, 1932-1970, Mabel was listed first as a loan manager for the Public Industrial Bank, then as an office manager at the Federal Housing Administration, then as a supervisor for the Colorado Industries for the Blind, and finally as a teacher. She retired after 1960, and her last listing was in 1970. Children:

1. Richard Hughes Jr., born ___, died probably in Denver, c. 1958; married Irene R. ___. In the Denver city directories, he was listed as a stocks and bonds broker and had his own company. His last listing was in 1958. Irene's listings continued until 1962.

2. Dorothy Hughes Johnson, born ___; perhaps married, c. 1950, Herbert T. Johnson who probably died 1981-4. In the Denver city directories, she was listed as a teacher until 1950. In 1969 a Dorothy and a Herbert Johnson were listed with her mother, and by 1984 Dorothy Johnson was listed alone.

B. Harvey Alexander Wilson, born Missouri, 1893; married Janetta Miller. They lived in Long Beach, California. According to the Long Beach city directory of 1951-2, he was a deputy of the United States Internal Revenue Service.

1. Eugene Wilson

2. Graham Wilson


5-40 WILSON THOMPSON GRAHAM,[31] born Morning Sun, Louisa County, Iowa, 15 October 1863, died of a stroke after a long illness in Omaha, Nebraska, 29 March 1939, buried Forest Lawn Cemetery, Omaha; married in Morning Sun, Iowa, 23 November 1887, ELIZABETH A. CUNNINGHAM (Lizzie), born Iowa, 21 June 1862, died in Omaha, 22 February 1931, buried Forest lawn Cemetery, Omaha, daughter of George Cunningham (born Ohio, 1828) and Mary A. Reed (born Pennsylvania, c. 1829).

Wilson and Lizzie were both graduated from Monmouth College. In about 1886 Wilson moved to Omaha, Nebraska, where he was a realtor. After he and Lizzie were married, he brought her back with him to Omaha where by 1895-96 he was an agent for the Bates-Smith Investment Company, but by 1897 he was again a realtor. He also later became a notary public and dealt in mortgages and loans as well as in real estate. By 1906 he was in partnership with William G. Ure, but the partnership may have been dissolved in 1908-9. By 1936 his son Harold came into the business with him. His obituary in the Omaha *Morning World-Herald,* 30 March 1939, p. 19, said that he was a past president of the Omaha real estate board, a member for more than thirty years of the University of Omaha board, an elder for forty years in the First United Presbyterian Church, and a leader in civic improvement and governmental reform. Children, all probably born in Omaha, Nebraska:

6-21 George Harvey, b. 20 June 1889

6-22 Harold Wilson, b. 5 August 1893

6-23 Victor Cunningham, b. 14 July 1896

6-24 Mary E., b. 6 October 1900

5-41 DALES YOUNG GRAHAM,[32] born Morning Sun, Louisa County, Iowa, 17 February 1866, died Morning Sun, 3 August 1927, buried Elmwood Cemetery; married in Morning Sun, 14 or 24 June 1893, LAURA ANGELINE TRUMBULL, born Linn Grove, Iowa, 30 October 1867, died Long Beach, California, 1 July 1947, daughter of the Rev. Charles DeWitt Trumbull (born Vermont, 1837, died probably Morning Sun, Iowa, 1914) and Mary Magdalene Sproull (born Pennsylvania, 1840, died probably Morning Sun, Iowa, 1912).

Dales was a physician. He was graduated from Monmouth College in 1887 and took his medical training at Morning Sun Academy and at Rush Medical College, Chicago. He practiced first at Nortonville, Kansas, then at Morning Sun, Iowa. In the 1910 census of Morning Sun, his mother was listed in his household. Child, born Nortonville, Kansas:

6-25 Wilmer Trumbull, b. 28 September 1894

CHILDREN OF 4-10 ARCHIBALD YOUNG GRAHAM
AND CATHARINE THIEROFF [33]


5-42 JANE WILSON GRAHAM CALDWELL (called Jennie), born Henderson County, Illinois, 18 April 1854, died Monmouth, Illinois, 25 November 1929, buried Monmouth Cemetery; married in Warren County, Illinois, 20 March 1884, FRANCIS MARION CALDWELL, born Ohio c. 1852, died Mishawaka, Indiana, ___, son of John Caldwell (born Cadiz, Ohio, 31 December 1813, died after 1886) and Mary A. McMehan (born Belmont County, Ohio, 26 March 1822, died after 1886).[34] Jennie was a nurse who worked in a doctor's office and in many homes. Francis was a traveling music teacher and left Monmouth early. Jennie died at her son's home in Monmouth, Illinois.[35] Child:

A. George Graham Caldwell, born Monmouth, Illinois, 16 December 1886, died 27 November 1960, buried Monmouth Cemetery; married 5-28H Arminta Amelia Cowden, born 1887, died 1964, daughter of 5-28 Elizabeth Jane Graham and George Henry Cowden. For child and grandchildren, see 5-28H.


5-43 NANCY M. GRAHAM BLAKE,[36] born Henderson County, Illinois, November 1855, died 17 September 1906; married in Warren County, Illinois, 19 October 1875, MELVILLE E. BLAKE, born Iowa, November 1853, died before 1904.

Nancy was graduated from Monmouth College in 1875. She and Melville lived in Burlington, Iowa, where Melville practiced law. According to the Burlington city directories, in 1890 he was in partnership with T. W. and T. G. Newman and William E. Blake (perhaps a brother). By 1894 Melville and William E. were in their own partnership. He and Nancy lived at 113 South Woodlawn.

According to their listing in the 1900 census, Nancy had had eight children, only six of whom were living. Known children, all born in Iowa:

A. Mary Ann Blake, b. c. 1876
B. Henry Y. Blake, b. c. 1877
C. Elmira L. Blake, b. December 1879
D. Wilson Blake, b. December 1882
E. Edgar Blake, b. August 1887
F. Ruth Blake, b. December 1890

A. Mary Ann Blake Jewell (called Minnie), born Iowa, c. 1876; married M. G. Jewell. He was a doctor practicing in Little York near Monmouth, Illinois. Children:

   1. Blake Jewell

   2. Merritt Jewell; married Louise ___. He is a retired optometrist, and they live in Monmouth.

   3. Melville Jewell. He was in Red Cross work.

B. Henry Y. Blake, born Iowa, c. 1877

C. Elmira L. Blake (called Myra), born Iowa, December 1879, died after 1951; unmarried. She was a high school math teacher in Burlington, Iowa. Her last listing in the city directories was in 1951.

D. Wilson Blake, born Iowa, December 1882, died after 1951; married (1) Inez ___ who perhaps died in about 1928; (2) Mary ___. According to the Burlington, Iowa, city directories, Wilson was a brakeman for the Chicago, Burlington, and Quincy Railroad. Inez was listed as his wife from 1916 to 1928 and Mary as his wife from 1935 to 1940. Mary was a beauty operator and had her shop in their home. Wilson's last listing in the city directories was in 1951.

E. Edgar Blake, born Iowa, August 1887; married Minor Waldo. Children:

   1. Melville Blake; married Rozanne Croft. He was in the embassy in Panama. Children:

      a. Melville Blake Jr.

      b. Mary Ann Blake

      c. John Waldo Blake

      d. Rebecca Blake

      e. Mary Blake

   2. Eve Blake. She lived in Decatur, Georgia.

   3. Waldo Blake; married Miriam Thompson. They lived in Silver Spring, Maryland. Children:

4-10 A.Y., 3-3 Matthew, 2-1 Andrew                                          5-43E3a

      a. James Blake

      b. Melissa Blake

      c. Dorothy Allison Blake

      d. Murray Blake

F. Ruth Blake Riegel, born Iowa, December 1890; married Leon Riegel.

    1. Nancy Riegel Blake; married ___ Blake.

    2. Ruth Ann Riegel Greau(?); married ___ Greau(?).


5-44 ELMIRA E. GRAHAM PATTERSON (Mira), born probably in Henderson County, Illinois, 25 June 1857, died in Burlington, Iowa, 9 August 1881, buried Monmouth Cemetery, Monmouth, Illinois; married in Warren County, Illinois, 19 November 1879, JAMES WILSON PATTERSON,[37] born 1849, died 1929, buried Monmouth Cemetery.

    They lived in Burlington, Iowa. In the 1880 census of Burlington, James's occupation was given as "provisions and grocery," and Mira's brother and sister 5-46 Edwin and 5-48 Mary were living with them. According to the 1908 Burlington city directory and 1910 federal census, James was then a traveling salesman for a soap company. He had married (2) c. 1884, Ella ___. Their children were Florence, born c. 1885; Clara, born c. 1887; and John, born c. 1891. Child of Mira and James:

A. Lena Patterson Smith Packard, born probably in Burlington, Iowa, c. 1881; married (1) Prosper Smith; (2) W. A. Packard. Child:

    1. Graham Smith; married Kathryn Thompson.


5-45 HARVEY MILLIGAN GRAHAM, born Henderson County, Illinois, 5 August 1859, baptized South Henderson United Presbyterian Church, 7 November 1859 (Session Minutes), died 21 November 1895; married, 4 June 1889, NETTIE B. MOORE, born Mount Carroll, Carroll County, Illinois, 31 March 1864, died 16 February 1895. In the 1880 census of Monmouth, Illinois, Harvey was listed in the household of his uncle 4-8 David Graham and was a clerk in a dry goods store.

4-10 A.Y., 3-3 Matthew, 2-1 Andrew          5-46

The following is from an obituary on Harvey:

> Harvey M. Graham, a well known business man of Monmouth, who for many years made his home with his uncle, David Graham, and also was associated with him in the dry goods establishment of D. Graham & Co., died November 21, 1896 [sic], at his home on East Detroit avenue. He had been ill for a month or so, but his death was not at all expected.
>
> Mr. Graham was born August 5, 1859, at Biggsville, and when he was but a few months old his parents moved to Monmouth, then when his father died in 1876 he began making his home with his uncle. On June 4, 1889, he married Miss Nettie Moore at Mount Carroll, and to them was born one son, Harold in 1890. Mrs. Graham died just a few months before her husband. He was a member and an elder in the Second United Presbyterian church, and also prominent in the work of the Y.W.C.A. His funeral was held at the Second church, conducted by Dr. W. T. Campbell, assisted by Dr. J. B. McMichael.[38]

Child, born in Monmouth, Illinois:

6-26 Harold M., b. 12 September 1890


5-46 EDWIN YOUNG GRAHAM, born Monmouth, Warren County, Illinois, 1862, died 1909; married ADAH HURD. In the 1880 census of Burlington, Iowa, he was listed in the household of his sister and brother-in-law 5-44 Mira and James Patterson. Children:

6-27 Leila                6-28 Ralph


5-47 ANDREW ARCHIE GRAHAM, born Monmouth, Warren County, Illinois, 1865, probably died young.


5-48 MARY LOUISE GRAHAM GLASS (or Lucy May; usually called May or Mary), born Monmouth, Warren County, Illinois, March 1870, died 1926; married in Warren County, Illinois, 19 February 1901, ROY T. GLASS, born Warren County, c. 1870, son of Seyum(?) Glass and

4-13 John M., 3-6 Robert C., 2-1 Andrew

Isabel Black (Warren County Marriage Records, Book E, p. 104). In the 1880 census of Burlington, Iowa, Mary was listed in the household of her sister and brother-in-law 5-44 Mira and James Patterson. After Mira died in 1881, Mary apparently returned to Monmouth, and after she married she and her husband moved to Kansas where they were listed in McPherson County in the 1910 census. Roy was a real estate agent. Children, all born in Illinois:

A. Frederick G. Glass, b. c. 1902
B. Madge L. Glass, b. 1908
C. Lois Glass, b. August 1909

---

A. Frederick G. Glass, born Illinois, c. 1902; married Gertrude Banks.

B. Madge L. (Louise?) Glass Morrison, born 1908; married Earl Morrison. Child:

1. Fred Morrison, born 1939

C. Lois Glass Fulzenhauer, born Illinois, August 1909; married Floris Fulzenhauer. Children:

1. Loretta Fulzenhauer, born 1928

2. Mary Fulzenhauer, born 1932


5-49 WILLIE GRAHAM, born Monmouth, Warren County, Illinois, died infancy, buried Monmouth Cemetery, Monmouth, Illinois.


## CHILDREN OF 4-13 JOHN MCKEE GRAHAM
## AND NANCY SOPHIA YOUNG


5-50 EDWARD YOUNG GRAHAM,[39] born Butler County, Ohio, 19 May 1843, died perhaps in New York City, 20 February 1910, buried in Mountain View Cemetery, Altadena, California; married AUGUSTA BENNETT, born Illinois or Ohio, c. 1854.

4-13 John M., 3-6 Robert C., 2-1 Andrew                                    5-51

Edward was in the prep class at Monmouth College, 1858-60, and the Sub Junior Science Class, 1864. Later he became a co-owner with 4-8 David Graham of Graham and Company in Monmouth, and in the 1880 census he was listed as a retail grocer living on East Garden Street, Monmouth.

Some time in the 1880's, Edward and Augusta moved to Pasadena, California, and in 1889 to San Francisco. There they ran a business called Graham Decorative Art, located on Post, and advertised that they did embroidery material of all kinds as well as stamping and designing. They changed their residence often: at first they lived on Post, then in 1891 they lived at 707½ Hyde, in 1893 at 1901 Baker, in 1894 at 1622 Fulton, in 1895 at 839 Post, in 1896 at The Renton, in 1897 at 147 San Jose Avenue, and in 1899-1901 at 928 Powell.

They may then have moved to New York City. The reason it is thought so is that Edward's will was in a safety deposit box at a bank in New York.

In his will, dated 23 June 1905 and filed 29 April 1910, he named his wife, Augusta, and their children as his heirs, appointed his wife as executrix, and instructed her to pay his brother 5-54 John M. Graham Jr. any balance due to him. The will was witnessed by a Madge Patton. When the will was filed, Augusta was using the address of their son Harry in San Francisco. Children, all born in Monmouth, Illinois:

6-29 Harry B., b. *c.* 1873        6-31 Elizabeth May, b. *c.* 1878
6-30 Alden Max, b. *c.* 1876


5-51 WILLIAM FRANCIS CLAYBAUGH GRAHAM,[40] born Butler County, Ohio, 15 May 1845, died Winterset, Madison County, Iowa, 29 July 1935, buried Chariton Cemetery, Lucas County, Iowa; married in Henderson County, Illinois, 4 October 1866, his first half-cousin once removed, 4-29 MARY MARGARET GRAHAM, born Henderson County, Illinois, 30 December 1844, died Winterset, Iowa, 1 December 1936, daughter of 3-8 William M. Graham and (2) Jane Popham. William and Mary Margaret were married by the Rev. J. A. P. McGaw.

Mary attended Monmouth College, Illinois, in 1862, and William was in the Sub Junior Science class there in 1864.

On 10 May 1864 while still a student, William enlisted as a private in Company D, 138th Illinois Volunteer Infantry, serving until 14 October 1864, and unfortunately suffering severe dysentery during most of his service. According to his description at the time of his enlistment, he was 5 feet 6 inches tall and had a fair complexion, blue eyes, and dark hair.

Mary joined the South Henderson U.P. Church on 26 July 1861. After she and William were married in 1866, they lived for a time in Biggsville, Henderson County, Illinois, where he was a farmer. In 1868 they moved to Winterset, Iowa, and in 1870 to Stuart, Iowa. Also in 1868 William became a locomotive engineer for the Chicago, Burlington, and Quincy Railroad, a job he held until 1897 although he continued to farm. By 1877 they were in Moberly, Missouri, and by 1878 in Newton, Kansas. The 1880 federal census listed them in Walton Township, Harvey County, Kansas, which is where Newton is located. In 1880 they were back in Winterset, Iowa, and in 1888 they moved to Chariton, Lucas County, Iowa, where they lived for many years.

William's eyesight began to fail in the late 1890's. As Mary testified later, the Chicago Great Western Railroad was about to hire him in 1897, but a physical examination showed that his vision was defective. Despite his affliction William continued to work, although no longer on the railroad, and in the 1900 and 1910 censuses William gave his occupation as cigar maker. He and Mary were still living in Chariton on 22 October 1918, but by 8 November 1921, according to William's pension records, they were in Fort Collins, Colorado, where their daughter Martha and son-in-law Leonard Wetzel also resided.

On 8 November 1921 Mary testified that William had been nearly blind for about eighteen months, and on 5 December 1929 she testified that he was totally blind in one eye and could barely distinguish outlines with the other. She had to help him dress and eat. On 27 January 1930 he, himself, testified that he could distinguish only daylight from darkness with one eye. He also seems to have suffered an incident of fainting and falling in September 1929. At that time they were living in Fort Collins, perhaps at the home of their daughter and son-in-law Martha and Leonard Wetzel. Their son Fred Y. and his wife were visiting. As Fred later testified, his father stepped out into the back yard at about 6 p.m. on 11 September 1929 and was found a few minutes later lying on his back unconscious. Fred and Martha's son, Orvil, carried William into the house where he regained consciousness and had no memory of what had happened. He injured his back in the fall.

At some time before 1930 William and Mary moved to Winter-

4-13 John M., 3-6 Robert C., 2-1 Andrew                                    5-52

set, Iowa, doubtlessly to be near another daughter and son-in-law Lela G. and John Crossley, where William and Mary lived out their few remaining years. On 30 July 1935 Lela applied for an official United States burial flag for her father's casket, and at Mary's death in 1936 her address, 614 North First Street in Winterset, was probably that of Lela's home. Children:

6-32 Charles M., b. IL, 11 August 1867
6-33 Fred Y., b. IA, 14 December 1868
6-34 Lillian Adeline, b. IA, 30 December 1870
6-35 Martha Ellen, b. IA, 4 October 1872
6-36 Sophia Jane, b. IA, 4 October 1874
6-37 Lela Elise, b. MO, 15 June 1878 (twin to next)
6-38 Lula Alice, b. MO, 15 June 1878 (twin to above)
6-39 William J., b. IA, 5 April 1885

5-52 DONALD M. GRAHAM,[41] born New York, *c.* 1848, died Los Angeles, California, 22 March 1890; married probably in Iowa or Illinois, *c.* 1870, MARGARET COLLIER, born Iowa, September 1850, died probably in South Pasadena, California, 17 January 1910, daughter of David Collier and Lydia Ann Lindsay (born Ohio, 16 November 1823, died South Pasadena, California, 10 November 1904).

In 1869 Donald was graduated from Monmouth College, subsequently becoming a lawyer, and was practicing in Los Angeles by 1874. He seems to have suffered a certain amount of ill health, however. In about 1876 he was driving a stage and mail line in order to be in the sun and open air as much as possible. He drove the line between Los Angeles and Pasadena, leaving Los Angeles at 9 a.m. every day and returning at 3 p.m. the same day. The following entertaining story about this period in Donald's life is from J. W. Wood's *Pasadena, California*:

> It was quite fitting that D. M. Graham, who, on account of flagging health, had come to the land of sunshine hoping to recover it, was the first officially authorized mail messenger between Pasadena and Los Angeles. Graham was a college man with some means, and did not accept the official post for its remuneration, for that need have tempted no man, being something like three hundred dollars per annum--nothing extra for horse feed! Graham had two pinto horses and an old carriage, and believed he needed open air exercise and a chance to absorb some of California's best climate. . . . On one occasion a news-

paper representative of the Philadelphia "Press" happening to ride with the owner of the carriage, entered into a discussion with him regarding the meaning of a certain Spanish name. Graham, out of his desire to assist the man, referred to the connection of the word with Latin and Greek, then the Hebrew! The Correspondent turned to him saying, "Say, I've ridden with many stage drivers, from Hank Monk down, but you are the first that could discuss Greek Roots!" But Greek roots did not interfere with Graham's enjoyment of the daily trip; he recovered his health, and lived for some years afterwards in active life.

As stated above, Donald recovered his health and as is known from another source soon sold out to a man named W. T. Vore. By 1879-80 Donald was a land and loan broker with an office in the Odd Fellows building in Los Angeles, and by 1881-2 he was a real estate agent. He also did newspaper work and was briefly connected with the *Evening Express* in Los Angeles. By 1883-4 Donald was in partnership with a man named William Riley. During this same period Donald became increasingly involved with Pasadena community affairs and in 1880 read a paper before the Shakespeare Club on "Pasadena as a Home." He also bought considerable land there as a business development and subsequently (*c.* 1885) built a two-story brick block in South Pasadena which became known as the Graham and Mohr block. (Mohr may have been a brother-in-law who married Margaret's sister Martha.) Pasadena's first library and reading room was established in this block. In about 1883 he and Margaret moved to Pasadena; this is known because Margaret later became a charter member of Pasadena's Pioneer Society which included only those who had moved there prior to 1 January 1884. In the 1888-9 Pasadena city directory, their home was listed as being on Monterey Road at Glendon Way, and Donald gave his occupation as "capitalist." Pasadena incorporated as a city in 1888, and Donald was the president of the board of five trustees named in the articles of incorporation.

He died soon after. The following is from his obituary as it appeared in *The Los Angeles Times*, 23 March 1890, p. 1:

> The remarkable thing about Mr. Graham's career is that, while his health was so poor that many a man under like circumstances would have considered himself unable to accomplish anything in business, he forged ahead and accumulated a fortune. . . .
>
> Mr. Graham was a man of high intellectual attain-

4-13 John M., 3-6 Robert C., 2-1 Andrew

ments, and he did not allow his interest in public affairs to flag even when confined to his room almost constantly for a year or more. His end was as peaceful as the going of life could be.

Donald's will, written on one page in pencil and dated 13 September 1882, was filed on 31 May 1890 (Probate #13157). In it he left his entire estate to his wife, Margaret. The estate was large because Donald, in partnership with William Collier and M. Chaney, owned a great amount of land in Southern California.

Margaret Collier Graham was herself unusual. She was graduated from Monmouth College in 1869 and later became the principal of an East Los Angeles grammar school. After she and Donald moved to Pasadena, she and her sister Jennie became active in the local Shakespeare Club and in Pasadena's Pioneer Society the first annual picnic of which (1898) was held on Margaret's grounds. She also became known as a writer of western stories, and in 1895 Houghton, Mifflin published them under the title of *Stories of the Foothills*. Other writings included somewhat feminist essays which were collected and published posthumously under the title of *Do They Really Respect Us?* (1912).

According to Donald's and Margaret's 1880 census listing in Los Angeles, Margaret's sister Jane E. (Jennie) Collier lived with them; in 1900 Margaret's sister Eliza A. Collier was listed in Margaret's household. Margaret also had another sister, Martha C. Mohr, and at least one brother, William Collier, a lawyer who lived in Riverside, California. There was also a David Collier, fruit grower, living in South Pasadena who may have been Margaret's father or another brother. Donald and Margaret had no known children.

5-53 ROBERT ALEXANDER GRAHAM (called Alexander),[42] born New York, 1850, died following an automobile accident near LaVerne, California, 16 February 1919, buried Mountain View Cemetery, Altadena, California; married (1) ANGELINE M. ___, born Iowa, 31 May 1858, died probably in South Pasadena, California, 12 November 1893, buried Mountain View Cemetery, Altadena, California; Alexander married (2) in Los Angeles, 26 May 1898, ELIZA WOLFE, born Sonora, California, October 1864, died at the San Marino Sanitarium, 22 August 1945, daughter of George Washington Wolfe (born Kansas) and Thomasina Marina Cofor (born Missouri). Alexander and Eliza were married by the Rev. L. O. Ferguson at the Church of Christ on Workman Street in Los Angeles.

4-13 John M., 3-6 Robert C., 2-1 Andrew                                    5-54

Alexander's grandfather 3-6 Robert C. mentioned Alexander in his will as Robert A., and Alexander appeared in the early censuses as Robert A., but the later censuses and his tombstone name him as Alexander R. Also, as Alexander Robert Graham he bought the east half of a lot in Mountain View Cemetery, Altadena, in which he and his first wife are buried as well as his parents, his son Oliver, and his brother Edward.

In the 1880 census Alexander and his first wife were listed in Center Point, Linn County, Iowa. In the 1900 census he and his second wife were listed in South Pasadena, California; he was a grocer. In the 1910 census he was listed as the proprietor of an apartment house in South Pasadena. His estate settlement totaled almost $38,000 and included a 240-acre ranch and farm equipment at Winchester, Riverside, California.

The newspaper article giving the account of the accident from which he died said that it occurred on 16 February 1910 at the Lincoln Avenue crossing of the Pacific Electric when his car was struck by a Los Angeles train going to San Bernardino. He was taken in critical condition to the Pomona Valley Hospital where he died soon after.

Eliza's official address at the time of her death was 1757 Rose Villa in Pasadena although she actually died at the San Marino Sanitarium to which she had been admitted thirty days earlier. The cause of her death was senile debility, arteriosclerosis, and chronic pernicious anemia.

Child of Alexander and (1) Angie M. ___:

6-40 Norma H., b. IA, c. 1878

Children of Alexander and (2) Eliza Wolfe, all born in California:

6-41 Oliver Howard, b. March 1899
6-42 Donald D., b. c. 1902
6-43 Pauline W., b. c. 1905
6-44 Earl A., b. c. 1907
6-45 Frank C., b. November 1909


5-54 JOHN MCKEE GRAHAM JR., born New York c. 1852. He was not listed with his parents in the 1880 census, but he was still alive on 23 June 1905 when his brother Edward wrote his will. In it Edward instructed that John be paid any balance owed to him. Nothing more is known of him.

5-55 ELLA GRAHAM, born New York *c.* 1854. She was listed with her parents in the 1880 census of Louisa County, Iowa.

5-56 MARGARET GRAHAM (MAGGIE), born New York *c.* 1857 or 1858. She was listed with her parents in the 1880 census of Louisa County, Iowa.

5-57 ANNE E. GRAHAM, born Illinois, *c.* 1863. She was listed with her parents in the 1880 census of Louisa County, Iowa.

CHILDREN OF 4-16 ANDREW EDWARD GRAHAM
AND MELCENA MARGARET GILLESPIE

5-58 JAMES GILLESPIE GRAHAM,[43] born Richland, Rush County, Indiana, 6 February 1852, died Greeley, Colorado, 24 October 1923, buried Linn Grove Cemetery, Greeley; married in Decatur County, Indiana, 23 December 1874, LOUIE JANE MAYNE, born Spring Hill, Indiana, 19 August 1853, died Greeley, Colorado, 9 May 1927, daughter of John Mayne (1824-1898) and Nancy Jane Dale (1834-1924).

Jim and Louie moved to Colorado in the latter half of the 1880's. He was a successful sheep rancher and was partly responsible for the introduction of irrigation ditches in the eastern part of the state. Children, the first three born in Richland, Indiana, the youngest born in Greeley, Colorado:

6-46 Mary T., b. 2 December 1878
6-47 Melcena M., b. 9 April 1882
6-48 Anna Dale, b. 2 April 1885
6-49 Myra Katharine, b. 15 April 1892

5-59 ROBERT FRANCIS GRAHAM (called Frank),[44] born Richland, Rush County, Indiana, 23 April 1853, died of a coronary in Greeley, Colorado, 13 September 1940, buried Linn Grove Cemetery, Greeley; married in Guide Rock, Nebraska, 7 April 1887, MYRA H. (SEARS) SPEAR, widow, born Boston, Massachusetts, *c.* 1851, died in Greeley,

4-16 Andrew E., 3-6 Robert C., 2-1 Andrew                                    5-59

Colorado, 23 August 1936, buried Linn Grove Cemetery, Greeley.

Frank was graduated from Indiana University in 1876, a classmate being George Banta, future brother-in-law of Frank's sister Martha. Frank then took medical training at the University of Cincinnati, interning at a hospital in Cleveland. In 1884-5 he practiced with his father in Rush County, Indiana, then moved to Greeley, Colorado. After his marriage in 1887, he built a house at 1129 Seventh Street which has since been declared an historic structure. In addition to his medical practice, he was a director and vice-president of the Weld County Savings Bank, had holdings in the First National Bank of Greeley, and owned a considerable amount of business and farm property. He and George Banta assumed the financial responsibility for the children of 5-62 Martha after she and her husband died.

The following is from Frank's obituary which appeared in *The Greeley Daily Tribune*, Friday, 13 September 1940, p. 1:

Dr. Robert F. Graham, 87 years old retired Greeley physician who began his practice of medicine here in 1885, died in his sleep at his home, 1129 Seventh street. His death was discovered Friday morning by Mrs. Jennie Luther, his housekeeper.

Dr. Graham had not been ill; Thursday afternoon he attended a meeting of the directors of the First National Bank. He had been a director of the bank since 1895 and at the time of his death was vice-president, a position he had held for many years. . . .

After one year's practice in Indiana, he came to Greeley in 1885 and established a practice in Greeley. He had his offices in several places, but most people remember his offices as being in the Coronado building.

He was married to Myra H. Spear . . . April 7, 1887 and they moved to the fine house at 1129 Seventh Street at that time one of the most pretentious of Greeley residences. For 53 years Dr. Graham lived in the house, located amid spacious lawns and gracious shade trees. Dr. Graham took an intense interest in making his lawn and garden attractive. . . .

At his residence here Dr. Graham kept horses in a stable and the old iron hitching post still stands in front of the house.

John Carlson and George Carlson, who was a governor of Colorado later, worked part of their way through college here by caring for Dr. Graham's horses. . . .

In addition to his holdings in the First National Bank, Dr. Graham owned the business property on Ninth avenue opposite the Sterling theatre known as the Harvard Block. He also owned a farm near Ault which he liked to inspect.

For 50 years, dating with the establishment of the Weld County Savings Bank, he was a director and vice-president of that institution, but in recent years, he had sold his interest in that bank. . . .

He was a long time member of Park Congregational Church of which he was a deacon emeritus.

Frank and Myra had no children.

5-60 KATHARINE M. GRAHAM LAMB (Kate),[45] born Richland, Rush County, Indiana, 11 April 1855, died of cancer in Greeley, Colorado, 24 May 1918, buried beside her husband in Aurora, Indiana; married in Richland, Indiana, 27 December 1882, LOUIS KOSSUTH LAMB, born Ohio County, Indiana, 15 October 1849, died probably in California, 1895, buried in Aurora, Indiana, son of Dr. James Lamb and Sarah Ann Carnine.

Kate attended Indiana University, 1873-4, and went to a music conservatory in Xenia, Ohio, for three years where she met her future husband. After her marriage in 1882, she and her husband moved to Tolono, Illinois, where he had been practicing medicine since 1879. He had studied with his father and attended the Ohio Medical College in 1871-2 and again in 1875-6, and was graduated in 1876. He practiced at Rising Sun, Indiana, 1876-9, then moved to Tolono, Illinois. In about 1893 they moved to California where he died in 1895, and in July of 1896 Kate moved to Greeley, Colorado, to be with her brothers and sister. She became a piano teacher and occasionally took in boarders. After her sister died in 1902, Kate reared her sister's children. She was a member of the Congregational Church in Greeley, the Kappa Alpha Theta Sorority, and the Daughters of the American Revolution.[46] Child:

A. James Graham Lamb (called Graham), born probably in Tolono, Illinois, 23 December 1883, died Denver, Colorado, 1938;

married (1) Margaret Taylor of Colorado Springs; (2) ___. Graham was graduated from the University of Colorado and later was the head chemist at the American Smelting and Refining Company at Pueblo, Colorado. In the 1920's he was a supervisor at the company's Mexican subsidiary, Peñoles Company at Torreon, Durango, Mexico. No children.

5-61 ANDREW EDWARD GRAHAM JR., born Richland, Rush County, Indiana, c. 1857, died 16 January 1871 (age 13), buried South Park Cemetery, Greensburg, Indiana.

5-62 MARTHA EVELYN GRAHAM BANTA (Matt or Mattie),[47] born Richland, Rush County, Indiana, 5 May 1861, died of tuberculosis in Greeley, Colorado, 29 January 1902, buried beside her husband in Greenlawn Cemetery, Franklin, Indiana; married in Richland, Indiana, 14 October 1885, CHARLES BANTA, born Franklin Indiana, 16 October 1859, died of malaria in Marion City, Indiana, 15 August 1897, buried Greenlawn Cemetery, Franklin, son of Judge David Demaree Banta (born Union Township, Johnson County, Indiana, 23 May 1833, died Franklin, Indiana, 9 April 1896) and Melissa Riddle (born Cheviot, Ohio, 27 March 1834, died Chicago, 1 May 1907).

Martha attended Indiana University, 1881-3, where she met her future husband whose father was the dean of the law school there. Charles was graduated from Indiana University in 1881. He studied law and taught school for a time, then became an insurance agent. After their marriage they moved to New York City where Charles was an inspector for several insurance companies and contributed articles to *Insurance World*. They lived in Mount Vernon, New York. In 1894-5 Mattie developed tuberculosis, and because her doctors suggested she move to a high, dry climate she moved with her children to Greeley, Colorado, where her brothers lived. In the meantime Charles switched to the Chicago office of the Continental Insurance Company of New York and did incessant traveling, leading to a run-down physical condition. He died of malaria in Marion, Indiana, while on a business trip in the summer of 1897, and Mattie died of tuberculosis four-and-a-half years later in Greeley, Colorado. Their children were reared by Mattie's sister, 5-60 Katharine (Kate) Graham Lamb. Mattie's brother 5-59 Robert Francis (Frank) Graham and her brother-in-law, George Banta, supported Mattie's children until they were graduated from college and married. Children:

4-16 Andrew B., 3-6 Robert C., 2-1 Andrew                               5-62A

- A. Katharine Banta, b. Franklin, IN, 30 July 1886
- B. Elizabeth Banta, b. Mount Vernon, NY, 21 August 1889
- C. Margaret Banta, b. Mount Vernon, NY, 22 July 1892

---

- A. Katharine Banta (Kathie), born Franklin, Indiana, 30 July 1886, died of typhoid in Greeley, Colorado, 8 November 1902, buried Linn Grove Cemetery, Greeley.

- B. Elizabeth Banta Tolle (Betty), born Mount Vernon, New York, 21 August 1889, baptized Mount Vernon, 13 April 1890, died in Birmingham, Michigan, 3 February 1975, buried White Chapel Cemetery, Troy, Michigan; married in Chicago, 25 December 1915, Oscar Sylvester Tolle (called Red), born near Hartford City, Indiana, 7 February 1888, died of a coronary in Dallas, Texas, 24 October 1954, buried Calvary Hill Cemetery, Dallas, son of ___ Tolle and Margaret ___ (Higgins?; born Indiana, November 1868, died probably in Bourbon County, Indiana, after 1927). Betty and Red separated in 1927 and were divorced c. 1932.

    Betty attended the State Normal at Greeley, Colorado, 1906-7, and Colorado College in Colorado Springs, 1907-8, then went east to Oberlin University where she earned a certificate in public school music, 1911. She then attended Indiana University, from which she was graduated in 1913, and earned a master's there in American history in 1914. She taught American history at the Manual Training High School, Indianapolis, 1914-15, and, after her marriage, moved to Dallas, Texas. Red was graduated from Indiana University in 1915, later working as a salesman of office furniture. After their separation in 1927, Betty moved with her children to Detroit to be near her sister. She taught music in the Detroit public schools for thirty years, retiring in 1960, and lived with her daughter from 1954 until her death. She was a member of the Delta Gamma sorority and was the president of her chapter during her senior year at Indiana University. Children:

    1. Charles Banta Tolle (born Charles Oscar Tolle), born Dallas, Texas, 8 November 1917, died of a coronary in Bloomfield Township, Michigan, 22 October 1955, ashes in White Chapel Cemetery, Troy, Michigan; married in Detroit, 15 June 1938, Jane Charlene Vallet (called Charlene), born Chicago, 11 June 1918, daughter of Victor Emil Vallet (1893-1980) and Mina Viola Robinson (1893-1970); Charlene

married (2) in Santa Barbara, California, 17 July 1977, James W. Snow, born Rochester, New York, 31 December 1918. Charles attended Indiana University, 1935-6, and the University of Michigan, receiving his M.D. degree in 1943. He then served for two years in the United States Navy and subsequently returned to the University of Michigan for training in internal medicine. In 1949 he became the head of the laboratory at Saint Joseph's Mercy Hospital in Pontiac, Michigan, and was making a name in blood diseases when he died suddenly at his home. Children:

a. Charles Vallet Tolle (called Mike), born Detroit, 30 April 1939; married (1) in Detroit, Sandra Kay Walker, born Detroit, 4 May 1941, daughter of Cecil Brodley Walker (1913-1963) and Ruth Virginia Donyea (1918- ). Mike and Sandy were divorced in 1979, and Mike married (2) in Van Nuys, California, 5 June 1983, Susan Allyn Jones, born c. 1962, since divorced. Mike was graduated from Michigan State University and in 1967 earned his master's from the University of California, Los Angeles, in computer systems. He has since worked in computers and lives in Van Nuys, California. Children: (a) Wendy Lee, born Birmingham, Michigan, 30 April 1959, married in Santa Barbara, California, 2 January 1988, Paul Walker; (b) Michael Charles (Mickey), born Birmingham, Michigan, 25 May 1960; and (c) Margaret Katharine (Maggie), born Encino, California, 30 June 1984.

b. Timothy Victor Tolle, born Detroit, 17 February 1944; married (1) Suzanne Leymann, since divorced; (2) on 10 June 1970, Rosemary Lynn Welch (called Lynn), born Laredo, Texas, 18 June 1944, daughter of Sidney Clois Welch (1911-1977) and Dorothy Lynn Smith (1919- ). This is Lynn's second marriage. Tim earned his Ph.D. in geography at Oregon State University in 1978 and is now a forest planning team leader for the United States Forest Service. He has served in Montana and Washington state. They live in Okanogan, Washington. Child: Charlene Elizabeth (called Molly), born Corvallis, Oregon, 30 April 1972. Lynn's child: Melissa Lynn Hammond (usually called Melissa Lynn Tolle), born Little Rock, Arkansas, 16 June 1964.

c. Patricia Mina Tolle Bohn, born Ann Arbor, Michigan, 17 January 1948; married and divorced (1) Dennis Johnston; (2) at Santa Barbara, California, 31 December

1973, Donald Rossiter, later divorced; (3) in August 1986, Dennis Bohn. Pat went to the University of the Seven Seas for a year. She lived in Hawaii for several years and is now in Seattle where she works as a court reporter. Child by first husband: Koshtra Tolle (Koshtra did not take her father's last name), born Santa Barbara, California, 14 September 1968.

2. Katharine Elizabeth Tolle Kell, born Indianapolis, Indiana, 18 September 1923; married in Chicago, 14 October 1944, Joseph Cass Kell, born Detroit, 23 August 1912, son of Joseph Kukielka (born Warsaw, Poland, 8 September 1878, died in Detroit, 30 March 1934) and Leokadia Komosinski (born Warsaw, Poland, 17 April 1887, died in Detroit, 23 January 1955). Katharine sang in the choir of "The Ford Sunday Evening Hour" until it went off the air in early 1942. Eventually she earned a Ph.D. in English and American literature at Wayne State University, Detroit, 1972, and has taught English at Wayne State and other colleges in the Detroit area. She wrote her dissertation on the American myth as it appears in twentieth-century American literature and has also published a few articles on folklore. She is now the librarian (volunteer) at her church. Joe was an X-Ray technician in the United States Army, 1941-5, and was graduated from Wayne State in 1950 with a major in eastern European studies. He has had considerable experience as a salesman in the Detroit area and in 1972 established his own business, Kamm and Company, in which he is a manufacturer's representative selling industrial tools. He also formerly sang tenor in the choir of his and Katharine's church, The Congregational Church of Birmingham. He and Katharine met at the home of their mutual voice teacher, Madame Göta Ljungberg, who sang at the Metropolitan Opera. They live in Birmingham, Michigan. Children:

a. Amy Elizabeth Kell, born Detroit, 30 April 1950; married in Bloomfield Hills, Michigan, 1 January 1979, Steven Richard Hoberman, born Jersey City, New Jersey, 4 November 1945, son of Hyman Hoberman (born Bayonne, New Jersey, 12 September 1907, died Livingston, New Jersey, 6 September 1976) and Florence Parnes (born Jersey City, New Jersey, 25 January 1912). Amy, who has retained her maiden name, was graduated from Oakland University, Michigan, in 1972, took graduate courses at Georgetown University, Washington, D.C., 1976-82, and earned an M.B.A. at the University of

Chicago in 1988. From 1974 to 1976 she worked for a landscape architect in Massachusetts and Florida. She then moved to Washington, D.C., where she held various positions in public housing, 1976-86. She has also written five books on public housing which are in official use. At present she is a mortgage loan officer with The Travelers Mortgage Company, formerly a subsidiary of The Travelers Insurance Company. Her hobby is gourmet cooking, and she has taken classes at *L'Academie de Cuisine*, Bethesda, Maryland. Steve was a petty officer in the United States Coast Guard Reserve, 1967-73, and was graduated in business administration from Northeastern University in 1973. He has since held a variety of computer-related jobs in Washington, D.C.; Rockville, Maryland; Rosslyn, Virginia; Cambridge and Boston, Massachusetts; and Chicago, Illinois. At present he is a manager in the information technology group of Price Waterhouse, southeast region. His hobby is motorcycling. He and Amy now live in Chevy Chase, Maryland.

b.  Joseph Mark Kell (called Mark), born in Detroit, 9 December 1951; married in Detroit, 10 October 1971, Carla Sue Bodner, born Detroit, 15 September 1952, daughter of Carl William Bodner (1925- ) and Margie May Cannon (1927- ); divorced 31 December 1980. Mark was in the United States Army as a specialist 4, 1971-1974, and was stationed in Germany for almost two years. He attended Arizona State University, 1975-82, and was eventually graduated from the New College of California, 1986. He also taught math at Heald College, Phoenix, Arizona, 1978-9, and computer programming at DeVry Institute of Technology, San Francisco, January to September 1984. He worked as a computer programmer at Sperry, 1979-82, and Motorola, 1982-3, both in Phoenix, then moved to San Francisco where he continued in computers at Metaphor, then at Hewlett Packard. In 1987 he switched to Unisoft where he was the director of product marketing and in September 1987 became the managing director of Unisoft GMbH, situated in Munich, West Germany. The next year he switched to Informix with whom he was the sales director for Germany, Austria, and Switzerland. In January 1989 he became a director at Softools located in The Netherlands and is now the managing director there. He lives in Zaltbommel, The Netherlands, and his chief hobby is photography.

c. Matthew Kenyon Kell, born Pontiac, Michigan, 30 March 1959; married in Bloomfield Hills, Michigan, 24 June 1989, Eileen Marie Fitzgerald, born Pontiac, 21 July 1955, daughter of John Michael Fitzgerald (born Pontiac, 22 October 1925) and Ruth Edna Fiedler (born Hamtramck, Michigan, 6 October 1925). Matt was graduated from Roeper City and County School for gifted children in 1977, later attended Oakland County Community College, and is now in the computer science program at Oakland University. Since 1984 he has also worked with his father as a manufacturer's representative and, as an avocation, has been the pianist and/or music director for many Detroit-area produced musicals including *A Funny Thing Happened on the Way to the Forum*, *Godspell*, *I Do! I Do!*, *Showboat*, *Gypsy*, *Pippin*, *The Sound of Music*, and others. His hobbies include tennis and chess playing, and he has won several trophies in chess tournaments. Eileen attended Oakland University, 1975-8, and earned a state license as an advanced emergency technician (paramedic) at Oakland County Community College. She used her license for only a short time. In 1981 she became a letter carrier for the United States Post Office in Pontiac. She has also performed in Detroit-area produced musicals including *Fiddler on the Roof*, *Peter Pan*, and *The Sound of Music* and has done much backstage work. She is on the board of directors of Pontiac Theater IV. Her hobbies include handicrafts, especially crocheting and knitting. Eileen's child: James Matthew John Fitzgerald, born Pontiac, 31 May 1975.

C. Margaret Banta Whitaker (Peg), born Mount Vernon, New York, 22 July 1892, died in Detroit, 13 September 1966; married in Chicago, 1917, Frank Birkett Whitaker (called Whit), born Buffalo, New York, 30 October 1892, died Detroit, 11 August 1957, son of Frederick Whitaker and Maybelle Giles; Peg and Whit were divorced in 1936. She was graduated from Indiana University in 1916. Later she was a piano accompanyist in the Detroit Public Schools, but she long fought mental illness. Child:

1. Margaret Frances Whitaker Chase, born Detroit, 13 December 1917; married Fred Crandall Chase, born Detroit, 4 September 1917, son of Percy Edwin Chase (1890-1950) and Elsie Crandall (1892-1966). Margaret earned a degree in later elementary education at Wayne State University in 1945 and has since been busy with her seven adopted children. Fred

was graduated from Wayne State and was in the Army Air Corps, 1941-5, and again in 1951-65, discharged as a colonel. He earned a doctorate in education at Stanford in 1954 and is now retired from Orange Unified School District, California, where he worked with handicapped children. Children (all adopted):

a.  Daniel William Chase, born Oakland, California, 10 December 1954; married Melody Anne Schobert, born Iowa, 17 May 1952, daughter of Joseph Schobert (1914- ) and Donna Corbey (1917- ). Dan earned a veterinarian's degree at Iowa State and has worked with the United States Department of Agriculture. He is presently in Nebraska. Children: (a) Allen Dunmore, born Ames, Iowa, 3 December 1973; and (b) Benjamin, born November 1981.

b.  Anne Louise Chase, born Richmond, Virginia, 4 June 1957. She works for the Great American Insurance Company and does occasional traveling.

c.  John Philip Chase, born Roanoke, Virginia, 25 May 1958. He is a skilled carpenter living in Riverside, California.

d.  Nancy Lee Chase Williams, born Washington, D.C., 7 April 1959; married, 1981, Wayne Williams, born c. 1960. Child: Brian, born September 1982.

e.  Scott Evan Chase, born Ottumwa, Iowa, 29 November 1964. He is retarded and deaf. He lives at home.

f.  Henry Martin Chase, born Washington, D.C., 15 June 1965. He is highly artistic and attended the California Institute of the Arts at Valencia, California, a school originally sponsored by Walt Disney.

g.  Jane Elizabeth Chase, born Los Angeles, 6 August 1967

## CHILD OF 4-22 ROBERT CULBERTSON GRAHAM
## AND MARY ELIZA MCDILL

5-63 ___ GRAHAM (boy), stillborn on 1 October 1871, buried South Henderson Cemetery.


## CHILDREN OF 4-23 JAMES THOMAS GRAHAM
## AND MELISSA JANE GILCHRIST [48]

5-64 ALVA EDSON GRAHAM (called Al), born Henderson County, Illinois, 25 December 1859, baptized South Henderson United Presbyterian Church, 2 April 1860 (Session Minutes), died perhaps in Almena Township, Norton County, Kansas, 7 July 1933; married, 1885, JANE P. or B. WINTER, born Indiana, 10 September 1862. At some time Al and Jane lived in Oregon where their second son, George, was born in 1891, and in 1897 they were in Missouri where their daughter, Ida, was born in April of that year. In the 1900 census, however, they were listed in Richland Township, Marshall County, Kansas, and in 1910 they were in Almena Township, Norton County, Kansas. Lorna Howard Cline (5-71B) writes, "Uncle Al was a farmer and had an old buggy in the yard. Sometimes when visiting, our cousin [6-50] Edgar, my sister [5-71C] Lorene, and I would get in this buggy and ride down an incline through a flock of chickens until our parents stopped us. We never killed a chicken and, as kids, it was fun." Children:

6-50 Edgar Lloyd, b. Kansas, 21 May 1887
6-51 George Raymond, b. Oregon, 6 November 1891
6-52 Ida Melissa, b. Missouri, 25 April 1897
6-53 Ralph A., b. Kansas, 9 August 1902


5-65 ANDREW RICHARD GRAHAM (called Dick), born Henderson County, Illinois, 18 October 1861, died 11 November 1940; married, c. 1901, BERTHA GERTRUDE SPRINGER, born Ohio, c. 1882, died in Burns County, Oregon, 26 March 1965. Shortly after their marriage they lived briefly in Geary County, Kansas, where their first child was born. Kathryn Patterson, wife of their son Frederick, writes that for a few years after 1902 Andrew and his brother Bill lived on a

4-23 J. Thomas, 3-8 William M., 2-1 Andrew

ranch at Hill City, Graham County, Kansas, and raised cattle. In the 1910 census Andrew and his wife were listed in Summerfield, Marshall County, Kansas. He was then a carpenter. Known children, all born in Kansas:

6-54 Henry Clay, b. 13 or 18 May 1902
6-55 Frederick Lawrence, b. 4 September 1904
6-56 Melvin R., b. 7 September 1907

6-57 John Howard, b. 8 October 1910
6-58 Etta Louise, b. 26 December 1915


5-66 WILLIAM MILLS GRAHAM (Bill), born Henderson County, Illinois, 27 December 1863, died Summerfield, Kansas, 5 April 1934; unmarried. Kathryn Patterson Graham, wife of 6-55 Frederick L. Graham, writes that for a few years after 1902 Bill and his brother Dick (5-65 Andrew R.) lived on a ranch at Hill City, Graham County, Kansas, and raised cattle. In the 1900 and 1910 censuses he was listed in Guittard Township, Marshall County, Kansas. Listed with him were his widowed cousin 5-82 Jessie Graham Schilling and her children.


5-67 HARRY WILFORD GRAHAM (called Had), born Henderson County, Illinois, 14 March 1866, died Anacortes, Washington, 8 August 1928, buried Anacortes, Washington; married, 27 December 1888, DORA ROSETTA SMITH, born Iowa, 25 May 1868, died Seattle, Washington, 4 August 1955, buried Anacortes, Washington. In about 1904 they moved to Anacortes where he owned a shingle mill. In 1922 he sold the mill and bought Fomo's grocery store which he ran until he retired. After that, his son Roy managed the store. His granddaughter 6-60B Arlene Propst Blackwell writes, "They lived just three blocks from us. . . . Grandpa had a grocery store the last years. He drove the delivery truck and older son Roy ran the store while Arlie clerked. He always went to town every Saturday night for a haircut. Grandma and he always drove by and picked up my sister and me. We waited in the car while Had had the haircut then we went to an ice cream parlor after. He was bald and just had a fringe to be cut around the edge. He loved picnics and we would go two or three times a week in summer after work. . . ." Children, all but the last born at Concordia, Kansas:

4-23 J. Thomas, 3-8 William M., 2-1 Andrew                                5-68

    6-59 Roy Edson, b. 19 October 1889
    6-60 Clara Lenore, b. 8 April 1891
    6-61 Lulu Maude, b. 28 June 1893
    6-62 Pearl Ward (boy), b. 1 August 1896
    6-63 Eda M. Blanche, b. 4 April 1898
    6-64 Stella Gladys, b. 24 March 1901
    6-65 Theodore Oscar, b. 3 July 1903
    6-66 Arlene Alice, b. Anacortes, WA, 14 July 1906

5-68 JOHN GILCHRIST GRAHAM,[49] born Henderson County, Illinois, 10 October 1868, died Summerfield, Kansas, 10 November 1948; married, 23 March 1892, CLARA BELLE CONARD, born Pawnee City, Nebraska, 11 August 1871, died Summerfield, Kansas, 23 June 1947, daughter of John Conard (1845-1937) and Elizabeth Winter (1842-1910). Clara Belle was a sister of Jessie F. Conard who married John's brother 5-69 Lawrence William Graham.

    When they were first married, John and Clara lived on the Nebraska farm where Clara had been born. It was about four-and-a-half miles west of Summerfield, Kansas, and was on the north side of the Kansas-Nebraska line. Not long after their first child was born, they moved to West Plains, Missouri, where John raised fruit trees and berries, but they soon returned to their first area and this time lived on the Kansas side of the line in Marshall County where they remained until their retirement. John was a successful farmer, an elected township trustee in 1914 and 1916, and a mail carrier. He was also a member of the Masons, the Modern Woodmen of America, and the Ancient Order of United Workmen. Lorna Howard Cline (5-71B) writes that he was among the first in the area to have electricity on his farm: "As children, we thought it great fun to have electric lights and to see them run the milk separator without having to turn the handle." Children:

    6-67 Ray William, b. Nebraska, 9 January 1893
    6-68 Ava Eola, b. Marshall Co., Kansas, 19 June 1895
    6-69 Iva Izetta, b. Nebraska, 13 December 1896
    6-70 Thelma Elizabeth, b. Nebraska, 3 October 1898
    6-71 Walter Ivan, b. Summerfield, Kansas, 18 December 1901

5-69 LAWRENCE WILLIAM GRAHAM (called Pete), born Adair County, Iowa, 4 August 1871, died 11 September 1963; married, 16 August 1893, JESSIE FLORENCE CONARD, born Nebraska, 3 February 1874, died 24

4-23 J. Thomas, 3-8 William M., 2-1 Andrew					5-70

April 1944, daughter of John Conard (1845-1937) and Elizabeth Winter (1842-1910). Jessie was a sister of Clara Belle Conard who married Pete's brother 5-68 John Gilchrist Graham. In the 1900 census Pete and Jessie were listed in Richland Township, Marshall County, Kansas. Listed with them was Pete's cousin 5-89 David. In the 1910 census they were listed in Mission Creek Precinct, Pawnee County, Nebraska. He was a farmer and, according to 5-71B Lorna Howard Cline, played the violin by ear. In the 1900 census Jessie said she had had three children by that time only two of whom were living. Known children:

6-72 Zella Lenore, b. Missouri, November 1894
6-73 Joseph C., b. Missouri, 17 December 1896
6-74 Everett McKinley, b. Kansas, 15 July 1900
6-75 Paul E., b. 5 July 1903
6-76 Arthur Marvin, b. Pawnee Co., NE, 28 April 1915

5-70 JAMES THOMAS GRAHAM JR. (called Doc), born Adair County, Iowa, 16 June 1874, died 7 May 1942, buried Mission Creek Cemetery, Pawnee County, Nebraska; married LILLIE PEARL CLARK, born 14 January 1894, died 4 May 1935, buried Mission Creek Cemetery, Pawnee County, Nebraska. Doc was a farmer. He and Lillie lived on the Kansas-Nebraska line between Marshall County, Kansas, and Pawnee County, Nebraska, but in the 1910 census they were listed in Pawnee County. Children, all born in Pawnee County, Nebraska:

6-77 Opal, b. 30 June 1908
6-78 Lola Marie, b. 14 May 1921
6-79 Pearl Arleen, b. 8 October 1923

5-71 IVA LENORE GRAHAM HOWARD, born Dexter, Iowa, 13 December 1876, died Franklin, Nebraska, 16 October 1965; married at Beattie, Kansas, 10 February 1897, JOHN HOWARD, born Ridge Farm, Illinois, 22 January 1869, died Franklin, Nebraska, 10 September 1965, son of William Riley Howard (born Tennessee, 15 January 1842, died Cherokee, Oklahoma, 19 February 1900) and Elmina Helen Stanley (born Henry County, Indiana, 29 August 1843, died Webber, Kansas, 14 August 1889).

Iva played the organ and piano and, according to her daughter Lorna, "took organ lessons on an old pump organ. One of her brothers would play what she had learned with variations. I can't remember what brother it was." John, who was a minister and a

4-23 J. Thomas, 3-8 William M., 2-1 Andrew　　　　　　　　　　　　　　5-71A

teacher, was graduated from Friends (Quaker) University, Wichita, Kansas, in its first class--1901. He, his brother, and his father acquired a farm in Oklahoma by running in the famous Cherokee Strip race in 1893. Later they helped establish the Friends Academy at Cherokee, Oklahoma, and John was the principal at one time. Children:

A. Cecil Frank Howard, b. Cherokee, OK, 16 May 1898
B. Lorna Veola Howard, b. Ingersall, OK, 3 March 1905
C. Olive Lorene Howard, b. Lawrence, KS, 16 January 1907

---

A. Cecil Frank Howard, born Cherokee, Oklahoma, 16 May 1898, died Lawrence, Kansas, 3 November 1952; married (1) Aline Karnes, an accomplished pianist; (2) Imogene Robertson. Cecil was a banker. His sister Lorna says he also had a beautiful baritone voice and sang on occasions while she accompanied him on the piano. Children.

1. Elinore June Howard (daughter of Aline)

2. Margaret Janice Howard Douglas (daughter of Imogene); married Lloyd Douglas who worked at the Reuter Organ Factory. Children:

    a. Mark Douglas

    b. Steven Douglas

    c. Cheryl Douglas

B. Lorna Veola Howard Cline, born Ingersall, Oklahoma, 3 March 1905; married at Sylvan Grove, Kansas, 27 August 1933, Elton W. Cline, born Guide Rock, Nebraska, 18 December 1908, died Pittsburg, Kansas, 3 June 1977, son of Arthur Washington Cline (born Pilot Mound, Boone County, Indiana, 18 July 1874, died North Branch, Kansas, 26 July 1937) and Emma Viola Hadley (born North Branch, Kansas, 24 September 1877, died Pittsburg, Kansas, 14 November 1955).

Lorna taught music and English in the North Branch, Kansas, Friends Academy, and had a piano class for many years. Elton was graduated from Asbury College, Wilmore, Kentucky. He taught chemistry and physics for ten years at Pittsburg, Kansas, High School, and for twenty years at Pittsburg State

4-23 J. Thomas, 3-8 William M., 2-1 Andrew

University in Kansas. Children:

1. Carole Ann Cline Jacques, born Sylvan Grove, Kansas, 19 April 1936; married at Pittsburg, Kansas, 5 August 1956, Richard Irwin Jacques, born 13 June 1930. Carole works in the Registrar's Office at Pittsburg State University, Kansas. Richard was in the United States Navy for almost four years and now teaches printing at Pittsburg State University, Kansas. Children:

    a. Marcia Ann Jacques Base, born Pittsburg, Kansas, 2 November 1960; married, 23 May 1981, Gregory Base. Marcia teaches retarded children at Andover, Kansas, and Gregory works at Foley's Tractor in Wichita.

    b. Michelle Lynn Jacques, born 10 December 1964. She attended Pittsburg State University, Kansas.

    c. Maureen Elizabeth Jacques, born 16 November 1966. She attended Pittsburg State University, Kansas.

    d. Mark Irwin Jacques, born c. 1971

2. Mariline Kay Cline Troth, born Holten, Kansas, 12 January 1940; married at Pittsburg, Kansas, 10 May 1970, Marion Earl Troth, born Pleasanton, Kansas, 11 September 1940. Mariline is a secretary at an insurance company. Earl, who was formerly in the United States Navy on active duty for six months then in the Naval Reserves, now sells insurance. Children:

    a. Angela Kay Troth, born Fort Scott, Kansas, 12 October 1972

    b. Thomas Craig Troth, born Pittsburg, Kansas, 15 October 1975

3. Shirley Lenore Cline Messenger, born Holten, Kansas, 8 September 1941; married at Pittsburg, Kansas, 8 June 1963, John Dudley Messenger, born Pittsburg, Kansas, 29 April 1940. Shirley teaches kindergarten, and John runs a lumber mill company which also does building and remodeling. Children:

    a. Mary Cathleen Messenger, born Pittsburg, Kansas, 26 November 1966. She attended Pittsburg State University.

4-23 J. Thomas, 3-8 William M., 2-1 Andrew                               5-71B3b

   b. Kristen Kay Messenger, born Pittsburg, Kansas, 3 May 1971

  C. Olive Lorene Howard Hafner (called Lorene), born Lawrence, Kansas, 16 January 1907; married at Liberal, Kansas, 24 June 1932, Orville Hafner. He is a retired counselor of Burr Oak, Jewell, and Lebanon High Schools, and Lorene is a retired teacher of home economics and Spanish. Children:

   1. Verna Jean Hafner Grover, born ___, died 11 April 1974; married (1) Manuel Casado, a contractor; (2) John Grover. Children:

    a. Bonnie Casado, born Wichita, Kansas

    b. Marty Casado

    c. Mark Casado

    d. Lisa Casado

   2. Howard Arlen Hafner, born Guide Rock, Nebraska, 7 February 1936; married Brenda Lawson. Howard was graduated from Fort Hays College and is now the co-head of prospective employees for insurance companies. Brenda is an X-ray technician. Children:

    a. Jason Hafner, born *c.* 1972

    b. Holly Hafner


5-72 GEORGE WASHINGTON GRAHAM, born Iowa, 10 December 1878, died probably in Denver, *c.* 1956-7; married CATHERINE MULHERN (called Kate). They lived in Denver where he worked at the Gates Rubber Company which manufactured tires. His last listing in the Denver city directories was in 1956, and in 1957-9 Kate was listed as a widow. She was not listed thereafter. Child:

  6-80 Georgia Genevieve(?)


5-73 FRANK IRWIN GRAHAM, born Marshall County, Kansas, 21 December 1885, died 13 February 1964; married, 4 December 1902, BERTHA PAULINE KLOXIN, born Marshall County, Kansas, 22 November 1884,

4-25 Matthew J., 3-8 William M., 2-1 Andrew                           5-74

died 25 August 1981, parents born in Germany. In the 1910 census they were listed in Center Township, Marshall County, Kansas. He was a farmer. Lorna Cline (5-71B) writes that he also played the violin by ear. She adds, "They lived near Marysville, Kansas. They had a small building over spring water running through it which kept milk and other foods cool. This was not far from the house. His wife was German and taught me to do Hardanger Embroidery." Children, all born near Marysville, Kansas:

6-81 Willis, b. 19 December 1908
6-82 ___ (boy), b. 1913, d. inf.
6-83 Violet Verene, b. 10 July 1915

## CHILDREN OF 4-25 MATTHEW JOSEPH GRAHAM
## AND MARY ELLEN ANDERSON [50]

5-74 GEORGE MILLS GRAHAM, born Henderson County, Illinois, 26 July 1868, died Wenatchee, Washington, 25 January 1961; married (1), *c.* 1892, LENORA WISEMAN, (called Nora), born in West Virginia, *c.* 1870; (2) MARTHA STEWART. He and his first wife were listed in Omaha, Nebraska, in the 1910 federal census. He was a traveling salesman. Later he lived for many years in Burbank, California. Children, all by (1) Nora:

6-84 Ralph W., b. Iowa, *c.* 1897
6-85 George M., b. Nebraska, *c.* 1902
6-86 Arthur H., b. Nebraska, *c.* 1908

5-75 CHARLES WESLEY GRAHAM, born Madison County, Iowa, 25 October 1870, died Glendale, California, April 1960; married ANNA PANFIELD, born ___, died after 1962.

5-76 FRANK LEONARD GRAHAM, born Madison County, Iowa, 18 August 1873, died in California, February 1954; unmarried. Apparently, this was the son who helped care for his aged father, 4-25 Matthew Joseph, at the home of Frank's sister 5-78 Mabel. Frank applied to the federal government for an official flag for his father's

4-25 Matthew J., 3-8 William M., 2-1 Andrew                                    5-77

coffin. Unfortunately, nothing more is known of him.

5-77  LEE ANDERSON GRAHAM, born Madison County, Iowa, 6 August 1875, died at Winterset, Iowa, 18 February 1966, buried Winterset, Iowa; married NELLE RUTH LEE, born Iowa, April 1879, died Winterset, Iowa, 5 June 1963. In the 1910 census of Winterset, he was listed as an artist and a photographer. Children, all born in Iowa:

    6-87 Harry Lee, b. 21 February 1900
    6-88 Joseph Donald, b. 5 June 1907
    6-89 Frederick, b. 1917

5-78  MABEL EVA GRAHAM PERCIVAL PAYTON, born Madison County, Iowa, 8 October 1879, died in Hollywood, California, c. 1980 (sic); married (1) c. 1906, LEO C. PERCIVAL, born Iowa c. 1875, died after 1936; (2) ___ PAYTON. After Mabel's father, 4-25 Matthew Joseph (called Joe), had grown extremely old and senile and his wife had died, he was moved into Mabel's home in Winterset, Iowa, where she, her brother (probably 5-76 Frank L.), and a maid took care of Joe. Because of Joe's government pension, the Veterans Administration was required to investigate the arrangement. The following is from the investigator's report:

> This pensioner was 98 years old on November 12, 1936. He is a widower, his wife having died about 4 years ago, since which time he has been making his home with his daughter. His daughter is the wife of Leo C. Percival, who is an attorney at law and his firm is said to have had the bulk of the better practice for the last two or three years. The Percivals have a very lovely home and as a matter of fact when I made inquiry at the post office as to where they lived, I was advised that I could pick out the nicest home on the street and that would be theirs [517 W. Jefferson Street, Winterset, Iowa]. . . . The downstairs or at least as much of it as I was able to see shows that it is the home of persons of considerable means.

It is not known whether Mabel had children.

5-79 MYRTLE IDA GRAHAM BECKER, born Madison County, Iowa, 8 January 1881, died Fresno, California, 9 December 1960, buried Winterset, Iowa; married DAVID BECKER, born ___, died after 1941. They lived in Fresno, California, where he was listed in the city directories as a carpenter, his last listing in 1941. By 1959 Myrtle was listed as a sales clerk at Rhodes. No known children.

5-80 ADA LENORE GRAHAM CALL, born Madison County, Iowa, 23 July 1886, died in Fresno, California, June 1937, buried Winterset, Iowa; married, after 1910, LA MONE CALL who died after 1942. He married (2) c. 1938, Grace ___. In the 1910 federal census of Winterset, Ada was listed with her parents and was a photographer. By 1935 she and her husband were living in Fresno, California, where he was listed in the city directories first as a carpenter then as a general contractor owning a business. His last listing was in 1942. He and Ada had no children.

CHILDREN OF 4-27 JOHN MILLS GRAHAM
AND (1) ELIZA A. COWDEN [51]

5-81 EFFIE JANE GRAHAM GLICK, born Henderson County, Illinois, 16 April 1869, died at a rest home in Madison, Kansas, 18 July 1964, buried Summerfield Cemetery, Summerfield, Kansas; married, probably in Marshall County, Kansas, 8 September 1887, ADAM W. GLICK, born Indiana, 1 September 1854, died in Topeka, Kansas, 21 October 1937, perhaps a son of Gideon Glick (born Ohio, February 1822) and Minerva ___ (born Pennsylvania, August 1827).

In the 1900 census Effie and Adam were listed in Richland Township, Marshall County, Kansas, and in about 1910 they moved to Topeka, Kansas, where in the 1910 census he was listed as a retired farmer. In the Topeka city directories, he was named as a carpenter and a sander. He and Effie lived in a house which was described as a modern, two-story frame with sixteen rooms, and they took in boarders. They also owned an apartment house called Glick Apartments. They were members of the First Methodist Church in Topeka. By 1960 Effie was living in Emporia, Kansas, probably with her daughter Ina. According to the 1900 census, Effie had had five children only four of whom were living. Known children,

4-27 John M., 3-8 William M., 2-1 Andrew                                    5-81A

all probably born in Marshall County, Kansas:

A. Ina M. Glick, b. January 1890

B. Louisa A. Glick, b. November 1892

C. Wilbur R. Glick, b. 26 August 1893

D. Grace Glick, b. December 1895

---

A. Ina M. Glick Schottler, born probably in Marshall County, Kansas, January 1890; married Martin Schottler. They lived in Emporia, Kansas, and had two sons.

B. Louisa A. Glick Lorts, born probably in Marshall County, Kansas, November 1892; married William J. Lorts. In the 1912 Topeka city directory, Louisa was listed as a clerk at Mills Dry Goods Company. When her father died in 1937 she and her husband were living in Emporia, Kansas, and by the time her brother died in 1961 they were living in Downey, California.

C. Wilbur R. Glick, born Summerfield, Marshall County, Kansas, 26 August 1893, died Topeka, Kansas, 4 April 1961; married Zola ___. In the 1912 Topeka city directory, Wilbur was listed as a messenger at the Palace Company. Later he became an electrician and was a member of the International Brotherhood of Electrical Workers. He was also a president of the American War Dads and worked actively with that organization in a Veterans Administration hospital. By 1962 Zola was listed in the Topeka city directories as an executive secretary, and by 1964 she was retired. She and Wilbur were members of the Kansas Avenue Methodist Church in Topeka. Known children:

1. Howard L. Glick. When his father died in 1961, he was living in Bellaire, Texas.

2. Wilbur R. Glick Jr. When his father died in 1961, he was living in Santa Fe Springs, California.

3. Pearl Grace Glick Lewkow; married ___ Lewkow. When her father died in 1961, she was living in Panama City, Florida.

D. Grace Glick Heil, born probably in Marshall County, Kansas, December 1895, died after 1964; married, c. 1921-4, Roy Heil, born ___, died c. 1960, probably a son of Peter Heil (died before 1921) and Susan Cox (died 1940-2). In the 1916-21 Topeka city directories, Grace was listed first as a clerk then as a stenographer at Capper Publishing Company. Roy was a dentist, and according to the 1924 city directory they were living then at her parents' house. Later they had their own home. Grace's last listing in the city directory was in 1964, Roy's last in 1960. Child:

1. Sarah Jane Heil; probably unmarried. In the 1946 Topeka city directory, she was listed as a student. Later she was a clerk then a secretary at the Menninger Foundation. She lived with her parents.

5-82 JESSIE LEONORA GRAHAM SCHILLING, born Biggsville, Henderson County, Illinois, 9 June 1870, died Beattie, Kansas, 27 May 1954, buried Union Cemetery, Beattie, Kansas; married, 2 April 1888, SIMON SCHILLING, born Kansas, died probably in Marshall County, Kansas, 1895-1900. Jessie was listed as a widow in the 1900 and 1910 censuses of Guittard Township, Marshall County, Kansas. Listed with her was her cousin 5-66 William M. By the time her brother Harry died in 1936, Jessie was living in Balsam Lake, Wisconsin. According to the censuses Jessie had had four children only three of whom were living. Known children:

A. Bertha S. Schilling, born Kansas, February 1890

B. Tolbert H. Schilling, born Kansas, February 1893

C. Simon O. Schilling, born Kansas, November 1895

5-83 MAE BELLE GRAHAM MARSHALL, born Biggsville, Henderson County, Illinois, 17 October 1871, died of a stroke near Beatrice, Nebraska, 30 December 1916, buried Evergreen Home Cemetery, Beatrice, Nebraska; married, 28 December 1892, JAMES MARSHALL, born Illinois, c. 1863. In the 1910 census of Gage County, Nebraska, James was listed as a farmer on a rented farm. Also in that census Mae was listed as having had four children only three of whom were living. Known children, all born in Nebraska:

A. Lela E. Marshall, born c. 1897

B. John M. Marshall, born c. 1899

C. Dale T. Marshall, b. c. 1901

4-27 John M., 3-8 William M., 2-1 Andrew                                    5-84

5-84 ROBERT COWDEN GRAHAM (called Bert), born Winterset, Iowa, 17 April 1873, died Beattie, Kansas, 20 September 1952, buried Saint Malachy Catholic Church, Beattie, Kansas; married in Marysville, Kansas, 15 August 1895, AMANDA AGNESS PETERMAN, born Jamesport, Missouri, 18 November 1873, died Beatrice, Nebraska, 16 August 1955, buried Saint Malachy Catholic Church, Beattie, Kansas, daughter of George Peterman and Margaret Morehart. In the 1910 census Robert was listed as a farmer in Richland Township, Marshall County, Kansas. According to the census, Amanda had had five children only two of whom were living. Since she is known to have had three more children after that time, she had at least eight children in all. Known children:

6-90 Pearl E., b. Beattie, KS, 1 January 1896
6-91 Thelma Agnes, b. Saint Joseph, MO, 5 December 1905
6-92 Robert Roy, b. Beattie, KS, 22 June 1911
6-93 Dorothy Margaret, b. Summerfield, KS, 13 February 1914
6-94 John William, b. Oketo, KS, 2 January 1916


5-85 GEORGE HENRY GRAHAM, born Madison County, Iowa, 26 October 1874, died 10 January 1960, buried Highland Cemetery, Winfield, Kansas; married, in 1901, EFFIE M. CUMMINGS, born Nebraska, *c.* 1883. In the 1910 census he was listed in Summerfield, Marshall County, Kansas, and was a carpenter. Known children, all born in Kansas:

6-95 Fleda B., b. *c.* 1903
6-96 George D., b. *c.* 1905
6-97 Keith, b. *c.* 1907
6-98 Leith, b. *c.* 1907


5-86 OLEY MILLS GRAHAM, born Madison County, Iowa, 3 June 1876, died 27 June 1949, buried Table Rock Cemetery, Table Rock, Nebraska; married, 26 October 1899, CARRIE E. WARNER, born Beattie, Kansas, 25 October 1882, died Pawnee County, Nebraska, 10 December 1956, buried Table Rock Cemetery, daughter of Alex Warner and Mary ___. In the 1910 census they were listed in Table Rock Precinct, Pawnee County, Nebraska. Oley was first a farmer then a carpenter in Pawnee County where he and Carrie lived all their lives. He was a member of the Odd Fellows Lodge, and he and Carrie were both members of the Pawnee City Christian Church. Known children, all born in Pawnee County, Nebraska:

4-27 John M., 3-8 William M., 2-1 Andrew                                    5-87

      6-99 Cecil Mary, b. *c.* 1902     6-103 Bail Robert, b. *c.* 1908
      6-100 Ira Florence, b. 7         6-104 Earl Lawrence, b. 4
          December 1903               January 1911
      6-101 Berniece Edna             6-105 Kenneth
      6-102 Arthur Bert, b. *c.* 1906


5-87 FLORENCE ELLA GRAHAM CLARK, born Madison County, Iowa, 8 March 1878, killed in an automobile accident near Falls City, Nebraska, 28 December 1941, buried Falls City Cemetery; married, *c.* 1900, SAMUEL BART CLARK (called Bart), born Nebraska, *c.* 1875, died after 1941. In the 1910 census of Summerfield, Marshall County, Kansas, Florence and Bart were listed immediately following the entries of her uncle 4-23 James Thomas and his wife, Melissa. Bart was a stock buyer. By the time her father died in 1926, Florence and Bart lived in Falls City, Nebraska. They had one adopted child:

    A. Marie Clark Hendrickson; married Chris W. Hendrickson and lived in Topeka, Kansas.


5-88 HARRY POPHAM GRAHAM, born Madison County, Iowa, 12 April 1880, died 4 July 1936, buried Summerfield Cemetery, Summerfield, Marshall County, Kansas; unmarried. When his father died in 1926, he was living in Springfield, Missouri. Later he returned to Summerfield, Kansas, where he was a plasterer.


5-89 DAVID ALBERT GRAHAM, born Winterset, Madison County, Iowa, 23 December 1881, died 21 November 1968, buried Cloverdale Cemetery, Boise, Idaho; married, 1900-6, MABEL L. WYMORE, born Kansas, *c.* 1886, died ___. In the 1900 census of Marshall County, Kansas, David was listed in the household of his cousin 5-69 Lawrence W. Graham. David was listed with his wife in Marshall County in the 1910 census. Listed with them in 1910 was David's brother 5-92 Frank. When his father died in 1926, David and Mabel lived in Perry, Oklahoma; by the time his brother Oley died in 1949, they lived in Casper, Wyoming; and by the time his sister Myrtle died in 1960, they were living in Boise, Idaho. Known child:

    6-106 Maxwell, b. Kansas,
        *c.* 1907

4-27 John M., 3-8 William M., 2-1 Andrew                                    5-90

5-90 MYRTLE IVA GRAHAM KONE, born Marshall County, Kansas, 4 July 1884, died at Saint Margaret's Hospital, Kansas City, Missouri, 16 December 1960, buried Bonner Springs Cemetery, Bonner Springs, Kansas; married, 22 November 1906, HENRY HOWELL KONE (called "Dad"), born Nebraska, c. 1878, died after 1960, son of John H. Kone (c. 1849- ) and ___. They were in the 1910 census of Summerfield, Marshall County, Kansas, where Henry was a merchant and a restaurant owner. Listed with them in the same census were his father and Myrtle's brother 5-93 Roy. In 1913 Myrtle and "Dad" moved to Marysville, Kansas, where they ran a furniture store and another restaurant named the Kone Café. In 1923 they moved to Bonner Springs, Kansas, where they owned a grocery store and later an upholstery business. No children.

5-91 ARAMINTA SIGNOR GRAHAM WARNER (called Minta), born Marshall County, Kansas, 15 April 1886, probably died before 1926; married B. S. WARNER. When Minta's father died in 1926, she was not named in his obituary as one of his survivors.

5-92 FRANK HARRISON GRAHAM, born Humboldt, Nebraska, 1 January 1888, died 31 January 1962, buried Marysville Cemetery, Marysville, Kansas; married, 20 November 1912, LUCY GEIGER. In the 1910 census of Summerfield, Marshall County, Kansas, Frank was listed in the household of his brother 5-89 David. Frank was a clerk. After he and Lucy were married, they lived a short time in Topeka where he was a motorman, and they then moved to Marysville, Kansas, where they owned a restaurant in partnership with Howell "Dad" Kone, husband of Frank's sister 5-90 Myrtle. The partnership was short-lived, however, and he and Lucy moved to Drumright, Oklahoma, where he worked in the oil fields. In 1915 they returned to Marysville, and he and Lucy bought a restaurant, but, believing he was about to be drafted into the army during World War I, they sold the restaurant, and he went to work as a brakeman on the Union Pacific railroad. Returning to the restaurant business in 1919, they first constructed a small building to house their café which in 1925 was considerably enlarged and which they continued to operate until 1945. At that time they bought the Elms Hotel. An avid golfer and a manager of a basketball club, Frank was also a musician and played in a local band. Child (adopted):

6-107 Marge

5-93 ROY GRAHAM, born Table Rock, Nebraska, 12 July 1891, died 4 April 1948, buried Sunset Memorial Park, Albuquerque, New Mexico; married, (1) on 30 May 1920, MAUDE SAMUELSON, born Monument, Kansas, 12 November 1892, died Albuquerque, New Mexico, 7 June 1932, buried Albuquerque, daughter of Peter Samuelson and ___; Roy married (2) c. 1935, OCTAVIA J. ___, born ___, died after 1981. In the 1910 census of Summerfield, Kansas, Roy was listed in the household of his sister 5-90 Myrtle. After he and his first wife, Maude, were married in 1920, they moved to Albuquerque, New Mexico, where he was a dentist. Prior to marriage she had been a teacher in Summerfield and Vermilion, Kansas. According to the 1949 Albuquerque city directories, Roy's second wife, Octavia, was then a student at the University of New Mexico. By 1952 she was a junior high school teacher, and by 1970 she was retired. Her last listing was in 1981. Roy's first wife, Maude, may have had one child who died in infancy. It is not known whether his second wife, Octavia, had children.

## CHILDREN OF 4-30 SAMUEL ALLISON GRAHAM AND ELIZABETH GRACE THOMSON [52]

5-94 WILLIAM ALLISON GRAHAM, born near Pitzer, Madison County, Iowa, 30 December 1870, died Spokane, Washington, 16 December 1959; married, 30 December 1896, ORA ALMA BONHAM, born Madison County, Iowa, 17 March 1876, died Spokane, Washington, 7 July 196_, daughter of William George Bonham and Susan Phillips. They lived in Macksburg, Madison County, Iowa, and in about 1913 moved to Fort Shaw, Montana. By 1918 they were living in Spokane, Washington, where, according to the city directories, he worked variously at Central Garage, Northwestern Supply Company, and Alta B. Collier, Realtor. They were members of the Metzger Methodist Church.[53] Children, the first five born in Macksburg, Iowa:

6-108 Mary Edna, b. 3 November 1897
6-109 Leslie Bonham, b. 10 June 1900
6-110 George Allison, b. 20 November 1903
6-111 Clarence Samuel, b. 3 August 1906
6-112 Merton, b. 26 July 1911
6-113 Ruby Ellen, b. Fort Shaw, MT, 3 August 1915
6-114 Chester William, b. Spokane, WA, 26 May 1920

4-30 Samuel A., 3-8 William M., 2-1 Andrew

5-95 THOMAS EDWARD GRAHAM (called Ed), born near Pitzer, Madison County, Iowa, 3 March 1872, died Long Beach, California, 6 March 1942; married in Creston, Iowa, 20 or 24 June 1908, CHARLOTTE MABEL JOHNSON (called Lottie), born Creston, Iowa, 4 June 1883, died Long Beach, California, 27 December 1968, daughter of Albert Alexander Johnson and Charlotte Hulda Peterson. They lived at Great Falls and Fort Shaw, Montana, and by 1938 were living in Long Beach, California. According to the Long Beach city directories, he was a plant operator for Lomita Gasoline Company. Children, all born in Montana:

6-115 Philip Edward, b. 18 December 1911
6-116 Gordon Albert, b. 8 July 1916
6-117 Robert Johnson, b. 5 October 1921

5-96 ROBERT CULBERTSON GRAHAM, born near Pitzer, Madison County, Iowa, 18 August 1873, died Creston, Union County, Iowa, 28 October 1948; married in Macksburg, Madison County, Iowa, 9 March 1897, MABEL ETHEL STEWART, born Macksburg, 26 July 1877, died Winterset, Iowa, 29 August 1943. Robert was a farmer. Children, all born in Macksburg, Iowa:

6-118 Arlie Harold, b. 3 April 1898
6-119 Earl Stewart, b. 19 August 1900
6-120 Dorothy, b. 17 November 1902
6-121 Lorene Mabel, b. 19 January 1906
6-122 Robert Russell, b. 9 March 1908
6-123 Wyman Lee, b. 1 January 1921

5-97 LILLIE MAUDE GRAHAM WIMMER, born near Pitzer, Madison County, Iowa, 30 June 1877, died Modesto, California, 2 December 1945, buried Fairmont Memorial Park, Spokane, Washington; married at Orient, Iowa, 2 July 1895, SAMUEL HOWELL WIMMER, born Adair County, Iowa, 30 October 1871, died Spokane, Washington, 14 March 1965, buried Fairmont Memorial Park, Spokane, son of John Calvin Wimmer (1841-1913) and Mary Howell.

After Lillie and Sam were married, he continued working on his father's farm then rented another farm nearby. In the summer of 1898 they decided to move to Yuma County, Colorado, so they set off in a horse-drawn wagon loaded with all their goods. The trip took over thirteen days, one reason being a long delay at a

one-lane bridge over the Platte River. A continuous line of
wagons crossing the bridge from the opposite direction delayed
their crossing until after midnight. They bought a farm near
Wray, Colorado, but a drought during the following year forced
them to spend all their savings, and they had to return to Iowa.
Two years later, October 1901, they moved to Turner County, South
Dakota, where they rented a farm about twelve miles southwest of
the town of Parker. In 1904, however, Lillie barely survived a
ruptured appendix, and because of her fragile condition they auc-
tioned their possessions on 13 December 1904 and again returned to
Iowa.

Fortunately, Lillie recovered her health the following year,
and they returned to South Dakota, this time buying an eighty-acre
farm two miles west of Parker. The farm prospered, but Sam developed crippling rheumatism because of the climate, so again they
sold out in May 1909 and moved to Leota, Kansas, where Sam worked
in a general store. A year later they heard of an opportunity to
homestead near Fort Shaw, Montana, and moved there in June-July
1910. There they farmed temporarily and opened a general store at
Fort Shaw which was instantly successful. They soon became involved in community life and built a two-story house on a four-
acre lot. They also joined with others in building a school and a
church, and Sam was the chief carpenter in both projects.

Fort Shaw was a rough town at the time, and a nearby hotel
and saloon lured rowdy men who often engaged in drunken brawls.
Since Lillie and Sam were outspoken prohibitionists, they began to
receive threats from the hotel owner, a man named Rohrbach. They
ignored the threats and continued talking against alcoholism, but
one morning just after Samuel stepped out of his store it was
blown up. Someone had saturated the second floor with gasoline
and ignited it at that moment. Sam barely escaped with his life.
Soon after, debtors came from all over to settle their accounts
and thus help Sam and Lillie to recover--which they did. They
soon bought a lot about a block away from the hotel-saloon and
built a larger store. Rohrbach's son-in-law built another store
as competition, but very few people patronized it. Therefore,
Sam's and Lillie's second store was blown up, and this time they
were deeply in debt. They had to sell all their possessions, and
Sam worked in the community for several months as a carpenter and
insurance salesman to pay their debts. In September 1916 they
moved to Great Falls, Montana, and in May 1917 to Spokane, Washington. Sam worked in lumber yards and later became a residence
building contractor. Lillie worked in the yard goods section of a
department store. Eventually they bought a home and spent time in
Long Beach and Modesto, California.

During most of her life, Lillie was active in church work, specifically in The Pitzer (Iowa) Associate Reformed Presbyterian Church (later the Pitzer United Presbyterian Church); the Methodist Church of Parker, South Dakota; The Congregational Community Church of Fort Shaw, Montana; and, from 1916 until her death in 1945, St. Paul's Methodist Episcopal Church of Spokane. She was also a member of The Order of the Eastern Star. Her son, Lyle, writes that her granddaughter, Ruth W. Leggett, possesses her New Testament which had been awarded to Lillie for Sunday school attendance and which includes in the back the Book of Psalms arranged in meter. It was arranged that way because no musical instruments were allowed in worship services. Children:

A. Max Rolland Wimmer, b. Adair Co., IA, 7 April 1896, d. 13 April 1896
B. Gladys Wimmer, b. Wray, Yuma Co., CO, 4 May 1899
C. Lyle Graham Wimmer, b. near Parker, SD, 23 June 1902

---

A. Max Rolland Wimmer, born prematurely, Adair County, Iowa, 7 April 1896, died of pneumonia and measles, 13 April 1896, buried Liberty Baptist Church Yard, Adair County, Iowa, next to his grandmother's grave monument.

B. Gladys Wimmer Haworth, born Wray, Yuma County, Colorado, 4 May 1899, still living in 1989; married at Spokane, Washington, 8 June 1921, Raymond Otis Haworth, born Belvedere, Nebraska, 1 March 1896, died Eugene, Oregon, 16 March 1973, buried Fairmont Cemetery, son of James Dennis Haworth and Elizabeth Livingston. They lived in Spokane, Washington, and Eugene, Oregon. Children:

1. Robert Lyle Haworth, born Spokane, Washington, 18 November 1922; married at Moscow, Idaho, 19 January 1944, Elizabeth Ann Woesner (called Betty Ann), daughter of Ray L. Woesner and Edith Van Wagenen. Robert and Elizabeth were graduated from the University of Idaho, and Robert later earned a master's at the University of Oregon. He is a veteran of World War II and was blown out of a foxhole during the Battle of the Bulge. Later he served in the rehabilitation of prisoners. At present he is a realtor and an insurance broker. Betty Ann inherited considerable timber property near Glacier National Park. They live in Springfield, Oregon. Children:

a. Robert Larry Haworth, born Spokane, Washington, 9 October 1946; married, 8 August 1970, Marguerite Anne DeReamer, born 6 March 1951. He was graduated from the University of California. Child: Graham Whitney Haworth, born 22 August 1972.

b. James Dennis Haworth, born Spokane, Washington, 19 October 1950; married, 29 December 1971, Priscilla Ann Pebley, born 8 January 1949. He was graduated from the University of Oregon. Children: (a) Benjamin Haworth, born 7 May 1974; and (b) Lindsay Haworth, born 16 August 1978.

c. Gary William Haworth (twin to next), born 10 August 1953; married, 31 August 1976, Penny Sue Lewellen, born 22 May 1951. He was graduated from the University of Oregon. Children: (a) Christopher Sean Haworth, born 11 July 1978; (b) Aaron Haworth, born 1980; (c) Gavin Haworth, born 1983; and (d) Holly Haworth, born July 1984.

d. Samuel Ray Haworth (twin to above), born 10 August 1953; unmarried. He was graduated from the University of Oregon.

2. Donald Raymond Haworth, born Spokane, Washington, 21 August 1926; married 3 June 1950, Jewel Virginia Smith, daughter of Jacob Ellsworth Smith and Ruth Brown. Donald and Jewel were both graduated from Washington State University. After serving in the United States Navy during World War II, he was employed by Sherry-Rand, Computer Division, in various managerial positions. Later he was the vice president of University Computers in Dallas, Texas; president and member of the executive committee of Greyhound Corporation, International Financial and Computer Division; and is now the president of Atlantic Bell, International. He and Jewel live in Dallas, Texas. Children:

a. Linda Katherine Haworth Nichols, born Spokane, Washington, 24 February 1952; married in Dallas, Texas, 1984, David Nichols. Child: Blaine Haworth Nichols, born September 1985.

b. Constance Lynn Haworth Hilliard, born Spokane, Washington, 7 July 1954; married in Dallas, Texas, 8 October 1972, Charles Wesley Hilliard IV. Children:

(<u>a</u>) Jennifer Lynn Hilliard; (<u>b</u>) Kimberly Ann Hilliard; (<u>c</u>) Michelle Leigh Hilliard; and (<u>d</u>) Charles Wesley Hilliard V.

    c. Julie Ann Haworth, born Seattle, Washington, 10 December 1957

3. Gerald Samuel Haworth, born Spokane, Washington, 21 October 1928, died of complications following a tonsillectomy in Spokane, Washington, 19 January 1936.

C. Lyle Graham Wimmer, born near Parker, South Dakota, 23 June 1902; married at Spokane, Washington, 17 September 1924, Mildred Bernice Roberts, born Spokane, Washington, 22 March 1902, daughter of Samuel Louden Roberts and Bertha Jane Hevener.

About his boyhood, Lyle writes:

The times my family lived on the ranch and in Fort Shaw, Montana, were probably the most pleasant and memorable years of my youth. I took all-day forays, exploring the wild mysteries of the cliffs, the gullies, and the rolling plains between, on, and around the several buttes near Fort Shaw. This was the terrain which the famed western artist Charles M. Russell used in many of his realistic paintings of early western life. (The Russell Memorial Museum is located in Great Falls, Montana.) My devoted, loyal, and alert companion was "Midget," a trained cow pony, truly a one-boy horse, who patiently grazed wherever I stopped, keeping track of my whereabouts by cocking her ears and pointing her eyes and nose at my location whether or not I was visible to her. In total darkness she could locate straying cattle and round them up. I would just sit in the saddle with loose reins and let her do her job. She could also smell or spot a rattlesnake and shy away from it. Coyote dens were along every cliff, a funeral pyre of a long-departed Indian chief was on top of Square Butte, and a buffalo run was on top of Shaw Butte where the Indians stampeded the buffaloes over the cliff to get their winter supply of meat. At the bottom of the cliff were piles of bones and horns. And of course it was fun for both boy and horse to sneak upward along a gully and then be outdistanced by a herd of antelope.

In 1920 when he was eighteen years old, Lyle began working at Fairbanks, Morse and Company, and for the next seven years he alternately worked for that company and attended college. He took course work at Whitworth College in Spokane, 1922-3, where he was on the basketball and track teams and was the president of the sophomore class. In 1927 he was graduated in electrical engineering from the University of Washington, and later completed additional studies at the University of California, 1937, and Golden Gate College in San Francisco, 1938. In 1926 he was elected to Tau Beta Pi, an honorary engineering society. During his college years his company also sent him variously to Indianapolis; Three Rivers, Michigan; and Beloit, Wisconsin. From 1927 to 1932 he was the manager of the Pacific Northwest Service Department for Fairbanks, Morse, and assistant manager of Diesel and Electrical Machinery Sales. In 1932 he decided to change careers and took a position at the Berkeley, California, office of Hartford Steam Boiler Inspection and Insurance Company. In 1940 Hartford transferred him to their main office in Connecticut, and in 1944 he switched to The Travelers Indemnity Company where he was the officer in charge of all underwriting and business development. He was the principal member of the Industry Committee for Contract Forms and Rating and a member of the Industry Canadian Executive Committee. He traveled extensively in the United States and Canada to encourage and maintain easy communication with and among Travelers employees as well as with brokers and agents. He also published many articles on boiler and machinery insurance and gave talks at conventions and conferences of industry executives and insurance managers. After retirement in 1967 he was a litigation consultant and special witness, an occupation which took him all over the United States, Canada, and Mexico. His clubs include the Hartford Club, the University Club, and the Farmington Country Club. Wherever he has lived he has also been active in church work and Christian education. This has included work at the Presbyterian church in Berkeley, California, and the Baptist church in West Hartford, Connecticut. In his other church work he has been chairman of the finance committee of the Greater Hartford Council of Churches, a member of the advisory committee for Hartford Seminary, president and trustee of the Denison Society at Mystic, Connecticut, and incorporator and first president of the Denison Pequot-Sepos Nature Center. In 1951 he was listed in *Who's Who in Insurance*. Since 1984 he and Mildred have lived in Boca Raton, Florida.

Mildred was graduated from a Washington teachers' college

which later became the University of Eastern Washington. Before marriage she taught school; since then has been very involved in church and committee work. Children:

1. Ruth Evelyn Wimmer Leggett, born Seattle, 6 March 1927; married at West Hartford, Connecticut, 15 October 1949, Richard Alexander Leggett, born 12 January 1919, son of Alexander Leggett and Margaret Thorne. Ruth was graduated in math from Middlebury College, Connecticut, and Richard was graduated from Trinity University in Hartford, Connecticut. Before retiring he was a vice-president and actuary of The Travelers Insurance Companies. Children:

   a. Elizabeth Roberts Leggett West, born Hartford, Connecticut, 1 April 1953; married, 1979, Corbett West. She was graduated from Denison College, Ohio, with a bachelor's in social science and is now the assistant director of university programs, Advanced Continuing Studies for Registered Nurses at Whitworth College, Spokane. Children: (*a*) Matthew Alexander West, born 1 January 1984; (*b*) Gillian Christine West, born 1 August 1985; and (*c*) Martha Lynn West, born 12 May 1987.

   b. John Graham Leggett, born Hartford, Connecticut, 21 September 1954. He was graduated with a bachelor's in music from Connecticut College and was in computer sales and programing. He is now with a computer export-import company.

   c. Jane Allison Leggett, born Hartford, Connecticut, 12 September 1956. She was graduated in environmental economics from Middlebury College and earned a master's in urban development at Harvard. She was with the United States Government EPA and later was stationed in Paris, France.

   d. Anne Sarah Leggett, born Hartford, Connecticut, 9 June 1959. She was graduated *magna cum laude* from Middlebury College with a degree in environmental economics. Later she earned a master's in botany at the University of Washington.

   e. Martha Starr Leggett, born Hartford, Connecticut, 18 April 1962. She was graduated from Dartmouth and was on the staff of a senator from Alaska. Later she earned a master's at the school of management, Yale

University.

2. Gordon Lyle Wimmer, born Seattle, 9 June 1929; married at Loudenville, New York, 1 February 1958, Grace Elizabeth Moloy, daughter of James Moloy and ___. He was graduated in engineering from Princeton and was with Westinghouse for fifteen years. He is now a certified consulting professional engineer. Children:

   a. John Gordon Wimmer, born 19 June 1959. He was graduated in accounting from Clarkson University, New York, and now works at Specialty Steel and Metals Manufacturing Company.

   b. James Lyle Wimmer, born 14 October 1960. He was graduated in accounting from Niagara College, New York, and is now a certified C.P.A. and a member of the accounting organization.

   c. Margaret Mary Wimmer, born 26 April 1963. She was graduated in economics from Colby College, Maine, and attended the London School of Economics. Later she earned a master's at the school of management at Duke University, and is now with a consulting firm in Washington, D.C.

5-98 ELIZABETH MARY GRAHAM JACOBSON (called Mary), born near Pitzer, Madison County, Iowa, 13 June 1879, died Creston, Union County, Iowa, 23 September 1956; married in Spaulding, Iowa, 2 or 12 June 1909, PETER WESLEY JACOBSON (called Wesley), born near Fairfield, Iowa, 16 April 1877, died Creston, Iowa, August 1963. They lived first in Spaulding, Iowa, and in 1910-14 near Towner, Colorado, but soon returned to Iowa where they lived near Afton, Union County. Children:

A. Helen Marjorie Jacobson, b. Spaulding, IA, 17 March 1910
B. Victor Graham Jacobson, b. Spaulding, IA, 16 June 1911
C. Wesley Cassel Jacobson, b. Towner, CO, 21 May 1913
D. Jeanette Eleanor Jacobson, b. near Afton, IA, 24 October 1914
E. Alden Dale Jacobson, b. near Afton, IA, 4 June 1916
F. Newell Edward Jacobson, b. near Afton, IA, 7 June 1918

4-30 Samuel A., 3-8 William M., 2-1 Andrew                                    5-98A

A.  Helen Marjorie Jacobson Sloan, born Spaulding, Iowa, 17 March 1910; married Roy Sloan. Children:

   1. Samuel Sloan

   2. Creighton Sloan

B.  Victor Graham Jacobson, born Spaulding, Iowa, 16 June 1911; married in Iowa City, 3 May 1943, Ella Margaret Peters. They live in Cedar Falls, Iowa. Child:

   1. Edward Graham Jacobson, born El Paso, Texas, 31 December 1944

C.  Wesley Cassel Jacobson, born Towner, Colorado, 21 May 1913; married (1) in Washington, D.C., 21 June 1947, Marian Margaret Mahoney who died before 1981; (2) Tess Dordal. They lived in Silver Spring, Maryland. Children:

   1. Carol Elizabeth Jacobson, born Washington, D.C., 5 February 1951

   2. Karen Jeanette Jacobson, born Washington, D.C., 1 December 1954

D.  Jeanette Eleanor Jacobson, born near Afton, Union County, Iowa, 24 October 1914, died Long Beach, California, 18 January 1989, buried Prairie Lawn Cemetery in Spaulding, Iowa; unmarried.

E.  Alden Dale Jacobson, born near Afton, Union County, Iowa, 4 June 1916; married (1) Elizabeth Berger; (2) at Homestead, Florida, 24 March 1968, Lillian Lorraine Suttle Dula, her second marriage, born Black Mountain, North Carolina, 20 May 1921. He is a retired lieutenant colonel in the United States Air Force and lives near Key Largo, Florida. Children, all by (1) Elizabeth Berger:

   1. Robert Dale Jacobson, born 21 April 1942; married in Indianola, Iowa, 14 June 1974, Connie Jean Richards. He is a lawyer living at Lumberton, North Carolina.

   2. Richard Wesley Jacobson, born 3 July 1944; married Gail Rodene Borovicki, her second marriage. Children:

      a. Deborah Jacobson, born Germany, 3 March 1970

4-30 Samuel A., 3-8 William M., 2-1 Andrew					5-98B2b

b. Julie Elizabeth Jacobson, born Germany, 16 July 1971

Gail also had two children by her first marriage: Linda and Daniel.

3. William Allison Jacobson, born 19 April 1948; unmarried. He lives in Honolulu.

4. Philip Alden Jacobson, born 1 August 1950; unmarried. He lives in Los Angeles.

Lillian also had two children by her first marriage: Chip and Peggy.

F. Newell Edward Jacobson, born near Afton, Union County, Iowa, 7 June 1918; married in Creston, Iowa, 22 June 1946, Dorothy May Myers, born 3 December 1919. He is a retired major in the United States Army and lives in Homestead, Florida. No children.

5-99 JANE GRACE GRAHAM BISHOP (Jennie), born Pitzer, Iowa, 9 February 1883; died Indianola, Iowa, 11 March 1959, buried Orient, Iowa; married in Spaulding, Iowa, 22 June 1904, CLAUDE O. BISHOP, born Stanton, Iowa, 6 October 1881, died Creston, Iowa, 2 November 1958, son of Tracy S. Bishop and Sara Nicetti Rogers. Children, all born in Orient, Iowa:

A. Myrle Graham Bishop, b. 19 June 1905
B. Straud Allison Bishop, b. 30 November 1906
C. Charlotte Mae Bishop, b. 19 July 1909
D. Elizabeth Mary Bishop, b. 17 February 1912

---

A. Myrle Graham Bishop, born Orient, Iowa, 19 June 1905, died in Chicago, 10 November 1964; married (1) in Chicago, 11 May 1929, Jeannette Ritter; (2) 16 December 1961, Inger Olson, born 27 June 1907. Children, both by (1) Jeannette:

1. Joanna Myrtle Bishop Hammerschmidt, born 19 June 1930; married Elmer Hammerschmidt. Children:

   a. Robert Hammerschmidt, born 1953

   b. Alan Hammerschmidt, born 1955

c. Lynda Marie Hammerschmidt, born 1960

2. Barbara Jean Bishop Markey, born 24 October 1932; married John Markey. In 1965 Barbara and John were living in Oceanside, California. Children:

a. Pamela Markey, born 1954

b. Patricia Markey, born 1956

c. Theresa Markey, born October 1963

B. Straud Allison Bishop, born Orient, Iowa, 30 November 1906, died Milwaukee, Wisconsin; married Betty ___. Children:

1. John Allison Bishop; married and has four children.

2. Mary Jane Bishop; married and has two children.

3. Thomas Bishop

4. Kenneth Bishop

C. Charlotte Mae Bishop Augustine, born Orient, Iowa, 19 July 1909, died Indianola, Iowa, 1975; married, 26 May 1935, Floyd Franklin Augustine. Children:

1. Claudette Jane Augustine, born Osceola, Iowa, 28 August 1936, died the same day.

2. Jim O. Augustine (adopted), born 1 January 1947. He is in the United States Marines Corps.

3. Jack G. Augustine (adopted), born 2 January 1948

D. Elizabeth May Bishop Morris, born Orient, Iowa, 17 February 1912; married in Chicago, 1 October 1934, Matthew Elmer Morris. Children:

1. Richard Alan Morris, born Berwyn, Illinois, 4 April 1941; married Judy ___. Children:

a. Michael Morris

b. ___ Morris (girl)

2. Peter Jon Morris, born Berwyn, Illinois, 23 October 1942

4-30 Samuel A., 3-8 William M., 2-1 Andrew                           5-100

5-100 WALTER NELSON GRAHAM, born near Macksburg, Madison County, Iowa, 13 October 1885, died at Vivian, Caddo Parish, Louisiana, 6 May 1979; married (1) at Spaulding, Union County, Iowa, 22 February 1911, OLIVE MAE STREAM (originally Stroehm), born at Macksburg, Madison County, Iowa, 19 February 1888, died Shreveport, Louisiana, 20 May 1962, buried Spaulding, Union County, Iowa, daughter of Fulton Stream and Ruth J. Richmond; (2) at Mooringsport, Caddo Parish, Louisiana, March 1963, ADELE SMITH.

Walter attended Colorado College at Colorado Springs where he joined the Kappa Sigma fraternity. Later he was a farmer, 1911-21, then became a banker in Iowa, 1921-39, and finally was a banker in Oil City, Louisiana, 1943-63. His nephew 5-97C Lyle Graham Wimmer writes that he was a "very interesting person." He was "a left-handed baseball pitcher" for Cutler Academy and Colorado College and was "an intrepid golfer, etc." His daughter says that golfing was indeed a strong avocation for him and that he helped establish at least two golf courses, one in Orient, Iowa, the other in Vivian City, Louisiana. The latter was named Monterey Country Club. Child:

6-124 Ruth Josephine, b. Creston,
      Union Co., IA, 5 October
      1916


5-101 SAMUEL ROSCOE GRAHAM (called Rock or Roscoe), born Macksburg, Iowa, 19 July 1888, died Long Beach, California, 2 February 1968, buried Masonic Cemetery, Des Moines, Iowa; married in Chariton, Iowa, 16 June 1908, ADDIE REED, born in Ida Grove, Iowa, 31 October 1887, died 3 September 1972, daughter of Elihu Reed and Lucetta ___. Addie had a twin sister, Ollie.

Rock worked in the credit department of the *Des Moines Register Tribune* for over fifty years and was the credit manager for over thirty years. He was a life member of the Crusade Masonic Lodge at Greenfield, Iowa, a member of the Des Moines Consistory, and a fifty-year member of the Waveland, Iowa, chapter of the Eastern Star.[54] He and Addie retired to Long Beach, California. Addie was one of sixteen children, but she and Rock had no children of their own. The executor of Rock's and Addie's estate was their nephew 6-115 Philip E. Graham.

4-32 Granville W., 3-9 Thomas P., 2-1 Andrew                                    5-102

## CHILDREN OF 4-32 GRANVILLE W. GRAHAM
## AND HELLEN NORA BURRUS [55]


5-102 THOMAS BURRUS GRAHAM, born in Kentucky, 11 July 1880, died in Denver, Colorado, January 1953, buried Mount Olivet Cemetery; married in Denver, Colorado, 3 August 1913, ELIZABETH BELLE MCGUIRE (called Bessie), born ___, died after 1962. They were married by Fr. Edward Barry at the Sacred Heart Church in Denver.

According to the Dallas city directories, Thomas was a fireman in 1906 and a carpenter from 1907 to 1916. He and Bessie then moved to Denver where he was a carpenter and a salesman. By 1932 he had a carpenter contracting business with a man named Ren DeBoer. Bessie's last listing in the city directory was in 1962. No children.


5-103 CHARLES WADDILL GRAHAM, born Kentucky, 10 October 1881, died in Dallas, Texas, 29 June 1942, buried Laurel Land Memorial Park; married, 26 April 1906, MAE ELLA UPCHURCH who died in 1970.

Charles was an electrician, and according to the Dallas city directories he worked for various firms: Egan-Farry Electric Company, 1907; Dallas Electric Construction Company, 1908; Lipscomb Electric Company, 1910; Electrical Contractors Association, 1915-16; and Builders Association, 1917. By 1925 he had his own firm, Graham Electric Company. In 1934-5 he was the executive secretary of National Electric Contractors, Dallas chapter. By 1936 he was with N. B. Busby and Company where he was a superintendant and by 1937 an assistant manager. He retired in 1937. Children:

6-125 Frank W.                    6-126 Mildred Rena


5-104 RENA MARY GRAHAM, born Kentucky, 25 August 1883, died 1953; unmarried. According to the Dallas city directories, Rena was a clerk at Sears, Roebuck, 1907-9; stenographer at Oak Cliff Furniture Company by 1915; secretary at Ruud-Humphrey Water Heater Company, 1916-18; cashier at Oak Cliff Building and Loan Association by 1925; assistant secretary at Continental Southland Savings and Loan Association, 1930; stock broker, 1934-35; stenographer at Busby and Company by 1938; and clerk at Holland's

4-32 Granville W., 3-9 Thomas P., 2-1 Andrew                        5-105

Magazine, 1947-50. She lived with her mother at 345 South Fleming, and her last address was 427 East Sixth.


5-105 NORA DAVIS GRAHAM SIMPSON, born Kentucky, 2 September 1885, died Dallas, Texas, 9 November 1971; married, 23 September 1908, RAYMOND RODELL SIMPSON, born near Cleburne, Texas, died in Dallas, 25 December 1940.

In the Dallas city directories, Nora was listed as a clerk at Sears, Roebuck, 1907, and as a cashier at Liquid Carbonic Company, 1908. Raymond's parents migrated in a covered wagon from Tennessee to Texas where they settled on the Brazos River below Cleburne. Children:

A. Raymond Rodell Simpson Jr.,   B. Virginia Helen Simpson,
   b. 24 July 1909                  b. 17 December 1911

---

A. Raymond Rodell Simpson Jr., born Dallas, Texas, 24 July 1909; married, 20 June 1942, Julia Higgins, daughter of Walter G. Higgins and Elta ___. In 1939 Raymond was graduated with a law degree from Southern Methodist University. Later he was the Dallas claims manager of Employers Group Insurance companies of Boston until August 1951 when his company transferred him to their San Antonio office where he and his wife have lived since. He retired in 1980. No children.

B. Virginia Helen Simpson Kauffman, born 17 December 1911, died Dallas, Texas, 8 February 1980; married Earl Kauffman, born ___, died in Missouri, c. 1973. They were divorced in 1939. Children:

1. Kenneth Kauffman, born 7 December 1937, died c. 1983; married Edie ___, later divorced. Children:

   a. Gregg Kauffman

   b. Kenneth Kauffman Jr.

   c. Kate Kauffman

   d. Karen Kauffman

2. John Kauffman, born c. 1939; married (1) ___ who died in

about 1980; (2) Betty ___. They live on Long Island, New York. Children, both by John's first wife:

a. Erica Kauffman

b. Gretchen Kauffman

## CHILDREN OF 4-33 ROBERT M. GRAHAM AND MARTHA E. HILTON

5-106 GEORGIA A. GRAHAM NORTHINGTON, born Kentucky, October 1870, died ___; married, c. 1889, ___ NORTHINGTON, who died probably c. 1895. Georgia and her children were listed with her widowed mother in the 1900 census of Ballard County, Kentucky. Children:

A. Mattie E. Northington, born Kentucky, September 1890

B. Gustavus Northington, born Kentucky, May 1892

5-107 THOMAS R. GRAHAM, born Kentucky, April 1874, died ___; married CARRIE ___, born Kentucky, August 1878. In the 1900 and 1910 censuses of Ballard County, Kentucky, Thomas was listed as a merchant. Known children, both born in Kentucky:

6-127 Robert M., b. c. 1905    6-128 Thomas R. Jr., b. c. 1908

## CHILDREN OF 4-38 ANDREW G. GRAHAM AND MARTHA CAROLINE FRANCIS

5-108 ___ GRAHAM (boy), born 11 November 1870, died 16 or 18 January 1871, buried Biggsville Cemetery, Henderson County, Illinois.[56]

4-38 Andrew G., 3-12 Andrew W., 2-1 Andrew                                    5-109

5-109 FRANK MILLS GRAHAM,[57] born Biggsville, Illinois, 7 October 1873, died ___, buried Biggsville Cemetery, Henderson County, Illinois; married (1) in Biggsville, 28 April 1897, ELIZABETH E. LYONS, born Pennsylvania, 26 October 1877, died 8 October 1898, buried Biggsville Cemetery, daughter of Benjamin W. Lyons and Margaret Johnston; Frank married (2) *c.* 1901, AMANDA ___, born Illinois, *c.* 1880. At the time of his first marriage, Frank's residence was Abington, Knox County, Illinois. In the 1910 census he was listed with his second wife in Biggsville, Henderson County, Illinois. He was a railroad operator. No children were listed.

5-110 CHARLES INMAN GRAHAM,[58] born Illinois, 9 September 1876, died 1953, buried Biggsville Cemetery, Henderson County, Illinois; married, *c.* 1900, MARY E. MCDILL, born Batavia, Iowa, 7 October 1877, died 1942, buried Biggsville Cemetery, daughter of David C. McDill (1847-1924) and Charlotta Thorpe (1850-1936). In the 1910 census of Biggsville, Charles was listed as a laborer. No children were listed.

5-111 MARY F. GRAHAM, born 24 September 1880, died 9 December 1880, buried Biggsville Cemetery, Henderson County, Illinois.[59]

5-112 RUSSELL ALEXANDER GRAHAM, born Biggsville, Illinois, 24 April 1885, died perhaps soon after 1910. He was listed with his parents in the 1900 census, but nothing more has been found on him. The reason it is known he died after 1910 is that his mother testified in the 1910 federal census that she had had five children only three of whom were living. Because the death dates of two of her children have been established as long before 1910, Russell must still have been alive then. Since nothing more has been found on him, however, he may have died shortly after 1910.

## SIXTH GENERATION

### CHILDREN OF 5-1 WILLIAM B. GRAHAM
### AND (1) MARTHA A. MCDILL

6-1 MARY FRANCES GRAHAM SPICER (called Fannie May),[1] born Henderson County, Illinois, 10 October 1864, died 23 March 1905, buried Monmouth, Illinois; married in Biggsville, Henderson County, Illinois, 9 April 1890, OLIVER ALEXANDER SPICER, born Burgess, Illinois, 23 September 1865, son of Alexander W. Spicer (died Warren County, Illinois, May 1911) and Flora Elliott. Oliver married (2), *c.* 1908, Margaret N. ___, born Iowa, *c.* 1871.

Fannie May joined the South Henderson United Presbyterian Church on 10 May 1879 and later was dismissed, probably to Monmouth (Church Register). In the 1910 federal census, Oliver was listed as a farmer; he and his second wife plus his four younger children were living in Monmouth Township, Warren County, Illinois. Children of Fannie May and Oliver, all born in Monmouth, Warren County, Illinois:

A. Ralph Wilson Spicer, b. 10 March 1891
B. ___ Spicer, b. 1 August 1894
C. Martha Lucille Spicer, b. 6 October 1895
D. Clarence Graham Spicer, b. 16 August 1898
E. Leland Ray Spicer, b. 24 October 1900
F. Wylie Braden Spicer, b. 27 September 1903

---

A. Ralph Wilson Spicer, born probably in Monmouth, Illinois, 10 March 1891, died 14 May 1893.

B. ___ Spicer, born in Monmouth, Illinois, 1 August 1894, died

5-1 William B., 4-2 Andrew, 3-3 Matthew, 2-1 Andrew

infancy.

C. Martha Lucille Spicer, born Monmouth, Illinois, 6 October 1895. She was an occupational therapist at the Mayo Clinic, 1921-5, and was with the United States Government Home Service, 1925-6. She lived in Monmouth, Illinois.

D. Clarence Graham Spicer, born Monmouth, Illinois, 16 August 1898, died 1977; married in Asheville, North Carolina, 25 September 1920, Grace Evelyn Sorrells. He served eleven months in France with the United States Aviation Corps. Later he was a farmer living at Tulia, Texas. Children:

1. Evelyn Marie Spicer Sivils, born Monmouth, Illinois, 23 November 1921; married "Buck" Sivils. They had a boy, Ronald, and three girls.

2. Ralph Graham Spicer, born Monmouth, Illinois, 24 March 1923, died during World War II.

3. Oliver Victor Spicer, born Azalea, North Carolina, 1 February 1930; married Frances ___. They had two sons and a daughter.

E. Leland Ray Spicer, born Monmouth, Illinois, 24 October 1900, died 1977; married in Galesburg, Illinois, 18 June 1924, Frances Marie McKelvie, daughter of Frank A. McKelvie and Pearl Wixson. He was a farmer near Monmouth, Illinois. Children:

1. Leland Ray Spicer Jr., born 22 August 1925; married Geraldine McCoy. Children:

   a. Rodney Spicer, born 1952; married Janice ___. Children: (**a**) Carrie, born 1971; and (**b**) Michael, born 1973.

   b. Julie Spicer Kumagai, born 1954; married Robert Kumagai. Children: (**a**) Philip, born 1974; and (**b**) Nathan, born 1977.

   c. Alan Spicer, born 1958; married Kathy ___.

   d. Ray Spicer, born 1961

2. Donald Wylie Spicer, born 26 July 1931; married Mona ___. Children:

   a. Blythe Spicer, born 1977

5-2 David W., 4-2 Andrew, 3-3 Matthew, 2-1 Andrew                6-1E2b

   b. Cherith Spicer, born 1978

 F. Wylie Braden Spicer, born Monmouth, Illinois, 27 September 1903; married Anne ___. He was a clerk with the Shell Oil Company at Wilmington, California, and lived in Long Beach.


6-2 ROBERT A. GRAHAM, born Biggsville, Illinois, July 1869, died ___; married, 5 February 1891, FRANCES B. SANDERSON, born April 1869, died ___, daughter of James Sanderson and ___ McLean. In September 1891 Robert, his parents, and his brother W. Wilson were dismissed by the South Henderson United Presbyterian Church to Sterling, Rice County, Kansas (Church Register). In the 1900 census Robert was listed in Sterling.


6-3 WILLIAM WILSON GRAHAM (called W. Wilson), born Henderson County, Illinois, 1872. In September 1891 he, his parents, and his brother Robert were dismissed by the South Henderson United Presbyterian Church to Sterling, Rice County, Kansas. He was married twice.[2] Known child:

7-1 Wilson Braden

   CHILD OF 5-1 WILLIAM B. GRAHAM
   AND (2) MARGARET WALLACE

6-4 ROSS W. GRAHAM, born Biggsville, Henderson County, Illinois, 6 January 1879.[3] He was listed with his parents in the 1900 census of Rice County, Kansas.



   CHILDREN OF 5-2 DAVID WILSON GRAHAM
   AND IDA ANSPACH BARNED


6-5 DAVID BARNED GRAHAM,[4] born Chicago, 9 April 1879, died in Summit, New Jersey, 15 July 1964; married in Chicago, 3 June 1910, MARY BURRELL, born Chicago, 9 September 1875, died Wilmette, Illinois, 24 December 1937, daughter of Louis Falger Burrell (born Freeport, Illinois, 1832, died Chicago, 1908) and Margaret Hamilton (born

5-2 David W., 4-2 Andrew, 3-3 Matthew, 2-1 Andrew       6-6

Bridgeport, Connecticut, died Chicago, 1885).

David was graduated from Princeton in 1902 and later was a businessman in the publication and distribution of greeting cards. His chief hobbies were tennis and reading. Mary attended the National Kingergarten College in Chicago and Pratt Institute in New York City. Later she was a kindergarten teacher in Chicago, a playground director in New York City, and a pottery instructor at the art institute in Chicago. She also worked with the Red Cross and the Women's City Club in Chicago. She and David lived most of their lives in Joliet, Illinois. They also owned a summer house in a resort called "Michillinda" in Michigan north of Muskegon which is on Lake Michigan. For three generations the house has been used for many family celebrations, reunions, and retreats. Child:

7-2 Margaret, b. Chicago,
    2 September 1912


6-6 EVARTS AMBROSE GRAHAM,[5] born Chicago, 19 March 1883, died Saint Louis, Missouri, 4 March 1957; married in Dubuque, Iowa, 29 January 1916, HELEN TREDWAY, born Dubuque, 21 July 1890, died Saint Louis, 4 April 1971, daughter of Harry Ellis Tredway (born Dubuque, 30 June 1861, died Saint Louis, 11 November 1944) and Marian McConnel (born Jacksonville, Illinois, 3 October 1863, died Dubuque, Iowa, 26 August 1940).

Evarts was graduated from Princeton in 1904 and earned his M.D. degree at Rush Medical College in 1907. In 1908-9 he was a fellow in pathology at Rush Medical College where he took additional training in surgery, and in 1910-14 he was an assistant in surgery at the same college as well as a member of the staff of Otho S. A. Sprague Memorial Institute for Clinical Research in Chicago, 1911-14. During World War I, he was a major in the United States Army, serving first at the School of Neurological Surgery in Chicago, then with the Empyeme Commission at Camp Lee, Virginia, and finally as the commanding officer of an evacuation hospital in France. After his discharge in 1919, he became a professor of surgery at the Washington University School of Medicine, Saint Louis, and surgeon-in-chief at Barnes Hospital and at Saint Louis Children's Hospital.

At Barnes Hospital in April 1933, Evarts made medical history by performing an operation which also made him famous: he successfully removed an entire lung of a Pittsburgh obstetrician who was stricken with lung cancer--the first time such an operation had succeeded on humans. Because of this new technique, many subsequent patients also afflicted with lung cancer were cured as was the Pittsburgh obstetrician. His other achievements included the development of a method of making the gall bladder visible on X-ray plates thus aiding diagnoses of gall bladder diseases, early surgery on the heart valve and the pancreas, and (with E. L. Wynder) early investigations of the connection between smoking and lung cancer. He also crusaded for improved medical standards and for the elimination of such questionable practices as fee splitting and "ghost surgery," a term used when a patient does not know the name of his operating doctor. He retired in 1953. In 1956 he joined with other doctors and scientists in calling public attention to the health threat of fallout from hydrogen bomb tests.

Evarts served on many national committees and was a member of many prestigious, world-wide medical and scientific organizations. He also received numerous honors among which was the Lister Medal, a British award given every three years, and he was the author of many articles as well as the editor of several medical journals.

Ironically, he died of lung cancer. He had been a smoker but had given up the habit ten years before he died. He was said to have been 6 feet tall and weighed 175 pounds. His hobby was gardening. In 1940 his address in Saint Louis was 4711 Westminster Place. Shortly thereafter he and Helen moved to Florissant, Missouri.

Helen Tredway Graham, herself an important civic leader and a distinguished scientist, was a professor of pharmacology at Washington University's School of Medicine in Saint Louis and continued in active research until she suffered a heart attack in her laboratory. She died a few days later.

Children:

7-3 David Tredway, b. Mason City, IA, 20 June 1917

7-4 Evarts Ambrose Jr., b. Saint Louis, 4 February 1921

5-8 Harvey W., 4-3 John W., 3-3 Matthew, 2-1 Andrew

CHILD OF 5-8 HARVEY WILSON GRAHAM
AND MARTHA AMANDA GLENN


6-7 HARVEY WILSON GRAHAM JR.,[6] born Sparta, Randolph County, Illinois, 20 December 1869, died Washington, D.C., 8 April 1947, buried Rock Creek Cemetery, Washington, D.C.; married at Santa Ana, Orange County, California, 13 July 1899, LENA HARRIET PARSONS, born Canton, Lewis County, Missouri, 12 October 1873, died Richmond, Virginia, 24 July 1955, buried Rock Creek Cemetery, Washington, D.C., daughter of Stephen Albert Parsons (born Miami, Missouri, 29 July 1849, died Canton, Missouri, 20 May 1890) and Lenora Howard Thomas (born Oxford, Oxford County, Maine, c. 1852, died Santa Ana, California, 30 April 1915). Harvey and Lena were married by the Rev. Bateman of Santa Ana Christian Church.

Most of Harvey's childhood was spent in Marissa, Saint Clair County, Illinois, where his mother had moved in 1872 from Sparta, Illinois. In 1887 Harvey joined in partnership with Robert Stuart Coulter and Professor McMichael to publish *The Marissa Messenger*. Coulter bought out Harvey and Professor McMichael soon after, and Harvey's mother and stepfather, Joseph W. Elder, moved to Beaumont, Riverside County, California, in the early part of 1888. Possibly Harvey also moved to California at this time.

During the 1890's Harvey worked at a newspaper in Santa Ana, California, where he met his future wife, Lena, who was employed there as a typesetter. Later Harvey took a civil service exam and acquired a position at the Government Printing Office in Washington, D.C. He and Lena moved to Washington shortly after their marriage. At first they lived at 40 New York Avenue NE, then in about 1906 moved to 14 T Street NE, and finally settled at 12 Rhode Island Avenue NE in 1912. These homes were all within a short distance of the Government Printing Office. Harvey worked as a printer and make-up until 1918 when he became a copy editor. In about 1933, however, he was forced into retirement because of the policies of the newly-elected Roosevelt administration.

At about the time of Thanksgiving in 1936, Harvey suffered a stroke while on a family automobile trip to Newport News, Virginia, to visit the family of his son Thomas H. The stroke affected his left side, and he was left-handed. Still, he could get around with a cane, but in about 1940 he suffered another stroke which caused him to be bedridden at his home until his death in 1947.

An amateur photographer interested not only in picture taking but also in film development, he also played the zither, receiving lessons from a musician in the Marine band. Both these activities were abandoned by 1912. Other activities not abandoned were carpentry and chess playing, and he was a member of a local chess club.

Lena's principal occupation was managing her home. Also, for several years she was on the board of the Episcopal Home for Children of the Diocese of Washington.

Harvey and Lena were members of the Church of the Advent at Second and U Street NW. This church was disbanded in about 1935, and they then transferred to Saint Paul's Rock Creek Church in Washington, D.C.

Children, all born in Washington, D.C.:

7-5 Daniel Parsons, b. 20 July 1900

7-6 Thomas Harvey, b. 6 November 1906

7-7 James Glenn, b. 22 October 1912


CHILDREN OF 5-30 JAMES ANDREW GRAHAM
AND MARY EMMA MARTIN [7]


6-8 DAVID GRAHAM, born near Biggsville, Henderson County, Illinois, died young.


6-9 MARY ELIZABETH GRAHAM BROOKS (called Beth), born near Biggsville, Henderson County, Illinois, 16 October 1887; married ORLOW BROOKS. Child:

A. Maribeth Brooks Ziebell, born 1918; married Edwin Ziebell. Children:

1. Deborah Ziebell Turriff, born 1948; married James Turriff.

2. Barry Ziebell, born 1950

6-10 **MELINDA E. GRAHAM BEARD** (called Linna), born near Biggsville, Henderson County, Illinois, 3 January 1890, died 1980; married WILLIAM H. BEARD, born 1889, died ___. They lived in Kansas City, Kansas, where, according to the city directories, he was the president of New Method Paint Company. Their last listing in the directories was in 1959. Children:

- A. Elizabeth Beard, b. 1918
- B. Margaret Jane Beard, b. 1920
- C. William Graham Beard, b. 1927

---

A. Elizabeth Beard Johnstone, born 1918, died 1954; married Alan Johnstone. Children:

1. Margaret Johnstone Krautzkampf, born 1940; married Larry Krautzkampf.

2. Kenneth Graham Johnstone, born 1944; married Judy Kane.

3. Susan Johnstone, born 1946 (twin to next)

4. Judy Johnstone, born 1946 (twin to above)

B. Margaret Jane Beard Fedoroff, born 1920; married George Fedoroff. Children:

1. Robert William Fedoroff, born 1949

2. Margaret Ann Fedoroff, born 1951

C. William Graham Beard, born 1927; married Mary Proctor, born 1928. In the Kansas City, Kansas, city directories, he was listed as a manager at Bankers Life Company and by 1975 was a vice-president at Mercantile Bank and Trust. He and his wife were not listed in the 1983 directory. Children:

1. Patricia Ann Beard, born 1950

2. Nancy Graham Beard, born 1953

3. Melinda K. Beard, born 1958

6-11 **JAMES H. GRAHAM**, born Biggsville, Illinois, *c.* 1896, died young.

## CHILDREN OF 5-35 EDWIN BROWN GRAHAM
## AND ELIZA M. LOURIE [8]

6-12 MARY CLARA GRAHAM EDMATON, born March 1877, died 1912; married GAIL EDMATON. In the 1900 census of Sioux City, Iowa, Mary was listed in her mother's household and was a stenographer. According to the city directories, she worked at S. C. Stock Yards Company, 1900-1, and at Edwards and Bradford Company, 1901-2. She was not listed in the directories after that time.

6-13 LAURA GRAHAM CAMPBELL, born January 1879; married JAMES CAMPBELL. In the Sioux City, Iowa, city directories, she was listed first as a student at Brown's Business College, 1900-1, then as a stenographer, 1901-3. She was not listed after that time. Children:

    A. Myrna Campbell, born 1906

    B. Thurlow Campbell, born 1908

    C. Margaret E. Campbell, born 1916

6-14 EDNA GRAHAM, born 1882, died 3 July 1882 (age 3 months, 10 days), buried Prospect Hill Cemetery, Omaha, Nebraska.

6-15 ELLA GRAHAM, born 1884, died 14 April 1884 (age 2 days), buried Prospect Hill Cemetery, Omaha, Nebraska.

6-16 LOIS GRAHAM EAKIN, born November 1892; married FRANK EAKIN. Children:

    A. Arthur Eakin, born 1908, died 1925.

    B. Frances Eakin, born 1914

    C. Lourie Eakin, born 1916

## CHILDREN OF 5-36 WILLIAM FRANKLIN GRAHAM
## AND DORA A. BUCK [9]

6-17 LESSIE JANE GRAHAM, born Atlantic, Iowa, 7 March 1889, baptized at the United Presbyterian Church in Atlantic, Iowa, 18 March 1890, died at Atlantic, 1 June 1900.

6-18 WILSON HARVEY GRAHAM (or Harvey Wilson), born Atlantic, Iowa, 30 September 1890, baptized at the United Presbyterian Church in Atlantic, 20 June 1891; married (1) MINONE LOWMAN; (2) ___. He moved to Nebraska c. 1921, and when his father died in 1927 he was living at Grand Island, Nebraska, where he worked at a telephone company.

6-19 XENOPHON ALEXANDER GRAHAM, born Atlantic, Iowa, 13 November 1892, baptized at the United Presbyterian Church in Atlantic, 26 May 1894. From 1920 to 1937 he was listed in the Omaha, Nebraska, city directories and was boarding at 620 South 28th. At first he was a clerk at National Cash Registers Company, next he was a clerk at Burgess-Nash Company, and finally he was an automobile mechanic. When his father died in 1927, however, he lived at Minden, Nebraska, and worked at a telephone company.

6-20 MARY M. GRAHAM EASTON, born Atlantic, Iowa, 26 February 1902, died after 1967; married GEORGE S. EASTON, born ___, died probably in Laguna Hills, California, after 1974. George was a dentist and taught at the University of Iowa in Iowa City. By 1962 he was a professor and dean of the College of Dentistry there. By 1970 he had retired to Laguna Hills, California. His last listing as a resident in the Iowa City directories was in 1967; from then until 1974 he was still listed in Iowa City, but his residence was given as Laguna Hills. Mary's last listing was in 1967. Known children:

A. James G. Easton

B. Alan G. Easton

## CHILDREN OF 5-40 WILSON THOMPSON GRAHAM
## AND ELIZABETH A. CUNNINGHAM [10]

6-21 GEORGE HARVEY GRAHAM, born probably in Omaha, Nebraska, 20 June 1889, died in Omaha, 25 August 1913, buried Forest Lawn Cemetery, Omaha; probably unmarried.

6-22 HAROLD WILSON GRAHAM, born probably in Omaha, Nebraska, 5 August 1893, died of a heart attack, 25 July 1965, cremated Forest Lawn Cemetery, Omaha; married JESSIE MCDONALD, born 29 January 1893, died of heart failure, 5 April 1979, cremated Forest Lawn Cemetery, Omaha, daughter of ___ McDonald and Emma E. ___ (born 2 April 1859, died 31 July 1944, buried Forest Lawn Cemetery, Omaha). According to the Omaha city directories, Harold joined his father's real estate business in about 1916, working first as a bookkeeper, then as a salesman, then as manager, and finally as owner. His last listing was in 1965; Jessie's last was in 1970. They lived at 5807 Pacific. Harold's grave marker says he was a second lieutenant in the United States Army during World War I. Jessie's cemetery record gives her occupation as executive secretary. Child:

7-8 Suzanne, b. 1934

6-23 VICTOR CUNNINGHAM GRAHAM, born Omaha, Nebraska, 14 July 1896, died 18 September 1966, buried Forest Lawn Cemetery, Omaha; married, probably after 1930, LYDA B. BLIZNAK (called Billye), born 22 June 1899, died 29 December 1984, buried Forest Lawn Cemetery, Omaha.

According to the Omaha city directories, in 1920 Victor was an accountant at the B & M Stock Remed Company, and in 1921 he was the office manager at Corn Derivatives Company. In 1923 he was a purchasing agent for Peters Trust Company, in 1925 he was a department manager at the same company, and by 1928 he was the secretary-treasurer at the Nebraska Savings and Loan Association. In 1929 he was a teacher at South High School, and in 1930 he was a private secretary. Although he was listed in the 1934-5 directory, his occupation was not given. The following is from his obituary in the Omaha *World-Herald*, 19 September 1966, p. 20:

5-40 Wilson T., 4-9 J. Harvey, 3-3 Matthew, 2-1 Andrew

Victor C. Graham, 70, the founder and organizer of First Federal Savings and Loan Association of Omaha, died in an Omaha hospital Sunday. He had been hospitalized for seven weeks.

Mr. Graham, who resided at 6008 Western Ave., was born in Omaha. His parents were early Omaha pioneers and his father, W. T. Graham who was active in the real estate and mortgage business, was co-founder of Omaha University. Mr. Graham entered the real estate and mortgage business when he was young and, except for a brief period when he served as administrator of the Passavent Hospital at Northwestern University in Chicago, continued in this field. Mr. Graham graduated from the University of Nebraska in 1919.

He founded First Federal Savings and Loan Association in 1934, serving as its president for several years preceding his retirement in 1962.

Mr. Graham was a veteran of World War I and was a member of American Legion Post No. 1. He was a board member of the Omaha Transit Company and a member of the Dundee Presbyterian Church.

He is survived by his wife Lyda B. (Billye) Graham.

When Lyda died her obituary in the *World-Herald*, 31 December 1984, p. 26, named her as "Graham--Lyda B. (Billye)." No children were mentioned in either obituary.

6-24 MARY E. GRAHAM WEETH, born probably in Omaha, Nebraska, 6 October 1900, died probably in Omaha, 6 April 1978, buried Forest Lawn Cemetery, Omaha; married RANDALL K. WEETH, born 27 March 1901, died 11 July 1986, buried Forest Lawn Cemetery, Omaha, son of Joseph C. Weeth (born 20 August 1865, died 24 May 1946, buried Forest Lawn Cemetery, Omaha) and Effie Francis ___ (born 26 November 1861, died 20 July 1942, buried Forest Lawn Cemetery, Omaha).

In 1926-1930 Mary was a teacher at South High School in Omaha and lived with her parents. In 1933 she was listed in the city directory as a musician, and in 1934 she was listed again as a teacher at South High School. Also according to the city directories, Randall worked in his father's business, Harmon and Weeth

Company, which dealt in coal, coke, wood, and fuel oil. By 1959 he was a manager at Byron Reed Company, and Mary was still a high school teacher. It is not known whether she had children.

### CHILD OF 5-41 DALES YOUNG GRAHAM AND LAURA ANGELINE TRUMBULL

6-25 WILMER TRUMBULL GRAHAM,[11] born Nortonville, Kansas, 28 September 1894, died ___; married at Monmouth, Illinois, 22 July 1922, FLORA ANN MORGAN, born Hubbel, Nebraska, 1 January 1899, daughter of Edwin E. Morgan and Stella Blanch Curran. Wilmer attended Monmouth College, 1912-14, taught at a country school in Morning Sun, Iowa, 1914-15, and was later graduated from the University of Chicago. He was an ordnance sergeant and attended the Field Artillery Officer's Training School of the United States Army in 1918. After the war he worked at Sweet's Catalogue Service in Chicago, 1919, and at Arkmo Lumber Company, Arkansas, 1920-23. He then joined the Rock Island Lumber Company and worked at branches in East Moline, Illinois, 1924-29; Davenport, Iowa, 1929-35; Saint Paul, Minnesota, 1936-45; and Portland, Oregon, 1945-47. Later he established the Graham Lumber Company in Morning Sun, Iowa, 1947, and Winfield, Iowa, 1948-66, retiring in 1967.

Wilmer had a strong interest in family history and wrote a vigorous though largely hypothetical Graham genealogy, copies of which he donated to various genealogical libraries. Subsequent research has revealed that Wilmer's hypotheses were incorrect, although he is to be commended for his enthusiasm and for his stimulation of interest in Graham family history.

Child:

7-9 James Wilmer, b. Moline, IL,
    3 December 1925

## CHILD OF 5-45 HARVEY MILLIGAN GRAHAM
## AND NETTIE B. MOORE

6-26 HAROLD M. GRAHAM,[12] born 12 September, 1890, died 17 February 1918, buried Monmouth Cemetery; unmarried. The word *Lt.*, probably meaning 'Lieutenant,' is inscribed on his gravestone.


## CHILDREN OF 5-46 EDWIN YOUNG GRAHAM
## AND ADAH HURD [13]

6-27 LEILA GRAHAM GRAY; married OLAN GRAY. Children:

    A. Chester Gray

    B. Martha Gray


6-28 RALPH GRAHAM; married LULU ___. Children:

    7-10 Adah            7-12 Leila K.
    7-11 Ralph Jr.       7-13 Joyce L.


## CHILDREN OF 5-50 EDWARD YOUNG GRAHAM
## AND AUGUSTA BENNETT

6-29 HARRY B. GRAHAM, born Monmouth, Illinois, *c.* 1873, died ___; married ___. In the 1889 San Francisco city directory, Harry was listed as a clerk in his parents' business, Graham Decorative Art. In the 1910 census he was listed as living at the Wellington Hotel, occupation "accountant," and he had been married once for sixteen years. In 1912 he and his mother lived at 208 Pacific Building on Market Street. His occupation as given in the city directory was clerk at Wayman and Henry Company, Insurance Agents. He did not appear in the directory thereafter.

6-30 ALDEN MAX GRAHAM (called Max), born Monmouth, Illinois, *c.* 1876. He was listed with his father in the 1900 census of San Francisco, his occupation given as "soldier USA." When his father died in 1910, Max was living in Walla Walla, Washington.

6-31 ELIZABETH MAY GRAHAM BREHM (called Bessie or Bess),[14] born Monmouth, Illinois, *c.* 1878, died Seattle, Washington, 24 August 1957; married, before 1910, GEORGE OTTO BREHM, born San Francisco, California, *c.* 1878, died Seattle, Washington, 29 March 1962.

Bessie was graduated from the University of California in 1901 and taught school for a short time at San Jacinta and Napa, California. After she and George moved to Seattle, she eventually became active with the girl scouts and was on the board of directors of the Seattle-King County Girl Scouts for many years. Also for many years she was a member of the first garden committee of the Children's Orthopedic Hospital. In her other activities she was a charter member of the Women's University Club, a member of the Lake Washington Garden Club, and a member of a Republican women's organization. George was graduated from the University of California and was listed in the 1901-2 San Francisco city directory as a cellarman at Eisen Vineyard Company. Soon after that time he spent two years in the consular service in China. Moving to Seattle in 1906, he was first a butter and egg broker and by 1909 was the president of the United Produce Company. By 1936 he owned a line of delicatessens in Seattle known as Brehm Food Stores. The business ceased operating probably in about 1959-60.

Children:

A. Katherine Brehm            B. Edward G. Brehm

A. Katherine Brehm Pohlman, born probably in Seattle, Washington, died perhaps in Atherton, California, before 29 March 1962; married Kingsley Pohlman. The reason it is thought she died before 29 March 1962 is that her father died then, and she was not mentioned in his obituary. She and her husband lived in

5-51 William F.C., 4-13 John M., 3-6 Robert C., 2-1 Andrew          6-31B

Atherton, California. She had children.

B. Edward G. Brehm (called Ed), born probably in Seattle, Washington, still alive in 1983; married (1) ___; (2), before 1960, Virginia ___. Ed was in joint ownership with his father of Brehm's Food Stores until the business ceased operating probably about 1960. In the Bellevue-Kirkland city directories (suburbs of Seattle), he was listed as a general contractor, 1960-71, and as occupied in "quantity surveying," 1972-83.

   Children by (1) ___:

   1. George A. Brehm; married Kathy ___. They were listed in the 1975-7 city directories of Bellevue-Kirkland, Washington, suburb of Seattle.

   2. Ellen Brehm

   Children by (2) Virginia ___:

   3. Karl F. Brehm; married (1) Joyia or Loyia ___; (2), c. 1983, Stephanie ___. In the 1970-2 city directories of Bellevue-Kirkland, Washington, Karl was listed as a student and was living with his parents. By 1975 he and his first wife had their own home, and he worked at Bon Marché. By 1976 he was a financial collector and by 1977 an assistant manager of public finance.

   4. Keith Brehm, born 1950. In the 1970-2 city directories of Bellevue-Kirkland, Washington, Keith was listed as a student and was living with his parents. In 1973 he was listed as a member of the United States Navy.


CHILDREN OF 5-51 WILLIAM FRANCIS CLAYBAUGH GRAHAM
AND 4-29 MARY MARGARET GRAHAM [15]


6-32 CHARLES M. GRAHAM, born Illinois, 11 August 1867, died 1953. He lived in LaGrande, Oregon.

6-33 FRED Y. GRAHAM, born Iowa, 14 December 1868, died after 1929; married in 1898, MELCENA (or Millie) ___, born Iowa, December 1876. They first lived in Chariton City, Lucas County, Iowa, where he was a cigar maker. In 1929, according to testimony in his father's pension records, they were living at Cresco, Howard County, Iowa, Children, all born in Iowa:

| | |
|---|---|
| 7-14 Lee W. (or William L.) b. October 1899 | 7-15 Richard C., b. *c.* 1904 <br> 7-16 Donald E., b. January 1910 |

6-34 LILLIAN ADELINE GRAHAM MAUK (called Addie), born Iowa, 30 December 1870, died 1952, buried Chariton Cemetery, Lucas County, Iowa; married WILLIAM A. MAUK, born 1870, died 1950, buried Chariton Cemetery, Lucas County, Iowa. Children:

A. Margaret Mauk Dixon, born 1900; married Raymond Dixon. They lived in Lucas County, Iowa.

B. Helen Mauk Bristow, buried Chariton Cemetery; married Harry Bristow.

C. Raymond Mauk. He lived in Omaha.

6-35 MARTHA ELLEN GRAHAM WETZEL (called Nelly), born Iowa, 4 October 1872, died 1967, buried Fort Collins, Colorado; married LEONARD A. WETZEL. Children:

A. Orvil Wetzel. He lived in California.

B. Mildred Wetzel, deceased.

6-36 SOPHIA JANE GRAHAM ISAACSON (called Jennie), born Iowa, 4 October 1874, died 1957; married in Warren County, Illinois, 19 February 1902, John A. ISAACSON (called Gus).[16] They lived in Clear Lake, Iowa. Known children:

A. Keith Isaacson

B. Mary Isaacson

6-37 LELA ELISE GRAHAM CROSSLEY MYERS (called Dot; twin to next), born Moberly, Missouri, 15 June 1878, died November 1961, buried Chariton Cemetery, Lucas County, Iowa; married (1) JOHN CROSSLEY; (2) ___ MYERS. Dot and her first husband had a business in Winterset, Iowa. No children.

6-38 LULA ALICE GRAHAM PATON (called Doll; twin to above), born Moberly, Missouri, 15 June 1878, died August 1967, buried Chariton Cemetery, Lucas County, Iowa; married, 29 October 1901, PETER T. PATON. Children:

- A. Paul Theodore Paton, b. 5 June 1902
- B. Robert Gerald Paton, b. 22 July 1905
- C. Martha K. Paton, b. 23 January 1911
- D. Ralph Thomas Paton, b. 9 June 1914
- E. Richard William Paton, b. 28 July 1918

---

A. Paul Theodore Paton, born 5 June 1902, died April 1954, buried Chariton Cemetery, Iowa; married Estaline Ross. Child:

1. Beverly Bayne Paton Clayton, born 1923; married ___ Clayton. They live in Des Moines.

B. Robert Gerald Paton, born 22 July 1905, died 1960, buried Glendale Cemetery, Des Moines, Iowa; married Mae Graham (no relation). Children:

1. Robert D. Paton, born 1933. He lives in Des Moines.

2. William Graham Paton, born 1935. He lives in Oskaloosa, Iowa.

3. Larry Paul Paton, born 1944

C. Martha K. Paton, born Chariton, Lucas County, Iowa, 23 January 1911; unmarried. Martha studied typing and shorthand at a business school in Omaha, Nebraska, then moved to Winterset, Iowa, where her aunt and uncle 6-37 Dot and John Crossley lived and had a business. At first Martha worked at the Percival and Wilkinson Law Office, then for Jim Silliman, a bill collector. In her capacity as receptionist she was shared by Silliman and Charles Van Werden, an attorney, and in April

1930 she began doing legal secretarial work for Van Werden. She was his legal secretary until his death in 1955 when Gordon Darling took over the firm with the stipulation that "I'll take over if Martha will stay." During her career Martha worked on many criminal and civil cases and compiled tax returns, and on 31 May 1986 she retired after fifty-six years as a well-known legal secretary. Her other activities have included the position of financial and church secretary for the First United Presbyterian Church in Winterset. She was also a secretary for thirty years and a member for fifty years of the Eastern Star, and a member of the Studious Moderns Club which she describes as "neither studious nor modern." She also sews and knits and in the eleven-year period from 1975 to 1986 made seventy-seven afghans all of which she gave away.

D. Ralph Thomas Paton, born 9 June 1914; married Leticia ___. They live in Alexandria, Virginia. Children:

1. John Melvin Paton

2. Richard Louis Paton

E. Richard William Paton, born 28 July 1918, died 1972, body to the University Hospital, Iowa City; married Betty Cox. Children:

1. Gwen Marie Paton, born 1945. She lives in Des Moines.

2. Jeanne K. Paton Roberts, born 1950; married ___ Roberts. She lives in Woodstock, New York.

6-39 WILLIAM J. GRAHAM, born Iowa, 5 April 1885, died 1909, buried Chariton Cemetery, Lucas County, Iowa.

## CHILD OF 5-53 ROBERT ALEXANDER GRAHAM AND (1) ANGELINE M. ___

6-40 NORMA H. GRAHAM COMPTON, born Iowa, c. 1878, died ___; married JAMES E. COMPTON, born California, c. 1868, died before 1914. In

5-53 R. Alexander, 4-13 John M., 3-6 Robert C., 2-1 Andrew 6-41

the 1906 Oakland, California, city directory, James was listed as a conductor for Oakland Traction. In the 1907-14 directories, he was listed as a car operator for the San Francisco, Oakland, and San Jose Railroad. His and Norma's home was on Manila. After James died, Norma was listed at 2209 Telegraph Avenue in 1915 and in 1916-17 at the Casadilla Apartments where she was the manager in 1916. When her father died in 1919, she was living at 6532 Dover Street, Oakland, California. No known children.

CHILDREN OF 5-53 ROBERT ALEXANDER GRAHAM
AND (2) ELIZA WOLFE

6-41 OLIVER HOWARD GRAHAM, born South Pasadena, California, March 1899, died South Pasadena, 21 July 1908, buried Mountain View Cemetery, Altadena, California.

6-42 DONALD D. GRAHAM, born South Pasadena, California, *c.* 1902. In the Pasadena city directories, Donald was listed as a clerk in 1920-23, a student in 1924, a clerk in 1926, and a salesman in 1930. He lived with his mother at 1757 Rose Villa.

6-43 PAULINE W. GRAHAM WALMSLEY, born South Pasadena, California, *c.* 1905; married in Pasadena, 31 July 1925, FRED F. WALMSLEY.[17] In the 1924 Pasadena city directory, Pauline was listed as a stenographer and in 1925 as a student.

6-44 EARL A. GRAHAM, born South Pasadena, California, *c.* 1907. Earl was listed in the Pasadena city directories from 1925 to 1941. He was a gardener and lived with his mother at 1757 Rose Villa.

6-45 FRANK C. GRAHAM, born South Pasadena, California, November 1909

5-58 James G., 4-16 Andrew E., 3-6 Robert C., 2-1 Andrew                                6-46

## CHILDREN OF 5-58 JAMES GILLESPIE GRAHAM
## AND LOUIE JANE MAYNE [18]


6-46 MARY T. GRAHAM BADGER (called Mamie), born Richland, Indiana, 2 December 1878, died Greeley, Colorado, 22 February 1940; married, c. 1904, HERBERT E. BADGER, born Colorado, c. 1878, later divorced. In the 1910 federal census, they were listed in Greeley, Colorado. He was a civil engineer. Children:

   A. Mary Badger, b. c. 1907    C. Robert E. Badger
   B. Alice Badger, b. c. September 1909

---

   A. Mary Badger Mitchell, born probably in Greeley, Colorado, c. 1907; married Nathaniel Mitchell. She is a retired teacher and guidance counselor. He is a retired maintenance worker at Aims Community College in Colorado. Child:

      1. Willis D. Mitchell, born c. 1933, died of a coronary in November 1976 at the age of 43. He was a principal of a school and moved to Alaska where he died. He married (1) ___; (2) Jan ___. He had three children by his first wife and two by his second:

         a. Anthony Mitchell

         b. Jacqueline Mitchell

         c. ___ Mitchell

         d. Cary Mitchell

         e. Amanda Mitchell

   B. Alice Badger Booth, born probably in Greeley, Colorado, c. September, 1909; married George Booth, deceased. She is a retired secretary living in Colorado; he was a train engineer. No children.

   C. Robert E. Badger, deceased; married Betty___ who lives in Colorado. Children:

      1. Barbara Badger Barker; married Samuel Barker. They live

5-58 James G., 4-16 Andrew E., 3-6 Robert C., 2-1 Andrew

in Trinidad, Colorado, where he is a wheat farmer.

2. Robert Badger, married and lives in Colorado.

6-47 MELCENA M. GRAHAM HOWARD, born Richland, Indiana, 9 April 1882, died Greeley, Colorado, 26 April 1955; married WELLINGTON HOWARD. Children:

| | | | |
|---|---|---|---|
| A. | Graham Howard | C. | James Howard |
| B. | Oliver Howard | D. | William Howard |

A. Graham Howard; married Dorothy ___. He is a farmer, and Dorothy is a guidance counselor in a junior high school. Formerly he worked as an engineer on a plantation in Haiti. Their three children were reared there. Children:

1. Wellington Howard (called Wix); married and has four children.

2. Robert Howard (called Tito); married and has twin boys.

3. Michael Howard; married and has two boys.

B. Oliver Howard, deceased; married Lucille Miller. He was a farmer in Colorado. Children:

1. Margaret Howard. She and her brother were killed at an auto racing track. They were walking along the fence when one of the cars crashed through, killing them.

2. ___ Howard (boy), killed at an auto racing track with his sister. See above.

3. Gary Howard; married Yvonne ___. They have four children, three boys and a girl, and live in Alaska.

4. Joseph Howard; married Joyce ___. She was married once before and has a daughter whom Joseph adopted. They also have another girl born to them both.

5. Charles Howard; married and has two children.

6. Wayne Howard

7. Martha Howard

C. James Howard; married Marian ___. He is a farmer in Colorado. Children:

1. Katharine Howard (Kathy); married and has two children.

2. Ann Howard; married ___.

D. William Howard; married Ruth ___. Children:

1. James Howard; married Susan ___. He does art work and layouts for magazines. No children.

2. John Howard

3. Thomas Howard

6-48 ANNA DALE GRAHAM SMILLIE, born Richland, Indiana, 2 April 1885, died San Fernando, Los Angeles County, California, 1 September 1961; married, c. 1909, JAMES DICKSON SMILLIE, born Colorado, c. 1885. In the 1910 federal census, they were listed in Eaton, Weld County, Colorado. He was a farmer. Children:

A. James Dickson Smillie Jr. (called Dick); married Margaret ___. They live in the Los Angeles area. Child:

1. Joan Smillie McCurran; married Henry McCurran and has one child.

B. John G. Smillie (Jack); married Ruth ___. He is a retired physician living in the Los Angeles area. They have several children.

6-49 MYRA KATHARINE GRAHAM AVERY, born Greeley, Colorado, 15 April 1892, died Greeley, 12 November 1978, buried Linn Grove Cemetery, Greeley; married in Storm Lake, Iowa, 6 December 1917, CHARLES DWIGHT AVERY (called Dwight), born Galesville, Wisconsin, 29 July 1877, died Takoma Park, Maryland, 1 February 1947, son of Dr. Henry Newel Avery and Catherine Sebring Fowler.

Myra was graduated from the University of Northern Colorado in 1912 and taught school for a time at Cheyenne, Wyoming. Dwight

5-58 James G., 4-16 Andrew E., 3-6 Robert C., 2-1 Andrew                6-49A

was a geological civil engineer working in Washington, D.C. After
he died Myra lived with her daughter, Nancy, in Brownsville,
Pennsylvania. In 1976 Myra moved with her daughter and her family
to Greeley, Colorado, where Myra had been born. Child:

A.  Nancy Avery Kuhl, born Cheyenne, Wyoming, 31 January 1919,
    died in Greeley, Colorado, after open heart surgery, 30 May
    1986; married in Takoma Park, Maryland, 20 June 1942, Charles
    Avery Kuhl, born Belle Vernon, Pennsylvania, 20 October 1917,
    son of Andrew Peter Kuhl (1893-1973) and Lenora Lillian
    Kohnfelder (1894-1984). Nancy was a teacher before she was
    married. In 1982 she earned an additional degree, bachelor of
    fine arts at the University of Northern Colorado. Charles is
    a retired metallurgist for Wheeling-Pittsburgh Steel. In 1976
    they moved to Greeley, Colorado, where they were active in the
    Friends of the Library and in historical societies. For
    several summers they also were Volunteers in Park for the
    National Park Service. Children:

    1.  Nancy Louise Kuhl Cochran Vasquez, born Pittsburgh, Penn-
        sylvania, 13 September 1943; married (1) at Greensville,
        South Carolina, 17 August 1962, Donald Sturgeon Cochran
        Jr., divorced 1976; she married (2) at Cherryfield, Maine,
        21 July 1979, William Vasquez. She is a teacher in a high
        school in Maine. Children, both by her first husband:

        a.  Nancy Lynn Cochran, born Clearfield, Pennsylvania, 22
            August 1964

        b.  Donald Andrew Cochran, born Homestead, Florida, 23 May
            1969

    2.  Barbara Jean Kuhl Roe, born Pittsburgh, Pennsylvania, 31
        January 1946; married at Monongahela, Pennsylvania, 15
        June 1967, Richard Lewis Roe. He was working on a
        doctorate in history at the University of Wisconsin but
        did not complete it. Later they both worked for the state
        of Wisconsin. They live in Madison, Wisconsin. Children:

        a.  Meghan Marie Roe, born Madison, Wisconsin, 19 December
            1971

        b.  Meredith Leigh Roe, born Madison, Wisconsin, 20 July
            1974

    3.  Dwight Charles Kuhl (called Dick), born Washington, Penn-
        sylvania, 25 January 1954; married in June 1983, Gayna

5-64 Alva E., 4-23 J. Thomas, 3-8 William M., 2-1 Andrew                6-49A4

Dawson. He was a salesman for a lumber company in Casper, Wyoming, and later worked in the oil fields there, his base being Casper. Gayna is a nurse.

4. Katharine Lynn Kuhl Faye (Kathy), born North Charleroi, Washington County, Pennsylvania, 16 August 1958; married in Dalton, Massachusetts, 3 July 1982, William Clifford Faye, son of Robert G. Faye and Christina ___. Kathy attended the University of Northern Colorado where she was the junior honorary president of Pi Mu Epsilon, a math honorary, and secretary of the American Chemistry Society. She then switched to Oregon State University, Corvallis, and earned her bachelor's in microbiology in 1980 and her master's in civil engineering (environmental) in 1981. Her husband earned his bachelor's at Southeastern Massachusetts University and his master's at Oregon State. In 1982 he was a mechanical engineer at Stone and Webster, Boston, while Kathy was doing medical research in blood clotting for Boston University. They live in Cambridge, Massachusetts.

CHILDREN OF 5-64 ALVA EDSON GRAHAM
AND JANE WINTER [19]


6-50 EDGAR LLOYD GRAHAM, born Kansas, 21 May 1887, died ___. He lived in Iowa.


6-51 GEORGE RAYMOND GRAHAM (called Scotchie), born Oregon, 6 November 1891, died ___; married RUBY SNYDER. In the 1910 census of Marshall County, Kansas, George was listed in the household of his uncle 5-73 Frank I. Graham. Children:

7-17 Virginia            7-19 Doris
7-18 Georgia


6-52 IDA MELISSA GRAHAM LINNEL, born Missouri, 25 April 1897; married RICHARD LINNEL. Children:

5-65 Andrew R., 4-23 J. Thomas, 3-8 William M., 2-1 Andrew        6-52A

    A. Richard Vaughn Linnel; married Beverly ___. Children:

        1. Richard Vaughn Linnel Jr.

        2. Vickie Diane Linnel

        3. Robin Linnel

        4. Kevin Lee Linnel

    B. Betty Jane Linnel Skoog; married Clifford Skoog. Children:

        1. Connie Skoog

        2. Gary Skoog

        3. Kim Skoog

    C. Iva Ann Linnel; married Westey Wegley. Children:

        1. Chris Wegley

        2. Thomas Wegley

        3. Annette Wegley

6-53 RALPH A. GRAHAM, born Kansas, 9 August 1902


CHILDREN OF 5-65 ANDREW RICHARD GRAHAM
AND BERTHA GERTRUDE SPRINGER [20]


6-54 HENRY CLAY GRAHAM, born Geary County, Kansas, 13 or 18 May 1902; married in Oklahoma, NORA ___.

6-55 FREDERICK LAWRENCE GRAHAM, born Hill City, Kansas, 4 September 1904, died Beattie, Kansas, 14 February 1973, buried Liberty, Nebraska; married, May 1933, KATHRYN PATTERSON, born 13 December

1908. Kathryn now lives in Omaha. Children:

7-20 Ruth Arlene, b. Beattie, KS, 10 July 1935
7-21 Marilyn Jo Ann, b. Marysville, KS, 12 July 1939
7-22 Charles Richard, b. Barneston, NE, 3 January 1944

6-56 MELVIN R. GRAHAM, born Hill City, Kansas, 7 September 1907, died Beattie, Kansas, 28 October 1964; unmarried.

6-57 JOHN HOWARD GRAHAM (called Howard), born Summerfield, Kansas, 8 October 1910, died Burns, Oregon, c. 1965; married in Idaho, 30 April 1941, EDNA BROADHEAD. Edna married (2) Don Bartell. Children:

7-23 Twila
7-24 Richard
7-25 Lester

6-58 ETTA LOUISE GRAHAM SUTTON BENSON (called Louise), born Summerfield, Kansas, 26 December 1915; married (1) in Kansas, ALFRED SUTTON; (2) DALE BENSON. In about 1982 Louise was living in Alliance, Nebraska. Known Children:

A. Carol Sutton

B. Charlene Sutton

C. Alfred Sutton Jr.

## CHILDREN OF 5-67 HARRY WILFORD GRAHAM AND DORA ROSETTA SMITH [21]

6-59 ROY EDSON GRAHAM, born Concordia, Kansas, 19 October 1889, died Aberdeen, Washington, 24 December 1969, buried Aberdeen; married in Anacortes, Washington, 5 December 1910, AMY ELIZABETH WADE,

5-67 Harry W., 4-23 J. Thomas, 3-8 William M., 2-1 Andrew       6-60

born Brownsburg, Quebec, Canada, 1 May 1892, died Anacortes, Washington, 25 September 1940, buried Anacortes, daughter of William John Wade (born Brownsburg, Quebec, 25 March 1865, died Anacortes, Washington, 28 August 1933) and Catherine Ann O'Byrne (born Brownsburg, Quebec, 27 March 1866, died Bellingham, Washington, 21 March 1938). Roy and Amy were divorced *c.* 1916, and he married (2) *c.* 1920, MRS. EDNA BULLOCK HOUSTON who was divorced or widowed. Edna had two children by her previous marriage: Jack and Louise. Amy married (2) in 1918, Dr. Earl Aurelius Sweet, a dentist at Mount Vernon, Washington.

Roy first worked as a shingle weaver in the shingle mill owned by his father, 5-67 Harry W. After Harry sold the mill in 1922, he bought Fomo's grocery in Anacortes which Roy managed until Harry died on 8 August 1928. That experience gave him the training he needed for the profession he followed for many years-- managing the Tradewell chain store. In 1942 he moved to Aberdeen, Washington, where he put his cooking expertise to profit by opening The Donut Bar located at a busy downtown intersection. It became a very popular breakfast and lunch spot for the Aberdeen business community. He was a life member of Anacortes Elks, Lodge 1204, and his hobbies included dancing, cooking, wood working, and fishing. He retired in 1963 at which time he especially pursued his interest in fishing.

Amy was a milliner before her marriage and a dental assistant from 1918 to 1933. She also had an operatic voice and sang on a Seattle radio station. Her hobbies included needlework and dancing. In 1933 she returned to Anacortes where she lived with her daughter until her death. Child of Roy and Amy, born Anacortes, Washington:

7-26 Erma Lorene, b. 13 May 1912


6-60 CLARA LENORE GRAHAM PROPST, born Concordia, Kansas, 8 April 1891, died Anacortes, Washington, 21 September 1980; married at Anacortes, 3 September 1910, WILLIAM VADEN PROPST, born West Virginia, 26 June 1890, died 2 October 1979. Children:

A. Verna Propst Moore Bowles, born 18 April 1911; married (1) ___ Moore; (2) Jack Bowles. Child:

   1. Rupert Vaden Moore

B. Arlene Propst Blackwell, born 9 June 1913; married Lyle

5-67 Harry W., 4-23 J. Thomas, 3-8 William M., 2-1 Andrew

Blackwell. They live in Lynnwood, Washington. Children:

1. Audre Blackwell Gilden, born 1931; married Elmer Gilden. Children:

   a. Claudia Gilden, born 1950

   b. Garth Gilden, born 1952; married ___ and has a child.

   c. Gene Gilden, born 1954; married ___ and has three children.

2. Gail Blackwell Field, born 1945; married George Field, since divorced. Children:

   a. Julie Renee Field, born 1960

   b. John Allan Field, born 1962

6-61 LULU MAUDE GRAHAM JONES (called Maude), born Concordia, Kansas, 28 June 1893, died Anacortes, Washington, 25 December 1975; married in Anacortes, 6 January 1920, BERT JONES. He owned a fishing boat and made trips to Alaska. Lorna Howard Cline (5-71B) writes that she never forgot the time he took her, her parents, and her sister Lorene out twelve miles on Puget Sound to watch a salmon trap lifted. They reared Marilyn Smith, daughter of Maude's sister 6-64 Stella. No children of their own.

6-62 PEARL WARD GRAHAM (boy; called Dutch), born Concordia, Kansas, 1 August 1896, died Redmond, Washington, 6 December 1981; married in Seattle, 8 April 1945, VICTORIA KROENER. No children.

6-63 EDA M. BLANCHE GRAHAM, born Concordia, Kansas, 4 April 1898, died Anacortes, Washington, 10 January 1912.

6-64 STELLA GLADYS GRAHAM SMITH, born Concordia, Kansas, 24 March 1901, died Anacortes, Washington, 16 March 1931; married at Anacortes, 8 March 1922, GEORGE D. SMITH. Children:

5-67 Harry W., 4-23 J. Thomas, 3-8 William M., 2-1 Andrew          6-64A

A.  Gordon Smith, born ___, died c. 1984.

B.  Ardelle Smith King; married ___ King, since divorced. She lives in Yakima, Washington, where she works in an insurance office. She has one daughter and two sons.

C.  Marilyn Smith Coberly, born 16 March 1931; married ___ Coberly. Marilyn's mother died at Marilyn's birth, and her aunt 6-61 Maude Graham Jones reared her. She has three daughters.

6-65 THEODORE OSCAR GRAHAM, born Concordia, Kansas, 3 July 1903, died Anacortes, Washington, 19 August 1976; married at Anacortes, 9 January 1946, J. ELVINA ERICKSON SETTERLAND, born Munising, Michigan, 3 January 1905, daughter of John Setterland (born Varmland, Sweden, February 1876, died Seattle, Washington, 1945) and Pauline Erickson (born Varmland, Sweden, 23 November 1882, died Anacortes, Washington, March 1970). In a letter dated 13 July 1989, Elvina wrote:

> I'm getting old, 84½ years, and have had two strokes three years ago and am living alone with no one to help me and I don't type and don't write very well. So maybe you can put the stuff I write in the right places. I met Ted in 1943 after he got out of the army. He was living with his mother as all the other children had left. I don't know anything about his army records. I know he was taken in when he was 39 years old and had just gotten home from Alaska on a fishing boat. They didn't keep him long, less than a year, as they needed fishermen, so he was sent home. Fishing was over for the season so he took a job in the butcher shop at Tradewell's stores. He was there for 1 year then in 1944 he worked at Anacortes Post Office carrying mail which he really enjoyed. After our marriage on January 9, 1946 he went to work in the Anacortes Plywood Mill till he retired 20 years later. Ted belonged to the Eagles, Elks, American legion, and helped the clubs out whenever he could. He went to Anacortes high school but didn't graduate but went to business college. Ted was the last to leave home and to get married. We had a boat and a camper (Chinook) so we traveled a lot. So I'd say we had a wonderful 30½ year life together. He was a wonderful man.

Elvina and Ted had no children.

6-66 ARLENE ALICE GRAHAM KRUG (called Arlie), born Anacortes, Washington, 14 July 1906, died Woodburn, Oregon, 13 December 1982; married at Reno, Nevada, 5 September 1931, ALVIN F. KRUG, born c. 1905. Alvin managed a Safeway store in Reno and later was a partner in Nevada Produce Company. He then spent three years in the United States Air Force. In 1945, he and Arlie moved to Seattle where he variously managed supermarkets, worked in drug supplies, and sold real estate. Arlie helped to handle their drug supply business and had a photography business of her own. No children. After Arlie died Alvin married (2) ___.

## CHILDREN OF 5-68 JOHN GILCHRIST GRAHAM
## AND CLARA BELLE CONARD [22]

6-67 RAY WILLIAM GRAHAM, born Nebraska, 9 January 1893, died Fairfield Bay, Arkansas, 21 October 1975, buried Eglantine Cemetery, Eglantine, Arkansas; married near Liberty, Nebraska, 14 September 1922, ANNA MARIA WITTMUSS, born Nebraska, 27 October 1897, still alive in 1989, daughter of Albert F. F. Wittmuss (born Germany, 18 July 1868, died Wymore, Nebraska, 1958) and Louisa Sophia Walker (born Germany, 23 October 1870, died Wymore, Nebraska, 1957).

During World War I Ray served in the Army Wagoneers, a group which transported ammunition. After he and Anna were married in 1922, they lived for two years on a rented farm called the Wherry place in Marshall County, Kansas, near the Kansas-Nebraska border. They then rented the Wagner farm, located near Ray's parents, where they lived for four years. In 1928 they bought 160 acres on the Nebraska side of the Kansas-Nebraska line and moved to it in 1929, living there for the next forty-six years. Some time later they bought 80 additional acres. The house had once belonged to Anna's Grandfather Walker and had been rented out for a lengthy time so that it had been neglected and required much repair. Fortunately, Ray had considerable mechanical and carpentry skills and not only repaired the house and farm buildings, but also was able to keep his machines in working condition during the Great Depression and did not have to buy expensive new machinery. When rural electricity finally arrived in 1936, he and his cousin 6-76 Marvin did most of the electrical wiring in the entire area. He and Anna were members of the North Elm Christian Church where he taught an adult Sunday school class, sang bass in the quartet,

and served as a deacon.  In 1947 and 1948 they moved first to
Pittsburg, Kansas, to help their son begin his business, then to
Summerfield, Kansas, to help care for Ray's ailing father and
invalid sister, Izetta.  Returning to the farm in late 1948, they
continued farming until about 1972 when they decided to retire and
sold their west 160 acres to a Robert Osterhaus on condition that
they continue to live there rent-free for as long as they wished.
The east 80 acres were rented to the Osterhaus family.  In 1970
they had bought a lot in Fairfield Bay, Arkansas, trading it for a
condominium there in 1972, and in 1975 they decided to move to
their condominium.  Unfortunately, Ray became ill during the
transactions and died a month after they moved to Arkansas.

Anna, Ray's wife, told his "biography" to their daughter, Rae
Graham Darner, who transcribed it in 1988 and distributed copies
to family members.  Included in the transcription were several
entertaining stories one of which pertained to the old frontier
custom of the shivaree which still prevailed in that area when Ray
and Anna were married in 1922:

> When Ray and Anna returned to Kansas [after their
> honeymoon], they found the community primed for the shi-
> varee they felt was owed them.  It was the custom for the
> neighbors to gather wherever the newlyweds were staying
> and make a big racket until the groom appeared to ask
> what it would take to make them stop.  The crowd would
> demand "the treats" usually specifying the kind they
> wanted--an oyster supper, an ice cream supper, etc.  The
> "treats" came out of the groom's pocket.
>
> Ray and Anna were staying at Ray's in-laws.  The
> threshing crew had been working there and the machinery
> was still in the barnyard.  When the day's work was done,
> the engineer of the steam engine stoked the fires to
> build up a full head of steam.  That evening when the
> crowd had gathered, the engineer drove the steam engine
> to the front of the house and tied the whistle down.  The
> ensuing shriek, plus the accompanying bell ringing and
> pot banging from the crowd, was deafening.  Since it
> wasn't sporting to give in too soon, Ray and Anna shut
> themselves in a closet and covered their ears.
>
> Anna's brother Louie and her Uncle George decided to
> create a diversion.  George put on a dress and the two of
> them slipped out into the twilight and ran from the house
> toward the timber.  The crowd let out a roar and it took
> them a few minutes to realize that their quarry had not

escaped after all. At last Ray stepped out and agreed to
the crowd's demand for an ice cream supper. The time and
place were set and everyone came up to offer congratula-
lations. The shivaree was over and the crowd dispersed.

Another story from Anna's account is as follows:

> The well had gone dry, and the farmstead was without
> water. All the time the search for a new source of water
> was taking place, Ray had to haul water for the stock
> tanks and for household use. After a long day in the
> fields, the water still had to be hauled. Water in abun-
> dant supply was finally found, but it was nearly a quar-
> ter of a mile from the house. Ray began the arduous task
> of digging a four-foot deep trench for a pipeline from
> the well site to the stock tanks. One morning North Elm
> church members arrived unannounced. The men brought
> their tools; their wives brought food. By the end of the
> day, the trench was finished. . . .
>
> The remoteness of the water supply turned out to be
> a blessing in disguise. Since the pipe line went by the
> house to reach the stock tanks, it took only a short spur
> line to put running water into the house. Had the water
> been found in either of the dry wells that were dug, Anna
> would have continued, like everyone else in the
> community, to carry water in from the pump.

Later Ray and Anna found an agreeable hobby in traveling:

> In 1961, Ray and Anna bought a travel trailer. It
> was a nineteen-foot Shasta with all conveniences and
> sleeping room for four--five, if you didn't mind crow-
> ding. For the first time in their lives, Ray and Anna
> were free to take winter vacations, and Ray enjoyed their
> trips immensely. They would hardly get home before he
> would ask, "Where shall we go next time?" Their trips
> took them into Texas, Arizona, California, Washington,
> into Canada, South Dakota, Florida, and the Carolinas.

Another hobby was singing. For many years they were part of
a quartet which sang at funerals, and Ray would hire someone to
take his place in the field so that he could sing in the quartet
when necessary. Anna still sings in the Methodist church choir.

Children:

5-68 John G., 4-23 J. Thomas, 3-8 William M., 2-1 Andrew                                    6-68

7-27 Calvin Wittmuss, b. Beat-        7-29 ___ (boy), b. and d.
     tie, KS, 11 October 1924              c. 1928
7-28 Rae Marie, b. Summerfield,
     KS, 13 June 1926


6-68 AVA EOLA GRAHAM SHUCK, born Summerfield, Marshall County, Kansas, 19 June 1895, died Springfield, Missouri, 16 June 1978; married, June 1920, ROBERT LEE SHUCK, born Fairburg, Nebraska, 1 July 1893, died Springfield, Missouri, 2 February 1972. Child:

A. Jack Dean Shuck, born Lincoln, Nebraska, 9 January 1924; married, 17 November 1945, Betty Jean Call, born Springfield, Missouri, 23 March 1922, daughter of Leslie Call and Julia ___. They live in Houston, Texas. Children:

1. Robert Leslie Shuck, born Maryville, Missouri, 17 August 1946; married (1) in November 1967, Rebecca Dixon, later divorced; (2) in 1973, Linda Phillips, divorced in 1976; (3) in September 1978, Priscilla Parker. They live in Beaumont, Texas.

   Child by (1) Rebecca Dixon:

   a. Richard Lee Shuck, born 18 August 1968. He lives in Connecticut.

   Child by (3) Priscilla Parker:

   b. Jason Dean Shuck, born 3 November 1979

2. Carol Jean Shuck Rodgers, born Springfield, Missouri, 5 December 1951; married, June 1974, Max Edwin Rodgers, divorced in November 1978.


6-69 IVA IZETTA GRAHAM, born Nebraska, 13 December 1896, died Summerfield, Kansas, 1 or 9 January 1949; unmarried. When she was eight years old, she developed a high fever which caused mental impairment. She never fully recovered.


6-70 THELMA ELIZABETH GRAHAM MCCLELLAN, born Pawnee County, Nebraska, 3 October 1898, died Summerfield, Kansas, 25 December 1982, buried

5-68 John G., 4-23 J. Thomas, 3-8 William M., 2-1 Andrew                6-70A

Summerfield, Kansas; married at Marysville, Kansas, 5 March 1927, EVERETT J. MCCLELLAN, born Huntington, Indiana, 7 November 1895, died at Pawnee, Nebraska, 10 July 1972. Thelma was a teacher. Children, all born in Armour, Nebraska:

A. Eugene Ray McClellan,
   b. 8 April 1929
B. Margie Marie McClellan,
   b. 8 August 1930
C. Richard Duane McClellan,
   b. 24 May 1932

---

A. Eugene Ray McClellan, born Armour, Nebraska, 8 April 1929; married at Venice, Ohio, 11 February 1956, Janet Anne Pooch, born Castalia, Ohio, 15 May 1933, daughter of William H. Pooch and Dorothy E. Krawetzki. Children:

1. Donald Eugene McClellan, born Pawnee City, Nebraska, 31 October 1956, died 16 August 1974.

2. William Everett McClellan, born Pawnee City, Nebraska, 2 September 1957; married, 20 April 1985, 6-83D1 Joni Lynn Whitebread, born 16 February 1962, daughter of Darel Gene Whitebread and 6-83D Nancy Elaine Grauer. Child:

   a. Christopher William McClellan, born 20 December 1986

3. Marla Kay McClellan, born Pawnee City, Nebraska, 28 April 1959. Child:

   a. Donald Michael McClellan, born 29 November 1982

4. Timothy Ray McClellan, born Pawnee City, Nebraska, 6 February 1961; married, 29 May 1982, Judy Weber, born 1 March 1963. Child:

   a. Samantha Ann McClellan, born 10 July 1986

5. Eugene Ray McClellan Jr., born Pawnee City, Nebraska, 5 February 1962; married (1) 11 February 1980, Karen Janssen, born 14 January 1961, since divorced; (2) 9 August 1982, Candace Berenstein, born 15 June 19__.

   Children by (1) Karen Janssen:

   a. Shawn Eugene McClellan, born 24 April 1980

b. Crystal Shay McClellan, born 25 June 1981

   Child by (2) Candace Berenstein:

c. Janet Louise McClellan, born 3 February 1983

6. Mark Allen McClellan, born Pawnee City, Nebraska, 25 November 1963

7. Barbara Jean McClellan, born Pawnee City, Nebraska, 17 March 1965

B. Margie Marie McClellan Hanson, born Armour, Pawnee County, Nebraska, 8 August 1930; married at Summerfield, Kansas, 7 August 1955, Elmer L. Hanson, born 17 May 1927, son of Oscar Emil Hanson and Emelia Eversina Walker. They live in McPherson, Kansas. Children:

1. Ronald Wayne Hanson, born McPherson, Kansas, 21 September 1957; married at Emporia, Kansas, 20 October 1979, Rebecca Lynn Notson. Child:

   a. Brady Wayne Hanson, born Emporia, Kansas, 17 September 1984

2. Richard Ward Hanson, born McPherson, Kansas, 28 January 1965

C. Richard Duane McClellan, born Armour, Nebraska, 24 May 1932; married at Summerfield, Kansas, 23 November 1973, Judy Dalton. Children (the first three adopted):

1. Diane McClellan Hoffman, born 7 August 1958; married, 11 March 1982, Tim Hoffman. Child:

   a. Shawn Michael Hoffman, born 2 April 1985

2. Roberta McClellan Siegel, born 30 August 1960; married, 12 April 1980, David Siegel. Children:

   a. Alicia Leah Siegel, born 11 June 1981

   b. Nicole Lynn Siegel, born 10 October 1984

3. Larry McClellan, born 20 December 1963; married, 15 August 1985, Carmen Johnson. Child:

5-69 Lawrence W., 4-23 J. Thomas, 3-8 William M., 2-1 Andrew          6-70C3a

    a. Danielle Rene McClellan, born 9 July 1986

  4. Duane Jay McClellan, born 8 November 1975

6-71 WALTER IVAN GRAHAM, born Summerfield, Kansas, 18 December 1901, died Seattle, Washington, 24 July 1979; married EDITH VIOLA RICHARDSON, born near Pawnee City, Nebraska, 26 February 1902, died Seattle, Washington, 18 September 1981. Edith was a sister of Velma Richardson who married 6-75 Paul E. Graham. Child (adopted):

7-30 Cynthia Rae


CHILDREN OF 5-69 LAWRENCE WILLIAM GRAHAM
AND JESSE F. CONARD [23]


6-72 ZELLA LENORE GRAHAM OLMSTEAD, born West Plains, Missouri, November 1894, died Raytown, Missouri, July 1987; married, September 1913, ALBERT OLIVER OLMSTEAD (called Bert), born Saint Joseph, Missouri, November 1892, died Pawnee City, Nebraska, January 1972, buried Mission Creek Cemetery. Bert was a farmer. Children, all born near Summerfield, Kansas:

A. Max Ray Olmstead,
   b. January 1915
B. Harold Graham Olmstead,
   b. November 1917
C. Rolland Wayne Olmstead,
   b. 9 March 1919
D. Carol Louise Olmstead, b. October 1921

---

A. Max Ray Olmstead, born near Summerfield, Kansas, January 1915, died March 1941, buried Mission Creek Cemetery.

B. Harold Graham Olmstead, born near Summerfield, Kansas, November 1917; married, September 1944, Marjorie Marie Kramer, born 10 September 1923, daughter of Roy Kramer (1894-1982) and Marie ___ (1894- ). They live in Omaha; Marjorie's mother lived with them. Children:

5-69 Lawrence W., 4-23 J. Thomas, 3-8 William M., 2-1 Andrew     6-72B1

1. Michael Hal Olmstead, born Beatrice, Nebraska, November 1946, died Omaha, Nebraska, August 1975, buried Omaha; unmarried.

2. Monte Kim Olmstead, born Beatrice, Nebraska, 25 December 1955. In 1986 he was living in Omaha with his parents and grandmother.

C. Rolland Wayne Olmstead (called Wayne), born Near Summerfield, Kansas, 9 March 1919; married, May 1941, Opal Williams, born Weldona, Colorado, July 1924, daughter of Marion Williams and Edith ___. They live in Raton, New Mexico. Children:

1. Kay Lorene Olmstead Grubelnik, born Summerfield, Kansas, February 1942; married, December 1962, David Grubelnik. They live in Raton, New Mexico. Children:

   a. Steve Grubelnik, born November 1964; married, December 1986, Susan Wiseman, born April 1967.

   b. Mark Grubelnik, born April 1967

   c. Chad Grubelnik, born September 1971, twin to next

   d. Brad Grubelnik, born September 1971, twin to above

2. James Leroy Olmstead (called Jim), born Weldona, Colorado, May 1943, killed in a traffic accident in Texas, December 1976, buried Raton, New Mexico; married at Raton, November 1960, Willie Elam who has since remarried and lives in Texas. Children:

   a. Laurie Kay Olmstead Jenkins, born August 1961; married ___ Jenkins. They live in California.

   b. Kimberly Ann Olmstead, born December 1963. She lives in Texas.

   c. Jamie Sean Olmstead, born January 1969. He lives in Texas.

D. Carol Louise Olmstead, born Summerfield, Kansas, October 1921; unmarried. She is retired from American Telephone and Telegraph and lives in Raytown, Missouri.

5-69 Lawrence W., 4-23 J. Thomas, 3-8 William M., 2-1 Andrew                    6-73

6-73 JOSEPH C. GRAHAM, born Missouri, 17 December 1896, died Barneston, Kansas, July 1968; married RELDA MOSER, born ___, died Barneston, Nebraska, October 1968. Children, all born in Summerfield, Kansas:

 7-31 Lawrence N.
 7-32 Velma Mary, b. 27 February 1923
 7-33 Myron Albert, b. 13 July 1925
 7-34 Ross G., b. 31 March 1931

6-74 EVERETT MCKINLEY GRAHAM, born Summerfield, Kansas, 15 July 1900; married, 20 July 1921, ETHEL R. E. LYNCH, born Liberty, Nebraska, 17 February 1901, died Beatrice, Nebraska, 18 June 1979. Children:

 7-35 Nelva Arlene, b. Summerfield, KS, 9 December 1921
 7-36 Wilma Maxine, b. Oketo, KS, 12 July 1923
 7-37 Donna June, b. Fairbury, NE, 15 June 1929
 7-38 Maurice Dean, b. Fairbury, NE, 7 October 1933

6-75 PAUL E. GRAHAM, born 5 July 1903, died 20 February 1986; married, 27 November 1923, VELMA IRENE RICHARDSON, born 27 March 1904, died 17 January 1986. Velma was a sister of Edith Richardson, wife of 6-71 Walter Ivan Graham. Children, the first five probably born in Summerfield, Kansas:

 7-39 Lynn
 7-40 Lowell Eugene, b. 12 December 1926
 7-41 Paul E. Jr., b. 7 February 1928
 7-42 Bonnie Lou
 7-43 Jessie Charlene, b. 16 October 1935
 7-44 Kae La Jeanne, b. Beatrice, NE, 8 February 1943

6-76 ARTHUR MARVIN GRAHAM (called Marvin), born Pawnee County, Nebraska, 28 April 1915, died April 1983, buried Mission Creek Cemetery; unmarried. He served in the army for four years, 1941-45.

5-70 James T. Jr., 4-23 J. Thomas, 3-8 William M., 2-1 Andrew                6-77

## CHILDREN OF 5-70 JAMES THOMAS GRAHAM JR.
## AND LILLIE PEARL CLARK [24]


6-77 OPAL GRAHAM HILL MITSCHLER, born Pawnee County, Nebraska, 30 June 1908, died 17 October 1978, buried Marysville, Kansas; married (1) BENNIE HILL; (2) WILFRED MITSCHLER, born 16 April 1907, died 15 January 1980, buried Marysville, Kansas. In the 1965 Marysville city directory, Opal was listed as an aide at Memorial City Hospital. Child:

    A. Donald Hill; married Marie ___. He is retired from Pacific Bell Telephone Company, and they live in Three Rivers, California. They are said to have eight children. Known children:

       1. Mickey Hill

       2. Marty Hill

       3. Donna Hill


6-78 LOLA MARIE GRAHAM CROSIER HABIG, born Pawnee County, Nebraska, 14 May 1921; married (1) on 2 September 1943, MILTON CROSIER, born 19 May 1889, died 20 January 1953, buried Wymore, Nebraska; (2) on 1 February 1955, CHAUNCEY HABIG, born 17 March 1906, died 20 July 1982, buried Marysville, Kansas. Lola lives in Marysville.

    Children by (1) Milton Crosier:

    A. Duane Crosier, b. 2 August 1944

    B. Judy Crosier, b. 9 August 1945

    Child by (2) Chauncey Habig:

    C. Dennis Habig, b. 14 March 1956

---

    A. Duane Crosier, born 2 August 1944; married, 6 October 1963, Lois Koch, born 29 August 1944. They live in Seneca, Kansas. Children:

       1. Laurie Crosier, born 2 March 1964

2. Scott Crosier, born 28 April 1965

3. Staci Crosier, born 8 April 1970

B. Judy Crosier Allerheiligen Ford, born 9 August 1945; married (1) on 16 August 1964, David Allerheiligen, since divorced; (2) on 1 September 1977, Jerry Ford, born 10 January 1934. She lives in Tucson, Arizona. Children:

1. Amy Allerheiligen, born 16 March 1968

2. Kevin Allerheiligen, born 28 April 1970

C. Dennis Habig, born 14 March 1956; married, 2 June 1979, Diana Feldhausen, born 29 March 1958. They live in Emporia, Kansas. Children:

1. Mandy Habig, born 4 November 1979

2. Daren Habig, born 6 July 1981

3. Aleah Habig, born 1 November 1983

6-79 PEARL ARLEEN GRAHAM PAGE HAMILTON, born Pawnee County, Nebraska, 8 October 1923, died 30 December 1985; married (1) on 11 February 1944, BRUCE F. PAGE, born 8 July 1914, died 20 April 1978, cremated; (2) on 18 March 1970, JOHN L. HAMILTON, born 16 March 1912, died 19 July 1980, buried Albuquerque, New Mexico. Children:

A. Linda Lee Page, b. Glendale, CA, 18 November 1944
B. Virginia Florence Page b. 5 October 1947
C. Bruce Patrick Page b. 2 November 1950

A. Linda Lee Page Bullock Bennett, born Glendale, California, 18 November 1944; married (1) on 15 September 1962, Charles Bullock, born 6 February 1944; (2) on 11 February 1966, George Bennett, born 4 July 1929. They live in Piedmont, Missouri.

Child by (1) Charles Bullock:

1. Toni Lynn Bullock, born 2 February 1965; married, 14 May

1982, Wayne Woods, born 20 June 1964. Children:

    a. Hannah Leigh Woods, born 23 July 1983

    b. Brandon Wayne Woods, born 16 December 1985

Children by (2) George Bennett:

2. Veronica Elaine Bennett, born 29 October 1966

3. David Michael Bennett, born 14 July 1968

B. Virginia Florence Page Biondo Mason, born 5 October 1947; married (1) on 12 December 1965, George Biondo, born 3 September 1946; (2) on 14 February 1983, Douglas Charles Mason, born 31 July 1961. Child by (1) George Biondo:

1. Erik Michael Biondo, born 1 September 1966

C. Bruce Patrick Page, born 2 November 1950; married, September 1968, Christine Rodriguez. They live in Albuquerque, New Mexico. Children:

1. Jason Lee Page, born 11 February 1971

2. Carrie Ann Page, born 30 September 1974

## CHILD OF 5-72 GEORGE WASHINGTON GRAHAM AND CATHERINE MULHERN

6-80 GEORGIA GENEVIEVE GRAHAM (or Genevieve Georgia), born ___, died probably in Denver, Colorado, c. 1983; probably unmarried. In some city directories of Denver, Colorado, she was listed as Georgia G.; in others she was listed as Genevieve G. She worked at Denver Dry Goods, and lived with her parents.

5-73 Frank I., 4-23 J. Thomas, 3-8 William M., 2-1 Andrew                        6-81

## CHILDREN OF 5-73 FRANK IRWIN GRAHAM
## AND BERTHA KLOXIN [25]

6-81 WILLIS GRAHAM, born near Marysville, Kansas, 19 December 1908; married, 23 February 1936, CAROLINE GRAUER, born 16 May 1910, died 28 January 1984. Children:

- 7-45 Charlene Ann, b. and d. 3 December 1938
- 7-46 Bette Lou, b. 26 October 1939
- 7-47 Mary Michelle, b. 20 June 1945

6-82 ___ GRAHAM (boy), stillborn 1913

6-83 VIOLET VERENE GRAHAM GRAUER, born near Marysville, Kansas, 10 July 1915; married, 10 February 1935, MERLIN GRAUER, born 18 April 1913, died 27 February 1972. Children:

- A. Shirley Ann Grauer, b. 31 October 1935
- B. Janice June Grauer, b. 23 June 1937
- C. Marilyn Dee Grauer, b. 15 April 1939
- D. Nancy Elaine Grauer, 12 November 1941
- E. Sherry Lea Grauer, b. 18 May 1948
- F. Jeffery Jay Grauer, b. 30 August 1956

---

A. Shirley Ann Grauer Schmidt, born 31 October 1935, died 17 February 1983; married, 28 December 1957, John Schmidt. Child:

1. Joya Kay Schmidt Siders, born 26 August 1958; married, 7 August 1977, Kevin Siders. Children:

    a. Jennifer Siders, born 1978

    b. Sara Siders, born 1979

    c. Shannon Siders, born 1982

B. Janice June Grauer, born 23 June 1937

5-73 Frank I., 4-23 J. Thomas, 3-8 William M., 2-1 Andrew

C. Marilyn Dee Grauer Krotzinger, born 15 April 1939; married, 17 May 1958, Francis John Krotzinger Jr., born 11 January 1939. Children:

1. Kyle Ray Krotzinger, born 16 January 1959; married, 24 April 1982, Diane Kay Lemke. Children:

   a. Heath Jonathan Krotzinger, born and died 10 October 1982.

   b. Kayla Rae Krotzinger, born 6 July 1984

   c. Eric John Krotzinger, born 22 June 1986

2. Kris Lee Krotzinger, born 11 February 1962

D. Nancy Elaine Grauer Whitebread, born 12 November 1941; married, 15 April 1961, Darel Gene Whitebread, born 29 September 1933. Children:

1. Joni Lynn Whitebread McClellan, born 16 February 1962; married, 20 April 1985, 6-70A2 William Everett McClellan, born 2 September 1957, son of 6-70A Eugene Ray McClellan and Janet Anne Pooch. For child see 6-70A2 William Everett McClellan.

2. Michael Gene Whitebread, born 14 August 1964

3. Jill Denise Whitebread Sparks, born 18 February 1969; married, November 1985, Riley Gene Sparks. Child:

   a. Joshua Gene Sparks, born 16 February 1986

E. Sherry Lea Grauer Carl, born 18 May 1948; married, 26 August 1967, Richard Douglas Carl, born 13 January 1947. Children:

1. David Scott Carl, born 16 April 1968

2. Barry Douglas Carl, born 20 May 1970

F. Jeffery Jay Grauer, born 30 August 1956; married Joyce Muck, born 8 July 1956. Children:

1. Jeffery Merle Grauer, born 8 February 1980

2. Jessica Dee Grauer, born 26 July 1982

## CHILDREN OF 5-74 GEORGE MILLS GRAHAM
## AND LENORA WISEMAN

6-84 RALPH W. GRAHAM, born Iowa, c. 1897

6-85 GEORGE M. GRAHAM, born Nebraska, c. 1902

6-86 ARTHUR H. GRAHAM, born Nebraska, c. 1908


## CHILDREN OF 5-77 LEE ANDERSON GRAHAM
## AND NELLE RUTH LEE [26]

6-87  HARRY LEE GRAHAM, born Iowa, 21 February 1900, died 1970, buried Winterset, Iowa. No children.

6-88  JOSEPH DONALD GRAHAM, born Iowa, 5 June 1907, died 1982, buried Winterset, Iowa. No children.

6-89 FREDERICK GRAHAM, born Iowa, 1917, died 1942 (said to have died in a hunting accident); married ___. Child:

    7-48 Susan Ann, b. 1940

5-84 Robert C., 4-27 John M., 3-8 William M., 2-1 Andrew

## CHILDREN OF 5-84 ROBERT COWDEN GRAHAM
## AND AMANDA AGNESS PETERMAN [27]

6-90 PEARL E. GRAHAM BULL, born Beattie, Kansas, 1 January 1896, died Marysville, Kansas, 15 April 1968, buried Deer Creek Cemetery, Oketo, Kansas; married at Marysville, Kansas, 6 February 1918, SIDNEY W. BULL, born near Marysville, Kansas, 27 January 1878, died Methodist Hospital, Omaha, Nebraska, 15 July 1933, buried Deer Creek Cemetery, Oketo, Kansas, son of Ruben Bull and Margaret McKay. Sidney was a merchant at Marietta and Oketo, Kansas. No children.

6-91 THELMA AGNES GRAHAM HEISERMAN, born Saint Joseph, Missouri, 5 December 1905; married at Summerfield, Kansas, 23 May 1922, FREDERICK D. HEISERMAN, born Beattie, Kansas, 8 February 1902, died Marysville, Kansas, 14 November 1962, buried Saint Gregory Catholic Cemetery, Marysville, Kansas, son of George Heiserman and Henrietta Breunsbach. Fred was a farmer deeply interested in soil conservation and in 1947 was named Marshall County's Outstanding Farmer by the county bankers. He and Thelma retired from farming in 1959 and moved to Marysville where he worked at the port of entry. He was a member of the Knights of Columbus. In the 1964 and 1965 city directories of Marysville, Thelma was listed as a housekeeper and a cook at Community Memorial Hospital. Children:

A. Nora Marie Heiserman, b. Beattie, KS, 10 February 1923
B. Dorothy Quorean Heiserman, b. Marysville, KS, 26 December 1923
C. Dale Frederick Heiserman, b. Marysville, KS, 10 September 1925
D. Mary Lou Heiserman, b. Beattie, KS, 7 June 1927
E. LeRoy Francis Heiserman, b. Beattie, KS, 4 September 1933

---

A. Nora Marie Heiserman, born Beattie, Kansas, 10 February 1923, died 22 July 1923.

B. Dorothy Quorean Heiserman, born Marysville, Kansas, 26 December 1923, died 20 August 1924.

C. Dale Frederick Heiserman, born Marysville, Kansas, 10 September 1925; married at Camp Walters, Weatherford, Texas, 26 May 1945, Charlotte Cudney, born Harrison, Arkansas, 31 December 1927, daughter of Leo Henry Cudney and Minnie Opal Slama. They live in Lawrence, Kansas. Children:

1. Dale Frederick Heiserman Jr., born Kansas City, Missouri, 11 October 1951; married, 11 February 1978, Jane Elsie Brunton.

2. Gary Lee Heiserman, born Beatrice, Nebraska, 29 August 1954; married, 3 May 1975, Lynn Bunce.

3. Linda Kay Heiserman, born McPherson, Kansas, 3 May 1959

4. Julie Ann Heiserman, born Council Grove, Kansas, 29 November 1960

D. Mary Lou Heiserman, born Beattie, Kansas, 7 June 1927, died 3 May 1959.

E. LeRoy Francis Heiserman, born Beattie, Kansas, 4 September 1933; married at First Christian Church, Marysville, Kansas, 5 June 1955, Marilyn Rose Cooper, born Marysville, Kansas, 28 July 1937, daughter of Arthur Clarence Cooper and Myrtle Irene Minger. They live at Oketo, Kansas. Children:

1. Bret Lee Heiserman, born Wichita, Kansas, 30 September 1958; married (1) on 20 January 1979, Linda Teresa Meador, since divorced; (2) on 24 September 1983, Janelle Wurm, born 3 October 1960.

2. Sherrie Lynn Heiserman Taylor, born Marysville, Kansas, 17 June 1962; married, 23 June 1984, Donald Abe George Taylor.

3. Larry Dean Heiserman, born Marysville, Kansas, 31 October 1963

6-92 ROBERT ROY GRAHAM (called Roy), born Beattie, Kansas, 22 June 1911, died Oketo, Kansas, 26 October 1977, buried Saint Malachy Catholic Cemetery, Beattie, Kansas; married at Catholic Parish house, Beattie, Kansas, 23 December 1933, EVA MAE TAYLOR, born Beattie, Kansas, 16 April 1914, daughter of James A. Taylor and Myrtie D. Smith. They lived at Oketo, Kansas. Children:

5-84 Robert C., 4-27 John M., 3-8 William M., 2-1 Andrew                              6-93

7-49 Jimmie Roy, b. Marysville, KS, 14 September 1934
7-50 Jo Ann Varda, b. Marysville, KS, 7 September 1935
7-51 Jimmy Darryl, b. Oketo, KS, 7 June 1938
7-52 Judith Marie, b. Marysville, KS, 13 October 1940


6-93 DOROTHY MARGARET GRAHAM RUYLE, born Summerfield, Kansas, 13 February 1914, died Beatrice, Nebraska, 5 November 1971, buried at Liberty, Nebraska; married (1) at Hiawatha, Kansas, 25 February 1933, OLIVER WILLIAM RUYLE, born Rockford, Nebraska, 23 May 1913, died Liberty, Nebraska, 7 October 1939, son of Lloyd Oliver Ruyle and Ina Cochran; Dorothy married (2) at Hiawatha, Kansas, 24 May 1946, her first husband's brother, THOMAS MILTON RUYLE, born Rockford, Nebraska, 15 May 1919, son of Lloyd Oliver Ruyle and Ina Cochran. Thomas Milton married (2) on 1 September 1978, Ilene Boehmer.

Children of Dorothy and (1) Oliver William Ruyle, all born in Liberty, Nebraska:

A. Robert Lloyd Ruyle, b. 26 March 1934
B. Jo Ann Ruyle, b. 13 March 1936
C. Shirley Lee Ruyle, b. 30 October 1937

Children of Dorothy and (2) Thomas Milton Ruyle, both born in Beatrice, Nebraska:

D. Donald Duane Ruyle, b. 10 January 1947
E. Thomas Kenton Ruyle, b. 4 September 1955

---

A. Robert Lloyd Ruyle, born Liberty, Nebraska, 26 March 1934; married at Wymore, Nebraska, 17 August 1957, Bernice Fay Vitosh, born Odell, Nebraska, 22 July 1936, daughter of Harry Joe Vitosh and Elsie C. Peterka. Children:

1. Sherri Lynn Ruyle Gartner, born North Kansas City, Missouri, 27 September 1958; married, 19 June 1982, Charles D. Gartner. Children:

    a. Nancy Rae Gartner, born Midland, Michigan, 17 February 1985

  b. Elizabeth Lynn Gartner, born Midland, Michigan, 20 August 1988

2. Nanci Ann Ruyle, born Gallup, New Mexico, 18 July 1960. On 11 May 1986 she earned an M.D. in pediatrics at the University of Nebraska, Omaha Medical Center, and was a resident at Shands Hospital, Gainesville, Florida, 1986-9.

3. Patricia Catherine Ruyle Schoettger, born Luverne, Minnesota, 7 December 1961; married at Lincoln, Nebraska, 28 August 1987, Scott M. Schoettger, born Lincoln, Nebraska, 28 May 1962.

4. Joan Clare Ruyle, born Lincoln, Nebraska, 4 March 1964. She was graduated from Bryan School of Nursing on 30 May 1986.

5. Robert Lloyd Ruyle Jr., born Lincoln, Nebraska, 24 February 1966

6. Steven Anthony Ruyle, born Lincoln, Nebraska, 19 November 1973

B. Jo Ann Ruyle Zvolanek Poutre, born Liberty, Nebraska, 13 March 1936; married (1) on 27 December 1956, James Jerry Zvolanek Jr., born 11 October 1934, died Liberty, Nebraska, 7 April 1969, buried Liberty, Nebraska; (2) at Saint Mary's Catholic Church, Wymore, Nebraska, 17 August 1971, Robert Michael Poutre, born Beatrice, Nebraska, 17 August 1940, son of Omer Armend Poutre and Alice Venita Moran. Robert had married (1) Polly Cheryl Yockel. Jo Ann and Robert live in Wymore, Nebraska. Children, all by (1) James Jerry Zvolanek Jr.:

1. James Allen Zvolanek, born Beatrice, Nebraska, 21 November 1957; married (1) in 1977, Debbie Flansburgh, since divorced; (2) in October 1986, Ellen ___. Children:

  a. Emily Jane Zvolanek, born Beatrice, Nebraska, 16 November 1976

  b. Jill Zvolanek, born Omaha, Nebraska, 2 June 1988

2. Jean Ann Zvolanek Windle, born Beatrice, Nebraska, 3 March 1959; married, 8 August 1980, Dean M. Windle, divorced in 1987. Children:

5-84 Robert C., 4-27 John M., 3-8 William M., 2-1 Andrew                6-93B2a

   a. Joseph Windle, born Nebraska City, Nebraska, 8 April 1984

   b. Ellie Jean Windle, born Nebraska City, Nebraska, 11 May 1985

3. Jon Oliver Zvolanek, born Beatrice, Nebraska, 16 July 1960

4. Jeffrey Lee Zvolanek, born Beatrice, Nebraska, 21 November 1962

5. Julie Marie Zvolanek, born Beatrice, Nebraska, 26 March 1966

Jo Ann's second husband, Robert Michael Poutre, had children by his first wife whom Jo Ann reared: Robert Paul Poutre, born Beatrice, Nebraska, 20 May 1960; Timothy John Poutre, born Minden, Nebraska, 20 February 1962; Judith Polly Poutre, born Beatrice, Nebraska, 21 May 1963; and Cynthia Kay Poutre, born 31 August 1964.

C. Shirley Lee Ruyle Duensing, born Liberty, Nebraska, 30 October 1937; married at Mount Calvary Lutheran Church, Marysville, Kansas, 5 November 1957, Clair V. Duensing, born Odell, Nebraska, 24 July 1937, son of August Duensing and Elsie Knabe. They live in Kansas City. Children:

   1. Timothy Lee Duensing, born Kansas City, Missouri, 11 October 1958; married, 7 March 1987, Teresa Diane Graham (no relation), born Texas, 4 July 1963.

   2. Daniel Gene Duensing, born Kansas City, Missouri, 31 January 1963

D. Donald Duane Ruyle, born Beatrice, Nebraska, 10 January 1947; married at Saint John's Lutheran Church, Beatrice, Nebraska, 5 April 1969, Diane F. Rice, born Beatrice, Nebraska, 22 March 1947, daughter of William M. Rice and Pauline C. Buss. Children:

   1. Rochelle Lynn Ruyle, born Beatrice, Nebraska, 18 October 1969

   2. Heather Lynn Ruyle, born Beatrice, Nebraska, 11 November 1973

E. Thomas Kenton Ruyle, born Beatrice, Nebraska, 4 September

1955; married at Wymore, Nebraska, 23 June 1984, Amy Keller, born 16 December 1960. Child:

1. Derek Clayton Ruyle, born Beatrice, Nebraska, 31 August 1987

6-94 JOHN WILLIAM GRAHAM, born Oketo, Kansas, 2 January 1916, died Bryan Hospital, Lincoln, Nebraska, 12 November 1980, buried Saint Gregory Catholic Cemetery, Marysville; married at Beattie, Kansas, 19 August 1936, LAURA MAXINE FLETCHER (called Maxine), born Marysville, Kansas, 9 January 1917, daughter of John Vardaman Fletcher and Laura Elizabeth Alderson. They lived at Beatrice, Nebraska, where they were listed in the city directories from 1950 to 1985. At first John was a mechanic at Lentz Motors then at Paul Henderson Motors. By 1966 he was a maintenance man at Holiday Inn, and by 1967 he worked at the Beatrice State Development Center. By 1979 he was retired. In 1981 Maxine was listed as working in quality control at Formfit, and by 1982 she was retired. Child:

7-53 John William Jr., b. Marysville, KS, 25 February 1947


CHILDREN OF 5-85 GEORGE HENRY GRAHAM
AND EFFIE M. CUMMINGS [28]


6-95 FLEDA B. GRAHAM, born Kansas, c. 1903. Acording to 5-71B Lorna Howard Cline, Fleda was "an excellent musician and studied piano in Europe. She played for radio and TV in Lincoln, Nebraska, for some time. The station offered a prize if she couldn't find the song that people called in for."

6-96 GEORGE D. GRAHAM, born Kansas, c. 1905

6-97 KEITH GRAHAM, born Kansas, c. 1907 (twin to next)

5-86 Oley M., 4-27 John M., 3-8 William M., 2-1 Andrew              6-98

6-98 LEITH GRAHAM, born Kansas, c. 1907 (twin to above)


CHILDREN OF 5-86 OLEY MILLS GRAHAM
AND CARRIE E. WARNER


6-99 CECIL MARY GRAHAM BATLEY, born Pawnee County, Nebraska, c. 1902; married ___ BATLEY. They lived in Pittsburg, Kansas.


6-100 IRA FLORENCE GRAHAM, born Pawnee County, Nebraska, 7 December 1903, died c. 1907-8.


6-101 BERNIECE EDNA GRAHAM PRICE, born Pawnee County, Nebraska; married ___ PRICE. They lived in Auburn, Kansas.


6-102 ARTHUR BERT GRAHAM, born Pawnee County, Nebraska, c. 1906, died 1952. He lived in Pawnee City, Nebraska.


6-103 BAIL ROBERT GRAHAM, born Pawnee County, Nebraska, c. 1908. He lived in Pawnee City, Nebraska.


6-104 EARL LAWRENCE GRAHAM, born Pawnee County, Nebraska, 4 January 1911. He lived in Pawnee City, Nebraska.


6-105 KENNETH GRAHAM, born Pawnee County, Nebraska

5-89 David A., 4-27 John M., 3-8 William M., 2-1 Andrew

## CHILD OF 5-89 DAVID ALBERT GRAHAM
## AND MABEL L. WYMORE

6-106 MAXWELL GRAHAM, born Marshall County, Kansas, c. 1907

## CHILD OF 5-92 FRANK HARRISON GRAHAM
## AND LUCY GEIGER

6-107 MARGE GRAHAM GODDARD; married TOM GODDARD. Child:

A. Roberta Goddard

## CHILDREN OF 5-94 WILLIAM ALLISON GRAHAM
## AND ORA ALMA BONHAM [29]

6-108 MARY EDNA GRAHAM EDWARDS (called Edna), born Macksburg, Iowa, 3 November 1897, died Spokane, Washington, 8 March 1976; married, 14 June 1933, EDWARD EDWARDS, born ___, died after 1976. Edna was graduated from Whitmore College. She and Edward lived variously in Spokane Valley, Hartline, and Spokane, Washington, where they were members of the United Methodist Church. Edna was also a Sunday school superintendant and was active in the women's society. Child:

A. Richard Lewis Edwards, born 19 November 1934; married Terrill Mudgett. They live in Wilbur, Washington. Children:

1. William Edwards. He is in the United States Air Force.

2. Michael Edwards. He lives in Hartline, Washington.

3. Yvonne Edwards, born 1957. She lives in Wilbur, Washington.

4. John Edwards, born 1961

6-109 LESLIE BONHAM GRAHAM, born Macksburg, Iowa, 10 June 1900, died Poulsbo, Washington, 23 February 1985; married (1) on 15 October 1928, MARGUERITE MILLER, born Walla Walla, Washington, 14 May 1903, died c. 1970; he married (2) in 1972, TERIA ___. The following is from an obituary on Leslie:

> Born June 10, 1900 in Marksbury [sic; should be Macksburg], Iowa, he moved to the Spokane area in 1917. While attending high school in Spokane, he became intrigued with the beginnings of radio. He was indirectly responsible for the first radio station in Spokane, and directed the first radio station show ever broadcast from a Spokane school. He worked with a crystal radio set, and made several innovations which were later used in the budding radio industry.
>
> Graham was among the first to be a ham radio operator when open spark transmitters were used, and installed a radio communications system in a National Guard airplane--the first radio equipment ever used in a plane in the Spokane area.
>
> He was a second lieutenant, signal, upon his honorable discharge from the National Guard. While in the guard, he received three local distinguished marksman awards and two national awards--the highest government award.
>
> He received a civil engineering license from the state of Washington in January, 1936. After working seven years for an independent telephone company, he joined Pacific Northwest Bell, from which he retired in Feb. 1963 after more than 31 years. One of his major accomplishments with the telephone company was the installation of an extensive telephone system at the World War II emergency shipyard in Vancouver.
>
> His favorite activity since moving to his Miller Bay home in 1951 was boating. He had been an active member of the Agate Pass United States Power Squadron since 1955 and was commander in 1961 and 1962. He was a charter member of the Pouslbo Yacht Club, and was responsible for the establishment of the Spokane United

States Power Squadron. He and Marguerite sailed their boat to Alaska in about 1960. His love of boating was demonstrated by his willingness to teach others about safe boating techniques.

He was a 50-year member of the Masons and the Order of the Eastern Star.

Leslie and Marguerite had no children.

6-110 GEORGE ALLISON GRAHAM, born Macksburg, Iowa, 20 November 1903, still alive in 1984; married (1) on 20 October 1928, EDITH AEBISHER(?); (2) on 12 December 1945, BERNICE LUCILE KIRK, born 2 August 1908. They live in Spokane, Washington. According to the Spokane city directories, he owned the George A. Graham Pipe Organ Sales and Service Company. Children, both by first wife:

    7-54 Fred                      7-55 Frances

6-111 CLARENCE SAMUEL GRAHAM, born Macksburg, Iowa, 3 August 1906, still alive in 1984; married (1) on 17 August 1928, WYNONA ___; (2) on 24 June 1961, LUCILE ADELAIDE BLAKE, born 18 November 1918. They live in Spokane, Washington, where according to the city directories he was the president of a food broker business, C. S. Graham Company. Wynona was the vice-president. Children:

    7-56 Diane                  7-57 Jacqueline

6-112 MERTON GRAHAM, born Macksburg, Iowa, 26 July 1911, died Fort Shaw, Montana, 25 January 1914.

6-113 RUBY ELLEN GRAHAM PHILLIPY, born Fort Shaw, Montana, 3 August 1915; married on 28 September 1935, ROY PHILLIPY. They live in Spokane, Washington, where according to the city directories he worked at the Great Northern Railroad. Children:

    A. Lawrence Phillipy, born 27 March 1937; married Evelyn Taylor (called Lynn). In the 1960 Spokane city directory, he was listed as a lineman for Pacific Telephone; Lynn was an IBM

5-95 Thomas E., 4-30 Samuel A., 3-8 William M., 2-1 Andrew       6-113B

operator.

B. David Allen Phillipy; married Joyce Benner.

C. Keith Phillipy; married Nancy Smith.


6-114 CHESTER WILLIAM GRAHAM, born Spokane, Washington, 26 May 1920; married on 14 May 1944, FRANCES MABERRY. In 1945 he was listed in the city directory of Spokane. Later he and his wife moved to Mineral Wells, Texas. Children:

7-58 William            7-59 ___ (girl)


### CHILDREN OF 5-95 THOMAS EDWARD GRAHAM
### AND CHARLOTTE MABEL JOHNSON [30]


6-115 PHILIP EDWARD GRAHAM, born Cascade, Montana, 18 December 1911; married (1) in 1931, WANITA VICKERS, born Mitchell, South Dakota, 21 April 1910, died California, 7 July 1937; (2) in Riverside, California, 4 August 1940, BERNICE MARGARET HAMMETT, born Pawnee, Nebraska, 19 November 1910, her second marriage. She had married (1) ___ Dobyns. Philip lived in Long Beach, California. According to the Long Beach city directories, he was a bookkeeper at Petrolane, Ltd., 1938-9; an employee at L. G. Company, 1940; credit manager at Desmond, 1943-4; insurance agent at another company, 1948-52; and by 1968 an accountant at Baash Ross. He was the executor of the estate of 5-101 Samuel Roscoe and Addie Graham.

Child of Philip and (1) Wanita Vickers:

7-60 Philip Edward Jr., b.
     7 July 1937

Child of Philip and (2) Bernice Margaret Hammett:

7-61 Mary Margaret, b. Long Beach,
     CA, 23 April 1943

Philip also reared his second wife's child by her first marriage: Patricia Louise Dobyns, born 4 April 1933; married, 11 June 1955, Edward Arthur Hinz Jr., born York, Nebraska, 1926. Children: Edward Arthur Hinz III, born 14 July 1962; and Steven Frederick Hinz, born 14 May 1964.

6-116 GORDON ALBERT GRAHAM, born Great Falls, Montana, 8 July 1916; married in Glendale, California, 8 July 1938, BETTY JUNE RICHESON, born Long Beach, California, 16 June 1916, daughter of Joseph Richeson and Laura Lucy Murray. They live in Jackson, Wyoming. Children:

7-62 Judith Lynne, b. Oakland, CA, 24 March 1941
7-63 Darleen Joan, b. San Jose, CA, 15 June 1945
7-64 Thais June, b. San Jose, CA, 14 October 1950

6-117 ROBERT JOHNSON GRAHAM, born Great Falls, Montana, 5 October 1921; married in Pomona, California, GLADYS KORSGARDEN, born Twin Valley, Minnesota, 24 January 1921. He is a retired pilot in the United States Marine Corps Air Force. Children:

7-65 Thomas Edward, b. Long Beach, CA, 11 January 1949
7-66 Christine Diane, b. Lexington Park, MD, 9 March 1952
7-67 Robert David, b. Corona, CA, 1 June 1954

CHILDREN OF 5-96 ROBERT CULBERTSON GRAHAM
AND MABEL ETHEL STEWART [31]

6-118 ARLIE HAROLD GRAHAM, born Macksburg, Iowa, 3 April 1898, died Des Moines, Iowa, 5 May 1934; married in Des Moines, 4 December 1917, RUTH MARY RITTER, born Afton, Iowa, 14 August 1897. Child:

5-96 Robert C., 4-30 Samuel A., 3-8 William M., 2-1 Andrew                    6-119

7-68 Robert Layman, b. Kanawha,
     IA, 11 August 1918


6-119 EARL STEWART GRAHAM, born Macksburg, Iowa, 19 August 1900, died
      Creston, Iowa, 25 or 27 February 1986; married (1) in Indianola,
      Iowa, 26 May 1926, HELEN BLACK, born Cumberland, Iowa, 22 April
      1902, died Omaha, Nebraska, 7 March 1969; (2) on 8 July 1970,
      BERNICE OSHEL FARQUHAR, born Orient, Iowa, 20 January 1899, died
      Creston, Iowa, 2 April 1982. Ruth Josephine Graham Butler
      (6-124) writes, "I have always considered Earl a sort of second
      father because he lived with us when I was a child, and he farmed
      later just six miles south of Orient, Iowa. . . ." Child:

      7-69 Margaret Karen, b. near Creston,
           IA, 18 December 1938


6-120 DOROTHY GRAHAM LIGHT VOGT, born Macksburg, Iowa, 17 November
      1902; married (1) at Leavenworth, Kansas, 22 October 1923, ARNOLD
      LIGHT, divorced in 1932; married (2) at Waterloo, Nebraska, 24
      October 1942, JOSEPH ROBERT VOGT, born Omaha, Nebraska, 23
      November 1903. Child:

      A. Raymond Earl Light, born Sioux City, Iowa, 14 November 1924;
         married at Kansas City, Missouri, 22 May 1955, Elaine Taylor.


6-121 LORENE MABEL GRAHAM ROSS, born Macksburg, Iowa, 19 January 1906,
      died Winterset, Iowa, 22 February 1960; married at Dunlap, Iowa,
      29 December 1934, JOHN WESLEY ROSS, born Macksburg, Iowa, 17
      January 1905, died Winterset, Iowa, 4 February 1966. Children:

      A. Carol Lee Ross, b. Winter-     C. John Edward Ross, b. Mount
         set, IA, 18 May 1936              Pleasant, IA, 12 May 1942
      B. Donald Frank Ross, b. Win-
         terset, IA, 17 February
         1938

      ------------------

      A. Carol Lee Ross Nahas, born Winterset, Iowa, 18 May 1936; mar-
         ried at Des Moines, Iowa, 2 June 1963, Richard Edward Nahas,
         born Des Moines, 12 August 1934. Children:

5-96 Robert C., 4-30 Samuel A., 3-8 William M., 2-1 Andrew                    6-121A1

      1. Richard Edward Nahas Jr., born Des Moines, 29 April 1964

      2. Lisa Michelle Nahas, born 28 June 1968, died 17 January 1977.

      3. John Minion Nahas, born 15 January 1970

  B. Donald Frank Ross, born Winterset, Iowa, 17 February 1938; married at Macksburg, Iowa, 27 July 1957, Annabelle Cameron, born Winterset, Iowa, 19 December 1936. Children:

      1. Kimberly Ann Ross Katch, born Des Moines, Iowa, 10 February 1960; married, 6 June 1981, Kurt Katch.

      2. Pamela Jean Ross, born Des Moines, 14 May 1962

      3. Susanna Kay Ross, born Des Moines, 25 July 1965

  C. John Edward Ross, born Mount Pleasant, Iowa, 12 May 1942; married in Los Angeles, Mary Ellen Anderson.


6-122 ROBERT RUSSELL GRAHAM, born Macksburg, Iowa, 9 March 1908; died Long Beach, California, 1974; married at Macksburg, Iowa, LUCILE JEANNETTE CONWAY, born Orange, California, 15 July 1908. Children:

    7-70 Margaret Jean, b. Macksburg, IA, 2 January 1928

    7-71 Betty Mae, b. Council Bluffs, IA, 13 April 1929

    7-72 Harold Edward, b. Greenfield, IA, 27 May 1934


6-123 WYMAN LEE GRAHAM, born Macksburg, Iowa, 1 January 1921; married at Pasadena, California, 7 December 1947, SHIRLEY LOUISE HAYMAN, born Glendale, California, 20 April 1924, daughter of Louis A. Haymon and Iva Belle Darby. They live near Orient, Iowa, where he is a farmer. Children:

5-100 Walter N., 4-30 Samuel A., 3-8 William M., 2-1 Andrew          6-124

7-73 Kenneth Lee, b. Creston, IA, 12 February 1949
7-74 William Robert, b. Greenfield, IA, 1 January 1952
7-75 Mary Louise, b. Creston, IA, 16 October 1958


CHILD OF 5-100 WALTER NELSON GRAHAM
AND OLIVE MAE STREAM


6-124 RUTH JOSEPHINE GRAHAM BUTLER (called Josephine),[32] born Creston, Union County, Iowa, 5 October 1916; married at Oil City, Louisiana, 25 May 1942, JERRY KEITHLEY BUTLER JR., born Mansfield, Louisiana, 27 December 1915, son of Jerry Keithley Butler and Mary Hylma Lawrence. Josephine was graduated from Grinnell College in 1938 and taught English in the high schools of Oto and Osceola, Iowa. Jerry is a former captain in the United States Marine Corps in which he enlisted on 10 March 1935 and from which he retired on 1 June 1958. He and Josephine have lived in California, North Carolina, and Hawaii and presently live in Oil City, Louisiana. Children:

A. Jerry Keithley Butler III, b. San Diego, CA, 19 October 1943
B. Robert Graham Butler, b. San Diego, CA, 28 May 1945
C. Ellen Ruth Butler, b. Cherry Point, NC, 19 August 1949
D. Lawrence Walter Butler, b. Bossier Parish, LA, 30 September 1952

---

A. Jerry Keithley Butler III, born San Diego, California, 19 October 1943; married (1) at Marshall, Texas, 8 February 1968, Mary Carolyn Joubert Soileau, born Ville Platte, Louisiana, 17 December 1946, daughter of Louis Joubert and Beatrice Jones; divorced c. 1975; Jerry married (2) on 7 January 1980, Deborah Ellen Patterson, born Tampa, Florida, 9 April 1940. Jerry was graduated from Louisiana Tech where he was a member of Kappa Sigma. He has served in the United States Air Force and has lived in California, North Carolina, Hawaii, Louisiana, Michigan, and Florida. Deborah is a professor of humanities at Edison College, Fort Myers,

Florida. She and Jerry live on Sanibel Island, Florida, and he works for a newspaper in Fort Myers. Child:

1. Geri Kaye Butler Savoie (called Kaye), born Ann Arbor, Michigan, 9 November 1969; married in Washington, Saint Landry Parish, Louisiana, 1 August 1987, Scott Christopher Savoie, born 18 December 1967, son of Bobby Glenn Savoie and Sandra Marie Elder. Scott is with the armed forces, and he and Kaye presently live at Eielson Air Force Base near Fairbanks, Alaska. Child:

    a. Christopher Ashton Savoie

B. Robert Graham Butler, born San Diego, California, 28 May 1945; married at Vivian, Louisiana, 19 February 1966, Melissa Dianne Idom, born Vivian, Louisiana, 19 March 1947, daughter of Harlin Avery Idom and Ada Oveline Jones. Robert was graduated from Louisiana Tech, is a member of Kappa Sigma, and presently is a salesman. Melissa sells real estate. They live in The Woodlands, Texas. Children:

1. Robin Melissa Butler, born Shreveport, Louisiana, 21 October 1966

2. Amanda Susan Butler, born Ruston, Louisiana, 22 November 1970

C. Ellen Ruth Butler Page, born Cherry Point, Craven County, North Carolina, 19 August 1949; married in Shreveport, Louisiana, 11 April 1969, Larry Elbert Page, born North Little Rock, Arkansas, 3 September 1938, son of Raymond Foster Page and Stella Irene Castor; Ellen and Larry were divorced in 1984. Children:

1. Matthew Corey Page, born Shreveport, Louisiana, 5 September 1972

2. Jeremy Foster Page, born Shreveport, Louisiana, 18 June 1979

D. Lawrence Walter Butler, born Barksdale Air Force Base, Bossier Parish, Louisiana, 30 September 1952; married (1) in Louisville, Kentucky, 27 October 1970, Jane Boyd West, divorced in January 1972; (2) at Shreveport, Louisiana, 19 October 1974, Barbara Ella Moore, born Oakland, California, 22 November 1958, daughter of Herman Ramon Moore and Mary Lucille Nix. Lawrence and Barbara have lived in Mooringsport, Louisiana, where he was a salesman, and they now live in North Fort Myers, Florida, where he is the block manager and machinery troubleshooter for a company which manufactures cement blocks. Children of Lawrence and Barbara:

1. Shawn Michael Butler, born Shreveport, Louisiana, 27 July 1974

2. Dawn Nicole Butler, born Shreveport, Louisiana, 6 January 1977


CHILDREN OF 5-103 CHARLES WADDILL GRAHAM
AND MAE ELLA UPCHURCH [33]


6-125 FRANK W. GRAHAM, born ___, died Kerrville, Texas, 1973; married (1) GRACE ___; divorced before World War II; (2) IRMA K. ___; (3) before 1951, CHARLOTTE ___. Frank was an electrician and in 1948-9 was the business manager of Maintenance Electrical Workers Local No. 1272. Later he was elected as business agent for the International Brotherhood of Electrical Workers (I.B.E.W.), Local Union No. 59. In 1951 he was appointed administrative assistant to the international president of I.B.E.W. in Washington, D.C., where he and Charlotte lived for the next twenty-one years. In 1972 they retired to Kerrville, Texas (near San Antonio). No children.


6-126 MILDRED RENA GRAHAM SMITH, born ___, died Dallas, Texas, 1972; married, c. 1934, THOMAS H. SMITH, born ___, died 1984-8. From 1932 to 1934 Mildred was a stenographer at the Universal Electric Company. Thomas worked for the Southwest Bell Telephone Company and by 1960 was a supervisor. They lived at 1418 Hollywood Avenue in Dallas. No children. Thomas married (2) Georgia ___.

5-107 Thomas R., 4-33 Robert M., 3-9 Thomas P., 2-1 Andrew                    6-127

## CHILDREN OF 5-107 THOMAS R. GRAHAM
## AND CARRIE ___

6-127 ROBERT M. GRAHAM, born Kentucky, c. 1905

6-128 THOMAS R. GRAHAM JR., born Kentucky, c. 1908

6-3 William W., 5-1 William B., 4-2 Andrew, 3-3 Matthew, 2-1 Andrew       7-1

## SEVENTH GENERATION

CHILD OF 6-3 WILLIAM WILSON GRAHAM
AND ___

7-1 WILSON BRADEN GRAHAM

CHILD OF 6-5 DAVID BARNED GRAHAM
AND MARY BURRELL

7-2 MARGARET GRAHAM PARKER (called Marnie),[1] born Chicago, 2 September 1912; married in Chicago, 10 June 1932, KENT HAMILTON PARKER, born Boston, Massachusetts, 21 June 1906, son of Frederic Charles Wesby Parker (born Worcester, Massachusetts, 1872, died Saint Petersburg, Florida, 1945) and Grace Elizabeth Reed (born New York City, 1873, died Saint Petersburg, Florida, 1966).

Marnie was graduated from the University of Chicago, 1934, and has since been active as a volunteer worker with the PTA, girl scouts, cub scouts, Presbyterian--Saint Luke's Hospital in Chicago, a local public library, and a local thrift shop. She also sews and knits and plays tennis and golf. Kent was graduated from the Illinois Institute of Technology, 1928, was an insurance actuary, 1929-71, and a consultant to Continental Insurance Company, 1971-5. He has been a member of a school board; president of the Winnetka, Illinois, Choir and Chorale Society; president of the Drug and Chemical Club, New York; board member of Olivet Institute, Chicago; and a member of Play Makers in Greenwich, Connecticut. He also plays tennis and golf and likes to garden. He and Marnie have lived in Chicago, Oak Park, and Winnetka, Illinois; as well as in Summit, New Jersey; Greenwich, Connecticut; and Sarasota, Florida. They now live in Chapel Hill, North Carolina.

Children, the first two born in Chicago, the others in Evanston, Illinois:

A.  Kent Hamilton Parker Jr. b. 11 December 1933
B.  David Graham Parker, b. 9 March 1936
C.  Sarah Parker, b. 26 October 1942
D.  Mary Parker, b. 24 January 1945
E.  Frederic W. Parker, b. 30 December 1946
F.  Margaret Parker, b. 18 July 1951
G.  Grace E. Parker, b. 25 November 1953
H.  Wesby Reid Parker, b. 10 November 1955

---

A.  Kent Hamilton Parker Jr., born Chicago, Illinois, 11 December 1933; unmarried. Kent was a specialist third class in the United States Army, 1955-58, and later was graduated from the University of Illinois, 1960, and from the National Graduate Trust School at Northwestern University, 1970. Since 1962 he has been a personal trust officer at Citibank, N.A. He is also a deacon at Fifth Avenue Presbyterian Church, New York City, a volunteer docent at Carnegie Hall, and a member of the American Numismatic Association.

B.  David Graham Parker, born Chicago, Illinois, 9 March 1936; married at Denver, Colorado, 24 December 1963, Kay Thomas, born Creston, Iowa, 22 January 1940, daughter of Harold Francis Thomas (born Afton, Iowa, 19 October 1913, died Creston, Iowa, 15 January 1955) and Thelma Peters Radevich (born Grand Island, Nebraska, 3 July 1916). David was graduated in electrical engineering from Iowa State University, 1958, and was a lieutenant, j.g., in the United States Naval Reserves, 1958-60. He has since worked as an electrical engineer. Kay was graduated from the University of Washington, 1964, and was a social worker, 1965-7, tour counselor, 1979-84, and product agent, 1987 to the present. She is a member of Pi Beta Phi and has done volunteer work at Focus on Part-Time Careers and at Hospice--Northwest Hospital. Child:

1.  Timothy Graham Parker, born Seattle, Washington, 22 April 1967. He was graduated in 1989 from Pacific Lutheran University, Takoma, Washington, with a major in communi-

cations.

C. Sarah Parker Robertson, born Evanston, Illinois, 26 October 1942; married at Summit, New Jersey, 20 June 1964, William Robertson, born Schenectedy, New York, 26 July 1941, son of Bruce Manson Robertson (born Waterloo, Iowa, 13 August 1915) and Mary Jo Gillam (born Memphis, Tennessee, 15 August 1915). Sarah was graduated from Skidmore in 1964 and has since done volunteer work with Rainbow Babies and Children's Hospital and the women's committee of the Cleveland Symphony. Her hobbies include golf, paddle tennis, skiing, and gardening. William was graduated from Colgate in 1964 and earned an MBA at Case Western University in 1967. He has been a banker since 1964. He has also been a member of the board of trustees of the College of Wooster and has done volunteer work with the Salvation Army, the Cleveland Ballet, and Saint Luke's Hospital. Among his hobbies are skiing, golf, and tennis. Children, all born in Cleveland, Ohio:

1. Deborah Graham Robertson, born 25 May 1966. She was graduated in 1988 from Duke University, majoring in pre-medicine and history.

2. John Robertson, born 23 January 1968. He attended Duke University, majoring in economics and political science.

3. Julie Robertson, born 4 May 1969. She is attending Colgate University and majoring in Russian and economics.

D. Mary Parker Ciancibella, born Evanston, Illinois, 24 January 1945; married at Shaker Heights, Ohio, 2 September 1970, Dominic Ciancibella Jr., born Cleveland, Ohio, 27 May 1945, son of Dominic Ciancibella (born Cleveland, 8 November 1915) and Lillian Murgel (born Cleveland, 25 July 1920). Mary was graduated from Smith College, 1967, and was an elementary school teacher, 1970-71, and a secretary, 1972-73. She has been active as a member of the school board, the library board, and the concert association, and has been a reading tutor and girl scout leader as well as a member of P.T.O. and the American Association of University Women. Dominic was graduated from the University of Dayton and the Dayton Art Institute and has been an instructor at Aspen School of Contemporary Art. He is presently a general contractor. In his volunteer activities he has been the president of a soccer association and has worked with the boy and cub scouts. Children, all born in Longview, Washington:

1. Allison Suzanne Ciancibella, born 20 June 1973

2. Dominic Parker Ciancibella, born 14 March 1976

3. Christopher David Ciancibella, born 13 June 1979

E. Frederic W. Parker, born Evanston, Illinois, 30 December 1946; unmarried. Frederic earned a bachelor's in aeronautical science at Embry-Riddle Aeronautical University, 1971, and has been with Associated Aviation Underwriters since 1973. He is also a commercial pilot. His chief hobby is sailing--he has received many sailing awards--and he is also a member of the Riverside, Connecticut, Yacht Club.

F. Margaret Parker Selbert, born Evanston, Illinois, 18 July 1951; married at Summit, New Jersey, 19 June 1971, Mark D. Selbert, born Kirkwood, Missouri, 17 December 1949, son of David Selbert and Laura ___; Margaret and Mark were divorced on 6 August 1982. Margaret was graduated from Lake Forest College, Illinois, 1973, and has since worked as a horse trainer, receiving several awards at horse shows. Her volunteer activities include working at her children's school, and her hobbies include needlepoint, aerobics, walking, and cooking. Mark was graduated from Lake Forest College, 1972, and is presently at Loyola University earning a master's in labor management. Children:

1. Parker David Selbert, born Elk Grove, Illinois, 20 September 1979

2. Logan H. Selbert, born Elk Grove, Illinois, 9 April 1982

G. Grace E. Parker, born Evanston, Illinois, 25 November 1953; unmarried. Grace earned a degree in nursing from the University of Washington, 1975, and took a master's in nursing in 1978. She has since been employed as a registered nurse and is a member of the American and Washington Nurses Association and of the American Pain Society. Her hobbies include mountaineering, skiing, swimming, dance skating, sewing, and knitting.

H. Wesby Reid Parker, born Evanston, Illinois, 10 November 1955; married at Verbank, New York, 9 August 1986, Lauren Gayle Mercer, born Darby, Pennsylvania, 13 April 1957, daughter of Vernon Swayne Mercer (born Mendenhall, Pennsylvania, 10 December 1923) and Frances Kathleen Phelps (born Galax, Virginia, 13 April 1925). Wesby was graduated from Rollins College,

Florida, 1977, and served as an electronics technician in the
United States Navy, 1983-86. He has been a data processor at
the Burlington, Vermont, News Agency and is now the manager.
Lauren was graduated from the State University of New York at
Albany, 1981, and has worked as a computer systems specialist
at Breen Systems Management and Healthcare. Child:

1. Rebecca Elizabeth Parker, born Burlington, Vermont, 18 May
   1988


## CHILDREN OF 6-6 EVARTS AMBROSE GRAHAM
## AND HELEN TREDWAY


7-3 DAVID TREDWAY GRAHAM,[2] born Mason City, Iowa, 20 June 1917, married in Prospect Park, Pennsylvania, 14 June 1941, FRANCES JEANETTE KEESLER, born Canastota, Madison County, New York, 1 August 1918, daughter of Clyde C. Keesler (born Galilee, Pennsylvania, 26 May 1891, died King of Prussia, Pennsylvania, 24 October 1961) and Norma Van Surdam (born Hoosick Falls, New York, 2 July 1892, died King of Prussia, Pennsylvania, 26 April 1967).

David earned his B.A. at Princeton in 1938, M.A. at Yale in 1941, and M.D. at Washington University, Saint Louis, in 1943. He later was a research fellow at Cornell University's College of Medicine, 1948-51; assistant professor of medicine at Washington University Medical School, 1951-7; and assistant professor of psychiatry there, 1956-7.

In 1957 he joined the faculty of the University of Wisconsin Medical School where he was an associate professor, then professor in 1963. He also was the assistant dean for admissions of the medical school, 1964-9; associate chairman of the department, 1969-71; and chairman, 1971-80. He became professor emeritus in 1986. Later that year he joined the faculty of the University of Delaware where he is now an adjunct professor of psychology. He is a member of many professional societies.

In 1968 he was an alternate delegate to the Democratic National Convention.

David's wife, Frances Keesler Graham, earned her B.A. at Pennsylvania State University in 1938 and her Ph.D. in psychology at Yale in 1942. She has been the acting director at the Saint Louis Psychiatric Clinic, 1942-44; an instructor at Barnard College, 1948-51; a research associate at the Washington University School of Medicine, 1942-48 and 1953-57; a research associate at the University of Wisconsin, 1957-64, as well as an associate professor there, 1964-68, and professor, 1968-86; a Hillside research professor, 1980-86; and is now a professor at the University of Delaware. She is a member of numerous organizations and associations and has published many articles in professional journals. In 1983 she received the Distinguished Alumna award from Pennsylvania State University. She has also been elected to the National Academy of Sciences. Children:

8-1 Norma Van Surdam, b. Saint Louis, 8 August 1944

8-2 Andrew Tredway, b. Philadelphia, 12 December 1945

8-3 Mary Brewster, b. Saint Louis, 6 February 1952

7-4 EVARTS AMBROSE GRAHAM JR.,[3] born Saint Louis, 4 February 1921; married in Pound Ridge, New York, 30 June 1951, FRANCES ADLER (called "Perugina," a pet name she preferred to Frances), born Chicago, 20 July 1920, died Washington, D.C., 30 April 1987, buried Santa Barbara, California, daughter of Herman Morris Adler (born New York City, 1876, died in Boston, 1935) and Frances Porter (died New York).

Evarts was graduated from Harvard in 1941 and worked for a year as a reporter and editor of the *Saint Louis Post-Dispatch*. In 1942 he was drafted as a private and was discharged in 1946 as a first lieutenant in the United States Air Force. After his discharge he returned to the *Saint Louis Post-Dispatch* with whom he remained until he retired in 1985. He has been its managing editor, 1968-79, and a contributing editor and Washington, D.C., columnist, 1979-85. He has also acted as president of various school and civic boards and has had assorted responsibilities for Harvard, the American Newspaper Guild, and the American Society of Newspaper Editors.

Perugina attended Scripps College in California, 1938-9, and was graduated from Radcliffe in 1942. In 1945-6 she was a civilian employee of the United States Army in Germany. In 1953 she earned a bachelor's in occupational therapy at Washington University, Saint Louis, and later worked as an occupational therapist and crafts instructor. Her father was a penologist and psychiatrist in Illinois and California, and her great-uncle, Felix Adler, was the renowned educator and founder of the Ethical Culture movement. Children, all born in Saint Louis:

8-4 Stephen Porter, b. 1 September 1954

8-5 Helen Evarts, b. 22 February 1957

8-6 Sarah Frances, b. 21 August 1962


CHILDREN OF 6-7 HARVEY WILSON GRAHAM JR.
AND LENA HARRIET PARSONS [4]


7-5 DANIEL PARSONS GRAHAM, born Washington, D.C., 20 July 1900; married (1) on 15 August 1928, EMMA AUDREY SPEAKE (called Audrey), born Charles County, Maryland, 5 October 1903, died Silver Spring, Maryland, 21 July 1960, buried Rock Creek Cemetery, Washington, D.C., daughter of Edwin Raymond Speake (born c. 1878, died Luray, Virginia, 1970) and Sarah Lavinia Brawner (born c. 1878, died Luray, Virginia, 1967). Audrey's sister Dorothy married Daniel's brother 7-6 Thomas. Daniel married (2) on 3 February 1962, CATHERINE LAPISH, born Washington, D.C., 10 March 1907, died Silver Spring, Maryland, 28 June 1979, buried Rock Creek Cemetery, Washington, D.C., daughter of Henry Lapish and Elizabeth ___.

While working at the Bureau of Standards in Washington, D.C., Dan attended night school at George Washington University for nine years, finally receiving his bachelor's in chemical engineering. He then joined the Bureau of Ship, Research, and Standards at the Navy Department from which he retired in 1960. From 1929 until 1983 he lived in Silver Spring, Maryland, and in 1983 he moved to McCoy, Virginia, where he has lived ever since. While in Silver Spring he and his wife were members of Grace Episcopal Church in which he served as senior warden for many years. Children, both by (1) Audrey, and both born in Washington, D.C.:

8-7 Daniel Parsons Jr., b. 14 December 1929

8-8 Richard Brawner, b. 30 September 1934

6-7 Harvey W. Jr., 5-8 Harvey W., 4-3 John W., 3-3 Matthew, 2-1 Andrew                    7-6

7-6 THOMAS HARVEY GRAHAM, born Washington, D.C., 6 November 1906, died Lynchburg, Virginia, 2 July 1987, buried Virginia Memorial Park, Bedford, Virginia; married, 30 August 1930, DOROTHY CLAGGETT SPEAKE (called Dot; sister of Audrey who married Thomas's brother 7-5 Daniel), born Charles County, Maryland, 17 February 1905, daughter of Edwin Raymond Speake (born *c.* 1878, died Luray, Virginia, 1970) and Sarah Lavinia Brawner (born *c.* 1878, died Luray, Virginia, 1967).

In 1929 Tom earned his bachelor's in civil engineering at the University of Maryland and in 1930 joined the Bell Telephone Company with whom he remained until he retired in 1970. He and Dorothy were members of Saint John's Episcopal Church, and his hobby was woodworking. They lived variously in Newport News, Hampton, Petersburg, Richmond, and Lynchburg, all in Virginia. Children:

8-9 David Harvey, b. Newport News, VA, 26 November 1931

8-10 Clara Claggett, b. Hampton, VA, 16 September 1934

8-11 Thomas Harvey Jr., b. Richmond, VA, 16 November 1946

7-7 JAMES GLENN GRAHAM, born Washington, D.C., 22 October 1912; married in Washington, D.C., 18 March 1946, LOIS MARGARET HOAG, born in Albert Lea, Freeborn County, Minnesota, 25 May 1916, daughter of the Rev. Arthur Joshua Hoag (born Howard Lake, Wright County, Minnesota, 9 May 1876, died Saint Paul, Minnesota, 10 May 1936) and Alice Margaret Misz (born Saint Paul, Minnesota, 27 December 1884, died Saint Paul, 2 December 1956).

James was graduated in zoology from the University of Maryland in 1935 and earned a master's in zoology from the same university in 1937. His thesis was entitled "Seasonal Attachment of Wharf Pile Organisms" and involved research done at the Chesapeake Biological Laboratory at Solomons Island, Maryland. From 1935 until 1942 he was a general science teacher at Hine Junior High School, Washington, D.C., and, from 1943 to 1973 he was principally a biology teacher at Saint Alban's School for Boys, Washington, D.C. Among other courses he also taught at Saint Alban's were general science, physics, physical geology, algebra, sacred studies, and ancient history. From 1973 until 1975 he was a general science teacher and assistant librarian at the International School, Washington, D.C., and for fifteen years he was also on the National College Board Summer Series for Examination Reviews.

In 1938 and 1940 James took a cruise to the Caribbean, visiting the Panama Canal and the northern coast of South America. After retirement he made four pilgrimages to England and Scotland.

As a member of Saint Paul's Rock Creek Church, James was the leader of a boy scout troop for two years. He recalls returning from a weekend camp and hearing on his car radio about the attack on Pearl Harbor. As a member of Saint John's Norwood Parish Church, Bethesda, Maryland, from 1947 to 1970, he served as librarian for twelve years and as vestry by appointment for one year. He is currently a member of Ascension and Saint Agnes Episcopal Church, Washington, D.C. He has also served as a verger at the Washington National Cathedral, 1943-73, and has recently volunteered to be a greeter at the cathedral. His other interests include stamp collecting and gardening.

Lois is a retired secretary at the Public Health Service and National Institute of Health, Bethesda, Maryland. She and James have lived in Bethesda since 1947.

Children, all born in Washington, D.C.:

8-12 John Robert, b. 10 July 1950

8-13 Joel Glenn, b. 27 August 1951

8-14 Elizabeth Margaret, b. 21 June 1953

8-15 Philip James, b. 4 December 1954

## CHILD OF 6-22 HAROLD WILSON GRAHAM AND JESSIE MCDONALD

7-8 SUZANNE GRAHAM CLEMENT HORNER, born 1934;[5] married (1) RAYMOND M. CLEMENT; (2) before 1979, ___ HORNER. She has lived in Omaha, Nebraska; Houston, Texas; and Punta Gorda, Florida. Children, all by (1) Raymond:

A. Graham Clement

B. Scott Clement

C. Kelly Clement

6-25 Wilmer T., 5-41 Dales Y., 4-9 J. Harvey, 3-3 Matthew, 2-1 Andrew          7-9

### CHILD OF 6-25 WILMER TRUMBULL GRAHAM
### AND FLORA ANN MORGAN

7-9 JAMES WILMER GRAHAM,[6] born Moline, Illinois, 3 December 1925; married in Fresno, California, 17 September 1949, CONNIE BAIRD. He was graduated in engineering from the University of California and was in the United States Air Corps. Children, both born in Fresno, California:

    8-16 Karen Lynn, b. May 1959    8-17 Jeff Baird, b. 2 February 1961

### CHILDREN OF 6-28 RALPH GRAHAM
### AND LULU ___ [7]

7-10 ADAH GRAHAM

7-11 RALPH GRAHAM JR.; married KATHERINE MCCUIE(?).

7-12 LEILA K. GRAHAM

7-13 JOYCE L. GRAHAM

### CHILDREN OF 6-33 FRED Y. GRAHAM
### AND MELCENA ___

7-14 LEE W. (or William L.) GRAHAM, born Iowa, October 1899

6-51 George R., 5-64 Alva A., 4-23 J. Thomas, 3-8 William M., 2-1 Andrew        7-15

7-15 RICHARD C. GRAHAM, born Iowa, c. 1904

7-16 DONALD E. GRAHAM, born Iowa, January 1910


CHILDREN OF 6-51 GEORGE RAYMOND GRAHAM
AND RUBY SNYDER [8]

7-17 VIRGINIA GRAHAM

7-18 GEORGIA GRAHAM

7-19 DORIS GRAHAM


CHILDREN OF 6-55 FREDERICK LAWRENCE GRAHAM
AND KATHRYN PATTERSON [9]

7-20 RUTH ARLENE GRAHAM BARNES, born Beattie, Kansas, 10 July 1935; married in Texas, 1 July 1955, MARVIN DALE BARNES, born 15 January 1934, since divorced. Children:

   A. Kathryn Arlene Barnes Marek, born Madrid, Spain, 4 December 1958; married in Texas, Wesley Marek, since divorced.

   B. Kenneth Dale Barnes, born Madrid, Spain, 9 March 1960

   C. John Gale Barnes, born Lincoln, Nebraska, 4 October 1961

7-21 MARILYN JO ANN GRAHAM BRADFORD, born Marysville, Kansas, 12 July 1939; married in Iowa, 29 July 1959, KENNETH BRADFORD, born Nebraska, 3 January 1935. Children, both born in Omaha, Nebraska:

- A. Darrel Dean Bradford, born 3 March 1961
- B. Bruce Eugene Bradford, born 6 April 1964; married in Texas, Sandra McDonald.

7-22 CHARLES RICHARD GRAHAM, born Barneston, Nebraska, 3 January 1944; married in Nebraska, 6 August 1966, CAROLE ANN RICHARDS, born Nebraska, 1 August 1944. Children, both born in Omaha, Nebraska:

8-18 Richard Wayne, b. 15 May 1967

8-19 Douglas Allen, b. 21 May 1970

## CHILDREN OF 6-57 JOHN HOWARD GRAHAM AND EDNA BROADHEAD [10]

7-23 TWILA GRAHAM; married ___ who was in the United States Air Force. They lived in Tacoma, Washington.

7-24 RICHARD GRAHAM; married ___. They lived in Burley, Idaho. Child:

8-20 Richard Jr.

7-25 LESTER GRAHAM, killed in a house fire some time before his father died in about 1965.

CHILD OF 6-59 ROY EDSON GRAHAM
AND AMY E. WADE [11]

7-26 ERMA LORENE GRAHAM MCCALLUM, born Anacortes, Washington, 13 May 1912; married at her home in Anacortes, 8 July 1938, WILLIAM GEORGE "Bill" MCCALLUM, born Anacortes, 20 January 1908, died Anacortes, 7 October 1985, son of William Hough McCallum (born Ontario, Canada, 1864, died Anacortes, Washington, 1933) and Mary Lanphear (born 1876, died Anacortes, 1942). Erma and Bill were married by the Rev. Donald Finlayson, minister of Westminster Presbyterian Church. In 1930-31 Erma attended Success Business College in Seattle then returned to Anacortes where she worked as a long distance operator for the West Coast Telephone Company from 1932 until about 1940. After marriage she worked part time in her husband's business until 1968 when she became a licensed real estate saleswoman, acquiring her real estate broker's license in 1971 and working full time until the business ceased in 1984. Since then she has been very active in real estate, working part time at Anacortes Realty, and for two years serving as a board member of the Skagit County Board of Realtors. She also was heavily involved in her husband's greatest business triumph, the securing of Shell Oil Company as the buyer of a 350-acre site for an oil refinery. This business coup brought thousands of jobs to Anacortes. Erma's many avocations include the following: she was a charter member of the Bessie Cook March Children's Hospital Guild, is a member of the Anacortes chapter of the General Federation of Women's Clubs, and is actively involved with the Westminster Presbyterian Church.

Bill attended the University of Washington in Seattle, 1927-1929, then returned to Anacortes to work in his father's real estate and insurance business of which Bill assumed ownership when his father died in 1933. He became so active in community affairs and was so well known and liked that when he and Erma were married in 1938 the local newspaper published a special edition with a three-inch headline saying, "MCCALLUM WEDS TODAY." In 1953 when he and Erma secured the Shell Oil contract, the newspaper published another special edition also with a three-inch headline and this time saying, "SHELL PICKS LOCAL SITE." He was the president of the Chamber of Commerce and was also a member of the Kiwanis Club, the Eagles, and the Elks, and was named honorary chief of the Junior Fire Marshall Program by the Anacortes Fire Department for providing fire hats and promoting fire prevention and safety education in the schools. But Bill's chief avocation was music. He played the saxophone and clarinet in a swing band called "The

Revelers" and was a member of the musician's union for fifty-two years. In tribute to his love for music, the William G. McCallum Memorial Fund was established at Anacortes High School to assist young musicians. Child:

A. Jennifer Lorene McCallum Juckett, born Anacortes, Washington, 3 March 1946; married in Everett, Washington, 7 July 1987, Russell Bernard Juckett Jr., born Hopkinsville, Kentucky, 26 October 1943, son of Russell Bernard Juckett (born Whittier, California, 29 November 1913) and Alice Barbo (born Bow, Washington, 16 November 1921). Jennifer was graduated from Stephens College, Columbia, Missouri, and in 1970-72 was the anchorwoman on KEET-TV. In 1974 she established her own business in Hollywood, California, in public relations and talent management. Her business is now entitled Juckett Sports and Entertainment, and she is the only woman negotiator in NFL draft choice contracts. Russell attended Shagit Valley College, 1961-63, was graduated from the University of Washington in 1965, and earned a doctor of laws degree at Vanderbilt University in 1971. In 1965-68, he was also a sergeant in the United States Army. He was a councilor-at-law in 1973-78, Everett city councilman in 1976, prosecuting attorney in 1978-82, and has since been a councilor-at-law. Children, (both adopted):

1. Lyle Bo Juckett, born Eureka, California, 9 November 1970

2. Lorene Andrea Juckett, born Eureka, California, 7 January 1972

## CHILDREN OF 6-67 RAY WILLIAM GRAHAM AND ANNA MARIA WITTMUSS [1,2]

7-27 CALVIN WITTMUSS GRAHAM, born Beattie, Kansas, 11 October 1924, baptized at Christian Church, Marysville, Kansas, 10 September 1933; married at Christian Church, Marysville, 5 October 1947, VELORES MAXINE KOLL, born near Oketo, Kansas, 8 March 1930, baptized Christian Church, Marysville, 29 March 1942, daughter of Edwin Frank Koll (born Marshall County, Kansas, 15 May 1891, died Marshall County, 11 December 1950) and Nettie Gibson (born Marshall County, 16 March 1900, died Marshall County, 8 April 1975).

6-67 Ray W., 5-68 John G., 4-23 J. Thomas, 3-8 William M., 2-1 Andrew          7-28

In 1942-43 Calvin attended Grand Island Business College, Grand Island, Nebraska, then joined the army but was soon discharged because of his severe asthma. He briefly had a roller skating business in Pittsburg, Kansas, and in 1948 began working at Boeing Aircraft in Wichita. In 1952 he switched to the aircraft plant operated by General Motors in Kansas City where he and Velores lived until 1956 when they moved to Columbus, Ohio. From 1956 to 1971 he worked at North American Rockwell at Columbus, and from 1971 to 1975 he was a real estate agent there. They then moved to Clinton, Arkansas, and established their own real estate business, Graham and Associates. Cal served as an elder, 1965-75, at Linden Church of Christ, Columbus, Ohio, which also gave him the Father-of-the-Year Award in 1965. He is now a member of the Clinton Zoning and Planning Commission, an officer of the Van Buren County, Arkansas, Livestock and Fair Association, and the president of the Van Buren County Board of Realtors. His chief hobby is music: he played the clarinet in high school and was a member of the choir and of the quartet at Linden Church of Christ. He also belonged to the Buckeye Barbershoppers and in about 1962 sang with a chorus in a competition in Dallas.

Velores has done volunteer work at Linden Church of Christ, Columbus, Ohio, worked at Riverside Methodist Hospital there, 1970-72, and earned a real estate license in 1973. In 1976 she received her broker's license in Arkansas and now works with her husband in their business, Graham and Associates, in Clinton, Arkansas. She was the secretary of Van Buren County, Arkansas, Realtors in 1978 and president of Clinton B. and P. W. in 1980. Since 1984 she has also served on the Van Buren County Fair board. Children, the first four born in Wichita, Kansas:

8-21 Jon Philip, b. 21 December 1948
8-22 Connie Rae, b. 21 January 1950
8-23 Gregg Edwin, b. 17 April 1951
8-24 Christopher Lee, b. 15 July 1952
8-25 Sue Ann, b. Kansas City, MO, 27 June 1955

7-28 RAE MARIE GRAHAM DARNER, born Summerfield, Kansas, 13 June 1926, baptized 1933; married in Pittsburg, Kansas, 31 October 1947, ROBERT DAYTON DARNER, born Omaha, Nebraska, 7 February 1924, baptized 1936, son of Clyde Otis Darner (born Overton, Nebraska, 22 December 1894, died Phoenix, Arizona, 2 November 1964) and Edna Louise Ranney (born Blue Hill, Nebraska, 16 May 1892).

6-67 Ray W., 5-68 John G., 4-23 J. Thomas, 3-8 William M., 2-1 Andrew                 7-28A

In 1943, Rae attended the Lincoln School of Commerce in Lincoln, Nebraska, and was the secretary to the dean of women at the University of Omaha, 1944-47. Later she was an administrative assistant at Good Shepherd Center for Exceptional Children, Flossmoor, Illinois, 1968-81. She and her husband retired to Fairfield Bay, Arkansas, in May 1981. She sings in the choir at the Methodist church, is a member of the P.E.O. sisterhood, and has done volunteer work not only with Outreach in the Hills, Fairfield Bay, but also with the United States Coast Guard Auxiliary.

Robert was a first lieutenant in the United States Air Force, 1943-46, and in 1948 was graduated from Iowa State University, Ames, Iowa, with a degree in industrial engineering. He then worked in marketing at the truck division of International Harvester Company from 1948 until 1981 when he and Rae retired to Fairfield Bay, Arkansas. In his volunteer work he has been a flotilla vice-commander, commander, and operations officer in the United States Coast Guard Auxiliary. He has also been a treasurer at the First Christian Church in Chicago Heights, a member of Tau Beta Pi (an honorary engineering fraternity), and a member of the Permanent Resident Property Owners Association in Fairfield Bay, Arkansas. Children:

A. Linda Rae Darner, b. Ames, IA, 6 June 1948
B. Cathy Louise Darner, b. Fremont, NE, 15 March 1950
C. Robert Graham Darner, b. Omaha, NE, 21 September 1951
D. David Richard Darner, b. Omaha, NE, 25 October 1952
E. Jeffrey Alan Darner, b. Fargo, ND, 19 October 1954

---

A. Linda Rae Darner Horelick Darley, born Ames, Iowa, 6 June 1948, baptized 1960; married (1) in Homewood, Illinois, 14 March 1971, Stephen A. Horelick, separated in 1978 and divorced in 1984; (2) in Ione, California, 29 April 1984, Paul Edward Darley, born Minneapolis, Minnesota, 17 November 1943, son of Ellis Fleck Darley (born Monte Vista, Colorado, 2 November 1915) and Katherine Delight Slusher (born Joplin, Missouri, 1 October 1916). Linda was graduated from Northern Illinois University in 1970 and from 1979 to the present has been the manager of Compensation and Benefits at Coopervision in California. Paul was graduated from the University of California at Davis, worked with the United States Public Service, 1968-70, and is now a research scientist at Alza

Corporation, 1971 to the present.

Child by (1) Stephen A. Horelick:

1. Devra Irene Horelick, born Saint Paul, Minnesota, 24 July 1972

Child by (2) Paul Edward Darley:

2. Elizabeth Delight Darley, born Palo Alto, California, 12 September 1984

B. Cathy Louise Darner Rezabek, born Fremont, Nebraska, 15 March 1950, baptized April 1962; married in Chicago Heights, Illinois, 27 December 1971, David Carl Rezabek, born Chicago, 15 January 1949, baptized February 1949, son of Raymond John Rezabek (born Berwyn, Illinois, 6 December 1927) and Marilyn Jean Ceranek (born Chicago, 1 May 1928). In 1974 Cathy was graduated from Northern Illinois University with a degree in textiles and clothing and presently is the secretary-treasurer in a business with her husband, Evergreen Interiors, Inc., which deals in tropical plants. She is a member of the P.E.O. sisterhood, the United Methodist Church, and the Parent-Teachers Association. David was a sergeant in the Illinois National Guard, 1971-77, and earned a bachelor's in education from Northern Illinois University in 1971. Later he earned two master's degrees: marketing (1973) and business administration (1975). He has had teaching experience at Morton High School, Berwyn, Illinois, and presently is a co-owner with his wife of Evergreen Interiors, Inc. Among his hobbies is water skiing. Children:

1. Jeffrey Ryan Rezabek, born Berwyn, Illinois, 5 August 1972

2. Janna Rae Rezabek, born Berwyn, Illinois, 28 November 1975

C. Robert Graham Darner, born Omaha, Nebraska, 21 September 1951, baptized 9 October 1964; married at West Dundee, Illinois, 5 October 1974, Joan Carol Netzbandt, born Elgin, Illinois, 22 March 1952, daughter of Ronald Earl Netzbandt (born Carpentersville, Illinois, 20 December 1920) and Arlene Mae Fierke (born Elgin, Illinois, 18 May 1920). Robert earned a bachelor's in psychology at the University of Illinois, 1973, attended the University of Illinois Law School, 1973-4, and earned his law degree at the Illinois Institute of Technology --Chicago Kent Law School, 1979. Until 1986 he practiced law in Chicago and is now a claims attorney in Bloomington, Illinois. Joan earned a bachelor's in journalism at the University of Illinois, 1974, and has had experience as a reporter and editor for an Illinois newspaper, 1976-82. Children, both probably born in Chicago:

1. Whitney Blake Netzbandt Darner, born 9 April 1982

2. Reagan Lorena Netzbandt Darner, born 5 September 1985

D. David Richard Darner, born Omaha, Nebraska, 25 October 1952, baptized 1964; married (1) on 6 September 1975, Donna Marie Dixon, divorced in 1981; (2) at Cicero, Illinois, 1 January 1983, Carol Jeanette Baldwin, born Kankakee, Illinois, 13 December 1953, baptized 1954, daughter of Earl Lee Baldwin (born Huntsville, Alabama, 22 May 1929) and Jeanette Tulcus (born Chicago, 23 May 1931). David earned a degree in psychology at the University of Illinois in 1974, was a catalogue buyer at Aldens, Inc. in Chicago until 1983, and is now the president and principal stockholder of Teksys Corporation. In his volunteer work he served on the pastor-parish relations committee of the Sheridan United Methodist Church in 1985 and was its chairman in 1986-87. Carol was a division control manager at Alden, Inc., 1971-83, and is presently the senior controller (inventory control) at Spiegel, Inc., in Oakbrook, Illinois. In 1987 she was part of the special study program at Kellogg Graduate School of Management. Children, all by (2) Carol:

1. David Lee Darner, stillborn at Morris, Illinois, 24 November 1983

2. Ashley Ann Darner, born Morris, Illinois, 27 November 1984

3. Rachel Leigh Darner, born Morris, Illinois, 11 February 1986

E. Jeffrey Alan Darner, born Fargo, North Dakota, 19 October 1954, baptized 1966; married at Saint Louis, Missouri, 21 October 1977, Linda Lee Craven, born Kansas City, Missouri, 23 July 1947, baptized 17 August 1947, daughter of Herman Reese Craven (born Kansas City, Missouri, 27 January 1920) and Margaret Aralee Aschwanden (born Kansas City, Missouri, 4 July 1924). This was Linda's second marriage, her first to ___ Robertson. Jeffrey was graduated in liberal arts from the University of Illinois, 1976, and has worked at International Harvester Company variously at Kansas City and Saint Louis, Missouri, and at Sioux City, Iowa, 1977-81. He is presently a manager in parts operations at Garden State International Trucks, San Jose, California. Linda was a trade show manager at Coopervision, 1982-7, and presently works at Octel Communications. Jeffrey and Linda have no children of their own although Linda had two children by her previous marriage: Tres Lee Robertson, born Belton, Missouri, 17 March 1968; and Jason Trent Robertson, born Fort Knox, Kentucky, 14 July 1971.

7-29 ___ GRAHAM (boy), born c. 1928, lived only a few hours

CHILD OF 6-71 WALTER IVAN GRAHAM
AND EDITH VIOLA RICHARDSON [13]

7-30 CYNTHIA RAE GRAHAM SHAW; married, September 1974, TERRY VINCENT SHAW.

CHILDREN OF 6-73 JOSEPH C. GRAHAM
AND RELDA MOSER [14]

7-31 LAWRENCE N. GRAHAM

7-32 VELMA MARY GRAHAM PALMER, born Summerfield, Kansas, 27 February 1923; married at Marysville, Kansas, 7 February 1944, GLENN ALBERT PALMER, born Summerfield, Kansas, 6 August 1922, son of William A. Palmer (born 26 May 1872, died 23 March 1946) and Zella Brown (born 20 November 1885, died ___). Children:

6-73 Joseph C., 5-69 Lawrence W., 4-23 J. Thomas, 3-8 William M., 2-1 Andrew        7-32A

- A. Jean Marie Palmer, b. 28 October 1945
- B. Keith Lynn Palmer, b. 30 May 1947
- C. Don William Palmer, b. 31 January 1949
- D. Glenda June Palmer, b. 14 June 1954
- E. Gary Dale Palmer, b. 14 November 1960

---

A. Jean Marie Palmer Kasten, born Beatrice, Nebraska, 28 October 1945; married at Emporia, Kansas, 13 February 1966, Dennis Dean Kasten, born 2 December 1943, son of Paul Kasten (born 26 January 1917) and Velova Koepse (born 26 March 1924). Child:

1. Victoria Renee Kasten Reynolds, born Emporia, Kansas, 28 September 1966; married at Emporia, 3 May 1986, Tony Reynolds, born 6 November 19__.

B. Keith Lynn Palmer, born Beatrice, Nebraska, 30 May 1947; married at Junction City, Kansas, 6 February 1965, Patricia Susan Sutter, born 21 March 1947. Child:

1. Paula Denise Palmer Hernandez, born Council Grove, Kansas, 10 August 1965; married in Puerto Rico, 11 December 198_, Hector Hernandez. Child:

    a. Julian Keith Hernandez, born 10 April 1987

C. Don William Palmer, born Beatrice, Nebraska, 31 January 1949; married, 22 March 1968, Margaret Wildman, born 11 August 1947 or 1948, divorced in 1984.

D. Glenda June Palmer, born 14 June 1954, died 25 July 1954.

E. Gary Dale Palmer, born Herington, Kansas, 14 November 1960; married at Parkerville, Kansas, 27 December 1985, Ella Mae Abernathy, born 5 June 1967, daughter of Thomas Abernathy and Valda Sams.

7-33 MYRON ALBERT GRAHAM, born Summerfield, Kansas, 13 July 1925; married, 29 September 1946, DONNA AMELIA BARGMAN, born Herkimer, Kansas, 3 November 1924. Children, all born in Beatrice, Nebraska:

8-26 Allen Eugene, b. 21 December 1947
8-27 Kathy Sue, b. 17 March 1954
8-28 Julie Lynne, b. 16 July 1957

7-34 ROSS G. GRAHAM, born Summerfield, Kansas, 31 March 1931; married at Barneston, Nebraska, 27 November 1958, DONNA RAE FREDERICKSON, born Beatrice, Nebraska, 31 May 1941, daughter of Daryl Frederickson (born ___, died Barneston, Nebraska, 30 October 1953) and Margaret ___. Children:

8-29 Jerald Ray, b. 16 November 1959
8-30 Janice Mae, b. 4 December 1961
8-31 Joe Alan, b. 18 March 1968

## CHILDREN OF 6-74 EVERETT MCKINLEY GRAHAM AND ETHEL R. E. LYNCH [15]

7-35 NELVA ARLENE GRAHAM ROBESON, born Summerfield, Kansas, 9 December 1921; married, 1 May 1946, LAWRENCE WILLIAM ROBESON, born Summerfield, Kansas, 24 September 1920. Children, all born in Nebraska:

A. Lawrence William Graham, b. Liberty, NE, 1 July 1943
B. Stephen Roy Robeson, b. Pawnee City, NE, 5 March 1957
C. Richard Dale Robeson, b. and d. 6 March 1959
D. Jo Lynne Robeson, b. Pawnee City, NE, 1 July 1960

---

A. Lawrence William Graham (Larry), born Liberty, Nebraska, 1 July 1943; married (1) on 20 July 1961, Sharon Lynn Wyman (Sherry), born Evansville, Illinois, 24 June 1941, divorced June 1967; (2) on 28 September 1968, Judith Ann McConaha, born Columbus, Ohio, 5 December 1938. Children by (1) Sherry:

1. Cynthia Lou Graham Helms (Cindy), born Albuquerque, New Mexico, 5 February 1962; married in 1981, Robert Helms,

separated in 1982.

2. Donald Eugene Graham, born Marysville, Kansas, 23 July 1964

Larry's second wife, Judy, had children by previous marriages: Rae Ann Newan, born Santa Maria, California, 24 June 1957; and Jody Lee Rodgers, born San Luis Obispo, California, 16 April 1961, adopted by Larry in 1970.

B. Stephen Roy Robeson, born Pawnee City, Nebraska, 5 March 1957; married, 5 May 1979, Julie Mae Husa, born 14 May 1960. Children, all born in Beatrice, Nebraska:

1. Jonathan Roy Robeson, born 6 October 1979

2. David William Robeson, born 11 July 1982

3. Jeffrey Voyne Robeson, born 23 September 1983

C. Richard Dale Robeson, born and died 6 March 1959

D. Jo Lynne Robeson Schwarz, born Pawnee City, Nebraska, 1 July 1960; married, 27 October 1978, Allen E. Schwarz (called Buck), born Marysville, Kansas, 6 April 1957. Children, both born in Marysville, Kansas:

1. April Marie Schwarz, born 28 April 1981

2. Jeremiah Edwin Schwarz, born 8 September 1984


7-36 WILMA MAXINE GRAHAM NAAF, born Oketo, Kansas, 12 July 1923; married at Fort Snelling, Minnesota, 2 August 1942, MERLIN PHILLIP NAAF, born Beattie, Kansas, 20 September 1918. Children:

A. Jerry Lee Naaf, b. Liberty, NE, 4 July 1943
B. Ronald Leroy Naaf, b. Manhattan, KS, 9 January 1948
C. Julienne Marie Naaf, b. Beatrice, NE, 17 December 1959

---

A. Jerry Lee Naaf, born Liberty, Nebraska, 4 July 1943; married, 9 September 1963, Doris Rinne, born 4 November 1943. Children:

6-75 Paul E., 5-69 Lawrence W., 4-23 J. Thomas, 3-8 William M., 2-1 Andrew          7-36A1

1. James Newman Naaf, born Lincoln, Nebraska, 26 January 1964

2. Thomas Frost Naaf, born Muscatine, Iowa, 27 April 1968

B. Ronald Leroy Naaf, born Manhattan, Kansas, 9 January 1948; married, 21 August 1983, Sharon Kay Stohs, born Marysville, Kansas, 17 September 1945. Child:

1. Sarah Elizabeth Naaf, born Beatrice, Nebraska, 28 October 1984

Sharon also had a child by a previous marriage: Stephanie Rachel Mansfield, born Topeka, Kansas, 14 September 1977.

C. Julienne Marie Naaf Freed (called Julie), born Beatrice, Nebraska, 17 December 1959; married, 17 December 1983, David Milton Freed, born Leavenworth, Kansas, 3 September 1958.

7-37 DONNA JUNE GRAHAM, born Fairbury, Nebraska, 15 June 1929, died September 1949.

7-38 MAURICE DEAN GRAHAM (called Bud), born Fairbury, Nebraska, 7 October 1933; married, 28 December 1956, SHIRLEY ANN BUCHER, born Omaha, Nebraska, 17 September 1936. Children, the first three born in Mobile, Alabama:

8-32 Lonnie Dean, b. 3 May 1958
8-33 Thomas Victor, b. 18 December 1960
8-34 Deborah Ann, b. 25 January 1962
8-35 Richard Dale, b. Beatrice, NE, 1 November 1964

CHILDREN OF 6-75 PAUL E. GRAHAM
AND VELMA IRENE RICHARDSON [16]

7-39 LYNN GRAHAM, born probably in Summerfield, Kansas ___, died of rheumatoid fever while still in high school, 17 January 1946.

7-40 LOWELL EUGENE GRAHAM, born Summerfield, Kansas, 12 December 1926; married (1) on 23 April 1954, BEVERLY JEAN BARTRAM, born Sabetha, Kansas, 27 December 1935, died 21 June 1977; (2) on 23 March 1979, NELDA JUNE OBERHELMAN, born Fairbury, Nebraska, 17 January 1938. Children, all by (1) Beverly:

8-36 Larry Eugene, b. 23 December 1954
8-37 Valerie Jean, b. Seattle, WA, 7 February 1956
8-38 Paula Sue, b. Beatrice, NE, 21 October 1958
8-39 Sheryl Ann, b. Seattle, WA, 24 June 1959
8-40 Gayle Larie, b. Seattle, WA, 23 October 1960
8-41 Lynda Kae, b. Seattle, WA, 13 March 1962

7-41 PAUL E. GRAHAM JR., born probably in Summerfield, Kansas, 7 February 1928; married, 9 February 1948, ROSE MARIE BUTLER, born 27 August 1929. Children:

8-42 Linda Marie, b. 23 June 1950
8-43 Paul James, b. 10 November 1954
8-44 Philip Eugene, b. 1 August 1957
8-45 Thomas Joseph, b. 26 October 1962

7-42 BONNIE LOU GRAHAM WILLIAMS, probably born in Summerfield, Kansas; married CAL WILLIAMS. They live in McPherson, Kansas.

7-43 JESSIE CHARLENE GRAHAM DUNTZ KOEPKE (called Charlene), born Summerfield, Kansas, 16 October 1935; married (1) at Junction City, Kansas, 5 November 1951, CARL LLOYD DUNTZ, born Smith Center, Kansas, 16 December 1927, divorced 14 February 1966; (2) ROLAND KOEPKE (called Kip). She lives in Lincoln, Nebraska. Children, all by (1) Carl and all born in Beatrice, Nebraska:

A. Terri Lea Duntz, b. 20 November 1951
B. Paul Neil Duntz, b. 19 January 1953
C. David Lee Duntz, b. 12 May 1954
D. Sheri Rae Duntz, b. 5 June 1958
E. Ricky Lynn Duntz, b. 29 May 1961

6-75 Paul E., 5-69 Lawrence W., 4-23 J. Thomas, 3-8 William M., 2-1 Andrew       7-43A

A.  Terri Lea Duntz, born Beatrice, Nebraska, 20 November 1951, died 9 December 1951.

B.  Paul Neil Duntz, born Beatrice, Nebraska, 19 January 1953; married at Lincoln, Nebraska, 31 August 1973, Janelle Maria Ray, born South Pasadena, California, 25 June 1953. Children:

   1. Stephanie Marie Duntz, born Lincoln, Nebraska, 17 June 1974

   2. Devin Jay Duntz, born Lyons, Kansas, 29 December 1976

C.  David Lee Duntz, born Beatrice, Nebraska, 12 May 1954; married (1) at Lyons, Kansas, 4 May 1974, Vencette Jan Pfister, born Sterling, Kansas, 4 May 1956, divorced 22 November 1979; (2) at Lincoln, Nebraska, 13 July 1985, Christine Jean Renner, born Crete, Nebraska, 17 December 1965.

   Children by (1) Vencette Pfister:

   1. Kristina Rae Duntz, born 2 January 1975

   2. Kevin William Duntz, born Lyons, Nebraska, 18 July 1978

   Children by (2) Christine Renner:

   3. Matthew David Duntz, born Crete, Nebraska, 2 February 1983

   4. Adam James Duntz, born Lincoln, Nebraska, 21 December 1986

D.  Sheri Rae Duntz LaFollette, born Beatrice, Nebraska, 5 June 1958; married at Burr, Nebraska, 5 June 1976, Gerald Leslie LaFollette, born Nebraska City, Nebraska, 8 July 1948. Children:

   1. Jason Lee LaFollette, born Syracuse, Nebraska, 24 October 1976

   2. Travis James LaFollette, born Syracuse, Nebraska, 12 September 1979

   3. Tyler Wade LaFollette, born Lincoln, Nebraska, 22 February 1986

E.  Ricky Lynn Duntz, born Beatrice, Nebraska, 29 May 1961; married at Lincoln, Nebraska, 13 July 1985, Debra Dawn Fienstra, born Platte, South Dakota, 29 April 1957. Child:

1. Andrea Lynne Duntz, born Syracuse, Nebraska, 22 November 1987

7-44 KAE LA JEANNE GRAHAM CINK, born Beatrice, Nebraska, 8 February 1943; married NORMAN LARRY CINK, born 18 January 1943. They live in Lincoln, Nebraska. Children:

A. Darren Jay Cink, born 23 December 1966

B. Dustin Shay Cink, born 16 November 1969


CHILDREN OF 6-81 WILLIS GRAHAM
AND CAROLINE GRAUER [17]


7-45 CHARLENE ANN GRAHAM, born and died 3 December 1938.

7-46 BETTE LOU GRAHAM PERRY, born 26 October 1939; married on 4 June 1967, ELTON ROGER PERRY. Children:

A. Kendra Jo Perry, born 28 June 1969

B. Roger Lee Perry, born 3 January 1976

7-47 MARY MICHELLE GRAHAM WHEELOCK HAECKER, born 20 June 1945; married (1) on 29 May 1964, DARREL WHEELOCK, born 10 June 1943; (2) on 19 June 1971, LEROY HAECKER, born 10 November 1941. Children, both by (1) Darrel Wheelock:

A. Michelle Marie Wheelock Milke, born 12 December 1964; married, 3 August 1984, Patrick Joseph Milke.

B. Gene Allen Wheelock, born 10 November 1965; married, 7 June 1986, Pamela Rae Edeal.

6-89 Frederick, 5-77 Lee A., 4-25 Matthew J., 3-8 William M., 2-1 Andrew

## CHILD OF 6-89 FREDERICK GRAHAM
## AND ___ [18]

7-48 SUSAN ANN GRAHAM, born 1940. In 1962 she was a registered nurse living in San Diego, California.

## CHILDREN OF 6-92 ROBERT ROY GRAHAM
## AND EVA MAE TAYLOR [19]

7-49 JIMMIE ROY GRAHAM, born and died in Marysville, Kansas, 14 September 1934.

7-50 JO ANN VARDA GRAHAM BARNHILL, born Marysville, Kansas, 7 September 1935; married at Saint Malachy Catholic Church, Beattie, Kansas, 7 April 1956, KENNETH JAMES BARNHILL, born Mullen, Nebraska, 3 November 1935, son of Lloyd K. Barnhill and Ethel May James. Children, all born in Beatrice, Nebraska:

A. Diane Lynne Barnhill Yousefi, born 2 May 1957; married, 2 January 1977, Reza Yousefi.

B. Lori Jo Barnhill, born 3 May 1958

C. Robert Kenneth Barnhill, born 6 May 1959

D. Michael James Barnhill, born 22 July 1960

E. Paul Jay Barnhill, born 19 October 1961

F. Dennis Gale Barnhill, born 4 July 1963

G. Darryl Joseph Barnhill, born 5 October 1965

H. David Todd Barnhill, born 10 August 1967

I. Chad Erin Barnhill, born 8 February 1975

7-51 JIMMY DARRYL GRAHAM, born Oketo, Kansas, 7 June 1938; married at Saint Malachy's Catholic Church, Beattie, Kansas, 1 July 1961, DIANE SEYMOUR, born Brattleboro, Vermont, 16 January 1940, daughter of William Russell Seymour and Merlene Phelps. They live at Englewood, Colorado. Children, both born in Denver, Colorado:

8-46 Sandra Kay, b. 2 May 1962

8-47 Douglas Roy, b. 6 January 1967

7-52 JUDITH MARIE GRAHAM MARSCHMAN, born Marysville, Kansas, 13 October 1940; married at Saint Thomas Aquinas Church, Lincoln, Nebraska, 11 August 1962, DALE DEAN MARSCHMAN, born Daykin, Nebraska, 14 March 1936, son of Edwin Marschman and Beulah Schmidt. They live at Littleton, Colorado. Children:

A. Leigh Ann Marschman, born Lincoln, Nebraska, 6 May 1963 or 1964

B. Daniel Dale Marschman, born Englewood, Colorado, 17 August 1965

C. Renae Lynette Marschman, born Englewood, Colorado, 15 August 1968

D. Kendra Marschman, born Englewood, Colorado, 1979

CHILD OF 6-94 JOHN WILLIAM GRAHAM
AND LAURA MAXINE FLETCHER [20]

7-53 JOHN WILLIAM GRAHAM JR., born Marysville, Kansas, 25 February 1947; married, 20 February 1970, SANDRA KAY CLEMENTS, born 15 January 1949. In the 1976-79 city directories of Lincoln, Nebraska, John was listed as a research technician at the University of Nebraska. Children:

8-48 Kristi Lynn, b. Tecumseh, NE, 10 October 1971

8-49 John D., b. Lincoln, NE, 7 April 1975

6-110 George A., 5-94 William A., 4-30 Samuel A., 3-8 William M., 2-1 Andrew

## CHILD OF 6-110 GEORGE ALLISON GRAHAM
## AND (1) EDITH AEBISHER(?) [21]

7-54 FRED GRAHAM

7-55 FRANCES GRAHAM

## CHILDREN OF 6-111 CLARENCE SAMUEL GRAHAM
## AND WYNONA ___ [22]

7-56 DIANE GRAHAM SMITH; married ___ Smith and has four children.

7-57 JACQUELINE GRAHAM; married and has two children.

## CHILDREN OF 6-114 CHESTER GRAHAM
## AND FRANCES MABERRY [23]

7-58 WILLIAM GRAHAM

7-59 ___ GRAHAM (girl)

CHILD OF 6-115 PHILIP EDWARD GRAHAM
AND (1) WANITA VICKERS [24]

7-60 PHILIP EDWARD GRAHAM JR., born 7 July 1937, died 9 July 1937.

CHILD OF 6-115 PHILIP EDWARD GRAHAM
AND (2) BERNICE MARGARET HAMMETT [25]

7-61 MARY MARGARET GRAHAM GABRIEL, born Long Beach, California, 23 April 1943; married, 24 February 1968, DONALD CASPER GABRIEL.


CHILDREN OF 6-116 GORDON ALBERT GRAHAM
AND BETTE JUNE RICHESON [26]

7-62 JUDITH LYNNE GRAHAM DUKATZ BAKER, born Oakland, California, 24 March 1941; married (1) in 1962, CARL FREDERICK DUKATZ; (2) MARK D. BAKER.

    Child by (1) Carl Dukatz:

A. Eric Dukatz

    Child by (2) Mark Baker:

B. Adam Gordon Samuel Baker


7-63 DARLEEN JOAN GRAHAM EXUM, born San Jose, California, 15 June 1945; married EDWARD SHERMAN EXUM. They live in Denver, Colorado. Children:

A. Amber Laura Exum, born 1974

B. Damon Edward Exum, born 1976


7-64 THAIS JUNE GRAHAM, born San Jose, California, 14 October 1950

## CHILDREN OF 6-117 ROBERT JOHNSON GRAHAM
## AND GLADYS KORSGARDEN [27]

7-65 THOMAS EDWARD GRAHAM, born Long Beach, California, 11 January 1949

7-66 CHRISTINE DIANE GRAHAM CROWDER, born Lexington Park, Maryland, 9 March 1952; married in 1979, RONALD CROWDER.

7-67 ROBERT DAVID GRAHAM, born Corona, California, 1 June 1954


## CHILD OF 6-118 ARLIE HAROLD GRAHAM
## AND RUTH MARY RITTER [28]

7-68 ROBERT LAYMAN GRAHAM, born Kanawha, Iowa, 11 August 1918; married at Little Rock, Arkansas, 12 August 1944, MARILYN LUYSCH(?), born Glenwood, Iowa, 11 March 1920. Children, all born in Omaha, Nebraska:

8-50 Kathleen, b. 3 March 1953
8-51 Arlene, b. 21 April 1955
8-52 Robert Layman Jr., b. 23 April 1957


## CHILD OF 6-119 EARL STEWART GRAHAM
## AND HELEN BLACK [29]

7-69 MARGARET KAREN GRAHAM TUSSEY, born near Creston, Union County, Iowa, 18 December 1938; married at Orient, Iowa, 7 June 1959, JAMES WILBUR TUSSEY, born Shannon City, Iowa, 5 January 1937. Children:

A. Jeffrey James Tussey, born Des Moines, Iowa, 24 September 1961; married at Greenfield, Iowa, 20 June 1981, Peni Jo Huddleson. Children:

1. Jill Tussey

2. Nick Tussey

B. Stephen Earl Tussey, born Des Moines, Iowa, 28 March 1964; married at Greenfield, Iowa, 23 July 1985, Teresa Jo Kingery. Child:

1. Thad Tussey


CHILDREN OF 6-122 ROBERT RUSSELL GRAHAM
AND LUCILE JEANNETTE CONWAY [30]


7-70 MARGARET JEAN GRAHAM KEYBURN, born Macksburg, Iowa, 2 January 1928; married at Compton, California, WILLIAM JOSEPH KEYBURN, born Norwalk, Connecticut, 17 March 1927. Children:

A. Robert George Keyburn, born Lynwood, California, 3 September 1954

B. Kathy Ann Keyburn, born Lynwood, California, 5 May 1957

C. Terri Lee Keyburn, born Lynwood, California, 1 April 1959

D. Thomas Edward Keyburn, born Harbor City, California, 28 December 1960


7-71 BETTY MAE GRAHAM BARR, born Council Bluffs, Iowa, 13 April 1929; married at Hollydale, California, JOHN HEROD BARR, born Paramount, California, 28 August 1929. Children, all born in Lynwood, California:

A. Sherry Lynn Barr, born 2 August 1953

B. Sharon Lee Barr, born 3 September 1954

6-123 Wyman L., 5-96 Robert C., 4-30 Samuel A., 3-8 William M., 2-1 Andrew          7-71C

C. Marianne Barr, born 28 December 1957

7-72 HAROLD EDWARD GRAHAM, born Greenfield, Iowa, 27 May 1934; married at Whittier, California, EILEEN ESTHER MCDONALD, born Canton, Ohio, 23 May 1935.

## CHILDREN OF 6-123 WYMAN LEE GRAHAM AND SHIRLEY LOUISE HAYMAN [31]

7-73 KENNETH LEE GRAHAM, born Creston, Iowa, 12 February 1949; married at Lenox, Iowa, 20 July 1969, ROSALIE ANN FREEMAN, born Creston, Iowa, 22 November 1950, daughter of Harry Freeman and Darlene Cole. Kenneth was in the United States Army and is now a farmer in Iowa. Children:

8-53 David Lee, b. Oceanport, NJ, 3 July 1971
8-54 Lori Ann, b. Creston, IA, 3 September 1973
8-55 Jennifer Lynn, b. Creston, IA, 3 September 1975

7-74 WILLIAM ROBERT GRAHAM, born Greenfield, Iowa, 1 January 1952

7-75 MARY LOUISE GRAHAM, born Creston, Iowa, 16 October 1958

# EIGHTH GENERATION

### CHILDREN OF 7-3 DAVID TREDWAY GRAHAM
### AND FRANCES JEANETTE KEESLER [1]

8-1 NORMA VAN SURDAM GRAHAM, born Saint Louis, Missouri, 8 August 1944; married at Eugene, Oregon, 6 July 1979, WAYNE WICKELGREN, born Hammond, Indiana, 4 June 1938, son of Herman Wickelgren (born Detroit Lakes, Minnesota, 26 October 1894, died Denver, Colorado, 1983) and Alma Emelia Larson (born Detroit Lakes, Minnesota, 12 November 1902).

Norma, who has retained her maiden name, was graduated from Stanford University in 1966, earned her Ph.D. at the University of Pennsylvania in 1970, and is presently a professor of psychology at Columbia University. Wayne was graduated from Harvard in 1960 and earned his Ph.D. at the University of California, Berkeley, in 1962. Children, all born in Eugene, Oregon:

A. Peter Wickelgren Graham, born 19 February 1980

B. Kirsten Graham Wickelgren, born 21 June 1981

C. Jeanette Graham Wickelgren, born 23 December 1985

8-2 ANDREW TREDWAY GRAHAM, born Philadelphia, Pennsylvania, 12 December 1945; married at Madison, Wisconsin, 8 June 1968, MARILYN SUZANNE HAACK, born Madison, Wisconsin, daughter of Herman Joseph Haack (born Madison, September 1913, died Madison, 1 May 1980) and Martha Anna Augusta Daellenbach (born Dorchester, Wisconsin, 8 October 1911). Andrew is a chemist at Dow Chemical in Midland, Michigan. Children, all born in Midland, Michigan:

9-1 James Tredway Graham, born 5 June 1978

9-2 Martha Daellenbach Graham, born 19 March 1982

9-3 Katharine Elizabeth Graham, born 6 June 1985


8-3 MARY BREWSTER GRAHAM, born Saint Louis, Missouri, 6 February 1952; married at Madison, Wisconsin, 29 December 1980, ROBERT FRANK SIMONS, born Kenosha, Wisconsin, 23 July 1946, son of Frank Edward Simons (born Chicago, 19 May 1903) and Florence Hughes (born Somers, Wisconsin, 17 August 1908, died Kenosha, Wisconsin, 1960).

Mary, who has retained her maiden name, was graduated from Stanford in 1974, took her master's at M.I.T. in 1978, and earned her LL.D. at Yale in 1982. She is presently practicing law at Wilmington, Delaware. Robert was graduated from the University of Wisconsin in 1968 and also earned his master's (1974) and Ph.D. (1980) at the University of Wisconsin. Child:

A. Laura Graham Simons, born Syracuse, New York, 29 November 1987


CHILDREN OF 7-4 EVARTS AMBROSE GRAHAM JR.
AND FRANCES ("Perugina") ADLER [2]


8-4 STEPHEN PORTER GRAHAM, born Saint Louis, 1 September 1954, died Saint Louis, 1970.


8-5 HELEN EVARTS GRAHAM, born Saint Louis, 22 February 1957; married in Arlington, Virginia, 30 June 1985, JAMES N. RETALLACK, born Montreal, Quebec, 2 July 1955, son of Norman F. Retallack and Lois Neill.

Helen, who has retained her maiden name, earned her bachelor's at Harvard in 1979. From 1979 until 1982 she was a Rhodes scholar at Oxford University where she earned an additional bachelor's in 1981 and a master's in 1982. In 1989 she earned her Ph.D. in agricultural economics at Stanford. She has been an assistant professor of economics at the University of Alberta, 1985-7, and at the University of Toronto, 1987-8. At present she is a staff member of Ontario's Minister of Treasury and Economics. James, who was also a Rhodes scholar, earned his Ph.D. in history at Oxford University, 1983. He was an instructor at the University of California at Santa Cruz, 1984-5, and an assistant professor at the University of Alberta, Canada, 1985-7. At present he is an assistant professor of history at the University of Toronto and is the author of *Notables of the Right: The Conservative Party and Political Mobilization in Germany, 1876-1918* (1988). Child:

A. Stuart Adler Graham Retallack, born Toronto, 26 July 1988

8-6 SARAH FRANCES GRAHAM, born Saint Louis, 21 August 1962; married in Saint Louis, 18 February 1989, JUAN A. IGLESIAS Y LOLI, born Lima, Peru, 21 September 1960, son of Juan Donato Iglesias y Calderon (born Lima, Peru) and Lastenia Loli (born Lima, Peru).

Sarah attended the Catholic University of Peru, 1982-3, and Tufts University from which she earned her bachelor's in 1984. She has been a writer for the Associated Press in Lima, Peru, 1984-6, and at Cheyenne, Wyoming, 1986-8, and has retained her maiden name. Juan attended the Catholic University of Peru, 1980-4, and is presently the export manager for Fabritex in Lima.

CHILDREN OF 7-5 DANIEL PARSONS GRAHAM
AND (1) EMMA AUDREY SPEAKE [3]

8-7 DANIEL PARSONS GRAHAM JR., born Washington, D.C., 14 December 1929. He lived in Maryland until 1977 and is now a resident at Stewart Home School, Frankfort, Kentucky.

8-8 RICHARD BRAWNER GRAHAM, born Washington, D.C., 30 September 1934; married at Blacksburg, Virginia, 22 September 1972, MARY ELLEN MORRIS, born Christiansburg, Virginia, 18 February 1944, daughter of William Howard Taft Morris and Virgie McCoy.

They live at McCoy, Virginia, where Dick is employed in maintenance at Virginia Polytechnic Institute and S.U. Children, both born in Radford, Virginia:

9-4 Faith Ellen Graham, born 6 October 1974

9-5 Joseph Brawner Graham, born 3 March 1979

## CHILDREN OF 7-6 THOMAS HARVEY GRAHAM
## AND DOROTHY CLAGGETT SPEAKE [4]

8-9 DAVID HARVEY GRAHAM, born Newport News, Virginia, 26 November 1931; married at Petersburg, Virginia, 26 July 1958, SARAH JANE ELLIS, born Petersburg, Virginia, 8 October 1934, daughter of Kenneth Nicholas Ellis (born Waverly, Virginia, 9 June 1893, died Petersburg, Virginia, 21 October 1970) and Orra Smith (born Java, Virginia, 25 June 1903, died Lynchburg, Virginia, July 1978).

David was a sergeant in the United States Army, 1952-4, and was stationed in Korea. Later he attended the Virginia Polytechnic Institute and in 1960 earned a bachelor's in industrial arts education. He has since taught industrial arts at the Lynchburg, Virginia, public schools and has also been a high school golf coach. He was the Golf Coach of the Year in 1986 and 1988. In addition to golfing his hobbies include fishing and hunting. Sarah attended Hollins College, 1952-3, then switched to the Richmond Professional Institute, a branch of William and Mary, where she earned a bachelor's in business administration in 1956. Since 1970 she has been a bookkeeper at Alan Pearson Drugs in Lynchburg, Virginia. Children:

9-6 Martha Burt Graham Lipscomb, born Radford, Virginia, 25 May 1960; married, Lynchburg, Virginia, 28 July 1984, Derrick Lee Lipscomb, born Lynchburg, 10 August 1960, son of Marcellus Pendleton Lipscomb (born 17 January 1934) and Nellie Faye Flint (born 27 December 1936). Martha earned a bachelor's and a master's at Radford University in 1983 and is now a speech and language pathologist at the Lynchburg public schools. Derrick attended Central Virginia Community College and since 1978 has been employed at Lynchburg Public Works. They are members of Saint John's Episcopal Church in Lynchburg. Child:

Emily Stuart Lipscomb, born Lynchburg, 30 May 1987

9-7 David Harvey Graham Jr., born Lynchburg, Virginia, 8 May 1963. He earned a bachelor's in mathematics at Lynchburg College and is now employed in the trust department at Central Fidelity Bank in Lynchburg. His hobby is golfing, and he has been an All-American Division golfer for the past three years. He is a member of Saint John's Episcopal Church.

8-10 CLARA CLAGGETT GRAHAM RENNICKS, born Hampton, Virginia, 16 September 1934; married in Maryland, 20 December 1953, ROBERT SMITH RENNICKS JR., born New Rochelle, New York, 13 January 1934, son of Robert Smith Rennicks (born Providence, Rhode Island, 20 February 1898) and Thora Smith (born Brooklyn, New York, 21 April 1900, died Petersburg, Virginia, 3 January 1963).

Clara attended PanAmerican Secretarial School, 1952-3, and presently works at Bellcore in New Jersey. In 1955 Robert earned a bachelor's at Virginia Military Institute and was a lieutenant in the United States Air Force until 1957. Later he earned a master's at Pace University and is now an engineer. They live in Westfield, New Jersey. Children:

A. Robert Smith Rennicks III, born Richmond, Virginia, 8 August 1955. He earned a bachelor's in mathematics and English at Dartmouth in 1977 and later earned his master's at Berkley. At present he is teaching and earning a doctorate there.

B. Jeffrey Graham Rennicks, born Dayton, Ohio, 13 March 1957, died 21 April 1974, buried Blandford Cemetery.

C. Elizabeth Brawner Rennicks, born Newport News, Virginia, 15 December 1958. She attended Lees-McRae College, North Carolina, in 1979 and earned a bachelor's at East Carolina University in 1981. Since 1982 she has worked at Bellcore in New Jersey and lives in Westfield. Her hobbies include soft ball. She was also in the Special Olympics Runs.

8-11 THOMAS HARVEY GRAHAM JR., born Richmond, Virginia, 16 November 1946; married at Richmond, 9 August 1969, FRANCES BRYANT MAYES, born Richmond, 16 December 1947, daughter of Bryant Cleveland Mayes (born Sussex County, Virginia, 12 December 1905, died Richmond, 12 December 1982) and Frances Harrington Blake (born Richmond, 11 August 1912).

In 1970 Thomas earned a bachelor's in business administration at Richmond Professional Institute, a branch of William and Mary in Richmond, then became a master sergeant in the United States Army Reserve Corps. Since 1980 he has been a sales engineer. His hobbies include woodworking, hunting, and fishing, and he is also interested in trains. Frances earned a bachelor's in education at Radford College in 1969 and was a teacher from 1969 until 1977 and again from 1987 to the present. She has also been active in the PTA, as a school volunteer, and as a Sunday school teacher in the United Methodist church of which she and Thomas are members. Children, all born in Richmond, Virginia:

9-8 Sarah Blake Graham, born 4 January 1978

9-9 Laura Speake Graham, b. 10 August 1979

9-10 Susan Ware Graham, born 23 November 1980

## CHILDREN OF 7-7 JAMES GLENN GRAHAM
## AND LOIS MARGARET HOAG [5]

8-12 JOHN ROBERT GRAHAM, born Washington, D.C., 10 July 1950; married at Saint Mark's Church, Bethesda, Maryland, 6 June 1982, MARJORIE JEAN BUCKINGHAM, born Rapid City, South Dakota, 1 March 1951, daughter of Porter Buckingham and Leita Snodgrass.

John was a sergeant in the United States Air Force, 1969-73, and was stationed in Thule, Greenland, and Vandenburg Air Force Base, California. In 1976 he was graduated in history from the University of Maryland and from 1977 to 1985 worked as a central service technician/receiver at Alexandria Hospital, Virginia. Since 1985 he has been the inventory control clerk for B'nai B'rith Women in Washington, D.C. As a member of Saint John's Episcopal Church in Bethesda, Maryland, John has been an acolyte, assistant director of acolytes, and Sunday school teacher. Since 1977 when he converted to the Orthodox church, he has been a Sunday school teacher and has twice been elected auditor of the financial records of Saint Mark's Church, Bethesda, Maryland. He has also maintained a strong interest in history, particularly the history of the American Civil War, and since 1978 has been a second lieutenant in a Civil War Living History Unit, the First Virginia Regiment. The activities of this group include battle reenactments, honor guards, parades, and first-person, living-history presentations to the public. Marjorie is a clerk at the FBI office in Washington, D.C. She and John live in Manassas, Virginia. Children, both born in Manassas:

9-11 Martin Garrett Graham, born 28 April 1985

9-12 David Michael Graham, born 4 January 1987


8-13 JOEL GLENN GRAHAM, born Washington D.C., 27 August 1951; says, "Ain't dead yet or married." Joel was graduated from Bethesda-Chevy Chase High School in 1969 and served in the United States Air Force, 1969-73, in the Forty-Ninth Tactical Fighter Wing in which he was an aircraft mechanic. Most of his military service was spent at Holloman Air Force Base near Almogordo, New Mexico, although he was sent on several tours to West Germany and on one tour to Thailand. Since 1975 Joel has been a member of the Izaak Walton League, B-CC Chapter, and is also a life member of the National Rifle Association. His hobbies include hunting, fishing, and target shooting. He works at Atlantic Guns in Silver Spring, Maryland.


8-14 ELIZABETH MARGARET GRAHAM THURBER (called Liz or Betty), born Washington, D.C., 21 June 1953; married, at Woodbury, New Jersey, 10 December 1977, TIMOTHY THURBER, born Barstow, California, 7 September 1954, son of Russel Thurber (born 5 October 1928) and Dolores Finizio (born 12 December 1928).

Liz was graduated from Bethesda-Chevy Chase High School where she was on the girl's field hockey team and was the president of the Girl's Sports Association. She was given the Golden Key Award. She was also in girl's hockey at Susquehanna University, Selinsgrove, Pennsylvania, from which she was graduated in biology in 1975. From 1975 to 1977 she was a veterinarian's assistant, first in the Philadelphia area, then in Montgomery County, Maryland. Since marriage she has worked part-time at a local produce stand and at a craft-garden store. Tim was graduated in Latin from Susquehanna University, Selinsgrove, Pennsylvania, and is presently a Latin and English teacher at a public high school in Easton, Maryland. He also coaches the school soccer team and works with the track team. Children, all born in Easton, Maryland:

A. Kurt Russel Thurber, born Maryland, 1 February 1979

B. Rebecca Leigh Thurber, born Maryland, 19 March 1981

C. Daniel James Thurber, born 28 October 1983


-15 PHILIP JAMES GRAHAM, born in Washington, D.C., 4 December 1954; unmarried. Phil was graduated from Bethesda-Chevy Chase High School in 1972. He attended Lycoming College, Williamsport, Pennsylvania, for one year before transferring to the University of Maryland, College Park, from which he was graduated in 1976 with a bachelor's in botany. In 1980 he earned a master's in plant pathology from Virginia Tech, Blacksburg, Virginia. His thesis dealt with the development of cylindrocladium black rot on peanuts and the survival of the causal organism in the soil. From 1980 to 1985 he was enrolled in the doctoral program in the Department of Plant Pathology at the University of Minnesota, Saint Paul, but did not complete it. Since 1985 he has lived in Bethesda, Maryland, and has worked not only as a part-time cashier for Giant Foods, but also as a seasonal gardener for Brookside Gardens in Wheaton, Maryland, and a bank teller for Sovran Bank. Recently he obtained a position with the National Park Service as a greenhouse technician. He is a member of the Bethesda First Baptist Church. Among his interests is research in family history and genealogy in general. In fact he is already being consulted by others for genealogical research.


CHILDREN OF 7-9 JAMES WILMER GRAHAM
AND CONNIE BAIRD [6]


-16 KAREN LYNN GRAHAM, born May 1959


-17 JEFF BAIRD GRAHAM, born 2 February 1961

## CHILDREN OF 7-22 CHARLES RICHARD GRAHAM
## AND CAROLE ANN RICHARDS [7]

8-18 RICHARD WAYNE GRAHAM, born Omaha, Nebraska, 15 May 1967

8-19 DOUGLAS ALLEN GRAHAM, born Omaha, Nebraska, 21 May 1970


## CHILD OF 7-24 RICHARD GRAHAM
## AND ___ [8]

8-20 RICHARD GRAHAM JR.


## CHILDREN OF 7-27 CALVIN WITTMUSS GRAHAM
## AND VELORES MAXINE KOLL [9]

8-21 JON PHILIP GRAHAM, born Wichita, Kansas, 21 December 1948; married at Columbus, Ohio, 8 May 1971, DONNELLE OLDAKER, born Columbus, 1 September 1948, daughter of Don L. Oldaker (born Ohio, 29 January 1916, died Columbus, Ohio, 31 October 1977) and Helen Yvonne Smith (born Ohio, 11 October 1919).

Jon earned a degree in business administration at Franklin University, Columbus, Ohio, and is presently a manager of financial planning at Memorial Mission Hospital in Ashland, North Carolina. Donnelle earned her degree at Ohio State University in 1970 and has had experience as a public school teacher, 1971-5 and 1985 to the present. Children:

9-13 Philip Jon Graham, born Columbus, Ohio, 22 April 1975

9-14 Andrew Jon Graham, born Lakeland, Florida, 7 May 1978

8-22 CONNIE RAE GRAHAM FORTLAGE (called Conrae), born Wichita, Kansas, 21 January 1950, baptized 1962; married (1) in January 1970, JOHN L. MERRILL, divorced October 1970; (2) in Columbus, Ohio, 9 August 1974, DAVID R. FORTLAGE, born Cleveland, Ohio, 14 April 1947, son of Herbert Fortlage (born Cleveland, 6 February 1917) and Phyllis Bethke (born Odessa, Minnesota, 15 November 1916).

Conrae attended Lincoln Christian College, 1969-70. After dropping out of college, she traveled through the South to California, living in several states and doing many different jobs such as selling encyclopedias, waiting on table, and assisting the cook on a fishing excursion boat in San Diego. In 1970 she took up sky diving but after four dives decided "the thrill was just too much." At present she is active not only in the Parent-Teachers Association, but also as a volunteer at public schools, as a Sunday school teacher, and as a member of the Homemaker's Club. David works at Hecht's where he has earned an award as an oustanding manager. He and Conrae both do scuba diving, and Dave is a dive master. She writes that they took their first night dive in Cozumel, Mexico, seeing barracuda and nursing sharks. They live in Columbia, Maryland. Children, all by (2) David Fortlage:

A. Tina Dee Conrae Fortlage, born Columbus, Ohio, 10 April 1975

B. Nathan David Graham Fortlage, born Toledo, Ohio, 30 July 1977

C. Michael Calvin Fortlage, born Columbia, Maryland, 22 October 1981


8-23 GREGG EDWIN GRAHAM, born Wichita, Kansas, 17 April 1951, baptized Linden Church of Christ, Columbus, Ohio, April 1963; married at Centralia, Missouri, 3 June 1973, SUSAN RAE LINCOLN, born Fayette, Missouri, 1 March 1954, baptized 1963, daughter of Roy Frank Lincoln (born 17 August 1935) and Patricia Mae Kempf (born Independence, Missouri, 22 May 1935).

Gregg was graduated from Lincoln Christian College, Lincoln, Illinois, in 1973 and served in the ministry in 1973-83. From 1983 until 1985 he was the director of development for Niños de Mexico and, 1985-6, the regional sales manager for Marketing and Management Corporation of America representing Innovative Sales and Retirement Programs. He is now the minister at Cherryvale Christian Church, Cherryvale, Kansas. He has been a substitute teacher and is a member of the Rotary and of a chess club. Marketing and Management Corporation awarded him the honors of top salesman for the company and top manager in the country. Susan attended Lincoln Christian College, 1972-3, and East Central College in Union, Missouri. In her many activities she has been a piano teacher since 1972, a choir director, a member of Crescendo Music Club in Cherryvale, Kansas, and a partner in The Basket Case in Cherryvale. She is related to Abraham Lincoln. Children:

9-15 Luke Christopher Graham, born Lebanon, Indiana, 31 December 1974

9-16 Katie Colleen Graham, born Lebanon, Indiana, 6 March 1977

9-17 Megan Michelle Graham, born Washington, Missouri, 12 March 1982


8-24 CHRISTOPHER LEE GRAHAM, born Wichita, Kansas, 15 July 1952, baptized July 1965; married at Trinity United Methodist Church, Anderson, South Carolina, 17 March 1984, KRISSI HARDER, born Williamsburg, Virginia, 5 March 1959, baptized 16 August 1982, daughter of Richard Harder (born Fairmont, Minnesota, 21 August 1931) and Burnus Meyer (born Fairmont, Minnesota, 20 April 1932).

Chris earned an associate degree in electrical engineering at Columbus Tech and a degree in business administration at Milligan College. He was an E-4 sergeant in the United States Air Force, 1972-6, and is presently an accountant with Consolidated Engraver's, Inc. In his volunteer work he has served with Habitat for Humanity. Krissi was graduated in chemistry from Stephen F. Austin State University, Texas, and since 1984 has been employed as a chemist at Sequa Chemicals, Inc. She and Chris are members of the First Baptist Church, Charlotte, North Carolina. Children:

9-18 Melissa Kristine Graham, born Charlotte, North Carolina, 26 December 1986

9-19 Joshua Koll Graham, born Charlotte, North Carolina, 27 July 1989


8-25 SUE ANN GRAHAM JONES, born Kansas City, Missouri, 27 June 1955; married at Edinburg, Illinois, 26 June 1977, JOHN K. JONES JR., born 27 June 1952, son of John K. Jones (born Pawnee, Illinois, 22 November 1924) and Betty Beatty (born Taylorville, Illinois, 13 November 1926).

7-33 Myron A., 6-73 Joseph C., 5-69 Lawrence W., 4-23 J. Thomas, 3-8 William M.    8-25A

Sue was graduated with a bachelor's in music from Lincoln Christian College in 1977, worked in a dentist's office in 1978 to 1982, and is now a piano teacher at Ozark Christian college. She also played for choirs in high school and college and has played for an Ozark College concert group which goes on tours. John was a sergeant in the United States Air Force, 1972-76. He earned his bachelor's in Christian ministries and Christian education at Lincoln Christian College and his master's there in the New Testament. He has had ministries at Ashland Church of Christ, 1977-78, Lake Fork Christian Church, 1978-82, and Windsor Road Christian Church, 1982-88. He is now a professor at Ozark Christian College. Children:

A. Lindsey Rae Jones, born Springfield, Illinois, 31 January 1982

B. Chelsea Ann Jones, born Champaign, Illinois, 6 February 1985


CHILDREN OF 7-33 MYRON ALBERT GRAHAM
AND DONNA AMELIA BARGMAN [10]


8-26 ALLEN EUGENE GRAHAM, born Beatrice, Nebraska, 21 December 1947; married, 15 February 1969, PEGGY LOU BETTES, born Lima, Ohio, 30 December 1947. Children, both born in Detroit, Michigan:

9-20 Susan Lynette Graham, born 5 October 1970

9-21 Barbara Michelle Graham, born 15 November 1973


8-27 KATHY SUE GRAHAM MORRISON, born Beatrice, Nebraska, 17 March 1954; married in Lawrence, Kansas, 17 September 1976, GARY MORRISON, born Lincoln, Nebraska, 28 February 1954.


8-28 JULIE LYNN GRAHAM CYRUS, born Beatrice, Nebraska, 16 July 1957; married, 29 August 1980, BURTON ROSS CYRUS, born Lincoln, Nebraska, 14 March 1958. Children, both born in Lincoln, Nebraska:

A. Nicholas Allen Cyrus, born 21 August 1982

7-34 Ross G., 6-73 Joseph C., 5-69 Lawrence W., 4-23 J. Thomas, 3-8 William M.　　　8-28B

B.  John Michael Cyrus, born 23 July 1986


CHILDREN OF 7-34 ROSS G. GRAHAM
AND DONNA RAE FREDERICKSON [11]


8-29 JERALD RAY GRAHAM, born 16 November 1959; married ___.  Children:

9-22 Morgan Rae Graham, born 29 December 1985

9-23 Benjamin Ross Graham, born 31 December 1986


8-30 JANICE MAE GRAHAM THOMAS, born 4 December 1961; married 24 July 1987, RONALD LYNN THOMAS.


8-31 JOE ALAN GRAHAM, born 18 March 1968


CHILDREN OF 7-38 MAURICE DEAN GRAHAM
AND SHIRLEY ANN BUCHER [12]


8-32 LONNIE DEAN GRAHAM, born Mobile, Alabama, 3 May 1958; married (1) on 11 March 1980, MELISSA SUSAN STAHL, born Beatrice, Nebraska, divorced 6 November 1983; (2) on 3 October 1986, PAMELA ANN KRUSKA, born 2 September 1964.  Children, both by (1) Melissa and both born in Beatrice, Nebraska:

9-24 Emily Louise Graham, born 3 October 1978

9-25 Sarah Elizabeth Graham, born 11 March 1980

7-40 Lowell E., 6-75 Paul E., 5-69 Lawrence W., 4-23 J. Thomas, 3-8 William M.          8-33

8-33 THOMAS VICTOR GRAHAM, born Mobile, Alabama, 18 December 1960


8-34 DEBORAH ANN GRAHAM FULTON, born Mobile, Alabama, 25 January 1962; married, 21 May 1982, LANCE ROBERT FULTON, born Beatrice, Nebraska, 26 February 1957. Children:

  A. Michael Robert Fulton, born Beatrice, Nebraska, 4 February 1981

  B. Kylee Ann Fulton, born Lincoln, Nebraska, 9 September 1982


8-35 RICHARD DALE GRAHAM, born Beatrice, Nebraska, 1 November 1964


CHILDREN OF 7-40 LOWELL EUGENE GRAHAM
AND (1) BEVERLY JEAN BARTRAM [13]


8-36 LARRY EUGENE GRAHAM, born 23 December 1954; married, 19 November 1977, LAURA KAE KUBES, born 4 July 1961. Children:

  9-26 Nicholas A. Graham, born 17 July 1980

  9-27 Timothy L. Graham, born 8 April 1982

  9-28 Amy M. Graham, born 19 December 1983


8-37 VALERIE JEAN GRAHAM KUBES, born Seattle, Washington, 7 February 1956; married, 16 February 1973, MICHAEL ALLEN KUBES, born 16 November 1954. Child:

  A. Candice A. Kubes (Candy), born 28 August 1972


8-38 PAULA SUE GRAHAM SHANAHAN, born Beatrice, Nebraska, 21 October 1958; married, 6 November 1976, WILLIAM ALLEN SHANAHAN, born 7

7-41 Paul E., Jr., 6-75 Paul E., 5-69 Lawrence W., 4-23 J. Thomas, 3-8 William M.     8-38A

August 1956. Children:

A.  Charles A. Shanahan, born 2 July 1976

B.  Corey S. Shanahan, born 4 October 1981


8-39 SHERYL ANN GRAHAM, born Seattle, Washington, 24 June 1959, died August 1971.


8-40 GAYLE LARIE GRAHAM WAGNER RICHARDSON, born Seattle, Washington, 23 October 1960; married (1) on 6 February 1976, MICHAEL L. WAGNER, born 24 June 1957; (2) on 13 April 1985, TERRY L. RICHARDSON, born 1 December 1964. Children, all by (1) Michael Wagner:

A.  Vickie L. Wagner, born 5 September 1977

B.  Christina M. Wagner, born 14 September 1979

C.  Randall E. Wagner, born 22 February 1983


8-41 LYNDA KAE GRAHAM LUZUM, born Seattle, Washington, 13 March 1962; married, 24 May 1977, THOMAS J. LUZUM, born 13 March 1958. Children:

A.  Jeremy J. Luzum, born 7 September 1977

B.  Shawndra L. Luzum, born 13 May 1981

C.  Bryan T. Luzum, born 8 November 1983


CHILDREN OF 7-41 PAUL E. GRAHAM JR.
AND ROSE MARIE BUTLER [14]


8-42 LINDA MARIE GRAHAM FOREHAND, born 23 June 1950; married on 2 March 1974, THOMAS C. FOREHAND, born 2 October 1951. They live in North

Lake, Illinois. Children:

A. Christina Marie Forehand, born 10 February 1977

B. Thomas Paul Forehand, born 11 June 1982


8-43 PAUL JAMES GRAHAM, born 10 November 1954; married, 12 September 1981, THERESA KOMAREK, born 14 August 1959. They live in Bella Vista, Arkansas. Child:

9-29 Daniel Eric Graham, born 6 August 1984


8-44 PHILIP EUGENE GRAHAM, born 1 August 1957; married, 22 March 1983, JOYCE ERICKSON, born 16 March 1957. They live in Manhattan, Kansas. Child:

9-30 Jason Graham, born 6 August 1986


8-45 THOMAS JOSEPH GRAHAM, born 26 October 1962. He lives in Manhattan, Kansas.


CHILDREN OF 7-51 JIMMY DARRYL GRAHAM
AND DIANE SEYMOUR [15]


8-46 SANDRA KAY GRAHAM, born Denver, Colorado, 2 May 1962


8-47 DOUGLAS ROY GRAHAM, born Denver, Colorado, 6 January 1967

CHILDREN OF 7-53 JOHN WILLIAM GRAHAM JR.
AND SANDRA KAY CLEMENTS [16]

8-48 KRISTI LYNN GRAHAM, born Tecumseh, Nebraska, 10 October 1971

8-49 JOHN D. GRAHAM, born Lincoln, Nebraska, 7 April 1975

CHILDREN OF 7-68 ROBERT LAYMAN GRAHAM
AND MARILYN LUYSCH(?) [17]

8-50 KATHLEEN GRAHAM, born Omaha, Nebraska, 3 March 1953

8-51 ARLENE GRAHAM, born Omaha, Nebraska, 21 April 1955

8-52 ROBERT LAYMAN GRAHAM JR., born Omaha, Nebraska, 23 April 1957

CHILDREN OF 7-73 KENNETH LEE GRAHAM
AND ROSALIE ANN FREEMAN [18]

8-53 DAVID LEE GRAHAM, born Oceanport, New Jersey, 3 July 1971

8-54 LORI ANN GRAHAM, born Creston, Iowa, 3 September 1973

8-55 JENNIFER LYNN GRAHAM, born Creston, Iowa, 3 September 1975

# NOTES

## INTRODUCTION

[1] Frank Adam, *The Clans, Septs, and Regiments of the Scottish Highlands*, 7th rev. ed. by Sir Thomas Innes of Learney (Edinburgh: W. and A. K. Johnston and G. W. Bacon, Ltd., 1965), p. 221; Charles A. Hanna, *The Scotch-Irish, or the Scot in North Britain, North Ireland, and North America*, 2 Vols. (N.Y.: G. P. Putnam, 1902), II, 415; and Margaret O. MacDougall, ed., *Robert Bain's the Clans and Tartans of Scotland*, 5th ed. (London: Collins, 1968), p. 108.

[2] Adam, p. 221.

[3] Madeleine Bingham, *Scotland under Mary Stuart: An Account of Everyday Life* (N.Y.: St. Martin's Press, 1971), pp. 16, 20, and 152ff.; James G. Leyburn, *The Scotch-Irish: A Social History* (Chapel Hill, N.C.: Univ. of North Carolina Press, 1962), pp. xv-xvi; T. C. Smout, *A History of the Scottish People, 1560-1830* (N.Y.: Charles Scribner's Sons, 1969), pp. 42ff.; Wayland F. Dunaway, *The Scotch-Irish of Colonial Pennsylvania* (Chapel Hill, N.C.: Univ. of North Carolina Press, 1944), pp. 13f.; James D. Scarlett, *Tartans of Scotland* (N.Y.: Hastings House, n.d. [c. 1972]), clan map in the frontispiece; and Adam, clan map in the frontispiece.

[4] Bingham, pp. 29ff.; Dunaway, p. 14; Leyburn, pp. 3ff.; Scarlett, *loc. cit*; Adam, *loc cit*; and Smout, pp. 104 and 135ff.

[5] Hanna, I, 400-2; R. L. Mackie, *A Short History of Scotland*, ed. Gordon Donaldson (N.Y: Frederick A. Praeger, 1962), pp. 89f.; and P. Hume Brown, *A Short History of Scotland*, new ed. by Henry W. Meikle (Edinburgh: Oliver and Boyd, Ltd., 1955), pp. 121-2.

[6] Hanna, I, 402.

[7] Robert Moffat, "Graham of Graham's Dyke?," *Scotland*, October 1967, pp. 19f.; and J. C. Beckett, *The Making of Modern Ireland: 1603-1923* (N.Y.: Alfred A. Knopf, 1966), p. 36.

[8] Bingham, pp. 61ff. and 95ff.; and Leyburn, pp. 16-35.

[9] Bingham, pp. 39ff. and 124ff.; Leyburn, pp. 48-51; Smout, pp. 54ff.; and Brown, pp. 179-80.

[10] Bingham, pp. 126-7.

[11] Bingham, pp. 129ff.; Leyburn, pp. 52ff.; and Smout, p. 60.

[12] Brown, pp. 170-6; Bingham, pp. 130-7; and Mackie, pp. 126-7.

[13] Two readable biographies of Knox are by Jasper Ridley, *John Knox* (N.Y.: Oxford University Press, 1968); and Geddes MacGregor, *The Thundering Scot: A Portrait of John Knox* (Philadelphia: Westminster Press, 1957). Although most encyclopedias give the date of John Knox's birth as 1505, persuasive evidence exists that the actual date was c. 1512-15. See the discussions in Ridley, pp. 531-4; and MacGregor, pp. 229-31.

[14] Ridley, pp. 292 and *passim*.

[15] Smout, pp. 53-61 and *passim*; Brown, pp. 179-83 and *passim*; Mackie, pp. 130-7 and *passim*; and Leyburn, pp. 54-61.

[16] J[ames] C[amlin] Beckett, *The Making of Modern Ireland* (N.Y.: Alfred A. Knopf, 1966), pp. 15ff. and 38ff.; Constantine Fitzgibbon, *Red Hand, The Ulster Colony* (Garden City, N.Y.: Doubleday, 1971), pp. 13ff. and 29ff.; Leyburn, pp. 83ff.; An t-Athair Tomas O'Fiaich, "The Beginnings of Christianity," *The Course of Irish History*, ed. T. W. Moody and F. X. Martin (N.Y.: Weybright and Talley, 1967), pp. 61-75; Kathleen Hughes, "The Golden Age of Early Christian Ireland," *The Course of Irish History*, ed. Moody and Martin, pp. 76-90; and G. A. Hayes-McCoy, "The Tudor Conquest," *The Course of Irish History*, ed. Moody and Martin, pp. 174-88.

[17] Beckett, pp. 21-24 and 43ff.; Leyburn, pp. 85-87; Fitzgibbon, pp. 13 and 19; Hayes-McCoy, *loc. cit.*; Henry Jones Ford, *The Scotch-Irish in America* (1915; rptd. N.Y.: Arno Press and The New York Times, 1969), p. 79; and Dunaway, p. 16.

[18] Beckett, pp. 35 and 43f.; Leyburn, pp. 85-7; Fitzgibbon, pp. 17-19; and Aidan Clarke, "The Colonisation of Ulster and the Rebellion of 1641," *The Course of Irish History*, ed. Moody and Martin, pp. 189f.

[19] Leyburn, pp. 87f.; Dunaway, pp. 19f.; Fitzgibbon, pp. 17ff. and 27-29; and Beckett, pp. 45ff. and 53ff.

[20] Beckett, pp. 82-102; Clarke, *The Course of Irish History*, ed. Moody and Martin, pp. 198-203; Leyburn, pp. 26f.; and Fitzgibbon, pp. 32-37.

[21] R. J. Dickson, *Ulster Emigration to Colonial America, 1718-1775* (London: Routledge and Kegan Paul, 1966), pp. 3-4; Beckett, p. 48; Fitzgibbon, p. 30; and Hanna, I, 615.

[22] Hanna, I, 614-5; Leyburn, pp. 164-8; Maude Glasgow, *The Scotch-Irish in Northern Ireland and in the American Colonies* (N.Y.: G. P. Putnam's Sons, 1936), pp. 128-31; Dunaway, pp. 31-3; Ford, pp. 186-7; and Dickson, pp. 38ff.

[23] Leyburn, pp. 142ff.; Dunaway, p. 12; and Fitzgibbon, p. 56.

[24] Fitzgibbon, p. 57; Dickson, pp. 7-12; and Ford, p. 185.

[25] Beckett, pp. 171ff.; Dickson, pp. 13-15, 42ff., and 70ff; Fitzgibbon, p. 58; Leyburn, p. 161; Dunaway, p. 29; and Ford, p. 186.

[26] Beckett, pp. 179-81; and Fitzgibbon, pp. 48-50 and 65.

[27] Dickson, pp. 20-23, 33f., 50f., and 57-9; Ford, p. 167; and Leyburn, p. 175. The historians differ considerably among themselves on the numbers of emigrants. Dickson's figures have been used herein because he seems to give the strongest evidence for their accuracy.

[28] Dickson, pp. 62-4 and 69ff.; Fitzgibbon, pp. 60-1; and Leyburn, p. 173.

[29] Jean Stephenson, *Scotch-Irish Migration to South Carolina, 1772 (Rev. William Martin and

*His Five Shiploads of Settlers)* (Washington, D.C.: the author, 1971), p. 2.

[30] W. Melancthon Glasgow, *History of the Reformed Presbyterian Church in America* (Baltimore: Hill and Harvey, 1888), p. 573.

[31] Stephenson, pp. 17-19 and 25-6; and Glasgow, pp. 572-3.

[32] Dickson, pp. 205-7 and 210-14.

[33] *Ibid.*, p. 253; and Stephenson, pp. 27 and 29.

[34] Dickson, pp. 206 and 254; and Stephenson, pp. 28 and 34.

[35] Dickson, p. 248; Stephenson, p. 28; and Janie Revill, *A Compilation of the Original Lists of Protestant Immigrants to South Carolina, 1763-1773* (Columbia, S.C.: The State Company, 1939), pp. 125-6.

[36] Dickson, p. 248; and Stephenson, p. 28.

[37] Dickson, p. 252; and Stephenson, p. 28.

[38] Stephenson, pp. 37-40; and Robert K. Ackerman, *South Carolina Colonial Land Policies* (Columbia, S.C.: Univ. of South Carolina, 1977), pp. 106-7.

[39] The bulk of Stephenson's book consists of a complete list of the people in Martin's party who went before the South Carolina General Assembly and the grants which they eventually received.--pp. 42-101. Revill also lists those who sailed on *Lord Dunluce, Hopewell, Pennsylvania Farmer,* and *Free Mason.*--pp. 121-27.

[40] Ackerman, p. 94.

[41] The sources for the information on Martin are W. Melancthon Glasgow, pp. 391-2 and 572-4; Stephenson, pp. 17-24; Mary Wylie Strange, *The Revolutionary Soldiers of Catholic Presbyterian Church, Chester County, South Carolina* (1946; rptd. York-Clover Printing Co., 1978), pp. 82-4; R[obert] Lathan, *A Historical Sketch of Union A.R.P. Church, Chester County, South Carolina* (1888; rptd. Richburg, S.C.: Chester County Genealogical Society, 1980), pp. 9-14 and 19-27; and Robert Lathan, *History of Hopewell A.R.P. Church, Chester County, South Carolina* (1879; rptd. Richburg, S.C.: Chester County Genealogical Society, 1981), pp. 5, 8, and 9.

[42] A clear account of the differences between the various Presbyterian groups is given by James Albert Woodburn, "The Scotch-Irish Presbyterians in Monroe County, Indiana," *Indiana Historical Society Publications*, IV, 8 (1910), 441-2 and 455-69. See also John Walker Dinsmore, *The Scotch-Irish in America* (Chicago: Winona Pub. Co., 1906), pp. 70-85.

[43] As quoted by Strange, pp. 83-4.

[44] W. Melancthon Glasgow, p. 574.

[45] Dickson, pp. 22-6; Ford, pp. 211, 221ff., 249ff., 260ff., and 379; Hanna, II, 29; Leyburn, pp. 219f.; Dunaway, pp. 46-9; Jack M. Sosin, *The Revolutionary Frontier, 1763-1783* (N.Y.: Holt,

Rinehart & Winston, 1967), pp. 43-5; E. Estyn Evans, "The Scotch-Irish: Their Cultural Adaptation and Heritage in the American Old West," *Essays in Scotch-Irish History*, ed. E. R. R. Green (London: Routledge & Kegan Paul, 1969), pp. 74ff.; and Solon J. Buck and Elizabeth Hawthorne Buck, *The Planting of Civilization in Western Pennsylvania* (Pittsburgh: Univ. of Pittsburgh Press, 1939), pp. 136f.

[46] Paul A. W. Wallace, *Pennsylvania, Seed of a Nation* (N.Y.: Harper & Row, 1962), p. 64.

[47] Evans, pp. 80f.

[48] Leyburn, p. 222; and Sosin, pp. 40 and 43.

[49] Hector St. John de Crèvecoeur, *Letters from an American Farmer* (1782; rptd. London: J. M. Dent & Sons, Ltd., 1911), pp. 51-2.

[50] *Ibid.*, pp. 62 and 64.

[51] Charles Woodmason, *The Carolina Backcountry on the Eve of the Revolution: The Journal and Other Writings of Charles Woodmason, Anglican Itinerant*, ed. Richard J. Hooker (Chapel Hill, N.C.: Univ. of North Carolina, 1953), p. 39.

[52] *Ibid.*, p. 15.

[53] *Ibid.*, p. 54.

[54] *Ibid.*, p. 14.

[55] *Ibid.*, pp. 16f.

[56] *Ibid.*, p. 30.

[57] Sosin, p. 186; and Esmond Wright, "Education in the American Colonies: The Impact of Scotland," *Essays in Scotch-Irish History*, ed. Green, p. 22.

[58] Woodmason, pp. 13, 15, 20, 41-3, and *passim*.

[59] Hanna, II, 116.

[60] Curtis P. Nettels, *The Roots of American Civilization: A History of American Colonial Life* (N.Y.: Appleton-Century-Crofts, 1938), pp. 126-7 and 516-21; and Louis B. Wright, *South Carolina: A Bicentennial History* (N.Y.: W. W. Norton, 1976), pp. 38-62.

[61] Ackerman, pp. 82, 90, 94, 106, and 110f.

[62] As quoted by David Duncan Wallace, *South Carolina, a Short History: 1520-1948* (Chapel Hill, N.C.: Univ. of North Carolina, 1951), p. 223.

[63] *Ibid., loc. cit.*

[64] *Ibid., loc. cit.*

⁶⁵ Stella H. Sutherland, *Population Distribution in Colonial America* (N.Y.: Columbia University, 1936), pp. 236-40; Wright, p. 98; and David Duncan Wallace, pp. 222-3.

⁶⁶ Richard J. Hooker, *The Carolina Backcountry on the Eve of the Revolution: The Journal and Other Writings of Charles Woodmason, Anglican Itinerant*, ed. Richard J. Hooker (Chapel Hill, N.C.: Univ. of North Carolina, 1953), pp. 170-2; and Wright, p. 98.

⁶⁷ David Duncan Wallace, pp. 226f.; Wright, pp. 98f.; and Hooker, pp. 172-80. Hooker prints Woodmason's petition to the council in full, pp. 213-33.

⁶⁸ Hooker, pp. 180-3.

⁶⁹ Woodmason, p. 209.

⁷⁰ Hooker, pp. 183f.

⁷¹ *Ibid.*, pp. 184-9; Wright, p. 99; David Duncan Wallace, p. 228-30; and Leyburn, pp. 304-5.

⁷² Thousands of books have been written on the American Revolution. For South Carolina during the Revolution, see especially Edward McCrady, *History of South Carolina in the Revolution, 1780-1783* (New York, 1902); Lyman C. Draper, *King's Mountain and Its Heroes* (Cincinnati, 1881); Kenneth Roberts, *The Battle of Cowpens: The Great Morale Builder* (New York, 1958); and Donald Barr Chidsey, *The War in the South: The Carolinas and Georgia in the American Revolution* (New York, 1969). Among the many comprehensive histories of the Revolution, the following may be mentioned: George F. Scheer and Hugh F. Rankin, *Rebels and Redcoats* (Cleveland, 1957), pp. 389-466; R. Ernest Dupuy and Trevor N. Dupuy, *The Compact History of the Revolutionary War* (New York, 1963), pp. 323-350 and 358-420; and Don Higginbotham, *The War of American Independence: Military Attitudes, Policies, and Practice, 1763-1789* (New York, 1971), pp. 352-376. Of course, South Carolina histories also include lengthy accounts of the Revolution in the state.

⁷³ Leyburn, pp. 304-5.

⁷⁴ David Duncan Wallace, pp. 298-9.

⁷⁵ W. Melancthon Glasgow, p. 390.

⁷⁶ David Duncan Wallace, p. 325.

⁷⁷ *Ibid.*, pp. 325-6.

⁷⁸ W. Melancthon Glasgow, p. 390.

⁷⁹ David Duncan Wallace, p. 329.

## FIRST GENERATION

¹ In the 1880 census both 3-7 Martha Graham Shanklin and 3-8 William M. Graham, children of David's son Andrew, listed Ireland as Andrew's place of birth. The Scottish migration to Ireland had

generally ceased by 1715. Since David did not die until 1795-1800, it is probable that he was born after 1715 and was therefore born in Ireland. Also, since he was probably a member of the Rev. William Martin's congregation in County Antrim, it is likely that he was born in that county.

[2] Council Journal, 6 January 1773 (British copy); also listed by Janie Revill, comp., *A Compilation of the Original Lists of the Protestant Immigrants to South Carolina, 1763-1773* (Columbia, S.C.: The State Co. 1939), p. 125; and Jean Stephenson, *Scotch-Irish Migration to South Carolina, 1772 (Rev. William Martin and His Five Shiploads of Settlers)* (Washington D.C.: the author, 1971), p. 74.

[3] *Chester County, South Carolina, Genealogical Society Bulletin,* I, 2 (June 1978), 11.

[4] Brent H. Holcomb and Elmer O. Parker, *Camden District, S. C., Wills and Administrations, 1781-1787 (1770-1796)* (Easley, S.C.: Southern Historical Press, 1978), p. 12.

[5] Recorded 29 August 1820, Book T, p. 265; also cited by Mary Wylie Strange, *The Revolutionary Soldiers of Catholic Presbyterian Church, Chester County, South Carolina* (1946; rptd. York-Clover Printing Co., 1978), p. 48.

[6] Brent H. Holcomb and Elmer O. Parker, *Chester County, South Carolina, Minutes of the County Court, 1785-1799* (Easley, S.C.: Southern Historical Press, 1979), p. 56.

[7] "Ferring books" were books on the blacksmith's trade. The modern spelling is "farring," and a farrier (someone who does farring) not only shoes horses, but also sometimes treats horse diseases.

## SECOND GENERATION

[1] The information herein on Andrew differs from that which the DAR has printed in its *DAR Patriot Index*, but the writers believe their information is correct. In its *Patriot Index* the DAR says the following: "Graham, Andrew, b c. 1734 d 1821 m (1)Margaret Coalton [sic] (2) Margaret Mary Chestnut." This data was taken from research done by someone at the DAR headquarters in Washington, D.C., who was working on Application #432472 submitted in 1954 by Mary Louise Bruington (great-granddaughter of 4-19 Martha Graham Hutchinson). The researcher penciled in (1) "Ireland" as Andrew's place of birth; (2) "c1753" as his date of birth then crossed out the date and wrote "c1734" above it, commenting that since Andrew had married a first wife in 1755 he must have been at least 21 years old then; and (3) "Mary Chestnut" as Andrew's second wife. (The researcher bracketed the name "Margaret" which Mrs. Bruington had typed as Andrew's second wife and penciled in the information that Margaret was the "3rd wife named in will." Apparently, when the *Dar Patriot Index* was compiled the researcher's addition of the second wife, "Mary Chestnut," and the typed-in "Margaret" as Mrs. Bruington's name for the second wife became telescoped into "Margaret Mary Chestnut." As to (1) above, the researcher was correct on Andrew's place of birth. This is known because Andrew's children 3-7 Martha and 3-8 William M. both gave Ireland as his birthplace in the 1880 census. As to (2) above, for three reasons the writers believe that Andrew was born not in c. 1734 but in c. 1753 as the researcher originally wrote. First, Andrew was unmarried when he came to America from Ireland in 1772. This is known because he received the single-person's warrant for 100 acres. If he had been married, he would have received warrants for an additional 50 acres for his wife and 50 more acres apiece for each child. Second, Andrew migrated to Kentucky in 1805-9; he would have been 71-5 years old then if he had been born in 1734--not an age when most people would travel several hundred

miles through the wilderness to settle. Third, he bought 340 acres in Todd County, Kentucky, in 1820 when he would have been 86 if he had been born in 1734--not an age when most people would invest in land. As to (3) above--that Andrew married (2) "Margaret Mary Chestnut"--no evidence whatever has been found in the South Carolina records to support this assertion. In fact, the only document on which the claim had been found is Mrs. Bruington's DAR application in the information penciled by the DAR researcher. Further, recent inquiries at the DAR headquarters in Washington, D.C., by Philip Graham have uncovered no clue as to why the researcher penciled in that information. The writers believe the marriage never took place.

[2] Letter, 26 August 1982, to Philip Graham from Frances Coulter, a descendant of Robert and Mary Coulter; and Eloise Ballard Triefenbach, Application #382021 for Membership in the DAR, 1949.

[3] According to the 1830 census, she was born no earlier than 1770; according to the 1800 census, she was born no later than 1774. The only evidence that her name may have been Mills is that she named her first son William Mills, and according to the naming customs of that time she probably would have named her first son after her father. Also, she named her first daughter Martha, so that may have been her mother's name.

[4] Council Journal, 6 January 1773 (British Copy); also listed by Janie Revill, comp., *A Compilation of the Original Lists of the Protestant Immigrants to South Carolina, 1763-1773* (Columbia, S.C.: The State Co., 1939), p. 126; and Jean Stephenson, *Scotch-Irish Migration to South Carolina, 1772 (Rev. William Martin and His Five Shiploads of Settlers)* (Washington, D.C.: the author, 1971), p. 80.

[5] *Chester County, South Carolina, Genealogical Society Bulletin*, I, 2 (June 1978), 11.

[6] Letter, 26 August 1982, to Philip Graham from Frances Coulter.

[7] Revolutionary War Accounts Audited 3024 Q479.

[8] A document dated 21 December 1778 which lists the names in this regiment is in the Andrew Richardson papers, South Caroliniana Library, University of South Carolina, Columbia, S.C. A copy of the document is reproduced on page 52 above.

[9] Brent H. Holcomb and Elmer O. Parker, *Camden District, S. C. Wills and Administrations, 1781-1787 (1770-1796)* (Easley, S.C.: Southern Historical Press, 1978), p. 12.

[10] Book A, p. 133.--Brent H. Holcomb and Elmer O. Parker, *Chester County, South Carolina, Minutes of the County Court, 1785-1799* (Easley, S.C.: Southern Historical Press, 1979), p. 51.

[11] *Ibid.*, p. 230.

[12] Robert McDill Woods and Iva Godfrey Woods, comps., *McDills in America* (Ann Arbor, MI: Edwards Bros., Inc., 1940), p. 152; and Holcomb and Parker, *Chester County Minutes*, p. 152.

[13] Book 1795-99.--Holcomb and Parker, *Chester County Minutes*, p. 362.

[14] Book 1795-99.--*Ibid.*, p. 360.

[15] Book 1795-99.--*Ibid.*, p. 403

[16] Book 1795-99.--*Ibid.*, p. 416.

[17] Book A, pp. 144, 182-8, and 245, and Book 1795-99.--*Ibid.*, pp. 56-7, 71-4, 97, and 402.

[18] Book B, pp. 80-1.--*Ibid.*, p. 188.

[19] Book B, p. 198.--*Ibid.*, p. 244.

[20] Willard Rouse Jillson, *The Kentucky Land Grants: A Systematic Index to All of the Land Grants Recorded in the State Land Office at Frankfort, Kentucky, 1782-1924*, Filson Club Publications, No. 33 (Louisville, KY: The Filson Club, 1925), p. 13.

[21] Register of the South Henderson United Presbyterian Church, Henderson Co., IL. This register is at the Presbyterian Historical Society, Philadelphia.

[22] Chester Co., S.C., *Genealogical Society Bulletin, loc. cit.*

[23] Council Journal, 6 January 1773 (British copy); Revill, p. 126; and Stephenson, p. 81.

[24] As stated in a letter, 23 April 1987, to Katharine Kell from Brent H. Holcomb, Certified Genealogist of Columbia, S.C.

[25] Bobby Gilmer Moss, *South Carolina Patriots in the American Revolution* (Baltimore: Genealogical Pub. Co., 1983), pp. 6 and 37; and A. S. Salley, ed., *Accounts Audited of Revolutionary Claims against South Carolina* (Columbia, S.C.: The Historical Commission of South Carolina, 1935), I, 86-8.

[26] Book A, pp. 27 and 324, and Book B, pp. 153 and 222.--Holcomb and Parker, *Chester County Minutes*, pp. 27, 131, 153, and 256.

[27] Except where noted in the text, the information on John and his descendants is from *Monroe County, Indiana, Family Heritage, 1987* (Bloomington, IN: Monroe County Historical Society, 1987), pp. 53 and 89-90; Charles Blanchard, ed., *1884 History of Monroe County, Indiana*, originally published as *History of Morgan, Monroe & Brown Counties* (1884; rptd. Knightstown, IN: The Bookmark, 1978), pp. 602-3 and 660; Ruth C. Carter, *Marriage Records, 1852-1859: Monroe County, Indiana* (Bloomington, IN: DAR, 1976), p. 26; Mrs. G. Kent Carter, *Marriage Records, 1859-1867: Monroe County, Indiana* (Bloomington, IN: DAR, 1978), p. 19; Ruth Carter, *Marriage Records: Monroe County, Indiana, 1882-1888* (Bloomington, IN: DAR, n.d.), p. 52; Ruth C. Carter, *Will Abstracts [from] Will Book IV, February, 1873 - February, 1890: Monroe County, Indiana* (Bloomington, IN: DAR, 1974), pp. 15f; Ruth C. Carter, *Will Abstracts, 1890-1904: Monroe County, Indiana* (Bloomington, IN: DAR, 1975), p. 31; Edith Bauer Cogswell, *An Index to Monroe County, Indiana, Marriage Records, 1818-1852* (n.p.: n. pub., 1954), pp. 2 and 68; Barbara S. Wolfe and Mary M. Morgan, *Cemetery Records: Monroe County, Indiana* (n.p.: DAR, 1987), pp. 25, 44, and 107; and federal censuses.

[28] Stephenson, pp. 50 and 72.

[29] Letter, 3 December 1987, to Katharine Kell from Brent H. Holcomb.

[30] Revolutionary War Audited Accounts, Number AA3030, Stub Indent Y444; and Applicant Pensions RW--National Genealogical Soc., Washington, D.C., James Graham, SC, Survivor No. 21786.

[31] Holcomb and Parker, *Chester County Minutes*, pp. 61, 113, 130, 132-3, 153-5, 172, 174, 202-3, 224, 243, 262, and 274.

[32] *Ibid.*, pp. 168, 207-8, 214-5, and 219.

[33] Book B, p. 264.--Holcomb and Parker, *Chester County Minutes*, p. 274.

[34] *Ibid.*, pp. 333, 360, 411, and 415.

[35] Mary Wylie Strange, *The Revolutionary Soldiers of Catholic Presbyterian Church, Chester County, South Carolina* (1946; rptd. York-Clover Printing Co., 1978), p. 50.

[36] There is no "Eighthly" in his will.

[37] Mrs. Don Short (Anita) and Mrs. Dale Bowers, *Cemetery Inscriptions, Preble County, Ohio*, 2 Vols. (DAR, 1969), I, 43.

[38] *Ibid., loc. cit.*

[39] Moss, p. 92.

[40] Except where noted in the text, the information on Molly Peggy is from Short and Bowers, I, 54 and 60.

[41] According to the 1830 census she was born in 1770-80; according to the 1820 census she was born no earlier than 1775.

[42] According to various censuses he was born 1760-70. Probably he was born in County Down, Ireland, because it is known that his brother, the Rev. William Blackstock, was born there.--William Melancthon Glasgow, *Cyclopedic Manual of the United Presbyterian Church of North America* (Pittsburgh: United Presbyterian Board of Education, 1903), p. 46. The date of Edward's death is given in the probate record of his estate, Henderson Co., IL, Box 2.

[43] Martha Bray Carson, *Chester County, South Carolina, Cemetery Inscriptions* (DAR, 1942), p. 33; and *Hopewell A.R.P. Church, Chester County, 1787--South Carolina--1982* (Chester County Genealogical Society, n.d.), p. 17. This latter source erroneously gives Elizabeth's date of death as 1855. The date on her tombstone is 1815.

[44] Except where noted in the text, the information on Edward is from "A Century of News," *The Herald-Independant* [of Winnsboro, S.C.], 6 March 1986, p. 2; Leona Bean McQuiston, *The McQuiston . . . Families, 1620-1937* (Louisville, KY: The Standard Press, 1937), p. 546; Fern Ainsworth, *Index to Naturalization Records, Chester County, South Carolina* (Natchitoches, LA: the author, n.d. [c. 1970]), p. 2; *The Story of South Henderson* (Henderson Co., IL: The South Henderson Cemetery Assn., 1940), p. 113; Lowell M. Volkel, *War of 1812: Bounty Lands in Illinois* (Thomson, IL: Heritage House, n.d. [c. 1977]), p. 300; and *The Bulletin* [of the] *Chester District Genealogical Society*, IX, 3 (September, 1986), 77.

[45] Letter, 15 June 1984, to Philip Graham from Mary Boulware, Research Genealogist of Blair, SC.

[46] As reprinted in *The Story of South Henderson*, pp. 61-2.

## THIRD GENERATION

¹ John Gleghorn's naturalization papers and the listings of his children in various 1880 federal censuses give Ireland as his place of birth, but in a short biography of one of his grandsons, 3-1F6 John M. Gleghorn, Scotland is erroneously stated to be the place.--*Biographical and Historical Memoirs of Northeast Arkansas* (Chicago: Goodspeed, 1889), p. 218.

² Chester County, South Carolina, Naturalized Citizens (1802-1835), Book A, pp. 184-5; also cited by Brent H. Holcomb, *South Carolina Naturalizations, 1783-1850* (Baltimore: Genealogical Pub. Co., 1985), p. 167.

³ "Autobiography of Matthew Elder, Jr.," as told to his daughter, Mary J. Elder, *Branching Out from St. Clair County, Illinois*, XIII, 1, 4-5.

⁴ *Ibid.*, pp. 2-3.

⁵ Mabel Abbott Tucker and Jane Warren Waller, comps., *Lincoln County, Tennessee Bible Records*, 6 Vols. (Batavia, IL: Lincoln County Tennessee Pioneers, 1971), II, 101.

⁶ Pressley Brown Gault and Elizabeth Pinkerton Leighty, *The William Gault Family History, 1735-1948* (Sparta, IL, n.d.), *passim*.--An unpub. ms. in the Sparta, IL, Public Library; bound copies are also at the Library of Congress and at the DAR library, Washington, D.C.

⁷ Timothy Richard Marsh and Helen Crawford Marsh, *Cemetery Records of Lincoln County, Tennessee* (Shelbyville, TN: Marsh Historical Publications, 1972), p. 59; and Tucker and Warren, *Bible Records*, II, 101.

⁸ *Ibid., loc. cit.*

⁹ Except where noted, the information on Andrew and his family is from *ibid.*, II, 100-2; Helen C. Marsh and Timothy R. Marsh, *Lincoln County, Tennessee, Official Marriage Records, 1838-1880* (Shelbyville, TN: Marsh Historical Publications, 1974), pp. 36, 160, and 179; Marsh and Marsh, *Cemetery Records*, p. 63; federal censuses; Katherine Reynolds, *The Jobe Family*, 6 Vols. (Houston, TX: n. pub., 1969-79), II, 340B-340Q; and letters to Katharine Kell from James L. Buckley Jr., a descendant of 3-1E Matthew Gleghorn.

¹⁰ In the 1880 federal census of Lincoln Co., TN, Mary and her daughter were listed in the home of W. H. Poindexter. Mary was specifically named as his daughter, and her daughter was named as his granddaughter.

¹¹ The information on Mary Ann and her family is from Reynolds, *loc. cit.*, Tucker and Warren, *Bible Records*, V, 39; Marsh and Marsh, *Marriage Records*, p. 9; Gault and Leighty, *Gault Family*, pp. 7-8; Marsh and Marsh, *Cemetery Records*, pp. 59-60; Helen Crawford Marsh and Timothy Richard Marsh, *Abstracts of Wills, Lincoln County, Tennessee, 1810-1895* (Shelbyville, TN: Marsh Historical Publications, 1977), p. 112; and federal censuses.

¹² The information on Nancy and her family is from Reynolds, *loc. cit.*; Marsh and Marsh, *Cemetery Records*, p. 64; Marsh and Marsh, *Marriage Records*, p. 33; Marsh and Marsh, *Abstracts of Wills*, p. 112; federal censuses; and James L. Buckley Jr.

[13] The information on Elizabeth and her family is from Reynolds, loc. cit, Marsh and Marsh, Cemetery Records, p. 59, Marsh and Marsh, Marriage Records, p. 53; Marsh and Marsh, Abstracts of Wills, p. 112; federal censuses; and James L. Buckley Jr.

[14] The information on Samuel W. and his family is from Reynolds, loc. cit., Marsh and Marsh, Cemetery Records, pp. 555-6; Marsh and Marsh, Marriage Records, p. 106; Compiled Service Records of Confederate Soldiers, National Archives, Washington, D. C.; and federal censuses.

[15] Marsh and Marsh, Abstracts of Wills, p. 52.

[16] Gault and Leighty, Gault Family History, p. 16.

[17] The information on John W. and his family is from a letter, 2 September 1987, to Katharine Kell from Dellawayne Gleghorn Watson who is a descendant; federal censuses; and Desmond Walls Allen, Index to the Tract Books for Izard and Stone Counties in Arkansas (Conway, AK: Rapid Rabbit Copy Co., n.d. [c. 1985]), p. 31.

[18] The information on Elizabeth Jane and her family is from Dellawayne Watson; Bobbie Jones McLane and Capitola Hensley Glazner, Hempstead County, Arkansas, Marriage Records, 1817-1875 (Hot Spring National Park, AK: the authors, 1969), p. 5.

[19] The information on Hugh and his family is from Dellawayne Watson; Allen, Tract Books, Izard Co., p. 31; Consolidated Index to Compiled Service Records of Confederate Soldiers; and federal censuses.

[20] The information on Mary E. is from McLane and Glazner, p. 136; and federal censuses.

[21] The information on Sarah S. is from Marsh and Marsh, Cemetery Records, p. 555; Marsh and Marsh, Marriage Records, p. 106; and federal censuses.

[22] Letter, 5 April 1989, to Katharine Kell from James L. Buckley Jr., a descendant of 3-1E Matthew.

[23] The information on Elgiva is from Dellawayne Watson; and federal censuses.

[24] Except where noted, the information on Matthew and his family is from letters, 14 and 24 February 1989, to Katharine Kell from James L. Buckley Jr. who is a descendant of Matthew's daughter Jane; McLane and Glazner, p. 25; and federal censuses.

[25] The information on James is from McLane and Glazner, p. 57; federal censuses; and James L. Buckley Jr.

[26] Except where noted, the information on John and his descendants is from a biography of his son John M. in Biographical and Historical Memoirs of Northeast Arkansas, p. 218; federal censuses; and James L. Buckley Jr.

[27] The information on Stephen T. is from Compiled Service Records of Confederate Soldiers; Frances T. Ingmire, Arkansas Confederate Veterans and Widows Pension Applications (St. Louis: the author, 1985), p. 148; and federal censuses.

[28] The information on John M. and his children is from *Biographical and Historical Memoirs of Northeast Arkansas*, p. 218; Compiled Service Records of Confederate Soldiers; and James L. Buckley Jr.

[29] Except where noted, the information on James and his descendants is from Gault and Leighty, p. 16; Compiled Service Records of Confederate Soldiers; federal censuses; *Navarro County Cemetery Records*, 5 Vols. (Corsicana, TX: Navarro County Genealogical Society, 1984), III, 66; and James L. Buckley Jr.

[30] Marsh and Marsh, *Lincoln Co. Marriages*, p. 42.

[31] McLane and Glazner, p. 57.

[32] *Ibid.*, p. 160.

[33] The information on David and his family is from Gault and Leighty, p. 37. The letter from Lyda Perkins Sproul was dated 18 March 1956 and was sent to Mrs. Guy D. Josserand of Dodge City, Kansas; a photocopy of this letter is in the possession of James L. Buckley Jr.

[34] Allen, *Tract Books, Izard Co.*, p. 31.

[35] *Ibid., loc. cit.*

[36] Except where noted, the information on Robert and his descendants is from *ibid*, p. 16; Dellawayne Gleghorn Watson; Compiled Service Records of Confederate Soldiers; federal censuses; and James L. Buckley Jr.

[37] McLane and Glazner, p. 149.

[38] *Ibid.*, p. 84.

[39] *Ibid.*, p. 2. In the marriage record listed by McLane and Glazner, his name is given as John J. Agee, but in the *Arkansas Genealogical Records* (Arkansas DAR, 1941), XXII, 2, his name is given as John A. Gee. This record was taken from a Bible in the possession of Mrs. S. B. Gee of Prescott, Hempstead Co., AR.

[40] The information on Ida is from the Gonzales County Historical Commission, *The History of Gonzales County, Texas* (Dallas, TX: Curtis Media Corp., 1986), I, 343; and federal censuses.

[41] Except where noted, the information on Elijah and his descendants is from Gault and Leighty, p. 16; Marsh and Marsh, *Lincoln Co. Marriages*, p. 6; Compiled Service Records of Confederate Soldiers; federal censuses; and James L. Buckley Jr.

[42] *Navarro County Cemetery Records*, III, 66.

[43] The information on William and his descendants is from Gault and Leighty, p. 16; Compiled Service Records of Confederate Soldiers; federal censuses; and James L. Buckley Jr.

[44] Marsh and Marsh, *Lincoln Co. Cemetery Records*, p. 60.

45 Inguire, *Arkansas Confederate Veterans and Widows Pension Applications*, p. 148.

46 Except where noted in the text, the information on Jennet and her descendants is from her father's will; and federal censuses.

47 As listed in a letter, 30 June 1970, to 4-19B5a Mary Louise Firoved Bruington from Mary Jane Harding of Arlington, VA. Mrs. Harding said she received the information from an aunt who had received it from relatives in Galveston, TX.

48 The information on William is from Nicholas Russell Murray, *Warren County, Mississippi, 1810-1900: Computer Indexed Marriage Records* (Hammond, LA: Hunting for Bears, Inc., n.d. [c. 1981]), p. 33; *Warren County Marriage Book D (January 15, 1826 - August 14, 1834)*, Vol. 1 of *Mississippi DAR Genealogical Records* (Vicksburg, MS: DAR, 1958), passim; federal censuses; and Todd Co., KY, tax lists.

49 The information on Samuel is from the federal censuses; and John Henry Brown, *Indian Wars and Pioneers of Texas* (Easley, S.C.: Southern Historical Press, 1978), p. 361.

50 The information on this Andrew Graham Mills and his descendants is from S. C. Griffin, *History of Galveston, Texas* (Galveston: A. H. Cawston, 1931), pp. 372-3; William Manning Morgan, *Trinity Protestant Episcopal Church [of] Galveston, Texas, 1841-1953* (Houghton and Galveston, TX: the author, 1954), pp. 339 and 753; J[ohn] C. Rietti, *Military Annals of Mississippi* (c. 1895; rptd. Spartanburg, S.C.: The Reprint Co., 1976), p. 74; and federal censuses.

51 The license was issued 20 December 1819.--Cordelia C. Cary, *Marriage Records, 1797-1850: Christian County, Kentucky* (n.p.: DAR, 1970), p. 71; and Elizabeth Prather Ellsberry, *Marriage Records of Christian County, Kentucky, 1795-1825* (Chillicothe, MO: DAR, n.d.), p. 35. Both are unpub. mss. in the NSDAR Library in Washington, D.C.

52 *History of Lincoln County, Missouri* (Chicago: Goodspeed Pub. Co., 1888), p. 564.

53 The information on Mary J. is from the Harding letter (footnote 47 above); federal censuses; and William S. Bryan and Robert Rose, *A History of the Pioneer Families of Missouri* (Saint Louis: Bryan, Brand & Co., 1876), p. 158.

54 The information on William is from *A Memorial and Biographical History of Johnson and Hill Counties, Texas* (Chicago: The Lewis Pub. Co., 1892), p. 351.

55 Nicholas Russell Murray, *Marshall County, Mississippi: Computer Indexed Marriage Records* (Hammond, LA: Hunting for Bears, Inc., n.d. [c. 1983]), p. 197.

56 *Biographical and Historical Memoirs of Mississippi*, 2 Vols. (Chicago: Goodspeed Pub. Co., 1891), I, 380-1; and Dunbar Rowland, *Military History of Mississippi, 1803-1898* (Spartanburg, S.C.: The Reprint Co., 1978), pp. 309-11.

57 Dunbar Rowland, *History of Mississippi, The Heart of the South*, 4 Vols. (Spartanburg, S.C.: The Reprint Co., 1978), II, 688.

58 The information on Nannie and her husband is from William S. Spear, ed., *The Encyclopedia of*

*the New West* (Marshall, TX: The U. S. Biographical Pub. Co., 1881), pp. 286-8; and federal censuses.

⁵⁹ The information on Minnie Knox and her family is from Griffin, pp. 241-3; *Texas Heroes Buried on Galveston Island* (Galveston: Sidney Sherman Chapter of the Daughters of the Republic of Texas, 1982), p. 53; and John Henry Brown, *Indian Wars and Pioneers of Texas* (1880; rptd. Easley, S.C.: Southern Historical Press, 1978), pp. 152-4.

⁶⁰ The information on Andrew is from James A. Creighton, *A Narrative of Brazoria County* [Texas] (Brazoria Co. Historical Commission, 1975), p. 68; and A[bigail] C[urlee], "Mills, Robert," *Dictionary of American Biography*, 20 Vols. (New York: Scribner's, 1934), XIII, 13-14.

⁶¹ The information on 3-1D Robert Mills and 3-1E David Graham Mills is from *ibid.*, *loc. cit.*; *Texas Heroes Buried on Galveston Island*, pp. 53-4; Creighton, pp. 68, 78, and 204-5; and *The Galveston Daily News*, 28 February 1886, p. 8, and 14 April 1888, p. 5.

⁶² *Dictionary of American Biography*, *loc. cit.* On 29 January 1839 Robert received a land grant of 320 acres in Harris County--Gifford White, *1840 Citizens of Texas, Vol. 1: Land Grants* (Saint Louis: Ingmire Pub., 1983), p. 176. Following his bankruptcy in 1873, he surrendered to creditors his plate, carriages, and mansion, although he could have claimed the protection of the homestead act because of the 1839 land grant.

⁶³ Murray, *Marshall Co. Marriage Records*, p. 225.

⁶⁴ *Ibid.*, *loc. cit.*

⁶⁵ Except where noted, the information on Matthew and Jane is from *History of Mercer and Henderson Counties* [Illinois], 2 Vols. (Chicago: H. H. Hill & Co., 1882), II, 1373; *Portrait and Biographical Album of Warren County, Illinois*, 2 Vols. (Chicago: Chapman Bros., 1886), II, 668; and Virginia Ross and Jane Evans, *Henderson County, Illinois, Cemeteries*, 2 vols. (Gladstone, IL: McDowell Publications, 1979), I, 54.

⁶⁶ Mrs. Don Short and Mrs. Dale Bowers, *Cemetery Inscriptions: Preble County, Ohio*, 2 Vols. (n.p.: DAR, 1969), I, 54.

⁶⁷ Except where noted, the information on Mary is from *Chester County, South Carolina, Cemetery Inscriptions* (Mary Adair Chapter of the DAR, 1942), p. 41--an unpub. ms. at the NSDAR Library in Wash., D.C.; and Mrs. Frank Torrens, *Narratives of Randolph County, Illinois*, 3 Vols. (n.p., n.d.), III, n.p.--unpub. ms. in the public library of Sparta, IL. Mrs. Torrens, who has compiled an extensive history of the McClurkin family, has found that a daughter of one James McClurkin (d. 1794-5) married (1) Andrew Young and (2), c. 1790, John Maben, father of Andrew Maben who married 3-4 Mary Graham. The daughter's name was Eleanor, as established in a court case cited herein on pp. 142-4. She was John's second wife and not the mother of Andrew Maben.

⁶⁸ *Hopewell A.R.P. Church, Chester County, 1787--South Carolina--1982* (Chester County Genealogical Society, n.d.), p. 11.

⁶⁹ J. H. Battle and W. H. Perrin, eds., *Counties of Todd and Christian, Kentucky* (Chicago: F. A. Battey Pub. Co., 1884), pp. 123-4.

⁷⁰ Janie Revill, comp., *A Compilation of the Original Lists of the Protestant Immigrants to*

*South Carolina, 1763-1773* (Columbia, S.C.: The State Co., 1939), pp. 122 and 125-6.

[71] Except where noted, the information on Sarah and her descendants is from Battle and Perrin, p. 291; letter, 13 April 1987, to Rosalie Heppner from Frances Fox, Certified Genealogist of Elkton, KY; and Mrs. J. C. (Celeste) Steger, "An Old Seceder Cemetery," *Bulletin* [of Chester Co., S.C., Genealogy Society], 3, 2 (June 1980), 32.

[72] Letters, 13 November 1985 and 13 April 1987, to Rosalie Heppner from Frances Fox.

[73] Except where noted in the text, the information on Margaret and her family is from Nanon Lucile Carr, *Marriage Records of Clay County, Missouri, 1822-1852* (n.p.: the author, 1957), pp. 14, 33, and 50; Elizabeth Prather Ellsberry, *Marriage Records of Clay County, Missouri . . . 1852-1900*, 3 Vols. (Chillicothe, MO, 1962), I, 36, 52, and 54; *The United States Biographical Dictionary and Portrait Gallery of Eminent and Self-Made Men: Missouri Volume* (New York: U.S. Biographical Pub. Co., 1878), pp. 324-7; and Nadine Hodges and Mrs. Howard W. Woodruff, *Genealogical Notes from the "Liberty Tribune,"* 7 Vols (Clay Co., MO: the authors, 1967-76), I, 5, 6, 21, 22, 44, and 99, II, 4, 21, 32, 57, 68, 104, and 123, III, 10, 43, 62, 91, and 111, IV, 13, 18, 37, 46, and 52, V, 10, VI, 77, and VII, 22, 71, and 81-2.

[74] Hoages and Woodruff, IV, 46.

[75] *Ibid.*, IV, 19; and Todd Co., KY, Marriage Records, Book A, p. 44.

[76] Mary Wylie Strange, *The Revolutionary Soldiers of Catholic Presbyterian Church, Chester County, South Carolina* (1946; rptd. York-Clover Printing Co., 1978), p. 44.

[77] Katherine Gentry Bushman, *Index to the First Plat Book of Clay County, Missouri, 1819-1875* (n.p., n.d.), p. 108.--unpub. ms. in the Allen Co. Public Library, Fort Wayne, IN.

[78] Except where noted, the names of these children and the information on them is from letters, 9 June and 19 June 1986, to Katharine Kell, from Vivian Cooper Shannon, granddaughter of 3-4C7 George Gilmer Gartin; federal censuses; and Elizabeth Prather Ellsberry, *Clay County, Missouri, Cemetery Records*, 2 Vols. (Chillicothe, MO: the author, 1962), II, 44.

[79] Hoages and Woodruff, I, 44.

[80] Nanon Lucile Carr, *Marriage Records of Clinton County, Missouri, 1833-1870* (n.p., 1955), p. 22.

[81] Hoages and Woodruff, II, 37; and Ellsberry, *Marriage Records of Clay Co.*, I, 52.

[82] Hoages and Woodruff, II, 5.

[83] In addition to Mrs. Shannon's information, the material on Anna and her family comes from *History of Clay and Platte Counties, Missouri* (Saint Louis: National Historical Soc., 1885), p. 876; and *Cemetery Records of Platte County, Missouri* (Platte Co. Historical Soc., 1945-60), p. 15.

[84] Hoages and Woodruff, I, 40.

[85] Cemetery Committee of the Warren Co., IL, Genealogical Society, *Tombstone Inscriptions--*

⁸⁵ *Spring Grove Township, Warren County, Illinois* (n.p., 1983), s.v. "Spring Grove Cemetery," p. 2. This is a pamphlet prepared by the society.

⁸⁶ *Ibid., loc. cit.*

⁸⁷ Letter, 17 August 1984, to Katharine Kell from William E. McKee, a descendant of John and Nancy McKee; and Short and Bowers, I, 55.

⁸⁸ The license was issued on 17 March 1812.--Cary, p. 46; and Ellsberry, *Marriage Records of Christian Co., KY*, p. 25.

⁸⁹ *The Scottish Tartans, with Historical Sketches of the Clans and Families of Scotland*, 2nd ed. (Edinburgh: W. and A. K. Johnston and E. K. Bacon, Ltd., 1945), p. 79.

⁹⁰ James Albert Woodburn, "The Scotch-Irish Presbyterians in Monroe County [Indiana]," *Indiana Historical Society Publications*, IV, 3 (1910), 498-9.

⁹¹ *Ibid.*, pp. 501-4.

⁹² Platte County [Missouri] Historical Soc., *Cemetery Records of Platte County, Missouri, Compiled . . . 1945-60*, 2 Vols. (n.p., n.d. [1968?]), II, 199.

⁹³ Margaret Sager Hohimer, et al., *Morgan County, Illinois, Marriages, Vol. I, 1827-1839* (Springfield, IL: Margaret Sager Hohimer, 1983), p. 35; and Morgan Co. Marriage Records, Book A, p. 14. In the Morgan Co., IL, files is an affidavit signed by 3-8 William M. Graham which says, "This is to certify that my Sister Martha Graham is above the age of Eighteen years. Given under my hand, this 3d Novr. 1831. Wm. M. Graham."

⁹⁴ Platte Co. Historical Soc., *loc. cit.*

⁹⁵ *An Illustrated Historical Atlas of Platte County, Missouri* (n.p.: Edwards Brothers, 1877), p. 12.

⁹⁶ *Ibid., loc. cit.*

⁹⁷ The information on Margaret and her children is from W. M. Paxton, *Annals of Platte County, Missouri* (Kansas City: Hudson-Kimberly Pub. Co., 1897), p. 626; 1880 federal census; *Cemetery Records of Platte Co.*, II, 194; *History of Clay and Platte Counties, Missouri* (St. Louis: National Historical Co., 1885), pp. 931-2; and letters to Vivian Cooper Shannon, descendant of 3-4C Jane Maben, from Margaret Knoop who is a descendant of Elijah Shanklin. Elijah's brother William Gartin Shanklin married 3-7 Martha.

⁹⁸ *Ibid.*; Platte County Historical Soc., *loc. cit.*; and *Cemetery Records of Platte Co.*, II, 199. This latter source incorrectly gives the dates of Martha Virginia's birth and death as 1917-1948; the actual dates were 1848-1917.

⁹⁹ Except where noted, the information on William M. is from Sarabelle O'Daniel, a descendant; and Mary Louise Bruington, Application #432472 for Membership in the National Society of the Daughters of the American Revolution, Washington, D.C., received 25 October 1954, accepted 10 December 1954.

[100] Richard Garten's short will, dated 2 February 1815 and proved June 1815, was recorded in the Christian Co., KY, Probate Records, Book C, p. 4. Unfortunately, it does not name his children, but an account in the local newspaper, *Weekly Messenger*, 19 August 1826, gave information on a suit filed by an Elijah Garten against the wife and heirs of Uriah Garten as well as the heirs of Richard Garten and another Elijah Garten. Listed among Richard Garten's heirs were "John Cordrey and Polly his wife, late Polly Garten, William Graham and Polly [sic] his wife, late Polly [sic] Garten."--as cited by Montgomery Vanderpool, *Logan County, Kentucky, Newspaper Genealogical Abstracts, Volume Four* (Russellville, KY: the author, 1987), p. 50. The latter "Polly" must have been a misprint since we know that the name of William's first wife was *Sally* Gartin (Garten). It should be noted, however, that Vivian Cooper Shannon, granddaughter of 3-4C7 George Gilmer Gartin, does not believe that Sally was Richard's daughter.

[101] For example, see the remarks of the Rev. Alexander Blaikie, one of the organizers (1835) of a Presbyterian synod in Illinois.--Talk reported in *The Story of South Henderson* (Henderson Co., IL: South Henderson Cemetery Assn., 1950), pp. 45-51.

[102] Hohimer, I, 16; Graves Registration WPA Project, *Tombstones Records of Madison County, Iowa* (n.p., n.d.), p. 58a; and Morgan Co., IL, Marriage Book A, p. 34, #1271. William and Jane were married by Jones Hedenberg.

[103] Wanda Warkins Allers and Eileen Lynch Gochanour, comps., *Morgan County, Illinois, Public Domain Land Tract Sales* (Springfield, IL: the authors, 1986), p. 36.

[104] *The Story of South Henderson*, pp. 7 and 15ff.

[105] Except where noted in the text, the information on Thomas is from Todd County Marriage Book A, p. 84; Anna Hunsaker Meador and Timothy Reeves Meador Sr., *Cemetery Records of [the] Southern Portion of Christian County, Kentucky* (Hopkinsville, KY: the authors, 1980), p. 282; Battle and Perrin, pp. 153 and 156; several letters to Philip Graham from Frances Fox, Certified Genealogist of Elkton, KY; federal censuses; Todd Co., KY, tax lists; and letters to Katharine Kell from Raymond Rodell Simpson of Dallas, TX, who is a descendant of Thomas.

[106] Marriage Book A, p. 25, #975; also listed by Eileen Gochanour, *Morgan County, Illinois, Marriages, Vol. I, 1827-1839* (Springfield, IL, 1983), p. 31.

[107] A John and Nancy McGregor were listed in the 1850 census of Linn County, Oregon. The census was transcribed and annotated by Lois M. Boyce, ed., *Linn County, Oregon, Early 1850 Records* (Portland, OR, n.d.), p. 7, and she gives the entry on John and Nancy as follows:

```
John McGregor   45   NY   DLC   1671 Linn, farmer
Nancy           42   SC   ( )   m. Aug 1847, Salem OT
J. Ann          16   IL
James           15   IL
William         10   IL
```

For the date and place of John's death, see *Genealogical Material in Oregon Donation Land Claims, Volume I* (Portland, OR: Genealogical Forum of Portland, 1957), p. 68.

[108] Morgan Co., IL, Deed Book I, p. 216.

109 As given in the Session Minutes of the South Henderson United Presbyterian Church; these minutes are in the Archives of the Presbyterian Historical Society, Philadelphia.

110 For example, see *Genealogical Material in Oregon Donation Land Claims, Volume I*, pp. 24 and 62; and Lottie L. Gurley, *Genealogical Material in Oregon Land Claims, Supplement to Volume I* (Portland, OR: Genealogical Forum of Portland, 1975), pp. 32, 38, 49, and 99.

111 Vol. 4, p. 340, as cited by Lottie LeGett Gurley, *Genealogical Material in Oregon Provisional Land Claims, Abstracted, Volumes I-VIII, 1845-1849* (Portland, OR: Genealogical Forum of Portland, 1982), p. 121.

112 The information on Bosworth is from the *Oregon Spectator Index*, 2 Vols (n.p.: WPA Project, 1941), I, 46.

113 Gurley, *Supplement to Vol. I*, p. 106.

114 Boyce, pp. 39 and 53.

115 Bushman, p. 108.

116 Except where noted in the text, the information on Julianna is from letters to Philip Graham from David A. Gwinn, a descendant; *Hopewell A.R.P. Church, Chester County, 1787--South Carolina--1982* (Chester County Genealogical Society, n.d.), p. 7; federal censuses; and Strange, pp. 28-31. Strange prints Julianna's will in full.

117 Except for references to legal documents, the information on Julianna's children is from David A. Gwinn.

118 The information on David and his family is from York Co., S.C., Court of Equity, File #24; Chester Co., S.C., Court of Equity, Petition #55; and the will (1826) of 3-15 James Graham Jr.

119 Martha Bray Carson, *Chester County, South Carolina, Cemetery Inscriptions* (Mary Adair Chapter of the DAR, 1942), p. 38.

120 The information on Esther and her descendants is from federal censuses; and letters to Philip Graham from James A. Smith, a descendant, and David A. Gwinn.

121 The information on the Rev. Thomas Peden Pressly is from *Centennial History of the Associate Reformed Presbyterian Church, 1803-1903* (Charleston, S.C.: Synod of the A.R.P. Church, 1905), pp. 313-4; James A. Smith; and David A. Gwinn.

## FOURTH GENERATION

1 Except where noted, the information on Martha and her family is from *Portrait and Biographical Album of Warren County, Illinois*, 2 Vols. (Chicago: Chapman Bros., 1886), II, 668; *History of Mercer and Henderson Counties (IL)*, 2 Vols. (Chicago: H. H. Hill & Co., 1882), II, 1380-1 (this source specifically states that Samuel was a brother-in-law of 4-2 Andrew); Robert McDill Woods and Iva Godfrey Woods, *McDills in America* (Ann Arbor, MI: Edwards Bros., Inc., 1940), pp. 71 and 73-5;

Virginia Ross and Jane Evans, *Henderson County, Illinois, Cemeteries*, 2 Vols. (Gladstone, IL: McDowell Publications, 1979 and 1981), I, 54-5; and Lottie L. Gurley, *Genealogical Material in Oregon Land Claims: Supplement to Volume I*, 5 Vols. (Portland, OR: Genealogical Forum, 1975), V, 48.

[2] Mrs. Stuart R. Bolin and Mrs. John S. Heaume, comps., *Early Marriage Bonds of Ohio: Preble County* (n.p.: DAR, n.d.), p. 98--unpub. ms. in the NSDAR Library. The Rev. Alexander Porter was born in Abbeville County, S.C., died Preble Co., OH, 29 March 1836. He was educated in South Carolina and at Dickerson College, PA, and was ordained on 18 October 1796. Subsequently he was the minister at Cedar Springs and Long Cane, Abbeville County, S.C., and in 1814 was called to the Hopewell Church, Israel Twp., Preble Co., OH. In 1833 he resigned because of illness although he continued to live in Preble County until he died.--*History of Preble County, Ohio* (Cleveland: H. Q. Williams and Bros., 1881), pp. 233-4 and 236; and James Brown Scouller, *A Manual of the United Presbyterian Church of North America, 1751-1887*, 2d ed. (Pittsburgh: United Presbyterian Board of Publications, 1887), p. 529.

[3] Except where noted, the information on James and his family is from his wife's Widow's Pension Record Application #59114, Certificate #32109, National Archives, Washington D.C.; Woods and Woods, pp. 73-4; Leona Bean McQuiston, *The McQuiston, McCuiston and McQueston Families, 1620-1937* (Louisville, KY: The Standard Press, 1937), pp. 521 and 523; J. N. Reece, *Report of the Adjutant General of the State of Illinois*, 9 Vols. (Springfield, IL, 1900), V, 163; Virginia Ross, *Henderson County, Illinois, 1841-1900 Marriages* (Gladstone, IL: Ross Research, 1984), p. 22; Ross and Evans, *Henderson County . . . Cemeteries*, I, 50, and II, 102; Marriage Book C, p. 36; federal censuses; and Elizabeth Caldwell Hallam who is a granddaughter of 5-28 Elizabeth Jane.

[4] Ross and Evans, *Henderson County . . . Cemeteries*, I, 50; and McQuiston, p. 523.

[5] Mrs. Don Short and Mrs. Dale Bowers, *Cemetery Inscriptions, Preble County, Ohio*, 2 Vols. (NSDAR, 1969), I, 54.

[6] *Ibid*, I, 54.

[7] The information on Andrew and his family is from his Pension Records, Application #1063575, Certificate #816296, and Widow's Application #1026551, Certificate #794119 TN, National Archives, Washington, D.C.; William Melancthon Glasgow, *Cyclopedic Manual of the United Presbyterian Church of North America* (Pittsburgh: United Presbyterian Board of Publications, 1903), p. 219; *The United Presbyterian*, 28 June 1888, p. 414; and Hugh Alexander Kelsey, *The United Presbyterian Directory* (Pittsburgh, n.d.), p. 216.

[8] The information on Maggie is from *The Daily Review Atlas* [of Monmouth, IL], 15 December 1908, p. 4.

[9] Except where noted, the information on Andrew is from Woods and Woods, p. 84; *History of Mercer and Henderson Counties*, II, 1362 and 1376-7; Ross and Evans, *Henderson County . . . Cemeteries*, I, 51, 54, and 63; *Historical Encyclopedia of Illinois and History of Henderson County*, 2 Vols. (Chicago: Munsell Pub. Co., 1911), II, 809; federal censuses; and Warren County, Illinois, Genealogical Society, *Warren County, Illinois, Female Marriage Index* (1985), p. 113.

[10] Except where noted, the information on John W. is from unpublished family records of Philip Graham who is a descendant; Ruth Slevin and Willard Heiss, *Preble County, Ohio, Marriages, 1808-1859* (Fort Wayne, IN: Fort Wayne and Allen County Public Library, 1965), Part 1, s.v. "Graham"; and Short

and Bowers, I, 44.

[11] Except where noted, the information on Robert C. is from Elizabeth Caldwell Hallam; federal censuses; and Martha E. Godbey, comp., *Henry County, Iowa, Grave Records* (Grinnell, IA: n. pub., 1936), p. 14--unpub. ms. in the Allen Co., Public library, Fort Wayne, IN. This latter source differs on some of the dates given in the censuses; where such differences occur, the census dates have been accepted.

[12] Except where noted, the information on William M. is from Glasgow, p. 140; Elizabeth Caldwell Hallam; and *General Catalogue of the Graduates and Former Students of Miami University . . . 1809-1909, During Its First Century* (Oxford, OH, 1909), p. 28.

[13] Except where noted, the information on Margaret and her family is from *History of Mercer and Henderson Counties*, II, 1253-4; federal censuses; Ross and Evans, *Henderson County . . . Cemeteries*, I, 49, 54, and 61; Ross, *Henderson County . . . Marriages*, pp. 3, 9, and 21; obituary of Sarah Cameron in *The Oquawka* [Henderson Co., IL] *Spectator*, 12 February 1902; Martha Hoffman Rising, "Monmouth College Graduates, Warren County, Illinois," *Illinois State Genealogical Society Quarterly*, XV, 4 (Winter, 1983), 236; and letter, 5 December 1984, to Philip Graham from Martha Hoffman Rising who is researching the Brown family.

[14] Except where noted, the information on Wilson M. is from Elizabeth Caldwell Hallam; letter, 22 January 1989, to Katharine Kell from 7-2 Margaret Graham Parker; and Ross and Evans, *Henderson County . . . Cemeteries*, II, 50.

[15] Except where noted, the information on David is from *Portrait and Biographical Album of Warren County*, II, 668; Luther E. Robinson, ed. *Historical and Biographical Record of Monmouth and Warren County, Illinois*, 2 Vols. (Chicago: Munsell Pub. Co., 1927), II, 367; *The Past and Present of Warren County, Illinois* (Chicago: H. F. Kett and Co., 1877), p. 160; Elizabeth Caldwell Hallam; and letter, 5 December 1984, to Philip Graham from Marsha Hoffman Rising.

[16] Except where noted, the information on James Harvey is from Arthur Springer, *History of Louisa County, Iowa*, 2 Vols. (Chicago: S. J. Clarke Pub. Co., 1912), I, 260; obituary of Harvey in *The United Presbyterian*, 8 July 1897, p. 434; Slevin and Heiss, *Preble County, OH, Marriages*, loc. cit.; letters, 22 July and 5 December 1984, to Philip Graham from Marsha Hoffman Rising; and WPA Graves Registration, *Tombstone Records of Louisa County, Iowa* (n.d.), p. 51.

[17] Except where noted, the information on A. Y. is from Hugh R. Moffet and Thomas E. Rogers, eds., *Historical Encyclopedia . . . and History of Warren County* [IL], 2 Vols. (Chicago: Munsell Pub. Co., 1903), II, 761-2; *Portrait and Biographical Album of Warren County*, II, 668; Ross, *Henderson County . . . Marriages*, p. 5; *Past and Present of Warren County*, p. 149; obituary in *The United Presbyterian*, 12 October 1876, p. 2; Monmouth College *Catalogue* and *Circulars*, 1857-71; and Elizabeth Caldwell Hallam who is a descendant of both A. Y. and his brother David.

[18] Except where noted, the information on Margaret and her family is from federal censuses; Barbara S. Wolfe and Mary M. Morgan, *Cemetery Records* [of] *Monroe County, Indiana* (n.p.: Indiana DAR, 1987), p. 109; *Portrait and Biographical Record of Ford County, Illinois* (Chicago: Lake City Pub. Co., 1892), p. 620; letter, 4 June 1896, to Philip Graham from Ethel Trego, Research Genealogist of Monmouth, IL; Marriage Book A, p. 200, as given by Edith Bauer Cogswell, *An Index to Monroe County, Indiana, Marriage Records, 1818-1852* (n.p.: n. pub., 1954), p. 52--unpub. ms. in the Allen County Public Library, Fort Wayne, IN (in this listing, Margaret's last name is spelled Grayham);

Warren County, IL, Probate Records, Box 208; and *Monmouth Daily Review*, 19 January 1906, p. 5.

[19] Ross, *Henderson County . . . Marriages*, p. 25.

[20] Reece, *Report of Adjutant General*, II, 526 and 538. James's pension was Application #942671, Certificate #663363; Cora's was Application #1208011, Certificate #941033.--National Archives, Washington, D.C.

[21] *The Prairie Farmers Reliable Directory of Farmers and Breeders: Warren and Henderson Counties, Illinois* (Chicago, 1918), p. 58; and Nicholas Russell Murray, *Warren County, Illinois, 1839-1869, Marriage Records*, 3 vols. (North Salt Lake, Utah: Hunting for Bears, 1988), I, 173.

[22] Ibid., p. 58. Since she was not listed in her father's household in the 1922 Monmouth city directory and was not named in her grandfather's will (1923), she had probably died before then.

[23] Except where noted in the text, the information on Edward is from Rising, "Monmouth College Graduates," p. 240; and letter, 13 September 1988, to Philip Graham from Martin W. Beerman, Research Genealogist of Omaha, Nebraska.

[24] The information on John is from Glasgow, p. 139; Quincy A. and Bella Warwick Davis, comps., *Early Marriage Records of Butler County, Ohio*, 3 Vols. (Butler Co., OH: DAR, n.d.), III, s.v. "Graham"; federal censuses; and *General Catalogue of Graduates and Former Students of Miami University*, p. 28.

[25] As listed in Marriage Book B, p. 124.--Cogswell, *loc. cit.* In his will, 3-6 Robert C. Graham specifically named a James Small as a son-in-law. This is the only James Small mentioned by Cogswell, and she gave his bride's name as Nancy C. Graham. The 1820 census of Todd Co., KY, and the 1830 census of Preble Co., OH, listed in Robert's household a girl, born 1812-15, and another girl, born 1815-20. It is known that the older girl was Margaret C. as confirmed by her listing in the 1850 census of Monroe Co., IN. Therefore, Nancy must have been the next older girl. The date of her birth has been set at 1817-20 because the second child, John McKee Graham, was born in 1816, as stated by Glasgow, p. 139.

[26] The others in the household were Robert (age 26, born Ireland), Nancy (age 40, born Ireland), Margaret (age 13, born Indiana), and Alexander (age 8, born Indiana).

[27] The information on Paulina is from McQuiston, p. 547; James Hemphill, *Hemphill Family Notes* (Charleston, S.C.: n. pub., 1894), p. 4; federal censuses; *Chester County, South Carolina, Cemetery Inscriptions* (Mary Adair Chapter DAR, n.d.), p. 40 (unpub. ms. in the NSDAR); Wolfe and Morgan, p. 109; James Albert Woodburn, "The Scotch-Irish Presbyterians in Monroe County [Indiana]," *Indiana Historical Society Publications*, IV, 3 (1910), 501-4; and divorce as listed in Book L-1846, p. 329, as given by Malinda E. E. Newhard, *Divorces Granted by the Indiana General Assembly Prior to 1852* (Harlan, IN: the author, 1981)--copyrighted, typewritten ms. in the Allen Co. Public Library, Fort Wayne, IN.

[28] The information on Martha and her family is from Warren County Marriage Records, Book B, p. 223; Glasgow, p. 261; *Past and Present of Warren County*, p. 183; federal censuses; *History of Mercer County* [IL] (Chicago: H. H. Hill & Co., 1882), p. 1182; John H. Montgomery's Pension Records, Application #529444, Certificate #399694, Widow's Application #1160827, Certificate #893141 NB, National Archives, Washington, D.C.; and John's obituary in *The United Presbyterian*, 5 August 1920, p. 21.

[29] the information on Andrew is from unpub. family records of Katharine Kell who is a descendant; Theophilus A. Wylie, *Indiana University, Its History from 1820, When Founded, to 1890* (Indianapolis: Indiana Univ., 1890), p. 408; G. W. H. Kemper, *A Medical History of the State of Indiana* (Chicago: American Medical Assn. Press, 1911), p. 384; and letter, 2 July 1911, to 5-60 Katharine Graham Lamb from Prof. James A. Woodburn (letter in the possession of Katharine Kell). Professor Woodburn is the one who wrote the article on the Scotch-Irish in Monroe County, IN, in which he gave the lengthy account of the quarrel which 3-6 Robert C. and his daughter 4-15 Paulina had with Paulina's in-laws and the local church authorities.

[30] The information on Mary and her husband is from federal censuses; Monmouth City Directories, 1874-1904; letter, 21 September 1984, to Katharine Kell from Phyllis Clark, Church Secretary, Faith United Presbyterian Church, Monmouth, IL; William A. Robison's death certificate, Book B, p. 70; *Monmouth Daily Review*, 12 December 1900, p. 1, and 5 March 1905, p. 8; Albert Nelson Marquis, *The Book of Chicagoans* (Chicago: A. N. Marquis Co., 1911), s.v. "Robison, John Albert"; *Past and Present of Warren County*, p. 220; and sources noted in the text.

[31] The information on John is from Marquis, *loc. cit.*; letter from Phyllis Clark; and the *Chicago Tribune*, 19 October 1942, p. 28.

[32] Except where noted, the information on Sarah and her family is from federal censuses; the will of her father; letter, 31 May 1983, to Katharine Kell from Ethel Trego, Research Genealogist of Warren Co., IL; Death Certificates of Warren Co., Book B, p. 180; *Monmouth Daily Review*, 26 April 1907, p. 1; *Cemetery Records of Ford County, Illinois*, 2 Vols. (Piper City, IL: DAR, 1962-64), II, 53; *Cemeteries of Ford County, Illinois* (n.p.: DAR, 1964), p. 53/55; and Cemetery Committee of the Warren Co., IL, Genealogical Society, *Tombstone Inscriptions--Spring Grove Township, Warren County, Illinois* (1983), s.v. "Spring Grove Cemetery," p. 3--unpub. ms. prepared by the society.

[33] Except where noted, the information on Martha and her descendants is from a letter, 15 June 1984, to Katharine Kell from Sarabelle Talbot O'Daniel who is a descendant; federal censuses; Ross, *Henderson County . . . Marriages*, p. 1; *History of Mercer and Henderson Counties*, II, 1366; and letter from Martin W. Beerman.

[34] The information on Ellen is from Sarabelle Talbot O'Daniel; Ross, *Henderson County . . . Marriages*, p. 12; *History of Henderson and Mercer Counties*, II, 1394-5; and federal censuses.

[35] *Oquawka Spectator*, 13 February 1868; and *Portrait and Biographical Album of Warren Co., Ill.*, II, 523.

[36] *Oquawka Spectator*, 9 April 1902.

[37] Except where noted, the information on Nancy and her descendants is from a letter, 10 March 1985, to Katharine Kell from Persis (Peggy) Ann Moss Blachly who is a descendant; and obituaries in the *Omaha World-Herald*, 14 August 1947, p. 17, and 15 March 1963, p. 54.

[38] The information on Andrew R. is from his pension records, Application #1118678, Certificate #961713, National Archives, Washington, D.C.; Sarabelle Talbot O'Daniel; *History of Henderson and Mercer Counties*, II, 1368; Ross and Evans, *Henderson County . . . Cemeteries*, I, 48 and 53; Church Register and Session Minutes of South Henderson United Presbyterian Church (Register now located at the Presbyterian Historical Society, Philadelphia, PA); Reece, *Report of the Adjutant General*, I, 492; and letter from Martin W. Beerman.

[39] The information on Robert is from his pension records, Application #287384, Certificate #260990, Widow's Application #769533, Certificate #548682 IL, National Archives, Washington, D.C.; Sarabelle Talbot O'Daniel; Woods and Woods, p. 91; federal censuses; Ross, Henderson County . . . Marriages, p. 5; Ross and Evans, Henderson County . . . Cemeteries, I, 53 and 57; Reece, Report of the Adjutant General, I, 494; Portrait and Biographical Album of Lancaster County, Nebraska (Chicago: Chapman Bros., 1888), p. 549; and sources noted in the text.

[40] Except where noted, the information on James Thomas is from a letter, 14 December 1985, to Katharine Kell from Velores Koll Graham whose husband, 7-27 Calvin W., is a descendant; Sarabelle Talbot O'Daniel; Elizabeth Caldwell Hallam; Emma E. Forter, History of Marshall County, Kansas (Indianapolis: B. F. Bowen & Co., 1917), p. 461; and Ross, Henderson County . . . Marriages, p. 16.

[41] The information on William is from his pension records, Application #1059477, Certificate #844929, National Archives, Washington, D.C.; Reece, Report of the Adjutant General, I, 492 and 493; Harriet Hughes Wright and Lydia Palmer Jones, The History of Summerfield (Summerfield, KS: n. pub., n.d. [c. 1980]), p. 18; Sarabelle Talbot O'Daniel; and Elizabeth Caldwell Hallam.

[42] The information on Matthew Joseph is from his pension records, Application #738219, Certificate #694149, National Archives, Washington, D.C.; Sarabelle Talbot O'Daniel; Elizabeth Caldwell Hallam; letter, 6 January 1986, to Katharine Kell from 5-97C Lyle Graham Wimmer who is a descendant of Joe's brother Samuel; Reece, Report of the Adjutant General, I, 492; and Graves Registration WPA Project, Tombstone Records of Madison County [IA] (n.d.), pp. 58A-59.

[43] The information on Sarah and her family is from B. F. Mundorff's pension records, Application #124679, Certificate #128410, Widow's Application #1106756, Certificate #840119 CA, National Archives, Washington, D.C.; Portrait and Biographical Album of Lancaster County, pp. 548-9; Ross, Henderson County . . . Marriages, p. 16; Reece, Report of the Adjutant General, I, 492; Lincoln-Lancaster Co. Genealogical Society, comps., Cemeteries of Lancaster County, Nebraska, 8 Vols. (n.p., 1977-83), II, 264 and 293; Lyle Graham Wimmer; and Sarabelle Talbot O'Daniel.

[44] The information on John M. is from letters, 14 December 1985 and 18 February 1986, to Katharine Kell from Velores Koll Graham; Monmouth College Catalogue and Circulars, 1862; Portrait and Biographical Album of Lancaster County, pp. 548-9; federal censuses; Reece, Report of the Adjutant General, V, 163 and 164; Wright and Jones, History of Summerfield, p. 18; Pension Application #967955, Certificate #777015, National Archives, Washington, D.C.

[45] Ross and Evans, Henderson County . . . Cemeteries, I, 61.

[46] The information on Samuel is from several letters to Katharine Kell from 5-97C Lyle Graham Wimmer who is a descendant; and Harry M. Switzer, comp., Madison County, Iowa, Early Marriages, 1849-1880 (Earlham, IA: n. pub., n.d.), s.v. "Graham." Elizabeth's parents were listed in the 1870 census of Jackson Twp., Madison Co., IA.

[47] Except where noted in the text, the information on Granville is from Todd County Marriage Book C, p. 68; Era W. Stinson, Todd County, Kentucky, Marriages (Bowling Green, KY: the author, 1985), s.v. "Graham, G. W."; Anna Hunsaker Meador and Timothy Reeves Meador Sr., Cemetery Records of [the] Southern Portion of Christian County, Kentucky (Hopkinsville, KY: the authors, 1980), p. 282; J. H. Battle and W. H. Perrin, eds., Counties of Todd and Christian, Kentucky (Chicago: F. A. Battey Pub. Co., 1884), p. 123; several letters to Philip Graham from Frances Fox, Certified Genealogist of Todd Co., KY; federal censuses; and letters to Katharine Kell from 5-105A Raymond Rodell Simpson of

Dallas, TX, who is a grandson.

[48] Except where noted, the information on Robert M. is from Todd County Marriage Book B, p. 291, #2528; Frances Fox; and federal censuses.

[49] Except where noted, the information on Mollie is from Stinson, s.v. "Daniel, W. B."; Marriage Book B, p. 281; federal censuses; and letter, 4 June 1988, to Philip Graham from Frances Fox.

[50] Except where noted, the information on Joanna is from Marriage Book C, p. 110; Frances Fox; and federal censuses.

[51] Except where noted, the information on Mary and her descendants is from Ross and Evans, *Henderson County . . . Cemeteries*, II, 86 and 106; Ross, *Henderson County . . . Marriages*, p. 12; *History of Mercer and Henderson Counties*, II, 1352 and 1371; federal censuses; *Prairie Farmers directory*, p. 149; Andrew's Pension Application #279140, Certificate #662752; and Mary's Widow's Application #887834, Certificate #662752, Washington, D.C.

[52] The information on Andrew G. is from his pension records, Application #207775, Certificate #259353, Widow's Application #769533, Certificate #548682, Washington D.C.; Ross and Evans, *Henderson County . . . Cemeteries*, I, 60, and II, 101; and *History of Mercer and Henderson Counties*, II, 1376.

## FIFTH GENERATION

[1] Except where noted, the information on William B. and his children is from Robert McDill Woods and Iva Godfrey Woods, *McDills in America* (Ann Arbor, MI: Edwards Bros., Inc., 1940), p. 88; *History of Mercer and Henderson Counties* [IL], 2 Vols. (Chicago: H. H. Hill & Co., 1882), II, 1377; Virginia Ross and Jane Evans, *Henderson County, Illinois, Cemeteries*, 2 Vols. (Gladstone, IL: McDowell Publications, 1979), I, 57; Henderson County, Illinois, Marriage Book C, p. 1; and federal censuses.

[2] The information on David is from Albert Nelson Marquis, ed., *The Book of Chicagoans* (Chicago: A. N. Marquis & Co., 1905), s.v. "Graham, David Wilson"; *Chicago Tribune*, 10 February 1925, p. 12; letters to Philip Graham from 5-28H1 Elizabeth Caldwell Hallam, granddaughter of 5-28 Elizabeth J., and from 6-25 Wilmer T. Graham; Chicago city directories; David's Pension Application #269594, Certificate #182704; and Ida's widow's Application #1229946, Certificate #961831.

[3] Anna Rothe and Evelyn Lohr, *Current Biography: Who's News and Why, 1952* (New York: H. W. Wilson, 1952), p. 220.

[4] Except where noted, the information on Martha Jane and her descendants is from Elizabeth Caldwell Hallam; Ross and Evans, I, 50; federal censuses; Monmouth College *Catalogue and Circulars*; *Oquawka Spectator*, 2 June 1870; Virginia Ross, *Henderson County, Illinois, 1841-1900 Marriages* (Gladstone, IL: Ross Research, 1984), p. 21; Church Register of the South Henderson United Presbyterian Church--register now in the archives of the Presbyterian Historical Society, Philadelphia; Woods and Woods, p. 102; and *Historical Encyclopedia of Illinois and History of Henderson County* (Chicago: Munsell Pub. Co., 1911), p. 899.

[5] The information on Matthew Y. is from Ross and Evans, I, 54; and Session Minutes of the South Henderson United Presbyterian Church.

[6] Except where noted, the information on the children of John W. is from unpublished family sources of Philip Graham who is a descendant.

[7] Mrs. Don Short and Mrs. Dale Bowers, *Cemetery Inscriptions, Preble County, Ohio*, 2 Vols. (n.p.: NSDAR, 1969), I, 43.

[8] *Ibid.*

[9] The information on Mike is from his Pension Records, Certificate #1144687; *Official Roster of the Soldiers of the State of Ohio in the War of Rebellion, 1861-1866*, 9 Vols. (Akron, OH: The Roster Commission, 1888), VI, 662; and Whitelaw Reid, *Ohio in the War*, 2 Vols. (New York: Moore, Wilstach and Baldwin, 1868), II, 487.

[10] *Official Roster . . . of Ohio*, IX, 374; and Reid, II, 697.

[11] Short and Bowers, I, 43.

[12] *Ibid.*

[13] The information on the children of Robert C. is from federal censuses; and Martha E. Godbey, *Henry County, Iowa, Grave Records* (n.p.: n. pub., 1936), p. 14--unpublished manuscript in the Allen County Public Library, Fort Wayne, Indiana.

[14] Except where noted, the information on the children of William Mills is from Elizabeth Caldwell Hallam.

[15] Marsha Hoffman Rising, "Monmouth College Graduates, Warren County, Illinois," *Illinois State Genealogical Society Quarterly*, XV, 4 (Winter, 1983), 240; and Monmouth College *Catalogue* and *Circulars*.

[16] Except where noted, the information on the children of Wilson M. is from Elizabeth Caldwell Hallam.

[17] The information on Jessie and her children is from Ross, *Henderson County Marriages*, p. 23; federal censuses; Alexander Moir, *Moir Genealogy* (Lowell, Mass.: the author, 1913), pp. 199 and 345-6; and Peoria, Illinois, city directories, 1908-1935.

[18] The information on Gus Campbell is from Chicago city directories; and Marquis, *s.v.* "Campbell, Alexander Fergus." This latter source gives 1916 as the date of his death, but the date on his grave marker is 1913.

[19] The information on William is from Marquis, *s.v.* "Montgomery, William Teel"; and Chicago city directories.

[20] The information on Will is from a letter, 27 August 1988, to Katharine Kell from 7-2 Margaret Graham Parker.

[21] The information on Elizabeth J. and her descendants is from Elizabeth Caldwell Hallam who is a granddaughter; Luther E. Robinson, ed., *Historical and Biographical Record of Monmouth and Warren County, Illinois*, 2 Vols. (Chicago: Munsell Pub. Co., 1927), II, 366-7; *History of Mercer and*

Henderson Counties, II, 1369; and Rising, p. 241.

[22] The information on Clara and her children is from her obituary in *The Daily Review Atlas* [of Monmouth, Illinois], 14 June 1916, p. 1; Death Records of Warren County, Illinois, Book 1, p. 147, and Book A, p. 145; federal censuses; William Melancthon Glasgow, *Cyclopedic Manual of the United Presbyterian Church of North America* (Pittsburgh: United Presbyterian Board of Education, 1903), p. 216; and Elizabeth Caldwell Hallam.

[23] Except where noted, the information on James is from obituaries in *The Monmouth Review*, 20 March 1937, p. 1, and *The Daily Review Atlas*, 18 October 1943, p. 3; and Elizabeth Caldwell Hallam.

[24] The information on Minnie and her family is from Elizabeth Caldwell Hallam; Rising, p. 245; and Warren County, Illinois, Genealogical Society, *Warren County, Illinois, Female Marriage Index, 1829 through 1915* (1985), p. 113.

[25] The information on Fannie and her husband is from John's Probate Record, General Number 3423; Fannie's Probate Record, General Number 4744; Warren County Marriage Book E, p. 125, as cited by *Warren County, Illinois, Female Marriage Index*, p. 114; Monmouth *Daily Review Atlas*, 24 May 1927 and 14 February 1942; and sources given in the text.

[26] Except where noted, the information on the children of James Harvey is from Elizabeth Caldwell Hallam; and federal censuses.

[27] The information on Clara and her family is from Rising, p. 243; WPA, *Grave Records, Louisa County, Iowa* (n.d.), pp. 77 and 98; Hugh Alexander Kelsey, *The United Presbyterian Directory* (Pittsburgh, n.d), p. 171; and Elizabeth Caldwell Hallam.

[28] The information on Edwin is from Louise Baumann, comp., *Prospect Hill Cemetery Records* (n.p.: Greater Omaha Genealogical Society, 1977), pp. 127 and 128; Rising, p. 243; James W. Savage and John T. Bell, *History of the City of Omaha; and South Omaha by Consul W. Bakerfield* (Chicago: Munsell & Co., 1894), p. 334; Elizabeth Caldwell Hallam; and Omaha, Nebraska, city directories, 1883-1895.

[29] The information on William F. is from *History of Cass County, Iowa* (Springfield, IL: Continental Historical Co., 1884), pp. 403-4; federal censuses; Elizabeth Caldwell Hallam; birth certificates of his children: Lessie Jane (called Tessie on the certificate--Birth Record 1, p. 187, Certificate 2405), Wilson Harvey (called Harvey Wilson on the certificate--Birth Record 1, p. 212, Certificate 2730), Xenophon Alexander (his first name was not given on the certificate--Birth Record 2, p. 21, Certificate 3366), and Mary M. (Birth Record 3, p. 32, no certificate number given); and letters, 13 and 19 March 1989, to Philip Graham from Wilma Symonds, Research Genealogist of Cumberland, Iowa.

[30] Except where noted, the information on Mary Ellen is from Elizabeth Caldwell Hallam; Nancy Avery Kuhl, daughter of 6-49 Myra Graham Avery who was reared in Greeley, Colorado where Mary Ellen lived; and the obituary of Mary Ellen's father, 4-9 James Harvey, in *The United Presbyterian*, 8 July 1897, p. 434.

[31] The information on Wilson is from *Portrait and Biographical Album of Louisa County, Iowa* (Chicago: Acme Pub. Co., 1889), p. 343; federal censuses; Elizabeth Caldwell Hallam; Omaha, Nebraska, city directories, 1886-1935 (some years missing); and letter, 24 September 1988, to Philip Graham from Martin W. Beerman, Research Genealogist of Omaha, Nebraska.

[32] The information on Dales Y. is from his son, 6-25 Wilmer T.; *Portrait and Biographical Album of Louisa County, Iowa*, pp. 171-2; WPA, *Grave Records, Louisa County, Iowa* (n.d.), p. 51; and Elizabeth Caldwell Hallam.

[33] Except where noted, the information on the children of A. Y. is from Elizabeth Caldwell Hallam who is a descendant.

[34] *Portrait and Biographical Album of Warren County, Illinois*, 2 Vols. (Chicago: Chapman Bros., 1886), I, 242.

[35] Obituary on Jenny in *The Daily Review Atlas*, Monday, 25 November 1929, p. 3; and 1880 federal census of Warren County, IL.

[36] The information on Nancy and her family is from Rising, p. 244; and Elizabeth Caldwell Hallam.

[37] Book D, p. 28.--*Warren Co., IL, Female Marriage Index*, p. 113.

[38] Obituary as given by Linda Gordon, comp., *Deaths and Obituaries Extracted from: Moffitt Book, Vol. VI*, 4 Vols. (Warren Co., IL, Genealogical Soc., 1985), II, 35-6.

[39] The information on Edward is from federal censuses; Genealogical Comm. of the California DAR, *Veteran's Grave Registration*, 2 Vols. (n.p: DAR, 1943), I, 342; J. N. Reece, *Report of the Adjutant General of the State of Illinois*, 9 Vols. (Springfield, IL, 1900), VII, 114; and his will filed in Los Angeles, 29 April 1910, Probate #16407.

[40] The information on William F. and Mary M. is from letters, 4 May 1985 and 10 November 1986, to Katharine Kell from 6-38C Martha Paton, a descendant; Monmouth College *Catalogue* and *Circulars*; William's Pension Records, Application #668253, Certificate #991608, National Archives, Washington, D.C.; federal censuses; Ross, *Henderson County Marriages*, p. 17; settlement of Mary's father's estate in Madison County, Iowa, 17 February 1882; Lucas County, Iowa, Genealogical Society, *Lucas County, Iowa, Cemetery Records* (Marceline, MO: Walsworth Pub. Co., 1981), pp. 135 and 142; and letter, January 1986, to Katharine Kell from 5-97C Lyle Graham Wimmer, son of 5-97 Lillie M.

[41] The information on Donald and his wife is from *The United Presbyterian*, Thursday, 6 April 1905, p. 27; Rising, p. 240; J. W. Wood, *Pasadena, California* (Pasadena: the author, 1917), pp. 109-10, 140, 378-9, and 476-7; William A. Spalding, *History and Reminiscences: Los Angeles City and County*, 3 Vols. (Los Angeles: J. R. Finnell & Sons, 1936), I, 246-7, 262, 315, and 373; Harold D. Carew, *History of Pasadena and the San Gabriel Valley*, 3 Vols. (Los Angeles: S. J. Clarke Pub. Co., 1930), I, 349-50; Lon F. Chapin, *Thirty Years in Pasadena* (Los Angeles: Southwest Pub. Co., 1929), Book 1, pp. 108-9 and 114-5, and Book 2, pp. 289-90; Los Angeles city directories; James D. Hart, comp., *A Companion to California* (New York: Oxford Univ. Press, 1978), p. 169; and Donald's obituary in *The Los Angeles Times*, Pasadena Edition, 23 March 1890, p. 1.

[42] The information on Alexander and his family is from his Probate Record, #42031, Los Angeles, filed 28 February 1919; Los Angeles Marriage Records, Book 46, p. 76, #538; federal censuses; *The Los Angeles Times*, 17 February 1910, Part 2, p. 3; and *The Los Angeles Times*, 18 February 1910, Part 1, p. 12.

[43] The information on James Gillespie Graham and his descendants is from Nancy Avery Kuhl who

was a granddaughter.

⁴⁴ The information on Frank is from unpublished family sources of Katharine Kell; letter, 29 October 1975, to Katharine Kell from Cheryl Arment, Secretary, Linn Grove Cemetery; and *The Greeley Daily Tribune*, 18 February 1885, 23 March 1887, 13 April 1887, and 13 September 1940.

⁴⁵ The information on Kate and her family is from unpublished family sources of Katharine Kell; Theophilus A. Wylie, *Indiana University: Its History from 1820, When Founded, to 1890* (Indianapolis: Indiana Univ., 1890), p. 409; *Portrait and Biographical Album of Champaign County, Illinois*, 2 Vols. (Chicago: Chapman Bros., 1887), II, 867; letter, 29 November 1975, to Katharine Kell from Clyde W. Morrison, Bartlesville, OK, a fraternity brother and long-time friend of Kate's son; letter, 28 September 1975, to Katharine Kell from Marion C. Moore, historian of Tolono, IL; and *The Greeley Daily Tribune and Greeley Republican*, 24 May 1918.

⁴⁶ She joined the DAR on her descent from her mother's maternal grandfather, John Hopkins (c. 1748-1814).

⁴⁷ The information on Mattie and her descendants is from unpublished family sources of Katharine Kell who is a granddaughter.

⁴⁸ Except where noted, the information on the children of James Thomas is from letters, 14 December 1985 and 8 January 1986, to Katharine Kell from Velores Koll Graham whose husband, 7-27 Calvin W., is a great-grandson; letters, 28 January 1986 and 3 April 1986, to Katharine Kell from Lorna Howard Cline, daughter of 5-71 Iva L.; letter, 9 September 1989, to Katharine Kell from Erma McCallum, granddaughter of 5-67 Harry W.; letters, 27 March and 15 April 1986, to Velores Koll Graham from Kathryn Patterson Graham, wife of 6-55 Frederick L., deceased; letter to Velores Graham from Alvin F. Krug, husband of 6-66 Arlie Graham Krug, deceased, who said he copied it from her mother's Bible; and federal censuses.

⁴⁹ The information on John G. is from letters, 8 January and 18 February 1986, to Katharine Kell from Velores Koll Graham; Emma E. Forter, *History of Marshall County, Kansas* (Indianapolis: B. F. Bowen & Co., 1917), pp. 861-3; and Anna Maria Wittmuss, "Ray William Graham," a biography as told to Anna's daughter, 7-28 Rae Graham Darner--unpublished family document.

⁵⁰ The information on the children of Matthew Joseph is from Martha Paton, 4 May 1985; 5-97C Lyle Graham Wimmer, January 1986; federal censuses; letter, 23 May 1987, to Velores Koll Graham from Elvina Graham, widow of 6-65 Theodore O.; and Harriet Hughes Wright and Lydia Palmer Jones, *The History of Summerfield* (Summerfield, KS: n. pub., n.d. [c. 1980]), p. 36.

⁵¹ Except where noted, the information on the children of John Mills is from Velores Koll Graham; and letter, 14 June 1989, to Katharine Kell from 6-93A Bernice Vitosh Ruyle whose husband is a great-grandson.

⁵² Except where noted, the information on the children of Samuel A. is from Lyle Graham Wimmer and 6-124 Ruth Josephine Graham Butler who are descendants.

⁵³ As stated in his obituary in *The Sportsman Review* [of Spokane, Washington], 19 December 1959, p. 12.

⁵⁴ As stated in his obituary in the *Des Moines Register*, 4 February 1968, local section, p. 4.

⁵⁵ The information on Granville's children is from letters to Katharine Kell from 5-105A Raymond R. Simpson Jr. and Charlotte Graham, wife of 6-125 Frank W. Graham; and from obituaries in *The Denver Post*, 31 January 1953, p. 11, and *The Dallas Morning News*, 30 June 1942, Section II, p. 7.

⁵⁶ Ross and Evans, II, 101.

⁵⁷ The information on Frank is from *ibid.*, *loc. cit.*; and Henderson County, Illinois, Marriage Records, Book C, p. 107.

⁵⁸ The information on Charles is from Woods and Woods, *McDills in America*, p. 92; and Ross and Evans, II, 101.

⁵⁹ *Ibid.*, *loc. cit.*

## SIXTH GENERATION

¹ The information on Fanny May and her family is from Robert McDill Woods and Iva Godfrey Woods, *McDills in America* (Ann Arbor, MI: Edwards Bros., Inc., 1940), pp. 91-2; and Elwilda Osborn and Ethel Trego, *Warren County, Illinois, Death Records, 1876 Through 1915* (Warren Co., IL, Genealogical Society, 1985), s.v. "Spicer, Fannie May Graham" and "Spicer, A. W."

² Woods and Woods, p. 92.

³ Henderson County, Illinois, Birth Records, Book 1, p. 73.

⁴ The information on David B. and his wife is from a letter, 25 February 1989, to Katharine Kell from their daughter, Margaret Graham Parker; and letter, 29 February 1988, to Philip Graham from their nephew 7-4 Evarts A. Graham.

⁵ The information on Evarts Ambrose is from Anna Rothe and Evelyn Lohn, eds., *Current Biography: Who's News and Why, 1952* (New York: H. W. Wilson Co., 1952), pp. 220-2; *Who Was Who among North American Authors, 1921-1929*, 2 Vols. (Detroit: Gale Research Co., 1940), pp. 608-9; and his obituary in *The New York Times*, 5 March 1957, p. 31.

⁶ The information on Harvey is from unpublished family sources of Philip Graham who is a grandson.

⁷ The information on the descendants of James Andrew is from Elizabeth Caldwell Hallam, granddaughter of 5-28 Elizabeth Graham Cowden.

⁸ The information on Edwin's descendants is from *ibid.*, and Louise Baumann, comp., *Prospect Hill Cemetery Records* (n.p.: Greater Omaha Genealogical Society, 1977), p. 127.

⁹ Except where noted, the information on William's descendants is from Elizabeth Caldwell Hallam; obituary on their father in the Atlantic, Iowa, newspaper; their birth certificates in Atlantic, Iowa (Lessie--Record 1, p. 187, certificate 2405; Harvey--Record 1, p. 212, certificate 273; Xenophon--Record 2, p. 21, certificate 3366; and Mary--Record 3, p. 32, certificate number not given); and letters, 13 and 19 March 1989, to Philip Graham from Wilma Symonds, Research Genealogist

of Cumberland, Iowa.

[10] Except where noted, the information on Wilson's children is from *ibid.*; and letter, 13 September 1988, to Philip Graham from Martin W. Beerman, Research Genealogist of Omaha, Nebraska.

[11] The information on Wilmer T. is from Wilmer, himself, letter to Philip Graham.

[12] The information on Harold is from Elizabeth Caldwell Hallam.

[13] *Ibid.*

[14] The information on Bessie and her family is from Bessie's will, filed in Seattle, WA, Vol. 702, p. 632; the will of her husband, George, Vol. 848, p. 166; Bessie's obituary in *The Seattle Times*, 25 August 1957, p. 30; George's obituary in *The Seattle Times*, 1 April 1962, p. 32; city directories of San Francisco and Seattle; and the federal censuses.

[15] Except where noted, the information on William F.'s descendants is from letters, 4 May 1985 and 10 November 1986, to Katharine Kell from 6-38C Martha Paton who is granddaughter; William's pension records, Application #668253, Certificate #991608, National Archives, Washington D.C.; and federal censuses.

[16] Martha Paton; and Warren County, Illinois, Genealogical Society, *Warren County, Illinois, Female Marriage Index, 1829 through 1915* (1985), p. 114.

[17] Letter, 22 July 1988, to Philip Graham from Pat Manusov, Certified Genealogist of Los Angeles, California.

[18] The information on the descendants of James G. is from letters to Katharine Kell from 6-49A Nancy Avery Kuhl who was a granddaughter.

[19] The information on Alva and his descendants is from a letter, 28 January 1986, to Katharine Kell from 5-71B Lorna Howard Cline who is a niece; and Velores Koll Graham, wife of 7-27 Calvin W.

[20] The information on Andrew R. and his descendants is from Lorna Howard Cline; and letters, 27 March and 15 April 1986, to Velores Koll Graham from Kathryn Patterson Graham, wife of 6-55 Frederick L. Graham.

[21] The information on Harry and his descendants is from a letter, 28 January 1986, to Katharine Kell from Lorna Howard Cline; letter, 23 May 1987, to Velores Graham from 6-65 Theodore; letter, 12 June 1987, to Velores from Alvin Krug, husband of 6-66 Arlene (Alvin said he copied the information from the Bible belonging to Arlene's mother); letter, 1 July 1987, to Velores from 6-60B Arlene Propst Blackwell; and letter, 9 September 1989, to Katharine Kell from Erma Graham McCallum, daughter of 6-59 Roy.

[22] The information on the descendants of John G. is from Lorna Howard Cline, letter, 28 January 1986; and Anna Maria Wittmuss Graham, "Ray William Graham," his biography as told to Anna's daughter, 7-28 Rae Graham Darner.--unpublished family document, 1988.

[23] The information on the descendants of Lawrence W. is from letters to Velores Graham from 6-72D Carol Olmstead.

[24] The information on the descendants of James Thomas Jr. is from letters, 14 December 1985 and 8 January 1986, to Katharine Kell from Velores Koll Graham; and letters to Katharine Kell, 28 January and 3 April 1986, from Lorna Howard Cline.

[25] The information on the descendants of Frank I. is from *ibid.*; and Velores Koll Graham.

[26] The information on the descendants of Lee A. is from a letter, 4 May 1985, to Katharine Kell from Martha Paton; and federal censuses.

[27] The information on the descendants of Robert C. is from letters, 26 March 1986 and 19 July 1989, to Katharine Kell from Bernice F. Ruyle, daughter-in-law of 6-93 Dorothy; and federal censuses.

[28] The information on the descendants of George Henry is from Velores Koll Graham; and federal censuses.

[29] Except where noted, the information on the descendants of William A. is from a letter, January 1986, to Katharine Kell from 5-97C Lyle Graham Wimmer; letter, January 1987, to Katharine Kell from 6-124 Ruth Josephine Graham Butler; and Edna's obituary in *The Spokesman Review* of Spokane, WA, 9 March 1976, p. 17.

[30] The information on the descendants of Thomas E. is from Lyle Graham Wimmer, January 1986.

[31] The information on the descendants of Robert C. is from *ibid.*; and Ruth Josephine Graham Butler, 5 January 1987.

[32] The information on Ruth Josephine Graham Butler is from Mrs. Butler, herself, letter to Katharine Kell, 5 January 1987.

[33] The information on the children of Charles W. is from his daughter-in-law, Charlotte Graham, wife of 6-125 Frank W.


## SEVENTH GENERATION

[1] The information on Margaret (Marnie) Graham Parker is from Marnie, herself, in letters to Katharine Kell.

[2] The information on David and his wife is from *Who's Who in America*, 44th ed. (Wilmette, IL: Macmillan Directory Division, 1987), I, 1085 and 1086.

[3] The information on Evarts is from *ibid.*, I, 1086; letters to Philip Graham from 6-25 Wilmer T. Graham; 5-28H1 Elizabeth Caldwell Hallam; and Evarts, himself, in letters to Katharine Kell.

[4] The information on the descendants of Harvey W. is from unpublished family sources of Philip Graham who is a grandson.

[5] The information on Suzanne is from her parents' obituaries in the *Omaha World-Herald*, 27 July 1965, p. 28, and 9 April 1979, p. 22; and from her aunt Mary Graham Weeth's obituary, *Omaha World-Herald*, 8 April 1978, p. 34.

[6] The information on James is from his father, Wilmer T., in letters to Philip Graham.

[7] All information is from Elizabeth Caldwell Hallam.

[8] All information is from Velores Koll Graham, wife of 7-27 Calvin Wittmuss Graham.

[9] The information on Frederick L. and his descendants if from letters, 27 March and 15 April 1956, to Velores Koll Graham from Kathryn Patterson Graham, widow of 6-55 Frederick L.

[10] *Ibid.*

[11] All information is from letters to Katharine Kell from 5-71B Lorna Howard Cline, 28 January 1986; and Velores Koll Graham, October 1988.

[12] Velores Koll Graham, October 1988.

[13] *Ibid.*

[14] *Ibid.*

[15] *Ibid.*

[16] *Ibid.*

[17] *Ibid.*

[18] Letter, 4 May 1985, to Katharine Kell from 6-38C Martha Paton.

[19] Letter, 26 March 1986, to Katharine Kell from Bernice F. Ruyle, wife of 6-93A Robert L. Ruyle.

[20] *Ibid.*

[21] Letters to Katharine Kell from 5-97C Lyle Graham Wimmer, January 1986, and 6-124 Ruth Josephine Graham Butler, January 1987.

[22] *Ibid.*

[23] *Ibid.*

[24] Lyle Graham Wimmer.

[25] *Ibid.*

[26] *Ibid.*

[27] *Ibid.*

[28] *Ibid.*; and Ruth Josephine Graham Butler.

[29] Lyle Graham Wimmer.

[30] *Ibid.*

[31] *Ibid.*

## EIGHTH GENERATION

[1] Letter, 29 February 1988, to Philip Graham from 7-4 Evarts A. Graham Jr.

[2] Letter, 27 May 1989, to Katharine Kell from 7-4 Evarts A. Graham Jr.

[3] All information is from unpublished family sources of Philip Graham.

[4] *Ibid.*

[5] *Ibid.*

[6] Letter to Philip Graham from 6-25 Wilmer T. Graham.

[7] Letters, 27 March and 15 April 1986, to Velores Koll Graham, wife of 7-27 Calvin W., from Kathryn Patterson Graham, widow of 6-55 Frederick L.

[8] *Ibid.*

[9] All information is from unpublished family sources of Velores Koll Graham and from each of her children in letters to Katharine Kell.

[10] *Ibid.*

[11] *Ibid.*

[12] *Ibid.*

[13] *Ibid.*

[14] *Ibid.*

[15] Letter, 26 March 1986, to Katharine Kell from Bernice Vitosh Ruyle, wife of 6-93A Robert L. Ruyle.

[16] *Ibid.*,

[17] Letters to Katharine Kell from 5-97C Lyle Graham Wimmer and 6-124 Ruth Josephine Graham Butler.

[18] Ruth Josephine Graham Butler.

# BIBLIOGRAPHY

PRIMARY SOURCES

City Directories

Deeds, birth and death certificates, probate records, and court records

Genealogical data sent by Graham family members

Newspapers, most of them on microfilm at the Library of Congress, Washington, D.C.:

*The Daily Review Atlas*, Monmouth, Illinois
*The Dallas Morning News*
*Denver Post*
*Des Moines Register*
*Galveston Daily News*
*The Greeley* [Colorado] *Daily Tribune*
*The Herald Independent*, Winnsboro, South Carolina
*Los Angeles Times*
*The Miami* [University] *Student*
*The New York Times*
*Omaha* [Nebraska] *World Herald*
*Oquawka* [Illinois] *Spectator*
*Spokesman Review*, Spokane, Washington
*The United Presbyterian*

Military and Pension Records at the National Archives, Washington, D.C.

Session Minutes and other records at the Presbyterian Historical Society, 425 Lombard Street, Philadelphia 19147

United States Federal Censuses, 1790-1910

SECONDARY SOURCES

Ackerman, Robert K. *South Carolina Colonial Land Policies.* Columbia, S.C.: Univ. of South Carolina, 1977.

Adam, Frank. *The Clans, Septs, and Regiments of the Scottish Highlands.* Revised by Sir Thomas Innes of Learney. 7th ed. Edinburgh: W. and A. K. Johnston and G. W. Bacon, Ltd., 1965.

Ainsworth, Fern. *Index to Naturalization Records: Chester County, South Carolina.* Natchitoches, La.: n. pub., n.d. [c. 1970].

Allen, Desmond Walls. *Index to the Tract Books for Izard and Stone Counties in Arkansas.* Conway, Arkansas: n. pub., 1985.

Battle, J. H., and Perrin. W. H., eds. *Counties of Todd and Christian, Kentucky.* Chicago: F. A. Battey Publishing Co., 1884.

Baumann, Louise, comp. *Prospect Hill Cemetery Burial Records from Earliest Known to December 31, 1975.* N.p.: Greater Omaha Genealogical Society, 1977.

Beckett, J[ames] C[amlin]. *The Making of Modern Ireland.* N.Y.: Alfred A. Knopf, 1966.

Bingham, Madeleine. *Scotland under Mary Stuart: An Account of Everyday Life.* N.Y.: St. Martin's Press, 1971.

*Biographical and Historical Memoirs of Mississippi.* 2 Vols. Chicago: Goodspeed Publishing Co., 1891.

*Biographical and Historical Memoirs of Northeast Arkansas.* Chicago: Goodspeed Publishing Co., 1889.

Bishop, Lois. *Warren County, Illinois, Will Index, 1831 through 1915.* N.p.: Warren County, Illinois, Genealogical Society, 1984.

Blanchard, Charles, ed. *1884 History of Monroe County, Indiana: Originally Published as History of Morgan, Monroe & Brown Counties.* 1884; rptd. Knightstown, IN: The Bookmark, 1978.

Bolin, Mrs. Stuart R., and Heaume, Mrs. John S., comps. *Early Marriage Bonds of Ohio: Preble County.* N.p.: Daughters of the American Revolution, n.d.

Boyce, Lois M., ed. *Linn County, Oregon: Early 1850 Records.* Portland, OR: Boyce-Wheeler Publishers, n.d.

Brown, John Henry. *Indian Wars and Pioneers of Texas.* Austin, TX: L. E. Daniell, 1880; rptd. Easley, S.C.: Southern Historical Press, 1978.

Brown, P. Hume. *A Short History of Scotland.* New edition by Henry W. Meikle. Edinburgh: Oliver and Boyd, Ltd., 1955.

Bryan, William S., and Rose, Robert. *A History of the Pioneer Families of Missouri.* Saint Louis: Bryan, Brand & Co., 1876.

Buck, Solon J., and Buck, Elizabeth Hawthorne. *The Planting of Civili-*

zation in Western Pennsylvania. Pittsburgh: Univ. of Pittsburgh Press, 1939.

Bushman, Katherine Gentry. *Index of the First Plat Book of Clay County, Missouri, 1819-1875.* N.p.: n. pub., n.d.--Unpublished manuscript at the Allen County Public Library, Fort Wayne, Indiana.

Carew, Harold D. *History of Pasadena and the San Gabriel Valley, California.* 3 Vols. N.p.: The S. J. Clarke Publishing Co., 1930.

Carson, Martha Bray. *Chester County Cemetery Inscriptions.* Chester Co., S.C.: Daughters of the American Revolution, 1942.

Carter, Ruth C. *Marriage Records, 1852-1859: Monroe County, Indiana.* Bloomington, IN: Daughters of the American Revolution, 1976.

--- (Mrs. G. Kent Carter). *Marriage Records, 1859-1867: Monroe County, Indiana.* Bloomington, IN: Daughters of the American Revolution, 1978.

---. *Marriage Records: Monroe County, Indiana, 1882-1888.* Bloomington, IN: Daughters of the American Revolution, n.d.

---. *Will Abstracts [from] Will Book IV, February, 1873 - February, 1890.* Monroe County, IN: Daughters of the American Revolution, 1974.

---. *Will Abstracts, 1890-1904: Monroe County, Indiana.* Bloomington, IN: Daughters of the American Revolution, 1975.

*Cemeteries of Ford County, Illinois.* N.p.: Daughters of the American Revolution, 1964.

*Cemeteries of Lancaster County, Nebraska.* 8 Vols. Lincoln, NE: Lincoln-Lancaster County Genealogical Society, 1977-83.

Cemetery Committee of the Warren County Genealogical Society, *Tombstone Inscriptions--Spring Grove Township, Warren County, Illinois.* N.p., 1983.--Unpublished manuscript prepared by the society.

*Cemetery Records of Ford County, Illinois.* 2 Vols. Piper City, IL: Daughters of the American Revolution, 1962-3.

*Cemetery Records of Platte County, Missouri.* 2 Vols. N.p.: The Platte County Historical Society, 1961 and 1968.

*The Centennial History of the Associate Reformed Presbyterian Church, 1803-1903.* Charleston, S.C.: The Synod, 1905.

Chapin, Lon F. *Thirty Years in Pasadena* [California]. 2 Vols. N.p.:

Southwest Publishing Co., 1929.

Cogswell, Edith Bauer. *An Index to Monroe County, Indiana, Marriage Records, 1818-1852: Compiled from the Original Records in the Office of the Monroe County Clerk.* N.p.: n. pub., 1954.--Unpublished manuscript in the Fort Wayne and Allen County Public Library, Fort Wayne, Indiana.

Creighton, James A. *A Narrative History of Brazoria County* [Texas]. Waco, TX: Brazoria County Historical Commission, 1975.

Crèvecoeur, Hector St. John de. *Letters from an American Farmer.* 1782; rptd. London: J. M. Dent & Sons, Ltd., 1912.

Dantell, L[ewis] E. *Personnel of the Texas State Government.* Austin, TX: the author, 1889.

Davis, Quincy A., comp. *Early Marriage Records of Butler County, Ohio.* 3 Vols. N.p.: Daughters of the American Revolution, n.d.

*Deaths and Obituaries Extracted from Moffitt Book, Vol. 5.* N.p.: Warren County, Illinois, Genealogical Society, 1985.

Dickson, R. J. *Ulster Emigration to Colonial America, 1718-1775.* London: Routledge and Kegan Paul, 1966.

*Dictionary of American Biography.* 20 Vols. Ed. Dumas Malone. N.Y.: Scribner's, 1932.

Dinsmore, John Walker. *The Scotch-Irish in America.* Chicago: Winona Publishing Co., 1906.

Dunaway, Wayland F[uller]. *The Scotch-Irish of Colonial Pennsylvania.* Chapel Hill, N.C.: Univ. of North Carolina, 1944.

Ellsberry, Elizabeth Prather. *Clay County, Missouri, Cemetery Records.* 2 Vols. Chillicothe, MO: the author, 1962.

---. *Marriage Records of Christian County, Kentucky, 1795-1825.* Chillicothe, MO: Daughters of the American Revolution, n.d.

---. *Marriage Records of Clay County, Missouri, 1852-1900.* N.p.: Daughters of the American Revolution, 1962.

Evans, E. Estyn. "The Scotch-Irish: Their Cultural Adaptation and Heritage in the American West." *Essays in Scotch-Irish History.* Ed. E. R. R. Green. London: Routledge & Kegan Paul, 1969. Pp. 69-86.

Fitzgibbon, Constantine. *Red Hand, the Ulster Colony.* Garden City,

N.Y.: Doubleday, 1971.

Ford, Henry Jones. *The Scotch-Irish in America*. 1915; rptd. N.Y.: Arno Press and The New York Times, 1969.

Forter, Emma E. *History of Marshall County, Kansas*. Indianapolis: B. F. Bowen & Co., 1917.

Gardner, John D., Paine, Tom Mimms, and Henson, Elizabeth. *Marriage Index of Todd County, Kentucky, 1820-1920*. Allensville & Hopkins-, ville, KY: n. pub., n.d. The authors write, "This was taken from the index of grooms prepared by the W.P.A. from the original Bonds. We have added the index for the brides."

Gary, Cordelia C. *Marriage Records, 1797-1850: Christian County, Kentucky*. N.p.: the author, 1970.

Gault, Pressley Brown, and Leighty, Elisabeth Pinkerton. *The William Gault Family History, 1735-1948*. 2 Parts: Part I in 1893 by Pressley Brown Gault, Part II in 1948 by Elisabeth Pinkerton Leighty. Sparta, IL: n. pub., n.d. [1948].

*Genealogical Material in Oregon Donation Land Claims*. Portland, OR: Genealogical Forum of Portland, Oregon, 1957.

*General Catalogue of the Graduates and Former Students of Miami University Including Members of the Board of Trustees and Faculty During Its First Century, 1809-1909*. Oxford, OH: Miami Univ., 1910.

Glasgow, Maude. *The Scotch-Irish in Northern Ireland and in the American Colonies*. N.Y.: G. P. Putnam's Sons, 1936.

Glasgow, William Melancthon. *Cyclopedic Manual of the United Presbyterian Church of North America*. Pittsburgh: United Presbyterian Board of Publication, 1903.

---. *History of the Reformed Presbyterian Church in America*. Baltimore: Hill & Harvey, 1888.

---. *A Supplement to the Cyclopedic Manual of the United Presbyterian Church of North America*. Pittsburgh: United Presbyterian Board of Publication, 1903.

Glazner, Mrs. Capitola, and McLane, Mrs. Gerald B., comps. *Hempstead County, Arkansas: United States Census of 1860*. N.p.: the authors, 1969.

Gochanour, Eileen, comp. *1836 Morgan County, Illinois, Tax List*. Springfield, IL: n. pub., 1986.

---. *Morgan County, Illinois, Marriages, Volume I: 1827-1839.* Springfield, IL: n. pub., 1983.

Godbey, Martha E., comp. *Henry County, Iowa, Grave Records.* Grinnell, IA: n. pub., 1936.

Gonzales County Historical Commission. *The History of Gonzales County, Texas.* Dallas, TX: Curtis Media Corp., 1986.

*Grave Records, Louisa County, Iowa.* N.p.: W.P.A., n.d.

Griffin, S. C. *History of Galveston, Texas.* Galveston, TX: A. H. Cawston, 1931.

Gurley, Lottie LeGett, comp. *Genealogical Material in Oregon Donation Land Claims.* 5 Vols. Portland, OR: The Genealogical Forum of Portland, Oregon, 1975.

---, comp. *Genealogical Material in Oregon Provisional Land Claims, Abstracted, Volumes I-VIII, 1845-1849.* Portland, OR: The Genealogical Forum of Portland, Oregon, 1982.

Hanna, Charles A. *The Scotch-Irish, or the Scot in North Britain, North Ireland, and North America.* 2 Vols. N.Y.: G. P. Putnam, 1902.

Harris, Mary Sue (Phillips), and McLane, Bobbie (Jones). *Independence County, Arkansas, Marriage Records, 1827-1877: Books A thru D.* N.p.: the authors, 1970.

Hart, James D. *A Companion to California.* N.Y.: Oxford Univ. Press, 1978.

Hemphill, James. *The Hemphill Family Notes.* Charleston, S.C.: n. pub., 1894.

*Historical Encyclopedia of Illinois . . . and History of Henderson County.* 2 Vols. Chicago: Munsell Publishing Co., 1911.

*Historical Encyclopedia of Illinois and History of Warren County.* 2 Vols. Chicago: Munsell Publishing Co., 1903.

*History of Cass County, Iowa.* Springfield, IL: Continental Historical Co., 1884.

*History of Clay and Platte Counties, Missouri.* Saint Louis: National Historical Co., 1885.

*History of Lincoln County, Missouri.* Chicago: The Goodspeed Publishing Co., 1888.

*History of Mercer and Henderson Counties* [Illinois]. 2 Vols. Chicago: H. H. Hill & Co., 1882.

*History of Mercer County* [Illinois] *Together with Biographical Matter, Statistics, Etc. . . . Containing also a Short History of Henderson County.* Chicago: H. H. Hill & Co., 1882.

*History of Preble County, Ohio, with Illustrations and Biographical Sketches.* Cleveland: H. Z. Williams & Bro., 1881.

Hodges, Nadine, and Woodruff, Mrs. Howard. *Genealogical Notes from the 'Liberty Tribune.'* Liberty, MO: Daughters of the American Revolution, 1967, printed 1975.

---, and Woodruff, Mrs. Howard W. *Missouri Pioneers.* N.p.: the authors, 1972.

Holcomb, Brent H., and Parker, Elmer O. *Camden District, S. C., Wills and Administrations, 1781-1787 (1770-1796).* Easley, S.C.: Southern Historical Press, 1978.

---, and Parker, Elmer O. *Chester County, South Carolina, Minutes of the County Court, 1785-1799.* Easley, S.C.: Southern Historical Press, 1979.

---, comp. *South Carolina Naturalizations, 1783-1850.* Baltimore: Genealogical Publishing Co., 1985.

Hooker, Richard J., ed. *The Carolina Backcountry on the Eve of the Revolution: The Journal and Other Writings of Charles Woodmason, Anglican Itinerant.* Chapel Hill, N.C.: Univ. of North Carolina, 1953.

*Hopewell A. R. P. Church, Chester County: 1787--South Carolina--1982.* Richburg, S.C.: Chester County Genealogical Society, n.d.

*An Illustrated Historical Atlas of Platte County, Missouri.* Philadelphia: Edwards Brothers of Missouri, 1877.

Ingmire, Frances T., comp. *Arkansas Confederate Veterans and Widows Pensions Applications.* Saint Louis: the author, 1985.

Jackson, Ronald Vern, ed. *Arkansas 1850 Census Index.* South Bountiful, UT: Accelerated Indexing Systems, Inc., n.d.

---, ed. *Mortality Schedules: Arkansas, 1860.* Bountiful, UT: Accelerated Indexing Systems, Inc., 1979.

---, ed. *Mortality Schedules: Arkansas, 1870.* Bountiful, UT: Accelerated Indexing Systems, 1979.

Jamison, Matthew H. *Recollections of Pioneer and Army Life.* Kansas City, MO: Hudson Press, 1911.

*Jefferson County, Indiana, Marriages, 1873-1899.* N.p.: Daughters of the American Revolution, n.d.

Jillson, Willard Rouse. *The Kentucky Land Grants: A Systematic Index to All of the Land Grants Recorded in the State Land Office at Frankfort, Kentucky, 1782-1924.* Louisville, KY: The Filson Club, 1925.

Kelsey, Hugh Alexander. *The United Presbyterian Directory: A Half-Century Survey, 1903-1958.* Pittsburgh: United Presbyterian Board of Publications, 1903.

Kemper, G. W. H. *A Medical History of the State of Indiana.* Chicago: American Medical Association Press, 1911.

Kennedy, Urban E. *Early History of Todd County, Kentucky.* N.p.: n. pub., n.d.

Langdon, Barbara. *York County Marriages, 1770-1869, Implied in York County, S. C., Probate Records.* Aitken, S.C.: the author, 1983.

Lathan, R[obert]. *A Historical Sketch of Union A. R. P. Church, Chester County, South Carolina.* 1888; rptd. Richburg, S.C.: Chester County Genealogical Society, 1980.

---. *History of Hopewell Associate Reformed Presbyterian Church, Chester County, S. C.* Yorkville, S.C.. Steam Presses of the Yorkville Enquirer, 1879; rptd. Richburg, S.C.: Chester County Genealogical Society, 1981.

Leyburn, James G[raham]. *The Scotch-Irish: A Social History.* Chapel Hill, N.C.: Univ. of North Carolina, 1962.

Lowry, R. E. *History of Preble County, Ohio: Her People, Industries and Institutions.* Indianapolis: B. F. Bowen & Co., 1915.

Lucas County Genealogical Society. *Lucas County, Iowa, Cemetery Records.* Marceline, MO: Walsworth Publishing Co., 1981.

MacDougall, Margaret O., ed. *Robert Bain's The Clans and Tartans of Scotland.* 5th ed. London: Collins, 1968.

MacGregor, Geddes. *The Thundering Scot: A Portrait of John Knox.* Philadelphia: Westminster Press, 1957.

Mackie, R. L. *A Short History of Scotland.* Ed. Gordon Donaldson. N.Y.: Frederick A. Praeger, 1962.

McLane, Bobbie Jones, and Glazner, Capitola Hensley, comps. *Hempstead County, Arkansas, Marriage Records: 1817-1875.* Hot Springs National Park, Arkansas: the authors, 1969.

McQuiston, Leona Bean, comp. *The McQuiston, McCuiston and McQuesten Families, 1620-1937.* Los Angeles: n. pub., 1937.

Marquis, Albert Nelson, ed. *The Book of Chicagoans: A Biographical Dictionary of Leading Living Men of the City of Chicago.* Chicago: A. N. Marquis & Co., 1911.

*Marriage Records of Henderson County, Illinois, Book I.* N.p.: Daughters of the American Revolution, n.d.

Marsh, Helen Crawford, and Marsh, Timothy Richard, comps. *Abstracts of Wills: Lincoln County, Tennessee, 1810-1895.* Shelbyville, TN: Marsh Historical Publications, 1977.

---, and Marsh, Timothy Richard. *Lincoln County, Tennessee, Official Marriage Records, 1838-1880.* Shelbyville, TN: Marsh Historical Publications, 1974.

Marsh, Timothy Richard, and Marsh, Helen Crawford. *Cemetery Records of Lincoln County, Tennessee.* Shelbyville, TN: Marsh Historical Publications, 1972.

Matson, Donald K., comp. *Rose Hill Cemetery* [of Bloomington, IN]. Bloomington, IN: Monroe County Genealogical Society, 1976.

*A Memorial and Biographical History of Johnson and Hill Counties, Texas.* Chicago: The Lewis Publishing Co., 1892.

Miles, John, and Milligan, Richard R. *Linn County, Oregon, Pioneer Settlers.* 5 Vols. Lebanon, OR: John Miles, 1984.

---, and Milligan, Richard R. *Oregon Territory Families in Linn County, Oregon, to 1855.* 5 Vols. Lebanon, OR: John Miles, 1983.

Moir, Alexander L. *Moir Genealogy and Collateral Lines with Historical Notes.* Lowell, Mass.: the author, 1913.

*Monmouth College Catalogue and Circular.* Monmouth, IL: Monmouth College, 1857-.

*Monroe County, Indiana, Family Heritage, 1987.* Bloomington, IN: Monroe County Historical Society, 1987.

Montague, E. J. *A Directory, Business Mirror, and Historical Sketches of Randolph County* [Illinois]. Alton, IL: Courier Steam Book and Job Printing House, 1859.

---. "The History of Randolph County, Illinois, Including Old Kaskaskia Island, 1859." Sparta, IL: copied by Elisabeth Pinkerton Leighty, 1948.

Moody, T. W., and Martin, F. X. *The Course of Irish History.* N.Y.: Weybright and Talley, Inc., 1967.

Morgan, William Manning. *Trinity Protestant Episcopal Church.* Galveston, TX: the author, 1954.

Moss, Bobby Gilmer. *Roster of South Carolina Patriots in the American Revolution.* Baltimore: Genealogical Publishing Co., 1983.

Murray, Nicholas Russell. *Marshall County, Mississippi, 1866-1900: Computer Indexed Marriage Records.* Hammond, LA: Hunting for Bears, Inc., 1983.

---. *Warren County, Illinois, 1839-1869: Computer Indexed Marriage Records.* North Salt Lake, UT: Hunting for Bears, Inc., 1988.

---. *Warren County, Mississippi, 1810-1900: Computer Indexed Marriage Records.* Hammond, LA: Hunting for Bears, Inc., 1981.

*Navarro County [Texas] Cemetery Records.* 5 Vols. Corsicana, TX: Navarro County Genealogical Society, 1984.

Neel, Eurie Pearl Wilford. *The Statistical Handbook of Trigg County, Kentucky: The Gateway to the Jackson Purchase in Kentucky and Tennessee.* Nashville, TN: Rich Printing Co., 1961.

Nettels, Curtis P. *The Roots of American Civilization: A History of American Colonial Life.* N.Y.: Appleton-Century-Crofts, 1938.

Newhard, Malinda E. E. *Divorces Granted by the Indiana General Assembly Prior to 1852.* Harlan, IN: the author, 1981.

*Official Roster of the Soldiers of the State of Ohio in the War of the Rebellion, 1861-1866.* 9 Vols. Akron, OH: General Assembly of the Roster Commission, 1888.

O'Neal, H. R., comp. *Lincoln County, Tennessee, Miscellaneous Court House Records, Volume 1.* Ardmore, TN: Russell O'Neal, 1986.

Osborn, Elwilda, and Trego, Ethel. *Warren County, Illinois, Death Records, 1876 through 1915.* N.p.: Warren County, Illinois, Genealogical Society, 1985.

---, and Trego, Ethel. *Warren County, Illinois, Female Marriage Index, 1829 through 1915.* N.p.: Warren County, Illinois, Genealogical Society, 1985.

---, and Trego, Ethel. *Warren County, Illinois, Male Marriage Index, 1829 through 1915.* N.p.: Warren County, Illinois, Genealogical Society, 1985.

*The Past and Present of Warren County, Illinois.* Chicago: W. F. Kett & Co., 1877.

Paxton, W. M. *Annals of Platte County, Missouri.* Kansas City, MO: Hudson-Kimberly Publishing Co., 1897.

*Portrait and Biographical Album of Champaign County, Illinois.* 2 Vols. Chicago: Chapman Brothers, 1887.

*Portrait and Biographical Album of Lancaster County, Nebraska.* Chicago: Chapman Brothers, 1888.

*Portrait and Biographical Album of Louisa County, Iowa.* Chicago: Acme Publishing Co., 1889.

*Portrait and Biographical Album of Wapello County, Iowa.* Chicago: Chapman Brothers, 1887.

*Portrait and Biographical Album of Warren County, Illinois.* 2 Vols. Chicago: Chapman Brothers, 1886.

*Portrait and Biographical Record of Ford County, Illinois.* Chicago: Lake City Publishing Co., 1892.

Posey, Walter Brownlow. *The Presbyterian Church in the Old Southwest, 1778-1838.* Richmond, VA: John Knox Press, 1952.

*Prairie Farmer's Reliable Directory of Farmers and Breeders, Warren & Henderson Counties, Illinois.* Chicago: Prairie Farmer, 1918.

Rawlins, Rosemary Guthrie, comp. *Deed Abstracts of Books A-B-C-D-E and F for Christian County, Kentucky, for Years 1797-1817.* Hopkinsville, KY: Christian County Genealogical Society, 1987.

Reece, J. N. *Report of the Adjutant General of the State of Illinois.* 9 Vols. Springfield, IL, 1900.

Reid, Whitelaw. *Ohio in the War: Her Statesmen, Her Generals, and Soldiers.* 2 vols. N.Y.: Moore, Wilstach & Baldwin, 1868.

Revill, Janie, comp. *A Compilation of the Original Lists of Protestant Immigrants to South Carolina, 1763-1773.* Columbia, S.C.: The State Company, 1939.

Reynolds, Katherine, comp. *The Jobe Family.* 6 Vols. Houston, TX: n. pub., 1969-79.

Ridley, Jasper. *John Knox.* N.Y.: Oxford Univ. Press, 1968.

Rietti, J[ohn] C., comp. *Military Annals of Mississippi.* C. 1895; rptd. Spartanburg, S.C.: The Reprint Co., 1976.

Rising, Marsha Hoffman. "Monmouth College Graduates, 1858-1876." *Illinois State Genealogical Society Quarterly,* XV, 4 (Winter, 1983), 236-45.

Robinson, Luther E., ed. *Historical and Bigraphical Record of Monmouth and Warren County, Illinois.* 2 Vols. Chicago: Munsell Publishing Co., 1927.

Ross, Virginia. *Henderson County, Illinois, 1841-1900 Marriages.* Gladstone, IL: Ross Research, 1984.

---, and Evans, Jane. *Henderson County, Illinois, Cemeteries.* 2 Vols. Gladstone, IL: the authors, 1979.

"Roster of Pi Alpha Chapter of Beta Theta Pi Fraternity, Monmouth College." *Prairie Pioneer,* VI, 1 (April-May 1986), 12-16. Published by the Warren County, Illinois, Genealogical Society.

Rothe, Anna, and Lohr, Evelyn, eds. *Current Biography: Who's News and Why, 1952.* N.Y.: H. W. Wilson Co., 1952.

Rowland, Dunbar. *History of Mississippi: The Heart of the South.* 4 Vols. Spartanburg, S.C.: The Reprint Co., 1978.

---. *Military History of Mississippi, 1803-1898.* Spartanburg, S.C.: The Reprint Co., 1978.

Rowland, George W. *Fathers of the Ridge: Genealogical Sketches of Greene and Clay Counties, Arkansas.* 4 Vols. Paragould, Arkansas: the author, 1980.

Salley, A. S., ed. *Accounts Audited of Revolutionary Claims against South Carolina.* Columbia, S.C.: Historical Commission of South Carolina, 1935.

Savage, James W., and Bell, John T. *History of the City of Omaha, Nebraska.* Chicago: Munsell & Co., 1894.

Scarlett, James D. *Tartans of Scotland.* N.Y.: Hastings House, n.d. [c. 1972].

*The Scottish Tartans, with Historical Sketches of the Clans and Families of Scotland: The Badges and Arms of the Chiefs of the Clans and Families.* 2d ed. Edinburgh: W. and A. K. Johnston and G. W. Bacon, Ltd., 1945.

Scouller, James Brown. *A Manual of the United Presbyterian Church of North America, 1751-1887.* Pittsburgh: United Presbyterian Board of Publication, 1887.

Short, Anita (Mrs. Don), and Bowers, Mrs. Dale. *Cemetery Inscriptions, Preble County, Ohio.* 2 Vols. N.p.: Daughters of the American Revolution, 1969.

---, and Bowers, Ruth. *Preble County, Ohio, Deed Records, 1808-1821: Deed Books 1 through 4.* N.p.: Daughters of the American Revolution, 1978.

--- (Mrs. Don), and Bowers, Mrs. Dale. *Preble County, Ohio, Marriage Records.* 2 Vols. N.p.: Daughters of the American Revolution, 1967.

*Simpson County, Kentucky, Records: The Censuses of 1820 and 1830, Family Bible Entries, Cemetery Headstone Inscriptions, Revolutionary War Veteran Pensions.* Franklin, KY: Simpson County Historical Society, 1975.

Slevin, Ruth, and Heiss, Willard. *Preble County, Ohio, Marriages, 1808-1859.* Fort Wayne, IN: Fort Wayne and Allen County Public Library, 1965.

Smout, T. C. *A History of the Scottish People, 1560-1830.* N.Y.: Charles Scribner's Sons, 1969.

Sosin, Jack M. *The Revolutionary Frontier, 1763-1783.* N.Y.: Holt, Rinehart & Winston, 1967.

Spalding, William A., comp. *History and Reminiscences: Los Angeles City and County, California.* 3 Vols. Los Angeles: J. R. Finnell & Sons, 1936.

Speer, William S., ed. *The Encyclopedia of the New West.* Marshall, TX: The United States Biographical Publishing Co., 1881.

Springer, Arthur. *History of Louisa County, Iowa.* 2 Vols. Chicago: S. J. Clarke Publishing Co., 1912.

Steers, Dorothy Donnell, comp. *Simpson County, Kentucky, 1819-1825: Circuit Court Orders.* Franklin, KY: the author, 1985.

Stephenson, Jean. *Scotch-Irish Migration to South Carolina, 1772: (Rev. William Martin and His Five Shiploads of Settlers).* Washington, D.C.: the author, 1971.

*The Story of South Henderson.* Galesburg, IL: The South Henderson Cemetery Assn., 1950.

Strange, Mary Wylie. *The Revolutionary Soldiers of Catholic Presbyterian Church, Chester County, South Carolina.* 1946; rptd. York-Clover Printing Co., 1978.

Sutherland, Stella H. *Population Distribution in Colonial America.* N.Y.: Columbia Univ. Press, 1936.

Switzer, Harry M., comp. *Madison County, Iowa, Early Marriages, 1849-1880.* Earlham, IA: n. pub., n.d.

*Texas Heroes Buried on Galveston Island.* Galveston, TX: Daughters of the Republic of Texas, 1982.

*Tombstone Records of Louisa County, Iowa.* N.p.: Graves Registration, W.P.A. Project, n.d.

*Tombstone Records of Madison County, Iowa.* N.p.: Graves Registration, W.P.A. Project, n.d.

Tucker, Mabel Abbott, and Waller, Jane Warren, comps. *Lincoln County, Tennessee, Bible Records.* 6 Vols. Batavia, IL: Lincoln County, Tennessee, Pioneers, 1971.

Vanderpool, Montgomery. *Logan County, Kentucky, Abstracts of Equity Cases.* Russellville, KY: the author, 1987.

---. *Logan County, Kentucky, Newspaper Genealogical Abstracts.* 4 Vols. Russellville, KY: the author, 1987.

*Veteran's Grave Registration, Los Angeles County to 1940.* 2 Vols. N.p.: Daughters of the American Revolution, 1943.

Walker, James D. *War of 1812: Bounty Lands in Illinois.* Thomson, IL: Heritage House, 1977.

Wallace, David Duncan. *South Carolina, a Short History: 1520-1948.* Chapel Hill, N.C.: Univ. of North Carolina, 1951.

Wallace, Paul A. W. *Pennsylvania, Seed of a Nation.* N.Y.: Harper & Row, 1962.

Wallace, W. Stewart, comp. *A Dictionary of North American Authors Deceased before 1950.* Toronto: The Ryerson Press, 1951.

Waller, Jane Warren, ed. *Lincoln County, Tennessee, Marriage Records: 1838-1839-1840.* Batavia, IL: Lincoln County, Tennessee, Pioneers, n.d.

---. *Lincoln County, Tennessee, Marriage Records: 1841-1842-1843.* Batavia, IL: Lincoln County, Tennessee, Pioneers, n.d.

White, Gifford, *Land Grants; Volume 1 of 1850 Citizens of Texas.*
Saint Louis: Ingmire Publ., 1983.

*Who Was Who among North American Authors, 1921-1939.* 2 Vols. Detroit: Gale Research Co., 1940.

*Who's Who in America.* 44th ed., 1986-1987. Wilmette, IL: Marquis, 1987.

Williams, Frances Marion. *The Story of Todd County, Kentucky, 1820-1970.* N.p.: the author, 1972.

Wolfe, Barbara S., and Morgan, Mary M. *Cemetery Records: Monroe County, Indiana.* N.p.: Daughters of the American Revolution, 1987.

Wood, J. W. *Pasadena, California, Historical and Personal: A Complete History of the Organization of the Indiana Colony.* N.p.: the author, 1917.

Woodburn, James Albert. "The Scotch-Irish Presbyterians in Monroe County, Indiana: A Paper Read before the Monroe County Historical Society, November and December, 1908." *Indiana Historical Society Publications*, IV, 8 (1910), 435-522.

Woodmason, Charles. See Hooker, Richard J.

Woods, Robert McDill, and Woods, Iva Godfrey, comps. *McDills in America: A History of the Descendants of John McDill and Janet Leslie of County Antrim, Ireland.* Ann Arbor, MI: Edwards Bros., 1940.

Wright, Esmond. "Education in the American Colonies: The Impact of Scotland." *Essays in Scotch-Irish History.* Ed. E. R. R. Green. London: Routledge & Kegan Paul, 1969. Pp. 18-45.

Wright, Harriet Hughes, and Jones, Lydia Palmer. *The History of Summerfield* [Kansas]. Summerfield, KS: n. pub., n.d. [c. 1980].

Wright, Louis B. *South Carolina: A Bicentennial History.* N.Y.: W. W. Norton & Co., 1976.

Wylie, Theophilus A. *Indiana University, Its History from 1820, When Founded, to 1890, with Biographical Sketches of Its Presidents, Professors and Graduates, and a List of Its Students from 1820 to 1887.* Indianapolis: Indiana Univ., 1890.

# INDEX

Abernathy, Alva Baskin...202,213
Abernathy, Beulah Griffith...213
Abernathy, Dollie I...202
Abernathy, Ella Mae...478
Abernathy, George T...213
Abernathy, Joseph W...202,213
Abernathy, Margaret Witherington..184
Abernathy, Thomas...478
Abernathy, Valda Sams...478
Abernathy, William M...184
Abernathy, William M. Jr...184
Acers, Ruth Baskin...208
Ackley, Zelma...335
Adams, Alexander...81
Adams, Allie C...79
Adams, Amanda Clark...80
Adams, Bancroft...80
Adams, Bertha Waldron...78
Adams, Blanche...79
Adams, Bridget Sherlock...79
Adams, Burt R...79
Adams, Carrie E...79
Adams, David (2-2B)...75,76,81
Adams, David (2-2A2)...78
Adams, Ed C...79
Adams, Elizabeth...79
Adams, Emma...78
Adams, Evert B...80
Adams, George...78
Adams, Grace...78
Adams, Guy...80
Adams, Indiana McQueen...78
Adams, infant...78
Adams, Isabella...80
Adams, James...79
Adams, Jane...80
Adams, Jean Graham...64,74-5
Adams, Jessie Deckard...79
Adams, Jessie E...79
Adams, John...74
Adams, John (2-2A)...76
Adams, John L...79
Adams, John S./L...79
Adams, Joseph...79
Adams, Joseph E...79
Adams, Joseph S...79
Adams, Laura...79
Adams, Laura Helms...79
Adams, Martha...75-6,81
Adams, Mary (2-2C)...75,76,81
Adams, Mary (2-2A1)...76
Adams, Mary Deckard...80
Adams, Mary M...78
Adams, Mary Simpson...76
Adams, May...80
Adams, Minerva Whisenand...79
Adams, Myrtle...79
Adams, Myrtle Prince...78
Adams, Ola...79
Adams, Perry...80
Adams, Pink L...80
Adams, Richard F...79
Adams, Rosanna...203
Adams, Roy L...79
Adams, Samuel...74-5
Adams, Samuel A...75-6,81
Adams, Sarah/Sallie...78
Adams, Sarah F...79
Adams, Susannah Woodman...81
Adams, Walter...80
Adams, Wilford C...79
Adams, William...78
Adams, William H...79
Adams, William J...79
Adkinson, Adaline Delashmit...217
Adkinson, Clemmie...217
Adkinson, George...179
Adkinson, James...178
Adkinson, Joseph F...217
Adkinson, Louisa...196
Adkinson, Margrete Easley...179
Adkinson, Mary ----...178
Adkinson, Mary F...178
Adler, Felix...465
Adler, Frances Perugina...464
Adler, Frances Porter...464
Adler, Herman Morris...464
Aebisher, Edith...450
Alderson, Laura E...446
Allen, Clement H...133
Allen, Elizabeth...228
Allen, Frances Gault...102
Allen, Jane W...180
Allen, Janine...272
Allen, Mattie...277
Allen, Minnie Hill...133
Allen, Sarah E...228
Allen, William...228
Allerheiligen, Amy...436
Allerheiligen, David...436
Allerheiligen, Judy Crosier...436
Allerheiligen, Kevin...436
Allison, Al...178
Allison, Hannah McBride...279
Allison, Hugh...279
Allison, Lorena McClerkin...178
Allison, Martha R...279,282
Allison, Nancy Graham...279
Allison, Sarah M...279
Allison, Thomas G...279
Allison, William E...279,282
Anderson, Clara...298
Anderson, Delvena...164
Anderson, Elizabeth...101
Anderson, Joanna Daniel...298
Anderson, John...101

Anderson, John...287
Anderson, Mary...298
Anderson, Mary E. (4-25)...287
Anderson, Mary E...454
Anderson, May...234
Anderson, Odessa...298
Anderson, Opal...278
Anderson, Ruth B...299
Anderson, Sophia...287
Anderson, William F...298
Andrews, Ann...107
Andrews, Cordillia Soden...107
Andrews, Delbert R...107
Andrews, Elizabeth Cleghorn...106
Andrews, Frank...107
Andrews, Jane...107
Andrews, John...107
Andrews, Joshua R...106
Andrews, Mary E...107
Andrews, Rebecca B...107
Andrews, Sarah...106
Andrews, Tilitha C...107
Andrews, Ulysses H...107
Anglin, Alice Goins...207
Anglin, Andrew J...207
Anglin, Sarah E.B...207
Anthony, Ada Hindman...188
Anthony, Margaret Whitley...188
Anthony, Thomas B...188
Anthony, William B...188
Apeling, Sarah...98,101,121
Appleby, Sarah A...247
Arnold, Mary M...116
Aschwanden, Margaret A...476
Ashby, Eva McClerkin...179
Ashe, Floyd W...218
Ashe, Mary O...190
Ashe, Robbie Cates...218
Atchison, Frances...153
Atkin, Edna...310
Atkins, Mary Cleghorn...104
Augustine, Charlotte Bishop...389,390
Augustine, Claudette J...390
Augustine, Floyd F...390
Augustine, Jack G...390
Augustine, Jim O...390
Avery, Charles D...418-9
Avery, Myra Graham...354,418-9
Avery, Nancy...419
Badger, Alice...416
Badger, Barbara...416
Badger, Betty...416
Badger, Herbert E...416
Badger, Mary...416
Badger, Mary Graham...354,416
Badger, Robert...417
Badger, Robert E....416
Bailey, Evelyn...278
Bailey, Jennie Cleghorn...100
Bailey, Porter...100
Bailey, Priscilla A...229
Bain, Ellen...270
Baird, Adele...282
Baird, Adele McHugh...282
Baird, Alice Kennard...281
Baird, Barbara...282

Baird, Bette...281
Baird, Claire J...282
Baird, Connie...468
Baird, Edgar A...281
Baird, Edgar A. Jr....281
Baird, Francis...189
Baird, Grace Staves...282
Baird, James...279
Baird, Jane...282
Baird, Janet...282
Baird, John L...177
Baird, Lynn...282
Baird, Margaret A...177
Baird, Mary E...280-1
Baird, Mary McAdam...279
Baird, Mary McGowan...189
Baird, Nancy McQuiston...176
Baird, Sarah Allison...279-80
Baird, Sarah E...175
Baird, Sarah L...281
Baird, Sarah McQuiston...177
Baird, Thomas P...282
Baird, William...176
Baird, William (4-20A)...279-80
Baird, William J...282
Baird, William J. Jr...282
Baker, Adam G.S...488
Baker, Amanda Saunders...131
Baker, John H...131
Baker, Judith Graham...452,488
Baker, Mark D...488
Baker, Mary Mills...131-2
Baker, Waller S...131-2
Baldwin, Carol J...476
Baldwin, Earl L...476
Baldwin, Jeanette Tulcus...476
Ballinger, Halley...132
Ballinger, Lucy...132
Ballinger, William P...132
Banks, Gertrude...347
Banks, Julia A.C...206,209,211,214
Banta, Charles...357
Banta, David D...357
Banta, Elizabeth...358-9
Banta, Katharine...358
Banta, Margaret...358,362
Banta, Martha Graham...265,357
Banta, Melissa Riddle...357
Barbo, Alice...472
Bargman, Donna A...478
Barker, Barbara Badger...416-7
Barker, Margaret...154
Barker, Samuel...416-7
Barned, Ida A...305
Barnes, Azel...155
Barnes, Guy...155
Barnes, James M...154
Barnes, Jamie...154
Barnes, John G...469
Barnes, Kathryn A...469
Barnes, Kenneth D...469
Barnes, Margaret A...176
Barnes, Martha Gartin...154
Barnes, Marvin D...469
Barnes, Mary...155
Barnes, Patsy...155

Barnes, Roy...154
Barnes, Ruth Graham...422,469
Barnett, Charles H...263
Barnett, Florence B...264
Barnett, Harold M...264
Barnett, Margaret Montgomery...263
Barnhill, Chad E...485
Barnhill, Darryl J...485
Barnhill, David T...485
Barnhill, Dennis G...485
Barnhill, Diane L...485
Barnhill, Ethel James...485
Barnhill, Jo Ann Graham...443,485
Barnhill, Kenneth J...485
Barnhill, Lloyd K...485
Barnhill, Lori J...485
Barnhill, Michael J...485
Barnhill, Paul J...485
Barnhill, Robert K...485
Barr, Betty Graham...454,490
Barr, John H...490
Barr, Marianne...491
Barr, Sharon L...490
Barr, Sherry L...490
Bartell, Don...422
Bartell, Edna Broadhead...422
Barton, Ada...188
Bartram, Beverly J...482
Base, Gregory...369
Base, Marcia Jacques...369
Baskin, Abner...208
Baskin, Ada Mills...211,214
Baskin, Alva E...202,213
Baskin, Andrew Jackson...196
Baskin, Andrew Jackson...209,214
Baskin, Andrew Jackson...210
Baskin, Artie L...213
Baskin, Cassanna Dacus...209,214
Baskin, Chesley...214
Baskin, Cynthia C...209,214
Baskin, Dallas A...214
Baskin, David J...196
Baskin, Du Pree...215
Baskin, Edward L...196
Baskin, Effie E...214
Baskin, Effie Elzoria...219
Baskin, Efford J...210
Baskin, Eliza J...213
Baskin, Elizabeth Coe...208
Baskin, Ermine E...215
Baskin, Ernest...197
Baskin, Etta Yount...197
Baskin, Eura Mills...210
Baskin, Faye E...208
Baskin, Geneva Gatlin..196
Baskin, George M...211,214
Baskin, George M.D...214
Baskin, Georgia M...215
Baskin, Georgia Williams...208
Baskin, Gertrude...196
Baskin, Hugh A...209,214
Baskin, infant...197,215
Baskin, Irene...215
Baskin, John F...197
Baskin, John H...207,208
Baskin, Joseph E...201

Baskin, Josephine Maddox...219
Baskin, Julia...196
Baskin, Julia E...214
Baskin, Julianna Mills...214
Baskin, Lee A...215
Baskin, Lelia E...208
Baskin, Leona...215
Baskin, Leslie E...208
Baskin, Lillie Tanner...201
Baskin, Lou A...209
Baskin, Louisa Adkinson...196
Baskin, Mahala Kelley...207,208
Baskin, Martha C...219
Baskin, Mary Caskey....196
Baskin, Mary Gwinn...208
Baskin, Mary Huffman...209,214
Baskin, Minerva Griggs...197
Baskin, Ola L...201
Baskin, Olien W...219
Baskin, Oma E...213
Baskin, Ottis B...214
Baskin, Ruby Taylor...215
Baskin, Ruth A...208
Baskin, Ruth E...196
Baskin, Sarah Hargett...214
Baskin, Sarah J...207,209
Baskin, Telitha Lavelle...210
Baskin, Warner...214
Baskin, Yerby...213
Batley, Cecil Graham...377,447
Beard, Elizabeth...403
Beard, Margaret J...403
Beard, Mary Proctor...403
Beard, Melinda Graham...331,403
Beard, Melinda K...403
Beard, Nancy G...403
Beard, Patricia A...403
Beard, William G...403
Beard, William H...403
Beatty, Betty...502
Beauchamp, C.R...146
Beauchamp, Margaret Shrader...146
Beaver, Cornelia Fuller...309
Beaver, Jack...309
Beaver, John...182
Beaver, John T...309
Beaver, Oma King...182
Beaver, Todd...309
Becker, David...373
Becker, Myrtle Graham...289,373
Beckham, Edwina Smith...110
Beckham, Soloman D...110
Belknap, Rebecca Hutchings...136
Belknap, W.B...136
Bell, Alice Hindman...188-9
Bell, Allie Darrell...106
Bell, Audie Artie...105
Bell, Ewart A...189
Bell, Johnnie Gault...102
Bell, Joseph P...106
Bell, Margaret Barnes...176
Bell, Mary E...176
Bell, Minnie Porter...116
Bell, Rebecca Dickey...189
Bell, Rebecca M...107
Bell, Robert B...176

Bell, William S...189
Benner, Joyce...451
Bennett, Augusta...347
Bennett, Dave...215
Bennett, David M...437
Bennett, George...436
Bennett, Georgia Baskin...215
Bennett, Linda Page...436
Bennett, Veronica E...437
Benson, Dale...422
Benson, Etta Graham...365,422
Bent, George...195
Bent, Oma Caskey...195
Benton, Rowena Knox...134
Benton, Samuel H...134
Benton, Samuel H. Jr...134
Benton, Willie...134
Berenstein, Candace...430
Berger, Elizabeth...388
Bergman, Fred H...275
Bergman, Gretchen Woods...275
Bergman, James E..275
Bergman, John M...275
Berlin, Diana...308
Bethke, Phyllis...501
Bettes, Peggy L...503
Bias, Marie...234
Billings, Bessie Gwinn...208
Billings, Carl R...182
Billings, George W...182
Billings, infant...182
Billings, Jane Walker...182
Billings, Leslie...208
Billings, Margaret McCormick...182
Billings, Massie Norman...182
Billings, Oma King...182
Billings, Paul K...182
Billings, Ruth E...182
Billings, W.W...208
Billings, Washington F...182
Biondo, Erik M...437
Biondo, George...437
Biondo, Virginia Page...437
Bishop, Barbara J...390
Bishop, Betty...390
Bishop, Charlotte M...389,390
Bishop, Claude O...389
Bishop, Elizabeth M...389,390
Bishop, Inger Olson...389
Bishop, Jane Graham...295,389
Bishop, Jeannette Ritter...389
Bishop, Joanna M...389
Bishop, John A...390
Bishop, Kenneth...390
Bishop, Mary J..390
Bishop, Myrle G...389
Bishop, Sara Rogers...389
Bishop, Straud A...389,390
Bishop, Thomas...390
Bishop, Tracy S...389
Bitle, Alicia...307
Bitle, Constance Whiteman..307
Bitle, Donald...307
Bittick, Elizabeth Stephens...232,233
Bittick, James...232,233
Bittick, Martha B...233

Blachly, Arthur T...281
Blachly, Persis Moss...281
Black, George...216
Black, Helen...453
Black, Isabel...347-8
Black, Nancy A...276
Black, Robbie Morton...216
Black, Violet...306
Blackstock, Edward...91
Blackstock, Elizabeth Wilson...91
Blackstock, Margaret Graham...64,91-4
Blackwell, Arlene Propst...423
Blackwell, Audre...424
Blackwell, Cleffie...211
Blackwell, Gail...424
Blackwell, Lyle...423-4
Blair, Virignia...230
Blake, Dorothy A...345
Blake, Edgar...343,344
Blake, Elmira L...343,344
Blake, Eve...344
Blake, Frances...496
Blake, Henry Y...343,344
Blake, Inez...344
Blake, James...345
Blake, John W...344
Blake, Lucile A...450
Blake, Mary...344
Blake, Mary A...343,344
Blake, Melissa...345
Blake, Melville...344
Blake, Melville Jr...344
Blake, Melville E...343
Blake, Minor Waldo...344
Blake, Miriam Thompson...344
Blake, Murray...345
Blake, Nancy Graham...254,343
Blake, Nancy Riegel...345
Blake, Rebecca...344
Blake, Rozanne Croft...344
Blake, Ruth...343,345
Blake, Waldo...344
Blake, Wilson...343,344
Blakely, Hattie M...232
Blanchard, James F...186
Blanchard, Katherine McCormick...186
Blankenship, Alva Wortham...209
Blankenship, Ardelle Wiseman...210
Blankenship, Bascom C...208,209,214
Blankenship, Bradie E...209
Blankenship, Eda C...209
Blankenship, Effie Baskin...209,214
Blankenship, Embry O...209
Blankenship, Eupha O...209
Blankenship, Iris...210
Blankenship, Jesse Farmer...209
Blankenship, Josie...216
Blankenship, Lavenia Owen...210
Blankenship, Leve B...209
Blankenship, Lillian Edmiston..209
Blankenship, Malinda Mills...208,209,214
Blankenship, Marvin B...209,214
Blankenship, Mary Huffman...209,216
Blankenship, Myrtle Rose...216
Blankenship, Naomi Dawson...215-6

Blankenship, Nettye English..209
Blankenship, Ottis H...209-10
Blankenship, Parrish...216
Blankenship, Robbie M...208,209
Blankenship, Robert O...216
Blankenship, Ruba G...216
Blankenship, Ruby Notgrass...216
Blankenship, Thomas...216
Blankenship, Thomas C...209,216
Blankenship, Thomas L...216
Blankenship, Vergie O...216
Blankenship, Vesper C...209
Bliznak, Lyda B...406-7
Bodner, Carl W...361
Bodner, Carla S...361
Bodner, Margie Cannon...361
Boeger, Howard...164
Boeger, Rosetta Hardesty...164
Boehmer, Ilene...443
Bogue, Ardelle Wiseman...210
Bohannon, Martha V...164
Bohn, Dennis...360
Bohn, Patricia Tolle...359-60
Boise, Elizabeth...310
Boling, Gus...100
Boling, Sadie Gleghorn...100
Bomar, John W....183,184
Bomar, John W. Jr...184
Bomar, Mary McCormick...184
Bomar, Myrtle Smith...183,184
Bonham, Ora A...379
Bonham, Susan Phillips...379
Bonham, William G...379
Bonner, Katherine...138
Bonner, Martha...131
Bonner, Ruth...138
Bonney, Addie Glenn...258
Bonney, Adeline L...258
Bonney, James H...258
Bookout, Jacob...127
Bookout, Mary Gleghorn...127
Bookout, William H...127
Booth, Alice Badger...416
Booth, George...416
Borovicki, Daniel...389
Borovicki, Gail Rodene...388-9
Borovicki, Linda...389
Boshears, Emma L...210
Boswell, Dorothy L...205
Boswell, Everett A...205
Boswell, Hazel Luttrell...205
Boswell, John W...205
Boswell, Mary Crouch...205
Boswell, Maude Wilson...205
Bowen, A.J...323
Bowen, Betty Landshur...323
Bowen, Brian R...323
Bowen, Clara Cowden...322
Bowen, David...323
Bowen, Deborah...323
Bowen, Dorothy Breiner...323
Bowen, Douglas...323
Bowen, Edith Hardesty...322-3
Bowen, Esther Patton...322
Bowen, Everett...322-3
Bowen, Fred A...322

Bowen, Gina...323
Bowen, Heidi E...323
Bowen, Jane L...323
Bowen, Jennifer...323
Bowen, Margaret L...322,323
Bowen, Marjorie E...322
Bowen, Mary E...323
Bowen, Michelle...323
Bowen, Patricia Maxey...323
Bowen, Richard...323
Bowen, Robert C...323
Bowen, Sally A...323
Bowen, Sarah Vinning...322
Bowen, Susan...323
Bowen, Warren...322
Bowles, Jack...423
Bowles, Lillian Gleghorn...100
Bowles, Verna Propst...423
Bowling, Rebecca E...101
Boyd, Frances...230
Boyse, David...88
Boyse, Elizabeth...88-9
Boyse, Jennet Graham...64,86,87-88
Boyse, Mary Margaret...88
Bradford, Bruce E...470
Bradford, Darrel D...470
Bradford, Kenneth...470
Bradford, Marilyn Graham...422,470
Bradford, Sandra McDonald...470
Bradley, Edna E...211
Brawley, James H...105
Brawley, Hugh P...105
Brawley, Mary E...105
Brawley, Tersie Gleghorn...105
Brawner, Sarah L...465,466
Brehm, Edward G...410,411
Brehm, Elizabeth Graham...348,410
Brehm, Ellen...411
Brehm, George A...411
Brehm, George O...410
Brehm, Joyia/Loyia...411
Brehm, Karl F...411
Brehm, Katherine...410-1
Brehm, Kathy...411
Brehm, Keith...411
Brehm, Stephanie...411
Brehm, Virginia...411
Breiner, Dorothy...323
Breunsbach, Henrietta...441
Brewer, Sarah K...196
Bridges, Emma Isom...217
Bridges, J.P...217
Brightwell, Susan P...112
Bringle, Sarah A...199
Bristow, Harry...412
Bristow, Helen Mauk...412
Broadhead, Edna...422
Brooks, Jennette F...107
Brooks, Maribeth...402
Brooks, Mary E...118
Brooks, Mary Graham...331,402
Brooks, Orlow...402
Brooks, Rosanna G...105
Brower, Elizabeth...332
Brown, Ardella J...216
Brown, Craig...310

Brown, Craig L...309
Brown, David M...310
Brown, Edna Atkin...310
Brown, Eleanor...245
Brown, Elizabeth...249
Brown, Elizabeth Mitchell...251
Brown, Elizabeth Porter...249
Brown, Gilbert A...185
Brown, Huldah Taylor...120
Brown, Imogene Caskey...195
Brown, James C...120
Brown, John...249
Brown, Joseph C...133
Brown, Laura...339
Brown, Louise...307
Brown, Maggie Smith...185
Brown, Marion H...120
Brown, Martha...125
Brown, Martha Lockart...216
Brown, Mary Hill...133
Brown, Mary J...251
Brown, Moore E...216
Brown, Nathan...251
Brown, Rhonda...310
Brown, Robert...195
Brown, Ruth...383
Brown, Ruth Fuller...309
Brown, Zella...477
Bruington, Donna J...273
Bruington, Elmer...273
Bruington, Everett M...273
Bruington, Jennifer M...273
Bruington, Marci Myers...273
Bruington, Mary Firoved...273
Bruington, Mina...273
Bruington, Todd S...273
Bruington, William E...273
Brunton, Jane E...442
Bryson, David B...331,332
Bryson, Elizabeth Brower...332
Bryson, infant...331,332
Bryson, James...331
Bryson, James...332
Bryson, James R...331,332
Bryson, Jessie Graham...331
Bryson, Mary E...331
Bryson, Mary Fay...332
Bryson, Mary Graham...331
Bryson, Nancy A...331
Bryson, Sara F...331
Bryson, William B...331
Bryson, William G...331
Buatte, Idile...121
Buchanan, Lela...230
Bucher, Shirley A...481
Buck, Cyrus L...337
Buck, Dora A...337
Buck, Julia A...337
Buckingham, Leita Snodgrass..497
Buckingham, Marjorie J...497-8
Buckingham, Porter...497
Buckler, Leonard...324
Buckler, Martha Cowden...324
Buckley, James L. Jr..110,112
Bulen, Barbara S...273
Bulen, Cynthia L...273

Bulen, Donald E...273
Bulen, Donald E. Jr...273
Bulen, George E...273
Bulen, Harold E...273
Bulen, Mary Saville...273
Bull, Margaret McKay...441
Bull, Pearl Graham...441
Bull, Ruben...441
Bull, Sidney W...441
Bullock, Charles...436
Bullock, Edna....423
Bullock, Linda Page...436
Bullock, Toni L...436-7
Bunce, Lynn...442
Bungle, Lou Joy...220
Bungle, Louise Hathcock...220
Bungle, Vernon...220
Burke, Cyndy Whiteman...307
Burke, Thomas...307
Burlison, Docia Evans...218
Burlison, Eurania M.T...218
Burlison, John E...218
Burmeister, Janet...325
Burns, Alice Caskey...195
Burns, Basil...195
Burns, Carl...195
Burns, Flora...195
Burns, Frank...195
Burns, Margaret...272
Burns, Paul...195
Burrell, Gene N...100
Burrell, Louis F...398
Burrell, Margaret Hamilton...398
Burrell, Mary...398-9
Burrell, Sadie Gleghorn...100
Burrow, Martha Phillips...186
Burrow, Ora...186
Burrow, Robert F...186
Burrus, Charles...295
Burrus, Charles H...295
Burrus, Charles R. or B...295
Burrus, Frances Sanders...296
Burrus, Hellen N...295
Burrus, Sarah M...295
Burrus, Zerilda...295
Burton, Julia E...210
Buss, Pauline C...445
Butler, Amanda S...456
Butler, Barbara Moore...456
Butler, Dawn N...457
Butler, Deborah Patterson...455
Butler, Ellen R...455,456
Butler, Geri K...456
Butler, Jane West...456
Butler, Jerry K...455
Butler, Jerry K. Jr...455
Butler, Jerry K. III...455-6
Butler, Lawrence W...455,456-7
Butler, Mary Joubert...455
Butler, Mary Lawrence...455
Butler, Melissa Idom...456
Butler, R. Josephine Graham...391,455
Butler, Robert G...455,456
Butler, Robin M...456
Butler, Rose M...482
Butler, Shawn M...457

Byrd, Lillian Smith...186
Byrd, Mary L...186
Byrd, Theo...186
Byrne, C.R...136
Byrne, Frances Hutchings...136
Caldwell, Arminta Cowden..322,326,343
Caldwell, Elizabeth J...326-7
Caldwell, Francis M...326,343
Caldwell, George G...326,343
Caldwell, Jane Graham...254,326,343
Caldwell, John...343
Caldwell, Mary McMehan...343
Call, Ada Graham...289,373
Call, Betty J...429
Call, Grace...373
Call, Julia...429
Call, La Mone...373
Call, Leslie...429
Callahan, Ruby...163
Callicotte, Cliff...163
Callicotte, Frances...163
Callicotte, George...163
Callicotte, Henry...163
Callicotte, Joseph W...163
Callicotte, Martha Hardesty...163
Callicotte, Mary Murray...163
Cameron, Annabelle...454
Cameron, Elizabeth A...246
Cameron, Lillian...233
Cameron, Sarah Graham...246
Cameron, William A...246
Campbell, Ada Barton...188
Campbell, Alexander F...319-20
Campbell, Allie Wiggins...111
Campbell, Brian E...278
Campbell, Carrie Graham...319
Campbell, Dennis P...278
Campbell, Emma C...111
Campbell, Evelyn Bailey...278
Campbell, J.W...278
Campbell, James...404
Campbell, James H...111
Campbell, John H...278
Campbell, John H. Jr...278
Campbell, Joseph C...278
Campbell, Joseph M...111
Campbell, Judith McKnight...278
Campbell, Laura Graham...337,404
Campbell, Madeline M...278
Campbell, Margaret E...404
Campbell, Martha E...111
Campbell, Martha Gleghorn...111
Campbell, Martha Hutchinson...278
Campbell, Mary Maben...319
Campbell, Mungo D...319
Campbell, Myrna...404
Campbell, Orville...111
Campbell, Pamelia...111
Campbell, Samuel...188
Campbell, Sarah...278
Campbell, Sarah J...111
Campbell, Susan B...188
Campbell, Thurlow...404
Campbell, Udora...111
Campbell, Valerian...111
Cannon, Eveline...212

Cannon, Margie M...361
Cannon, Nina...317
Carl, Barry D...439
Carl, David S...439
Carl, Richard D...439
Carl, Sherry Grauer...438,439
Carnahan, Margaret...262
Carnine, Sarah A...356
Carpenter, C.C...101
Carpenter, Lili B...101
Carpenter, Sallie Gleghorn...101
Carter, Gertrude...213
Cartwright, Anthony W...154
Cartwright, Kenneth G...154
Cartwright, Rhonda Cooper...154
Cartwright, Timothy R...154
Casado, Bonnie...370
Casado, Lisa...370
Casado, Manuel...370
Casado, Mark...370
Casado, Marty...370
Casado, Verna Hafner...370
Cashion, Agnes Hindman...189
Cashion, Alexander B...189
Cashion, James F...189
Cashion, Margaret McLister...189
Caskey, Agnes/Nancy Marion...192-3
Caskey, Alice B...195
Caskey, Alta McRoberts...195
Caskey, Arthur W...194
Caskey, Carmi Norrick...194
Caskey, Clarence E...194
Caskey, Daisy O'Nell...195
Caskey, Dana Miley...195
Caskey, David...195
Caskey, Della...195
Caskey, Edward A...199
Caskey, Elizabeth...194
Caskey, Elizabeth E...175,220
Caskey, Ella F...198
Caskey, Elvis A...195
Caskey, Erma E...195
Caskey, Ernest B...194
Caskey, Esther...174
Caskey, Esther (3-13E)...175,205-6
Caskey, Ethel...200,204
Caskey, Eula M...195
Caskey, Euphemia R...199
Caskey, Francis M...200
Caskey, Glenn...195
Caskey, Harold H...195
Caskey, Harvey T...195
Caskey, Howard C...196
Caskey, Hugh W...193
Caskey, Imogene...195
Caskey, infant...194,199
Caskey, James (3-13D)...175,193
Caskey, James Jr (3-13D3)...192,196
Caskey, James A...194
Caskey, James J...193
Caskey, Jane Hindman...192,196
Caskey, Joanna (3-13G)...175,220
Caskey, Joanna (3-13D7)...200,210,218
Caskey, John...174
Caskey, John (3-13C)...175,192-3
Caskey, John (3-13D3)...196

Caskey, Joseph S...200
Caskey, Julianna Graham...86,174
Caskey, Letitia J...199
Caskey, Letitia Wilson...193
Caskey, Lidy J...195
Caskey, Logan S...198
Caskey, Margaret...194
Caskey, Margaret W...203
Caskey, Martha E...205
Caskey, Mary...175
Caskey, Mary A...204
Caskey, Mary B...193-4
Caskey, Mary J...196
Caskey, Mary McWilliams...194,200
Caskey, Mary R...194-5
Caskey, Matilda Wallace...193
Caskey, Odelia C...195
Caskey, Oma O...195
Caskey, Ora E...194
Caskey, Robert C...199-200,204
Caskey, Robert N...195
Caskey, Rosa C...195
Caskey, Rosanna W...175,192
Caskey, Rosetta P...199
Caskey, Ruth May...195
Caskey, Sarah (3-13D1b)...193
Caskey, Sarah (3-13D2d)...195
Caskey, Sarah (3-13D12)...204
Caskey, Sarah L...197,207,211
Caskey, Tabitha Wilhite...194
Caskey, Thomas (3-13D1)...193
Caskey, Thomas...174-5
Caskey, Thomas Jr.(3-13H)..175,221
Caskey, Thomas L...195
Caskey, William (3-13D1a)...193
Caskey, William 3-13D2)...194
Caskey, William F...198
Caskey, William G...195
Castor, Stella I...456
Cates, Alice M...218
Cates, Artie Baskin...213
Cates, Cora Dawson...218
Cates, Elma F...218
Cates, George A...213
Cates, Herbert R...213
Cates, Margaret Huffman...218
Cates, Nannie Griffith...213
Cates, Robbie B...218
Cates, Thomas V...218
Cates, Virginia I...218
Cates, William B...218
Caughron, Sallie Jobe...103
Cerenak, Marilyn J...475
Chadwick, Bertha B...105
Chadwick, Boyse A...106
Chadwick, C.A...105,106
Chadwick, Loma Gleghorn...106
Chadwick, Nancy Wagoner...105,106
Chapman, Marie...220
Chase, Allen D...363
Chase, Anne L..363
Chase, Benjamin...363
Chase, Daniel W...363
Chase, Elsie Crandall...362
Chase, Fred C...362-3
Chase, Henry M...363

Chase, Jane E...363
Chase, John P...363
Chase, Margaret Whitaker...362-3
Chase, Melody Schobert...363
Chase, Nancy L...363
Chase, Percy E...362
Chase, Scott E...363
Chesnut, A.W...144
Chesnut, Alexander...142
Chesnut, Jane...144
Chesnut, John...142-4
Chesnut, Margaret...236,240
Chesnut, Mary E...144
Chesnut, Ruth Vance...142
Chesnut, Sarah Maben...142-4
Chesnut, Sarah Meek...142
Childress, Helen L...183
Ciancibella, Allison S...462
Ciancibella, Christopher D...462
Ciancibella, Dominic...461
Ciancibella, Dominic Jr...461
Ciancibella, Dominic P...462
Ciancibella, Lillian Murgel...461
Ciancibella, Mary Parker...460,461
Cink, Darren J...484
Cink, Dustin S...484
Cink, Kae Graham...434,484
Cink, Norman L...484
Clanahan, Jane Knapp...311
Clanahan, Steven...311
Clark, Adah Snyder...277
Clark, Amanda...80
Clark, Amy D...277
Clark, Barbara E...277
Clark, Beverly Sprout...277
Clark, Bradley D...277
Clark, Brenda K...277
Clark, Brian L...277
Clark, Flora Hutchinson...276
Clark, Florence Graham...293,377
Clark, Gerald L...277
Clark, James Whyte...201
Clark, James William...277
Clark, Lillie P...367
Clark, Louis L...276
Clark, Maggie Nerren...103
Clark, Maria L...277
Clark, Marie...377
Clark, Samuel B...377
Clark, Tara L...277
Clark, Velma McWilliams...201
Clark, Virginia Livingston...277
Clark, William D...277
Clayton, Beverly Paton...413
Clement, Graham...467
Clement, Kelly...467
Clement, Raymond M...467
Clement, Scott...467
Clement, Suzanne Graham...467
Clements, Benjamin L...190
Clements, Bessie M...190
Clements, Magnolia Roberts...190
Clements, Sandra K...486
Clendenin, Mary A...313
Clifton, Ethel Deckard...79
Clifton, Leonard L...79

Cline, Arthur W...368
Cline, Carole A...369
Cline, Elton W...368-9
Cline, Emma Hadley...368
Cline, Lorna Howard...368-9
Cline, Mariline K...369
Cline, Shirley L...369
Coats, Adrian...220
Coats, Sarah C...198,212,215
Coats, Werdner Hathcock...220
Cobb, Edna Morton..216
Cobb, Jake...216
Coberly, Marilyn Smith...425
Coburn, Arlene...324
Cochran, Andrew...238
Cochran, Boyd...238
Cochran, Christina...238
Cochran, Clarence W...238
Cochran, David...238
Cochran, Donald A...419
Cochran, Donald E...238
Cochran, Donald S...419
Cochran, Donna Johnson...238
Cochran, Dorothy Pendarvis..238
Cochran, Eloris Puckett...238
Cochran, Francis...238
Cochran, Frank...238
Cochran, Gary...238
Cochran, Ina...443
Cochran, infant...238
Cochran, James W...237
Cochran, Jan...238
Cochran, Jane Menely...238
Cochran, John D...237
Cochran, John R...238
Cochran, John R. Jr...238
Cochran, Karen...238
Cochran, Katherine...238
Cochran, Kathy...238
Cochran, Kenneth M...238
Cochran, Loren Lee...238
Cochran, Lynn...238
Cochran, Mabel Johnston...238
Cochran, Martha McDill...237
Cochran, Nancy Kuhl...419
Cochran, Nancy L...419
Cochran, Naomi Godfrey...237-8
Cochran, Norma...238
Cochran, Paul...238
Cochran, Pearl Myers...238
Cochran, Rachel J...237
Cochran, Ruth Miller...238
Cochran, Steven...238
Cochran, Stuart A..238
Cochran, Suzanne....238
Cochran, Walter R...238
Cochran, William H...237
Cochran, William K...238
Cockrell, Mary...186
Cockrell, Sarah Tipton...186
Cockrell, Thomas E.S...186
Coe, Elizabeth...208
Coffee, Fred...100
Coffee, Minnie Gleghorn...100
Cofor, Thomasina M...352
Cole, Clemmie E...206

Cole, Darlene...491
Coleman, Sciscilda/Sisley...114
Collier, David...350
Collier, Lydia Lindsay...350
Collier, Margaret...350
Collins, Nancy...156
Commer, Jimmie...207
Compton, James E...414
Compton, Norma Graham...353,414-5
Conard, Clara B...366
Conard, Elizabeth Winter...366,367
Conard, Jessie F...366
Conard, John...366,367
Conway, Lucile J...454
Cooper, Arthur C...442
Cooper, David C...323
Cooper, DeWitt T...154
Cooper, Elizabeth M..154
Cooper, Gilmer D...154
Cooper, James O...154
Cooper, Jestina Webb...154
Cooper, John E...323
Cooper, Katherine J...323
Cooper, Marie Mitts...154
Cooper, Marilyn R...442
Cooper, Mary Bowen...323
Cooper, Myrtle Minger...442
Cooper, Rhonda K...154
Cooper, Thelma V...154
Cooper, Virginia Gartin..153-4
Cooper, Vivian E...154
Cooper, Ward...323
Cotton, Mary J...178
Coulter, Margaret...65
Coulter, Mary Stuart...65
Coulter, Robert...65
Coupal, Laurent...323
Coupal, Melissa...323
Coupal, Renee...323
Coupal, Sally Bowen...323
Cousar, Odell Adkins...214
Cousar, Pattie M...219
Cowden, Arlene Coburn..324
Cowden, Arminta A...322,326,343
Cowden, Billy...324
Cowden, Clara C...322
Cowden, David G...324
Cowden, David H...322,324
Cowden, Debbie...325
Cowden, Dorothy Smith...328
Cowden, Earl W...322,328
Cowden, Eliza A...292
Cowden, Elizabeth Graham...251,321-2
Cowden, Elsie Parker...324
Cowden, Eunice Signor...292,321
Cowden, George D...324
Cowden, George G...322,324
Cowden, George H...321
Cowden, George W...292,321
Cowden, Holly...324
Cowden, Janet Burmeister...325
Cowden, Jessie E...322,324
Cowden, Jo Anne...325
Cowden, John...325
Cowden, Laura Flowers...324
Cowden, Laurie...324

Cowden, Lillian Dale...324
Cowden, Margaret L...322,323
Cowden, Marian F...325
Cowden, Martha E...324
Cowden, Mary Jones...324
Cowden, Mary M...322,325
Cowden, Matthew W...238
Cowden, Nancy...324
Cowden, Norma Murphy...325
Cowden, Ralph W...322,324
Cowden, Ralph W. Jr...325
Cowden, Ralph W. III...325
Cowden, Robert P...325
Cowden, Roland...328
Cowden, Rosalind M...328
Cowden, Ruth Roland...328
Cowden, Suzanne C...324
Cowley, Agnes Gault...102
Cox, Betty...414
Cox, Elizabeth...186
Cox, Estelle...114
Cox, George W...220
Cox, James R...220
Cox, Judith...220
Cox, Mary Mills...220
Cox, Nancy G.F...220
Cox, Susan...374
Crandall, Elsie...362
Crank, Joe S...112
Crank, Lou Gleghorn...112
Craven, Herman R...476
Craven, Linda L...476
Craven, Margaret Aschwanden...476
Crawford, Andrew...99
Crawford, Mary...99
Crawford, Ollie...100
Crenshaw, Edris Dawson..216
Crenshaw, Louis...216
Creswell, Mary...275
Crews, Albert M...110
Crews, E...109
Crews, Eliza Gleghorn...109
Crews, Martha J...109
Crews, Robert M...109
Crews, Sarah L...109
Crews, William...110
Crist, Catharine...253
Crockett, Bessie E...229
Crockett, Bessie Tucker...229
Crockett, Cora...229
Crockett, Cora Hogue..229
Crockett, David...229
Crockett, Harry H...229
Crockett, Harry W...230
Crockett, Ida Tucker...229
Crockett, James S...229
Crockett, Julie Fox...230
Crockett, Katherine Hellis...229
Crockett, Lee...229
Crockett, Mary Farrester...229
Crockett, Mary Smith..228-9
Crockett, Mildred...229
Crockett, Paul A...229
Crockett, Paul A. Jr...230
Crockett, Paul S...229
Crockett, Sarah...229

Crockett, Thomas M...229
Croft, Rozanne...344
Crosby, Carrie...309
Crosby, David...309
Crosby, James...309
Crosby, Jeff...309
Crosby, Karen Fuller...309
Crosier, Duane...435
Crosier, Judy...435,436
Crosier, Laurie...435
Crosier, Lois Koch...435
Crosier, Lola Graham...367,435
Crosier, Milton...435
Crosier, Scott...436
Crosier, Staci...436
Cross, Margaret Shannon...154
Cross, Matthew S...154
Cross, Quincy R...154
Cross, Ray L...154
Crossley, John...413
Crossley, Lela Graham...350,413
Crouch, Mary J...205
Crowder, Christine Graham...452,489
Crowder, Ronald...489
Cudney, Charlotte...442
Cudney, Leo H...442
Cudney, Minnie Slama...442
Cummings, Effie E...376
Cunningham, Bob H...230
Cunningham, David C...230
Cunningham, Elizabeth A...341
Cunningham, George...341
Cunningham, Harry Crockett...230
Cunningham, Helen DeWitt...230
Cunningham, John T...230
Cunningham, John T. Jr...230
Cunningham, Mary Reed...341
Cunningham, Montell Hooper...230
Cunningham, Virginia Water...230
Curle, Avery A...219
Curle, Vivian Hathcock...219
Curran, Stella B...408
Currie, Hugh...229
Currie, Ruth Oates...229
Curtis, Ruth...209
Cyrus, Burton R...503
Cyrus, John M...504
Cyrus, Julie Graham...479,503
Cyrus, Nicholas A...503
Dacus, Bessie Etheridge...214
Dacus, Cassanna...209,214
Dacus, Elizabeth...215
Dacus, Henry F...214
Dacus, James L...213-4
Dacus, Odell Adkins...213
Dacus, Trilby Mills...213-4
Daellenbach, Martha A.A...492
Dahltorp, Bruce...309
Dahltorp, Jeff...309
Dahltorp, Sally Fuller...309
Dahltorp, Timothy...309
Dailey, Beatrice M...210
Dailey, Ida Laskey...210
Dailey, Jesse...210
Dale, Lillian...324
Dale, Nancy J...354

Dalton, Judy...431
Daniel, Annie R...299
Daniel, Horace...298,299
Daniel, Inez P...298-9
Daniel, Jane Millen...298
Daniel, Joanna...298
Daniel, Leona B...299
Daniel, Mary Graham...298
Daniel, Richard E...298,299
Daniel, Robert L...298,299
Daniel, Ruth Anderson...299
Daniel, William B...298
Daniels, Elma Deckard...79
Daniels, Eugene...79
Darby, Iva B...454
Darley, Elizabeth D...475
Darley, Ellis R...474
Darley, Katherine Slusher...474
Darley, Linda Darner...474-5
Darley, Paul E...474-5
Darnell, Helen Woods...274
Darnell, Morris...274
Darnell, Samuel..274
Darner, Ashley A...476
Darner, Carol Baldwin...476
Darner, Cathy L...474,475
Darner, Clyde O...473
Darner, David L...476
Darner, David R...474,476
Darner, Donna Dixon...476
Darner, Edna Ranney...473
Darner, Jeffrey A...474,476-7
Darner, Joan Netzbandt...475
Darner, Linda Craven...476
Darner, Linda R...474-5
Darner, Rachel L...476
Darner, Rae Graham...429,473
Darner, Reagan L.N...476
Darner, Robert D...473
Darner, Robert G...474,475-6
Darner, Whitney B.N...476
Darrell, Allie E...106
Davidson, Harold G...231
Davidson, Laura Jack...135
Davidson, Mary J...257
Davidson, Robert V...135
Davidson, Sue Trobaugh...231
Davis, Alice Laurence...208
Davis, Bessie...212
Davis, David W...240
Davis, Elizabeth A...297
Davis, Faye Baskin...208
Davis, Hannah F...240
Davis, Helen...282
Davis, Joseph J...208
Davis, Margaret A...153
Davis, Oscar G...208
Davis, Rachel A...240
Davis, Ruth Baskin...208
Davis, Thomas G...208
Dawson, Annie Hathcock...220
Dawson, Ardella Brown...216
Dawson, Boyce W...218
Dawson, Catherine Sherrod...217
Dawson, Clemmie Adkinson...217
Dawson, Cora E...218

Dawson, Edris V...216
Dawson, Eicy...217
Dawson, Eliza J...215,217
Dawson, Estelle...219
Dawson, Florence Rose...218
Dawson, Gayna...419-20
Dawson, Hugh L...220
Dawson, Hugh L. Jr...220
Dawson, Ida Wortham...218
Dawson, infant...216
Dawson, Jesse F...201,217
Dawson, LeRoy...218
Dawson, Liza E...216
Dawson, Margie McWilliams...202-3
Dawson, Martha Mills...201,217
Dawson, Mary Shelly...220
Dawson, Mattie Smith...218
Dawson, Nancy McWilliams...201,217
Dawson, Naomi O...215-6
Dawson, Nicholas C...201,217-8
Dawson, Nola J...219
Dawson, Onie F...219
Dawson, Ony Joiner...216
Dawson, Pawnee B...216
Dawson, Pearl...217
Dawson, Robert C...217
Dawson, Robert T...203
Dawson, Rosanna Mills...215
Dawson, Saphronia A...216-7
Dawson, Sarah A...218
Dawson, Trotty M...217
Dawson, Willard H...217
Dawson, William B...215,217
Dawson, William Bradley...215
Dawson, William Bradley...216
Dawson, William L...216
Dawson, Willie E...219
Dawson, Zona B...216
Deckard, Charles...79
Deckard, David...79
Deckard, Elma...79
Deckard, Ethel H...79
Deckard, Frances Kelly...79
Deckard, Jessie...79
Deckard, Laura Adams...79
Deckard, Lawrence...79
Deckard, Mary...80
DeCourcey, Mary Thompson...146
DeCourcey, T.W.W...146
Deen, Elbert L...207
Deen, Elma Cates...218
Deen, Jeremiah...207,218
Deen, Mary McWilliams...201
Deen, Melville O...218
Deen, Ollie Gwinn...207
Deen, Robert...201
Deen, Susan Townsend...207,218
Dekin, Elmer...151
Dekin, Emma Gartin...151
Delameter, Sarah...269
Delancy, Marie...199
Delashmit, Adaline G...217
Dennis, D. N...136
Dennis, Margaret Knox...136
Denton, Elvira...77
Denton, Zera V...77

DeReamer, Marguerite A...383
Dewese, Effie D...178
DeWitt, Helen...230
Dickey, Alice A...207
Dickey, Aubrey E...212
Dickey, Elizabeth A...104
Dickey, Elizabeth Gleghorn...103
Dickey, J.C...103
Dickey, John S...103
Dickey, Julia Mills...212
Dickey, Laura Myers...207,212
Dickey, Martha D...103
Dickey, Mary J...103
Dickey, R.N...103
Dickey, Rebecca S...189
Dickey, Samuel...103
Dickey, Thomas A...103
Dickey, Thomas E...103
Dickey, William H...207,212
Digby, Eleanor Hayes...229
Digby, Thomas E...229
Dixon, Donna M...476
Dixon, Margaret Mauk...412
Dixon, Raymond...412
Dixon, Rebecca...429
Dobyns, Bernice Hammett...451
Dobyns, Patricia L...452
Donyea, Ruth V...359
Dordal, Tess...388
Dorimus, Elsie...335
Doudna, Janet Fuller...309
Doudna, Laura A...309
Doudna, William...309
Doudna, William S...309
Douglas, Cheryl...368
Douglas, Claryce Roane...219
Douglas, Lloyd...368
Douglas, Margaret Howard...368
Douglas, Mark...368
Douglas, Nola Dawson...219
Douglas, Steven...368
Douglas, William...219
Douglas, William S...219
Dowden, Donna Bruington...273
Dowden, John L...273
Dowden, Kristie Holm...273
Dowden, Nancy E...273
Dowden, Sally J.A...273
Dowden, Steven H...273
Drennan, Elizabeth...258
Drennan, Nancy I...259
Drennan, Philip...258
Drew, Emily W...145
Duensing, August...445
Duensing, Clair V...445
Duensing, Daniel G...445
Duensing, Elsie Knabe...445
Duensing, Shirley Ruyle...443,445
Duensing, Tersea Graham...445
Duensing, Timothy L...445
Duerson, Eleanor Waddill...298,299
Duerson, Granville...299-300
Duerson, Inez Daniel...298-9
Duerson, Joanna Graham...169,299-300
Duerson, Lawrence W...298
Duerson, Thomas...298,299

Dugdale, Allison...282
Dugdale, Eunice...282
Dugdale, Grant...282
Dugdale, Helen Davis...282
Dugdale, Martha Allison...279,282
Dugdale, William...282
Dukatz, Carl F...488
Dukatz, Eric...488
Dukatz, Judith Graham...452,488
Dula, Chip....389
Dula, Lillian Suttle...388
Dula, Peggy...389
Duncan, Jeptha...144
Duncan, Mary Chesnut...144
Duntz, Adam J...483
Duntz, Andrea L...484
Duntz, Carl L...482
Duntz, Christine Renner...483
Duntz, David L...482,483
Duntz, Debra Fienstra...483
Duntz, Devin J...483
Duntz, Janelle Ray...483
Duntz, Jessie Graham...434,482
Duntz, Kevin W...483
Duntz, Kristina R...483
Duntz, Matthew D...483
Duntz, Paul N...482,483
Duntz, Ricky L...482,483
Duntz, Sheri R...482,483
Duntz, Stephanie M...483
Duntz, Terri L...482,483
Duntz, Vencette Pfister...483
Durham, Hannah W...232
Durham, Margaret L...232
Durham, Ruby Peeler...232
Durham, Willie...189
Durr, Mildred...186
Eakin, Arthur...404
Eakin, Frances...404
Eakin, Frank...404
Eakin, Lois Graham...337,404
Eakin, Lourie...404
Earp, Donald...278
Earp, Gerald...278
Earp, Marian Hess...278
Earp, Marilyn J...278
Earp, Wayne...278
Easley, James D...179
Easley, Margrete...179
Easley, Mary Pickard...179
Easton, Alan G...405
Easton, George S...405
Easton, James G...405
Easton, Mary Graham...338,405
Eaton, G.E...307
Eaton, Opal...307
Eckman, Esther A...256
Edeal, Pamela R...484
Edmaton, Gail...404
Edmaton, Mary Graham...337,404
Edmiston, John...120
Edmiston, Lillian M...209
Edmiston, Nancy Gleghorn...120
Edwards, Edward...448
Edwards, Mary Graham...379,448
Edwards, Michael...448

Edwards, Richard L...448
Edwards, Terrill Mudgett...448
Edwards, William...448
Edwards, Yvonne...448
Elam, Willie...433
Elder, Ada G...314
Elder, Eva M...314
Elder, Joseph R...314
Elder, Joseph W...314
Elder, Robert B...314
Elder, Sandra M...456
Elleat, Nancy Smith...232
Elleat, Robert B. Jr...232
Elliott, Ethel...307
Elliott, Flora...396
Elliott, Minerva G...130
Ellis, Kenneth N...495
Ellis, Orra Smith...495
Ellis, Sarah J...495
English, Margaret J...189
English, Nettye...209
Erickson, Donna Oaks...276
Erickson, Eric W...276
Erickson, John W...276
Erickson, Joyce...507
Erickson, Linda R...276
Erickson, Paula S...276
Erickson, Pauline...425
Erwin, Robert P...218
Erwin, Virginia Cates...218
Escue, Albert H...190
Escue, Albert J...190
Escue, Myrtle Hindman...190
Etheridge, Bessie F...214
Eudaukas, Elizabeth Riddick...232
Eudaukas, Peter...232
Evans, Absalom H...208
Evans, Andrew J...208
Evans, Annie...151
Evans, Belle...151
Evans, Claude...208
Evans, Docia M...218
Evans, Eliza...208
Evans, Elizabeth Dacus...215
Evans, Eula Gwinn...208
Evans, George...151
Evans, Ida Norris...151
Evans, Irene Baskin...215
Evans, John...151
Evans, John H...215
Evans, Julia Gwinn...208
Evans, Lucy...151
Evans, Margaret...151
Evans, Marvin O...215
Evans, Mary Gartin...150-1
Evans, Rebekah Ricketts...208
Evans, Richard...151
Evans, Richard P...150
Evans, Roger M...208
Evans, Sallie...151
Evans, Virgie...151
Ewing, Lila...114
Exum, Amber L...488
Exum, Damon E...488
Exum, Darleen Graham...452,488
Exum, Edward S...488

Faires, Elizabeth...183
Faires, Margaret J...183
Faires, William J...183
Faris, Elizabeth D...234
Farmer, Jessie...209
Farmer, Lou Baskin..209
Farmer, Otie Q...209
Farquhar, Bernice O...453
Farrester, Mary...229
Faucett, Emily C...212
Faulk, Alice M...212
Faulk, Anna P...234
Faulk, Elizabeth Faris...234
Faulk, Joel B...234
Fay, Mary...332
Faye, Christina...420
Faye, Katharine Kuhl...420
Faye, Robert G...420
Faye, William C...420
Fedoroff, George...403
Fedoroff, Margaret A...403
Fedoroff, Margaret Beard...403
Fedoroff, Robert W...403
Feldhausen, Diana...436
Ferguson, Jennette Brooks...107
Ferguson, W...107
Fiedler, Ruth E...362
Field, Gail Blackwell...424
Field, George...424
Field, John A...424
Field, Julie R...424
Field, Kae...164
Fienstra, Debra D...483
Fierke, Arlene M...475
Fike, Aileen...316
Fillman, Cynthia L...327-8
Fillman, Martha Kersey...328
Fillman, William...327-8
Filter, Gina Bowen...323
Filter, Greg...323
Findley, Agnes Ritchey...236
Findley, Alexander...236
Findley, Nancy...236
Finizo, Dolores...498
Firoved, Anna B...272
Firoved, Bruce M...272
Firoved, Donald B...272
Firoved, Edna M...272
Firoved, Frank M...273
Firoved, Horace E...271
Firoved, Iris Long...272
Firoved, Isabella Sprout...271
Firoved, Jeffrey...271
Firoved, Leona Permenter...271
Firoved, Loure Salzmann...271
Firoved, Margaret Burns...272
Firoved, Mary L...273
Firoved, Nancy McLaughlin...273
Firoved, Nellie P...273
Firoved, Nettie M...272
Firoved, Robert E...271
Firoved, Roberta L...272
Firoved, Rose Smith...271
Firoved, Sarah Hutchinson...270,271
Firoved, Simon...271
Firoved, Susan E...271-2

Firoved, William...271
Firoved, William G...271
Firoved, William G...271
Firoved, Wilma A...271
Fitzgerald, Eileen M...362
Fitzgerald, James M.J...362
Fitzgerald, John M...362
Fitzgerald, Ruth Fiedler...362
Flansburgh, Debbie...444
Fleming, Alice Lavelle...218-9
Fleming, Bertha Griffin...204
Fleming, Cora Dawson...218
Fleming, Don...218
Fleming, Herman M...204
Fleming, Mary E...231
Fleming, Thomas...218-9
Fleming, Veda M...219
Fleming, Willie M...210
Fletcher, John V...446
Fletcher, Laura Alderson...446
Fletcher, Laura M...446
Flint, Nellie F...495
Flowers, Laura...324
Flowers, Myrtie...213
Forbes, Donald G...274
Forbes, Donna A...274
Forbes, George...274
Forbes, Hazel Plant...274
Forbes, Lila Kirk...274
Forbes, Marla E...274
Forbes, Merrill L...274
Forbes, Michael R...274
Forbes, Randolph G...274
Forbes, Robert L...274
Forbes, Ronald D...274
Forbes, Tonya M...274
Forbes, Virginia Woods...274
Ford, Effie...191
Ford, Jerry...436
Ford, Judy Crosier...436
Fordyce, Esther...306
Forehand, Christina M...507
Forehand, Linda Graham...482,506-7
Forehand, Thomas C...506
Forehand, Thomas P...507
Forsythe, Joseph...180
Forsythe, Margaret Sherrill...180
Forsythe, Sarah Eunice...180-1
Fortlage, Connie Graham...473,501
Fortlage, David R...501
Fortlage, Herbert...501
Fortlage, Michael C...501
Fortlage, Nathan D.G..501
Fortlage, Phyllis Bethke...501
Fortlage, Tina D.C..501
Fortner, Edna Bradley...211
Fortner, James H...211
Fortner, Nina E...211
Fouad, Hesham...275-6
Fouad, Martha Oyler...275
Fouad, Miriam...275
Fouad, Sarah...275
Fouad, Youssef...275
Fox, Julie...230
Fox, Sallie Gleghorn...101
Francis, Martha C...301

Franklin, Johanna Fuller...309
Franklin, Laura S..309
Franklin, Willard...309
Fraser, Hugh W...153
Fraser, Margaret Gartin...153
Frasier, Emma Funk...152
Frasier, Frank...152
Fredrickson, Daryl...479
Fredrickson, Donna R...479
Fredrickson, Luther A...184
Fredrickson, Margaret...479
Fredrickson, Mary McCormick...184
Freed, David M...481
Freed, Julienne Naaf...480,481
Freeman, Darlene Cole...491
Freeman, Harry...491
Freeman, Rosalie A...491
Freitag, Beverly Shannon...154
Freitag, Elizabeth A...154
Freitag, Jack E...154
Friedman, Bart...310
Friedman, Brian...310
Friedman, Cassandra Fuller...310
Friedman, Gerold...310
Fryer, Annie Gwinn...197
Fryer, Mary Reed...197
Fryer, Richard...197
Fryer, William E...197
Fuller, ---...309
Fuller, Alice Jackson...291
Fuller, Byron...310
Fuller, Cassandra...310
Fuller, Catherine...309
Fuller, Cornelia...309
Fuller, David...309
Fuller, Dean G...308
Fuller, Dean G...309
Fuller, Dick G...310
Fuller, Donald G...308
Fuller, Eileen Gans...310
Fuller, Elizabeth Boise...310
Fuller, Ethel Hartsock...308
Fuller, Everett M...310
Fuller, Frances Mahaffey...308
Fuller, Fritz...308
Fuller, George H...309
Fuller, Grace Martin...308
Fuller, Guy C...308
Fuller, Harry...309
Fuller, Harvey...308
Fuller, Helen Scheder...309
Fuller, Hiram C...291
Fuller, Jack...309
Fuller, James...308
Fuller, Jane...309
Fuller, Janet R...309
Fuller, Jason...310
Fuller, Jerome...308
Fuller, Johanna...309
Fuller, Judith McKechnie...309
Fuller, Karen...309
Fuller, Laura...308
Fuller, Laura McMillan...308
Fuller, Lois Nelson...310
Fuller, Lola Mock...309
Fuller, Marcella Gombert...309

Fuller, Martha L...309
Fuller, Marvin L...308
Fuller, Mary Opstad...308
Fuller, Mia...308
Fuller, Michael...308
Fuller, Myra Tucker...309
Fuller, Pamela...309
Fuller, Patricia Peters...309
Fuller, Paul...309
Fuller, Rachel G...310
Fuller, Richard...309
Fuller, Ruth F...309
Fuller, Sally J...309
Fuller, Stuart M...310
Fuller, Tiffanie...310
Fuller, Tom...308
Fuller, Toni Spann..308
Fulton, Deborah Graham...481,505
Fulton, Kylee A...505
Fulton, Lance R...505
Fulton, Michael R...505
Fulzenhauer, Floris...347
Fulzenhauer, Lois Glass..347
Fulzenhauer, Loretta...347
Fulzenhauer, Mary...347
Funk, Annie Jenkins...152
Funk, Annie L...152
Funk, Earl...153
Funk, Eliza Gartin...152
Funk, Emma...152
Funk, Gillie...152
Funk, Harry...152
Funk, Jacob R...152
Funk, Jane Baird...282
Funk, John...152
Funk, John A...152
Funk, Lute/Lutie...152
Funk, Lydia Richardson...152
Funk, Mary...152
Funk, Mattie...152
Funk, Nancy Rice...152
Funk, Pink...152
Funk, Sallie...152
Funk, Sarah Gartin...152
Fuqua, Annie M...191
Furgerson, Margaret A...184
Furgerson, Marguerite Hewitt...184
Furgerson, W. Lanier...184
Futch, Franklin R...248
Futch, Margaret Porter...248
Futch, Wilton...248
Futch, Wilton Jr...248
Gabriel, Donald C...488
Gabriel, Mary Graham...451,488
Gahlgren, Belle Pressly..233
Gahlgren, David M...233
Gailor, Martha B...183
Gans, Eileen...310
Gant, Henry C...147
Gant, James D...147
Gant, Minerva Thompson...147
Gardner, Mary Rowell...104
Garland, Barbara Whiteman...307
Garland, Edward...307
Garland, Edward O...307
Garland, Robert H...307

Garland, Sara J...307
Garson, Lynn Baird...282
Gartin, ---...172
Gartin, Andrew K...143,148-50
Gartin, Anna Kincaid...148,164
Gartin, Annie...151
Gartin, Archie...151
Gartin, Bess Seaton...151
Gartin, Betty R...153
Gartin, Carol L...153
Gartin, Charles...151
Gartin, Clara Schuster...151
Gartin, Eliza...152
Gartin, Elva...151
Gartin, Emily Rankin...150
Gartin, Emma...151
Gartin, Enid Keeny...153
Gartin, Fannie...151
Gartin, Frances...162
Gartin, Frances Atchison...153
Gartin, Frank W...153
Gartin, George G...153
Gartin, George G. Jr...153
Gartin, George G. III...153
Gartin, Gladys Wilson...153
Gartin, Howard P...153
Gartin, Imogean Hiatt...153
Gartin, James...150
Gartin, James A...153
Gartin, James W...151
Gartin, Jane/Jennet...153
Gartin, Jane Maben...142,148-50
Gartin, John...151
Gartin, John A...155
Gartin, John P...153
Gartin, Kate Gore..153
Gartin, Lillie...151
Gartin, Margaret A...153
Gartin, Margaret Davis...153
Gartin, Margaret E...151
Gartin, Margaret V...153
Gartin, Martha V...154
Gartin, Mary E...153
Gartin, Mary F...150-1
Gartin, Mary Miller...151
Gartin, Maude Patrick...153
Gartin, Nellie L...153
Gartin, Paul M...153
Gartin, Richard...148,164
Gartin, Richard M..150
Gartin, Sally C...164,525 note 100
Gartin, Sarah J...152
Gartin, Thomas...151
Gartin, Virginia M...153-4
Gartner, Charles D...443
Gartner, Elizabeth L...444
Gartner, Nancy R...443
Gartner, Sherri Ruyle...443
Gatlin, Geneva...196
Gault, Agnes...102
Gault, Albert...102
Gault, Andy...101
Gault, Carl...102
Gault, Charlie...102
Gault, Clarence...102
Gault, Eliza...121

Gault, Elizabeth...121
Gault, Elizabeth Anderson...101
Gault, Elizabeth Porter...102
Gault, Frances...102
Gault, Fred...101
Gault, Frederick...102
Gault, Grace...98,104,117,122,124,126
Gault, Henry C...101
Gault, Henry C Jr...102
Gault, Herbert...102
Gault, Hubert...102
Gault, James H...121
Gault, Jane L...121
Gault, John C...121
Gault, John W...122
Gault, John Wood...102
Gault, Johnnie Mae...102
Gault, Lewis S...102
Gault, Lloyd...101
Gault, Lois...101
Gault, Macie...102
Gault, Maggie...102
Gault, Martha J...102
Gault, Martha T...122
Gault, Mary A...102
Gault, Mary E...121
Gault, Mary Emma...102
Gault, Mary Gleghorn...101
Gault, Maude...102
Gault, Myrtle...101
Gault, Nancy...98,120
Gault, Nancy E...102
Gault, Robert...122
Gault, Robert L...102
Gault, Samuel B...101
Gault, Sarah...121
Gault, Sarah A...102
Gault, Sarah Apeling...98,101,121
Gault, Sarah E...122
Gault, Sarah Gleghorn...98,121
Gault, Thomas...98,101,121
Gault, Thomas C...122
Gault, Tom...102
Gault, William...121
Gault, William O...121
Gault, William T...101
Gay, Bernice I...199
Gay, Mary A...201
Gee, James R...190
Gee, John H...124
Gee, Martha Gleghorn...124
Gee, Mary Ashe...190
Gee, Nora E...190
Geiger, Lucy...378
George, Mittie F...179
Gibbs, Lillian...316
Gibson, Nettie...472
Giddings, Rena...332
Gilchrist, Melissa J...284
Gilden, Audre Blackwell...424
Gilden, Claudia...424
Gilden, Elmer...424
Gilden, Garth...424
Gilden, Gene...424
Giles, Maybelle...362
Gillam, Mary Jo...461

Gillespie, Catharine Hopkins...264
Gillespie, Jesse M...264
Gillespie, Melcena M...264
Gillihan, Andrew J...196
Gillihan, Gertrude Baskin..196
Gillihan, Sarah Brewer...196
Gillihan, Vera V...197
Gillihan, William H...196
Gilpin, Lucille Griffin...204-5
Gladden, Mary B...206,207
Glass, Frederick G...347
Glass, Gertrude Banks...347
Glass, Isabel Black...347-8
Glass, James...212
Glass, Letitia E...212
Glass, Lois...347
Glass, Madge L...347
Glass, Mary Graham...254,346
Glass, Mary Raynor...212
Glass, Roy T...346
Glass, Seyum...346
Glaze, Alvin...218
Glaze, Nelle Lavelle...218
Gleghorn, Abraham...120
Gleghorn, Albert E...101
Gleghorn, Albert E...113
Gleghorn, Alfred S...127
Gleghorn, Amanda...116
Gleghorn, Andrew (3-1B)...98,104-5
Gleghorn, Andrew...101
Gleghorn, Andrew C...100
Gleghorn, Andrew J...107
Gleghorn, Andrew W...119
Gleghorn, Annie L...101
Gleghorn, Archie V...105
Gleghorn, Arthur R...101
Gleghonr, Arvel...127
Gleghorn, Asa V...119
Gleghorn, Audie Bell...105
Gleghorn, Austin W...105
Gleghorn, Baron D...113
Gleghorn, Belle...101
Gleghorn, Benjamin E...123
Gleghorn, Bernard...127
Gleghorn, Bertha Chadwick...105
Gleghorn, Bertha Greer...100
Gleghorn, Bertha Haley...100
Gleghorn, Beulah...100
Gleghorn, Canaan E...107
Gleghorn, Caroline...117
Gleghorn, Chalmers...104
Gleghorn, Charley E...117
Gleghorn, Christine...127
Gleghorn, Claris...127
Gleghorn, Clarissa Scott...119
Gleghorn, Clark...101
Gleghorn, Claude...100
Gleghorn, Cobburn...108
Gleghorn, Coleburn...118
Gleghorn, Count P...112-3
Gleghorn, Count P. (3-1E7)...113
Gleghorn, Count P....113
Gleghorn, David (3-1H)...98,120
Gleghorn, David...124
Gleghorn, David W...115
Gleghorn, Delina...127

Gleghorn, Dellaphine Johnson...105
Gleghorn, Docksey D...117
Gleghorn, Dolphes...119
Gleghorn, Earl E...106
Gleghorn, Edith...116
Gleghorn, Edna...112
Gleghorn, Edythe Oldfield...105
Gleghorn, Effie Hogue...100
Gleghorn, Elbert...119
Gleghorn, Eldee...126
Gleghorn, Elgiva...108
Gleghorn, Elijah...98,120,124
Gleghorn, Eliza...109
Gleghorn, Eliza...127
Gleghorn, Eliza A...118
Gleghorn, Eliza J...126
Gleghorn, Eliza Jane...125
Gleghorn, Eliza U...120,125
Gleghorn, Eliza Wilson...98,126
Gleghorn, Elizabeth...127
Gleghorn, Elizabeth B...103
Gleghorn, Elizabeth Graham...74,95-7
Gleghorn, Elizabeth J...123
Gleghorn, Elizabeth Jane...106
Gleghorn, Ellen...117
Gleghorn, Ellen (Eileen?)...116
Gleghorn, Ellen Powell...113
Gleghorn, Emma O/I...113
Gleghorn, Ernest M...112
Gleghorn, Etta...117
Gleghorn, Etta (Hattie)...116
Gleghorn, Evalee...106
Gleghorn, Evaline...118
Gleghorn, Frances...119
Gleghorn, Frances ---...113
Gleghorn, Frances Resinover...101
Gleghorn, Frank...124
Gleghorn, Gertrude...101
Gleghorn, Golda A...107
Gleghorn, Guynell...112
Gleghorn, Hardy C...117
Gleghorn, Harriet C...126
Gleghorn, Helen...101
Gleghorn, Henry B...124
Gleghorn, Hiram M...113
Gleghorn, Homer...127
Gleghorn, Hugh...107
Gleghorn, Hugh E...105
Gleghorn, Huldah Taylor...98,120
Gleghorn, Ida...124
Gleghorn, infant/child...106,126,127
Gleghorn, J.A...101
Gleghorn, James (3-1G)...98,117-8,125
Gleghorn, James...119
Gleghorn, James Andrew (3-1E4)..111-2
Gleghorn, James Andrew...112
Gleghorn, James D...101
Gleghorn, James E...105
Gleghorn, James Johnson...107,118
Gleghorn, James K.P...117
Gleghorn, James L...105
Gleghorn, James R...116
Gleghorn, Jane see also Janette,
  Jennette, Jiney
Gleghorn, Jane (3-1D)...98,109
Gleghorn, Jane (Jeannette)...110

Gleghorn, Jane...126
Gleghorn, Janette...106
Gleghorn, Jennette Brooks...107
Gleghorn, Jennie...100
Gleghorn, Jesse...100
Gleghorn, Jiney...117
Gleghorn, John (3-1F)...98,114
Gleghorn, John...116
Gleghorn, John...117
Gleghorn, John...125
Gleghorn, John A...122
Gleghorn, John Andrew/Matthew...112
Gleghorn, John C...113
Gleghorn, John Diemer...101 two
  entries
Gleghorn, John F...120
Gleghorn, John H...125
Gleghorn, John Matthew (3-1)...95-7
Gleghorn, John Matthew/Andrew...112
Gleghorn, John Mobley...115-6
Gleghorn, John T...116
Gleghorn, John T./F....120
Gleghorn, John W...105
Gleghorn, John Y...127
Gleghorn, Johnson...118
Gleghorn, Jonathan...120
Gleghorn, Joseph C...101
Gleghorn, Josephine...119
Gleghorn, Kilbert V...106
Gleghorn, L.A...124
Gleghorn, Lavona Herriott...105
Gleghorn, Lee...125
Gleghorn, Leila...100
Gleghorn, Letha S...106
Gleghorn, Lila...100
Gleghorn, Lillian...100
Gleghorn, Lillie Owens...100
Gleghorn, Lillie Moxley...112
Gleghorn, Lindsey C...116
Gleghorn, Lizzie Williams...101
Gleghorn, Logan H.R...127
Gleghorn, Loma J...106
Gleghorn, Lou I...112
Gleghorn, Louis C...117
Gleghorn, Lucretia M...115
Gleghorn, Lucy A...116
Gleghorn, Lucy B...101
Gleghorn, Lucy E...117
Gleghorn, Luther...116
Gleghorn, Luther...118
Gleghorn, Luther L...114
Gleghorn, Luther L...116
Gleghorn, Maggie...127
Gleghorn, Margaret (3-1C)...98,108
Gleghorn, Margaret...101
Gleghorn, Margaret C...123
Gleghorn, Margaret Hamilton...111
Gleghorn, Margaret Jones...118
Gleghorn, Margaret L...101
Gleghorn, Marietta A...117
Gleghorn, Martha...111
Gleghorn, Martha...125
Gleghorn, Martha...126
Gleghorn, Martha A...112
Gleghorn, Martha E...104
Gleghorn, Martha H...124

Gleghorn, Martha M...108
Gleghorn, Martha Smith...109
Gleghorn, Mary...119
Gleghorn, Mary ---...113
Gleghorn, Mary (Marietta) A...117
Gleghorn, Mary Ann...98,101
Gleghorn, Mary Arnold...116
Gleghorn, Mary Brooks...118
Gleghorn, Mary C...115
Gleghorn, Mary C...127
Gleghorn, Mary Coborn...114
Gleghorn, Mary Crawford...99,108
Gleghorn, Mary E...124
Gleghorn, Mary E...126
Gleghorn, Mary Elender...108
Gleghorn, Mary Elizabeth...112
Gleghorn, Mary J...116
Gleghorn, Mary Johnson...98,117,125
Gleghorn, Mary L...127
Gleghorn, Mary Poindexter...100
Gleghorn, Mary R...104
Gleghorn, Mary S...117
Gleghorn, Mary Susan...121
Gleghorn, Mary Shannon...106
Gleghorn, Matthew/Mathew (3-1E)..98, 109
Gleghorn, Matthew...118
Gleghorn, Matthew...125
Gleghorn, Maud G...100
Gleghorn, Melissa...115
Gleghorn, Melissa E...123
Gleghorn, Minnie...100
Gleghorn, Minnie Porter...116
Gleghorn, Moses...126
Gleghorn, Nancy...117
Gleghorn, Nancy ---...119
Gleghorn, Nancy E...120
Gleghorn, Nancy E. ---...127
Gleghorn, Nancy J...115
Gleghorn, Narcissus Lampkin...107
Gleghorn, Noble...127
Gleghorn, Ola...100
Gleghorn, Olis...112
Gleghorn, Ollie Crawford...100
Gleghorn, Opal Reeves...106
Gleghorn, Otis...112
Gleghorn, P.E...119
Gleghorn, Parlee...119
Gleghorn, Plesants...101
Gleghorn, Rachel...127
Gleghorn, Ralph...100
Gleghorn, Ralph...127
Gleghorn, Rebecca...107,108
Gleghorn, Rebecca Bowling...101
Gleghorn, Rebecca E...119
Gleghorn, Rebecca Elgiva...106
Gleghorn, Rebecca Johnson..98,104
  two entries
Gleghorn, Retta Pincard...100
Gleghorn, Rhoda E...114
Gleghorn, Robert...98,122
Gleghorn, Robert A...100
Gleghorn, Robert L...100
Gleghorn, Robert Y...100
Gleghorn, Rosa L...127
Gleghorn, Rosaline...101

Gleghorn, Rosanna Brooks...105
Gleghorn, Ruby...116
Gleghorn, Ruth A...113
Gleghorn, Sadie...100
Gleghorn, Sallie...101
Gleghorn, Sallie (Lila)...100
Gleghorn, Sallie Hampton...100
Gleghorn, Sallie Hines...100
Gleghorn, Samuel...98,99
Gleghorn, Samuel M...104
Gleghorn, Samuel W...104,108
Gleghorn, Samuel Wiley...100
Gleghorn, Sarah (3-1I)...98,121
Gleghorn, Sarah...127
Gleghorn, Sarah B...113
Gleghorn, Sarah E...117
Gleghorn, Sarah Eliza...121
Gleghorn, Sarah F...112
Gleghorn, Sarah G...106
Gleghorn, Sarah S...104,108
Gleghorn, Sarah V...113
Gleghorn, Sarah White...100
Gleghorn, Sciscilda/Sisley
  Coleman...114
Gleghorn, Stephen C...115
Gleghorn, Susan Brightwell...112
Gleghorn, Susan Wilson...98,120,124
Gleghorn, Terry M...107
Gleghorn, Tersie E...105
Gleghorn, Theodore...100
Gleghorn, Thomas F...125
Gleghorn, Thomas I...112
Gleghorn, Thomas L...112
Gleghorn, Thomas U...100
Gleghorn, Thomson S...104
Gleghorn, Tommie Terrell...101
Gleghorn, Troy R...106
Gleghorn, Ursula...108
Gleghorn, Ursula Wilson...98,122
Gleghorn, Vera...112
Gleghorn, Vernila V...119
Gleghorn, Walker...108
Gleghorn, Walter...116
Gleghorn, Walter V...127
Gleghorn, Warren...119
Gleghorn, William (3-1L)...98,126
Gleghorn, William...113
Gleghorn, William...116
Gleghorn, William...127
Gleghorn, William A...120,125
Gleghorn, William B...117
Gleghorn, William B. (3-1J2)..122-3
Gleghorn, William F...100
Gleghorn, William G...126
Gleghorn, William W...100
Gleghorn, Willie J...117
Gleghorn, Wood...100
Gleghorn, Young M...126
Glenn, Addie V...258
Glenn, Cora M...257
Glenn, Cora Small..256
Glenn, Edward G...255,258-9
Glenn, Edward M...258
Glenn, Edward P...259
Glenn, Elizabeth...258
Glenn, Elizabeth Drennan...258

Glenn, Elizabeth Mosher..258
Glenn, Elsie...258
Glenn, Emma...258
Glenn, Harvey E...257
Glenn, Harvey E. Jr...257
Glenn, Helen E...257
Glenn, Helen N...257
Glenn, infant...255,259
Glenn, James H...255-6
Glenn, James W...313
Glenn, Jessie...258
Glenn, John...254-5
Glenn, John A...257
Glenn, John H...257
Glenn, Lorene D...257
Glenn, Margaret Graham...161,254-5
Glenn, Martha Amanda...313
Glenn, Martha Ann...255
Glenn, Mary Clendenin...313
Glenn, Mary E...256
Glenn, Nancy...254
Glenn, Nelle Roberson (Robinson?).257
Glenn, Ruth E...258
Glenn, Ruth S...258
Glenn, Sarah Adeline...255,259
Glenn, Sarah Annabel...256-7
Glenn, Theophilus M...255,258
Glenn, Theophilus M. Jr...258
Glenn, Vergie Blankenship...216
Glenn, Walter B...216
Glick, Adam W...373
Glick, Effie Graham...293,373
Glick, Gideon...373
Glick, Grace...374-5
Glick, Howard L...374
Glick, Ina M...374
Glick, Louisa A...374
Glick, Minerva...373
Glick, Pearl G...374
Glick, Wilbur R...374
Glick, Wilbur R. Jr...374
Glick, Zola...374
Goddard, Marge Graham...378,448
Goddard, Roberta...448
Goddard, Tom...448
Godfrey, Naomi...237-8
Godwin, Eliza T...105
Goforth, Alvin P...215
Goforth, Ina Mills...211-2
Goforth, Lee Baskin...215
Goforth, Lillie M...197-8
Goforth, Lois Miller...210
Goforth, Russell L...211-2
Goforth, Sarah Coats...198,212,215
Goforth, William M...198,212,215
Goins, Alice E...207
Gombert, Marcella...309
Goodlett, Ardelle Hindman...188
Goodlett, Dudley K...188
Goodlett, Gordon...188
Gore, Kate...153
Gouch, David...117
Gouch, Mary/Marietta Gleghorn...117
Gourley, Elizabeth R...192
Gourley, Hugh...192
Gourley, James...192

Gourley, John...192
Gourley, Mary...192
Gourley, Robert...192
Gourley, Rosanna Caskey...175,192
Gowdy, E. Emma...239
Graff, Charles...203
Graff, Pauline McWilliams...203
Graham, ---(first name unknown)...86,
   221,451,487
Graham, Ada L...289,373
Graham, Adah...409,468
Graham, Adah Hurd...346
Graham, Addie Reed...391
Graham, Adele Smith...391
Graham, Alden M...348,410
Graham, Allen E...479,503
Graham, Alva E...286,364
Graham, Amanda...395
Graham, Amanda Peterman...376
Graham, Amy M...505
Graham, Amy Wade...422-3
Graham, Andrew (2-1)..34-6,39-45,51-
   2,57,64-74,514 note 1. See also
   Grimes (Grimbs, Grumbs), Andrew.
Graham, Andrew (4-2)...140,240-1
Graham, Andrew A...254,346
Graham, Andrew E...161,264-5
Graham, Andrew E. Jr...265,357
Graham, Andrew G...173,301-2
Graham, Andrew J...500
Graham, Andrew Richard (4-21)...167,
   282-4
Graham, Andrew Richard (5-65)...286,
   364-5
Graham, Andrew T...464,492
Graham, Andrew W...74,172-3
Graham, Angeline M...352-3
Graham, Anna...292
Graham, Anna D...354,418
Graham, Anna Panfield...371
Graham, Anna Wittmus...426-8
Graham, Anne E...260,354
Graham, Araminta S...293,378
Graham, Archibald Y...140,253-4
Graham, Arlene...489,508
Graham, Arlene A...366,426
Graham, Arlie H...380,452
Graham, Arthur B...377,447
Graham, Arthur H...371,440
Graham, Arthur M...367,434
Graham, Augusta Bennett...347-8
Graham, Ava E...366,429
Graham, Bail R...377,447
Graham, Barbara M...503
Graham, Benjamin R...504
Graham, Bernice Farquhar...453
Graham, Bernice Hammett...451
Graham, Bernice Kirk...450
Graham, Berniece E...377,447
Graham, Bertha Kloxin...370-1
Graham, Bertha Springer...364
Graham, Bette L...438,484
Graham, Betty M...454,490
Graham, Betty Richeson...452
Graham, Beverly Bartram...482
Graham, Bonnie L...434,482

Graham, Calvin W...429,472-3
Graham, Carole Richards...470
Graham, Caroline Grauer...438
Graham, Carrie...394
Graham, Carrie S...249,319-20
Graham, Carrie Warner...376
Graham, Catharine Thierolf...253-4
Graham, Catherine Lapish...465
Graham, Catherine Mulhern...370
Graham, Cecil M...377,447
Graham, Charlene A...438,484
Graham, Charles I...302,395
Graham, Charles M...350,411
Graham, Charles R...422,470
Graham, Charles Waddill...297,392
Graham, Charles Wesley...289,371
Graham, Charlotte...457
Graham, Charlotte Johnson...380
Graham, Chester W...379,451
Graham, Christine D...452,489
Graham, Christopher L...473,502
Graham, Clara Cecilia...251,328-9
Graham, Clara Claggett...466,496
Graham, Clara Conard...366
Graham, Clara J...253,334-5
Graham, Clara L...366,423
Graham, Clarence S...379,450
Graham, Clinton W...245,317
Graham, Connie Baird...468
Graham, Connie R...473,501
Graham, Cornelia McConnell...264-5
Graham, Cynthia L...479
Graham, Cynthia R...432,477
Graham, Dales Y...253,342
Graham, Daniel E...507
Graham, Daniel P...402,465
Graham, Daniel P. Jr...465,494
Graham, Darleen J...452,488
Graham, David (1-1)...34-7,46-7,61-4.
 See also Grimes (Grimbs), David.
Graham, David (3-5)...74,155-6,222
Graham, David (3-15)...86,174,221-4,
 226
Graham, David (4-8)...140,249-51,253
Graham, David (6-8)...331,402
Graham, David A...293,377
Graham, David B...305,398-9
Graham, David H...466,496
Graham, David H. Jr...496
Graham, David L...491,508
Graham, David McDill...167,293
Graham, David Michael...498
Graham, David T...400,463-4
Graham, David W...242,315
Graham, David Wilson...241,305
Graham, Deborah A...481,505
Graham, Diane...450,487
Graham, Diane Seymour...486
Graham, Donald D...353,415
Graham, Donald E...412,469
Graham, Donald Eugene...480
Graham, Donald M...260,350-2
Graham, Donna Bargman...478
Graham, Donna Frederickson...479
Graham, Donna J...434,481
Graham, Donnelle Oldaker...500

Graham, Dora Buck...337
Graham, Dora Smith...365
Graham, Doris...420,469
Graham, Dorothy...380,453
Graham, Dorothy M...376,443
Graham, Dorothy Speake...466
Graham, Douglas A...470,500
Graham, Douglas R...486,507
Graham, Earl A...353,415
Graham, Earl L...377,447
Graham, Earl S...380,453
Graham, Eda M.B...366,424
Graham, Edgar L...364,420
Graham, Edith Aebisher...450
Graham, Edith Richardson...432
Graham, Edna...337,404
Graham, Edna Broadhead...422
Graham, Edna Bullock...423
Graham, Edward Y...260,347-8
Graham, Edwin B...253,335-7
Graham, Edwin Y...254,346
Graham, Effie Cummings...376
Graham, Effie J...293,373
Graham, Eileen McDonald...491
Graham, Eleanor McCreight...155
Graham, Eliza Cowden...292
Graham, Eliza E...169,295
Graham, Eliza Lourie...335,337
Graham, Eliza Wolfe...352-3
Graham, Elizabeth (3-1)...74,95-7
Graham, Elizabeth...221
Graham, Elizabeth Brown...249
Graham, Elizabeth Cunningham...341
Graham, Elizabeth J...251,321-2
Graham, Elizabeth Lyons...395
Graham, Elizabeth Margaret..467,498-9
Graham, Elizabeth Mary...295,387
Graham, Elizabeth May....348,410
Graham, Elizabeth McGuire...392
Graham, Elizabeth Robison...244
Graham, Elizabeth Thomson...293-4
Graham, Ella (5-55)...260,354
Graham, Ella (6-15)...337,404
Graham, Elmira E...254,345
Graham, Elvina Setterland...425
Graham, Elvira Wilson...248-9
Graham, Emily L...504
Graham, Emma Speake...465
Graham, Erma L...423,471-2
Graham, Esther...82
Graham, Esther (3-17)...86,227-8
Graham, Ethel Lynch...434
Graham, Etta L...365,422
Graham, Eva Taylor...442
Graham, Evarts A...305,399-400
Graham, Evarts A. Jr...400,464-5
Graham, Everett M...367,434
Graham, Faith E...495
Graham, Fleda B...376,446
Graham, Flora Morgan...408
Graham, Florence E...293,377
Graham, Frances...450,487
Graham, Frances Adler...464-5
Graham, Frances Keesler...463-4
Graham, Frances M...251,332-4
Graham, Frances Maberry...451

Graham, Frances Mayes...496-7
Graham, Frances Sanderson...398
Graham, Frank C...353,415
Graham, Frank H...293,378
Graham, Frank I...286,370-1
Graham, Frank L...289,371-2
Graham, Frank M...302,395
Graham, Frank W...392,457
Graham, Frank Y...242,314-5
Graham, Fred...450,487
Graham, Fred Y...350,412
Graham, Frederick...372,440
Graham, Frederick L...365,421-2
Graham, Gayle L...482,506
Graham, George A...379,450
Graham, George D...376,446
Graham, George Harvey...342,406
Graham, George Henry...293,376
Graham, George M...371,440
Graham, George Mills...289,371
Graham, George R...364,420
Graham, George W...286,370
Graham, Georgia...420,469
Graham, Georgia A...298,394
Graham, Georgia G...370,437
Graham, Gertrude S...249,320
Graham, Gladys Korsgarden...452
Graham, Glenn F...317
Graham, Gordon A...380,452
Graham, Grace...457
Graham, Granville W...169,295-7
Graham, Gregg E...473,501-2
Graham, Grizzella Milligan...241-2
Graham, Harold E...454,491
Graham, Harold M...346,409
Graham, Harold W...342,406
Graham, Harriet E...245,316-7
Graham, Harry B...348,409-10
Graham, Harry L...372,440
Graham, Harry P...293,377
Graham, Harry W...286,365
Graham, Harvey M...254,345-6
Graham, Harvey W...242,313-4
Graham, Harvey W. Jr...314,401-2
Graham, Helen Black...453
Graham, Helen E...465,493-4
Graham, Helen Tredway...399,400
Graham, Hellen Burrus...295-7
Graham, Henry C...365,421
Graham, Ida Barned...305
Graham, Ida M...364,420
Graham, infant...225,242,284,302,303, 315,364,371,394,429,438,477
Graham, Ira F...377,447
Graham, Irma K...457
Graham, Iva I...366,429
Graham, Iva L...286,367-8
Graham, Jacqueline...450,487
Graham, James (2-4)...34-6.48-56,58- 60,64,82-6. See also Grimes (Grimbs), James.
Graham, James....246
Graham, James Jr...86,225-7
Graham, James A...251,329-31
Graham, James Gillespie...265,354
Graham, James Glenn...402,466-7

Graham, James H...331,403
Graham, James Harvey...140,251-2
Graham, James Thomas...167,284-6
Graham, James Thomas Jr...286,367
Graham, James Tredway...493
Graham, James W...408,468
Graham, Jane see also Janet,Jean, Jennet.
Graham, Jane...156,254
Graham, Jane A. Wilson...337-8
Graham, Jane G...295,389
Graham, Jane McGaw...314-5
Graham, Jane Popham...165-7,348
Graham, Jane W...254,326,343
Graham, Jane (Jennette) Wilson...89, 139-40
Graham, Jane Winter...364
Graham, Janet. See also Jane, Jean, Jennet.
Graham, Janet...61,64
Graham, Janice M...479,504
Graham, Jason...507
Graham, Jean. See also Jane, Janet, Jennet.
Graham, Jean...35-6,39,64,74-5. See also Grimes (Grimbs), Jean.
Graham, Jeff B...468,499
Graham, Jennet. See also Jane, Janet, Jean.
Graham, Jennet (2-6)...64,87-8
Graham, Jennet (3-2)...74,127-8
Graham, Jennette Wilson. See Graham, Jane (Jennette) Wilson.
Graham, Jennifer L...491,508
Graham, Jerald R...479,504
Graham, Jessie C...434,482
Graham, Jessie Conard...366-7
Graham, Jessie E.(5-21)..249,318
Graham, Jessie E...331
Graham, Jessie L...293,375
Graham, Jessie McDonald...406
Graham, Jimmie R...443,485
Graham, Jimmy D...443,486
Graham, Jo Ann V...443,485
Graham, Joanna...169,299-300
Graham, Joe A...479,504
Graham, Joel G...467,498
Graham, John (2-5)...64,86-7
Graham, John (5-22)...249,319
Graham, John D...486,508
Graham, John G...286,366
Graham, John H...244,315
Graham, John Howard...365,422
Graham, John M...245,317
Graham, John McKee...161,259-60
Graham, John McKee Jr...260,353
Graham, John Milligan...242,312
Graham, John Mills...167,292
Graham, John Mitchell...253,338
Graham, John R...467,497-8
Graham, John W...140,241-2
Graham, John William...376,446
Graham, John William Jr...446,486
Graham, Jon P...473,500
Graham, Joseph B...495
Graham, Joseph C...367,434

Graham, Joseph D...372,440
Graham, Joshua K...502
Graham, Joyce Erickson...507
Graham, Joyce L...409,468
Graham, Judith L...452,488
Graham, Judith M...443,486
Graham, Judith McConaha...479
Graham, Julianna...86,174-5
Graham, Julie L...479,503
Graham, Kae L. J...434,484
Graham, Karen L...468,499
Graham, Kate Pierson...283
Graham, Katharine E...493
Graham, Katharine M...265,356
Graham, Katherine...321
Graham, Katherine McCuie...468
Graham, Kathleen...489,508
Graham, Kathryn Patterson...421-2
Graham, Kathy S...479,503
Graham, Katie C...502
Graham, Keith...376,446
Graham, Kenneth...377,447
Graham, Kenneth L...455,491
Graham, Krissi Harder...502
Graham, Kristi L...486,508
Graham, Larry E...482,505
Graham, Laura (5-14)...245,315-6
Graham, Laura (6-13)...337,404
Graham, Laura E...253,338-9
Graham, Laura Fletcher...446
Graham, Laura Kubes...505
Graham, Laura S...497
Graham, Laura Trumbull...342
Graham, Lawrence N...434,477
Graham, Lawrence W. (5-69)..286,366-7
Graham, Lawrence W. (7-35A)...479
Graham, Lee A...289,372
Graham, Lee W...412,468
Graham, Leila...346,409
Graham, Leila K...409,468
Graham, Leith...376,447
Graham, Lela E...350,413
Graham, Lena Parsons...401-2
Graham, Lenora Wiseman...371
Graham, Leslie B...379,449-50
Graham, Lessie J...338,405
Graham, Lester...422,470
Graham, Lillian A...350,412
Graham, Lillie Clark...367
Graham, Lillie'M...295,380-2
Graham, Linda M...482,506-7
Graham, Lois...337,404
Graham, Lois Hoag...466-7
Graham, Lola M...367,435
Graham, Lonnie D...481,504
Graham, Lorene M...380,453
Graham, Lori A...491,508
Graham, Louie Mayne...354
Graham, Lowell E...434,482
Graham, Lucile Blake...450
Graham, Lucile Conway...454
Graham, Lucy A...169,298
Graham, Lucy Geiger...378
Graham, Luke C...502
Graham, Lula A...350,413
Graham, Lulu...409

Graham, Lulu M...366,424
Graham, Lyda Bliznak...406-7
Graham, Lynda K...482,506
Graham, Lynn...434,481
Graham, Mabel E...289,372
Graham, Mabel Stewart...380
Graham, Mabel Wymore...377
Graham, Mae...413
Graham, Mae B...293,375
Graham, Mae Upchurch...392
Graham, Margaret (2-8)...64,91-4
Graham, Margaret (3-10)...74,169
Graham, Margaret (4-6)...140,245
Graham, Margaret (5-56)...260,354
Graham, Margaret (7-2)...399,459-60
Graham, Margaret C...161,254-5
Graham, Margaret Collier...350-2
Graham, Margaret Coulter...65-7
Graham, Margaret J...454,490
Graham, Margaret K...453,489
Graham, Margaret Mills...65
Graham, Margaret Wallace...304
Graham, Marge...378,448
Graham, Marguerite Miller...449,450
Graham, Marilyn Haack...492
Graham, Marilyn J...422,470
Graham, Marilyn Luysch...489
Graham, Marjorie Buckingham...497-8
Graham, Martha...74,162,524 note 93
Graham, Martha Ann (4-19)..167,269-70
Graham, Martha Ann (4-42)...225,303
Graham, Martha B...495
Graham, Martha D...493
Graham, Martha E...245,317
Graham, Martha Ellen...350,412
Graham, Martha Evelyn...265,357
Graham, Martha Francis...301
Graham, Martha Glenn...313-4
Graham, Martha Hilton...297
Graham, Martha J...241,306
Graham, Martha McDill...240
Graham, Martha McDill...304
Graham, Martha McKee...156-8,161
Graham, Martha Richie...243-4
Graham, Martha Stewart...371
Graham, Martha W...140,236
Graham, Martin G...498
Graham, Mary (2-7)...64,89-90
Graham, Mary (3-4)...74,140-3
Graham, Mary Anderson...287-9
Graham, Mary B...464,493
Graham, Mary Brown...251-2
Graham, Mary Burrell...398-9
Graham, Mary C...337,404
Graham, Mary E...342,407-8
Graham, Mary Edna...379,448
Graham, Mary Elizabeth...331,402
Graham, Mary Ellen....253,340
Graham, Mary F...302,395
Graham, Mary Frances...305,396
Graham, Mary H...225,303
Graham, Mary Louisa...251,331
Graham, Mary Louise (5-48)...254, 346-7
Graham, Mary Louise (7-75)...455,491
Graham, Mary M. (4-35)...169,298

Graham, Mary M. (4-37)...173,300
Graham, Mary M. (6-20)...338,405
Graham, Mary Margaret (4-29)...167, 293,348-50
Graham, Mary Margaret (7-61)...451, 488
Graham, Mary Martin...329-31
Graham, Mary McDill...284
Graham, Mary McDill...395
Graham, Mary McQuown...283
Graham, Mary Michelle....438,484
Graham, Mary Morris...494-5
Graham, Mary S...161,266-7
Graham, Mary T...354,416
Graham, Mary Waddill...167-8
Graham, Matthew (Mathew,2-3)...34-6, 39,64,81-2. See also Grimes (Grimbs), Matthew (Mathew).
Graham, Matthew (3-3)...74,89,139-40
Graham, Matthew J...167,287-9
Graham, Matthew Y...241,311
Graham, Maude M...249,320-1
Graham, Maude Samuelson...379
Graham, Maurice D...434,481
Graham, Maxwell...377,448
Graham, Megan M...502
Graham, Melcena...412
Graham, Melcena Gillespie...264-5
Graham, Melcena M...354,417
Graham, Melinda E...331,403
Graham, Melissa Gilchrist...284-6
Graham, Melissa K...502
Graham, Melissa Stahl...504
Graham, Melvin R...365,422
Graham, Merton...379,450
Graham, Mildred R...392,457
Graham, Mina...317
Graham, Minone Lowman...405
Graham, Mitchell M...242,312-13
Graham, Morgan R...504
Graham, Myra K...354,418-9
Graham, Myra Sears...354
Graham, Myron A...434,478
Graham, Myrtle Ida...289,373
Graham, Myrtle Iva...293,378
Graham, Nancy...173,303
Graham, Nancy C. (3-11)...74,169-72
Graham, Nancy C. (4-14)...161,260-1
Graham, Nancy E...167,279
Graham, Nancy M...254,343
Graham, Nancy Wilson...246
Graham, Nancy Young...259-60
Graham, Nelda Oberhelman...482
Graham, Nelle Lee...372
Graham, Nelva A...434,479
Graham, Nettie Moore...345
Graham, Nicholas A...505
Graham, Nina Cannon...317
Graham, Nora...421
Graham, Nora D...297,393
Graham, Norma H...353,414-5
Graham, Norma V.S...464,492
Graham, Octavia J...379
Graham, Oley M...293,376
Graham, Olive Stream...391
Graham, Oliver H...353,415

Graham, Opal...367,435
Graham, Ora Bonham...379
Graham, Pamela Kruska...504
Graham, Paul E...367,434
Graham, Paul E. Jr...434,482
Graham, Paul J...482,507
Graham, Paula S...482,505-6
Graham, Paulina J...161,261-2
Graham, Pauline W...353,415
Graham, Pearl A...367,436
Graham, Pearl E...376,441
Graham, Pearl W...366,424
Graham, Peggy Bettes...503
Graham, Peter W...492
Graham, Philip Edward...380,451
Graham, Philip Edward Jr...451,488
Graham, Philip Eugene...482,507
Graham, Philip James...467,499
Graham, Philip Jon...500
Graham, Rachel Davis...240-1
Graham, Rae M...429,473-4
Graham, Ralph...346,409
Graham, Ralph Jr...409,468
Graham, Ralph A...364,421
Graham, Ralph W...371,440
Graham, Ralph Walter...251,332
Graham, Ray W...366,426-8
Graham, Relda Moser...434
Graham, Rena M...297,392-3
Graham, Richard...422,470
Graham, Richard Jr...470,500
Graham, Richard B...465,494
Graham, Richard C...412,469
Graham, Richard D...481,505
Graham, Richard W...470,500
Graham, Robert...245,317
Graham, Robert A...305,398
Graham, Robert Alexander...260,352-3
Graham, Robert C. (3-6)..74,156-61
Graham, Robert C. (4-4)...140,242-4
Graham, Robert Cowden...293,376
Graham, Robert Culbertson (4-22)... 167,284
Graham, Robert Culbertson (5-96)... 295,380
Graham, Robert D...452,489
Graham, Robert F...265,354-6
Graham, Robert J...380,452
Graham, Robert L...453,489
Graham, Robert L. Jr...489,508
Graham, Robert M. (4-33)...169,297
Graham, Robert M. (6-127)...394,458
Graham, Robert Roy...376,442
Graham, Robert Russell...380,454
Graham, Rosalie Freeman...491
Graham, Rose Butler...482
Graham, Ross G...434,479
Graham, Ross W...305,398
Graham, Roy...293,379
Graham, Roy E...366,422-3
Graham, Ruby E...379,450
Graham, Ruby Snyder...420
Graham, Russell A...302,395
Graham, Ruth A...422,469
Graham, Ruth J...391,455
Graham, Ruth Ritter...452

Graham, Sally...249,320
Graham, Sally Gartin...164-5,525 note 100
Graham, Samuel A...167,293-4
Graham, Samuel R...295,391
Graham, Sandra Clements...486
Graham, Sandra K...486,507
Graham, Sarah...246
Graham, Sarah B...497
Graham, Sarah Burrus...295
Graham, Sarah E...161,268
Graham, Sarah Elizabeth...504
Graham, Sarah Ellis...495
Graham, Sarah F...465,494
Graham, Sarah J...167,289-90
Graham, Sharon Wyman...479
Graham, Sheryl A...482,506
Graham, Shirley Bucher...481
Graham, Shirley Hayman...454
Graham, Sophia J...350,412
Graham, Stella G...366,424
Graham, Stephen P...465,493
Graham, Sue A...473,502-3
Graham, Susan A...440,485
Graham, Susan L...503
Graham, Susan Lincoln...501-2
Graham, Susan W...497
Graham, Suzanne...406,467
Graham, Teresa D...445
Graham, Teria...449
Graham, Thais J...452,488
Graham, Thelma A...376,441
Graham, Thelma E...366,429-30
Graham, Theodore O...366,425
Graham, Theresa Komarek...507
Graham, Thomas B...297,392
Graham, Thomas Edward (5-95)...295,380
Graham, Thomas Edward (7-65)..452,489
Graham, Thomas H...402,466
Graham, Thomas H. Jr...466,496-7
Graham, Thomas J...482,507
Graham, Thomas P...74,167-9
Graham, Thomas R...298,394
Graham, Thomas R. Jr...394,458
Graham, Thomas V...481,505
Graham, Timothy L...505
Graham, Twila...422,470
Graham, Valerie J...482,505
Graham, Velma M...434,477
Graham, Velma Richardson...434
Graham, Velores Koll...472-3
Graham, Victor C...342,406-7
Graham, Victoria Kroener...424
Graham, Violet V...371,438
Graham, Virginia...420,469
Graham, Walter I...366,432
Graham, Walter N...295,391
Graham, Wanita Vickers...451
Graham, William (5-12)...244,315
Graham, William (7-58)...451,487
Graham, William Alexander..167,286-7
Graham, William Allison...295,379
Graham, William Andrew...242,312
Graham, William B...241,304
Graham, William F...253,337-8
Graham, William F.C...260,293,348-50

Graham, William I...245,317
Graham, William J...350,414
Graham, William Mills (3-8)..74,164-7, 348
Graham, William Mills (4-5)..140,244-245
Graham, William Mills (5-66)..286,365
Graham, William R...455,491
Graham, William W...249,321
Graham, William Wilson...305,398
Graham, Willie...254,347
Graham, Willis...371,438
Graham, Wilma M...434,480
Graham, Wilmer T...342,408
Graham, Wilson B...398,459
Graham, Wilson H...338,405
Graham, Wilson M...140,248-9
Graham, Wilson T...253,341-2
Graham, Wyman L...380,454
Graham, Wynona...450
Graham, Xenophon A...338,405
Graham, Zella L...367,432
Grauer, Caroline...438
Grauer, Janice J...438
Grauer, Jeffery J...438,439
Grauer, Jeffery M...439
Grauer, Jessica D...439
Grauer, Joyce Muck...439
Grauer, Marilyn D...438,439
Grauer, Merlin...438
Grauer, Nancy E...430,438,439
Grauer, Sherry L...438,439
Grauer, Shirley A...438
Grauer, Violet Graham...371,438
Graves, Frances Callicotte...163
Graves, Gilbert...163
Gray, Chester...409
Gray, Isophene...106
Gray, Leila Graham...346,409
Gray, Martha...409
Gray, Olan...409
Gray, Sue...212
Greau, Ruth Riegel...345
Green, JoAnne...311
Greer, Bertha...100
Greggs, Willie T...201
Griffin, Bertha M...204
Griffin, Ethel Caskey...200,204
Griffin, infant...204
Griffin, Lucille...204-5
Griffin, Maurice...205
Griffin, William R...204
Griffith, Beulah E...213
Griffith, Charles F...213
Griffith, Cynthia F...213
Griffith, Gertrude Carter...213
Griffith, Hugh J...213
Griffith, John J...213
Griffith, Nannie A...213
Griffith, Sarah Smith...213
Griffith, Slonney Mills...212-3
Griffith, Zuma...213
Griggs, Henderson P...197
Griggs, Lilli Gwinn...207
Griggs, Minerva I...197
Griggs, Oscar...207

Griggs, Vera Gillihan...197
Grigsby, J.T...217
Grigsby, Lena Isom...217
Grimbs, see Grimes
Grimes (Grimbs, Grumbs), Andrew...34-36,39-42,44,51-2. See Graham, Andrew (2-1).
Grimes (Grimbs), David...35-7,46-7,61. See Graham, David (1-1).
Grimes (Grimbs), James...35-6,48-56,58-60. See Graham, James (2-4).
Grimes (Grimbs), Jean...35-6,39. See Graham, Jean.
Grimes (Grimbs), Matthew (Mathew)...35-6,39. See Graham, Matthew (Mathew, 2-3).
Grissom, Hester...106
Grover, John...370
Grover, Verna Hafner...370
Grubelnik, Brad...433
Grubelnik, Chad...433
Grubelnik, David...433
Grubelnik, Kay Olmstead...433
Grubelnik, Mark...433
Grubelnik, Steve...433
Grubelnik, Susan Wiseman..433
Grumbs, see Grimes.
Guinn see also Gwinn
Guinn, Estes M...198
Guinn, Eula Huffman...197,211
Guinn, Henrietta...197
Guinn, Robert L...197,211
Gwinn see also Guinn
Gwinn, Alice Dickey...207
Gwinn, Amanda A...197
Gwinn, Annie M...197
Gwinn, Beryl Walton...198
Gwinn, Bessie B...208
Gwinn, Beulah B...208
Gwinn, David A...198
Gwinn, Ella J...219
Gwinn, Eula D...208
Gwinn, George O...198
Gwinn, Hugh A...197,207,211
Gwinn, James M...208
Gwinn, Julia A...208
Gwinn, Lillie Goforth..197-8
Gwinn, Lillie M...207
Gwinn, Margaret E...208
Gwinn, Martha E...207
Gwinn, Mary J...208
Gwinn, Mary Mills...197,206
Gwinn, Melvin A...197
Gwinn, Modenia P...197
Gwinn, Ollie L...107
Gwinn, Reatha D...198
Gwinn, Regie L...207-8,209
Gwinn, Robbie Blankenship...208,209
Gwinn, Robert M...197,206
Gwinn, Roscoe M...207
Gwinn, Russell W...207
Gwinn, Samuel A...198
Gwinn, Sarah A...206
Gwinn, Sarah Anglin...207
Gwinn, Sarah Baskin...207,209
Gwinn, Sarah Caskey...197,207,211

Gwinn, William...206
Gwinn, William T...207,209
Haack, Herman J...492
Haack, Marilyn S...492
Haack, Martha Daellenbach...492
Habig, Aleah...436
Habig, Chauncey...435
Habig, Daren...436
Habig, Dennis...435,436
Habig, Diana Feldhausen...436
Habig, Lola Graham...367,435
Habig, Mandy...436
Hackett, Ollie...151
Hackett, Sallie Evans...151
Hadley, Emma V...368
Haecker, LeRoy...484
Haecker, Mary Graham...438,484
Hafner, Brenda Lawson...370
Hafner, Holly...370
Hafner, Howard A...370
Hafner, Jason...370
Hafner, Olive Howard...368,370
Hafner, Orville...370
Hafner, Verna J...370
Haley, Bertha...100
Hall, Ethel Inman...229
Hall, Spencer...229
Hallam, Allyson S...328
Hallam, Anna Robb...326
Hallam, Charles T...327-8
Hallam, Cynthia Fillman...327
Hallam, David Mark...327
Hallam, David Milton...326-7
Hallam, David W...328
Hallam, Elizabeth Caldwell...326-7
Hallam, Erika L...327
Hallam, George M...326
Hallam, John R...327
Hallam, Laura Terry...327
Hallam, Peter G...328
Hallam, Sean C...327
Hamilton, A.W...111
Hamilton, Amy...308
Hamilton, Elizabeth...111
Hamilton, Ivy B...178
Hamilton, James W.B...178
Hamilton, John L...436
Hamilton, Kent...308
Hamilton, Margaret...398
Hamilton, Margaret M...111
Hamilton, Mary Cotton...178
Hamilton, Pearl Graham...367,436
Hamilton, Susan Kelly...308
Hamilton, William T...308
Hammerschmidt, Alan...389
Hammerschmidt, Elmer...389
Hammerschmidt, Joanna Bishop...389
Hammerschmidt, Lynda M...390
Hammerschmidt, Robert...389
Hammett, Bernice M...451
Hammond, Melissa L...359
Hampton, Sallie...100
Hancock, Eliza Gleghorn...118
Hancock, William A...118
Handson, Brady W...431
Hanks, Autry Isom...217

Hanks, James...217
Hanks, Lillie M...213
Hanson, Claire...316
Hanson, Elmer L...431
Hanson, Emelia Walker...431
Hanson, Margie McClellan...430,431
Hanson, Mary...316
Hanson, Oscar E...431
Hanson, Rebecca Notson...431
Hanson, Richard W...431
Hanson, Ronald W...431
Harder, Burnus Meyer..502
Harder, Krissi...502
Harder, Richard...502
Hardesty, Billy M...163
Hardesty, Billy S...164
Hardesty, Charley...164
Hardesty, Deloris Lillihaug...163
Hardesty, Devena Anderson...164
Hardesty, Edith...322-3
Hardesty, Fannie Slaughter...163
Hardesty, Hazel F...163
Hardesty, Hope...164
Hardesty, infant...163
Hardesty, John C...164
Hardesty, Kae Field...164
Hardesty, LaDel...164
Hardesty, Lily O...163
Hardesty, Lois...164
Hardesty, Lowell S...164
Hardesty, Lowell S. Jr...164
Hardesty, Margaret Shanklin...162-3
Hardesty, Martha J...163
Hardesty, Martha V...163
Hardesty, Milton P...164
Hardesty, Opal Robertson...163
Hardesty, Richard D...164
Hardesty, Richard H...163
Hardesty, Rosetta D...164
Hardesty, Ruby Callahan...163
Hardesty, Sharron Z...164
Hardesty, Thomas E...163
Hardesty, Thomas P...163
Hardesty, Verda Wills...163
Hardesty, Willa Hunt...164
Hardesty, William R...163
Hargett, Sarah E...212,213
Hargett, Sarah E...214,218
Harley, Gail Knapp...311
Harley, Robert...311
Harley, Sarah J...311
Harrell, Amanda...80
Harrell, Arthusa J...80
Harrell, Edward...80
Harrell, Ethel...80
Harrell, James...80
Harrell, Jane Adams...80
Harrell, Jane Holland...80
Harrell, John P...80
Harrell, Joseph...80
Harrell, Lena M...80
Harrell, Marshall...80
Harrell, Mary Thrasher...80
Harrell, Maud...80
Harrell, Ralph K...80
Harrell, Samuel...80

Harrell, Susie...80
Harrell, Tabitha...80
Harrell, William O...80
Harrington, Lucille Griffin...204-5
Harris, John W...136
Harris, John W. Jr...136
Harris, Minnie Hutchings...136
Harrison, Anita J...309
Harrison, Jane Fuller...309
Harrison, Laura...134
Harrison, Wilkes D...309
Harrison, Will D...309
Harsha, Hannah E...280
Hart, Mary L...180
Hartsfield, Telitha...218
Hartsock, Ethel...308
Hathcock, Annie E...220
Hathcock, Estelle Dawson..219
Hathcock, James...219,220
Hathcock, James C...219
Hathcock, James W...220
Hathcock, Kitty Kinney...219
Hathcock, Louise...220
Hathcock, Lula Hodges...219-20
Hathcock, Miskel Huffman...220
Hathcock, Vivian...219
Hathcock, Werdner...220
Hathcock, William T...219
Hathcock, Willie Dawson...219
Hawkinson, Cynthia Hinckley...272
Hawkinson, Edna Firoved...272
Hawkinson, John E...272
Hawkinson, Newton W...272
Hawkinson, Thomas N...272
Hawks, Henry...100
Hawks, Leila Gleghorn...100
Haworth, Aaron...383
Haworth, Benjamin...383
Haworth, Chrisopher S...383
Haworth, Constance L...383
Haworth, Donald R...383
Haworth, Elizabeth Livingston...382
Haworth, Elizabeth Woesner...382
Haworth, Gary W...383
Haworth, Gavin...383
Haworth, Gerald S...384
Haworth, Gladys Wimmer...382
Haworth, Graham W...383
Haworth, Holly...383
Haworth, James D...382
Haworth, James D...383
Haworth, Jewel Smith...383
Haworth, Julie A...384
Haworth, Linda R...383
Haworth, Linsay...383
Haworth, Marguerite DeReamer...383
Haworth, Penny Lewellen...383
Haworth, Priscilla Pebley...383
Haworth, Raymond O...382
Haworth, Robert Larry...383
Haworth, Robert Lyle...382
Haworth, Samuel R...383
Hayes, Alice Shankle...229
Hayes, Bessie Crockett...229
Hayes, Eleanor E...229
Hayes, James G...229

Hayes, Priscilla Bailey...229
Hayes, Samuel B...229
Hayes, Samuel B. Jr...229
Hayman, Iva Darby...454
Hayman, Louis A...454
Hayman, Shirley L...454
Heil, Grace Glick...374-5
Heil, Peter...374
Heil, Roy...374-5
Heil, Sarah J...375
Heil, Susan Cox...374
Heinemeyer, Ellen...124
Heiserman, Bret L...442
Heiserman, Charlotte Cudney...442
Heiserman, Dale F...441,442
Heiserman, Dale F. Jr...442
Heiserman, Dorothy Q...441
Heiserman, Frederick D...441
Heiserman, Gary L...442
Heiserman, George...441
Heiserman, Henrietta Breunsbach...441
Heiserman, Jane Brunton...442
Heiserman, Janelle Wurm...442
Heiserman, Julie A...442
Heiserman, Larry D...442
Heiserman, LeRoy F...441,442
Heiserman, Linda K...442
Heiserman, Linda Meador...442
Heiserman, Lynn Bunce...442
Heiserman, Marilyn Cooper...442
Heiserman, Mary L...441,442
Heiserman, Nora M...441
Heiserman, Sherrie L...442
Heiserman, Thelma Graham...376,441
Hellis, Katherine...229
Helms, Cynthia Graham...479-80
Helms, Laura B...79
Helms, Robert...479-80
Hemphill, Jennet McQuiston...261
Hemphill, Martha E...262-3
Hemphill, Paulina Graham...161,261-2
Hemphill, Robert...261-2
Hemphill, William...261
Hendrickson, Chris W...377
Hendrickson, Marie Clark...377
Henry, Nancy...133
Henson, Beulah Gleghorn...100
Herbert, Frances Graham...251,332-4
Herbert, John B...332-4
Herbert, John T...332
Herbert, Rena Giddings...332
Herdman, Emma Mitchell...272
Herdman, James H...272
Herdman, John N...272
Herdman, Nettie Piroved...272
Hernandez, Hector...478
Hernandez, Julian K...478
Hernandez, Paula Palmer...478
Herring, Belle Gleghorn...101
Herriott, Elizabeth Ross...105
Herriott, George R...105
Herriott, Lavona A...105
Hess, Allen H...278
Hess, Betty...278
Hess, Billie A...278
Hess, James H...278

Hess, Linda R...278
Hess, Louise Torley...278
Hess, Marian R...278
Hess, Mary Hutchinson...277
Hess, Mattie Allen...277
Hess, Opal Anderson...278
Hess, Richard L...278
Hess, T.M...277
Hess, Theola M...277
Hess, Theola M. Jr...278
Hess, Thomas...277
Hevener, Bertha J...384
Hewitt, Marguerite...184
Hiatt, Imogean...153
Higgins, Elta...393
Higgins, Julia...393
Higgins, Margaret...358
Higgins, Walter G...393
Hill, Alexander...133
Hill, Bennie...435
Hill, David C...133
Hill, Donald...435
Hill, Donna...435
Hill, James H...133
Hill, Lucerne...133
Hill, Malcolm H...133
Hill, Marie...435
Hill, Marty...435
Hill, Mary...133
Hill, Mary A...133
Hill, Mary Knox...133
Hill, Mary Randall...133
Hill, Mattie...133
Hill, Mickey...435
Hill, Minnie A...133
Hill, Minnie J...133
Hill, Nancy Henry...133
Hill, Nannie...133
Hill, Nannie L...133
Hill, Opal Graham...367,435
Hill, Rowena B...133-4
Hilliard, Charles Wesley IV...383
Hilliard, Charles Wesley V...384
Hilliard, Constance Haworth...383
Hilliard, Jennifer L...384
Hilliard, Kimberly A...384
Hilliard, Michelle L...384
Hills, Mae...274
Hilton, Elizabeth Davis...297
Hilton, George...297
Hilton, Martha E...297
Hinckley, Cynthia...272
Hindman, Ada R...188
Hindman, Agnes N...189
Hindman, Alexander S...179-80
Hindman, Alice M...188-9
Hindman, Alice Randolph...181
Hindman, Ardelle...188
Hindman, Bessie Clements...190
Hindman, Charles E..189-90
Hindman, Clemmie E...177
Hindman, Cora L...189
Hindman, Elizabeth J.A...181-2
Hindman, Elizabeth McClerkin...179
Hindman, Gerald P...188
Hindman, Grace Smith...189

Hindman, James...175
Hindman, James F...180
Hindman, James G...175-6
Hindman, James H...180-1
Hindman, James H.C...176
Hindman, James R...176
Hindman, Jane H...192,196
Hindman, John A...176
Hindman, John H...180-1
Hindman, Joseph A...181
Hindman, Leroy E...188
Hindman, Lindsay S...176-7
Hindman, Luther E...177
Hindman, Margaret Baird...177
Hindman, Margaret McCullough..187-8
Hindman, Martha E...181
Hindman, Martha Moore...177
Hindman, Mary A...180
Hindman, Mary Bell...176
Hindman, Mary Caskey..175
Hindman, Mary J...190-1
Hindman, Maude E...181
Hindman, Myrtle R...190
Hindman, Nora Gee...190
Hindman, Robert Olien...189
Hindman, Robert Orrell...189
Hindman, Rosa Miller...180
Hindman, Rosanna W...177
Hindman, Ruth Sacra...188
Hindman, Sarah...175
Hindman, Sarah Baird...175
Hindman, Sarah Forsythe...180
Hindman, Sarah Lynn...175-6
Hindman, Sarah S...185
Hindman, Sidney A...180
Hindman, Susan Campbell..188
Hindman, Thomas K...180
Hindman, Thomas Sidney...190
Hindman, Thomas Sidney Jr...190
Hindman, Thomas Stewart...187-8
Hindman, William...175
Hindman, William C...181
Hindman, William P...176
Hindman, William S...188
Hindman, Willie B...188
Hindman, Willie Durham...189
Hines, Belle Evans...151
Hines, Sallie...100
Hines, William...151
Hinton, Christine McWilliams...203
Hinton, Walt...203
Hinz, Edward A. Jr...452
Hinz, Edward A. III...452
Hinz, Patricia Dobyns...452
Hinz, Steven F..452
Hise, Eupha Blankenship...209
Hise, Martha Ladd...209
Hise, Marvin A...209
Hise, William H...209
Hoag, Alice Misz...466
Hoag, Arthur J...466
Hoag, Lois M...466
Hoberman, Florence Parnes...360
Hoberman, Hyman...360
Hoberman, Steven R...360
Hodges, Lula...219,220

Hoffman, Diane McClellan...431
Hoffman, Shawn M...431
Hoffman, Tim...431
Hogue, Cora...229
Hogue, Effie...100
Hogue, James...229
Hogue, Jemima Moffatt...229
Hohlfeldt, Bradley...310
Hohlfeldt, David...310
Hohlfeldt, Elizabeth McMillan...310
Hohlfeldt, Erin E...310
Holland, Jane...80
Holly, Ozella Jobe...102
Holm, Kristie...273
Holmes, Howard...164
Holmes, Lois Hardesty...164
Hook, Lorena M...276
Hooper, Montell...230
Hopkins, Catharine C...264
Horelick, DeVra I...475
Horelick, Linda Darner...474-5
Horelick, Stephen A...474
Horner, Suanne Graham...406,467
House, Arnold...309
House, Catherind A...309
House, Johanna Fuller...309
House, Mary E...231
Houston, Edna Bullock...423
Howard, Aline Karnes...368
Howard, Ann...418
Howard, Cecil F...368
Howard, Charles...417
Howard, Dorothy...417
Howard, Elinore J...368
Howard, Elmina Stanley...367
Howard, Gary...417
Howard, Graham...417
Howard, Imogene Robertson..368
Howard, Iva Graham...286,367-8
Howard, James (6-47C)...417,418
Howard, James...418
Howard, John (5-71)...367-8
Howard, John...418
Howard, Joseph...417
Howard, Joyce...417
Howard, Katharine...418
Howard, Lorna V...368-9
Howard, Lucille Miller...417
Howard, Margaret...417
Howard, Margaret J...368
Howard, Marian...418
Howard, Martha...418
Howard, Melcena Graham...354,417
Howard, Michael...417
Howard, Olive L...368,370
Howard, Oliver...417
Howard, Robert...417
Howard, Ruth...418
Howard, Susan...418
Howard, Thomas...418
Howard, Wayne...417
Howard, Wellington...417
Howard, William...417,418
Howard, William R...367
Howard, Yvonne...417
Howell, Mary...380

Hoy, Maxine...275
Huddleson, Peni J...490
Huffman, Albert...211
Huffman, Anna M...210
Huffman, Annie Marshall...207
Huffman, Ardelle...206
Huffman, Bessie M...201,211
Huffman, Cora Morrison...206
Huffman, Eris...219
Huffman, Eula A...197,211
Huffman, Fentress M...177
Huffman, Hugh G...207
Huffman, Hugh M...177
Huffman, James C...207
Huffman, Jimmie Commer...207
Huffman, John F...197,201,211
Huffman, Johnnie L...211
Huffman, Julia Banks...206,209,211, 214
Huffman, Lillian Vaughan...219
Huffman, Lindsey B...206
Huffman, Lynn U...207
Huffman, Margaret J...218
Huffman, Martha E...209
Huffman, Martha Moore...177
Huffman, Mary A...209,214
Huffman, Mary E...209,216
Huffman, Minnie C...207
Huffman, Miskel...220
Huffman, Nancy Marshall...207
Huffman, Neverette L...207
Huffman, Nina Fortner...211
Huffman, Nora L...206-7
Huffman, Raymond M...211
Huffman, Rosanna Mills...197,201,211
Huffman, Sarah Gwinn...206
Huffman, Thelma Marshall...206
Huffman, Turner E...219
Huffman, William Alexander...177
Huffman, William Alexander..206,209, 211,214
Huffman, William C...206
Huffman, William V...206
Huggins, Lena F..199
Hughes, Barbara A...277
Hughes, Dorothy...341
Hughes, Florence...493
Hughes, Irene E...341
Hughes, Mabel Wilson...340-1
Hughes, Richard...341
Hughes, Richard Jr...341
Humphrey, Beverly Shannon..154
Humphrey, Melvin...154
Hunt, Willa D...164
Hunter, Mary S...281
Hurd, Adah...346
Husa, Julie M...480
Hutchings, Commadore...136
Hutchings, Elizabeth...136
Hutchings, Frances...136
Hutchings, George B...136
Hutchings, John H...135-6
Hutchings, John H. Jr...136
Hutchings, Lelia C...136
Hutchings, Mary....136
Hutchings, Mary ---...136
Hutchings, Mary M...136
Hutchings, Minnie K...136
Hutchings, Minnie Knox...135-6
Hutchings, Rebecca...136
Hutchings, Robert M...136
Hutchings, Sealy...136
Hutchings, Sealy Jr...136
Hutchings, William...136
Hutchinson, Donald...277
Hutchinson, Elizabeth J...270,274
Hutchinson, Ellen...270
Hutchinson, Flora B...276
Hutchinson, Frederick M...278
Hutchinson, Graham...277
Hutchinson, Harley E...277
Hutchinson, James C...269
Hutchinson, Lillian E...279
Hutchinson, Martha E...278
Hutchinson, Martha Graham..167,269-70
Hutchinson, Mary...270,276
Hutchinson, Mary Ruby...277
Hutchinson, Mary Ruby...278
Hutchinson, Mary Swinney...276
Hutchinson, Mildred...277
Hutchinson, Myrl Sprout...278
Hutchinson, Samantha...270,275
Hutchinson, Samuel...269-70
Hutchinson, Samuel W...277
Hutchinson, Sarah D...270,271
Hutchinson, Sarah Delamater...269
Hutchinson, William G...270,276
Idom, Ada Jones...456
Idom, Harlin A...456
Idom, Melissa D...456
Iglesias y Calderon, Juan D...493
Iglesias y Loli, Juan A...493
Iglesias, Lastenia...493
Ingalls, David...311
Ingalls, Jennifer...311
Ingalls, Margaret Leslie...311
Inman, Cora Crockett...229
Inman, Ethel L...229
Inman, Harry...229
Inman, John...229
Inman, Melissa A...230
Inman, William...229
Ipock, Macie Gault...102
Isaacson, John A...412
Isaacson, Keith...412
Isaacson, Mary...412
Isaacson, Sophia Graham...350,412
Isom, Autry j...217
Isom, Emma J...217
Isom, Lena M...217
Isom, Margaret C...217
Isom, Mary E...217
Isom, Nathaniel...217
Isom, Nathaniel Jr...217
Isom, Trotty Dawson...217
Isom, Vera D...217
Isom, William B...217
Jack, David M...135
Jack, Hallie B...135
Jack, Laura H...135
Jack, Laura Harrison...134
Jack, Nannie Knox...134

Jack, Thomas M...134-5
Jack, Thomas M. Jr...135
Jack, William H...134
Jackson, Alice B...291
Jackson, Clara M...291
Jackson, Florence Mundorff...290
Jackson, George O...290
Jackson, Jane V...203
Jacobson, Alden D...387,388
Jacobson, Carol E...388
Jacobson, Connie Richards...388
Jacobson, Deborah...388
Jacobson, Dorothy Myers...389
Jacobson, Edward G...388
Jacobson, Elizabeth Berger...388
Jacobson, Elizabeth Graham...295,387
Jacobson, Ella Peters...388
Jacobson, Gail Rodene...388
Jacobson, Helen M...387,388
Jacobson, Jeanette E...387,388
Jacobson, Julie E...389
Jacobson, Karen J...388
Jacobson, Lillian Suttle...388
Jacobson, Marian Mahoney...388
Jacobson, Newell E...387,389
Jacobson, Peter W...387
Jacobson, Philip A...389
Jacobson, Richard W...388
Jacobson, Robert D...388
Jacobson, Tess Dordal...388
Jacobson, Victor G...387,388
Jacobson, Wesley C...387,388
Jacobson, William A...389
Jacques, Carole Cline...369
Jacques, Marcia A...369
Jacques, Mark I...369
Jacques, Maureen E...369
Jacques, Michelle L...369
Jacques, Richard I...369
James, Elizabeth Oates...229
James, Ethel M...485
James, Jock T...229
James, Lula E...216
Janssen, Karen...430
Jeans, George W...201
Jeans, Minerva Ladd...201
Jeans, Minnie L...201,211
Jenkins, Annie...152
Jenkins, Laurie Olmstead...433
Jewell, Blake...344
Jewell, Jestina...154
Jewell, Louise...344
Jewell, M.G...344
Jewell, Mary Blake...343,344
Jewell, Melville...344
Jewell, Merritt...344
Jobe, Alvin L...102
Jobe, Arlena L...103
Jobe, Elizabeth J...103
Jobe, Eugene...103
Jobe, Florette...102
Jobe, Frank...102
Jobe, Grady G...102
Jobe, James K...102
Jobe, James L...103
Jobe, John...103

Jobe, John H...102
Jobe, John H...103
Jobe, Joseph...103
Jobe, L.M...103
Jobe, Mary -----...102
Jobe, Mary Dale...103
Jobe, Mary Gault...102
Jobe, Mary R...103
Jobe, Nancy A...103
Jobe, Nancy E...103
Jobe, Nancy Gleghorn...102
Jobe, Nancy L...103
Jobe, Ozella...102
Jobe, P.Y...103
Jobe, Rebecca...102
Jobe, Riley...103
Jobe, Sallie...103
Jobe, Samuel...102
Jobe, Samuel...103
Jobe, Velma...102
Jobe, Virgil...102
Jobe, Walter S...103
Jobe, Zederick...102
Joffyees see Coffee
Johnson, Albert A...380
Johnson, Bertha...77
Johnson, Carmen...431
Johnson, Charlotte M...380
Johnson, Charlotte Peterson...380
Johnson, Clara M...77
Johnson, David...76-7
Johnson, Dellaphine...105
Johnson, Donna...238
Johnson, Dorothy Hughes...340,341
Johnson, Eliza Godwin...105
Johnson, Elvira N...77
Johnson, Emma...77
Johnson, Emma...134
Johnson, Florence...77
Johnson, Frances...77
Johnson, Frank...77
Johnson, Grace Gault...98,104,117
Johnson, Herbert T...341
Johnson, Hester K...77
Johnson, James...98,104,117
Johnson, Lucy E...77
Johnson, Martha J...77
Johnson, Mary...77
Johnson, Mary (3-1G)...98,117,125
Johnson, Mary A...77
Johnson, Mary Adams...76-7
Johnson, Mary E...77
Johnson, Mildred L...77
Johnson, Olive...77
Johnson, Rebecca...98,104
Johnson, Robert R...77
Johnson, Samuel D...105
Johnson, Samuel E...77
Johnson, Sarah Stipp...77
Johnson, William G...77
Johnson, Zera Denton...77
Johnston, Dennis...359
Johnston, Mabel...238
Johnston, Patricia Tolle...359-60
Johnstone, Alan...403
Johnstone, Elizabeth Beard...403

Johnstone, Judy...403
Johnstone, Judy Kane...403
Johnstone, Kenneth G...403
Johnstone, Margaret...403
Johnstone, Susan...403
Joiner, Joe...216
Joiner, Lula James...216
Joiner, Nellie...219
Joiner, Ony G...216
Jones, Ada O...456
Jones, Beatrice...455
Jones, Becky J...154
Jones, Bert...424
Jones, Betty Beatty...502
Jones, Chelsea A...503
Jones, Elizabeth Cooper...154
Jones, John K...502
Jones, John K. Jr...502-3
Jones, Lee...113
Jones, Linsey R...503
Jones, Lorena McClerkin..178
Jones, Lucretia Gleghorn...115
Jones, Lulu Graham...366,424
Jones, Margaret A...118
Jones, Mary...324
Jones, Rae G...154
Jones, Ronald...154
Jones, Sarah Gleghorn...113
Jones, Sue Graham...473,502-3
Jones, Susan A...359
Jones, William...115
Joubert, Beatrice Jones...455
Joubert, Louis...455
Joubert, Mary C...455
Joy, Lou A...220
Juckett, Alice Barbo...472
Juckett, Jennifer McCallum...472
Juckett, Lorene A...472
Juckett, Lyle B...472
Juckett, Russell B...472
Juckett, Russell B. Jr..472
Kahman, Betty Stuckey..153
Kahman, Howard...153
Kahman, Howard Jr...153
Kahman, Jerry...153
Kane, Judy...403
Karnes, Aline...368
Kasten, Dennis D...478
Kasten, Jean Palmer...478
Kasten, Paul...478
Kasten, Velova Koepse...478
Kasten, Victoria R...478
Katch, Kimberly Ross...454
Katch, Kurt...454
Kauffman, Betty...394
Kauffman, Earl...393
Kauffman, Edie...393
Kauffman, Erica...394
Kauffman, Gregg...393
Kauffman, Gretchen...394
Kauffman, John...393-4
Kauffman, Karen...393
Kauffman, Kate...393
Kauffman, Kenneth...393
Kauffman, Kenneth Jr...393
Kauffman, Virginia Simpson...393

Keeny, Enid E...153
Keesler, Clyde C...463
Keesler, Frances J...463
Keesler, Norma Van Surdam...463
Kehoe, Ardelle Huffman...206
Kehoe, Christopher J...206
Keister, Ethel Elliott...307
Keister, George...307
Keister, Sarah E...307
Kell, Amy E...360-1
Kell, Carla Bodner...361
Kell, Eileen Fitzgerald...361
Kell, Katharine Tolle...360
Kell, Joseph C...360
Kell, Joseph M...361
Kell, Matthew K...362
Keller, Amy...446
Kelly, Brian...308
Kelly, Diana Berlin...308
Kelly, Frances...79
Kelly, John R...308
Kelly, Mahala K...207,208
Kelly, Margaret Whiteman...308
Kelly, Melinda...308
Kelly, Ollie Smith...308
Kelly, Owen...308
Kelly, Rollyn G...308
Kelly, Shannon...308
Kelly, Susan J...308
Kempf, Patricia M...501
Kennard, Alice F...281
Kennedy, Clara Graham...253,334-5
Kennedy, Edwin J...335
Kennedy, Elsie Dorimus...335
Kennedy, James A...334-5
Kennedy, Joan B...335
Kennedy, Joseph P...335
Kennedy, Mary...335
Kennedy, Mary C...334
Kennedy, Patricia...335
Kennedy, Paul...335
Kennedy, William...334
Kennedy, William G...335
Kennedy, Zelma Ackley...335
Kent, Mary...105
Kersey, Martha...328
Keyburn, Kathy A...490
Keyburn, Margaret Graham...454,490
Keyburn, Robert G...490
Keyburn, Terri L...490
Keyburn, Thomas E...490
Keyburn, William J...490
Kidd, Mary Dickey...103
Kidmore, Sarah...319
Kifer, Ella Heinemeyer...124
Kifer, Howard B..124
Kifer, Ida Gleghorn...124
Kifer, Lee...124
Kileen, Andrea Smith...275
Killabrew, Anna McWilliams...203
Killabrew, William...203
Kincaid, Anna...148,164
Kindle, Mildred...310
King, Ardelle Smith...425
King, Oma...182
King, Sarah Crockett...229

King, Walter B...229
Kingery, Teresa J...490
Kinney, Eula Lockart...199,201
Kinney, Kitty M...219
Kinney, Obadiah...201
Kinney, Thurman...199,201
Kinney, Willie Greggs...201
Kirk, Bernice L...450
Kirk, Lila J...274
Kirkpatrick, Clara McCoy...329
Kirkpatrick, Elizabeth Lowe...329
Kirkpatrick, Francis A...329
Kirkpatrick, Gilbert E...329
Kloxin, Bertha P...370
Knabe, Elsie...445
Knapp, Ann...311
Knapp, Gail...311
Knapp, H.D...311
Knapp, Jane E...311
Knapp, John...311
Knapp, Patricia McMillan...311
Knight, Anne...282
Knight, Eunice Dugdale...282
Knox, Hannah Mills..130,132-3
Knox, James..133
Knox, James Jr...133
Knox, Jane McElroy...133
Knox, John...133
Knox, Lucy...136
Knox, Margaret...136
Knox, Mary J...133
Knox, Minnie...135-6
Knox, Nancy Mills...132-3
Knox, Nannie...134
Knox, Rowena G...134
Knox, Sarah...193
Knox, Virginia...134
Knox, William J...133
Koch, Lois...435
Koepke, Jessie Graham...434,482
Koepke, Roland...482
Koepse, Velova...478
Kohnfelder, Lenora L...419
Koll, Edwin F...472
Koll, Nettie Gibson...472
Koll, Velores M...472
Komarek, Theresa...507
Komosinski, Leokadia...360
Kone, Henry H...378
Kone, John H...378
Kone, Myrtle Graham..293,378
Korsgarden, Gladys...452
Kramer, Marie...432
Kramer, Marjorie M...432
Kramer, Roy...432
Krautzkampf, Larry...403
Krautzkampf, Margaret Johnstone..403
Krawetzki, Dorothy E...430
Kroener, Victoria...424
Krotzinger, Diane Lemke...439
Krotzinger, Eric J...439
Krotzinger, Francis...439
Krotzinger, Francis Jr...439
Krotzinger, Heath J...439
Krotzinger, Kayla R...439
Krotzinger, Kris L...439

Krotzinger, Kyle R...439
Krotzinger, Marilyn Grauer...439
Krug, Alvin F...426
Krug, Arlene Graham...366,426
Kruska, Pamela A...504
Kubes, Candice A...505
Kubes, Laura K...505
Kubes, Michael A...505
Kubes, Valerie Graham...482,505
Kuhl, Andrew P...419
Kuhl, Barbara J...419
Kuhl, Charles A...419
Kuhl, Dwight C...419-20
Kuhl, Gayna Dawson...419-20
Kuhl, Katharine L...419
Kuhl, Lenora Kohnfelder...419
Kuhl, Nancy Avery...419
Kuhl, Nancy L...419
Kukielka, Joseph...360
Kukielka, Leokadia Komosinski...360
Kumagai, Julie Spicer...397
Kumagai, Nathan...397
Kumagai, Philip...397
Kumagai, Robert...397
Lackland, John W...123
Lackland, Maggie...123
Lackland, Margaret Gleghorn...123
Lackland, Martha...123
Lackland, Mary...123
Lackland, Robert A...123
Ladd, Annie M...198
Ladd, Martha E...209
Ladd, Minerva A...201
LaFollette, Charles...151
LaFollette, Elva Gartin...151
LaFollette, Gerald L...483
LaFollette, Jason L...483
LaFollette, Sheri Duntz...482,483
LaFollette, Travis J...483
LaFollette, Tyler W...483
Lamb, James...356-7
Lamb, James G...356
Lamb, Katharine Graham...265,356
Lamb, Louis K...356
Lamb, Margaret Taylor...357
Lamb, Sarah Carnine...356
Lambright, Eliza Gleghorn...125
Lambright, Josiah M...125
Lampkin, Narcissus J...107
Landshur, Betty...323
Lang, Sara C...271
Lanneau, A.S...146
Lanneau, Minnie Shrader...146
Lanphear, Mary...471
Lant, Charles E...248
Lant, Lulu Porter...248
Lapish, Catherine...465
Lapish, Elizabeth...465
Lapish, Henry...465
Larimer, David...152
Larimer, Sallie Funk...152
Larimore, Mary A.E...182
Larson, Alma E...492
Laskey, Ida...210
Lathan, Sarah...177
Laurence, Alice...208

Lavelle, Alice M...218-9
Lavelle, Alton H...218
Lavelle, Bridgett...218
Lavelle, Effie Baskin...219
Lavelle, Eris Huffman...219
Lavelle, Eurania Burlison...218
Lavelle, Gladys V...219
Lavelle, Herbert L.V...219
Lavelle, Herman G...219
Lavelle, James E...219
Lavelle, James F...218
Lavelle, James N...218
Lavelle, James Nathan...218
Lavelle, Jessie B...218
Lavelle, Lawrence R...219
Lavelle, M.A...218
Lavelle, Manon F...218
Lavelle, Marion Roberge...218
Lavelle, Marshall E...219
Lavelle, Martha Baskin...219
Lavelle, Mary S...218
Lavelle, Nelle...218
Lavelle, Nellie Joiner...219
Lavelle, Olien E...219
Lavelle, Onie Dawson...219
Lavelle, Pattie Cousar...219
Lavelle, Robbie Merritt...219
Lavelle, Roy E...219
Lavelle, Sarah Dawson...218
Lavelle, Telitha Agnes...218
Lavelle, Telitha Ann...210
Lavelle, Telitha Hartsfield...218
Lavelle, Thomas...219
Lavelle, Veda Fleming...219
Lawrence, Bernice Gay...199
Lawrence, Ella Caskey...198-9
Lawrence, James G.K...199
Lawrence, Lena Huggins...199
Lawrence, Marie Delancy...199
Lawrence, Mary H...455
Lawrence, Thomas J...198-9
Lawson, Brenda...370
Leach, Anna Huffman...210
Leach, Annie Evans...151
Leach, John...151
Leach, Margaret H...210
Leach, Oscar S...210
Ledford, Margaret Gleghorn...101
Lee, Nelle Ruth...372
Leggett, Alexander...386
Leggett, Anne S...386
Leggett, Elizabeth E...386
Leggett, Jane A...386
Leggett, John G...386
Leggett, Margaret Thorne...386
Leggett, Martha S...386
Leggett, Richard A...386
Leggett, Ruth Wimmer...386
Lemke, Diane K...439
Leslie, Bill...310
Leslie, Charles...310
Leslie, David...310
Leslie, Jane McMillan...310
Leslie, Joe...310
Leslie, Margaret J...311
Leslie, Mildred Kindle...310

Leslie, Stacie...310
Leslie, Steven...310
Leslie, Susan O'Neal...310
Leslie, Thomas H...310
Leslie, William J...310
Lethem, Charles...116
Lethem, Minnie Porter...116
Lewellen, Penny S...383
Lewis, James O...325
Lewis, Marian Cowden...325
Lewis, Scott...325
Lewis, Sean...325
Lewis, William...325
Lewkow, Pearl Glick...374
Leymann, Suzanne...359
Light, Arnold...453
Light, Dorothy Graham...380,453
Light, Elaine Taylor...453
Light, Raymond...453
Lightfoot, Oma King...182
Liles, Ida M...185
Lillihaug, Deloris...163
Lincoln, Abraham...502
Lincoln, Col. George...147
Lincoln, George...147
Lincoln, Harriett Shanklin...164
Lincoln, James...147
Lincoln, Lucy...147
Lincoln, Patricia Kempf...501
Lincoln, Robert...147
Lincoln, Roy F...501
Lincoln, Sarah Thompson...147
LIncoln, Stephen...147
Lincoln, Susan R...501-2
Lincoln, Walter...164
Linderman, Clifton E...232
Linderman, Harriett Smith...232
Lindsay, Lydia A...350
Linnel, Betty J...421
Linnel, Beverly...421
Linnel, Ida Graham...364,420
Linnel, Iva A...421
Linnel, Kevin L...421
Linnel, Richard...420
Linnel, Richard V...421
Linnel, Richard V. Jr...421
Linnel, Robin...421
Linnel, Vickie D...421
Lipes, Barbara J...279
Lipes, Betsy J...279
Lipes, Bonnie J...279
Lipes, Gerald...279
Lipes, Jerry E...279
Lipes, Lillian Hutchinson...279
Lipscomb, Derrick L...495
Lipscomb, Emily S...496
Lipscomb, Marcellus P...495
Lipscomb, Martha Graham...495
Lipscomb, Nellie Flint...495
Livingston, Elizabeth...382
Livingston, Virginia A...277
Lockart, Allie Wiseman...201
Lockart, Annie J...201
Lockart, Edith...201
Lockart, Eula G...199,201
Lockart, James E...201

Lockart, Jane Stephenson...201
Lockart, John B....201
Lockart, Martha A...216
Lockart, Mary Gay...201
Lockart, Mary McWilliams...201
Lockwood, G.A...319
Lockwood, James E...319
Lockwood, Jane...319
Lockwood, Mabel Moir...319
Lockwood, Robert...319
Lockwood, Sarah Kidmore...319
Lofton, Blanche...191
Lofton, Effie Ford...191
Lofton, John...191
Loli, Lastenia...493
Long, Elizabeth..234
Long, Iris...272
Lorts, Louisa Glick...374
Lorts, William J...374
Lourie, Eliza M...335
Love, Anna Thompson...148
Love, James...148
Lowe, Elizabeth...329
Lowe, Jennie...152
Lowe, Margaret Gartin...151
Lowe, Nellie...152
Lowe, Percival G...151
Lowe, Percival G. Jr...152
Lowe, Wilson...151
Lowman, Minone...405
Ludwig, Jo Anne Cowden...325
Ludwig, John...325
Lungren, Angela L...275
Lungren, John...275
Lungren, Richard...275
Lungren, Sharon Welch...275
Luttrell, Hazel...205
Luysch, Marilyn...489
Luzum, Bryan T...506
Luzum, Jeremy J...506
Luzum, Lynda Graham...506
Luzum, Shawndra L...506
Luzum, Thomas J...506
Lyles, Helen...183
Lyles, Margaret Isom...217
Lyles, Ruth Billings...182
Lyles, Thomas...217
Lyles, Walter W...182,183
Lynch, Ethel R. E...434
Lynn, Alexander...247
Lynn, Elizabeth McQuiston...175
Lynn, Elmer J...203-4
Lynn, Emma McDougal..203-4
Lynn, infant...204
Lynn, James A...203
Lynn, Jane Jackson...203
Lynn, John...175
Lynn, John C...204
Lynn, John P...203
Lynn, Margaret Caskey...203
Lynn, Marietta...247
Lynn, Martha E...203
Lynn, Rosanna A...203
Lynn, Rosanna Adams...203
Lynn, Sarah Appleby...247
Lynn, Sarah J...175

Lynn, William D...204
Lyons, Elizabeth E...395
Maben, Andrew...140
Maben, Jane/Jennet...142-4,148-9
Maben, John...140
Maben, Margaret...142-5
Maben, Mary A...319
Maben, Mary Graham...74,140-3
Maben, Sarah...142-4
Maberry, Frances...451
MacRobert, Elizabeth...293
Maddox, Josephine...219
Mahaffey, Frances...308
Mahoney, Marian M...388
Mansfield, Sharon Stohs...481
Mansfield, Stephanie R...481
Marek, Kathryn Barnes...469
Marek, Wesley...469
Marine, Marianne...306
Marion, Agnes/Nancy...192-3
Marion, Jennet Stewart...192
Marion, William...192
Markey, Barbara Bishop...390
Markey, John...390
Markey, Pamela...390
Markey, Patricia...390
Markey, Theresa...390
Marschman, Beulah Schmidt...486
Marschman, Dale D...486
Marschman, Daniel D...486
Marschman, Edwin...486
Marschman, Judith Graham...443,486
Marschman, Kendra...486
Marschman, Leigh A...486
Marschman, Renae L...486
Marshall, Annie M...207
Marshall, Dale T...375
Marshall, James...375
Marshall, James A...206,207
Marshall, John M...375
Marshall, Lela E...375
Marshall, Mae Graham...293,375
Marshall, Mary Gladden...206,207
Marshall, Nancy E...207
Marshall, Thelma...206
Martin, Andrew W...300
Martin, Ann Taylor...300
Martin, Annie B...300,301
Martin, Cynthia Griffith...213
Martin, Dorinda J...300,301
Martin, Grace...308
Martin, Ida M..300,301
Martin, John B...300,301
Martin, Lucinda...212
Martin, Martha Dickey...103
Martin, Mary E...329
Martin, Mary Graham...173,300
Martin, Preston...300
Martin, Samuel P...300,301
Martin, Welton...213
Martin, Rev William...14-15,17-19
Mason, Douglas C...437
Mason, Virginia Page...437
Massengill, Ardella G...213
Massie, George W...216
Massie, Saphronia Dawson...216-7

Mauk, Helen...412
Mauk, Lillian Graham...350,412
Mauk, Margaret...412
Mauk, Raymond...412
Mauk, William A...412
Maxey, Patricia...323
Maxwell, Augusta...230
Maxwell, Barbara Hughes...277
Maxwell, Basil B...230
Maxwell, Beth M...231
Maxwell, Ellen...247
Maxwell, Fitz L...231
Maxwell, Frances C...231
Maxwell, Frances McDougall...247
Maxwell, Frances Smith...230
Maxwell, Henry L...277
Maxwell, Howard...247
Maxwell, Howard E...277
Maxwell, Howard S...231
Maxwell, Howard S...231
Maxwell, James...247
Maxwell, Jean...247
Maxwell, Jennie S...230
Maxwell, John Basil...230
Maxwell, John Bonner...231
Maxwell, John Bonner Jr...231
Maxwell, Lantye Turnage...230
Maxwell, Lela Buchanan...230
Maxwell, Luther M...230
Maxwell, Maria Clark...277
Maxwell, Martha...247
Maxwell, Martha W...230,231
Maxwell, Mary House...231
Maxwell, Medora W...230,231
Maxwell, Neva McGregor...231
Maxwell, Thomas H...277
Maxwell, William H...277
May, M.D...124
May, Mary Gleghorn...124
May, Ruth L...195
May, W.G...124
Mayes, Bryant C...496
Mayes, Frances B...496-7
Mayes, Frances Blake...496
Mayne, John...354
Mayne, Louie J...354
Mayne, Nancy Dale...354
Mayo, Leonard...163
Mayo, Martha Hardesty...163
McAdam, Mary J...279
McAlister, Mary V...212
McBride, Hannah...279
McBride, Lilly Ada...182
McBride, Mary Larimore...182
McBride, William W...182
McCalla, Agnes...192
McCalla, Virgin...183
McCallum, Erma Graham...423,471-2
McCallum, Jennifer L...472
McCallum, Mary Lanphear...471
McCallum, William G...471-2
McCallum, William H...471
McCarroll, Nancy...205
McClaery, Carl...194
McClaery, John...194-5
McClaery, Mary Caskey...194-5

McClellan, Barbara J..431
McClellan, Candace Berenstein..430
McClellan, Carmen Johnson...431
McClellan, Christopher W...430
McClellan, Crystal S...431
McClellan, Danielle R...432
McClellan, Diane...431
McClellan, Donald E...430
McClellan, Donald M...430
McClellan, Duane J...432
McClellan, Eugene R...430,439
McClellan, Eugene R. Jr...430
McClellan, Everett J...430
McClellan, Janet L...431
McClellan, Janet Pooch...430,439
McClellan, Joni Whitebread...430,439
McClellan, Judy Dalton...431
McClellan, Judy Weber...430
McClellan, Karen Janssen...430
McClellan, Larry...431
McClellan, Margie M...430,431
McClellan, Mark A...431
McClellan, Marla K...430
McClellan, Richard D...430,431
McClellan, Roberta...430
McClellan, Samantha A...430
McClellan, Shawn E...430
McClellan, Thelma Graham...366,429-30
McClellan, Timothy R...430
McClellan, William E...430,439
McClerkin, Alice...179
McClerkin, Ann McQuiston...179,185
McClerkin, Annie Turnage...179
McClerkin, Charles M...179
McClerkin, Elizabeth M...179
McClerkin, Eva...179
McClerkin, Eva E...178
McClerkin, Gussie Price...179
McClerkin, Herbert H...178
McClerkin, Inez...179
McClerkin, infant...178
McClerkin, Ivy Hamilton...178
McClerkin, J.M...179
McClerkin, James C...178-9
McClerkin, James C. Jr...179
McClerkin, James M...177
McClerkin, James Martin...177
McClerkin, John M...179,185
McClerkin, Lorena...178
McClerkin, Margrete Easley...179
McClerkin, Martha...178
McClerkin, Mary Adkinson...178
McClerkin, Mary E...178
McClerkin, Mary J...177,187
McClerkin, Nancy M...185
McClerkin, Ola Williams...179
McClerkin, Rosanna Hindman...177
McClerkin, Samuel T...178
McClerkin, Sarah E.B...178
McClerkin, Sarah Lathan...177
McClerkin, Sidney E...179
McClerkin, William E...179
McClerkin, Willie I...178
McConaha, Judith A...479
McConnel, Marian...399
McConnell, Cornelia...264

McConnell, David G...339
McConnell, George W...264
McConnell, Graham S...339
McConnell, Helen...339
McConnell, Helen Slagle...339
McConnell, Hugh...338-9
McConnell, John S...339
McConnell, Laura Brown...339
McConnell, Laura Graham...253,338-9
McConnell, Luther G...339
McConnell, Marjorie B...339
McConnell, Martha...338
McConnell, Martha T...339
McConnell, Mary...339
McConnell, Mary E...339
McConnell, Sarah...339
McCormick, Agnes McCalla...192
McCormick, Allen M...185
McCormick, Alta Simmons...191
McCormick, B.M...186
McCormick, Blanche Lofton...191
McCormick, Carl W...187
McCormick, Charles...186
McCormick, Clara McCullough...186
McCormick, Clarence L...192
McCormick, Claude H...184
McCormick, Claudius...183
McCormick, Clifton T...183
McCormick, Cora McQuiston...191
McCormick, Elizabeth Cox...186
McCormick, Elizabeth Hindman...181-2
McCormick, Elizabeth Teasley...191
McCormick, Estes V...187
McCormick, Everett R...191
McCormick, Faires R...183
McCormick, Fay...186
McCormick, George N...185
McCormick, Grover N...185
McCormick, Helen Lyles...183
McCormick, infant...182,183,185,187, 192
McCormick, Ivee Sheppard...187
McCormick, James R...183
McCormick, James S...184
McCormick, James W...184
McCormick, Jennie Lowe...152
McCormick, John L...190
McCormick, John W...183
McCormick, Katherine...186
McCormick, Laura E...182-3
McCormick, Laura F...186
McCormick, Laura Paine...185
McCormick, Leslie E...184
McCormick, Lilly McBride...182
McCormick, Lloyd...152
McCormick, Lomas E...191
McCormick, Lorenzo T...187
McCormick, Lucia E...185
McCormick, Lucy Yancey...183
McCormick, Margaret Abernathy...184
McCormick, Margaret Fairies...183
McCormick, Margaret Furgerson...184
McCormick, Margaret R.A...182
McCormick, Margaret Witherington..184
McCormick, Margie Simonton...184
McCormick, Marvin E...186

McCormick, Mary A...184
McCormick, Mary Byrd...186
McCormick, Mary Cockrell...186
McCormick, Mary J...184
McCormick, Mary Hindman...190-1
McCormick, Mary R...186
McCormick, Mary Rainey...181,185,191
McCormick, Mary W...184
McCormick, Mildred Durr...186
McCormick, N. Bate...185-6
McCormick, Nancy G...191
McCormick, Nancy McClerkin...185
McCormick, Nathaniel R...181-2
McCormick, Norris R...183
McCormick, Olive E...184-5
McCormick, Ora Burrow...186
McCormick, Oscar B...186
McCormick, Oscar W...186
McCormick, Othello S...184
McCormick, Pearl...187
McCormick, Ralph N...186
McCormick, Robbie Moore..187
McCormick, Roscoe M...191
McCormick, Rudolph B..186
McCormick, Sadie ---...183
McCormick, Sadie M...183
McCormick, Sam E...186
McCormick, Samuel...181,185,190-1
McCormick, Sarah Hindman...185
McCormick, Viola G...191
McCormick, Virgin McCalla...183
McCormick, Virginia Murphy...184
McCormick, Willard C...191
McCormick, William S...186
McCormick, William T...182
McCormick, Winnie Norris...183
McCoy, Albert G...328-9
McCoy, Albert G. Jr...329
McCoy, Clara E...329
McCoy, Clara Graham...251,328-9
McCoy, Estelle...329
McCoy, Geraldine...397
McCoy, Hugh W...329
McCoy, James...275
McCoy, James A...329
McCoy, Laura E...275
McCoy, Louella M...276
McCoy, Mary Creswell...275
McCoy, Patsy...329
McCoy, Samantha Hutchinson...270,275
McCoy, Virgie...494
McCoy, William...275
McCreight, Eleanor...155
McCreight, Nancy...155
McCreight, Robert...155
McCuie, Katherine...468
McCullough, Clara...186
McCullough, Elizabeth Moore..188
McCullough, John L...185
McCullough, Margaret R...187-8
McCullough, Pauline Smith...185
McCullough, Robert B...188
McCurran, Henry...418
McCurran, Joan Smillie...418
McDaniel, Fountain P...230
McDaniel, Frances Boyd...230

McDaniel, Howard M...230,231
McDaniel, Hurdle E...230,231
McDaniel, Hurdle E. Jr...230
McDaniel, Margaret L...232
McDaniel, Martha Maxwell..230,231
McDaniel, Melissa Inman...230
McDaniel, Rebecca Riddick...230,231
McDaniel, Virginia Blair...230
McDill, Andrew T...237,239
McDill, Charlotte Thorpe...395
McDill, David C...395
McDill, E. Emma Gowdy...239
McDill, Elizabeth...306
McDill, infant...237
McDill, James...236,240
McDill, James C...237
McDill, John A...240
McDill, Lee H...239
McDill, Lydia A...240
McDill, Margaret...237
McDill, Margaret Chesnut...236,240
McDill, Margaret E...237,240
McDill, Martha...240
McDill, Martha A...304
McDill, Martha C...240
McDill, Martha E...237
McDill, Martha Graham...140,236
McDill, Martha J...237,238
McDill, Mary E...395
McDill, Mary Eliza...284
McDill, Mary Porter...284,304
McDill, Matthew H...237,238
McDill, Nancy Findley...236
McDill, Noveen...239
McDill, Ora...239
McDill, Quintin...240
McDill, Ray...239
McDill, Ray ---...239
McDill, Robert...284,304
McDill, Robert R...240
McDill, Samuel...236-7
McDill, Samuel F...240
McDill, Sarah McQuiston...237
McDill, William J...240
McDill, William W...239
McDonald, Eileen E...491
McDonald, Emma E...406
McDonald, Jessie...406
McDonald, Sadie McCormick...183
McDonald, Sandra...470
McDonald, William H...183
McDougal, Bertha Wilson...203
McDougal, Emma A...203-4
McDougal, Harold...203
McDougal, James H...203
McDougal, Lucille Miller...203
McDougal, Martha Lynn...203
McDougal, William J...203
McDougall, Alice Porter...246
McDougall, Clifford...276
McDougall, Daniel...247
McDougall, Ellen Bain...270
McDougall, Ellen Hutchinson...270
McDougall, Frances...247
McDougall, Frederica...247
McDougall, James...270

McDougall, John...271
McDougall, John H...270
McDougall, John W...247
McDougall, Louella McCoy...276
McDougall, Luetta...270
McDougall, Maggie Thompson...270
McDougall, Martha Stevenson...247
McDougall, Pear...276
McDow, Mary McCormick...186
McDow, Thomas...186
McDowell, David...138
McDowell, Edward...138
McDowell, Eliza...138
McDowell, James...138
McDowell, James R...138
McDowell, Jane/Jennette...138
McDowell, Jane Mills...130,138
McDowell, Katherine Bonner...138
McDowell, Mary...138
McDowell, Rose...138
McDowell, Ruth Bonner...138
McDowell, William...138
McElmurry, Fannie...106
McElroy, Jane...133
McFerrin, Nancy Jobe...103
McGaw, Jane E...314-5
McGowan, Cora Hindman...189
McGowan, Dorothy Watts...189
McGowan, Joseph B...189
McGowan, Justin B...189
McGowan, Laurie T...189
McGowan, Margaret English...189
McGowan, Mary G...189
McGowan, William O...189
McGregor, John...169,171-2
McGregor, Nancy Graham...74,169-72
McGregor, Neva...231
McGuire, Elizabeth B...392
McHugh, Adele...282
McIntosh, Dean...301
McIntosh, Dorinda Martin...300,301
McIntosh, Jack...301
McIntosh, John M...301
McIntosh, Marjorie...301
McIntosh, Maude...301
McKay, Margaret...441
McKechnie, Judith...309
McKee, Janet...127
McKee, John...156
McKee, Martha B...156-7,161
McKee, Nancy Collins...156
McKelvie, Frances N...397
McKelvie, Frank A...397
McKelvie, Pearl Wixson...397
McKnight, Judith...278
McLaughlin, Goldie Smith...185
McLaughlin, John...178
McLaughlin, John...185
McLaughlin, Joseph...273
McLaughlin, Margaret Wilson...178
McLaughlin, Mary...273
McLaughlin, Mary A...184
McLaughlin, Mary McClerkin...178
McLaughlin, Nancy...273
McLaughlin, William R...178
McLean, ---...398

McLister, Effie Dewese...178
McLister, Emily Faucett...212
McLister, John C...212
McLister, Julia Mills...212
McLister, Lizzie A.V...189,207
McLister, Lucius Q.C.L...212
McLister, Margaret E...189
McLister, Waldo A...178
McLister, William A...178
McLister, Willie McClerkin...178
McMartin, Barbara Baird...282
McMartin, Ray...282
McMartin, Richard...282
McMartin, W.J...282
McMehan, Mary A...343
McMillan, Anna M...306
McMillan, Edward A...306,310
McMillan, Elizabeth...310
McMillan, Florence Watson...310
McMillan, Graham W...310
McMillan, Jane...310
McMillan, Jessie B...306
McMillan, JoAnne Green...311
McMillan, John...306
McMillan, Laura...306,308
McMillan, Martha Graham...241,306
McMillan, Mary A...310
McMillan, Mary Ross...310
McMillan, Mary Senseman...311
McMillan, Michelle...311
McMillan, Patricia...311
McMillan, Robert...311
McMillan, Robert T...306
McMillan, Steven...311
McMillan, Walter W...306,311
McMillan, Wendy...311
McNeel, Elizabeth...137
McNicol, Marilyn...306
McPeak, Bradie Blankenship...209
McPeak, Clarence...209
McQueen, Indiana...78
McQuiston, Ann...179,185
McQuiston, Calpuria Raymond...191
McQuiston, Cora J...191
McQuiston, Elizabeth...175
McQuiston, James...237
McQuiston, James A...180
McQuiston, Jane...89
McQuiston, Jane Allen...180
McQuiston, Jennet...261
McQuiston, Margaret McDill...237
McQuiston, Mary Hindman...180
McQuiston, Nancy J...176
McQuiston, Sarah...237
McQuiston, Sarah A...177
McQuiston, Thomas C...191
McQuiston, William H...180
McQuown, Arthur O...283
McQuown, Mary A...283
McQuown, Nancy Smith...283
McRobert see MacRobert
McRoberts, Alta...195
McWilliams, Anna E...202
McWilliams, Anna M...203
McWilliams, Anna Pinner...202
McWilliams, Bessie Huffman...201,211

McWilliams, Bryce W...202,203
McWilliams, Christine...203
McWilliams, Clyde (two people)...202
McWilliams, Clyde...210
McWilliams, David C...194,200
McWilliams, Dollie Abernathy...202
McWilliams, Elizabeth...194,200
McWilliams, Ernest E...202
McWilliams, George P...201,211
McWilliams, Grace Mills...202,203,213
McWilliams, infant...200,202
McWilliams, James H...203
McWilliams, James W...202
McWilliams, Joanna Caskey..200,210,
  218
McWilliams, John F...202,203,213
McWilliams, Kirby T...202
McWilliams, Malcomb...203
McWilliams, Margie L...202-3
McWilliams, Mary...201
McWilliams, Mary E...201
McWilliams, Mary J...194,200
McWilliams, Minnie Jeans...201,211
McWilliams, Nancy B...201,217
McWilliams, Norma...201
McWilliams, Ola Baskin...201
McWilliams, Ola I...202
McWilliams, Olvi G...202
McWilliams, Oma Rose...202
McWilliams, Pauline...203
McWilliams, Pressly B...200,210,217
McWilliams, Robert J...201
McWilliams, Ruth...201
McWilliams, Tabatha Wilson...203
McWilliams, Thelma L...202,203
McWilliams, Velma...201
McWilliams, Walter A...201,211
Meador, Linda T...442
Meek, Sarah...142
Meier, Emma Caskey...195
Meier, Otto...195
Melton, Effie F...202,210
Mench, Clara McCoy...329
Mench, Jack L..329
Menely, Jane...238
Mentz, Barbara...291
Mentz, Clara Jackson...291
Mentz, Elizabeth...291
Mentz, Walter T...291
Mercer, Frances Phelps...462
Mercer, Lauren G...462
Mercer, Vernon S...462
Merrill, Connie Graham...473,501
Merrill, John L...501
Merritt, Ella Gwinn...219
Merritt, Forest Edward...154
Merritt, Forest Eugene...154
Merritt, Robbie...219
Merritt, Robert W...219
Merritt, Thelma Cooper...154
Messenger, John D...369
Messenger, Kristen K...370
Messenger, Mary C...369
Messenger, Shirley Cline...369
Meyer, Burnus...502
Meyers, Edith G...274

Meyers, Lulu...274
Miley, Dana...195
Milke, Michelle Wheelock...484
Milke, Patrick J...484
Millen, Jane...298
Miller, Clarence...256
Miller, Esther Eckman...256
Miller, George...256
Miller, George E...256
Miller, J. Ed...256
Miller, Janetta...341
Miller, John G...180
Miller, John M...199
Miller, Lois...210
Miller, Lucille...203
Miller, Lucille...417
Miller, Marguerite...449,450
Miller, Martha Williams...180
Miller, Mary F...151
Miller, Mary Glenn.256
Miller, Rosa A...180
Miller, Rosetta Caskey...199
Miller, Ruth...238
Miller, Sarah Bringle...199
Miller, Walter B...199
Milligan, Grizella...241
Milligan, Jane Mitchell..241
Milligan, John...241
Mills, Ada F...211,214
Mills, Adam...127-30
Mills, Alice Faulk...212
Mills, Alton E...213
Mills, Andrew G. (3-2C)...130,136-7
Mills, Andrew G. (3-2A2)...132
Mills, Anna...206
Mills, Annie Gleghorn...101
Mills, Ardella Massengill...213
Mills, Ballinger...132
Mills, Ballinger Jr...132
Mills, Basil F...213
Mills, Beatrice Dailey...210
Mills, Bertha Rose...213
Mills, Blanche L...212
Mills, Bonnie S...213
Mills, Cecil D...210-1
Mills, Charles F...197
Mills, Cleffie Blackwell...211
Mills, Clifton W...213
Mills, Clyde McWilliams..202,210
Mills, Cynthia Baskin...202,209,214
Mills, David G. (3-2E)...130,137-8
Mills, David G. (3-2A3)...132
Mills, Donnie...213
Mills, Elizabeth Caskey...175,220
Mills, Elizabeth McNeel...137
Mills, Ernie M...210
Mills, Erskine L...210
Mills, Esther Caskey...175,205-6
Mills, Eula Richardson...210
Mills, Eura G...210
Mills, Evy Waters...132
Mills, Glenn R...212
Mills, Grace E...202,203,213
Mills, Hannah...130,132-3
Mills, Hugh J...202,210
Mills, Hugh M...205-6

Mills, Ina K...211-2
Mills, Jane M...130,138
Mills, Janet McKee...127
Mills, Jennet Graham...74,127-8
Mills, John...206
Mills, John C...220
Mills, John L...220
Mills, John M...210
Mills, John S...202,209,214
Mills, John V...210
Mills, Julia Burton...210
Mills, Julia C...212
Mills, Julianna E...214
Mills, Leno R...210
Mills, Lois Miller...210
Mills, Lora L...212
Mills, Lucy Ballinger...132
Mills, Malinda C...208,209,214
Mills, Mamie Williams...211
Mills, Margaret...65,67,73
Mills, Margaret Leach...210
Mills, Martha...65
Mills, Martha A...201,217
Mills, Martha Bonner...131
Mills, Mary A...197,206
Mills, Mary J...220
Mills, Mary M. (3-2G)...130,139
Mills, Mary M. (3-2A1a)...131-2
Mills, Mary Solomon...220
Mills, Mary Whitesides...210
Mills, Minerva Elliott...130
Mills, Modenia Gwinn...197
Mills, Myrtie Flowers...213
Mills, Nancy...130,132-3
Mills, Nora Tracy...211
Mills, Oma Baskin...213
Mills, Randall S...210
Mills, Richard T...212
Mills, Robert...130,137-8,522 note 62
Mills, Rosanna...197,201,211
Mills, Rosanna J...215
Mills, Ruth E...212
Mills, Samuel D...131
Mills, Sarah E...212
Mills, Sidney C...211
Mills, Slonney E...212-3
Mills, Sue Gray...212
Mills, Trilby R...213-4
Mills, Velma Zenar...213
Mills, William...65
Mills, William...127
Mills, William (3-2A)...130-1
Mills, Willie Fleming...210
Mills, Y.B...213
Mills, Yerby S...211
Minger, Myrtle I...442
Mink, Candace...310
Mink, Craig...310
Mink, Rhonda Brown...310
Misz, Alice M...466
Mitchell, Amanda...416
Mitchell, Anthony...416
Mitchell, Cary...416
Mitchell, Elizabeth...251
Mitchell, Emma J...272
Mitchell, Jacqueline...416

Mitchell, Jan...416
Mitchell, Jane...241
Mitchell, Mabel...274
Mitchell, Mary Badger...416
Mitchell, Nathaniel...416
Mitchell, Willis D...416
Mitschler, Opal Graham...367,435
Mitschler, Wilfred...435
Mitts, Marie...154
Mock, Lola...309
Moffatt, James E...191
Moffatt, Jemima...229
Moffatt, John H...191
Moffatt, Nancy McCormick...191
Moffatt, Willard E...191
Moir, Jessie Graham...249,318
Moir, John...318
Moir, John G...318-9
Moir, Mabel M...318,319
Moir, Mary Nicol...318
Moir, Robert...318
Moir, Robert (5-21B)...318,319
Moloy, Grace E...387
Moloy, James...387
Montgomery, Alfred C...263
Montgomery, Archibald...262
Montgomery, Charles A...263
Montgomery, David W...263
Montgomery, Isaac...320
Montgomery, John H...262-3
Montgomery, John P...107
Montgomery, Margaret Carnahan...262
Montgomery, Margaret J...263
Montgomery, Martha Hemphill..262-3
Montgomery, Mary B...263
Montgomery, Mary P...263
Montgomery, Mary Teel...320
Montgomery, Maude Graham...249,320-1
Montgomery, Tilitha Andrews...107
Montgomery, William T...320
Moore, Barbara E...456
Moore, Carol Thompson...276
Moore, Elizabeth...188
Moore, Herman R...456
Moore, James...208
Moore, James W...276
Moore, John A...177,187
Moore, Lucille Nix...456
Moore, Martha E...177
Moore, Mary Gwinn...208
Moore, Mary McClerkin...177,187
Moore, Nettie B...345
Moore, Robbie M...187
Moore, Rupert V...423
Moore, Verna Propst...423
Moran, Alice V...444
Morehart, Margaret...376
Morgan, Edwin E...408
Morgan, Elizabeth...332
Morgan, Flora A...408
Morgan, infant...331
Morgan, Sara Bryson...331
Morgan, Stella Curran...408
Morgan, W. Gerald...331
Morgan, William...331
Morris, Elizabeth Bishop...389,390

Morris, Judy...390
Morris, Mary E...494-5
Morris, Matthew E...390
Morris, Michael...390
Morris, Peter J...390
Morris, Richard A...390
Morris, Virgie McCoy...494
Morris, William H.T...494
Morrison, Clemmie Cole...206
Morrison, Cora O...206
Morrison, Earl...347
Morrison, Fred...347
Morrison, Gary...503
Morrison, John G...206
Morrison, Kathy Graham...479,503
Morrison, Madge Glass...347
Morrissey, David W...279
Morrissey, Fredrick J...279
Morrissey, Mary Hutchinson...278
Morrissey, William T...278
Morseman, Sarah Baird...281
Morseman, Truman...281
Morton, Andrew J...212
Morton, Callie Swindle...212
Morton, Dessie M...216
Morton, Edna E...216
Morton, Elsie J...216
Morton, Estes C...216
Morton, Eveline Cannon...212
Morton, Finis E...212
Morton, Floyd...212
Morton, George...216
Morton, infant...216
Morton, John E...216
Morton, Letitia Glass...212
Morton, Liza Dawson...216
Morton, Lora Mills...212
Morton, Lytle E...212
Morton, Robbie...216
Morton, Ruby...216
Morton, Theodore...216
Morton, William H...212,216
Moser, Cephas W...106
Moser, Rebecca Gleghorn...106
Moser, Relda...434
Mosher, Alexander...258
Mosher, Elizabeth...258
Mosher, Elizabeth ------...258
Moss, James H...281
Moss, Mary E...281
Moss, Mary Hunter...282
Moss, Mervyn E...281
Moss, Paul M...281
Moss, Persis A...281
Moss, Sarah Patton...281
Moxley, Lillie...112
Moyers, Maggie Gault...102
Muck, Joyce...439
Mudgett, Terrill...448
Mulhern, Catherine...370
Mundorff, Arthur A...290,291
Mundorff, Benjamin F...289-90
Mundorff, David...289
Mundorff, David F...290,291
Mundorff, Elma...291
Mundorff, Ethel...292

Mundorff, Florence E...290
Mundorff, Maude M...291
Mundorff, Sarah Graham...167,289-90
Mundorff, Sarah Stailey...289
Mundorff, T. Dean...292
Mundorff, Verna M...291-2
Mundorff, William M...290,291
Murgel, Lillian...461
Murphy, Dutes E...218
Murphy, Hilliard...184
Murphy, Michael F...196
Murphy, Norma...325
Murphy, Ruth Baskin..196
Murphy, Telitha Lavelle...218
Murphy, Virginia R...184
Murray, Laura L...452
Murray, Mary A...163
Myers, Dorothy M...389
Myers, Laura A...207,212
Myers, Lela Graham...413
Myers, Marci...273
Myers, Pearl L...238
Naaf, Doris Rinne...480
Naaf, James N...481
Naaf, Jerry L...480
Naaf, Julienne M...480,481
Naaf, Merlin P...480
Naaf, Ronald L...480,481
Naaf, Sarah E...481
Naaf, Sharon Stohs...481
Naaf, Thomas F...481
Naaf, Wilma Graham...434,480
Nahas, Carol Ross...453
Nahas, John M...454
Nahas, Lisa M...454
Nahas, Richard E...453
Nahas, Richard E. Jr...454
Neill, Lois...493
Nelson, James S...108
Nelson, Lois...310
Nelson, Martha Gleghorn...108
Nelson, Melissa...323
Nelson, Michelle Bowen...323
Nerren, Ben...103
Nerren, John...103
Nerren, Maggie...103
Nerren, Mary Jobe...103
Netzbandt, Arlene Fierke...475
Netzbandt, Joan C...475
Netzbandt, Ronald E...475
Newan, Judith McConaha...479,480
Newan, Rae A...480
Nichols, Blaine H...383
Nichols, David...383
Nichols, Elizabeth Long...234
Nichols, Elizabeth Pressly...233
Nichols, Elizabeth Sale...233-4
Nichols, Herbert S...233
Nichols, Herbert S. Jr...234
Nichols, James E...233
Nichols, Linda Haworth...383
Nichols, Sarah Pressly...233
Nichols, Thomas E...233
Nicol, Mary...318
Nix, Mary L...456
Nixon, Laura Terry...327

Norman, Massie...182
Norrick, Carmi...194
Norris, Ida...151
Norris, Winnie...183
Northington, Georgia Graham...298,394
Northington, Gustavus...394
Northington, Mattie...394
Notgrass, Ruby...216
Notson, Rebecca L...431
Oaks, Donna J...276
Oaks, Hazel M...275
Oaks, Helen L...275
Oaks, Jayne E...276
Oaks, John M...275
Oaks, Karen Sellers...276
Oaks, Laura McCoy...275
Oaks, Laurence O...276
Oaks, Lorena Hook...276
Oaks, Margaret A...276
Oaks, Melissa N...276
Oaks, Nancy Black...276
Oaks, Patricia R...276
Oaks, Stefanie K...276
Oaks, Susan L...276
Oaks, William L...276
Oaks, William S...276
Oates, Elizabeth...229
Oates, James L...229
Oates, Lee Crockett...229
Oates, Louise W...229
Oates, Pauline...229
Oates, Ruth...229
Oberhelman, Nelda J...482
O'Byrne, Catherine A...423
O'Daniel, Emily...272
O'Daniel, James A...272
O'Daniel, James C...272
O'Daniel, Janine Allen...272
O'Daniel, John A...272
O'Daniel, John W...272
O'Daniel, Meghan...272
O'Daniel, Sarabelle Talbot...272
Oldaker, Don L...500
Oldaker, Donnelle...500
Oldaker, Helen Smith...500
Oldfield, Allen...106
Oldfield, Edythe M...105
Oldfield, James P...105
Oldfield, Janette Gleghorn..106
Oldfield, Mary Kent...105
Olmstead, Albert O...432
Olmstead, Carol L...432,433
Olmstead, Harold G...432
Olmstead, James L...433
Olmstead, Jamie S...433
Olmstead, Kay L...433
Olmstead, Kimberly A...433
Olmstead, Laurie K...433
Olmstead, Marjorie Kramer...432
Olmstead, Max R...432
Olmstead, Michael H...433
Olmstead, Monte K...433
Olmstead, Opal Williams...433
Olmstead, Rolland W...432,433
Olmstead, Willie E...433
Olmstead, Zella Graham...367,432

Olson, Inger...389
O'Neal, Susan...310
O'Nell, Daisy...195-6
Opstad, Mary...308
Orr, Aileen Fike...316
Orr, Eva...316
Orr, Laura Graham...245,315
Orr, Leila...316
Orr, Marian...316
Orr, Myrtle Sald...316
Orr, Robert...316
Orr, Samuel Y...315-6
Orr, William G...316
Orr, William G. Jr...316
Ott, Blanch...234
Owen, Anna McWilliams...202
Owen, Effie Melton...202,210
Owen, Lavenia F...210
Owen, Richard L...202,210
Owen, Riley B...202
Owens, Dock...110
Owens, Emma Scott...110
Owens, Lillie...100
Oyler, Helen Oaks...275
Oyler, James L...275
Oyler, Martha A...275
Packard, Lena Patterson...345
Packard, W.A...345
Page, Bruce F...436
Page, Bruce P...436,437
Page, Carrie...437
Page, Christine Rodriguez...437
Page, Ellen Butler...455,456
Page, Jason L...437
Page, Jeremy F...456
Page, Larry E...456
Page, Linda L...436
Page, Matthew C...456
Page, Pearl Graham...367,436
Page, Raymond F...456
Page, Stella Castor...456
Page, Virginia F...436,437
Paine, Laura K...185
Palmer, Don W...478
Palmer, Ella Abernathy...478
Palmer, Gary D...478
Palmer, Glenda J...478
Palmer, Glenn A...477
Palmer, Jean M...478
Palmer, Keith L...478
Palmer, Margaret Wildman...478
Palmer, Patricia Sutter...478
Palmer, Paula D...478
Palmer, Velma Graham...434,477
Palmer, William A...477
Palmer, Zella Brown...477
Panfield, Anna...371
Parker, Bud...153
Parker, David G...460
Parker, Elsie...324
Parker, Frederic C.W...459
Parker, Frederic W...460,462
Parker, Grace E...460,462
Parker, Grace Reed...459
Parker, Helen Gleghorn...101
Parker, Kay Thomas...460

Parker, Kent H...459-60
Parker, Kent H. Jr...460
Parker, Lauren Mercer...462
Parker, Margaret...460,462
Parker, Margaret Gartin...153
Parker, Margaret Graham...399,459-60
Parker, Mary...460,461
Parker, Priscilla...429
Parker, Rebecca E...463
Parker, Sarah...460,461
Parker, Timothy G...460-1
Parker, Wesby R...460,462-3
Parks, Velma Jobe...102
Parnes, Florence...360
Parsons, Lena H...401-2
Parsons, Lenora Thomas...401
Parsons, Stephen A...401
Paton, Betty Cox...414
Paton, Beverly B...413
Paton, Estaline Ross...413
Paton, Gwen M...414
Paton, Jeanne K...414
Paton, John M...414
Paton, Larry R...413
Paton, Leticia...414
Paton, Lula Graham...315,413
Paton, Mae Graham...413
Paton, Martha K...413-4
Paton, Paul T...413
Paton, Peter T...413
Paton, Ralph T...413,414
Paton, Richard L...414
Paton, Richard W...413,414
Paton, Robert D...413
Paton, Robert G...413
Paton, William G...413
Patrick, Maude...153
Patterson, Alex...100
Patterson, Deborah E...455
Patterson, Ella...345
Patterson, Elmira Graham...254,345
Patterson, Frances Gleghorn...119
Patterson, James...119
Patterson, James W...345
Patterson, Kathryn...421
Patterson, Lena...345
Patterson, Louiza...119
Patterson, Maud Gleghorn...100
Patton, Carey S...280
Patton, Esther...322
Patton, Hannah Harsha...280
Patton, Mary Baird...280-1
Patton, Paul H...280-1
Patton, Sarah E...281
Payton, Mabel Graham...289,372
Pearson see Pierson
Pebley, Priscilla A...383
Peden, Sarah B...231,232
Peeler, Ruby...232
Pendarvis, Dorothy...238
Percival, Leo C...372
Percival, Mabel Graham...289,372
Peregoy, Edith Lockart...201
Peregoy, Ernest P...201
Perkins, Ephraim...121
Perkins, Idile Buatte...121

Perkins, Jeremiah C...121
Perkins, Lyda...121
Perkins, Mary Gleghorn...121
Permenter, Leona...271
Perring, Clinton...78
Perring, Sarah Adams...78
Perry, Bette Graham...438,484
Perry, Elton R...484
Perry, Kendra J...484
Perry, Roger L...484
Peterka, Elsie...443
Peterman, Amanda A...376
Peterman, George...376
Peterman, Margaret Morehart...376
Peters, Ella M...388
Peters, Patricia...309
Peterson, Charlotte H...380
Peva, Margaret Caskey...194
Pfister, Vencette J...483
Phelps, Frances K...462
Phelps, Merlene...486
Phillips, Linda...429
Phillips, Martha...186
Phillips, Susan...379
Phillips, Vera Isom...217
Phillips, Walter D...217
Phillipy, David A...451
Phillipy, Evelyn Taylor...450
Phillipy, Joyce Benner...451
Phillipy, Keith...451
Phillipy, Lawrence...450
Phillipy, Nancy Smith...451
Phillipy, Roy...450
Phillipy, Ruby Graham...379,450
Pickard, Mary J...179
Pickle, Lucy Gleghorn...101
Piercy, Roger...112
Piercy, Sarah Gleghorn...112
Pierson, Kate A...283
Pilger, Britta N...271
Pilger, Emilie K...271
Pilger, Sara Lang...271
Pilger, Sue A...271
Pilger, Theodore R...271
Pilger, Vernon D...271
Pilger, Wilma Firoved...271
Pincard, Retta...100
Pinner, Anna L...202
Plant, Hazel A...274
Pohlman, Katherine Brehm...410-1
Pohlman, Kingsley...410
Poindexter, Mary...100
Poindexter, Sallie...100
Poindexter, W.H...100
Pollaschek, Fred...310
Pollaschek, Rachel Fuller...310
Pooch, Dorothy Krawetzki...430
Pooch, Janet A...430,439
Pooch, William H...430
Pool, Ann E...114
Pool, Colman J...115
Pool, Daniel...114
Pool, George A...115
Pool, Granville M...115
Pool, James W...114
Pool, John A...115

Pool, John W...115
Pool, Mary C...114
Pool, Melissa Gleghorn...115
Pool, Rhoda Gleghorn...114
Pool, Robert T...115
Pool, Samuel...114
Pool, Walter L...115
Pope, Margaret...268
Popham, Ezekiel...165,169-71
Popham, J. Ann...172
Popham, James...172
Popham, Jane...165-7,169,348
Popham, Nancy Graham...74,169-72
Popham, William T...172
Porch, Sarah Gleghorn...121
Porter, Alexander L...245
Porter, Alice E...246-7
Porter, Anna...247
Porter, Anna M...248
Porter, Eleanor Brown...245
Porter, Elizabeth...102
Porter, Elizabeth...249
Porter, Frances....464
Porter, Frank M...246,247-8
Porter, Hugh...245
Porter, infant...246
Porter, James E...248
Porter, John...246,247
Porter, Lauretta L...246
Porter, Lulu K...248
Porter, Marella...247
Porter, Margaret...248
Porter, Margaret Graham...140,245
Porter, Marietta Lynn...247
Porter, Mary...284,304
Porter, Minnie...116
Porter, Sarah Graham...246
Porter, William R...246,247
Porter, Wilson G...246,247
Posey, Ruth Billings...182
Posey, William F...182
Postlewaite, Edward...246
Postlewaite, Frank...246
Postlewaite, Isabel...246
Postlewaite, James F...246
Postlewaite, John J...246
Postlewaite, Lauretta Porter...246
Postlewaite, Margaret...246
Postlewaite, Russell...246
Potter, Frank...306
Potter, Lillian...306
Potter, Violet Black...306
Poutre, Alice Moran...444
Poutre, Cynthia K...445
Poutre, Jo Ann Ruyle...443,444
Poutre, Judith P...445
Poutre, Omer A...444
Poutre, Polly Yockel...444
Poutre, Robert M...444
Poutre, Robert P...445
Poutre, Timothy J...445
Powell, Charles H...133
Powell, Ellen A...113
Powell, Flossie...114
Powell, Hiram...113
Powell, Mattie Hill...133

Powell, Ora...114
Powell, Sarah R...113
Pressly, Belle B...233
Pressly, David...231,232
Pressly, David P...233
Pressly, Dora Smith...232
Pressly, Elizabaeth S...233
Pressly, Elizabeth Stephens...232,233
Pressly, James W...233
Pressly, Lillian Cameron...233
Pressly, Martha Bittick...233
Pressly, Peden B...233
Pressly, Sarah B...233
Pressly, Sarah Peden...231,232
Pressly, Sunie M...231
Pressly, Thomas J...233
Pressly, Thomas P...232
Price, Berniece Graham...376,447
Price, Gussie...179
Prince, Myrtle...78
Proctor, Mary...403
Propst, Arlene...423-4
Propst, Clara Graham...366,423
Propst, Verna...423
Propst, William V...423
Puckett, Eloris...238
Pyott-Love, Adeline J...267
Radevich, Thelma P...460
Rainey, Mary...181,185,191
Rainey, Maude Gault...102
Ralph, Mary Gay...201
Ramsey, Benton...134
Ramsey, Emma Johnson...134
Ramsey, Felix...134
Ramsey, Knox...134
Ramsey, Mildred...134
Ramsey, Rowena Hill...133-4
Ramsey, Sam...134
Ramsey, William F...133-4
Randall, Mary L...133
Randolph, Alice...181
Rankin, Emily...150
Ranney, Edna L...473
Ray, Florette Jobe...102
Ray, Janelle M...483
Raymond, Calpuria...191
Raynor, Mary J...212
Reed, Addie...391
Reed, Elihu...391
Reed, Grace E...459
Reed, Lucetta...391
Reed, Mary A...341
Reed, Mary J...197
Reedy, --- Graham...86,221
Reedy, John...221
Reeves, Charles...106
Reeves, Hester Grissom...106
Reeves, Opal E...106
Renner, Christine J...483
Rennicks, Clara Graham...466,496
Rennicks, Elizabeth B...496
Rennicks, Jeffrey G...496
Rennicks, Robert S...496
Rennicks, Robert S. Jr...496
Rennicks, Robert S. III...496
Rennicks, Thora Smith...496

Resinover, Frances...101
Retallack, James N...493
Retallack, Lois Neill...493
Retallack, Norman F...493
Retallack, Stuart A.G...494
Reville, Minnie Rowell...104
Reynolds, Hugh R...237
Reynolds, Margaret J...238
Reynolds, Sarah McQuiston..237
Reynolds, Tony...478
Reynolds, Victoria Kasten...478
Rezabek, Cathy Darner...474,475
Rezabek, David C...475
Rezabek, Janna R...475
Rezabek, Jeffrey R...475
Rezabek, Marilyn Ceranek...475
Rezabek, Raymond J...475
Rhode, Elizabeth G...231
Rhorer, Alvin K...78
Rhorer, Emma Adams...78
Rhorer, Henry C...78
Rhorer, Martha...78
Rhorer, Russell...78
Rice, Diane F...445
Rice, Dora P...218
Rice, Nancy...152
Rice, Pauline Buss...445
Rice, William M...445
Richard, Carl...114
Richard, Estelle Cox...114
Richard, Flossie Powell...114
Richard, Fred...114
Richard, Gordon...114
Richard, James A...114
Richard, Lila Ewing...114
Richard, Mary Gleghorn...114
Richard, Ora Powell...114
Richard, William...114
Richards, Carole A...470
Richards, Connie J...388
Richardson, Clayton M...210
Richardson, Edith V...432
Richardson, Emma Boshears...210
Richardson, Eula C...210
Richardson, Fannie McElmurry...106
Richardson, Gayle Graham...482,506
Richardson, Gladys Lavelle...219
Richardson, John...106
Richardson, Letha Gleghorn...106
Richardson, Lydia...152
Richardson, Terry L...506
Richardson, Tollye J...106
Richardson, Velma I...434
Richardson, Warner L...219
Richeson, Betty June...452
Richeson, Joseph...452
Richeson, Laura Murray...452
Richmond, Ruth J...391
Ricketts, Margaret Shanklin...162
Ricketts, Rebekah...208
Ricketts, T.B...163
Riddick, Dorathy...232
Riddick, Elizabeth K...232
Riddick, Eudora Smith...232
Riddick, Medora Maxwell...230,231
Riddick, Patricia M...231

Riddick, Prentice...230,231
Riddick, Rebecca H...230,231
Riddick, Sidney O...232
Riddle, Melissa...357
Riegel, Florence Witherhold...325
Riegel, Leon...345
Riegel, Lewis E...325
Riegel, Mary Cowden...322,325
Riegel, Nancy...345
Riegel, Robert E...325
Riegel, Ruth A...345
Riegel, Ruth Blake...343,345
Rinne, Doris...480
Ritchie, Agnes...236
Ritchie, Martha...243
Ritter, Jeannette...389
Ritter, Ruth M...452
Roane, Claryce...219
Roane, Sarah...211
Robb, Anna...326
Roberge, Marion...218
Roberson see Robinson
Roberts, Bertha Hevener...384
Roberts, Jeanne Paton...414
Roberts, Mildred B...384
Roberts, Magnolia Z...190
Roberts, Ruth...145
Roberts, Samuel L...384
Robertson, Bruce M...461
Robertson, Deborah G...461
Robertson, Imogene...368
Robertson, Jason T...477
Robertson, John...461
Robertson, Julie...461
Robertson, Katie...215
Robertson, Linda Craven...476-7
Robertson, Mary Gillam...461
Robertson, Opal...163
Robertson, Sarah Parker...460,461
Robertson, Tres L...477
Robertson, William...461
Robeson, David W...480
Robeson, Jeffrey V...480
Robeson, Jo L...479,480
Robeson, Jonathan R...480
Robeson, Julie Husa...480
Robeson, Lawrence W...479
Robeson, Nelva Graham...434,479
Robeson, Richard D...479,480
Robeson, Stephen R...479,480
Robinson, Mina V...358
Robinson, Nelle E...257
Robison, Adeline Pyott-Love..267
Robison, Elizabeth A...244
Robison, infant...268
Robison, John...266
Robison, John A...267-8
Robison, Magdaline...266
Robison, Mary Graham...161,266-7
Robison, William A...266-7
Rodene, Gail...388
Rodgers, Carol Shuck...429
Rodgers, Jody L...480
Rodgers, Judith McConaha...479,480
Rodgers, Max E...429
Rodgriguez, Christine...437

Roe, Barbara Kuhl...419
Roe, Meghan M...419
Roe, Meredith L...419
Roe, Richard L...419
Rogers, Sara N...389
Roland, Ruth...328
Roll, Edward...147
Roll, Fannie Shrader...146-7
Roll, Harry...147
Roll, Henry E...146-7
Rose, Bertha G...213
Rose, E.L...215
Rose, Edward W...215
Rose, Erskine L...202
Rose, Eunice E...215
Rose, Florence A...218
Rose, Henry H...202
Rose, Ina Mills...211-2
Rose, infant...215
Rose, James F...212,213,214,218
Rose, Julia Baskin...214
Rose, Katie Robertson...215
Rose, Leona Baskin...215
Rose, Lula Wiseman...214,216
Rose, Mary Wilson...215
Rose, Myrtle B...216
Rose, Nan Wiseman...202
Rose, Olvi McWilliams..202
Rose, Oma B...202
Rose, Oscar L...212
Rose, Samuel S...214,216
Rose, Sarah Hargett...212,213,214,218
Rose, Walter E...214
Rose, William J...215
Rosier, Asa...152
Rosier, David...152
Rosier, infant...152
Rosier, Lute/Lutie Funk..152
Rosier, Richard...152
Rosier, Russell...152
Rosier, Vincent...152
Ross, Anabelle Cameron...454
Ross, Carol L...453
Ross, Donald F...453,454
Ross, Elizabeth C...105
Ross, Estaline...413
Ross, Fanny C...304
Ross, John E...453,454
Ross, John W...453
Ross, Kimberly A...454
Ross, Lorene Graham...380,453
Ross, Mary...310
Ross, Mary Anderson...454
Ross, Pamela J...454
Ross, Susanna K...454
Rossiter, Donald...360
Rossiter, Patricia Tolle...459-60
Rowell, Elizabeth Dickey...104
Rowell, Knox R...104
Rowell, Mary E...104
Rowell, Minnie R...104
Russell, Ida Scott...110
Russell, Jasper N...110
Russell, Mary E...110
Ruyle, Amy Keller...446
Ruyle, Bernice Vitosh...443

Ruyle, Derek C...446
Ruyle, Diane Rice...445
Ruyle, Donald D...443,445
Ruyle, Dorothy Graham...376,443
Ruyle, Heather L...445
Ruyle, Ilene Boehmer...443
Ruyle, Ina Cochran...443
Ruyle, Jo Ann...443,444
Ruyle, Joan C...444
Ruyle, Lloyd O...443
Ruyle, Nancy A...444
Ruyle, Oliver W...443
Ruyle, Patricia C...444
Ruyle, Robert L...443
Ruyle, Robert L. Jr...444
Ruyle, Rochelle L...445
Ruyle, Sherri L...443
Ruyle, Shirley L...443,445
Ruyle, Steven A...444
Ruyle, Thomas K...443,445-6
Ruyle, Thomas M...443
Sacra, Ruth...188
Sald, Myrtle...316
Sale, Elizabeth...233-4
Sale, Laura Sanford...234
Sale, William H.W...234
Salter, David P...270
Salter, George....270
Salter, Gertrude....270
Salter, Guy...270
Salter, Josephine...270
Salter, Luetta McDougall...270
Salter, Margaret...270
Salter, Sarah E...271
Saltzmann, Loure E...271
Sams, Valda...478
Samuelson, Maude...379
Samuelson, Peter...379
Sanders, Frances S...296
Sanderson, ---- McLean...398
Sanderson, Frances B...398
Sanderson, James...398
Sanford, Laura K...234
Sarten, Dixie...196
Sarten, Geneva Gatlin...196
Saunders, Amanda...131
Saville, Edgar S...273
Saville, Mary A...273
Saville, Sarah White...273
Savoie, Bobby G...456
Savoie, Geri Butler...456
Savoie, Sandra Elder...456
Savoie, Scott C...456
Sawyer, Rosie M...183
Sawyers, Valerian Campbell...111
Scheder, Helen...309
Schilling, Bertha...375
Schilling, Jessie Graham...293,375
Schilling, Simon...375
Schilling, Simon O...375
Schilling, Tolbert H...375
Schmidt, Beulah...486
Schmidt, John...438
Schmidt, Joya K...438
Schmidt, Shirley Grauer...438
Schmitz, Iris Blankenship...210

Schobert, Donna Corbey...363
Schobert, Joseph...363
Schobert, Melody A...363
Schoettger, Patricia Ruyle...444
Schoettger, Scott M...444
Schoonover, Eula Caskey...195
Schoonover, Richard...195
Schottler, Ina Glick...374
Schottler, Martin...374
Schuster, Clara...151
Schwarz, Allen E...480
Schwarz, April M...480
Schwarz, Jeremiah E...480
Schwarz, Jo Robeson...479,480
Scott, Alice Smith...110
Scott, C.M....316
Scott, Carol A...316
Scott, Carolyn...316
Scott, Clarissa B...119
Scott, Emma V...110
Scott, Frank...316
Scott, Ida D...110
Scott, Leila Wilson...316
Scott, Marian...316
Scott, Mary Hanson...316
Scott, William W...110
Sears, Myra H...354
Seaton, Bess...151
Selbert, David...462
Selbert, Laura...462
Selbert, Logan H...462
Selbert, Margaret Parker...460,462
Selbert, Mark D...462
Selbert, Parker D...462
Sellers, Karen J...276
Senseman, Mary E...311
Setterland, Elvina E...425
Setterland, John...425
Setterland, Pauline Erickson...425
Sewalt, Evaline Gleghorn...118
Sewalt, L.L....118
Seymour, Diane...486
Seymour, Merlene Phelps...486
Seymour, William R...486
Shamblee, Eunice Rose...215
Shamblee, Harvey L...215
Shanahan, Charles A...506
Shanahan, Corey S...506
Shanahan, Paula Graham...482,505-6
Shanahan, William A...505-6
Shankle, Alice...229
Shanklin, Frances Gartin...162
Shanklin, Harriett M...164
Shanklin, Joseph...162
Shanklin, Margaret E...162-3
Shanklin, Martha Bohannon...164
Shanklin, Martha Graham...74,162,524 note 93
Shanklin, Nancy...162
Shanklin, Robert G..162,164
Shanklin, William G...162
Shannon, Beverly L...154
Shannon, Isophene Gray...106
Shannon, John B...106
Shannon, Lynwood...154
Shannon, Margaret A...154

Shannon, Margaret Barker...154
Shannon, Mary E...106
Shannon, Orville L...154
Shannon, Vivian Cooper...154
Shaw, Cynthia Graham...432,477
Shaw, Terry V...477
Shelley, M.H...220
Shelley, Marie Chapman...220
Shelley, Mary S...220
Shelton, Pearl Tate...102
Shepp, Carrie Adams..79
Sheppard, Ivee...187
Sherlock, Bridget...79
Sherlock, Malinda...79
Sherlock, Stephen...79
Sherrill, Margaret E...180
Sherrod, Catherine...217
Sherrod, Fredrick S...217
Shipp, Mary E...197
Shrader, Eliza Thompson...146
Shrader, Fannie...146
Shrader, Harry...147
Shrader, James W...146
Shrader, Margaret...146
Shrader, Minnie...146
Shrader, Stephen R...146
Shuck, Ava Graham...366,429
Shuck, Betty Call...429
Shuck, Carol J...429
Shuck, Jack D...429
Shuck, Jason D...429
Shuck, Linda Phillips...429
Shuck, Priscilla Parker...429
Shuck, Rebecca Dixon...429
Shuck, Richard L...429
Shuck, Robert Lee...429
Shuck, Robert Leslie...429
Siders, Jennifer...438
Siders, Joya Schmidt...438
Siders, Kevin...438
Siders, Sara...438
Siders, Shannon...438
Siegel, Alicia L...431
Siegel, David...431
Siegel, Nicole L...431
Siegel, Roberta McClellan...431
Signor, Eunice M...292,321
Simmons, Alta...191
Simons, Florence Hughes...493
Simons, Frank E...493
Simons, Laura G...493
Simons, Robert F...493
Simonton, Margie...184
Simpson, Julia Higgins...393
Simpson, Martha McClerkin...178
Simpson, Mary...76
Simpson, Nora Graham...297,393
Simpson, Raymond R...393
Simpson, Raymond R. Jr...393
Simpson, Virginia H...393
Sivils, Buck...397
Sivils, Evelyn Spicer...397
Sivils, Ronald...397
Skinner, Bonnie F...111
Skinner, Clinton...111
Skinner, Dewey...111

Skinner, Etta Smith...110
Skinner, George...110
Skinner, Grace...111
Skinner, Idell...111
Skinner, James P...111
Skinner, John W...111
Skinner, Lester...111
Skinner, Mary Smith...111
Skinner, Maude...111
Skinner, Una...111
Skoog, Betty Linnel...421
Skoog, Clifford...421
Skoog, Connie...421
Skoog, Gary...421
Skoog, Kim...421
Slagle, Helen...339
Slama, Minnie O...442
Slaughter, Belle A...163
Slaughter, Edward C...163
Slaughter, Fannie M...163
Sloan, Mrs ---...179
Sloan, Creighton...388
Sloan, Helen Jacobson...387,388
Sloan, Roy...388
Sloan, Samuel...388
Slusher, Katherine D...474
Small, Cora L...256
Small, James...260
Small, Joseph...261
Small, Matilda...261
Small, Nancy Graham...161,260-1
Small, Nancy J...261
Smillie, Anna Graham...354,418
Smillie, James D...418
Smillie, James D. Jr...418
Smillie, Joan...418
Smillie, John G...418
Smillie, Margaret...418
Smillie, Ruth...418
Smith, Adele...391
Smith, Alexander...227-8
Smith, Alexander D...232
Smith, Alexander H...228,235
Smith, Alice...110
Smith, Andrea L...275
Smith, Ann...110
Smith, Anna Faulk...234
Smith, Annie Lockart...201
Smith, Ardelle...425
Smith, Augusta W. Jr...189,207
Smith, Blanch Ott...234
Smith, Bridgett Lavelle...218
Smith, Clement...110
Smith, Constance Whiteman...307
Smith, David H...201
Smith, Diane Graham...450,487
Smith, Don...220
Smith, Dora A.L...232
Smith, Dora R...365
Smith, Dora Rice...218
Smith, Dorothy...328
Smith, Dorothy L...359
Smith, Edith C...275
Smith, Edward S...182-3
Smith, Edwina...110
Smith, Emaline...201

Smith, Esther Graham...86,227-8
Smith, Etta...110
Smith, Eudora B...232
Smith, Faris M...234
Smith, Fitz J.L...234
Smith, Frances B.H...230
Smith, George B...307
Smith, George D...424
Smith, George T...218
Smith, Georgia...457
Smith, Goldie..185
Smith, Gordon...425
Smith, Grace P...189
Smith, Graham...345
Smith, Harriett E...232
Smith, Harry A...185
Smith, Harry G...275
Smith, Harry G. Jr...275
Smith, Hattie Blakely...232
Smith, Hazel Oaks...275
Smith, Helen Y...500
Smith, Henrietta...218
Smith, Ida Liles...185
Smith, infant...185,234
Smith, J.G...234
Smith, Jacob E...383
Smith, James...147
Smith, James A...110
Smith, James Allen...232
Smith, James C...232
Smith, James G...228
Smith, James O...234
Smith, Jane/Jeannette Gleghorn...110
Smith, Jane W...228,234
Smith, Janice O...275
Smith, Jerusha Walker...182,184
Smith, Jewel V...383
Smith, John A...182,184
Smith, John C. (3-17C)...228,235
Smith, John Calvin...110
Smith, John D...231
Smith, John W...275
Smith, John W.A...231
Smith, Joseph A...234
Smith, Julia Baskin...196-7
Smith, Kathryn Thompson...345
Smith, Laura McCormick...182-3
Smith, Lena Patterson...345
Smith, Leslie E...185
Smith, Lillian...186
Smith, Lizzie McLister..189,207
Smith, Louie P...231
Smith, Lucy Lincoln...147
Smith, Luther A.D...234
Smith, Maggie L...185
Smith, Margaret Durham...232
Smith, Margaret McDaniel...232
Smith, Marie Bias...234
Smith, Marilyn...425
Smith, Martha...109
Smith, Mary Gleghorn...108
Smith, Mary J.W...228-9
Smith, Mary L...111
Smith, Mary Russell...110
Smith, Mattie B...218
Smith, Maxine Hoy...275

Smith, May Anderson..234
Smith, Michael H...275
Smith, Mildred Graham...392,457
Smith, Myrtie D...442
Smith, Myrtle C...183,184
Smith, Nancy...451
Smith, Nancy ----...110
Smith, Nancy E...110
Smith, Nancy S...283
Smith, Nancy Suzanne...232
Smith, Nora Huffman...206-7
Smith, Norman E...206
Smith, Olive McCormick...184-5
Smith, Ollie...308
Smith, Ora...495
Smith, Pauline...185
Smith, Prentiss L...201
Smith, Prosper...345
Smith, Richard...275
Smith, Rodney...183
Smith, Roger B...183
Smith, Rose L...271
Smith, Rosie Sawyer...183
Smith, Ruth Brown...383
Smith, Samuel E...197
Smith, Sarah Allen...228
Smith, Sarah F...213
Smith, Sarah Wiseman...201
Smith, Stella Graham...366,424
Smith, Sunie Pressly...231
Smith, Susan...275
Smith, Theo...218
Smith, Thomas H...457
Smith, Thora...496
Smith, Velna...185
Smith, Wallace G...234
Smith, Werdner Hathcock...220
Smith, William...109
Smith, William A...108
Smith, Wyatt A...182,184-5
Snodgrass, Jo Anne Cowden...325
Snodgrass, Leita...497
Snodgrass, Michael...325
Snodgrass, Richard...325
Snow, James W...359
Snow, J. Charlene Vallet...358-9
Snyder, Adah B...277
Snyder, Ruby...420
Soden, Cordillia...107
Soileau, Mary Joubert...455
Solomon, Mary E...220
Sorrells, Grace E...397
Spann, Toni...308
Sparks, Jill Whitebread...439
Sparks, Joshua G...439
Sparks, Riley G...439
Speake, Dorothy C...466
Speake, Edwin R...465,466
Speake, Emma A...465
Speake, Sarah Brawner...465,466
Spear, Myra Sears...354
Spencer, J.S...136
Spencer, John H...136
Spencer, Mary Hutchings...136
Spicer, Alan...397
Spicer, Alexander W...396

Spicer, Anne...398
Spicer, Blythe...397
Spicer, Carrie...397
Spicer, Cherith...398
Spicer, Clarence G...396,397
Spicer, Donald W...397
Spicer, Evelyn M...397
Spicer, Flora Elliott...396
Spicer, Frances...397
Spicer, Frances McKelvie...397
Spicer, Geraldine McCoy...397
Spicer, Grace Sorrells...397
Spicer, infant...396
Spicer, Janice...397
Spicer, Julia...397
Spicer, Kathy...397
Spicer, Leland R...396,397
Spicer, Leland R. Jr...397
Spicer, Margaret N...396
Spicer, Martha L...396,397
Spicer, Mary Graham...305,396
Spicer, Michael..397
Spicer, Mona...397
Spicer, Oliver A...396
Spicer, Oliver V...397
Spicer, Ralph G...397
Spicer, Ralph W...396
Spicer, Ray...397
Spicer, Rodney...397
Spicer, Wylie B...396,398
Springer, Bertha G...365
Sproul, C.E...121
Sproul, Lyda Perkins...121
Sproull, Mary M...342
Sprout, Beverly D...277
Sprout, Isabella...271
Sprout, Myrl E...278
Stahl, Melissa S...504
Stailey, Sarah...289
Stancill, Jesse C...185
Stancill, Lucia McCormick...185
Stanley, Elmina H...367
Stark, Emma Gleghorn...113
Stark, S.N...113
Starnes, Lelia Baskin...208
Starnes, Thomas T...208
Staves, Grace...282
Stebbins, Naomi Dawson...215-6
Stebbins, R.H...216
Stephens, Elizabeth...232,233
Stephens, Harold...164
Stephens, Jerry...232
Stephens, LaDel Hardesty...164
Stephens, Martha Taylor...232
Stephenson, Jane...201
Stevenson, Martha...247
Stewart, Jennet...192
Stewart, Mabel E...380
Stewart, Martha...371
Stinson, Elsie Morton...216
Stinson, Roy...216
Stipp, George...77
Stipp, Sarah E...77
Stohs, Sharon K...481
Stott, Brooke...309
Stott, Martha Fuller...309

Stratton, Frances...307
Stream, Fulton...391
Stream, Olive M...391
Stream, Ruth Richmond...391
Strong, Martha L...181
Stuart, Mary...65
Stucky, Betty E...153
Stucky, Claiborn...153
Stucky, Nellie Gartin...153
Sutherland, Harriet...307
Sutter, Patricia S...478
Suttle, Lillian...388
Sutton, Alfred...422
Sutton, Alfred Jr...422
Sutton, Carol...422
Sutton, Charlene...422
Sutton, Etta Graham...365,422
Swigert, Sue Pilger...271
Swigert, Tom...271
Swindle, Callie B...212
Swindle, Mary McAlister...212
Swindle, Thomas E...212
Swinney, Mary E...276
Sympson, C...247
Sympson, Frederica McDougall...247
Sympson, Robert F...247
Talbot, Anna Firoved...272
Talbot, Sarabelle...272
Talbot, William C...272
Tanner, Lillie M...201
Tate, Arch...102
Tate, J. Norman...102
Tate, Martha Gault...102
Tate, Pearl...102
Tate, Pressley...102
Tate, Sarah Gault...102
Taylor, Ammon...202
Taylor, Ann...300
Taylor, Donald A...442
Taylor, Elaine...453
Taylor, Eva M...442
Taylor, Evelyn...450
Taylor, Huldah...98,120
Taylor, James A...442
Taylor, Joe R...212
Taylor, John C...98,120
Taylor, Joseph J...212
Taylor, Lucinda Martin...212
Taylor, Margaret...357
Taylor, Martha A...232
Taylor, Myrtie Smith...442
Taylor, Nancy Gault...98,120
Taylor, Ola McWilliams...202
Taylor, Ruby E...215
Taylor, Sarah Mills...212
Taylor, Sherrie Heiserman...442
Teasley, Annie Fuqua...191
Teasley, Elizabeth F...191
Teasley, John O...191
Teel, Mary...320
Tennant, Henry O...193-4
Tennant, Inez McClerkin...179
Tennant, Mary Caskey...193-4
Tennant, Odie E...179
Tennant, William T...194
Terrell, Tommie...101

Terry, Dorothy...327
Terry, James...327
Terry, Laura...327
Teter, Beverly Shannon...154
Teter, Robert M...154
Thierolf, Catharine...253
Thierolf, Catharine Crist...253
Thierolf, Johannes G...253
Thomas, Harold F...460
Thomas, Irene...307
Thomas, Janice Graham...479,504
Thomas, Kay...460
Thomas, Lenora H...401
Thomas, Ronald L...504
Thomas, Thelma Radevich...460
Thompson, Amanda Gwinn...197
Thompson, Anna R...148
Thompson, Carol J...276
Thompson, David R...147
Thompson, Eliza...146
Thompson, Emily Drew...145
Thompson, Gideon...144
Thompson, Harold G...276
Thompson, James P...147
Thompson, James T.V...143,144-6
Thompson, John D...148
Thompson, John L...197
Thompson, Kathryn...345
Thompson, Knox...133
Thompson, Maggie...270
Thompson, Margaret...147
Thompson, Margaret Maben...142,144-5
Thompson, Mary J...146
Thompson, Mary K...133
Thompson, Minerva...147
Thompson, Miriam...344
Thompson, Nannie Hill..133
Thompson, Patricia Oaks...276
Thompson, Robert...147
Thompson, Rowena...133
Thompson, Ruth Roberts...145
Thompson, Samuel...147
Thompson, Sarah...147
Thomson, Elizabeth G...293
Thomson, Elizabeth MacRobert...293
Thomson, Samuel...293
Thormod, Gary...311
Thormod, Margaret Leslie...311
Thormod, Tyler...311
Thorne, Margaret...386
Thorpe, Charlotte...395
Thrasher, Mary...80
Thurber, Daniel J...499
Thurber, Dolores Finizio...498
Thurber, Elizabeth Graham...467,498-9
Thurber, Kurt R...499
Thurber, Rebecca L...499
Thurber, Russel...498
Thurber, Timothy...498-9
Tinkler, David R...181
Tinkler, Martha Hindman...181
Tinkler, Martha Strong...181
Tinkler, Neil D...181
Tipton, Sarah...186
Todd, Charley E...80
Todd, Pink Adams...80

Tolle, Charlene E...359
Tolle, Charles B...358-9
Tolle, Charles V...359
Tolle, Elizabeth Banta...358-9
Tolle, J. Charlene Vallet...358-9
Tolle, Katharine E...360
Tolle, Koshtra...360
Tolle, Margaret Higgins...358
Tolle, Margaret K...359
Tolle, Melissa L...359
Tolle, Michael C...359
Tolle, Oscar S...358
Tolle, Patricia M...359-60
Tolle, Rosemary Welch...359
Tolle, Sandra Walker...359
Tolle, Susan Jones...359
Tolle, Suzanne Leymann...359
Tolle, Timothy V...359
Tolle, Wendy L...359
Torley, Louise...278
Townsend, Susan...207,218
Tracy, Nora E...211
Tredway, Harry E...399
Tredway, Helen...399,400
Tredway, Marian McConnel...399
Trobaugh, Elizabeth Rhode...231
Trobaugh, Jesse D...231
Trobaugh, John C...231
Trobaugh, Louie Pressly...231
Trobaugh, Mary Fleming...231
Trobaugh, Sue B...231
Trobaugh, William S...231
Troth, Angela K...369
Troth, Mariline Cline...369
Troth, Marion E...369
Troth, Thomas C...369
Trumbull, Charles...342
Trumbull, Laura A...342
Trumbull, Mary Sproull...342
Tucker, Bessie...229
Tucker, Ida M...229
Tucker, Myra...309
Tulcus, Jeanette...476
Turley, Lili Carpenter...101
Turnage, Annie P...179
Turnage, John A...179
Turnage, Lantye...230
Turnage, Mittie George...179
Turriff, Deborah Ziebell...402
Turriff, James...402
Tussey, James W...489
Tussey, Jeffrey J...490
Tussey, Jill...490
Tussey, Margaret Graham...453,489
Tussey, Nick...490
Tussey, Peni Huddleson...490
Tussey, Stephen E...490
Tussey, Teresa Kingery...490
Tussey, Thad...490
Tyree, D.F...123
Tyree, J.D...123
Tyree, J.H...123
Tyree, J.J...123
Tyree, John B...123
Tyree, M.U...123
Tyree, Melissa Gleghorn..123

Tyree, R.G...123
Tyree, S.M...123
Upchurch, Mae E...392
Vallet, J. Charlene...358-9
Vallet, Mina Robinson...358
Vallet, Victor E...358
Van Overmeiren, Frank...323
Van Overmeiren, Ileanna M...323
Van Overmeiren, Jane Bowen...323
Van Overmeiren, Robert S...323
Van Surdam, Norma...463
Van Wagenen, Edith...382
Vance, John...142
Vance, Ruth...142
Vasquez, Nancy Kuhl...419
Vasquez, William...419
Vaughan, Lillian...219
Vickers, Wanita...451
Vinning, Sarah...322
Vitosh, Bernice F...443
Vitosh, Elsie Peterka...443
Vitosh, Harry J...443
Vogt, Dorothy Graham...380,453
Vogt, Joseph R...453
Vroman, Helen...274
Waddill, Eleanor G...298,299
Waddill, Granville...167
Waddill, Mary P...167
Wade, Amy E...422
Wade, Catherine O'Byrne...423
Wade, J. Warren...196-7
Wade, Julia Baskin...196-7
Wade, Lois Gault...101
Wade, William J...423
Wagner, Christina M...506
Wagner, Gayle Graham...482,506
Wagner, Michael L...506
Wagner, Randall E...506
Wagner, Vickie L...506
Wagoner, Nancy M...105,106
Waldo, Minor...344
Waldron, Bertha...78
Walk, Claude L...205
Walk, Dorothy Boswell...205
Walk, Jerusha...205
Walk, Oscar C...205
Walker, Cecil B...359
Walker, Emelia E...431
Walker, Jane L...182
Walker, Jerusha D...182,184
Walker, Louisa S...426
Walker, Paul...359
Walker, Ruth Donyea...359
Walker, Sandra K...359
Walker, Wendy Tolle...359
Walkup, Annie Gartin...151
Walkup, Fannie Gartin...151
Walkup, George...151
Walkup, James...151
Wallace, Clyde...276
Wallace, David...304
Wallace, Fanny Ross...304
Wallace, James A...185
Wallace, John C...276
Wallace, LeRoy...276
Wallace, Margaret...304

Wallace, Mary Hutchinson...270,276
Wallace, Matilda...193
Wallace, Sarah Knox...193
Wallace, Velna Smith...185
Wallace, William...193
Walmsley, Fred F...415
Walmsley, Pauline Graham...353,415
Walton, Annie Ladd...198
Walton, Beryl I...198
Walton, George A...198
Walton, Henrietta Smith...218
Walton, Ida Wortham...218
Walton, William D...218
Ward, Dorothy Woods...277
Ward, Janel E...277
Ward, Merrill C...277
Ward, Merrill J...277
Warner, Alex...376
Warner, Araminta Graham...293,378
Warner, B.S...378
Warner, Carrie E...376
Warner, Mary...376
Washburn, Donald...308
Washburn, Elizabeth Whiteman...307
Washburn, Kristopher...308
Water, Virginia...230
Waters, Elizabeth...204
Waters, Evy S...132
Waters, infant...204
Waters, John Y...204
Waters, Lodd M...132
Waters, Mary Caskey...204
Waters, Thomas...204
Watson, Dellawayne Gleghorn...106
Watson, Florence...310
Watts, Dorothy...189
Waugh, Aaron...323
Waugh, Bruce...323
Waugh, Michelle Bowen...323
Weakly, Joan...307
Webb, Jestina J...154
Weber, Judy...430
Weed, Elizabeth H...257
Weed, Frances A...257
Weed, Mary Davidson...257
Weed, Robert H...257
Weed, Samuel H...257
Weed, Sarah Glenn...256
Weeth, Effie F...407
Weeth, Joseph C...407
Weeth, Mary Graham...342,407-8
Weeth, Randall K...407-8
Wegley, Annette...421
Wegley, Chris...421
Wegley, Iva Linnel...421
Wegley, Thomas...421
Wegley, Westey...421
Welch, Dorothy Smith...359
Welch, James W...275
Welch, James W. Jr...275
Welch, Janice Smith...275
Welch, Myrtle Gault...101
Welch, Rosemary L...359
Welch, Sharon...275
Welch, Sidney C...359
West, Artmer...195

West, Corbett...386
West, Elizabeth Leggett...386
West, Gillian C...386
West, Jane B...456
West, Martha L...386
West, Matthew A...386
West, Rosa Caskey...195
Wetzel, Leonard A...412
Wetzel, Martha Graham...350,412
Wetzel, Mildred...412
Wetzel, Orvil...412
Wheelock, Darrel...484
Wheelock, Gene A...484
Wheelock, Mary Graham...438,484
Wheelock, Michelle M...484
Wheelock, Pamela Edeal...484
Whisenand, Minerva J...79
Whisnand, Anna...268
Whisnand, Isaac...268
Whisnand, James C...268,269
Whisnand, Lucy A...268,269
Whisnand, Margaret Pope...268
Whisnand, Martha M...268,269
Whisnand, Mary B...268,269
Whisnand, Robert B...268,269
Whisnand, Sarah Graham...161,268
Whisnand, William C...268
Whisnand, William E...268,269
Whitaker, Ernest...201
Whitaker, Frank B...362
Whitaker, Frederick...362
Whitaker, Margaret Banta...358,362
Whitaker, Margaret F...362-3
Whitaker, Maybelle Giles...362
Whitaker, Norma McWilliams...201
White, George E...273
White, Nellie Firoved...273
White, Sarah...100
White, Sarah D...273
Whitebread, Darel G...430,439
Whitebread, Jill D...439
Whitebread, Joni L...430,439
Whitebread, Michael G...439
Whitebread, Nancy Grauer..430,438,439
Whitehorn, Bessie Davis...212
Whitehorn, Blanche Mills...212
Whitehorn, Edgar...186
Whitehorn, Mary McCormick...186
Whitehorn, Nelson F...212
Whitehorn, Stanley W...212
Whiteman, Alexander F...306
Whiteman, Amanda...307
Whiteman, Angela...308
Whiteman, Barbara J...307
Whiteman, Carol...308
Whiteman, Charles R...307
Whiteman, Cheri K...307
Whiteman, Connie L...307
Whiteman, Constance J...307
Whiteman, Cyndy L...307
Whiteman, David...306
Whiteman, Dean...306
Whiteman, Donald G...307
Whiteman, Douglas S...307
Whiteman, Edith P...307
Whiteman, Elizabeth McDill...306

Whiteman, Elizabeth S...307-8
Whiteman, Esther Fordyce...306
Whiteman, Frances Stratton...307
Whiteman, Frank P...306
Whiteman, Garth...306
Whiteman, Harold M...306
Whiteman, Harriet Sutherland...307
Whiteman, Henry M...306
Whiteman, Howard G...308
Whiteman, James...308
Whiteman, James N...307
Whiteman, Jennie L...306
Whiteman, Jessie McMillan...306
Whiteman, Joan Weakly...307
Whiteman, Kirk D...306
Whiteman, Laurie P...307
Whiteman, Lillian Potter...306
Whiteman, Louise Brown...307
Whiteman, Lucille Zimmerman...307
Whiteman, Margaret J...308
Whiteman, Marianne Marine...306
Whiteman, Marilyn McNichol...306
Whiteman, Michael...308
Whiteman, Nancy A...307
Whiteman, Opal Eaton...307
Whiteman, Ralph E...307
Whiteman, Richard...307
Whiteman, Robert H...307
Whiteman, Russell E...307
Whiteman, Sarah Keister...307
Whiteman, Scott...307
Whiteman, Teresa...308
Whiteman, Thomas...307
Whiteman, Wendell F...307
Whiteman, Wendy L...307
Whitesides, Mary A...210
Whitesides, Sarah Wright...210
Whitesides, William R...210
Whitley, Margaret E...188
Wickelgren, Alma Larson...492
Wickelgren, Herman...492
Wickelgren, Jeanette E...492
Wickelgren, Kirsten G...492
Wickelgren, Wayne...492
Wickersham, Lucy Evans...151
Wiggins, Allie...111
Wildman, Margaret...478
Wilhite, Tabitha...194
Williams, Annie Lockart...201
Williams, Bonnie Graham...434,482
Williams, Brian...363
Williams, Cal...482
Williams, Edith...433
Williams, Georgia...208
Williams, Inez McClerkin...179
Williams, James T...179
Williams, Lizzie...101
Williams, Mamie L...211
Williams, Marion...433
Williams, Martha J...180
Williams, Mary Andrews...107
Williams, Nancy Chase...363
Williams, Ola...179
Williams, Opal...433
Williams, Richard...106-7
Williams, Richard...211

Williams, Sarah Andrews...106-7
Williams, Sarah Roan...211
Williams, Vincent G...107
Williams, Wayne...363
Williams, William P...201
Wills, Verda...163
Wilson, Alvin...307
Wilson, Bertha T...203
Wilson, C.S...316
Wilson, Claire Hanson...316
Wilson, Constance Whiteman...307
Wilson, Eliza L...98,126
Wilson, Elizabeth...91
Wilson, Elvira J...248
Wilson, Esther J...340
Wilson, Eugene...316
Wilson, Eugene...341
Wilson, Eula...316
Wilson, Gladys...153
Wilson, Grace Gault...98,122,124,126
Wilson, Graham...341
Wilson, Harvey A...340,341
Wilson, infant...205
Wilson, James H...340
Wilson, Jane (Jennette)...89,139-40
Wilson, Jane A...337
Wilson, Jane McQuiston...89
Wilson, Janetta Miller...341
Wilson, Jennette...139
Wilson, John...89,139
Wilson, John...98,122,124,126
Wilson, John W...91
Wilson, Leila...316
Wilson, Letitia...193
Wilson, Lillian Gibbs...316
Wilson, Mabel E...340-1
Wilson, Margaret...178
Wilson, Marian Orr...316
Wilson, Martha...89,139
Wilson, Martha Caskey...205
Wilson, Mary Boyse...88-9
Wilson, Mary Graham...253,340
Wilson, Mary S...215
Wilson, Matthew...89
Wilson, Maude L...205
Wilson, Nancy...246
Wilson, Nancy McCarroll...205
Wilson, Nellie Lowe...152
Wilson, Paul M...316
Wilson, Rebecca Gleghorn...119
Wilson, Robert T...307
Wilson, Samuel...152
Wilson, Samuel S...119
Wilson, Susan C...98,120,124
Wilson, Tabatha...203
Wilson, Thomas T...340
Wilson, Ursula...98,122
Wilson, William H...205
Wilson, William L...205
Wimmer, Gladys...382
Wimmer, Gordon L...387
Wimmer, Grace Moloy...387
Wimmer, James L...387
Wimmer, John C...380
Wimmer, John G...387
Wimmer, Lillie Graham...295,380-2

Wimmer, Lyle G...382,384-6
Wimmer, Margaret M...387
Wimmer, Mary Howell...380
Wimmer, Max R...382
Wimmer, Mildred Roberts...384
Wimmer, Ruth E...386
Wimmer, Samuel H...380-2
Windle, Dean M...444
Windle, Ellie J...445
Windle, Jean Zvolanek...444
Windle, Joseph...445
Winham, Allen...201
Winham, Lloyd...201
Winham, Ruth McWilliams...201
Winham, Velma McWilliams...201
Winter, Elizabeth...366,367
Winter, Jane P/B...364
Wiseman, Allie...201
Wiseman, Ardelle...210
Wiseman, Elgiva Gleghorn...108
Wiseman, Emaline Smith...201
Wiseman, Isaac...201
Wiseman, John...108
Wiseman, Lenora...371
Wiseman, Lula...214,216
Wiseman, Nan...202
Wiseman, Sarah...201
Wiseman, Susan...433
Witherhold, Florence E...325
Witherington, James B...184
Witherington, Margaret L...184
Witherington, Mary McLaughlin...184
Wittmus, Albert F.F...426
Wittmus, Anna M...426-8
Wittmus, Louisa Walker...426
Wixson, Pearl...397
Woesner, Edith Van Wagenen...382
Woesner, Elizabeth A...382
Woesner, Ray L...382
Wolfe, Eliza...352-3
Wolfe, George W...352
Wolfe, Thomasina Cofor...352
Wood, Adele Baird...282
Wood, Ted...282
Woodman, Susannah...81
Woods, Arthur W...274
Woods, Barbara Clark...277
Woods, Brandon W...437
Woods, Clarence J...277
Woods, Dora...274
Woods, Dorothy J...277
Woods, Edith Meyers...274
Woods, Elizabeth Hutchinson...270,274
Woods, Gretchen M...275
Woods, Hannah L...437
Woods, Helen M...274
Woods, Helen Vroman...274
Woods, Isaac...274
Woods, Lulu Meyers...274
Woods, Mabel Mitchell...274
Woods, Mae Hills...274
Woods, Melville L...274
Woods, Randolph N...274
Woods, Ross H.H...274
Woods, Samuel D.E...274
Woods, Toni Bullock...436-7

Woods, Virginia...274
Woods, Wayne...437
Wortham, Alva...209
Wortham, Brent H...209
Wortham, Henrietta Smith..218
Wortham, Ida...218
Wortham, Nathaniel...218
Wortham, Ruth Curtis...209
Wright, Eliza Gleghorn...118
Wright, George A...118
Wright, Lucy Knox...136
Wright, Sarah E...210
Wright, Wilbur W...136
Wurm, Janelle...442
Wyman, Sharon L...479
Wymore, Mabel L...377
Yancey, Lucy O...183
Yancey, Martha Gailor..183
Yancey, Rufus W...183
Yarbrough, Elgrim W...202
Yarbrough, Ola McWilliams...202
Yockel, Polly C...444
Young, Nancy S...259
Yount, Etta P...197
Yount, James M...197
Yount, Mary Shipp...197
Yousefi, Diane Barnhill...485
Yousefi, Reza....485
Zenar, James O...213
Zenar, Lillie Hanks...213
Zenar, Velma...213
Ziebell, Barry...402
Ziebell, Deborah...402
Ziebell, Edwin...402
Ziebell, Maribeth Brooks...402
Zimmerman, Irene Thomas...307
Zimmerman, Lucille...307
Zimmerman, Thomas...307
Zvolanek, Debbie Flansburgh...444
Zvolanek, Ellen...444
Zvolanek, Emily J...444
Zvolanek, James A...444
Zvolanek, James J. Jr..444
Zvolanek, Jean A...444
Zvolanek, Jeffrey L...445
Zvolanek, Jill...444
Zvolanek, Jo Ann Ruyle...443,444
Zvolanek, Jon O...445
Zvolanek, Julie M...445

# Family of John Paul Jones

STUART

1. Levi Stuart, born , died ; married .

[cites: Deed E, page 263 Chester County SC]

Children of Levi Stuart:
1. Elizabeth Stuart
2. Mary Stuart
3. Margaret/Margarette Stuart
4. Sarah Stuart

## CHILDREN OF LEVI STUART

1. Elizabeth Stuart Paul, born , died 9 September 1827 SC; married William Paul.

Children:
1. John Paul, born 1780 SC

2. Mary Stuart, born ca 1729 Scotland, died ca 1790 Chester County SC; married ca 1750 Ireland to Robert Coulter, born 1720/5 Ireland, died ca 1783 Chester County SC

Children of Robert Coulter & Mary Stuart:
1. Archibald Coulter, born Ireland 1753 Ireland, died 1824 Todd Co KY; married about 1771 probably Chester Co SC to Mary or Ann ---, died 1823 Todd County KY?.
2. Mary Coulter, born Ireland c 1754 probably Ireland, died c 1825 probably in Todd County KY; married by 1780 to JOHN STEVENSON SR, born 20 December 1750 Ireland, died 27 April 1851 Whitfield Co GA.
3. Margaret Coulter, born probably in Ireland, died about 1792/6 Chester County SC; married about 1774 Chester County SC to ANDREW GRAHAM, born about 1753 Ireland, died 1821 Todd County KY, son of David Graham and Janet. Andrew Graham married (2) to Margaret ---, died around 1840 probably in Henderson County IL.
4. Elizabeth Coulter, born probably in Ireland; married ---- KELL.
5. Robert Stuart Coulter, born 1760 Gabinheough County Tyrone Ireland, died 1821 Madison Co IL, buried near Highland, Madison Co IL; married about 1785 Winnsboro Co SC to MARGARET FLEMING, born 1764 Winnsboro Co SC or VA, died 1825 Madison County IL, daughter of George Fleming and Mrs Sidneh (Rosine) Brown.

3. Margaret Stuart, born ca 1714 County Antrim, Ireland, died ; married Alexander Morton, born ca 1710 County Antrim, Ireland, died .

Children:
1. Thomas Morton, born 1736 County Antrim, Ireland
2. Jane Morton, born 1738
3. Elizabeth Morton, born 1740
4. Margaret Morton, born 1747, died January 1820
5. John Morton, , born 1749
[Family Search website]

1. Thomas Morton, born 1736 County Antrim Ireland, died (29 August 1790) 25 August 1806 Chester County SC, buried Paul's Graveyard, Chester County SC; married Elizabeth Paul.

# Family of John Paul Jones

"Heritage History of Chester County SC", 1982, page 314-5:
Thomas Morton born in County Antrim Ireland; fought in Revolution as one of Gen. Francis Morton's men in SC; elder at Rocky Creek Covenanter Church; may have moved to TN with son Alexander. Alexander twin of Margaret. Alexander Morton moved from Chester County SC to TN, later of Walnut Hill, Marion County IL, near Salem, buried in Old Covenanter Cemetery, Salem, IL.


Children of Thomas Morton & Elizabeth Paul:
(1) Alexander Morton, born 1775/6 Chester County SC, died 18 August 1829 Marion, IL buried Old Covenanter Cemetery, Walnut Hill, IL, married Martha Phoebe Blair born 1 June 1773 Chester County SC, died 11 January 1844 same, daughter of James Blair & Margaret Junkin/Jenkins (note 6 children between 1807 to 1818 born in Lincoln, TN)
(-) Margaret Morton, born 1775; married William Blair, son of James Blair & Margaret Junkin. Moved with husband from Chester County SC to TN, where he died, later she moved with a daughter of Randolph County IL, buried in Old Bethel Cemetery, Randolph County IL.
(2) Martha Morton, born 1776(9) or 1780 SC, died 8 April 1850 IL, married James Weir Gillespie, son of John Gillespie & Sarah Weir. In 1830 James, his wife, and all of their family moved from Chester County SC to IL and settled in three adjoining counties - Perry, Randolph & Washington.
(3) Mary Morton, born 1786 SC, died 27 August 1843, married 1802 SC to John Paul, born 1780, died 1841.
(-) Thomas Morton jr

2. Jane Morton, born 1738 Scotland or Ireland, died 28 January 1817, 79 yrs, Chester County SC, buried Pauls Graveyard; married in Ireland to John Kell, born 1736 Scotland or Ireland, died 2 November 1819 Chester County SC, buried Paul's Graveyard, Chester County SC.

[Kell-
1. John Kell, bon 1736, died 2 November 1819 Chester Co SC; married Jane Morton.
2. Archibald Kell, born ab1738
3. Jannet Kell, born ab 1740
4. Matthew Kell, born ab 1742, died in Revolutionary War.
5. James Kell, born ab 1744 County Antrim, Ireland, died August 1813 Chester County SC]

Children:
(1) Alexander Kell, born 1770 Ireland, died Princeton IN;
(2) John Kell, born 1772, died Princeton IN;
(3) Thomas Kell, born 16 November 1774 Rocky Creek, Chester County SC, died 21 March 1844 Marion County IL, buried Walnut Hill Cemetery, Salem, IL, married ab 1799 Margaret Ann Gaston.

1. John Paul, born 1780 SC, died 27 October 1841 Washington County IL; married 1802 SC to Mary Morton, born 1786 SC, died 27 August 1843 Washington County IL, daughter of Thomas Morton (born ca 1755, died ca 1830) & Elizabeth/Betsey Paul, born ca 1755, died ca 1830.

Children:
1. Eli McClod Paul, born 1808 SC


1. Eli McClod Paul, born 1808 SC, died 1871 Washington County IL; married 19 Jauary 1837 Lincoln County TN to Charlotte Robinson, born October 1816 AL, died October 1881 IL,

# Family of John Paul Jones

daughter of ---- (born Scotland, Baptist Preacher).

1840 census Lincoln Co TN; 1850 census Washington County IL.

Children:
1. Adrian Paul, born 28 May 1838 TN
2. Mary Paul, born 6 November 1839 TN
3. John Paul, born 11 February 1841 TN


John Paul Jones:

John Paul, married Jean MacDuff

Children:
4. John Paul, born 6 July 1747 estate of Arbigland, SW Scotland,


4. John Paul (later added Jones)

# Descendants of Andrew Graham

## SECOND GENERATION

2-1 ANDREW GRAHAM, (also written *Grumbs, Grimbs,* and *Grimes*, pages 65-74 in the genealogy), born probably in County Antrim Ireland, c. 1753, died in Todd County, Kentucky, between 11 March and May 1821 (dates of writing and probate of his will); married (1) in Chester County, South Carolina, c. 1774 to MARGARET COULTER, born probably in County Tyrone, Ireland, died in Chester County South Carolina, 1792-6, daughter of Robert Coulter and Mary Stuart; married (2) possibly MARY CHESNUT; married (3) MARGARET [PHILLIPS], born Ireland, 1770-4, died Henderson County, Illinois, after 1840.

Andrew, listed in the South Carolina Council Journal as Andrew Grumbs, came to America with his parents and siblings on the ship Pennsylvania Farmer which left Belfast on 16 October 1772 and arrived at Charleston, South Carolina, on 19 December 1772. He was part of the Rev. William Martin's group of five shiploads of settlers. On 6 January 1773 he went with the others before the South Carolina General Assembly to request land and on 17 March 1775, as Andrew Grimbs, received the single-person's grant of 100 acres. The land was in Craven (later Chester) County on Rocky Creek and was bounded by the lands of James Knox, Francis Henderson, Benjamin Mitchell, and Laird Burns (Royal Grant, Vol. 35, p. 307; and Colonial Plats, Vol. 16, p. 243).

Andrew may have married Margaret Coulter shortly before he received his land since their first child, Elizabeth, could have been born as early as 1775. On 6 February 1773 Margaret had been warranted 100 acres as a single person in Craven County on Rocky Creek on land bounded by that of Mary Ann Coulter (Margaret's sister) and Joseph Carley, other boundaries vacant (Colonial Plats, Vol. 14, p. 202). This 100 acre tract was later sold on 3 July 1791 by Andrew and Margaret Graham to Hugh McMillian (Book E, p. 263). Margaret Coulter Graham had the following siblings: (a) Archibald, born Ireland, c. 1753, died Todd County, Kentucky 1824; (b) Mary Ann, died Todd County, Kentucky, c. 1825, married John Stevenson; (c) Elizabeth, married ____ Kell; and (d) Robert Stuart, born County Tyrone, Ireland, c. 1760, died Madison County, Illinois, 1821, married in South Carolina, c. 1798, Margaret Fleming. Both Archibald and Robert S. had Revolutionary War records, and both, plus Mary Ann, received warrants in Craven County, South Carolina (Colonial Plats, Vol. 14, pp. 202-3).

During the Revolution Andrew fought in militias and provided beef for them, and on 24 May 1785 he filed a claim in the amount of 1 pound, 11 shillings, 5 pence sterling for his services. One militia he fought in was that of Capt. John Turner in Colonel Winn's regiment. Another was that of Capt. Alexander Turner belonging to the Upper Battalion of Colonel Richardson's Regiment under the command of Major Joseph Brown. Among those in the company were his brother 2-4 James as well as James Willson, John Madill, Alexander Chesnut, and John, Matthew, and Thomas McClurken -- all names associated with the Grahams.

During the war Andrew's name appeared on at least one land document: on 27 October 1779 he witnessed a deed of sale from Samuel and Frances Fulton to Robert McCullough (Book E, pp. 168-170). After the war Andrew's name appeared often on deeds and other documents in Chester County: (1) on 19 September 1785, Andrew Graham and Archibald Coulter were named as executors of the will of John Caskey, witnesses by Andrew as well as his father, David, and brother John: (2) July 1786, Andrew Grimes was paid 10 shillings for four days in court as a witness for Thomas McClurkin in his suit against John Holeman; (3) 5 January 1790, Andrew and Margaret Graham sold to Lard (sic) Burns, for 15 pounds, 100 acres granted to Andrew Grimbs on 17 March 1775 (Book B, pp. 576-8); (4) 7 May 1791, John Cameron sold to Andrew Graham 200 acres on Rocky Creek, Chester County (recorded 23 July 1799, Book G, pp. 94-7); (5) 3 July 1791, Andrew and Margaret Graham sold to Hugh McMillian 100 acres warranted to

# Descendants of Andrew Graham

Margaret Coulter in 1773 (Book E, p. 263); (6) January 1792, Andrew Graham gave an indenture of lease and release to Lard (sic) Burns (Order Book B, p. 167); (7) 22 November 1792, Andrew Graham and Robert Caskey witnessed two deeds of sale to John McKee from Matthew and Jenny McQuiston (Book F, pp. 142-6); (8) 28 November 1794, Andrew Graham, James Brown, and James Chesnut were witnesses to the will of Thomas McDill of Chester County; (9) 25 January 1797, a release from Andrew Graham to Hugh McMillen; (10) 24 January 1797, Andrew Graham, Matthew McClurken, and John Mabin were named as witnesses to the will of David Weir; (11) 25 January 1799, Andrew Graham was paid for three days at court as a witness on behalf of James Boyd in his suit against William Reedy and David Bell; (12) 9 May 1799, Andrew Graham, his son Matthew Graham, and his son-in-law Adam Mills were witnesses to two deeds of sale to another son-in-law, John Gleghorn (Book W, pp. 3-5); (13) 24 July 1799, Andrew Graham, James Cooper, and Adam Mills appeared in court as witnesses to the will of John McKee. John McKee was probably the future father-in-law of Andrew's third son, Robert C. Graham; and (14) Andrew sold 200 acres in Chester County on 24 October 1805 to John McClurkin for $900 (Book L. page 249–incidentally, in this deed Andrew identified himself as a blacksmith as was his father before him).

Andrew also served on the jury in the Chester County court at the January and July terms of 1787 and the July term of 1799, and in tow court cases he acted as foreman of the jury. (Before July 1787 he was listed as Andrew Grimes in the court records; after that time he was called Andrew Graham.) Also, in April 1790 Andrew was one of the men appointed as overseers for the construction of a north-south road beginning at the York County line on the North and continuing to Fairfield County on the South. Andrew's section was large: it began near Bull Run which is near the center of the county and continued south to the Fairfield County line. In September 1792, however, Andrew was relieved of his duty as overseer, and William Reedy was appointed in his stead. It is thought that Andrew's wife, Margaret Coulter, became ill or died at about this time, and her illness or death may have accounted for his being released from duty.

It is uncertain if Andrew had two or three marriages. The records in South Caroline and Kentucky only indicate two marriages: first to Margaret Coulter and the second to a Margaret whose maiden name is unknown. According to a family history compiled in the early 1900s by Bates McFarland Allen (1875-1969), a descendant of Andrew through his daughter Jennet Graham Mills (wife of Adam Mills), Andrew had three marriages. The first wife as Margaret "Coulton", second wife was Mary Chesnut, and the third wife was Margaret Phillips. This same information of the three wives of Andrew Graham was stated in a 1970 letter written by a Mrs. Lynn B. (Mary Jane) Harding, of Arlington VA, to 4-19B5a Mrs. Mary Firoved Bruington. Mrs Harding is/was a relation of Bates Allen.

Andrew and his family moved from Chester County, South Carolina to Kentucky in 1805-6 because the last deed transaction by Andrew in Chester County South Caroline was in 1805 and 1806 was the earliest year in which his name appeared on the Kentucky Tax Rolls. Andrew Graham's name did appear on two documents in Chester County South Caroline after 1805. He proved two land deeds to his son-in-law John Gleghorn on 1 November 1806. Since these deeds were not recorded until 17 October 1825 (Book W, pp. 3-5), the 1806 was probably an error on the part of the recording clerk, and the actual date of Andrew's proof of the two deeds was 1 November 1805.

Andrew was listed in 1806 Logan County Tax Rolls with an estate of 200 acres of "second rate land", on the Elk Fork, and owned one slave and three horses or mules. Matthew Graham [3-3], Andrew's son, and Adams Mills, Andrew's son-in-law husband of 3-2 Jennet Graham, also first appeared on the Logan-Christian County Tax Rolls in 1806. Another whose name first appeared on the Christian County Tax Rolls in 1806 was John McKee, probably the father of Martha B.

# Descendants of Andrew Graham

McKee who later married Andrew's son 3-6 Robert C. Graham. Probably several families, including the Grahams, Mills, Wilsons, and McKees migrated as a group from South Carolina to Kentucky in the winter of 1805-6.

The earliest known recorded land purchase by Andrew in Kentucky was in September 1809

Andrew continued to be listed in Logan County Tax Rolls until 1817. In the 1807 Tax Rolls Andrew's property was described as 238 acres of "third rate land", owned one slave and had two horses or mules. In 1810 he owned 238 acres of "third rate land" and had a slave and five horses, etc. In 1815 he paid taxes on 109 acres patented to B. Allen plus 138 acres of "third rate land." He also had a slave and four horses, etc. In 1815 his land was valued at $5 an acre, and the total value of his property including his slave and his horses was $1,740. In 1816 his "third rate land" consisted of 238 acres, with a total value of $1,730, and he still owned one slave and four horses. In 1817 he owned the same amount of land plus one slave and five horses or jacks, with a total value of $1,897.

No tax list is extant for Logan County in 1818. In 1819, Andrew was listed in Christian County (then next to Logan County). He owned 240 acres of "second rate" land, one slave, five horses, etc., totaling $2,955. Later in 1819, the area in Christian County where Andrew and his family lived became part of the newly established Todd County. The 1820 tax record for Todd County was the last Kentucky listing for Andrew Graham: he still owned 240 acres of "second rate" land, one slave, five horses, etc, totaling $2,825.

Will Book A, page 15

In the name of God Amen March the 11th Eighteen hundred & twenty one. I Andrew Graham of Todd county & State of Kentucky being very Sick & weak of body but of perfect mind & memory Thanks be to god. Therefore Calling to mind the mortality of my Body & knowing that it is appointed for all men once to die do make & constitute this to be my last Will and Testament that is to Say principally & first of all I give & recommend my Soul unto god who gave it & my body I recommend to the Earth to be buried in a decent & Christian manner at the Discretion of my Executors nothing doubting but at the general Resurrection I shall receive the same again by the mighty power of God touching Such worldly estate whereof it has pleased god to bless me in this life I Give devise & dispose in the following manner Viz, I will & bequeath my plantation containing near five hundred acres to my three Sons William M. Graham Thomas Graham & Andrew to be equally divided between them according to the valuation my Sone Andrew is to have his part laid off in the middle lot so as to include all my improvements also the Timber part of my land I wish in the Division to be equally divided between my three sons if any of them should die in their non age the land to be divided between the surviving heirs my son William is to have the mare which he calls his & is to pay thirty dollars to my wife and Daughter at the expiration of two years from this date which money is to be equally divided between my wife & three daughters my wife Margaret is to have decent support off my farm after paying my Just Debts all the balance of my property is to be equally divided between my wife and three daughters (to wit) my wife Margaret & Martha Margaret & Nancy my 3 daughters my wifes part at her death is to be equally divided between my three daughters above mentioned my widowed daughter Mary Maben is not to be disturbed in her possession which she may choose to keep them or until the land is sold my Book to be equally divided to all the above mentioned except my son Andrew is to have my large bible for his share of Books. I will & bequeath to Elizabeth Graham one Dollar also to the heirs of Jennet Mills deceased one dollar also to Mathew Graham one dollar also to Mary Maben one dollar also to David Graham one dollar also to Robt C. Graham one dollar with respect to my negro man Sandy my will is that my Executors should have the power of choosing his master if he must be hired out with I wish to be awarded if

# Descendants of Andrew Graham

possible all the profits arising from sd negro is to be divided equally divided between my wife & three daughters above mentioned (to wit) Martha Margaret & Nancy   I likewise make & ordain my two sons Mathew Graham & Robt C. Graham and William McKee the sole executors of this my last will & Testament & I hereby revoke & disavow all former wills & Testaments in witness whereof I have hereunto set my hand & seal this 11th day of May 1821

Andrew Graham (seal)

Signed sealed in presence of
Joseph C. Frazer
Hugh Brown

Recorded May 1821.

 Andrew died between March and May of 1821, but not until 1824 when his estate was settled did his widow, Margaret, appear on the Todd County tax rolls. At that time no land was listed in her name, but she did own one slave, one horse, etc., at a total value of $775.

 William McKee, brother-in-law of 3-6 Robert C. Graham, appeared as executor to the estate of Andrew Graham in the Todd County Tax Rolls between 1821-23. In 1821 Andrew Graham's estate consisted of 346 acres, one slave, four horses, etc.; and in 1822 the estate consisted of the same amount of land plus three horses, etc., but no slaves. By 1823 the estate amounted to 220 acres on Rain Lick Creek, no slave, one horse, etc., totaling $1,360. In 1824 William was no longer listed as Andrew's executor, presumably because the estate had been settled.

 It is interesting that William did not list Andrew's slave, Sandy, in 1822 and 1823. Andrew bequeathed Sandy to his widow and daughters, but they did not emancipate Sandy until 1829. In the 1837 & 1838 Todd County Tax Rolls, Sandy Graham was listed as a free black.

 The following accounts are selections from the probate records of the estate of 2-1 Andrew Graham (Todd County Court House Will Book A p. 169-175). Andrew Graham apparently continued to work in the blacksmith trade up until his latter years as two of these accounts were due the estate for blacksmith work.

-March 1822, Robert E Acock received $10 from Robert C Graham, administrator of the estate of Andrew Graham, for the schooling of Thomas Graham, son of Andrew Graham decd.

-Due to W.B. Scott, December 1820, $1.25 for 2 lb of coffee "lent to the old man" and 25 cents "lent to by sugar" ... received in full of Robert Graham 24 July 1822.

-Due to Alexander Thompson $3 for the tuition of two "schollars" 97 days during the lifetime of said decedent Andrew Grimes (sic) ... received payment 5 August 1822.

-Due to Shadrach Mims an account of $3.75: 15th September 1820 to 1 1/4 gallons of whs [whiskey] at 4/6 per gal for $00.93 3/4; 17th November 1820 to 2 ½ gallons of whs for $1.87 ½; 18th December to 1 1/4 gallons whs for $00.93 3/4  - total $3.75 ... received payment 28th day August 1822.

-Due to Joseph C. Frazer, 1820, to one gallon whiskey at 75 cents, also to one pint "Do" [whiskey] to 50 cents ... received 22 July 1822.

-Due to James Cordry to making one coffin at $2.00 ... received 23 July 1822.

# Descendants of Andrew Graham

-Due from Joseph C. Frazer, 10th June 1820, for Smith work: to Laing (?) of 1 shovel at 0.23, to sharping of 1 shovel plow at 0.40, to sharping of 2 shovel plow at 0.16, total $00.75 ... received by estate 22nd April 1822.

-Due from Samuel Lowry, paid 28 April 1823
    3rd August 1820:

| | |
|---|---:|
| to repairing waggon | $2.03 1/4 |
| to welding & putting on 2 tyre | 1.50 |
| April 1821: | |
| to working done by son John in Shop | 0.50 |
| to a balance of leather for the year 1819 | 0.25 |
| to a balance of leather for 1820 | 1.25 |
| to work done to boys | 0.37 1/2 |
| | $7.40 3/4 |
| | |
| Credit by Sandy 5 1/2 days at 50 cents per day | 2.75 |
| Paid to Wm Shankling | 4.60 3/4 |
| Todd City fee | 0.50 |
| | 5.18 3/4 |

-1821 Mr R. C. Graham with W. R. Bean, December 20th to making 1 pair coarse shoes for Sandy, 00.75, 11th January 1822 to making 1 pair fine shoes for Nancy 1.00 ... $1.75 Total.

-One day after state I promise to pay unto William Mills an order three hundred and fifty six dollars for value received of him given under my hand and seal this 20th December 1819 ... Andrew Graham, seal.

-Due to James L. Glenn, Box Ointment to William at 00.50, to "emetyet cathly" for sister at 1.25, received payment in full 25th July 1822.

-Due to Joseph Roberts, 1822

| | |
|---|---:|
| To one Quart of Whisky | 00.25 |
| To one do | 00.25 |
| To three gallons whisky | 1.87 1/2 |
| | 2.37 1/2 |
| The exrs of A Graham two gallons whisky | 1.25 |
| | 3.62 1/2 |

-Received of Robert C. Graham two Dollars for meeting house seat with other expenses August 8th 1823 ... James Chesnut. (Probably for the Hopewell Associate Reform Church in Todd County of which James Chesnut was a trustee).

-Andrew Graham indebted to John Campbell for one hundred weight of Tobacco at $4 dollar per hundred, received in the year 1820.

Personally appeared Joseph Roberts before me a Justice of the peace in & for said County [Todd] & made oath that the within acct is just and remains unpaid as written stated Given under my hand this 12th day of January 1825. J. C. Frazer JP.

The following is the appraisal bill of the estate of 2-1 Andrew Graham dated 23 May 1821 and

# Descendants of Andrew Graham

presented to the June Term 1821 Todd County Court (Todd County Will Book A p. 23-24). This bill gives a good overview of what items were of use to the Graham family at this time period.

| | |
|---|---:|
| 1 black cow & calf | 10.00 |
| 1 brindle cow & calf | 10.00 |
| 1 bell cow | 10.00 |
| 1 black cow & calf | 10.50 |
| 1 red cow & calf | 10.00 |
| 1 white face cow & calf | 12.00 |
| 1 white cow & calf | 8.00 |
| 2 white year old heifers | 8.00 |
| 1 black year old heifers | 4.00 |
| 16 head of hogs | 33.00 |
| 2 sows & 10 pigs | 11.00 |
| | 126.50 |
| 1 bay horse | 85.00 |
| 1 blaze face sorrel mare | 65.00 |
| 1 sorrel mare | 75.00 |
| 1 Waggon hind gear (unreadable) | 130.00 |
| 1 black man Sandy | 700.00 |
| | 1151.50 |
| 2 Ewes & lambs | 4.00 |
| 1 barshear plow | 7.00 |
| 1 shear plow | 3.00 |
| 1 shear plow | 3.00 |
| 1 bull toung plow | 1.75 |
| 1 horse harrow | 4.00 |
| 2 mallocks | 5.50 |
| 2 iron wedges | 2.00 |
| 2 weeding hoes | 2.00 |
| 1 foot edge & sprouting hoe | 1.50 |
| 1 pair of hackles 2 single trees | 1.50 |
| 1 Lott of Iron | 1.00 |
| amount of first column | $1217.73 |
| 4 old axes | 6.00 |
| 1 do | 1.00 |
| 1 log chain | 3.50 |
| 2 hammers & s(?) | 1.00 |
| 1 pitch fork | 0.50 |
| 2 blind bridles | 3.50 |
| 1 Lott of Bridles & --- | 11.50 |
| 2 pairs of gear & 2 shuck collars | 7.00 |
| 1 double tree & single tree & 2 clev-- | 3.50 |
| 3 augers & chizzles | 1.75 |
| 1 saddle & bridle | 7.00 |
| 1 do | 7.50 |
| 1 side saddle & bridle | 12.00 |
| | 54.25 |
| 1 lott sheep shears Jack plain branding iron | 1.00 |
| 1 brass buckle and iron do | 6.00 |
| 2 flat irons | 2.00 |
| ---- spools and cork shell | 1.25 |

# Descendants of Andrew Graham

| | |
|---|---|
| 1 stone jug & 2 old bridles | 1.25 |
| -- bells & collars | 5.00 |
| 1 grind stone | 1.00 |
| 1 hand saw | 2.00 |
| 1 sickle | 0.25 |
| 1 coffee mill | 0.50 |
| 3 halter chains | 3.00 |
| 5 barrels, 1 churn & basket | 3.00 |
| 3 milk crocks 1 flat (kit?) | 1.00 |
| 1 saddle bag | 2.00 |
| 1 rasp gimblet & horse sleams(?) | 1.25 |
| 3 flax wheels | 9.00 |
| 2 common chests | 1.50 |
| 1 churn & 2 water pails & strainer | <u>1.50</u> |
| Amount of second column | 97.20 |
| 1 Table & Bred [bread?] tray | 2.50 |
| 1 setter (?) & half bushel 2 old bags | 1.50 |
| 1 bedstead bed & furniture claimed by widow | 45.00 |
| 1 bed do & do claimed by Martha | 45.00 |
| 1 bed do & do claimed by Margaret | 45.00 |
| 1 bed do without furniture claimed by Nancy | 10.00 |
| 1 Press | 25.00 |
| 1 kettle & pot hooks | 3.00 |
| 1 Tea kettle | 2.00 |
| 1 small pot & skillet | 1.75 |
| 2 ovens & lids | 4.00 |
| 1 pair of hand irons | 2.50 |
| 2 [Patracks?] | 3.50 |
| 1 skillet | <u>1.25</u> |
| | 192.00 |
| cupboard furniture | 12.00 |
| 1 Dining table & linnen | 12.00 |
| 1 bureau | 20.00 |
| 1 brass candle stick & small trunk | 2.00 |
| 1 looking glass & cotton wheel | 3.00 |
| 5 chairs | 2.00 |
| Five Dogs tongs shovel & | 1.00 |
| 1 side saddle | <u>15.00</u> |
| | 259.00 |
| | 1217.75 |
| | <u>97.25</u> |
| Total amount | $1574.00 |

J. Brown, J.D. (Goren?), John McKee appraisers and Wm McKee, Matthew Graham, Robt C. Graham executors.


The sale bill of the estate of Andrew Graham is recorded in Todd County Will Book A p. 25-27, dated 30 May 1821. Those involved in the sale included family members & neighbors of the Grahams including: Adams Mills, William Mills, Robert C. Graham, Matthew Graham, John McKee, William McKee, Matthew Wilson, & John Coulter.

# Descendants of Andrew Graham

Children of Andrew Graham & Margaret Coulter, born Chester County SC:
3-1 ELIZABETH GRAHAM, born about 1775-7
3-2 JENNET GRAHAM, born about 1777-9
3-3 MATTHEW GRAHAM, born 17 January 1780
3-4 MARY GRAHAM, born about 1784
3-5 DAVID GRAHAM, born about 1787
3-6 ROBERT C. GRAHAM, born 11 July 1792

Children of Andrew Graham & either Mary Chesnut or Margaret Phillips:
3-7 MARTHA GRAHAM, born Chester County SC 23 August 1798
3-8 MARGARET GRAHAM, born Chester County SC about 1800
3-9 WILLIAM MILLS GRAHAM, born Chester County SC 26 September 1801

Children of Andrew Graham & Margaret Phillips:
3-10 THOMAS PHILLIPS GRAHAM, born Chester County SC, about 1803
3-11 NANCY GRAHAM, born Logan County KY, about 1807
3-12 ANDREW W. GRAHAM, born Logan County KY, bout 1809

2-2 JEAN/JANE GRAHAM ADAMS, born Ireland, died SC 1820-22; married SAMUEL ADAMS.

2-3 MATHEW GRAHAM, born probably Ireland, died in South Carolina, 1775-8.

It is not known beyond question whether 1-1 David Graham had a son named Matthew because no one of that name is mentioned in David's will (written 1795). On the other hand, a Matthew Grimbs was named immediately after 2-1 Andrew Grumbs and 2-2 Jean Grimbs on the list of people who had recently come from Belfast on the Pennsylvania Farmer and who on 6 January 1773 went before the South Carolina General Assembly to request land.

On 17 March 1775 (the same day on which Andrew Grimbs and Jean Grimbs were granted their land), Matthew was granted 100 acres in Craven (Chester) County on Rocky Creek. Matthew's land was bounded by lands of Samuel Willson, John McDonald, and Alexander Turner, the other sides vacant (Vol. 35, page 294). His name also appeared on two other documents: on 6 January 1773 William Fairy was warranted 200 acres in Chester County, and the land he later received in his grant by then was bounded by that of Matthew Grimbs, William Boyd, David Chesnut, John Pike, and Elisha "Garets." On the same day, John Smith was warranted 250 acres in Chester County, and the land he later received in his grant by then was bounded by that of Matthew Grimbs, Elisha Garret, William Hood, Thomas Hickling, and Jasper Rogers. Nothing more about Matthew appears in the records after 1775, however, so it is thought that he died soon after. Andrew named his first son Matthew, born 17 January 1780; perhaps the son was named for a deceased brother.

2-4 JAMES GRAHAM, born Ireland, 1761, died Tipton County TN, 1837; married (1) to unknown; married (2) in Chester County SC after 1785 to ESTHER ____. Esther had married (1) John Caskey, died 1785 Chester County SC.

Children of James Graham & unknown:
3-13 JULIANNA GRAHAM, born SC about 1785

Children of James Graham & Esther:
3-14 DAVID GRAHAM, born SC 1787-1797
3-15 JAMES GRAHAM jr, born SC about 1793

# Descendants of Andrew Graham

**3-16 ESTHER GRAHAM, born SC 1796**

**2-5 JOHN GRAHAM**, born Ireland, about 1767, died Chester County, South Carolina, between 30 August 1809 and 1 December 1809 (dates of writing and probate of his will); unmarried.

[The date of his birth is established at about 1767 or earlier because John witnessed with his brother 2-1 Andrew and his father, 1-1 David, the will of John Caskey dated 19 September 1785. John would have had to be at least eighteen years old to witness a legal document]

On 22 September 1795, a John Graham (perhaps unrelated to the Graham family in this study) received a deed of conveyance from Samuel Lowrie, and on 31 October 1796 a John Graham and a William Graham entered security for court costs in a lawsuit by William Rice versus Sherwood Nance. A John Graham sued Charles Atterberry on 1 February 1799 and was awarded $4 plus costs. A John Graham also served on a jury on 16 April 1799. The 1800 census of Chester County, South Carolina, showed two men named John Graham, therefore, these law cases may have referred to the unrelated man of that name.

For several years John was an elder in the Catholic Presbyterian Church in Chester County, serving until his death in 1809. He and his sister 2-7 Mary inherited most of their father's property.

John's will is transcribed verbatim as follows:

In The Name of God Amen.
I John Graham of Chester District State of South Carolina Being Sick of Body; But Sound of Memory & Judgement; & Calling to mind that it is Appointed for All men once to die– Therefore I do hereby make & ordain this as my last Will & Testament in Manner & form following this 30$^{th}$ Day of Augt in the Year of our Lord one Thousand eight Hundred & Nine: That is to Say

First I leave & Commit my Soul to the Hands of Almighty God who gave it; and my Body to my friends & Executors to be Decently Buried — Secondly (after the full payment of all my Just & Lawful Debts) I leave & Bequeath to my Niece Martha Adams the Sum of one Hundred Dollars to be taken equally off the whole of my Estate & paid her by my Executors.

Thirdly I leave & Bequeath to my Brother Andw Grahams the Sum of one Dollar and no more.

Fourthly I leave & Bequeath to Jane Adams Wife of Samuel Adams the Sum of One Dollar and no more.

Fifthly I leave & Bequeath to Jennet Boyse formerly the Wife of David Boyse the Sum of one Dollar & no more.

Sixthly I leave & Bequeath to my Brother James Grahams the Sum of one Dollar & no more.

Seventhly I leave & Bequeath the whole of the Remainder of my whole estate equally Betwixt my two Sisters Mary Grahams and Margaret Grahams by an equal Division.

Ninthly, and lastly I leave Constitute and Ordain James Chesnut and Robert Hamilton the Soal Executors and Administrators of this my last Will and Testament. Given under my Hand & Seal ths Day & Year above written.
   his
John T Graham L.S.

# Descendants of Andrew Graham

mark

Robert Wilson
Samuel adams [?]
John willson

This document was proved 1 December 1809 and recorded in Book D, page 434. It is located in Apartment No. 21.

2-6 JENNET GRAHAM BOYSE, (called Jane or Jenny), born Ireland about 1769, died Preble County Ohio, 10 March 1849, buried Hopewell Cemetery, Israel township, Preble County Ohio; married in South Carolina to DAVID BOYSE, born about 1763, died Union County Indiana 22 July 1827 (64 years and 7 days), buried Hopewell Cemetery, Preble County Ohio, son of David Boyse & Jane Archer.

No record of the Boyse family in Chester County SC. David Boyse & Jane Archer were residents of Abbeville 96 district SC

Jennet is mentioned in the will of her father & two siblings of Chester County South Carolina. In her father's will, written 2 April 1795, she was named as "Jinat Boys wife of david Boys." In the will of her brother 2-5 John, written 30 August 1809, she was mentioned as "Jennet Boyse formerly the wife of David Boyse." The will of her sister 2-7 Mary, written 21 January 1822, she is mentioned along with her two daughters "my niece Molly Peggy Boyse daughter of David Boyse of the state of Ohio the sum of sixty dallors ... bequeath to Elizabeth Boyse daughter of said David Boyse forty dallors ... to my sister Jane Boyse ten dallors.

Mary Graham's will shows that the family of David Boyse moved to Ohio as early as 1822. He is known to have been in Israel township Preble County Ohio by 1824 because he bought land from Martha Foster on 1 June 1824. The deed (Book 6, page 136) involved 60 acres in township 6 range 1 east section 2 in the northwest quarter for $120. The witnesses were John Ramsey and Thomas McDill. Later that year he moved to Union County Indiana which is across the border from Preble County. There is a record of a mortgage deed dated 31 December 1824 in the Preble County deed books (Book 6, page 245) by Miers Miller of Preble County to David Boyse of Union County Indiana. David and "Jenny" Boyse, of Union County Indiana, sold the land to Miers Miller on 31 December 1825 (Preble County deed Book 6, page 311).

David Boyse died in Union County Indiana 22 July 1827, where his will is recorded (Bk -, pages 53-4, dated 25 June 1827, proved 3 September 1827). He left all property & rights to "my beloved wife Jenny Boyse" and my two daughters "Polly P & Elizabeth Boyse." David appointed as executors of the will his brothers James Boyse & Robert Boyse, both of Preble County Ohio. Witnesses were John Pinkerton & Elizabeth M. Boyse.

Jennet and her daughters probably moved back to Preble County Ohio although Jennet, herself, did not die until 10 March 1849. On her tombstone is inscribed "Fell asleep on Sabbath 10th March 1849, Jennet Graham, wife of David Boyse at the age of 4 score years."

Children, probably born in South Carolina:
A. Mary Margaret Boyse, born 1795
B. Elizabeth Boyse, born about 1798

A. Mary Margaret Boyse Wilson (Molly P. or Molly Peggy or Mary P.), born probably South Carolina, 1795, died Preble County Ohio 28 September 1853, 59 years, buried Hopewell

# Descendants of Andrew Graham

Cemetery, Preble County Ohio; married in Preble County Ohio, 8 December 1841, to Matthew Wilson, born Ireland, about 1780, died in Preble County Ohio, 24 June 1863, buried Hopewell Cemetery, Preble County Ohio, son of John Wilson (died Chester County SC 20 November 1807) & Martha ___ (died Preble County Ohio, 10 December 1849, 88 years, buried Hopewell Cemetery).

Matthew Wilson had married (1) in Christian County, Kentucky, 9 March 1809, Jane or Jennet McQuiston (died Preble County Ohio 24 May 1837, 47 years, buried Hopewell Cemetery), daughter of William McQuiston & Jane Chesnut. Matthew moved to Preble County, Ohio, from Todd County, Kentucky, in 1829, about the same time that 3-3 Matthew Graham and 3-6 Robert C. Graham moved there with others from Kentucky. Matthew Wilson was a brother of Jennette Wilson who married 3-3 Matthew.

On 29 December 1851 Mary Boyse Wilson, her husband, Matthew Wilson, and her sister, Elizabeth Boyse, all of Preble County, Ohio, sold land to 4-3 John W. Graham, of Preble County Ohio for $2360 (Book 39, page 605). The land was in two sections of township 6 range 1 east: first in section 16, east half of southeast quarter consisting of 107 acres; second in section 21, part of northeast quarter consisting of 60 acres. Witnesses were David McDill & Nathan Brown.

B. Elizabeth Boyse, born probably in South Carolina, died after 1851, probably unmarried.

2-7 MARY GRAHAM, born probably Ireland, died Chester County, South Carolina, between 21 January 1822 and 7 October 1822 (dates of writing and probate of her will); unmarried.

2-8 MARGARET GRAHAM BLACKSTOCK, born Chester County SC, about 1775-80, died SC about 1836; married Chester County SC to Captain EDWARD BLACKSTOCK.

# Descendants of Jean Graham and Samuel Adams

ADAMS

First Generation

1-1 John Adams,

Second Generation

2-1 Jean (Jane) Graham Adams, born probably County Antrim, Ireland, 1754-8, died Chester County, South Carolina, perhaps 1820-2; married Samuel Adams, born in Ireland, died Chester County, South Carolina, 1822-7.

Sources list him as "Capt" Samuel Adams.

Children:
3-1 John Adams, born Chester County, South Carolina, 12 August 1785
3-2 Martha Adams, born Chester County, South Carolina, 1786-94
3-3 Mary Adams, born Chester County, South Carolina, 1786-95
3-4 Samuel Adams, born Chester County, South Carolina, 1786-94
3-5 David Adams, born Chester County, South Carolina, 1795-1800

Third Generation

CHILDREN OF JOHN ADAMS & JANE GRAHAM

3-1 John Adams, born Chester County, South Carolina, 12 August 1785, died Perry Township, Monroe County, Indiana, 4 January 1853, buried United Presbyterian Church Cemetery, in Bloomington Township, Monroe County, Indiana; married in South Carolina, Mary Simpson, born Chester County, South Carolina, ca May 1792, died Perry Township, Monroe County, Indiana, 3 April 1878, buried Clear Creek Cemetery, Monroe County, Indiana.

Monroe County IN Deed Index: Book 3 (mostly 1853-59)
-David Adams et al to 28 [record number] Joseph Adams, 18540306 [date deed] Bk P, p. 117
-Joseph Adams et al to 30 David Adams, 18560306 P 118
-Joseph Adams 91 David Adams, 18560719 Q 396
-David Adams guar, 93 Joseph Adams, 185607199 Q 397
-Mary Adams et al Benjamin F. Adams, 18540301 P 157

1850 census, District 132 Perry Township, Monroe County, IN, page 308-9, line 40, 208/208
John Adams, 65, farmer, 2500, SC
Mary Adams, 58, SC
Jane Adams, 27, SC
David Adams, 25, farmer, SC - next page
Joseph Adams, 23, SC
Jane Adams, 20, SC
Isabella Adams, 19, SC
Alexander Adams, 18, SC

1860 census, Perry Township, Monroe County, IN, p.o. Bloomington, page 553 [113], line 7, 802/777
David Adams, 38, farmer, 3000/1000, SC
Mary Adams, 61 or 69, SC
Jane Adams, 25, SC
Isabella Adams, 24, SC

# Descendants of Jean Graham and Samuel Adams

1870 census, Perry Township, Monroe County, IN, p.o. Bloomington (page 7) Smithville (page 8), page 387-8 [7-8], line 39, 48/45
David Adams, 49, farmer, 1500/1800, SC
Indiana Adams, 39, keeping house, IN
Sarah Adams, 5, at home, IN - next page
Emma Adams, 3, at home, IN
Mary Adams, 79, at home, SC, parents of foreign birth, can not write

Children:
4-1 Mary [Jane] Adams, born South Carolina, ca 1825 [1823?]
4-2 David Adams, born South Carolina, 4 October 1821
4-3 Joseph Adams, born South Carolina, September 1823
4-4 Jane Adams, born South Carolina, 15 February 1829
4-5 Isabella Adams, born South Carolina, 17 October 1831

3-2 Martha Adams, born Chester County, South Carolina, 1786-94

3-3 Mary Adams, born Chester County, South Carolina, 1786-95

3-4 Samuel Adams, born Chester County, South Carolina, 1786-94

1850 census, Chester County, SC, page 11, line 32, 166/166
Saml Adams, 50, farmer, 3000, SC
David Adams, 48, farmer
Mary Adams, 35, SC

3-5 David Adams, born Chester County, South Carolina, 1795-1800

1850 census, Chester County, SC, page 11, line 32, 166/166
Saml Adams, 50, farmer, 3000, SC
David Adams, 48, farmer
Mary Adams, 35, SC

1850 Slave Schedule, Chester County, SC, page 883, column 1, line 3
David Adams, 1 48 f B, 2 12 m B

1860 Federal Census Mortality Schedule, Chester District, SC, page [4], line 29
-David Adams, 63 yrs, male, married, born SC, died October, farmer, excessive drinking, number of days ill 7

Fourth Generation

CHILDREN OF JOHN ADAMS & MARY SIMPSON

4-1 Mary Adams, born South Carolina, ca 1825, died probably Monroe County, Indiana, after 1880; married in Monroe County, Indiana, 4 March 1847, David Johnson, born South Carolina, ca 1822, died Monroe County, Indiana, between 2 March and 26 May 1877 (dates of writing and probate of will).

1850 census, Salt Creek Township, Monroe County, IN,
page 316 [631], line 15, 67/67 -[page is crossed out with "see page 721"]
page 361 [721], line 15, 891/891 - [ "see page 631"]

# Descendants of Jean Graham and Samuel Adams

David Johnson, 28, farmer, 800, SC
Mary A. Johnson, 25, SC
Martha J. Johnson, 2, IN

1860 census, Perry Township, Monroe County, IN, p.o. Bloomington, page 581 [141], line 17, 1005/993
David Johnson, 39, farmer, 2800/1000, SC
Mary Johnson, 34, SC
Mary C. Johnson, 15, IL
Geo Johnson, 14, IN
Martha Johnson, 13, IN

Mary Johnson, 10, IN
Emma Johnson, 7, IN
Robt Johnson, 3, IN
Jane Johnson, 40, SC

1870 census, Perry Township, Monroe County, IN, p.o. Bloomington, page 396 [25], line 1, 181/170
David Johnson, 48, farmer, 500, SC
Mary Johnson, 23 [sic], keeping house, SC
Mary E. Johnson, 19, at home, IN
Emma Johnson, 16, IN
Robert Johnson, 13, at home, IN, can not read or write, idiotic
Frank Johnson, 10, at home, IN
Willie Johnson, 6, IN

1880 census, Perry Township, Monroe County, IN, ed 285, page 98 [3C], line 15, 22/22
Mary Johnson, 53, widow, keeping house, SC, SC, SC
Robert R. Johnson, 23, son, single, at school, blind, can not read or write, IN, SC, SC, - all
Frank N. Johnson, 20, son, single, at home
Willie G. Johnson, 16, son, at home
Samuel A. Johnson, 8, son,
Mary J. Johnson, 22, niece, single, at home,

Children:
A. Martha J. Johnson, born ca 1848
B. Mary Johnson, born ca 1850
C. Emma Johnson, born ca 1853
D. Robert R. Johnson, born 1857
E. Frank N. Johnson, born July 1860
F. William G. Johnson, born May 1864

---------

A. Martha J. Johnson, born ca 1848

B. Mary Johnson, born ca 1850

C. Emma Johnson, born ca 1853

D. Robert R. Johnson, born 1857

E. Frank N. Johnson, born July 1860, died after 1930; married in Monroe County, Indiana, Zera Vilula

# Descendants of Jean Graham and Samuel Adams

Denton, born Indiana, May 1865, died after 1930, daughter of Richard Denton (born Maryland, died Indiana) & Elivra (Hightower) (born Tennessee, October 1827, died after 1910).

1850 census, District 132 Bloomington, Monroe County, IN, page 292, line 27, 14/14
Richard N. Denton, 27, plasterer, 400, MD
Elvira Denton, 22, TN
William O. Denton, 1, IN
Laura Denton, 3/12, IN
Unicy Hightower, 69, NC
[household 11/11 - William Denton 56, bricklayer, MD, Elizabeth Denton, 57, MD]

1860 census, Bloomington Township, Monroe County, IN, page 702 [78], line 4, 183/183
Richard N. Denton, 38, plasterer, 800/75, MD
Elvira J. Denton, 34, TN
Wm O. Denton, 11, IN
Joseph M. Denton, 6, IN
Richard L. Denton, 4, IN
John Denton, 2, IN
Eunice Hightower, 78, TN

1870 census, Bloomington, Bloomington Township, Monroe County, IN, page 332 [17], line 19, 116/147
Richard Denton, 48, plasterer, 1000/800, MD
Elvira Denton, 42, keeping house, TN
William Denton, 21, plasterer, IN
Joseph Denton, 16, farmer, IN
Richard Denton, 14, at home, IN
Lula Denton, 5, IN
Lyda M. Denton, 3/12, IN, March

1880 census, Perry Township, Monroe County, IN, ed 285, page 102 [11C], line 42, 105/105
Richard Denton, 57, farmer, MD, MD, MD
Elvira J. Denton, 52, wife, keeping house, TN, NC, TN
William Denton, 30, son, single, laborer, IN, MD, TN - all
Richard Denton, 24, son, single, laborer
John Denton, 22, son, single, laborer
Lulu Denton, 15, daughter, at school

1900 census, Perry Township, Monroe County, IN, ed 98, page [7B], line 76, 139/141
Frank N. Johnson, head, July 1860, 39, marr 12, IN, SC, SC, farmer, o, m, f
Zera V. Johnson, wife, May 1865, marr 12, 4/4, IN, MD, TN
Mary E. Johnson, daughter, Nov 1889, 10, IN, IN, IN, at school
Elvira N. Johnson, daughter, Nov 1891, 8, IN, IN, IN, at school
Hester K. Johnson, Feb 1894, 6, IN, IN, IN, at school
Mildred L. Johnson, daughter, Oct 1895, 4, IN, IN, IN
Elivra J. Denton, mother-in-law, Oct 1827, 72, widow, 11/4, TN, TN, SC
William Denton, brother-in-law, Jan 1849, 51, single, IN, MD, TN, farmer, r, f, f

1910 census, Perry Township, Monroe County, IN, ed 137, page [8B], line 51, 158/161
Frank N. Johnson, head, 49, m1 22, IN, SC, SC, night watchman, ??rating plant, o, f, f
Zera Vilula Johnson, wife, 44, m1 22, 4/4, IN, MD, TN
Emily Johnson, daughter, 20, IN, IN, IN

# Descendants of Jean Graham and Samuel Adams

Norene Johnson, daughter, 18, IN, IN, IN
Catherine Johnson, daughter, 16, IN, IN, IN
Mildred Johnson, daughter, 14, IN, IN, IN
Elvira J. Denton, mother-in-law, 83, wd, 4/4, TN, TN, TN
William Denton, brother-in-law, 60, single, IN, MD, TN, farm laborer, works farm

1920 census, Perry Township, Monroe County, IN, ed 166, page [3B], line 68, 63/67
Frank N. Johnson, head, 59, IN, SC, SC, farmer, general farm
Zera A. Johnson, wife, 54, IN, MD, TN, none
Emila Johnson, daughter, 30, single, IN, IN, IN, none
Lovina Johnson, daughter, 28, single, IN, IN, IN, none
Catharine Johnson, daughter, 26, single, IN, IN, IN, sewing, tailor shop
Millard Johnson, son, 24, single, IN, IN, IN, teacher, public school
William D. Denton, brother-in-law, 70, single, IN, MD, TN, none

1930 census, Perry Township, Monroe County, IN, ed 18, page [15B], line 69, 335/346
Frank N. Johnson, head, 69, marr 28, IN, SC, SC, farmer, farm
Zera B. Johnson, wife, 64, marr 23, IN, MD, TN, none
Emily Johnson, daughter, 41, single, IN, IN, IN, none
Kathryn Johnson, daughter, 36, single, IN, IN, IN, clerk, dry goods store
Norene Kraft, daughter, 39, marr 30, IN, IN, IN, stenographer, law firm
Margarite Kraft, grand daughter, 8, IN, IN, IN, none
Richard R. Denton, brother-in-law, 72, D, IN, MD TN, plasterer, building

F. William G. Johnson, born May 1864

1900 census, Perry Township, Monroe County, IN, ed 98, page [13A], line 5, 255/257
William G. Johnson, head, May 1864, 36, marr 11, IN, SC, SC, farmer, o, f, f
Sarah E. Johnson, wife, Jan 1870, 30, marr 11, 6/4, IN, IN, SC
Mary A. Johnson, daughter, Jun 1891, 8, IN, IN, IN, at school
Clara M. Johnson, daughter, Apr 1893, 7, IN, IN, IN, at school
Lucy E. Johnson, daughter, Mar 1897, 3, IN, IN, IN
Florence Johnson, daughter, Nov 1888 [sic], 1, IN, IN, IN
George Stipp, father-in-law, Nov 1824, 75, widow, IN, KY, VA,

--------

4-2 David Adams, born South Carolina, 4 October 1821

Monroe County Deed Index:
Singleton Wm Comr 4177 [record #] Adams David 18611121 Bk U, page 103
State of IN 4214 Adams David 18630117 Bk U, page 229

1860 census, Perry Township, Monroe County, IN, p.o. Bloomington, page 553 [113], line 7, 802/777
David Adams, 38, farmer, 3000/1000, SC
Mary Adams, 61 or 69, SC
Jane Adams, 25, SC
Isabella Adams, 24, SC

1870 census, Perry Township, Monroe County, IN, p.o. Bloomington (page 7) Smithville (page 8), page 387-8 [7-8], line 39, 48/45
David Adams, 49, farmer, 1500/1800, SC
Indiana Adams, 39, keeping house, IN

# Descendants of Jean Graham and Samuel Adams

Sarah Adams, 5, at home, IN - next page
Emma Adams, 3, at home, IN
Mary Adams, 79, at home, SC, parents of foreign birth, can not write


4-3 Joseph Adams, born Chester County, South Carolina, 13 September 1823, died Monroe County, Indiana, 11 February 1905, 82 yrs; married Minerva Jane Whisenand, born Monroe County, Indiana, ca 1832, died Salt Creek, Monroe County, IN, 24 February 1894, daughter of Peter Whisenand (born ca 1809 Washington County, VA, died September 1857 Salt Creek, Monroe County, Indiana) & Elizabeth McGuire Myer (born 21 March 1807, died 16 April 1881 Coles, IL - note has her married to George Whisenand 1815-1875).

1860 census, Perry Township, Monroe County, IN, page 553 [113], line 2, 801/776
Joseph Adams, 37, farmer, 2000/1500, SC
Minerva Adams, 29, IN - all
Eliz Adams, 7
John L. Adams, 5
Milford Adams, 2
[next household - David Adams]

1870 census, Perry Township, Monroe County, IN, page 386 [6], line 31, 41/38
Joseph Adams, 47, farmer, 4000/1115, SC
Minerva J. Adams, 38, keeping house, IN
Lizzie Adams, 17, at home, IN
John L. Adams, 15, farm laborer, IN
Wilford Adams, 12, at home, IN
Joseph E. Adams, 9, at home
William Adams, 7, at home, IN
Pink Adams, 1, at home, IN

1880 census, Perry Township, Monroe County, IN, ed 285, page [8D], line 35, 74/74
Joseph Adams, 56, marr, farmer, SC, SC, SC
Minerva J. Adams, 48, wife, keeping house, IN, IN, KY
Elizabeth J. Adams, 26, daughter, single, at home, IN, SC, IN - all
Wilfred Adams, 21, son, single, works on farm
Edgar Adams, 19, son, single, school teacher
William Adams, 17, son,
Pink Adams, 12, daughter, at school
Evart B. Adams, 9, son

1900 census, Perry Township, Monroe County, IN, ed 98, page [2B], line 51, 34/36
Joseph Adams, head, Sept 1823, widow, Sc, Ireland, Ireland, farmer, o, f, f
Pink L. Todd, daughter, Oct 1869, 30, marr, 2/1, IN, SC, IN, house keeper
Charley E. Todd, son, March 1898, 2, IN, IN, IN

Indiana Deaths, 1882-1920:
-Joseph Adams, date 11 February 1905, Monroe County, 82 years, male, white, City Health Offic Bloomington.

Monroe County IN Deed Index:
William Bender 383 [record number] to Joseph Adams, 18610323 Bk T, p. 238

# Descendants of Jean Graham and Samuel Adams

Children, born Indiana:
5-Elizabeth J. Adams, born 1853,
5- John Lewis Adams, born 10 October 1854, died Bloomington, Indiana, 12 December 1930; married Sarah Payne, born Indiana, 10 December 1860, died Bloomington, Indiana, 12 January 1929, buried Clear Creek Cemetery, daughter of Jesse R. Payne & Margaret E. Shook. Child: 6- Joseph Simpson Adams, born 8 March 1887, died Bloomington, 26 November 1931, married Lyril Bell Pope, born Centrailia, Missouri 20 November 1892, died Bloomington, Indiana, 26 November 1971. Child: 7- Erma Virinda Adams, married Irvin M. Deckard.
5-Wilford C. Adams, born July 1858, died Monroe County, Indiana, 3 January 1913; married Monroe County, Indiana, 5 November 1890, Bridget Sarah Sherlock, born Clear Creek, Monroe County, Indiana, 17 April 1862, died Monroe County, Indiana, 3 September 1935.
5- Joseph Edgar Adams, born 1861
5- William H. Adams, born April 1863
5- Bancroft Adams, born ca 1865
5- Pink L. Adams, born October 1869
5- Evart B. Adams, born 1873
[OneWorldTree]


4-4 Jane Adams, born South Carolina, 15 February 1829

4-5 Isabella Adams, born South Carolina, 17 October 1831

# Descendants of ELIZABETH GRAHAM GLEGHORN

## GLEGHORN

[1-1]    DAVID GRAHAM, born probably in Ireland, died in Chester County, SC, about 1800; married probably in Ireland to JANET ____, born probably in Ireland, died Chester County, South Carolina, 1800-9.

Children of David Graham and Janet:
[2-1] Andrew Graham, born probably in County Antrim, Ireland, c. 1753


[2-1]    ANDREW GRAHAM, born probably in County Antrim, Ireland, c. 1753, died Todd County, Kentucky, 1821; married (1) in Chester County, South Carolina, to MARGARET COULTER, born probably in County Tyrone, Ireland, died Chester County, South Carolina, 1792-6, daughter of Robert Coulter & Mary Stuart; married (2) possibly Mary Chesnut; married (3) probably in Chester County, South Carolina, c. 1797, MARGARET [Phillips?], born Ireland 1770-4, died Henderson County, Illinois, after 1840.

Children of Andrew Graham and Margaret Coulter:
[3-1] Elizabeth Graham, born Chester County, South Carolina, 1775-77

## FIRST GENERATION

1-1    ELIZABETH GRAHAM GLEGHORN (pp. 95-8 in the genealogy as 3-1), born Chester County, South Carolina, 1775-1777, died probably in Lincoln County, Tennessee, 1830-40; married in Chester County, South Carolina, c. 1794, JOHN MATTHEW GLEGHORN, born Ireland, 1770-1775, died probably in Lincoln County, Tennessee, 1832-1840.

1830 census, Lincoln County, TN, page 169 or 259, line 24
John Gleghorn, Males; 1 10 to 15 yrs, 2 15 to 20 yrs, 2 20 to 30 yrs, 1 60 to 70 yrs; Females; 1 15 to 20 yrs, 2 20 to 30 yrs, 1 50 to 60 yrs

On 22 October 1831 John Gleghorn sold 86 acres in Lincoln County to Robert Meek for $530 (Book I p. 234). The tract was on Cold Water Creek and bordered property owned by William Smith among others. William Smith was the father-in-law of John's and Elizabeth's son 2-5 Matthew. John signed this deed with his mark. It was witnessed by William Smith and by John's and Elizabeth's sons 2-2 Andrew Gleghorn and 2-9 David Gleghorn.

Several children of John & Elizabeth (Graham) Gleghorn were members of either Prosperity Associate Reform Presbyterian Church, Bethel Associate Reform Presbyterian Church or the Hephzibah/Swann Creek Reformed Presbyterian Church all in Lincoln County Tenneesee[1].

The first families of Associate Reform Presbyterians were reported to have moved from the area of Abbeville, Chester, and Fairfield Counties South Carolina to Lincoln County Tenneesee around 1827. Some of these families settled ten miles south of Fayetteville and organized the Prosperity congregation, while other families settled about six miles west of Fayetteville and organized the Bethel congregation.

# Descendants of ELIZABETH GRAHAM GLEGHORN

Rev. Dr. Henry Bryson was installed as the first pastor of Prosperity Church on 17 May 1828 and served the congregation until April 1847. An amusing story concerning the early history of the Prosperity congregation is from The Centennial History of the Associate Reform Church:

> Prosperity had three houses of worship. The first was a log house built in 1828 and used for some time with only the dirt floor. During a protracted meeting one summer this log house was too small for the accommodation of the congregation, and they went to a grove in the graveyard. While they were preaching in the graveyard some young people got together and danced in the log church without floor. When they got through dancing the boys decided to have some fun at Dr. Bryon's expense, and sent for him to come in the church to talk with a young man (pretending to be) under conviction of sin and seeking for light. Dr. Bryson came and found the young man crying and feigning deep penitence. At once divining the situation he ordered the boys all to their knees and to prayer. Having done this Dr. Bryson began the prayer by asking God to convert the young man if his penitence was sincere, but if not sincere to strike him dead at once. The young man jumped up in great fright and got away. A few days later he came to Dr. Bryson, saying in earnest he was converted and joined the church.

Bethel Associate Reform Presbyterian congregation was organized also under Rev. Henry Bryson. The Bethel Church was consolidated with New Hope ARP Church (organized in 1850) in 1895 to form Elk Valley Assoicate Reform Presbyterian Church.

Hephzibah Reform Presbyterian Church was situated along the Elk Creek River, near Fayetteville. The congregation was organized 12 June 1812 as the Elk Congregation by Rev. John Reilly. The church changed names several times as it was also called the Swan Creek Reformed Presbyterian Church during the 1830s[2].

As mentioned in the genealogy, the Gleghorns were closely associated with the families of Thomas Gault, Grace Gault Johnson Wilson, and Nancy Gault Taylor, all children of William Gault & Rebecca Coffey. Pressley Brown Gault recounts some his hand stories of these families during 1800s as the author of the first Part of the The William Gault Family History[3]. He was a grandson of William & Rebecca (Coffey) Gault and nephew of John & Grace (Gault) Wilson. Pressley was born in --- and died in 1890 Sparta IL.

William Gault was born in Pennsylvannia about 1735 and settled in the Waxhaw area of North Carolina in the 1760s. He married Rebecca Coffey who was born in Virginia and they had 13 children. Soon after William Gault died, about 1803, Rebecca Coffey Gault moved to Williamson County Tenneesee with some of her family. After a few years members of this family moved again to Lincoln County TN and settled 5 miles west of Fayettsville.
According to Pressley Brown Gault, his Uncle John Wilson & Aunt Grace moved with three of their Gleghorn sons-in-law from Lincoln County TN to Sparta, Randolph County, Illinois in the spring of 1841. They stayed there in Sparta through the summer and moved back to Lincoln County TN in the fall. The next spring, all five of the Gleghorn sons-in-law moved with John & Grace (Gault) Wilson to Arkansas.

A different account of the move west by the Gleghorns was collected by Johnnie Karr Hairfield[4], who has done primary research in Arkansas. A Nolan Gleghorn of Izard County Arkansas tells the following story about how the Gleghorns came to settle near Franklin in

# Descendants of ELIZABETH GRAHAM GLEGHORN

that county.

A wagon train which included three Gleghorn cousins from Nashville, Tennessee, reached the Mississippi River. Most turned back but the Gleghorns persevered and built rafts to cross the torrent. When across, according to the story, they settled near Franklin.

A relative of this Nolan Gleghorn is a man named Devon, son of 5-96 Walter V. and Vesta B. Gleghorn. Devon was with Nolan when he repeated the story to Johnnie Hairfield's informant, and said the story was correct but that it was about four Gleghorn brothers, not three Gleghorn cousins, and two cousins named Harvey accompanied them.

1850 census, Subdivision 1, Lincoln County, TN, page 146, line 4, 552/552
Jno Wilson, 65, [?] carpenter, VA
Elizabeth Wilson, 34, TN
Ellen D? Wilson, 33, TN
James Wilson, 23, farmer, TN
William Wilson, 20, farmer, TN
Nancy Taylor, 10, TN
Constant E. Smith, 30, TN
[note: same page as Gleghorns & Gaults]

Children of John Gleghorn and Elizabeth Graham:
2-1 Samuel Gleghorn, born 19 November 1795
2-2 Andrew Gleghorn, born c 1798
2-3 Margaret (?) Gleghorn, born 1795-1804
2-4 Jane(?) Gleghorn, born 1800-4
2-5 Matthew Gleghorn, born c. 1802
2-6 John Gleghorn, born c. 1810
2-7 James Gleghorn, born c. 1810
2-8 David Gleghorn, born 1810-1815
2-9 Sarah Gleghorn, born c. 1814
2-10 Robert Gleghorn, born c. 1814
2-11 Elijah Gleghorn, born c. 1818
2-12 William Gleghorn, born c. 1820

# Descendants of Alexander Chestnut

Sources:
-Daniel L. Chesnut Rt 1, Box 51, Byars, OK, 74831-9736 <chesnut@ionet.net> webpage www.familtreemaker.com/users/c/h/e/Daniel-sr-L-Chesnut/index.html
-Lawrence Glenn Hardin <lawrencehardin@netscape.net> webpage via rootsweb connection.
-Cindy Taylor <ctmgm@earthlink.net> webpage via rootsweb connection

## CHESNUT/CHESTNUT

### First Generation

1. Alexander Chesnut, born Isle of Wight, died 1690; married unknown.

Child:
1. Alexander Chesnut, born 1672

### Second Generation

1. Alexander Chesnut, born 1672, died 1749 Frederick County VA; married in County Antrim Ireland to Mary Adrian O'Draine.

Children:
1. William Chesnut, born ab 1712 County Antrim, Ireland, died bef 24 February 1783 Rockingham County VA/ now Highland County VA; married unknown. Children: John, William & Samuel.
2. David Chesnut, born 1713 County Antrim Ireland
3. John Chesnut, born 1715, died ; married unknown. Child: William
4. James Chesnut, born 1717, died 1754/5 near Winchester, Frederick County VA; married Margaret Cantey, born Feb 1722/3 Ireland. Children: 1. Margaret Chestnut, married James/Alexander Irwin; 2. Col. John Chesnut, born 18 June 1743 Shanandoah Valley VA, died 1 April 1813, buried Knights Hill, near Camdem, SC, married 1770 Camden, SC to Sarah Cantey; 3. James Chesnut, born 1745, died 8 December 1772.

### Third Generation

1. DAVID CHESNUT, born 1713 County Antrim, Ireland, died about 1779 Chester County SC; married Jane/Jannette Brown, born [1735 Ireland], died [1798 SC], daughter of Alexander Brown (born 1685 Ireland, died Chester County, SC) & Margaret McDill.

Land grant for David Chesnut of 200 acres on Rocky Creek on 3 February 1773.

Will of David Chesnut, planter, Rocky Creek, Chester County SC, dated 22 April 1778, proved December 1779. [Apt 8, pkt 122].

Children of David Chesnut & Jane Brown:
1. Alexander Chesnut, born 4 July 1759 Ireland
2. Samuel Chesnut, born 1739/40 Ireland
3. Margaret Chesnut, 1 November 1739 Ireland
4. Martha Chesnut, born before 1748 Ireland
5. Barbara Chesnut, born December 1748 Ireland
6. James Chesnut, born, born 1752/7 Ireland
7. Janet Chesnut, born ab 1760 Ireland

# Descendants of Alexander Chestnut

["The Revolutionary Soldiers of Catholic Presbyterian Church, Chester County, South Carolina", 1978, Mary Wylie Strange. Page 32]["Heritage History of Chester County SC", 1982, Chester County Heritage History Committee.]

Fourth Generation

1. Alexander Chesnut, born 4 July 1759 County Antrim Ireland, died 9 May 1809 Christian County (now Todd County) KY, buried Chesnut or Old Seceder Cemetery, Todd County KY; married Sarah Meek, born 1766 Ireland, died 13 July 1831 Todd County KY, about 65 yrs, buried Chesnut Cemetery or Old Seceder Cemetery, Todd County KY, daughter of James Meek (will in Chester County SC) & Martha.

Alexander Chesnut served in Revolutionary War as private in Col. Winn's Regt SC militia. Bronze plaque with information on Alexander Chesnut at the Chesnut Cemetery on Traughber Road, off highway 102 in Todd County.

Christian County KY Deeds
Bk C, page 180, dated 28 September 1810:
John Lowry & Sally, wife, for $950 paid by Administrators of Alexander Chesnut, deceased, Sarah Chesnut & James Chesnut are Ad. Inv., 400 acres in Christian County. Signed John Lowry & Sally Lowry.
Bk C, page 370, dated 1812:
Samuel Lowry & ---- Chesnutt for $157 a parcel of land, 45 acres, on east fork of Red River. Signed Samuel Lowry.

History of Todd County, Kentucky, ed. J. H. Battle, 1884, F. A. Battey Publishing Co., 1884, pp. 318-19.    [Trenton Precinct]

THE CHESNUT FAMILY. Among the prominent families who early immigrated to Todd County in the pioneer days, may justly be mentioned the one appearing at the head of this brief sketch. Near the beginning of the present century the widow Chesnut removed from North Carolina to Todd County, Ky., and settled on the Elk Fork of the Red River. With her came her sons, Samuel James, John and Alexander. They were zealous members of the old Seceder Church. Of these sons, Samuel, born in North Carolina, 1793, was a valiant soldier in the war of 1812, and died in 1866. His son, William A. Chesnut, was born October 4, 1819, in Princeton, Ky.; removed to Todd County with his parents in 1828, where he married Margaret M., daughter of David N. and Lydia (McElwain) Russell, of this county, where he died January 30, 1879. Mrs. Margaret M. Chestnut [sic] was born September 24, 1822, and is still living. Their children are: Lydia A. (deceased), Samuel D., James W. and Martha J. (Burge). Samuel David Chesnut was born August
2, 1857, at the place of his present residence, in Todd County, Ky., where he has all his life retained his residence. He was favored with a fine classical education, and is still an intelligent student of standard works, and the current literature of the day. He is actively engaged in farming and stock-raising, superintending the family homestead of 540 acres of valuable land, which he successfully cultivates. He is a member of the Masonic Fraternity, and also of Cumberland Presbyterian Church. James W. Chesnut, Trenton, is a native of Todd County, where he was born August 20, 1862, and where he has all his life resided. He is the son of William A. and Margaret (Russell) Chesnut. He early obtained a good education, and in the midst of active duties finds time to devote to reading. In 1881, he commenced merchandising in Trenton (firm style Chesnut & Russell) at which he has been fairly successful. He is extensively engaged in the implement trade, and the firm handle a fair proportion of the produce shipped from

# Descendants of Alexander Chestnut

Trenton. In religion he is a Cumberland Presbyterian, and in politics a Democrat.

Children of Alexander Chesnut & Sarah Meek:
1. Jennet Chesnut, born SC
2. David Chesnut, born 3 March 1785
3. Elizabeth Chesnut, born 1 May 1808
4. Louise Chesnut
5. Martha Chesnut
6. Sarah Chesnut
7. William Chesnut
8. James Chesnut, born 1780/90
9. Samuel Chesnut, born 17 June 1783 Chester County SC
10. Margaret Chesnut, born 1787
11. John Chesnut, born 25 July 1795 Chester County SC
12. Alexander Chesnut, born 1800
["The Revolutionary Soldiers of Catholic Presbyterian Church, Chester County, South Carolina", 1978, Mary Wylie Strange. Page 37]["American Descendants of John "Jean" Gaston", 1997, Max Perry, page 222]

2. Samuel Chesnut, born , died before 14 July 1817; married unknown.

Child:
1. William Chesnut, ; married Margaret McDill, born October 1772, daughter of Thomas McDill & Margaret Chesnut.

3. Margaret Chesnut, born 1 November 1739 Ireland, died 6 December 1827, buried; married Thomas H. McDill, born 1725 Broughnow, Ballymena Parish, County Antrim Ireland, died 4 December 1794, son of John McDill & Janet Leslie.

Children:
1. John McDill, born 1760 Ireland, died 3 November 1848, buried Moffatt-Strong-McDill Cemetery, Chester County SC: married Mary Brown, born 1771, died 2 December 1832.
2. David McDill, born 17 March 1763 Ireland, died 7 March 1843, buried Hopewell Cemetery, Preble County OH; married Isabella McQuiston, born 1773 SC, died 6 August 1829. Moved from SC to OH in 1806.
3. Samuel McDill, born 1767 Ireland, died 2 December 1851, buried OH; married Jennet Bonner, born 1772, died 23 May 1847, buried OH. Moved from SC to IN in 1816.
4. James McDill, born 20 December 1769 Ireland, died 21 November 1854, buried South Henderson Cemetery, Henderson County IL; married Margaret Chestnut, born 25 December 1778. Moved from SC to Rossville OH in April 1807; 1809 to Preble County OH; 1846 to South Henderson IL.
5. Margaret McDill, born October 1772, died SC; married William Chesnut.
6. Thomas McDill, born 8 March 1775 SC, died 13 June 1813 of a disease contracted while serving in the War of 1812; married Mary Young. Moved to Preble County OH from SC in 1807. Buried in Hopewell Cemetery.
7. George McDill, born 3 September 1777 SC, died 14 December 1864 Henderson County IL; married Margaret Douglas, born 2 November 1779, died 2 August 1847. Ten children, four of whom died in one month in 1840 of "prairie fever".. Moved from SC to Newton GA in 1825, where he helped found Hopewell APR Church. In April 1837, moved to Henderson County IL in covered wagons because opposition to slavery. Both buried in South Henderson Cemetery.
8. Alexander McDill, born March 1780 SC, died 12 March 1838, buried Moffatt-Strong-McDill

# Descendants of Alexander Chestnut

Graveyard, Chester County SC.
9. Jane McDill, born 11 December 1785 SC, died 29 January 1870; married 1811 to Alexander Brown.

4. Martha Chesnut; married John Barber

5. Barbara Chesnut, born 1748, died 6 September 1829, buried Moffatt-Strong-McDill Graveyard, Chester County SC; married William Moffatt, born 1738, died 20 January 1794, buried same, son of Samuel Moffatt & martha McCully.

Children:
1. Samuel Moffatt, born , died 9 February 1854, 85 yrs, buried Moffatt-Strong-McDill Graveyard, Chester County SC; married Mary Curry, born 1770, died 10 August 1819, buried same; married (2) Jane Telford, born 1806, died 1878
2. James Moffatt, born , died 8 May 1805 buried Moffatt-Strong- McDill graveyard, Chester County SC; married unknown.
3. Martha Moffatt, born 1777, died 2 February 1837, buried Fishing Creek Presbyterian Church, Chester County SC; married John Millen, born 1776 SC, died 31 July 1844, buried same, son of Robert Millen (born 1746 Coleraine, County Antrim Ireland, died 29 April 1806 Fishing Creek Cemetery) & Margaret Elizabeth Wilson (born 1753, died 2 September 1785, 72 yrs, buried Fishing Creek Cemetery)..

6. James Chesnut, born died 1 September 1822, buried Moffatt-Strong-McDill graveyard, Chester County SC; married Esther Stormont, died 24 September 1821, 68 yrs, buried same.

Children:
1. James Chesnut
2. Jeannette Brown Chesnut, born 22 April 1790, died 31 July 1864 Xenia, OH
3. Martha Chesnut, died 3 January 1860 Cederville Twp, Greene County OH
4. Esther Chesnut, born 4 January 1796, died 2 February 1826 Chester County SC

7. Janet Chesnut, born , died ; married George Cherry, died 1806, son of Robert Cherry & Mary Riley.

## Fifth Generation

### Children of Alexander Chesnut & Sarah Meek

1. Jennet Chesnut, born SC

2. David Chesnut, born [13] 3 March 1785 Camden District, SC, died [28 April or 28 March] 25 November 1837 in Newton County GA, buried Hopewell ARP Cemtery, Newton County GA; married ca 1804 SC to Jane [Gaston] Gladney, [born 1 March 1785 Fairfield County, SC, died 15 January1865 Chamblee, De Kalb County, GA], buried Prosperity Cemetery, De Kalb County, GA, daughter of Robert Gladney (born 1741 Kinbally County Antrim, Ireland, died 2 August 1793 Winnsboro, Fairfield County, SC) & Janet Strong (born 1757 County Antrim, Ireland, died 22 September 1833 Winnsboro, SC).

Moved to Newton County GA in 1829. Probably buried in New Hopewell ARP Church Cemetery in GA.

# Descendants of Alexander Chestnut

Children:
1. Mattie Chesnut
2. William Roseborough Chesnut, born 23 February 1805 Fairfield, SC
3. Sarah Chesnut, born 19 September 1806 Fairfield, SC
4. Jennet G Chesnut, born 8 January 1808
5. Alexander James Chesnut, born 27 August 1809
6. Martha Elizabeth Chesnut, born 30 May 1811
7. J. I. Chesnut, born 1813 DeKalb County, GA
8. Letitia Strong Chesnut, born 1815
9. Margaret Chesnut, born 1817
10. Richard Gladney Chesnut, born 1819
11. David Chesnut, born 1821
12. Samuel J. Chesnut, born 1826
13. Malinda Jane Chesnut, born 1826
14. Charles Gladney Chesnut, born 1829
["The Revolutionary Soldiers of Catholic Presbyterian Church, Chester County, South Carolina", 1978, Mary Wylie Strange. Page 37]["American Descendants of John "Jean" Gaston", 1997, Max Perry, page 222]

3. Elizabeth Chesnut, born 1 May 1808 SC, died 1820 Todd County KY, buried "Old Seceder" or Chestnut Cemetery Todd County KY; married in Todd County KY to John Millen.

4. Louise Chesnut

5. Martha Chesnut, born , died Todd County KY; married 31 January 1828 Todd County KY to Walter W. Price.

6. Sarah Chesnut,

7. William Chesnut

8. James Chesnut, born 1780/90 SC, died ; married Elizabeth Stevenson, born , died prior to 1854, daughter of John Stevenson & Mary Ann Coulter.

Moved to Macoupin County Illinois by 1854.

1850 census, Cartinville, Macoupin County, IL, page 175, line 21, [1/1] - Hotel
John A. Chesnut, 34, lawyer, 10000, KY

Children:
1. John A. Chesnut
2. Daughter ; married G.B. Waller
3. Daughter ; married M.F. Wood.

9. Samuel Chesnut, born 14 June 1783 Chester County SC, died 5 October 1866 Todd County KY, buried Chesnut Cemetery or Old Seceder Cemetery, Todd County KY; married 17 December 1818 Christian County KY to Martha (Patsy) B. Wimms..

Samuel Chesnut was a private in 10th Regt Ky Mounted Milita in War of 1812.

1850 census, District No 2, Todd County KY, page 270, line 6, 341/341

# Descendants of Alexander Chestnut

Samuel Chesnut, 57, famer, 2200, SC
Martha B. Chesnut, 50, VA
William Chesnut, 30, farmer, 1600, KY - all
Patterson do, 19, student
Louisa do, 17
James do, 14
David do, 11
[previous household - previous page, John Chesnut, 54, Ruth, 37]

1860 census, Todd County, KY, p.o. Elkton, page [22], line 20, 146/146
Samuel Chesnut, 67, farmer, 10000/10000, SC
Martha B. Chesnut, 60, VA
Jas Chesnut, 23, farmer, -/200, KY
David Chesnut, 21, KY

History of Todd County, Kentucky, ed. J. H. Battle, 1884, F. A. Battey Publishing Co., 1884, pp. 318-19.    [Trenton Precinct]

THE CHESNUT FAMILY. Among the prominent families who early immigrated to Todd County in the pioneer days, may justly be mentioned the one appearing at the head of this brief sketch. Near the beginning of the present century the widow Chesnut removed from North Carolina to Todd County, Ky., and settled on the Elk Fork of the Red River. With her came her sons, Samuel, James, John and Alexander. They were zealous members of the old Seceder Church. Of these sons, Samuel, born in North Carolina, 1793, was a valiant soldier in the war of 1812, and died in 1866. His son, William A. Chesnut, was born October 4, 1819, in Princeton, Ky.; removed to Todd County with his parents in 1828, where he married Margaret M., daughter of David N. and Lydia (McElwain) Russell, of this county, where he died January 30, 1879. Mrs. Margaret M. Chestnut [sic] was born September 24, 1822, and is still living. Their children are: Lydia A. (deceased), Samuel D., James W. and Martha J. (Burge). Samuel David Chesnut was born August 2, 1857, at the place of his present residence, in Todd County, Ky., where he has all his life retained his residence. He was favored with a fine classical education, and is still an intelligent student of standard works, and the current literature of the day. He is actively engaged in farming and stock-raising, superintending the family homestead of 540 acres of valuable land, which he successfully cultivates. He is a member of the Masonic Fraternity, and also of Cumberland Presbyterian Church. James W. Chesnut, Trenton, is a native of Todd County, where he was born August 20, 1862, and where he has all his life resided. He is the son of William A. and Margaret (Russell) Chesnut. He early obtained a good education, and in the midst of active duties finds time to devote to reading. In 1881, he commenced merchandising in Trenton (firm style Chesnut & Russell) at which he has been fairly successful. He is extensively engaged in the implement trade, and the firm handle a fair proportion of the produce shipped from Trenton. In religion he is a Cumberland Presbyterian, and in politics a Democrat.

Children:
1. William Chesnut, born [1831] 1820 KY
2. Patterson Chesnut, born 1831 KY
3. Louisa Chesnut, born 1833
4. James Chesnut, born 1836
5. David Chesnut, born 1839 KY

10. Margaret Chesnut, born 1787, died 1844 [4 May 1836 Macoupin County, IL; married Robert Stevenson, born [1778 Mecklinburg, NC], died 19 April 1852 Macoupin County IL, son of John

# Descendants of Alexander Chestnut

Stevenson & Mary Ann Coulter.

1850 census, Macoupin, Macoupin County, IL, page 213, line 12, 3/3
W.R. Cass, 33, farmer, 1500, OH
Margaret J. Cass, 29, KY
Henry M. do, 7, IL
Caroline do, 5, IL
Ambrose B. do, 3, IL
Heneretta I? do, 1/12, IL

Children:
1. Daughter ; married W.R. Cass.

11. John Chesnut, born 26 July 1796 [25 July 1795] Chester County SC, died 1 January 1873 [14 January 1873) Todd County KY, buried Chesnut Cemetery or Old Seceder Cemetery, Todd County KY; married (1) 4 October 1821 Todd County KY to Sarah Maben/Maybin, born 9 July 1804 SC, died 30 January 1835, buried Chesnut Cemetery or Old Seceder Cemetery Todd County KY, daughter of Andrew Maben & Mary Graham; married (2) 13 June 1836 Todd County KY to Ruth Wilson Vance, born 7 November 1812 Mecklenberg, SC?, died 1 January 1873 Todd County KY, buried Chesnut Cemetery or Old Seceder Cemetery, Todd County KY, daughter of John Vance & Martha Davidson.

1850 census, District No 2, Todd County KY, page 270, line 35, 340/340
John Chesnut, 54, farmer, 3000, SC
Ruth do, 37, KY - all
Washington do, 27
Jane do, 25
Mary E. do, 23
John W. A. do, 13
James A. do, 11 - next page
Samuel M. do, 9
Franklin do, 7
Martha L. do, 5
John W. do, 3

Children by first wife:
-A. Washington Chesnut, born 1823, died ; married 26 May 1856 Todd County KY to M F Belamy. Resident of Paducah, McCracken County KY, in 1884.
-Jane Chesnut, born 1825
-Mary Chesnut, born 5 January 1827, died 13 November 1861 Todd County KY, buried Chesnut Cemetery; married 15 February 1855 Todd County KY to Jeptha Hollingsworth Duncan.

Children:
-John William Alexander Chesnut, born 1837, after 1850 Ballard County KY [18 December 1857]
-James Augustus Chesnut, born 1839
-Samuel Massena Chesnut, born 24 March 1842, died 20 August 1865 buried Chesnut or Old Seceder Cemetery, Todd County KY.
-Franklin Marion Chesnut, born 23 February 1844, died 1910; married 6 October 1870 Todd County KY to Joyce Josephine Drake.
-Martin Luther Chesnut, born 1845 Todd County KY, died 9 November 1904 Marshall County KY, buried Provine Cemetery; married Laura L. Beaty, born 1848 KY; married (2) 16 January 1901 to Addie Houston

# Descendants of Alexander Chestnut

-Underwood Porter Chesnut, born 1848 Todd County, KY, died 22 February 1883; married Ollie Morrison [Olive (Sarah) Morrison], born May 1850 Montgomery County TN, died 1 May 1900, daughter of James Morrison & Elgantine Emily Walton.
-Sarah Ellen Chesnut, born 1851 ; married 18 February 1873 Todd County KY to Robert H. Coleman
-Margaret Jane Chesnut, born 1853; married Charles Connor, born TN

12. Alexander Chesnut, born [28 December 1799 SC] 1800, died 17 April 1881 Doraville, GA.

Chesnut Cemetery has: "In Memory of Alexander Chesnut, died May 1859, aged about 50 years, erected by Samuel Chesnut".

1860 census, Todd County, KY, p.o. Elkton, page [3], line 35, 22/22
Alexander Chesnut, 60, farmer, 2200/4000, SC
El. J. Chesnut, 37, KY - all
A. T. do, 8, (m)
A. P. do, 7, (m)
Jas. W.. Do, 5, (m)

1870 census, Elkton Precinct, Todd County, KY, p.o. Elkton, page 352 [50], line 17, 270/265
Alexander Chesnut, 70, farmer, 2000/3000, SC
Elizabeth J. do, 47, keeping house, KY
Andrew T? do, 18, farm laborer, -/100, KY
Alexander P. do, 17, farm laborer, KY
James W. do, 15, farm laborer, KY

# Emigration Led by Reverend William Martin in 1772

"Presbyterian Emigrations from Ulster to South Carolina; the Cahans Exodus from Ballybay to Abbeville in 1764" by Hugh McGough

http://magoo.com/hugh/cahans.html

Emigration Led by Reverend William Martin in 1772

Several Presbyterian pastors led their congregations in emigrations from Ulster to American in the decade following Doctor Clark's emigration from Ballybay in 1764. The most notable of these was the emigration of Covenanter Presbyterian in 1772 from the area of Kellswater in central county Antrim. Were are interested in Reverend Martin because he settled in the general area of Abbeville, South Carolina (Rocky Creek in Chester County), and after his church was burned by the British in 1780, he took refuge in Mecklenburg County, North Carolina.

The emigrants led by Reverend Martin traveled to Charleston, South Carolina, in five ships from Belfast, Larne, and Newry, and settled throughout western South Carolina, many in the Abbeville area. The story is told in "Scotch-Irish Migration to South Carolina, 1772: Reverend William Martin And His Five Shiploads of Settlers" by Jean Stephenson (Shenandoah Publishing House 1970).

The background of the Rev. William Martin is in "History of Kellswater Reformed Presbyterian Church: A Short History" by Robert Buchanan. He was born the oldest son of David Martin of Londonderry. The Rev. Martin was the only Covenanter minister in counties Down and Antrim at the time. In 1760 he resided at Kellswater. He had oversight responsibility for societies at Cullybackey, Laymore, Cloughmills, and Dervock. He preached also in Londonderry and Donegal. The Presbytery was founded in 1743 and Kellswater became the center in 1760.

See also: Kellswater Reformed Presbyterian Church. Chapter X: Irish and Emigrant Places and Lineages: [or "Back to 'Bonnie Kellswater'", by Eull Dunlop (of the Cambridge House Boys' Grammar School, Ballyemena, Co. Antrim), in Familia, the Ulster Genealogical Review, Vol. 2, No. 5 (1989), page 87:]

"First things first. Where is Kellswater? The name, is unofficial and not found on the maps, is wholly familiar to folk in Mid-Antrim. Local authorities suggest that it is most accurately applied to the district which lies between Ross's Factory, on the Antrim-Ballymena 'line', and Kellswater railway station, truly the 'terminus ad quem'. Here, in other words, is a general name, for an area beginning in the townland of Ballymacvea, but crossing the burn into Tullynamullan. What, then, about Kellswater Reformed Presbyterian church, the Covenanters' meeting-house at 'the back of the Water', above the Shankbridge, in the townland of Carnaughts. This oldest congregation (1760) in its denomination, the 'capital of Covenanting' in the phrase of Principal Adam Loughridge, is some miles distant. As the late Superintendent Robert Buchanan (R.U.C.) pointed out in his recently-published Short History, the congregation of Kellswater (like the sister cause of Faughan, county Londonderry) . . . does date its title from a river, but no fastidious local (as opposed to anyone using 'Kellswater' in imprecise association) would apply the name to that place."

" Kellswater is in the townland of Carnaghts in the Parish of Connor. See Kellswater Reformed Presbyterian Church, Co. Antrim, A Short History, by Robert Buchanan, published by The Congregational Committee, Kellswater Reformed Presbyterian Church, 21 Grove Road, Shankbridge, Ballymena, Northern Ireland, BT42 3DP, June 1989. The Rev. William Martin is listed as the Minister from 1760 to 1772." County Antrim, Ireland to Chester County, South Carolina to Randolph County, Illinois—Dispersal of Some of the Descendants of John LYNN and

# Emigration Led by Reverend William Martin in 1772

Jennet MALCOLM by James H. Lynn.

From "Back to 'Bonnie Kellswater, 2'", by Eull Dunlop (of the Cambridge House Boys' Grammar School, Ballymena, Co. Antrim), in Familia, the Ulster Genealogical Review, volume 2, number 6 (1990), pages 91, 94:

"The Presbyterian preponderance in the parish of Connor has already been emphasised, but how many of those who emigrated from Kellswater in the last century (the 19th) were also ... members of the Orange Order?.... even today, men of senior years remark how, in their own youth, striplings in a homogeneous community 'rode the goat' (were initiated) as a matter of hereditary course. How much more so in the last century when, despite the transatlantic travel under discussion, the world was small and, as local marriage registers show, many married within their own townlands? What, on the other hand, about the mobility of the privileged class that was the Presbyterian ministry?.... Had not the Covenanting minister of Kellswater, Rev. William Martin, gone to South Carolina in 1772, taking with him five shiploads of settlers? While Jean Stephenson's volume (1971) on Scotch-Irish Migration presumes that Martin's fellow travellers were drawn from north as well as mid-Antrim, inspection of surnames reveals no small number (e.g. Allen, Dunlop, Hanna, McKee, Miller) that are still typical of the parish of Connor. From Maccadoo to Muddy Creek?"

[a couple of interpretive notes: "burn" - a small river; "R.U.C." - Royal Ulster Constabulary Note also, the Orange Order mentioned above did not exist in Rev. Martin's day. It was formed in the aftermath of the Rising of (17)'98, from the ashes of the United Irishmen movement, discussed below, in which many Ulstermen of both Catholic and Protestant hues participated in an abortive uprising against the British Crown. The discussion does illustrate the homogeneity of the Kellswater community, however.]

Jean Stephenson expands the territory of those who emigrated with Reverend Martin to the north of Kellswater:says that Reverend Martin's congregation was from and :

"The majority of them were probably from the vicinity of Ballymoney, Ballymena, Kellswater, and Vow, County Antrim." (page 15).

Ballymoney is a town in north Antrim, on the east side of the Lagan River, not far south of Coleraine.

There were five ships in the emigration led by Reverend Martin. All sailed in 1772. The first two sailed from Larne, the next two from Belfast, and the last one from Newry. For a map of the emigration ports from Ulster in the 17th and 18th century, go to Brian Orr's Emigration—the Ulster-Scots (Scots-Irish): What made them seek a better land?

The James and Mary sailed first on August 25 from Larne. There was smallpox on board (five children died) when they arrived in Charleston harbor on October 16, and they were required to remain on board in quarantine, lying off Sullivan's Island for over seven weeks, until the first part of December. Dickson, Ulster Emigration to Colonial America: 1718–1775, page 253. English America: American Plantations & Colonies, by Thomas Langford, contains ship lists of voyages to English America from 1500 to 1825. The site may be searched both by the name of a ship or by the port of destination. See also The Vessels, Voyages, Settlements, and People of English America 1500 - 1825.

The next ship to sail was the Lord Dunluce that left Larne on October 4 and arrived in Charleston on December 20. This is the only ship that listed "Rev. Wm. Martin (Kellswater)" as

# Emigration Led by Reverend William Martin in 1772

an agent. The original sailing date was to have been August 15. The sailing was delayed until August 20, and then rescheduled for September 22. On August 28, the ship announced that passengers must give earnest money by September 5 since a greater number had offered to go than could be taken. On September 15, the ship advertised that, since some families had drawn back, two hundred more passengers could be accommodated. Reverend Martin was on this ship when it finally sailed on October 4. One man and several children died of small pox on the trip. (Dickson, page 254).

The Pennsylvania Farmer, whose destination had originally been advertised as Philadelphia, sailed from Belfast on October 16 and arrived in Charleston on December 19. (Dickson, page 248). The Hopewell sailed from Belfast on October 19 and arrived in Charleston on December 23. (Dickson, page 248). The Freemason sailed from Newry on October 27 and arrived in Charleston on December 22 (Dickson, page 252).

The five ships and the people who came with the Rev. Martin are discussed on the English-America website. A web site that is no longer active, <http://homepages.rootsweb.com/~merle/Rm/RMIndex.htm>, can be accessed through the Internet Archives Wayback Machine. The names of the emigrants have been reconstructed from letters written home to Ulster and published in the paper and from extractions of the South Carolina Quarter Session Minutes, by Janie Revill and Jean Stephenson.

There is a Surname Summary of those who came with the Rev Martin.

There were five Patersons aboard the Hopewell, part of the emigration led by Reverend William Martin in 1772: Agnes (350 acres), Janet (100 acres), John (250 acres), John (100 acres), William (350 acres). Aboard the FreeMason were: Samuel Patterson (350 acres) and Mary Patterson (100). Aboard the Pennsylvania Farmer was Andrew Paterson (250 acres). A Long Cane Settlers List in the Abbeville/Long Cane Research Archives shows that Samuel Patterson filed a plat on 100 acres on Long Cane Creek (Bold Branch) on September 3, 1772.

Sketches of North Carolina, Historical and Biographical, Illustrative of the Principles of a Portion of Her Early Settlers by William Henry Foote Electronic Edition.

In 1750 Presbyterians from Octoraro, Virginia, and North Carolina, came to South Carolina and settled at Rocky Creek. By 1755 Irish immigrants, many of them Covenanters, began arriving. Various groups (Associate, Covenanter, Burgher, Anti-Burgher, Seceders) formed the "Catholic" (meaning a union of various groups of Presbyterians) church on Rocky Mount Road, 15 miles southeast of Chester. In 1770 Covenanters began holding society meetings and wrote to Ireland for a minister. Reverend William Martin answered the call in 1772, and preached many times at the Catholic church. In 1774 the Covenanters, under the leadership of Reverend William Martin, withdrew from the Catholic congregation and built their own meeting house, a log building on the same road as the Catholic church, and two miles east of it. (See Emigration Led by Reverend William Martin in 1772, above, and Stephenson, page 20).

"In County Down Ireland, James Blair's family was part of the congregation of Rev. William Martin, called the 'seceders' they were a splinter Presbyterian group. In 1772, Reverend Martin received a 'call' to South Carolina; about one thousand seceders, five shiploads, went with him. James Blair's ship was the Lord Dunluce, which left Larne Ulster, 4 Oct. 1772 and it arrived at Charleston, South Carolina on 2 Dec. 1772, after sailing against contrary winds. The land in America was to cost five pounds, and the acreage was determined by family size. If the immigrant had no money the land was free. Since, these were Scotsman and thrifty with their money, the book says not too many of them could come up with the five pounds. This was a large group, and

# Emigration Led by Reverend William Martin in 1772

as such they were scattered around the Abbeville district of South Carolina. James was given 230 acres on the shores of Fishing Creek near Rev. Martin in Craven County, later Chester County." Blair Ancestors of Barbara Blair Feldhaus.

See also: Porter, Howard Leonard (1985). Destiny of the Scotch-Irish: an account of a migration from Ballybay...to Washington County..., Winter Haven Fla.: Porter Co. P.O. Box 7533, Winter Haven.

# JENNET GRAHAM MILLS

## MILLS/MCDOWELL

[1-1]     DAVID GRAHAM, born probably in Ireland, died in Chester County, SC, about 1800; married probably in Ireland to JANET ____, born probably in Ireland, died Chester County, South Carolina, 1800-9.

Children of David Graham and Janet:
2-1 Andrew Graham, born probably in County Antrim, Ireland, c. 1753

[2-1]     ANDREW GRAHAM, born probably in County Antrim, Ireland, c. 1753, died Todd County, Kentucky, 1821; married (1) in Chester County, South Carolina, to MARGARET COULTER, born probably in County Tyrone, Ireland, died Chester County, South Carolina, 1702-6, daughter of Robert Coulter & Mary Stuart; married (2) probably in Chester County, South Carolina, c. 1797, MARGARET ___, born Ireland 1770-4, died Henderson County, Illinois, after 1840.

Children Andrew Graham and Margaret Coulter:
3-2 Jennet Graham, born Chester County, South Carolina, 1777-79

## FIRST GENERATION

1-1     JENNET GRAHAM MILLS (Janet, Jane -- pp. 127-130 in the genealogy as 3-2), born South Carolina, 1777-79, died Christian County, Kentucky, c 1817; married in Chester County, South Carolina, c. 1798, ADAM MILLS, born Ireland, died Todd County, Kentucky, between 1824 and 14 February 1825, son of William Mills and Janet (Jane) McKee.

   An account of the early Mills family from a 1970 letter written by Mrs. Lynn B. (Mary Jane) Harding then of Arlington VA to 4-19B5a Mrs. Mary Firoved Bruington contains some inaccurate data but may have some factual basis.

   The Harding letter begins the Mills family with a William Mills who was born in England 1715 and died in County Antrim Ireland.  He married Janet McKee who was born Scotland 1725 and died probably in South Carolina.  The children of William & Janet (McKee) Mills were: (1) William, born 1752, died at sea, (2) Adam Mills, born 1755, (3) Matty Mills, born 1759.  Janet McKee Mills emigrated from Ireland to South Carolina with her two children and settled in Union County SC.

   The Harding letter continues with an accurate listing of the children of Adam & Janet (Graham) Mills and additional information on the lines of the families of James & Hannah Nancy (Mills) Knox [2-2] and Malcolm & Mary Jane (Knox) Hill [3-7].

   In the 1806 Tax Rolls of Logan County, Kentucky, Adam Mills was listed as the owner of 200 acres of "third rate land" on the Elk Fork.  In the 1807 Tax Rolls he had the same 200 acres in Logan County and also was the owner of 400 acres of "third rate land" in Christian County, Kentucky.  He owned the same land in 1810 but apparently sold some of his Christian County holdings before 1815.  In that year he was listed as owning only 200 acres in Christian County; the land had a value of $4 an acres.  He still had his 200 acres on the Elk Fork in Logan County, however; this land was valued at $5 an acre and the total value of his property which included one slave and four horses was $3,500.  In 1817 he still had 200 acres of "second rate" land in Christian County.  He also owned four slaves and eight horses or mules, and the total value of his property was $3,446.

# JENNET GRAHAM MILLS

The area of Christian County where Adam lived became Todd County in 1819, and in the 1821 Todd County tax list, he was assessed for 338 acres of "second rate" land, three slaves, and three horses, etc, with a total value of $4,167. Gradually, however, he divested himself of his land and other property so that by 1822 he was assessed for 178 acres, one slave, and two horses, etc, and in 1823 his tax assessment was for 160 acres on Spring Creek and one slave, totaling $1,510. Probably, after 1819 he was deeding land to his sons as they matured. In his last listing in the 1824 Todd County Tax Records, the household of Adam Mills consisted of 1 white male over 21, 1 black male over 16 with 2 blacks total, and 2 horses; 176 acres on West Fork, valued at $8, totaling $2658.

In his will dated 20 Febrauary 1823, Adam Mills named as his executors William Harlan, 3-3 Matthew Graham, and 3-6 Robert C. Graham. The will was proved in Todd County Court on 14 February 1825, and Robert C. Graham was required to post a bond of $3,000 with William Harlan and Matthew Graham as securities (Todd County Court Orders Book B, pp 356-7).

Following is the account of the sale of items of the estate of Adam Mills found in Todd County Kentucky Will Book A pages 280-2, dated 18th February 1825.

An Amount of the Sales of Real & Personal property of Adam Mills decd on Febry 18th 1825

| Allen McPhail | 1 table | 0.50 |
| --- | --- | --- |
| same | 1 Pail & Noggin | 0.06 1/4 |
| same | 1 kittle & skillet | 0.06 1/4 |
| Mathew Graham | 1 oven & pot hooks | 1.50 |
| Robt Cunningham | 1 skillet & lid | 1.50 |
| same | 1 Lote tin ware | 0.50 |
| William Brooks | 1 piggin & noggin | 0.50 |
| Phillips Allen | 2 Pails | 0.50 |
| William McKee | 1 soap tub | 0.12 ½ |
| John McKee | 1 Slate | 0.26 |
| Jas Allen | 1 ditto | 0.23 3/4 |
| Wm Bean | 1 looking glass | 0.50 |
| Wm McKee | Knives forks & spoons | 0.62 ½ |
| same | Cups & saucers | 0.12 ½ |
| Jno Pendleton | 5 plates | 0.37 ½ |
| same | 1 Lin pan | 0.62 ½ |
| Jno James | 1 drawing knife | 0.75 |
| James Chesnut | 1 basket & | 1.00 |
| Wm Linsley | 1 lote old bridle | 0.50 |
| Jas Chesnut | 1 shovel Chissell & | 0.50 |
| Wm McKee | 1 brand iron | 0.50 |
| John McKee | 1 Hammer & Bell | 1.10 |
| Is H Boone | 1 Box & salt | 0.81 1/4 |
| Wm McKee | 1 Lott of Leather | 1.56 1/4 |
| Telb Ewing | 1 pr Clenses & collar | 2.37 ½ |
| Wm McKee | 1 collar | 0.25 |
| Same | 1 keg Tallow | 0.75 |
| Mathew Wilson | Parcel of cotton | 2.37 ½ |
| Leroy Taliferno | 1 matlock | 1.00 |
| William McKee | 1 meal barrel & | 0.06 1/4 |
| Robt Andrews | 1 keg lard | 0.50 |
| Mathew Wilson | 1 keg lard | 1.00 |

# JENNET GRAHAM MILLS

| | | |
|---|---|---|
| Telb Ewing | 1 pair plough gear | 3.37 ½ |
| John Peden | 1 saddle & Bridle & | 1.06 1/4 |
| John Janard | 1 do blankett | 2.37 ½ |
| John Pendleton | 1 bed & furniture | 26.00 |
| Hugh Brown | 1 singletree & | 0.62 ½ |
| Wm McKee | 1 sted | 0.31 1/4 |
| Is H Boone | 1 Clevis & Singletree | 1.37 ½ |
| Wm Simpson | 1 grind stone | 1.99 |
| Wm McKee | Soap & | 0.50 |
| Wm Simpson | 1 hand saw | 2.28 |
| John Gay | Lote of Irons | 0.75 |
| Wm Parker | Lad Irons & | 0.56 1/4 |
| Wm Smith | 2 asces | 2.18 3/4 |
| John McKee | 1 do do | 1.75 |
| Samuel L Duval | 1 do do | 1.50 |
| Wm Hooser | 1 ditto | 1.62 ½ |
| James Cordery | Iron square | 0.37 ½ |
| John Edington | 2 hoes | 1.06 1/4 |
| Miles Foster | 1 do do | 0.31 1/4 |
| Wm Hooser | 2 iron wedges | 1.81 1/4 |
| Jno Pendleton | 1 pr ano irons | 3.06 1/4 |
| Wm Hooser | 3 plains | 0.31 1/4 |
| Robt Millen | 1 crose | 0.12 ½ |
| Mat Wilson | 1 lott books | 0.25 |
| same | 1 ditto | 0.50 |
| same | 1 ditto | 0.06 1/4 |
| same | 1 ditto | 0.43 1/4 |
| Wm Graham | 1 book | 1.00 |
| Hugh Brown | 1 ditto | 0.75 |
| Wm McKee | 1 ditto | 0.75 |
| Mathew Graham | 1 ditto | 1.31 1/4 |
| Mat Graham | 2 Books | 1.62 ½ |
| Reuben Grady | 1 anville | 2.00 |
| Wm Graham | Case razors | 0.75 |
| Bennett Ballard | 1 bed stead | 0.50 |
| Wm McKee | 1 bridle & knife | 0.37 ½ |
| John Young | 3 chains | 2.56 1/4 |
| same | 3 do | 1.50 |
| Wm McKee | 1 wire sifter | 2.56 1/4 |
| Wm Hooser | 1 lot awls | 0.12 ½ |
| Jas Allen | 1 sugar chest | 2.31 1/4 |
| Jno McKee | 2 drawing chains | 2.10 |
| Mat Wilson | 1 lott silver tea spoons | 9.25 |
| Same | 1 work bench | 0.25 |
| Wm Hooser | Bull tongue plough | 1.00 |
| Same | Barshear do | 2.43 3/4 |
| Robt Andrews | 1 cairy do | 3.50 |
| Is H Boone | 1 cairy do | 6.39 |
| Robt Cunningham | 200 lbs bacon | 12.37 ½ |
| Andrew Coulter | 1 pickling tub | 0.87 ½ |
| Spots Smith | 200 lbs bacon | 14.06 1/4 |
| Wm B Scott | ballance at $8 pr 100 lbs | 6.24 |

# JENNET GRAHAM MILLS

| | | |
|---|---|---|
| Isa H. Boone | 10 bls corn | 10.00 |
| Same | 10 ditto at $1.12 ½ | 11.25 |
| Jos Deeds | 10 ditto at $1.12 ½ | 11.25 |
| Major Cheatham | 10 do do $1.09 | 10.90 |
| Same | 10 do $1.17 | 11.70 |
| Same | 10 do $1.15 | 11.50 |
| Same | 10 do $1.13 | 11.50 |
| Same | 3 do $1.15 | 3.45 |
| Jno P Hice | 2 sows & 13 pigs | 13.75 |
| Jas Hice | 2 do with pig | 9.00 |
| Geo Cross | 5 first choice hogs | 18.00 |
| Wm B Scote | 6 snd choice do | 15.00 |
| Jer Barker | 2 steers | 5.00 |
| Same | 1 ditto | 4.00 |
| Robt Andrews | 1 heifer | 2.06 1/4 |
| Mat Wilson | 1 cow & calf | 16.31 1/4 |
| same | 1 heifer | 8.00 |
| Reuben Grady | 1 bull cow & bell | 14.12 ½ |
| Axnum Brake | 1 red steer | 8.50 |
| Jno Edington | 1 do heifer | 8.50 |
| Axnum Brake | 1 white steer (stray) | 9.06 1/4 |
| Mat Wilson | Cross Flax | 0.80 |
| P Andreson | 1 lott fodder | 3.25 |
| Same | 1 do | 3.00 |
| Littby Royster | 1 roan horse | 120.00 |
| John Edington | 1 sorrel do | 34.25 |
| Mat Wilson | 1 silver watch | 3.06 1/4 |
| Willis Lewis | 1 bed stead | 0.50 |
| William Mills | 1 negro Boy | 710.00 |
| Robt Andrews | 178 acres land | 1051.50 |
| John Gay | 1 well bucket | 1.50 |
| Wm Smith | 2 yds Cambrick | 1.50 |
| Wm B. Scote | 1 parcel of beef | 1.00 |

The above is a true account of the sales of the real & personal estate of Adams Mills Decd sold as above Given under my hand & seal this ---- day of ---- 1825.  Robt C. Graham, executor

1790 census - not listed

1800 census, Chester County, SC, page
Adam Mills, free white males, 1 under 10,1 16-25; free white females 2 under 10, 1 26-44

1810 census, Logan County, KY, page 194
Adam Mills, free white males, 2 under 10, 1 10-15, 1 26-44; free white females, 1 under 10, 1 26-44,1 +45, Slaves 1

1820 census, Todd County, KY, page 129
Adam Mills, free white males -,1 10-16,-,-,-,1 +45; free white females, 2 to 10; male Slaves, 1 under 14

Children of Adam Mills and Janet Graham:
2-1 William Mills, born Chester Co., SC, c. 1800

# JENNET GRAHAM MILLS

2-2 Hannah (Nancy) Mills, born Union Co., SC, 1803?
2-3 Andrew Graham Mills, born Logan Co., KY, c. 1805
2-4 Robert Mills, born Logan Co., KY, 9 March 1809
2-5 David Graham Mills, born Logan Co., KY, c. 1811
2-6 Jane McKee Mills, born Logan Co., KY, September 1815
2-7 Mary Margaret Mills, born Logan Co., KY, c. 1817

# Notes to Mills

## NOTES

### SECOND GENERATION

1. Information on William Mills is from: "Hutchings Family" file, Rosenberg Library, Galveston TX; Betty Couch Wiltshire, comp., Marriages and Deaths from Mississippi Newspapers, 4 vols. (n.p.: Heritage Books, Inc., 1989), vol II p. 4; vol III p.172; Simpson County, Kentucky 1819-1825 Circuit Court Orders, compiled by Dorothy Donnell Steers (Mrs Roy L Steers), 1985, printed by Printers Inc., Franklin, KY, p. 99 (Book A p. 407); Simpson County, Kentucky 1826-1831 Circuit Court Orders and 1826 Tax List, Dorothy Donnell Steers (Mrs Roy L Steers), 1990, printed by Printers Inc, Franklin KY, pp. 3, 23, & 217; Warren County Mississippi Marriage Records, Book E, p. 48; Mississippi Newspapers, 1805-1940 (Jackson, MS: The Mississippi Historical Records Survey, Service Division of the W.P.A., 1942) p. 246; a letter, 16 October 1991, to Philip Graham from Mary Lois Ragland, Research Genealogist of Vicksburg, Mississippi; and Hubert Horton McAlexander, The Prodigal Daughter: A Biography of Sherwood Bonner. 1981. Baton Rouge, LA: Louisiana State Univ., pp. 39-40).

2. Information on the family of James Knox and Hannah Nancy Mills is from: "Portrait and Biographical Record of St. Charles, Lincoln and Warren Counties Missouri", 1895, Chicago, Chapman Publishing, pages 239-40 pioneer taxpayers in 1821; pages 397-8, sketch on William W. Knox; "History Lincoln County Missouri", 1888, Chicago: The Goodspeed Publishing Co., pages 515-6 sketch of Ephraim Cannon, pages 564-5 sketch of Joseph A. Knox; "The Cannon Book", 1958, by Clarence Cannon (n.p.), pages 38-9; "Hutchings Family" file, Rosenburg Library, Galveston TX. The Knox Genealogy The Knox Family, A Genealogical and Biographical Sketch of the Descendants of John Knox of Rowan County, North Carolina and Other Knoxes. 1905. Hattie S. Goodman. Whittet & Shepperson, Richmond VA. pp. 113-8, 131-134, lists James Knox sr as the son of Robert Knox, grandson of James Knox (born 1752 NC, died 1794) & Lydia Gillespie, great grandson of John Knox (born 1708 Ireland, died 1758) & Jean Gracy (died 1772). This probably is an error. James Knox sr (1776-1846) was born & married in Ireland and arrived to America in the 1790s.

3. Information on Andrew Mills is from: Simpson County Kentucky, 1826-1831, Circuit Court Orders & 1826 Tax List, Dorothy Donnell Steers, compiler, Franklin KY, 1990, pp. 104, 113, 125.

4. Information on Robert Mills is from: Galveston Daily News, 14 April 1888, p. 8, obituary for Robert Mills; History of the Island and the City of Galveston, Charles W. Hayes, 2 vols. (Cincinnati, 1879; rptd. Austin TX: Jenkins Garrett Press, 1974), II, 924-8; Texas Heroes Buried on Galveston Island, (Galveston, TX: Sidney Sherman Chapter of the Daughters of the Republic of Texas, 1982), pp. 53-4; and The Prodigal Daughter: A Biography of Sherwood Bonner, Hubert Horton McAlexander, (Baton Rouge, LA: Louisiana State Univ., 1981), p. 108.

5. Information on David Graham Mills if from: Galveston Daily News, 28 February 1885, p. 8)

6. Information on the family of James McDowell and Jane Mills McDowell is from: David McDowell, "Panola County [MS] Family Histories--The Coles", Panola County Story, IX, 3 (July 1980), p. 16; Marriages and Deaths from Mississippi Newspapers, Betty Couch Wiltshire, 4 vols. (n.p.: Heritage Books, Inc., 1989), III, 169; The Prodigal Daughter: A Biography of Sherwood Bonner, Hubert Horton McAlexander, (Baton Rouge, LA: Louisiana

# Notes to Mills

State Univ., 1981), pp. 212-2 and 141; Laurel Hill Cemetery Records, Philadelphia, PA.

7. Information on Mary Margaret Mills is from: Cemetery Records, DAR, p. 39; and "Hutchings Family" file in the Rosenberg Library, Galveston TX; and The Prodigal Daughter: A Biography of Sherwood Bonner, Hubert Horton McAlexander, (Baton Rouge, LA: Louisiana State Univ., 1981), pp 108-9.

## THIRD GENERATION

1. Information on Samuel Mills is from: Peggy Gregory, comp., Record of Interments of the City of Galveston, 1859-1872 Houston, Texas, 1976, p. 61; and the "Hutchings Family" file, Rosenberg Library, Galveston, Texas.

2. Only source for John Mills is the "Hutchings Family" file at the Rosenberg Library, Galveston, Texas.

3. Information on Green Mills is from: Military Annals of Mississippi. Military Organizations Which Entered The Service of the Confederate States of America, compiled by John C. Riette, reprinted by The Reprint Company, Publishers, Spartanburg SC, 1976, pp. 73, 76-77; and the "Hutchings Family" file at the Rosenberg Library, Galveston, Texas.

4. Information on Andrew Graham Mills is from: Cemetery Records [of] Galveston, Texas, Missouri State Society of the DAR, March 1941, restored and retyped 1985, p. 39; Texas Heroes Buried on Galveston Island, (Galveston, TX: Sidney Sherman Chapter of the Daughters of the Republic of Texas, 1982), pp. 5-7; Military Annals of Mississippi. Military Organizations Which Entered The Service of the Confederate States of America, compiled by John C. Riette, reprinted by The Reprint Company, Publishers, Spartanburg SC, 1976, pp. 74-5; and the "Hutchings Family" file at the Rosenberg Library, Galveston, Texas.

5. Information on David G. Graham is from: the "Hutchings Family" file at the Rosenberg Library, Galveston, Texas; and census material.

6. Information on the family of William Knox and Sarah L. Browning is from: The Nevada County Chronicles: Brides of the Gold Rush (1851-1859), 1987, David Allen Comstock, Comstock Bonanza Press, Grass Valley, CA. p. xi, 131; The Knox Family, A Genealogical and Biographical Sketch of the Descendants of John Knox of Rowan County, North Carolina and Other Knoxes, 1905, Hattie S. Goodman, Whittet & Shepperson, Richmond VA, pp. 131-134; Index of Oak Hill Cemetery, San Jose CA from records of the Santa Clara County Historical & Genealogical Society, Santa Clara CA, obtain January 1994; Genealogy of the Brownings in America from 1621 to 1908, Edward Franklin Browning, reprinted by Higginson Book Co, Salem Mass, pp. 482 & 541.

7. Information on the Bean family is from: History of Santa Clara County with Biographical Sketches ... 1922, Eugene T. Sawyer, Historic Record Company, Los Angeles CA, pp. 270, 880, & 1362; Nevada County Vital Statistics. June 1850 to June 1859, 1986, David A Comstock & Ardis H Comstock, Comstock Bonanza Press, Grass Valley CA, p. 6; federal census 1870 Nevada County CA, 1880 & 1900 San Jose CA; and The Knox Family, A Genealogical and Biographical Sketch of the Descendants of John Knox of Rowan County, North Carolina and Other Knoxes. 1905. Hattie S. Goodman. Whittet & Shepperson, Richmond VA. pp. 131-134.

8. Information on the Benton family is from: Cemeteries of Marshall County, Mississippi.

# Notes to Mills

Bobby Mitchell, comp., (Ripley, MS: Old Timer Press, 1983), p. 20; Genealogical Narrative of the Hart Family in the United States, compiled by Mrs Sarah S Young, 1882, private printing, p. ?(82); The Knox Family, A Genealogical and Biographical Sketch of the Descendants of John Knox of Rowan County, North Carolina and Other Knoxes, 1905, Hattie S. Goodman, Whittet & Shepperson, Richmond VA, pp. 131-134.

9. Information on the Hutchings family is from: Galveston Daily Press, 21 December 1915, p. 3, obituary of Minnie Knox Hutchings; the"Hutchings Family" file at the Rosenberg Library, Galveston, Texas; and Cemetery Records [of] Galveston, Texas, Missouri State Society of the DAR, March 1941, restored and retyped 1985, p. 13.

10. Information on the Wright family is from: The Knox Family, A Genealogical and Biographical Sketch of the Descendants of John Knox of Rowan County, North Carolina and Other Knoxes, 1905, Hattie S. Goodman, Whittet & Shepperson, Richmond VA, pp. 131-134; Index to Oak Hill Cemetery, San Jose CA, obtained from the Santa Clara County Historical & Genealogical Society, Santa Clara CA. January 1994.

11. Information on the Dennis family is from: A History of Wharton County [Texas], 1846-1961, 1964, Annie Lee Williams, pp. 65, 133-8, 367, and 372-3; A History of Texas and Texans, 1914, Frank W. Johnson, The American Historical Society, Chicago & NY, 5 vols, 5:2383; The Knox Family, A Genealogical and Biographical Sketch of the Descendants of John Knox of Rowan County, North Carolina and Other Knoxes, 1905, Hattie S. Goodman, Whittet & Shepperson, Richmond VA. pp. 131-134. Dennis, Isaac N. The Handbook of Texas Online. Http://www.tsha.utexas.edu/handbook/online/articles/view/DD/fde41.html.

12. Marriages and Deaths from Mississippi Newspapers, Betty Couch Wiltshire, 4 vols. (n.p.: Heritage Books, 1989), 3:151.

13. Bobby Mitchell, comp., Cemeteries of Marshall County, Mississippi, (Ripley, MS: Old Timer Press, 1983, pp. 26 & 32; federal censuses; and Biographical and Historical Memoirs of Mississippi, 2 Vols. (rptd. Spartanburg, SC: The Reprint Co., 1978), II, 285; and McAlexander, p. 153.

14. The information of James R. Jr. and his family is from: Vicksburg Daily Tribune, 2 July 1878, p. 22; letter, 16 October 1991, to Philip Graham from Mary Lois S. Ragland, Research Genealogist, Vicksburg MS; Nicholas Russell Murray, Warren County, Mississippi, 1810-1900, Computer Indexed Marriage Records (Hammond, LA: Hunting for Bears, Inc., 1981), p. 31; Madison Parish Marriage Record Book (1869-1880) p. 116 and Madison Parish Marriage Bonds Book (1869-1880) p. 83 for marriage of Rosa Dancy to A. Bynum Amis; Letter, 23 May 1994, to Philip Graham from Millard Miles, Santa Rosa CA, who is researching the Amis Family.

15. Hubert Horton McAlexander, The Prodigal Daughter: A Biography of Sherwood Bonner (Baton Rouge, LA: Louisiana State University, 1981), p.22.

16. Information on the family of Edward McDowell is from: Hubert Horton McAlexander, The Prodigal Daughter: A Biography of Sherwood Bonner (Baton Rouge, LA: Louisiana State University, 1981), pp. 5-6, 39, 166, and 181; Bobby Mitchell, comp., Cemeteries of Marshall County, Mississippi (Ripley, MS: Old Timer Press, 1983), p. 21.; and William Baskerville Hamilton, Holly Springs, Mississippi, to the Year 1878 (Holly Springs: The Marshall County Historical Soc., 1984), p. 97).

# Notes to Mills

17. McAlexander, pp. 40-43, 166, and passim.

18. McAlexander, pp. 101 et passim.

19. McAlexander, p.17.

20. McAlexander, pp. 116-18; Hamilton, p. 97.

21. McAlexander, pp. 141-2 and 146.

22. McAlexander, pp. 160-1, 166, 168, 172, et passim.

23. McAlexander, pp. 180-1.

24. McAlexander, pp. 211-3.

25. McAlexander, pp. 212-3.

26. Information on the Fort family is from: Cemeteries of Marshall County, Mississippi, (Ripley, MS: Old Timer Press, 1983), pp. 4, 29, and 44; James Fort Daniel, Recollections of Things Past: Holly Springs, Mississippi (n.p.: the author, 1947?), nonpaged; and letter to Philip Graham from Harris Gholson II, Holly Springs MS, September 1991. and Golsan, Golson, Gholson, Gholston Families in America.

27. Recollections of Things Past: Holly Springs, Mississippi, by James Fort Daniel, (n.p.: the author, 1947?), nonpaged.

28. Hubert Horton McAlexander, The Prodigal Daughter: A Biography of Sherwood Bonner (Baton Rouge, LA, Louisiana State Univ., 1981), p. 85.

29. McAlexander, pp. 141-2.

30. Hubert Horton McAlexander, The Prodigal Daughter: A Biography of Sherwood Bonner (Baton Rouge, LA: Louisiana State University, 1981) pp. 4 and 7.

31. McAlexander, pp. 85-6, 103, 113, and 141.

32. McAlexander, pp. 159, 163, and 166.

33. McAlexander, pp. 163, and 168-73.

## FOURTH GENERATION

1. Information on 4-1 Ballinger Mills is from: Texas City Ancestry Searchers, Galveston County Tombstone Inscriptions, 3 vols. (Texas City, TX: Moore Memorial Park Library, 1990). III, p. 129-130.

2. Information on 4-2 Virginia knox Maddox is from: The Knox Family, A Genealogical and Biographical Sketch of the Descendants of John Knox of Rowan County, North Carolina and

# Notes to Mills

Other Knoxes. 1905. Hattie S. Goodman. Whittet & Shepperson, Richmond VA. pp. 131-134.

3. Information on the children of 3-8 Virgina Knox Beans is from: The Knox Family, A Genealogical and Biographical Sketch of the Descendants of John Knox of Rowan County, North Carolina and Other Knoxes. 1905. Hattie S. Goodman. Whittet & Shepperson, Richmond VA. pp. 131-134; and History of Santa Clara County with Biographical Sketches ... 1922. Eugene T. Sawyer. Historic Record Company, Los Angeles CA. p.270, 880, 1362.

4. Information on the children of 3-9 Rowena Knox Benton is from: Bobby Mitchell, comp., Cemeteries of Marshall County, Mississippi. (Ripley, MS: Old Timer Press, 1983), p. 20; and Genealogical Narrative of the Hart Family in the United States. compiled by Mrs Sarah S Young. 1882. private printing 82p.

5. Cemetery Records [of] Galveston, Texas, Missouri State Society of the DAR, March 1941, restored and retyped 1985, p. 13.

6. From the obituary of 4-18 Minnie Hutchings Harris in the Galveston Daily News, 15 May 1922, p.3.

7. Cemetery Records [of] Galveston, Texas, Missouri State Society of the DAR, March 1941, restored and retyped 1985, p. 12.

8. McAlexander, pp. 40, 85, 213, and 223-226.

9. Information on the family of 4-42 Janet Fort Gholson is from: Cemeteries of Marshall County, Mississippi, (Ripley, MS: Old Timer Press, 1983), pp. 4, 29, and 44; James Fort Daniel, Recollections of Things Past: Holly Springs, Mississippi (n.p.: the author, 1947?), nonpaged; Harris Gholson II, Holly Springs MS, in a letter to Philip Graham, September 1991; and Golsan, Golson, Gholson, Gholston Families in America.

10. Bobby Mitchell, comp., Cemeteries of Marshall County, Mississippi. (Ripley, MS: Old Timer Press, 1983), p. 26.

11. Information on the family of 4-45 David McDowell jr is from an article written by his son David McDowell II: David McDowell, "Panola County Family Histories", In The Panola Story, Vol IX, No 3 (July 1980), 16-17.

12. Information on 4-46 Ruth McDowell Stephenson is from: McAlexander p. 226; and Cemeteries of Marshall County, Mississippi, (Ripley, MS: Old Timer Press, 1983), p. 3-4.

13. Cemeteries of Marshall County, Mississippi, (Ripley, MS: Old Timer Press, 1983), p. 3.

# Descendants of John Popham

## POPHAM FAMILY

Gilbert de Popham, married 1200 Joan/Jane Clarke
|
Robert Popham
|
Hugh Popham, married Joan Kentisbury le Blount
|
Hugh Popham
|
John Popham, married Alexandria Horsey
|
Hugh Popham, married Hawise Brent
|
Richard Popham of Alfoxton
|
John Popham
|
John Popham, married Margaret Houndons or Gaye
|
Walter Popham, married Agnes Hatch
|
Walter Popham, died 1582, married Elizabeth Berry
|
Richard Popham, born about 1559, died 1628, married Jane Osborne, died 1661
|
Hugh Popham, born 1599, died 1678, married Joan Rowle, died 1678/9
|
Richard Popham, of Barnstaple, born 1631, probably was the Richard Popham who emigrated to Maryland in 1661.
[Morrison, Theron V. 1983. The Popham Ancestral Line ...]

Richard Popham emigrated from England to Maryland in 1661 & settled in Calvert County MD. By law he was indentured for four years to Thomas Sichworth & was to receive 50 acres of land upon his release. On 16 September 1662 Thomas Sichworth of Calvert County MD secured a right to 500 acres of land in the names of Robert Brooks & Richard Popham both imported 1661.
[Morrison, Theron V. 1983. The Popham Ancestral Line ... pages 57-64]

This Richard Popham may have been connected to the John Popham of Westmoreland County VA. Other Pophams in Maryland from Revolutionary War records include: Benjamin Popham of Frederick MD, Frances Popham, Samuel Popham of Prince Georges County MD who died in Baltimore MD.
[Morrison, Theron V. 1983. The Popham Ancestral Line ...]

First Generation

1. JOHN POPHAM, died about 1739 Westmoreland County VA; married c1683 RACHELL ---, died after 11 December 1755. Rachell Popham married (2) James Maxwell.

John Popham was a resident of Washington Parish, Westmoreland County VA, in the early 1700s. The first record of John Popham is his purchase 100 acres on 3 August 1713 in Washington Parish, Westmoreland County VA (Bk 5 part 1 p233). John Popham was listed as a "cooper" in

# Descendants of John Popham

this deed.

Further purchases of John Popham include:
-purchase 126 acres in King George County VA 21 January 1722 at a price of 10,000 pounds of "good tobacco in cask" (Bk 1 folio 116). Here John Popham was listed as a "planter" & resident of Washington Parish, Westmoreland County VA.
-purchased 105 acres on 5 October 1733 in Westmoreland County VA for 10,000 pounds of "good tobacco" (Bk 8 pt 2 p226).
-purchased 100 acres 8 September 1736 in Washington Parish, Westmoreland County VA for 4,000 pounds of tobacco & 10 pounds of current money ( Bk 8 part 2 p 291).

Over a 23 year period John Popham amassed 431 acres - 3 tracts in Westmoreland County & 1 tract in King George County. These tracts are assumed to have strattled the county line.

John Popham's will is dated 31 October 1738 & probated 27 March 1739 (Bk 9, p15). This will mentions a 500 acre tract in Prince William County VA near Frying Pan Run as well as several personal slaves.

Rachel Popham married a second time to James Maxwell. Rachel Popham Maxwell died after 11 December 1755 when her son, Job Popham, reserved her right of dower in the original tract of land that John Popham purchased in 1713 (Deed Bk 12, p299)

Children of John Popham & Rachell:
1. Job Popham, born 1709
2. John Popham, born 1711; married Elizabeth ---. moved to Goochland County VA.
3. Sophia Popham, born 1713
4. Mary Popham, born 1715
5. Anne Popham, born 1717; married William Nolle, lived near Job Popham, in Culpeper Co VA.
6. daughter, married --- Littleton.
[Morrison, Theron V. 1983. The Popham Ancestral Line ... pages 66 - 103; will of John Popham on pages 92-4][IGI]

## Second Generation

1. JOB POPHAM, born [c1709] Westmoreland County VA, died about 1781 Brumfield Parish, Culpeper County VA; married [c1709] ANN ( possibly Evans or Evins), born , died 4 March 1825 Culpeper County VA.

Sometime prior to 4 September 1755, Job Popham moved from Westmoreland County to Culpeper County VA. Job Popham sold the 200 acres of land in Washington Parish, Westmoreland County VA that he inherited from his father, John Popham. Job Popham received 27 pounds 2 shillings for the land - this may indicate the land had been worn out by repeated tobacco planting. This deed mentions a burial place on the land.

Job Popham was constable for Culpeper County sometime prior to 1763 as on March 18 1763 a George Goggins was appointed to replace him.

Deed Records of Job Popham:
-Job Popham, of Brumfield Parish, Culpeper County VA, sold 100 acre tract in Westmoreland County VA on 23 December 1778 for 250 pounds - deed recorded 4 March 1778(?).
-Purchased 150 acres on Gourd Vine Fork of the Rappahannock River, Brumfield Parish, Culpeper County VA for 35 pounds (Bk C p. 267)

# Descendants of John Popham

-15 March 1773 land estate sale of James Tutt Jr.
-20 December 1773 land estate sale of William Meldrum
-one of three executors of the will of Richard Ship, 9 February 1781, probated 20 August 1781

On 21 January 1782 inventory appraisal of estate of Job Popham by John Long, William Pierce, and James Branham. Widow served as administrix of estate. The final settlement of estate not recorded until 20 November 1809.

On 19 April 1790, Ann Popham, widow of Job Popham, purchased from William Nolle & Ann, of Culpeper County, 100 acres in the Brumfield parish on Gourd Vine Fork of Rappahannock River, for 50 pounds.

Ann Popham died 4 March 1825, inventory of estate made 21 March 1825. Her will dated 13 March 1822 (Will Book 1, p 348).

Children of Job Popham & Ann (Evins/Evans), Culpeper County VA:
1. Elizabeth Popham, born 1761
2. Humphrey Popham, born 1763
3. Thomas Popham, born
4. Rachel Evins Popham, born 1765
5. Nancy Popham, born 1767
6. Gerard Popham, born 1768
7. John Popham, born 1770
8. James Popham, born 1772
9. Job Popham, born 1774
10. Mary Popham, born 1778
[Morrison, Theron V. 1983. The Popham Ancestral Line ... pages 104-114][IGI]

## Third Generation

1. ELIZABETH POPHAM, born 1761 Culpeper County VA; married --- SPARKS.
[Morrison, Theron V. 1983. The Popham Ancestral Line ...]

2. HUMPHREY POPHAM, born 1763 Culpeper County VA, died ; married 2 November 1788 Culpeper County VA by William Mason (Baptist minister) to BETSEY/BETTY HAWKINS, born c1762 Culpeper County VA, died , daughter of Matthew Hawkins & Elizabeth Maxwell.

Humphrey Popham, of Brumfield Parish, Culpeper County VA, purchased 100 acres for 31 pounds on south side of "Huse's River" on 20 February 1792 (Bk Q, p454). He sold this tract on 19 October 1794 for 50 pounds (Bk 2, p93).

Nelson County KY:
-11 September 1809 Cornelius Yager to Elizabeth Popham, husband of Humphrey Popham, of Nelson County KY 60 acres on the waters of Neelys Run, a branch of Beech Fork, for 50 pounds (Bk 12 p 15). A clarification of the above deed was dated September 1816 in Nelson County KY.
-17 March 1810, the Pophams sold the above land to Joseph Norris (Bk 9, p38) & on same date bought 50 acres from Joseph Norris (Bk 9, p 40).
-21 January 1817, Pophams sold the above land (Bk 12, p149) - at this time moved from Nelson County KY to Washington County KY.

In the 1820 census for Washington County KY three families listed: Humphrey, Jacob, & William.

# Descendants of John Popham

In a deed dated 13 September 1824 Humphrey & Elizabeth Popham, of Washington County KY, sold to Aaron House, of Madison County VA, 94 & ½ acres in Madison County VA which had been made from Culpeper County in 1792/3. [note this is the last record Morrison has on this family].

Humphrey Popham was a witness to the marriage of Nancy Popham to William Ray in Franklin County KY on 17 August 1818.

Moved to Edgar County Illinois by 1830. Deed record of Edgar County IL, Book 1 p. 297: Humphrey & Elizabeth Popham, Edgar County, to Stephen B. Shelleday, 80 acres, E ½ of SE 1/4 section 27 T14 R12, dated 16 April 1830, recorded October 1830. Humphrey Popham listed in 1840 census (p. 22) along with an Ezekiel Popham (p28). No record in Will Book (1829-1853) or Estate Records (1823-1963) for Humphrey Popham or Elizabeth/Betsey Popham.

Children of Humphrey Popham & Betsey Hawkins:
1. William Nolle Popham, born 1789 Culpeper Co VA
2. Mary Popham, born 9 August 1792 Culpeper Co VA
3. Elizabeth Popham, born between 1794 & 1800 Culpeper Co VA
4. Lucy Popham, born between 1794 & 1800 Culpeper Co VA
5. Job or Jacob Popham, born 1796 Culpeper Co VA
6. John Popham, born 1798 Culpeper Co VA
7. Ezekiel Popahm, born between 1800 & 1810
8. Nancy C. Popham, born between 1800 & 1810
9. Jane Popham, born 12 April 1809 Virginia
10. daughter, born between 1800 & 1810
[IGI][Culpeper County VA Marriage Records][Culpeper County VA Marriages 1780-1853 by John Vogt & T. William Kethley jr. 1986. p87][Morrison, Theron Vasco. 1983. The Popham Ancestral Line of Theron Vasco Morrison. address: 3727 SE 18th Ave, Cape Coral FL, 33904. pages 123, 135-137+]

3. THOMAS POPHAM, born , died ; married PHEBE HAWKINS, daughter of Matthew Hawkins & Betty Maxwell.

Thomas Popham was one of three witnesses to the will of Benjamin Hawkins, grandfather of Thomas's wife, Phebe Hawkins Popham. Dated 1 August 1793 (Bk D p 100).

Thomas Popham moved to Hardin County KY where he was listed in the 1820 census.

Children of Thomas Popham & Phebe Hawkins:
1. John Popham, born 29 May 1792 Culpeper County VA, died 7 October 1877 Meade County KY; married 1813 Hardin County KY to Rebecca Setzer.
2. James Popham, born 1793 VA
3. Thomas Popham, born 1798 VA; married 1804 Washington County KY to Mary McCullam.
4. Job Popham, born 1786; married 1813 Hardin County KY Elizabeth Setzer.
5. Eleanor Popham, born 1800/10, died ; married Daniel Westfall, Meade County KY
[Morrison, Theron V. 1983. The Popham Ancestral Line ... pages 131-4][The Popham Newsletter. March 1985. article by Richard R. Popham "Westward Movement of our Ancestors"]

4. RACHEL EVINS POPHAM, born 1765 Culpeper Co VA; married 3 August 1786 Slate Mills, Culpeper County VA by William Mason (Baptist minister) to MOORE SCOTT, born 3 January 1758 Cupar, Fife, Scotland, died 3 July 1848, son of Henry Scott & Sarah.

# Descendants of John Popham

[Morrison, Theron V. 1983. The Popham Ancestral Line ...][Culpeper County VA Marriage Records][Culpeper County VA Marriages 1780-1853 by John Vogt & T. William Kethley jr. 1986. p185]

5. NANCY POPHAM, born 1767 Culpeper Co VA; married 26 May 1788 Culpeper County VA to HEDGMAN TRIPLETT.
[Morrison, Theron V. 1983. The Popham Ancestral Line ...]

6. GERARD POPHAM, born 1768 Culpeper Co VA; married 11 December 1795 Culpeper County VA by Lewis Conner (Baptist minister) to KEZIAH VAUGHN or BAUGHAN.

An estate settlement for a Gerard Popham was filed in Boone County KY 24 July 1848 with Nancy Snyder as administrix.
[Morrison, Theron V. 1983. The Popham Ancestral Line ...][IGI][Culpeper County VA Marriage Records][Culpeper County VA Marriages 1780-1853 by John Vogt & T. William Kethley jr. 1986. p87]

7. JOHN POPHAM, born 1770 Culpeper Co VA, died 1813 or 1817; married 27 December 1795 Culpeper County VA by Lewis Conner (Baptist minister) ELIZABETH BROWN.

On 22 May 1824 the Court ordered appraisement of Negroes belonging to the estate of John Popham.
[Morrison, Theron V. 1983. The Popham Ancestral Line ...][IGI][Culpeper County VA Marriage Records][Culpeper County VA Marriages 1780-1853 by John Vogt & T. William Kethley jr. 1986. p87]

8. JAMES POPHAM, born 1772 Culpeper Co VA

James Popham listed in the 1810 census for Culpeper County VA.
[Morrison, Theron V. 1983. The Popham Ancestral Line ...]

9. JOB POPHAM, born 1774 Culpeper Co VA

10. MARY POPHAM, born 1778 Culpeper Co VA

### CHILDREN OF HUMPHREY POPHAM & BETSEY HAWKINS

1. William Nolle Popham, born 1789 Culpeper Co VA; married 1816 in Nelson Co KY to Mary (Polly) Davis, daughter of Traver Davis & Frances Melton.

Children:
1. Mary (Polly) Popham, born 9 August 1792
2. Elizabeth (Betsey) Pophamborn ca 1794\1800
3. Lucy Popham, born 1794\1800
[Morrison, Theron Vasco. 1983. The Popham Ancestral Line of Theron Vasco Morrison.]

2. Mary Popham, born 9 August 1792 Culpeper Co VA; married 24 September 1811 in Nelson County KY to Reuben Morgan
[Morrison, Theron Vasco. 1983. The Popham Ancestral Line of Theron Vasco Morrison.]

3. Elizabeth Popham, born between 1794 & 1800 Culpeper Co VA; married 15 April 1813 in Nelson County KY to William B. Ferguson

# Descendants of John Popham

Moved to Washington County KY by 1830
[Morrison, Theron Vasco. 1983. The Popham Ancestral Line of Theron Vasco Morrison.]

4. Lucy Popham, born between 1794 & 1800 Culpeper Co VA; married 15 April 1813 in Nelson County KY to George Morrison

Moved to Malden VA near what is now Charleston WVA by 1818; this is the line of Theron Vasco Morrison.
[Morrison, Theron Vasco. 1983. The Popham Ancestral Line of Theron Vasco Morrison.]

5. Job or Jacob Popham, born 1796 Culpeper Co VA, died 1863; married .

By 1830 to Boone County KY, where listed in the 1850 census.

Children:
1. Albert Popham, married Jemima Turner in 1842 by Lewis Conner (same Baptist minister from Culpeper Co VA)
[Morrison, Theron Vasco. 1983. The Popham Ancestral Line of Theron Vasco Morrison.]

6. John Popham, born 1798 Culpeper Co VA; married (1) 13 September 1840 in Boone County KY to Mary Hood; married (2) 24 January 1847 to Elizabeth Conrad by Lewis Conner.

Listed in 1850 census Boone County KY
[Morrison, Theron Vasco. 1983. The Popham Ancestral Line of Theron Vasco Morrison. address: 3727 SE 18th Ave, Cape Coral FL, 33904. pages 123, 135-137+]

7. Ezekiel Popham, born between 1800 & 1810, died 20 August 1847 Salem, Champoeg County OR; married 17 October 1833 Morgan County IL to Nancy C. Graham, born 1807 Logan County KY, died after 1860 perhaps in Linn County OR, daughter of Andrew Graham (b. 1758 Ireland, d. 1821 Todd County KY) & Margaret --- (d. 1840s Henderson County IL).

Ezekiel Popham was a bondman & witness to the marriage of his sister, Nancy Popham, to William Ray in Franklin County KY 17August 1818.

Ezekiel & Nancy (Graham) Popham moved from Morgan County IL to Henderson County IL in 1836 with other members of the Graham family. Their son, William Thomas Popham, was baptized in the South Henderson Presbyterian Church on 1 June 1840. In the late 1840s the Pophams moved to Oregon where Ezekiel Popham had a claim to 640 acres in Champoeg County in 1847. Ezekiel Popham was killed in a fight over his son. Nancy Graham Popham married second to John McGregor, who died September 1851.

In the Edgar County IL probate records is listed an estate record for Ezekiel Popham Box #169.

Children:
1. J. Ann Popham, born c 1834
2. James Popham, born c 1835
3. William Thomas Popham, born 1840 Henderson County IL.

8. Nancy C. Popham, born , married 17 August 1818 in Franklin County KY to William Ray.

The 100 pound bond for the marriage of William Ray & Nancy Popham was paid by Ezekiel

# Descendants of John Popham

Popham & William Ray, residents of Franklin County KY. Witnesses to the marriage included Ezekiel Popham & Humphrey Popham.

1840 census Edgar County IL: Nancy Ray
1850 census Edgar County IL: Nancy Ray, widow, listed next to her brother-in-law John E. Ray.

Edgar County IL deed records:
Bk 3 p. 804 - Jane Popham to James Ray, part sec 1 T12R11, dated Sept 1837, recorded June 1839. Bk 4 p. 4 - Jane Popham, John Ray & Eliza wife, & Mary Ray all of Edgar County to William Black, land in town of Elbridge, dated March 1838, recorded May 1839.
Bk 4 p. 476 - Jane Popham of Clark Co IL to Simon Taylor, part east half of sw quarter sec 1 T12R11, dated July 1840, recorded November 1840.
[Ronald Walker, Kansas City MO, via Mrs. Theron Morrison]

9. Jane Popham Graham, born 12 April 1809 Virginia, died 14 December 1893 Winterset, Madison County, IA; married 13 March 1835 Morgan County IL to William Mills Graham, born 26 September 1801 Chester County SC, died 28 January 1882 Winterset Iowa, son of Andrew Graham (b. 1758 Ireland, d. 1821 Todd County KY) & Margaret --- (d. 1840s Henderson County IL.

William M. Graham had married first in Todd County KY in 1823 to Sally Gartin (1798-1833). William Graham was an elder in the Presbyterian Church near Jacksonville IL. The Grahams moved from Morgan County IL to Henderson County IL in 1836, joined the South Henderson Presbyterian Church. Jane Popham Graham was reared a Baptist and formerly joined the Presbyterian Church when she was baptized at the Sunday service on 27 May 1836. In December 1870, William & Jane (Popham) Graham moved to Winterset, Madison County, Iowa along with several of their children.

Children of William Graham & Jane Popham:
1. James Thomas Graham, born 8 October 1836
2. William Alexander Graham, born 26 September 1837
3. Sarah Jane Graham, born 3 September 1840
4. John Mills Graham, born 27 March 1842
5. David McDill Graham, born February 1843
6. Mary Margaret Graham, born 30 December 1844
7. Samuel Allison Graham, born 18 March 1848.

10. daughter, born between 1800 & 1810
[Morrison, Theron Vasco. 1983. The Popham Ancestral Line of Theron Vasco Morrison.]

## OTHER POPHAMS

1. ---- Popham, married 1750 Culpeper County VA to John Triplett.

1. Hawkins Popham, married 21 April 1817 Culpeper County VA by Daniel James to Rebecca Hawkins.
[IGI][Culpeper County VA Marriage Records][Culpeper County VA Marriages 1780-1853 by John Vogt & T. William Kethley jr. 1986. p87]

1. Ann Popham, married 15 March 1821 Culpeper County VA by Daniel James to Presley Brown.

# Descendants of John Popham

1. Rebecca Popham, married 1822 Culpeper County VA to John Story.

1. Hiram Popham, married 27 December 1832 Culpeper County VA by Wm F. Broadus to Lucy Brown.

1. John Popham, married 10 January 1833 Culpeper County VA by Wm F. Broadus to Elizabeth Harris.

------

### HAWKINS FAMILY

1. BENJAMIN HAWKINS, born c1718 Culpeper County VA; married c1739 Culpeper County VA to JUDA/JUDITH ---.

Will of Benjamin Hawkins, dated/probated 1 August 1793 (Bk D p100).

Children, born Culpeper County VA:
1. Matthew Hawkins, born c1740+
2. Benjamin Hawkins, born c1744
[IGI][Morrison, Theron V. 1983. The Popham Ancestral Line ...]


1. MATTHEW HAWKINS, born c1740 Culpeper County VA, died ; married c1761 Culpeper County VA ELIZABETH MAXWELL, daughter of James Maxwell. James Maxwell married Rachel Popham, widow of John Popham.

Children, born Culpeper County VA:
1. Betsey/Betty Hawkins, born c 1762; married Humphrey Popham
2. Job Hawkins, born c1764
3. Phebe Hawkins, born 1770; married Thomas Popham
4. John Hawkins, born c1774
[IGI][Morrison, Theron V. 1983. The Popham Ancestral Line ...]

# Children of John Stevenson & Mary Coulter

## STEVENSON

### FIRST GENERATION

1. JOHN STEVENSON SR, born 20 December 1750 County Antrim, Ireland, died 27 April 1851 Murray, Whitfield County, GA; married by 1780 to MARY (ANN) COULTER STEVENSON, born c 1754 probably Ireland, died c 1825 probably in Todd County KY, daughter of Robert Coulter & Mary Stuart.

John Stevenson sr migrated to America in 1772, landing at Charleston SC. Shortly thereafter, he moved to the Waxhall settlement where his land was literally on the dividing line between Mecklenburg County NC and Lancaster County SC. John Stevenson stated in his Revolutionary War Pension that he went from Mecklenburg County NC about 1803 to Pendleton District SC. After about 11 years he went to what became Todd County KY, where he stayed for another 11 years. This would make him to Todd County about 1814 to 1825. After her death John returned to South Carolina. His daughter, Mary, and her husband decided to follow two of their sons who had gone to DeKalb County, GA, and sent such glowing reports of the area. John also went, living there for a while and helping establish the Prosperity ARP church. Then at the age of 90 decided again to move with his grandson, William, and his wife, to Murray County, GA, in the northern part of the state. It is now Whitfield County and that is where John is buried.

Robert Stevenson, a grandson of John & Mary (Coulter) Stevenson, left a "ledger" with family information. He stated that the wife of John Stevenson was Ann Coulter and that she died in Todd County KY of cancer of the face and that after she died John returned to SC. This would mean that Ann Coulter Stevenson died between 1814 and 1825 but probably closer to 1825 as her death is suppose to be the reason that John returned to SC. John Stevenson later moved to Georgia where he died in Murray County 27 April 1851.

Children of John Stevenson & Mary Coulter:
1. Robert Stevenson, born
2. Andrew Stevenson, born 30 August 1783 Mecklenburg Co NC
3. William Stevenson, born
4. John Stevenson, born 23 December 1785 NC/SC
5. Mary Stevenson, born
6. Elizabeth Stevenson, born
7. Margaret Stevenson, born
[Revolutionary War - AA 7378, X310][Pension R10142][Mrs Francis Coulter, Coulterville IL] [James Buckley data]["The Stevenson Family Record", by Charles Perry Stevenson, 1981,]

### SECOND GENERATION

### CHILDREN OF JOHN STEVENSON & MARY/ANN COULTER

1. ROBERT STEVENSON, born [ca 1778], died 19 April 1852 Macoupin County IL, buried Sulphur Springs Cemetery, Nilwood Twp, Macoupin County IL; married MARGARET CHESNUT, born 1787, died 1844, daughter of Alexander Chesnut & Sarah Meek.

Children of Robert Stevenson & Margaret:
- daughter; married W.R. Cass of Sangamon County IL in 1854.
- daughter; married Wm M. Maddox of Macoupin Co IL in 1854.
- Alexander C. Stevenson, of Macoupin Co IL in 1854
- daughter ;married John Rodgers of Montgomery Co IL in 1854

# Children of John Stevenson & Mary Coulter

- David C. Stevenson, of Macoupin Co IL in 1854
- daughter ; married John R. Cunningham of IL in 1854
- William J. Stevenson, of IL in 1854
- John Stevenson of IN in 1854
- daughter; married A.C. Wood of Sangamon County IL in 1854
- Robert Y. Stevenson, died prior 1854 Macoupin Co IL; married Virginia E. --- (children: Emorila F. Stevenson, Virginia C. Stevenson, Robert Y. Stevenson).
["The Stevenson Family Record", by Charles Perry Stevenson, 1981,]

2. ANDREW STEVENSON, born 30 August 1783 Mecklenburg Co NC, died 10 July 1857 Anderson Co SC, buried Old Concord Cemetery; married (1) JANE ROGERS, died 1817 (Anderson Co SC); (2) about 1822 to ELIZABETH MOOREHEAD, born 29 January 1797, died 14 September 1870, buried Old Concord Cemetery, daughter of James Moorehead & Mary Polly Jones.

Family moved to Anderson County SC about 1803 & lived in a log house with plank windows shutters two miles north of Anderson on one of the two places bought by his father.

Children of Andrew Stevenson & Jane Rodgers:
1. Mary Stevenson, ; married John McElroy, to Cross County Arkansas in 1848.
2. Elizabeth Stevenson, ; married --- Holt.
3. William Stevenson, ; married Sara McElroy, to Whitfield County GA.
4. John Stevenson, ; married Pauline Richey.
5. Anna Stevenson, ; married Samuel Bell, to Falls County TX.
6. Jane Stevenson, ; married (1) --- Parker; married (2) Reuben Richey of Anderson Co SC, later to TX.
Children of Andrew Stevenson & Elizabeth Moorehead:
7. Nancy Stevenson, born 28 July 1822, died 6 April 1900; marreid James E. Dobbins, buried Old Concord Cemetery.
8. Violet Stevenson, born 22 May 1826, died 4 November 1904; married William Barr Bailey, buired Midway Church, five miles north of Anderson SC.
9. James Stevenson, born 22 May 1826, died about 1856/8.
10. Robert Stevenson, born 4 January 1829, died 5 November 1905.
11. Ebenezer Stevenson, born 1832 ; married Tennessee Parks, went to Dalton GA, later to Walker County TX in 1859.
["The Stevenson Family Record", by Charles Perry Stevenson, 1981,]

3. WILLIAM STEVENSON, born [ca 1782], died .

4. JOHN STEVENSON, born 23 December 1785 [near Waxhaw, Mecklenburg County, NC] NC/SC, died [11 September] 6 October 1835 Macoupin County IL, 49 yrs 8 mo 18 days, buried Stevenson Cemetery, North Otter Twp, Macoupin County IL; married 6 October 1811 Christian County KY to JANE GRAYHAM, born [16] 15 February 1790 NC, died 6 June 1849 Macoupin County IL, 59 yrs 3 mo 21 days, buried Stevenson Cemetery, North Otter Twp Macoupin County IL, daughter of Thomas Grayham (born 1764, NC) & Rebecca — (born 1768 NC).

Children of John Stevenson & Jane Grayham:
1. Mary Ann Stevenson, born 23 November 1812 KY
2. James Young Stevenson, born 28 July 1814 KY
3. infant, born 1 March 1816
4. Nancy Graham Stevenson, born 5 Jly 1817 KY
5. Elizabeth Moorehead Stevenson, born 27 February 1819 KY

# Children of John Stevenson & Mary Coulter

6. William Steward Stevenson, born 9 November 1820 KY
7. Margaret Jane Stevenson, born 1824 KY
8. John Wilson Stevenson, born 17 April 1828 KY
9. Andrew Thomas Stevenson, born 10 February 1831 KY
[Mrs. Ralph (Esther) Bigham, Vista CA]

5. MARY STEVENSON MCELROY, born , died , buried DeKalb County GA; married SAMEUL MCELROY, born , died , buried DeKalb County, GA.

Resident Murray County GA.

Children:
1. Andrew Jackson McElroy, born , died ; married Margaret McCloud McDonald. Andrew was a Presbyterian minister.

6. ELIZABETH STEVENSON CHESNUT, died prior to 1854; married JAMES CHESNUT, bonr 1780/90 SC, son of Alexander Chesnut (b. 4 July 1759, d. 9 May 1809 Christian Co KY) & Sarah Meek (d. 13 July 1831 Todd Co KY, 65 yrs).

Family moved to (Macoupin Co) Illinois by 1854.

Children of James Chesnut & Elizabeth Stevenson:
- John A. Chesnut
- daughter ; married G.B. Waller
- daughter ; married M.F. Wood

7. MARGARET STEVENSON, born , died 1835.

Never married but had one child out of wedlock, named Margaret Jane (called Jane). Andrew may have helped raised Jane. Eventually, Jane went to Macoupin County, IL.

Andrew Stevenson was executor of his sister Margaret's will, which gave Jane (daughter of Andrew) 100 acres of land.

## CHILDREN OF JOHN STEVENSON & JANE GRAYHAM

1. MARY ANN STEVENSON GRAHAM, born 23 November 1813 [1812 Christian County] KY, died 4 February 1898 [Macoupin County, IL] Dallas Township, Marion County IA, buried Gosport Cemetery, Knoxville, Dallas Township, Marion County, IA; married 11 May 1830 Todd County KY to THOMAS [Isaac] GRAHAM, born 5 August 1805 [NC] SC, died 20 December 1881 Marion County IA, buried Gosport Cemetery, Marion County IA (parents born in Ireland).

Todd County KY Deeds:
- Book F, p. 10: 21 April 1827, John & Nancy McKee to Thomas Graham & John M. Graham, for land on Elk Fork of Red River, 107 1/2 acres, bounding Peter Perkin's purchase of John Carpenter in Moody Grubbs line & John Stephenson's line, $250.
- Book G, p. 495-6: 11 Sept 1832, Thomas & Mary Ann Graham to John M. Graham, born $254, land above.

By 1835, Thomas & Mary Ann (Stevenson) Graham had moved to North Otter Township, Macoupin County IL. There, on 28 May 1835, Thomas bought 40 acres, section 17 twp 12 range 7 west, and on 20 November 1835 he bought 80 additional acres, section 28 twp 12 range 7 west.

# Children of John Stevenson & Mary Coulter

On 6 November 1847 he bought 40 more acres, section 17 twp 12 range 7 west. In the 1850 census Thomas Graham gave his total assests as $4,000; in 1860 he gave them as almost $10,000.

Some time in the 1860's Thomas & Mary Ann moved to Marion County IA.

Notes Children:
-John Gaddis Graham - Civil War veteran from Illinois. A letter from Fern Graham Erhens to Leona Appleyard Stull states that the first Methodist Church in the Edgar area was formed in the Graham home by a Circuit rider minister.

Children of Thomas Graham & Mary Stevenson:
1. John Gaddis Graham, born 26 June 1831 Todd County, KY, died perhaps [21 March 1900] in Nuckolls Co NB; married Nancy J. Johnston, daughter of Isaac Johnston & Elizabeth King.
2. James William Graham, born 20 February 1834 Virden, Macoupin County, IL, died 1862 Carlinville, Macoupin Co IL; married 1858 Lucinda C. Johnston, daughter of Isaac Johnston & Elizabeth King.
3. Nancy J. Graham, born 4 November 1836 Macoupin County, IL, died 1837.
4. Elizabeth O. Graham, born 8 August 1838 Virden, Macoupint County, IL, died 16 January 1876; married Henry Ballard.
5. Mary Margaret Graham, born 1 June 1841 Virden, IL, died 21 April 1884 Chariton, Lucas County, IA; married John B. Tucker, born 1 May 1840 Giles, Hardin County, TN, died 3 February 1912 Chariton, Lucas County, IA.
6. Louisa W. Graham, born 16 June 1844 Virden, IL; married James Y. Berry.
7. Nancy Jane Graham, born 6 June 1847 Virden, IL; died 2 November 1928 Marion County IA; married Benjamin Franklin Wilson, born 1844 Lincoln County, NC, son of Robert Wilson & Mary.
8. Virginia Harden Graham, born 14 June 1850 Virden, IL, died 25 April 1920; married Samuel Benjamin Imel.
9. A.S. Graham, born 26 December 1854 Virden, IL, died 26 December 1854.
10. Thomas J. Graham, b 3 May 1856 Virden, IL, died 18 May 1856.
[Esther Wilson Bigham][Todd County KY Marriage Book A p. 58]["The Stevenson Family Record", by Charles Perry Stevenson, 1981,]["Tombstone Revelations in Macoupin County Illinois", 1983, compiled by Wanda Warkins Aller & Eileen Lynch Tochanour]["Macoupin County, Illinois, Original Purchasers of Land", 1985, by Littleton T. Bradley][Federal Census records]

2. JAMES YOUNG STEVENSON, born 28 July 1814 KY, died 10 July 1892; married 19 September 1837 Macoupin County, IL to SARAH DAVIDSON.

3. infant, born 1 March 1816, died 27 March 1816 [Todd County, KY].

4. NANCY GRAHAM STEVENSON CLOUD, born 5 Jly 1817 KY, died 25 April 1866 Marion County, IA; married 14 January 1836 Macoupin County IL to GEORGE AUGUSTUS W. CLOUD.

5. ELIZABETH MOOREHEAD STEVENSON HAGLER, born 27 February 1819 KY, died 16 August 1854; married 15 November 1838 Macoupin County, IL to JOHN GRAHAM HAGLER.

6. WILLIAM STEWARD STEVENSON, born 9 November 1820 KY, died 18 April 1888; married 14 February 1844 Macoupin County, Ilto MARY KRUMP; married (2) SARAH E IRI--(?).

7. MARGARET JANE STEVENSON, born 28 November 1823 KY, died 13 May 1849 Macoupin

# Children of John Stevenson & Mary Coulter

County IL, 25 yrs, 3 mo 15 days, buried Stevenson Cemetery, North Otter Twp, Macoupin County IL.

8. JOHN WILSON STEVENSON, born 17 April 1828 KY, died 20 December 1854, buried Stevenson Cemetery, North Otter Twp, Macoupin County IL.

9. ANDREW THOMAS STEVENSON, born 10 February 1831 KY, died 7 October 1859, buried Stevenson Cemetery, North Otter Twp, Macoupin County IL.

# Descendants of William Gartin

## GARTIN FAMILY

### FIRST GENERATION

-William Garten, born about 1649 England, died December 1709 Christ Church, Lancaster County VA; married Hanah Margaret Angell, born about 1670 VA, died, daughter of William Angell.

-Uriah Garten, born about 1675, died 1755 Spotsylvania County VA; married Winifred ---.

1. ELIJAH GARTIN, Sr., born about 1727, d St. George's Parish, Spotsylvania County, Virginia, about 1774; married 5 March 1752 FRANCES DICKENSON, born ca 1731, died Todd County, Kentucky, about 1825, daughter of Nathaniel Dickenson & Elizabeth Mansfield. Frances Dickenson Gartin married (2) 25 August 1778 Rockingham County Virginia to John Brown.

Will of Elijah Gartin, sr., probated in Spotsylvania County VA Court May 1774.

Frances Dickenson Garten moved to the area of Todd County KY with her brother Elijah Dickenson & his family. Will of Frances Brown dated 1 May 1824, probated in Todd County KY 14 March 1825 in Will Book A. pages 271-2. Her son, John Brown jr, was executor.

Children of Elijah Gartin & Frances Dickenson:
1. William Gartin, born about 1756
2. Elijah Gartin, born Spotsylvania County VA, 12 November 1758
3. Nathaniel Gartin, born Orange County, VA, 11 August 1759
4. Richard Gartin, born Spotsylvania County, VA, about 1760
5. Uriah Gartin, born
6. Frances/Fanny Gartin, born Virginia, about 1770
7. Elizabeth Gartin, born
8. Griffith Gartin, born 17 September 1763 Orange County VA
[Don Dickerson - Ddickerson@aol.com - via rootsweb][webpage ju5tdew1t@yahoo.com - information from William Garten - stops at Richard Garten & Anna Kincaide]

### SECOND GENERATION

### CHILDREN OF ELIJAH GARTIN & FRANCES DICKENSON

1. WILLIAM GARTIN, born about 1756, died 1837 Todd County KY; married (1) 2 March 1786 Greenbriar County, VA to Jane Miller March; married (2) 1813 Todd County KY to MATILDA SHREVE.

2. ELIJAH GARTIN, jr, born Spotsylvania County VA, 12 November 1758, died Fayetteville, Lawrence County, IN, 1840, buried Shiloh Cemetery, Eureka, IN; married 16 March 1782 Augusta County VA to SARAH BOYD, born 12 May 1761, died .

3. NATHANIEL GARTIN, born Orange County, VA, 11 August 1759, died Monroe County, VA, 7 March 1840; married Mary ---.

Nathan Garten served in the Revolutionary War; filed a petition in Monroe County VA 1834.

4. RICHARD GARTIN, born Spotsylvania County, VA, about 1752 or 1760, died Christian County, KY, 1815; married Greenbrier County, VA, 2 August 1792 to ANNA KINCAID, born Greenbriar

# Descendants of William Gartin

County VA about 1775, died Kentucky after 1 May 1824, daughter of Andrew Kincaid & Mary.

Richard Gartin moved to the area of what is now Todd County KY about 1809. He received a land patent, dated 16 January 1816, in Christian/Logan County. This tract of land was on the Elk Fork of the Red River.

Will of Ana Kincaid Gartin dated 1 May 1824. Andrew Kincaid(e), will written 9 June 1810 Greenbriar County VA, Book 1 page 276.

Children of Richard Gartin & Anna Kincaid:
1. Frances/Fanny Gartin, born about 1793 VA
2. Mary/Polly Gartin, born 1 June 1795
3. Elizabeth Gartin, born 1797 Elkton, Christian County, KY
4. Sally C. Gartin, born KY, 29 November 1798 [Todd County,] KY
5. Anna Gartin, born 25 February 1801 [Greenbriar County, VA]
6. Elizabeth Gartin, born
7. Elijah Gartin, born 28 January 1803 [Orange, VA]
8. Andrew Kincaid Gartin, born Greenbriar County VA, 31 December 1805
9. Nathaniel Gartin, born 26 January 1808 [Orange County, VA]
10. Richard Gartin, born 1810 [Orange County, VA]
11. William Harvey Gartin, born 30 June 1812 Christian County, KY
[OneWorldTree - lists child Virginia Gartin with no dates]

URIAH GARTIN, born 1760 Orange County AV, died Washington County, KY, 1818; married (1) 1785 Rockingham County VA to Margaret Devier; married (2) 1787 Rockingham County VA to Sarah Houston..

FRANCES/FANNY GARTIN SHANKLIN, born Virginia, about 1770, died Syracuse, Morgan County, Missouri, after 1850; married in the New Providence Church (Presbyterian), VA, about 1791 to JOSEPH SHANKLIN, born perhaps in Virginia, died Christian County, KY, about 1815 to 1818, son of Edward Shanklin.

The Shanklins were owned land adjoining that of the family of 2-1 Andrew Graham in Todd County KY during the 1820's. In 1830, Fanny Gartin Shanklin moved to Cooper County, Missouri, with her children, William Shanklin, Thomas Jefferson Shanklin, Jeanette Shanklin, and Elizabeth Shanklin. They came in a four horse drawn wagon. The Shanklins, of Cooper County, MO, sold land in Todd County KY to John Foster for $400 (Todd County KY Deed Book K p. 10. This land in Todd County KY was described as from the estate of Joseph Shanklin, deceased.

1850 census, Richland Township, Morgan County, MO, page 242, line 31, 311/311
Thomas J. Shanklin, 38, farmer, 400, KY
Hantippa? Shanklin, 37, KY
Tabitha Shanklin, 9, MO
Frances Shanklin, 80, VA


Children of Joseph Shanklin & Fanny Gartin:
1. William Gartin Shanklin, born Virginia, 4 July 1802
2. Gilbert David Shanklin,
3. Elijah Shanklin,
4. Thomas Jefferson Shanklin

# Descendants of William Gartin

5. Jeanette Shanklin
6. Elizabeth Shanklin

-----

1. William Gartin Shanklin, born Virginia, 4 July 1802, died Platte County, MO, 27 May 1891, buried Second Creek Cemetery, Platte County, MO; married in Morgan County, IL, 3 November 1831 to Martha Graham, born probably in Chester County, SC, 23 August 1798, died near Linkville, Platte County, MO, 26 August 1887, buried Second Creek Cemetery, Platte County MO, daughter of Andrew Graham & Margaret.

see Graham history under 3-7 Martha Graham Shanklin page 162.

1850 census, Carrol Township, Platte County, MO, page 411-2, line 39, 124/124
Wm G. Shanklin, 48, farmer, 1900, VA
Martha Shanklin, 47, SC
Nancy Shanklin, 17, MO
Margaret Shanklin, 15, MO
Robt Shanklin, 10, MO - next page
Nancy F. Graham, 2, MO

1880 census, May Township, Platte County, MO, ed 99, page 188 [13C], line 17, 119/119
William G. Shanklin, 77, farmer, VA, VA, VA
Martha Shanklin, 76, wife, housework, SC, Ireland, Ireland
Nancy F. Shanklin, 47, daughter, single, house work, MO, VA, SC

2. Gilbert David Shanklin, died in KY in 1815.

3. Elijah Shanklin, born Kentucky, 1796, died ; married Ann Roberts, born Kentucky, 1799, died , daughter of Joseph Roberts & Luvinia Brooks.

Elijah & Ann (Roberts) Shanklin & Joseph & Luvinia Roberts came to Booneville, Cooper County, MO in 1828.

1830 census, Cooper County, MO, page 221 - Elijah Shanklin [next page has William Steel, & John Cordry]

1840 census, Richland Township, Morgan County, MO, page 181 - Thomas J. Shanklin, Elijah Shanklin

1850 census, Richland Township, Morgan County, MO, page 243, line 24, 318/318
Elijah Shanklin, 54, farmer, 1000, KY
Ann Shanklin, 51, KY
John Shanklin, 17, labourer, MO - all
Cordelia Shanklin, 15
Mary Ann Shanklin, 13
Davis Shanklin, 9
Ivy McCoy Shanklin, 26 (f)
Alexander Shaanklin, 8

1860 census, Mill Creek Township, Morgan County, MO, p.o. Syracuse, page [106], line 30, 755/719

# Descendants of William Gartin

Elijah Shanklin, 61, farmer, 4000/5960, VA
Ann Shanklin, 61, KY
Ivy Shanklin, 37, KY
John Shanklin, 24, MO
Mary A. Shanklin, 21, MO
Elijah Shanklin, 19, MO
M. McCoy, 16 (m), MO

1860 census, Slave Schedule - 9 slaves - Elijah Shanklin

Land Patents - Millcreek Township, Cooper County, MO
-Elijah Shanklin: 1843 -04-01, Township 45 N, Range 18 W, section 9, NESE: MO0510_.079
-William H. Shanklin: 1833-07-30, Township 45N, Range 18W, section 9, NWNE, NENE, SWNE & SENE: MO0510_. 079
-Nathaniel Gartin: 1835-11-04, Township 45 N, Range 18W, section 9 SENW, 80 acres: MO0530_. 168
-Elijah Shanklin: 1835-11-14, Township 45N, Range 18W, section 10, NWSW & SWSW, MO0540_.113
-William Shanklin: 1833-06-08, Township 45N, Range 18W, section 10, NESW & SESW, MO0500_.151
-Thomas J. Shanklin: 1837-11-02, Township 45N, Range 18W, section 10, NWSE, MO2650_.345
-William Steel: 1840-01-10, Township 45N, Range 18W, section 10, SENE, NWNE & NENE, MO2680_.391 & MO2780_.143

Morgan County, MO, Marriages:
-John Logan to Cordelia Shanklin, 11 January 1859, Book 1
-George Kennedy to Mary A. Shanklin, 17 May 1864 Book 2
-Alexander McCoy to Ivy Shanklin, 12 October 1842

Children of Elijah Shanklin:
A. David Shanklin, died in Federal Pen. in IL during Civil War.
B. John Shanklin
C. Robert Shanklin, went to California in the Gold Rush.
D. Jory Shanklin ?
E. Caldelia Shanklin ?
F. Mary Ann Shanklin

4. Thomas Jefferson Shanklin, born Kentucky, 1812, died ; married 6 April 1837 Cooper County, MO to Xantippia Lampton, born 20 December 1811 Clark County, KY, died 1871 Morgan County, MO, daughter of John Lampton (born 8 June1766 Spotsylvania County, VA, died 22 December 1827 Clark County KY) & Tabitha Taylor (born KY, died April 1837 Cooper County, MO).

Moved to Cooper County MO in 1830.

1850 census, Richland Township, Morgan County, MO, page 242, line 31, 311/311
Thomas J. Shanklin, 38, farmer, 400, KY
Hantippa? Shanklin, 37, KY
Tabitha Shanklin, 9, MO
Frances Shanklin, 80, VA

1870 census, Millcreek Township, Morgan County, MO, p.o. Versailles, page 173 [13], line 4,

# Descendants of William Gartin

100/100
Thomas Shanklin, 59, farmer, 1000/1200, KY
Hamputia? Shanklin, 58, keeping house, KY
Tabitha Shanklin, 30, MO
Eller Shanklin, 13, (f), at school, MO
Frederick Shanklin, 8, MO


Children:
-Tabitha Shanklin, born 1840
-Ella Shanklin, born 1857, Morgan County, MO
-Frederick Shanklin, born 1862 Morgan County, MO
[OneWorldTree - not list parents of Thomas J. Shanklin]

5. Jeanette [Janet] Shanklin Carpenter, Kentucky, 5 January 1805, died 24 May 1862; married 8 August 1837 in MO to Thomas Carpenter, born Todd County, Kentucky, 11 April 1817, died Morgan County, Missouri, 24 September 1883, son of John Carpenter (born 17 June 1790 Lincoln County, NC, died 23 April 1878 Morgan County, MO) & Jane Gallahan (born 15 October 1796, NC, died 3 February 1888 Morgan County, MO). Thomas Carpenter married (2) in Morgan County, MO to Helena Westlake, born Morgan County, MO, 1837, died 1930.

1850 census, Richland Township, Morgan County, MO, line 18, page 243, line 18, 326/324
Thomas Carpenter, 33, farmer, 230, KY
Jane Carpenter, 38, KY
John J. Carpenter, 11, MO
[previous household, John J. Carpenter, 29, KY; next previous John Carpenter, 60, NC & Jane, 55, NC]

1860 census, Mill Creek Township, Morgan County, MO, p.o. Syracuse, page [105], line 16, 747/711
Thomas Carpenter, 43, farmer, 5600/1123, KY
Jeanet Carpenter, 49, KY
John Carpenter, 21, MO
[line 37, 750/714 - John Carpenter, 70, farmer, NC, Jane, 63, NC, Sarah, 26, MO]

1870 census, Mill Creek Township, Morgan County, MO, p.o. Versailles, born [18], line 18, 141/141
Thomas Carpenter, 53, farmer, 3000/1400, KY
Lena Carpenter, 33, keeping house, VA
Mary Carpenter, 3, MO
Charles Carpenter, 10/12, MO

1880 census, Mill Creek Township, Morgan County, MO, ed 192, page 217 [26B], line 30, 227/261
Thomas Carpenter, 63, farmer, KY, NC, NC
Hellen Carpenter, 43, wife, keeping house, VA, VA, VA
John Carpenter, 41, son, single, wood mecanic?, MO, KY, KY
Mary J. Carpenter, 12, daughter, at school, MO, KY, VA
Charles W. Carpenter, 11, son, single, at school, MO, KY, VA
James H. Carpenter, 5, son, MO, KY, VA
Armina? Westlake, 50, sister-in-law, single, at home, VA, VA, VA

Child by first wife:

# Descendants of William Gartin

-John J. Carpenter, born 1839, died single
Children by second wife -3
[OneWorldTree]

6. Elizabeth Shanklin - moved to Cooper County MO in 1830.

-----

ELIZABETH GARTIN DOUGLASS, born 1765 Augusta County VA, died ; married 1787 Rockingham County VA to JOSEPH DOUGLASS.

They lived in the part of Augusta County VA that became part of Rockingham County VA in 1778. They moved to Washington County KY in 1813.

GRIFFITH GARTIN, born 17 September 1763 Orange County VA, died 27 April 1835 Monroe County VA; married 19 September 1787 Monroe County, Viriginia, to HANNAH MILLER.
[Don Dickerson - Ddickerson@aol.com - via rootsweb]

## THIRD GENERATION

### CHILDREN OF RICHARD GARTIN & ANNA KINCAID

FRANCES/FANNY GARTIN CULBERTSON, born ca 1793 VA, died 1880 MO; married 22 March 1813, Christian County, KY, to DANIEL CULBERTSON, born 1783 Rowan County, NC, died about [8 March] 1847 Todd County KY, son of John Culbertson (born 1746 PA, died Rowan County, NC) & Elizabeth McConnell (born 1745, died 1800 Rowan County, NC)..

Andrew Gartin & Jane, his wife, and Daniel Culbertson & Fanny, his wife, late heirs of Richard Gartin deceased of Todd County KY sold to Robert Grady, of Todd County KY, their portion of the tract of land of Richard Gartin in Todd County on the Elk Fork of the Red River. Recorded in Todd County KY Deed Book J, page 476, dated 21 May 1836.

Daniel Culbertson, will written 1 February 1842, probated 8 March 1847 Todd County KY.

1850 census, District No. 1, Todd County, KY, page 234, line 28, 572/576
Frances Culbertson, 56, 525, VA
John do, carpenter, KY - all
Lucinda do, 18
Patterson do, 14 (m)
Andrew do, 13
Sally do, 9
line 34, -/577
Jeptha Tull?, 25, waggon marker, KY
Sarah do, 20, KY

1860 census, Tremont Township, Buchanan County, MO, p.o. Rock House Prairie?, page [225], line 3, 1508/1508
William Garden, 48, farmer, 11775/3250, KY
Martha J. Garden, 40, TN
Richard B. do, 14, MO
Elizabeth A. do, 12, MO
Sarah F. do, 9, MO

# Descendants of William Gartin

Flora Jane do, 7, MO
William C. do, 5, MO
Mary M. do, 2, MO
Budda do, 8/12 (m), MO
Elizabeth Graves, 63, TN
Melvina E. Gravies, 12, MO
Frances Culbertson, 66, VA

1870 census, Jackson Township, Gentry County, MO, p.o. Albany, page 628 [25], line 8, 177/180
Harrison Ballard, 50, farmer, 2400/1340, KY
Frances do, 48, keeping house, KY
Ellen do, 18, KY
Mary do, 16, KY
Andrew L. do, 14, KY
Lucian do, 12, (m), KY
John P. do, 9, MO
Viola do, 4, MO
Vicoria? do, 4, (f), MO
Lucinda do, 2, MO
Frances Culbertson, 78, 1000, VA

1880 census, Platte Township, Buchanan County, MO, ed 77, page [2B-3C], line 44, 20/20
J.W. Gartin, 45, farmer, KY, VA, KY
Mary F. Gartin, 42, wife, keeping house, IL, KY, KY
Archie J. Gartin, 18, son, single, farmer, MO, KY, IL
Charles do, 15, son, farmer, MO, KY, IL
Fannie do, 12, daughter, MO, KY, IL
Thos do, 10, son, MO, KY, IL
Elva do, 7, daughter, MO, KY, IL
Emma Gartin, 3, daughter, MO, KY, IL - next page
Frances Culventson,, 91, grand ma, widow, VA, VA, VA
G. G. Gartin, 36, bro-in-law, farmer, MO, VA, KY
M.A. Gartin, 33, sister-in-law, keeping house, MO, KY, VA
Nellie Gartin, 7, daughter, MO, MO, MO
George Gartin, 5, son, MO, MO, MO


Children:
A. Margaret Elliot Culbertson, born 1815 KY, died 1856; married 19 December 1833 Todd County, KY to Patterson Hawk, born , died 1834 Todd County, KY.
B. Mary Ann Culbertson, born 23 January 1816, KY, died 15 August 1849 Buchanan County, MO; married 8 March 1836 Todd County, KY to Archibald Millen, born July 1814, KY, died 10 June 1847 Buchanan County, MO, son of Archibald Millen. Child: Mary Frances Millen, born 12 July 1837 Jacksonville, Morgan County, Illinois. Married (2) 29 March 1848 Buchanan County, MO to Samuel L. Jones, born 15 March 1820, died 15 June 1849 Buchanan County, MO.
C. Martha Jane Culbertson, born 1819, KY, died 1880 CA; married 3 March 1842 Buchanan County, MO to Hiram Shartzer, born 1818, VA, died 1880.
D. Emily Stewart Culbertson, born 19 November 1822 Todd County, KY, died 13 May 1856 Hopkins County, KY; married Thomas Jefferson Bone, born 7 February 1799 Wilson County, TN, died 1874 Memphis, TN.
E. Frances Elizabeth Culbertson, born 9 September 1826 Todd County, KY, died 26 December 1897 Stanberry, Gentry County, MO; married 31 March 1845 Todd County, KY to Harrison

# Descendants of William Gartin

Ballard, born 19 August 1819, Christian County, KY, died 6 February 1886 Stanberry, Gentry County, MO.
F. John Richard Culbertson, born 22 January 1828 Todd County, KY, died 7 May 1919 St. Louis, MO; married (1) 14 July 1855 Macoupin County, IL to Rhoda Ann McGregory, born 1833, IL, died 1877; married (2) 20 January 1876 Carrollton, Carroll County, MO to Virginia Merriamn, born 1846 IN, died 1935 San Bernardino, CA.
G. Jane Culbertson, born 1829 KY, died .
H. Sarah Caroline Culbertson, born 12 July 1831, Todd County, KY, died 1900 MO; married married 13 March 1850 Todd County, KY to Jeptha Riggin Tull, born 28 March 1825, KY, died 26 December 1887, Harrison, MO.
I. Lucinda Ellen Culbertson, born 28 August 1833, Todd County, KY, died 19 April 1913 Tremont, Buchanan County, MO; married 15 May 1860 Buchanan County, MO to William Lane Gibson, born 4 January 1818, AL, died 21 September 1891 Tremont, Buchanan County, MO.
J. Patterson, Culbertson, born 1832, Todd County, KY, died 18 December 1856 Buchanan County, MO.
H. Andrew D. Culbertston, born 1837, Todd County, KY, died 23 March 1855 Todd County, KY.
I. Sally Culbertson, born 1841 Todd County, KY, died .
[OneWorldTree]

MARY/POLLY GARTIN CORDRY, born Virginia, 1 June 1795, died after 1860; married in Christian County, KY, 28 February 1815 to JOHN CORDRY, born in Virginia, about 1790, died possibly in Buchanan or Henry County, MO, about 1844, son of John Cordry (born Frederick County, VA, 1760, died Christian County, KY, 1815) & Catherine Mann (born VA 1764, died Cooper County, MO, 2 July 1836).


New Lebanon Cemetery, Cooper County, MO - Cooper County genealogy webpage: CORDRY, CATHERINE (old) born 1764 died July 2, 1836. [Catherine Mann was the wife of John Cordry. She was born in Va., married and started her family there, pioneered with her husband in what is now western Ky., and pioneered once again with her children in Missouri John Cordry served as a Pvt. in Capt. Joseph Crockett's County, 7th Va. Regt. of Foot commanded by Alexander McClenachan from Dec. 28. 1776 to June 30, 1777. John and Catherine Cordry had nine children: Charles Cordry born Mar. 6, 1784: Hannah Cordry born 1785-6: William Cordry born c1788; John Cordry born c1790: Elizabeth Cordry born c1792; James Cordry born Nov. 20, 1795; Mary Cordry born c1798; Sally Cordry born May 1, 1801; and Elijah Cordry born 1805. Also see DVKM. I

John Cordry served in the War of 1812. He substituted for his brother, William Cordry, on 8 October 1812 as a private in Captain Benjamin H. Reeves' Company, 6th Regiment KY Detached Militia at Henderson, KY, and is shown as such until 23 December 1812 - although at the latter date he is designated a "drumer" at a rate of pay of 7 dollars 33 cents per month. John Cordry appears on a muster roll of a detachment from the 6th Regiment of KY D. Militia at Vincennes, Indiana Territory, from 24 December 1812 to 9 January 1813.

In 1827, John Cordry sold 44 acres of land in Todd County KY to James Vaughan. He was the first of his family to move from Todd County KY to Cooper County MO but the exact date of arrival is not known. John Cordry entered his first 80 acres in Cooper County MO on 28 May 1829 & appears on the 1830 census of Cooper County. In 1836, John Cordry, along with Nathaniel Gartin, Elizabeth Gartin, Richard Gartin, and William Gartin, sold their interest in the estate of Richard Gartin to Andrew Gartin. Recorded in Todd County KY Deed Book K, page 3, dated 18 June 1836.

# Descendants of William Gartin

On 28 April 1845, the heirs of John Cordry sold 40 acres or more of land in Buchanan County MO to Archibald Millen for $200, as recorded in Book C, pages 32-3. The heirs were named as: Mary Cordry, Margaret Cordry, Green R. Cordry & Eliza, his wife, Joseph Y Steele & Martha, his wife, and Andrew W. Graham & Joranda, his wife. On 14 July 1846, the heirs of John Cordry sold 80 acres of additional land in Buchanan County to Martha Gartin for $700 as recorded in Deed Book D, page 464. Note that Elijah G. Cordry was not listed in these deeds as an heir of the estate of John Cordry.

1860 census, Rochester Township, Andrew County, MO, page [86-7], line 29, 631/616
Elijah Cordry, 34, farmer, -/500, KY
Mary Cordry, 40, IN
Susan do, 11, MO - all
Eliza do, 9
Jane do, 8
Roburn? do, 6 (m)
Belle do, 4
Tabitha do, 2
Samuel do, 6/12
Mary Cordry, 65, VA
Mary A. Cordry, 36, KY
Albert Cordry, 18, farmer, MO
Martha Graham, 14, MO - next page


Children of John Cordry & Mary Gartin:
1. Green Rayourn Cordry, born KY, 11 December 1816
2. Joranda Jane Cordry, born KY, 1818
3. Martha Ann Cordry, born 27 July 1819, Cooper County, MO
4. Margaret Brown Cordry, born 23 October 1820 Cooper County, MO
5. Mary E. Cordry, born 1823 Cooper County, MO
6. Elijah G. Cordry, born 1825, Cooper County, MO
[Cordry, Eugene, Allen. 1973. Descendants of Virginia, Kentucky, and Missouri Pioneers.]
[OneWorldTree]

------

1. Green Rayourn Cordry, born near Elkton, now Todd County, KY, 11 December 1816, died New Lebanon, Cooper County, MO, 7 December 1896, buried New Lebanon Cemetery; married in Cooper County, MO, 11 August 1839, to Eliza Jane Steele, born Cooper County, MO, 26 September 1820, died Cooper County, MO, 11 February 1911, buried New Lebanon Cemetery, daughter of William Addison Steele (born 13 August 1791 Greene County, TN, died 23 January 1864 Otterville, Cooper County, MO, buried New Lebanon Cumberland Presbyterian Church Cemetery, Cooper County, MO) & Jane Kirkpatrick (born 25 September 1793 Lancaster County, SC, died 5 August 1854 Otterville, Cooper County, MO, buried New Lebanon Cumberland Presbyterian Church Cemetery, Cooper County, MO).

New Lebanon Cemetery, Cooper County, MO - Cooper County Genealogy web page:
-CORDRY, GREEN R. (LB-43) born Dec. 11, 1816 died Dec. 7. 1896. [Green Raybourn Cordry was born in Todd County Kentucky and came to Cooper County Missouri no later than 1829, see DVKM.]

1850 census, Tremont Township, Buchanan County, MO, page 66a-b, line 41, 916/916
Green R. Cordry, 35, farmer, 1500, KY
Eliza do, 30, KY

# Descendants of William Gartin

Mary Cordry, 12, MO - all - next page
Martha Cordry, 10
William Cordry, 8
Margaret Cordry, 6
John Cordry, 3
[previous household Elijah G. Cordry; next household Nathaniel Gartin]

Children:
-Mary Jane Cordry, born 23 February 1841 Cooper County, MO, died 25 September 1888 Cooper County MO; married Abraham Crites, born 8 February 1838 Jackson County, [WV], died 28 February 1907 Blairstown, MO.
-Missouri Cordry, born 6 October 1842 Cooper County, MO, died 1 November 1842.
-Martha Ellen Cordry, born 10 November 1843 Cooper County, MO, died 20 January 1849.
-Margaret Ann Cordry, born 11 December 1847 Syracuse, Morgan County, MO, died 23 July 1936 Sedalia, Pettis County, MO; married 19 February 1868 Cooper County, MO to John W. Steele, born 1846 New Lebanon, Cooper County, MO, died 27 January 1893 Byberry, Cooper County, MO, son of Green Steele & Margaret Kivitt, grandson of William Steele & Jane Kirkpatrick.
-John Rayburn Cordry, born 9 April 1850 Cooper County, MO, died 14 February 1915 Otterville, Cooper County, MO; married 19 October 1871 Cooper County, MO to Sophia Olive Downs, born 13 March 1848 Frankfort, Clinton County, IN, died 24 August 1925 Otterville, MO.
-Lycurgus Malcolm Cordry, born 18 January 1855 Syracuse, Morgan County, MO, died 28 December 1928 Otterville, MO; married 14 November 1883 Otterville, MO to Ella Medora Brownfield, born 14 April 1857, MO, died October 1935 Otterville, MO.
-Alice Medora Cordry, born 24 February 1857 Otterville, Cooper County, MO, died 8 April 1925.
-Rosie Belle Cordry, born 15 August 1860 Syracuse, Cooper County, MO, died 11 May 1926 Sedalia, Pettis County, MO; married 4 August 1881 Cooper County, MO to George Washington King, born 6 October 1852 Centertown, Cole County, MO, died 1926 Sedalia, MO.
-Elijah Ray Cordry, born 16 February 1862 Syracus, Morgan County, MO, died 28 September 1938 Otterville, MO; married Missouri Abigail King, born 25 December 1860 Centertown, Cole County, MO, died 8 April 1937, Cooper County, MO.
[OneWorldTree]

2. Joranda Jane Cordry Graham, born probably Christian County, KY, died in Clinton or Buchanan County, MO, about 1849; married probably in MO, about 1842, to Andrew W. Graham, born Logan County, KY, 1807, died perhaps in CA after 1849, son of Andrew Graham & Margaret ---.

see Graham history under 3-12 Andrew W. Graham.

OneWorldTree - Zuranda Z Cordry married to Vinnie Shaw
[OneWorldTree]

3. Martha Ann Cordry Steele, born 27 July 1819 Cooper County, MO, died 14 February 1861 Cooper County, MO; married 1845 Cooper County, MO to Joseph Young Steele, born 8 September 1822 Cooper County, MO, died 13 December 1863 Cooper County, MO, son of William Steele & Jane Kirkpatrick.

Andrew Graham & Joranda, of Buchanan County, MO, sold 40 acres in Clinton County MO to Joseph Young Steele recorded in Clinton County MO Deed Book C, pages 397-8, recorded 19 August 1845.

# Descendants of William Gartin

1850 census, District 23, Cooper County, MO, page 144, line 25, 1055/1055
Joseph Y. Steel, 27, farmer, 1000, MO
Martha A. Steel, 25, KY
Mary Steel, 8, MO - all
William H. Steel, 6
Martha Steel, 4
Clementina Steel, 2
[next household, John A. Steel, 31, KY; then Robert Steel, 21, MO; previous household, Green Steel, 25, MO; then William Steel, 59, TN & Jane Steel, 27, SC]

1860 census, Lebanon Township, Cooper County, MO, p.o. Otterville?, page [16], line 15, 96/96
J.Y. Steele, 37, farmer, 1300/800, MO
Martha A. do, 41, KY
M.F. do, 15 (f), MO - all
W. H. do, 13 (m)
M. J. do, 12, (f)
C.B. do, 11, (f)
John C. do, 10
Joseph R. do, 8
E.E. do, 6 (f)
Geo W. do, 3

1870 census, Lebanon Township, Cooper County, MO, page 479 [50], line 2, 341/337
William Steele, 24, farmer, -/500, MO - all
Rebecca A. Steele, 27, keeping house
Martha A. Steele, 2
John H. Steele, 1
Clementine B. Steele, 21, keeping house
Joseph R. Steele, 17, works on farm
George Steele, 12, works on farm

Children, born Cooper County, MO:
-Mary Frances Steele, born 1843, died 1913; married 1872 Cooper County, MO to Henry Ruby Burnett, born 1841 Cooper County, MO, died 1921.
-William Harvey Steele, born 10 July 1845, died 15 March 1903 Cooper County, MO; married 1866 Cooper County, MO to Rebecca Ann Cordry, born 25 April 1839 Cooper County, MO, died 12 May 1923 New Lebanon, Cooper County, MO, daughter of John Bailey Cordry & Mary E. Wear.
-Clementine Steele, born 1848, died ; married 1873 Cooper County, MO James H. Neal.
-John Cordry Steele, born 22 May 1851, died 7 April 1913; married 1873 Vernon County, MO to Mary Ann Lee, born 1852 Macoupin, IL, died 8 January 1929 Long Island, KS.
-Joseph R. Steele, born 1852, died ; married 1874 to Amy ?.
-Eliza Ellen Steele, born 1855, died 1927 New Lebanon, Cooper County, MO; married 1877 George P. Downs, born 1848 Frankfort, IN, died 1892 New Lebanon, MO.
-Robert C. Steele, born 1856, died
-George Steele, born 1857, died 15 March 1915 Hunt County, TX; married Ella McKee.
[OneWorldTree]

4. Margaret Brown Cordry [Mullin] Millen, born 23 October 1820 Cooper County, MO, died 18 September 1888 Gentry County, MO; married Buchanan County, MO, 29 December 1846 to Elias S. [Mullin] Millen, born 13 November 1814 [Gentry, MO], died 18 November 1884 Gentry County, MO.

# Descendants of William Gartin

Note - Ancestry.com tree submitted by Michael Rice:
Elias L. Millen married Margaret B. Cardy. One child listed.

1860 census, Township, No. 61, Gentry County, MO, p.o. Gentryville, page [29], line 24, 186/186
Elias Millen, 45, farmer, 5600/1000, KY
Margaretta do, 36, KY
Mary do, 12, IL
John do 10, IL
Harrietta do, 8, IL
Elias do, 6, IL

1880 census, Township 61 Range 32 Jackson Twp, Gentry County, MO, ed 278, page 541 [27C], line 21, 229/232
Elias L. Millen, 58, farming, KY, KY, KY
Margaret Millen, 58, wife, house keeping, MO, MO, MO
Elias Millen, 19, son, single, farm laborer, MO, KY, MO
[previous household, Samuel Millen, 64, & Emily 55]

Children:
-Mary H. Millen, born 7 November 1847, died 6 December 1915 Gentry County, MO; married Madison Caldwell, born 12 August 1843, Montgomery County, VA, died 6 June 1892 King City, Gentry County, MO.
[OneWorldTree - birth date, no marriage listed]

5. Mary E. Cordry, born 1823 Cooper County, MO, died.
[OneWorldTree]

6. Elijah G. Cordry, born ca 1826 KY, died ; married Buchanan County, MO, 16 March 1848 to Mary Morgan.

1850 census, Tremont Township, Buchanan County, MO, page 66a, line 35, 915/915
Elijah G. Cordry, 23, farmer, 500, KY
Mary do, 30, Ten?, can not read or write
Susan do, 1, MO
Mary do, 5/12, MO
Mary do, 50, VA, can not read or write
Mary Do, 22, KY, can not read or write
[next household Green R. Cordry, 35]

1860 census, Rochester Township, Andrew County, MO, page [86-7], line 29, 631/616
Elijah Cordry, 34, farmer, -/500, KY
Mary Cordry, 40, IN
Susan do, 11, MO - all
Eliza do, 9
Jane do, 8
Roburn? do, 6 (m)
Belle do, 4
Tabitha do, 2
Samuel do, 6/12
Mary Cordry, 65, VA
Mary A. Cordry, 36, KY

# Descendants of William Gartin

Albert Cordry, 18, farmer, MO
Martha Graham, 14, MO - next page

1880 census, Nodaway Township, So. Div., Andrew County, MO, ed 41, page [4D] 257, line 29, 36/38
Elijah Cordry, 54, farmer, KY, KY, VA
Mary Cordry, 60, wife, house keeping, IN, VA?, ?
Ann B. Cordry, 24, daughter, single, at home, MO, KY, IN
Francis Cordry, 22, daughter, single, at home, MO, KY, IN
Samuel Cordry, 20, son, single, at home, MO, KY, IN
Mary J. Corry, 57, sister, single, at home, [blind & idiotic, cannot read or write], KY, KY, VA
Elijah Cogdell, 10, grandson, MO, MO, MO
William do, 8, grandson, MO, MO, MO
Arch do, 6, grandson, MO, MO, MO

Elijah G. Cordry was not listed among the heirs of the estate of John Cordry in the Missouri deed records. He is said to have been a Methodist Minister, who moved to DeKalb County, MO, in the 1850s.
[OneWorldTree - no marriage listed]

------

3. ELIZABETH GARTIN CORDRY, born Christian County, KY, 1797, died Cooper County, MO, 15 September 1843, buried New Lebanon Cemetery; married in Cooper County, MO, 25 October 1840 to JAMES CORDRY, born Christian County, KY, 20 November 1795, died Cooper County, MO, 18 April 1860, son of John Cordry (born Frederick County, VA, 1760, died Christian County, KY, 1815) & Catherine Mann (born VA 1764, died Cooper County, MO, 1836). James Cordry married (1) in Christian County, KY, 27 December 1814 to Margaret Murphy, born 21 March 1797 SC, died 6 July 1840 New Lebanon, Cooper county, MO, daughter of William Murphy (born 1772 Charleston, SC, died ) & Mary A. Kates; married (3) in Todd County KY, 1843 or 1845, to Catharine Murphy Nichols, born 1805, SC, died , daughter of William Murphy & Mary A. Kates, sister of Margaret Murphy.

James Cordry moved from Todd County KY to Cooper County MO sometime before 1836. James Cordry was church clerk for Regular Baptist Church of Christ called West Fork Pettite Saline, in Cooper County MO.

Elizabeth Gartin sold her interest in the estate of Richard Gartin to Andrew Gartin in a deed recorded in Todd County KY Deed Book K page 3, dated 18 June 1836.

New Lebanon Cemetery, Cooper County, MO - Cooper County genealogy webpage:
-CORDRY, ELIZABETH (old) died Sept. 18, 1843 Second wife of James Cordry. [James Cordry married secondly Oct. 25, 1840 Clay County Missouri Elizabeth Garton born 1797 Christian County Kentucky and had no children., see DVKM.]
-CORDRY, JAMES (old) died Apr. 18, 1860 aged 64 years 5 months 28 days. [He was born Nov. 20, 1795 near Elkton, Christian County (now Todd County) Kentucky and came to Cooper County Missouri in the fall of 1830. He married Margaret Murphy and had nine children: (1) William Langston Cordry born Jan. 15, 1816; (2) Thomas Murphy Cordry born Nov. 13, 1817; (3) Mary Ann Cordry born Nov. 18, 1819 (married George Decater Wear); (4) Catherine Elizabeth Cordry, born Sept. 3, 1823 (married Jonathan Warren Weir: (5) son born Jan. 21, 1825 died Jan. 21, 1825: (6) James Francis Marion Cordry born May 27, 1827: (7) son born Aug. 12,

# Descendants of William Gartin

1829 died Sept. 1, 1829; (8) Bathsheba Adeline Cordry (married Samuel Calvin Rankin): and (9) John Mann Cordry born May 23 1833. Also see HHCC and DVKM.]
-CORDRY, MARGARET (old) died July 6, 1840 aged 4:t years. [Margaret Murphy was born Mar. 21, 1797 in South Carolina daughter of William Murphy; she married Dec. 27, 1814 Christian County Kentucky James Cordry born Nov. 20, 1795.1

1850 census, District 23, Cooper County, MO, page 139, line 36, 985/985
James Cordry Sen, 52, farmer, 2000, KY
Cathrine do, 38, KY
John do, 14, MO
John Nichols, 23, laborer, KY
Simeon do, 20, do, KY
Thomas do, 15, do, KY
Franklin do, 13
[other Cordry families on this page]

Cooper County, Missouri, Cemetery Records, Vol 1-12
Location: Center NE 1/4 of Section 21; T-46-N; R-18-W; on the Forest Lewis Farm Note: August, 1978 Mr. Lewis informed Mr. Gene Cordry that recently some grave stones had been discovered when he and his sons were cultivating land at this site. He had not known of a burial plot there. They took the stones to his home and stacked them near the house. Mr. Cordry and Mr. and Mrs. W. R. Mitzel were invited to his home and recorded these names:
-William L.(angston) Cordry, 15 January 1816, 26 Dec 1903

Children of James Cordry & Margaret Murphy:
-William Langston Cordry, born 15 January 1816 Fayette, Howard County, MO, died 26 December 1903, buried New Lebanon Cumberland Presbyterian Church Cemetery, Cooper County, MO.
-Thomas Murphy Cordry, born 13 November 1817 Elkton, Christian County, KY
-Mary Ann Cordry, born 18 November 1819 Elkton, KY
-James Francis Cordry, born 27 May 1821 Elkton, KY
-Catherine Elizabeth Cordry, born 3 September 1823 Elkton, KY
-Bathsheba Adeline Cordry, born 13 January 1831 Cooper County, MO
-John M. Cordry, born 1833 Cooper County, MO
[OneWorldTree]

SALLY C. GARTIN GRAHAM, born KY, 29 November 1798, died Jacksonville, Morgan County, Illinois, 29 July 1833; married in Todd County, KY, 23 December 1823 to WILLIAM MILLS GRAHAM, in Chester County, SC, 26 September 1801, died in Winterset, Madison County, IA, 28 Janaury 1882. William M. Graham married (2) in Morgan County, IL, 13 March 1835 to Jane Popham, born Virginia, 12 April 1809, died Winterset, IA, 14 December 1893.

See Graham history under 3-8 William Mills Graham.

ANNA GARTIN/Garton MILLEN, born 25 February 1801 Greenbrier County, VA, died 17 April 1875 Albany, Gentry County MO; married 25 February 1823 Christian County, KY to JOHN Gameliel MILLEN, born 12 February 1803 SC, died 14 March 1886 Gentry County, MO, son of Archibald Millen.

1860 census, Township No. 61, Gentry County, MO, p.o. Gentryville, page [27], line 19, 172/172
John Millen, 57, farmer, 14000/4000, SC
Ann Millen, 59, VA

# Descendants of William Gartin

Didemia Millen, 32, KY
Fannie Millen, 29, MO
Richard Millen, 22, farmer, MO
Julia Millen, 20, MO
Julius Rena?, 14, farm laborer, OH
[household 175/175 - Samuel Millen ,47, & Emily, 34, both KY]

1870 census, Albany, Athens Township, Gentry County, MO, page [7], page 547, line 7, 53/59
John G. Millen, 67, farmer, 8500/3720, SC
Ann Millen, 69, keeping house, VA
Diadema Millen, 46, at home, 0/600, KY
Frances E. Millen, 39, at home, 0/600, MO

Children:
A. Diedamia Millen, born 27 December 1823 Todd County, KY, died 1 November 1879 Gentry, MO.
B. Andrew G. Millen, born 1825 KY, died ; married 19 March 1857 Morgan County, IL to Sarah E. White, born 1829 IL, died 1880.
C. Sarah Millen, born 1829 MO, died 13 December 1896 Denver, CO; married 26 December 1850 Morgan County, IL to John D. Antrobus, born 1831, IL, died .
D. Frances E. Millen, born 16 April 1831, MO, died 29 September 1879 Gentry, MO.
E. Mary A. Millen, born 1 April 1833, IL, died 12 October 1888 Gentry, MO; married George Purnell Taylor, born 22 June 1828 Nicholas County, KY, died 15 June 1898 St. Joseph, Buchanan County, MO.
F. Marion Lafayette Millen, born 14 May 1835, Morgan County, IL, died 13 February 1905 Gentry County, MO; married Viriginia B. Smith, born 24 September 1844 Gentry County, MO, died 26 January 1899 Albany, Gentry County, MO.
G. Archibald Richard Millen, born 28 August 1837, Morgan County, IL, died 9 July 1883 Gentry County, MO; married Mary M.Cranor, born 2 April 1841 Williamsburg, Wayne County, IN, died 3 January 1900 St. Joseph, MO
H. Juliet Millen, born 1839, IL, died 1886.
I. Margaret Millen, born 1843, IL, died Carthage, Jasper County, MO; married John M.Whedbee, born 1833, NC, died .
[OneWorldTree]

-----------

A. Diedamia Millen, born 27 December 1823 Todd County, KY, died 1 November 1879 Gentry County, MO.
[OneWorldTree]

B. Andrew G. Millen, born 1825 KY, died 1880; married 19 March 1857 Morgan County, IL to Sarah E. White, born 1829, IL, died 1880.

Children:
(1) Ann Millen, born 1858 Gentry County, MO
(2) Margarita Millen, born 1861, Gentry County, MO
(3) John Millen, born 7 September 1863, Gentry County, MO
(4) Thomas W. Millen, born 1867, MO
(5) Harriett F. Millen, born 1873, MO
[OneWorldTree]

C. Sarah Millen, born 1829 MO, died 13 December 1896 Denver, Worth County, CO; married 26

# Descendants of William Gartin

December 1850 Morgan County, IL to John D. Antrobus, born 1831, IL, died .
[OneWorldTree]

D. Frances E. Millen, born 16 April 1831, MO, died 29 September 1879 Gentry County, MO.
[OneWorldTree]

E. Mary A. Millen, born 1 April 1833, IL, died 12 October 1888 Gentry County, MO; married 24 October 1898 Gentry County, MO to George Purnell Taylor, born 22 June 1828 Nicholas County, KY, died 15 June 1898 St. Joseph, Buchanan County, MO.

Children:
(1) daughter Taylor, born Gentry County, MO
(2) Katie A. Taylor, born 6 April 1858 Gentry County, MO
(3) John J. Taylor, born 21 September 1863 Gentry County, MO
[OneWorldTree]

F. Marion Lafayette Millen, born 14 May 1835, Morgan County, IL, died 13 February 1905 Gentry County, MO; married 7 March 1861 Gentry County, MO to Virginia B. Smith, born 24 September 1844 Gentryville, Gentry County, MO, died 26 January 1899 Albany, Gentry County, MO.

Children, born Gentry County, MO:
(1) Orion L. Millen, born 1866
(2) Annie L. Millen, born February 1870
(3) Richard A. Millen, born 1872
(4) Jennie W. Millen, born 12 November 1874
[OneWorldTree]

G. Archibald Richard Millen, born 28 August 1837, Morgan County, IL, died 9 July 1883 Gentry County, MO; married 22 September 1864 Gentry County, MO to Mary M. Crannor, born 2 April 1841 Williamsburg, Wayne County, IN, died 3 January 1900 St. Joseph, Buchanan County, MO.

Children, born Gentry County, MO:
(1) William Manlove Millen, born 27 November 1865
(2) John Holt Millen, born 25 February 1868
(3) Ella A. Millen, born 8 April 1871
(4) Ernest Richard Millen, born 7 March 1880
(5) Frank Millen, born 1883
[OneWorldTree]

H. Juliet Millen, born 1839, IL, died 1886.
[OneWorldTree]

I. Margaret Millen, born 1843, IL, died Carthage, Jasper County, MO; married John M. Whedbee, born 1833 NC, died .
[OneWorldTree]

----------

ELIZABETH GARTIN, born , died ; unmarried in 1826.

ELIJAH GARTIN, born [Orange County, VA] 28 January 1803, died 20 April 1881 Oktibcha,

# Descendants of William Gartin

Kemper County, Mississippi; married (1) in Todd County, KY, 13 September 1827 to SARAH BROOKS, born , died in KY 1829/1830; married (2) to ANN T. ----, born in TN 1810/11 , died in Mississippi between 1870 & 1880; married (3) to ELIZABETH ---, born Mississippi in 1837/8.

Elijah Gartin & Ann, his wife, of Oklebbeha County, Mississippi, sold their interest of land inherited from the estate of Richard Gartin to Andrew Gartin in a deed recorded in Todd County KY Deed Book K page 11, dated 21 September 1838.

1850 census, Oktibbeha County, MS, page 268, line 23, 170/170
Elijah W. Garton, 47, farmer, 480, VA
Ann do, 39, TN
Permelia do, 21, KY
Sarah do, 17, AL
Brown, do, 15, none, MS
James do, 13, MS
Bentley do, 11, MS
Andrew do, 9, MS
Jordan do, 7, MS
Robert do, 5, MS
Mary do, 1, MS

1860 census, Oktibbeha County, MS, p.o. Starkville, page [33], line 23, 244/212
Elisha W. Gartin, 57, farmer, 4300/10500, VA
Ann do, 47, TN
James do, 23, MS
Bentley do, 20, MS
Andrew do, 18, MS
Jordan do, 17, MS
Robert do, 14, MS
Mary Ann do, 12, MS
Ellen do, 7, MS
Thomas L. Jones, 26, teacher of English & ancient branches, AL

Bethesda Baptist Church, southeast corner of Oktibbeha County, five miles west of Crawford, MS:
-Elijah Gartin, 22 January 1803 to 20 April 1881
-James William Gartin, 23 July 1870 to 11 July 1920
-Permelia F. Gartin, 4 March 1851 to 15 May 1872, 24 yrs 2 mos 10 days. of W.R. & Arepsey Brooks.
-M.E. Mallory, dau of E.W. & A. T. Gartin, 27 Oct 1848 to 10 July 1869

Children of Elijah Gartin:
1. Permelia Gartin, born 1829
2. Sarah Gartin, born Alabama 1832/3
3. John Brown Gartin, born Mississippi 1834/5
4. James William Gartin, born MS 1836/7, died 10 November 1862
5. Bently G. Gartin, born MS 1838/9, died 19 January 1862
6. Elijah Andrew Gartin, born MS 1840/1
7. Burl Jordan Gartin, born 1843
8. Robert F. Gartin, born 1844/5
9. Mary E. Gartin, born 27 October 1848, died 10 July 1869
10. Ellen Gartin, born

# Descendants of William Gartin

ANDREW KINCAID GARTIN, born Greenbriar County VA, 31 December 1805, died Barry, Clay County, Missouri, 21 March 1875; married 11 August 1838 to JANE or JENNET MABEN, born Kentucky, 7 December 1808, died Barry, Clay Count, MO, 30 September 1876, daughter of Anrew Maben (died KY 1810) and Mary Graham (born SC about 1784, died KY about 1835).

Andrew Gartin obtained the interest of his father's estate from his siblings in two deeds recorded in Todd County KY: Book K page 1, dated 21 September 1836, and Book K page 3, dated 18 June 1836. Andrew Gartin & Jane, and Daniel Culbertson & Fanny, all of Todd County, sold this land (about 270 acres) to Robert Grady, of Todd County, for $1300 in a deed recorded in Book J page 467, dated 21 May 1836.

see Graham History, under 3-4C Jane/Jennet Maben Gartin; supplement under Maben section under 2-3 Jane/Jennet Maben Gartin.

NATHANIEL GARTIN, born 26 January 1808, died Gentry County, MO, 22 June 1882, 76 yrs 4m 14d; married in Todd County, KY, 17 November 1830 or Cooper County, MO, 15 February 1831 to CLEMENTINE B. STEELE, born Kentucky, 23 February 1814, died Gentry County, MO, 9 February 1887, daughter of William Steele (born 13 August 1791, died 23 January 1864, buried New Lebanon Cemetery, Cooper County MO) & Jane Kirkpatrick (born 25 September 1793, died 5 August 1854, buried New Lebanon Cemetery, Cooper County MO).

The Steeles moved from Todd County KY to Cooper County MO sometime bebore 1836 with the Cordrys & Gartins. Nathaniel Gartin & Clementine sold their interest in the estate of Richard Gartin to Andrew Graham in a deed recorded in Todd County KY Book K page 3, dated 18 June 1836.

Land Patents:
Millcreek Township, Morgan County, MO:
-Nathaniel Gartin: 1835-11-04, Township 45 N, Range 18W, section 9 SENW, 80 acres: MO0530_.168
Richland Township, Morgan County, MO:
-Nathaniel Gartin, 1854-03-10, Township 45N, Range 19W, section 21, MO3080_.094


1850 census, Tremont Township, Buchanan County, MO, page 67a, line 6, 917/917
Nathaniel Gartin, 43, farmer, 6000, VA
Clementine do, 37, KY
Francis do, 16, MO - all
Wellington do, 14
Elilzabeth do, 12
Didama? do, 10 (f)
William do, 9
Andrew do, 7
Lindsey do, 6 (m)
John do, 3
Newton do, 1
Cynthia do, 17
[previous household - Green Cordry]

1860 census, Township No 62, Gentry County, MO, p.o. Gentryville, page [49-50], line 31, 315/313
Nathl Gartin, 52, farmer, 12000/4765, KY

# Descendants of William Gartin

Clementine do, 45, KY
William do, 18, farmer, MO
Andrew do, 16, farmer, MO
Linya? do, 14 (m), MO
John do, 12, MO
Newton do, 10, MO
Maranda Gartin, 6, MO - next page
James Gartin, 4, MO
Marion Gartin, 11/12, MO
Richard do, 50, KY

1870 census, Miller Township, Gentry County, MO, p.o. Albany, page [50], line 18, 360/380
Nathaniel Garton, 63, farmer, 5400/1875, VA
Clementina B. do, 56, keeping house, KY
Newton K. do, 20, farm hand, 1600/200, MO - all
Maranda E. do, 17
James G. do, 14, school
Marion P. do, 11 (m), do
line 24, 361/381
John Garton, 23, farmer, 2800/835, MO
Balinda C. do, 19, keeping house, MO


Children:
-Mary Jane Gartin, born 30 June 1832 Cooper County, MO, died 27 November 1888, Buchanan County, MO; married 18 March 1847 Buchanan County, MO to Calvin Morgan Graves, born 25 May 1827 Claiborne County, TN, died 5 December 1898 Home Grower, Clinton County, MO.
-Minerva Frances Gartin, born 1 August 1834 Buchanan County, MO, died 11 May 1882 San Joaquin County, CA; married 30 April 1851 Buchanan County, MO to Randal Morgan, born 1830, TN, died .
-Lindsay Jones Gartin, born 20 December 1845 Gentry County, MO, died 24 April 1869; married 1876 (sic) Gentry County, MO to Anna Maria Crow, born 1851 Gentry County, MO, died 24 March 1914 Darlington, Gentry County, MO.
-John Richard Gartin, born 16 November 1848 Buchanan County, MO, died 4 February 1927; married 7 April 1869 Gentry County, MO to Belinda Caroline Morgan, born 15 July 1850 Gentry County, MO, died 27 September 1934.
-Miranda Ellen Gartin, born 8 October 1853 MO, died ; married Nelson Clark, born 1856, TN, died .
-James Griffith Gartin, born 15 June 1857 MO, died 3 January 1933; married Josie E. Ray, born 1862, MO, died .
-Marion Pattison Gartin, born 17 July 1859 Gentry County, MO, died ; married Sarah Crow, born 1861, MO, died .
[OneWorldTree]

0. **RICHARD GARTIN**, born 1810, died ; married 30 August 1832 Cooper County, MO to **ANNA ELIZA (Adeliza?) Elliott**, born 1815, died .

Richard Gartin moved from Todd County KY to Cooper County MO sometime before 1836 with other members of his family. Richard Gartin & Anna Eliza sold their interest in the estate of Richard Gartin to Andrew Gartin in a deed recorded in Todd County KY Book K page 3, dated 18 June 1836.

# Descendants of William Gartin

Children of Richard Gartin & Ann Elliott, born MO:
1. John R. Gartin, born 1834
2. William H. Gartin, born 1836
3. Margaret J. Gartin, born 1838
4. James A. Gartin, born 1839
5. Alvin S. Gartin, born 1842
6. Newton Franklin Gartin, born July 1850
[OneWorldTree]

LLIAM HARVEY GARTIN, born 30 June 1812 Christian County, Kentucky, died 10 July 1893 Jordan Valley, Wheeler County, Oregon; married 13 March 1845 Buchanan County MO to MARTHA Jane GRAVES, born June 1820 Claiborne County, TN, died 16 January 1892 Buchanan County, MO.

William Gartin moved from Todd County KY to Cooper County MO sometime before 1836 with other members of his family. William Gartin sold his interest in the estate of Richard Gartin to Andrew Gartin in a deed recorded in Todd County KY Book 3, dated 18 June 1836.

1850 census, Tremont County, Buchanan County, MO, page 63b, line 1, 866/866
William Garton, 38, farmer, 5000, KY
Martha do, 30, TN
Boston do, 4, (m), MO
Eliza do, 2, MO
Eliza Graves, 55, KY

Children of William Gartin & Martha Graves, born Buchanan County, MO:
1. Richard Boston Gartin, born 19 December 1846, died 26 August 1917 Gower, Clinton County, MO; married 1 October 1868 Buchanan County, MO to Katherine Moore, born 25 August 1852 Buchanan County, MO, died 7 April 1935 Gower, MO.
2. Elizabeth A. Gartin, born 29 May 1848, died 8 April 1865.
3. Sarah Gartin, born 1851 Gower, Buchannan County MO, died 1929 Glendora, LA, CA; married Joe Williamson [not on OneWorldTree]
4. William C. Gartin, born 1852/5, died 23 April 1906 West Baden, Orange County, IN
5. Lizzie Gartin, born 1854 [not on OneWorldTree]
6. Flora Gartin, born 1856; married Thomas Kincaid [not on OneWorldTree]
7. Mary Melvina Gartin, born 9 April 1858, died 30 September 1905 Rice, Stevens County WA; married 3 January 1884 Frazier, MO to Charles Montgomery Deakins, born 22 September 1853 Washington County, TN, died 18 April 1926 Long Beach, CA.
8. James Gilmore Gartin, born 1 January 1860 Gower, Buchannan County MO, died 5 December 1929 Caldwell, Idaho; married Ella Louise Woodruff. [not OneWorldTree]
[OneWorldTree]

# *Descendants of DAVID GRAHAM (1788-1844)*

### THIRD GENERATION

3-15    DAVID GRAHAM[7], (pp. 221-5 in the genealogy) born Chester County, South Carolina, c. 1788-1792, died ; married in York County, South Carolina, 4 March 1819, ELIZABETH ---.

It is now believed that David Graham moved from Chester County SC to Lowndes County AL by the 1830s. The two daughters of David Graham married in Lowndes County AL in 1837 & 1839. David Graham (age 40-50 yrs) is listed in the 1840 census for Lowndes County. No further information on David Graham can be found in the public records for Lowndes County AL.

David Graham & Elizabeth, his wife, had a stormy marriage which ended in permanent separation by 1823. Elizabeth Graham remained in York County SC with her father, while David Graham moved to Chester County where he owned land. Elizabeth Graham went before the York County Equity Court, 9 January 1824, to request alimony. This case was further complicated when on 15 June 1826 in the Chester County Court of Equity David Graham was declared "deranged or that he is a lunatic" by a panel of 15 men. Thomas Caskey, David's brother-in-law & husband of Julianna Graham, was appointed David's guardian to manage his estate. The court ordered Thomas Caskey to pay Elizabeth Graham $120 per year on behalf of David on 13 August 1827. This case of Elizabeth Graham against the estate of David Graham dragged at least to June of 1844. According the initial court records of 9 January 1824, David & Elizabeth had three children: Mary H., Martha Ann, and a son. A statement made by Elizabeth Graham to the court in 27 June 1836 implied that one of the children had died. Further details of the court case between David Graham & his wife, Elizabeth, can be found in the genealogy.

Further information concerning both David Graham & Elizabeth, his wife, is vague. There is a family account that David Graham went from Lowndes County AL to Tipton County TN where some of his siblings had moved from Chester County SC. Another family rumor is that David Graham went to East Texas with his daughter, Jane Graham Furrh, and son, M. William Graham, in 1853. It is not known when David Graham or Elizabeth Graham died or where they were buried.

Children of David Graham & Elizabeth, born probably in York County SC:
4-40 Mary Hannah Graham, born 1819
4-41 M. William Graham, born c. 1820
4-42 Annie Jane Graham, born 2 February 1821

### NOTES

7. The information on David Graham and his family is from: York County SC, Court Equity file #24; Chester County SC, Court of Equity petition #55; census records; and family research compiled by Dr. K. Edwin Graham, Gulfport, MS, who is a descendant

### FOURTH GENERATION

#### CHILDREN OF 3-15 DAVID GRAHAM[5] & ELIZABETH ---

4-40    MARY HANNAH GRAHAM FURRH, born 1819 probably in York County SC, died ; married in Lowndes County, AL 19 January 1837 to GEORGE FURRH, jr, born about 1791, died , son of George Furrh, sr.

# *Descendants of DAVID GRAHAM (1788-1844)*

George Furrh, jr, had married three times. He had three children by his first wife, whose name is unknown: (1) a son, born 1811, (2) a daughter, born 1813, and (3) a daughter, born 1815. George Furrh, jr, had two sons by this second wife, whose name is also unknown: (1) John William Furrh, who married 4-42 Janie Graham, sister of Mary Hannah Graham, and (2) Jacob Furrh. His third marriage was to Mary Hannah Graham.

It is reported that the family of George Furrh, jr, moved to Shelby County AL in 1839 & lived in Tuscaloosa & Montgomery County AL. The name was spelled "Farr" in the 1840 census. Between 1840 & 1850 the family returned to Lowndes County AL and settled near where they had lived before.

Child of George Furrh, jr, & Mary Hannah Graham:
A. Alexander Furrh, born 1839

4-41    M. WILLIAM GRAHAM, born c. 1820 probably in York County SC, died in Hattiesburg, Old Perry County, MS, 2 September 1872, buried Jones Cemetery, Hattiesburg, MS; married February 1844 to ELIZABETH (Betty) POUNCEY, born 29 January 1829, died in Seminary, Covington County, MS, 18 October 1908, buried Seminary Cemetery, Covington, MS, daughter of Samuel A. P. Pouncey, jr & Elizabeth Higdon..

There is also the date of 20 August 1818 given for the birth of M. William Graham. Jones Cemetery is located at the northeast corner of Highway 49 and Interstate 59 in Hattiesburg, MS.

It is believed that his father, David Graham, brough his children to Lowndes County AL from Chester or York County SC sometime after 1826. M. William met his wife Betty Pouncey after he took her home with him for lunch one day.

Later, M. William Graham and his sister, Jane Graham Furrh, moved to eastern Texas in 1853. Jane Graham Furrh settled in Panola County TX, near Carthage. In 1862, M. William Graham and his wife, Betty Pouncey Graham, moved back to Lowndes County AL from Texas because Betty was lonely for her family. Their son, James Morgan Graham, was born in Louisiana enroute back to Alabama. M. William Graham later moved his family to Old Perry County Mississippi some time before 1870.

1850 census, Covington County, AL, page 134, line 20, 93/93
William Graham, 32, farmer, 200, SC
Elizabeth Graham, 23, AL
Alexander do, 6, AL
William do, 3, AL
Rosan? do, 8/12, (f), AL

1870 census, On Bowie, Perry County, MS, page [29], line 5, 182/285
William Graham, 52, farmer, 100/450, SC
Elizabeth do, 42, keeping house, AL
Eliza do, 18, at home, AL
James do, 7, MS

1880 census, Subdivision district 2, Covington County, MS, ed 123, page [22B], line 20, 176/176
Elizabeth Graham, 52, widow, planter, AL, GA, GA

# *Descendants of DAVID GRAHAM (1788-1844)*

James do, 17, son, single, works on farm, LA, GA, AL

Children of M. William Graham & Betty Pouncey:
5-John Alexander Graham, born 21 November 1844 Hattiesburg, MS
5-William McDaniel Graham, born 5 October 1846
5-Eliza Ann Graham, born 18 April 1852 AL
5-James Morgan Graham, born 5 October 1862 LA

4-42    ANNIE JANE GRAHAM FURRH (called "Janie"), born 5 February 1821 probably in York County SC, died in Furrh, Panola County TX, 22 February 1904, buried Carter Cemetery, Carthage, TX; married in Lowndes County AL, 26 November 1839, to JOHN WILLIAM FURRH, born Lowndes County AL, 6 January 1821, died Furrh, Panola County TX, 12 January 1899, buried Carter Cemetery, Carthage TX, son of George Furrh, jr, by his second wife.

Annie Jane's sister, 4-40 Mary Hannah Graham, was the third wife of George Furrh, jr.

John Furrh & Janie Graham Furrh moved from Alabama to the area of Carthage, Panola County TX around 1853, along with the family of 4-41 M. William Graham. The Grahams later moved back to Alabama in 1862.

Jane & her husband became very successful in east Texas. John Furrh owned a ranch, a grist mill, a saw mill and the community store and post office. A town in Panola County was named "Furrh" but it is no longer listed on current maps. It was near Carlisle.

1860 census, Beat No 1, Panola County, TX, p.o. Bethany, page 352 [17], line 26, 111/111
John Furrh, 38, farmer, 4500/9000, AL
Jane do, 36, house k., SC
Sarah do, 17, do, AL - all
Martha do, 15, do
Jame do, 13
Mary do, 11
Amanda do, 9
Lenia do, 7
Narcissus do, 5 (f)
Lucy do, 2

Children of John W. Furrh & Janie Graham:
A. James Madison Furrh, born 19 November 1845 Fort Deposit, Lowndes County AL
B. John William Furrh, born 1848 Lowndes County, AL
C. Sally Furrh, born
D. Amanda Furrh, born
E. Mary Furrh, born
F. Narcisis Delilah Furrh, born
G. Bettie Furrh, born
H. Lucy C. Furrh, born 6 February 1858
I. Gertrude Furrh, born
J. Levy (Jane) Furrh, born

------

A.    James Madison Furrh, born 19 November 1845 Fort Deposit, Lowndes County AL,

# *Descendants of DAVID GRAHAM (1788-1844)*

died 1936 Elysian Fields, TX, buried Elysian Fields Cemetery, TX; married Sara Elizabeth Holland, born Panola County TX, died 1930 Elysian Fields, TX, buried Elysian Fields Cemetery, TX.

Mrs LaGRone history says his name was Matthew.

Children of James Furrh & Sara Holland:
(1) Ewing Furrh, born 1880
(2) John DeWitt Furrh, born 1883 Elysian Fields, TX
(3) James Brooke Furrh, born 21 April 1885 Elysian Fields, TX
(4) Junnis M. Furrh, born 1887
(5) Ruth Furrh, born 1891
(6) William Kirkpatrick Furrh, born 1893
(7) Janie Furrh, born 1899

(1) Ewing Furrh, born 1880, died ; married W.C. Tenney.

(2) John DeWitt Furrh, born 1883 Elysian Fields, TX, died ; married Zuma Perkins.

(3) James Brooke Furrh, born 21 April 1885 Elysian Fields, TX, died 14 September 1969 Marshall, TX, buried Elysian Fields Cemetery, TX; married Margaret Hagan, born 12 October 1899 Mt. Clinton, VA, died , daughter of William C. Hagan & Mary Howard Johnson.

Children of James Furrh & Margaret Hagan:
(a) Mary Elizabeth Furrh, born 1 July 1923 Marshall TX; married --- Cooke
(b) James Brooke Furrh, jr, born ; married Mary Lee ---.

(4) Junnis M. Furrh, born 1887, died ; married Marie Haggerty.

(5) Ruth Furrh, born 1891, died ; married Grafton Lathrop.

(6) William Kirkpatrick Furrh, born 1893, died ; married Winifred Brownreig.

(7) Janie Furrh, born 1899, died ; married Julian M. Pitts.

B.	John William Furrh, born 1848 Lowndes County, AL, died Marshall, TX; married --- Leigh.

Children of John Furrh & --- Leigh, born Waskon, TX:
(1) John William Furrh, jr, born
(2) James Furrh, born
(3) Graham Furrh, born
(4) Bernice Furrh, born
(5) Margaret Furrh, born

   C.	Sally Furrh, born , died; married --- Steele.

   D.	Amanda Furrh, born , died.

   E.	Mary Furrh, born , died ; married --- Holt.

# Descendants of DAVID GRAHAM (1788-1844)

F.  Narcisis Delilah Furrh, born , died; married --- Bryson.

G.  Bettie Furrh, born , died ;married --- Leach.

H.  Lucy C. Furrh, born 6 February 1858, died 1957; married (1) Dr. Charles B. O'Brien, born , died ; married (2) Killis Walton Holt.

Helene H. Heidtman LaGrone, (wife of Wayne LaGrone), daughter of Elizabeth Holt Heidtman, granddaughter of Lucy Furrh Holt, wrote the Panola County TX at the historical society in Carthage TX.

Child of Charles O'Brien & Lucy Furrh:
(1) Charlie O'Brien.
Children of Killis Holt & Lucy Furrh:
(2) Elizabeth Holt; married --- Heidtman
(3) Thomas Madison Holt
(4) Lucy Leigh Holt; married --- Heidtman.

I.  Gertrude Furrh, born , died ; married --- Holt.

J.  Levy (Jane) Furrh, born , died ; married --- Griswold.

Texas notes indicate she may have been Levy Jane Furrh.

------
## NOTES

5. Information on the family line of 3-15 David Graham & Elizabeth is from Dr. Kenneth Edwin Graham, of Gulfport, MS, a descendant.

### FIFTH GENERATION

### CHILDREN OF 4-41 M. WILLIAM GRAHAM[17] & BETTY POUNCEY

5-  JOHN ALEXANDER GRAHAM, (called Alex), born in Hattiesburg, MS, 21 November 1844, died 25 April 1926, buried Seminary Cemetery, Seminary, MS; married (1) 8 October 1869 to SARAH ANN BENNETT, born 17 July 1849, died 18 May 1914, buried Seminary Cemetery, Covington, MS; married (2) 22 July 1919 to JOANNA MILLER JONES, born 6 September 1859, died 21 January 1925, buried Oakvale Meth., Seminary, MS.

There are also dates of 20 November 1844 for his birth & 26 April 1925 for his death date. His tombstone shows dates listed above. One record indicate that his wife was Sarah Ann Collier but the old family bible records Bennett as her surname. Joanna Miller Jones had married (1) about 1855 or 1857 to Phillip Jones.

Alex Graham did not have any children but the 1880 census shows that he had a son, Albert. Albert was not listed with Alex Graham in the 1890 census, but it showed he had a foster daughter, Jane?. These are believed to be Watts children. Alex Graham is said to have adopted nine children and gave each of them a farm.

Alex & Sarah (Bennett) Graham, John Pickering, James P. Johnson, Hugh Graham, Mahala Pickering, H.R. Curtis, and James L. Finley organized the Concord Baptist Church near Graham's mill on Curry Creek in the Double Branches Community of the County on

# *Descendants of DAVID GRAHAM (1788-1844)*

December 3 1886 (Seminary Baptist Church). They later moved it to Seminary in 1897 to an old school building on the current James M. Graham property on Oak Street. A new church building was erected in 1901.

Child of Alex Graham & Sarah Bennett:
6-Albert Graham, born about 1871

5-     WILLIAM MCDANIEL GRAHAM, (called Mack), born Hattiesburg, MS, 5 October 1846, died 12 January 1925, buried Restland Cemetery, Olney, TX; married (1) 13 August 1867 to MARTHA ELIZABETH MIXON, born 28 January 1846, died 1930, buried Seminary Cemetery, Seminary, MS; married (2) CELIA JANE COX, born LA or TX, 26 February 1855, died 2 February 1937 Ingleside Com., Olney, Young County TX, buried Restland Cemetery, Olney, TX, daughter of Richard Cox & Mary Ann Hall.

The family bible lists him as William McDaniel Graham but in Texas the records show him as William McDonald Graham.

William McDaniel (Mack) Graham was first married to Elizabeth Mixon who had difficulty establishing a stable home. It is reported that Mack provided two or three different homes and she would become dissatisfied and return to her parents until he arranged another house for them. She also had maintained relationships with other male friends, in particular a Dr. Wheeler. She would accompany him in his buggy on long trips when he made calls on patients. There was much talk in the community about this matter.

One man in particular, Mr. Knight, was a community gossip and often talked about Elizabeth to other men. Mack Graham talked with him several times, finally telling him that if he did not stop talking about his wife he would kill him. Later, when they were attending services at Providence Church, near Bowie River and the community of Richmond in Covington County, some friends told Mack that Mr. Knight had been talking about Elizabeth again. Several persons were gathered at the well (or spring) on the church grounds. Mack was there with his child Azaline in his arms when Mr. Knight appeared. Mack asked him if he had said things about Elizabeth and he said yes and made other remarks. Mack handed Azaline to a friend, pulled out his gun and shot him.

When his mother, Betty Pouncey Graham, heard about it she advised Mack to take a horse and leave. He went west to the home of his Aunt Jane Graham Furrh in Panola County TX. Enroute across Mississippi he met a family moving west and travelled with them. When they reached the Mississippi river he told them he was afraid the police would be checking the border, so he was hidden between the mattresses on the wagon while they crossed the river on the ferry.

Mack worked on the ranch with his Aunt Jane & Uncle John Furrh. A detective finally tracked him to the ranch. He got a job & worked along side of Mack for several weeks trying to get an opportunity to arrest him for murder, but Mack always carried two guns. One day after they were soaked in a rainstorm, Mack placed his two guns on the mantle and left the room to change clothes. When Mack returned the detective had taken his guns and arrested him for murder.

John Furrh was a prominent leader in the community (later called Furrh) and he demanded a hearing in Texas before the detective took Mack to Mississippi. John Furrh paid Mack's bond and while they were awaiting the hearing, Jane Furrh gave her nephew her horse. He rode out the back lane between the rail fences and went west. The Furrhs did not know

# Descendants of DAVID GRAHAM (1788-1844)

where Mack went and never saw him again.

It is reported that Mack returned to Mississippi in secret four times to try to persuade his wife, Elizabeth, and daughter, Azaline, to come to Texas with him. Each time they refused. Elizabeth continued her lifestyle and her mother played an active role in rearing Azaline.

Mack's mother, Betty Pouncey Graham, was always concerned about her son and she asked her other two sons to try to find him. John Alexander (Alex) Graham & James Morgan Graham went to Texas and finally found Mack and had their picture made together to bring back to their mother. Betty Pouncey Graham died within weeks in October 1908 and James Morgan died in April 1909 a few months after his return from Texas. It is alos thought that Mack came by train to New Orleans once to meet other family members who joined him there but it cannot be confirmed.

Child of Mack Graham & Elizabeth Mixon:
6-Edith Azaline Graham, born 18 October 1868 Old Perry County, MS
Children of Mack Graham & Celia Cox:
6- John Monroe Graham, born 1882 TX
6- William Terrell Graham, born 4 February 1884 Terrell, Kaufman County TX
6- Theodosia Graham, born 2 March 1886
6- Effie Mae Graham, born 11 November 1888 Decatur, Wise County TX
6-James Madison Graham, born 1890 Decatur, Wise County TX
6-Samuel David Graham, born 4 March 1892 Pleasant Ridge, Montague County TX
6-Homer Graham, born 5 September 1894 Montague, Montague County TX
6- Mary Elizabeth Graham, born 1895
6- Della Graham, born 26 May 1897 Pleasant Ridge, Montague County TX
6- Minnie Lee Graham, born 20 February 1899 Montague County TX

5-      ELIZA ANN GRAHAM WATTS, born 18 April 1852 AL, died 7 November 1920, buried New Hope Baptist, Covington County MS; married 2 December 1874 to GEORGE CLAIBORNE WATTS.

Children of George Watts & Eliza Ann Graham, born Covington County MS:
A. Jane K. Watts, born 9 August 1875
B. William France Watts, born 9 September 1876
C. Martha E. Watts, born 4 January 1878
D. Mary Watts, born 23 January 1879
E. Sarah Artesia Watts, born 22 February 1880
F. John Watts, born 13 August 1883
G. Amanda Olevia Watts, born 8 July 1884
H. Minnie G. Watts, born 17 February 1885

-----

A.      Jane K. Watts, born 9 August 1875, died 25 December 1966, buried P. Watts or New Hope Cemetery, Seminary, MS; married Frank Robbins, born 1885, died 1929.

Children of Frank Robbins & Jane Watts:
(1) Leuna Robbins
(2) Mary Robbins; married --- Graham.
(3) Edna Robbins; married Plez Herrin

B.      William France Watts, born Covington County, MS, 9 September 1876, died

# *Descendants of DAVID GRAHAM (1788-1844)*

Hattiesburg, MS 12 June 1942, buried New Hope Baptist Church, Covington County MS; married (1) 1896 to Edna Thames, born 1878, died 1904; married (2) 1909 to Nancy Elizabeth Miller, born Covington County, MS, 1 January 1885, died Hattiesburg, MS, 5 July 1966, buried Highland Park, Hattiesburg, MS, daughter of William Miller & Angelia King.

Edna Thames Watts died in childbirth.

Children of William Watts & Edna Thames:
(1) Charlie Watts, born 1898
(2) Bertha Watts, born 1899
(3) Howard Watts, born 1901
(4) George Clyde Watts, born 1904, died 1975, buried New Hope Baptist Cemetery, MS.
Children of William Watts & Nancy Miller, born Covington County MS:
(5) Stella Pauline Watts, born 23 February 1910; married 3 January 1932 Fred Wheeler McGrew, born 1902, died 1990.
(6) Romeo Maxwell Watts, born 26 February 1913; died 16 December 1964; married Doris Cunningham.
(7) Lorene Vermont Watts, born 28 July 1914; married Stanley Williams.
(8) Curtis P. Watts, born 27 October 1916; married Judy Brady.
(9) Erma Lee Watts, born 13 November 1919; married Arthur Sullivan.
(10) Junie Jewell Watts, born 1 June 1923, died June 1984, buried Highland Park, Hattiesburg, MS.
(11) Jacqueline Frances Watts, born 1 June 1923; married Hebron Samford.

C.   Martha E. Watts (called "Tete"), born 4 January 1878, died 1958, buried New Hope Baptist Church, Covington County MS; married Ben Aultman, born 1877, died 1955, buried New Hope Cemetery, Covington County MS.

Children of Ben Aultman & Martha Watts:
(1) Delia Aultman, married --- Wilkes.
(2) Clifford Aultman, buried New Hope Baptist Cemetery or P. Watts Cemetery, Seminary, MS; married Nannie Mae Watts.

D.   Mary Watts, born 23 January 1879, died 25 April 1965, buried New Hope Baptist Church, Covington County MS; married G.W. Aultman (called "Doc"), born 29 January 1872, died 30 January 1855, buried New Hope Cemetery, Covington County MS.

Children of G.W. Aultman & Mary Watts:
(1) Ernest Aultman, married Letha Powell
(2) Jennings Aultman, married Bennie Fortenberry
(3) Bertie Lee Aultman, married --- Messer. Lives in Pascagoula, MS. No children.

E.   Sarah Artesia Watts (called "Art"), born 22 February 1880, died 29 December 1967, buried New Hope Baptist Church, Covington County MS; married ---- Lott.

Children of Sarah Watts Lott:
(1) Claude Lott
(2) Mailer Lott, married --- Massengale
(3) Carrie Lott, twin of Harry.
(4) Harry Lott, twin of Carrie.
F.   John Watts, born 13 August 1883, died 22 January 1966, buried Roseland Park, Hattiesburg, MS; married Mrs. John Watts.

# Descendants of DAVID GRAHAM (1788-1844)

Children of John Watts:
(1) "Shuck" Watts
(2) Felda Watts

G.     Amanda Olevia Watts, born 8 July 1884, died 16 January 1978, buried Highland Park, Hattiesburg, MS; married --- Fullingame.

Childrenof Amanda Watts Fullingame:
(1) William "Willie" Fullingame. There is a grave in New Hope Cemetery of a daughter of W.E. Fullingame who died in 1940. Apparently an infant.
(2) Gladys Fullingame
(3) Winford Fullingame

H.     Minnie G. Watts, born 17 February 1885, died 11 May 1963, buried New Hope Baptist, Covington County MS; married Samuel A. Pouncey, born 17 November 1885, died 7 December 1934, buried New Hope Cemetery, Covington County, MS, son of Peter A. Pouncey & Texana Crawford.

-----

5-     JAMES MORGAN GRAHAM, born LA in 5 October 1862, died Seminary, Covington County MS 15 April 1909, buried Seminary Cemetery, Covington County MS; married 18 October 1883 to HULDAH JANE SHORT, born Pass Christian, Harrison County MS, 20 January 1867, died Seminary, Covington County MS ,16 July 1947, buried Seminary Cemetery, MS, daughter of Thomas Prosser Short & Frances Josephine Hall.

James Morgan Graham was born in Louisana as his parents were returning from Panola County, Texas to Alabama because his mother was lonely for her family. His father later moved to Old Perry County (now Hattiesburg) MS.

James M. Graham ran a store and post office in Richmond (on Bowie River) and then moved the store and post office to Seminary about 1903. A former black slave, "Uncle Wyche" Watts, who was 12 years old when the Civil War was over, lived with the Grahams and helped them for the rest of his life. James Morgan refused to join the KKK (White Caps) and they tried to chase his blacks away. He gave the blacks guns and helped them keep the KKK away in their attempts to beat the blacks.

In 1905 James Morgan Graham organized the Bank of Seminary with $30,000 of capital and served as the first president of the bank.

Children of James Morgan Graham & Huldah Short:
6-Louella Graham, born 28 September 1884
6-William McDaniel Graham, born 2 October 1886
6-Samuel David Graham, born 12 October 1888, Seminary, MS
6-John Buford Graham, born October 1890
6-Mollie Esther Graham, born 9 January 1893
6-Alma Lucille Graham, born 11 December 1894
6-Vermont Graham, born 13 April 1898 Covington County, MS
6-Oma Graham, born 20 April 1899
6-Robert Earl Graham, born 23 May 1901 Seminary, MS
6-Arthur Short Graham, born

# *Descendants of DAVID GRAHAM (1788-1844)*

### NOTES

17. Information on these family lines is from research collected by Dr. K. Edwin Graham, Gulfport, MS.

### SIXTH GENERATION

### CHILD OF 5- MACK GRAHAM & ELIZABETH MIXON[13]

6-      EDITH AZALINE GRAHAM HEMETER, born Old Perry County, MS, 18 October 1868, died Seminary, Covington County MS, 16 Decmeber 1955, buried Seminary Cemetery, MS; married GEORGE SCOGGINS HEMETER, born about 1864, died 1953, buried Seminary Cemetery, MS.

Edith Azaline Graham graduated from Blue Mountain College. She tagheter in Forrest County Schools. George Hemeter was a banker in Seminary, MS, well educated. Bookkeeper at Hemeter Co.

Children of George Hemeter & Edith Graham:
A. Leslie Hall Hemeter, born 1 October 1895, died 15 September 1967, buried Seminary Cemetery, MS; married Frances Corrine Pope, born 1899.
B. Mildred Lee Hemeter, born about 1903, living in 1991 in a nursing home in Hattiesburg, MS. Never married.
C. Leo Elizabeth Hemeter, born 19 July 1905, died 31 March 1969, buried Seminary Cemetery, MS; married Kenneth Charles Davis, born 1901, died 1973.
D. Infant Hemeter, born 31 July 1909
E. George Graham Hemeter, born 21 February 1911, died Natchez, MS, 28 July 1987, buried Seminary Cemetery, MS; married Samantha Purnell.

### CHILDREN OF 5- MACK GRAHAM & CELIA COX[13]

6-      JOHN MONROE GRAHAM, born TX, 1882, died 1882.

6-      WILLIAM TERRELL GRAHAM, born Terrell, Kaufman County TX , 4 February 1884, died Milpitas, CA, 10 January 1969, buried Fremont, CA; married 14 January 1912 to ALSIE REYNOLDS, born Emory, Rains County, TX, 8 February 1885, died Milpitas, CA, 30 September 1971, buried Fremont, CA, daughter of E. C. Reynolds & Mary Lou Shipley.

Will Graham was the only child to get a college education. He went to Decatur Baptist College in Wise County, TX. Two other dates given for birth of Alsie Reynolds, 2 August 1883 and 4 February 1885.

Children of William Graham & Alsie Reynolds:
7-Alfred Graham, born 1 January 1913, Olney, Young County TX
7-Terrell Graham, born 22 May 1914, Olney, Young County TX
7-John Patrick Graham, born 25 October 1916, Olney TX
7-Barbara Jewell Graham, born 11 May 1918 Olney TX
7-Beatrice Graham, born 2 December 1920 Megarel, Archer County TX
6-      THEODOSIA GRAHAM PARCHMAN, born 2 March 1886, died Lubbock, TX, 22 January 1954, buried Ralls, Crosby County, TX; married Olney, Young County, TX, in 8 June 1909 to GEORGE W. PARCHMAN, born Blossom Prarie, Lamar County, TX, 24

# *Descendants of DAVID GRAHAM (1788-1844)*

January 1882, died Lubbock, TX, 25 October 1973, buried Ralls, Crosby County TX, son of Aquilla Henderson Parchman & Caroline Ellis.

Children of George Parchman & Theodosia Graham:
A. George Welman Parchman, born Lorenzo, Crosby County TX, 1 July 1911; married 4 Febraury 1940 to Delma Pierot.
B. Alton Harrell Parchman, born Olney, Young County, TX, 12 August 1914.
C. Pauline Marie Parchman, born Lorenzo, Crosby County, TX, 12 August 1917; married 5 August 1939 to Delman Davis.
D. Roger Maurice Parchman, born Lorenzo, Crosby County, TX, 1 June 1920; married 18 January 1943 to Mary Ellen Lowe.
E. Arnold Truitte Parchman, born Lorenzo, Crosby County, TX, 28 July 1923; married 16 January 1949 to Nadeen Weldon.
F. Richard Dalton Parchman, born Lorenzo, Crosby County, TX, 14 February 1926; married 21 May 1954 to Anna Mae Shapley.
G. Wilma Jean Parchman, born Lorenzo, Crosby County, TX, 13 September 1929; married 8 June 1947 to W.E. Graver.

6-     EFFIE MAE GRAHAM HERRING, born Decatur, Wise County TX, 11 November 1888, died 24 January 1958, Hamlin, Jones County TX, buried Hamlin East Cemetery, TX; married in Olney, TX, 22 November 1910 to MARCUS EUGENE HERRING (called Mark), born Groonsbeck, Limestone, TX, 14 April 1886, died Hamlin, TX, 26 December 1935, buried Hamlin East Cemetery, TX, son of Charles Abraham Herring & Linda Alice Garrett.

Children of Mark Herring & Effie Mae Graham:
A. Alma Eugenia Herring, born 24 August 1911 in Ingleside, Young County TX, died 25 January 1969; married 1 August 1931 to Thomas Charles Carter.
B. Clifford William Herring, born 25 August 1913 in Ingleside, Young County TX, died 7 October 1932.
C. Howard Graham Herring, born 11 July 1915 in Ingleside, Young County TX; married 15 July 1939 to Ruby Inez Watts.
D. Charles Woodrow Herring, born 9 March 1917 in Ingleside, Young County TX; married 3 September 1938 to Wauldean Pope.
E. Winnie Mae Herring, born 2 August 1918 in Tulia, Swisher County TX, died 16 June 1967; married 9 April 1934 to Edward Pringle Moore.
F. Lawrence Leonard Herring, born 29 January 1920 in Tulia, Swisher County TX; married 1 June 1940 to Opal Frances Waldrop.
G. Kermit Willard Herring, born 10 June 1921 in Tulia, Swisher County TX; married 2 December 1940 to Jacqueline Leana Blackburn.
H. Washington Merrill Herring, born 7 April 1924 in Tulia, Swisher County TX; married 5 December 1961 to Kikue Hamada.
I. Dorothy Maxine Herring, born 12 December 1925 in Tulia, Swisher County TX; married 6 May 1944 to Jack Everett Townley.

6-     JAMES MADISON GRAHAM, born Decatur, Wise County, TX, 1890, died 1890, 6 months old.

6-     SAMUEL DAVID GRAHAM, born Pleasant Ridge, Montague County, TX, 4 March 1892, died Fort Worth, TX, 1 May 1975, buried Restland Cemetery, Olney, Young County TX; married 1915, (later divorced) to VIOLA WILBURN. Married for 4 years.

6-     HOMER GRAHAM, born 5 September 1894 Montague, Montague County TX, died

# *Descendants of DAVID GRAHAM (1788-1844)*

Longview, TX, 1 June 1969; married (1) GRACE ---; married (2) Olney, Young County, TX, 3 September 1920 to WINNIE NELL MULLINAX.

Children of Homer Graham & Winnie Mullinax, born Ingleside, Young County, TX:
7-Gerald Mack Graham, born 9 June 1921
7-Johnnie Bell Graham, born 16 April 1923
7-John Pat Graham, born 9 March 1924

6-	MARY ELIZABETH GRAHAM, born TX, 1895, died 1895, 9 months old.

6-	DELLA GRAHAM PHILLIPS, born Pleasant Ridge, Montague County, TX, 26 May 1897, died Portales, NM, 21 August 1928; married 1916 to RUFUS YOUNG PHILLIPS, born Pooleville, TX, 27 September 1890, died Lockney, TX, August 1930.

Children of Rufus Phillips & Della Graham:
A. Junia Rudell Phillips, born Young County, TX, 19 April 1918; married 22 April 1944 to Waymond K. Moore.
B. Carroll McDonald Phillips, born Lorenzo, Crosby County, TX, 1 April 1922; married 13 December 1941 to Helen Ray Ballard.

6-	MINNIE LEE GRAHAM VAUGHT KOLB, born Montague County, TX, 20 February 1899; married (1) 24 November 1917 to JAMES ELBERT VAUGHT (called "Gus"), born Leon County, TX, 15 May 1899, died Arlington, TX, 14 December 1971, buired Moore's Memorial Garden; married (2) WILLIAM "Bill" KOLB.

Minnie Graham Vaught Kolb resident of Arlington, TX.

Children of Gus Vaught & Minnie Graham, born Olney, Young County, TX:
A. Joy Graham Vaught, born 13 August 1919
B. Kenneth Alwyn Vaught (called "Bill"), born 2 October 1922, died 5 June 1944.
C. Janes Edell Vaught, born 23 September 1925
D. Doris Jeanne Vaught, born 26 May 1934

CHILDREN OF 5- JAMES MORGAN GRAHAM & HULDAH SHORT[13]

6-	LOUELLA GRAHAM LOTT, born 28 September 1884, died 18 June 1985, buried Seminary Cemetery, Seminary, MS; married 8 November 1903 to LOUIS BROWN LOTT, born 10 January 1883, died 6 February 1968.

Children of Louis Lott & Louella Graham, born Seminary, MS:
A. Erma L. Lott, born 21 July 1904, died Collins, MS, 24 May 1994; married (1) 2 July 1924 to Ernest Madison Kelly, died 1926; married (2) 31 December 1930 Archie W. Morris, born 1882, died 1956.
B. Infant Lott, born & died 22 September 1906
C. Myrna Estelle Lott, born 6 February 1907, died 21 February 1980, buried Seminary Cemetery, MS; married 8 November 1923 to Frank C. Napier, born 1902, died 1981.
D. Allen Graham Lott, born 24 November 1909, died 28 July 1975, buried Seminary Cemetery, MS; married Kileen, TX, to Juanita Whizzenat, died 1958.
E. Lois Lott, born 9 October 1915; married 26 December 1940 to Morris G. McLemore, born 1913, died 1976.
F. Mary Nell Lott, born 7 July 1917; married El Dorado, AR, 3 November 1959 to Robert A. Sims, born 1918, died 1991.

# Descendants of DAVID GRAHAM (1788-1844)

6-       WILLIAM MCDANIEL GRAHAM, (called "Mack"), born 2 October 1886, died 5 March 1933, buried City Cemetery, Collins, MS; married to CAROLYN WYCHE, born 6 April 1886, buried City Cemetery, Collins, MS.

Children of William Graham & Carolyn Wyche:
7- Infant Graham, born & died 20 January 1922.

6-       SAMUEL DAVID GRAHAM, born Seminary, Covington County, MS, 12 October 1888, died 13 February 1980, buried Marion King Cemetery, Jefferson Davis County, MS; married 26 September 1909 to ALICE IRENE KING, born Bassfield, Jefferson Davis County, MS, 12 April 1891, died 2 October 1985, buried Marion King Cemetery, MS, daughter of Jefferson Marion King & Sarah Elizabeth Coulter.

Children of Samuel Graham & Alice King:
7-James Marion Graham, born 2 May 1911, Seminary, Covington County, MS
7-Huldah Ruth Graham, born 22 March 1913
7-Vera Nell Graham, born 28 June 1914 Bassfield, Jefferson Davis County, MS
7-Homer Hall Graham, born 5 February 1916 Covington County, MS
7-Claude Ray Graham, born 12 February 1917
7-Clyde Ford Graham, born 4 April 1918
7-Harold Graham, born 14 September 1920
7-Nellie Graham, born 20 December 1921
7-Samuel David Graham, born 2 October 1923 Jefferson Davis County, MS

6-       JOHN BUFORD GRAHAM, born October 1890, died 27 June 1957, buried Methodist Cemetery, Mantua, NJ; married 2 July 1915 to MARGUERITE BERNICE MAITLAND (called "Peg"), born Morgan City, LA, 21 January 1888, died June 1967, buried Methodist Cemetery, Mantua, NJ, daughter of Robert Smith Maitland & Julia Barbara Westerling, of Morgan City, LA.

Children of John Graham & Marguerite Maitland:
7-Huldah Barbara Graham, born 14 May 1916
7-Sarah Marguerite Graham, born 23 March 1918 Morgan City, LA

6-       MOLLIE ESTHER GRAHAM PICKERING, born 9 January 1893, died 17 September 1994, Jackson, MS, buried Lakewood Cemetery, Jackson MS; married HERBERT PICKERING, son of James M. Pickering & Lutter L.

Child of Herbert Pickering & Mollie Graham:
A. Mary Graham Pickering, born Laurel, MS, 7 January 1923; married (1) 16 August 1947 (later divorced) Allen Bernice Wilson, born 1915, died 1964; married (2) 12 January 1974 Philip Levereault, born 1912.

6-       ALMA LUCILLE GRAHAM CONNER, born 11 December 1894; married 15 December 1921 to MARTIN SENNETT CONNER, born Hattiesburg, MS, 31 August 1891, died Jackson, MS, 16 September 1921 or 1950, son of Oscar Weir Conner, sr, & Holly Gertrude Sennett.

Martin Sennett Conner was a govenor of Mississippi.

Child of Martin Conner & Alma Graham:

# *Descendants of DAVID GRAHAM (1788-1844)*

A. Lady Rachel Conner, born 24 October 1922; married 10 July 1950 to Robert Alanson Biggs, jr.

6-      VERMONT GRAHAM LIGHTSEY, born Covington County, MS, 13 April 1898, died Houston, TX, 31 December 1985, buried Catholic Cemetery, Houston, TX; married 14 June 1918 (later divorced) to ADREN CHESTER LIGHTSEY, born Paulding, Jasper County MS, 22 February 1895, died San Francisco, CA, January 1965, buried Veterans Cemetery, San Francisco, CA.

Family friends from the state of Vermont visited the family of James Morgan Graham while Huldah Jane was pregnant. The mother named the baby "Vermont".

Children of Adren Lightsey & Vermont Graham, born Laurel, MS:
A. Betty Jane Lightsey, born 8 April 1920; married Washington D.C. 1 July 1942 to William Henry Ramsden Crooks, born 1912.
B. Louise Lightsey, born 30 August 1924, died Houston, TX, 23 July 1989; married 1958 (later divorced) Clyde B. Stephens.

6-      OMA GRAHAM, born 20 April 1899, died 16 September 1906, buried Seminary Cemetery, Covington County, MS. Oma Graham died of malaria at age 7.

6-      ROBERT EARL GRAHAM, born Seminary, Covington County, MS, 23 May 1901, died Jackson, Hinds County, MS, 4 December 1967, buried Jackson, MS; married in Burns, Smith County, MS, 19 October 1924 to FANNIE ELLENDER ROBINSON, born Burns, Smith County, MS, 1 March 1903, died 26 August 1994.

Children of Robert Graham & Fannie Robinson:
7-Bobbye Frances Graham, born 14 August 1925 Seminary, Covington County MS
7-Patricia Ann Graham, born 14 July 1927 Burns, Smith County, MS
7-Billy Mack Graham, born 4 December 1930 Hattiesburg, MS

6-      ARTHUR SHORT GRAHAM (called "Jinx"), born , died ; married Jackson, Hinds County, MS, to ADA B. STEPHENS.

Arthur Graham got his nick name "Jinx" when one of his siblings looked into his crib when he was an infant & said "you little Jinx" after hearing an older relative say that his birth had been a jinx.

## NOTES

13. Information on these family lines are from Dr. K. Edwin Graham, Gulfport, MS.

### SEVENTH GENERATION

#### CHILDREN OF 6- WILLIAM GRAHAM & ALSIE REYNOLDS[5]

7-      ALFRED GRAHAM, born Olney, Young County, TX, 1 January 1913; married June 1939 to KATHERINE FERRY.

7-      TERRELL GRAHAM, born Olney, Young County, TX, 22 May 1914; married 18 January 1944 to SALLY NORVELL.

# *Descendants of DAVID GRAHAM (1788-1844)*

7-      JOHN PATRICK GRAHAM, born Olney, Young County, TX, 25 October 1916; married 22 June 1946 to MARY ELIZABETH WINSTON.

7-      BARBARA JEWELL GRAHAM, born Olney, Young County, TX, 11 May 1918, died March 1924, buried Megarel, Archer County, TX.

7-      BEATRICE GRAHAM WAKEFIELD, born Megarel, Archer County, TX, 2 December 1920; married November 1943 (later divorced) to DOYLE WAKEFIELD.

### CHILDREN OF 6- HOMER GRAHAM & WINNIE MULLINAX[5]

7-      GERALD MACK GRAHAM, born Ingleside, Young County, TX, 9 June 1921; married 22 December 1946 to FRANCES LOUISE BYRD.

7-      JOHNNIE BELL GRAHAM BURGE, born Ingleside, Young County, TX, 16 April 1923; married 11 February 1942 to LOUIS JAMES BURGE.

7-      JOHN PAT GRAHAM, born Ingleside, Young County, TX, 9 March 1924; married December 1954 to AGNES GOLDEN.

### CHILDREN OF 6- SAMUEL GRAHAM & ALICE KING[5]

7-      JAMES MARION GRAHAM, born Seminary, Covington County, MS, 2 May 1911, died Hattiesburg, Forrest County, MS, 6 February 1992, buried Marion King Cemetery, Bassfield, Jefferson Davis County, MS; married Bassfield, MS, 10 August 1929 to MYRTLE DELILAH MCRANEY, born Collins, Covington County, MS, 29 September 1910, died Hattiesburg, MS, 9 January 1988, buried Marion King Cemetery, Bassfield, MS, daughter of .

Children of James Graham & Myrtle McRaney:
8-Kenneth Edwin Graham, born 17 August 1930, Bassfield, Jefferson Davis County, MS
8-Joseph Maxwell Graham, born 2 June 1932 Bassfield, Jefferson Davis County, MS
8-David Eugene Graham, born 19 April 1934 Bassfield, Jefferson Davis County, MS
8-Nannie Katherine Graham, born 28 October 1935 Bassfield, Jefferson Davis County, MS
8-Nellie Carolyn Graham, born 8 February 1939 Collins, Covington County, MS
8-Huldah Jane Graham, born 21 December 1942 Collins, Covington County, MS
8-Billy Sam Graham, born 24 October 1944 Collins, Covington County, MS

7-      HULDAH RUTH GRAHAM BROWN, born 22 March 1913; married Hattiesburg, Forrest County, MS, 21 September 1952 to JOHN FRANKLIN BROWN.

7-      VERA NELL GRAHAM KING, born Bassfield, Jefferson Davis County, MS, 28 June 1914; married Williamsburg, Covington County, MS, 13 May 1933 to GEORGE CORLEY KING.

7-      HOMER HALL GRAHAM, born Covington County, MS, 5 February 1916, died Gulfport, MS, 13 September 1978, buried Flower Hill Cemetery, Gulfport, MS; married BESS MAGEE, born 1919, died 1985.

7-      CLAUDE RAY GRAHAM, born 12 February 1917, died 2 July 1989, buried Marion King Cemetery, Jefferson Davis County, MS; married (1) VIVIAN MAUREEN BURKETT, born 1917; married (2) ETHEL MERLE BASS, born 1925; married (3) 13 July 1957 to IDA MAE STEWART, born 1921.

# *Descendants of DAVID GRAHAM (1788-1844)*

7-      CLYDE FORD GRAHAM, born 4 April 1918, died 3 February 1980, buried Marion King Cemetery, Jefferson Davis County, MS; married MARIAN BURKETT, born 1920.

7-      HAROLD GRAHAM, born 14 September 1920, died 16 August 1922, buried Marion King Cemetery, Jefferson Davis County, MS.

7-      NELLIE GRAHAM, born 20 December 1921, died 20 August 1922, buried Marion King Cemetery, Jefferson Davis County, MS.

7-      SAMUEL DAVID GRAHAM, born Jefferson Davis County, MS, 2 October 1923, died Collins, Covington County, MS, 18 August 1980, buried Cold Springs Cemetery, Collins, MS; married (1) GWENDOLYN DAVIS; married (2) 22 May 1950 to NELL LOTT, born 1927.

### CHILDREN OF 6- JOHN GRAHAM & MARGUERITE MAITLAND[5]

7-      HULDAH BARBARA GRAHAM BAKLEY (called "Bobbie"), born 14 May 1916; married 8 November 1937 to CHARLES GEORGE BAKLEY, born 1915, died 1975.

7-      SARAH MARGUERITE GRAHAM BUSH (called "Titter"), born Morgan City, LA, 23 March 1918; married Manuta, NJ, 6 April 1946 to CARL EUGENE BUSH, born 1916, died 1986.

Sarah Marguerite Graham attended Camden Commerical College, Camden, NJ, and worked in Camden, Philadelphia and Washington D.C. She worked for the Department of Justice, then the Army where she worked in legal and procurement departments.

### CHILDREN OF 6- ROBERT GRAHAM & FANNIE ROBINSON[5]

7-      BOBBYE FRANCES GRAHAM BRANTLEY, born Seminary, Covington County, MS, 14 August 1925; married Jackson, Hinds County, MS, 1 June 1950 to ROBERT JACKSON BRANTLEY, born 1922, died 1983.

7-      PATRICIA ANN GRAHAM GABLE, born Burns, Smith County, MS, 14 July 1927; married October 1952 to GERALD PHILLIPS GABLE.

Patricia Ann was born in Burns during a campaign trip of her father. The family did not live in Burns at the time.

7-      BILLY MACK GRAHAM, born Methodist Hospital, Hattiesburg, Forrest County, MS, 4 December 1930; married Forrest County, MS, 30 August 1959 to DOUGLAS ANN STEVENS, born 1934.

### NOTES

5. Information on these family lines are from Dr. K. Edwin Graham, Gulfport, MS.

### EIGHTH GENERATION

### CHILDREN OF 7- JAMES GRAHAM & MYRTLE MCRANEY

# *Descendants of DAVID GRAHAM (1788-1844)*

8-       KENNETH EDWIN GRAHAM, born Bassfield, Jefferson Davis County, MS, 17 August 1930; married Crystal Springs, Copiah County, MS, 17 August 1949 to JO ANN EADY, born Crystal Springs, Copiah County, MS, 23 March 1930, daughter of Henry Lewis Eady & Merle Orene Crews.

Children of K. Edwin Graham & Jo Ann Eady:
9-Kenneth Andrew Graham, born 8 August 1953 Atlanta, Fulton County, GA
9-Charlyn Elizabeth Graham, born 14 January 1958 McComb, Pike County, MS
9-Mark Edwin Graham, born 14 July 1960 St. Louis, MO

8-       JOSEPH MAXWELL GRAHAM, born Bassfield, Jefferson Davis County, MS, 2 June 1932; married McComb, Pike County, MS, 13 April 1952 to MARY VIRGINIA COTTEN.

8-       DAVID EUGENE GRAHAM, born Bassfield, Jefferson Davis County, MS, 19 April 1934; married 2 November 1956 to EDWINA R. SHOEMAKE.

8-       NANNIE KATHERINE GRAHAM ABERCROMBIE, born Bassfield, Jefferson Davis County, MS, 28 October 1935; married 12 November 1954 to ISAAC HARDY ABERCROMBIE.

8-       NELLIE CAROLYN GRAHAM SMITH, born Collins, Covington County, MS, 8 February 1939; married 12 February 1960 to JOHNNY DOYLE SMITH.

8-       HULDAH JANE GRAHAM PURSER CHRISTIANSEN, born Collins, Covington County, MS, 21 December 1942; married (1) 26 January 1963 (later divorced) to FRED EARL PURSER; married (2) 26 October 1980 to JARVIS CHRISTIANSEN.

8-       BILLY SAM GRAHAM, born Collins, Covington County, MS, 24 October 1944; married 28 September 1968 to LINDA RUTH BOUNDS.

NOTES

. Information on these family lines are from Dr. K. Edwin Graham, Gulfport, MS.

NINTH GENERATION

CHILDREN OF 8- K. EDWIN GRAHAM & JO ANN EADY

9-       KENNETH ANDREW GRAHAM, born Atlanta, Fulton County, GA, 8 August 1953; married Long Beach, CA, in 1980 to MARLA MCQUARRIE.

9-       CHARLYN ELIZABETH GRAHAM, born 14 January 1958 McComb, Pike County, MS

9-       MARK EDWIN GRAHAM, born St. Louis, MO, 14 July 1960; married Kensington, Montgomery County, MD, 1 May 1993 to SUSAN MARIE MCLAUGHLIN.

Notes

. Information is from Dr. K. Edwin Graham, Gulfport, MS.

Made in the USA
San Bernardino, CA
27 April 2017